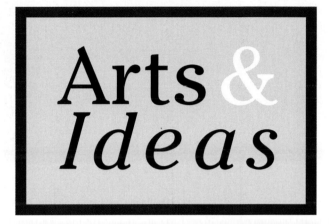

Arts & Ideas

TENTH EDITION

Mary Warner Marien
Syracuse University

William Fleming

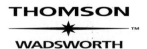
THOMSON
™
WADSWORTH

Australia • Canada • Mexico • Singapore • Spain
United Kingdom • United States

THOMSON
WADSWORTH

Publisher: Clark Baxter
Acquisitions Editor: John R. Swanson
Development Editor: Sharon Adams Poore
Assistant Editor: Amy McGaughey
Editorial Assistant: Brianna Brinkley
Technology Project Manager: Melinda Newfarmer
Marketing Manager: Mark Orr
Marketing Assistant: Annabelle Yang
Signing Representative: Tim Kenney
Senior Project Manager, Editorial Production: Paul Wells
Art Director: Maria Epes
Print/Media Buyer: Karen Hunt
Permissions Editor: Stephanie Lee

Production Service: Graphic World Inc.
Text Designer: Sue Hart
Photo Researcher: Sandra Lord
Copy Editor: Graphic World Inc.
Cover Designer: Jeanne Calabrese
Cover Image: Henry Matisse. *Interior with a Violin,* 1917–1918. DOWIC Fotografi. Statens Museum for Kunst, Copenhagen. © 2004 Succession H. Matisse, Paris/Artists Rights Society (ARS), New York
Cover Printer: Phoenix Color Corp
Compositor: Graphic World Inc.
Printer: Courier Corporation/Kendallville

For more information about our products, contact us at:
Thomson Learning Academic Resource Center
1-800-423-0563
For permission to use material from this text or product, submit a request online at
http://www.thomsonrights.com.
Any additional questions about permissions can be submitted by email to thomsonrights@thomson.com.

Library of Congress Control Number: 2004107621
Student Edition: ISBN 0-534-61371-3
Instructor's Edition: ISBN 0-534-61381-0

Thomson Wadsworth
10 Davis Drive
Belmont, CA 94002-3098
USA

Asia
Thomson Learning
5 Shenton Way #01-01
UIC Building
Singapore 068808

Australia/New Zealand
Thomson Learning
102 Dodds Street
Southbank, Victoria 3006
Australia

Canada
Nelson
1120 Birchmount Road
Toronto, Ontario M1K 5G4
Canada

Europe/Middle East/Africa
Thomson Learning
High Holborn House
50/51 Bedford Row
London WC1R 4LR
United Kingdom

Latin America
Thomson Learning
Seneca, 53
Colonia Polanco
11560 Mexico D.F.
Mexico

Spain/Portugal
Paraninfo
Calle Magallanes, 25
28015 Madrid, Spain

CREDITS

Preface National Science Foundation.
Chapter Opener 1 Slide No. 27. Photo Jean Clottes. Lions hunting on the main panel in the End Chamber. Scenes are rare in Paleolithic art. This one is unique. Document elaborated with the support of the French Ministry of Culture and Communication, Regional Direction for cultural Affairs—Rhone-Alpes, Regional Department of Archaeology; **1.1** Hans Hinz; **1.2** Slide No. 27. Photo Jean Clottes. Document elaborated with the support of the French Ministry of Culture and Communication, Regional Direction for cultural Affairs—Rhone-Alpes, Regional Department of Archaeology; **1.3** Giraudon/Art Resource, NY; **1.4** Naturhistorisches Museum, Vienna; **1.5** British School of Archaeology in Jerusalem; **1.6:** Arlette Mellaart; **1.7** © Sergio Pitamitz/SuperStock; **1.8** Erwin Böhm; **1.9** HIP/Scala/Art Resource, NY; **1.10** Courtesy of The Oriental Institute of the University of Chicago; **1.11** © Adam Woolfitt/Corbis; **1.12** Reunion des Musées Nationaux/Art Resource, NY; **1.13** British Museum, London; **1.14** Bildarchiv Preussischer Kulturbesitz/Art Resource, NY; **1.15** Copyright © The British Museum; **1.16** Scala/Art Resource, NY; **1.17** Robert Harding Picture Library; **1.18** K. Scholz/SuperStock; **1.19** Michael Holford, Loughton, England; **1.20** Bildarchiv Preussischer Kulturbesitz/Art Resource, NY; **1.21** SuperStock; **1.22** Studio Kontos; **1.23, 1.24** Scala/Art Resource, NY; **1.25** Erich Lessing/Art Resource, NY.
Chapter Opener 2 Scala/Art Resource, NY; **2.1** Photo by Raymond V. Schoder, copyright 1987 by Bolchazy-Carducci Publishers, Inc.; **2.3** photo Henri Stierlin; **2.4A** Studio Kontos; **2.5** Summerfield Press; **2.6. 2.7, 2.8** Scala/Art Resource; **2.10** © Susanna Pashko/Envision; **2.11** A. F. Kersting, London; **2.12, 2.13** British Museum, London. Reproduced by courtesy of the Trustees; **2.14** Erich Lessing/Art Resource, NY; **2.15** Studio Kontos; **2.16, 2.17, 2.18, 2.19** Hirmer Fotoarchiv, Munich; **2.20** Vanni/Art Resource, NY; **2.21** Scala/Art Resource, NY; **2.22** SuperStock; **2.23, 2.24** Erich Lessing/Art Resource, NY; **2.25** Scala/Art Resource, NY; **2.26** Photo Reunion des Musées, Nationaux/Art Resource, NY; **2.27** Antikensammlung, Staatliche Museum, Berlin; **2.28** Erich Lessing/Archiv fur Kunst und Geschichte, Berlin; **2.29** Alinari/Art Resource, NY; **2.30** Scala/Art Resource, NY; **2.31** Museo Nazionale Archeologico, Naples; **2.32** Bildarchiv Preussischer Kulturbesitz/Art Resource, NY; **2.33** Erich Lessing/PhotoEdit; **2.34** Bildarchiv Preussischer Kulturbesitz/Art Resource, NY; **2.36** Nimatallah/Art Resource, NY; **2.37** Saskia Ltd. Cultural Documentation; **2.38** Scala/Art Resource, NY; **2.39** Dr. Mauro Pucciarelli, Rome.
Chapter Opener 3 Scala/Art Resource, NY; **3.1** Ministry of Culture, Archaeological Receipts Fund, Athens, Greece; **3.2** Art Resource, NY; **3.3, 3.4** Bildarchiv Preussischer Kulturbesitz/Art Resource, NY; **3.5** Summerfield Press, Ltd.; **3.6** Photo Giovanni Lattanzi **3.7, 3.8, 3.9;** Bildarchiv Preussischer Kulturbesitz/Art Resource, NY; **3.10** Scala/Art Resource, NY; **3.11** Bildarchiv Preussischer Kulturbesitz/Art Resource, NY; **3.12** Photo Vatican Museums; **3.13** Canali Photobank, Milan; **3.14** Alinari/Art Resource, NY; **3.15** Archiv fur Kunst und Geschichte, Berlin; **3.16, 3.17** Scala/Art Resource, NY; **3.18** Metropolitan Museum of Art, New York; **3.19** Dr. Mauro Pucciarelli, Rome; **3.20, 3.21** Alinari/Art Resource, NY.
Chapter Opener 4 Erich Lessing/PhotoEdit; **4.1** Copyright © M. Sarri/Photo Vatican Museums; **4.2** Scala/Art Resource, NY; **4.3** Alinari/Art Resource, NY; **4.4** Saskia Ltd. Cultural Documentation; **4.5** © David Lees/Corbis; **4.6** Copyright © Mike Andrews/Ancient Art & Architecture Collection Ltd.; **4.7A** Museo della Civilta Romana, Rome; **4.8** De Masi/Canali Photobank, Milan; **4.9** Photo Marcello Bertinetti/White Star; **4.10A** Dr. Mauro Pucciarelli, Rome; **4.11** Alinari/Art Resource, NY; **4.12** Dr. Mauro Pucciarelli, Rome; **4.13** Alain Lonchampt/CNMHS © Artists Rights Society (ARS) New York/SPADEM, Paris; **4.14** Erich Lessing/PhotoEdit; **4.15** Photo Vatican Museums; **4.16** Fototeca; **4.18** © Carmen Redondo/Corbis; **4.19** Oliver Benn/Getty Images; **4.20A** Jan Halaska/Photo Researchers, New York; **4.21** © 1993 National Gallery of Art, Washington; **4.23** Courtesy of the heirs of Salvatore Aurigemma; **4.24** Scala/Art Resource, NY; **4.25** Fototeca Unione at the American Academy in Rome.
Chapter Opener 5 Scala/Art Resource, NY; **5.1** Scala/Art Resource, NY; **5.2** Foto Archivio Fabbrica di San Pietro in Vaticano; **5.3, 5.4, 5.5A** Scala/Art Resource, NY; **5.7, 5.8** Scala/Art Resource, NY; **5.9A** Fotocielo, Rome; **5.10** Scala/Art Resource, NY; **5.12** Alinari/Art Resource, NY; **5.13A** Alan Oddie/PhotoEdit; **5.14** photo Henri Stierlin; **5.15, 5.16** Canali Photobank, Milan; **5.17** Ara Güler, Istanbul; **5.18** Photo Vatican Museums; **5.19** Cameraphoto Arte, Venice/Art Resource, NY; **5.20** Scala/Art Resource, NY; **5.21** Reproduction by kind permission of the Trustees of the Chester Beatty Library, Dublin; **5.22A** Yoram Lehmann, Jerusalem; **5.23** A. F. Kersting, London; **5.25** Saskia Ltd. Cultural Documentation; **5.26** Scala/Art Resource, NY; **5.27** photo Henry Stierlin; **5.28** The Metropolitan Museum of Art, New York. Gift of Alexander Smith Cochran, 1913; **5.29** Alinari/Art Resource, NY; **5.30** Scala/Art Resource, NY; **5.31** TAP Service, Athens; **5.32** Dr. Harold Busch; **5.33** The Board of Trinity College, Dublin, Ireland/Bridgeman Art Library.
Chapter Opener 6 The Pierpont Morgan Library/Art Resource, NY; **6.1** Ancient Art & Architecture Collection; **6.3** Reunion des Musées Nationaux/Art Resource, NY; **6.4** Art Resource, NY; **6.5** Jean Dieuzaide; **6.6** Cliche de la Reunion des Musees Nationaux, Paris; **6.7** Scala/Art Resource, NY; **6.8** Ancient Art & Architecture Collection; **6.9** Marburg/Art Resource, NY; **6.10** The Pierpont Morgan Library/Art Resource, NY; **6.11** From Illuminations of Hildegard of Bingen, p. 114, courtesy Otto Mueller Verlag, Salzburg; **6.12** Vanni/Art Resource, NY; **6.13, 6.14** Farinier Museum of the Abbey at Cluny; **6.15** By permission of Goslar Tourist Information Office, Germany; **6.16** Scala/Art Resource, NY; **6.17** Caisse Nationale des Monuments et des Sites, Paris, © Artists Rights Society (ARS), New York/SPADEM, Paris; **6.18** Erich Lessing/Art Resource, NY; **6.19:** © Archivo Iconografico, S.A./Corbis; **6.20** Erich Lessing/Art Resource, NY; **6.21** Art Resource, NY; **6.22** Aerofilms Ltd., Borehamwood, England; **6.23A** British Tourist Authority; **6.24** A. F. Kersting, London; **6.25** Marvin Trachtenberg; **6.26** Ancient Art & Architecture Collection; **6.27** Bibliotech Nationale Paris. B.N.; **6.28** J. Feuillie/Caisse Nationale des Monuments et des Sites, Paris. Copyright Artists Rights Society (ARS), New York/SPADEM, Paris; **6.29** © Sandro Vannini/Corbis; **6.30** © Hulton Deutsch Collection/Corbis.
Chapter Opener 7 © Sonia Halliday Photographs; **7.1** Copyright © Könemann GmbH/Photo: Achim Bednorz; **7.2** Pubbli Aer Foto; **7.3A** French Government Tourist Office; **7.4** © Sonia Halliday and Laura Lushington; **7.5A** C. Bibollet/Agence TOP, Paris; **7.6** Caisse Nationale des Monuments et des Sites, Paris. Copyright Artists Rights Society (ARS), New York/SPADEM, Paris; **7.8** © Sonia Halliday Photographs; **7.9** Index, Firenze; **7.10** © Sonia Halliday Photographs; **7.11** Marburg/Art Resource, NY; **7.12** © Vanni Archive/Corbis; **7.13** © Dean Conger/Corbis; **7.14** © Angelo Hornak Library; **7.15** Giraudon/Art Resource, NY; **7.16** Marburg/Art Resource, NY; **7.17** Giraudon/Art Resource, NY.
Chapter Opener 8 HIP/Scala/Art Resource, NY; **8.1** A. F. Kersting, London; **8.2** Aerofilms Ltd., Borehamwood, England; **8.3** A. F. Kersting, London; **8.4** Réunion des Musées Nationaux/Art Resource, NY; **8.5** Archive fur Kunst und Geschichte, Berlin; **8.6** Copyright © Konemann GmbH/Photo: Achim Bednorz; **8.7** Foto Marburg/Art Resource, NY; **8.8** Scala/Art Resource, NY; **8.9, 8.10** Alinari/Art Resource, NY; **8.11, 8.12, 8.13, 8.14, 8.15, 8.16** Scala/Art Resource, NY; **8.17** Canali Photobank, Milan; **8.18** Summerfield Press, Ltd.; **8.19** Alinari/Art Resource, NY; **8.20, 8.21** Scala/Art Resource, NY; **8.22** New York Public Library/Art Resource, NY; **8.23** HIP/Scala/Art Resource, NY.
Chapter Opener 9 Canali Photobank, Milan; **9.1A** Vanni/Art Resource, NY; **9.2A** Scala/Art Resource, NY; **9.3A** Alinari/Art Resource, NY; **9.4** Scala/Art Resource, NY; **9.5** Alinari/Art Resource, NY; **9.6, 9.7** Wadsworth Collection; **9.8** Alinari/Art Resource, NY; **9.9** Scala/Art Resource, NY; **9.10** Alinari/Art Resource, NY; **9.11** Ralph Lieberman; **9.12** Alinari/Art Resource, NY; **9.13** Canali Photobank, Milan; **9.14** Alinari/Art Resource, NY; **9.15, 9.16, 9.17** Canali Photobank, Milan; **9.18** © Massimo Listri/Corbis; **9.19** Bildarchiv Preussischer Kulturbesitz/Art Resource, NY; **9.20** Erich Lessing/Art Resource, NY; **9.21** Canali Photobank, Milan; **9.22** Alinari/Art Resource, NY; **9.23** Scala/Art Resource, NY; **9.24** Summerfield Press, Ltd.; **9.25** The National Gallery, London; **9.26** Réunion des Musées Nationaux/Art Resource, NY; **9.27** AP/Wide World Photos; **9.28** Alinari/Art Resource, NY; **9.29** The Royal Collection © 1994 Her Majesty Queen Elizabeth II; **9.30** Canali Photobank, Milan; **9.31** Image @2004 Board of Trustees, National Gallery of Art, Washington; **9.32** Reunion des Musées Nationaux/Art Resource, NY.
Chapter Opener 10 Photo Vatican Museums; **10.1** Guido Alberto Rossi/The Image Bank; **10.3** Scala/Art Resource, NY; **10.2** The National Gallery, London; **10.4** Alinari/Art Resource, NY; **10.5** Scala/Art Resource, NY; **10.6** © Stefano Bianchetti/Corbis; **10.7, 10.8** Scala/Art Resource, NY; **10.9** Copyright © Nippon Television Network Corporation, Tokyo; **10.10, 10.11** Photo Vatican Museums; **10.12** Copyright © Bracchietti-Zigrosi/Photo Vatican Museums; **10.13** Copyright © M. Sarri/Photo Vatican Museums; **10.15** Erich Lessing/Art Resource, NY; **10.17** Leonard von Matt/Photo Researchers; **10.18** Canali Photobank, Milan.
Chapter Opener 11 Ailsa Mellon Bruce Fund. Image © 2004 Board of Trustees, National Gallery of Art, Washington; **11.1** © The National Gallery, London; **11.2** Ailsa Mellon Bruce Fund. Image © 2004 Board of Trustees, National Gallery of Art, Washington; **11.3** Giraudon/Art Resource, NY; **11.4** Photo copyright © Metropolitan Museum of Art. All rights reserved; **11.5** Artothek; **11.6** © The National Gallery, London; **11.7, 11.8** Scala/Art Resource, NY; **11.9** Erich Lessing/Art Resource, NY; **11.10** Kuntshistorisches Museum, Vienna; **11.11** © Francis G. Mayer/Corbis; **11.12** Bridgeman Art Library; **11.13** Scala/Art Resource, NY; **11.14** Giraudon/Art Resource, NY; **11.15** Erich Lessing/Art Resource, NY; **11.16** © The National Gallery, London; **11.17** By permission of the Folger Shakespeare Library; **11.18** Conjectural reconstruction by C. Walter Hodges; **11.19** Marginal drawing for the last page of Erasmus's 1515 Basel printing of In Praise of Folly, facsimile reproduced from the original in the Offentliche Kunstsammlung Basel, published by H. Oppermann in 1931. The George Arents Research Library at Syracuse University; **11.20** Erich Lessing/Art Resource, NY; **11.21** Artothek.
Chapter Opener 12 Corbis; **12.1, 12.2** Scala/Art Resource, NY; **12.3** Alinari/Art Resource, NY; **12.4A** © Yann Arthus-Bertrand/Corbis; **12.5A** A. F. Kersting, London; **12.6** Erich Lessing/Art Resource, NY; **12.7** Alinari/Art Resource, NY; **12.8** © 1994 National Gallery of Art, Washington; **12.9** Scala/Art Resource, NY; **12.10** The Royal Collection copyright © 2000, Her Majesty Queen Elizabeth II; **12.11** © 1987 M. Sarri/Photo Vatican Museums; **12.12** Scala/Art Resource, NY; **12.13** Erich Lessing/Art Resource, NY; **12.14** Canali Photobank, Milan; **12.15, 12.16** Scala/Art Resource, NY; **12.17** Canali Photobank, Milan; **12.18** Jean Bernard Photographe; **12.19** Photo Vatican Museums; **12.20, 12.21** Scala/Art Resource, NY; **12.22** Summerfield Press, Ltd.; **12.23** © The National Gallery, London; **12.24** © Alinari Archives/Corbis; **12.25** © The National Gallery, London; **12.26** Kunsthistorisches Museum, Vienna; **12.27** Timothy McCarthy/Art Resource, NY; **12.28** Scala/Art Resource, NY; **12.29, 12.30** Scala/Art Resource, NY; **12.31** Art Resource, NY; **12.32** © Andrea Jemolo/Corbis; **12.33** © Wolfgang Kaehler/Corbis.
Chapter Opener 13 Erich Lessing/Art Resource, NY; **13.1** Photo Vatican Museums; **13.2A** Alinari/Art Resource, NY; **13.3** Scala/Art Resource, NY; **13.4A** Canali Photobank, Milan; **13.5** Alinari/Art Resource, NY; **13.6** Scala/Art Resource, NY; **13.7** Canali Photobank, Milan; **13.8** Scala/Art Resource, NY; **13.9** Summerfield Press Ltd., Florence; **13.10** SEF/Art Resource, NY; **13.11** Scala/Art Resource, NY; **13.12** Gabinetto Fotographico Nazionale, ICCD, Rome; **13.13** Canali Photobank, Milan; **13.14** Institut Amatller d'Art Hispanic, Barcelona; **13.15** Art Resource, NY; **13.16** Arxiu MAS Ampliaciones y Reproducciones; **13.17** The Art Archive/Dagli Orti; **13.18** Monasterio del Escorial; **13.19** Giraudon/Art Resource, NY; **13.20** © National Gallery Collection; by kind permission of the Trustees of the National Gallery, London/Corbis; **13.21** Victoria & Albert Museum, London/Art Resource, NY; **13.22** Erich Lessing/Art Resource, NY; **13.23** © Charles & Josette Lenars/Corbis; **13.24** Copyright © Justin Kerr; **13.25** Photo by Hillel Burger; **13.26** © Charles & Josette Lenars/Corbis.
Chapter Opener 14 Reunion des Musées Nationaux/Art Resource, NY; **14.1** Reunion des Musées Nationaux/Art Resource, NY; **14.2** © SuperStock; **14.3** Aerofilms, Ltd.; **14.4** Caisse Nationale des Monuments et des Sites, Paris © Artists Rights Society (ARS), New York/SPADEM, Paris; **14.5** Henri Dauman, NY; **14.6** New York Public Library/Art Resource, NY; **14.7, 14.8** Reunion des Musées Nationaux/Art Resource, NY; **14.9** Giraudon/Art Resource, NY; **14.10** Scala/Art Resource, NY; **14.11** Artothek **14.12** Metropolitan Museum of Art, New York. Harris Brisbane Dick Fund, 1946; **14.13, 14.14** Photo Reunion des Musées Nationaux/Art Resource, NY; **14.15** Metropolitan Museum of Art, New York. Harris Brisbane Dick Fund, 1930; **14.16** © Philippa Lewis; Edifice/Corbis; **14.17, 14.18A** A. F. Kersting; **14.19** By courtesy of the Board of The Trustees of the Victoria and Albert Museum/The Bridgeman Art Library, London; **14.20, 14.21, 14.22** A. F. Kersting; **14.23** ©University Library, Hamburg, Germany/SuperStock.
Chapter Opener 15 © Bettmann/Corbis; **15.1** Copyright the Frick Collection, New York; **15.2** Museum Boymans-van Beuningen, Rotterdam; **15.3** The Toledo Museum of Art, Toledo (purchased with funds from the Libbey Endowment, gift of Edward Drummond Libbey); **15.4** Board of Trustees, National Gallery of Art, Washington, DC; **15.5** Erich Lessing/Art Resource, NY; **15.6** Copyright © Rijksmuseum, Amsterdam; **15.7** Art Resource, NY; **15.8** Gemaldegalerie Alte Meister, Staatliche Kunstsammlungen Dresden, NY; **15.9** © 2004 Board of Trustees, National Gallery of Art, Washington, DC; **15.10** Erich Lessing/Art Resource, NY; **15.11** Scala/Art Resource, NY; **15.12** Guildhall Art Gallery, Corporation of London; **15.13** Rijksmuseum, Amsterdam; **15.14** Photo copyright © Mauritshius, The Hague; **15.15** Scala/Art Resource, NY; **15.16** Copyright The Frick Collection, New York; **15.17** Erich Lessing/Art Resource, NY; **15.18** © Bettmann/Corbis; **15.19** Scala/Art Resource, NY.
Chapter Opener 16 SuperStock; **16.1** Scala/Art Resource, NY; **16.2:** Cooper-Hewitt National Design Museum, Smithsonian Institution; **16.3** Ancient Art & Architecture Collection; **16.4** Scala/Art Resource, NY; **16.5** Hirmer Fotoarchiv, Munich; **16.6** A. F. Kersting, London; **16.7** Wallace Collection, London; reproduced by courtesy of the Trustees; **16.8** Metropolitan Museum of Art, New York. Bequest of William K. Vanderbilt, 1920; **16.9** SuperStock; **16.10** Art Resource, NY; **16.11** Photo copyright © 1990 Metropolitan Museum of Art. All rights reserved; **16.12** Scala/Art Resource, NY; **16.13** Erich Lessing/Art Resource, NY; **16.14** © The Phillips Collection, Washington; **16.15** © National Gallery Collection; by kind permission of the

Brief Contents

CONTENTS

LISTS OF MAPS
AND CHRONOLOGIES

MAPS

CHRONOLOGIES

PREFACE

At the beginning of the twenty-first century, scientists began vigorously debating an idea that humanists have long assumed to be true: we became fully human when we became creative and capable of symbolic thinking. This does not mean that the arts made, or make, us human but rather that we have been art-makers for as long as we have been human. Of course, scientists frame the argument differently than humanists. They focus on image and symbol making as indicators of advanced brain development. We look at early human artifacts, such as the piece of red ocher from South Africa (Fig. P.1) that dates to about 77,000 years ago and recognize deliberate repetition of overlapping triangular patterns as evidence of self-consciousness and intentional composition. Here is a design that surpasses the fulfillment of immediate needs such as food and shelter. These marks, whether they were intended to record time, convey religion, or even if they are merely fanciful doodles, are recognizably human. They sprang from a self-identity that early primates do not seem to have possessed. Humans and some animals make tools and adapt their environment to make it more hospitable and safe. Humans and some animals indulge in play, for its own sake, and not as practice for skills such as hunting. But only humans create symbols for themselves and for other humans.

The first art that we know about is probably not the first art to be created. Decorations placed on bodies or on clothing would have perished, along with many kinds of transformed organic materials, such as wood. But rocky overhangs and caves in Africa, Asia, and Europe preserved decorated tools, jewelry, sculpture, and of course, some astonishing paintings.

With the first art came cultural centers. Semi-nomadic Ice-Age dwellers returned for hundreds of years to the same locations. They decorated the walls of rocky overhangs with animal sculptures, and although they did not live in the caves, they kept up the paintings there and often added to them. Caves were cultural centers like the more diverse Gothic cathedral towns. Nevertheless, they may have served many of the functions found in later, larger cultural centers. They were hubs for multiple kinds of human expression, ranging from family or clan identity to religion, storytelling, political persuasion, record storage, and entertainment. Throughout history, cultural centers have been places where artists and audiences came together to create interpretations of human experience and the world around them. *Arts & Ideas* dwells on the visual art, music, literature, and architecture created in cultural centers in the West, and it identifies concepts underlying these expressions. One cannot pursue meaning in the art of the present or the past without taking into consideration the nature of the art medium. As the arts evolved, so too did their vocabulary. Throughout this text, art terms are defined in relation to spe-

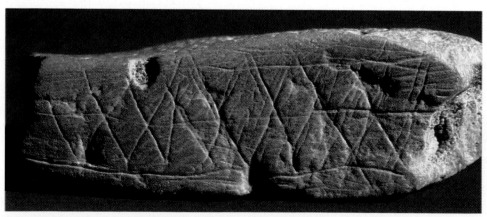

P.1 Engraved ochre from Blombos Cave.

cific art works so that students can see and hear what a term means and how it is used. A glossary is included at the end of the book, and students can access art terms, as well as other learning aids online.

This book is a place to begin to recognize the historical and social interactions of the arts in Western culture. The arts may not make us human, but they can make us aware of how humans have understood their lives, their societies, and the world. To ask what is art is to find out what is human.

NEW TO THIS EDITION

The Tenth Edition is now available in a two-volume split. Volume I covers prehistory to through the Renaissance (Chapters 1–12), Volume II covers the Renaissance to the present (Chapters 9–23). In addition:

- Thoroughly revised and updated, the text reflects current research and works. A new Introduction provides students with a thorough background to understanding the arts. Increased coverage of women and other marginalized authors, artists, and works is also presented.

- More than 200 new works of art and a predominantly 4-color design provides a beautiful presentation.

- New maps better illustrate the discussions of important historical places.

- New discussions of photography, film, and mass media add to the book's currency.

- Boxed sections present contrasts between the past and the present, giving students a more historical perspective.

- A resource list at the end of each chapter directs students to valuable resources.

AN EXPANDED SUPPLEMENT PACKAGE

FOR STUDENTS

- **Exploring Humanities CD-ROM** Packaged free with every new copy of this book, the Exploring Humanities CD-ROM includes a collection of interactive learning modules, online timelines, and links to Web sites that focus on a full range of humanities topics—music, literature, theater, philosophy, and art.

- **Audio CD** Also available is a text-specific audio CD that contains the music discussed in the text.

- **Study Guide** This brief new addition to the supplements package includes chapter-by-chapter reviews and questions to help students absorb and comprehend the material.

- **InfoTrac® College Edition Workbook** Covering many of the core topics discussed in **Arts & Ideas,** this booklet provides in-depth exercises that ask students to use their free subscription to the *InfoTrac College Edition* online library.

- **InfoTrac® College Edition** Instructors and students automatically receive 4 months of FREE access to *InfoTrac College Edition,* an online library that offers complete articles from nearly 5,000 scholarly and popular publications. Updated daily and going back more than 20 years, *InfoTrac College Edition* is a great homework tool or for catching up on the news. NEW! Students now have instant access to critical thinking and paper writing tools through *InfoWrite.*

- **Book Companion Web Site,** http://art.wadsworth.com/fleming10/ The new Book Companion Web Site for **Arts & Ideas, Tenth Edition,** offers students numerous resources to help their study of the humanities. Students will find tutorial quizzing; *InfoTrac College Edition* exercises; Internet activities; chapter-specific links to readings covered in the text; a glossary and flashcards with pronunciations; annotated Web links; and other music, art, and philosophy-related resources.

- **The Museum Experience** This is a practical handbook that will enrich students' understanding of the museum experience, including a primer on museum etiquette, a guide to writing an exhibition review, and an extensive listing of museums across the United States.

- **ArtBasics: An Illustrated Glossary and Timeline** This handy reference includes a brief introduction to basic terms, styles, and time periods.

FOR INSTRUCTORS

- **WebTutor™ Advantage . . . on Blackboard and WebCT** Ready to use as soon as you log on, *WebTutor Advantage* is a complete course management and communication tool preloaded with content from **Arts & Ideas,** organized by chapter for convenient access. It includes illustrations, outlines and summaries, practice quizzes, online tutorials, interactive modules in art and literature, and much more.

- **_Instructor's Manual and Test Bank_** The _Instructor's Manual_ provides a summary of the lecture content for each chapter, key words, and topics for discussion. The _Test Bank_ includes multiple-choice, essay, and identification questions.

- **_Slide Set_** The slide set contains seventy-five carefully selected, high-quality images from the text.

- **_ExamView®_** _ExamView_ computerized testing (on a cross-platform CD-ROM) allows instructors to easily customize the _Test Bank_ provided in the _Instructor's Manual_ or create tests.

ACKNOWLEDGMENTS

William Fleming's classic text, _Arts & Ideas,_ was one of the first works to introduce college students to the interplay of philosophy and art practice that occurs in the creation, performance, and viewing of the arts. The many letters he received during his nearly 90 years indicate that generations have been enriched by Fleming's learning and perceptions.

I was one of his students who later became his friend. Yet, like many who knew him as a teacher, he remained my mentor. I struggled to call him Bill, but it ultimately seemed too presumptuous. He was Professor Fleming, and I was honored beyond words when he asked me to take on the next edition of _Arts & Ideas._

No book of this scope can be revised and updated without taxing the goodwill of scholarly friends. My greatest debt is to Professor Frank Macomber, who collaborated with Professor Fleming on their book, _Musical Arts and Styles._ Frank's enthusiasm for music is matched by his extraordinary command of the literature and by a penetrating wit that readily deflates the pomposity of those who would make the arts obscure. The revised music sections owe to his scholarship. Throughout the updating of this book, Dr. Randall I. Bond, librarian extraordinaire, never failed to find a fact, suggest a book, or point me toward an informative Web site. His recent retirement leaves many of us to ponder how fortunate we were to interact with him professionally and to know him as a friend. Edward Gokey, an able member of Randy's staff in the Syracuse University library, came to my rescue many times and took on the task of date-checking with his customary skill and good humor. Similarly, the library's Laura Levin sprang into action when she received yet another of my phone inquiries.

In the Department of Fine Arts at Syracuse University, Professor Wayne Franits not only let me learn from his then-unpublished book, _Dutch Seventeenth-Century Genre Painting: Its Stylistic and Thematic Evolution,_ but also in his role as chair allowed me to take the time necessary to launch this edition. Linda Straub and Corinne Willis made it possible for me to continue as the department's Graduate Director while in the midst of writings.

Thomson Wadsworth drew together a talented group of individuals that I came to think of as the Thomson Team. In the book's initial stages, John Swanson, Rebecca Green, and Brianna Brinkley were helpful—and patient beyond the call of duty. Sharon Adams Poore, who took on the role, if not the title, of development editor, coached, cajoled, and best of all, slew all the dragons, great and small, that sprang up to interrupt the writing of the book. Carolyn Smith edited the initial text with an enviable eye and ear for clear language. Paul Wells supervised the book's production process, and Suzanne Kastner, no stranger to dragon slaying, ably wedded words and images as she prepared the manuscript for print. She was ably assisted by John May, who typeset each page with unparalleled attention to detail. Sandra Lord, ably assisted by Cheri Throop, fearlessly tracked down new and better images from a large number of sources. And, as always, I am awed by the keen eye and mind of Michael Marien, my live-in editor, who managed to proof most of the book in airport lounges and the tight confines of tourist-class seats.

I am also indebted to the following reviewers, who carefully considered the book and gave me many suggestions.

James S. Allen, Southern Illinois University–Carbondale

Carole C. Barnett, Jacksonville University

Beth D. Biron, Dalton State College

Robert W. Brown, University of North Carolina–Pembroke

James Busby, Houston Baptist University

Allen J. Christenson, Brigham Young University

Ann Fairbanks, University of St. Thomas

Gary M. Guinn, John Brown University

Catherine Hubbard, State University of New York, College at Brockport

Gerard P. NeCastro, University of Maine at Machias

Peter G. Potamianos, College of DuPage

Robert Prescott, Bradley University

Benjamin W. Redekop, Kettering University

Daniel Robinson, Penn State University

Doris L. Salis, The University of Findlay

Thomas E. Schirer, Lake Superior State University

Jon M. Suter, Houston Baptist University

Joan M. Watson, Virginia Polytechnic Institute and State University

Edward W. Wolner, Ball State University

INTRODUCTION

Imagine a tightrope walker gracefully and confidently treading a wire strung between two poles. Now let's add two more poles and string another wire about a foot from the first. The tightrope walker easily takes up the dare and hops from wire to wire. But we're not finished testing this performer's agility. Bring on more poles and more wire, and put one new wire higher than the existing two and one lower. The shrewd performer calls for a balance beam; but as long as the four wires run in the same direction, the tightrope walker can negotiate turns and jump from level to level. What we need to create a taxing challenge are many more wires, running at odd angles through the existing four. At the sight of them, the tightrope walker drops the balance beam. In the irregular web we have concocted, it has become a liability that could easily flick our performer to the ground. Navigating this multidimensional network, the tightrope walker will have to rely on many resources: skill, training, judgment, and balance.

Just looking and listening to the arts is like walking a single wire. It requires careful attention and offers rewards. But adding more wires—that is, accounting for the multiple, crisscrossing aspects of art-making—brings increased challenges, which, in turn, yield greater understanding of other people, times, and places and a deeper sense of accomplishment.

Everyone readily agrees that humans absorb the ideas of their time. How else would we conduct our daily lives and communicate with others? Language itself is time bound: it is of a place and a particular moment. Look at the opening line of John Dowland's love song, composed more than 400 years ago: "My thoughts are wingde with hops" (see Fig. 11.17). Because spelling was not standardized then, it was acceptable to write "winged" as "wingde." But what about "hops"? Is the singer really sending warm thoughts to a lover with a package of the grain used as the basic flavoring ingredient of beer? Unlikely. "Hops" is an alternative spelling of "hopes"; thus the singer's thoughts are winged with hopes. Like language, the vocabularies of all the visual and tonal arts are needed to be understood as they were in their times.

A related question concerns the extent to which an artist's personal thoughts and unique experiences counter the tug of the dominant culture. For art—and life—this remains an intriguing conundrum, but we can illuminate some of its features.

During much of Western history, visual artists, architects, composers, and playwrights were considered craftspeople who worked for royals, leaders, and the wealthy. The struggle for individual recognition began in earnest during the Renaissance, but the patronage system was still thriving in the eighteenth century, especially in music, where it hung on longer than in the other arts. For example, during his short life, Mozart struggled against the constraints of patronage, but he did not succeed in making a living without giving music lessons and taking on commissions from royals who felt free to criticize his compositions. His most famous complaint came from Emperor Joseph II, who is said to have grumbled, "too many notes, my dear Mozart, too many notes." Of course, society has recognized some extraordinarily talented individuals in the past, like Imhotep in Egypt and Praxiteles in Greece (Fig. Intro.1), who were singled out for special treatment and acclaim. But the average artist could look forward to an apprenticeship with a master artist, much as a would-be carpenter would train in the workshop of an accomplished woodworker. The young artist might eventually gain a small commission for a specific work, such as a portrait, and would have to pay close attention to the patron's instructions about how to paint it. Similarly, a composer or a poet had to heed carefully the suggestions of the patron for a specific form of music or literature, such as an epithalamium, which is a song or a poem for a wedding, or an elegy, which is a reflection on sorrow written to memorialize someone who has died. In works such as these, self-expression or social commentary were either out of the question or driven so deep into the work's symbols and juxtapositions that their meaning was obscured.

In prohibitive circumstances such as these, artists, writers, and composers tended to distinguish themselves through technical excellence: for example, Praxiteles developed ways to make marble look like flesh, and Zeuxis is said to have achieved such an illusion of reality in one of his paintings that the birds came to peck at a bunch of grapes he depicted.

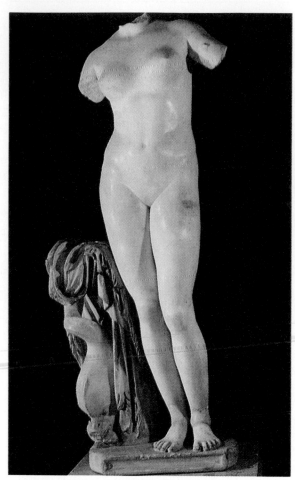

Intro.1 *Aphrodite of Cyrene.* Roman copy of c. 100 BCE. After Praxitelean original, found at Cyrene, North Africa. Marble, height 5′. Museo Archeologio Nazionale, Rome.

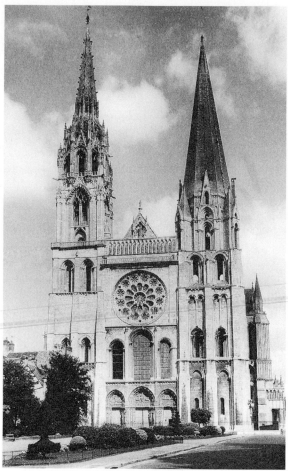

Intro.2 West facade, Chartres Cathedral. Portals and lancet windows, c. 1145; south tower (right), c. 1180, height 344′; north spire (left), 1507–1513, height 377′. Length of cathedral 427′, width of facade 157′.

If we want to understand how art is an expression of the ideas and values of the time in which it was created—indeed, how the arts actively shaped the perceptions of people living in a particular historical period—we must consider that for most of Western history, the arts have been an indirect account of the worldview held by a powerful few and interpreted through the talents of anonymous others. Unidentified persons built the pyramids and the Gothic cathedrals (Fig. Intro.2). From time to time, they slipped in a fanciful figure, but mostly, they labored under the direction of a builder. The builder took orders from a master-builder, who paid close attention to the whims and wishes of a member of the court or the church.

As wealth spread to more people, especially people who were outside court and church circles, the arts found that new patrons and artists often could entertain new ideas and technical approaches. One sees the influence of freshly minted wealth in the art of seventeenth-century Holland, where merchants and bankers identified them-

selves as a class different and more progressive than the landed aristocracy (Fig. Intro.3). Painters became entrepreneurs like their new patrons. They developed signature styles and worked in particular genres, such as portraiture or landscape painting. They also began a practice that is universal today: they made paintings "on spec," meaning they created canvases before they knew whom the buyers would be.

One of the greatest changes in Western art occurred in the late eighteenth and early nineteenth centuries, during the Romantic Movement, when artists, writers, and composers actively redefined themselves as people whose art sprang from special sensibilities and deep feelings. Because the Romantics believed art was rooted in their uniqueness, they did not want to be told how and what to create. This revolution could not have taken place without the multifaceted social upheaval in which the power of the aristocracy and the church were rapidly replaced by the increasing middle class, who demanded political power and educational

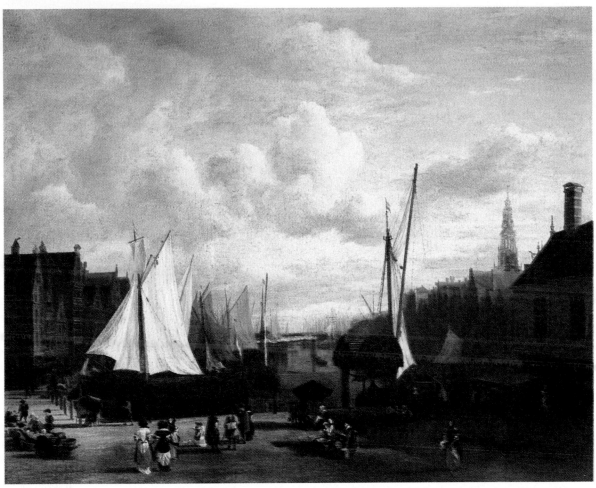

Intro.3 Jacob van Ruisdael. *Quay at Amsterdam,* c. 1670. Oil on canvas, 1′8¾″ × 2′2″.

advantages in accord with their commercial success and industrial ingenuity. In an important sense, the middle classes were the first Romantics, relying not on tradition but on imagination. Despite the poet William Butler Yeats's 1931 assertion that he and his generation of writers were the last Romantics, Western culture is still enamored by the self-made individual who appears to be a pathbreaker. The transition from the Romantic poet to the Romantic engineer and the Romantic computer geek has been a smooth one. Artists today mostly operate with the Romantic assumption that their work needs to be different—to have a signature style—that stood apart from that of other artists. For most of the past, this idea would have been judged foolish or fanatical.

No one has defined the number of people necessary to promote the development of art. Bands of seminomadic Ice-Age people may have included no more than thirty individuals, yet they generated extraordinary art and kept it going for centuries. This book is organized around the notion of cultural centers, such as cities, palaces, churches, and monasteries, where some of the most influen-

tial Western art and music was created. In recent decades, cultural historians have looked beyond many of the dominant towns and courts, identifying art, architecture, and music of significant originality created outside the most studied cultural centers, such as Paris, London, Rome, and New York. They have invented a lively new history and sociology of the arts that is enriching and enlarging the humanities.

They have also made it difficult to imagine how a history of the arts of the West could fit between two covers! *Arts & Ideas,* then, is not intended as an exhaustive survey but rather as a sampling of the ways in which the Western arts interacted and how they reverberate with the central ideas of specific times and places. As William Fleming explained in the ninth edition of this book: "the whole concept is not to present a chronologically complete history, but to select and study in depth the major styles and works within the periods and cultures that produced them." Readers should keep in mind that this approach and scope represent a fraction—albeit a familiar one—of the world's art.

Studying the Western arts in this way is not, in itself, a slight to other art practices and histories. Most of the readers of this text live in the midst of Western culture and values. Consequently, they need the analytical and critical tools with which to understand how cultural history continues to have a bearing not only on the arts today but also on contemporary society. By emphasizing how various cultural centers defined and developed the arts, *Arts & Ideas* becomes a platform from which readers can proceed to look at Western and non-Western art without falling prey to the prejudice that art is a universal impulse that fully transcends the boundaries of time and culture. Indeed, recent scholarship suggests that our sense of fair play, combined with our excitement about the arts in other cultures, has led to a serious, if well-meaning, distortion of art-making in those very cultures. For example, as Craig Clunas argues in his study on the arts of China, the notion of a collective entity called the arts is a relatively recent invention there. No one living during that land's long history before the nineteenth century would think of putting painting, sculpture, and ceramics in the same field of inquiry, even though China has a venerable tradition of arts criticism and collecting.[1]

Although this book highlights the intellectual terrain shared by artists and their times, it is important to keep in mind that sharing ideas does not mean that art objects are otherwise alike. Art media, like cultures, differ. They respond to, present, and inhabit ideas differently. When writers, composers, and architects create, they generally do so with the expectation that they can enlarge themes over time. In effect, they orchestrate the emergence of ideas for listeners and viewers. By contrast, many sculptors and painters plan their works to be taken in their entirety, and then, perhaps, examined in their particular parts. Of course, there are similarities between these two groups. The facade of a building may be viewed much as a painting is, and a series of sculptures or paintings may be programmed much in the way a play is. Nevertheless, in some of the most meaningful art, form cannot be separated from idea. Splashes of blood-red paint spattering a canvas carry meanings for which there are no words (Fig. Intro.4). The triumphant thump of a dancer's feet hitting the stage's floor is heard by the ear and perceived by the kinesthetic sense, that is, the body's awareness and identification with another human form. The scintillating, verbal barrage of a play by Shakespeare is simultaneously an auditory and intellectual experience in which form and

idea have merged. Different art media exist because the scope of human responsiveness and the intricacy of thought are so broad that one or two media would fail to express their range or subtleties. The arts, developed so closely in relation to the senses, are remarkably alike across cultures, even though the contexts in which they are practiced vary widely, for instance, from religion to entertainment.

When he wrote *Arts & Ideas,* William Fleming used the word style in a particular sense, defined by cultural historian Meyer Schapiro. Rather than suggesting superficial fashion, style is "a system of forms with a quality and a meaningful expression through which the personality of the artist and the broad outlook of a group are visible." It is also, Schapiro wrote, "a vehicle of expression within the group, communicating and fixing certain values of religious, social, and moral life through the emotional suggestiveness of forms."[2] At the same time, the lifetimes of the ideas and art forms related by style do not necessarily correspond with momentous historical events. For instance, Renaissance experimentation with perspective and study of the human form continued despite wars that toppled the rulers of Italian regions and cities. Moreover, in any historical moment, the arts are not synchronized like a row of clocks. Conventions—think of the wedding march by Felix Mendelssohn—become entrenched and are expected to be part of ceremonies that take place decades, even centuries later. As a result, some arts remain closely tied to tradition, while social circumstances allow others to be more innovative. Also, contact between and among the arts, especially before modern communications and transportation, cannot be assumed. For centuries, artists in Ireland were unaware of Greek sculpture. Conversely, the frequent, multiple invasions of Cyprus gave artists Phoenician, Greek, and Roman influences, to name just a few.

Whether through custom or taste, certain art objects are considered to transcend their immediate purposes and circumstances. Ever since Rome, Greek art, literature, and philosophy have been deemed enduringly worthwhile and ripe for reinterpretation through contemporary thoughts and conditions. For example, in 2003, more than 1,000 readings of Aristophanes's ancient Greek play, *Lysistrata,* were performed in fifty-nine countries in a global antiwar effort. Audiences today find Mozart's music a profound humanistic statement that was probably not there for his eighteenth-century listeners, perhaps because they felt free to talk, flirt, or eat during the per-

[1]Craig Clunas, *Art in China* (New York: Oxford University Press, 1997), pp. 9–15.

[2]Meyer Schapiro, "Style" in *Theory and Philosophy of Art: Style, Artist, and Society* (New York: George Braziller, 1994), pp. 51–52.

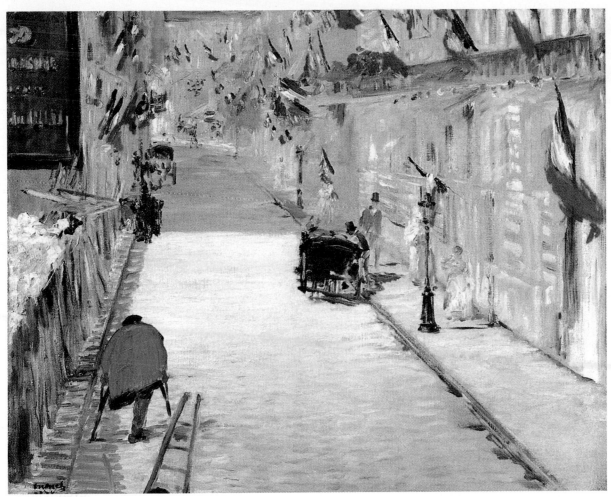

Intro.4 Édouard Manet. *Rue Mosnier, Paris, Decorated with Flags on June 30, 1878*, 1878. Oil on canvas, 2′1½″ × 2′7½″.

formances. Perhaps the greatest examples of timeless art are Shakespeare's plays. *Romeo and Juliet* has been made as a film about contemporary life several times. During the rise of Hitler, *Richard III* was set in a future fascist England; and *Macbeth* was staged during the Vietnam War, with the characters dressed in modern military garb.

As compelling and imaginative as these efforts are, they belong more to the present that recasts them than to the past that invented them. As Erwin Panofsky, one of the most influential cultural historians, wrote, to be a historian one must remain sharply aware that one's "cultural equipment . . . would not be in harmony with that of people in another land and of a different period."[3] Few of us today would argue that the cultures and values that shape the people of the world could be easily disregarded. But when it comes to comprehending the past, and the arts in particular, we are often willing to believe that understanding art is simply a matter

of reacting to it. No one can deny that powerful emotional reactions to paintings, music, theater, architecture, film, photography, dance, and the other arts are sometimes life-altering experiences that draw us in and make us want to know more. Yet to grant a work of art its due means attempting to recreate the circumstances of its creation, knowing full well that—barring the invention of a time machine equipped with instant language translators—one will always fall short of complete understanding.

Aboard a 5AM plane to Egypt's Luxor and the Valley of the Kings, watching the dawn color the Nile River, or standing on the windswept hill of Pergamon in western Turkey, where the Altar of Zeus once stood high above the sea, are exhilarating experiences that I recall with great contentment. Equally thrilling was the way in which reading the works of the pioneering Egyptologists and classicists enriched and broadened my understanding of those places and their pasts. History, as William Fleming wrote, can be joyous and adventuresome. It is my hope that this book brings you knowledge mixed as it ought to be with pleasure and excitement.

[3]Erwin Panofsky, "The History of Art as a Humanistic Discipline," in *Meaning in the Visual Arts* (Garden City, NJ: Doubleday Anchor, 1955), p. 17.

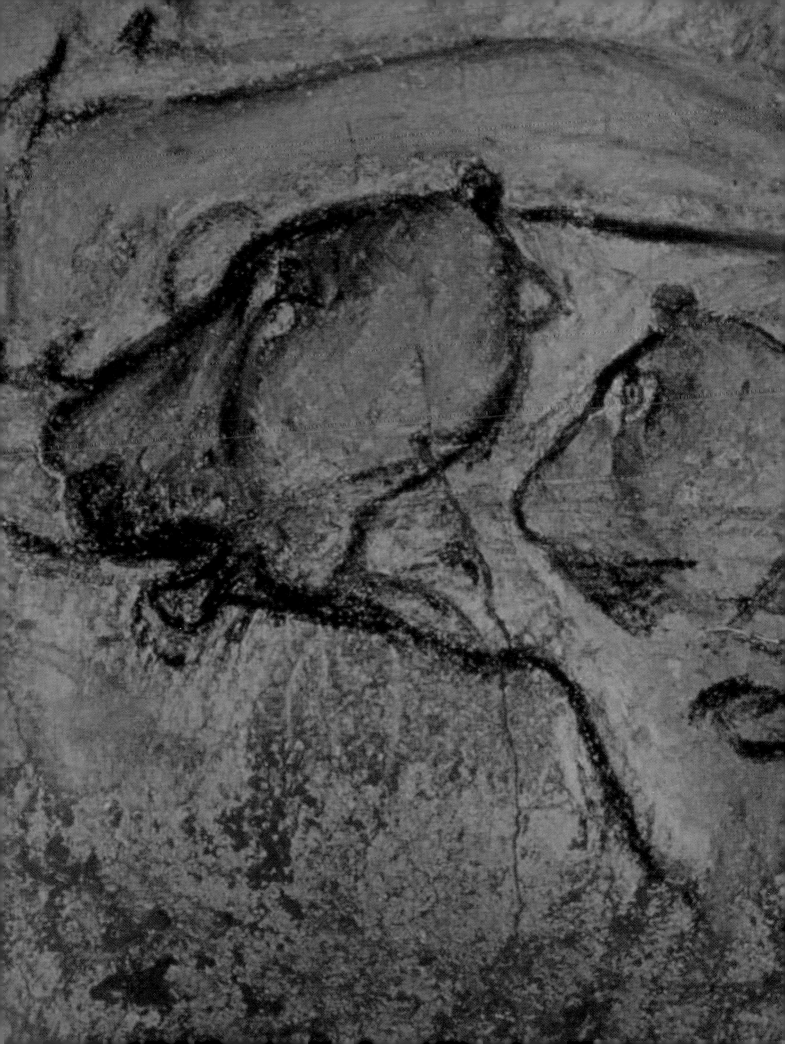

C H A P T E R

THE ORIGINS OF WESTERN ART

THE FIRST ART MAY be older than we humans are. Millions of years ago, a proto-human living in Africa or Asia might have pick up a stick and admired it, not as a tool but as an object of pleasing proportions. That same stick may have served to remind the *hominid,* as proto-humans are called, of an event in the past, or it might have signified a force of nature, such as lightning. Scholars think that certain very early tools were shaped with such attention to design that the craft of making them developed into an art before hominids became fully human.

Some questions about the origins of art may never be answered. The earliest instance of art made by *Homo sapiens*—that is, people like us—is only a little clearer. The skeletal remains of *Homo sapiens* have been dated to about 100,000 years ago in Africa and a bit later in southwestern Asia. If these people fashioned images in sand or wood, decorated their bodies with paint, or contrived intricate dances, their efforts necessarily perished in the course of time. The first imagery that survived in abundance was made by a group of humans called *Cro-Magnons,* named after the town in France where their remains were found in 1868.

THE CRO-MAGNONS

The Cro-Magnons lived a seminomadic life in the cold climate of the Ice Age, whose glaciers had already waxed and waned for more than 1.5 million years. People of this Ice Age followed the seasonal migrations of herds of animals, such as reindeer, goats, and bison. They used stone-tipped lances to hunt, sharpened stone blades for cutting, and fashioned bone harpoons to spear fish. They also gathered fruits and seeds. Humans during this time discovered how to make fire to warm the shallow cavelike areas beneath rocky overhangs, in which they lived and to which they seem to have returned over many generations as they coped with the advancing and retreating ice shield that drove the animals they hunted to new grasslands.

Despite the name given them in the nineteenth century, Cro-Magnons did not arise in what is now France; rather, they seem to have originated in western Asia. In fact, several types of early humans may have coexisted in Europe, Africa, and Asia. One of the mysteries of the past is what ultimately became of these people. For example, a less developed group of humans was named *Neanderthal* for the place in Germany where evidence of their existence was located in 1856. Like the Cro-Magnons, they lived not only in Europe but also in parts of central and southwestern Asia. Recent evidence from Neanderthal dwelling sites indicates that they were not the savage brutes of horror movies and cartoons. They enjoyed family relations that included caring for disabled and elderly members of their clans. Research suggests that Cro-Magnons and Neanderthals lived in Europe at the same time, about 40,000 years ago, and that they had contact with each other. Neanderthals seem to have died out about 30,000 years ago, just at the point when the Ice Age art of the Cro-Magnons appeared. They may have been destroyed by the Cro-Magnons, or they may have perished because they could not compete with the Cro-Magnons for scarce resources. Another possibility is that they were simply absorbed into the Cro-Magnon population. Much speculation has centered on whether the Neanderthals had the physical and mental capacity for complicated speech and symbol-making that the Cro-Magnons enjoyed. Amid so much conjecture, we are certain of one profound difference between the Neanderthals and the Cro-Magnons. Both groups developed tools, used fire, decorated their bodies with red ochre, lived migratory lives, and buried their dead, sometimes leaving small memorials. But only the Cro-Magnons created an extensive art that is rich in signs and description. Recent theories suggest that the great concentration of European cave art was created in the most populated areas. Thus, the repeated images and symbols could indicate that the people in the area shared cultural values and ideas.

CAVE ART

Deep inside the twisting limestone caves of south-central France, cave artists drew what they saw with such accuracy and immediacy that later literate societies have never surpassed the sheer strength of the pictorial record they left. The herds of beasts painted and carved on cave walls and ceilings capture the essence of animality and the precarious place of these people in a world dominated by brutish forces. At Lascaux (Fig. 1.1), lively animals, seen mostly from the side, face off in a circular space that was continually repainted for hundreds of years by artists using bits of moss and naturally occurring mineral pigments and working by the light of small, hand-held oil lamps. They placed puzzling dots of pigment above the nose of the spotted bovine and what looks like a representation of a spear on the shoulder of the huge facing bull.

The 1994 discovery of the Chauvet cave in France also revealed paintings in a sophisticated style (Fig. 1.2). Forms are shaded and overlap one another to give the appearance of **perspective.** In addition, the areas above the lions' heads were deliberately scraped down to the cave's white, chalky walls to create contrast with the broad black outlines. The artists often took advantage of the natural contours of the cave surfaces so that the animal figures appear in **relief.** It is as if the natural formations of the stone suggested the

particular animal forms. Like those at Lascaux, the walls at Chauvet display abstract signs such as dots and stripes.

Why were these images created? There is no convincing evidence that the people of the Ice Age actually lived in the decorated areas of the caves. In fact, the decorated areas may have been difficult to reach. Many scholars believe that the animals may have been symbols representing the processes of nature. The making of such lifelike images might have been a means to discuss, understand, and pass down ideas about the world. The caves may also have been sanctuaries for magical rituals or initiation ceremonies for young hunters as they reached maturity and independence.

Signs that lances were hurled at the paintings point to primitive hunting rites. For the cave people, the images may have been substitutes for the animal themselves. By assaulting these images with their spears, the hunters may have hoped that they could magically subdue their real quarry. Other theories hold that the paintings may have constituted a record of seasonal animal migrations or that the beasts may have been totemic figures representing various tribal families, just as modern sports teams adopt the names of animals to symbolize strength and endurance. In addition, one cannot rule out the possibility that these amazing images may have been created simply for the sheer pleasure of making a likeness of the world the artists saw around them. In any case, the people of the Ice Age

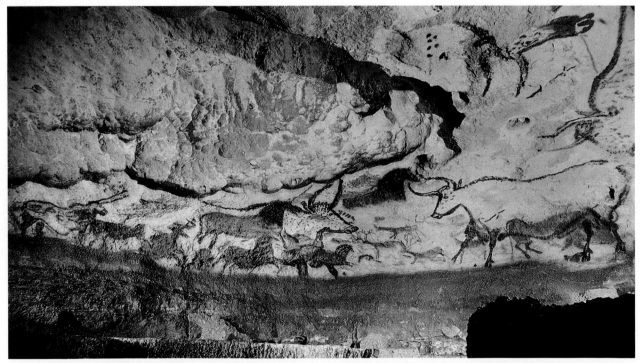

1.1   Hall of Bulls (left wall), c. 15,000–10,000 BCE. Largest bull approx. 11′6″ long, Lascaux (Dordogne), France.

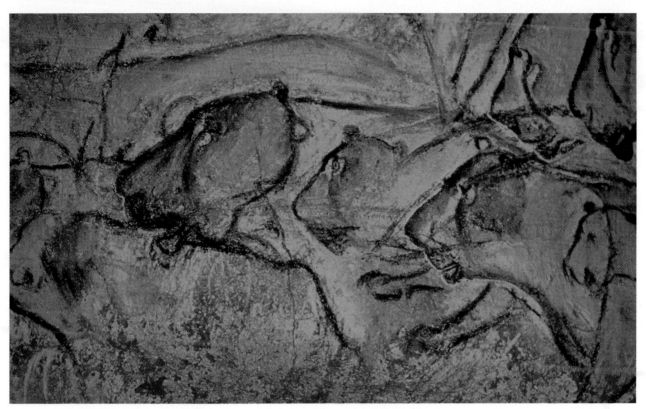

1.2   Detail of group of lions at Chauvet-Pont-d'Arc Cave. Lions hunting on the main panel in the End Chamber, Chauvet Cave, France. Scenes are rare in Paleolithic art. This one is unique.

produced art that embraced naturalism and realism, abstraction and expressionistic distortion.

Cave paintings have been discovered primarily in France and Spain, but decorated tools and portable works of art have been found throughout the huge landmass that extends from Europe to the far reaches of Siberia. A fascinating piece of broad reindeer antler found in the French Pyrenees (Fig. 1.3) is sensitively engraved with the image of deer that seem to be crossing a waterway while salmon are

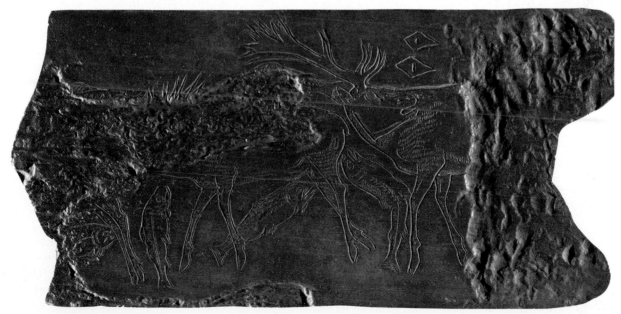

1.3   Reindeer antler decorated with a procession of stags with salmon jumping between their limbs. Musée des Antiquites Nationales, Saint-Germain-en-Laye, France.

swimming upstream. Like cave images, this picture does not have a ground line or background, yet the artist carefully etched tiny lines around the shoulders of the deer and on the fish to indicate the texture of hair and scales. To create this image, the artist must have keenly observed animal appearance and behavior. The large deer turns its head and opens its mouth, perhaps to make a sound to those who follow. This pose is repeated in other instances of Ice Age art. Above the deer's shoulder are two diamond shapes containing a small, single vertical line. Such combinations of natural observation and abstract symbols occur regularly. Although it may not constitute writing, the choice of a particular seasonal moment and the use of signs suggest that the intent was to communicate.

THE WOMAN OF WILLENDORF

Throughout the Ice Age, representations of humans are rare compared with animal images and signs. When people do appear, they usually are not treated as naturalistically as the animals. One figure, less than 5 inches tall, is the Woman of Willendorf (Fig. 1.4). Her head is crowned with small stylized curls or braids above a featureless face. She clasps huge breasts with tiny arms as she gazes downward at her swollen, possibly pregnant belly. These exaggerated sex characteristics suggest how much early people, who struggled with scarcity, would have valued health and fertility. The statue also alludes to aesthetic values. The whole compact composition can be seen as a set of cones, curves, and spheres. Even more abstract female figures than the Woman of Willendorf have been found through Europe and Russia, hinting that early people may have had contact with each other through seasonal migrations and trade.

THE TRANSITION TO AGRICULTURE

In the nineteenth century, the term **Paleolithic,** meaning "old stone," was used to describe the culture of the people of the Ice Age. These nomadic hunter-gatherers made stone tools but lacked features of more advanced life, such as pottery, settled communities, and elaborate systems of writing. However, a steady stream of research findings suggests that Paleolithic people, although they did not permanently settle in one place, regularly returned to sites such as Lascaux, used as-yet-undeciphered symbols in a manner approaching writing, and may even have done some rudimentary farming and taming of animals. Al-

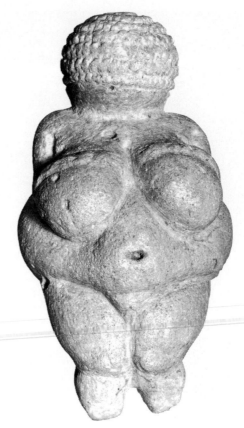

1.4   *Woman of Willendorf,* c. 30,000–25,000 BCE. Limestone, height 4¼". Naturhistorisches Museum, Vienna, Austria.

though now proved to be inaccurate, the term *Paleolithic* continues to be used because it provides a rough contrast between people of the Ice Age and the cultures that developed in the **Neolithic,** or "new stone" age, when farming, domestication of animals, and comprehensive systems of writing were developed. Of course, this vast transition, sometimes called the *agricultural revolution,* took place slowly and unevenly over thousands of years. Some remote cultures did not emerge from the Paleolithic until the twentieth century.

In an area known as the *Fertile Crescent* (see Map 1.1), the soil was more productive than that in the surrounding areas and the climate was favorable to irrigation-assisted agriculture. The Fertile Crescent extended from the Persian Gulf through the land between the Tigris and Euphrates Rivers, and then turned south, running along the Mediterranean coast and down the Nile valley. This area witnessed the transition from hunting and gathering to the beginnings of agriculture and town life.

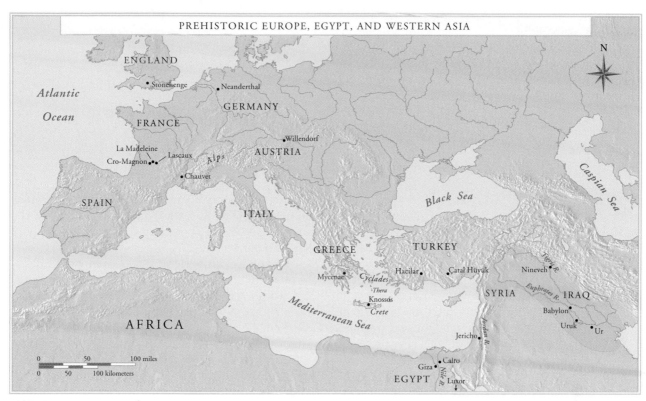

PREHISTORIC EUROPE, EGYPT, AND WESTERN ASIA

MAP 1.1

Over the course of millennia, plant cultivation and animal husbandry gradually replaced hunting and food gathering, with the result that people could live year-round in stable settlements. Similar development took place about 4,000 years ago in the Indus River valley in what is now Pakistan, as well as in the river valleys of China.

Excavations at Jericho near the Jordan River reveal that people may been attracted to the site by a natural spring thousands of years before they settled there permanently and built mud-brick houses, in about 7000 BCE. The area's location in a fertile river valley and along trade routes may have encouraged village life and the diverse occupations that come with it. The residents of Jericho built thick protective walls (although these are not the walls that came tumbling down in the Bible story) and a stone tower. Agricultural life and trade allowed citizens to accumulate surplus wealth that they needed to protect themselves from invaders, hence the walls and tower. This wealth also led to the development of more elaborate burial practices. For example, human skulls were carefully filled in and modeled with plaster. They were given seashell eyes, and pigment was sometimes added to simulate living flesh and hair (Fig. 1.5).

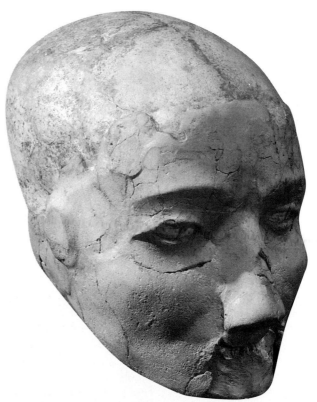

1.5   Modeled head from Jericho, c. 7000–6000 BCE, Archeologicial Museum, Amman, Jordan.

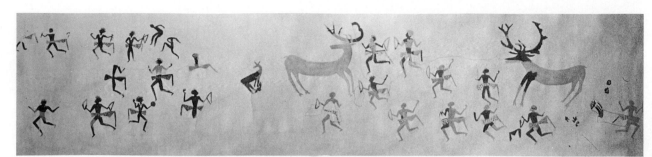

1.6   Deer hunt, detail of a copy of a painting from Level III, Çatal Hüyük (modern Turkey), c. 5750 BCE.

Whereas Ice Age art was concerned largely with renderings of animals and signs, human images appeared more frequently in these early settlements. At Çatal Hüyük, the largest known Neolithic settlement in what is now Turkey, 8,000 people built 2,000 houses with shared walls. The houses could be entered only through openings in the flat roofs. Invaders would have to drop down into the houses, where they might be trapped. Some of the houses at Çatal Hüyük seem to have been used as shrines, where artists represented groups of people in what seems to be an early attempt to tell a story (Fig. 1.6). Some anthropologists estimate that the wall paintings at Çatal Hüyük were repainted more than 100 times. One theory holds that as the sedentary lifestyle of agricultural people became more common, occupational specialization and specific gender roles became more pronounced. But at Çatal Hüyük, recent excavations in the 1990s revealed no conclusive evidence that gender determined roles in society.

Outside the Fertile Crescent, hunting and gathering may have supplemented agriculture for a long time before settled town life appeared. Across the same large European and Asian landmass where Ice Age female figures were found—but several millennia later when the climate had moderated—people built intriguing stone structures. One of these, con-

centric stone circles in southern England known as Stonehenge (Fig. 1.7), was laid out so as to allow the sun to rise over a special stone on the first day of the summer solstice.

Of course, an agricultural people would be interested in observing and predicting the seasons, but would they have labored for years simply to construct a device that would be just as useful if it were smaller? Stonehenge would have taken many years and a great deal of labor, far more effort than would logically have been expended for a calendar. Some of Stonehenge's **megaliths,** or large stones, were brought almost 200 miles to the site. The stones were shaped, and a peglike projection was fashioned on the top of each. The stones were then set up vertically, perhaps by first dragging each stone into a pit and then pulling it upright. Capping stones, with holes that fit the projections on the tops of the upright stones, were raised and placed snugly down on the pegs. This type of construction is called ***post and lintel.***

MESOPOTAMIAN CIVILIZATIONS

The earliest Near Eastern settlements were established in the region known as Mesopotamia, a Greek word meaning the land between the two

1.7   Stonehenge, c. 2550–1600 BCE. Circle is 97′ diameter; trilithons approx. 24′ high. Salisbury Plain, Wiltshire, England.

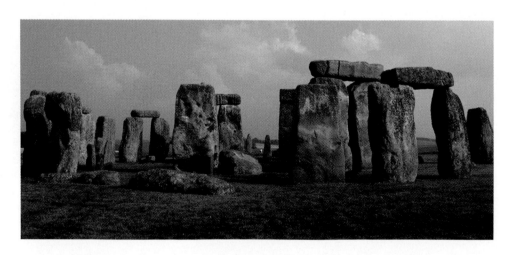

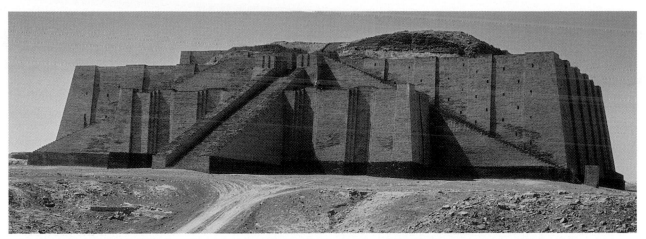

1.8 Ziggurat (northeastern facade with restored stairs), Ur (modern Tell Muqayyar), Iraq, c. 2100 BCE.

rivers, specifically, the Tigris and Euphrates, whose generous waters were brought under control by a system of dikes and irrigation canals. In about 4000 BCE, the land of Sumer (in what is now southern Iraq) was inhabited by a people who developed a highly organized society capable of public works projects such as dams. The Sumerians invented an early numerical system and also devised a form of writing on clay tablets with wedge-shaped characters called **cuneiform.**

THE SUMERIANS

The Sumerians believed in a pantheon of gods who personified the creative and destructive forces of nature. In their cities they typically built low temple complexes at ground level and a high temple called a **ziggurat,** which means "mountain" or "pinnacle." These massive, terraced structures were conceived as dwelling places of the gods who watched over the fortunes of the town. They were also the center of a powerful priesthood, where scribes kept records, accounts, and inventories of food and supplies. In the flat surrounding countryside, these multistoried structures rose so high that they were thought, as recorded in the Bible (Gen. 11:3–4), to "reach unto heaven." The nearly 300-foot ziggurat at Babylon, the tallest ever built, was the legendary Tower of Babel, but only the foundation remains. The ziggurat at Ur (Fig. 1.8), dating from about 2100 BCE, was also an imposing pile. The broad base of the ziggurat did not have interior rooms but was usually filled with rubble and faced with decorative brickwork. It was approached by three great stairways of 100 steps, each leading to the gatehouse some 40 feet above ground level. The corners of the massive oblong base are oriented toward the four points of the compass. Inward-sloping walls rise to

make a platform for the second stage, which in turn supported a now ruined temple at the top.

Beginning in 1922, a rich treasure of art came to light during archeological digs at the royal tombs of Ur, the biblical Ur of the Chaldees and traditional birthplace of Abraham. The jewelry, headdresses, musical instruments, and other artifacts reveal an extraordinary quality of craftsmanship. The reconstructed harp (Fig. 1.9) has a marvelously wrought

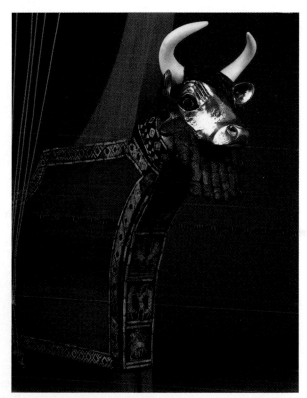

1.9 Bullheaded lyre or harp, from Ur, c. 2600–2400 BCE. Wood with gold, lapis lazuli, and shell inlay. British Museum, London, England.

golden bull's head facing the sound box. The tips of the horns, the hair, the eyes, and the human beard are carved of lapis lazuli, a precious blue stone imported from Afghanistan. The four panels below are decorated with a delicate inlay of shell and gold leaf depicting mythological scenes.

Other excavations have unearthed statuettes that were probably left by worshippers at shrines and temples (Fig. 1.10). Made of gypsum, these votive figures are not portraits but stand-ins who were to continue praying after the worshiper had left a sacred site. Their wide eyes, filled with bits of shell or lapis lazuli are characteristic of Mesopotamian art. Their large eyes have never been fully explained, but they may have been intended to register an intense religious experience. The statues are **stereotyped,** that is, made in a similar pattern. The different sizes may indicate the greater or lesser social status of the worshipers. Gudea, the devout ruler of the city of Lagash, is shown in Figure 1.11, depicted in one of many such statues that were set in temples around his city. The work is carved of diorite, a hard stone that takes a high polish and resists decay and destruction. From all accounts, Gudea was a serious but benevolent man who considered himself the "faithful shepherd" of his people. He is always shown as pensive or prayerful. In one version he is depicted with a building plan, probably the wall of a temple precinct, on his lap.

Later, from about 1791 to 1750 BCE, Hammurabi ruled a kingdom that united most of Mesopotamia. He commands a secure place in history as the codifier of the influential body of laws that were inscribed on a tall **stele** of polished black stone (Fig. 1.12). The top is a sculptured relief of Hammurabi as "the favorite shepherd" of the enthroned, flame-shouldered sun god Shamash, whose wishes were that "justice should prevail in the land" and that "the strong might not oppress the weak." Hammurabi's code did not strictly enforce equal justice for all: the upper classes and the royals enjoyed greater privileges and leniency. Slaves could be bought, sold, and readily killed. However, the code was designed to protect widows and orphans and to see that children supported their aged parents. Although a woman's first duty was to give her husband legitimate offspring, she was otherwise an independent person, free to borrow and lend money as well as to own, buy, and sell land; in some instances, women even ran businesses. Adulterous wives and their lovers, however, were sentenced to be lashed together and drowned in the river.

In Sumerian literature, the outstanding *Epic of Gilgamesh* predates Homer's *The Iliad* by some 1,500 years, and it still makes for compelling reading. Gilgamesh was a legendary hero who ruled at Uruk, the biblical Erech, in about 2700 BCE. The story is about the age-old human quest for the meaning of life in the face of death, the conflict be-

1.10   Statuettes of worshippers from the Square Temple at Eshnunna (modern Tell Asmar), Iraq, c. 2700 BCE. Gypsum inlaid with shell and black limestone, tallest figure approx. 2′6″ high. Iraq Museum, Baghdad, and Oriental Institute, University of Chicago.

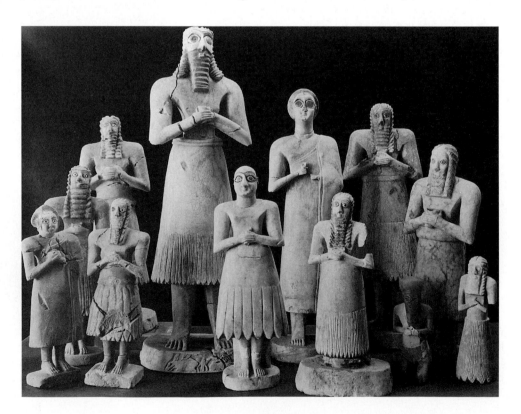

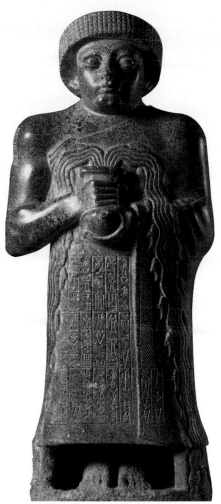

1.11   Green calcite statue of Gudea, Diorite, c. 2150 BCE, height 2′4″. Louvre, Paris, France.

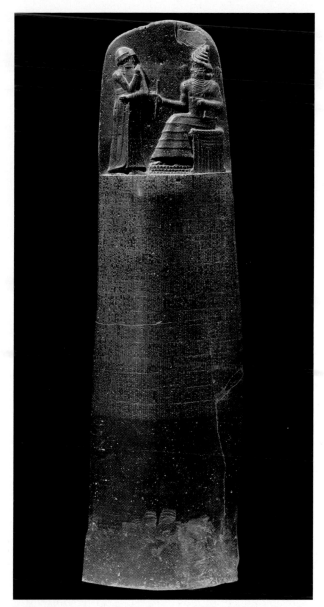

1.12   Hammurabi Stele, Susa, c. 1792–1750 BCE. Basalt, height of entire stele 7′4″. Louvre, Paris, France.

tween gods and mortals, and the consolations of love and friendship. While searching for his lost youth and immortality, Gilgamesh encounters Utnapishtim, who has survived a mighty flood by building an ark and assembling all manner of birds and beasts within it. From him Gilgamesh receives a miraculous plant that magically restores youth, only to have a wily serpent snatch it from his grasp. The epic ends with the words, "He was wise, he saw mysteries and knew secret things, he brought us a tale of the days before the flood. He went a long journey, was weary, worn out with labour, and returning engraved on a stone the whole story."

Thus, the journey ends tragically in death and disillusionment as Gilgamesh "goes back through the gate by which he came." The reader is left with the impression that the purpose of the journey may have been the journey itself and that in such a quest for self-understanding it is perhaps better to ask

questions than to receive answers. It is interesting to note that some of these tales and images would later find their way into the Book of Genesis. Among them are the stories of Noah and the flood, Nimrod the hunter, and the building of the Tower of Babel.

Music played a strong role in Mesopotamian life, from the songs of shepherds to the music rooms found in some temples. Like other rulers, Gudea encouraged musical performances. Early Mesopotamian music is represented by a complete song dating from about 1400 BCE. It was discovered in archeological excavations at ancient Ugarit (the modern Ras Shamra on the Mediterranean coast of

Syria). Recorded in cuneiform script on clay tablets, the lyrics are in the Hurrian language, which has yet to be fully deciphered. Enough is known, however, to reveal that the song is a cult hymn in praise of the mother goddess Nikkal, wife of the moon god. Texts dealing with various tuning systems for musical instruments, dating to about 1800 BCE and found in the excavations at Ur, proved helpful to the musicologists who reconstructed the melodic intervals of the song. Quite surprisingly, the scale closely approximates our major mode, that is, the modern arrangement of musical notes in an octave. Even more astonishing was the discovery that there were two different pitches meant to be sounded simultaneously: one for the voice, with words, and the other for an accompanying stringed instrument such as a harp or lyre (Fig. 1.13). Before this discovery it had been assumed that all music before the medieval invention of counterpoint was **monophonic,** that is, music consisting of a single line.

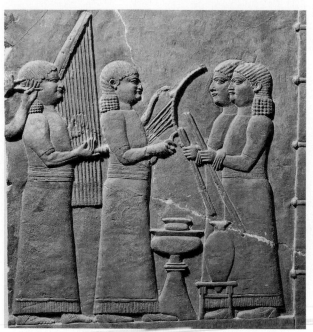

1.13 *Musicians Playing at Ashurbanipal's Banquet,* detail of a relief from the North Palace of Ashurbanipal at Nineveh, 668–627 BCE. Limestone, 1′11″ × 4′7″. British Museum, London, England.

THE ISRAELITES

After the fall of the Sumerians, Mesopotamia was dominated in turn by the Akkadians and the Assyrians. Meanwhile, nearer the Mediterranean coast the Hebrew-speaking nomadic tribe of Israel, a small but tenacious people, established a kingdom under Saul and his successors David and his son Solomon, who built a noted temple and an impressive palace in Jerusalem. After Solomon's death the kingdom was divided in two; the northern part was called Israel and the southern part Judah. In 722 BCE, Israel was conquered by the Assyrians, while Judah fell in 587 BCE to the Babylonians under Nebuchadnezzar: "And he burnt the house of the Lord, and the king's house, and all the houses of Jerusalem, and every great man's house burnt he with fire" (II Kings: 25:8–9). Among the captured Israelites was their king Jehoiachin and the prophet Ezekiel. Their lament is echoed eloquently in the words of Psalm 137:

> By the rivers of Babylon, there we sat down,
>   yea, we wept, when we remembered Zion.
> We hanged our harps, upon the willows in the
>   midst thereof.
> For there they that carried us away captive
>   required of us a song; and they that wasted
>   us required of us mirth, saying, Sing us one
>   of the songs of Zion.

Music making under such circumstances can be seen in the carved panel relief from Ashurbanipal's palace at Nineveh (Fig. 1.13). At this time,

Nebuchadnezzar's Babylon had once again become a prosperous and resplendent city, with its fabled Hanging Gardens. There were also a grand royal palace and an impressive temple complex surrounded by a magnificent wall and approached by spacious processional ways. The surviving Ishtar Gate (Fig. 1.14) was faced with enameled and molded brick that gleamed in the sun. The portal is decorated with fabulous beasts, with the dragon of Marduk and the bull of Adad, in white with yellow details, marching in solemn procession.

But as ever, pride goes before a fall. As the prophet Daniel declaimed:

> The king spake, and said, Is not this great
>   Babylon, that I have built for the house of
>   the Kingdom by the might of my power, and
>   for the honour of my majesty?
> While the word was in the king's mouth, there
>   fell a voice from heaven, saying, O king
>   Nebuchadnezzar, to thee it is spoken; The
>   kingdom is departing from thee. (Dan. 4:30–31)

True enough, after the king's death the city was soon under siege, and this time the Neo-Babylonian empire fell to the Persians under Cyrus.

In the arts the Israelites were bound by the commandment from God to Moses: "Thou shalt not make unto thee any graven image, or any like-

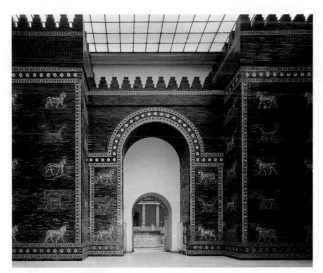

1.14 Ishtar Gate (restored), from Babylon, Iraq, c. 575 BCE. Enameled baked brick, height 48′9″. Antikensammlung, Staatliche Museen zu Berlin, Berlin, Germany.

ness of any thing that is in heaven above, or that is in earth beneath, or that is in the water under the earth" (Ex. 4:20). This effectively ruled out the representative arts of sculpture and painting. The Israelites did, however, build temples and palaces, all of which have perished in the course of time. Their creative thinking was channeled into the world of letters with the compilation of the Old Testament, the first part of which, from the Book of Genesis to II Kings, achieved its present form in the late fifth century BCE.

THE EGYPTIANS

Through monumental buildings, magnificent statues and murals, and representations of priestly ceremonies and royal processions, the Egyptians dramatically portrayed the concepts of divinity, kingship, and priestly authority. Egyptian artists, like those in Mesopotamia, were compelled to follow formulas in depicting the body and indicating social rank. Nevertheless, the paintings on the walls of Egyptian tombs show a keen eye for informal activities and naturalistic detail. As can be seen in the tomb of Nebamun (Fig. 1.15), the artist was concerned mostly with the picture plane, not with creating illusions of depth, modeling the figures in three dimensions, or showing them against a background. In accordance with the formulas, the heads are always drawn in profile, but the eyes are represented as if facing forward. The torsos are frontal, but the arms and legs offer a side view. Although the figures are shown from the side, they

have two left feet so that both big toes are toward the front. If a pool or river is included in a landscape, the view of it is from above, but fish, ducks, plants, and trees in and around it are shown sideways. Important persons always appear larger than their families, followers, or servants.

Once these formulas are taken into consideration, the scenes appear remarkably lifelike. Naturalistic detail is rendered so accurately that botanists and zoologists can recognize each species of plant or animal life represented. The Egyptian artist also knew how to portray the fur and feathers of animals and birds by breaking up the color surfaces with minute brushstrokes of various hues. When Nebamun, an Egyptian official, had himself depicted hunting fowl in the marshes, he was demonstrating that he would eternally enjoy sports while fulfilling his obligation to maintain the waterways and keep them free from crocodiles and hippopotamuses. Egyptian tomb art is thus a re-creation of life as it was experienced in the flesh, and these still-vital, colorful murals provide an amazingly complete and comprehensive picture of how people behaved in an ancient civilization.

SOCIAL STRUCTURE

Together with literature and other types of written records, tomb decorations offer a glimpse of everyday life. As might be expected, peasants spent much of their time in farming, herding, housekeeping, and food preparation. Although

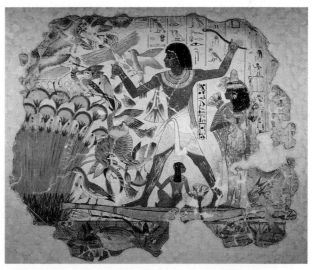

1.15 *Fowling in the Marshes,* tomb of Nebamun, Thebes, Egypt, Dynasty XVIII, c. 1400–1350 BCE. Fresco on dry plaster, approx. 2′8″ high. British Museum, London, England.

women in all classes of society achieved part of their status through male relatives, they also had legal rights of inheritance like Mesopotamian women. Land and wealth passed down through the female line, and women could manage property independent from their spouses. Powerful Egyptian gods were female as well as male. Occasionally a woman like Queen Hatshepsut ruled the country, in fact if not in title. Often, women were represented as having lighter skin than men (see Fig. 1.18). The custom probably indicated that affluent women did not work in the fields, where the sun would darken their skin like that of peasant women. On the other hand, women of all classes were not restricted to the home but were seen in markets, shops, and public events. They were depicted in wall paintings and other media accompanying men to review farm and labor activities, as well as celebrating at feasts and funerals. Women worked as priests, midwives, professional mourners, and musicians and dancers.

Egyptian society was like a pyramid. At the base were the peasants, then came the landowners and nobility, near the top was the priestly caste, and at the apex, the pharaoh. Because they were viewed as gods, pharaohs were also burdened with the responsibility to keep the universe balanced and orderly. They could be blamed for droughts and famines. Sometimes pharaohs responded to the obligation by creating socially beneficial public works, like the building of canals and irrigation systems along the Nile, which overflowed its banks each year and deposited rich, black soil on the adjacent farmland. The famous pyramids at Giza, outside the modern city of Cairo, were built not only as the most imposing structure in a complex of buildings used for the pharaoh's funeral rites and burial but probably also as a project to keep a large part of the population actively employed and fed during the annual Nile flood.

The Pyramid of Khufu (*Cheops* in Greek) is the largest and grandest of funerary monuments, meant to last forever (Fig. 1.16). Its statistics are staggering. Combining the basic geometrical forms of the square and the triangle, it was built of 2.3 million blocks of stone, each weighing about 2.5 tons. The stupendous structure covers more than 13 acres, encloses a volume of 85 million cubic feet, and is completely solid except for two small burial chambers. To line it up with the four corners of the world, it was surveyed so accurately that each of its 755-foot sides faces one of the cardinal points of the compass. The stone is so skillfully cut that joints are scarcely visible. For centuries the pyramids served as convenient quarries, so now the original smooth facing of varicolored sandstone and granite remains in only a few places.

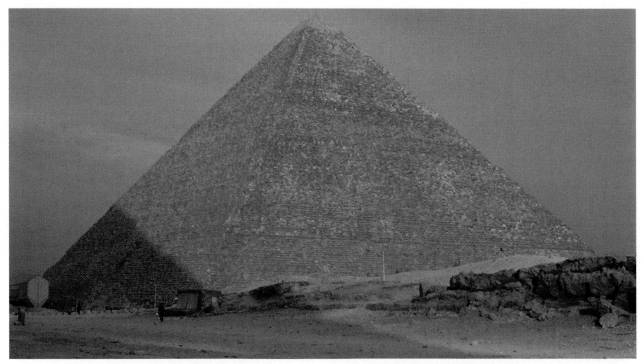

1.16   Pyramid of Khufu, Giza, Egypt.

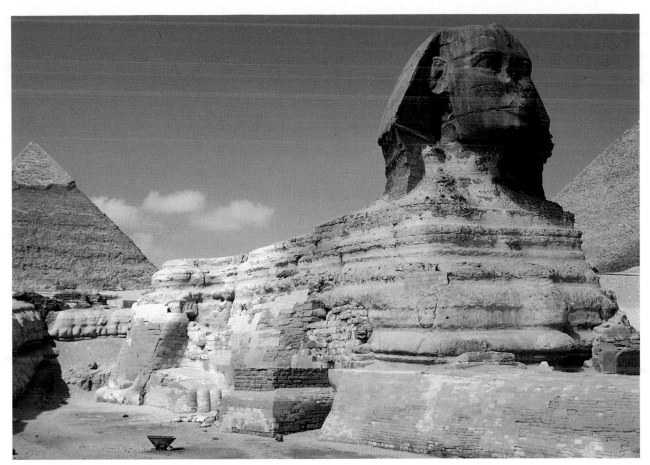

1.17 *Sphinx,* Giza, Egypt, c. 2520–2494 BCE.

The companions of this mighty monument are the pyramids of Khufu's dynastic successors and lesser members of the royal line, along with the Sphinx (Fig. 1.17), which combines the crouching body of a lion with a human head. It was placed near a temple that was connected to the pyramid of King Khafre, son of Khufu. Facing the rising sun, the Sphinx's body symbolizes immortality, while the face is thought to be a portrait of the deified King Khafre.

CONCERN WITH DEATH AND THE AFTERLIFE

The dominant concern of upper-class Egyptians was death and the afterlife. Their most important surviving literary legacy is the *Book of the Dead.* Their art forms, including mummy cases, stone sarcophagi, death masks, sculptured portraits, pyramids, temples, and tombs, were all associated with death. The main purpose of this art was not to gladden the eye of the living but to provide for the needs of the dead in the after-

life. Death for prominent Egyptians did not mean extinction but rather a continuation of life beyond the grave. To achieve immortality the body had to be preserved and, especially in later dynasties, the tomb elaborately furnished. The inner walls, floors, and ceilings were covered with hieroglyphic inscriptions that identified the deceased, recounted his or her titles and honors, and portrayed the deceased surrounded by family and friends or occupied with his or her favorite pursuits. The activities of everyday life—sowing and reaping crops, caring for farm animals, baking bread—were commonly depicted because these activities were to continue as usual in the afterlife. The wealthy and powerful had themselves depicted in various pursuits, such as hunting and fishing, supervising work in the fields, and making offerings to the gods.

After the mummy itself, the next most important object in the tomb was the image of the deceased. Such a statue was considered the vessel of

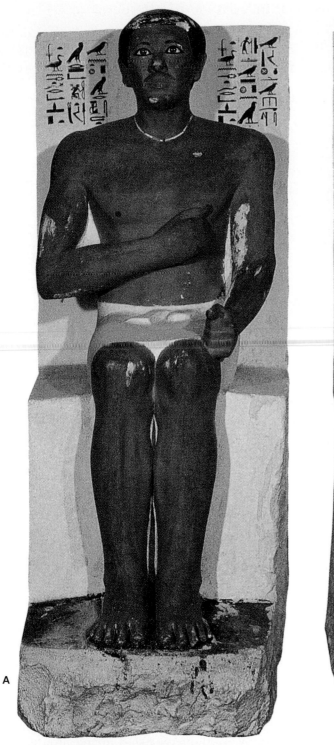
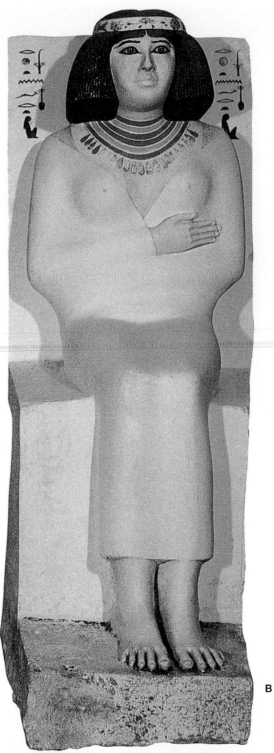

1.18   (A) Prince Rahotep and (B) Nofret, c. 2610 BCE. Painted limestone, height 3′11¼″. Egyptian Museum, Cairo, Egypt.

the deceased's immortal other self, or ***ka.*** A pair of these ka statues represent Prince Rahotep and his wife Nofret (Fig. 1.18). Even after thousands of years, they preserve their original freshness. Statues like these might have found a temporary spot in a royal home, but these works were intended primarily for the tomb.

TEMPLES AND TEMPLE DECORATION

The priestly caste had a major influence on the design and decoration of Egypt's temples. From its origins in the practice of occult magic, this group gradually gained in scientific knowledge and social influence. The priests were skilled in geometry and mathematics, knew the heavens and the movements of stars, and could predict the time when the Nile would overflow and bring renewed life to fields and gardens. Only the priests and the well-to-do were allowed within temple precincts. The privileged worshipers approached the temples by broad avenues and entered through massive **pylons,** or gateways, into a forecourt. **Hypostyle** halls of giant columns lay beyond. These columns were often carved with hieroglyphic inscriptions, as in the Temple of Amon (Fig. 1.19). The colossal statues of Ramses II flanking the entrance to this temple typify the aloof, rigid, unchangeable images of the pharaohs. These sculptured forms provide no suggestion of movement to disturb their majestic calm, on which the tranquility of the universe was thought to depend. Strict convention dictated the pose, with its severe frontality, stylized ceremonial beard, and hands placed upon the knees. As the direct descendant of Horus, god of the skies, the pharaoh appeared as the absolute ruler.

AKHENATON AND TUTANKHAMEN

An exception to these rigid and stylized representations of pharaohs occurred during the reign of Amenhotep IV, who rejected the many gods and rituals of his ancestors, adopted monotheism, and changed his name to Akhenaton ("Beneficial of the Aton," the universal and sole god of the sun). Akhenaton's vision is expressed in his eloquent *Hymn to the Sun,* which begins:

> Thou appearest beautifully on the horizon of
>   heaven, Thou living Aton, the beginning
>   of life.
> When thou art risen on the eastern horizon,
>   Thou hast filled every land with thy beauty.
> Thou art gracious, great, glistening, and high
>   over every land; Thy rays encompass the
>   lands to the limit of all thou hast made.

An unfinished bust of Akhenaton's beautiful queen, Nefertiti, was found at Tel el Amarna, the new town Akhenaton built to give a fresh start to his religion (Fig. 1.20). Despite the royal

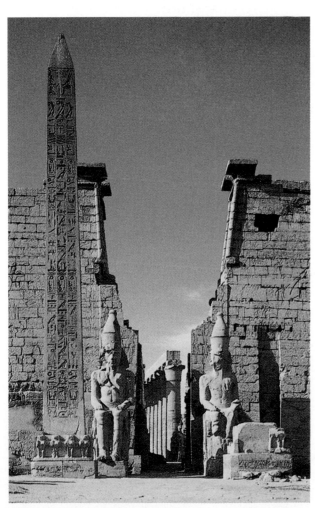

1.19   Temple of Amon. Luxor, Egypt, 1290–1224 BCE.

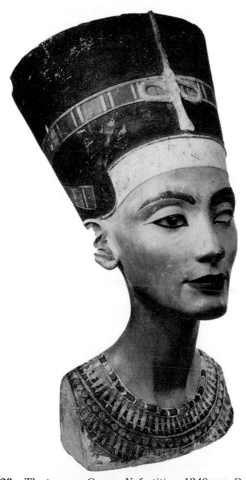

1.20   Thutmose. *Queen Nefertiti,* c. 1340 BCE. Painted limestone with inlaid glass eye, height 1′8″. Aegyptische Sammlung, Staatliche Museen, Berlin, Germany.

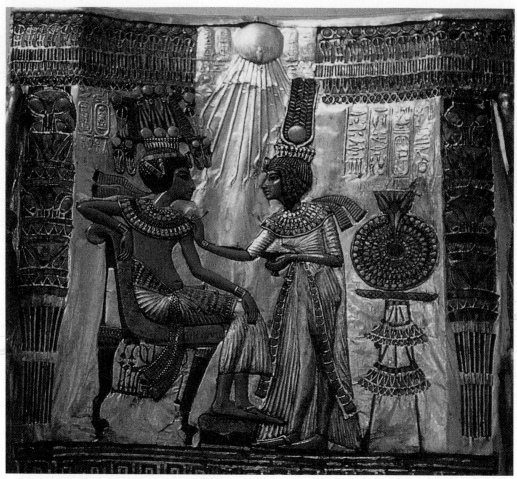

1.21 Back of Tutankhamen's throne, from Thebes, c. 1300 BCE. Wood covered with gold leaf and colored inlays of faience, glass, and stone; back width 1′9″. Egyptian Museum, Cairo, Egypt.

headdress, regal dignity, conventional elongated neck, and bright paint, the queen's official sculptor, Thutmose, let the personality of his subject show through. Breaking with precedent, Akhenaton allowed himself to be portrayed informally as he offered his queen a flower and caressed his baby daughter, with Nefertiti holding two infant princesses on her lap.

Akhenaton's death resulted in the restoration of polytheism as Egypt's official religion, but the relative informality of the art he preferred carried over briefly into the reign of his successor, King Tutankhamen, famous because his is the only Pharaonic tomb found in modern times almost intact and unplundered. On the back of Tutankhamen's throne (Fig. 1.21), the king is shown in a relaxed attitude talking with his wife while the sun god bestows his divine blessing with many raylike hands.

THE AEGEAN

Other important ancient civilizations arose in the Aegean region: the Minoan on the island of Crete as well as on the Cycladic Islands, and later the Mycenaean on the Peloponnesian peninsula of mainland Greece. The residents of Crete were mobile, seafaring folk who developed a prosperous import–export economy based on trade. The gentle Mediterranean climate enabled them to produce enough food to be self-sufficient, and even to create surplus products. They traded olive oil, wine, pottery, and finely wrought crafts such as gold and silver cups, jewelry, and vases for other supplies. In the process they also gathered knowledge about other civilizations, their histories and lore, and their ideas and ways of life.

THE MINOANS

About 1700 BCE, the people known as Minoans for the mythological king Minos began to rebuild palaces that had been destroyed by an earthquake. These palaces functioned both as royal residences and as business centers. The palace complex at Knossos was constructed around a rectangular central courtyard that could be entered only by circuitous routes through the rooms surrounding it. This confusing layout may have given rise to the legend of the labyrinth or maze that was thought to have contained an inner courtyard where the Minotaur, a half-man/ half-bull monster who fed on hapless youths, was found and slain by the Athenian hero Theseus with the help of a thread spun by the Minoan princess Ariadne.

Large areas of the palace were set aside for storage of wine and oil. Its interior walls were decorated with lively *frescoes,* including a fascinating scene that seems to show a bronze skinned acrobat tumbling over the back of a bull (Fig. 1.22). The much-restored wall painting portrays light-skinned figures, possibly women, on either side of an animal that looks more like a child's rocking horse than the aggressive bulls of Ice Age art. If the two light-skinned figures are female and the tumbler male, the artist has employed the conventional body colors used in Egyptian art to signify that males worked outdoors in the sun while upper-class women were sheltered in the home.

Unlike the people of Mesopotamia and Egypt, the people of Crete and the Cycladic Islands did not have to fear invasion by land armies. Although their palaces did not include large defensive barriers, some fortifications have been found for protection against naval attacks. They do not seem to have had an organized religious life, as the Egyptians did. Along roadsides, in caves, or on mountaintops there were small shrines with votive figures dedicated to heroes or local deities.

Minoan culture, and perhaps political and economic dominion, spread northward to the Cycladic Islands. There the Minoans would have encountered traces of an agricultural people whose artists had been creating marble figures ranging in size from a few inches tall to life size.

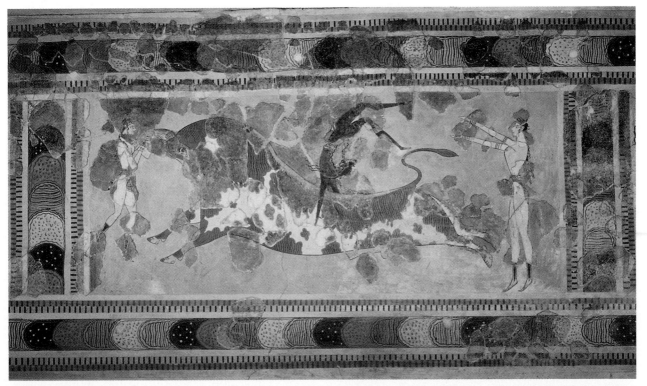

1.22 *Bull-leaping* fresco, from the palace at Knossos (Crete), Greece, c. 1450–1400 BCE. Approx. 2′8″ high, including border. Archeological Museum, Herakleion, Greece.

The statues (Fig. 1.23), which were first made about 3000 BCE, were shaped like flattened ovals. Moreover, they could not stand on their own. Like the ka statues of Egypt, they were mostly found in tombs. Their strange, shield-shaped faces tilt back in the manner of the heads of Mesopotamian worshipping figures. Most of the pigment that was applied to the figures has worn off, and we cannot guess how they were painted. Were these carved figures goddesses, fertility cult forms, guides to the underworld, or spirits of the dead?

On the island of Thera (also called Santorini), frescoes at the town now named Akrotiri are among the best preserved Minoan examples. Entering some of the rooms must have been like walking into a flower garden filled with songbirds on the wing (Fig. 1.24). In some scenes, one sees cats chasing ducks on riverbanks or lion and bull hunts in progress. Other scenes depict dancing figures in gauzy drapery. The subjects were mostly everyday events, technically known as **genre** scenes: fishing, women at their daily chores, children playing, and sporting activities such as a youthful boxing match. All are done with a lightness of touch, a lively line, a love of bright colors, and a fondness for capturing the fleeting moment.

THE MYCENAEANS

The decline of the Minoan civilization, once thought to have been provoked by a violent volcanic explosion on Thera about 1500 BCE that darkened the area with ash for hundreds of miles, was accompanied by the rise of the Mycenaeans on the Greek mainland. The Mycenaeans challenged the Minoan command of the seas and eventually took over Crete, apparently without much of a struggle. Mycenaean culture was shaped by their harsh environment and the need to defend themselves on land by the sword. Stout fortifications enclosed their palace complexes; the farming folk lived outside the walls in mud-brick or wooden houses with earthen floors. Among the most renowned Mycenaean structures still surviving is the Lion Gate at Mycenae (Fig. 1.25), which dates from about 1250 BCE. It was the entrance portal to the fortified citadel. Twin rampant lions carved in bold relief appear above the doorway. The workmanship seems rough, but the heraldic image signifying power and strength undoubtedly outweighed the need for sculptural refinement. The nearby beehive-shaped royal tombs, however, with their 44-foot-high domes, are marked by finely dressed and skillfully joined stone masonry, obviously built to last for the ages.

Mycenae flourished during the period vividly described in Homer's epic poems about the Trojan War. The descendants of the royal line founded by King Atreus of Mycenae found their way into Greek

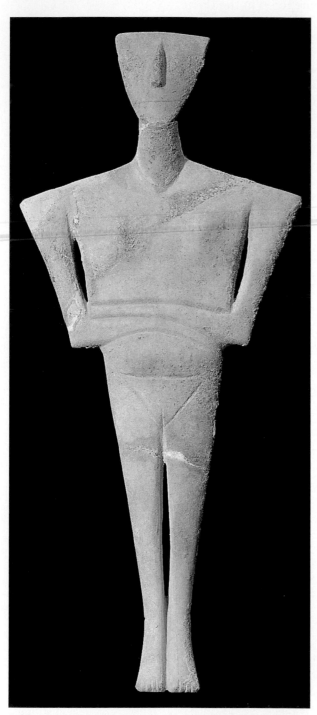

1.23   Cycladic figure, Greece, c. 2500–2300 BCE. Marble, approx. 1′6″ high. National Archaeological Museum, Athens, Greece.

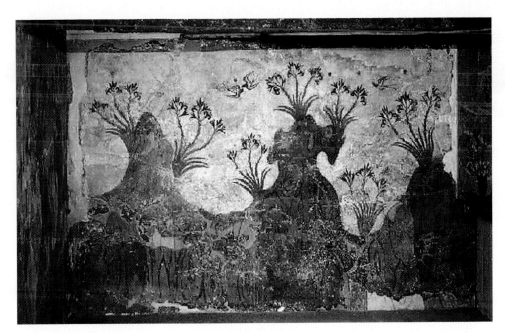

1.24 Mural from Thera. Room with landscape frescoes, House Delta, Thera. Minoan, c. 1500 BCE. National Archaeological Museum, Athens, Greece.

legends and folklore, and especially the plays of the major Athenian dramatists—Aeschylus, Sophocles, and Euripides. Their monumental tragedies tell how one of Atreus's sons, Agamemnon, married his cousin Clytemnestra and fathered Orestes, Electra, and Iphigenia. The other son, Menelaus, married the beauteous Helen, who was abducted by the Trojan prince Paris; this action was the reputed cause of the Trojan War as described by Homer in *The Iliad.*

When the Dorian Greeks migrated from the north in the twelfth century BCE, the Mycenaean settlements were burned and pillaged, thus bring-ing their culture to an abrupt end. In historical perspective, Mycenaean civilization can be considered either as a postscript to the Minoan or as a transitional time pointing toward the classical period of Greek and Roman civilization.

IDEAS

We may never know how and where art first began, but once it was established, Western art's early uses were remarkably alike across cultures and time periods. From cave paintings to the

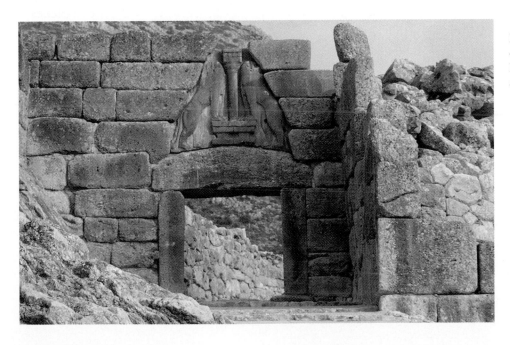

1.25 Lion Gate at Mycenae, Greece, c. 1300–1250 BCE. Limestone, relief panel approx. 9′6″ high.

Bull Leaping fresco at the Minoan palace of Knossos (Fig. 1.22), art was closely related to religious activity, ceremonies of initiation, and group identity. Art was also used to show power, wealth, and position in society. Someone approaching the Ishtar Gate of Babylon (Fig. 1.14) could not help but be struck by the figures of dragons and bulls alternating on its facade and, by implication, the authority of the city's ruler to command that such works be created.

The physical appearance and distinctive character traits of individuals were seldom the subjects of early art. The Woman of Willendorf is not a particular person but a symbol of human regeneration. Sumerian worshipper figures (Fig. 1.10) are somewhat differentiated in their appearance and garb, yet their faces and expressions are very similar. Even the slim, modeled face of Nefertiti (Fig. 1.20), which looks so much like a modern woman, may have resulted from the art principles of the time, which required artists to elongate forms, especially the head and neck.

In early societies, individuals seem to have been selected at a young age for their ability to draw, sculpt, plan buildings, or play music. Pharaohs and kings fostered training in the arts and sponsored schools where techniques were passed from one generation to the next. Along with olive oil and wine, the Minoans traded useful and decorative pottery and fine gold pieces treasured throughout the Aegean area. Eventually, Minoan artists also migrated to fulfill demand for their jewelry.

It is reasonable to assume that being an artist was one of the earliest occupations. Nevertheless, artists and musicians were considered workers. Their low status is evidenced by the fact that they usually did not sign their work. On the other hand, pharaohs like Akhenaton wrote poetry, and well-to-do Mesopotamians prided themselves on their ability to compose music.

Naturalism—that is, depiction of the world as the eye sees it—made a fleeting appearance in Egyptian art, for instance, in the birds and foliage portrayed in the wall painting from the tomb of Nebamun (Fig. 1.15). It also arose sporadically in classical art, but it did not begin its steady development until the Renaissance. In other words, realistic representation is relatively new in Western art. Its development took place in tandem with the advancement of science and technology, as well as with the expansion of Western commercial interests in other parts of the world.

For much of human history, naturalistic depiction was rejected in favor of rich symbolic meaning and suggestion. For some, realistic description was a distraction from the search for eternal truth; for others, it was an insult to the Creator. In sum, the idea that one should paint a bird that could fool the eye would have been as ill considered as making music that only imitated birdsong.

YOUR RESOURCES

- *Exploring Humanities CD-ROM*
  - Interactive Map: Prehistoric Europe and the Near East

  - Readings—*Epic of Gilgamesh, The Iliad, The Odyssey, Law Code of Hammurabi*

- *Web Site*

  http://art.wadsworth.com/fleming10

  - Chapter 1 Quiz

  - Links

Origins of Western Art (all dates approximate)

	Key Events	Architecture	Visual Arts	Writing	Music
33,000 BCE	**250,000–10,000 Paleolithic Period** (Old Stone Age); Cro-Magnon peoples **6,000–3,000 Neolithic Period** (New Stone Age)	Houses of brick and mud; wattle and daub construction **7700–5700 First cities** appear at Çatal Hüyük (Turkey), Jericho (Palestine)	**30,000 Woman of Willendorf** **15,000–10,000 Cave paintings and carvings** **Stone carving** (weapons and flint axes)		Bone whistles, primitive drums
4000 BCE					

Mesopotamia

	Key Events	Architecture	Visual Arts	Writing	Music
4000 BCE	**3000–2000 Sumerian Kingdom** **2000 Old Babylonian empire** **1792–1750 Hammurabi** reigned **1600–1200 Hittite empire** **2000–612 Assyrian empire** **612–539 Neo-Babylonian empire** **625–539 Nebuchadnezzar II** reigned	**2100 Ziggurat** at Ur built **575 Ishtar Gate** at Babylon built	**Beginnings of Sumerian art**; metalworking, bronze casting **3300 Female head** from Uruk carved **2100 Gudea** from Tello carved **1760 Stele of Hammurabi** carved	**2400 Cuneiform writing** invented **1750 Law Code of Hammurabi** **1500 Alphabetic writing** invented in Syria **1200 *Epic of Gilgamesh*** recorded **650 King Ashurbanipal** collected library of 22,000 clay tablets	**2600 Sumerian harp** from royal tombs at Ur **1800 Test for tuning system** written on clay tablets **1400 Cult song from Ugarit** written with notation on clay tablets
333 BCE					

Egypt

	Key Events	Architecture	Visual Arts	Writing	Music
3000 BCE	**3000 Egypt** united under one pharaoh **2575–2150 Old Kingdom** **2008–1630 Middle Kingdom** **1540–1075 New Kingdom** **1479–1458 Queen Hatshepsut** reigned **1353–1336 Amenhotep IV** reigned **1332–1323 Tutankhamen** reigned **1279–1213 Ramses II** reigned **304–30 Ptolemaic Dynasty**	**2630 Imhotep built step pyramid** for King Zoser **2551–2528 Pyramid of Khufu** built **2520–2494 Pyramid of Khafre** built **1473–1458 Temple of Amon** at Karnak built **1390 Temple of Amon** at Luxor built **1350 New capital** at Tel el Amarna built **323 City of Alexandria** built	**2580 Statues of Prince Rahotep and wife Nofret** carved and painted **2520–2494 Great Sphinx** carved **2040–1640 Golden age** of arts and crafts **1360 Bust of Queen Nefertiti** carved and painted **1330 Tutankhamen's throne** constructed **1260 Colossal statues of Ramses II** carved	**3100 Hieroglyphic writing** invented **2600–2300 Collections of Egyptian religious literature** carved in pyramids **1580–1350 *Book of the Dead*** existed in pyramid inscriptions **663–525 *Book of the Dead*** assumed present form **1350 Akhenaton's *Hymn to the Sun*** written **320 Great library of Alexandria** assembled	**4000–3500 Harps and flutes** played in Egypt **3500–300 Lyres and reed instruments** added **1420 Musicians** playing instruments painted for Tomb of Nakht
30 BCE					

Cycladic Islands, Crete, and Mycenae

	Key Events	Architecture	Visual Arts	Writing	Music
3000 BCE	**2500–1400 Minoan culture** flourished **1400–1100 Mycenaean culture** flourished **1230 Troy** destroyed by Mycenaeans **1100 Dorian** invasion of Greece **1100–750 Dark Age**	**1750 Early palace** built at Knossos, Crete **1250 Lion Gate** of palace at Mycenae built	**3000–2000 Cycladic Island idols** carved	**2000 Phoenician alphabet** developed **700 Homeric poems** *The Iliad* and *The Odyssey* composed	
1000 BCE					

Israel

	Key Events	Architecture	Visual Arts	Writing	Music
1025 BCE	**1025–1000 Saul** **1000–968 David** **968–937 Solomon** **922–597 Two kingdoms;** Israel to 437, Judah to 589 **722 Israel** conquered **587 Judah** fell to Babylonians	**950 Temple of Solomon** built	**700 Frieze for Sennacherib's palace** at Nineveh carved depicting procession of war prisoners, including Palestinians	**587 Early books of Old Testament** assembled during Babylonian captivity	**1000 David's Psalms** sung with lyre accompaniment
587 BCE					

35,000 BCE

Late Paleolithic period, c. 35,000 BCE
First Paleolithic paintings and sculptures, c. 30,000 BCE

3500 BCE

Invention of the wheel, c. 3500 BCE
Union of Upper and Lower Egypt, c. 3000–2920 BCE
Development of writing and the beginnings of recorded history, c. 2900 BCE
Khufu, Khafre, and Menkaure, builders of the Great Pyramids, c. 2551–2472 BCE

1800 BCE

Hammurabi, r. c. 1792–1750 BCE
Hatshepsut, r. 1473–1458 BCE
Akhenaton and the Amarna period, 1353–1335 BCE
Tutankhamen, r. 1333–1323 BCE
Ramses II, r. 1290–1224 BCE

800 BCE

First Olympic Games, 776 BCE
Foundation of Rome by Romulus, 753 BCE
Homer, fl. c. 150–100 BCE
Tarquinius Priscus, first Etruscan king of Rome, 616 BCE

500 BCE

Darius I, r. 522–486 BCE
Xerxes, r. 486–465 BCE
Socrates, 469–399 BCE
Peloponnesian War, 431–404 BCE
Plato, 429–347 BCE

300 BCE

Aristotle, 384–322 BCE
Alexander the Great, r. 336–323 BCE
Alexander the Great conquers Persia and Egypt, 332 BCE
Battle of Issus, 331 BCE
Death of Alexander the Great, 323 BCE

31 BCE

Battle of Actium, 31 BCE
Augustus, first emperor of Rome, r. 27 BCE–14 CE
Vitruvius, *The Ten Books of Architecture*, c. 25 BCE

PART ONE

CLASSICAL PERIOD

The Greco-Roman era, later called the classical period, spanned about 1,000 years. It began with the age of Pericles, when Greek culture reached its zenith; witnessed the expansion of Greek settlements far and wide under Alexander the Great; saw the rise of Roman power, the grandeur of the Roman Empire, and its eventual decline and fall; and ultimately beheld the rise of Christianity as a social, political, and religious force. The period may be divided into a purely Hellenic phase, a more expansive and widespread Hellenistic continuation, the era of the Roman Republic and Empire, and the Early Christian period.

Instead of blindly accepting mythological and religious explanations of their world, Greek philosophers examined the physical world for themselves. In the sixth century BCE, Pythagoras proposed that there was a unity in nature based on numbers. As the heavenly bodies described their mathematically predictable orbits, they were thought to create a musical harmony of the spheres. Socrates's eloquent pursuit of the goals of truth, goodness, and beauty inspired his pupil Plato, for whom the world of ideas was preeminent. Aristotle's more down-to-earth approach brought together all current knowledge of logic, ethics, politics, poetics, physics, and metaphysics. His thinking was to remain influential for the next 2,000 years.

The Romans, in turn, were adept at applying general principles to practical problems. They developed public works projects and architectural engineering. At the pinnacle of its power, Roman practicality and administrative ability brought most of Europe and parts of Asia and Africa under its dominion. In later antiquity, Roman forms and institutions found their way into the Early Christian tradition in both the eastern Byzantine sector at Constantinople and the Western section with its capital at Ravenna.

Throughout these phases and in various cultural centers, the arts flourished and interacted brilliantly. In architecture, the Greeks carried the post-and-lintel system to perfection in their gleaming temples. The Romans, building for larger cities and populations, brought the arch-and-vault method to its peak. Sculpture, based on the expressive power of the human body, achieved lifelike plasticity and fluidity, and large-scale murals and mosaics provided a pictorial dimension.

Music played a prominent role in ancient social and religious life. Greek musical theory laid the basis for all future musical development in the West. Greek and Roman epic, lyric, and dramatic writing mirrored the ancients' search for self-understanding and self-awareness. Drama in particular provided insights into human character and its motivations. Greek tragedy explored the heights and plumbed the depths of human potential and spirit.

In Western thought, the period was given the title "classical," for the excellence of its art, philosophy, and literature. To this day, classical architecture endures as a model and a set of ideas to be emulated.

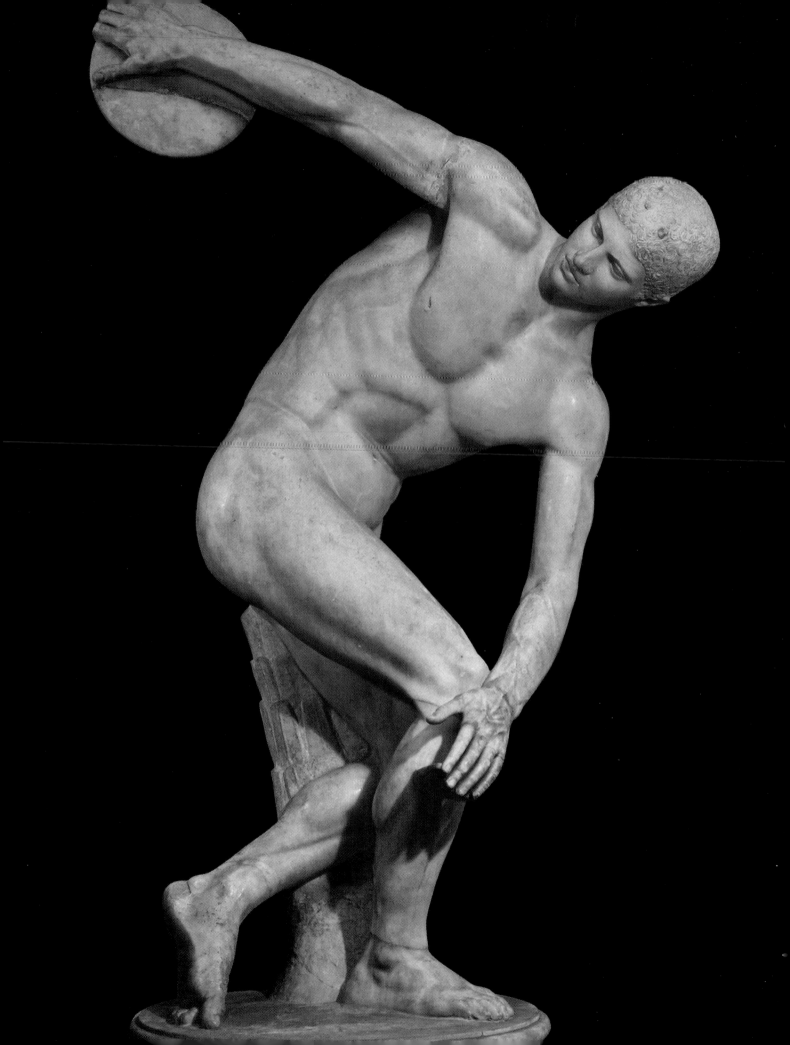

CHAPTER

ATHENS IN THE FIFTH CENTURY BCE

IN THE LAND OF HELLAS, as the Greeks called their country, a small city-state dedicated to Athena, goddess of wisdom, saw the birth of a new spirit. There for a brief time were concentrated the creative energies of many outstanding politicians, philosophers, and artists. Among them were leaders who secured victory for Athens in the struggle to dominate the Mediterranean world (Map 2.1); statesmen with the perception to make Athens a protodemocracy in an era of tyrants; philosophers committed to the search for an understanding of the physical, social, and spiritual nature of the environment

they lived in; and artists who conceived daring expressions in stone, word, and tone. Here the statesman Pericles and the philosopher Socrates heard the wisdom of Anaxagoras, who taught that the universe was governed by a supreme mind that brought form out of the chaos of nature. He also taught that people, by thinking for themselves, could likewise bring order into human affairs.

Without hereditary rulers, the government of Athens rested on the shoulders of the citizen class, and rule by the **demos,** the "people," was the order of the day. Unique in its time, Athenian

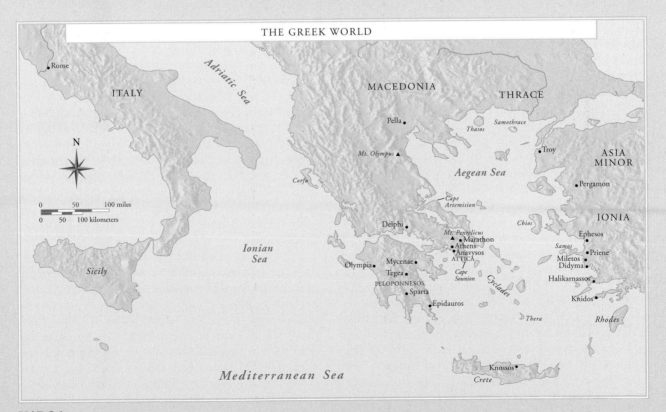

MAP 2.1

citizenship was still limited. As inspiring as it has been in Western culture, Athenian democracy extended only to property-owning men. In effect, democracy was enjoyed by only 25,000 to 30,000 people, ranging from the wealthy to the marginally successful. Women, foreign nationals, and slaves were not legally allowed to participate in Athenian democracy. Paradoxically, citizenship depended on a child being born of two Athenians, putting women in the odd legal situation of both being and not being Athenians.

Other contradictions characterized life in Athens, some of them having to do with notions of gender. A powerful female goddess, Athena, watched over the city. Indeed, Greek mythology teemed with strong women, although they were occasionally dangerous, like the all-female barbarians called Amazons or the beautiful Pandora, who unleashed evil on humankind. Plato considered women capable of being Guardians, leaders of the ideal society he depicted in *The Republic*. In Aristophanes's comedy *Lysistrata*, married women from several Greek cities, including Athens, join forces and capture the Athenian Acropolis. From this hilltop stronghold of Athenian politics and religion, they create a strike, refusing men sexual favors until the men choose peace rather than war. Pitched against these favorable, or at least vivid images of active, outgoing women, there are multiple text sources that paint a different picture. They suggest that Athenian women, at least those above the poverty level, were not allowed to leave their homes. Indeed, researchers once concluded that the Athenians considered women a burden—required for reproduction and housework, but little else.

These contradictions have absorbed contemporary scholars. They question the idea that women did not cross the threshold of the house and did not participate in the economic, civic, and cultural life of the Athenian city-state. Insights from anthropology and other fields suggest a gap between what was sometimes written about women and how women actually lived. With that concept in hand, thinkers are now conjecturing a fuller life for Athenian women. For example, women were often responsible for weaving and might have developed the craft into an art. Moreover, in his *Natural History,* the Roman historian Pliny the Elder intriguingly described the work of six female artists who gained fame later, in the Hellenistic and Roman eras. Unfortunately, we may never confidently know whether the artistic talents of some Athenian women were encouraged and developed. In the fifth century BCE, most works of art and craft were not signed.

ATHENS REBUILDS

In 480 BCE, Athens drove its powerful Persian enemies from the Greek mainland and the Aegean Sea. During the war with Persia, Athens's monuments had been reduced to rubble. After the war, many Greek states and islands formed an alliance to protect themselves from further Persian invasions. They called themselves the Delian League, after the sacred island of Delos. With funds that the League stored in Athenian treasuries, Pericles launched a new building program, one that would serves as a model for Western architecture to this day.

Like many other ancient cities, Athens had developed around an *acra,* or "high place," originally found suitable as a military vantage point. Victory centuries earlier on this fortified hilltop, known as the **Acropolis** (Fig. 2.1), had been attributed to the help of the gods. This caused the people to regard the acra as a sacred place, one that should be crowned with appropriate monuments. In Greece, religious sites such as the Athenian Acropolis were also public spaces and symbols of civic pride. As buildings, palaces, and temples were erected on the Acropolis, the people in the city below looked up toward the structures that recorded their history; represented their aspirations; and had become the center of their religious, cultural, and civic ceremonies.

From the beginning, the Athenian Acropolis was never static, and its successive buildings reflected the city's changing fortunes. Once it had been the site of a palace for the legendary king Erechtheus. Later it was transformed from a military citadel and royal residence into a religious shrine, sacred especially to Athena, the city's protector. This change is described by the poet Homer in *The Odyssey:* "Therewith gray-eyed Athene departed over the unharvested seas, left pleasant Scheria, and came to Marathon and wide-wayed Athens, and entered the house of Erechtheus."

Spreading out from the base of the Acropolis was the *agora* (Fig. 2.2), a meeting and marketplace, with rows of columns, public buildings, market stalls, gardens, and shade trees. This 10-acre square was the center of the city's bustling business, social, and political life. Here country folk sold their wares, citizens discussed the news, foreign visitors exchanged stories, and magistrates conducted routine city affairs.

On a typical day, the philosopher Socrates could be heard arguing with the Sophists, whom he called "retailers of knowledge." As his pupil,

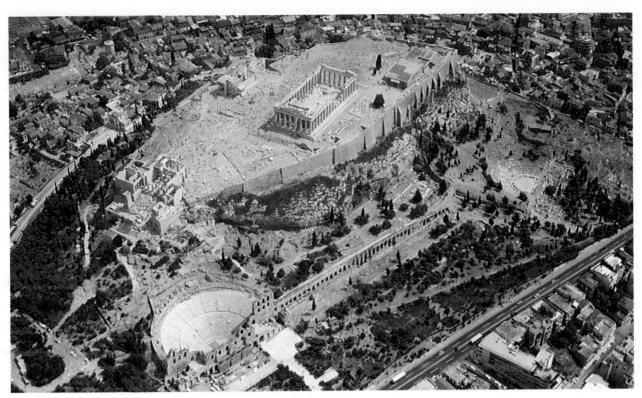

2.1 Aerial view of the Acropolis, Athens, Greece.

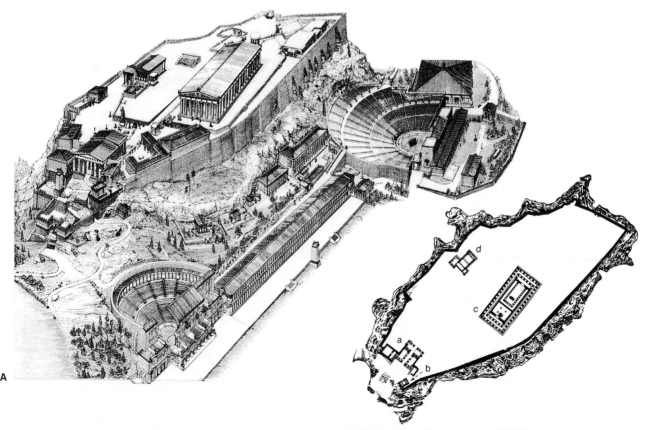

2.2 *Acropolis, Athens.* Reconstruction drawings as of the end of the second century CE. (A) Upper right, Theater of Dionysus, fourth century BCE; lower left, Odeion of Herodes Atticus, second century CE. Reconstruction by A. N. Oikonomides. (B) Plan of Athenian Acropolis, with Propylaea (a), Temple of Athena Nike (b), Parthenon (c), and Erechtheum (d).

Plato, would eventually point out, merchandizing in the agora was "partly concerned with food for the use of the body, and partly with food of the soul which is bartered and received in exchange for money." The Sophists were concerned primarily with the art of persuasive speech, but some professed to teach wisdom as well. As manipulators of public opinion, they often became intellectual opportunists who would use any argument to make a point. In his disputations, Socrates showed that sophistry was more a matter of quibbling over words than of penetrating the world of ideas. By pricking some of the Sophists' pretensions with the sting of his wit, Socrates gained his immortal reputation as the "gadfly" of Athens.

On the southern slope of the Acropolis was the Theater of Dionysus (Fig. 2.2, upper right), a sanctuary dedicated to the god of wine and revelry, who was also the patron deity of drama. Here, more than 2,000 years before Shakespeare, the Athenians gathered to marvel at plays that mirrored their worldview in dramatic form. Annually, through their applause, they chose the winner of the coveted poetry prize, which had been won no less than thirteen times by Aeschylus, the founder of heroic tragedy. Sophocles, his successor and the principal poet of the Periclean period, quickened the pace of Greek drama by adding more actors and action. Euripides, the last of the great tragic poets, explored the full range of emotions, endowing his plays with such passion and pathos that they rose to the heights and plumbed the depths of the human spirit. After the Periclean age, the comedies of Aristophanes, such as *Lysistrata,* proved that the Athenians still were able to see the humor and absurdity of life. Today we are likely to read Greek plays rather than see them performed, which makes it easy to forget that the Greek dramatists were more than writers—they were also directors who had to choreograph the movements of actors and the entrances of the chorus while keeping in mind the diverse interests of the audience.

Above the theater, on the rocky plateau of the Acropolis, was a site about 1,000 feet long and 445 feet wide where the temples were constructed (Fig. 2.2). Under Cimon and his successor Pericles, this was a place of ceaseless activity by builders, sculptors, and painters. Later the Roman historian Plutarch declared in his biography of Pericles that as the buildings rose, stately in size and fair in form, the artists were "striving to outvie the material and the design with the beauty of their workmanship, yet the most wonderful thing of all was the rapidity of their execution. Undertakings, any one of which

singly might have required . . . for their completion, several successions and ages of men, were every one of them accomplished in the height and prime of one man's political service." This rivalry among artists reflected the dominant spirit of the period, in which mental gymnastics and intense debate helped refine philosophy, science, and mathematics. The cultural emphasis on intelligence and reasoning shows how the Athenians put their faith in human abilities. They fashioned accounts of human nature, society, and the material world that were not due to the unpredictable actions of the gods.

Pericles had the wisdom to foresee that the unity of a people could rest on philosophical ideas and artistic leadership as well as on military might and material prosperity. A seafaring folk, the Athenians had always looked beyond the horizon for ideas as well as goods to enrich their way of life. In the Delian League, once the Persian threats ended, the Athenians joined with the broader community of Greek-speaking peoples of the mainland, the Aegean Islands, and the coast of Asia Minor to defend themselves and achieve cultural unity.

Athens quickly became a city whose acknowledged wealth consisted not only of material goods but also of its intellectual and artistic riches: the dramatists Aeschylus, Sophocles, and Euripides; the architects Ictinus, Callicrates, and Mnesicles; the sculptors Myron and Phidias; and painters such as Polygnotus and Apollodorus.

The Acropolis itself was both the material and spiritual treasury of the Athenians, the place that held both their worldly gold reserves and their religious and artistic monuments. Work continued with undiminished enthusiasm until the end of the fifth century BCE. By then, the Acropolis had become a sublime setting, one worthy of the goddess of wisdom and beauty. It was also the pedestal that proudly bore the shining temples dedicated to her.

In this chapter, we examine the major arts from the era called Hellenic (from the word *Hellenes,* by which the Greeks referred to themselves). The principal ideas that thread their way through the arts are summarized and coordinated. We will see that **humanism**—the idea that human beings are the primary measure of all things—is one of the underlying principles of Hellenic art; even the Greek gods are conceived of in human form. We will also see how **idealism** is exalted over reality, as revealed in perfect forms that exclude blemishes and shortcomings in representing the human figure, and how **rationalism** and eternal principles prevail over the emotional and transitory phases of human life.

ARCHITECTURE

THE ACROPOLIS AND THE PROPYLAEA

On festive occasions, the Athenians would leave their modest homes to walk along the Panathenaic Way (Fig. 2.2), the main avenue of their city, toward the Acropolis. A panel from the ionic frieze on the Parthenon probably portrays this event. Towering above the celebrants was the supreme shrine—the Acropolis—where they worshiped their gods, commemorated their heroes, and recreated themselves. Accessible only by a single zigzag path up the western slope, the ascent was never easy. In *Lysistrata,* a chorus of old men bearing olive branches to kindle the sacred fires chants as they mount the hill: "But look, to finish this toilsome climb only this last steep bit is left to mount. Truly, it's no easy job without beasts of burden and how these logs do bruise my shoulder!"

As the procession nears the top, the exquisite little Temple of Athena Nike appears on a parapet to the right (see Fig. 2.10). Ahead was the mighty Propylaea, the imposing gateway to the Acropolis (Fig. 2.3). Pericles entrusted the design of this entranceway, undertaken shortly after the completion of the Parthenon, to the architect Mnesicles. The principal architect of the Parthenon, Ictinus,

also may have had a hand in planning the Propylaea, whose aesthetic relationship to the Parthenon is revealed in the proportions of its forms, in the presence of certain features of the **Ionic** order in a dominantly **Doric** structure (see Fig 2.9), and in the main axis that the Propylaea shares with the larger monument.

The Propylaea was built mainly of Pentelic marble from nearby Mt. Pentelicus, except for some dark, contrasting Eleusinian stone. It was a spacious gateway with wings extending on either side to an overall width of about 156 feet. An enclosure on the left was a picture gallery, and an open room on the right contained statues. In the center was the porch, consisting of six Doric columns with the middle two spaced more widely apart, as if to invite entrance. Between the columns looking toward the city and the corresponding ones on the opposite side facing the Acropolis plateau was an open vestibule with columns of the more slender Ionic order, which permitted greater height and space for exhibitions and the waiting crowds (Fig. 2.3).

Through the gateway of the Propylaea the procession entered the sacred area. Amid the revered monuments to the gods and heroes and looming above them was a colossal gold and ivory statue of Athena, said to have been fash-

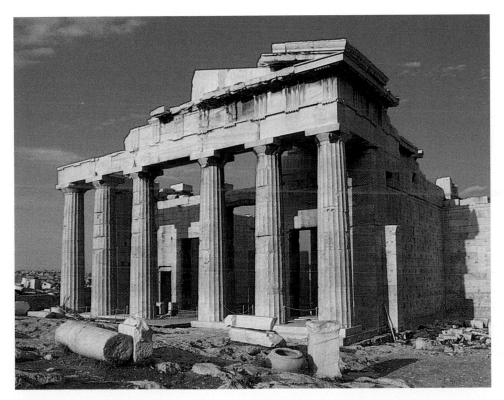

2.3 *Mnesicles,* Propylaea (view from the northeast). Acropolis, Athens, Greece, 437–432 BCE.

ioned by Phidias from the bronze shields of defeated Persian enemies. The tip of her spear is said to have gleamed brightly enough to guide homecoming sailors over the seas toward Athens. On the right was the majestic Parthenon; on the left, the graceful Erechtheum.

THE PARTHENON

DORIC ORDER.   At first glance, the Parthenon seems to be a typical Doric temple (Fig. 2.4A). Such a shrine was originally conceived of as an idealized dwelling to house the image of a deity. Under a low-pitched gabled roof, the interior was a windowless rectangular space called the *cella,* which sheltered the cult statue of the deity to whom the temple was dedicated. The *portal,* or doorway, to the cella was on one of the short ends, which extended outward in a *portico,* or porch, faced with columns to form the *facade,* or front. Sometimes columns were erected around the building in a series known as a *colonnade.* (For other details, see Fig. 2.4B.)

The strict rules of the Doric order were based on a ratio of 1:2. According to the philosopher Pythagoras, who worked out the proportions of the musical intervals (see p. 50), the harmony of the universe was based on the perfect interval of the octave (1:2). Therefore, a temple dedicated to a divinity should reflect these perfect proportions. This meant that the ground plan should be twice as long as it was wide. When the front had four columns, the side must have eight, and so on with all the details of the building.

The harmonious proportions of the Parthenon have long been attributed to some subtle and obscure system of mathematical ratios. But despite close study and analysis, no geometric formula has so far been found that fits all the evidence, and the scholarly discussion continues to this day. However, the proportion 9:4 occurs repeatedly. This proportion has been noticed in the length of the building (228 feet relative to its width of 104 feet), when measured on the **stylobate,** or top step; in the width of the **cornice** contrasted to the height of the **raking cornice** at the center; in the distance between the center of one column and that of the next (about 14 feet) as compared with the diameter of the column at its base; and in the bottom diameter of the columns relative to the width of the **triglyphs.**

DEVIATIONS FROM REGULARITY.   At the same time, many irregularities defy mathematical logic. Any visitor to the Parthenon can observe that the columns stand somewhat closer together at the corners. Also apparent is the gentle arching of the stylobate from corner to corner. Above the columns, the **architrave** supporting the **entablature** echoes this curve. Noticeable too is the slight outward swelling of the column shafts as they rise and a tapering off toward the top, producing a curved effect known as *entasis.* Entasis creates the impression of elasticity, as if the "muscles" of the columns bulged a bit in bearing the load imposed by the building's superstructure (Fig. 2.4B). Because the Parthenon was to serve both as a shrine to Athena and as a treasury of the Delian League, the plan called for a double cella, that is, two inner rooms. The larger room on the east was to house Phidias's magnificent gold-and-ivory statue of Athena, and the room on the west was to

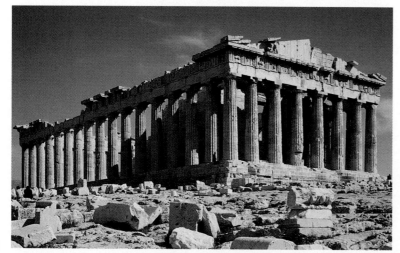

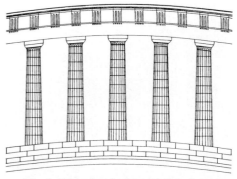

A   B

2.4   (A) *Ictinus and Callicrates,* Parthenon, Athens, 447–432 BCE. Pentelic marble; height of columns 34 feet, length 228′ × 104′. (B) Schematic rendering of the Parthenon exaggerating the curvature and irregularities in the scale.

be the treasury. It was this western cella that technically was the ***parthenon,*** or chamber of the virgin goddess. Later the name was given to the whole building. The outer four walls of the cella were embellished by a continuous frieze, a decorative device borrowed from the Ionic order.

The master builder Ictinus labored to avoid the rigidity and repetitiveness of the strict Doric order and to make the Parthenon organically coherent rather than merely mechanically regular. The building can be thought of as a monumental sculpture, compact and firmly structured but resilient and elastic in the relationships among its component parts. This invests the whole with an organic quality like that of life itself. Considered in this way, the Parthenon becomes more visual than logical, more the work of inspired stonemasons than that of mathematicians. Far from being a cold abstraction, the Parthenon is a work of art.

Except for such details as the wooden roof beneath the marble tiles and the wooden doors with their frames, the entire Parthenon was built of Pentelic marble. When freshly quarried, this fine-grained stone was cream colored, but as it has weathered through the centuries, its minute veins of iron have oxidized, so today the color varies from light beige to darker golden tones, depending on the light.

In the original design, bright colors played an important part. Ancient sources tell us that the triglyphs were tinted dark blue and parts of the molding were red. The sculptured parts of the **metopes** were left cream colored, but the backgrounds were painted. In the frieze along the cella walls, the reins of horses were bronze additions, and the draperies of figures here and on the **pediments** were painted. Facial features such as eyes, lips, and hair were done in natural tints.

For the sheer technical skill of its construction, the Parthenon is astonishing. No mortar was used; the stones were cut so exactly that when fitted together they form a single smooth surface. The columns, which appear to be monoliths of marble, actually are constructed of sections called **drums,** so tightly fitted by square plugs in the center that the joinings are scarcely visible.

In its time the Parthenon stood out as a proud monument to Athena and her people and the attainment of Pericles's ideal of "beauty in simplicity." Begun in 447 BCE as the first edifice in the building program, it was dedicated during the Panathenaic festival 10 years later. It and its companion buildings on the Acropolis would be standing today, with only the usual deteriorations of time, were it not for a disaster that occurred in 1687. At that time, a Turkish garrison was using the Parthenon for ammunition storage. During a siege by the Venetians, a random bomb ignited the stored gunpowder, blowing out the temple's central section. Ever since, the Parthenon has been a noble ruin. Today, after numerous partial restorations, its outline is still clear. In its incomparable proportions and reserved poise, it remains one of the great achievements of the human mind.

Other impressive Doric temples can be found as far afield as Agrigento in Sicily and Paestum in southern Italy (Fig. 2.5). In Athens itself, on a low hill near the Acropolis, is the Hephaesteum, one of the best preserved of all Greek temples. It overlooks the quarter where the metal workers and potters had their shops. Appropriately, it was dedicated to both Hephaestus, the blacksmith of the gods, and Athena, the goddess of knowledge.

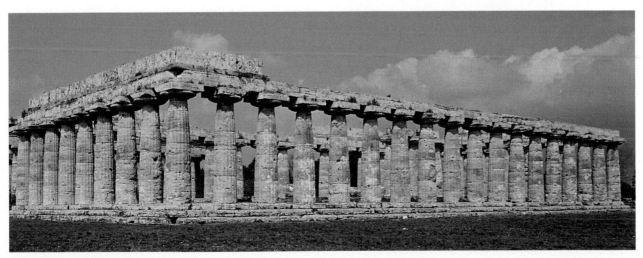

2.5 Temple of Hera at Paestum, Italy, c. 550 BCE.

2.6 *Mnesicles (?),* Erechtheum, Athens, Greece, c. 421–405 BCE. Pentelic marble; length 37′, width 66′.

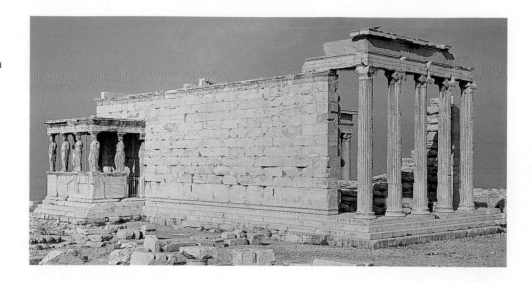

THE ERECHTHEUM

After Phidias's gold-and-ivory statue was so handsomely housed in the Parthenon, the city's leaders wished to provide a place for an older wooden statue of Athena that was thought to have fallen miraculously from the sky. They also wished to venerate the other heroes and deities that formerly shared the Acropolis with her. Hence, they erected a new building of the Ionic order (Fig. 2.6), described in the city records as "the temple in the Acropolis for the ancient statue."

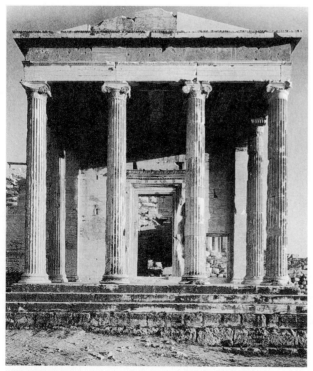

2.7 *Mnesicles (?),* north porch of Erechtheum, Athens, Greece. Width 35′2″.

The site chosen was where Erechtheus, the legendary founder of the city, had once dwelt. As recounted by Homer, Erechtheus was born from Earth, the grain giver, and was befriended and fostered by Athena, who "gave him a resting place in Athens in her own rich sanctuary; and there the sons of the Athenians worship him with bulls and rams as the years turn in their courses."

The Erechtheum, as the building was called, was also the spot where Athena and the sea god Poseidon were said to have held their contest for the patronage of Athens and the surrounding area called Attica. This story is depicted in the sculptures on the west pediment of the Parthenon. As the two deities asserted their claims, Poseidon brought down his trident on a rock, from which sprang a horse, his gift to humanity. A spring of saltwater gushed forth to mark the event. When Athena's turn came, she produced an olive tree, and the gods awarded her the victory. Later, Erechtheus, whom she protected, tamed the horse and cultivated an olive that gave the Athenians oil for cooking, a spread for their bread, ointment for their bodies, and fuel for their lamps.

Because the sacred olive tree, the salt spring, the mark of Poseidon's trident on the rock, and the tomb of Erechtheus were all in the same sacred precinct but not on the same plane, the architect, thought by some scholars to be Mnesicles, had to design a multileveled temple. Combining these areas makes the plan of the Erechtheum as complex as that of the Parthenon is simple. The rectangular interior had four rooms for the various shrines, which were built on two different levels. Projecting outward from three of the sides were porticoes, each different in size and design. The east porch has a row of six Ionic columns almost

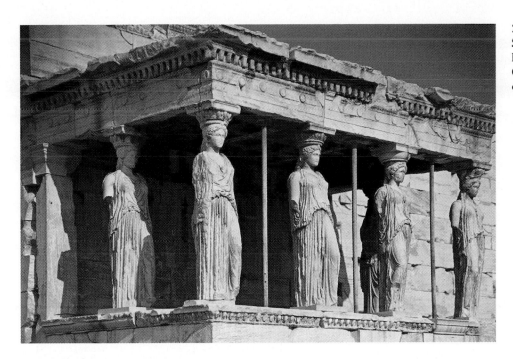

2.8 Mnesicles (?). South porch of Erechtheum, Athens, Greece. Height of caryatids 7'9".

22 feet high. The north porch (Fig. 2.7) has a like number, but with four in front and two on the sides, while the smaller porch on the south (Fig. 2.8) is famous for its six *caryatids,* the sculptured maidens who replace the customary columns.

THE IONIC ORDER

Ionic columns (Fig. 2.9), unlike those of the Doric order, are more slender and have their greatest diameter at the bottom. Their shafts rest on a

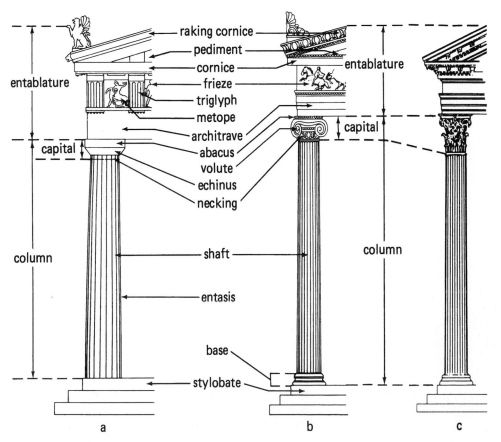

2.9 Comparison of Greek orders: Doric (a), Ionic (b), Corinthian (c).

molded base instead of directly on the stylobate, and they have 24 flutings instead of 20. Most striking, however, is the Ionic capital with its **volutes,** or scroll-like ornaments. The fine columns of the north porch (Fig. 2.7) rest on molded bases carved with a delicate design. The necking has a band decorated with a leaf pattern. Above this is a smaller band decorated with the egg-and-dart motif, followed by the volutes and then a thin **abacus** carved with eggs and darts. The columns support an architrave that is divided horizontally into three bands, each receding slightly inward. The architrave thus consists of a continuous carved frieze rather than the alternating triglyphs and metopes of the Doric order. Above rises a shallow pediment without sculpture. A richly decorated doorway leads into the cella of the Erechtheum. The lintel above it is framed with a series of receding planes and combines the decorative motifs that appear elsewhere in the building.

SOUTH PORCH.   Facing the Parthenon, the south porch of the Erechtheum, with its caryatids (Fig. 2.8), is smaller than the others. Above three steps rises a parapet on which the six maidens, about one and a half times larger than life, are standing. To preserve the proportions of the building and not appear to overburden the figures, the frieze and pediment were omitted.

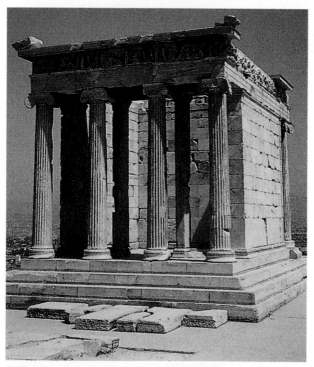

2.10   *Callicrates,* Temple of Athena Nike, Athens, Greece, c. 427–424 BCE. Pentelic marble; length 17′9″, width 26′10″.

Grouped as if in a procession, the figures seem engaged in a stately forward motion, with those on one side lifting their right legs and those on the other, their left. They originally carried libation bowls in their right hands. The folds of their draperies suggest the fluting of columns. Although the maidens seem solid enough to carry their loads, there is no stiffness in their stance.

On the Acropolis, the Athenians brought to the highest point of development two distinct Greek building traditions—the Doric with the Parthenon and the Ionic with the Erechtheum and the Temple of Athena Nike (Fig. 2.10). By combining the two architectural orders in the Propylaea and displaying them separately in the Parthenon and the Erechtheum, the Athenians made symbolic reference to their city as the place where the Dorian people of the Greek mainland and the Ionian people of the islands and the coast of Asia Minor had lived together in relative peace and harmony for centuries.

THE CORINTHIAN ORDER

In the following century, another order was added: the Corinthian (Fig. 2.9). The columns of the Corinthian order are taller and more treelike than the Ionic. They are distinguished by their ornate capitals with double rows of acanthus leaves and fernlike fronds rising from each corner and terminating in miniature volutes. Too ornate for the generally restrained Hellenic taste, the Corinthian order had to wait for Hellenistic and Roman times to reach its full development, as can be seen in the ruins of the Temple of Olympian Zeus (Fig. 2.11).

SCULPTURE

THE PARTHENON MARBLES

The Parthenon sculptures rank high among the surviving originals of the fifth century BCE. The statuary that has survived falls into three groups: the high-relief metopes of the Doric frieze, the low-relief cella frieze, and the freestanding pediment figures. Phidias's celebrated gold-and-ivory cult statue of Athena has long since disappeared, and inferior later copies convey little of the splendor attributed to it by ancient sources.

As architectural sculpture, the friezes and pediments should not be judged apart from the building they embellished. By providing curved and diagonal accents and irregular masses, as well

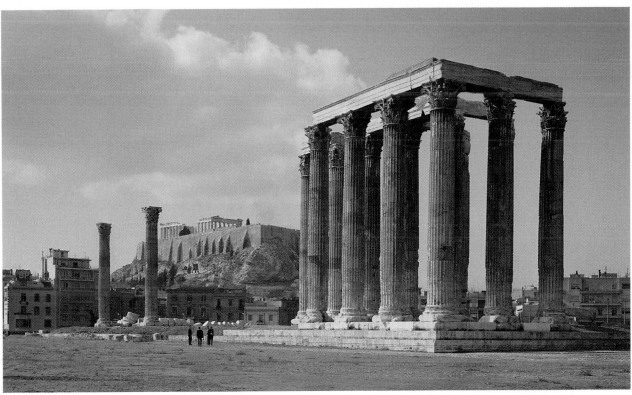

2.11 *Temple of Olympian Zeus,* Athens, Greece, 174 BCE–130 CE. Pentelic marble; height of columns 56′6″.

as figures in motion, they offset the vertical and horizontal balance of the structural parts. The original location of these sculptures must also be kept in mind: they were meant to be seen outdoors in the intense Greek sunlight and from the ground some 35 feet below. Although some of the frieze work is still in place, most of it is now in museums, where it is seen in dim artificial light and at eye level.

THE METOPES OF THE DORIC FRIEZE.   The metopes of the Doric frieze play an important part in the architectural design of the Parthenon: they provide a welcome variety of figures to relieve the structural unity. Their predominantly diagonal lines contrast well with the alternating verticals of the triglyphs and the long horizontals of the architrave and cornice just below and above them. To take full advantage of the bright sunlight, the sculptors chiseled these metopes in **high relief,** a technique by which the figures are deeply carved so as to project boldly outward from the background plane.

The subject of the figures in the south frieze is the battle of the Lapiths, legendary people who lived in the north of Greece, and centaurs, powerful half-man/half-horse creatures. The battle took place after a drunken centaur kidnapped a Lapith bride at a wedding feast. In one of the most skillfully executed metopes (Fig. 2.12), the rich spreading folds of the mantle form a fine unifying framework for the splendid human figure. In turn, both make a striking contrast with the awkward centaur.

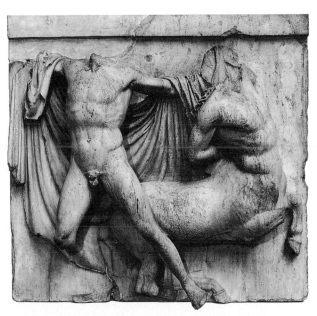

2.12 *Lapith and Centaur,* metope from Parthenon frieze, 447–441 BCE. Marble, 3′11″ × 4′2″. British Museum, London, England.

2.13 *Horsemen,* detail of Parthenon north frieze, c. 447–438 BCE. Marble, height 3′6″. British Museum, London, England.

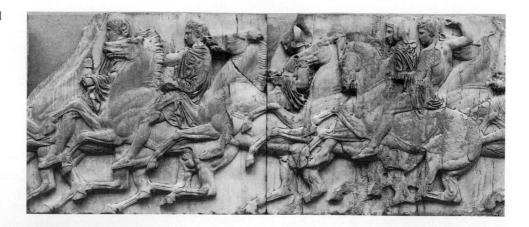

THE CELLA FRIEZE. The inner frieze (Figs. 2.13 and 2.14) that ran along the outer walls of the cella was a continuous band that included some 600 figures. Because this frieze was placed behind the colonnade and directly below roof level, where it had to be viewed from up close and at a steep upward angle, some sculptural adjustments were called for. The technique used was **low relief,** in which the figures are shallowly carved. The handling of space, however, is so deft that as many as six horsemen are shown riding abreast without confusing the separate spatial planes. All the heads, whether the figures are afoot or on horseback, have been kept on the same level to preserve unity of design and to provide a parallel with the horizontal lines. (This principle, known as **isocephaly,** will also be encountered later in Byzantine art [see Figs. 5.15 and 5.16]).

The cella frieze, unlike the traditional mythological subjects portrayed elsewhere in the

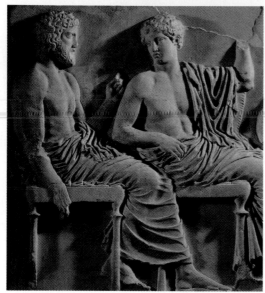

2.14 *Poseidon and Apollo,* detail of Parthenon east cella frieze, c. 440 BCE. Marble, height 43″. Acropolis Museum, Athens, Greece.

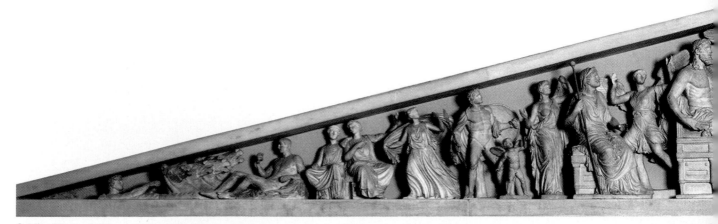

2.15 *Birth of Athena.* Reconstruction of Parthenon east pediment. Acropolis Museum, Athens, Greece.

Parthenon sculptures, depicts the Athenians themselves participating in the festival of their goddess. One of the oldest and most important festivals, the Panathenaea, took place every 4 years. Larger than the annual local procession because it included delegations from other Greek cities, the Greater Panathenaea was a prelude to poetical and oratorical contests, dramatic presentations, and games.

On the western side (Fig. 2.13) of the Parthenon, last-minute preparations for the parade are in progress as the riders ready their horses. The action, appropriately enough, starts just at the point where the live procession, after passing through the Propylaea, would have paused to regroup. The parade then splits in two, one file moving along the north side and the other along the south. The charioteers follow the bareback riders, and as the procession approaches the eastern corners, the marshals slacken the tempo to a more dignified pace. Here are musicians playing lyres and flutes, youths bearing wine jugs for libations, and maidens walking with stately steps. The two files meet again on the east side, where magistrates would be waiting to begin the ceremonies.

Even the gods, as seen in the panel depicting Poseidon and Apollo (Fig. 2.14), are present to bestow their Olympian approval on the proceedings. The high point of the ritual comes in the center of the east side with the presentation of the **peplos,** the saffron and purple mantle woven by chosen maidens to drape over the ancient image of Athena.

Several scholars have recently questioned whether the procession on the frieze represents the Panathenaea. They suggest that it may depict the bloodcurdling story of King Erechtheus, who was told by the oracle at Delphi that he must sacrifice his three daughters if he wished to secure Athens's triumph over an invader. In this alternative interpretation, the peplos of Athena becomes the cloth in which the daughter will be brought to the altar for sacrifice.

THE PEDIMENTAL SCULPTURES. In contrast to the friezes, the pedimental sculptures are freestanding figures, carved in the round and placed in the pediment. The themes of both pediments have to do with Athena. The one on the west, facing the city, depicts her triumph over Poseidon. The one on the east (Fig. 2.15) recounts the amazing story of her birth, the event that was celebrated each summer at the Panathenaea. Although only a few fragments of the Western pediment remain, enough of its eastern counterpart survives to allow us to estimate what might be represented. But because individual statues or groups may have been given by different patrons, a specific narrative was probably not depicted.

From various sources, it is known that the eastern scene is Mount Olympus and that Zeus, the father of the gods, was seated in the center. On one side stood the fire god Hephaestus, who is splitting open the head of Zeus to let Athena spring forth fully grown and fully armed. The sudden appearance of the goddess of wisdom, like a brilliant idea from the mind of its creator, disturbs the Olympian calm. As the news spreads from the center to the sides, all the figures affected by the presence of divine wisdom in their midst,

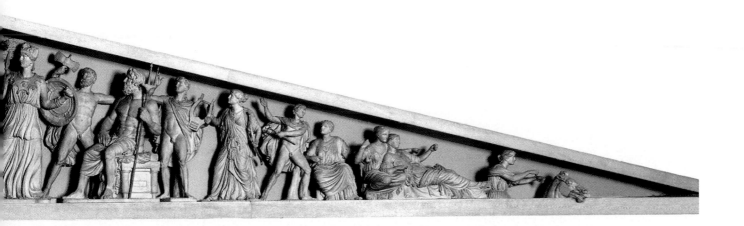

2.16 *Demeter, Persephone, and Iris.* From Parthenon east pediment, c. 438–432 BCE. Marble, larger than life-size. British Museum, London, England.

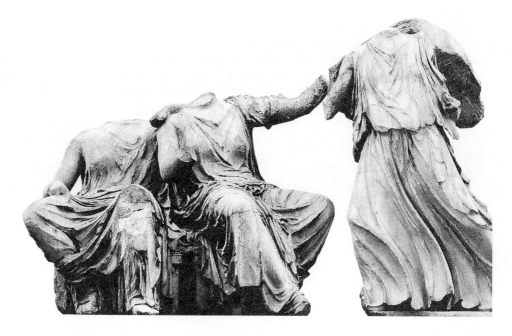

Iris, the messenger of the gods, who often traveled on a rainbow (Fig. 2.16), rushes toward the left with a rapid motion revealed by her windswept drapery. Seated on a chest, Demeter and Persephone turn toward her, and the rich folds of their costumes reflect their attitudes and interest. The reclining figure, usually identified as Dionysus, with his panther skin and mantle spread over a rock (Fig. 2.17), is awakening and looking toward the sun god Helios, the horses of whose chariot are just rising from the foaming sea at dawn.

Three goddesses (Fig. 2.18) on the opposite side have postures that bring out their relationship to the composition. The one nearest the center of the pediment, aware of what has happened, is about to rise. The middle figure is starting to turn

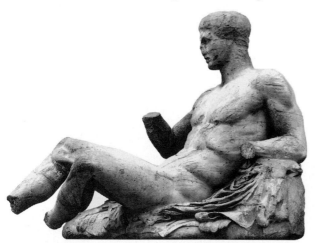

2.17 *Dionysus/Hercules,* from Parthenon east pediment, c. 438–432 BCE. Marble, larger than life-size. British Museum, London, England.

toward her. The reclining figure at the right, still in repose, is unaware of the event, as is her counterpart, Dionysus, on the far left. Like the female group on the left, these figures form a unified episode in the composition, and their relationship to the whole is made clear in the lines of their flowing robes. This undulating linear pattern and the way it reveals the anatomy of the splendid bodies beneath mark a high point in the art of sculpture.

At the far right of this group, the chariot of the moon goddess Selene is seen descending. Now only the expressive downward-bending horse's head (Fig. 2.19) remains to show by his spent energies that it is the end of the journey.

Perhaps the most admirable aspect of the entire composition is the ease and grace with which each piece fills its assigned space. Fitting suitable figures into a low isosceles triangle while maintaining an uncrowded yet unified appearance was a problem that long occupied Greek designers. An oversized standing figure usually dominated the center, with seated or crouching figures on either side and reclining ones in the acute side angles. Here the chariots of the rising and setting sun and moon define the time span as that of a single day. Moreover, the background of Mount Olympus and the single event portrayed identify time, place, and action, in keeping with the classical unities (a principle that will be discussed more fully later in the chapter).

The ascending and descending chariots give a contrasting upward and downward movement on the extreme ends, while the reclining and seated figures lead the eye to the apex, where the climax takes place.

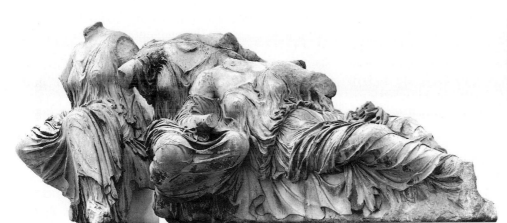

2.18 *Three Goddesses* from Parthenon east pediment, c. 438–432 BCE. Marble, life-size. British Museum, London, England.

THE OVERALL SCULPTURAL PROGRAM. Taken as a whole, the Parthenon marbles present the scope of fifth-century aspirations. The Athenians tried to interpret ancient myths in the light of their history and philosophy.

The metopes on the east frieze portray the primeval battle between gods and giants for control of the world. The triumph of the Olympian gods hailed the coming of order out of chaos. The metopes on the south frieze show the oldest inhabitants of the Greek peninsula, the Lapiths, subduing the half-human/half-horse centaurs with the aid of the Athenian hero Theseus. This victory signaled the ascendancy of human ideals over the animal side of human nature. In the north group, the Homeric epic of the defeat of the Trojans by the Greeks is told, while in the west metopes, the Greeks are seen overcoming the Amazons, female warriors who symbolized the Greeks' Asiatic enemies and, in this case, who allude to the Athenian defeat of the Persians at Marathon. In the east pediment, the birth of the city's patroness, Athena, is seen, while the west pediment tells the story of the rivalry of Athena as goddess of the intellect and Poseidon as patron of maritime trade, suggesting a conflict between two ways of life—the search for wisdom and the pursuit of material wealth.

The Panathenaic procession portrayed on one of the cella walls brings Greek history up to date by depicting a contemporary subject. Here the proud Athenians could look upward and see their own images carved on a sacred temple, an echo of the living procession that marched along the sides of the temple on feast days. The climax came after they had gathered at the east porch and the portals of the temple were opened to the rays of the rising sun, revealing the image of the goddess herself. With Athena's help, Greek civilization had overcome the ignorance of the barbarians. The bonds between the goddess and the citizens of

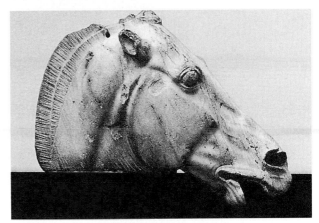

2.19 *Moon Goddess's Horse,* from Parthenon east pediment, c. 438–432 BCE. Marble, life-size. British Museum, London, England.

her city were thus periodically renewed, and the Parthenon as a whole glorified not only Athena but the Athenians as well.

THE RETURN OF WAR

Dark clouds began to gather on the Athenian political horizon, even while the buildings on the Acropolis were being erected. By developing an empire and expending the funds of the Delian League on the Acropolis, Athens excited the wrath of some of the rival city-states. Their exaltation of themselves over other Greeks and the depiction of themselves in the presence of the Olympian gods in the Parthenon frieze added fuel to the argument. When Phidias carved Pericles's and his own self-portrait on the sacred shield of the cult statue of Athena, he went too far, even for an Athenian. Such demonstrations of Athenian military power and political dominance laid the foundation for the Peloponnesian

War between Athens and Sparta, which broke out only 1 year after the Parthenon was completed.

Another, more modern battle involving the Athenian Acropolis continues today. Figures from the east pediment (see Figs. 2.16, 2.17, and 2.18) of the Parthenon as well as from the building's friezes were brought to England by Lord Elgin in 1801–1803, when Greece was under the rule of the Ottoman Empire. The so-called Elgin Marbles were likely saved from ruin during a period of strife. The return of the collection, now exhibited in London's British Museum, has long been sought by Greece, most recently in heated exchanges during preparations for the 2004 Olympic games in Athens.

THE COURSE OF HELLENIC SCULPTURE

A tremendous change took place in Greek sculpture from the archaic, or preclassical, phase to the end of the Hellenic period in the midfourth century. It can best be illustrated by comparing examples from successive periods.

MALE FIGURES.   The *kouros* (plural, *kouroi*) (Fig. 2.20) is an archaic sculptural type depicting a youthful nude male. During the 150 years of its popularity, beginning in the midseventh century, it may have served multiple purposes: as a funeral memorial, a **votive** statue, or an acknowledgment of victory in athletic games. The large feet, the advancing left leg, and the clenched hands attached to the body are reminiscent of Egyptian sculpture, in which movement was more symbolic than physically accurate.

Nevertheless, the nude body did not occur in conventional Egyptian sculpture. Moreover, Egyptian figures were more naturalistically depicted. Here, the long vertical line from the neck to the navel divides the chest, while the diamond-shaped abdomen is defined by four almost-straight lines, a heritage of the formal geometric conventions of the preclassical, archaic period. The wide shoulders and long arms provide a rectangular framework for the statue. About a century later, a similar figure (see Fig. 2.36) reveals how the rigid posture has been softened, the muscles relaxed, and the spirit enlivened.

In contrast, the *Doryphorus,* or *Spear Bearer,* by Polyclitus (Fig. 2.21) moves with great poise and freedom. Originally in bronze, it is now known only through marble copies. Polyclitus won fame in ancient times for his attempts to formulate a **canon,** or body of rules, for the proportions of the human figure. Exactly how Polyclitus's theory worked is not known, but the Roman architect Vitruvius mentions that beauty consists "in the proportions, not of the elements, but of the parts, that is to say, of finger to finger, and of all the fingers to the palm and wrist, and of these to the forearm, and of the forearm to the upper arm, and of all . . . to each other, as . . . set forth in the Canon of Polyclitus."

Whether the **module** (unit of measure) was the head, the forearm, or the hand apparently varied from one statue to another. Yet once the module was adopted, the whole and all its parts could be expressed in multiples or fractions of it. As Vitruvius

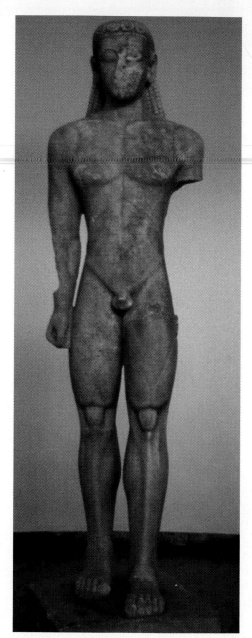

2.20   Kouros from Sounion, c. 615–590 BCE. Marble, height 11′. National Archaeological Museum, Athens, Greece.

illustrated the canon, the head would be one-eighth the total height. The face would be one-tenth, subdivided, in turn, into three parts: forehead, nose, and mouth and chin. The forearm would be one-fourth the height, and the width of the chest would be equal to this length of forearm. Like the optical refinements of the Parthenon, however, Polyclitus's canon was not a strict mechanical formula. It allowed for some flexibility; the dimensions could be adjusted for a figure in movement or for one designed to be seen from a certain angle.

The poised and polished *Hermes and the Infant Dionysus* (Fig. 2.22), which has traditionally been attributed to Praxiteles, was sculpted at the close of the Hellenic period. The sculptor was reputed to be among the wealthiest of Athenians. Unlike other artists, who worked from one commission to the next, Praxiteles could afford to make models for statues before they were commissioned by a patron. Praxiteles's good fortune indicates the rising status of artists in late Hellenic times.

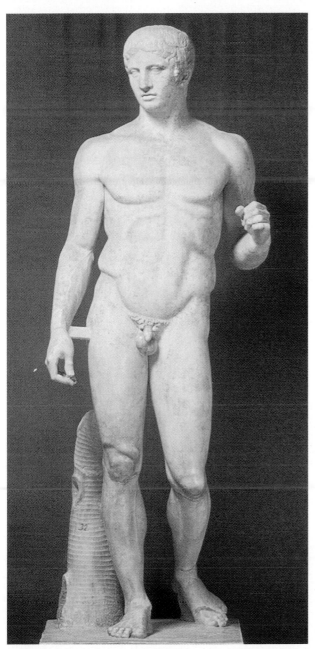

2.21 Polyclitus. *Doryphorus (Spear Bearer)*. Roman copy of original of c. 450–440 BCE. Marble, height 6′6″. Museo Nazionale, Naples, Italy.

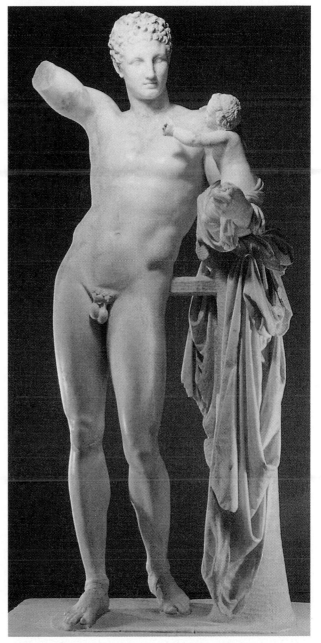

2.22 Praxiteles (?). *Hermes and the Infant Dionysus*, c. 340 BCE. Marble, height 7′1″. Archaeological Museum, Olympia, Greece.

Unlike the rather restrained *Doryphorus,* Praxiteles's Hermes rests his weight easily on one foot. The relaxed stance throws the body into the familiar S-curve, a Praxitelean pose that was widely copied in later Hellenistic and Roman statuary. From the stiffness of the stolid archaic *Kouros* and the strength of the stocky *Doryphorus,* Praxiteles arrived at a more sensual treatment of his material. Through the soft modeling and suave surface treatment, he suggests the blood, bone, and muscles beneath the skin and gave his cold marble material the vibrancy and warmth of living flesh.

Two rare Hellenic bronze originals, the *Charioteer* found buried in the ruins of Delphi (Fig. 2.23), and the *Zeus* found in the sea off Cape Artemision (Fig. 2.24), along with the Roman marble copy of Myron's lost bronze *Discobolus,* or *Discus Thrower* (Fig. 2.25), reveal a transition in style from quiet monumentality to energetic action that took place within a 20-year span in the midfifth century. The splendid *Charioteer* once was part of a larger group that included a chariot and several horses. Although in action, the figure has something of the monumentality and equilibrium of a fluted column due to the vertical folds of its lower garment. The statue probably commemorated an individual's win in a chariot race and also served to honor the god Apollo.

The commanding figure of *Zeus,* poised to throw a thunderbolt, reveals in its powerful musculature the massive reserves of strength of a truly godlike physique. In Greek religion and art,

2.23   *Charioteer.* From Sanctuary of Apollo, Delphi, Greece, c. 470 BCE. Bronze, height approx. 5'11". Archeological Museum, Delphi, Greece.

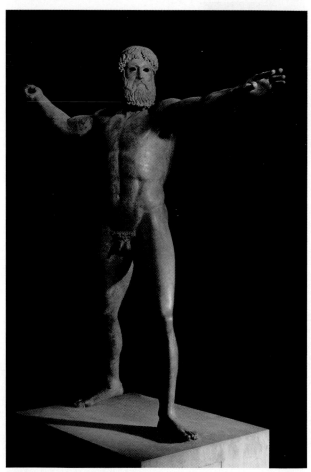

2.24   *Zeus (Poseidon?),* from the Artemisium at Cape Sounion, c. 460–450 BCE. Bronze, height 6'10". National Archaeological Museums, Athens, Greece

the gods were envisioned as humans, not forces of nature or combinations of human and animal aspects, as in Egypt and Mesopotamia. Some contemporary scholars speculate that many statues of Zeus about to throw his thunderbolt were placed at Olympia, the site of the original Olympic games. One punishment for athletes who cheated at the games was being required to commission such a statue and have pious statements inscribed on it.

In his *Discobolus,* Myron faced the challenge of expressing movement in static terms. His inspired solution was to choose a pose in which the taut yet elastic muscles of the athlete are poised momentarily after his backswing and before his forward lunge. The whole backward–forward movement is thus captured in this one "Myronic moment." The vigorously stretched tight point in the action is admirably displayed by the tension between the curving arch of the body and the extended curve of the outstretched arms.

FEMALE FIGURES. The so-called Lady of Auxerre, named for the French town in whose museum she was mysteriously found in 1909 (Fig. 2.26), may have originated in Crete during the early seventh century. Her cinched waist is reminiscent of the body as it was portrayed by the Minoans (see Fig. 1.22), and her large wig recalls an Egyptian

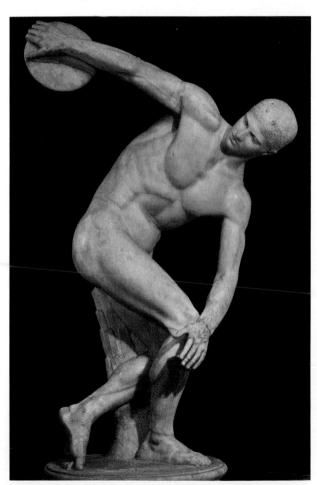

2.25 Myron. *Discobolus (Discus Thrower).* Roman copy after bronze original of c. 450 BCE. Marble, life-size. Museo Nazionale Romano, Rome, Italy.

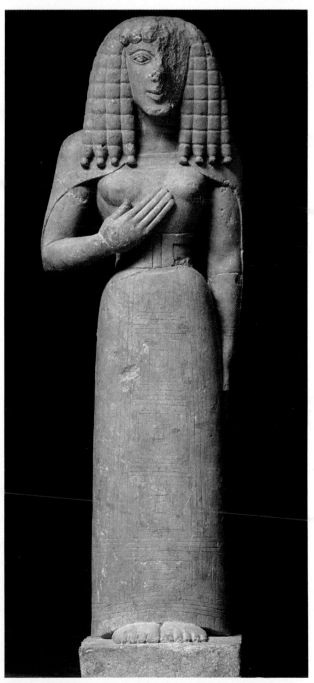

2.26 *Lady of Auxerre,* statue of a goddess or kore, c. 650–625 BCE. Limestone, approx. 2′1½″ high. Louvre, Paris, France.

hairstyle. The mix of styles used indicates how cosmopolitan life was for the seafaring Greeks, especially those who lived and operated trading stations on the many islands that stretch south and west from the Greek mainland to what is now modern Turkey. The purpose of this statue is unknown, but her large hand, which is attached to the body, may have been posed as if to suggest that she was extending it forward. The awkward gesture might be read as a greeting or a plea, in which case the statue could be a votive figure placed at the shrine of a god or goddess.

At about the same time, life-size and larger than life-size figures of clothed girls and women called *kore* (plural, *korai*) were first made. An archaic *Kore* from Samos (Fig. 2.27) is one of many figures of girls or women, originally in a temple courtyard, carrying small animals as votive offerings. Inscriptions tell us that she was dedicated to the goddess Hera. The statue's severely cylindrical figure is quite abstract. Everything extraneous has been eliminated and only the essential formal and linear elements have been retained. The rhythmically repeated lines of the

skirt contrast with the curves of the upper drapery to create a pleasing linear design.

It is interesting to note that the *kore* figures are more varied, especially in dress, than the *kouros* figures, leading some scholars to speculate that the male figures had a more universally understood meaning, perhaps as symbols of mental and physical excellence. The korai statues, on the other hand, may have had meanings specific to their garb.

The *Athena Lemnia* (Fig. 2.28) is a marble copy of Phidias's original bronze statue, which once

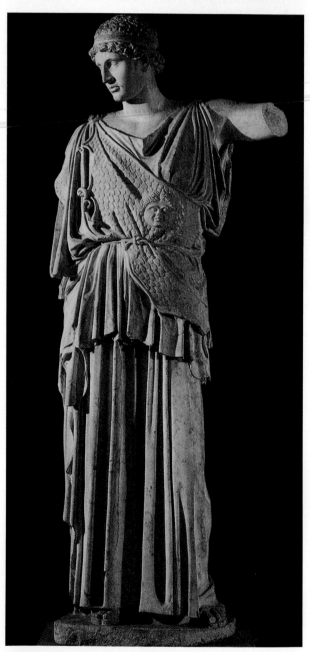

2.28   Phidias (?). *Athena Lemnia*. Roman copy after original of c. 450 BCE. Marble, height 6′6″. Body, Albertinum, Dresden, Germany; head, Museo Civico, Bologna, Italy.

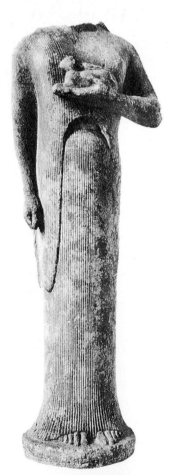

2.27   Kore from Samos, c. 550 BCE. Marble, height 5′3″. Antikensammlung, Staatliche Museum, Berlin, Germany.

stood on the Athenian Acropolis. In it Phidias created a mood that is more lyrical than heroic. In ancient sources, the original statue was often referred to as "the beautiful." The serene profile, softened by the subtle modeling, approaches the ideal of chaste classical beauty.

Praxiteles's *Aphrodite of Cnidos* was proclaimed by Greco-Roman critics to be the finest statue in existence. Known only through inferior copies such as the one shown in Figure 2.29, the statue may have been the first large female nude in Greek art. The "smile playing gently over her parted lips" and the "soft melting gaze of the eyes with their bright and joyous expression" that the Roman writer Lucian so admired in the original can now only be imagined. Praxiteles, however, departed from the draped goddesses of the previous century by boldly portraying the goddess of love in the nude. By so doing, he created a **prototype,** or original model, that influenced all subsequent treatments of the undraped female figure.

VASE PAINTING

Like early Greek sculpture, early Greek pottery depicted rigid angular human figures. However, the shape of early painted vases and other pottery forms was often very graceful and sophisticated. The *François Vase* (Fig. 2.30), found in an Etruscan tomb (see pp. 92–93), was not meant for everyday use but rather was a ritual object and an art form. Its Athenian painter, Kleitias, and potter, Ergotimos, both signed the work, indicating the extent to which they had achieved a reputation for uniqueness and excellence. Created at about the same time as the Kouros from Sounion (Fig. 2.20), the black figures on the François Vase share with the kouros a stiffness and simplification of muscle structure.

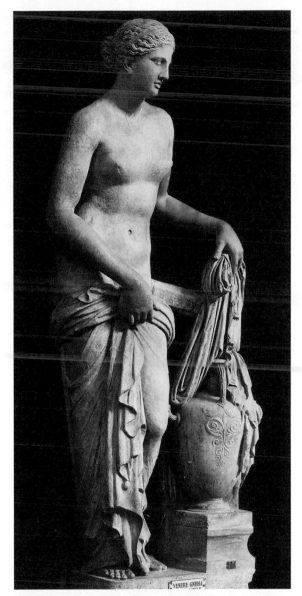

2.29   Praxiteles. *Aphrodite of Cnidos.* Roman copy after original of c. 340 BCE. Marble, height 6′8″. Vatican Museums, Rome, Italy.

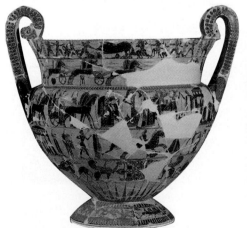
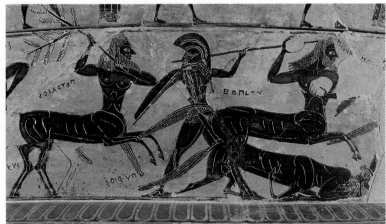

2.30   *François Vase.* Its Athenian painter, Kleitas, and potter, Ergotimos, both signed the work. From Chiusi, Italy, c. 570 BCE. Museo Archeologico, Florence, Italy.

Later potters developed a technique that rendered the figures red. Red-figure pottery often simplified the narrative to one crucial scene. Its figures are agile and better proportioned anatomically than those of the François Vase. Facial and drapery details are picked out in thin black lines. Because virtually no wall painting remains from classical Greece, we have only ancient texts and the indirect, controversial evidence of painted pottery to testify to the quality and interests of Greek painters (Figs. 2.31 and 2.32).

DRAMA

Greek drama was a distillation of life represented in poetic form on the stage. Through the **chorus,** members of the audience became vicarious participants in events happening to a group of people at another time and in another place.

Like all great works of art, Greek drama can be approached on many different levels. At one level, it can be a thrilling story of violent action and bloody revenge. At another, it is a struggle between human ambition and divine retribution or a conflict between free will and predestined fate. At still another level, it becomes a moving experience that affects the viewer through fine language and inspired poetry.

Plots were taken from mythology, heroic legends, or stories of royal houses. Because these age-old themes were forms of popular history, known in advance to the audience, the dramatist could concentrate more on poetry than on plot, provide dramatic commentaries on old tales, and reinterpret them in the light of recent events. The playwright could thus inspire by conjuring up the heroic past, as Aeschylus did in *The Persians;* express individual sentiments in the light of universal experience, as Sophocles did in *Antigone;* invite reexamination of ancient superstitions, as Euripides did in *The Bacchae;* or place current problems in broader historical perspective.

THE ORIGINS OF GREEK DRAMA

Greek drama had its roots in the ancient tradition of heroic verse, in which the storyteller might impersonate an epic hero. It was also associated with the worship of Dionysus (Bacchus in Roman mythology), the god of wine and revelry, whose cult festivals coincided with planting and harvesting seasons. Beginning as primitive magical practices, the rituals became more refined until they became a vehicle for powerful creative expression. When theaters were built, they were located in a precinct sacred to Dionysus. His altar occupied the center of the circular **orchestra,** where the chorus sang and danced. The audience paid tribute to him by their presence.

The theater of Dionysus at Athens (Fig. 2.2), like the better-preserved one at Epidaurus (Fig. 2.33)

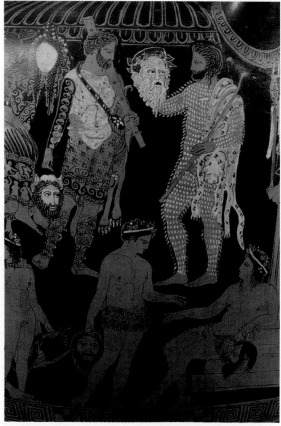

2.31   Pronomos Painter. *Actors Holding Their Masks.* Detail of red-figured painting showing the cast of a satyr play on exterior of volute krater. Ruvo, Italy, c. 410 BCE. Terra cotta, height 2′5½″. Museo Nazionale Archeologico, Naples, Italy.

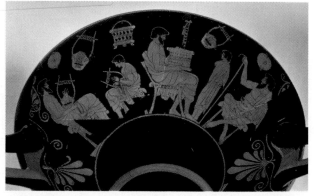

2.32   Douris. *Instruction in Music and Grammar in an Attic School.* Red-figured painting on exterior of kylix, from Cerveteri, c. 480 BCE. Clay, 11³⁄₁₆″ diameter. Antikensammlung, Staatliche Museum, Berlin, Germany.

on the Peloponnesus, was built around the time of Alexander the Great (see pp. 63–64). It had an **auditorium** hollowed out of a hillside that could accommodate approximately 12,000 spectators. The semicircular tiers of seats half surrounded the orchestra and faced the *skene,* a permanent architectural facade with three doors for the actors. The chorus entered and exited at the corners below.

The stylized facade of the skene, suggesting a temple or palace, was suitable for most dramatic situations, because the action almost always took place in the open. The chorus, for example, usually represented worshipers at a shrine, townspeople or petitioners before a palace, a mob, or a group of prisoners. The actors moving in and out of the portals above took the parts of priests, heroes, or members of royal families. When the situation demanded another setting, the chorus or an actor would "paint" the scene with a few words, so other sets were not necessary.

THE STRUCTURE AND SCOPE OF GREEK DRAMA

A typical Greek play opens with a **prologue** spoken by one of the actors. The prologue sets the scene, outlines the plot, and provides a taking-off point for the action. The substance of the drama then unfolds in a sequence of alternating choruses and episodes (usually five episodes enclosed by six choruses) and concludes with the **exodus** of the chorus and an **epilogue.** Actors wore masks (Fig. 2.31) of general types that the audience could recognize instantly. The size and outdoor location of the theaters made facial expressions ineffective, and the swift pace of Greek drama required the player of a king or shepherd to establish a type and character instantly. Masks also proved useful when an actor took more than one part, bringing him immediate acceptance in either role.

Restraint and simplicity were the rule in Greek staging. As with the later Elizabethan theater, scenery was conspicuous by its absence. The only visual illusion seems to have been the *mechane,* a crane that lowered to the stage actors who were portraying gods. In later times, this *deus ex machina,* or "god from the machine," became an easy way of solving dramatic problems that were too complex to be worked out by normal means.

Direct action never occurred onstage. Any violent deed took place elsewhere and was reported by a messenger or another character. The plays proceeded by narration, commentary, speculation, dialogue, and discussion. All these devices—

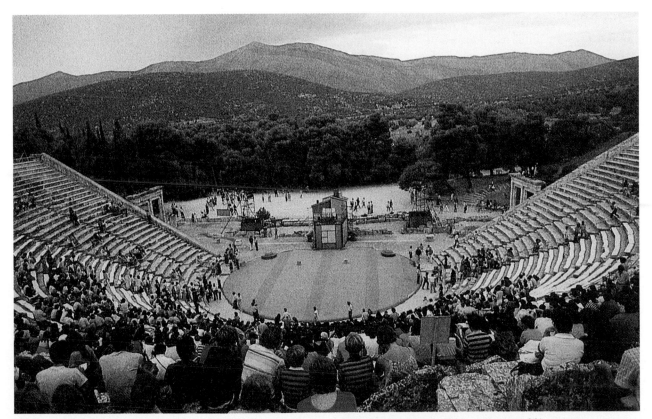

2.33 Polyclitus the Younger. Theater, Epidaurus, Greece, c. 440 BCE. Diameter 373', orchestra 66' across.

plot known in advance, permanent stage setting, use of masks, offstage action—served two principal purposes: to accentuate the poetry of the play and to give the greatest possible scope to the spectator's imagination. Greek drama unfolds as a sequence of choral song, group dances, mimed action, and dialogue coordinated into a dramatic whole. Poetry, however, always remains the central dramatic agent.

The scope of Greek drama was tremendous. It extended from majestic tragedy of heroic proportions, through the pathos of **melodrama** (in its proper meaning of "drama with melody"), all the way to the riotous **comedies** of Aristophanes. Conflict, however, was always the basis for dramatic action. The playwrights created tensions between such forces as murder and revenge, crime and retribution, cowardice and courage, protest and resignation, and pride and humility. When, for instance, a hero is confronted with his destiny, the obstacles he encounters are insurmountable and yet must be surmounted. In the conflict that follows, the play runs the gamut of human emotions and explores the heights to which human life can soar and the depths to which it can sink. In Sophocles's *Oedipus the King,* the hero starts at the peak of his kingly powers and ends in the abyss of human degradation. In Euripides's *Bacchae,* Pentheus, a pillar of respectability, is first made ridiculous and then destroyed.

The **protagonist,** or central character, of a Greek play can fulfill the requirements of tragedy only when portraying some noble figure—one who is "highly renowned or prosperous," as Aristotle argues—who is eventually brought to grief through a personal flaw or by some inevitable stroke of fate. The reasons for this must be made apparent to the audience gradually through the process of "causal necessity." A common person's woes might bring about a pathetic situation but not a tragic one in the classical sense. When a virtuous hero is rewarded or the evil designs of a villain receive their just desserts, obviously there is no tragic situation. When a blameless person is brought from a fortunate to an unfortunate condition or when an evil person rises from misery to good fortune, there is likewise no tragedy because the audience's moral sense is outraged.

AESCHYLUS. According to its founder Aeschylus, Greek tragedy was an instrument through which mortals might comprehend the mystery of the divine will. In his *Oresteia,* a trilogy (three related plays), gods and mortals interact as they seek vengeance for real and perceived wrongs. By establishing a working relationship between mortals and gods, Aeschylus's tragedies also sought to find a basis for personal and social justice. The implications of the early Aeschylean tragedy were thus strongly ethical, showing clearly that in his mind the drama was still identified with theological thought.

SOPHOCLES. The forms of Sophocles's plays were distinguished by their flawless construction, while their lofty content was based on the course of human destiny as seen in light of the moral law of the universe. Aristotle hailed *Oedipus the King* as the greatest of Greek tragedies, both for the nobility of its conception and for the inexorable logic of its plot. Because everyone in Sophocles's audience knew the story, he was free to write a new play on an old theme.

Unknown to himself at the time, Oedipus had violated two of the most basic taboos in any society—murdering his father and marrying his mother. Modern audiences may find this all the more shattering because of Freud's teaching that this dilemma mirrors our own secret desires and fears. "It is that fate of all of us," wrote Freud in his *Interpretation of Dreams,* "to direct our first sexual impulses towards our mother and our first hatred and . . . murderous wish against our father [the Oedipus complex]. Our dreams convince us that this is so."

Like Pericles, Oedipus was a master politician in full control of the state. But he was determined to seek the truth about his origins. The heroic aspect of Oedipus's character is not that his life is predestined by fate or by the will of the gods but that he is free to pursue the truth wherever it might lead. Oedipus commands both admiration and sympathy as he brings the full force of his intelligence, courage, and relentless perseverance to the quest. In this progressive unmasking of himself, the audience sees the hero as his own destroyer, as a detective who discovers that the criminal is himself. The closer he comes to his imminent downfall, the higher his stature rises. The true tragic grandeur then comes when he and the audience recognize that he must bear full moral responsibility for his life and acts. To make amends for his crimes, he calls for his sword to kill himself. Then, in a moment of bitter irony, he seizes his wife Jocasta's golden pin and pierces his eyeballs, saying that when he could see he was blind, so only in blindness can he really see: "Be dark from now on, since you saw before what you should not, and knew not what you should."

The audience in fifth-century Athens was inevitably caught up in the web of the plot, enthralled with its relentless progress while identifying with the plight of the characters whose fate was unraveling. When the awful truth was revealed, Oedipus's catastrophe was perceived as the tragedy of the Athenians themselves as they in turn became aware of their own ignorance. Instead of humans being the measure of all things, perhaps it was they who were being measured, tried in the balance, and found wanting.

EURIPIDES. Aristotle observed that Euripides sought to show people as they are, whereas Sophocles had depicted them as they ought to be. In some ways, the works of Euripides may not be so typical of the Hellenic style as those of Aeschylus or Sophocles, but his influence on the subsequent development of the drama, both in Hellenistic and in later times, was incalculably greater.

The *Bacchae,* the last of Euripides's surviving plays, was written toward the end of the disastrous Peloponnesian War, a time of disillusionment for Athenian intellectuals. In it he gives voice to some of the doubts and uncertainties of his time. The play's theme is the complex interplay between the human and divine wills, as well as between the known and the unknown. The pale self-righteousness of Pentheus is crushed by the implacable, terrifying wrath of the god Bacchus. Agave, Pentheus's mother, is led to murder her own son because she voluntarily surrenders her reason to an irrational cult. Pentheus's downfall comes because his reason is not strong enough to comprehend the emotional and irrational forces that motivate the members of his family and his subjects. Because Pentheus cannot understand these forces, he cannot bring them under control and thus lacks the wisdom and tolerance required of a successful ruler.

Like most masterpieces, the *Bacchae* is in some respects atypical, but in others it seems to stem from the deepest roots of theater. Despite some inner inconsistencies and a certain elusiveness of meaning, the *Bacchae* has all the formal perfection and poetic grandeur of the loftiest tragedies. The strange, wild beauty of its choruses and the magic of its poetry give this drama all the necessary ingredients of theater at its best.

ARISTOTLE ON THEATER. After the great days of Aeschylus, Sophocles, and Euripides had passed, Aristotle, with knowledge of their complete works instead of the relatively few examples known today, wrote a perceptive analysis of tragedy and more broadly of art in general. In his treatise *Poetics,* he argues that true drama—and indeed all works of art—must have form in the sense of a beginning, a middle, and an end.

Unity of time, place, and action is also desirable. Sophocles's *Oedipus Rex,* for example, takes place in a single day (albeit a busy one); all the scenes are set in front of the palace at Thebes; and the action is direct and continuous, without subplots. Other Greek plays encompass a longer span of time and have several settings. As Aristotle pointed out, these unities were useful but by no means hard-and-fast rules.

Custom held that three actors onstage at one time was the maximum desirable. If the play required six parts, the roles were usually apportioned among three actors. As the action proceeds, the conflict between protagonist and antagonist emerges, and the play rises to its climax in the middle episode. Through the tragic necessity, the hero's downfall occurs because he carries the seeds of his own destruction within his breast. After this turning point, the well-planned anticlimax resolves the action into a state of equilibrium.

Tragedy, according to Aristotle, had to be composed of six necessary elements, which he ranked as follows: *plot,* "the arrangement of the incidents"; *character,* "that which reveals moral purpose"; *thought,* "where something is proved to be or not to be"; *diction,* "the metrical arrangements of the words"; *song,* which "holds the chief place among the embellishments"; and *spectacle.* Finally, Aristotle summed up his definition of *tragedy* as "an imitation of an action that is serious, complete, and of a certain magnitude; in language embellished with each kind of ornament, the several kinds being found in separate sections of the play; in the form of action, not of narrative; with incidents arousing pity and fear, wherewith to accomplish its **katharsis** ["purgation"] of the emotions."

MUSIC

The word *music* implies a fully mature and independent art. It must be remembered, however, that symphonies, chamber music, and solo instrumental compositions, in which the focus is almost entirely on abstract sound, are relatively modern forms. *Music* covers the union of sound with many other elements, as in the case of popular songs, dance music, military marches, and church hymns. It also describes the combination of sound with lyric and narrative poetry, as in songs and ballads; with step and gesture, as in dance; and with drama, as in opera.

In ancient Greece, music in its broadest sense meant any of the arts and sciences that came under the patronage of the Muses, mythological maidens who were the daughters of the heavenly Zeus and the earthly Mnemosyne. Because Zeus was the creator and Mnemosyne, as her name implies, the personification of memory, the

Muses and their arts were thought to be the results of the union of the creative urge and memory, half divine, half human. This was a way of saying that the arts were thought of as recorded inspiration.

As Greek civilization progressed, the number of Muses gradually increased to nine, all of whom were under the patronage of Apollo, god of prophecy and enlightenment. The arts and sciences over which they presided came to include all the intellectual and inspirational disciplines that sprang from the fertile minds of a creative people—lyric poetry, tragic and comic drama, choral dancing, and song. Astronomy and history were also included. The visual arts and crafts, on the other hand, were protected by Athena and Hephaestus—symbolizing intellect tempered by fire. Plato and others placed music in opposition to gymnastic or physical pursuits, and its meaning in this sense was as broad as our use of the general terms *liberal arts* or *culture.*

The Greeks also used *music* more narrowly, in the sense of the tonal art. But music was always intimately bound up with poetry, drama, and dance and was usually found in their company. At one place in the *Republic,* Socrates asks: "And when you speak of music, do you include literature or not?" The answer is yes. Thus, although the Greeks did have independent instrumental music apart from its combination with words, evidence suggests that the vast body of their music was connected with literary forms.

This does not imply, of course, that music lacked a distinct identity or that it was swallowed up by poetry—rather it had an important and honored part in poetry. Plato, for instance, remarks: "And I think that you must have observed again and again what a poor appearance the tales of the poets make when stripped of the colours which music puts upon them, and recited in simple prose. . . . They are like faces which were never really beautiful, but only blooming; and now the bloom of youth has passed away from them."

MUSIC AND LITERATURE

Greek music must therefore be considered primarily in its union with literature, as illustrated in the vase painting *Instruction in Music and Grammar in an Attic School* by Douris (Fig. 2.32). The clearest statement of this is found in the *Republic,* where it is pointed out that "melody is composed of three things, the words, the harmony [the sequence of melodic intervals], and the rhythm." In discussing the relative importance of each, Plato states that "harmony and rhythm must follow the words." The two arts thus are united in the single one of **prosody**—that is, the melodic and rhythmic setting of a poetic text.

Greek melodies and rhythms are known to have been associated with specific moods, or **modes**—scales constructed by adjusting the pitch of tones within the octave. The modern major scale, or mode, can be found on the piano by playing the white keys from middle C to the next C above (eight tones, or an **octave**). Similarly, the melodic minor scale, or mode, goes from A (two white keys below middle C) to the A above. The ancient Greek Dorian mode can be approximated by the white keys from E (two white keys above middle C) to the E an octave above.

The great variety of Greek modes allowed poets and dramatists to elicit a wide range of emotional responses from their audiences. Although ethical and emotional orientations have changed over the centuries, the basic modal and metrical system of the Greeks has, in effect, continued through all subsequent periods of Western music and poetry.

Music, in both its broadest and narrowest senses, was woven into the emotional, intellectual, and social life of the ancient Greeks. The art was also considered to have a fundamental connection with the health and well-being of individuals, as well as with their social and physical environment. There is no more eloquent tribute to the power of art in public affairs than that attributed to Socrates: "When modes of music change, the fundamental laws of the State always change with them."

Ideal education for young people in Greece consisted of a balanced curriculum of music for the soul and gymnastics for the body. Even the welfare of the soul after death had musical overtones, because to many Greeks immortality meant being somehow in tune with the cosmic forces and being at last able to hear the "music of the spheres."

All these notions had to do with the physical world being in some way in harmony with the world of the spirit—the metaphysical world—and the soul was in tune with the body. According to the Greek myth of Orpheus, who is depicted in a fine red-figured vase of the early fifth century BCE (Fig. 2.34), music even had the miraculous power to overcome death.

MUSIC THEORY

The Greeks' most important contribution to music is without doubt a theoretical one—that of coordinating the mathematical ratios of melodic inter-

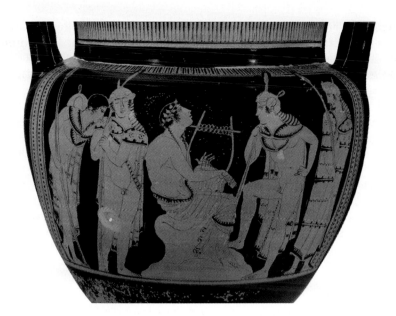

2.34 *Orpheus among the Thracians.* Attic red-figure vase, c. 440 BCE.

vals with their scale system. The discovery, attributed to Pythagoras, showed that intervals such as the octave, fifth, and fourth have a mathematical relationship (Fig. 2.35). This can easily be heard when a tuned string is stopped off exactly in the middle. The musical interval between the tone of an unstopped string and the one that is divided into two equal parts is an octave, and the mathematical ratio is $1:2$. If a segment of the string divided into two parts is compared with a segment of a string divided into three parts, the resulting interval will be a fifth, and the ratio, $2:3$. If one compares the tone of the triply divided string with that of a string divided into four parts, the interval will be a fourth, and the ratio $3:4$. Hence, $1:2$ mathematically equals the octave; $2:3$, the fifth; $3:4$, the fourth; $8:9$, the whole tone; and so on. Because of these mathematical relationships, to Pythagoras and his followers music was synonymous with order and proportion, and it rested on a demonstrably rational basis.

MUSIC AND DRAMA

Knowledge of Greek music must be gleaned from a variety of sources, such as occasional literary references, poetry and drama, visual representations of musical instruments and music making in sculpture and painting, theoretical treatises, and some very fragmentary surviving examples of the music itself. When all the sources are combined, we can gain a faint notion of what Greek music was actually like. Music's highest development undoubtedly was in its union with the drama. Athenian dramatists were by tradition responsible for the

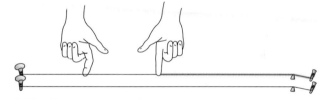

2.35 Demonstrating the octave.

music, the training of the chorus, and the staging of their plays, as well as for the writing of the script. In addition, they often played some of the roles. With all their other activities, the great dramatists had to be composers as well as poets, actors, playwrights, and producers.

In reconstructing the Greek drama, one must imagine an audience to whom the drama was a lively audio and visual experience, consisting of choral singing and dancing, vocal and instrumental music, as well as dialogue and dramatic sequences. Music itself was a full partner in conveying the poet's meaning. Today, with the choruses and dances missing, a performance of a play like *The Suppliants* by Aeschylus is like the text of an opera being read instead of sung. In Euripides's *Bacchae,* the emotional intensity of the individual scenes often rises to such a pitch that music must take over where the words leave off—just as when a person is so overcome with feeling that words fail and inarticulate sounds and gestures are all that remain.

THE CHORUS. The weight of musical expression fell primarily on the chorus, which was the original basis of the dramatic form and from which all the other elements of the drama evolved. The chorus performed both in stationary positions and in motion. As the chorus circulated around the altar of Dionysus in the center of the orchestra, its song was accompanied by appropriate gestures. The forms of the choruses were metrically and musically very elaborate and were written with such variety and invention that repetitions, either within a single play or in other plays by the same poet, were very rare.

Interestingly enough, the sole surviving relic of Greek music from the fifth century BCE is a fragment of a choral **stasimon,** or "stationary chorus," from Euripides' *Orestes*. All ancient Greek manuscripts have come down through the ages from the hands of medieval scribes, who omitted the musical notation of earlier copies because it was no longer comprehensible to them. In the Euripides fragment, the musical notation was included, but all that is left is a single sheet of poorly preserved papyrus.

Fragmentary though this scrap of evidence is, these few notes are enough to tell their own story. Euripides's choruses were musically complex, requiring highly skilled singers who could master the Mixolydian mode, which Aristotle described in his *Politics* as "mournful and restrained." The words that accompany the fragment perfectly express this sentiment, and when properly performed, the fragment still conveys this mood. Other than this single relic of choral recitative, the music of the fifth century must remain mute to our ears.

IDEAS

Each of the arts—architecture, sculpture, painting, poetry, drama, and music—is a distinct medium of expression. Each has its own materials, whether stone, bronze, pigments, words, or tones. Each has its skilled artists, who have disciplined themselves through years of study so that they can mold their materials into meaningful forms. But every artist, whether architect, sculptor, painter, poet, dramatist, or musician, also lives in a specific time and place.

No art exists in isolation, and thus it is no accident that the Greeks thought of the arts as a family of sister Muses. Architecture, to complete itself, must rely on sculpture and painting for embellishments. Sculpture and painting must search for congenial architectural surroundings. Drama embraces poetry, song, and dance in the setting of a theater.

This interdependence of the arts was quite clear in ancient times, as Plutarch quoting Simonides indicates: "Painting is silent poetry; poetry is painting that speaks." When Plato and Aristotle examined the arts, they looked for common elements that applied to all. And they were just as keen in their search for unity in the arts as they were for unity among all the other aspects of human experience.

Certain recurring themes appear in each of the arts of the Hellenic period as artists sought to bring their ideals to expression. Out of these themes emerges a trio of ideas—humanism, idealism, and rationalism—that recur continually in Athenian thought and action. These three ideas, both separately and in their interaction, provide a framework that surrounds the arts and encloses them in such a way that they come together into a significant unity.

HUMANISM

"Man," said Protagoras, "is the measure of all things." And as Sophocles observed, "Many are the wonders of the world, and none so wonderful as man." This, in essence, is humanism. The Greeks conceived their gods and goddesses as idealized beings, immortal and free from physical infirmities but, like themselves, subject to human passions and ambitions. The gods, likewise, were personifications of human ideals: Zeus stood for masculine creative power, Hera for maternal womanliness, Athena for wisdom, Apollo for youthful brilliance, and Aphrodite for feminine desirability. Because of this perceived resemblance to the gods, the Greeks gained greatly in self-esteem.

The principal concern of the Greeks was with human beings—their social relationships, their place in the natural environment, and their stake in the universal scheme of things. In such a small city-state as Athens, civic duties fell upon the individual. Every responsible citizen had to be concerned with politics, which Aristotle considered the highest of all pursuits. Participation in public affairs was based on the need to subordinate personal aspirations to the good of the state. A person endowed with great qualities of mind and body was honor-bound to exercise these gifts in the service of others. Aeschylus, Socrates, and Sophocles were men of action, who served Athens on the battlefield as well as in public forums and theaters. One responsibility of a citizen was to foster the arts. Under Athenian democracy, the state itself, meaning the citizenry, became the principal patron of the arts.

Politically and socially, the life of Athenian citizens was balanced between aristocratic conservatism and liberal individualism, a balance that was maintained by the democratic institutions of their society. Their arts reflected a tension between this aristocratic tradition, which resisted change and emphasized austerity, restraint, and stylization in the arts, and the new dynamic liberalism, which put greater emphasis on emotion, the desire for ornateness, and a taste for naturalism. The genius of Phidias was his ability to achieve a middle road between these opposites; the incomparable Parthenon was the result.

Humanism also expressed itself in kinship with nature. Although they conceived their gods in the image of humans, the Greeks also tried to come to terms with unpredictable natural phenomena and explain the inexplicable, **personifying** many animate and inanimate entities. Their forests were populated with elusive nymphs and satyrs, their seas with energetic tritons, and their skies with capricious zephyrs. All were imaginative explanations and personifications of forces beyond their control. Attempting to create an imaginary world that is also a poetic image of the real world will always be one of the chief pursuits of the artist. Moreover, the Greeks thought of art as a ***mimesis***— that is, an imitation or representation of nature. Because this also included human nature, it implied a re-creation of life in the various mediums of art.

The art of sculpture was congenial to this humanistic mode of thought. With the human body as the point of departure, divinities such as Athena and Apollo appeared as idealized images of perfect feminine and masculine beauty. Equally imaginative were such deviations from the human norm as the goat-footed Pan, the half-human/half-horse centaurs, and the many fanciful creatures and monsters that symbolized the forces of nature.

The Greeks were more thoroughly at home in the physical world than the later Christian peoples, who believed in a separation of flesh and spirit and strongly favored the spirit. The Greeks greatly admired the beauty and agility of the human body at the peak of its development. In addition to studying literature and music, Greek male youths were trained from childhood for competition in the Athenian and Olympic games. Women may have been allowed to train, but they could not enter the games. Because it was through the perfection of their bodies that human beings most resembled the gods, the culture of the body was a spiritual as well as physical activity.

The nude male body in action at gymnasiums was a fact of daily experience, and sculptors had ample opportunity to observe its proportions and musculature. The *Kritios Boy* (Fig. 2.36), a kouroi found on the Athenian Acropolis, is one of the rare marble originals of this period. The slight turn of

the head and the easy stance with the weight placed on one foot give the figure a supple grace and animation. In Western art appreciation, he became a symbol of the balance between body and soul so admired by the Greeks. In a lesser way, this idea was also attributed to well-known examples such as the *Doryphorus* (Fig. 2.21) and the *Discobolus* (Fig. 2.25). As an instrument of expression, the male nude reached a high point in the fifth century BCE. The female form, however, had to wait until the next century for similar inspired treatment.

Any humanistic point of view assumes that life here and now is good and is meant to be enjoyed.

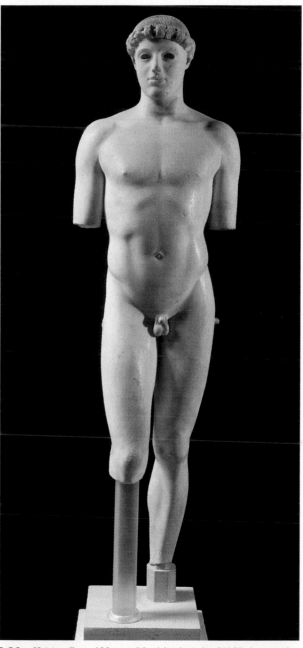

2.36 *Kritios Boy,* 480 BCE. Marble, height 2′10″. Acropolis Museum, Athens, Greece.

This attitude is the opposite of medieval self-denial, which viewed the joys of this life as snares of the devil (see Fig. 6.1) and held that true good could be attained only in the unseen world beyond the grave. Although the Greeks had no single belief about life after death, a typical one is found in the underworld scene of Homer's *The Odyssey,* in which the spirit of the hero's mother explains that "when first the breath departs from the white bones, flutters the spirit away, and like to a dream it goes drifting." In the same scene, the ghost of Achilles tells Odysseus that he would rather be the slave of the poorest living mortal than reign as king over the underworld. Greek *steles,* or grave-stones, usually depicted the deceased in some characteristic worldly attitude—a warrior in battle, a hunter with his favorite horse or dog, or a lady choosing her jewelry for the day's adornment (Fig. 2.37). The grave stele or grave marker of Hegeso offers an idealization of a good wife and mother, who produced model Athenian citizens. She is more elaborately dressed and coifed than the woman, probably a slave, who assists her. At the same time she is calm and introspective, showing some of the serenity of the three goddesses from the Parthenon (Fig. 2.18).

The spiritual kingdom of the Greeks was definitely of this world. They produced no major religious prophets and had no divinely imposed creeds, no sacred scriptures as final authority on religious matters, and no single organized priesthood. The mottoes inscribed on the sacred stones of Delphi, such as "Know thyself" and "Nothing in excess," were suggestions that bore no resemblance to the thunderous "Thou shalt nots" of Moses's Ten Commandments.

Knowledge of their gods came to the Greeks from Homer's epics and Hesiod's book of myths. The character and action of these gods, however, were subject to a variety of interpretations, as is clear from the commentaries of the fifth-century drama. This nonconformity indicated a broad tolerance that allowed free speculation about the nature of the universe. Indeed, the Greeks worked hard to penetrate the divine mind and to interpret its meaning in human affairs. Ultimately, their ethical principles were embodied in four virtues: *courage,* meaning physical and moral bravery; *temperance,* in the sense of nothing too much or, as Pericles put it, "our love of what is beautiful does not lead us to extravagance"; *justice,* which meant rendering to each person what was due him or her; and *wisdom,* the pursuit of truth.

HUMANISM AND THE ARTS. Just as Greek religion sought to capture the godlike image in human form, so the arts tried to bring the experience of space and time within human grasp. Indefinite space and infinite time meant little to the Greeks. The modern concept of a nation as a territorial or spatial unit, for instance, did not exist for them. Expansion of their city-state had less to do with lines on a map than with a cultural unit consisting of independent people who shared a common language and set of ideals. The Greeks had little knowledge of or concern with an accurately dated historical past. This is seen in the imperfection of their calendar and in the fact that their best-known historians, Herodotus and Thucydides, were really chroniclers of almost-contemporary events.

For the Greeks, geometry was designed to measure static rather than moving bodies, and their visual arts emphasized poise and calm. Greek architecture humanized the experience of space by organizing it so that it was neither too complex nor too grand to be comprehended fully. The Parthenon's success rests on its power to humanize the experience of space. Through its geometry, such visual facts as repeated patterns, spatial progressions, and distance intervals are made easy to see and understand. The simplicity and clarity

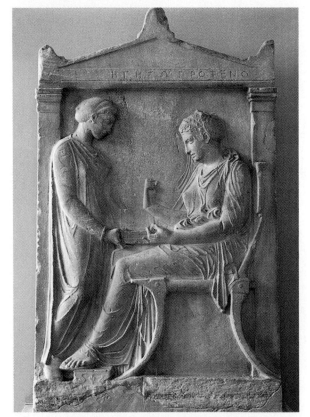

2.37 Grave stele of Hegeso, c. 410–400 BCE. Marble, height 4'11". National Archaeological Museum, Athens, Greece.

of Greek construction were always evident to the eye, and by defining the indefinite and imposing a sense of clarity and order on the chaos of space, the architects of Greece made their conceptions of space both articulate and intelligible.

Just as architecture humanized the perception of space, so the arts of dance, music, poetry, and drama humanized the experience of time. These arts fell within the broad meaning of *music,* and their humanistic connection was emphasized in the education of youth. For as Plato said, "rhythm and harmony find their way into the inward places of the soul, on which they mightily fasten, imparting grace, and making the soul of him who is rightly educated graceful."

The triple unities of time, place, and action observed by the dramatists brought the flow of time within definite limits and are a striking contrast to the shifting scenes and continuous narrative styles of later periods. The essential humanism of Greek drama is found in its creation of distinctive human types; in its use of the chorus to provide a collective commentary on the actions of gods and heroes; in its treatment of human actions in such a way that they rise above individual limitations to the level of universal principles; and above all, in the creation of tragedy, in which the great individual is shown rising to the highest estate and then plunging to the lowest depths, thereby spanning the limits of human experience.

In sum, all the arts of Greece became the generating force by which Athenians consciously or unconsciously identified with other citizens and with the entire rhythm of life around them. Through the arts, human experience was evaluated and dignified.

IDEALISM

When artists face the practical problem of representation, they may follow one of two courses. They can choose to represent objects either as they appear to the physical eye or as they appear to the mind's eye. In one case, they would emphasize nature, in the other, imagination; in one the world of appearances, in the other, the world of essences; in one, the real, in the other, the ideal. The avowed realist is more concerned with rendering the actual, tangible object, with all its particular and peculiar characteristics. The idealist, on the other hand, accents abstraction, eliminating all extraneous accessories and concentrating on the essential qualities of things. A realist, in other words, seeks to represent things as they are, an idealist, as they might or should be. Idealism as a creative viewpoint gives precedence to

the idea or mental image, tries to transcend physical limitations, aspires toward a fulfillment that goes beyond actual observation, and seeks a concept closer to perfection.

Both courses were followed in the Hellenic style. One of Myron's most celebrated works was a bronze cow said to be so natural that it aroused amorous reactions in bulls and calves tried to suckle it. Such a work would certainly have been in line with the Greek definition of art as the imitation of nature. The striving to represent the world of natural appearances is well exemplified in the astonishing likeness of a warrior, a fifth-century BCE Greek original bronze found off the coast of southern Italy (Fig. 2.38). The naturalistic

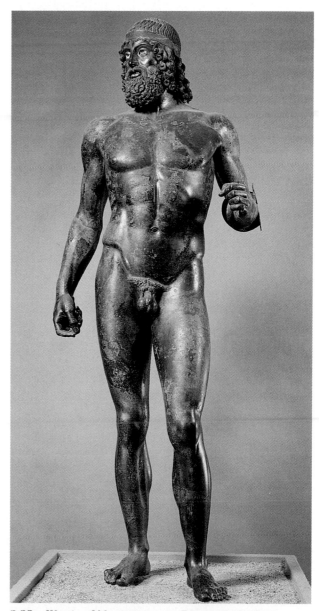

2.38 *Warrior,* fifth century BCE. Bronze with glass, bone, silver, and copper inlay, height 6′6″. Museo Archeologico Nazionale, Reggio Calabria, Italy.

representation is fortified by the use of bone and glass for the eyes; copper for the eyelashes, lips, and nipples; and silver for the teeth. These embellishments remind us that the Greeks preferred polychrome, or colored statues, and that the association of pure white marble with Greek civilization is a much later, and mistaken, impression.

The distance from stylization to realism can be measured by comparing the bronze warrior with the earlier kouros (Fig. 2.20). On the other hand, the difference between realism and idealism can also be seen when this warrior is compared with the representation of Zeus in Figure 2.24.

PLATO AND ARISTOTLE'S IDEAL FORMS. The case for idealism is argued in depth in Plato's dialogues. He assumes a world of eternal verities and transcendental truths but recognizes that perfect truth, beauty, and goodness can exist only in the world of forms and ideas. Phenomena observed in the visible world are but lesser versions of these invisible forms.

Plato's *Republic* is an attempt to describe an ideal society and explore its consequences. No one knew better than Plato that such a society did not exist and probably never would. But this did not lessen the value of imagining it and discussing it. The important thing was to establish goals that would approach Plato's ideal more closely than did any existing situation. "Would a painter be any the worse," he asks, "because, after having delineated with consummate art an ideal of a perfectly beautiful man, he was unable to show that any such man could ever have existed? . . . And is our theory a worse theory because we are unable to prove the possibility of a city being ordered in the manner described?"

Plato's idealistic theory, however, leads him into a rather strange position regarding the activities of artists. When, for instance, they fashion a building, a statue, or a painting, they are imitating, or representing, specific things that, in turn, are imitations of ideal forms; hence their products are thrice removed from the truth. The clear implication is, of course, that art should try to get away from the accidental and accent the essential to avoid the transitory and seek the permanent. This point was also made in the *Republic,* in the allegory of the cave. Plato asks us to imagine a dark cavern in which prisoners are chained in such a way that they cannot turn around and look toward the daylight outside. They are forced to watch stories told by shadow puppets. Just as these tales become real to the prisoners, so the experience of everyday life seems real to us. But neither the shadow puppets nor what we see with our eyes is eternal.

Aristotle, on the other hand, distinguished among various approaches in art. In his *Poetics* he observes that "we must represent men either as better than in real life, or as worse, or as they are. It is the same in painting. Polygnotus depicted men as nobler than they are, Pauson as less noble, Dionysius drew them true to life. . . . So again in language, whether prose or verse unaccompanied by music. Homer, for example, makes men better than they are; Cleophon as they are; Hegemon the Thasian, the inventor of parodies, . . . worse than they are." Aristotle applied the same standard to drama, pointing out, "Comedy aims at representing men as worse, Tragedy as better than in actual life." In the visual arts, he distinguishes between an idealized image, a realistic image, or a caricature. Aristotle clearly implies that idealism, as expressed in Homer's heroic poetry, Polygnotus's noble paintings, and Sophocles' moving tragedies, constitutes the highest form of art.

IDEALISM AND THE ARTS. At its high point in the second half of the fifth century BCE, Hellenic art was dominated by idealism. The Greek temple was designed as an idealized dwelling place for a perfect being. Through its logical interrelationship of lines, planes, and masses, it achieves a sense of permanence and stability in the face of the transitory and random state of nature.

In portraying an athlete, a statesman, or a deity, the Hellenic sculptor concentrated on typical or general qualities rather than on the unique or particular. This was in line with the Greek idea of personality, which was thought to be better expressed in the dominating traits than in individual oddities.

In sculpture, as in all the other arts, the goal was to rise above transitory sensations and capture the permanent, the essential, the complete. Thus, the sculptor avoided representing the human being in infancy, infirmity, or old age, because such representations would imply incompleteness or imperfection and hence were incompatible with the concept of ideal types. The range of representations extends from athletes in their late teens through images of Hermes, Apollo, and Athena, who are conceived of as being in their early maturity, to Zeus, father of the gods, who appears as the fully developed patriarch in all the power of mature manhood. It must also be remembered that few of the Hellenic sculptors' works were intended to represent human beings as such. Most were fashioned to represent gods, who, if cast in human form, must have bodies of transcendent beauty.

In some way, even the intangible tones of music participated in the ideal world by way of the mathematical relationships on which they are based. A melody, then, might have something more permanent than its fleeting auditory nature would indicate.

One of the main functions of drama was to create ideal types, and although the typical was always opposed to the particular, somehow the one arose from the other. The interpretation of this interplay was assigned to the chorus, and the drama as a whole shared with the other arts the power of revealing how the permanent could be derived from the impermanent; how the type could be found in the many specific cases; and how the **archetype,** or highest type, could arise from the types.

In the extreme sense, the ideal and real worlds represent perfect order and blind chaos. Because the one was unattainable and the other intolerable, it was necessary to find a middle ground. Glimpses of truth, beauty, and goodness could be caught occasionally, and these glimpses should help people steer a course from the actual to the ideal. By exercising the faculties of reason, judgment, and moral sense, human beings could subdue the chaotic conditions of their existence and come closer to perfection.

The Socratic theory of education, expressed in the balance between gymnastics for the body and music for the soul, was designed as a curriculum leading toward this end. The Greek temple, the nobly proportioned sculptural figures, the hero of epic and tragedy, and the orderly relationships of the melodic intervals in music are all embodiments of this ideal. As Socrates said, "Let our artists rather be those who are gifted to discern the true nature of the beautiful and graceful; then will our youth dwell in a land of health, amid fair sights and sounds, and receive the good in everything; and beauty, the effluence of fair works, shall flow into the eye and ear, like a health-giving breeze from a purer region, and insensibly draw the soul from earliest years into likeness and sympathy with the beauty of reason."

RATIONALISM

Rationalism is a concept and a way of life that rests on the idea that the rule of reason should prevail in human affairs. In the *Republic,* Plato sought to demonstrate that the mind could illuminate the ways and means of ordering human life

as well as governing the state through the application of reason. He divided the human constitution into three parts—appetitive, emotional, and rational—which were located in the abdomen, the chest, and the head, respectively. Likewise, human life could rise from its initial stage of ignorance, through a period of constantly changing opinion, to the final security and stability of knowledge together with the contemplation of the eternal verities—truth, goodness, and beauty. The clear implications are that the intellect is the highest human faculty and that through education men and women can rise to the point where reason rules their lives.

From the time Pythagoras discovered the exact mathematical ratios of the musical intervals, Greek thinkers were convinced that the universe was knowable because it was founded on rational and harmonic principles. Plato recounts in the *Republic* the story of a fallen warrior, Er, who returned to life and told of what he had seen in the otherworld. He said that he had beheld the heavenly bodies moving together to form a single harmony, "and round about, at equal intervals, there is another band, three in number, each sitting upon her throne: these are the Fates, daughters of Necessity, . . . Lachesis and Clotho and Atropos, who accompany with their voices the harmony of the sirens—Lachesis singing of the past, Clotho of the present, Atropos of the future."

Following the Pythagorean theory that "all things are numbers," Socrates and Plato taught that human inquiries and endeavors could serve as a mirror of the cosmic order. It also followed that beyond the changing and shifting world of appearances there was an underlying permanent and orderly continuity in both cosmic and human affairs and that it was based on logic and reason.

In the Hebraic and Christian traditions, original sin lay in breaking the moral law, but to the Greeks, the greatest error was lack of knowledge. The tragedy of Oedipus in Sophocles's *Oedipus the King* is his ignorance, because it prevents him from knowing that he is murdering his father, marrying his mother, and begetting children who are also his siblings. His downfall therefore comes through his ignorance, and his fate is the price he has to pay for it. The entire Greek philosophical tradition concurred in the assumption that without knowledge and the free exercise of reason, there is no ultimate happiness.

By thinking for themselves in the spirit of free intellectual inquiry, the Greeks, to a great extent, formulated rules for the conduct of life and its creative forces. This faith in reason also imparted to the arts an inner logic of their own, because when an artist's hands are guided by an alert mind, the work can penetrate the surface play of the senses and plunge to deeper levels of universal experience. For later periods, this balance between the opposites of reason and emotion, form and content, reality and appearance becomes the basis for revivals of classical style. For subsequent classical movements such as those of the Renaissance and the late eighteenth and early nineteenth centuries, the guiding principles were symmetry, proportion, and unity based on the interrelationship of parts with one another and with the whole.

HARMONIC PROPORTIONS. In the *Timaeus,* Plato theorized that God had created the world by making successive divisions of matter and placing in space the seven heavenly bodies known to the Greeks. As the planets moved in their orbits, they were thought to create cosmic music in the manner of the division of the octave into the seven tones of the diatonic scale. All this accorded with the discoveries of Pythagoras and the doctrine of the music of the spheres. This doctrine survived into the Middle Ages and the Renaissance through the writings of Galileo and Kepler (see pp. 411–412), who still maintained that the planets created a music of the spheres in a kind of sonic counterpoint to the laws of planetary motion. According to Plato, God created the human soul as the mirror image of this universal soul and endowed human beings with rational faculties so that they could aspire to immortality "by learning the harmonies and revolutions of the universe."

Because God composed the universe according to musical and geometric laws, it followed that human architecture and sculpture ought to mirror the cosmic order. At Agrigentum in Sicily, the largest of all Doric temples was dedicated to Zeus. Zeus was the lord of the skies, hence the two porches have seven columns each (an allusion to the seven planets) and the lateral columns number fourteen in the octaval proportion of $1:2$. Near Athens on the island of Aegina, a temple to a local goddess, Aphaia, is also in the Doric order and has six columns on the front and back and twelve on the sides, again in the proportion of $1:2$. On the mainland, however, by the midfifth century the proportions had shifted to $1:2$ plus 1, possibly for greater elegance and less rigid mathematical regularity. This is seen in the temple of Zeus at Olympia and the Hephaesteum in Athens. Both are framed by six frontal and thirteen lateral columns in the ratio of $6:13$; the ratio of columns in the Parthenon is $8:17$. Later, the geometry of the Pantheon in Rome was also based on exact harmonic proportions (see Fig. 4.22A).

Polyclitus thought along the same lines when he formulated a rational theory of the proportions of the human body. It was based on a modular system in which all parts become multiples or fractions of a basic common measure. His long-lost book was known to the Roman architectural theorist Vitruvius, who pointed out that because the head would be one-eighth the total height of an idealized figure, the human body itself would fit into the octave relationship of the musical intervals.

Vitruvius, for his own part, showed how the human body fits into the two most perfect geometric forms: the circle and square. The drawing in Figure 2.39 by Leonardo da Vinci is based on the theories of Vitruvius. Both hark back to Plato's *Timaeus,* in which the cosmic soul is the macrocosm of the universe and the human soul the microcosm.

RATIONALISM AND THE ARTS. Hellenic artists were as much concerned as were Plato and Aristotle with the pursuit of an ideal order, which they believed could be grasped by the mind through the medium of the senses. Greek architecture, in retrospect, turns out to be a high point in the rational solution for building problems. The post-and-lintel system of construction, as far as it goes, is reasonable and completely comprehensible. All structural members fulfill their logical purpose. The orderly principle of repetition on which Greek temple designs are based is as logical in its way as one of Euclid's geometry propositions or Plato's dialogues. It accomplishes for the eye what Plato tries to achieve for the mind.

The tight unity of the Greek temple met the Greek requirement that a work of art be complete in itself. Its carefully controlled but flexible relationships of verticals and horizontals, solids and voids, structural principles and decorative embellishments give it a relentless internal consistency. Moreover, the harmonic proportions of the Parthenon reflect the Greek image of a harmoniously proportioned universe quite as much as a logical system does.

Sculpture likewise avoided the pitfalls of rigid mathematics and succeeded in working out principles adapted to its specific needs. When Polyclitus said that "the beautiful comes about, little by little, through many numbers," he was stating a rational theory of art in which the parts and whole of a work could be expressed in mathematical proportions. But he also allowed for flexible application

2.39 Leonardo da Vinci. *Study of Human Proportions According to Vitruvius,* c. 1485–1490. Pen and ink 1′1½″ × 9¾″. Galleria dell'Accademia, Venice, Italy.

of the rule, depending on the pose or line of vision. By such a reconciliation of the opposites of order and freedom, he reveals the kinship of sculptors with their philosophical and political colleagues who aspired to do the same for other aspects of Athenian life.

Rational and irrational elements were present in both the form and content of Greek drama, just as they were in the architecture of the time. In the Parthenon, the structurally regular triglyphs were interspersed with panels showing centaurs and other mythological creatures. The theme of these sculptures was the struggle between the Greeks as champions of enlightenment and the forces of darkness and barbarism. In the drama, the rational Apollonian dialogue existed alongside the Dionysian chorus, with its interests in altered states of consciousness. In the union of mythological and rational elements, tragedy could mediate between the irrational and rational, that is, the Dionysian and Apollonian principles.

Yet the intricate metrical schemes and the complex arrangements partake of rationalism and convey the dramatic content in a highly ordered composition. In the dialogue of a Greek tragedy, the action of the episodes must lead inevitably and inexorably toward the predestined end. The different elements must achieve a coherence that meets Aristotle's critical standard of "a single action, one that is a complete whole in itself with a beginning, middle, and end, so as to enable the work to produce its proper pleasure with all the organic unity of a living creature."

Just as the harmony of the Parthenon depended on the module taken from the Doric columns, so Polyclitus derived his proportions for the human body from the mathematical relationships among its parts. In similar fashion, melodic lines in music were based on the subdivisions of the perfect intervals derived from the mathematical ratios of the fourth, fifth, and octave. So also the choral sections of the Greek drama were constructed of intricate metrical units that added up to the unity of the drama. In none of these cases, however, were rational proportions the whole story. In the architecture of the Hellenic style; in the statues of Polyclitus; in the dramas of Aeschylus, Sophocles, and Euripides; and in the dialogues of Plato, the rational approach was used as a process for presenting human and aesthetic dilemmas, not as a goal in itself.

It was also the Greeks who insisted that music, like drama and the other arts, was a midpoint between the divine madness of an inspired musician, such as Orpheus, and the solid mathematical basis on which the art rested. The element of inspiration had to be tempered by an orderly theoretical system that could demonstrate mathematically the arrangement of its melodic intervals and metrical proportions.

Finally, it should be remembered that the chief deity of Athens was the goddess of knowledge and wisdom. Even the veneration of Dionysus tended constantly toward increased rationalism and abstract thought. Although Athena, Dionysus, and Apollo were all born out of myth, their destinies found a common culmination in the supreme rationalism of Socrates and Plato, who eventually concluded that philosophy was the highest music.

THE HELLENIC HERITAGE

"We are all Greeks." So said Shelley in the preface to his play *Hellas.* "Our laws, our literature, our religion, our arts, have their roots in Greece." Merely the mention of such key words as *mythology, philosophy,* and *democracy* points immediately to their Greek source. Similarly, the familiar forms of architecture, sculpture, painting, poetry, drama, and music began in Hellas, the land where the Hellenic style was nurtured and brought to fruition. Although circumstances conspired to bring about a decline of its political power, Athens was destined to remain the teacher of Greece, Rome, and later Western societies. Ultimately, Hellas was not simply a country or even a time period, but a worldview that focused on the nature of human civilization.

─────── **YOUR RESOURCES** ───────

- ***Exploring Humanities CD-ROM***

  ○ Interactive Map: The Greek World

  ○ Readings—Plato, *Republic;* Aristotle, *Politic;* Sappho, *Four Poems*

  ○ Philosophers and Their Works

- ***Web Site***

  http://art.wadsworth.com/fleming10

  ○ Chapter 2 Quiz

  ○ Links

THE HELLENIC PERIOD

Key Events	Architecture and Visual Arts	Literature and Music
c. 800–c. 650 **Geometric period; Homer; Eastern contacts**		
776 **First Olympic games;** beginning of Greek calendar		
c. 750 **Hesiod** wrote *Theogony* (basis of Greek mythology)		c. 750 **Hesiod** ◆
c. 650–c. 500 **Archaic period**		c. 700 **Homer** ◆
	c. 650 **Ionic temple of Artemis** built at Ephesus	
	c. 600 **Kouroi (youths) from Sounion** carved	c. 600 **Sappho** ◆
	570–560 **Kleitias ▲,** painter, primarily of pottery	c. 582–c. 507 **Pythagoras** ○
	570–560 **Ergotimos ▲,** potter	c. 525–456 **Aeschylus** ◆
	c. 550 **Korai (maidens) of Samos** carved	
	c. 530 **Archaic Doric temples** built at Athens, Delphi, Corinth, Olympia	

500

Key Events	Architecture and Visual Arts	Literature and Music
		c. 500–c. 428 **Anaxagoras** ○
c. 494 **Persians** under Darius invaded Greece	c. 490–c. 432c. **Phidias** ●	c. 496–406 **Sophocles** ◆
c. 490 **Athenians** defeated Persians at Marathon	c. 489 **Doric treasury of Athenians** built at Delphi	c. 495–c. 425 **Herodotus** ✪
480 **Persians** under Xerxes defeated Spartans at Thermopylae	c. 480 **Temple of Olympian Zeus** built at Agrigentum, Sicily	c. 485–411 **Protagoras** ○
Athens sacked and burned; Athenians defeated Persian fleet at Salamis	c. 480–430 **Polygnotus ▲** noted for perspective drawing	c. 480–406 **Euripides** ◆
477 **Delian League** against Persians set up under Athenian leadership	c. 475 ***Charioteer of Delphi*** cast in bronze	c. 469–c. 399 **Socrates** ○
468–450 **Cimon** (c. 510–450), general leader of conservative aristocratic party, dominated Athenian politics	c. 465–c. 457 **Temple of Zeus** built at Olympia	c. 460–c. 395 **Thucydides** ✪
	c. 460 *Zeus* cast in bronze	
	c. 460–c. 450 **Myron active** ●	
456 **Athenian land empire** reached greatest extent	c. 460–c. 440 **Polyclitus active** ●	
454 **Delian League treasury** moved to Athens	c. 450 **Myron** cast *Discobolus* in bronze	
449–429 **Pericles** (c. 490–429), leader of popular party, ruled Athens	c. 450 **Phidias** carved *Athena Lemnia*	
	450 **Phidias** appointed overseer of works on Athenian Acropolis	
	448–440 **Temple of Hephaestus (Theseum)** built	
	447–432 **Parthenon** built by Ictinus; Parthenon sculptures carved under Phidias: metopes, 447–442; inner frieze, 442–438; Phidias' cult statue of Athena dedicated in 438; pediments, 438–332	c. 444–c. 380 **Aristophanes** ◆
	c. 440 **Apollodorus ▲,** the shadow painter, modeled figures in light and shade, flourished	c. 434–c. 355 **Xenophon**
431–404 **Peloponnesian War** between Athens and Sparta	437–432 **Propylaea** built by Mnesicles	
	427–424 **Temple of Athena Nike** built by Callicrates	427–347 **Plato** ○
	421–409 **Erechtheum,** thought by some to have been built by Mnesicles	
413 **Athenians** defeated at Syracuse, Sicily		
404 **Athens** fell to Sparta; end of Athenian Empire		

400

Key Events	Architecture and Visual Arts	Literature and Music
399 **Socrates** sentenced to death	c. 390–c. 330 **Praxiteles** ●	
387 **Plato** founded Academy		384–322 **Aristotle** ○
359–336 **Philip of Macedon** gained control of Greek peninsula	c. 350–c. 300 **Lysippus active** ●	**Plato's dialogues and Aristotle's treatises** deal extensively with musical theory, practice, and ethical implications of music in education and life
336 **Alexander the Great** succeeded Philip as king of Greece	c. 340 **Praxiteles** carved *Hermes and Infant Dionysus, Aphrodite of Cnidos*	
335 **Aristotle** founded Lyceum	334 **Choragic monument of Lysicrates** built; first external use of Corinthian order	
335–323 **Alexander** conquered Near East, Asia Minor, Persia; India reached		c. 321 **Aristoxenus of Tarentum ◆,** wrote treatise on Greek music
146 **Corinth** destroyed by Romans		c. 300 **Euclid ◆,** wrote treatise on music
86 **Athens** sacked by Romans under Sulla		

▲ - Painter   ○ - Philosopher   ● - Sculptor   ◆ - Writer   ✪ - Historian

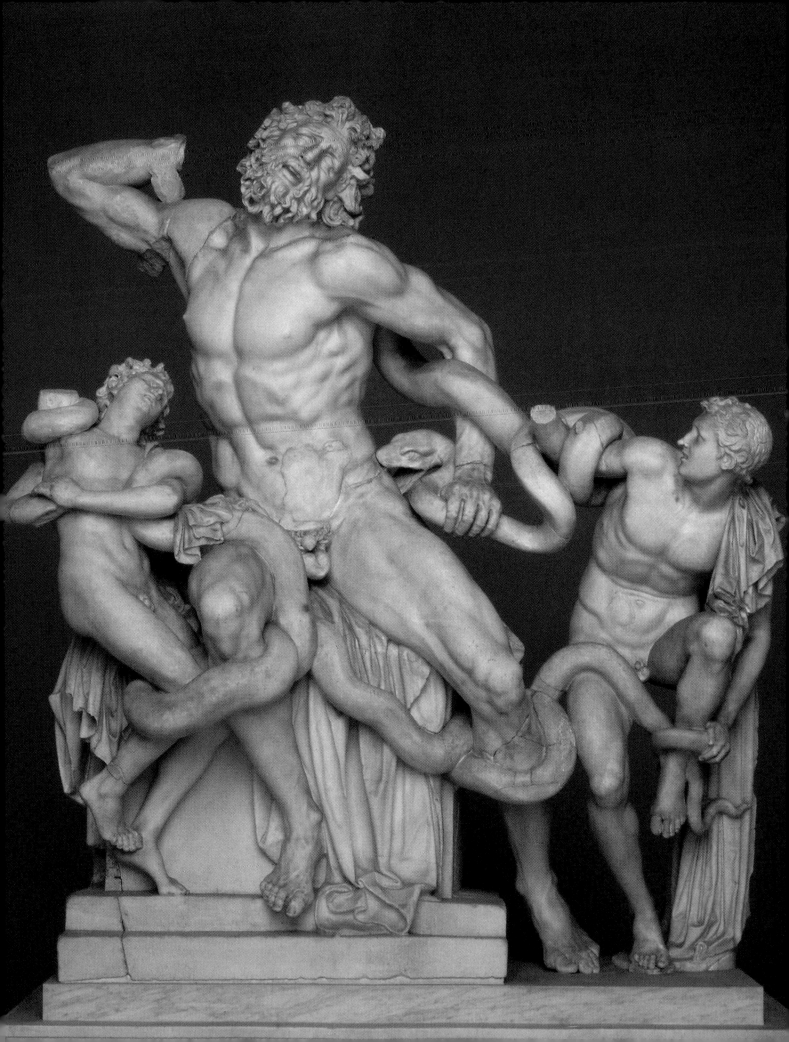

CHAPTER

3

HELLENISTIC STYLE

ATHENS WAS THE ACKNOWLEDGED CENTER of the Greek world in the fifth century BCE, but after the defeat of Athens by the Spartans in 404 BCE, a new political and cultural hub arose: Macedon. The Macedonians may have been a Greek tribe, like the people who founded Athens. They spoke and wrote in Greek, prized Greek art, and hosted the famous Greek painter Zeuxis and the playwright Euripides. The celebrated Greek painter Apelles is thought to have painted portraits of both King Philip and his son, Alexander.

At Pella, the capital, mythological scenes were depicted in floor mosaics made from water-smoothed river pebbles (Fig. 3.1). One of these scenes was signed by its designer, Gnosis, indicating that the skill had become so advanced that it boasted well-known craftspeople. The Macedonian admiration for Greek sculptural form is evident in the careful modeling of the bodies of the hunters, which have been outlined with thin strips of lead and clay. Nevertheless, the action and fierceness of the hunters' attack is foreign to the Athenian preference for restraint and tranquility. Lion hunting was a popular theme in the art of rulers in the Asian territories to the east of Greece. Its presence in the Macedonian capital may indicate contact with these people—and perhaps their defeat at the hands of the Greeks. The scene hints at the aggressive consolidation strategy advocated by King Philip of Macedon. He assembled a disciplined, well-equipped army and united the entire Greek peninsula into one kingdom, bringing to an end the independent rule of the city-states.

The precocious Alexander accompanied his father on his campaign in southern Greece, learning the art of war along the way. Alexander the Great's exploits became legendary (Fig. 3.2). He is said to

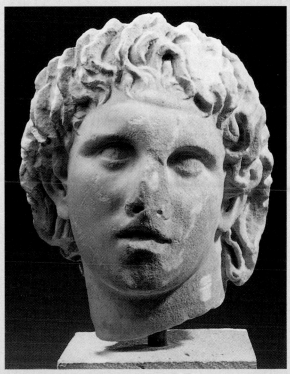

3.1   Gnosis, Stag Hunt, from Pella, Greece, c. 300 BCE. Pebble mosaic, figural panel 10′2″ high. Archeological Museum, Pella, Greece.

3.2   Head of Alexander the Great, from Pella, Greece, c. 200–150 BCE. Marble, approx. 1′ high. Archeological Museum, Pella, Greece.

have tamed the wild horse Bucephalus, whereupon his father lightheartedly observed that Alexander would have to conquer his own kingdom because Macedonia was too small for both of them.

Alexander was tutored in his youth by the philosopher Aristotle, who may have given the boy his copy of *The Iliad,* Homer's epic poem about the Trojan War. When his father was assassinated in 336 BCE, Alexander set out to quell rebellion in the south and ultimately to conquer his own kingdom. Legend has it that throughout his travels, he carried Aristotle's copy of *The Iliad* with him. Eventually the vast territory from Egypt and Mesopotamia to Persia and the borders of India succumbed to his rule. One of the shrewdest generals of all time, Alexander also saw himself as the champion of Hellenism, and he brought the authority of Greek culture with him wherever he went. Greek art influenced Buddhist stone reliefs and sculpture in what is now Pakistan and Afghanistan. Indian figures of the Buddha took on the facial expressions and drapery of Greek sculpture, which, in turn, migrated farther east into China, Korea, and Japan.

When Alexander died at Babylon in 323 BCE, his empire was divided among his generals—the Ptolemies in Egypt and the Seleucids in Babylonia and Anatolia. After breaking away from the Seleucids, the Attalid dynasty, named for the ruler Attalus I, developed a flourishing economic and cultural capital city at Pergamon. The height of the Hellenistic period spans the time from the death of Alexander to the Roman conquest of Corinth in 146 BCE. During these two centuries, cultural leadership remained in the hands of the Greeks, but as they came in contact with the variety of influences in the lands they controlled, their culture became progressively more multiethnic. They picked up ideas from Asia and Africa and adapted them to their Greek heritage. Hence we make the distinction between the earlier and self-consciously purer Hellenic culture of Greece, and the later, more eclectic Hellenistic or Greek-like styles that arose in Asia Minor. Although in decline, the Hellenistic period continued through a transitional Greco-Roman era until 31 BCE, when Rome became master of the Western world.

During the Hellenistic period the Hellenic emphasis on eternal truths yielded to more practical and hedonistic philosophies. Idealism shifted toward realism, and rationalism gave way to more emotional expression.

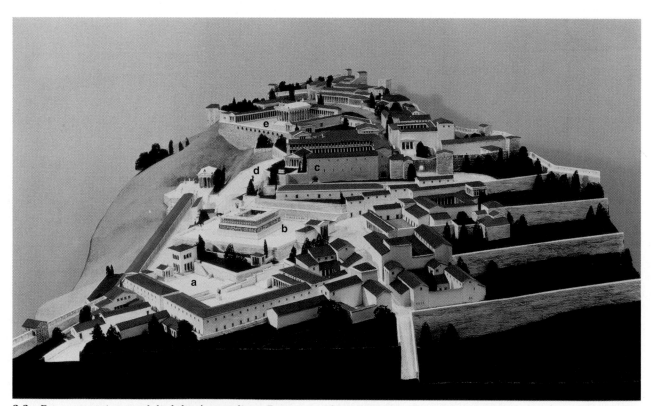

3.3 Reconstruction model of the Acropolis at Pergamon. Complete view from the south, 3 CE. (a) Upper Agora. (b) Altar of Zeus. (c) Temple of Athena Polias, courtyard, and library. (d) Theater. (e) Temple of Trajan and palace precinct. Antikensammlung, Staatliche Museen zu Berlin, Berlin, Germany.

PERGAMON: SECOND CENTURY BCE

Like the earlier city of Athens, Pergamon (or Pergamum) in Asia Minor developed around its acra, the high, fortified hilltop that one ancient writer described as being shaped like a pineapple. The Pergamene acropolis, a site with even greater natural advantages than the Acropolis of Athens, played a significant role in the growth of the city. Strategically located on a plain near the Aegean Sea, Pergamon developed a prosperous export trade. The fertile plain, formed by the flowing together of three rivers, was easily defensible from the hill. The city itself, surrounded as it was by the sea, high mountains, and precipitous ravines, was unassailable except from the south. Here, in an unusually dramatic setting, grew the cultural center that was to play such an important role in the Hellenistic period.

Unlike the Athenian Acropolis, which was primarily a religious and civic site, the acropolis in Pergamon was where the city's rulers built palaces, temples, gymnasiums, and public markets (Fig. 3.3). New plays were performed in the theater, poets read their works aloud, and philosophers presented their ideas. Unlike Athens, Pergamon integrated religious, civic, cultural, educational, and daily life. The city also welcomed non-Greeks more readily than Athens had in the fifth century.

The planning of Greek cities apparently goes back no further than the middle of the fifth century BCE. The fame of "wide-wayed Athens" rested on its Panathenaic Way, a street about 12 feet wide. Just large enough for five or six people to walk abreast, it was the route followed by processions to the Acropolis, theaters, and marketplace. Athens's other streets were narrow alleys barely broad enough to permit the passage of a driver with a donkey cart. Wide, open spaces could be found only in the agora and on the Acropolis, but even here buildings were planned with more attention to their individual logic than to their interrelationships as a group.

Hellenistic city plans, although a vast improvement over their haphazard predecessors, were based on the application of a crisscrossing grid pattern that paid little or no attention to the irregularities of the natural site. When a hill was within the city limits, the streets sometimes became so steep that they could be climbed only by series of stairways. Greek cities in Asia Minor, such as Miletus and Priene, were rebuilt according to this grid system (Fig. 3.4). The residential sections of the ancient city of Pergamon also tried to follow a regular plan. Under Eumenes II, the city reached its greatest extent, and the thick wall he built around it enclosed more than 200 acres of ground—more than four times the territory included by his

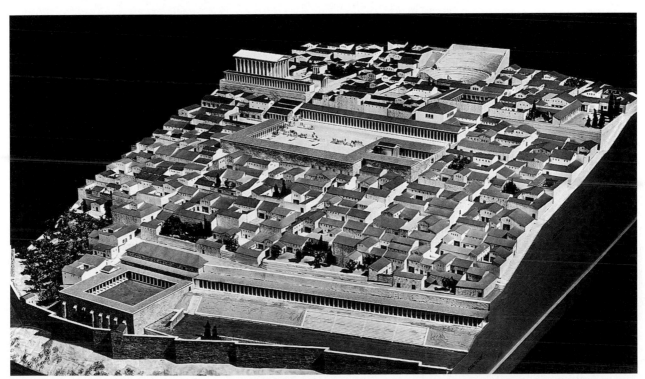

3.4 Model of the City of Priene, Turkey, fourth century BCE and later. Staatliche Museen, Berlin, Germany.

predecessor. Aqueducts brought in ample water from nearby mountain springs to supply a population of 120,000. The system was the greatest of its kind prior to the Roman aqueducts.

The main entrance to Pergamon was from the south, through an impressive arched gateway topped by a pediment with a triglyph frieze. Traffic was diverted through several vaulted portals, which led into a square where a fountain refreshed travelers. From here the road led past the humbler dwelling places toward the lower marketplace, which bustled with the activities of peddlers and hucksters of all sorts. This market was a large open square surrounded on three sides by a two-story colonnade, behind which were rows of rooms that served as shops. Moving onward, the road went past buildings that housed the workshops and mills for pottery, tiles, and textiles. The homes of wealthier citizens were located higher on the hill off the main streets, and they overlooked the rest of the city. At the foot of the acropolis was another square, which boasted a large fountain and a fine view.

Then, on a dramatic, windswept site almost 1,000 feet above the surrounding countryside, rose the Pergamene acropolis (Fig. 3.3), a stronghold that ranked among the most imposing in the Greek world. Up the slopes of the hill, on terraces supported by massive retaining walls and fortifications, were the buildings and artifacts that gave the city its reputation as a second Athens. Through the ingenious use of natural contours, the Pergamenes had developed attractive settings for a number of buildings, which not only were outstanding as individual edifices but also were grouped into a harmonious whole by means of connecting roadways, ramps, and open courtyards. On a succession of rising levels were marketplaces, gymnasiums, athletic fields, temples, public squares, wooded groves, and an amphitheater. Above them all, flanked by watchtowers, barracks, arsenals, storage houses, and gardens, stood the residence of the kings of Pergamon.

ARCHITECTURE

THE UPPER AGORA AND THE ALTAR OF ZEUS

Approaching the acropolis was the highest of the marketplaces (Fig. 3.3A), an open square that served both as an assembly place and as a market for quality merchandise, such as the renowned Pergamene pottery and textiles. Above this agora spread the broad marble-paved terrace on which stood a great altar that tradition and scant textual sources suggest was dedicated to Zeus (Fig. 3.3B);

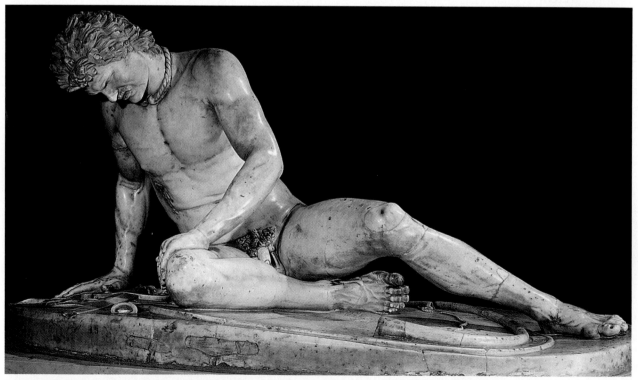

3.5 Epigonos (?). *Dying Gaul.* Roman copy after bronze original of c. 230–220 BCE. Marble, approx. 3′½″ high. Museo Capitolino, Rome, Italy.

its famous frieze depicted the battle of the gods as personifications of light and order against the giants as representatives of darkness and chaos. Conventionally dated from about 180 BCE, this artistic triumph of the reign of Eumenes II was considered by some Hellenistic and Roman authorities to be one of the seven wonders of the ancient world. Because both its structure and sculptures are of major importance, this edifice will be discussed in more detail later in the chapter.

THE ATHENA PRECINCT AND THE THEATER

Above the Altar of Zeus was a precinct dedicated to Athena Polias, or Athena, protectress of cities and guardian of laws and city life. Her shrine (Fig. 3.3C) was a graceful Doric temple, smaller than the Parthenon, with six-columned porches on either end and ten columns on each side. The temple was framed by an L-shaped, two-story colonnade that formed an open courtyard in which stood the bronze monument that celebrated the victory of Attalus I, Eumenes' father, over the Gauls (Figs. 3.5 and 3.6). This colonnade also served as the facade of the great library of Pergamon, which appropriately was placed here in the precinct of Athena, goddess of reason, learning, contemplation, and wisdom. The most precious part of the library was housed in four rooms on the second level that stretched over an area about 145 feet long and 47 feet wide. On their stone shelves, some of which still exist, rested the ancient scrolls, estimated to have numbered about 200,000 at the time of the Attalids.

The Pergamon library ranked with that of Alexandria in Egypt as one of the two greatest libraries of antiquity. The English word *parchment* derives from the Latin word *pergamena*. It is said that parchment originated in Pergamon when the Ptolemies in Alexandria, jealous that the Pergamon library would exceed their own, refused to send additional papyrus. Later, after the major portion of the Alexandria library's collection of half a million volumes was burned in an uprising against Caesar, Mark Antony made a gift to Cleopatra of the entire library of Pergamon.

Below the Athena precinct was the theater (Fig. 3.3D), constructed under Eumenes II about 170 BCE. The auditorium, with 80 semicircular tiers of stone seats, was carved out of the hillside and could hold 10,000 spectators. In the center was a circular section of the orchestra, where the chorus performed around a small altar dedicated to Dionysus, and a rectangular scene platform for the actors.

THE ROYAL RESIDENCE

Just as the Attalid kings dominated the life of their city and constituted the apex of the Pergamene social pyramid, the royal residence crowned the highest point in their capital city. Later, after the realm came under the domination of Rome, part of the palace was destroyed to make way for a large Corinthian temple honoring the Emperor Trajan (Fig. 3.3E).

From their hilltop residence, the kings of Pergamon could survey much of their rich domain. The mountains to the north yielded silver and copper for their coins, which were essential for promoting trade and paying soldiers. From the same region came supplies of pitch, tar, and timber—needed for building ships—as well as marble for buildings and sculptures. A panorama thus unfolded around the people of Pergamon, starting with the heights of Mount Ida and the surrounding range all the way to the bright waters of the Aegean Sea, beyond which lay the shores of the Greek mainland.

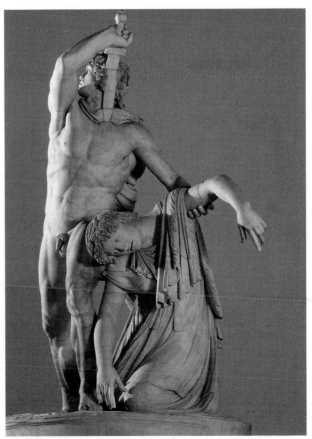

3.6 Epigonos (?). *Gaul and His Wife.* Roman copy after bronze original of c. 230–220 BCE. Marble, height approx. 6'11". Museo Nazionale Romano-Palazzo Altemps, Rome, Italy.

The planning of Pergamon cleverly promoted the idea of the monarchy towering above it. At the top, topographically as well as politically, stood the king, aloof from his people and associated by them with the gods. Even while living, he was accorded such divine prerogatives as a cult statue with perfumed grain burning on an altar before it and an annual celebration in his honor. This semi-divine status, connected with the king's right to rule, served the practical social purposes of commanding obedience to his laws, facilitating the collection of taxes (often under the guise of offerings to the deities), and uniting the peoples and factions who lived under him. Assisting in this deification were the scholars and artists he attracted to his court, whose works were regarded with awe by locals and foreigners alike.

The pomp and display that marked Hellenistic life was a distinct departure from the simplicity and nobility of the more austere fifth century BCE. Grandeur became grandiosity, and many monuments were erected not to revere the gods but to honor kings. The accent was no longer on abstract ideals but on the glorification of individuals.

With the changing times, however, definite advances in the art of building were taking place. Domestic architecture was emphasized, and Pergamene architects went beyond the simple post-and-lintel system of the Hellenic period and employed the arch and vault in city gates and underground water and sewer systems. Architecturally as well as culturally, Pergamon forged an important link between the Greek idealism and Roman practicality.

SCULPTURE

Although sculptural works of all kinds existed in profusion throughout Pergamon, the examples that claim the attention of posterity were located on two terraces of the acropolis. In the Athena precinct just below the royal residence, bounded by the temple on one side and the L-shaped colonnade of the library on two others, was a spacious courtyard in which Attalus I erected sculptural monuments commemorating his victories. The groups he commissioned were in place during the last quarter of the third century BCE. In the first quarter of the second century BCE, his son and successor Eumenes II built the Altar of Zeus (see Fig. 3.7), with its famous frieze on the terrace below.

The two periods have been distinguished as the First and Second Schools of Pergamon. Because they were separated by less than half a cen-tury, however, some sculptors may have worked on both projects; if not, they must have had a hand in training their successors. All the bronze originals of the First School have disappeared and can be studied only in marble copies made by later Hellenistic or Roman artists. Most of the sculptures from the Second School survive and may be seen today in the Pergamon Museum in Berlin.

THE FIRST SCHOOL

The principal works of the First School were two large monuments in bronze, each composed of many figures. One commemorated the victories of Attalus over the neighboring Seleucid kingdom. Only a few details of this group survive. The other honored his earlier and greater victory over the nomadic tribes of Gauls, who swept down from Europe across the Hellespont (as the Greeks called the Dardanelles, the narrow waterway that divides Europe from Asia) and into the region north of Pergamon. From this province, called Galatia after them, the Gauls were a constant threat to the Greek cities to the south. While his predecessor had bought them off by paying tribute, Attalus I refused to do so. He met their invasion with an army, and the outcome of the battle was decisive enough to repel the Gauls for a generation. The consequences were felt far and wide, and all the cities and kingdoms of the Greek world breathed a little easier.

The fierce Gauls had inspired such general terror in the popular mind that their defeat came to be seen as an extraordinary event. The name of Attalus was everywhere acclaimed as *Soter* ("Savior," the victor), and after incorporating the lands he had gained, he assumed the title of king. Thereafter, as King Attalus the Savior, he continued to capitalize on his fortunes by embarking on a program to beautify the city, enlisting the services of the best available Greek artists. Sharing the same patroness, Athena, Pergamon began to acquire the status of a second Athens, and its ruler, that of a political and cultural champion of Hellenism.

Parts of the monument that Attalus erected to commemorate his victory over the Gauls can be seen in numerous museums. The *Dying Gaul* (Fig. 3.5) and the *Gaul and His Wife* (Fig. 3.6) survive in Roman copies of what were likely bronze originals. The *Dying Gaul* is a fine example of Hellenistic emotional expression. He is the trumpeter who sounded the call for relief. Mortally wounded, the warrior has agonizingly dragged himself out of the battle to struggle alone against death. His eyes are fixed on the ground, where his sword, the trumpet, and other pieces of his equipment are lying. He supports himself weakly with one arm, proud and defiant to the end, while his life's blood flows out of the gaping wound in his side. The anguished expression on his face has an intensity not encountered in prior Greek art, which prized emotional balance and composure. The strong but rough musculature of his powerful body, so different from that of the supple Greek athletes, marks him as a barbarian. Further evidence of his origin is found in the collar of twisted gold he wears around his neck and in the look of his hair, which is greased so heavily that it is almost as thick as a horse's mane.

All these carefully recorded details show the interest of the period in individuals as such, in the features that distinguish one person or group from another, and in the portrayal of non-Greek types as heroic in size and fearsome in battle. The very strength and bravery the Pergamenes attributed to their enemies made their victory seem all the more impressive. In addition, the artist tried to awaken the sympathy of the observer and thereby involve him or her in the situation. The viewer might have felt both attraction and repulsion toward such a subject and hence might have experienced a strong emotional reaction. The sword and trumpet lying beside the Gaul, as well as other realistic details, convey a sense of immediacy to the beholder. At the same time, the viewer is invited to look beyond the physical wounds and behold the spiritual anguish of the proud but defeated warrior, so reluctant to accept his fate.

The expressive impact of the *Gaul and His Wife* (Fig. 3.6) is no less powerful. It was customary for women and children to travel with the

Gauls on their campaigns. Realizing his defeat and being too proud to be taken as a slave, this Gaul has just killed his wife. He looks apprehensively over his shoulder at the approaching enemy as he plunges his sword into his own neck. The mood of despair is heightened by the sweeping lines of the woman's drapery, which droops downward in deep folds, casting dark shadows. Strong feeling is aroused in the observer by these noble figures who stare death in the face so directly and courageously.

THE SECOND SCHOOL AND THE ALTAR OF ZEUS

To the Second School of Pergamon are assigned all the works that fall within the reign of Eumenes II, the patron under whom Pergamon achieved its greatest power and glory. Like his father before him, Eumenes II had victories over the Gauls, and in the Altar of Zeus (Fig. 3.7) he continued the tradition of erecting commemorative works. The altar was at once the city's greatest single monument and one of the supreme architectural and sculptural works of the Hellenistic period. It was intended to glorify Eumenes' contribution to Hellenism in the struggle against the barbarians.

Beginning in 1873, each fragment was unearthed, and after a half-century of study, the entire monument was reconstructed in the Pergamon Museum in Berlin. As with the Parthenon sculptures in the British Museum (see Figs. 2.16 and 2.17), cultural ownership of the Altar of Zeus is loudly contested. Just as contemporary Greece strongly wants the Parthenon sculptures returned, so too do modern Turks and Greeks lay claim to the Altar of Zeus. Famed throughout the ancient world, the altar was described in the early

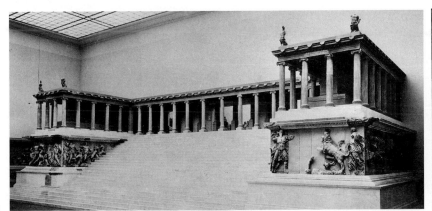
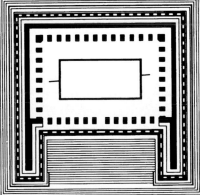

3.7 (A) Altar of Zeus, Pergamon (restored). Begun c. 180 BCE. Marble. Antikensammlung, Staatliche Museen zu Berlin, Berlin, Germany. (B) Plan of Altar of Zeus.

years of the Christian era by St. John as "Satan's seat" (Rev. 2:13). The reference seems to have been prompted by the structure's resemblance to an immense throne and by the animated pagan gods and demons depicted in the frieze.

THE STRUCTURE. The actual altar on which animal sacrifices and other offerings were burned was a large stone podium standing in the inner courtyard (Fig. 3.7A). The building rested on a **podium,** or platform, with five steps, above which was the great frieze, more than 7 feet high and 450 feet long. It ran continuously around the entire podium, bending inward on either side of the stairway and diminishing in size as the steps rose. Below, the frieze was framed by a molding; above, by a **dentil range** (Figs. 3.8 and 3.9), that is, a series of small projecting rectangular blocks. These bricklike blocks served also to support an Ionic colonnade that surrounded the structure and paralleled the frieze. Above the colonnade appeared a

friezeless entablature with a second dentil range supporting the roof. Crowning the whole was a series of freestanding statues of deities and mythological animals placed at various points along the outer edges of the roof.

The concept of space that informed the Altar of Zeus differs from that of the fifth century. In the earlier period, the altar was placed outside the temple and rituals took place against the exterior colonnades. In the Hellenistic period, the new concept of space included a greater interest in depth. Thus, in the Altar of Zeus the spectator looked into a courtyard that enclosed the altar, not toward a background plane. The wider space between the columns also invited the eye toward the interior, whereas the more closely spaced columns of the fifth century promoted the continuity of the plane.

The general effect produced by the Altar of Zeus is that of a traditional Greek temple turned upside down. The simple formality of older Doric

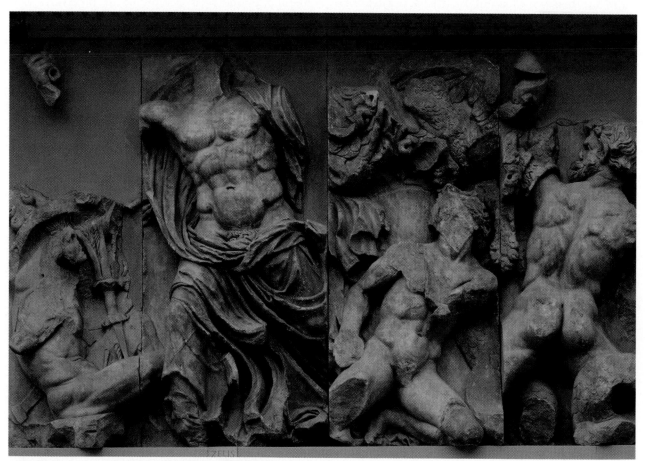

3.8 *Zeus Hurling Thunderbolts.* Detail of Altar of Zeus frieze, c. 180 BCE. Marble, height 7′6″. Antikensammlung, Staatliche Museen zu Berlin, Berlin, Germany.

temples—the Parthenon, for example—depended on the structural and visual integration of their parts. The columns served the logical purpose of supporting the upper members, and the sculptured sections were high above, where they embellished but did not dominate the design. At Pergamon, the traditional order was inverted. Considered more important than the columns, the decorative frieze was put a little above eye level in order to be seen more easily. For the sake of tradition, the colonnade was included, but it was placed above the frieze, where it had no structural purpose. The guiding principle of structural clarity yielded to decoration for its own sake, and the art of architecture gave way to the art of sculpture. In the Parthenon, the decorative frieze was included to give some variety to what might otherwise have been monotonous unity. In the Altar of Zeus, on the other hand, the variety of the frieze was so overwhelming that the regularity of a colonnade was needed to preserve unity.

THE FRIEZE. The subject of the frieze is the familiar battle between gods and giants. In the typical depiction of this scene, it was customary to include the twelve Olympians and an equal number of opponents, but here the unprecedented length of available space demanded more participants. Perhaps scholars working in the library were called on to compile a catalogue of divinities, together with their attendants and attributes, in order to have enough figures to go around. Lettered inscriptions were liberally used to identify the less familiar figures and to make the narrative more vivid. These program notes supplied many associational meanings and made it possible to both read the frieze and view it.

Scholarly influence is also suggested in the allegorical treatment of the ancient battle theme. In Pergamon, literal belief in the gods was largely a thing of the past, and local scholars interpreted the gods as personifications of benign and orderly forces of nature. By contrast, the giants represented

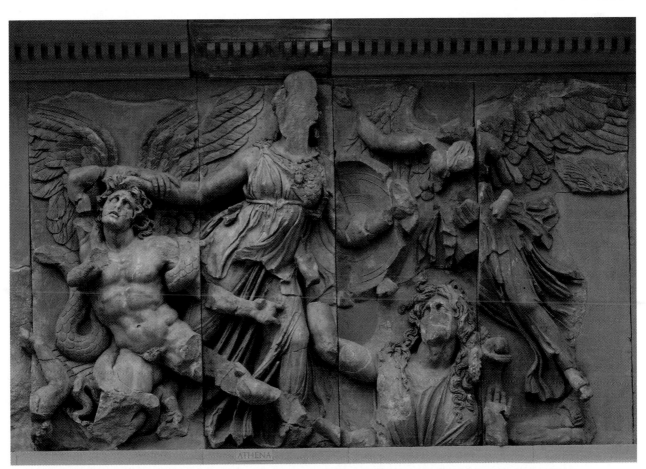

3.9 *Athena Slaying Giant.* Detail of Altar of Zeus frieze, *c.* 180 BCE. Marble, height 7′6″. Antikensammlung, Staatliche Museen zu Berlin, Berlin, Germany.

such calamities as earthquakes, hurricanes, and floods. In addition, the battle scenes make implicit reference to the fifth-century defeat of the Persians by the Athenians and the warding off of the Gauls by Attalus I.

The narrative begins on the inner part of the right podium, facing the stairs. Moving parallel with the descending stairs, it proceeds along the south side and around the corner to the east. Along the way the principal characters in the drama are introduced: Zeus and his fellow gods in mortal combat with Chronos, father of Zeus, and his supporters, the wicked titans and giants. There are also Helios, the sun god; Hemera, the winged goddess of day; her brother Aether, the spirit of air; and the moon goddess. Hecate, goddess of the underworld; Artemis, the heavenly huntress; and Hercules, father of Telephus, the legendary founder of Pergamon, are included as well. The struggle is between the forces of darkness and the spirits of light.

In the four panels reproduced in Figure 3.8, Zeus is seen, appropriately, in combat with no less than three titans at once. His powerful figure, wrapped in a swirling mantle, is rearing back to smite the giants with his spear and thunderbolts. Most of Zeus's right arm is missing, but his hand is seen in the upper left corner of the panel. The titan in the lower left has already been overcome by a thunderbolt, which is shown as a pointed spear with a handle of acanthus leaves. The second giant is on the other side, his body tense with terror before the blow falls. In the slab to the right, Porphyrion, king of the titans, is shown from the back. From his animal ears to his serpent legs, he is a fearsome sight as he shields himself with a lion skin from both Zeus's eagle above and the additional thunderbolts that the mighty god is about to hurl.

Next is the final group, depicting the part played by Athena, protectress of Athens and Pergamon (Fig. 3.9). Her figure is shown in the second slab. Bearing a shield on her left arm, she grasps a winged giant by the hair with her right hand and forces him to Earth, where her sacred serpent can inflict the mortal wound. A moment of pathos is provided by the giant's mother, the earth goddess Gaea, who is seen as a torso rising from the ground. Although she is on the side of the gods, she implores Athena with her eyes to spare the life of her rebellious son. Gaea's attributes are seen in the horn of plenty she carries in her left hand, a cornucopia filled with the fruits of the earth: apples, pomegranates, and grapes with vine leaves and a pine cone. The goddess Nike, symbolizing victory, hovers over Athena.

From this climax in the sky, the action on the shadowy north side of the frieze gradually descends into the realm of the water spirits. They drive the fleeing giants around the other corner of the stairway into the sea, where they drown. Here, likely enough, are representations of the rivers of Greece. Around the face of the west side and up the stairs are other creatures of the sea. The tumultuous action opens on the right side with the divinities of the land and ends on the left with those of the sea. They are separated by the wide stairs as well as by their placement at the beginning and end of the dramatic conflict between the forces of good and evil.

The frieze as a whole is a technical feat of the first magnitude. It was executed by a school of sculptors, many of whose names are inscribed below it. In addition to the figures, details such as swords and belt buckles, saddles and sandals, and clothing are carved and polished to simulate the textures of metal, leather, and textiles, respectively. The bold high-relief carving, the deep undercutting that allows the figures to stand out almost in the round, and the rich modeling effects that make full use of light and shadow reveal complete mastery of the material.

The swirl of struggling forms and violent movement is sustained over the entire frieze. By contrast, the traditional Doric frieze depended for unity on the alternation of action in the metopes with calm in the triglyphs. At Pergamon, unity is generated by the continuity of the motion itself. The slashing diagonal lines and sharp contrasts of movement are grouped into separate episodes by the device of coiling snakes. Winding in and out, they are at once the visual punctuation marks that separate the scenes and the connecting links of the composition. They lead the eye from one group to another and promote a sense of constant writhing motion. Athena's posture was taken directly from that on the Parthenon's east pediment; that of Zeus is derived from the Poseidon of the west pediment. There the Athenians had defeated the Persians, while here the Pergamenes had vanquished the Gauls. In both instances the cities and their rulers had become the champions of Greek culture against barbarian invasion. Pergamon was pictured as the new Athens, a shining cultural center directly under the protection of the goddess Athena.

EVOLUTION OF STYLE

Comparing the great frieze with the *Dying Gaul* and the *Gaul and His Wife,* one notes a change in style from the First to the Second School. Both allude to the constant wars between the Pergamenes and Gauls, but in contrast to the earlier monuments' preoccupation with pain, the gods on the Altar of Zeus slay the giants with frenzied abandon. Instead of having sympathy and even admiration for their enemies, the viewer now marvels at the many ingenious ways in which the gods dispatched their foes.

All the monuments accentuate pathos, but whereas in the earlier examples the compassion of the observer is awakened simply and directly, the great frieze deals with its subject as a thinly disguised allegory for the war between the Pergamenes and the Gauls. In the guise of the gods, the Pergamenes become superhuman figures, whereas the giants, whose features closely resemble earlier Gallic and other non-Greek types, are rendered as monsters.

Instead of the frank realism of the previous generation, the tale is told in the language of melodrama accompanied by visual bombast. It is put on the stage, so to speak, with theatrical gestures and postures. The emotional range is correspondingly enormous, beginning with the stark horror of monsters with enormous wings, animal heads, snaky locks, long tails, and serpentine legs. After being terrorized by the sight of such bestial forms, viewers must have melted into sympathy for the earth mother pleading for mercy for her monstrous offspring, and perhaps gone from tears to laughter at the inept antics of some of the clumsy giants. And after hissing the villains, they may have applauded the gods coming to the rescue. This theatrical exaggeration of reality extends to the representation of bodily types. The functional physique of the *Dying Gaul* has evolved into the power of the professional strongman who finds himself more at home in the arena than on the battlefield.

The perception of deeper space entered into the sculptural composition of the Altar of Zeus as well as into its architectural composition. Just as when viewing the architectural composition the eye is drawn into an enclosed interior, when viewing the sculpture the eye not only moves from side to side, as in a plane, but is constantly led back and forth into spatial depth. To escape the plane, some of the figures project outward in such high relief as to be almost in the round; others even step outward from the frieze and support themselves by kneeling on the edge of the steps. The heavy shadows cast by the high-relief carving intensify this effect. At Pergamon, the two-dimensional plane of the Hellenic style was expanded here to suggest more recession in depth.

A general comparison of Hellenistic art with the Athenian art of the fifth century BCE leaves one with the impression of discord rather than harmony; emotionalism in the place of a rational presentation; virtuosity triumphing over dignified refinement; melodrama superseding drama; variety in the place of unity. The Athenian culture, in short, placed its trust in exceptional human beings; the Hellenistic, in superbeings. No longer the masters of their fate, Hellenistic people seem engulfed in the storms and stresses of circumstances beyond their control.

PAINTING AND MOSAIC

As a consequence of the enduring qualities of stone, more ancient sculpture has survived than art works in any other form. Buildings were torn down for their materials and replaced by others. Statues of bronze, precious metals, and ivory were often too valuable in their essential materials to survive. Libraries either were burned or saw their volumes disintegrate over time, so their books survive only in imperfect copies made by medieval scribes or as fragmentary quotations in other volumes. The musical notation contained in ancient manuscripts could not be understood by these copyists, who eventually omitted it. Mosaics and pottery have fared better, but for the most part they, too, were either broken up or carried off by conquerors and collectors.

PERGAMENE PAINTING AND ROMAN ADAPTATIONS

Of all the major visual arts in antiquity, painting has suffered most from the ravages of time. So few examples survive that we can gain only a hint of what this art must have been at its best, and it is easy to arrive at the incorrect impression that sculpture was the most important of all the arts. Literary sources, however, verify the effectiveness of painting and the high esteem in which it was held.

Pausanias, a writer of Roman times, described the works of the legendary fifth-century BCE Athenian painters Polygnotus and Apollodorus. The former worked out the principles of perspective drawing, and the latter was renowned for his use of light and shadow and fine gradations of color. Pausanias also mentioned many paintings at Pergamon, including some by Apollodorus. The excavated fragments there reveal that the interior walls of temples and public buildings frequently were painted with pictorial panels and had streaks of color that imitated the texture of marble. Other scattered fragments of paintings show that the Pergamenes favored bright colors, such as yellows, pinks, and greens, which contrasted with deep reds, blues, and browns.

The palace paintings used motifs of actual animals, such as lions and charging bulls, and imaginary ones, such as tritons and griffins. Interiors of rooms were often decorated with painted friezes similar to sculptural ones, and walls, especially of small rooms, were painted with panels and columns that included realistic shadows to create the illusion of spaciousness. The writers of antiquity mention that the subjects of paintings were often drawn from mythology or from literary sources such as Homer's *The Odyssey*. It is also known that Hellenistic painting commonly dealt in **genre scenes,** that is, casual, informal subjects from daily life.

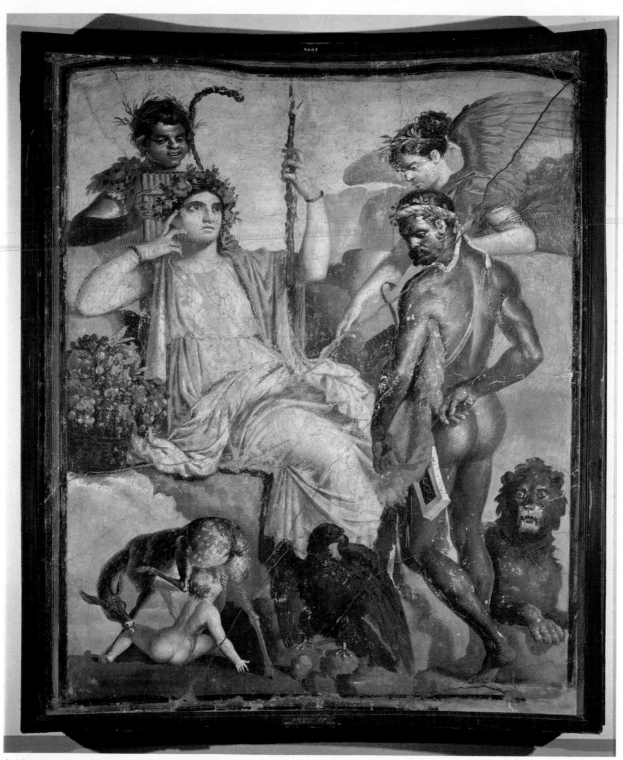

3.10   *Hercules Finding His Infant Son Telephus,* c. 70 CE. Fresco from Herculaneum, probably a copy after a Pergamene original of second century BCE. Museo Archeologico Nazionale, Naples, Italy.

Although the original paintings no longer exist and only fragments of mosaics and vase painting survive, well-preserved copies of Pergamene work have been found in the Greek cities of southern Italy, notably Herculaneum. This city supposedly was founded by Hercules, whose son Telephus founded Pergamon. A "family" relationship thus existed between the two centers. Herculaneum, in fact, became a later middle-class version of the earlier aristocratic Pergamon.

Both Herculaneum and nearby Pompeii were suddenly buried in a rain of cinders and a hail of volcanic stone that accompanied the eruption of Mount Vesuvius in 79 CE. When rediscovered in the eighteenth century, the two cities yielded many paintings and mosaics preserved almost intact. The prevailing taste was Hellenistic, and the well-to-do patrons, preferring traditional subjects, usually commissioned copies of famous paintings rather than original works of art.

Hercules Finding His Infant Son Telephus (Fig. 3.10) is an adaptation of a Pergamene original. The winged figure in the upper right is pointing out to Hercules his son Telephus, who is seen in the lower left among wild animals, suckling a doe. The place is the legendary fertile land of Arcadia, personified by the stately seated figure. Beside her are the fruits of the land, and at her back a playful faun is holding a shepherd's crook and blowing the panpipes. The coloring for the most part is sepia and reddish brown, relieved by lighter blue, green, and whitish tints. The figures appear against the background plane of the sky, which projects them forward in the manner of relief sculpture. The drapery and modeling of the flower-crowned Arcadia recall the carving of a marble relief, while the powerful musculature of Hercules's body is cast in the manner of a bronze statue in the round.

Because ancient sculpture usually was painted in vivid colors and reliefs sometimes had landscapes painted in their backgrounds, the arts of painting and sculpture obviously were closely identified in the Hellenistic mind, and they should perhaps be thought of more as complementary arts than as independent media. Paintings were more adaptable to interiors, whereas weather-resistant stone made marble reliefs better for the open air. The existing evidence clearly shows that the visual intention and expressive effect of both arts were closely associated and that neither could claim aesthetic supremacy over the other.

MOSAIC

Mosaic, an art that dates to remote antiquity, was highly favored at Pergamon for the flooring of interiors and for wall paneling. As with later Roman work, geometric patterns were often preferred for floors, whereas representations of mythological subjects, landscapes, and genre scenes were used for floors and murals. Such compositions are formed of small cubes or pieces of stone, marble, or ceramic, known as **tesserae,** which are set in cement.

A mosaic by the artist Hephaistion covered the entire floor of a room (Fig. 3.11). It has a blank center surrounded by a colorful geometric design

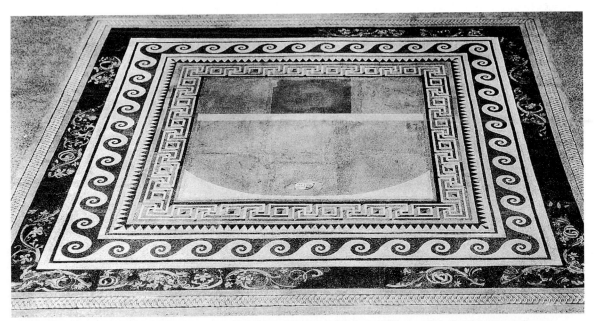

3.11   Hephaistion. Mosaic from Palace of Attalus II at Pergamon, c. 150 BCE, 28′. Antikensammlung, Staatliche Museen zu Berlin, Berlin, Germany.

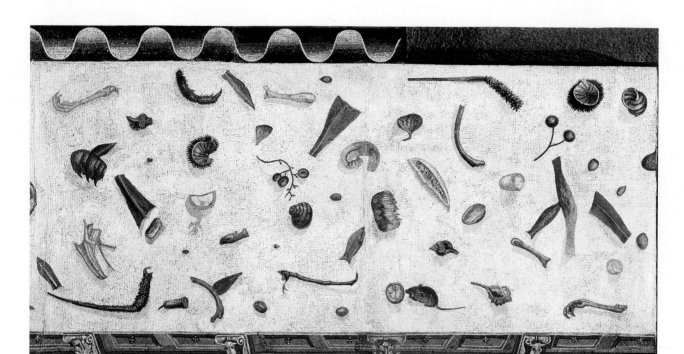

3.12   After Sosus. *Unswept Dining Room Floor.* Detail of later Roman copy of original Pergamene mosaic of second century BCE. Museo Gregoriano Profano, Vatican Museums, Rome, Italy.

of black, gray, red, yellow, and white marble tesserae. Beyond this is a wavelike pattern of black and white. Enclosing the whole is a border about a yard wide with a foliated, or leaflike, design of such rich variety that in its 44-foot expanse there is no repetition. Against a dark background are intertwined colored flowers, exotic lilies, vine leaves, and various fruits, all with delicate shadings. In some places, grasshoppers are feeding on acanthus leaves; in others, small winged *putti,* or Cupid-like boys symbolizing love, are playing among the vines.

According to the Roman writer Pliny the Elder, the most famous mosaicist of antiquity was Sosus, who worked at Pergamon. Among his most widely copied designs was one of doves drinking from a silver dish. A favorite design of his for the floors of dining rooms showed vegetables, fruit, fish, a chicken leg, and in the lower left corner, a mouse gnawing on a nut (Fig. 3.12). Shadows and highlights increase the illusion of three-dimensionality.

A quality mosaic copy of an earlier Hellenistic painting was found at Pompeii. It depicts the youthful Alexander's triumph in the *Battle of Issus* (Fig. 3.13), a scene of epic sweep and unprecedented vividness. The subject is the climactic moment when the Persians realize that defeat is imminent and are about to turn and flee. The dauntless Alexander advances on his horse, Bucephalus (whose name means ox head). The inside of the horse's ear has been rendered in white to resemble an ox horn. Alexander presses forward directly into the phalanx of bending spears. Darius, the king of kings, looks older and frightened. He extends his hand in a gesture that indicates a plea for mercy, while his charioteer's whip gives the signal for retreat. The brilliant lighting allows the swords and armor to gleam and the skillfully modeled figures to cast shadows on the ground. Note also the fallen Persian warrior on the right, cowering between the two horses and staring at his own face reflected in his polished bronze shield.

MUSIC

Pergamon adapted the musical traditions of the nearby region of northern Asia Minor known as Phrygia, which had its own characteristic idioms, modes, rhythms, scales, and instruments. As early as the fifth century BCE, Athenians were divided regarding the merits of the Dorian musical tradition of the Greek mainland and were increasingly influ-

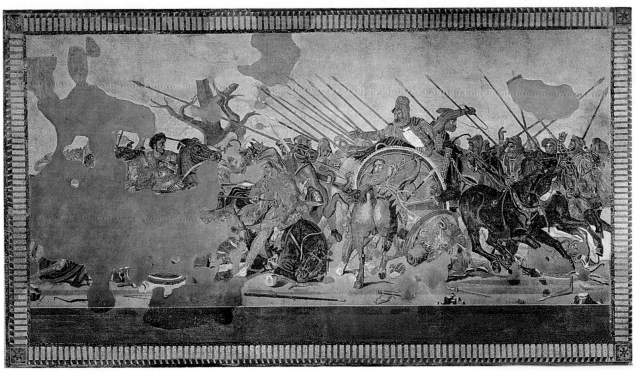

3.13   *Battle of Issus,* from House of the Faun, Pompeii, Italy, c. 310 BCE. Mosaic, 8′10″ × 16′9″. Mosaic copy of painting from c. 320–311 BCE. Museo Nazionale, Naples, Italy.

enced by the music of foreign cultural centers. During the Hellenistic period, the exciting music of Phrygia gained popular favor.

PHRYGIAN VERSUS DORIAN MUSIC

Melodies in the Phrygian mode apparently induced strong emotional reactions. The musical instrument called the Phrygian pipe was said to stir the senses. This pipe, known as the ***aulos,*** was a reed instrument with a peculiarly penetrating sound. English translations from ancient Greek incorrectly render the aulos as a "flute." Marsyas plays a double version in Figure 3.14, at the right. Dorian music, by contrast, was associated with stringed instruments such as the lyre and the ***cithara*** (Fig. 3.14, left), the latter often mistranslated as a "harp."

Both the lyre and the cithara in the Dorian musical tradition and the aulos in the Phrygian were used principally to accompany songs, melodies, and choruses and, to a much lesser extent, were played as solo instruments by skilled performers. In the Dorian tradition, lyre playing was especially associated with the cult of Apollo. The Greeks attributed to this body of music the quality of ***ethos,***

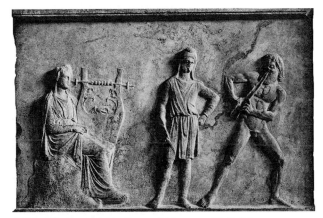

3.14   *Contest of Apollo and Marsyas.* Relief from Mantineia, Greece, c. 350 BCE. Marble, height 38′¼″. National Museum, Athens, Greece.

or ethical character. The aulos, the instrument of Dionysus, was associated with ***pathos,*** or strong emotional feeling, and had a sensuous quality conducive to enthusiasm. To the Athenians, this indicated a division in their aspirations and ideals: one instrument and mode of singing were associated with clarity, restraint, and moderation, the other with emotional excitement and aroused passions.

MUSICAL CONTESTS.   This division of musical opinion was expressed in the many sculptural representations of the musical contest between the Olympian Apollo and the Phrygian satyr Marsyas. According to myth, Athena was the inventor of the aulos. One day as she was playing, however, she caught sight of her reflection in a pool of water. She was so displeased with the facial grimaces the aulos caused her to make that she threw it away in disgust. Marsyas, happening along, found it and was so enchanted by its sounds that he challenged Apollo, the immortal patron of the Muses, to a contest. The god chose to play on the dignified lyre, won the contest easily, and proved once again that mortals are no match for the gods. As a punishment, Apollo had his challenger skinned alive.

A relief from Mantineia, of the school of Praxiteles, represents the contest in progress (Fig. 3.14). On one side, calmly awaiting his turn, is the seated Apollo with his lyre; on the other, Marsyas is ecstatically blowing on the aulos. Between them is the judge, or music critic, standing patiently but with knife in hand.

MUSIC IN HELLENISTIC LIFE

Although there are few remnants of the actual musical life of Pergamon, it is known that here, as in other Hellenistic centers, the practice of music was given a high place in the arts. Gymnastic and musical festivals in honor of the Pergamene kings were held annually. Both boys and girls received musical instruction and sang hymns as they marched in processions or participated in religious observances. The curriculum included musical notation and the chanting of poetry to the accompaniment of the cithara. Among his other duties, the chief educator of the city, the *gymnasiarch,* was expected to arrange for appearances by visiting poets and musicians.

Tralles, a city of the Pergamene kingdom, provides one of the best examples of ancient music. A tombstone bearing an inscription consisting of some four lines of poetry accompanied by musical notation was unearthed there. The inscription, an epitaph by a man named Seikilos for the departed Euterpe, turned out to be the words and music of a short but intact tune in the Phrygian mode from the first century BCE. Unlike the typical wild and orgiastic Phrygian music, the mode of this song is melancholy. The little song, almost 2,000 years old, was of a popular type known as a *skolion,* or drinking song. It urged listeners, "Oh laugh while you may / Keep toil and trouble at bay. / For life is short and in its day / the night of death soon takes you away." The song was sung

after dinner by the guests as a cup was passed around for toasts and offerings to the gods.

The word *skolion* is derived from the Greek meaning "zigzag." It referred to the manner in which the lyre and cup were passed back and forth, crisscrossing the table as each of the reclining guests sang in turn. The simplicity of this song marks it as the type of tune expected in the repertory of every acceptable guest rather than as one of the more elaborate ballads intended to be sung by professional entertainers. In spirit and mood it is not unlike the New Year's Eve song, "Auld Lang Syne."

IDEAS

There were many striking differences between the Hellenistic and earlier Hellenic styles. Although both styles are Greek, the Hellenic was a more concentrated development in the small city-states of the Greek mainland, whereas the Hellenistic is a combination of native Greek and regional influences from western Asia, North Africa, Sicily, and Italy. In fact, the spread of Hellenistic art over several centuries and the entire Mediterranean world makes any quest for stylistic unity difficult.

The contrast between Hellenic and Hellenistic styles resembles a tilting of the cultural scale in one direction or another. The generalized social humanism of Athens becomes the particularized **individualism** of Pergamon and other centers. Hellenic idealism breaks down into a **realism** that looks at the world more in terms of immediate experience than under the aspect of eternity. The uncompromising rationalism of Socrates and Plato yields to the **empiricism** of scientists, scholars, and artists who are interested more in the development of methods and techniques and the application of knowledge to practical affairs than in the spirit of free inquiry. The tendencies that underlie the various art enterprises at Pergamon in particular and the Hellenistic period in general, then, are to be found in a pattern of interrelated ideas, of which individualism, realism, and empiricism are the most significant parts.

INDIVIDUALISM

The individualistic bias of Hellenistic life, thought, and art was an aspect of humanism, but it contrasted with that of the Hellenic period. In politics, rough-and-tumble public discussions of Athenian citizens and decisions arrived at by voice vote were superseded at Pergamon by the rule of a small group headed by a king who enjoyed semidivine status. Another indication of Hellenistic individualism was the cult of hero worship that started with

Alexander the Great and continued with the kings who succeeded him in the various parts of his far-flung empire. It was reflected in the popular biographies of great men and in the building of lavish temples and monuments glorifying not the ancient gods but monarchs and military heroes. The famous Mausoleum (Fig. 3.15) for King Mausolus of Halicarnassus, thought to be one of the wonders of the ancient world, is a good example. Individualism was also reflected in the sculptor's accent on individual characteristics, personality traits, and ethnic differences. In the earlier Hellenic centers, poets, playwrights, and musicians were mainly skilled amateurs; even in sports the emphasis was on active participation. In the Hellenistic period, however, a rising spirit of professionalism can be seen in the fame of individual writers, actors, musical performers, and athletes. As a result, more people became passive spectators rather than active participants.

STOICISM AND EPICUREANISM. Two contrasting philosophies—Stoicism, with its emphasis on world order and determinism, and Epicureanism, with its accent on chance and personal freedom—dominated Hellenistic thought. The founder of Stoicism was Zeno, who taught in the stoa of the Athenian agora and whose thought took the greatly expanded world of Alexander's empire into account. Hellenistic Greece was no longer a collection of city-states with a common language and geography. Instead, it was an empire that dominated the known parts of western Asia, North Africa, and Mediterranean Europe.

Like Plato in his *Timaeus,* Zeno believed that the human race had been fashioned by the creator in the image of the world soul. He envisaged humanity as one people, citizens of one state, with each individual as part of the world soul observing universal laws and living in harmony with fellow beings. As his follower, the Phrygian philosopher Epictetus, observed, every person is like an actor in a play in which God has assigned the parts, and it is our duty to perform our parts worthily, whatever they may be.

With a world empire to be taken into account, the Stoic ideal of kinship with nature and world

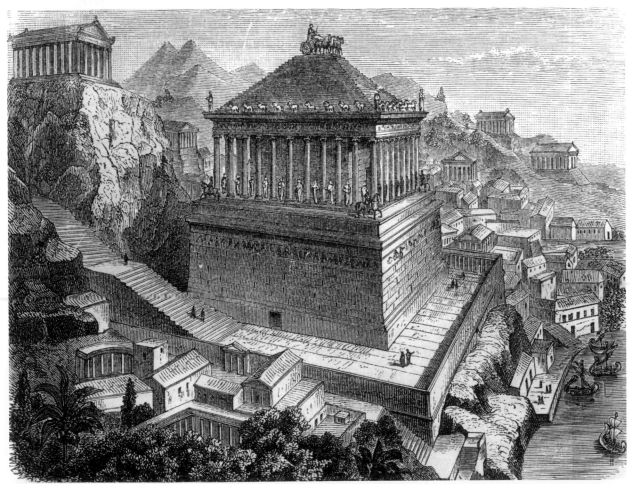

3.15 Pythios. Mausoleum at Halicarnassus, 359–351 BCE. Length 106′, width 86′. Reconstruction drawing. Archiv fur Kunst und Geschichte, Berlin, Germany.

citizenship found fertile soil in later Roman thought. Seneca, a dramatist, politician, and philosopher, counseled that a wise man cannot meet with misfortune because all experience of evil is only an instrument to train the mind. Evil is also a challenge to exercise the powers of endurance and a means of showing the world a person's indifference to external conditions. Later, the Roman emperor Marcus Aurelius, in his *Meditations,* attempted to rationalize his philosophy with his exalted position by declaring that he was *in* the world, not *of* it. His thought embraced recognition of the interdependence of all people and the cultivation of fortitude and endurance. In sum, the Stoics believed that true good lies within oneself. Only by cultivating virtue, accepting duty, and maintaining human dignity in the face of adversity can true freedom and mastery of life be attained.

Epicurus's theory that pleasure was the highest good found ready acceptance in the rich cities of Asia Minor. His materialistic worldview was based on **atomism,** the belief that all is brought about by the haphazard collision and conjunction of tiny particles. Everything is perpetually changing as atoms come together and then separate to form new patterns. There is, then, no afterlife, no future reward or punishment, because death is simply the dissolution of a person's collection of atoms. The life here and now should thus be lived to the fullest, and the object is "freedom from trouble in the mind and from pain in the body."

The lofty idealism and rigorous logic of Socrates gave way to a tendency toward a comfortable **hedonism,** the belief that pleasure is the chief goal in life. But because too much physical pleasure can lead to pain, moderation should prevail. And because some pleasures exceed others, the mind and critical faculties are needed to identify those that give more lasting satisfaction. Epicurus also held that happiness for the individual lay in the simple life, self-sufficiency, and withdrawal from public affairs. This view in effect denied the social responsibilities of citizenship and encouraged escapism and extreme individualism. These different philosophies had considerable influence on the various modes and manners of depicting both gods and men and their expressive attitudes.

PHILOSOPHY AND THE ARTS

Because the state was wealthy, many Hellenistic people could enjoy comfortable personal and home lives. By contrast, poverty, or at least self-deprivation, was considered honorable in ancient Athens, where both rich and poor lived as neighbors in modest homes. Hellenistic prosperity, however, allowed a more luxurious standard of living for a larger percentage of the population. Hellenistic architects took a special interest in domestic dwellings. Painters and mosaicists were called on to decorate the houses of the well-to-do. Sculptors created figurines with informal, sometimes humorous, subjects, because they were more adaptable to the home than the monumental formal works found in public places. Together with potters and other craftspeople, artisans contributed to the life of luxury and ease of a frankly pleasure-loving people.

Hellenistic artists were interested in exceptions more than rules, in the abnormal more than the normal, in diversity more than unity. In portraiture, they noted the physical peculiarities that set an individual apart more than those he or she shared with others. Even the gods were personalized rather than generalized, and the choice of subjects from daily life showed artists' increased preoccupation with informal, casual, everyday events. They were also more concerned with societal influences on the human condition than with the ability to rise above one's limitations. Hellenistic artists, by recognizing the complexity of life, gave their attention

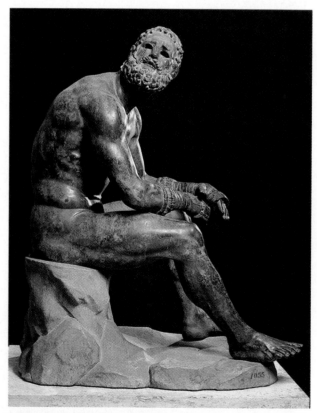

3.16 Seated Boxer, c. 100–50 BCE. Bronze, approx. 4′2½″. Museo Nationale Romano, Rome, Italy.

to shades of feeling and to representing the infinite variety of the world of appearances.

Hellenistic thought was oriented toward emotional life. Instead of looking for universal aspects of experience that could be shared by all, Hellenistic philosophers held that each person has feelings, ideas, and opinions that are entirely different from those of others. Thus, each must decide what is good and evil, true and false. Instead of seeking a golden mean between opposites such as harmony and discord, as did their Hellenic predecessors, Hellenistic philosophers became psychologists, analyzing the self and laying bare the causes of inner conflict, as in the expression of the *Seated Boxer* (Fig. 3.16). He sits partially slumped, displaying facial wounds, a broken nose, and missing teeth. Bright drops of copper blood drip down his face. This is not a calm, fearless Hellenic athlete such as the *Doryphorus* (see Fig. 2.21), but a defeated competitor conscious of his slacking powers. The self-satisfaction and pride of accomplishment with which the Hellenic gods and athletes were depicted were social emotions to be shared by all. The sorrow, anguish, and suffering of Hellenistic wounded warriors and defeated giants were private, personal feelings that separated a person from the group and invited inward reflection. At the same time, Hellenistic representations of conquest, or even old age (see Fig. 3.18) invite a voyeuristic fascination with imperfection and misery that Hellenic culture disparaged.

Exploring this orientation, Hellenistic artists turned from the ideal of self-mastery to that of self-expression, from the concealment of inner impulse to outbursts of feeling—in short, from ethos to pathos. It was said of Pericles that he was never seen laughing and that even the news of his son's death did not alter his dignified calm. A strong contrast to this Olympian attitude is provided by the *Laocoön Group* (Fig. 3.17), in which reason seems about to be overcome by emotion. Recent speculation on the long-debated originality of the piece

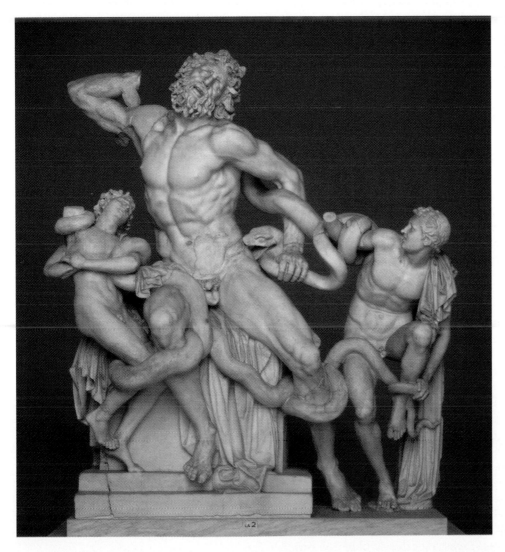

3.17 Agesander?, Athenodorus?, and Polydorus of Rhodes? *Laocoön Group.* Early first century CE. Marble, height 8′. Vatican Museums, Rome, Italy.

argues that it is not a copy, but a late Hellenistic work. It shows the torment of Laocoön, a priest of Troy whom the gods are punishing for warning citizens that the Greeks, whom the gods favored, had sinister motives for leaving the now-famous wooden Trojan horse to tantalize them just outside the gates of Troy. The scene, which seems to have been taken directly from Virgil's *Aeneid,* shows the priest and his sons mortally attacked by fierce, venomous sea snakes. Translated into marble, the blood-curdling event from Virgil's text seems somewhat restrained in its depiction of agony. However twisted in pain, the bodies recall the Hellenic idea. Yet the subject of physical and psychological agony is purely Hellenistic. Could it be, as the eighteenth-century German critic Gotthold Lessing suggested, that Greek culture had a more permissive attitude toward the depiction of pain in literature and plays than in the visual arts? Whatever the cause, the *Laocoön Group* seems to hover between Hellenic idealism and Hellenistic realism.

The preoccupation of Pergamene artists with painful and agonizing subjects such as the defeated Gauls, the punishment of Marsyas, and the battle of gods and giants reveals the deliberate intention to involve the spectator in a kind of emotional orgy. Misfortune becomes something that can be enjoyed by the fortunate, who participate in the situation with a kind of morbid satisfaction.

In the spirit of Stoic philosophy, life and suffering were to be endured with a benign resignation and acceptance of misfortunes that one can do nothing about. The artists of the frieze of the Altar of Zeus, for instance, were incredibly inventive in the ways they found for the gods to inflict pain and death. The composition approaches encyclopedic inclusiveness in the various modes of combat by the gods and the capacity for suffering by the giants. Nothing like it appears again until the Romanesque Last Judgments (see Fig. 6.1) and Dante's *Inferno* (see pp. 232–234).

REALISM

The increasing complexity and quicker pulse of Hellenistic life weakened the belief in the underlying unity of knowledge and abiding values that had produced the poise of Hellenic figures and the unemotional calm of their facial expressions. The world of concrete experience was more real to the Hellenistic mind than the world of abstract ideals. Taking a more relativistic view of things, people now looked to variety rather than unity and took into account individual experiences and differences. The decline of idealism was not so much the result of decadence as it was a matter of placing human activities in a new frame of reference, reexamining the goals and redefining the basic values of humanity. Confronted with the variety and multiplicity of this world, Hellenistic artists made no attempt to reduce its many manifestations to the simplicity of types and archetypes.

Hellenic artists portrayed their subjects standing aloof and rising above their environmental limitations, but in Hellenistic art, men and women find themselves beset by natural and social forces and are inevitably conditioned by them. The writhing forms on the great frieze reveal some of the conflicts and contradictions of Hellenistic thought. The gods in this work can be seen as projections of human psychological states. The earlier Hellenic gods appeared to have the world well under control, and the calm, poised Zeus in Figure 2.24 exhibits no sign of strain as he hurls his thunderbolt. The deities on the Altar of Zeus, however, are fighting furiously, and the struggle verges on getting out of hand.

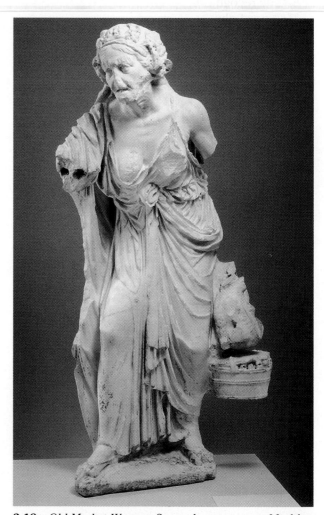

3.18 *Old Market Woman.* Second century BCE. Marble, approx. 7′10½″ high. Metropolitan Museum of Art, New York.

REALISM AND ARCHITECTURE. In Athenian architecture of the fifth century BCE, each building, however well suited to its site, was an independent unit, and the architects were little concerned with any precise relationship to nearby buildings. Indeed, to have admitted that one structure was dependent on another in a group would have diminished its status as a self-contained whole and thus rendered it incomplete by Hellenic standards. On the Athenian Acropolis, each temple had its own axis and its independent formal existence, in keeping with the conception that each separate work of art must be a logical whole made up of the sum of its own parts. Only such concessions to nature as were necessary, like the multiple levels of the Erectheum on the Athenian Acropolis, were made. The perfection of each building stood as a monument to the human mind as it rose above its material environment rather than be bound by it.

Hellenistic architecture moved away from the isolated building as a self-contained unit and toward a realistic recognition that nothing is complete in itself but must always exist as part of an interrelated pattern. City planning is in this sense a form of realism, and Hellenistic buildings were considered part of the community as a whole. In the case of the Pergamene acropolis, the position of each building was carefully calculated, with regard to not only its surroundings but also its place in the group.

REALISM AND SCULPTURE. In sculpture, the members of each group were likewise subject to their environment, and the individual was portrayed as an essential part of the surroundings. Incorporating painted backgrounds and higher relief, Hellenistic sculpture relied on changing light and shadow for its expressive effect, allowed for movement in more than one plane, and suggested greater depth in space. In Hellenic sculpture, a figure always bore the stamp of a type, and personality was subordinate to the individual's place in society. A warrior, for example, had a well-developed physique, but his face and body bore no resemblance to those of a specific person. He could be identified by a spear or shield and was more a member of a class than a person in his own right.

The Hellenistic desire to render human beings as unique personalities and not as types required a masterly technique that was capable of reproducing such particular characteristics as the twist of a mouth, wrinkles of the skin, physical blemishes, and individualized facial expressions. Faces, moreover, had to appear animated and lifelike so that the subject of a realistic portrait could be distinguished from all others. Faithfulness to nature also meant accurate rendering of anatomical detail. Like a scientist, the sculptor carefully observed the musculature of the human body so as to render every nuance of the flesh. The *Old Market Woman* (Fig. 3.18), for example, reveals the body of a person worn down by toil. The bent back, sagging breasts, and knotty limbs are the results of the physical and social conditions under which she has had to live. A portrayal such as this would have been unthinkable to an earlier artist, whose clients treasured a state of equilibrium between youth and age.

In the handling of materials, the older Hellenic sculptors never forgot that stone was stone, but their realistic zeal often led later Hellenistic craftspeople to force stone to simulate the softness and warmth of living flesh. The story of the legendary sculptor Pygmalion, who chiseled his marble maiden so realistically that she came to life, could have happened only in the Hellenistic period, and the sensuous figure of the *Aphrodite of Cyrene* (Fig. 3.19) surely bears this out. The easy grace

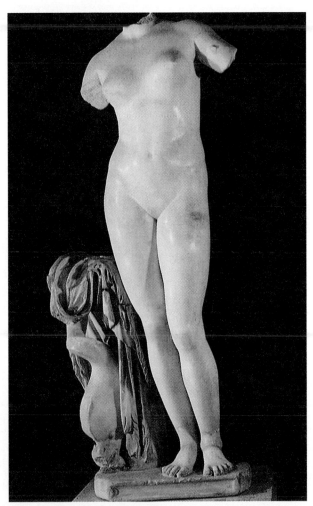

3.19 *Aphrodite of Cyrene.* Roman copy of c. 100 BCE. After Praxitelean original, found at Cyrene, North Africa. Marble, height 5′. Museo Archeologio Nazionale, Rome, Italy.

with which Praxiteles rendered his gods and goddesses (see Fig. 2.29) reaches a climax in such elegant and polished figures as this Aphrodite and the famous *Apollo Belvedere* (Fig. 3.20). Other masterpieces from this period include the great *Winged Victory of Samothrace* and the *Venus of Milo*. Hellenistic emphasis on realism appealed greatly to the forthright Roman conquerors of Greece. Its appeal was largely responsible for the survival of the Pergamene art known to us today.

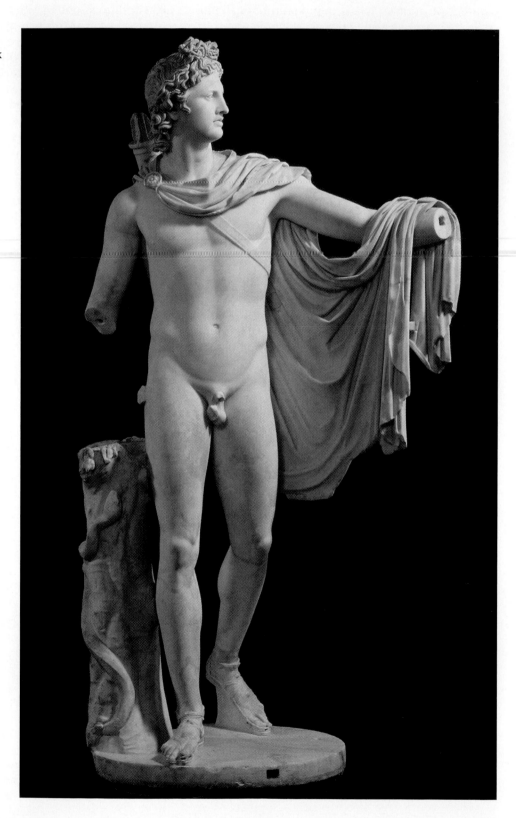

3.20 *Apollo Belvedere.* Roman copy after Greek original of late fourth century BCE. Marble, height 7′4″. Museo Pio Clementino, Vatican Museums, Rome, Italy.

EMPIRICISM

The rationalism of Hellenic thought as developed by Socrates, Plato, and Aristotle emphasized the spirit of free intellectual inquiry in a quest for universal truth. Epicureanism and Stoicism, by contrast, were practical philosophies for living. The abstract logic of the earlier period yielded to an empiricism that was concerned more with science than with wisdom. It focused on bringing together the results of isolated experimentation and applying scientific knowledge to the solution of practical problems. More broadly, it stressed gathering facts, cataloguing source materials, conducting research, collecting art works, and developing criteria for judging the arts.

Epicurus, by eliminating the notion of divine intervention in human affairs and offering physical explanations of natural phenomena, led the way toward a scientific materialism. The scientific achievements of the period were truly impressive. Hellenistic mathematics extended as far as conic sections and trigonometry, and astronomers and physicists such as Archimedes and Hero of Alexandria knew the world was round and its approximate circumference and diameter. Hellenistic scientists devised a solar calendar of 365¼ days, invented a type of steam engine, and worked out the principles of steam power and force pumps. Similarly, commercial developments led to new sources of wealth. Indeed, more devices might have been developed in Hellenistic times had not slave labor, the product of conquest and expansion, been so cheap and abundant.

The scientific attitude of Hellenistic thought found brilliant expression in the development of the theoretical bases of music. Although philosophers and mathematicians of the earlier period had made many discoveries and had brilliant insights into the nature of music, it remained for the Hellenistic mind to systematize them and construct a full and coherent science of music. Under Aristoxenos of Tarentum, a disciple of Aristotle, and under the great geometrician Euclid, the science of music reached a formulation so complete and comprehensive that it became the foundation for Western music theory. It is impossible to go into the intricacies of the Greek musical system here, but it was in the theoretical field more than any other that the lasting musical contribution of the period was made.

THE RISE OF ANTIQUARIANISM. After establishing his great library, Eumenes II gathered about him many outstanding Greek scholars. They were dedicated to the task of preserving the literary masterpieces of former days, making critical editions of the works of ancient poets and dramatists, selecting material for anthologies, cataloguing collections, copying manuscripts, writing grammatical treatises, and compiling dictionaries. In their scholarly endeavors, they often held earlier works above those of their own time. As a consequence, their literary production began to be addressed to scholars.

This was a period of **antiquarianism,** or concern with things old and rare, of scholarly rather than creative writing, of book learning instead of inspiration. Only systematic, exhaustive research, for instance, could have produced the program of the great frieze encircling the Altar of Zeus, which is a veritable catalogue of Greek mythology, complete with footnotes and annotations. The Attalids not only collected art but actually engaged in archeological excavations, another antiquarian activity. For the first time, living sculptors and painters were confronted with museums filled with noted works from the glorious past. As a result, copying the masterpieces of Myron, Phidias, and others became an industry that thrived throughout antiquity until the coming of organized Christianity. The age raised the social position of the artist. As in literature and music, it established the history of art and formulated aesthetic standards, so now art was worthy of attention in intellectual and social circles.

THE ROAD TO ROME

A reputation for learning had direct bearing on the political purposes of the Pergamene government. The more famous their capital became for its intellectual and cultural enterprises, the higher its prestige in the Greek world would rise. The career of Eumenes II's brother, who eventually succeeded him as Attalus II, is a case in point. As a skillful general, he was invaluable to the Pergamene regime, yet at the conclusion of a successful war, he took 5 years off to study philosophy at the academy in Athens. Moreover, the proudest boast of the Attalids after their military victories was that they had saved Hellenism from the barbarians. This claim, of course, had to be fortified by the development of their capital as a center of arts and letters.

To advertise the cultural achievements of his realm, Eumenes II chose his librarian, the famed grammarian Crates of Mallus, as his ambassador to Rome. By defending humanistic learning and stimulating Roman desire for more knowledge of Greek

3.21   Arch of Trajan.
Benevento, Italy, 114 CE.

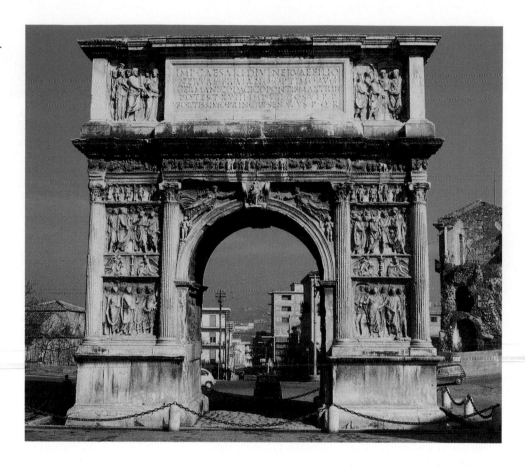

philosophy, literature, and art, Crates made a lasting impression on the future world capital.

With literary talents being diverted to the editing of manuscripts, scholars delving into the history of the past, art collectors digging for buried treasure, and musicians writing theoretical treatises, Pergamon was well on its way to becoming an archive and a museum. In time, this antiquarianism was bound to reduce artistic developments to a system of academic formulas and rules, all of which is symptomatic of a hardening of the artistic arteries and the eventual decline of creative powers. When Attalus III willed his kingdom to Rome in 133 BCE he was actually presenting that city with a living museum. The vast art holdings of the Attalids soon were on their way to Italy, where the interest and admiration they commanded, when shown in public exhibitions, were destined to have a powerful effect on the taste of the Romans. With them went the Hellenistic craftspeople who would embellish the new world capital with a wealth of public buildings, carvings, murals, and mosaics.

Southern Italy and Sicily had long been sites of important Greek settlements. In the sixth and fifth centuries BCE, there were thriving settlements on the mainland, such as Naples, Paestum, and Tarentum, as well as on Sicily at Syracuse and Agrigentum. Greek influence still prevailed in late Hellenistic times in these places and also at Pompeii and Herculaneum. When Greece came under Roman political control, Greece took over Rome with its philosophy, literature, and art. The emperor Trajan's Arch at Benevento (Fig. 3.21), which celebrated the completion of a highway from Rome to the seaport that linked it with the main centers of the east, is a reminder of the route by which the heritage of the classical Mediterranean world became a part of the Western cultural tradition. The road between Greece and Rome was thus smoothly paved, both literally and figuratively.

YOUR RESOURCES

- **Web Site**

  http://art.wadsworth.com/fleming10

  ○ Chapter 3 Quiz

  ○ Links

- **Audio CD**

  ○ *Skolion of Seikolos*

HELLENISTIC PERIOD, FOURTH TO FIRST CENTURIES BCE

Key Events	Architecture	Visual Arts	Literature and Music
359–336 **Philip of Macedon** in control of Greece			
352–350 **Artemisia,** queen of Caria, reigned	c. 350 **Mausoleum** at Halicarnassus built under Queen Artemisia: Pythios, architect; frieze carved by Scopas and others		
336 **Philip** assassinated; succeeded by son, Alexander the Great			c. 341–c. 270 **Epicurus,** founder of Epicureanism
334–323 **Alexander's conquests** in Near East, Asia Minor, India	350 **Theater at Epidaurus** built by Polyclitus the Younger		c. 336–c. 264 **Zeno of Citium,** founder of Stoicism
333 **Battle of Issus,** conquest of Persia		c. 330 **Apelles,** court painter to Alexander, flourished	c. 321 **Aristoxenus of Tarentum,** musical theorist, flourished
331 **City of Alexandria,** Egypt, founded			
323 **Alexander the Great** died in Babylon			
323–275 **Alexander's generals** divided empire: Ptolemies in Egypt, Seleucids in Syria and Palestine, eventually the Attalids in Pergamon			
323–31 **Hellenistic period;** great centers of culture at Alexandria, Pergamon, Antioch, and Rhodes; 146–31 transitional Greco-Roman period		c. 310 *Battle of Issus* painted, now lost except for mosaic copy from Pompeii	
300			c. 300 **Euclid** flourished
			c. 287–212 **Archimedes**
269–197 **Attalus I,** king of Pergamon; defeated Gauls in Galatia, allied kingdom with Rome, erected monument commemorating victory over Gauls, patron of First School of Pergamene sculpture		c. 280 **Colossus of Rhodes** cast in bronze by Chares	
		c. 230–c. 220 **First School of Pergamene sculpture:** Attalus I's monument celebrating victory over Gauls	
200			
197–159 **Eumenes II,** king of Pergamon; defeated Gauls, founded Pergamene library, commissioned Altar of Zeus, patron of Second School of Pergamene sculpture. Power of kingdom at zenith	183–179 Eumenes II built **Altar of Zeus at Pergamon:** Menocrates of Rhodes, architect	c. 200 **Boethos** active: Statue of *Boy with Goose*	
		c. 190 *Winged Victory of Samothrace* carved	
159–138 **Attalus II,** king of Pergamon; patron of painting	c. 150 **Stoa of Attalus** built at Athens	c. 180–c. 160 **Second School of Pergamene sculpture:** Altar of Zeus frieze carved	
146 **Roman** conquest of Corinth			
138–133 **Attalus III,** king of Pergamon; willed kingdom to Rome			
120 **Pergamon** became a Roman province		c. 120 *Venus of Milo (Aphrodite of Melos)* carved	
100			
		c. 100 *Laocoön Group* carved	c. 50 CE **Skolion of Seikilos,** complete melody with Greek words carved on tombstone
			c. 50–138 CE **Epictetus**
			c. 205–270 CE **Plotinus,** founder of Neoplatonism

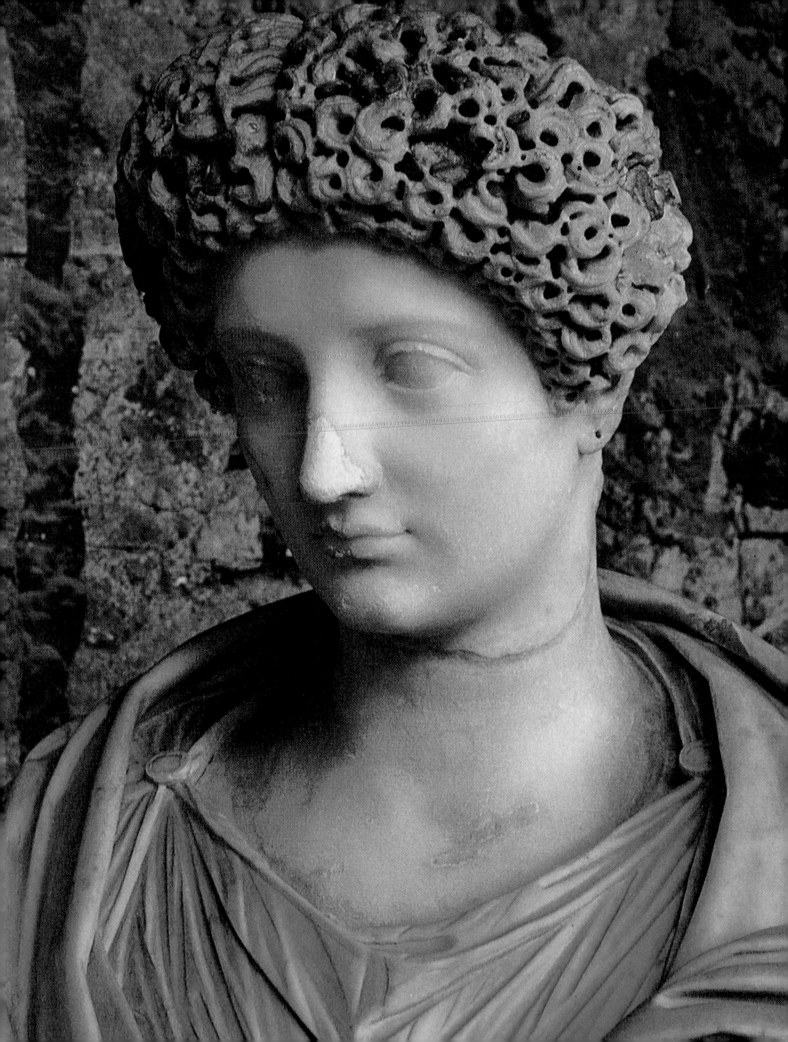

C H A P T E R

4

ROMAN STYLE

ROMAN EMPIRE

When Octavian, later Augustus Caesar, defeated the combined forces of Antony and Cleopatra at the Battle of Actium in 31 BCE, he soon became the sole ruler of the Roman world. His early life had been that of a warrior, and that is how he is portrayed in an imposing statue found at Prima Porta (Fig. 4.1). His posture is that of an **imperator,** or commander-in-chief, addressing his troops. Augustus probably stood 5 feet, 7 inches tall, but the statue is almost 7 feet tall. The idealized face and slightly tousled hair recall images of Alexander the Great, whom Roman rulers revered (see Fig. 3.2). Augustus seems to have actively encouraged comparisons between himself and Alexander. Like many men of the Roman elite, he visited Alexander's grave in Egypt. He also used a signet ring with Alexander's portrait to sign official documents.

Carved on the **cuirass,** or metal breastplate, of Augustus's armor are scenes in low relief recounting the outstanding achievements of his reign together with pictures of gods and goddesses who conferred favors upon him. Below is a cupid astride a dolphin, a double reference to the goddess Venus, mother of Aeneas, the legendary founder of Rome to whom Augustus traced his ancestry. The dolphin is a reminder that Venus was born of the sea, and the cupid symbolizes her status as the goddess of love. After Augustus, emperors made frequent use of symbols to indicate their superhuman associations. Indeed, they were like Egyptian pharaohs, controlling the economy and civil life of their huge domain. The power of the Roman Senate, once the governing body of Rome from which its two consuls or ruling magistrates were chosen, significantly diminished.

Augustus sought to establish what came to be known as the **Pax Romana,** a lasting peace after almost a century of civil and foreign wars. Assuming the title Augustus Caesar (he was the grand-nephew of Julius Caesar), he turned his energies to restoring civilian morale and rebuilding the city of Rome. By fostering literature in Latin, rather than Greek, he awakened the pride of his people in their own historical past and present. One such work was Virgil's *Aeneid,* an epic poem written in the same manner as Homer's *The Odyssey.* Augustus also undertook an ambitious building plan that

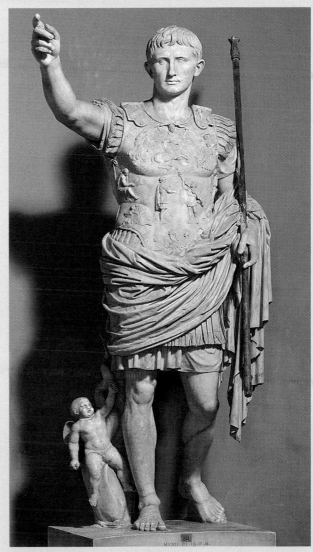

4.1 Augustus of Prima Porta, Italy, early first century CE copy of bronze original c. 20 BCE. Marble, height 6'8". Vatican Museums, Rome, Italy.

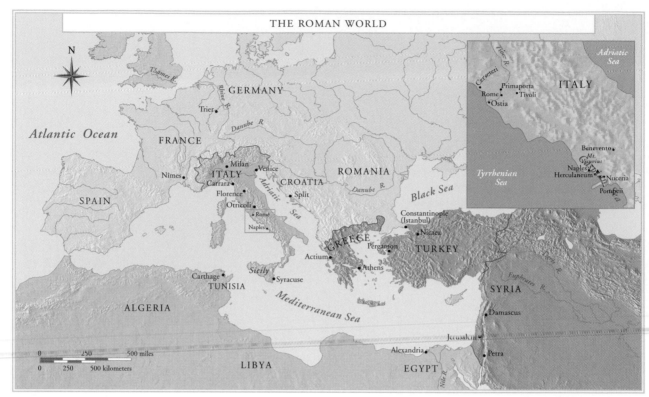

THE ROMAN WORLD

MAP 4.1

included a new forum and numerous other public edifices; the gem among them was the *Ara Pacis Augustae,* an altar dedicated to the spirit of peace.

The frieze on the north and south sides of the *Ara Pacis* (Fig. 4.2) recalls the Panathenaea, the Athenian procession depicted on the Parthenon, as well as figures on the Altar of Zeus at Pergamon (see Figs. 2.13 and 3.7A). Nevertheless, it differs from them in depicting a specific and recent historical event, using portraits of people whom viewers would recognize. The altar's outer walls are embellished by elegantly wrought, high-relief

4.2 *Ara Pacis Augustae* (Augustus's Altar of Peace), c. 13 BCE. Marble, 36′ high, 33′ wide. Museum of the Ara Pacis, Rome, Italy.

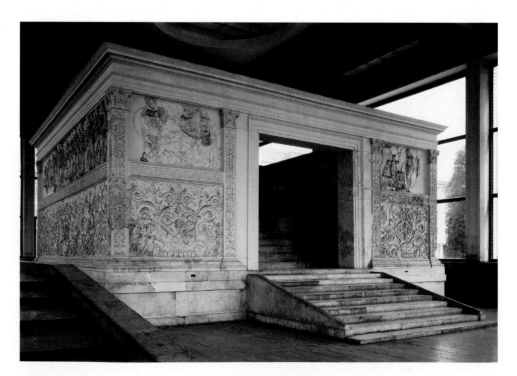

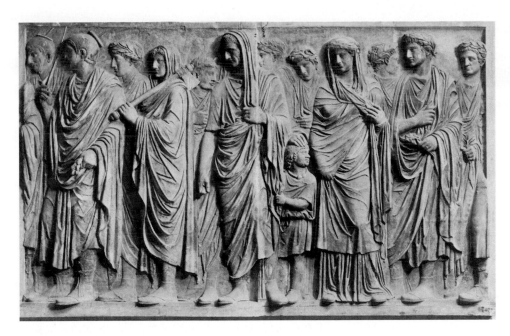

4.3 *Priests and the imperial family led by Marcus Agrippa* (south frieze). Roman relief, 13–9 BCE. Museum of the Ara Pacis, Rome, Italy.

sculptured panels that picture the original dedicatory ceremony. The sculptor of the *Ara Pacis* cleverly implied recessive space by using high relief for the figures closest to the viewer and low relief for those in the background.

Augustus, whose depiction is highly damaged, leads the group, followed by priests who will perform the sacrifice. Farther down the line, the man who has veiled his head is Agrippa, a favorite advisor who died before the altar was dedicated (Fig. 4.3). The child tugging the fabric of Agrippa's garment is probably Gaius, Agrippa's son. When Augustus's second wife was determined to be unable to have children, Augustus asked Agrippa to di-

vorce his wife and marry Julia, Augustus's daughter. Their child, Gaius, was adopted by Augustus as his son and heir. Sadly, however, Gaius died in his early twenties. The woman next to Gaius is probably Julia. The solemnity of the dedication scene is undercut by the restlessness of Gaius. In fact, several children appear on the *Ara Pacis,* suggesting the importance of family lineage in Roman life and politics.

The climax of the handsome design is seen in a panel that may depict the seated earth goddess, Tellus, from whose name the word *Italy* is derived (Fig. 4.4). She is shown in the midst of sheaves of grain, flocks of sheep, and other bounty of the earth. At her breast are two infants, possibly

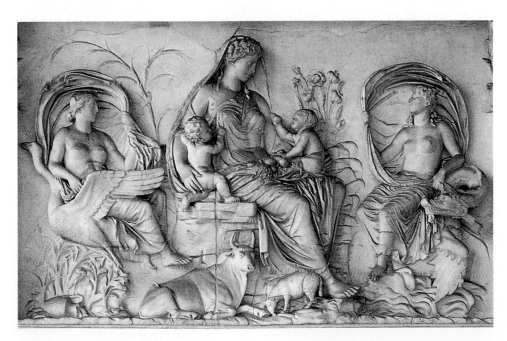

4.4 Female personification (Tellus?), panel from the east facade of the *Ara Pacis Augustae,* Rome, Italy, 13–9 BCE. Marble, height approx. 5'3".

Romulus and Remus, the legendary founders of Rome. At her left is a bird on the wing and a female figure with a blowing mantle, both representing the sky. On the right, above a gushing stream, reclines a river god. In combination, they represent three of the basic elements: earth, air, and water.

In the second century CE, Rome had a sequence of rulers—Nerva, Trajan, Hadrian, Antoninus Pius, and Marcus Aurelius—who were called the "Five Good Emperors" for their continued support of the public welfare and the arts. In his classic book *The Decline and Fall of the Roman Empire,* historian Edward Gibbon declared that "the empire of Rome comprehended the fairest part of the earth and the most civilized portion of mankind." He attributed Rome's emergence as a cultural center to the Romans' talent for law and order, their cultivation of tolerance and justice, and their capacity for wise government.

ARCHITECTURE AND SCULPTURE

Before the founding of the Roman Republic in about 500 BCE, a thriving but mysterious culture known as the Etruscans flourished in Italy. These people lived in the region between the Tiber River in the south and the Po valley in the north. The area surrounding the modern city of Florence is still known as Tuscany. Eventually Rome prevailed over the Etruscans, and all that remains are the fragments and outlines of their temples and the items found in their excavated tombs, which contain both sculptures and wall paintings. Their pottery techniques were derived from those of the Greeks, who inhabited Italy south of Rome. In fact, the Etruscans were great collectors of Greek pottery and other objects that they encountered during their extensive trading ventures in the Mediterranean Sea, and even into the Baltic Sea. Their temples (Fig. 4.5) bear some resemblance to the Greek Doric order, although they regularly divided the cella (that is, the inner room for cult statues) into three areas, unlike the singular cella usually found in Greek temples. In addition, Etruscan temples were more frontally oriented. They were placed on a raised **podium,** or masonry platform, with only one small stairway allowing visitors to enter the deep porch.

Surviving Etruscan sculpture is mostly **terra cotta,** or baked clay. The forms range from urns made to contain cremated remains to brightly colored funerary **sarcophagi** (singular, **sarcophagus**). A famous example probably represents a husband and wife reclining on a banqueting couch (Fig. 4.6). The man holds his palm up and flat; perhaps some gift or other item was to have been placed on it. The woman may have been holding a round object in her outstretched hand. It is interesting to ponder what their Greek acquaintances would have thought of a representation that showed such public ease and rapport between a man and woman. In Greek society, only men attended banquets. In Rome, women's fate was often determined by the *paterfamilias,* or father of the family. But recent research suggests that Etruscan women enjoyed unprecedented freedom. They are shown in art driving chariots. Moreover, they could run businesses and inherit money.

4.5 Reconstruction of a typical Etruscan temple of the sixth century as described by Vitruvius. Museo delle Antichità Etrusche e Italiche, Università di Roma "La Sapienza," Rome, Italy.

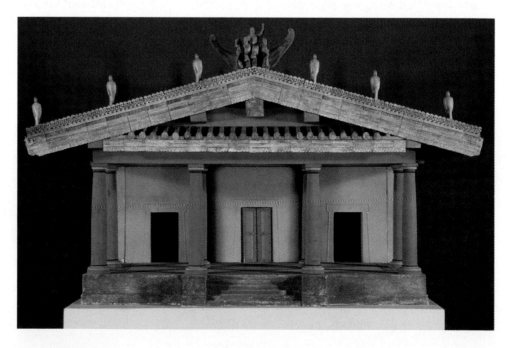

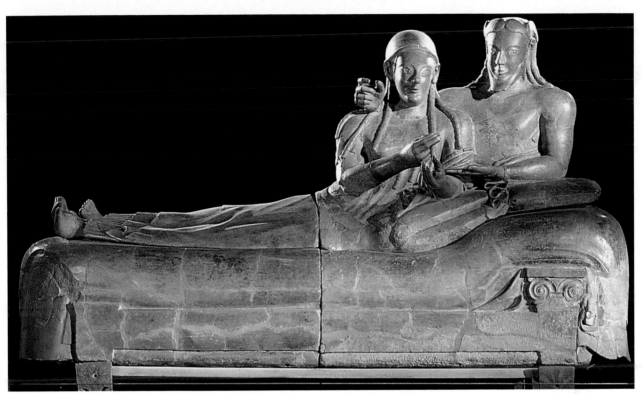

4.6 Sarcophagus, from Cerveteri, Italy, c. 520 BCE. Painted terra cotta, approx. 3′9½″ high. Museo Nazionale di Villa Giulia, Rome, Italy.

When the Romans defeated the Etruscans, much of the Etruscan culture was absorbed into the Roman orbit. Etruscan engineering helped the Romans construct bridges and aqueducts. The architecture of the Romans was thus a synthesis of the Etruscan and Greek traditions, with significant elements and ideas of their own. By Trajan's time, Rome had not only departed from Hellenistic precedents but also absorbed arts and ideas

from the entire Mediterranean world. The result was a new and distinctive Roman style.

THE FORUM OF TRAJAN

Following his accession as emperor in 98 CE, Trajan began a grandiose project in Rome: the construction of a new forum (Fig. 4.7). Just as the empire had grown in his time to its greatest extent, the

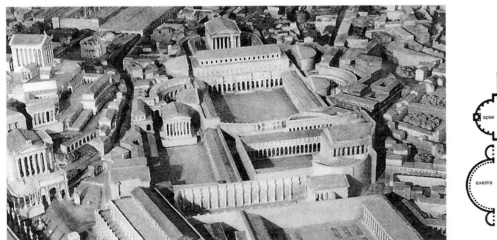

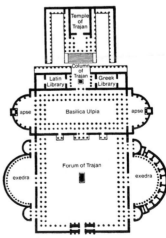

A   B

4.7 (A) Apollodorus of Damascus. Forum of Trajan, Rome, c. 113–117 CE. Length 920′, width 51′8″. Reconstruction to scale 1:250 by Italo Gismondi, 1937–1977. Museo della Civiltà Romana, Rome, Italy. (B) Plan of Forum of Trajan.

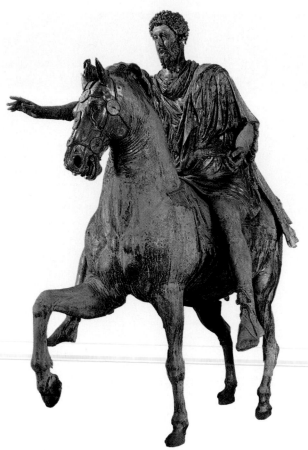

4.8　Equestrian statue of Marcus Aurelius, from Rome, Italy, c. 175 CE. Gilt bronze, approx. 11′6″ high. Musei Capitolini, Rome, Italy.

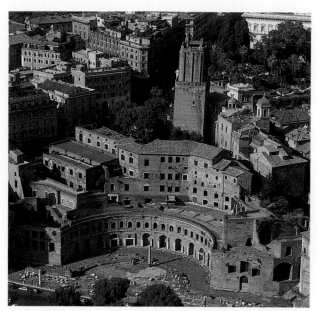

4.9　Apollodorus of Damascus. Forum of Trajan, Rome, northeast exedra and market hall, c. 113–117 CE.

population of Rome had increased to more than 1 million people, creating a need for larger buildings. The old Roman forum of the republic and that of Augustus had long been inadequate. Trajan's project, however, was so ambitious that it equaled all previous forums combined, bringing the total area covered by such structures to more than 25 acres. The magnificence of the new forum was in every way comparable to its size. Trajan entrusted the project to Apollodorus, a Greek architect-engineer from Damascus, who was already famous for the construction of a stone bridge over the widest part of the Danube.

Typically Roman in conception, a forum was a system of interrelated courtyards and buildings. The reconstruction drawing of the Athenian Acropolis (see Fig. 2.2) shows that the Parthenon and Erechtheum had little in common beyond the site on which they stood. But no part of a forum existed in isolation. The whole was conceived organically from the beginning and constructed on a grand scale, with an eye to symmetry and proportion. Trajan's forum, as seen in the ground plan (Fig. 4.7B), was divided by a central axis running

from the center of an arched gateway, through the middle of the open square, through the entrance to the basilica (whose axis is at right angles to that of the whole forum), to the base of the monumental column (see Fig. 4.10A), and finally up the steps of the temple to the altar at the back.

Visitors came into the forum through a majestic triple archway that led to the large paved rectangular courtyard. The courtyard was enclosed on three sides by a wall and colonnade and on the fourth by the Basilica Ulpia, whose entrances stood opposite those of the archway. Standing in the exact center of the open square was an impressive bronze statue of Trajan on horseback. Although no longer in existence, it is known to have resembled the bronze equestrian portrait of Marcus Aurelius (Fig. 4.8), who sits astride his splendid mount with a sense of balance and a thoughtful appearance worthy of the patient Stoic philosopher and author of the *Meditations* (see p. 198). In the original version, a conquered barbarian cowered beneath the horse's raised hoof, offsetting the tranquility of the emperor's face. Many such equestrian statues of emperors and military leaders once existed, and recent scholarship suggests that this fiery steed may have been intended for another, smaller rider. On the other hand, the Romans sometimes used scales symbolically, depicting people as larger than the horses they rode or the boats in which they sailed (see Fig. 4.11).

Flanking the square on the east and west were semicircular recesses known as ***exedrae,*** which were outlined by tall Doric columns. On one side,

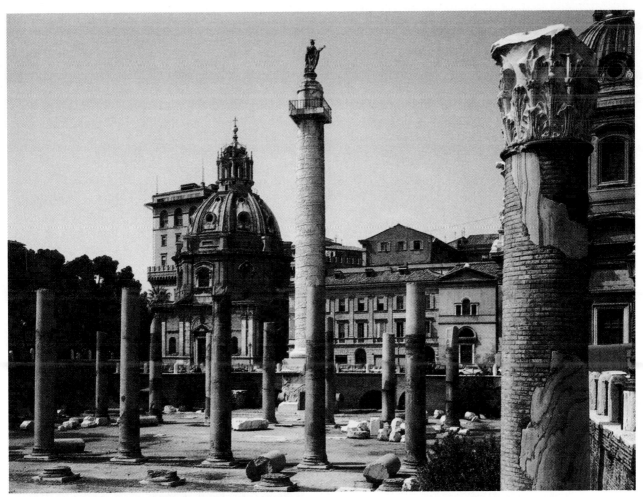

A

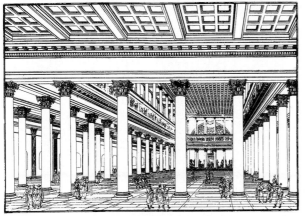

B

4.10   (A) Apollodorus of Damascus. Column of Trajan and ruins of Basilica Ulpia, Rome. Column of Trajan, 106–113 CE. Marble, height of base 18′, height of column 8′1″. (B) Apollodorus of Damascus. Basilica Ulpia, Forum of Trajan, Rome, 113 CE. Reconstruction drawing of interior.

THE BASILICA ULPIA

Adjacent to the open square was the Basilica Ulpia (Fig. 4.10A), of which only rows of broken columns remain. In Roman times, the term **basilica** was applied generally to large public buildings. It is approximately equivalent to our use of the word *hall* to refer to a meeting place. Because court sessions were also held in a basilica, the term **hall of justice** is likewise related to one of its functions. As an architectural form, the Roman basilica is one link in the long chain of Mediterranean structures that had its beginning with domestic dwellings, Egyptian hypostyle halls, and Greek temples, and continued later with Christian basilicas.

The large rectangular interior of the Basilica Ulpia, named for Trajan's family, was marked by a double colonnade in the Corinthian order that

cut into the Quirinal hill, was a market complex, a precursor of the modern megamall, constructed of brick and rising some six stories (Fig. 4.9). On the first floor were stalls for fresh produce; above were large vaulted halls where wine and oil were stored. Spices and imported delicacies were sold on the third and fourth floors. The fifth floor was used to distribute food and money from the imperial treasury. On the top floor there were tanks that were supplied with fresh water from an aqueduct and that housed live fish to be bought.

ran completely around the building. It supported a balcony and a second tier of columns that, in turn, supported the beams of the timbered roof (Fig. 4.10B). This large central hall served as a general meeting place and a business center. The semicircular interior recesses, called **apses,** housed the law courts. They were probably roofed over with hemispherical vaults, as seen in the reconstruction, and they may have been set apart from the central hall by screens or curtains.

TRAJAN'S COLUMN

Beyond the basilica were two libraries, one for Greek scrolls and the other for Latin scrolls. They were separated by a courtyard that enclosed the base of Trajan's Column. The column's location between two libraries demonstrates the Roman concern for public education and underscores the idea that history could be learned from pictorial sources as well as from Greek and Latin writings.

To commemorate Trajan's victories in the two campaigns to subdue the Dacian people of the lower Danube region, a monumental column was erected in the emperor's forum by the Senate and people of Rome. The structure rose to a height of 128 feet. Inside the column is a circular staircase that winds upward to the top and is lighted by small windowlike slits cut into the frieze. According to tradition, Trajan chose the monument as the site of his burial, and his ashes were placed in a chamber under the column.

The column is constructed in several sections of white marble. A spiral band carved in low relief covers the entire surface. Reading from left to right, the story of the two Dacian campaigns unfolds in a continuous strip about 4 feet, 2 inches wide and 218 yards long. More than 2,500 human figures make their appearance in this visual narrative, in addition to horses, boats, vehicles, and equipment of all kinds.

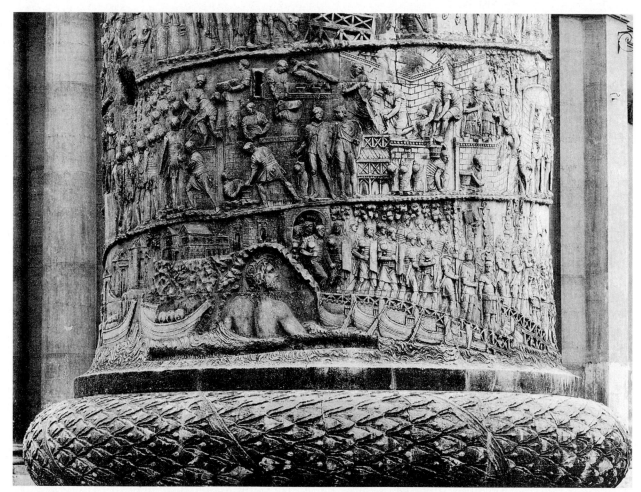

4.11   *Trajan's Campaign against the Dacians,* detail of Trajan's Column, 106–113 CE. Marble, height of frieze band 4′2″.

The hero of the story is, of course, the soldierly Trajan, who is shown fulfilling his imperial mission as the defender of Rome against the advances of the barbarians. The empire was always willing to include any people who accepted the values of Mediterranean civilization, but it could tolerate no challenge. When an important barbarian kingdom was founded in Dacia, Trajan regarded it as a threat and set out to bring it under Roman control. It took two campaigns to do the job, and the lasting result of this Romanizing process can be seen in the name of one of the nations of the conquered region: modern Romania.

Trajan's skill as a commander was well known, and on this column and other similar monuments, his reputation did not suffer for lack of public advertisement. In the frieze, he is portrayed as a bold, steady figure in complete command of the situation, whatever its nature. Sharing top billing with their general are the Roman soldiers. Opposite them are Trajan's antagonists, the Dacian king Decebalus and his barbarian hordes.

The campaign begins on the banks of the Danube in a Roman camp guarded by sentries and supplied by boats (Fig. 4.11). As the Romans set forth across a pontoon bridge, a river god personifying the Danube rises from a grotto and lends his support by holding up the bridge. From this point the action moves with singular directness toward the inevitable climax: the triumph of Roman arms. The scenes show Trajan holding a council of war, clad in a toga while pouring a sacrificial drink to the gods, and standing on a platform as he addresses his troops (Fig. 4.12). The army is shown pitching a camp on enemy soil, burning a Dacian village, and engaging in battle. At this key moment, Jupiter appears in the sky, throwing thunderbolts at the enemy to disperse them in all directions. The aftermath is then shown, with the victorious soldiers crowding around the

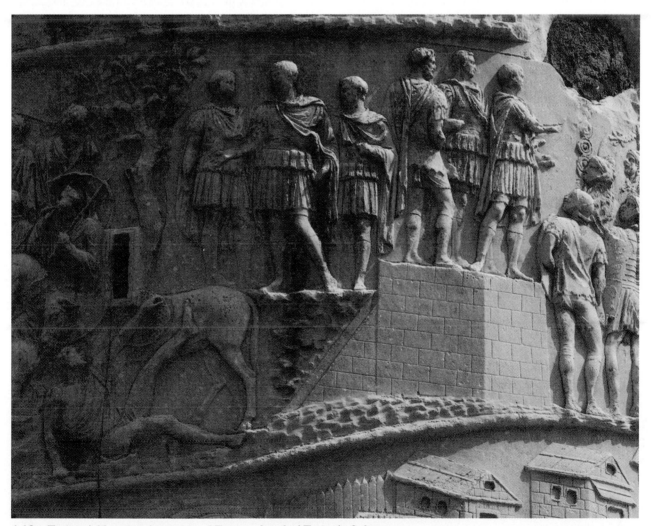

4.12 *Trajan Addressing Assembly of Troops,* detail of Trajan's Column.

emperor and holding up the severed heads of the enemy; surgeons are seen caring for the wounded, and winged Victory makes her appearance.

The scenes are designed to promote the continuous flow of action as smoothly as possible, but for reasons of clarity, the episodes have to be differentiated. The artist does this through some ninety separate portrayals of Trajan, each of which signals a new activity. Other devices used include an occasional tree to distinguish one scene from another, and new backgrounds, such as a mountain or a group of buildings.

This type of spiral relief has been compared with the unfolding papyrus and parchment scrolls that educated Romans were accustomed to reading in the nearby libraries. Trajan is known to have written an account of his Dacian campaigns, much as Julius Caesar had done in the case of the Gallic Wars, but the document is lost. Because commentaries on this bit of history are so fragmentary, the column has become one of the principal sources of information about it. The column may have been originally surrounded by a colonnade that supported an upper gallery from which views of the story in stone could be obtained. For those willing to circle the column again and again, the impression would have been vivid and comprehensive, because the scenes were designed to capture and hold viewers' attention and give them a shorthand experience of having been on the campaign with Trajan.

The reliefs have a definite likeness to literature in their manner of telling a story through visual narration. The methods the Romans used in such cases have been distinguished as the *simultaneous* and the *continuous*. The simultaneous method is the same as that used by the Greeks in the east pediment and frieze of the Parthenon, for example, where all the action takes place at a given moment that is frozen into sculptural form. It thus observes the classical unities of time, place, and action. The Romans developed the continuous, or cyclic, method for just such a series of scenes as Trajan's wars. Unity of action is obtained through the telling of a life story, or as in this instance, it can be broadened to include a couple of military campaigns. The unities of time and place are sacrificed as far as the whole composition is concerned but are preserved in the separate scenes. Whereas the origin of this continuous style is still a subject of scholarly dispute, no one has challenged the effective use the Romans made of it. It reflects their keen interest in

historical and current events, and its value for the purposes of state propaganda is obvious.

Despite the direct narrative content of the spiral frieze, the style is not realistic. For effects, the artist depended on a set of symbols that were as carefully worked out as the words used by writers of epics. A series of undulating lines, for example, indicates water. A jagged outline on the horizon stands for a mountain. A large figure rising up out of the water represents a river. A wall can mean either a city or a camp. A female figure whose draperies are folded in the shape of a crescent moon informs the observer that it is night.

With such symbolism, liberties with perspective inevitably occur, and it is quite usual to find a man taller than a wall or an important figure, such as the emperor, much larger than those around him. This technique does not rule out such clearly recognizable things as the banners of certain Roman legions as well as the details of their shields and armor. The Trajan frieze points unmistakably in the direction of the pictorial symbolism used later by Early Christian and medieval artists, who doubtless were influenced by it.

Much of the work might seem crude to the Hellenistic artists who were still active in Rome, but this relief is an example of Roman popular art. As such it was addressed to the large segment of the populace that was not accustomed to getting its information and enjoyment from books. The elegant and placid forms of Greek gods were not apt to arouse the emotions of ordinary Romans who sought amusement in the gladiatorial contests held in the Colosseum. The Roman Empire needed an educated elite to run its affairs. This minority seems to have admired dignity and restraint in sculpture. Nevertheless, most people were used to being roused by "bread and circuses," that is, free food and fast-paced entertainment. They relished such an energetic, action-filled story as shown in Trajan's frieze, involving people like themselves having adventures. Thus viewed, the frieze is fresh, original, and astonishingly alive.

The artist who designed the frieze was clearly a master of relief sculpture, able to depict with ease, in extremely low relief, whole armies, pitched battles, and the surrounding landscapes and sky. Care was taken in the execution throughout; even though the reliefs at the top were almost certainly out of view, the quality remains the same.

Standing in its prominent location from Trajan's time to the present, this column and the similar one of Marcus Aurelius had an incalculable influence on later art. The continuous mode of visual narration was imitated in the catacomb paintings of the early Roman Christians, as well as in illuminated manuscripts, religious sculptures, and the stained glass of the medieval period. And it can still be found in the comic strips of daily newspapers. Even modern films owe a certain debt to the technique worked out in Rome in the second century CE. Examples of the direct influence of this narrative mode include the Roman Christian tomb of Junius Bassus (see Fig. 5.2); the mosaics relating the story of Christ in the church of Sant' Apollinare Nuovo in Ravenna (see Fig. 5.5); the Bayeux Tapestry, which tells the story of the Norman conquest of England (see Fig. 6.17); and the studious duplication of Trajan's Column made under Napoleon for the Place Vendôme in Paris.

THE TEMPLE OF TRAJAN

After Trajan's death his adopted son and successor, Hadrian, built a Corinthian temple at the end of the main axis of the forum; the temple, dedicated to Trajan, climaxed the grand design and, architecturally, was a version of an earlier Roman temple at Nîmes in southern France, called the *Maison Carrée* (Fig. 4.13). Like other Roman temples, the *Maison Carrée* rested on a podium and had porches only in the front. These porches were much more prominent than those of Greek temples, owing perhaps to the influence of the Etruscans (Fig. 4.5). In the well-preserved example at Nîmes, only the columns of the porch are freestanding; the rest are attached to the cella. This indicates that columns were needed less for structural strength than for embellishment.

The practice of deifying rulers and erecting temples to them was widespread in Hellenistic

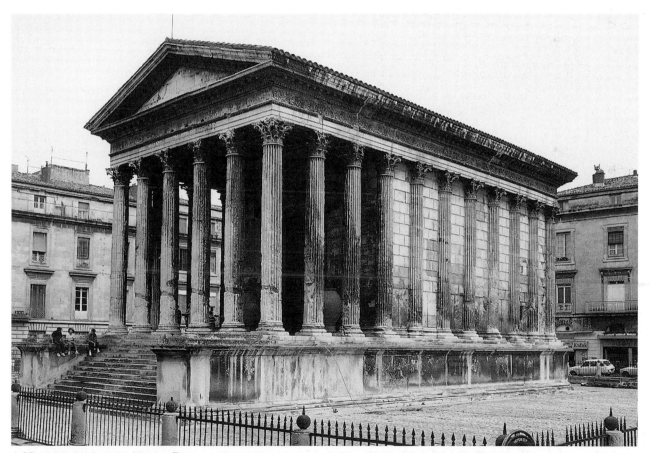

4.13   Maison Carrée, Nîmes, France, 16 BCE. Marble, base 117′ × 59′, height of podium 11′, height of columns 30′6″.

PAST AND PRESENT

Walking to Work

A clerk walking to work in ancient Rome or Ostia, its prosperous harbor city, would encounter several examples of art. Cutting through the forum of Trajan on his way to a government job, the clerk could glance at Trajan's column (see Fig. 4.10) and find among the figures depicted there someone whose garments reminded him of his home in one of Rome's distant provinces. Talking with friends in the office, the clerk might smile as he recalls the spectacular sea battle he saw enacted the day before in the coliseum. On his return home from work, the clerk may notice an advertising sign that shows a woman handing a fruit or vegetable to a customer and he may respond by buying groceries for the evening meal.

A clerk in a modern American city, on her trek from the subway station to the government building where she works, might take a shortcut through a plaza and take a fresh look the contemporary sculpture placed prominently in the center of the plaza. As she walks to the building's elevator, which carries her hundreds of feet above the street level to an office, she might glance into a courtroom where foreigners who had studied the English language and American history are about to be sworn in as citizens. On her walk home from work, the clerk could choose to put on her earphones and adjust her MP3 player to listen to the music she downloaded on her home computer the evening before. Music of all kinds, from rock to classical, is inescapable in the modern city; it plays in elevators, restaurants, offices, and even in the public restrooms. In addition, during her walk to and from the subway, colorful billboards, bus placards, electric signs, newspapers, and magazines—all designed to promote and enhance products, news, and events—compete for her attention.

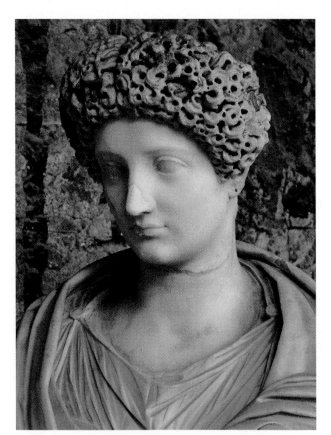

4.14 *Portrait of a Roman Lady,* c. 90 CE. Marble, lifesize. Musei Capitolini, Rome, Italy.

times and began in Rome as early as the reign of Augustus. The type of statue that stood in such a temple can be seen in the portrait of Augustus that was found near Prima Porta, the villa belonging to Augustus's wife Livia (Fig. 4.1).

Much of Roman religion was a family affair, honoring the living **paterfamilias,** or "father of the family," as well as near and remote ancestors. A room in every residence was set aside for this purpose, and the custom was responsible for a uniquely Roman type of portrait sculpture. Examples range from the elegantly poised, fashionable young Roman matron (Fig. 4.14) to the calm gravity and dignity of the patrician couple who are the honored elders of their family (Fig. 4.15). In contrast to the generalized and idealized image of Augustus as statesman and imperator, these living likenesses of everyday Roman personalities are remarkably vivid and realistic. Both kinds of sculpture, however, served the same purpose: they were portraits to be honored with reverence and respect.

The emperor was believed to deserve the universal reverence of the whole Roman family because he was considered **pater patriae,** or "father of his country." Erecting a temple to a distinguished Roman emperor was done in much the same spirit as building the Washington Monument

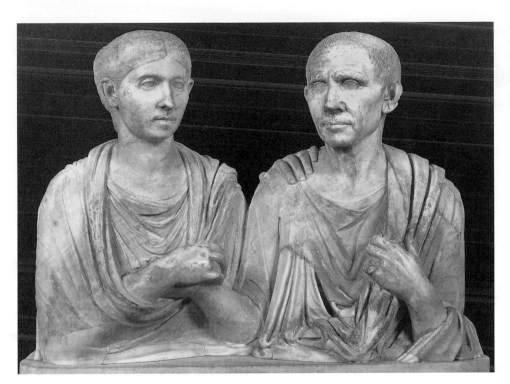

4.15 *Porcia and Cato (?),* portrait of a Roman couple, c. first century BCE. Marble, height 2′3″. Vatican Museums, Rome, Italy.

or the Lincoln Memorial in Washington, D.C. In ancient Rome, certain days were set aside for the offering of food and drink in simple family ceremonies. On the day for honoring the emperor, the rites at his temple were more formal, occasionally including animal sacrifice, a procession, festivities, and amusements. Religion to the Romans was the tradition and continuity of the family and, in the larger sense, the history and destiny of Rome itself.

With the exception of the temple, the Forum of Trajan was completed during his lifetime and was dedicated by him for the use of the people of Rome in 113 CE. Its many parts—the triumphal entrance archway, the courtyard and its equestrian statue, the market buildings, the Basilica Ulpia, two libraries, a monumental column, and the temple—add up to an architectural composition on a grand scale, designed to accommodate activities on many levels. Beginning with a shopping center and place to transact business, the forum continued with a general meeting place and the halls of justice; moved on to places for quiet contemplation, such as study in the libraries or reading history in visual form on the column; and came to rest in the precinct for honoring the emperor and worshiping the gods.

THE IMPERIAL BATHS

One of the duties of every emperor was to provide for public amusement out of his private purse. The ability to provide grand entertainments, such as re-creations of famous sea battles in the **amphitheater,** served to prove the emperor's right to rule. Only the very wealthy could afford entertainment in their own homes, so ordinary people looked beyond the home for recreation. To this end, many public baths, theaters, and stadiums were built throughout the city. To this day, the highest praise that can be given an elaborate public festival is to call it a *Roman holiday.*

The imperial baths provided far more than hot, cold, and tepid swimming pools. They also offered dressing rooms, gymnasiums, restaurants, bars, and shady walks. In addition, guests could attend plays, witness athletic contests, listen to public lectures, read in one of the libraries, or stroll about the galleries or gardens where paintings and statues were exhibited. The baths were, in short, the people's palaces. Favored also as places to show the booty and souvenirs from foreign conquests, they are the sites where much ancient statuary has been found.

Trajan added a large establishment, also built by Apollodorus, to the already existing public

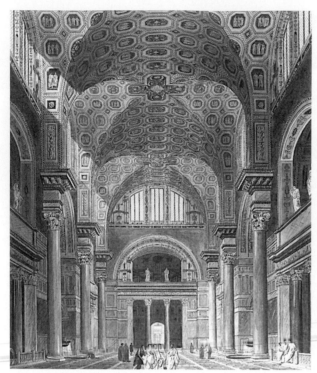

4.16   Reconstruction drawing of the central hall, Baths of Caracalla, Rome, Italy, 212–216 CE. Reconstruction drawing by Spiers.

baths. Although the ruins of his ***thermae*** (baths) are less well preserved than the later Baths of Caracalla and Diocletian, enough is known to establish a clear picture of what they were like. The large central hall was the earliest known use of concrete **cross vaulting,** which can be studied in Figure 4.22 and in the similar central hall of the

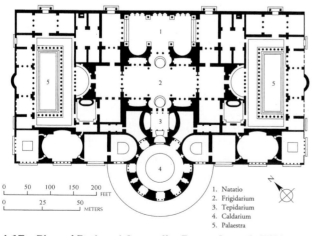

1. Natatio
2. Frigidarium
3. Tepidarium
4. Caldarium
5. Palaestra

4.17   Plan of Baths of Caracalla, Rome. Length 750′, width 380′.

Baths of Caracalla (Figs. 4.16 and 4.17). It measured 183 feet in length and was 79 feet wide. From the illustration, it can be seen that the barrel vault that runs lengthwise is intersected three times at right angles by shorter vaults extending across the width of the hall. Besides spanning larger interior spaces without the obstruction of supporting piers and columns, this type of construction offered the advantage of ample lighting through a **clerestory,** a row of windows in the upper part of a wall, which used thin strips of translucent yellow marble in place of glass. When erecting such huge edifices as Union Station in Washington, D.C., and Grand Central Terminal in New York City, modern architects found no better models among large secular structures than these Roman baths.

THE COLOSSEUM AND THE AQUEDUCTS

The Colosseum (Fig. 4.18), which dates from the late first century, was the scene of flamboyant forms of mass entertainment, including gory gladiatorial contests between men and wild beasts. It was called an *amphitheatre* (from the Greek words for "around" plus "theater") because its oval shape surrounded an arena. The Colosseum covers about 6 acres and could seat about 50,000 spectators. Around its circumference run some eight archways, which served so efficiently as entrances and exits that the entire bowl could be emptied in a matter of minutes. The Roman talent for organization not only is evidenced here in such practical respects but also extends to the structure and decorative design. Three architectural orders are combined in the successive stories of the same building. The attached columns on the lower range are the "homegrown" variation of the Doric, known as the Tuscan. Those on the second tier are Ionic, and those on the third, Corinthian. On the fourth tier, which rises to a height of 157 feet, are shallow, flat piers known as **pilasters,** which were executed in the Corinthian style. Between the pilasters runs a row of sockets for poles over which a canvas awning could be rolled out to protect spectators from sun and rain.

The building material of the Colosseum was a concrete made from broken pieces of brick, small rocks, volcanic dust, lime, and water. Concrete could be poured into molds of any desired shape, including channels for use in aqueducts. Originally, marble facing covered the Colosseum's exterior. The structure would be in good condition had it not been used as a quarry for building ma-

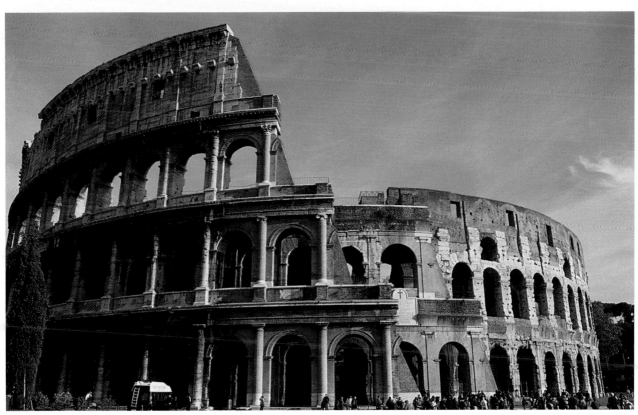

4.18 Colosseum, Rome, 72–80 CE. Long axis 620′, short axis 513′, height 160′.

terials right up to the eighteenth century. Today it is jostled by vibrations from the numerous automobiles that pass nearby. Still, the Colosseum is one of the most impressive ruins to survive from Roman times. One can see its enduring popularity as a model in football stadiums found on college campuses.

To provide enough water for his public bathing establishments, Trajan found it necessary to improve the old system of aqueducts and add a new one 35 miles long. A fine example of a Roman aqueduct is the Pont du Gard at Nîmes (Fig. 4.19), which survives from the first century CE. A system of underground and open concrete channels was

4.19 Pont du Gard, Nîmes, France, early first century. Length 902′, height 161′.

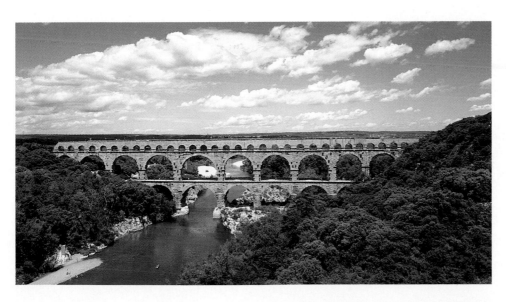

constructed to bring water from mountain sources to the town 25 miles away. Functioning on the principle of gravity, the ducts were sloped in the desired direction. In this instance the water was carried almost 300 yards across the valley at a height of more than 160 feet. The graceful lower range of arches supports a bridge, whereas the upper series of large and small arches carries the water channel.

THE PANTHEON

The Roman sense of social organization extended into the field of religion with the Pantheon (Fig. 4.20). Whereas the name might imply a temple to all the gods, in effect the Pantheon became a mirror of the Roman understanding of ideal world order. Statues were placed in niches to personify the planetary deities: Jupiter, Saturn, Venus, Mars, Mercury, the sun, and the moon. The emperor Hadrian himself is said to have had a hand in the design of this edifice, and he occasionally presided over meetings of the Roman Senate held in its splendid interior.

The Pantheon's geometry is based on the conjunction of the circle, the cylinder, and the sphere. The dome is an exact hemisphere. If completed, the whole sphere would fit precisely into the allotted interior space (Fig. 4.20B and 4.20C). It covers a circular area 144 feet in diameter, and the height of the structure is the same, thus creating the closest of all harmonic proportions, 1:1. The cylindrical base is also the height of its own radius, 72 feet, in the proportion of 2:1, thus yielding the musical octave. The proportions of the Pantheon echo the musical aspect of Plato's universe (see p. 56), as interpreted by the influential Roman author Vitruvius.

The inner surface of the dome is indented with **coffers,** panels that serve the dual purpose of diminishing the weight of the concrete and furnishing the basis for its decorative scheme. In the center of each coffer was a gilded bronze rosette or star, a motif that related the dome to the sky. A column of light descends through the **oculus,** or eye of the dome (Fig. 4.21). Like a searchlight beam signifying the all-seeing eye of heaven, it moves around the interior, varying with time of day and season, illuminating the seven planetary deities on their altars.

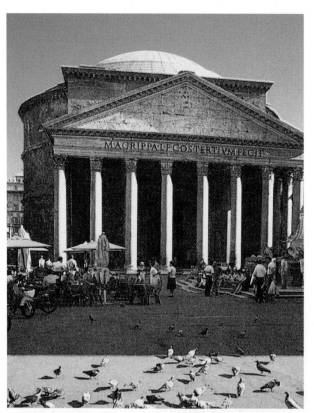

A

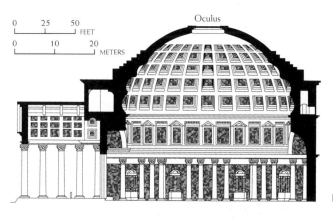

B

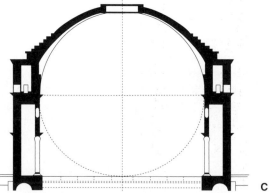

C

4.20   (A) The Pantheon, Rome, c. 120 CE. Height of portico 59′. (B) Plan of the Pantheon. (C) Cross section of the Pantheon.

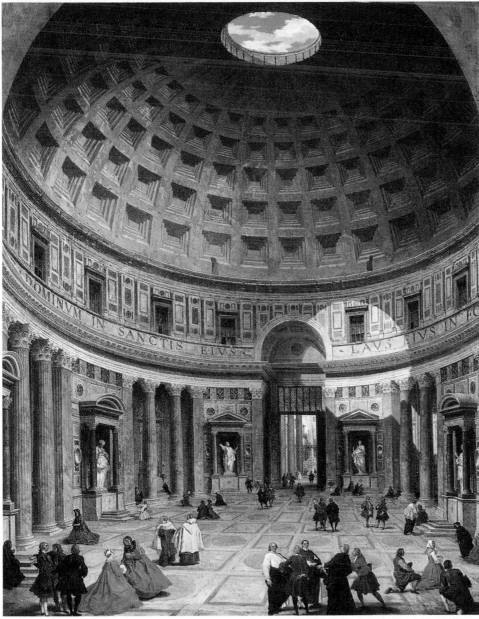

4.21 Giovanni Paolo Pannini. *The Interior of the Pantheon, Rome.* Oil on canvas, 4′2½″ × 3′3″. National Gallery of Art, Washington, D.C., Samuel H. Kress Collection, 1939.

After the fall of the Roman Empire, the Pantheon was converted into a Christian church, which accounts for its fine state of preservation. Much of the once-elegant interior, with its marbles of glowing ocher with red, green, and black contrasts, is still in place. Gone, however, are the gilt bronze rosettes that once spread across the coffered inner dome like an expanse of stars. The exterior marble veneer, the bronze plates of the portico ceiling, and the gilt bronze sheath that once covered the dome's exterior have also long since disappeared, and the stairs used by visitors are now below street level. The Pantheon's appropriateness as a place of worship, whether pagan or Christian, is clear to all who enter. The worshiper is free to ponder the nature of the seen and the unseen and to contemplate the dome as an image of heaven. Indeed, the dome and half-dome became symbols of the universe, and the forms were incorporated into countless later Christian churches.

Despite the vicissitudes of time, the Pantheon is the best-preserved single building from the ancient world and the oldest structure of large proportions with its original roof intact. It still holds its own as one of the world's most impressive domed buildings, despite such outstanding competition as Hagia Sophia in Constantinople (see Fig. 5.14), the Cathedral in Florence (see Fig. 9.2A), St. Peter's in Rome (see Fig. 10.17), and St. Paul's in London (see Fig. 14.18). Its descendants are many: the Villa Rotonda (see Fig. 12.4), Thomas Jefferson's home at Monticello, the rotunda he designed for the University of Virginia (see Fig. 17.11), the Pantheon in Paris, certain features of the Capitol rotunda in Washington, D.C., and the Low Memorial Library at Columbia University in New York.

THE ROMAN CONTRIBUTION TO ARCHITECTURE

The Romans' contribution to architecture was fourfold: they excelled in conceptualizing and constructing buildings for practical use. They developed the arch and vault as a structural principle. This, in turn, allowed their buildings to reach new heights. Finally, they designed interiors that responded to particular needs of the people. In the first case, Roman architecture was marked by a shift in emphasis from religious buildings to the civil engineering projects that had such an important bearing on the solutions of the practical problems of the day. Of course, buildings like the Pantheon indicate that the Romans did not neglect their shrines and temples or lack religious feeling. In the practical category, they built basilicas, aqueducts, roads, bridges, and even sewer systems, which admirably met their needs.

Second—and perhaps most important—was the Roman exploitation of the possibilities inherent in the arch. The construction of a true arch by means of wedge-shaped blocks (a process known as *voussoirs*), as well as some of the implications of the system, can be seen more easily in Figure 4.22 than explained in words. When such arches are placed in a series side by side, the resulting **arcade** can be used for such structures as aqueducts and bridges, as seen in the Pont du Gard (Fig. 4.19). When placed in a series from front to back, the result is a **barrel vault** (also called a **tunnel vault**), which can be seen in the Arch of Trajan at Benevento (see Fig. 3.21) and was useful for roofing interiors. When two barrel vaults intersect each other at right angles, as seen in Figure 4.16, the result is a **cross vault** (or **groin vault**). When a series of arches span a given space by intersecting each other around a central axis, the result is a dome, as exemplified in the Pantheon (Fig. 4.22A). Briefly put, these constitute the technical principles behind the Roman architectural achievement.

Third, through their technical advances, the Romans were able to increase the height of their buildings in proportion to the growing size of their large structures. The six-story market buildings of Trajan's Forum were an impressive demonstration of the practical advantages of such verticality, which made possible the combination of many small shops into a single structure in a crowded city location. The multifamily, multistory apartment houses in Rome and its port city of Ostia were also cases in point. The trend was to be seen, too, in the great height of the halls such as the Baths of Trajan and Caracalla and the Pantheon. The pleasing proportions resulting from such height were made possible by cross vaulting and the dome.

Last, the enclosing of large units of interior space was made necessary by the expansion of the city's population. The direction of architectural thought in meeting this need can easily be

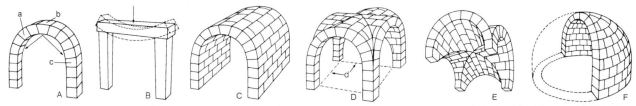

4.22 An arch is a curved structural member used to span a space between two vertical elements, such as posts (piers) or walls (A). Wedge-shaped blocks, called voussoirs (a), give the arch its form and stability by virtue of their compressed relationship to each other and to the keystone (b) at the apex of the semicircle. The curve of the arch rises from the springing on either side of the opening (c). The compression of its stone is better able to resist the downward thrust of the load above than the tensile strength of a lintel on posts (B). It does this by directing the weight in a lateral direction and by transmitting the load to the ground through the arch and the vertical elements supporting it. Placed one after the other, a series of arches make a barrel vault, or tunnel vault (C). Two tunnel vaults intersecting each other at right angles (D) create a cross vault, also known as a groin vault (so called for the groin line [E] along which the vaults join). The square or rectangular space they define is called a bay (d). Intersecting each other around a central axis, a series of arches forms a dome (F).

seen by contrasting a Greek agora (see Fig. 2.1, flat area in the upper left corner) with the Forum of Trajan, a Hellenistic theater (see Figs. 2.33 and 3.3D) with the Colosseum, or the Parthenon with the Pantheon. Special attention to space and lighting are evident in the planning of such interiors as those of the Basilica Ulpia, the Pantheon, and the halls of the great baths. In all instances, the Romans treated space as a tangible reality to be molded into significant designs.

MUSIC

The practice of poetry and music enjoyed higher favor among educated Roman amateurs than did dabbling in the visual arts. Suggesting a plan for a building or some of its decorative details was all right for a member of the patrician, or upper, class, but from then on it was the architect's and carpenter's business. Women of the patrician class may also have participated in such activities. Although women could not marry or divorce without permission from their fathers, they did enjoy authority and influence within the family. The materfamilias might run the family's investments and to a certain extent inherit money. Although there is little reliable evidence about the daily lives of poor women and men, it is certain that members of both sexes worked as artisans and in the manual trades. With sculpture and painting, wealthy people could make an impression as collectors, but the actual chiseling and painting were occupations for artisans and slaves.

When it came to writing verse or singing to the accompaniment of the lyre, however, amateurs were plentiful in the highest ranks of Roman society, including the emperors themselves. Elite women were educated and wrote poetry. Whereas Trajan's recreations seem to have been as strenuous as some of his military activities, those of his immediate successors included literary and musical pursuits. Hadrian wrote poetry in both Greek and Latin, but it remained for Marcus Aurelius to build an enduring reputation as a writer and philosopher. The emperors Hadrian, Antoninus Pius, and Caracalla were proficient on the cithara and hydraulic organ.

INSTRUMENTS AND PERFORMING GROUPS

Whereas much is known about Roman literature, no examples of Roman music survive. Our knowledge about it must be gathered from surviving musical instruments and occasional literary references, as well as portrayals of music-making in sculptures, mosaics, and wall paintings. From these sources, it is clear that the Romans heard a great deal of music and that no occasion, public or private, was complete without it.

A mosaic showing a small Roman instrumental ensemble performing in an amphitheater during a gladiatorial contest was found in excavations in North Africa (Fig. 4.23). One musician is shown playing the long, straight brass instrument known as the

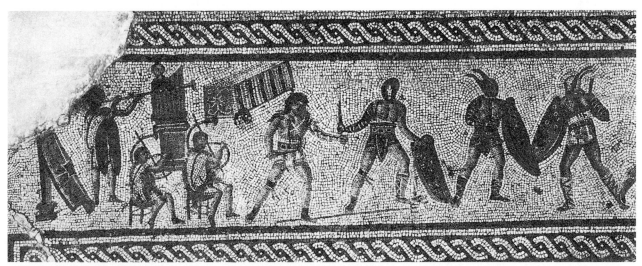

4.23 *Gladiatorial Contest,* showing orchestra with hydraulic organ, trumpet, and horn players. Mosaic from Zliten, North Africa, c. 70 CE.

tuba, or trumpet. Two others are playing the circular **cornu,** or horn. Still another is seated at the **hydraulus,** or water organ. Equipped with a rudimentary keyboard and stops, this highly ingenious instrument produced sounds by forcing air compressed by two water tanks through a set of bronze pipes. Some hydrauli were 10 feet high. They were used mainly in open-air arenas, where their tone must have resembled that of the more modern calliope, which was popular in circus parades and which played tunes for merry-go-rounds.

In keeping with the Roman idea of grandeur, the size of music groups and instruments increased greatly. The writer Marcellinus described an open-air performance by hundreds of players, some of whom were said to have performed on "lyres as big as chariots." An ever-increasing volume of sound was demanded of wind instruments owing to their usefulness in warfare. Battle signals, such as advances and retreats, were relayed by means of trumpet calls. The more numerous the legions, the bigger and brassier the sound. This intensification of sound was verified by the philosopher and teacher Quintilian, who asks a typical rhetorical question and proceeds to answer it with a characteristic flourish: "And what else is the function of the horns and trumpets attached to our legions? The louder the concert of their notes, the greater is the glorious supremacy of our arms over all the nations of the earth."

MUSIC IN SPEECH AND DRAMA

Quintilian also points out some of the practical applications of music to the art of oratory. He particularly emphasizes the development of the voice, because "it is by raising, lowering, or inflexion of the voice that the orator stirs the emotions of his hearers." He describes a great speaker who had a musician standing behind him while he gave his speeches. The musician's duty was to give the speaker "the tones in which his voice was to be pitched."

Music was also a part of every theatrical performance. Whereas the Roman drama omitted the chorus that the Greeks had stressed, its dialogue was interspersed with songs accompanied by the **tibia,** an ancient wind instrument originally fashioned from the leg bone (that is, the tibia) of an animal. Such musical portions, however, were not directed by the dramatists, as they had been in Athenian dramas, but were delegated to specialists. The importance of choruses and bands for military morale was not overlooked, and a func-

tional type of military music existed in addition to trumpet calls. Popular groups played music at games and contests, and strolling street musicians were part of the everyday scene.

The fact that not a single note of any of this music exists today testifies to the fact that Roman music was primarily a performing art. Whereas practicing musicians may have composed their own songs or created variations on traditional tunes, they seem not to have been concerned with writing them down. If they had done so, the later church fathers would very likely have had these pagan melodies committed to the flames. Like much folk music that existed only in oral tradition until the coming of modern notation and recording devices, the art of Roman music died with the people who practiced it.

LITERATURE

Roman literature was slow in gaining momentum during the republic because the educated classes preferred Greek writers. That taste continued during the period of the empire. Although thoroughly Roman in its no-nonsense reflections on duty, the brevity of human life, and aversion to pleasure, Marcus Aurelius wrote his *Meditations* in Greek. Like emperors before him, he appreciatively toured Alexandria and Athens.

Early Roman playwrights, such as Plautus and Terence, wrote plays in the Greek tradition for their Latin-speaking audiences. The outstanding dramatist of the empire, Seneca, also used Greek plays as his models. After the invention of printing in the fifteenth century, these Roman playwrights enjoyed renewed popularity. English translations were made in the Elizabethan era, and Shakespeare paid tribute to Plautus by borrowing material from him for an early play, *The Comedy of Errors.*

Eventually, Roman literature shed some of its slavish imitation of Greek models and came into its own in the early years of the empire. There were philosophical authors, such as Cicero, with his expansive orations and penetrating essays, and Lucretius, with his masterly *On the Nature of Things,* which explored the scientific world in poetic meter and lordly language. There were also numerous historians. Julius Caesar's account of the Gallic Wars and Livy's *History of Rome* were required reading until the end of the nineteenth century. Tacitus provided insights into Roman life and customs, and Suetonius offered anecdotal biographies in *Lives of the Twelve Caesars.* Poetry also excelled in Horace's lyric odes; Catullus's sensuous love lyrics; and Ovid's *Metamorphoses,* ardent love poems, and erotic *Art of Love,* which tells readers how to attract and keep a lover.

A special Roman development is found in the art of satire, as exemplified in the witty twists of Martial's epigrams and the pungent verses of Juvenal. Satire, with its ironic bite and neat turns of phrase, makes for lively and amusing reading. It also became a potent weapon for writing disguised as social and political criticism. Satiric wit and wisdom continued in the prose of Petronius, who was Emperor Nero's arbiter of elegance. His *Satyricon,* a tale of three adventurers, contains the hilarious scene of Trimalchio's feast. Trimalchio, the object of the lampoon, is a newly rich braggart who provides an extensive meal for his scoffing acquaintances. During the dinner, as he cleans his teeth with a silver toothpick, he bores them with his rags-to-riches story. The *Satyricon* was followed by Apuleius's popular *Golden Ass,* the only Latin novel to survive intact. Both works were commentaries on the follies and foibles of Nero's reign. Later picaresque stories (episodic adventure tales), such as Cervantes's *Don Quixote* and John Fielding's *Tom Jones,* owe much to the techniques developed by Petronius and Apuleius.

The climactic figure of Latin letters, however, was Publius Vergilius Maro, known to history as Virgil. His elegant *Eclogues,* or *Bucolics,* were cast in the form of dialogues sung by idyllic shepherds dwelling in an ideal rural landscape called Arcadia. It became a model for all future pastoral poetry. The *Georgics* were paeans of praise to the beauties of nature, the joy of living and working with the soil, and the importance of the farmer in the social scheme of things. Their visual counterpart can be found in the Tellus panel of the *Ara Pacis* (Fig. 4.4). Both the *Georgics* and Virgil's masterpiece, the *Aeneid,* were commissioned by Augustus, who was seeking to establish a national literature in the native tongue that would rival that of Greece.

The *Aeneid* conjures up a legendary past for Rome through the exploits and adventures of its reputed founder, the Trojan prince Aeneas. As myth has it, Aeneas's father Anchises was so handsome that he attracted the attention of the goddess Venus, and Aeneas was the fruit of their union. After the fall of Troy, the gods commanded Aeneas to abandon the flaming ruins of the city and set forth across the sea to Italy, where he was destined to found a great empire that would one day rule the world. Virgil, who was educated by Greek tutors, found his model in Homer's *The Odyssey,* and like *The Odyssey,* the *Aeneid* may be read as a voyage of the spirit. Aeneas, like Ulysses, is beset on his journey by all manner of ogres and temptresses. Despite such distractions, however, he never loses sight of his stern duty.

The epic opens with the stirring words "Arma virumque cano" (Of war and a man I sing). This opening has gripped readers ever since and is still repeated, in Latin, in contemporary science fiction tales about wars with other galaxies. In contemporary English, the poem reads:

> I sing about war and the hero who first from
>   Troy's frontier,
> Displaced by destiny, came to Lavinian shores,
> To Italy—a man much travailed on sea and land
> By the powers above, because of the brooding
>   anger of Juno,
> Suffering much in war until he could found a
>   city
> And march his gods into Latium, whence rose
>   the Latin race,
> The royal line of Alba and the high walls of
>   Rome.

Aeneas is telling his tale at a feast given by Dido, the founder of Carthage, where he has been driven by a raging storm stirred up by the jealous goddess Juno. Here, after finding the love of his life, he is once more called on by Jupiter to pursue his destiny and sail onward. Dido then takes her own life, and his ship is lighted out of the harbor by the flames of her funeral pyre. Aeneas later descends into the underworld, where he learns from the shade of his dead father the shape of Rome's future:

> Let others fashion from bronze more lifelike
>   breathing images—
> For so they shall—and evoke living faces from
>   marble;
> Others excel as orators, others track with their
>   instruments
> The planets circling in heaven and predict
>   when stars will appear.
> But, Romans, never forget that government is
>   your medium!
> Be this your art:—to practice man in the habit
>   of peace,
> Generosity to the conquered, and firmness
>   against aggressors.

At long last, Aeneas lands on Latium's shore near the mouth of the Tiber to fulfill his mission as an empire builder.

Topical allusions to the Emperor Augustus's times were plentiful in the *Aeneid*. Roman readers would have seen Aeneas as the ancestor of the first emperor, who played the role of pater patriae (Fig. 4.1), while his people became the new Trojans. Dido has been portrayed sympathetically in many later plays and operas (see p. 468) as the tragic queen abandoned by her faithless lover. But to the Romans, she was the temptress who tried and failed to seduce a Roman hero and divert him from his imperial destiny.

In her farewell to her people, Dido cursed Aeneas and called for someone to rise up and avenge her. The Romans had only to recall Hannibal, the fearsome Carthaginian warrior who crossed the Alps with his army (including elephants) on the way to laying siege to Rome itself. They would also have recalled Cato's thunderous words to the Roman senate: "Carthago delenda est" (Carthage must be destroyed). The Romans would have interpreted the burning of the city when Aeneas left as a prophecy of their ultimate victory in the Punic Wars, when Carthage was once more laid in ruins. Dido could also have been seen as a legendary version of Cleopatra, who had seduced another Roman hero, Anthony. In addition, Aeneas's exploits could have been read as an allusion to Augustus's campaign in the east, which included his triumph over Cleopatra at the Battle of Actium. Most critics have pointed out the part the poem played as imperial propaganda. This is true, but it does not dim the conception and the magnificence of the writing. In the Latin original, Virgil's majestic **hexameters** create haunting rhythms akin to magical incantations. The *Aeneid* was aptly hailed by the modern poet T. S. Eliot as the supreme classic of Western literature.

IDEAS

Roman civilization shared many of the basic ideas that produced the Hellenic and Hellenistic styles. In fact, the prevailing philosophy of the Roman patrician class was that of Stoicism and, to a lesser extent, Epicureanism (see pp. 79–80). Here, however, the discussion will center on how Roman thought affected the arts.

The Romans widened the scope of the arts to include not only works aimed at the expert but also those with mass appeal. The two ideas that differentiate the Roman style from earlier classical styles are a genius for organization and a frank spirit of utilitarianism. Both conceived of the arts as a means of popular enjoyment and the solution to practical problems.

ORGANIZATION

The Roman ability to organize is shown in the building of a systematic world order that embraced a single language, a unified religion, a unified body of laws, and a unified civilization. Military conquest was, to be sure, one of the means used. However, the allowance of a maximum of self-government to subject peoples and the latitude given to local customs, even to tribal and cult religions, demonstrate the Romans' realistic approach to governing. Their desire for external unity did not imply internal uniformity, and their frank recognition of this fact was at the root of their success as administrators.

ARCHITECTURE

With their ability to organize religious, legal, social, and governmental institutions, the Romans' greatest contribution in the arts clearly appears in architecture. This organizational spirit, moreover, is revealed most decisively in their undertaking of large public works projects, such as roads, ports, and aqueducts. The expression, "all roads lead to Rome," referred to the fact that a central milestone marked the center of the Roman Empire. Organization is also seen in their manner of grouping buildings on a common axis, as in the Forum of Trajan, which was so directly in contrast to the Hellenic idea of isolated perfection. The technical application and development of all the possibilities of construction inherent in the arch and vault is another example, as is the combination of the Ionic and Corinthian capitals to form the Composite order, the only distinctive Roman contribution to the classical orders. The Roman combination of three orders on the exterior of the same building, as in the Colosseum, also illustrates Roman organization. The development of the multifamily apartment house, the attention given to the efficient assembling and dispersing of large numbers of people in such buildings as the Colosseum, and the invention of the supermarket or mall, as in the six-story market in Trajan's Forum, are equally impressive in this regard. A final example is the erection of a supertemple to the principal gods, as in the Pantheon.

EXPANSION OF INTERIOR SPACE. The same organizational spirit is reflected in the gradual expansion of interior space, as in the Basilica Ulpia, the Pantheon, and the great halls of the baths, to accommodate ever-larger numbers of people. The Greeks had defined space in planes. Thus, the exteriors of their temples were designed as backdrops for processions and religious ceremonies. In this sense, Greek architectural space was not shaped or organized in complex relationships to other buildings. In the Pantheon, however, interior space was enveloped and made palpable. The Romans recognized the possibilities of molding three-dimensional space, enclosing it and giving it significant form.

The Romans sought to enhance this spatial feeling in many ways. They exhibited sensitivity to scale and tended to design buildings in related structural units. They exploited color through the use of **polychrome,** or many-colored, marbles, which enlivened interiors and added to the perception of depth. They used illusionistic wall paintings to suggest the third dimension (Fig. 4.24). Furthermore, they gave increased attention to lighting in buildings and in paintings.

And they accomplished all this without sacrificing the classical clarity of form.

The same attitude was carried over into sculptural reliefs, where the tangibility of the spatial environment is provided in the backgrounds by means of buildings and landscapes that suggest depth. The fifth-century BCE Greek style, by contrast, consciously omitted any such frame of reference. In addition, the organization of time into a continuum, as in the spiral series on the Column of Trajan, shows a new concept of sequential order translated into a pictorial medium.

THE BROADENING APPEAL OF THE ARTS

The Roman organizational ability flourished in programs that catered to a wide range of taste in the arts. There were styles that appealed to the educated elite and styles that held the attention of the middle and lower classes. The conservative tastes of the elite embraced the tried-and-true values of Greek art. Members of the elite either collected antique statues and paintings or

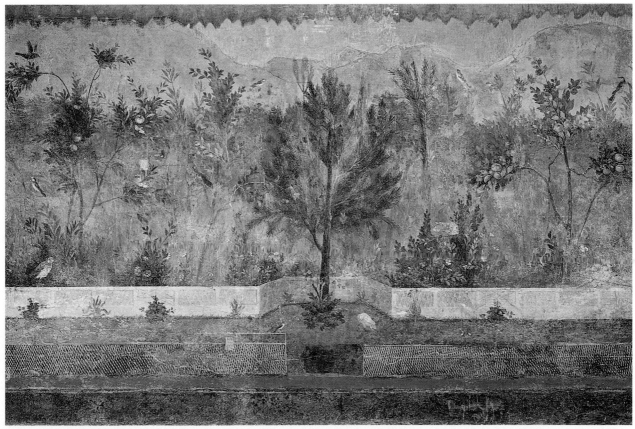

4.24   View of a Garden, c. 20 BCE. Wall painting from Villa of Livia at Prima Porta, height, 6′7″. Museo Archeologico Nazionale, Rome, Italy.

commissioned new works to be executed in the older style. Exquisite Greek craftsmanship held little interest for the majority, who preferred spectacular public objects, like a large bronze equestrian statue or a monumental triumphal arch. In Trajan's Forum, allowances were made for variations in taste. Between the Greek and Latin libraries, Trajan's column told the story of his campaigns in a carefully worked-out popular visual language of symbols designed to engage the curiosity of the multitude.

The disdain of the conservative group for popular art was defended by Athenaeus, a Greek scholar and teacher who lived in Rome around 200 CE. He upheld the virtues of the older cultural tradition and often made unflattering comparisons between the higher standards of past times and those that prevailed in his own day. "In early times," he wrote, "popularity with the masses was a sign of bad art; hence, when a certain aulos-player once received loud applause, Asopodorus of Phlius, who was himself still waiting in the wings, said 'What's this? Something awful must have happened!' The player evidently could not have won approval with the crowds otherwise. . . . And yet the musicians of our day set as the goal of their art success with their audiences."

Just as in the case of architecture, sculpture, and painting, the Romans were heirs to the Greek

musical tradition. The ancient theories survived in philosophical speculation, and Greek music teachers were employed in the homes of the wealthy. The only musical compositions to survive from this period are three hymns by Mesomedes, a Greek musician attached to Hadrian's court. Those who cultivated this more austere style believed that music was meant primarily to educate and elevate the mind.

Popular taste lay in quite another direction from the restraint and earnest soul-searching evident in Greek plays (see pp. 46–49). The music that Athenaeus scorned was obviously the very kind that the majority of Romans enjoyed at their public festivals, military parades, games, sporting contests, races, and to some extent, the theater. The modern parallel would be the split that exists between audiences interested in chamber music, symphony concerts, and the opera and those attracted to marching bands, Broadway musicals, rock, and rap. What the Romans' diversity accomplished was to broaden the appeal of the arts and gear them to different types of audiences. They thus succeeded in providing for the entertainment of a large city population, just as their buildings and civil engineering projects took care of the physical needs of the populace.

UTILITARIANISM

Instead of theorizing about the nature of the ideal state, as Plato did, the Romans pursued the practical aspects of governing. Speculating about the eternal verities could uplift the mind, but understanding human behavior had more immediate rewards. The Romans reached a balance based on acceptance of the Stoic doctrine of "live and let live" and the Epicurean idea of pleasure as an index of the highest good. The transfer of these concepts to the forms and policies of government meant a high degree of tolerance and the recognition that the standard of excellence in either a law or a work of art was the greatest good for the greatest number.

The construction of elegantly proportioned temples was therefore less important than the building of bridges (Fig. 4.25). Maintaining a luxurious private palace was secondary to providing public baths and theaters. A private collection of sculpture was subordinate to public exhibitions in city squares and galleries, where the statues could be seen and enjoyed by many. A play, poem, or piece of music that awakened only the sensibilities of the cultured minority did not rank as high

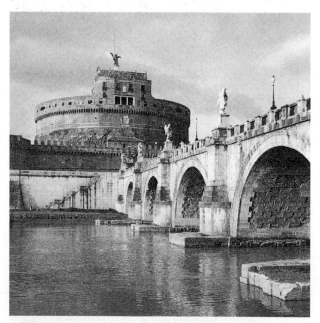

4.25   Bridge of the Angels (Pons Aelius), Rome, 134 CE. Hadrian's Tomb (Castel Sant' Angelo), 135–139 CE.

on this scale as those that were applauded by the multitude. In short, the practical arts were favored over the decorative arts, material goods superseded spiritual blessings, and utility was valued over abstract beauty (although the two are by no means mutually exclusive).

Because the Romans were little concerned with ideal forms, it was not an accident that their greatest successes occurred in the art of government rather than in the fine arts. Consequently, the art that proved most congenial to Roman aspirations was that of architecture, especially its utilitarian aspects. Building a 200-mile highway over the mountains, moving part of a hill more than 100 feet high to make way for a forum, providing a sewer system for a city of more than 1 million inhabitants, bridging the Danube at its widest point, perfecting a new building material such as concrete—all these were taken in stride.

When it came to sculpture, the Romans saw that subject matter served the purposes of the state by praising the virtues and deeds of the emperors. Epic poems such as Virgil's *Aeneid* performed a similar service in the literary medium. As Quintilian pointed out, the loud sounds of brass instruments proclaimed the glory of Roman arms.

Other applications of this utilitarianism are found in the brilliant exploitation of technical devices such as the arch and vault. The Romans' success in solving practical problems is proved by the many surviving roads, aqueducts, and bridges. In sculpture, the application of the continuous-narrative method provided a practical and psychologically functional way of telling a story. This method promoted a sense of continuity in time and anticipated later Christian and secular pictorial forms (see, for example, Figs. 8.1B and 9.19).

Effective as utilitarianism was, it had its price. The Romans built and decorated well, but the two activities somehow failed to achieve a harmonious interrelationship. This is well illustrated by the somewhat hollow claim of Augustus that he found Rome a city of brick and left it a city of marble. Actually, Rome was still a city of brick, stone, and concrete under an Augustan marble veneer. None of these materials needs a disguise, or even an apology, as is proved by the rhythmic grace of the functional arches of the Pont du Gard. Hence, Augustus had no need to imply that Roman structures such as the Pantheon were solid marble like the Greek Parthenon. As a whole, then, Roman architecture was at its best when it stuck to its forthright utilitarianism, undertook vast engineering projects, and successfully solved practical problems of construction.

THE ETERNAL CITY

Rome became an empire long before Augustus assumed the title of emperor. To maintain the lavish lifestyles of the wealthy, the Romans adopted an expansionist policy toward foreign cultures. Expansion allowed the Romans to gather riches in the form of tribute and property, as well as the many foreign slaves who were forced to work the large agricultural estates that provided food for the burgeoning city of Rome. It has been estimated that 2 million of the 6 million inhabitants of Italy were slaves. During the second century, the empire reached its greatest extent, covering most of Europe, North Africa, and western Asia. It influenced even more people beyond its official borders, who were drawn to the outskirts of the empire to provide goods and services for an ever-increasing population.

The more restrained classical purity of older cultural centers, such as Athens and Pergamon, did not exert much influence on the forms of Western art until the archeological discoveries of the eighteenth and nineteenth centuries. All intervening phases of classicism, if not content, were, in effect, revivals of the Roman style. With the establishment of Roman building methods, Western architecture was firmly set on its course, and it steered in substantially the same direction until the technological discoveries of the nineteenth and twentieth centuries made new approaches to architecture possible. Consequently, it must again be emphasized that Rome was the gateway through which all the styles, forms, and ideas of Mediterranean civilization passed in review. After being transformed by the process of selectivity—and flashes of genuine originality—into a uniquely Roman expression, they proceeded by way of the new Roman imperial capitals of Byzantium in the East and Ravenna in the West.

Rome in imperial times was also the western center of Christendom after the first century. Because Christians were occasionally persecuted, Christian art was often hidden in underground passages known as **catacombs.** Later, when Constantine legalized Christianity with the Edict of Milan in 313, large churches known as basilicas were built. Surviving from this time are many elaborately carved marble tombs, or sarcophagi, depicting biblical subjects (see Fig. 5.2).

When Rome declined as the center of world empire, it still remained the capital of Christendom. As objects of pilgrimages, its architectural, sculptural, and literary monuments were bound to exert a massive influence on those who were drawn toward the city. Because of this enduring preeminence, no important Western city exists without a bit of Rome in it. It is therefore with full justification that Rome has been and continues to be called the Eternal City.

YOUR RESOURCES

- ***Exploring Humanities CD-ROM***

  ○ Interactive Map: The Roman World

  ○ Readings—Virgil, Book 1 *Aeneid;* Horace, *Ode 11;* Livy, Book I of the *Histories;* Tacitus, *Annals of Imperial Rome*

- ***Web Site***

  http://art.wadsworth.com/fleming10

  ○ Chapter 4 Quiz

  ○ Links

ROMAN PERIOD: REPUBLIC AND EARLY EMPIRE

Key Events	Architecture	Literature
753 BCE Legendary date of **Rome's founding** 616–c 509 BCE **Etruscan period;** Tarquin kings reigned c. 509 BCE **Roman Republic** founded; Tarquins dethroned		

500

Key Events	Architecture	Literature
c. 450 BCE **Romans** colonized Italy 390 BCE **Gauls** sacked Rome 280–275 BCE **Greek power** in Italy weakened 264–241 BCE **First Punic War;** Rome annexed Sicily, Corsica, Sardinia 218–201 BCE **Second Punic War;** Hannibal invaded Italy, Carthage ceded Spain to Rome		c. 254–184 BCE **Plautus,** comic poet and dramatist

200

Key Events	Architecture	Literature
150–146 BCE **Third Punic War;** Carthage destroyed, African province created 133 BCE **Pergamon** bequeathed to Rome		c. 185–159 BCE **Terence,** Roman senator and writer of comedies 106–43 BCE **Cicero,** statesman, orator, essayist

100

Key Events	Architecture	Literature
100–44 CE **Julius Caesar;** conquered Gaul (58–51); crossed Rubicon, occupied Rome, became dictator (49); founded Julian family dynasty of future emperors; campaigned in Egypt, Asia Minor, Africa, Spain (48–45); Julian calendar (45); assassinated (44) 43 BCE **Second Triumvirate** formed; Anthony, Octavian, Lepidus 31 BCE **Naval battle at Actium; Anthony and Cleopatra** defeated; Octavian master of Rome 27 BCE–14 CE **Roman Empire** founded; **Octavian** reigned as Caesar Augustus 4 BCE **Birth of Jesus**	c. 48 BCE **Forum of Julius Caesar** begun 27 BCE–14 CE **Augustus** built new forum, *Ara Pacis,* Mausoleum of Augustus, Baths of Agrippa, Theater of Marcellus, Basilica Julia c.16 BCE **Maison Carée** built at Nîmes, France	c. 100–44 BCE **Julius Caesar,** military leader and historian, wrote *Gallic Wars* c. 96–55 BCE **Lucretius,** poet, philosopher, wrote *On the Nature of Things* c. 84–54 BCE **Catullus,** lyric poet 70–19 BCE **Virgil,** wrote the *Aeneid, Eclogues, Georgics* 65–8 BCE **Horace,** wrote *Odes* 59 BCE–17 CE **Livy,** wrote *History of Rome* 43 BCE–17 CE **Ovid,** wrote *Art of Love, Metamorphoses* c. 50–c. 10 BCE **Vitruvius** active, wrote treatise *De architectura* 3 BCE–65 CE **Seneca,** philosopher, dramatist

CE

Key Events	Architecture	Literature
54–68 CE **Nero** reigned 70 CE **Titus** took Jerusalem; temple destroyed 79 CE **Vesuvius** erupted; destroyed Pompeii, Herculaneum 79–81 CE **Titus** reigned 96–180 CE **Antonine Age,** or "Era of Five Good Emperors"; Roman Empire at height of power 98–117 CE **Trajan** reigned; Dacian campaigns (101–106); conquered Armenia, Parthia; Empire extended to Persian Gulf and Caspian Sea (113–117)	c. 10 CE **Pont du Gard** built at Nîmes, France c. 60 CE **Nero** built Domus Aurea, Baths of Nero c. 80 CE **Titus** finished Colosseum; built Temple of Vespasian, Arch of Titus	c. 20–66 CE **Petronius,** wrote *Satyricon* 23–79 CE **Pliny the Elder,** naturalist, encyclopedist c. 50–138 CE **Epictetus,** Stoic philosopher 35–c. 96 CE **Quintilian,** Institutes of Oratory 40–c. 102 CE **Martial,** epigrammatist c. 46–120 CE **Plutarch,** wrote *Parallel Lives* 55–c. 117 CE **Tacitus,** historian, wrote *Annals, Germania* c. 60–c. 127 CE **Juvenal,** wrote *Satires* 62–113 CE **Pliny the Younger,** writer, administrator; delivered Panegyric to Trajan before Roman Senate (100) c. 67–c. 140 CE **Suetonius,** wrote *Lives of the Caesars*

100

Key Events	Architecture	Literature
	c. 100–c. 120 CE **Apollodorus of Damascus,** architect, active c. 50 CE **Harbor at Ostia** constructed 105 CE **Apollodorus of Damascus** constructed bridge over Danube River c. 110 CE **Trajan** constructed Via Trajana from Benevento to Brindisi; Baths of Trajan built; Forum and Column of Trajan erected 113 CE **Arch of Trajan** at Benevento begun 117 CE **Temple of Olympian Zeus** at Athens completed under Hadrian	
117–138 CE **Hadrian** reigned 138–161 CE **Antoninus Pius** reigned 161–180 CE **Marcus Aurelius** reigned	c. 120 CE **Pantheon** built at Rome 120–127 CE **Villa of Hadrian** at Tivoli built 135 CE **Hadrian's Tomb** built in Rome 211–217 CE **Baths of Caracalla** built in Rome c. 298–306 CE **Baths of Diocletian** built in Rome	c. 160 CE **Apuleius** flourished, philosopher, wrote *Golden Ass* c. 175 CE **Marcus Aurelius,** wrote *Meditations*

300

Edict of Milan, 313
Foundation of Constantinople, 324

400

Honorius moves capital of Rome to Ravenna, 404

500

Saint Benedict establishes Benedictine Rule for monasteries, 529

700

Muslims defeat Visigoths in Spain, 711
Charles Martel defeats Muslims at Poitiers, 732
Charlemagne, r. 768–814, crowned emperor in Rome, 800

900

Cluniac order founded, 910

1000

Norman conquest of England (Battle of Hastings), 1066
Pope Urban II preaches the First Crusade, 1095
Crusaders capture Jerusalem, 1099

PART TWO

AFTER ROME: EARLY CHRISTIAN, BYZANTINE, AND MEDIEVAL STYLES

Historians once used the phrase "Dark Ages" to refer to the 1,000-year span between the fall of Rome and the revival of classical learning in the Renaissance. Of course, the era was not dark in the sense of being unknowable or unprogressive. It did, however, seem like a near-void separating the classical world of Greece and Rome from the revival of classical learning in the Renaissance. Happily, the notion of the Dark Ages was whittled away over time as research defined a rich post-Roman era.

This period was characterized by multiple and shifting cultural and political centers, whose instability can be traced to the division of the empire at the height of its powers. In the second century, Emperor Diocletian separated the empire into eastern and western divisions. Soon after Constantine officially recognized Christianity, he moved the capital from Rome to Byzantium, which was renamed Constantinople. The East Roman Empire remained a powerful force until Constantinople fell to the Ottoman Turks in 1453.

The move to the east further weakened the economy and public services of the city of Rome. Germanic tribes, whom the Romans had called barbarians, flourished in proximity to the Empire's margins. As the western Empire weakened and could not defend its borders, the tribes took advantage of the power vacuum and settled in Roman territory. Often, they converted to Christianity. The Germanic tribes moved farther inward as waves of other migratory peoples, such as the Huns, moved into middle Europe. The power of the western empire continued to erode, especially when Emperor Honorius abandoned the city of Rome. Soon after, in 410, one of the barbarian tribes, the Goths, lay siege to Rome and sacked the city.

In the West, the development of Early Christian art overlaps the apex, decline, and fall of the western empire. The history of the former western empire includes an unsettled period of migration and war (550–1100) as Germanic tribes set up kingdoms and people from the north, known as Vikings (or Norsemen, and eventually Normans), plundered the western coasts of Europe. Islam, which dates to 622, when the prophet Muhammad fled Mecca for Medina, expanded during the next two centuries throughout Arabia and North Africa and extended eastward all the way to India. In Europe, it expanded into Spain and parts of France. In what is now Germany, the Carolingian and Ottonian empires (750–1000) emerged. The Romanesque phase (1000–1150) witnessed the growth of church power throughout Europe. During the next period, the Gothic (1150–1400), the power of the church combined with the influence of prosperous towns to create unique European landmarks known as Gothic cathedrals.

Although imprecise, the word *medieval* is generally used to describe this cluster of developments in western Europe from about 500 to about 1300, which includes the rise of monasticism, feudalism, the building of cities, the beginnings of the Crusades, and the emergence of national monarchies. Art was almost exclusively under the patronage of the church. Yet new voices could be woven around the traditional tunes, a practice that allowed musicians wide latitude.

The Romanesque period saw people embarking on pilgrimages to shrines in Rome, Jerusalem, and Santiago de Compostela. Gothic times witnessed the rise of cities in northern Europe. Here merchants and artisans became distinct social groups, organizing into guilds, similar to trade unions, that regulated prices, established codes governing business practices, and ensured quality of production.

This era mirrors the inventive power and inspired spirit of the people who participated in it. The creation of such marvels as the immense abbey churches, the organization of the Crusades that initiated contact and conflict between the peoples of the Christian West and Muslim East, the building of the soaring Gothic cathedrals, the intricate logic of scholastic treatises that systematized the articles of faith into monumental edifices, the founding of universities, the invention of liturgical dramas and miracle plays, the fiery magic of stained glass that transformed natural light into supernatural visions, and the otherworldly sounds of plainchant all combine into a magnificent panorama of the arts.

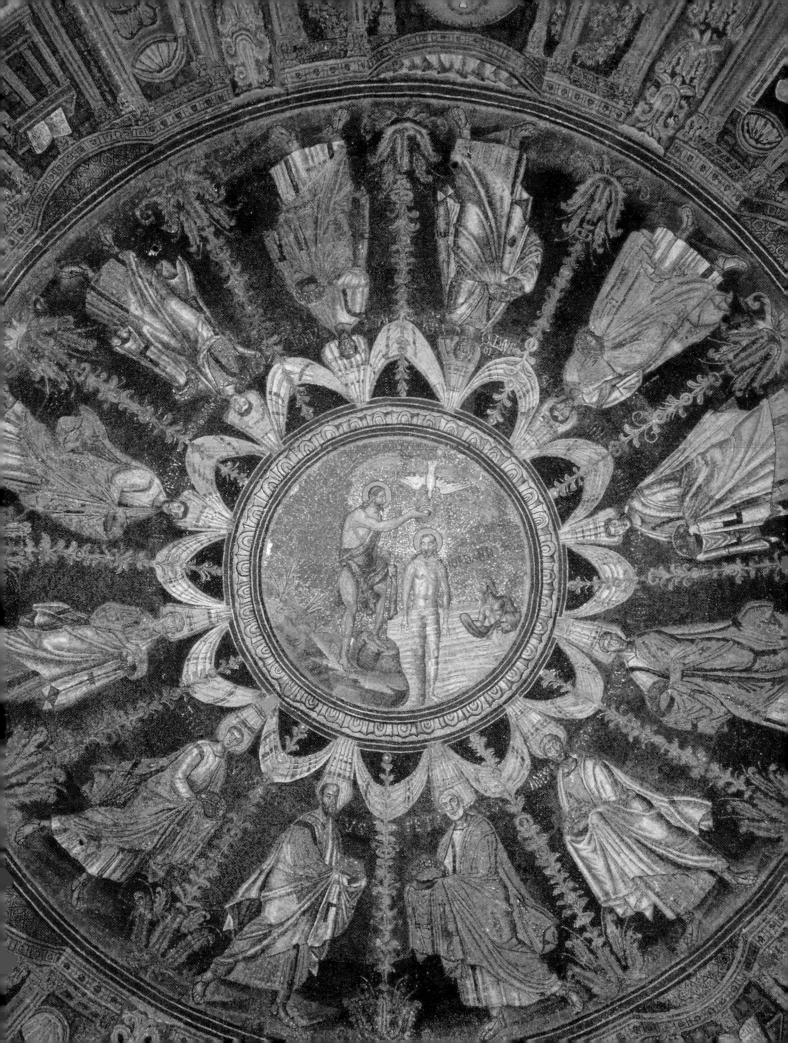

CHAPTER

EARLY CHRISTIAN, BYZANTINE, AND ISLAMIC STYLES

IN THE EARLY DAYS OF the empire, Christianity was to the Romans only one of many mystery cults that promised a better life beyond the grave. Eventually it was the only one to survive. It spread gradually beyond Italy into North Africa, Spain, France, and Britain. Early converts were mainly from the dispossessed and downtrodden masses, although some were drawn from the patrician and educated classes. With the acceptance of slaves and women into their communities, Christians gained momentum until their religion became a force to be reckoned with. Because Christians believed in peace and goodwill, most refused to pay homage to the emperor or serve in the imperial armies. Consequently, they were periodically persecuted.

In 303, in an attempt to stem the rapid spread of Christianity among his subjects, Emperor Diocletian launched the final official suppression of the faith. Just 10 years later his successor, Constantine, issued the Edict of Milan, which recognized Christianity as one of the official state religions of the empire. It was now possible for Christians to worship openly. With Constantine's financial support, an extensive building program was undertaken in Rome that included the

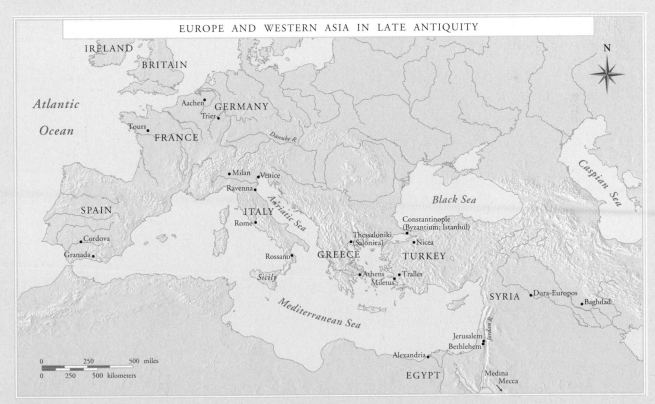

EUROPE AND WESTERN ASIA IN LATE ANTIQUITY

MAP 5.1

basilicas of St. Peter in the Vatican (see Fig. 5.6) and St. Paul Outside-the-Walls. The church of Santa Maria Maggiore, built by Pope Sixtus III, also used the Roman basilica plan. Thus, Christian art, architecture, and music became more visible to the citizens of Rome.

THE ART OF THE EARLY CHRISTIAN ERA

At first, Christianity was of necessity an underground religion, both literally and figuratively. Believing in the resurrection of the body, Christians departed from the Roman practice of cremation. Nevertheless, they followed the Roman practice of extending aboveground cemeteries into underground facilities and dug burial chambers in catacombs. Although meetings were held mostly in private homes, during periods of persecution, the underground burial chambers were also used as meeting places for secret communal meals. Decorative art not only was beyond the financial means of Early Christians but also was considered too worldly. Some slave converts, however, had artistic skills, and they were allowed to paint the walls with Christian symbols and visual versions of Old and New Testament stories that illustrated the teachings of the church for those who could not read (Fig. 5.1).

Favorite subjects were Christ as the good shepherd leading his flock, as in the Twenty-third Psalm, vineyard scenes that referred to the communion wine, and Old Testament stories that were reinterpreted with new meaning. The story of Abraham sacrificing Isaac was seen as a prophecy of Christ's sacrificial mission. The tale of Jonah being thrown overboard, spending 3 days in the belly of a great fish, and finding himself on a peaceful shore under the shade of a green gourd vine was seen as the journey of the soul after death toward refuge in heaven. Daniel's rescue from the lions' den, like that of the three youths from the fiery furnace, meant redemption through suffering and deliverance through the power of faith.

Some sarcophagi carved after Christianity became legal show a consummate craftsmanship

5.1 *The Good Shepherd,* c. fourth century. Painted ceiling, Catacomb of Saints Pietro and Marcellino, Rome, Italy.

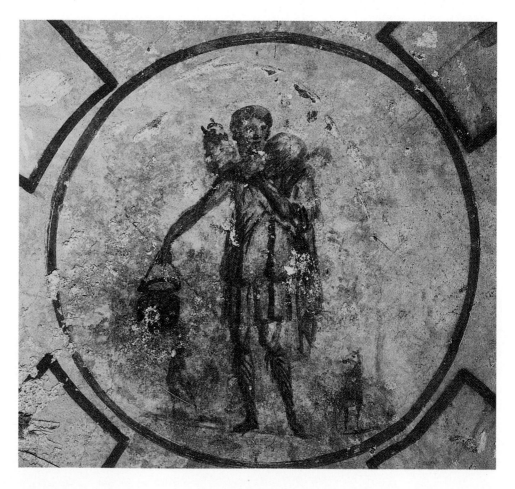

that set them apart from catacomb paintings and forged a link between pagan Roman and Early Christian art. The sarcophagus of Junius Bassus, a Roman prefect, is a prime example (Fig. 5.2). In the upper register, from left to right, are high-relief panels showing Abraham as his hand is stayed by a messenger from God, the arrest of Peter, and Christ enthroned in majesty between Sts. Peter and Paul. Under Christ's feet is the canopied Roman sky god, Coelus, who signified the firmament or, in Christian terms, the heavenly realm. Here, a specific Roman god has been brought into a Christian work. The Roman use of scale to indicate social stature (see p. 89) has been employed, particularly in the image of Christ in the center of the lower register.

The crucifixion of Christ, central to the idea of redemption, was seldom represented in Early Christian art. Still, it was alluded to in the sarcophagus of Junius Bassus, in the upper fourth and fifth panels from the right, which depict Jesus being judged by Pontius Pilate. On the lower left are panels showing Job's sufferings, as well as Adam and Eve with the tree of knowledge and the serpent between them. The scene makes reference to original sin by showing Adam and Eve nude but ashamed of their bodies, as they were not in Paradise. Next come Christ's triumphal entrance into Jerusalem, Daniel in the lions' den, and finally, St. Paul being led to his execution. For clarity, the scenes are framed by classical colonnettes. All the figures except Adam and Eve are draped in Roman togas. Christ, however, is accorded the honor of the Greek *pallium,* a robe associated in classical times with teachers and philosophers. The youthful representation of Jesus also recalls images of the young Apollo (see, for example, Fig. 3.20).

A decisive event in Early Christian history was the convening of the Council of Nicaea (now Iznik, Turkey) by Constantine in 325. Here the basic tenets of the Christian faith were debated and coordinated by leaders from both the West and the East. The most controversial issues were the nature of the godhead and the doctrine of the Trinity. Was Jesus, as the only begotten son of God, of one substance with the Father and hence purely divine? Or, because he was begotten, was he both divine and human? Or was he all human? As professed in the Nicene Creed,

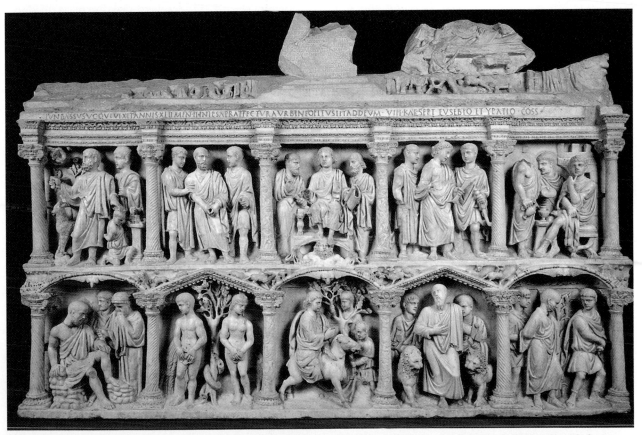

5.2 Sarcophagus of Junius Bassus, c. 359. Marble, 3′10½″ × 8′. Museo Storico del Tesoro della Basilica di San Pietro, Rome, Italy.

Jesus was believed to be "of one substance with the Father, by whom all things were made."

The major dissenter was Arius of Alexandria, who held that Jesus was the most perfect of men but not of one substance with the Father. Arius was excommunicated, and his followers were declared heretics. The Arians, however, continued to make converts, especially among the peoples of the Danube Valley, including the Ostrogoths. Their leaders at the time were Odoacer and Theodoric, who finally brought about the fall of the Western Roman Empire by capturing Ravenna, its capital city. The Eastern Roman Empire survived, but it was challenged by the birth of a powerful new religious movement, Islam. Both religions established a structure that favored authoritarian leadership and, at the same time, relied on otherworldly mysticism.

RAVENNA IN THE LATE FIFTH AND EARLY SIXTH CENTURIES

Many old Roman coins bear the inscription *Ravenna Felix* (Happy Ravenna). By a felicitous stroke of fate, this previously unimportant little town on Italy's Adriatic coast became the cultural center where many of the great political, religious, and artistic dramas of a century and a half of world history were enacted.

Ravenna was, in turn, the seat of the last Roman emperors of the West, the capital of a barbarian Ostrogothic kingdom, and the western center of the Eastern Roman Empire. A more inhospitable site can hardly be imagined. To the east lay the Adriatic Sea, to the north and south were wide deltas of the Po River, and the only land approach was through marshes and swamps. Yet when the barbarian hordes had Rome under almost constant siege, it was this very isolation that led Emperor Honorius to abandon the city in 402 and seek at Ravenna a fortress where his hard-pressed legions could be supplied by the Eastern Roman Empire through the nearby port of Classe.

Even with all its natural advantages, Ravenna could hold out against the barbarians only until 476. Odoacer then succeeded in entering the all-but-impregnable city and putting an end to the Western Roman Empire. The Ostrogothic kingdom of Theodoric, Odoacer's successor, was even more short-lived. Ravenna fell once again in 540, when the armies of the Eastern Roman Empire under Justinian conquered the Italian peninsula and for a brief time reunited the old empire. Meanwhile, a third force, the more enduring

power of the Roman papacy, was becoming increasingly influential. Despite its opposition to the Roman Empire, Catholicism eventually emulated the orderliness and hierarchy that had allowed Rome to maintain its vast domain. With the decline and fall of Rome, the Catholic Church emerged as an international organization, with Latin as its international language and Roman roads providing its means of communication. Like Rome, the Catholic Church struggled with the pressures of diverse cultures and interests.

Distinct historical traditions as well as great distances separated Rome in the west, Byzantium in the east, and the nomadic Ostrogoths in the north. Early in the fourth century, after making Christianity an official state religion, Emperor Constantine moved his court to Byzantium, christening the city the "new Rome." This second capital was later renamed Constantinople in his honor. Soon the Eastern and Western Roman Empires went their separate ways. With the encroachment of northern barbarians, a three-way struggle for power began among Justinian, Theodoric, and the pope.

Much more than the sea stretched between Ravenna and Constantinople; high mountains stood between it and the restless northern barbarians, and great obstacles separated it from Rome. As the foundations of Christian belief were being drawn up, theological barriers, in fact, proved more impassable than seas or mountains. The controversies in Ravenna foreshadowed the later separation of Christianity into Eastern Orthodox and Roman Catholic. Paralleling the political and religious controversies, a conflict of art styles took

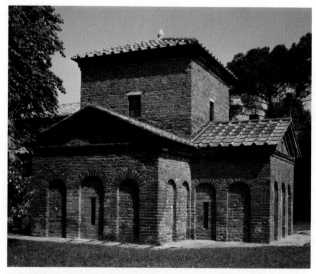

5.3   Mausoleum of Galla Placidia, Ravenna, Italy, c. 425.

place within Ravenna as successive rulers built and embellished the city. In the sixth century, Ostrogothic Arian heretics, Byzantine patriarchs, and members of the Roman hierarchy, together with the schools of artists each patronized, had different cultural heritages, aesthetic goals, and ways of viewing the world.

When the Roman Empire was united, cultural influences came from all parts of the Mediterranean world, and with due allowance for regional diversity, Roman art achieved a recognizable unity. But with the disintegration of Roman power, the adoption of Christianity as an official religion, and the separation of the empire into eastern and western centers, a reorientation in the arts took place. Although they shared a common heritage, two distinct styles began to emerge. The term *Early Christian* designates the Western art of this time, and its Eastern counterpart is referred to as *Byzantine.*

Ravenna's replacement of Rome as the capital city demanded successive building programs, which transformed a minor provincial town into a major metropolis. No ruler could afford to be outdone by his or her predecessors. Each embarked on a vigorous building program. Empress Galla Placidia, for instance, sponsored a church, one part of which was long thought to be her tomb (Fig. 5.3). Although she probably was not buried there, the little chapel continues to be known by its traditional designation. The unadorned brick exterior of the Mausoleum of Galla Placidia does not hint at the ornate interior of this architectural gem, which is completely lined with mosaic work of surpassing brilliance. The area over an entrance is decorated with a portrayal of the youthful Christ as the Good Shepherd in the midst of his flock (Fig. 5.4). Later, when Theodoric came to power, he sought to be more Roman than the Romans. As he wrote to an official in Rome, he wished his age to "match the preceding ones in the beauty of its buildings." After the Byzantine conquest, Justinian made architectural contributions matching his imperial rank.

RECTANGULAR CHURCHES

Theodoric included in his building program a church that would serve his own Arian sect. Originally dedicated by him to "Our Lord Jesus Christ,"

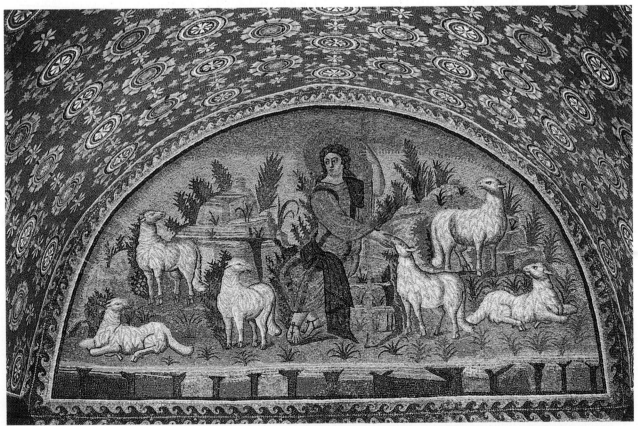

5.4 *Christ as the Good Shepherd,* mosaic above entrance portal, interior of mausoleum of Galla Placidia, Ravenna, Italy, 425–450.

this church (Fig. 5.5A) today bears the name of Sant' Apollinare Nuovo, honoring Apollinaris, the patron saint of Ravenna and, by tradition, a disciple and friend of St. Peter. The floor plan is severely simple (Fig. 5.5B). The space is divided into a vestibule entrance, known as the *narthex;* a central area for the congregation to assemble, known as the *nave,* which is separated from the side aisles by two rows of columns; and a semicircular *apse,* which framed the altar and provided seats for the clergy.

Older pagan temples, with their small, dark interiors, were not suitable models for Christian churches that had to house large congregations. Ancient Greek ceremonies took place outdoors around an altar with the temple as a backdrop. The principal architectural and decorative elements of the classic temples—colonnades, friezes, and pediments—faced outward. The Christian basilica turned the Greek temple outside in, leaving the exterior plain and focusing attention on the interior colonnades and the painted or mosaic embellishments of the walls and semidomed apse.

The most monumental of these Early Christian basilicas was Old St. Peter's (Fig. 5.6), so called because it was destroyed in the sixteenth century to make way for the present basilica created by Bramante, Michelangelo, and Maderno (see Fig. 10.1). Planned from the year 324, when it was dedicated by Constantine, built over the presumed tomb of the Apostle, and the largest church of the period, Old St. Peter's ranked as the key monument of Western Christendom until its demolition. It could hold 3,000 to 4,000 worshipers, some of whom would have been pilgrims who traveled to see the relics of St. Peter.

To provide for all Christian liturgical activities, Old St. Peter's intertwined elements of Roman domestic, civic, and temple architecture in a new harmonious composition. Approached by a flight of steps, the open **atrium** was entered through an arched gateway. This courtyard, derived from Roman country villas, was surrounded by roofed **arcades,** or series of arches, supported by columns. It provided space for congregations to gather, facilities for the instruction of converts, and offices for church officials. In its center was a fountain for the ceremonial washing of hands. The side of the atrium toward the church became the narthex, which served as a frontispiece to the church proper. Through the portals of the **narthex,** one entered into the nave and the side aisles. This spacious nave was 80 feet wide and resembled the rectangular law courts of Roman public basilicas (see Fig. 4.10B). It was flanked on either side by two aisles, each 30 feet wide, and a procession of columns that led the eye along its 295-foot length to the **triumphal arch** (so called because of its derivation from similar Roman imperial structures, such as that in Fig. 3.21). Beyond this was the wide **transept,** "arms" set at right angles to the nave and an area that functions as a second nave, followed by the semicircular apse. In sum, the ground plan was

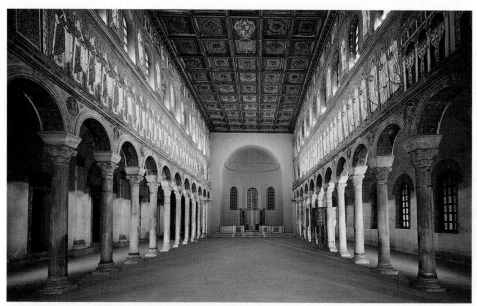

A

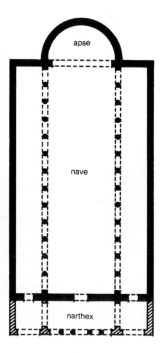

B

5.5   (A) Interior, Sant' Apollinare Nuovo, Ravenna, Italy, c. 493–526. (B) Plan of Sant' Apollinare Nuovo.

roughly T-shaped or cruciform, resembling a long Latin cross with short arms. From beginning to end, the design of Old St. Peter's swept along a horizontal axis of 835 feet and opened out at its widest point in the 295-foot transept.

A basilica rises vertically above the nave colonnades through an intermediate area called the ***triforium.*** Above this is the **clerestory,** with rows of windows to light the interior and masonry to support the wooden beams of the shed roof. In keeping with the sheltered and inward orientation of these early basilicas, no windows offered views of the outside world. Those in the clerestory were too high and deeply set to allow even a glimpse of the sky. It was inner radiance of the spirit rather than natural light that was sought.

EARLY CHRISTIAN AND BYZANTINE MOSAICS

Unlike Old St. Peter's, which had to accommodate a standing congregation of 4,000 or more, Sant' Apollinare Nuovo (Fig. 5.5A) is small. It was originally designed as the private chapel of Theodoric's palace. Only the nave remains intact; all other parts are restorations or later additions. Its modest architecture would attract only passing attention. However, the magnificent mosaics that decorate its nave wall are of major importance in art history.

The art of mosaic depends for its effectiveness on directing the flow of light from many tiny reflectors. After the placement of the panels, the design, and the colors have been determined, the

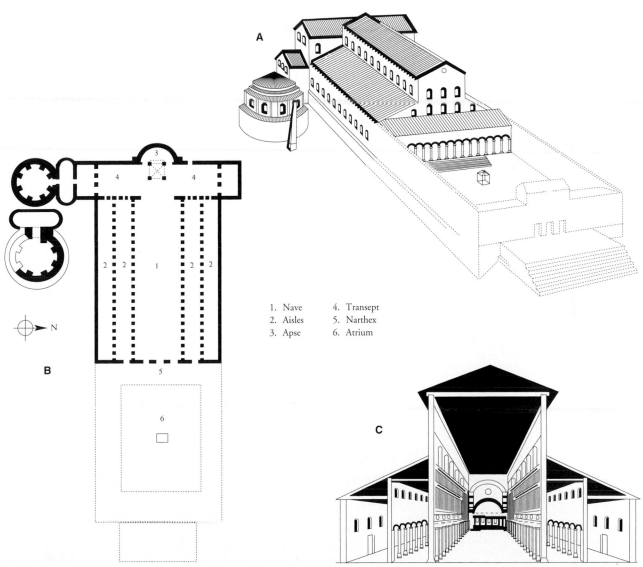

1. Nave
2. Aisles
3. Apse
4. Transept
5. Narthex
6. Atrium

5.6   Reconstruction of Old St. Peter's Basilica, Rome, c. 333. Length of grand axis 835′, width of transept 295′. (A) Restored view. (B) Floor plan. (C) Interior section.

mosaicist must take into account both the natural source of light from windows and artificial sources from lamps or candles. Accordingly, the mosaicist fits each *tessera,* or small cube made of glass, marble, shell, or ceramic, onto an adhesive surface, tilting some this way, others that, so that a shimmering luminous effect is obtained.

Although they present a harmonious design, the mosaics at Sant' Apollinare Nuovo actually were made in two different phases and styles. The mosaics of the earlier period were commissioned by Theodoric and made in the style of Early Christian art in Rome. Through his secretary Cassiodorus, Theodoric wrote to an official in Rome that he should send "some of your most skilled marble workers, who may join together those pieces which have been exquisitely divided, and connecting together their different veins of color, may admirably represent the natural appearance." After Justinian's conquest, the church was rededicated and references to Arian beliefs and Theodoric's reign were removed. Half a century later, part of the frieze above

the nave arcade was replaced by mosaics in the Byzantine style.

Completely covering both walls of the nave, the mosaic work is divided into three bands (Fig. 5.5A). Above the nave arcade and below the clerestory windows, a wide, continuous mosaic strip runs the entire length of the nave in the manner of a frieze. It depicts two long files of saints (the Byzantine part) moving in a majestic procession from representations of Ravenna on one side to its seaport Classe on the other (the Early Christian part). The second band fills the space on either side of the clerestory windows with a series of standing toga-clad figures.

At the top level, panels depicting incidents in the life of Christ alternate with simulated canopy-like niches over the figures standing below. The middle and upper bands are of Roman craftsmanship. The scenes in the upper band constitute the most nearly complete representation of the life of Christ in Early Christian art. On one side, the story of the parables and miracles is told, among them

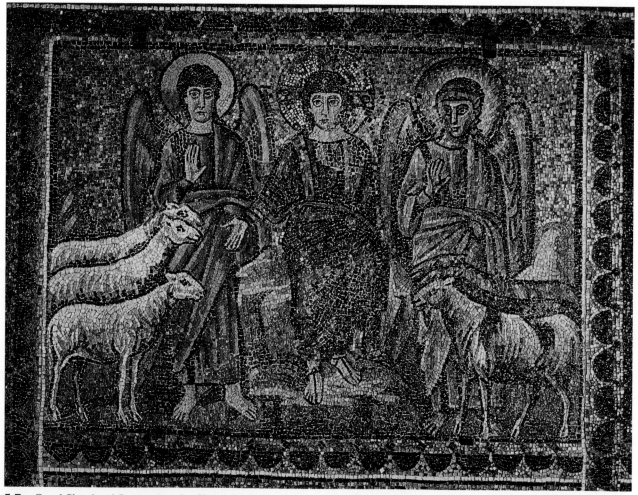

5.7   *Good Shepherd Separating the Sheep from the Goats,* c. 520. Mosaic, Sant' Apollinare Nuovo, Ravenna, Italy.

the *Good Shepherd Separating the Sheep from the Goats* (Fig. 5.7), a reference to the Last Judgment. In this and other scenes, Christ appears youthful and unbearded, with blue eyes and brown hair. The opposite side presents scenes of the Passion and Resurrection. The *Last Supper* (Fig. 5.8) shows Christ as a mature and bearded figure reclining with the apostles in the manner of a Roman banquet. In all instances, Christ has a cruciform halo with a jewel on each arm of the cross to distinguish him from the attending saints and angels. His dignified demeanor and purple cloak show him in royal majesty.

Standing like statues on their pedestals, the figures in the middle band are modeled three-dimensionally in light and shade and cast diagonal shadows. They apparently were once identified by inscriptions over their heads. The removal of their names suggests that they may have been prophets and saints revered by the Arian Christians.

The great mosaic frieze above the nave arcade starts to the left and right of the entrance with representations of Classe and Ravenna, respectively. In a crescent-shaped harbor with three Roman galleys riding at anchor, Classe is seen between two lighthouses. Above the city walls, some of the ancient buildings are discernible, and from the gate issues a procession of virgin martyrs.

On the opposite side is Ravenna, with Theodoric's palace in the foreground. Under the word *Palatium* (palace) is the central arch, where there once was a portrait of Theodoric on horseback. Under the other arches, outlines and traces of heads and hands indicate that members of his court were also portrayed, and Theodoric was again depicted in the city gate at the right. When the Ostrogothic kingdom came to its abrupt end, these personages were replaced by simulated Byzantine textile curtains. Above the palace are several of Theodoric's

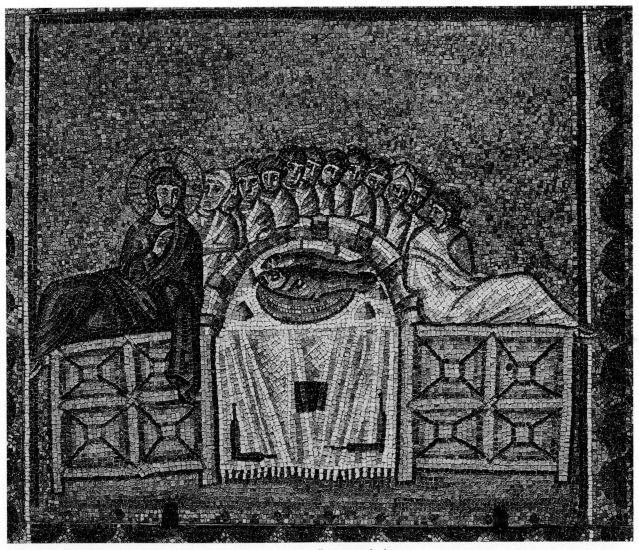

5.8 *Last Supper,* c. 520. Mosaic, Sant' Apollinare Nuovo, Ravenna, Italy.

buildings, with the Church of Sant' Apollinare Nuovo itself on the left.

According to early custom, the congregation gathered in the side aisles, with women on one side and men on the other. At the offertory they went forward through the nave to the altar, carrying gifts of bread and wine for the consecration. In a stylized way, the procession frieze reenacts this part of the service on a heavenly level. On the left, twenty-two virgins are led forward by the Three Wise Men to the throne of the Virgin Mary, who holds the Christ child on her lap. Arrayed in white tunics with richly jeweled mantles, the virgins carry their crowns of martyrdom in their hands as their votive offerings.

In a similar manner, twenty-five male martyrs on the right are escorted by St. Martin of Tours into the presence of Christ, who is seated on a lyre-backed throne. The eye is led along by the upward folds and curves of their costumes as they step along a flowered path lined with date palms, which symbolize both Paradise and their martyrdom. All is serene, and no trace of their earthly suffering is seen. Their heads, although tilted differently to vary the design somewhat, are all on the same level, in keeping with the Greco-Byzantine convention of isocephaly (see p. 36). Only St. Agnes is identified by her attribute, the lamb. Otherwise, the faces reveal so little individuality that they cannot be recognized without the inscriptions above their heads.

When these Byzantine figures are compared with the earlier Roman work in the bands above, the differences between Roman and Byzantine work are revealed. The lines of the Byzantine design form a frankly two-dimensional pattern, whereas the garments of the Roman personages fall in natural folds that model the forms they cover in three-dimensional fashion. All the figures in the upper two bands wear simple unadorned Roman togas, but the saints below are clad in luxurious, ornate Byzantine textiles decorated with gems. The Roman figures appear against natural three-dimensional backgrounds, such as the Sea of Galilee, hills, or a blue sky. The Byzantine virgins and martyrs, however, are set against a shimmering gold backdrop with uniformly spaced stylized palms. By the sixth century, gold was the preferred background, crowding out or pushing to the side naturalistic observations of nature. The candor, directness, and simplicity with which the Roman scenes are depicted contrast strikingly with the impersonal, aloof, and symbolic Byzantine treatment of the nave frieze. Differences in theological outlook also influenced stylistic decisions. The Arian–Roman panels accentuate the Redeemer's worldly life and human suffering, whereas the Byzantine frieze visually stresses his divinity and remoteness from worldly matters.

CENTRAL-PLAN CHURCHES

Little more than a year elapsed between the death of Theodoric and the accession of Justinian as emperor in Constantinople. Almost immediately, Justinian decided to build the church of San Vitale at Ravenna (Fig. 5.9A). In the politics of the times, building a church that would surpass anything undertaken by Theodoric served both as an assertion of Justinian's authority in Italy and as evidence of the weakening power of Theodoric's Ostrogothic successors.

At first, the project languished because Justinian's position in the capital of the Western Roman Empire was anything but certain. Ultimately, he used force to assert his Italian claims, and his armies entered Ravenna in 540. Thereafter, construction of San Vitale proceeded swiftly. Seven years later the church was ready for its dedication by Archbishop Maximian. Its plain red-brick exterior shows that as little attention was paid to the outside of San Vitale as to that of any other church of the period. But with its multicolored marble walls, carved alabaster columns, pierced marble screens, and sanctuary mosaics, the Church of San Vitale is a veritable jewel box.

Architecturally, San Vitale is a highly developed example of the central-plan church (Fig. 5.9B), differing radically from Sant' Apollinare Nuovo. Still, it has all the usual features of the basilica, including a narthex entrance, a circular nave, surrounding side aisles, and a triumphal arch leading into a sanctuary with an apse and two side chambers. The striking difference, however, between an oblong basilica and a centralized church is the direction of its axis. In the former, the axis runs horizontally through the center of the building, dividing the church lengthwise into halves and leading the eye toward the apse. In the central-plan building, the axis is vertical, leading the eye upward from the central floor space to the dome. Were it not for the addition of the oblong narthex on the west and the apse and side chapels on the east, the ground plan of San Vitale would be a simple octagon.

The two side chambers of the apse are usually associated with Eastern Orthodox churches. Their presence here points to the fact that San Vitale was designed as a theater for the Byzantine liturgy. The northern chamber was designated the ***prothesis,*** to indicate its use as the place to prepare the communion bread and wine for the altar. In Eastern Orthodox usage, the sacrificial aspect of the mass assumed a dramatic character, and the sacramental bread was symbolically "wounded, killed, and buried" on the table of the prothesis before it appeared on the altar, where it symbolized the resurrection of the body. The southern chamber was called the **diakonikon.** It served as the vestry and as a place to store the sacred objects used in the orthodox service.

To understand the history of San Vitale and central-plan churches, one must examine similar buildings at Ravenna and elsewhere. Whereas the ancestors of the rectangular basilica were Roman domestic and public buildings, the centralized church is derived from ancient circular tombs, such as Hadrian's colossal monument on the banks of the Tiber. The ancient preference for the circular mausoleum can be explained partly by its symbolism. Immortality was often represented by the image of a serpent biting its tail, that is, a living creature whose end was joined to its beginning. Another ancestor is the round classical temple, such as the Pantheon (see Fig. 4.20A).

The idea of a church built in the same form as a tomb is by no means as somber as it might seem. In the Christian sense, such a church symbolized the Easter tomb, reminding all of the res-

urrection of Christ. Churches were dedicated to martyrs and saints, who were believed to be partaking of the heavenly life with Christ, just as the faithful hoped they themselves would one day be doing. The Roman cult of Orpheus, the Greek god whose music resurrected his wife from the underworld, stressed the idea of the body being the tomb of the spirit. Hence, death and resurrection were aspects of the same idea, and the martyr's death was a mystical union with Christ. Indeed, the altar itself was a tomb or repository for the sacred relics of the saint to whom the church was dedicated. Early altars in the catacombs actually were sarcophagi that also served as communion tables. Thus, in the rites of the church, the earthly past of Christ and his apostles, saints, and martyrs was commemorated, and at the same time the glorious heavenly future was anticipated.

BAPTISTRIES

The eight-sided Christian baptistry was modeled directly on the octagonal bathhouses found in ancient Roman villas. There the bathing pool was usually octagonal, and the structure around it assumed that shape. Early Christian baptisms required total immersion, and the transition from

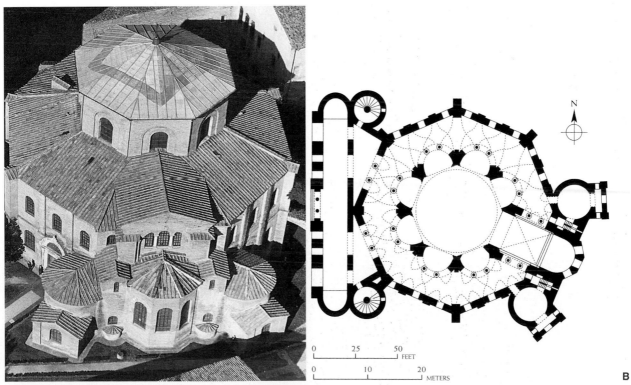

5.9   (A) Exterior of apse, San Vitale, Ravenna, c. 526–547. Diameter 112′. (B) Plan of San Vitale, Ravenna.

bathhouse to baptistry was easy. Because baptism was a personal and family affair, not calling for the presence of a congregation, baptistries usually were small.

The Arian Baptistry was built in Theodoric's time in the same style as the earlier "Neonian" Baptistry of the Roman Christians. Both are domed structures with fine interior mosaics. Both have similar representations of the baptism of Christ on the interior surfaces of their *cupolas,* or domes. That of the Arian Baptistry (Fig. 5.10) shows the ceremony being performed by St. John the Baptist, while the river Jordan is personified as an old man in the manner of the ancient river gods (see Fig. 4.11, lower left).

Around the central scene are the twelve apostles, who move in a procession toward the throne of Christ. Just as the virgins and martyrs reenact the offertory procession above the nave arcade of Sant' Apollinare Nuovo, so the apostles here mirror the baptismal rites on a more heavenly level. They group themselves around the center above, where Christ is being baptized, just as the clergy, family, and sponsors gathered about the font below for the baptism of a Ravenna Christian. Here is yet another example in which the **iconography,** or subject matter, of the decorative scheme reflects the liturgical activity that took place within the building.

DOME CONSTRUCTION

During the sixth century, architects were preoccupied with balancing domes over square or octagonal supporting structures. The Romans had found one solution in the case of the Pantheon—resting the dome on supporting cylindrical walls—but builders in Ravenna found two other solutions. The exquisite little Mausoleum of Galla Placidia (Fig. 5.3), which dates from about 425, was built in the form of an equal-winged Greek cross. Its dome rests on **pendentives,** concave spherical triangles of masonry rising from the square corners and bending inward to form the circular base of the dome (Fig. 5.11). The role of the pendentives is to encircle the square understructure and make the transition to the round domed superstructure. The Ravenna baptistries exemplify the same pendentive solution, but their domes rest directly on octagonal understructures.

Another solution stemming from the same early period is based on a system of **squinches,** pieces of construction placed diagonally across the angles of the square or octagonal walls of the understructure to form a proper base for a dome (Fig. 5.11). This was the method used for the doming of San Vitale. The eight piers of the arcaded central room culminate in an octagonal drum on which, by means of squinches, the dome rests. Above the nave arcade and beneath the dome, the

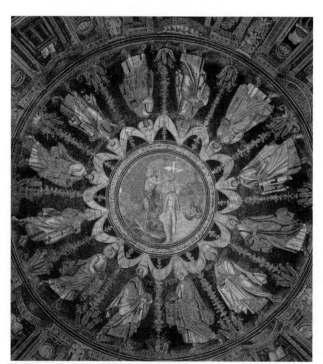

5.10 *Baptism of Christ Surrounded by the Twelve Apostles,* c. 458. Dome mosaic, Baptistry of the Orthodox, Ravenna, Italy.

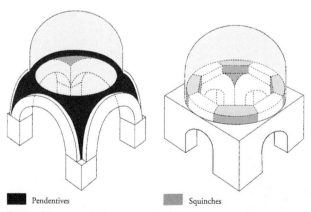

◼ Pendentives   ▨ Squinches

5.11 Circular domes can be raised over rectangular buildings by *pendentives* or *squinches*. Pendentives are vaults in the form of spherical triangles that connect arches springing from corner piers and unite at the apex of the arches to form a circular base upon which the dome rests. Squinches are stone lintels placed diagonally across corners to form a continuous base for masonry built up in wedge or arch formation.

builders of San Vitale included a vaulted triforium gallery running around the church and opening into the nave (Fig. 5.12). This gallery, which was called the **matroneum,** was for the use of women, who were strictly segregated in Byzantine rites.

Eastern parallels of San Vitale are found in Justinian's churches at Constantinople, including the church of Sts. Sergius and Bacchus. The magnificent Hagia Sophia ("Sancta Sophia," or "Holy Wisdom") is also a central-plan church under a

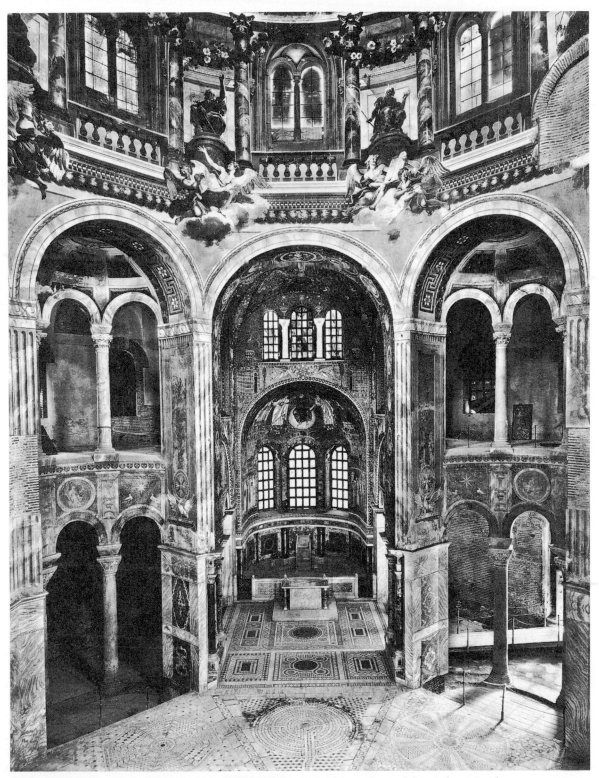

5.12 Interior, San Vitale, Ravenna, Italy, 527–547 (clerestory decorations, eighteenth century).

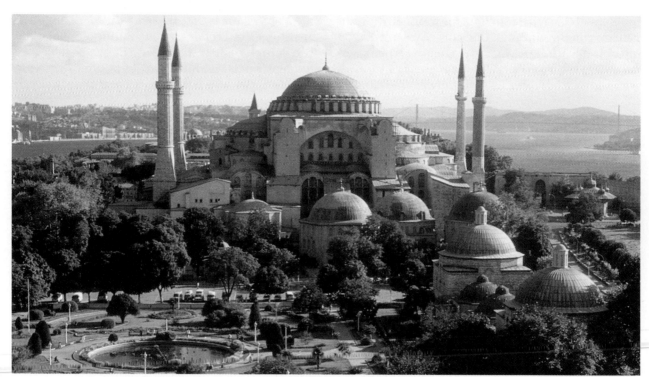

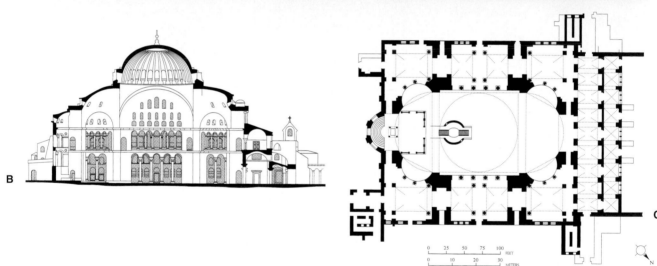

5.13 (A) Anthemius of Tralles and Isidorus of Miletus. Hagia Sophia, Istanbul (Constantinople), Turkey, 532–537 (minarets after 1453), 308′ × 236′. (B) Section of Hagia Sophia. (C) Plan of Hagia Sophia.

large dome. Justinian chose two scholars from the cultural centers of Tralles and Miletus in Asia Minor to help him achieve a dramatic visual statement of his rule. As a combination of great art and daring engineering, the Hagia Sophia, conceived by Anthemius of Tralles and Isidorus of Miletus, remains impressive (Fig. 5.13). Externally, it is practically square, with bulging **buttresses,** or masonry supports, and swelling half-domes mounting by means of pendentives to a full dome on top. Internally, from the narthex entrance on the west, the space opens into a large nave. Above, the huge dome seems to float on the diffused sunlight brought in by forty windows. Although the eye is led horizontally to the apse in the east (Fig. 5.14), it is important to note that in the rites of the Eastern Church an elaborately embroidered curtain would have kept the mass from being viewed by congregants other than priests and the emperor. In later Eastern churches, an **iconostasis,** or wall, served this function. Whereas the most ambitious Gothic cathedral nave never spanned a width of more than 55 feet, the architects of Hagia Sophia achieved an open space 100 feet wide and 200 feet long.

The psychological effect of the dome in central-plan churches is to bring the separate parts into a unified whole. In the interiors of both Hagia Sophia and San Vitale, the dome and its supports are clearly visible and the structure is therefore self-explanatory. Ironically, the dome of San Vitale can be seen from the interior only because on the outside its octagonal base has

been continued upward and roofed over. Psychologically, the equilibrium found in central-plan churches creates a restful effect that is in direct contrast with the restless interiors of later Gothic cathedrals. In the cathedrals the dynamic surge upward psychologically depends, in part, on the fact that the crucial structural element, the exterior buttressing, is not apparent to the viewer from the inside of the church.

MOSAIC PORTRAITURE

In the apse of San Vitale, facing the altar from opposite sides, are two mosaic panels that portray the leading figures of early Byzantine rule in Ravenna. On one, Emperor Justinian appears in the midst of

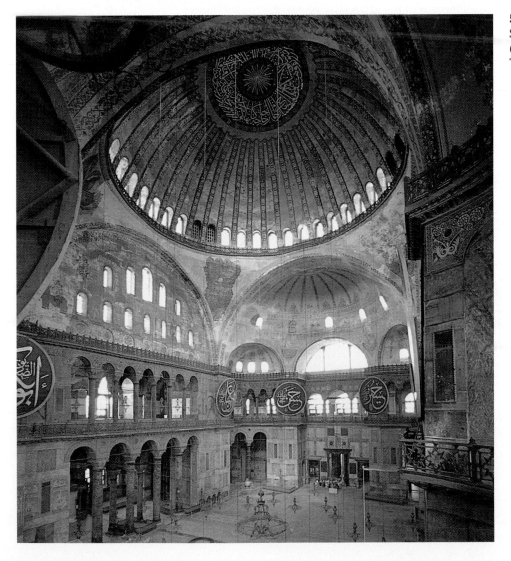

5.14 Interior of Hagia Sophia, Istanbul (Constantinople), Turkey.

his courtiers (Fig. 5.15). On the other, facing him as an equal, is Empress Theodora (Fig. 5.16). They are portrayed as if they were making a procession through the church.

It is significant that the finest existing portrait of the great emperor should be in mosaic rather than in the form of a sculptured bust, a bronze figure on horseback, or a colossal statue as it might have been in Rome. Mosaic conveyed the union of temporal and spiritual power situated at Ravenna. Justinian based his rule on skillful use of legal and theological formulas, as well as on military might. He helped codify Roman law, presided at religious councils, and reconciled different political points of view. He chose to be represented as a symbol of unity between the force of the church on one hand and the power of the state on the other.

Preceding Justinian in the procession are the clergymen, among whom only Archbishop Maximian is identified by name above his head. His crucifix is held up as an assertion of his power as the spiritual and temporal lord of Ravenna. On the emperor's other side are his courtiers and honor guard, holding their jeweled swords aloft. The shield with its Chrismon insignia points to the status of the soldiers as defenders of the faith. The Chrismon was a widely used monogram of the time, made up of the Greek letters *chi* (χ) and *rho* (ρ), which together form the first two letters of the Greek word *Christo,* meaning "anointed one." To those who read Latin, the Greek-derived chi–rho symbol was also interpreted as the word *pax,* or peace. Somewhat more allegorically, the letters of the chi–rho symbol could be viewed as a combination of the cross and the shepherd's crook, which symbolize the Savior's death and pastoral mission. In addition, Christians used the first and the last letters of the Greek alphabet, *alpha* and *omega,* to indicate that their God and their faith encompassed everything.

Justinian stands in the center of the procession, magnificently clothed and crowned with the imperial diadem. The observer knows immediately that this is no ordinary royal personage but rather one who could sign his name as Emperor Caesar Flavius Justinianus, Alamanicus, Francicus, Germanicus, Anticus, Alanicus, Vandalicus, Africanus, Pious, Happy, Renowned, Conqueror, and Triumpher, ever Augustus. Great as Justinian's military exploits were, however, it is

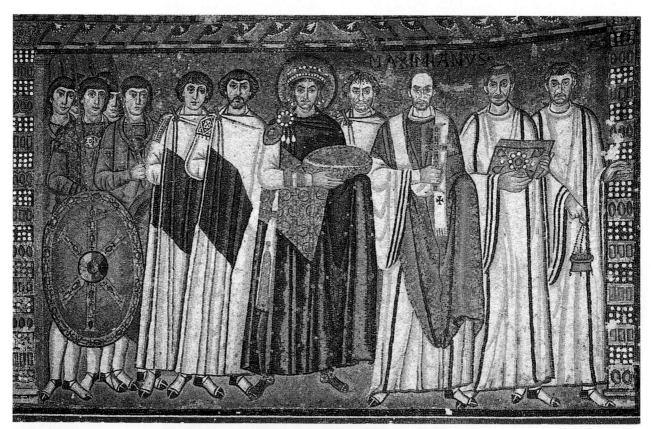

5.15   *Emperor Justinian and Courtiers,* c. 547. Mosaic, San Vitale, Ravenna, Italy.

his works of peace that endured. In addition to a vast building program, the Byzantine emperor is remembered for his monumental code, the *Digest of Laws,* whose influence was felt for centuries throughout the Western world.

On her side, Empress Theodora (Fig. 5.16), richly jeweled and clad in imperial purple, is depicted as she is about to enter the church from the narthex. Possibly because of her humble origins and early career as an actress, Theodora may have wished to appear more royal than the king. Her offering recalls a caustic remark by the hypocritical Procopius, chronicler of Justinian's reign. He said that she fed the geese of the devil while on the stage and the sheep of Christ while on the throne. On the hem of her robe, the offertory motif is carried out in the embroidered figures of the Three Wise Men, the first bearers of gifts to Christ. Because the Wise Men, like Justinian and Theodora, came from the East, this motif served as a reminder to the people of Ravenna that the source of wisdom and power lay in that direction.

These two mosaic portraits are especially valuable because they are among the few surviving visual representations of vanished Byzantine courtly ceremonies. The regal pair appear as if participating in the offertory procession at the dedication of the church, which took place in 547, although neither was actually present on that occasion. Such ceremonial entries were part of the elaborate Byzantine liturgy, and both the emperor and the empress are shown as bearers of gifts. Justinian is carrying the gold **paten,** which was used to hold the communion bread at the altar, while Theodora is presenting the chalice that contains the wine. Because their generosity was responsible for the building, decoration, and endowment of San Vitale, the allusion is to gifts of gold as well.

In keeping with the rigid conventions of Byzantine art, all the heads appear in one plane. Those of Justinian and Theodora are distinguished by their halos, which not only refer to their awesome power but also are a carryover of the semidivine status claimed by earlier Roman emperors. Even though they are moving in a procession, Justinian and Theodora are portrayed frontally in the manner of imperial personages accustomed to receiving the homage of their subjects. Despite the stylized medium, the eye can

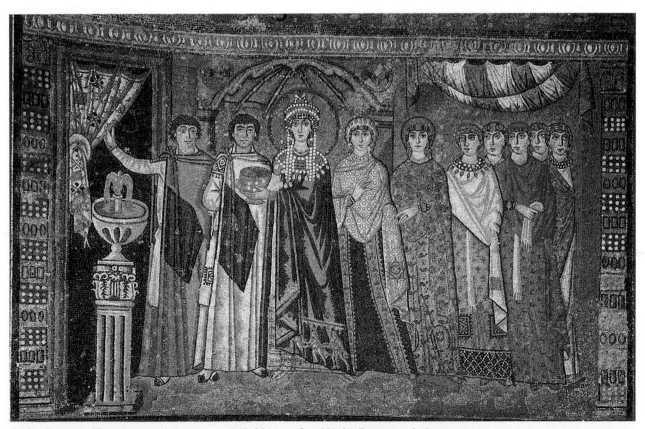

5.16   *Empress Theodora and Retinue,* c. 547. Mosaic, San Vitale, Ravenna, Italy.

follow the procession as it moves in dignified measure, carried forward by the linear pattern in the folds of the garments. The elegant, luxurious costumes add to the richness of the scene.

The decorative design of San Vitale also includes carved alabaster columns, polychrome marble wall panels, pierced marble choir screens, and many other details. The capitals of the columns are carved with intricate patterns (Fig. 5.17). The harmonious proportions of the building as a whole combine with the rich optical effects of the mosaics, polychrome marble, and ornamental sculptures. Along with Hagia Sophia, San Vitale is the high point of Byzantine art in the West.

SCULPTURE

From its status as a major art in Greco-Roman times, sculpture declined to a relatively modest place in the ranks of Early Christian arts. It became primarily the servant of the architectural and liturgical forms of the church. Even its classical three-dimensionality was in eclipse, and sculpture tended

to become increasingly pictorial and symbolic as it assumed a teaching role in Early Christian usage.

When sculpture moved indoors, it underwent necessary changes. For instance, a statue in the round was either placed against a wall or stood in a niche, which prevented its being seen from all sides. The closeness in time and place to the pagan art served to channel Christian visual expression in other directions. With one of the Ten Commandments expressly forbidding the making of

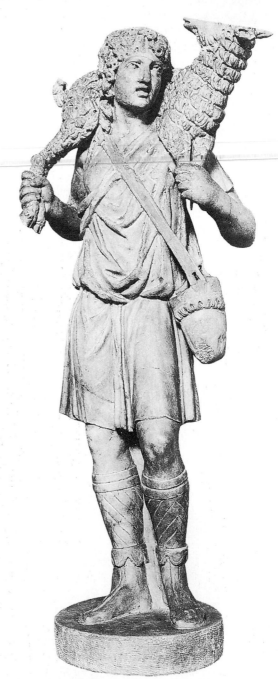

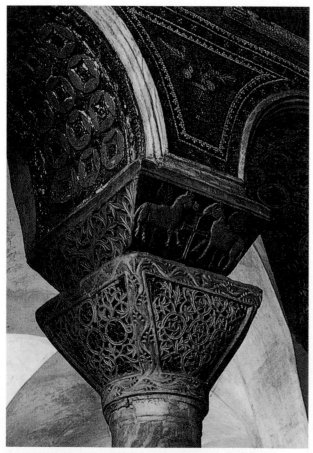

5.17 Byzantine capital (with horses), c. 547. San Vitale, Ravenna, Italy.

5.18 *Good Shepherd,* c. 300. Marble, height 3'3". Vatican Museums, Rome, Italy.

"graven images," it is remarkable that the art survived as well as it did.

A rare example of three-dimensional Early Christian sculpture is the *Good Shepherd* (Fig. 5.18). Figures of peasants carrying calves or sheep to market are commonly found in ancient Greek and Roman genre sculpture. In the Christian interpretation, however, the shepherd is Christ and the sheep are the congregation of the faithful; when a jug of milk is included, the whole image refers to the Eucharist.

CHRISTIAN FORMS AND SYMBOLS

Architectural sculpture proved adaptable to the new demands placed on it. Capitals of columns, decorative relief panels, carved wooden doors, and to some extent, statues in niches continued, with appropriate Christian modifications. The principal emphasis, however, shifted toward objects that were central to Christian worship, such as altars, pulpits, pierced marble screens, and carved ivory reliefs. Smaller items, such as precious metal boxes for relics, lamps, incense pots, communion chalices, jeweled book covers, and patens, all with delicately worked designs, were closer to the province of jewelry than to that of grand classical art.

One of the strongest influences on Early Christian design was the new orientation of thought toward symbolism. As long as the religions of Greece and Rome were focused on the human form, sculptors could represent the gods as idealized human beings. But Christians were challenged to represent in concrete form such abstractions as the Trinity, the Holy Spirit, the salvation of the soul, and the idea of redemption through participation in the Eucharistic sacrifice. The solution came through the use of parables and symbols. Thus, the Christian idea of immortality could be rendered through several biblical scenes of deliverance: Noah from the flood, Moses from the land of Egypt, Job from his sufferings, Daniel from the lions' den, the youths from the fiery furnace, and Lazarus from his tomb.

In Early Christian relief panels, plant and animal motifs were included less for naturalistic reasons than to convey symbolic meaning. The dove represented the Holy Spirit, the peacock stood for Paradise, and so on. The cross is seldom found in Early Christian art, because it recalled a punishment used for the lowest type of criminal. Instead, the Chrismon symbol already seen on the shield of Justinian's soldiers (Fig. 5.15) was used. A fish, or the Greek word for it, *ichthys,* is often found as a reference to Jesus's making his disciples fishers of men. The letters of the word also constituted an abbreviation for "Jesus Christ Son of God, Savior." In effect, symbols and lettered inscriptions carried special meaning and mystical significance for initiated worshipers.

CARVED STONE TOMBS

One of the chief forms of Early Christian sculpture is the carved stone sarcophagus. A special Christian incentive came from the desire for interment within the sacred precincts of the church. The relics of saints reposed in the altar. Tombs of bishops and other dignitaries were housed in the church. Those of the laity were usually placed in the atrium. The latter custom survives in modern times, with burials of famous people taking place in vaults below the church floor.

A fine example is provided by the sarcophagus of Archbishop Theodore (Fig. 5.19). The front panel shows the combination of the Chrismon symbol with an alpha and an omega, another

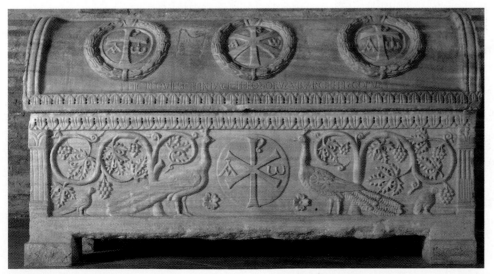

5.19 Sarcophagus of Archbishop Theodore, sixth century. Marble, 3'3½" × 6'9". Sant'Apollinare in Classe, Ravenna, Italy.

reference to Christ, taken from his statement that he was both the beginning and the end. Their inclusion here on a tomb indicates the end of the earthly life and the beginning of the heavenly one. Flanking the symbols are two peacocks, symbolizing Paradise, and on either side, a graceful vine pattern in which small birds feeding on grapes refer symbolically to communion. The inscription reads in translation, "Here rests in peace Archbishop Theodore." On the lid are repetitions of the Chrismon monogram, surrounded by the conventional laurel wreath symbolizing immortality.

THE ARCHBISHOP'S CHAIR

By far, the most impressive single example of sculpture of this period is a chair that is thought to be that of Archbishop Maximian (Fig. 5.20), Justinian's

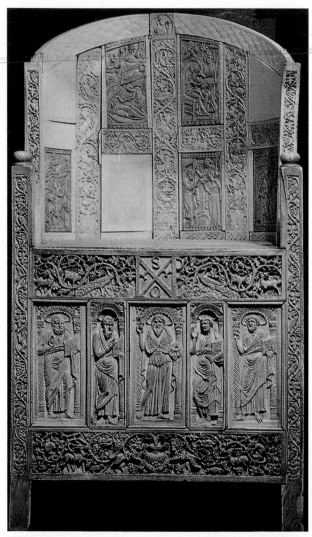

5.20   Cathedra of Maximian, c. 546–556. Ivory panels on wood frame, 5′11″ × 1′11⅝″. Museo dell'Arcivescovile, Ravenna, Italy.

viceroy, who is portrayed beside him in the mosaic panel in San Vitale (Fig. 5.15). Such an episcopal, or bishop's, throne is called a **cathedra,** and the church in which it is housed is termed a **cathedral.** When a bishop addresses his congregation from it, he is said to be speaking **ex cathedra.** A cathedra may also be called a *sedes* (the Latin word for "seat"), from which is derived the noun *see,* which once meant the seat of a bishop but was extended to indicate the territory in the charge of a bishop. Originally *sedes* meant a chair denoting high position. Roman senators used such chairs on public occasions, and modern politicians still campaign for a "seat" in the senate or legislature. Both Jewish rabbis and Greek philosophers sometimes taught from a seated position, hence the reference in modern colleges to a "chair" of philosophy or history.

Maximian's cathedra consists of a set of ivory panels, delicately carved and carefully joined together. Originally, there were thirty-nine pictorial panels, some of which told the Old Testament story of Joseph and his brethren, and the others, the story of Jesus. The chair is thought to have been presented to Maximian by Justinian, and the different techniques used in the various panels indicate collaboration by craftspeople from Anatolia, Syria, and Alexandria. On the front panel, below Maximian's monogram, is a representation of St. John the Baptist flanked on either side by the Evangelists. The Baptist holds a medallion on which a lamb is carved in relief, and the Evangelists hold the Gospels attributed to them.

The elegant Byzantine carving of the front panel—with its complex grapevine motif intertwined with birds and animals denoting the tree of eternal life, the peacocks symbolizing heaven, the symmetrically arranged saints, and the luxuriant linear pattern of their classical drapery—lends itself best to just such a static, formal, stylized design. In the story of Joseph illustrated on the side panels, however, the overriding concern is with an active narrative related in a series of episodes. Content and vivid detail rise above formal considerations. Because monumentality is neither possible nor desirable in ivory carvings, such details as these, handled with precision, are richer and more satisfying than the work as a whole.

MUSIC

Knowledge about the status of musical thought in sixth-century Ravenna can be gained from the writings of Theodoric's ministers Boethius and Cassiodorus. Both were deeply learned in Greek and Roman culture, which remained central to the education of elites. Like the writings of the church fathers and other literary figures of the day, however, Boethius and Cassiodorus reveal much about the theory of the art but little about its practice.

THEORETICAL DISCUSSIONS OF MUSIC

Boethius was a tireless translator of Greek philosophical and scientific treatises into Latin, among which were no less than thirty books by Aristotle. When he fell from favor and was imprisoned, Boethius wrote *The Consolation of Philosophy,* which became one of the most influential books of medieval times. The *Consolation* later found its way into English via translation by Chaucer and Queen Elizabeth. Boethius had a universal mind, capable of discoursing on anything from the mechanics of water clocks to the science of astronomy.

Over time, Boethius's treatise on music became the source of most medieval essays on the subject. It transmitted the gist of ancient Greek musical theory and developed into the foundation of Western musical thinking. Like the Greeks, Boethius believed that "all music is reasoning and speculation," and hence he more closely allied with mathematics than with actual musical practice.

Boethius divided music into three classes, the first of which was the "music of the universe," by which he meant the unheard astronomical "music" of planetary motion. The second was "human music," which referred to the attunement of the mind and body, or the rational and irrational elements of the human constitution, in the manner of the Greek notion of the harmony of opposites. The third was instrumental music and song, of which he had the philosopher's usual low opinion, considering only the theoretical aspects of the art as pursuits worthy of a gentleman and scholar. The only true "musician" in Boethius's opinion was one "who possesses the faculty of judging, according to speculation or reason, appropriate and suitable to music, of modes and rhythms and of the classes of melodies and their mixtures . . . and of the songs of the poets."

Cassiodorus, a senator and advisor to Theodoric, wrote in a similarly learned vein. Even after he retired from public life to his monastery at Vivarium, he remained involved in the lives of the powerful. For example, Clovis, king of the Franks, requested that he recommend a **citharoedus,** that is, a singer who accompanied himself on a type of lyre known as the cithara (see Figs. 3.12 and 5.31). In search of such a musician, Cassiodorus turned to Boethius, who was in Rome at the time. His letter launches into a flowery discourse on the nature of music, which he describes as the "Queen of the senses." It continues with discussions of its curative powers, how David cast out the evil spirit from Saul, the nature of the modes, the structure of the Greek scale system, and the history of the art. It then turns to the lyre, which Cassiodorus calls "the loom of the Muses." After going off on more learned tangents, Cassiodorus finally makes his point. "We have indulged ourselves in a pleasant digression," he writes, making a classic understatement, "because it is always agreeable to talk of learning with the learned; but be sure to get us that Citharoedus, who will go forth like another Orpheus to charm the beast-like hearts of the Barbarians. You will thus obey us and render yourself famous."

CHURCH MUSIC

Knowledge about the church music of Ravenna is based on conjecture and must be gathered from a variety of sources. Church writings demonstrate that great importance was attached to music in connection with divine worship. The problem was how to create a proper body of church music out of the crude idioms of popular music on one hand and the highly developed but pagan art music of Rome on the other. From St. Paul and the Roman writer Pliny the Younger, in the first and second centuries, respectively, scholars once surmised that the earliest Christian music was directly adapted from the ancient Jewish singing of psalms. Recent research questions this sole source.

Nevertheless, a mix of Hebrew, Greek, and Latin sources must have provided the basis for Early Christian music, just as they had done for theology and the visual arts. Out of these diverse elements, along with original ideas of their own, the Christians of the Eastern and Western churches gradually worked out a synthesis that resulted in a musical art of great power and beauty. The sixth century witnessed the culmination of many early experimental phases. At its close, the Western form of the art consisted primarily of **plainsong** or **plainchant.** In its various changes and restorations, as well as in its theoretical aspects, this system remained the official basis of Roman Church music up to the Second Vatican Council, which ended in 1965. Closely related forms are still in use throughout the Christian world, where free adaptations of these melodies have enriched the hymn books and liturgies of nearly every denomination.

ARIAN LITURGY. Knowledge of the Arian liturgy, such as that practiced at Sant' Apollinare Nuovo during Theodoric's reign, is obscure because all sources were destroyed when the Orthodox Christians gained the upper hand and stamped out the Arian heresy. From a few negative comments, however, it is known that hymn and psalm singing by the congregation as a whole was included among Arian practices.

Arius, the founder of the Arian sect, was accused of insinuating his religious ideas into the minds of his followers by means of hymns sung to melodies derived from drinking songs and theatrical tunes. Such hymns were frowned upon because they were too closely allied with popular music. Moreover, the Arian way of singing them was described as loud and raucous, which must have grated on the sensitive ears of the devout Roman Christians.

AMBROSIAN LITURGY. The popularity of Arian musical practices helped the Arians make many converts. In the spirit of fighting fire with fire, St. Ambrose, bishop of Milan, where the Arians were strong, compromised by introducing hymn and psalm singing into the Milanese church service.

A firsthand account of this practice is contained in a passage from St. Augustine's *Confessions*. In the fourth century, when Bishop Ambrose was engaged in one of his many power plays and doctrinal disputes with Byzantine Empress Justina, he and his followers at one point had to barricade themselves in a church for protection. "The pious people kept guard in the church, prepared to die with their bishop," wrote St. Augustine. "At the same time," he continues, "it was here first instituted after the manner of the eastern churches, that hymns and psalms should be sung, lest the people should wax faint through the tediousness of sorrow: which custom being retained from that day to this, is still imitated by divers, yea, almost by all thy congregations throughout other parts of the world."

During the following century, the practice of hymn and psalm singing spread widely and was incorporated into the Roman Catholic liturgy. Because Ravenna was the neighboring see, or bishopric, to that of Milan, musical practices there may have been similar.

Some half-dozen hymns can be attributed to St. Ambrose. Whether he also composed the melodies is not as certain, but they date from his time. The example of *Aeterne Rerum Conditor* confirms the extreme simplicity and metrical regularity of these vigorous Ambrosian hymns, which made them especially suitable for congregational singing.

The psalms were sung either antiphonally or responsorially. When two choruses sing alternate verses, then join together in a refrain on the word *alleluia* after each verse, the practice is referred to as **antiphonal psalmody.** When the priest or leader chants one verse as a solo and the choirs perform the next verse as a choral response, it is called **responsorial psalmody.** Both practices were widespread in the Western church, including Ravenna.

BYZANTINE LITURGY. Because Sant' Apollinare Nuovo and San Vitale were designed for different congregations and liturgies, it follows that their music must also have differed. As part of the Byzantine liturgy, the music heard at San Vitale would have been like that of the cathedral in Constantinople. As in the West, congregational singing was included at first, as part of the offertory procession. When the procession was abandoned, congregational singing was gradually replaced by that of a professional choir. Music for congregational singing must always be kept relatively simple. By contrast, professional groups, which have special musical knowledge and rehearsal time, can explore and develop the art.

San Vitale, like Hagia Sophia, was under the direct patronage of the emperor, and because both formed a part of Justinian's grand design, provision for a group capable of performing the music of the Byzantine liturgy could hardly have been overlooked. The principal difference between the music of the Eastern and Western churches is that between a contemplative and an active attitude. The contemplative aspect of the Eastern liturgy is illustrated by a remark of St. John Chrysostom, who said, "One may also sing without voice, the mind resounding inwardly, for we sing not to men, but to God, who can hear our hearts and enter into the silences of the mind." This attitude contrasts strongly with that of St. Ambrose, who said, in connection with the congregation's participation in

Musical Example 5.1
Aeterne Rerum Conditor   (Hymn of St. Ambrose)

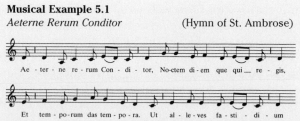

Ae - ter - ne re - rum Con - di - tor, No-ctem di - em que qui __ re - gis,

Et tem - po-rum das tem - po - ra. Ut al - le - ves fa - sti - di - um

song, "If you praise the Lord and do not sing, you do not utter a hymn. . . . A hymn, therefore, has these three things: song and praise and the Lord."

In a static form of worship, greater rhythmic freedom is possible, whereas the chant that accompanies a procession must have greater metrical regularity. The singing of a professional choir, moreover, implies an elaborate and highly developed art, whereas the practice of congregational singing avoids technical difficulties. The difference, then, is the difference between the sturdy Ambrosian **syllabic** hymn—that is, with a syllable allotted to each note—and the more elaborate **melismatic** alleluia of Byzantine origin—that is, with each single syllable prolonged over many notes in the manner of a **cadenza.**

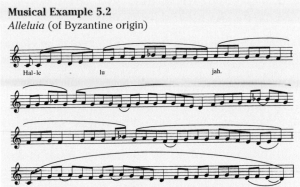

Musical Example 5.2
Alleluia (of Byzantine origin)

Byzantine music had a distinctive style, comparable in this respect to that of the visual arts. The elaborate melismas of Byzantine music would have been heard in San Vitale and other Byzantine churches at the end of the sixth century. It was these florid alleluias that were ruled out by the Gregorian reform that occurred in the early seventh century, which will be discussed later in this chapter.

ISLAMIC STYLE

In the early seventh century, a new dynamic force appeared on the horizon: *Islam,* an Arabic word signifying submission to the word of God. Born around 570, Mohammed, its founder, was a member of a merchant family in Mecca. At about age 40, he experienced a revelation indicating that he had been chosen by God to be the prophet of a new religion. Throughout his lifetime, he continued to receive such revelations, many of which were recorded after his death in the Koran. Written in clas-

sical Arabic, the Koran became the bible of Islam, and like the Bible itself, it became an influential book in world history. For the Islamic faithful, the Koran (Fig. 5.21) was literally the word of God as revealed through the Angel Gabriel to the Prophet Mohammed, who had been chosen as his messenger. It covered all aspects of life—religious, legal, political, social, and personal.

Mohammed held that Jews, Christians, and Arabs were descended from Abraham. He recognized Jesus, along with ancient prophets such as Moses and Isaiah, as authentic prophets and called himself the final prophet. However, he rejected the concept of the Trinity and hence the divinity of Christ. His belief is stated most succinctly in the motto, "There is no God but Allah, and Mohammed is his prophet." In the beginning there was considerable resistance from the then-polytheistic Arabs. Plots on Mohammed's life led him to journey (the famous *hegira*) to the city of Yathrib, which then was renamed Medina, meaning the city of the prophet. The year was 622, a date that later became the first year of the Islamic calendar.

Almost immediately after Mohammed's death, Islam spread with astonishing rapidity in both the

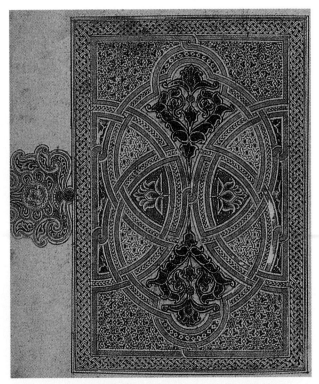

5.21   Illuminated page from Koran, by Ali ibn Hilal, known as Ibn al-Bawwab, Baghdad, Iraq, eleventh century. Paper, 6.9″ × 5.3″. Dublin, Chester Beatty Library, ms. 1431, folio 285 recto.

religious and the military senses. Arab armies swept eastward, capturing Palestine, Syria, Iraq, Persia, and other territories as far as the Indus valley in India. In the West, Egypt and all North Africa fell to them. They then occupied the island of Sicily and most of Spain. After crossing the Pyrenees Mountains in 732, they got as far as Poitiers in France, where they were defeated in a decisive battle by King Charles Martel, Charlemagne's grandfather. Recent research reveals that the Christians living in Islamic strongholds in southern Spain were enthralled with Arab intellectual accomplishments and their fine holdings of books.

To counter Islamic encroachments into Europe, the Normans (see Chapter 6) drove them out of southern Italy and Sicily in the eleventh century. This action was followed intermittently by Crusades that challenged the Islamic conquest of the Holy Land. For a brief time, a short-lived Kingdom of Jerusalem ruled. Thereafter, the city was reclaimed by the Muslims, who continued to besiege Constantine's Byzantine Empire until they finally captured Constantinople in 1453, renaming it Istanbul. In the end, Spain defeated the last Islamic stronghold in Granada in 1492. The rest of the territories in North Africa, the Near East, and Asia have remained dominantly Islamic to this day, except for the establishment of the Jewish state of Israel after World War II.

Islamic civilization sponsored advanced learning that included preserving and translating Greco-Roman treatises. These included the works of Aristotle, Euclid, Archimedes, and Ptolemy. Islamic thinkers covered the scholarly spectrum from astronomy, mathematics, chemistry, pharmacology, and surgery to philosophy and music. In the wake of the Crusades, European scholars found they had much to learn from their Muslim counterparts. Many traveled to Spain to read and translate various treatises into Latin for use in European universities. In mathematics, to cite one vital example, Arabic numerals quickly replaced their clumsy Roman equivalents. Soon Arabic numbers were adopted by merchants and bankers for their calculations; later they were accepted worldwide. Arabic scholars also introduced the concept of *zero*, an Arabic word, as well as such terms as *cypher, algebra, almanac,* and *zenith.*

THE DOME OF THE ROCK AND THE GREAT MOSQUE OF CORDOVA

The first major monument of Islam was the Dome of the Rock (Fig. 5.22A), located at the high point of Mount Moriah in Jerusalem. In Judaic tradition, this was the site where God commanded Abraham to sacrifice his only son, Isaac. At the last moment, Abraham's hand was stayed by an angel. Later the rock was enclosed in the sacred precincts of King Solomon's temple. For Muslims, this was the high point from which Mohammed rose on his fiery steed to make a night's journey into the heavens. The Dome of the Rock functioned as a visible political state-

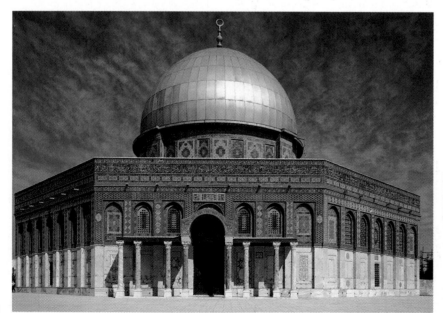

A

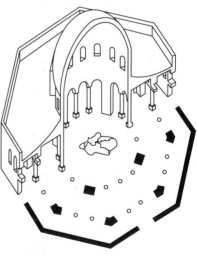

B

5.22 (A) The Dome of the Rock (Qubbat As-Sakhrah), Jerusalem, late seventh century. (B) Perspective of the Dome of the Rock.

ment that asserted Islamic control of the Holy Land. After Mecca and Medina, Jerusalem became the third most sacred site in Islam and a point of pilgrimage for the faithful.

Caliph Abd al-Malik built the structure, which was completed in 691; it has survived almost intact except for the exterior mosaics. At that early point in history there was no distinctive Islamic architectural style. Here, as elsewhere, Muslim buildings used familiar regional buildings as points of departure. Precedents could be found in the nearby church of the Holy Sepulchre and two edifices of Emperor Justinian's time: Sts. Sergius

and Bacchus in Constantinople and San Vitale in Ravenna (see pp. 128–129). Like the floor plans of these structures, the Dome of the Rock (Fig. 5.22B) is octagonal.

Because the Dome of the Rock was conceived of as a shrine rather than a mosque, no large space was needed for prayer and instruction. The interior is a domed rotunda with eight interior columns separating two ambulatories, while four inner pillars surrounding the rock rise to support the gilded wooden dome, which rests on a circular drum (Fig. 5.22B). The interior walls (Fig. 5.23) were decorated with mosaics and

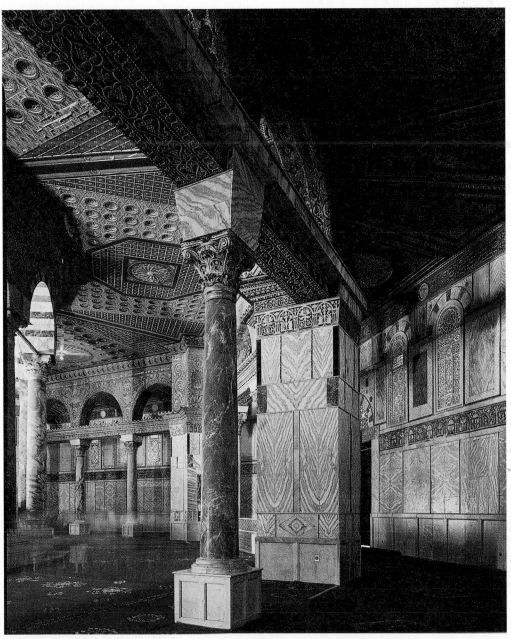

5.23   Interior of the Dome of the Rock. Note colored marble and filigree.

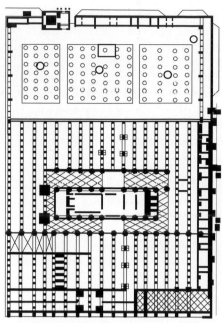

5.24 Plan of the Great Mosque of Cordova.

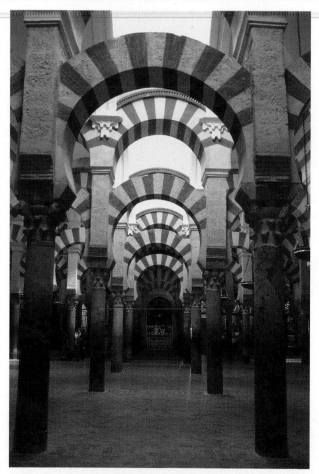

5.25 Interior of the Mosque of Córdoba, Spain, begun 786.

marble paneling. Since Mohammed accepted Moses's commandment forbidding graven images, this ruled out portraiture as well as naturalistic representation. Therefore, here as elsewhere, the decor is based on an infinite variety of geometric principles and ingenious abstract designs. The patterns in this case recall Roman acanthus scrolls and floral patterns similar to those of San Vitale (see Fig. 5.12). One interesting device was cutting slabs of marble in half so that the two halves seem to open like a book.

After the conquest of Spain in 785, Cordova was chosen as the site of a great mosque, which was steadily enlarged in succeeding centuries. The ground plan (Fig. 5.24) shows a large open central courtyard adjacent to a covered hall of prayer. Shapely columns crowned with carved gilded capitals support splendid polychrome arches with alternating red and white marble voussoirs (Fig. 5.25). At regular intervals quartets of columns are surmounted by low-rising cupolas that form the roof. When originally lighted by metallic lamps and with the floor covered with colorful carpets, the interior must have been even more awesome than it is today.

The Alhambra and the Taj Mahal

By the fifteenth century, the Islamic rulers in Spain were long past the peak of their power and Christians were gradually reclaiming various territories. One final note of beauty and grandeur, however, was sounded by the Alhambra Palace in the hills above Granada in southern Spain. The stark, fortresslike brick exterior conveys no outward promise of the dreamlike interior, with its exquisite courtyards set amid lush formal gardens (Fig. 5.26). The walls are faced with rhythmic patterns of abstract design in marble and stucco, and fountains and intricately devised waterways cool the courtyards and interior spaces.

One of the most celebrated buildings in the world—India's famed Taj Mahal—is also of Islamic origin (Fig. 5.27). Although shaped like a domed mosque with four surrounding minarets, it is actually a mausoleum begun in 1632 by the ruler Shah Jahan as a shrine to honor his beloved wife Mumtag-i-Mahal ("chosen one of the palace"). By inference, it is also a tribute to women. Nowhere is she portrayed, for that would have been a violation of Muslim law. Only in the serene and elegant proportions and

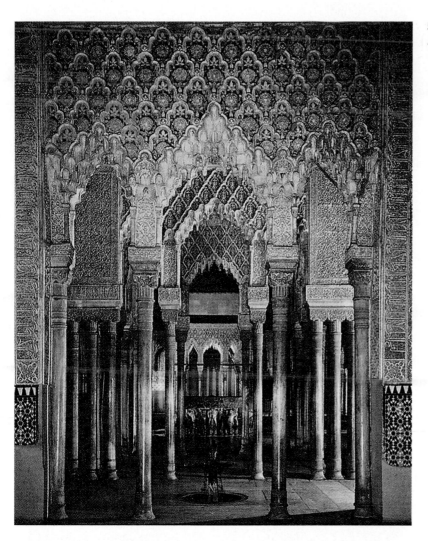

5.26 Court of the Lions, the Alhambra, Granada, Spain, 1343–1391.

5.27 Taj Mahal, Agra, India, 1631–1648.

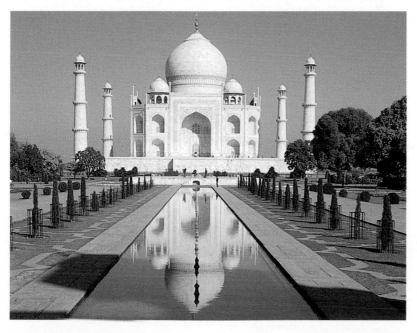

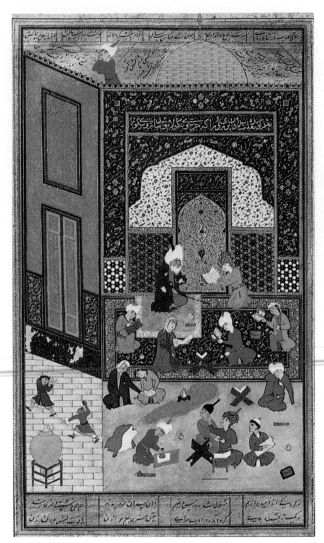

5.28 *Lalia and Majnun at School,* miniature from a manuscript of the *Khamsa of Nizami,* 1525. Ink, colors, and gold on paper. Metropolitan Museum of Art, New York.

abstract geometric decor could his love be expressed. Set in formal gardens on the banks of the Jumna River, the shapely central dome rises amid four smaller cupolas. The contours of this central dome allude to a Hindu symbol of femininity, a lotus bud rising from the water. It is the product of a team of architects, including the shah himself, who was later laid at her side. Symmetry abounds, with each of the four broader sides facing the points of the compass while combining with the four lesser sides to form an irregular octagon. The exterior is faced with mul-

ticolored marble and sandstone carved in stylized floral patterns, and the door frames quote verses from the Koran. The interior focuses on the tombs of the royal pair; the walls are carved with intricate abstract designs.

These major architectural masterpieces of Islamic art exist alongside a full range of other forms. Among them are manuscript illuminations (Fig. 5.28), drawings, paintings, carvings in ivory and wood, sculptural works for tombs, ceramic and glass objects, carpeting, textile designs, all manner of metal work, jewelry, and calligraphy. As for general decor in geometric and abstract designs, the very word *arabesque* points to a distinctive Islamic style.

IDEAS

All the surviving monuments of Early Christian art are oriented toward religion. Consequently, liturgical purposes, as well as patronage and geographic location, determine the forms of architecture, the iconography of mosaics, the designs of sculpture, and the performance practices of music.

The Early Christian and Byzantine styles were both Christian, and all the arts of the time lived, moved, and had their being within the all-embracing arms of the church. But the church's western and eastern arms pointed in different stylistic directions. The disintegration of Roman power in the West led to a decentralization of authority and allowed a wide range of local and regional styles, whereas the Byzantine emperors maintained tight autocratic control of all phases of secular and religious life. Early Christian art in the West was an expression of the people. It involved all social levels, its quality varied from crude to excellent, and it was simpler and more direct in its approach. Byzantine art, however, was under the personal patronage of a powerful and prosperous emperor who ruled as both a Caesar and a religious patriarch. Only the finest artists were employed, and the arts, like the vertical axis of a centralized church, directed attention to the highest level and tended to become further removed from the people and more purely symbolic.

Islamic art at first took on the local practices of the time and place where it developed. It later crystallized into a distinctive style of its own. As the arts of both West and East pass by in review, two ideas seem offer clues to their understanding: authoritarianism and mysticism.

AUTHORITARIANISM

Ravenna in the sixth century was the scene of a three-way struggle among a barbarian king who was a champion of Roman culture, a Byzantine emperor who claimed the prerogatives of the past golden age, and a Roman pope who had little military might but a powerful influence based on spiritual authority. Conflict arose from the clash among worldly liberalism, traditionalism based on a divinely ordered social system, and a new spiritual institution with a genius for compromise.

In the course of the century, the Ostrogothic kingdom was vanquished by the Byzantine Empire. However, after a brief period of domination, Byzantine power in the West crumbled and the political and military weakness that followed became the soil that nurtured the growth of the new Rome. By the end of the century, Gregory the Great had succeeded in establishing the papacy as the authority that would eventually dominate the medieval period in the West, whereas the Eastern Roman Empire continued in its traditional Byzantine forms of organization.

The principle of authority was by no means foreign to Christianity, which grew to maturity in the latter days of the Roman Empire. With Christianity an official state religion under the protection of the emperors, Christian organization increasingly reflected the authoritarian character of the imperial government. Theologians accepted the authority of the divinely inspired Scriptures and the commentaries on them by the early church fathers. The same is true in the world of Islam, where supreme authority was vested in the Koran.

Authoritarianism also colored the educational picture. Both Cassiodorus and Boethius were major classical scholars who served as officials in Theodoric's government. Both were key figures in the transition from Greco-Roman paganism to Christianity. Boethius was especially influential, with his lucid Latin translations of treatises such as Nichomachus's on arithmetic, Ptolemy's on astronomy, and Archimedes's on physics and mechanics. All became basic texts in the schools and universities of the Middle Ages. His translation and commentary on Aristotle's *Organon* were especially important and set the

tone for logical argumentation in succeeding centuries. His own *The Consolation of Philosophy* unfolds like a Platonic dialogue in prose and poetry. In it he seeks to reconcile capricious turns of fortune and misfortune with the benevolent role of Providence in human affairs.

Over the centuries, many Greek texts, including works of Plato and Aristotle, had been lost in the West. Islamic scholars, however, preserved them and made them available to intellectuals and universities in the later Middle Ages.

The thought of the period was expressed in constant quotations and interpretations of ancient Hebrew, Greek, Latin, and Early Christian authors. No one seemed willing or able to assume complete and independent authority for a position; on all issues one had to cite established sources. The intellectual climate this reliance on precedents produced eventually paved the way for a mighty future struggle for political and spiritual authority.

AUTHORITARIANISM AND THE ARTS. Justinian, who claimed the authority and semidivine status of the Roman emperors, lived in an atmosphere so unchanging and conservative that at his court the words *originality* and *innovation* were used as terms of reproach. Yet some variety and freedom were to be found in the arts, even though the art of both church and state was under the sole patronage of the emperor. It was thus remarkable that the flowering that produced Hagia Sophia in Constantinople and San Vitale in Ravenna could have taken place. In both of these instances, the methods of construction were experimental and the solution developed in response to the architectural and decorative problems seems unconstrained and bold.

The Byzantine concept of authority was embodied in the architectural and decorative plans of both Hagia Sophia and San Vitale. The central-plan church, with its sharp hierarchical, or ranked, divisions that set aside places for men and women, clergy and laity, aristocrat and commoner, was admirably suited to convey the principle of imperial authority. The vertical axis culminated in a dome that overwhelmed Byzantine subjects by reminding them of their humble place in the scheme of things. The august imperial portraits in the sanctuary showed them that, outside the clergy, only the emperor and empress and those who occupied the top rungs of the social ladder might approach the altar.

5.29 Exterior of apse, Sant' Apollinare in Classe, Ravenna, Italy, c. 530.

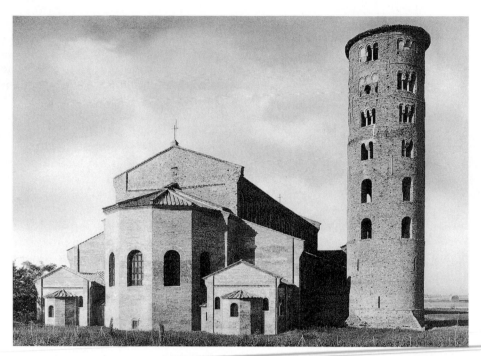

5.30 Interior of apse, Sant' Apollinare in Classe, Ravenna, Italy, c. 530.

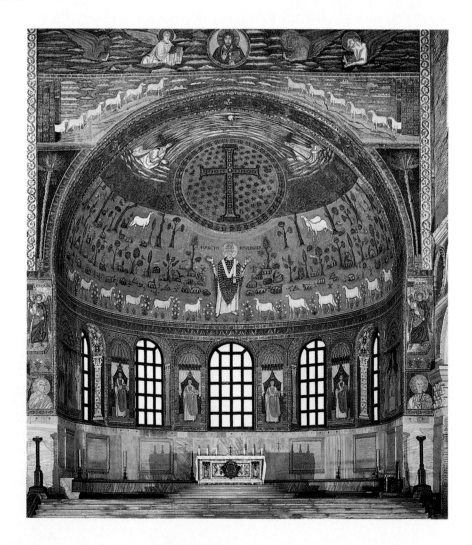

On the other hand, as typical forms of the basilica, Sant' Apollinare Nuovo and its companion, Sant' Apollinare in Classe (Figs. 5.29 and 5.30), indicated a contrasting conception of both God and humanity. As the twin rows of columns on either side of the nave marched forward, they carried the eyes of the faithful with them. The approach to the sacred precincts was encouraged rather than forbidden, and even the gift of the poor widow's pittance (Mark 12:41–42; Luke 21:2) was acknowledged in one of the mosaic panels.

MYSTICISM

The art of the sixth century in Ravenna, like that of other important centers such as Constantinople and Rome, marked the transition from classical Greco-Roman to the medieval world. Although some of the ancient grandeur remained, the accent on symbolism laid the foundation for the coming medieval styles. The physical was replaced by the psychical, the outer world of reality by the inner world of the spirit, and the rational road to knowledge by intuitive revelation.

A WORLD OF SYMBOLS. Many of the older art forms were carried over and reinterpreted in a new light. The Roman bathhouse became the Christian baptistry, where the soul was cleansed of original sin, and the public basilica was redesigned for church mysteries. Mosaics, formerly used for Hellenistic and Roman floors and pavements, became the mural medium for mystical visions. The shepherd of classical genre sculpture became symbolically the Good Shepherd. Classical bird and animal motifs became symbols for the soul and the spiritual realm. Music became a reflection of the divine unity of God and mortals, and the classical lyre, because of its stretched strings on a wooden frame, was reinterpreted by St. Augustine as a symbol of the crucified flesh of Christ. Orpheus, by means of the lyre's sounds, had descended into the underworld and overcome death. Christ as the new Orpheus is therefore often represented as playing a lyre (Fig. 5.31), and at Sant' Apollinare Nuovo, he is seated on a lyre-backed throne.

The concept of space turned from the classical three-dimensional representation of the natural world to an infinite Christian two-dimensional symbolic world. Invisible things rose in importance above those that could be seen, just as the mathematics of music was thought to surpass mere musical performance.

Whereas the classical mind regarded the world objectively from without, the Early Christian mind contemplated the soul subjectively from within. St. Augustine observed that "beauty cannot be beheld in any bodily matter." Such mystical visions were best represented through symbols. Natural science had been the foundation of ancient philosophy, but symbolic theology became the basis of Christian philosophy. Whereas Greek drama (which was a form of religious experience) had reached its climax step by step with remorseless logic, the Christian drama (as expressed in the liturgy) kindled the fires of faith and arrived at its mystical climax through suggestion and emotion. The denial of the flesh and the conviction that only the soul can be beautiful doomed the classical nude and exalted bodilessness. Instead of capturing and clothing the godlike image in flesh and blood, art now attempted to release the spirit from the bondage of the flesh. Similarly, Islam developed a complex symbolic language that permeates all its visual arts.

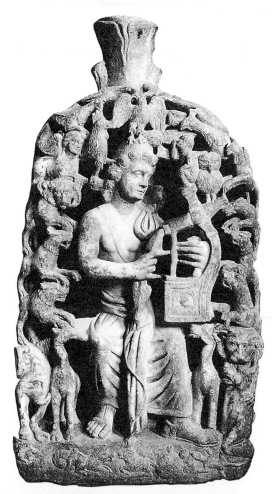

5.31 *Christ as Orpheus,* fourth century. Marble, height 3'4¼". Byzantine Museum, Athens, Greece.

Liturgy as the Embodiment of Mysticism. The liturgy was an all-inclusive medium shaped to convey the otherworldly vision. The thought, action, and sequence of rites in Constantinople, Ravenna, Rome, and other cultural centers shaped the architectural plans of churches, the symbolism of mosaics, and the forms of sculpture and music. Centuries of theoretical speculation united with the practical efforts of countless generations of writers, builders, decorators, and musicians to produce the Byzantine liturgy in the East and the synthesis of Gregory the Great in the West. Removed from its primary religious association and seen in a more detached aesthetic light, the liturgy as a work of art embodies a profound and dramatic insight into the deepest longings and highest aspirations of the human spirit.

The Early Christian and Byzantine styles were responses to the need for new verbal, visual, and auditory modes of expression. In both cases there was a shift from forms designed to represent this world to those capable of conjuring up otherworldly visions. In the church liturgy, through the poetry of language, the dancelike patterns of step and gesture, and the exalted melodies of the chant, the gripping drama of humanity was enacted in awe-inspiring theaters. These sacred theaters were furnished with an impressive array of stage settings, decor, costumes, and props created by the finest craftspeople and artists of the time. The liturgy is, moreover, a continuous pageant that unfolds in a sequence of solemn and joyful feasts throughout the year.

THE ROAD NORTHWARD

In the East, the Byzantine Empire, so powerful from the time of Constantine through that of Justinian, gradually began to crumble as various parts of it fell to the armies of Islam. In the West, after the fall of Ravenna and Rome, the center of gravity gradually shifted northward and a period once known as the Dark Ages descended on Europe. Time did not stop, of course, but the spread of Christianity was accompanied by struggle and strife among contending migratory tribes and local factions, which resulted in a power vacuum. One of the first lights to shine through the prevailing disorder was the kingdom of the Franks in the Rhine valley. The Franks, who later gave their name to the whole of France, were Christians faithful to the pope as bishop of Rome. They gradually took over much of the Roman system of government.

The riches of Ravenna and the fame of San Vitale reached the court of the Frankish king, Charles the Great, known to history as Charlemagne. During his prodigious lifetime, he conquered most of Western Europe, and in 800, he was crowned Holy Roman Emperor by the pope in St. Peter's Basilica. Thereafter, his eyes turned eastward, and he established more or less friendly relations with the Byzantine Empire. He even sent ambassadors by elephant as far afield as Baghdad, to the court of Harun-al-Rashid, the famed caliph of the *Arabian Nights*. In his capital city of Aachen (Aix-la-Chapelle), he built a sumptuous palace that included the Imperial Chapel, designed by Odo of Metz (Fig. 5.32), whose plan was based on the octagonal contours of San Vitale.

In addition to his military conquests and the building of palaces and churches, Charlemagne took pleasure in the company of scholars. His cultural center at Aachen was eventually nicknamed the "Ravenna of the North." He gathered around him some of the wisest and most eminent scholars from Italy, Ireland, and England. Among them was Alcuin of York, who came to Aachen to head Charlemagne's Palatine (that is, palace) School. Here he restored a purified form of Latin

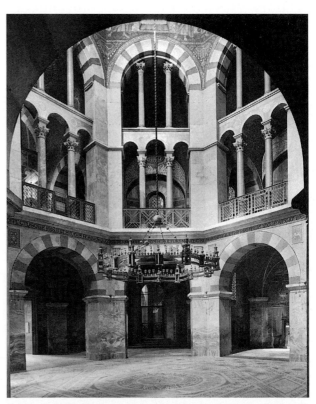

5.32   Capella Palatina (Charlemagne's Chapel), 792–805. Aachen (Aix-la-Chapelle), Germany.

as the primary literary language, systematized the curriculum, and promoted study of the liberal arts.

Charlemagne improved the education not only of the clergy but also of youth. He urged priests in every town to establish free schools for the children of the rich and poor alike. Christian doctrine, plainsong, and grammar were to be taught. Education in monastery and cathedral schools was more rigorous and elaborate, sometimes including the works of Cassiodorus (see p. 138) and Boethius (see p. 139). In effect, Charlemagne made Latin the language of an educated class that, like the Roman elite, was familiar with Roman bureaucratic structure and prepared to administer an empire. Like Rome, the Holy Roman Empire readily integrated non-Christian beliefs. For example, Christmas Day grew out of pagan German celebrations of midwinter and the lengthening of the daylight hours.

Aachen represents one kind of cultural hub, based on the centralization of political power, which in turn fostered education, book collecting, and the copying of ancient manuscripts. At the same time, another sort of cultural center had taken root in Ireland, a territory that was never directly under Roman rule. Christianity spread from England to Ireland in the fifth century. Unlike the religious scholars who were called to Aachen to study and teach, the Irish did not integrate religion and city life. Instead, they founded some of the earliest monasteries, that is, self-sufficient religious refuges isolated from worldly temptations. Their art developed in relative independence from Roman and Roman Christian traditions. Illuminated (that is, decorated) manuscripts like the *Book of Kells* (Fig. 5.33) stressed geometric intricacy and colorful abstraction rather than storytelling. However far removed they were from the Holy Roman Empire, the Irish were still

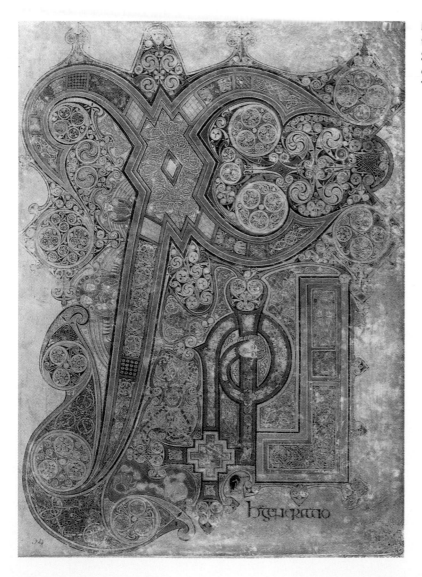

5.33 Chi-rho-iota page, folio 34 recto of the *Book of Kells,* probably from Iona, Scotland, late eighth or early ninth century. Tempera on vellum, 1′1″ × 9½″. Trinity College Library, Dublin, Ireland.

involved in continental European affairs. They had accepted the challenge of the pope to be missionaries to the Germanic tribes, and they visited the famous religious and scholarly facilities at Aachen.

Charlemagne's long and productive reign has gone down in history as the Carolingian Renaissance. It was more precisely a restoration of Greco-Roman learning and Roman authority rather than a movement that used the revival of traditional learning to chart new paths, as did the Italian Renaissance. Carolingian influence was felt not just in Germany but from the Baltic Sea to the Adriatic. Charlemagne's accomplishments, along with those of Otto the Great, who reigned as Holy Roman Emperor in the succeeding century, did much to pave the way for the future florescence of the Romanesque period.

YOUR RESOURCES

- *Exploring Humanities CD-ROM*

  ○ Interactive Map: Europe and the Near East in Late Antiquity

  ○ Architectural Basics: The Islamic Mosque

  ○ Reading—Einhard, *Life of Charlemagne*

  ○ Images—*Mosaic from Hagia Sophia, Mosaic from Justinian I*

- *Web Site*

  http://art.wadsworth.com/fleming10

  ○ Chapter 5 Quiz

  ○ Links

- *Audio CD*

  ○ *Hymn of St. Ambrose*

  ○ *Alleluia*

EARLY CHRISTIAN CENTURIES, ISLAM

Rome

Key Events	Architecture	Literature and Music
300 306–337 **Constantine,** emperor 313 **Edict of Milan** legalized Christianity 325 **First Council of Nicaea;** Arian heresy condemned c. 340–397 **St. Ambrose,** bishop of Milan from 374 402 **Rome** abandoned by Emperor Honorius as capital of the Western Roman Empire 410 **Visigoths** under Alaric sacked Rome 476 **Odoacer** conquered Italy; fall of the Western Roman Empire 590–604 **Gregory the Great** established papacy as political power **600**	c. 313 **Lateran Basilica** begun on site of present San Giovanni in Laterano c. 324–c. 333 **Old St. Peter's Basilica** begun on Vatican Hill c. 330–c. 350 **Tomb of Santa Costanza,** daughter of Constantine; later rededicated as a church 385 **San Paolo fuori le Mura** ("St. Paul's outside the Walls") **Basilica** built; destroyed by fire 1823 and rebuilt c. 432–c. 440 **Santa Maria Maggiore Basilica** begun	340–420 **St. Jerome;** translated Latin Vulgate Bible 354–430 **St. Augustine,** bishop of Hippo (North Africa); author of *Confessions* (c. 400), *City of God* (c. 412) c. 524 **Boethius** wrote authoritative treatise *De musica* c. 600 **Pope Gregory the Great** codified church liturgy and chant

Ravenna, Aachen

Key Events	Architecture	Literature and Music
360 c. 368 **Justina** becomes the second wife of Emperor Valentinian I 410 **Ravenna,** under Emperor Honorius, became capital of the Western Roman Empire 476 **Odoacer** conquered Ravenna; fall of the Western Roman Empire 476–493 **Odoacer** established Ostrogothic kingdom in Ravenna, also ruled Italy 493–526 **Theodoric the Great** reigned as king of Ostrogoths, also ruled the Western Roman Empire 523–540 **Cassiodorus** served as prime minister to Theodoric and successors 535 **Belisarius** invaded Italy in name of Emperor Justinian 546 **Maximian,** archbishop of Ravenna; ruled as Justinian's representative 732 **Charles Martel** defeated Muslims in battle of Tours and Poitiers, France 768–814 **Charlemagne** ruled at Aachen; Carolingian Period 781 **Charlemagne** established Palace School 792–805 **Odo of Metz** designed and built the Palatine Chapel for Charlemagne 800 **Charlemagne** crowned Holy Roman Emperor by **875** pope in Rome	c. 400–450 **"Neonian" Baptistry** for Roman Christians c. 425 **Mausoleum of Galla Placidia** 493 **Church of Sant' Apollinare Nuovo** begun c. 520 **"Arian" Baptistry** c. 526 **Mausoleum of Theodoric** built c. 527 **Church of San Vitale** begun at Ravenna 547 **San Vitale** completed c. 549 **Church of Sant' Apollinare** in Classe completed 556 **Ivory throne of Maximian** finished at Ravenna c. 792–800 **Centula monastery** built by Charlemagne c. 796–804 **Palatine Chapel** at Aachen built by Charlemagne	c. 386 **Bishop Ambrose of Milan** arranged hymns and psalms for congregational singing; body of choral music, Ambrosian chant (plainsong), is attributed to him 524 **Boethius** wrote *Consolation of Philosophy* c. 540 **Cassiodorus** founded monastery at Vivarium, Italy, for preserving and copying manuscripts, wrote *History of Goths* 560–636 **Isidore of Seville** collected Greek and Latin writings 730 **Venerable Bede** wrote *Historia Ecclesiastica Gentis Anglorum* (Ecclesiastic History of the English People) 735–804 **Alcuin of York;** from 782 active at Charlemagne's court c. 750 **Organs** powered by wind replaced water organs 760 **Book of Kells** (Latin Gospels) illuminated in Ireland 790 **Schools for Church music** founded at Paris, Cologne, Soisson, and Metz 870 *Musica enchiriadis,* a treatise using Latin letters for musical notation

Byzantium (Constantinople)

Key Events	Architecture	Literature and Music
320 c. 324–330 **Constantine** made Byzantium capital of the Eastern Roman Empire 325 **First Council of Nicaea** 518–527 **Justin,** Eastern Roman emperor 527–565 **Justinian the Great,** Eastern Roman emperor **570** 570–632 **Mohammed**	c. 527 **Church of Sts. Sergius and Bacchus** begun 532–537 **Church of Hagia Sophia** built by architects Anthemius of Tralles and Isidorus of Miletus	329–379 **St. Basil,** bishop of Caesarea and liturgist of Eastern Orthodox Church c. 345–407 **St. John Chrysostom,** patriarch of Constantinople and liturgist of Eastern Orthodox Church 529 **Justinian** issued Code of Civil Law c. 564 **Byzantine historian Procopius** died

Islam

Key Events	Architecture	Literature and Music
600 622 **Hegira,** Mohammed's flight to Yathrib, renamed Medina (city of the prophet) 622 **Year 1** of Islamic calendar 630 **Mecca conquered,** becomes religious center of Islam, Koran (Quran) begins to be compiled 732 **Charles Martel** defeated Muslims in Battle of Tours, France c. 750 **Islamic empire** spread from Asia Minor to North Africa, Spain **1654**	691 **Dome of the Rock** begun at Jerusalem 705 **Mosque at Damascus** begun 785 **Mosque at Cordova** begun 1309–1354 **Alhambra Palace** built at Granada, Spain 1631–1648 **Taj Mahal** built at Agra, India	

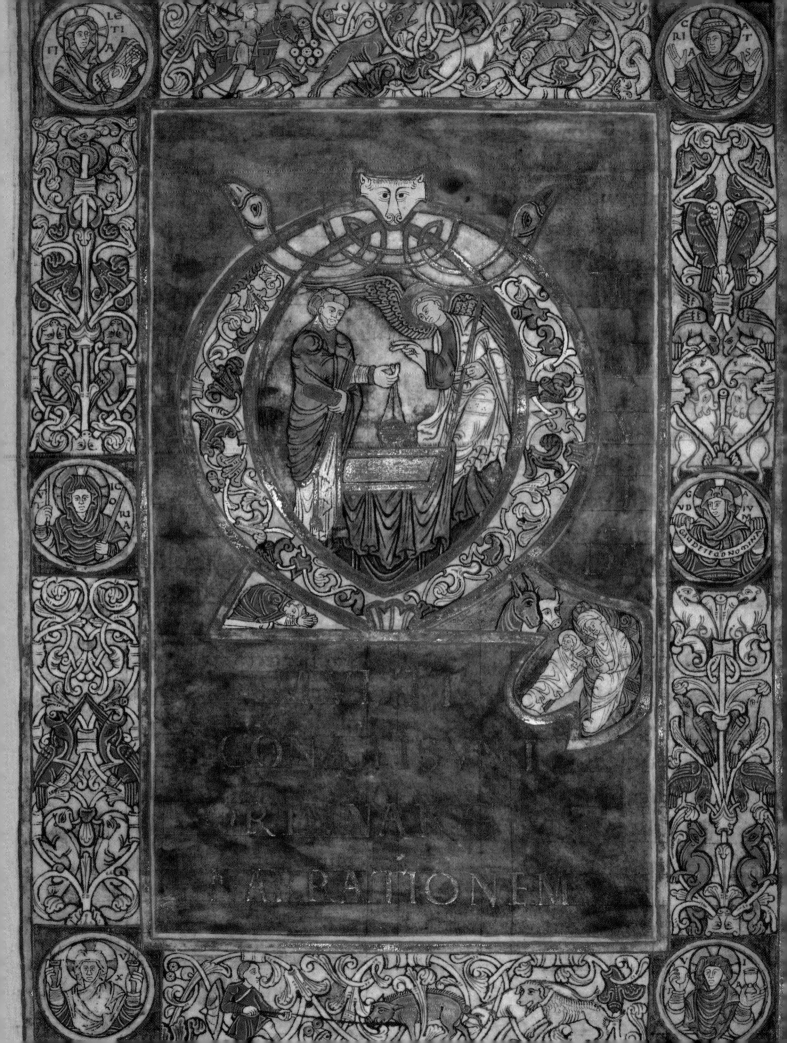

CHAPTER

ROMANESQUE STYLE

As CHRISTIANITY SPREAD NORTHWARD AFTER the fall of the Western Roman Empire, southern classical forms met and merged with those of the northern barbarian peoples. The older, settled, newly Christianized Roman civilization, with its notions of centralized power, literacy, and organization, confronted various tribes whose migratory ways had changed to semisettled lives on the fringes of the old Roman Empire. These so-called barbarians had greater allegiance to local leaders and family affiliations than to centralized governments. Owing to their migratory customs, their art was necessarily small and portable.

Although the Roman Empire had collapsed, the Church of Rome did not. In fact, it expanded beyond the boundaries of the Roman world, bringing with it an international organization, the increased authority of the pope, and a transnational identity for believers. Indeed, in Europe the church called itself "Catholic," which means universal, in direct contrast with both the Eastern Church, centered in Constantinople, and with Islam, which was spreading in the Holy Land and North Africa.

The most significant cultural centers of the Romanesque period were the monastery and the castle. One was a refuge and sanctuary where life was a prelude to a heavenly hereafter; the other was a fortress concerned mainly with security and survival in the troubled world of the here and now. The monastic way of life dated from the Early Christian period, when hermits and groups of religious men and women rejected worldly temptations to live simply in out-of-the-way or inhospitable places. In the sixth century, after Cassiodorus had served in Theodoric's Ostrogothic kingdom, he retired to his country estate at Vivarium, where he founded a monastery that was noted for preserving and copying classical and Christian manuscripts (see p. 139). The basic rules of monasticism, codified by St. Benedict, were widely accepted by the seventh century. The movement gradually gained momentum and eventually reached its climax in Romanesque times, and with it came the development of a typical style that reached maturity between the years 1000 and 1150. The spread of cultural centers in the form of widely scattered monastic communities lent a peculiar intensity and wide variety to the expressive forms of the Romanesque.

Lacking the security of strong central governments and not having the advantages of flourishing cities and towns, the monastic movement sought peace of mind in the abbey or monastery as a haven from the prevailing chaotic social surroundings. These centers off the beaten path were miniature worlds that contained a cross section of Romanesque life. Besides serving as religious shrines where pilgrims could gather to revere sacred relics, monasteries were the manufacturing and agricultural centers of their regions, as well as seats of learning and the places where the only libraries, schools, and hospitals of the time were to be found. Like cultural centers before them, monasteries preserved learning while inventing new forms of architecture, sculpture, and music.

SOCIAL STRUCTURE

The social structure of Romanesque society was built upon the strict hierarchical principle of feudalism. Under feudalism, every person was presumed to have a predetermined status, based primarily on the circumstances of his or her birth and only partially on individual ability. A key feature of feudalism was *primogeniture,* in which the firstborn son inherited all the family's property to prevent land from being subdivided over the generations. Younger brothers of the heir usually had just two choices: to carve out careers in the church or to enlist as soldiers of fortune.

The lives of noble and wealthy women were shaped by their families' economic and political positions. Their marriages were arranged to the best advantage of their families, and their primary duty was to bear children. If unmarried, they could stay in the family household as dependents, reside in nunneries as paying guests, or join the ranks of nuns. Convents provided women access to education as well as other intellectual and artistic pursuits. By contrast, peasant women and women living in towns entered marriages that were understood to be economic partnerships. They were freer than the rich to choose mates, and they appear to have made more mutual decisions about family assets and businesses.

Despite legal and conventional restrictions, women were involved in a surprisingly large number of enterprises. Wealthy women administered large estates when their husbands departed, often for a decade, to fight in the Crusades. Charlemagne attempted to provide universal schooling (see p. 151) to educate boys and girls using the same curricula. Some women, usually those whose parents could spare them from household duties, went on to advanced training in the liberal arts. Convent life also encouraged teaching and learning. Secular and religious women routinely tutored children. Occasionally a townswoman worked as a full-time professional artist, but nuns were more commonly employed to copy and illuminate books. Similarly, although there were professional women musicians (see Hildegard of Bingen and the Countess de Dia, later in this chapter), most were amateurs whose achievements rose above the routine requirements of their education. Crafts such as embroidery cut across class lines. Textile- and carpet-making were family businesses in which women excelled. Rarely, as in the case of ribbon-makers living in French cities like Paris, women founded their own guilds.

The Romanesque economy was based primarily on agriculture, which made possession of land all-important. At the bottom of the social ladder were the serfs, who did most of the hard labor on the land. Technically they were not slaves, but most were tied to the soil. In the system of feudal loyalties, the serfs were responsible to tenant farmers, who rented land from the lord of the manor. He, in turn, was beholden to a regional baron, duke, or leader, whose territories were allotted him by the king. In church circles, the chain of command rose from curate or chaplain to parish priest, bishop, archbishop, and pope. In the monastery, individual monks owed allegiance to their priors or abbots, who in turn reported to the pope. Over all of them was the all-embracing figure of God the Father.

THE ROMANESQUE WORLDVIEW

During the Romanesque period, the figure of Christ changed from the Good Shepherd of Early Christian times (see Figs. 5.1 and 5.4) to a mighty king, crowned and enthroned in the midst of his heavenly courtiers and sitting in judgment on the entire world. At the French cathedral of Saint-Lazare in Autun, the **tympanum** (a half-moon-shaped space over a door) displays a chilling Last Judgment scene (Fig. 6.1). Souls are weighed and then either sent to heaven, at Christ's right hand, or thrown into hell by snarling devils, on his left. Chiseled along the bar that separates the souls of the dead from the judgment scene are words that threaten sinners with hell in the afterlife. On the same bar, the name of the tympanum's sculptor, Giselbertus, proclaims

6.1 Gislebertus. *Last Judgment,* west tympanum of Saint-Lazare, Autun, France, Autun Cathedral, c. 1130–1135. Marble, approx. 21′ wide at base.

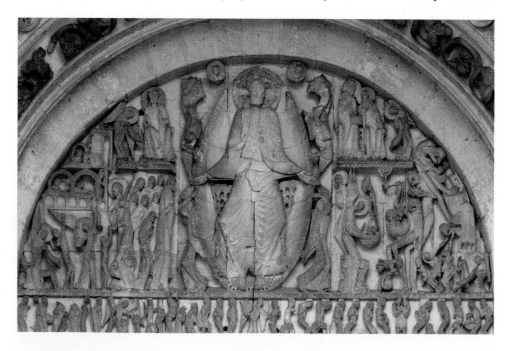

that he made the work, an unusual public assertion of artistic identity in a period when knowing one's place was paramount.

In the Romanesque worldview, all life had to be brought into an organized plan that would conform to the cosmic scheme of things. The stream of authority, descending from Christ through Peter to his papal successors, flowed out from Rome. The Holy Roman emperor received his crown from the hands of the pope; in turn, all the kings of the Western world owed him homage, as did everyone below them, from the great lords to the humblest serfs, for all had a preordained place in the great cosmic plan.

This hierarchical principle, moreover, applied not only to the social and ecclesiastical levels but also to basic thought processes. Authority for all things rested firmly in the Scriptures and interpretations of them by the early church fathers. Scholarship consisted not so much in exploring new intellectual paths as in interpreting traditional sources. For the educated, this process took the form of learned commentaries; for the uneducated, it was expressed in the cult of relics. In the arts, this veneration of the past made mandatory the continuance of such traditional forms as the Early Roman Christian basilica and the music of the plainchant.

Another key feature of the Romanesque period was the religious pilgrimage. In the broad band at the bottom of the tympanum at Autun (Fig. 6.1) are two figures on the viewer's left carrying walking staffs. They are well-traveled pilgrims (see Map 6.1 for pilgrimage routes). One has a seashell badge, symbolizing that he has visited Santiago de Compostela, and the other has a cross, signifying that he has been to Jerusalem. Thousands traveled the dusty pilgrimage roads across France to Spain to touch the revered tomb of the Apostle James at Compostela. Fewer went to Jerusalem, but that number increased in the late eleventh century with the beginning of the Crusades (see later discussion).

RELIGIOUS ROMANESQUE

The largest and grandest of all Romanesque monasteries, the abbey at Cluny, was also a major cultural center. Its appearance at the pinnacle of its

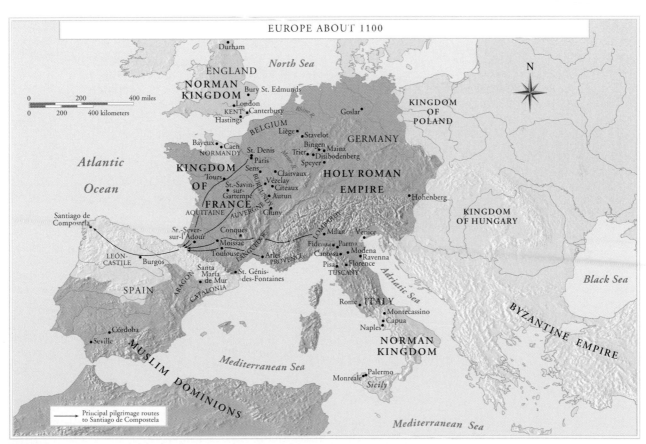

MAP 6.1

power and fame has been reconstructed in Figure 6.2. The world within these walls was populated principally by professed monks devoted to prayer and contemplation. It also housed some world-weary men of action who sought to escape life in the unsettled society outside the abbey's precincts.

By taking the triple vows of poverty, chastity, and obedience, the monk renounced such worldly pursuits as individual material rewards, the pleasures of the senses, the personal satisfactions of family life, and even the exercise of his own free will. According to the Rule of St. Benedict, the founder of Western European monasticism, a monk "should have absolutely not anything; neither a book, nor tablets, nor a pen—nothing at all . . . it is not allowed to the monks to have their own bodies or wills in their power."

To provide such a life, a monastery had to be planned such that the monks would have all that was necessary for both their bodily sustenance and their spiritual nourishment. The Benedictine Rule did not prescribe the exact form that a monastic building should take, and nominally each abbey was free to solve its problems according to its needs, the contours of its site, and the extent of its resources. But tradition often operated as rigidly as rules, and most monasteries followed a common pattern with local variations. If one allows for its exceptional size and complexity due to its status as mother house of a great order, the plan of Cluny can be accepted as reasonably typical.

Because the life of a monk was one of almost continuous religious duties alternating with periods of prayer and meditation, the soul of the

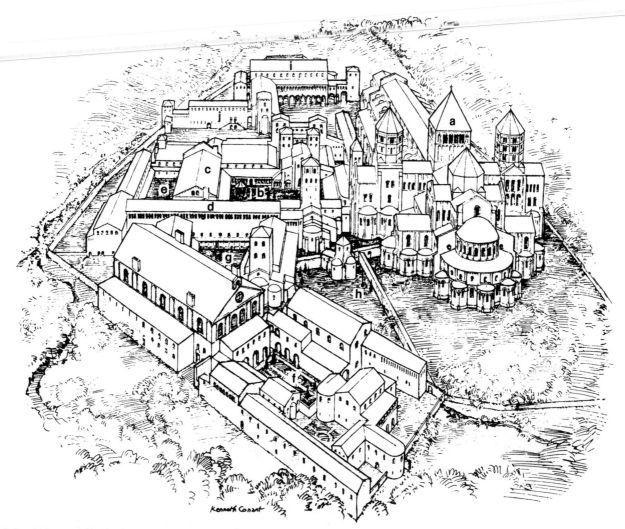

6.2 Abbey of Cluny, from southeast, c. 1157. Reconstruction by Kenneth J. Conant. Third Abbey Church, with lantern tower over crossing of nave and major transept (a); Cloister of Pontius, main cloister (b); refectory (c); monks' dormitory (d); novices' cloister (e); visitors' cloister (f); Cloister of Notre Dame (g); monks' cemetery (h); hospice (i); craftspeople's quarters and stables (j).

monastery was in its abbey church, and its heart was in its cloister. The church at Cluny, the largest in Europe, served primarily as the scene of the constant devotional activities of the monks day and night throughout the year. Only secondarily was it a shrine for the streams of pilgrims who arrived from near and far to revere relics of saints.

Cluny was rich in such relics, and on feast days of the saints, pilgrims flocked there as they did to other famous shrines, such as that of the Apostle James at Santiago de Compostela in Spain. European pilgrimage routes were traveled mainly by foot. **Hospices** (guesthouses) or inns at 20-mile intervals provided places where travelers could eat and sleep after a day's journey. Pilgrims from England had to cross the English Channel. Those from Germany traveled south by way of the Alpine passes. Pilgrims to the Holy Land went by ship from Genoa, Venice, or Sicily, with stops at Cyprus, Constantinople, or Rhodes.

Next in importance to facilities for church services was provision for the contemplative life, which centered on the cloister. Typically, a cloister was found in the center of the abbey, south of the nave of the church. The other monastic buildings clustered around it. The usual cloister was an open quadrangular garden plot enclosed by a covered arcade on all four sides. The somewhat irregular shape of the cloister at Cluny in the twelfth century resulted from the ambitious building program required by the monastery's rapid growth. Because this renowned marble-columned cloister no longer exists, the one at St. Trophîme at Arles will serve as an example (Fig. 6.3).

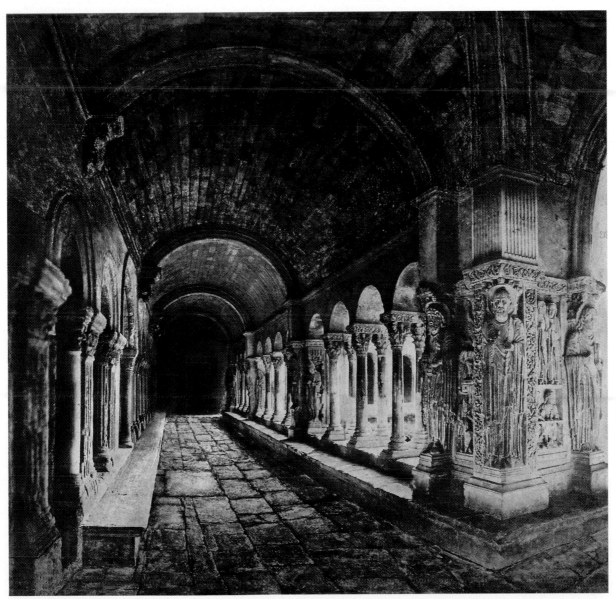

6.3 Cloister, Abbey of St. Trophîme, Arles, France, c. 1100.

A complete abbey like the one at Cluny had to provide for many functions in addition to worship and meditation. The daily life of the monks demanded a refectory, or dining room, where they could eat their meals, plus kitchens, bakeries, and storage space. Abbeys also provided a chapter hall, where they could transact their communal business, and a dormitory adjacent to the church, because services were held during the night as well as by day. Three small cloisters were included: one for the education of novices (young future members of the order); another for visiting monks and religiously inclined laymen who sought refuge from the world; and a third, near a cemetery, for aged and infirm brothers. The hospice provided accommodations for visitors, who flocked in during the pilgrimage season. There were also quarters for blacksmiths, carpenters, cobblers, and the like, as well as stables for dairy cattle and other domestic animals. Such monasteries also held large tracts of land, including forests that provided building material and wood for heat. Some of the soil was worked by the monks themselves, whereas other tracts were rented to tenant farmers.

The plan of the abbey at Cluny was a coherent system of adjoining quadrangles that embraced courts and cloisters whose variation in size and importance accommodated the differing activities they were designed to serve. Altogether, it was a highly complex yet logical plan for a complete community. It took into account the ideals, aspirations, practices, and everyday activities of a group that gathered to work physically and spiritually toward a common end.

ARCHITECTURE

Hugh of Semur, the greatest of the Cluniac abbots, succeeded to his position in 1049. Under him, Cluny attained a period of such splendor that it was described by an enthusiastic chronicler as "shining on the earth like a second sun." Taking as his model the accepted feudal organization of society, in which smaller and more dependent landowners swore allegiance to the larger and more powerful landlords in return for protection, Hugh brought many of the traditionally independent Benedictine monasteries into the Cluniac orbit. With the express approval of the popes, Hugh gradually concentrated the power of the whole order in his hands and transformed Cluny into a vast monastic empire that extended from Scotland in the north to Portugal in the west,

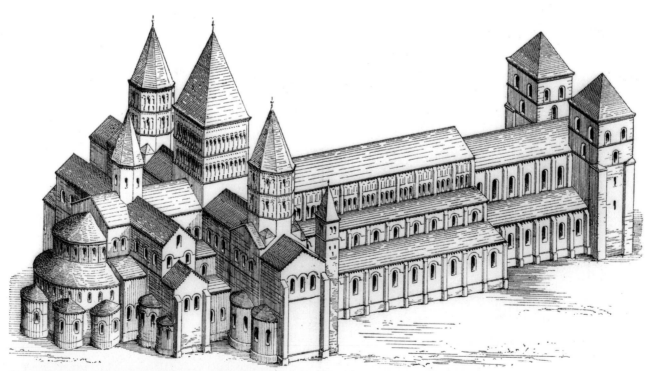

6.4   Reconstruction of the third church of Abbey at Cluny, view from the northeast, c. 1120.

Jerusalem in the east, and Rome in the south. In the church hierarchy, he was outranked only by the pope. In the secular world, he was the peer of kings. Like the feudal nobles, the monastery at Cluny amassed a vast fortune, making it influential in the worldly affairs it had originally renounced. Indeed, the church was probably the biggest landowner in Europe, owing in part to generous bequests and in part to the fact that the clergy's higher ranks were increasingly populated by wealthy individuals who brought wealth and influence with them.

Cluny figured prominently in the historical events of the day. For example, Hugh acted as an intermediary between an emperor and a pope on the famous occasion when Henry IV came to Canossa in Italy to beseech Gregory VII for forgiveness. Hugh's greatest moment, however, came when Pope Urban II, who had received training as a monk at Cluny under Hugh's personal guidance, was present to dedicate the high altar of his great new abbey church. Honor after honor was bestowed on the monastery by this Cluniac pope.

THE THIRD ABBEY CHURCH AT CLUNY. With such a rapidly expanding monastic order, Hugh had to undertake a massive building program. The ever-increasing number of Cluniac monks and the growing importance of Cluny as a pilgrimage center made the older second church inadequate. To rival the legendary temple of Solomon and eclipse all other churches in Western Christendom, Hugh and the monk Hezelo, whom some believe was the architect for the project, began the immense Third Abbey Church. It became the largest church in Christendom.

In contrast to the Early Christian basilicas, Romanesque abbey churches show remarkable extensions before and beyond the nave (Fig. 6.4). The three-aisled narthex entrance grew to the size of a large church. It was, in fact, called variously the "church of the pilgrims" and the "minor nave." Besides accommodating visitors, the narthex was the assembly place for the clergy who marched in the grand processions on high holidays, such as feast days of saints.

The spacious five-aisled nave allowed pilgrims and townspeople to gather for religious services, whereas the space beyond was expanded for the large monastic community. Instead of a single transept, there were now two. Extending outward from both the major and minor transepts were chapels dedicated to various saints, each the size of a small church. In addition, the apse was enlarged to accommodate the huge high altar, and an **ambulatory,** or passage for pilgrims and processions, was provided to reach the **apsidal chapels** that radiated outward from the apse. An exterior view of the apsidals is shown in Figure 6.5.

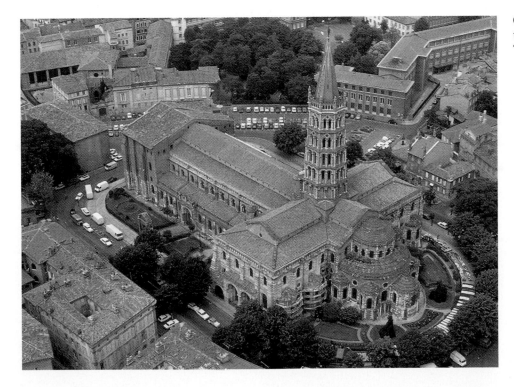

6.5 Aerial view from the southeast, St. Sernin, Toulouse, France, c. 1080.

On entering the nave (Fig. 6.6), one noticed at once the mighty proportions of the huge basilica. The entire horizontal axis from front to back, including the narthex, reached an overall length of 615 feet. The nave itself had eleven **bays,** or arched units, between the supporting columns. Each bay was separated by a group of columns clustered around supporting piers.

Early Christian basilicas were horizontally directed, whereas Romanesque churches had a more vertical emphasis. Gradually the vertical space increased, creating new areas for architectural innovation and decoration. At Cluny, a double row of windows above the nave served as the clerestory for illumination.

The nave at Cluny was spanned by ribbed barrel vaults, 32 feet wide, supported by slightly pointed arches. Rising a full 98 feet above the pavement, the vaults were the highest that had been achieved up to this time. Sadly, the emotional drive to achieve height outran the engineering knowledge needed to maintain it, and a part of the Cluny vaulting soon collapsed. Out of this accident came experimentation with **buttressing,** or external supports. When the vaults were rebuilt, a range of buttresses with open round arches was placed outside. With its high nave vaults supported by external buttressing and its pointed arches, the great abbey church at Cluny set the stage for future Gothic cathedrals, which would bring these features into a unified, systematic whole.

The decorative plan of the church was carried out on a scale comparable in quality to the grandeur of its spatial dimensions. More than 1,200 sculptured capitals surmounted the columns of the structure, and carved moldings outlined the graceful pointed arches of the nave arcade. Most of the sculpture was painted in rich colors that gave an added glow to the splendor of the interior, and mosaic floors inlaid with images of saints and angels or with abstract designs paved the entire church.

All this magnificence did not go unchallenged. St. Bernard, a vigorous opponent of the Cluniac order, disapproved violently of such extravagances. By expressing his disapproval in writing, he inadvertently left a firsthand account of the glory of Hugh's church soon after it was finished. In a letter to one of the Cluniac abbots, Bernard deplored (with Cluny in mind) "the vast height of your churches, their immoderate length, their superfluous breadth, the costly polishings, the curious carvings and paintings which attract the worshiper's gaze and hinder his attentions." His feeling was that "at the very sight of these costly yet marvelous vanities men are more kindled to offer gifts than to pray. . . . Hence the church is adorned with gemmed crowns of light—nay, with lustres like cart-wheels, girt all round with lamps, but no less brilliant with precious stones that stud them. Moreover we see candelabra standing like trees of massive bronze, fashioned with marvelous subtlety of art, and glistening no less brightly with gems than with the lights they carry. What, think you, is the purpose of all this? The compunction of penitents, or the admiration of beholders?"

Cluny Abbey stood proudly until the tumultuous years following the French Revolution, when a wave of anticlericalism led to the sacking and burning of the abbey. In 1809, most of the buildings, except for a single transept wing, were blown up by gunpowder, and the rubble was sold as common building stone. Some sculptural fragments survive, and the spirit of the great monastery lives on in the influence it exerted on related structures, such as St. Trophîme at Arles (Fig. 6.3), St. Sernin in Toulouse (Fig. 6.5), and La Madeleine at Vézelay (Figs. 6.7, 6.8, and 6.9).

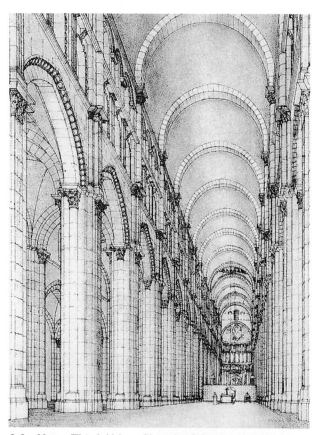

6.6 Nave, Third Abbey Church of Cluny, 1088–1130. Reconstruction by Kenneth J. Conant.

SCULPTURE AT VÉZELAY

Some of the first sculpture dating from the period of Cluny's grandeur is found in the abbey church of La Madeleine at Vézelay. The nave and narthex are contemporary with Hugh's church at Cluny, and restoration in the nineteenth century by the French archeologist Viollet-le-Duc accounts for their present good condition. Although its proportions are considerably smaller than those of the great basilica at Cluny, La Madeleine today is the largest Romanesque abbey church in France. Rich in historical associations, in medieval times it attained its principal fame as the repository of the relics of St. Mary Magdalene. Of chief interest at Vézelay, however, is its wealth of sculptured capitals. Unlike the statuary of antiquity, which was made of marble or bronze, French Romanesque capitals were usually of soft sandstone and limestone. The plasticity of these materials responded more quickly to the imaginative demands made on them than a harder stone could have. Above all, the relief compositions over the three internal portals leading from the narthex into the nave and side aisles illustrate the historical and symbolic significance of La Madeleine. Here Pope Urban II proposed to launch the First Crusade. Bernard of Clairvaux urged a Second Crusade here. The Third Crusade, launched by Richard the Lionhearted of England in conjunction with King Philip Augustus of France, set out from Vézelay in 1190.

Unlike the plain exteriors of Byzantine churches (see pp. 122 and 129), important sections of Romanesque churches were decorated with sculpture. A visitor entering the main door of the narthex of La Madeleine could look up at the tympanum and its surrounding **archivolts,** the series of arches that frames the tympanum, and be visually reminded of the power of Christ and of the church's long association with the Crusades.

THE TYMPANUM. The splendid semicircular tympanum over the central portal of the narthex at Vézelay (Fig. 6.7) dates from the first quarter of the twelfth century. Here as elsewhere, Romanesque designers and sculptors looked for their subjects in the drawings and miniature paintings that illustrated the texts of the Scriptures in monastic libraries. Such illuminated manuscripts provided convenient models that the monks could show to the sculptors who were to carry out the projects. At Vézelay, the robes of Christ and the apostles reveal a pattern of clear, sharp, swirling lines that derive from pen drawings in manuscripts of the time.

The interpretation and iconography of the tympanum scene may be discovered in the vision of St. John as recorded in Revelation (22:1–2):

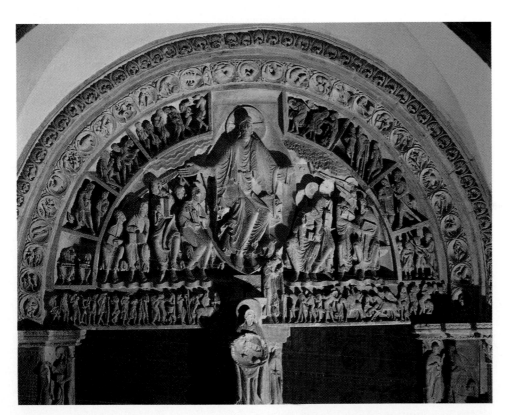

6.7 Tympanum of the center portal of the narthex, La Madeleine, Vézelay, France, c. 1120–1132.

"And he showed me a pure river of water of life, clear as crystal, proceeding out of the throne of God and of the Lamb. In the midst of the street of it, and on either side of the river, was there the tree of life, which bare twelve manner of fruits, and yielded her fruit every month: and the leaves of the tree were for the healing of the nations."

The figure of Christ dominates the composition; he is seated, as St. John says, on "a great white throne," but not so much to judge mortals as to redeem them. The streams issuing from his fingers descend on the barefoot apostles, who bring spiritual understanding through the books they hold and physical healing through the divine mercy they transmit to humanity. On one side of Christ's head, the water referred to in the quotation flows forth, whereas on the other are the branches of the tree. The mission of the apostles to convert heathens would also have been read by visitors as a reference to the goal of the Crusades to capture the Holy Land.

The Crusades and the mission of the apostles are also alluded to in the eight compartments of the archivolts surrounding the tympanum. At the top left, next to the head of Christ, appear two strange dog-headed men, whom the Spanish scholar Isidore of Seville, in his *Etymologies,* called the "Cynocephaloi," a tribe that was supposed to have inhabited India. The corresponding compartment on the right side shows the crippled and bent figure of a man and that of a blind woman taking a few halting steps as she is led forward. The other compartments depict the lame supported on crutches, along with lepers who point toward their sores.

Along the lintel below, a parade of the nations converges toward the center. Among these peoples who populate the remote regions of the Earth are a man and woman (in the far right corner) with enormous ears and feathered bodies. Next to them is a group of dwarfs or pygmies so small that they have to mount a horse by means of a ladder. On the far left, half-naked people hunt with bows and arrows, and toward the left center some heathens are shown leading a bull to sacrifice.

The Archivolts. The twelve fruits, one for each month of the year, are found among the twenty-nine medallions in the middle band of archivolts. A figure treading grapes, for example, represents September; October is symbolized by a man gathering acorns for his pigs. The months themselves, besides being connected with such labors, are symbolized by the signs of the zodiac, which were intended to remind Christians of the very limited time they have in which to attain salvation. A few

of the other medallions picture strange beasts taken from **bestiaries,** books that recounted lore about animals, both actual and fabulous. A survival from antiquity can be noted in the medallion (lower right) that depicts a centaur.

Capitals. At Vézelay, the imaginative scope displayed in the abundance of sculptured capitals is breathtaking. Biblical scenes, incidents from the lives of the saints, allegorical commentaries, and the play of pure fantasy are found throughout the narthex and the nave. One of the capitals shows the angel of death striking down the eldest son of Pharaoh (Fig. 6.8). Another shows a bearded figure pouring grain into a hand mill being turned by a barefoot man (Fig. 6.9). The real meaning of this scene would be lost to posterity were it not for a chance remark in the writings of Suger, the abbot of St. Denis near Paris, who visited Cluny and Vézelay before rebuilding his own abbey church. He noted that the corn is the old law, which is poured into the mystic mill by an ancient Hebrew prophet, probably Moses, and ground into the meal of the new law by St. Paul.

Romanesque sculpture remained an integral part of architectural design and is inseparable from the whole. The walls, ceiling, portals, col-

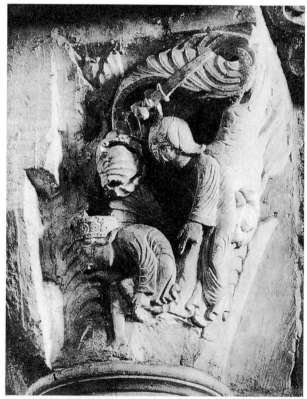

6.8 Nave capital sculpture, Church of La Madeleine, Vézelay, France, c. 1130. Angel of Death Killing Eldest Son of Pharaoh.

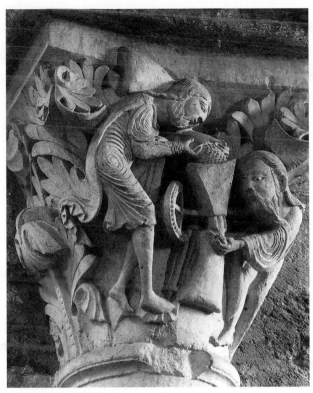

6.9 Nave capital sculpture, Church of La Madeleine, Vézelay, France, c. 1130. Mystic Mill: Moses and St. Paul Grinding Corn.

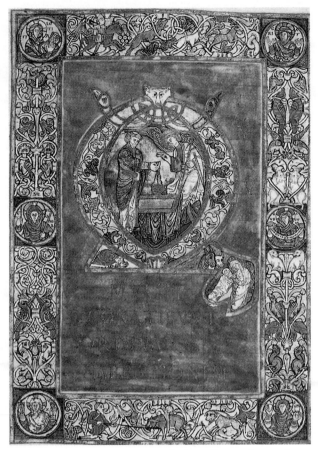

6.10 Initial page with letter Q, from Evangeliary of Abbey at St. Omer, c. 1000. Manuscript illumination. The Pierpont Morgan Library, New York.

PAINTING

At one extreme of the art of painting in the Romanesque period were miniatures of modest proportions on the parchment pages of books; at the other were monumental murals in the apses of abbey churches. The one craft that the monks are known to have consistently practiced is the copying, illustrating, and binding of books, activities that took place in a large communal room called the **scriptorium.** This tradition, which dates from the time of Cassiodorus, was followed by all Benedictine houses, and those in the Cluniac order fostered it with both diligence and enthusiasm.

Although the Cluniac copyists were known for the beauty of their lettering and the accuracy of their texts, a monk who was skilled in his craft would certainly not have been content merely to copy letters all his life. A blank place in the manuscript provided both the opportunity and the challenge to fill it in. At first these areas contained

umns, and capitals were not merely mute structural necessities. They were places where carved images communicated messages and meanings, where stone spoke to monk, nun, and pilgrim alike in the eloquent language of form, line, and color.

nothing more than fanciful little pen drawings or elaborate initial letters at the beginning of a paragraph. Gradually the drawings grew into miniature paintings, and the initial letters became highly complex designs.

The development of this art of illustrating, or *illuminating,* manuscripts seems to have been one compensation for the austerity of Benedictine life. As the practice became more widely accepted, specialists in the various phases were designated. A painter of small illuminated scenes was called a **miniator,** whereas one who did initial letters was known as a **rubricator.**

Cluniac manuscripts were illustrated with the utmost delicacy. Miniatures were painted in many colors, and the halos of saints or crowns of kings were made with thin gold leaf. The letter Q in an evangeliary from St. Omer is an intricate example of the illuminator's art (Fig. 6.10).

Convents offered a unique environment for female artists, who were also involved in manuscript illumination. A remarkable example was Hildegard of Bingen, who was educated in a Benedictine double monastery (that is, one providing facilities for nuns as well as monks) and later became the abbess of a convent near Bingen. She wrote Latin poetry and composed words and music for more than seventy hymns. Her morality play, *Ordo virtutum*, dramatizes a contest between the virtues and the devil to gain a Christian soul. Her vision of heaven in seven circles was illustrated by artists under her supervision (Fig. 6.11). Mary is its majestic queen, holding the orb and scepter. Just below, an angelic choir is singing, while other circles enclose patriarchs, prophets, apostles, and saints.

Flourishes of the pen by expert copyists and the gradual refinement of the art of illumination had effects far beyond the medium for which either was originally intended. They became the models for the large murals that decorated the walls and apses of churches and for the sculpture that embellished the spaces above portals and columns.

Later they became the prototypes for the design of stained-glass windows in Gothic cathedrals.

Contrasting with the diminutive illuminations in manuscripts were the huge frescoes painted on the surfaces of the barrel-vaulted ceilings, arches, and semidomed apses of churches of the Romanesque period. Except for a few fragments, all the large paintings at Cluny itself have disappeared. Notable examples are found elsewhere, however. In a chapel at nearby Berzé-la-Ville (a residence built for Hugh in his last years), there is an apse mural modeled after the one in the Third Abbey Church (Fig. 6.12). Christ is clothed in a robe of white, over which is draped a red mantle. With his right hand he blesses the surrounding apostles and saints, while with his left he gives St. Peter a scroll containing the law. The heavenly setting is suggested by the dark blue background of the

6.11 Hildegard of Bingen's vision of heaven in seven circles. Manuscript illumination.

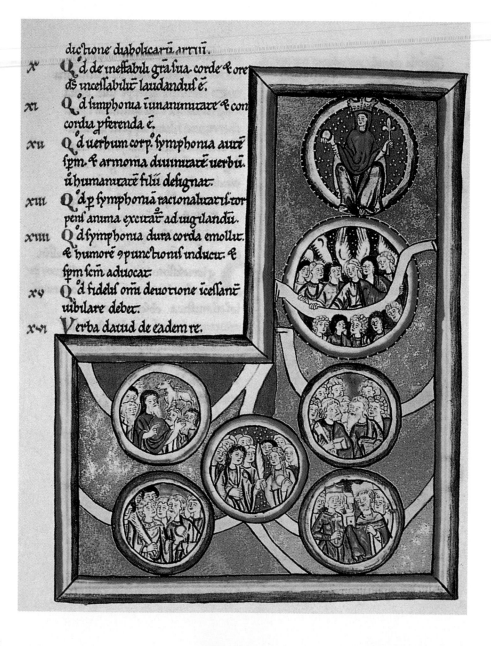

mandorla, an almond-shaped halo or glory, which is studded with golden stars, and by the hand of God the Father, which hovers above Christ, holding a crown.

MUSIC

Odo of Cluny, who served as the second abbot from 927 to 942, brought the monastery its earliest musical distinction by actively fostering choral music. Documents tell of more than 100 psalms being sung at Cluny daily in his time. On his tours of inspection to other monasteries, he devoted much of his energy to the instruction of choirs. His great success made it necessary for his teaching methods to be written down, and from this circumstance, something about the early status of music at Cluny can be ascertained.

THE DEVELOPMENT OF NOTATION. Odo's great accomplishments include arranging the tones of the scale into an orderly progression from A to G, an early system of Western musical notation. Odo's method, as expounded in a treatise often ascribed to him, included the mathematical measurement of **intervals,** the difference in pitch between tones, on a musical instrument called a **monochord.** Consisting of a single string stretched over a long wooden box with frets for varying the length of the string, the monochord made it possible to demonstrate the relationships between string lengths and intervals.

Before Odo's time, the chants used in the sacred service had to be learned laboriously by rote. If any degree of authenticity was to be achieved, chants had to be taught by a graduate of the Schola Cantorum, the school for teaching chants that had been founded by Pope Gregory I in Rome. Odo's treatise declares that when singers were taught to perform by reading notes, they soon "were singing at first sight and extempore and without a fault anything written in music, something which until this time ordinary singers had never been able to do." Odo's system of notation made songbooks possible and enabled the transmission of music from one generation to the next.

In the eleventh century, another monk, Guido of Arezzo, refined Odo's method. His treatise, which was in the library of Cluny, made it clear that he embraced the Cluniac musical reforms. He also freely acknowledged his debt to the Abbot Odo, "from whose example," he said, "I have departed only in the forms of the notes." This slight departure by Guido was actually the invention of the basis for modern musical notation on a staff of lines, where tones of the same pitch always appear on the same line or space. Odo's work also led to Guido's system of **solmization,** which assigned certain syllables, derived from a hymn to St. John, to each degree of the scale. Later the syllable *si,* compounded from the first two letters of the Latin form of "St. John" *(Sancte Ioannes),* was added as the seventh degree of the scale. In France, these syllables are still used as in Guido's time. In Italy and elsewhere, the first note, *ut,* was replaced by the more singable, and familiar, *do.*

Musical Example 6.1
Hymn to St. John the Baptist   Guido of Arezzo

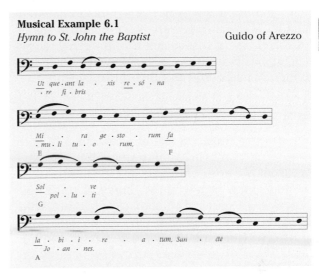

Ut que·ant la . xis re·só · na
·re fi·bris

Mi . ra ge·sto · rum fa
·mu·li tu · o · rum,
E   F

Sol . ve
pol·lu·ti
G

la . bi·i·re . a·tum, Sun·cte
Jo·an·nes.
A

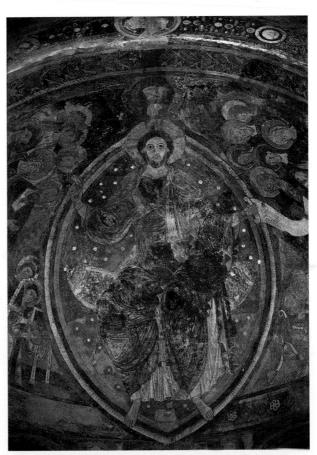

6.12 *Christ in Majesty,* c. 1103. Fresco (apse mural), height 13′. Chapelle des Moines, Berzé-la-Ville, France.

The most remarkable fact about Odo's and Guido's treatises is that both describe music as an art designed to praise the Creator and enhance the beauty and meaning of prayer. Previously, Boethius, along with most early writers on music, had considered music a branch of mathematics that could reveal the secrets of the universe. Guido, however, made a point of stating that the writings of Boethius were "useful to philosophers, but not to singers." Both Odo and he intentionally omitted heavenly speculations. Cluny, therefore, emerged as a center of practical music-making rather than as a place where scholars pondered music only as a theoretical science.

MUSIC PICTURED IN SCULPTURE

The story of music at Cluny was also told with compelling beauty in sculptured capitals that survive from the apse of Hugh's great church. In the sanctuary, the architectural climax of the whole edifice, was a series of columns grouped in a semicircle around the high altar. One capital portrayed on its four faces the theological virtues; another, the cardinal virtues. On a third were pictured the cycles and labors of the monk's year in terms of the four seasons. His hopes for the hereafter were portrayed by the four rivers and trees of Paradise. Finally, his praise for the Creator was expressed with figures to symbolize the eight tones of sacred psalmody.

On the first of the eight faces of these twin capitals (Fig. 6.13) is inscribed, "This tone is the first in the order of musical intonations." The figure is that of a solemn-faced youth playing a lute. Here the symbolism of the stringed instrument stems from the belief in the power of music to banish evil, as David had cast out Saul's evil spirit when he played to him. Another figure (Fig. 6.14) shows a young man playing a set of chime bells. The accompanying inscription notes that he is playing a lament. The Latin word *planctus* denotes a funeral dirge. The practice of ringing bells at burials is pictured in the contemporary representation of the burial procession of Edward the Confessor in the Bayeux Tapestry, in which the figures accompanying the bier carry small bells.

EARLY FORMS OF POLYPHONY

Gregorian plainsong was a purely melodic style and continued to be practiced as such, but during the Romanesque period the choral responses began to show variations in the direction of singing in several parts at different levels of pitch. The ninth, tenth, and eleventh centuries thus saw the tentative beginnings of the **polyphonic,** or "many-voiced," style that was to flourish in the Gothic period and in the Renaissance.

Unfortunately, the polyphonic practice of the pre-Gothic period is known only through theoretical treatises. However, from the rules they give for the addition of voices to the traditional chant, some idea of the early forms of polyphony can be determined. As might be expected, mathematics and Pythagorean number theory influenced the musical usages of the time (see pp. 51 and 58). The perfect intervals of the octave, fifth, and fourth

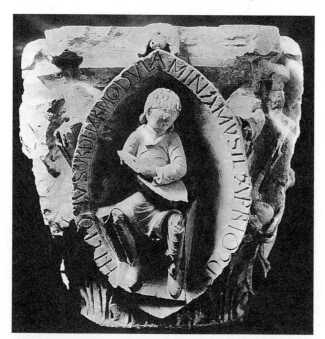

6.13   Side of ambulatory capital, Great Third Abbey Church of Cluny, 1088–1095. *First Tone of Plainsong.*

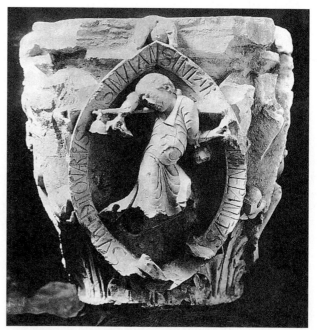

6.14   Other side of ambulatory capital, Great Third Abbey Church of Cluny. *Fourth Tone.*

were preferred over all others, because their mathematical ratios indicated a closer correspondence with the divine order of the universe.

PARALLEL ORGANUM (TENTH CENTURY)

In a treatise from the beginning of the tenth century, the type of choral response known as **parallel organum** is discussed. The original Gregorian melody was maintained intact. However, the principal voice was paralleled at pitch levels of the fourth, fifth, and octave above and below by so-called organal voices. Parallel organum, like buttresses in architecture, built a mighty fortress of choral sound around the traditional Gregorian line of plainsong. By thus enclosing it within the stark but strong perfect intervals, parallel organum achieved a massive and solid style quite in the spirit of the other Romanesque arts.

Musical Example 6.2
Parallel Organum (tenth century)

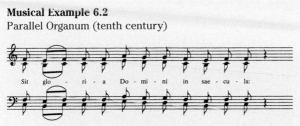

Sit glo - ri - a Do - mi - ni in sae - cu - la:

The music of this time was yet another expression of the praise of God. When related to the great buildings, the richly carved sculpture, the illuminated manuscripts, and painted murals, it fits into the picture as a whole. Consequently, when the choir section of a monastic church was being planned, every effort was made to provide a resonant, acoustically vibrant setting for the perpetual chant. Hugh's great church was especially famous for its acoustics. The curved ceiling vaults and the great variety of angles in the wall surfaces of the broad transepts and cavernous nave gave the

chant there a characteristic tone color that can be reproduced only in a similar setting. The effect of a monastic choir of several hundred voices performing joyous songs must have been overwhelming.

Cluny's sculptured capitals depicting the tones of plainsong represent an obvious synthesis of the arts of sculpture, music, and literature into an appropriate architectural setting. Their expressive intensity, moreover, bespeaks both the motion and the emotion typical of Romanesque style in general. As such, they are representative products of a people capable of the long and difficult pilgrimages and fantastic effort associated with the organization of the First Crusade. These sculptures reveal something of that unconquerable energy, and especially a vigorous attitude toward the act of worship that must have been channeled into a performance style that was emphatic in feeling. They are, in fact, the embodiment of the spirit expressed by St. Augustine, who called upon the faithful to "Sing with your voices, and with your hearts, and with all your moral convictions, sing the new songs, not only with your tongue but with your life."

WORLDLY ROMANESQUE

Whereas a monastery was a haven of peace, a feudal manor was an armed fortress. And whereas the monk was a man of prayer, the landed baron was a man of war.

The treasures of a monastery or cathedral were always under the watchful eye of the clergy, and religious restraints against raiding church property usually were strong enough to prevent wanton destruction. The same cannot be said for secular property. Feudal castles were constantly subject to siege, and those that survived often were remodeled in later centuries according to the changing fortunes of their successive owners. Among the best preserved of these Romanesque residences are the Imperial Palace near Goslar, Germany (Fig. 6.15),

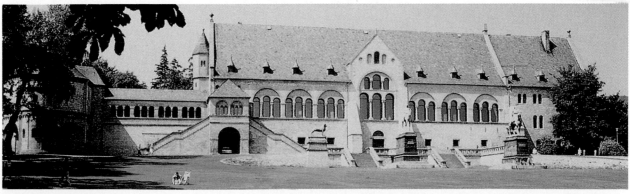

6.15 Imperial Palace at Goslar, Lower Saxony, Germany, begun 1043, rebuilt 1132. Chapel of St. Ulrich (far left), eleventh century.

and parts of the Palace of the Normans in Sicily, notably the Dining Hall of Roger II, with its emblematic animals and traditional symbols of feudal heraldry (Fig. 6.16).

Towns grew up in the protective shadows of castles, monasteries, or cathedrals, but only a few urban dwellings remain, such as those at Cluny (Fig. 6.17). Their arched doorways facing the street were sometimes decorated by sculptured hunting scenes or representations of an artisan's trade—a cobbler bending over his workbench, for example, or a merchant showing cloth to a customer. Of interior decorations—mural paintings, wall hangings, furniture, and the like—almost nothing is left. And because poetry and music were intended to be heard rather than read, little of either was written down.

History, however, is filled with accidents. For example, the single large-scale example of secular pictorial art, the famous Bayeux Tapestry, survives because it was designed for a church instead of a castle. The only French epic poem before the Crusades, the *Song of Roland,* owes its present existence to some monastic scribe who happened to write it down, either for a minstrel with a poor memory or because he wanted to preserve it after it had ceased to be sung. The one authentic melody to which such poetry was chanted exists because it was included as a jest in a thirteenth-century musical play. The so-called Tower of London, a **keep,** or fortress, that William the Conqueror constructed, is still intact because of its later use as a royal residence and prison and because it housed an important chapel.

THE BAYEUX TAPESTRY AND THE NORMAN CONQUEST

The most nearly complete example of pictorial art is the Bayeux Tapestry, which tells the story of how the English crown was won by William the Conqueror at the Battle of Hastings in 1066. Not a

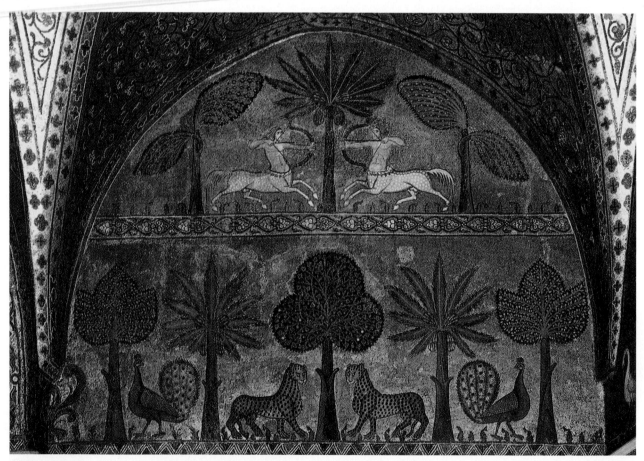

6.16 Mosaic of centaurs, leopards, and peacocks from Dining Hall of Roger II, c. 1132. Palace of Norman Kings, Palermo, Italy.

true tapestry but a work of embroidery, it presents a vivid picture of the life and attitudes of the feudal period. Such cloth decorations were used to cover the bare stone walls of castles. The work's extraordinary dimensions—1 foot, 8 inches high and 231 feet long—and its possession over the centuries by the Bayeux Cathedral indicate that it was intended to cover the plain strip of masonry over the nave arcade of that building. The designer remains unknown, but it was probably embroidered by skilled women in one of the renowned workshops of the period. Apparently it was completed about 20 years after the great battle it so vividly describes. As a continuous narrative, the Bayeux tapestry resembles Trajan's Column (see Figs. 4.10A, 4.11, and 4.12), which recorded relatively recent history from the point of view of the victor.

On the English side of the Channel, Harold, an English duke, claimed the throne on the recommendation of Edward the Confessor and his election by the Saxon barons. Besieged in the north by the Danes, he had won a complete victory near York less than 3 weeks before he had to face William in the south at Hastings. The long, forced march tired his men, but they still fought from dawn to dusk on that fateful day. The Saxon foot soldiers were both outnumbered and outmaneuvered by the swift Norman cavalry. In the course of the battle, Harold's two brothers were killed and Harold himself was fatally struck by a chance arrow, leaving the English side leaderless. By nightfall the English had retreated, and William had won one of the most momentous battles in history.

The tapestry tells the story from the Norman point of view. The central figure is, of course, William the Conqueror, who indelibly stamped his powerful personality on the north European scene throughout the second half of the eleventh century. The span of time is from the closing months of the reign of Edward the Confessor to

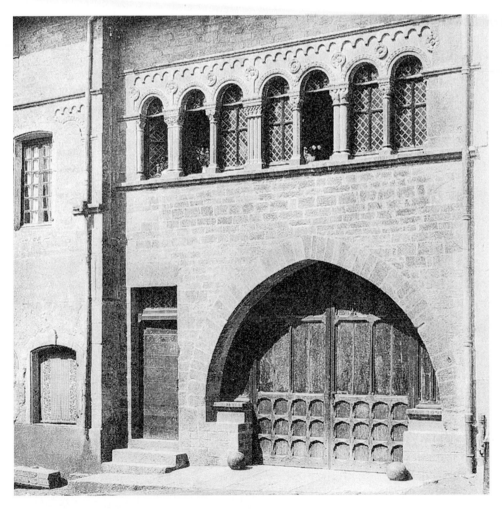

6.17 Romanesque house, Cluny, France, c. 1159.

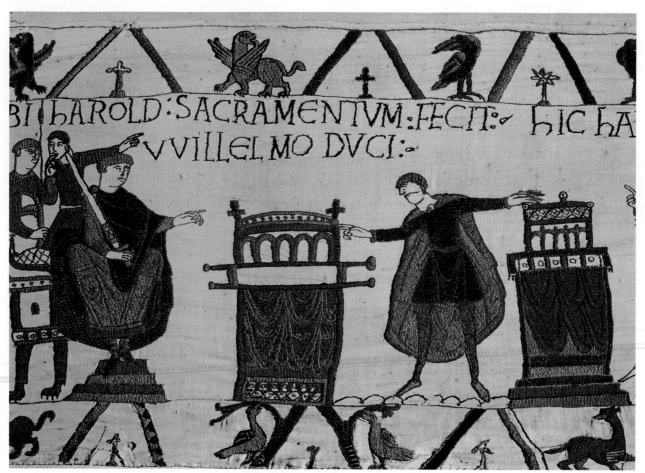

6.18 *Harold Swears Fealty to William,* detail of Bayeux Tapestry, c. 1073–1088. Wool embroidery on linen, height 1′8″, entire length 231′. Musee de la Tapisserie, Bayeux, France.

the day the Conqueror made good his claim to the throne at the Battle of Hastings.

In its surviving state, the Bayeux Tapestry is divided into seventy-nine panels, or scenes. The first part (panels 1–34) is concerned with William's reception of Harold, whose mission to Normandy allegedly was to tell William that he would succeed Edward the Confessor as king of England. In one of these scenes, William and Harold are shown at Bayeux (Fig. 6.18), *where Harold took an oath to Duke William.* (The italics here and later are literal translations of the Latin inscriptions that run along the top of the tapestry above the scenes they describe.) Placing his hands on the reliquaries that repose on the two altars, Harold seems to swear to uphold William's claim, although the exact nature of the oath is left vague. This is, however, the episode that later be-

came William's justification to make war on England, because Harold, contrary to his supposed sworn word, had himself crowned king.

In the upper and lower borders of these early panels, a running commentary on the action continues a tradition begun in manuscript illuminations. Here the commentary is in the form of animal figures that were familiar to people of the time from bestiaries and folktales. Others allude to certain fables of Aesop. The choice of the fox and crow, the wolf and stork, and the ewe, goat, and cow in the presence of the lion all have to do with deception and violence. They point out the supposedly treacherous character of Harold.

The main course of the action in the Bayeux Tapestry moves like the words on a printed page—from left to right. At times, however, it was necessary to represent a pertinent episode apart from the

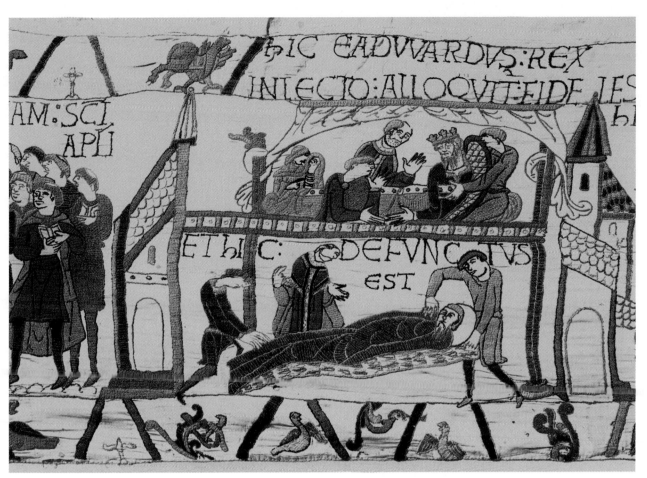

6.19 *Burial Rights for Edward the Confessor,* detail of Bayeux Tapestry, c. 1073–1088. Wool embroidery on linen, height 1′8″, entire length 231′. Musee de la Tapisserie, Bayeux, France.

principal action. In these instances the pictorial narrator simply reversed the usual order and moved the scene from right to left, thus, in effect, achieving a kind of visual parenthesis and avoiding confusion with the flow of the story.

Such a reversal is used in the scene depicting the death and burial of the Confessor (Fig. 6.19). On one side of the king's bed is a priest; Harold is on the other, while the queen and her lady-in-waiting are mourning at the foot of the bed.

When William received word that Harold had been crowned king, he immediately resolved to invade, and the second part of the tapestry (panels 35–53) is concerned with the preparations for his revenge. After all was in readiness, he set sail. The ships seen in the tapestry are similar to those in which William's restless Viking ancestors invaded the French coast two centuries be-

fore. It was in just such ships that Leif Eriksson and his fellow mariners apparently reached the eastern coast of North America earlier in the same century.

After the landing, the grand finale begins with the assembling of forces for the great battle (panels 54–79). The Norman side has both archers on foot and knights on horseback, whereas the English infantry fight in close formation with immense battle-axes, small spears, and clubs with stone heads. The Normans move in from left to right and the English from the opposite direction. The climax of the battle is reached in a wild scene at a ravine, where men and horses are tumbling about while the *English and French fall together in battle.* Shortly after, Harold is killed, and the fighting concludes with *English turned in flight.* The lower border in these scenes spares none of the horrors of warfare.

Dismembered limbs are strewn about, scavengers strip coats of mail from the bodies of the fallen, and naked corpses are left on the field.

The design of the Bayeux Tapestry is dominantly linear and, like the illuminated manuscripts of the time, is rendered in two dimensions, with no suggestion of spatial depth. The coarseness of the linen and the thickness of the wool, however, create interesting textural contrasts. The eight shades of woolen yarn—three blues, light and dark green, red, buff yellow, and gray—make for a vivid feeling of color, which is not used for natural representation but to enliven the design. Some men have blue hair, others have green hair, and horses often have two blue legs and two red ones. Faces are merely outlines, although some attempt at portraiture is made in the various likenesses of William (Fig. 6.20).

Details such as costumes, armor, mode of combat, and deployment of troops in battle are, by contrast, done with great accuracy. For this reason, the tapestry is a never-ending source of amazement and one of the most important sources of information about life in the eleventh century—so much so that its historical value is often allowed to overshadow its quality as a work of art.

The Bayeux Tapestry is a work of infinite variety. After a slow beginning with frequent digressions, the designer went on in the middle panels to the rather feverish preparations that culminated in the breathless climax of the battle. In both tempo and organization, the tapestry can stand up to comparison with the best works in narrative form, visual or verbal. The details, whether in the main panels or in the upper or lower borders, are handled so imaginatively that they not only embellish the design but also add visual accents, comment on the action, and advance the flow of the plot. Scenes are separated from one another by buildings that figure in the story and by such devices as stylized trees, which are mere conventions. So skillfully are these arranged that the continuity of the whole is never halted, and the observer is hardly aware of their presence.

THE SONG OF ROLAND

Epic poems were popular sagas based on the mighty deeds of legendary heroes, replete with blood feuds, gory vengeance, and black magic. The Anglo-Saxon *Beowulf* and the Germanic *Nibelungenlied (Song of the Nibelungs),* which Richard Wagner revived for his *Ring* cycle of music dramas in the nineteenth century (see pp. 497–498), were set in dark forests populated with lurking dragons

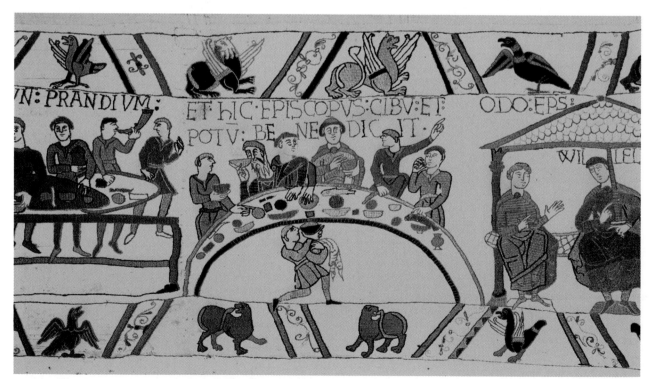

6.20 *William's Feast,* detail of Bayeux Tapestry. Musee de la Tapisserie, Bayeux, France.

and bloodthirsty monsters. Their French counterpart, the *Chanson de Roland (Song of Roland)* is cast in the mold of a **chanson de geste,** or song of deeds, an action story in poetic form derived from tales told by storytellers long ago and sung by a minstrel accompanied by a viol or lyre. It was written in Old French, the vernacular medieval language of the French people, rather than in scholarly Latin. Narrated in an abrupt, direct manner, the transitions between episodes are sudden and unexpected. A warlike atmosphere surrounds the characters, including the fighting Archbishop Turpin and the Archangels Gabriel and Michael, who, like the Valkyries in the *Song of the Nibelungs,* swoop down onto the battlefield to bear the souls of fallen warriors to heaven.

Although set in an earlier time (the actual event took place in 778), the *Song of Roland* is, both in form and spirit, a product of the warlike eleventh century. In fact, various recorders of historical events of that time mention it in connection with the Battle of Hastings. Guy of Amiens, one of William the Conqueror's courtiers, was the author of a Latin poem about a **jongleur,** or singing actor, by the name of Taillefer. This "minstrel whom a very brave heart ennobled," Guy relates, led William's forces into the battle throwing his sword in the air, catching it again, and singing a song of Roland. The English historian William of Malmesbury, writing about 50 years after the battle, relates that William began to sing the *Song of Roland* "in order that the warlike example of that hero might stimulate the soldiers."

The *Song of Roland* is an action-packed story set in the time of Charlemagne. It relates incidents from the campaign in northern Spain, where that emperor had been battling the Islamic armies and the troublesome Basques for 7 years. Roland, Charlemagne's favorite nephew, and the twelve peers, the flower of French knighthood, have been left in charge of the rear guard, while Charlemagne and the main body of the army are crossing the Pyrenees back into France. Roland is betrayed by his own stepfather, the wicked Ganelon, who has violated his vow of fidelity to Charlemagne and loyalty to his own family. The situation would have been read by the Normans as William's betrayal by Harold. Roland is attacked near Roncesvalles by overwhelming Muslim forces. The outnumbered rear guard is cut to pieces, and Roland, before dying a hero's death, sounds his ivory horn, summoning his uncle and his army from afar.

The latter part of the poem speaks of Charlemagne's vengeance, just as the corresponding section of the Bayeux Tapestry relates that of William. All is action and heroism, with swords flashing, helmets gleaming, drums beating, horns blowing, banners snapping, and steeds prancing. The story of the battle proceeds in what amounts to a blow-by-blow account, echoing frequently with such statements as "fierce is the battle and wondrous grim the fight."[1]

First one hears the preparations in the camp of Charlemagne. Using a cumulative technique, the poet describes the ten battalions one by one. Knight is added to knight, battle group to battle group, weapon to weapon, in order to build up the monumentality of the occasion in the listeners' imaginations. The forces of Western Christendom are eventually drawn up on Charlemagne's side— the French, Normans, Bavarians, Germans, Bretons, and so on. The virtues of the men invariably are bravery, valor, and hardiness. They have no fear of death, they never flee the battlefield, and their horses are swift and good.

Suddenly, and without any transition, the reader is in the midst of the attacking Saracens, whose battalions are described. To show how the Christians were outnumbered, yet another ten are added to the twenty battalions of the opposition. The fearsomeness of the enemy, however, is due not to their numbers alone but to their ferocious character. The only admirable quality allowed them is that of being good fighters; otherwise, they are hideous to behold, fierce and cruel, and lovers of evil. Yet despite this, the poet can say of both forces, "Goodly the armies."

The physical appearance of the people from these strange lands is fantastically exaggerated, as it was at Vézelay (Fig. 6.7). The Myconians, for instance, are men "Upon whose backs all down the spine in rows, / As on wild boars, enormous bristles grow." Of the warriors of the desert of Occian, it is said, "Harder than iron their hide on head and flanks, / So that they scorn or harness or steel cap." Later, during the battle, these same men of Occian "whinny and bray and squall," whereas the men of Arguille "like dogs are yelping all."

The religious life of the enemy is scorned as much as their appearance. They are represented

---

[1]All quotations from *Song of Roland* translated by Dorothy L. Sayers, published by Penguin Books. © Executors of Dorothy L. Sayers, 1937, 1957.

as polytheists who worship as strange an assortment of gods as was ever assembled—Apollyon, Termagant, and Mahound. When things are not going well from their point of view, they upbraid these gods. The statue of Apollyon is trampled underfoot; Termagant is robbed of his carbuncle, a precious stone; and Mahound is cast "into a ditch . . . For pigs and dogs to mangle and befoul." Later, when Marsilion, the king of Spain, dies, the listener hears that he "yields his soul to the infernal powers." Such fanciful descriptions could not have been written after the Crusades had brought Western warriors into contact with Muslim culture. Like the foreigners depicted on the Vézelay tympanum, the imagery of the *Song of Roland* is filled with naïve ethnocentrism.

With the lines of battle thus drawn, the setting is described in a single line: "Large is the plain and widely spread the wold." Then, as the conflict begins, battalion falls on battalion, hewing and hacking. Christian knights hurtle against Muslim knights throughout the day until the battle is reduced to a personal encounter between Charlemagne and his opposite, Baligant the Emir:

> At the Emir he drives his good French blade,
> He carves the helm with jewel-stones ablaze,
> He splits the skull, he dashes out the brains,
> Down to the beard he cleaves him through the
> face,
> And past all healing, he flings him down, clean
> slain.
> After this the pagans flee, and the day is won.

The lines of the original Old French proceed according to a rhyming scheme of **assonance,** in which the final syllables of each line correspond roughly in sound:

> Carlon the King, our Emperor Charlemayn,
> Full seven years long has been abroad in Spain.
> He's won the highlands as far as to the main;
> No castle more can stand before his face,
> City nor wall is left for him to break,
> Save Saragossa in its high mountain place;
> Marsilion holds it, the king who hates God's name,
> Mahound he serves, and to Apollyon prays:
> He'll not escape the ruin that awaits.

Much of the direct character and rugged strength of the poem is due to rigid avoidance of literary embellishment. Nothing is allowed to block the progress of these sturdy military monosyllables. So consistent is this quality of starkness throughout the poem that it even extends to the portrayal of the characters themselves. Each is the embodiment of a single ideal and human type: Ganelon is all treachery and hatred; Roland is bravery to the point of rashness; Oliver, Roland's close companion, is reason and caution; and Charlemagne, outstanding in his solitary grandeur, represents the majesty of both church and state. Through each of these devices singly and combined, the poem as a whole rises to the heights of epic art. Its language, style, and form thus fit the brave deeds of the heroic men with whom its narrative is concerned.

Under the patronage of the feudal nobility, Gothic poetry and music bloomed from the eleventh through thirteenth centuries. Courtly tournaments, brave knights winning fair ladies, and aristocratic poets making music with minstrels also enlivened the nobles' entertainments (Fig. 6.21). The jongleurs were not of noble birth, as were most of the later troubadours and their northern French and German counterparts, the **trouvères** and **minnesingers,** who were welcomed in every castle and abbey. The most famous of the latter was the early thirteenth-century minnesinger and poet Walter von der Vogelweide ("Walter the Birdcatcher"). The Crusades spawned many musical works designed to stir men to join the cause. One such is von der Vogelweide's *Palestine Song,* whose twelve verses encourage military bravado. It marches onward, eloquently articulating the joys felt at the first sight of the city of Jerusalem, with its rich heritage for "Christians, Jews and Heathens."

Records reveal that some women were included in the ranks of jongleurs and troubadours. Little is known about the life of the Comtessa de Dia, a French composer. Nevertheless, the one song and melody that remain show that the theme of lovesickness, which pervaded this courtly art, was not strictly limited to male singers.

Secular music forms that emerged in the eleventh century were no doubt modeled on formulas used in the performance of church music. The simple repetitive melodies used to recite the epic secular chansons de geste melded with the insistent rhythms of the poetry and must have had much in common with the litany, although, of course, the subject matter differed radically. At the end of each poetic stanza was a melodic appendage that served as a refrain, much like the *alleluias* between the verses of psalms and hymns. The best-known *chanson,* the *Song of Roland,* has been preserved only in its text version; no music survives. Although jongleurs could refresh their memories of longer epics from the manuscripts they carried with them in leather pouches, these manuscripts included no musical parts. It is assumed that the melodies were so simple that there was little need to write them down.

NORMAN ROMANESQUE ARCHITECTURE

The architecture of the Normans, the descendants of the Norsemen or Vikings, was sufficiently distinctive to give one aspect of the Romanesque style the name Norman. The building done in eleventh-century Normandy, in northwestern France near the English Channel, had a lasting effect on that region and reached a logical conclusion in the fortresses, castles, abbeys, and cathedrals that the Normans later built in England. Because the Romanesque style in England dates from the Norman Conquest, it is still referred to there as the Norman style.

Norman architecture, like many other facets of Norman culture, resulted from the union of Viking themes and ideas with the Christian remnants of the disintegrated Carolingian empire. Their architecture is noted for its blunt strength and forthright character.

Both the Carolingian and Viking societies were seminomadic. Charlemagne and his successors, as well as the dukes of Normandy down to William's time, frequently shifted their residences. Moreover, the insecurity of the times discouraged large

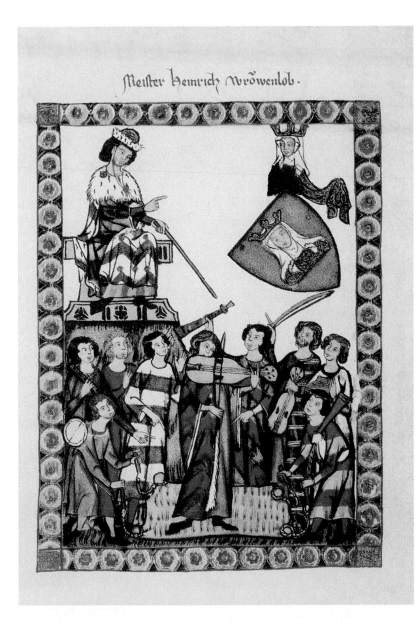

6.21 *Heinrich Frauenlob Directing a Minstrel Performance,* from the Manesse Manuscript of German minnesingers, fourteenth century. University Library, Heidelberg, Germany.

6.22   Tower of London, aerial view, c. 1078–1097.

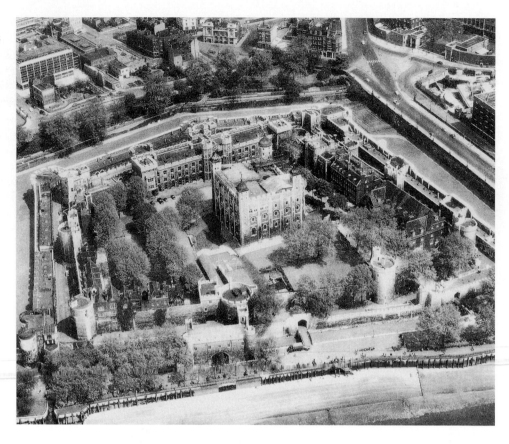

building schemes. But as the feudal system reached its mature stage and a more settled order became possible, instead of seeking further conquests, the Norman conquerors developed the vast new lands they had acquired. Earlier, William had discouraged the construction of castles and sanctioned only monasteries; now he proposed to impress his new subjects with solid and unconquerable fortresses as well as feats of arms. In other words, William's policy shifted from offensive to defensive.

6.23   (A) Tower of London (White Tower), c. 1078–1097. Height 92′. (B) Plan of the White Tower. (a) Banqueting hall; (b) Presence chamber; (c) Chapel.

A

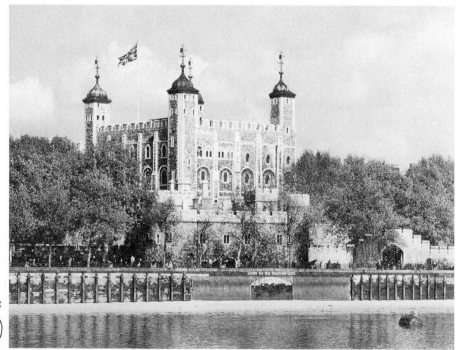

B

THE TOWER OF LONDON. The Tower of London (Fig. 6.22), or more specifically the White Tower (Fig. 6.23A), was begun by William the Conqueror in about 1078 and finished by his successor; its purpose was to defend and dominate the town. Its form was that of a Norman keep, and as such it was something new to England. The White Tower is simply a massive, square, compact stone building divided into four stories that rise 92 feet, with a turret at each corner. A glance at the plan (Fig. 6.23B) reveals some of its many irregularities. Its four sides, for instance, are unequal in length, and its corners therefore are not exactly right angles. Three of its turrets are square, and one is round. The walls vary from 11 to 15 feet in thickness. In addition, a wall that runs from north to south divides the interior into two unequal parts.

The bareness of its original exterior, which has been changed over the centuries, was well suited to the White Tower's function as a fortress. The austerity of the interior offers a glimpse of the general lack of physical comforts in medieval life. The tower was divided into four stories by means of wooden floors, and its darkness was relieved only by narrow, slitted, glassless windows that were more important as launching sites for arrows than as sources of light and air.

After Norman times, other buildings were added until the whole became a system of outward-spreading fortifications with the old Norman keep as its heart. From William's time on, the tower has been in continuous use as a fortress, palace, or prison.

The main floor of the White Tower has three divisions: a large council chamber that doubled as a banqueting hall, a smaller presence chamber, and the well-preserved St. John's Chapel (Fig. 6.24). Like

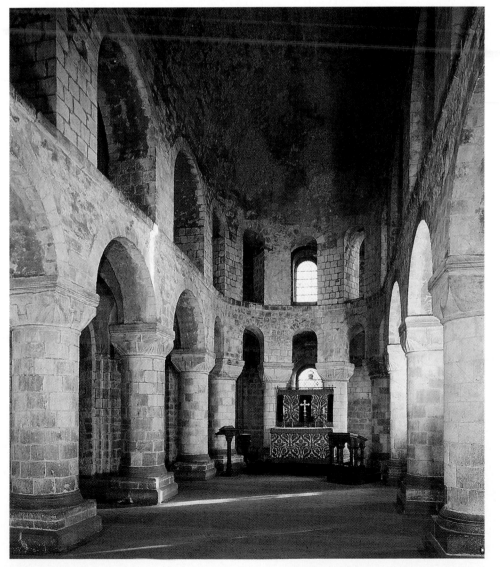

6.24 Interior, St. John's Chapel, White Tower, London, England, 1078–1097.

a miniature church, this chapel has a barrel-vaulted nave with four bays. On either side are aisles that command interest because of their early use of cross vaulting. The columns of the nave arcade are thick and stubby, and the cushionlike capitals have only simple scalloped carving by way of decoration. Above is a triforium gallery that was used by the queen and her ladies. Its slitlike windows serve as a clerestory.

THE ABBEY CHURCHES AT CAEN. At Caen, in Normandy, two buildings were under the personal protection of William and Queen Matilda and designated as their respective burial places: St. Étienne (Abbaye-aux-Hommes; Fig. 6.25) and Ste. Trinité (Abbaye-aux-Dames). Because both were abbey churches, they properly belong in a discussion of the monastic Romanesque style. They were, however, not commissioned by the church itself but rather by two worldly donors.

Begun just before the Norman Conquest, St. Étienne has a well-proportioned west facade. Four prominent buttresses divide the section below the towers into three parts that correspond to the central nave and two side aisles of the interior. Vertically, the facade rises in three stories, with the portals matching the level of the nave arcade inside. The two rows of windows above are at the gallery and clerestory levels, respectively. The windows, mere openings, are quite undistinguished. The functional honesty in this correspondence between the exterior design and interior plan was a Norman innovation that came into general use during the Gothic period.

The twin towers belong to the original design, but their spires are later additions. As with the usual Norman church, the towers are square and in three stories. Thus, they repeat on a higher level the triple division of the facade below. The first story is of solid masonry. The second has alternating blind (that is, blank) and open arches. The greater open space of the third story contributes to its function as a belfry and relieves the general heaviness of the structure. The bareness of the exterior is a fitting prelude to the gloomy grandeur of the interior (Fig. 6.26). The church as a whole is as rugged as its founder and typifies the spirit of the Norman people and their forceful leader.

Lack of decoration was a conscious part of the design of St. Étienne and the Tower of London. One facade impresses by its bold outlines, sturdiness, and straightforward honesty; the other, by its strength and bluntness. Nevertheless, in their churches, although the clerestory windows were small, the Normans achieved better lighting than in previous Romanesque structures. In addition, the Normans achieved more unified interiors by connecting the three levels of the nave arcade, gallery, and clerestory with single vertical shafts running from floor to ceiling. Both these features, as well as the harmonious spatial divisions of a facade like that of St. Étienne, were incorporated into the Gothic style.

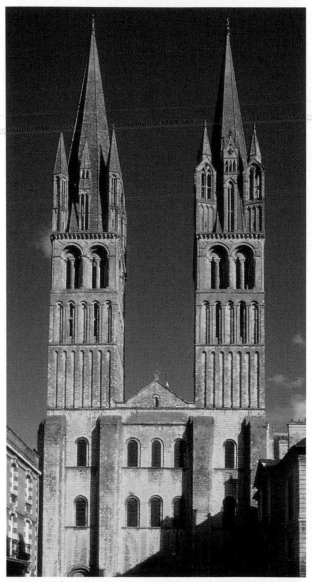

6.25 St. Étienne (Abbaye-aux-Hommes), Caen, France, c. 1067–1135. Nave 157′6″ × 32′1″, height of towers 295′.

On the other hand, when the work of the Normans is placed alongside that of their Burgundian contemporaries, it seems crude by comparison. The Normans were as blunt and brash as the Cluniacs were ingenious and subtle. The difference, in short, is that between action and contemplation. Soon the Norman accent on structure rather than embellishment would be altered by Islamic influences (see pp. 141–145) brought back by the Crusaders.

IDEAS

The key to understanding the Romanesque as a living and active art style is knowledge of the opposing forces that created it. As Christian influence spread northward, its conservative reiterations of classical sources encountered the more asymmetrical, restless art forms that originated with the former barbarian tribes, which they incorporated in their art when they converted to

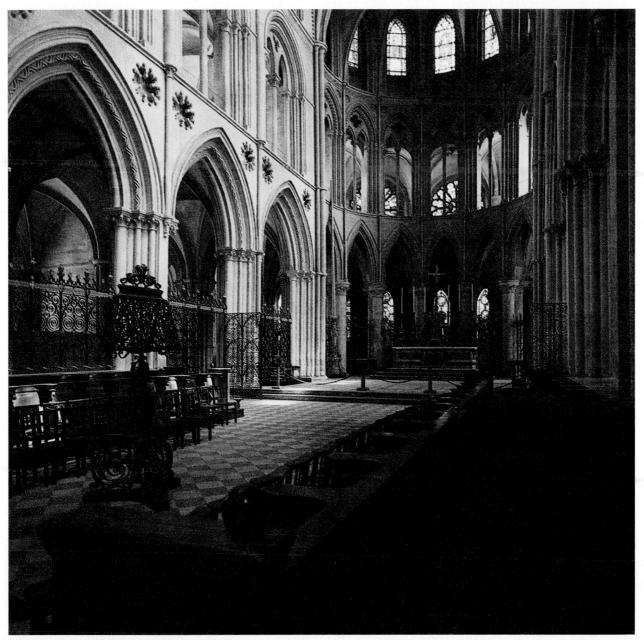

6.26 Interior, St. Étienne, Caen, France.

Christianity (Fig. 6.27). In effect, a church that respected and admired tradition and encouraged an unchanging order was absorbing peoples who preferred new twists and turns in forms that seemed to break out of their frames.

For example, builders combined the horizontal Early Christian basilica with northern towers and spires, taking the first step toward Romanesque architecture. A musical counterpart was formed when the Mediterranean tradition of singing one melody in unison met the northern custom of singing in several parts. The result was the experimentation with counterpoint and harmony that characterized the music of the Romanesque period.

This meeting of southern unity with northern variety slowly matured over the centuries and was ultimately responsible for the first truly pan-European (all-European) art style: the Romanesque. As Romanesque art took shape, two opposing ways of life evolved: sacred and secular, otherworldly and worldly. In fact, the underlying themes of the Romanesque cluster around these divisions. The religious side found its ful-

fillment in contemplation, whereas the secular aspect was expressed mainly in action.

THE CONTEMPLATIVE LIFE

The monastic way of life demanded the seclusion of the countryside as an escape from the distractions of the world. Because the monk conceived earthly life as only a stepping stone to the life beyond, living in this world required only the barest essentials. Rural isolation was nonetheless enhanced by the reading and copying of books. The very severity of monastic life stimulated imaginative experience at the same time that individual self-denial reinforced communal energies. The turn away from the world found architectural expression in plain exteriors. The rich interiors of monastic churches symbolized the wealth of spiritual life.

Two favorite Cluniac saints were Paul and Anthony, who, in Early Christian times, had gone into the forbidding African desert, where they had the most fantastic visions and the most dreadful and horrifying temptations. The arts, conse-

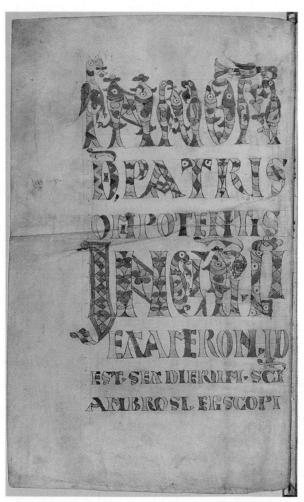

6.27 Example of Merovingian script, probably written at Canterbury, c. 1120.

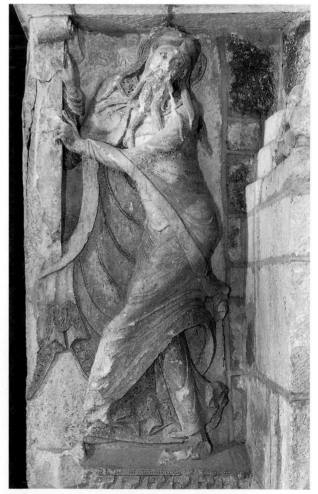

6.28 *Isaiah,* west portal, Church of Notre Dame, Souillac, France, c. 1110.

quently, were not intended to mirror the natural world or to decorate the dwelling place of an earthly ruler but rather to conjure up otherworldly visions of divine majesty and hellish monsters. The arts found common ground in their attempts to depict aspects of the world beyond.

At first the cloistered monks and nuns developed an art of elaborate symbolism addressed to an educated community that was familiar with sophisticated and intricate allegories. The growth of such a symbolic language—whether in architecture, sculpture, painting, or music—could have been promoted only by an abbot like Hugh, who favored higher learning. By contrast, the succeeding Gothic arts were directed more toward the unlettered people in the growing towns. The sculpture and stained glass of the Gothic cathedrals were destined to become the Bible portrayed in stone and glass for the poor. This does not mean that Romanesque art was overly intellectualized and remote from the experience of those to whom it was addressed. On the contrary, it was very directly related to the intensity of the inner life and the visionary otherworldly focus of the religious communities that developed it.

Greco-Roman sculpture was successful in its way precisely because the classical mind had conceived of the gods in human form. When godhood was conceived of as an abstract principle, a realistic representation of it became essentially impossible. Mathematical proportions were of no help to the Romanesque mind, because it was considered impossible to understand God fully through the intellect. God had to be felt through faith rather than comprehended by the mind. Only through the intuitive eye of faith could His essence be grasped. Physical substance was secondary and soul primary, but the latter could be depicted only in the imagination.

A life so abstractly oriented and motivated by such deep religious convictions could never have found its models in the natural world. The eccentric treatment and distortions of the human body in Romanesque sculpture, the unnecessarily elaborated initials in the manuscript illuminations, and the ornate melismas added to the syllables of the chant all signified a rejection of the natural order of things and its replacement by the supernatural. The most admired book of the Bible was Revelation, containing as it does the apocalyptic visions of St. John. It is not surprising, then, that the pictorial element in sculpture and painting in both large and small forms reflected Romanesque emotions with such intensity that the human figures sometimes seem to be consumed by the inner fires of their faith. Reason seeks to persuade through calm or serene attitudes, but such animated figures as those of the prophets at Souillac (Fig. 6.28) and Moissac seem to be performing spiritual dances in which their slender forms stretch to unnatural heights with gestures more convulsive than graceful.

The Romanesque monks and nuns dwelt in a dream world where the trees that grew in Paradise, the angels who populated the heavens, and the demons of hell were more real than anyone or anything in everyday life. Indeed, the monsters whose fearsome characteristics were described in the bestiaries and represented in manuscripts and sculptures had a moral and symbolic function far more real than any animal of mere physical existence. All these imaginary creatures existed together in a rich jungle of the imagination where the abnormal was the normal and the fabulous became the commonplace (Fig. 6.29).

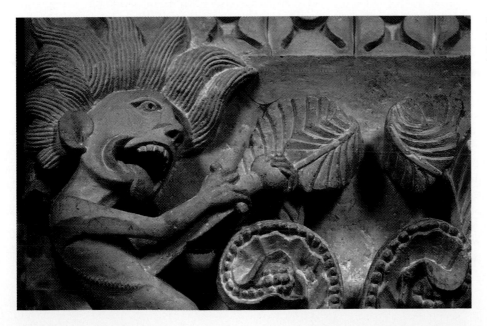

6.29 *Demon of Luxury*, nave capital sculpture, Church of La Madeleine, Vézelay, France, c. 1130.

A strict hierarchical social structure of society prevailed throughout the Romanesque period. It was as rigid in its way inside the monastery as was the feudalism outside the cloistered walls. It supported a worldview grounded in the assumption of a divinely established order of the universe and the church's authority to interpret it. The majestic figure of Christ in Glory carved over the entrance portals of the Cluniac abbey churches proclaimed this concept. As if to lend emphasis to this doctrine, St. Peter, said to have been the first pope, is seen at Berzé-la-Ville receiving a scroll containing the divine laws from the hands of Christ. The papacy of medieval days found its most powerful support in the Cluniac order, and through such aid, it succeeded in establishing a social order based on this mandate from Christ.

The authority of the church was nowhere better expressed than in these monumental sculptural and mural compositions, which warned those who beheld them of their position on the road to either salvation or damnation. The milestones marking the path were placed there by the church, whose clergy alone could interpret them and assure the penitent that he or she was on the way to the streets of gold instead of the caldrons of fire. The frequency with which the apocalyptic vision of St. John was represented, with apostles and elders surrounding the throne of Christ, was evidence of the reverence for the protective father image in the form of the bearded patriarch.

The Romanesque abbey church was organized according to a rigid hierarchical plan that mirrored the strict order of precedence in the liturgical processions for which it was the setting. Through its insistence on visible proportions, it signified the invisible plan of a divinely ordered world. The monastic buildings that surrounded it were similarly significant in their regularity. They were designed to enclose those who were willing to conform to such a regulated life and thus to reflect the divinely established plan for salvation.

The very spaciousness of the abbey church was far in excess of anything that was needed to accommodate the few hundred people who normally worshiped there. It was, however, the monument that mirrored the unshakable religious convictions of the Romanesque mind, and as the house of the Lord and Ruler of the universe, it became a palace surpassing that of any king on the face of the Earth. In the insecurity of the feudalistic world, Romanesque people built fortresses for their faith that were designed to withstand the attacks of heretics and heathens as well as the more elemental forces of wind, weather,

and fire. Moreover, the abbey church was the place where the heavenly Monarch held court; it was where his subjects could pay Him homage in the divine services that went on day and night, year in and year out.

Romanesque structures, whether churches or castles, never became types, as Greek temples, Byzantine churches, and the later Gothic cathedrals did. Each building and each region sought its own solutions. Through constant experimentation, Romanesque architects found the key to new structural principles, such as their vaulting experiments. By gradually achieving command of their medium, they progressed in their building techniques from earlier heavy, fortresslike structures to later edifices of considerable elegance.

Meanwhile, the decorators slowly groped toward restoring monumental sculpture and mural painting. The need for larger and better choirs likewise led to the invention of notational systems, and the emotional exuberance in worship led to many modifications of the traditional chant, which eventually culminated in the art of counterpoint. In all, the creative vitality exhibited in each of the Romanesque arts is a constant source of astonishment.

THE ACTIVE LIFE

The virtues of the active life were courage and loyalty to both peers and superiors. Whatever one's station in life, everybody was a vassal of some lord, a relationship that involved mutual obligations. As a vassal, one was bound to swear an oath of **fealty,** or fidelity, that promised loyalty to the immediate superior. Central governments were weak, and the main function of kings was to raise armies to defend their realms against foreign invaders. Local governments were powerful in enforcing laws, raising taxes, and settling disputes.

Factional and regional confrontations involving treachery or defection from the feudal code had to be decided by personal combat or on the field of battle, with God awarding victory to the righteous cause. Enemies, however, were granted the distinctions of honor and bravery; otherwise, it would have been socially impossible to do battle with them. In the *Song of Roland,* no one below the rank of baron figures with any prominence; similarly, the abbeys of William and Matilda were intended primarily for men and women of rank, and by founding these churches, the royal pair pledged their feudal oath to God.

Both the Bayeux Tapestry and the *Song of Roland* are set in a masculine world of clear-cut loyalties and moral and physical certainties. In each, chivalry is based on the ways of fighting men. The code of Roland was clearly, "My soul to God, my life to the king, and honor for myself." It remained for the Gothic period to add, "My heart to the ladies." Roland's dying thoughts, for instance, are occupied with his family and lineage; his king, Charlemagne; his country, France; and his sword, Durendal. Typically, he makes no mention of the woman he has promised to marry, the Lady Aude.

Earlier, his exasperated friend Oliver reproached Roland for his rashness in not summoning aid sooner, and at that time he swore:

> Now by my beard . . . if e'er mine eyes
> Again behold my sister Aude the bright,
> Between her arms never you think to lie.

No true or courtly love is this, but only the feudal baron bestowing his female relatives, like his goods and property, on those whose faith and courage he has cause to admire. Later, after Charlemagne returns to France, the poor Lady Aude inquires about the fate of her fiancé. The king tells her of his heroic death, and as a consolation prize, he offers her the hand of his son, Louis, whereupon the lady falls dead at his feet. Whether she dies of grief for Roland or the indelicacy of Charlemagne's suggestion is left open to conjecture. Because scarcely more than a dozen of the 4,000-odd lines of the poem are devoted to her, the historian Henry Adams was fully justified in observing, "Never after the first crusade did any great poem rise to such heroism as to sustain itself without a heroine."

Curiously enough, on the Islamic side, after the king of Spain is incapacitated, the queen takes an important part in the affairs of state. Nowhere on the Christian side is a woman given anything close to similar status. In the Bayeux Tapestry, a woman is mentioned by name in one place only—the enigmatic inscription *Where a cleric and Aelfgyva*, which was apparently introduced to provide a motive for the minor episode describing an invasion of Brittany. Although a few female figures are found in the borders and in attendance at the death of the Confessor (Fig. 6.19), none has any prominence. Both works are thus as bold and direct as the poetry and art of the coming Gothic period was delicate and subtle. Roland and his counterparts in the tapestry fought for king and country. In later literature, the knightly hero entered the list of war recruits in exchange for a loving glance from his lady's eyes, a fleeting smile, or a fragrant rose tossed from his lady's chamber.

The Romanesque in general, and its worldly side in particular, were characterized by the process of forming, experimenting with, and reaching out toward new modes of expression. The emphasis in the tapestry on representations of castles, fortifications, and specific buildings, like the Bayeux Cathedral and the abbey churches at Caen, suggests that the Romanesque created a busy builder's world, full of innovation. The forthright, direct narration of deeds in the *Song of Roland* and the Bayeux Tapestry finds its architectural counterpart in the functional honesty of the White Tower and William's church at Caen. Just as the action-filled stories of the *Song of Roland* and the Tapestry take precedence over literary form and decorative flourish, so the structural honesty of the building process, as exemplified by the White Tower and St. Étienne, becomes the leading characteristic.

The Norman secular world inherited the Viking adventurer's clear-headed and boisterous outlook. The Normans caught on quickly to any progressive development of the time, whether it was the discarding of their rather inflexible mother tongue in favor of the more expressive French or the adopting of many of the Cluniac moral and architectural reforms. Whatever the Normans did, they did with characteristic determination and energy. Thus, the rugged man of action, William the Conquerer, finds a parallel in the military monosyllables of the *Song of Roland,* the frank, almost comic-strip directness of the Bayeux Tapestry, and the rough-hewn stones of the White Tower. Each was concerned with forms of action, and whether in picture, word, or stone, the epic spirit is present. Deed on deed, syllable on syllable, stitch on stitch, image on image, stone on stone—each builds to a robust presence.

TRADITION AND INNOVATION

The veneration of past traditions figured strongly in Romanesque thought. The divine order of their world had been handed down in the Scriptures, where the word of God was manifest. Curiously enough, this traditionalism never led to stagnation or uniformity. In making learned commentaries on the Scriptures, the writers unconsciously, and sometimes consciously, interpreted them in the light of contemporary views. And as the untaught populace traveled about Europe on pilgrimages and later went to the Near East on the Crusades, they absorbed new ideas that eventually were to transform the provincialism of feudal times into a more dynamic social structure.

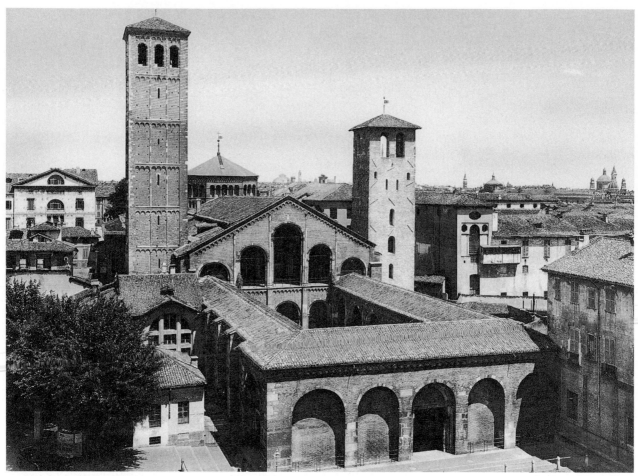

6.30 Sant'Ambrogio, Milan, Italy, from west, c. 1181. Length, including atrium, 390′; width 92′.

Diversity rather than unity was the rule of Romanesque architecture. Regional building traditions and the availability of craftspeople and materials contributed to the varied pattern. St. Mark's in Venice (see Fig. 12.1) combines the multidomed Byzantine style with Greek cross ground plans. Moorish influence was felt in Spain. In northern Italy, Sant'Ambrogio in Milan (Fig. 6.30) has the rich red brickwork and square belfry towers typical of Lombardy. In central Italy, the Romanesque was characterized by zebra-striped exteriors composed of alternating strips of dark green and cream-colored marbles, as at the Baptistry of Florence and the Cathedral of Pisa. In sum, all the arts of the period exhibited extraordinary inventiveness and such rich variety as to make the Romanesque one of the most spontaneous and original periods in history.

YOUR RESOURCES

- ***Exploring Humanities CD-ROM***
  - ○ Interactive Map: Europe about 1100
  - ○ Architectural Basics: The Romanesque Portal
  - ○ Readings—*Song of Roland*

- ***Web Site***

  http://art.wadsworth.com/fleming10
  - ○ Chapter 6 Quiz
  - ○ Links—Online Reading: *Beowulf*

- ***Audio CD***
  - ○ *Hymn to St. John*
  - ○ *Parallel Organum*
  - ○ Vogelweider, *Palestine Song*

THE ROMANESQUE PERIOD

Key Events	Architecture and Visual Arts	Literature and Music
c. 480–c. 547 **St. Benedict,** founder of Western monasticism; c. 540 formulated monastic rules	c. 529 **St. Benedict** built abbey at Monte Cassino, Italy	

800

Key Events	Architecture and Visual Arts	Literature and Music
841 **Vikings** invaded and colonized northern France 910 **Abbey of Cluny** in Burgundy, France, founded	c. 820 **St. Gall** (Switzerland) monastery, plan drafted	c. 800–850 *Beowulf,* epic poem composed; earliest manuscript c. 1000 840–912 **Notker Balbulus,** poet and hymn writer 927–942 **Odo,** abbot of Cluny, reputed author of musical treatises 980 **Organ with 400 pipes** constructed at Winchester, England c. 995–c. 1050 **Guido of Arezzo,** author of musical treatises; inventor of staff notation

1000

Key Events	Architecture and Visual Arts	Literature and Music
c. 1000 **Leif Eriksen,** Viking navigator, reached North America (?) 1035 **William** (c. 1027–1087) succeeded as Duke of Normandy after father's death on pilgrimage to Jerusalem 1041–1066 **Edward the Confessor,** king of England 1049–1109 **Hugh of Semur,** abbot of Cluny 1051 **Duke William** visited England; probably received promise of English succession from Edward the Confessor 1053 **William** married his cousin Matilda, daughter of Count of Flanders, who traced lineage from Alfred the Great 1057 **Normans** arrive in southern Italy 1059 **Pope** granted dispensation for marriage of William to Matilda 1064 **Duke Harold of England** visited Normandy; presumably upheld William's claim to English throne 1061–1091 **Norman** conquest of Sicily under Roger I (1031–1101) 1066 **Death of Edward the Confessor;** coronation of Harold as successor; invasion of England by William the Conqueror; Battle of Hastings, Harold killed; William crowned king of England 1066 **William, Duke of Normandy** conquered England 1066–1087 **William the Conqueror** reigned as king of England 1077 **Emperor Henry IV** bowed to Pope Gregory VII at Canossa; Abbot Hugh of Cluny mediated 1085 **Domesday Survey,** census and land as basis for taxation 1088–1099 **Urban II of Cluny** became pope; 1095 preached First Crusade 1095 **First Crusade** 1098 **Cistercian order** founded by St. Bernard of Clairvaux; principal opposition to Cluniac order	1037–1066 **Abbey Church of Notre Dame** at Jumiège built in early Norman Romanesque style 1043 **Imperial Palace** of Holy Roman emperors built near Goslar 1065 **Westminster Abbey** in Norman style dedicated by Edward the Confessor; later rebuilt in Gothic style 1063 **Pisa Cathedral** begun; 1153 Baptistry added c. 1064 **Church of St. Étienne** (Abbaye-aux-Hommes) begun at Caen, under patronage of William; Church of Ste. Trinité (Abbaye-aux-Dames) begun at Caen under patronage of Matilda c. 1075 **Pilgrimage church** at Santiago de Compostela, Spain, begun c. 1073–1088 **Bayeux Tapestry** embroidered in English workshop 1078 **Tower of London** begun by William c. 1080 **Church of Sant'Ambrogio** begun in Milan c. 1088–1160 **Church of St. Sernin** built at Toulouse, France 1088–1130 **Great Third Church at Cluny** built under Hugh of Semur, perhaps by architect Hezelo; 1088–1095 capitals depicting tones of plainsong carved; 1095 apse dedicated by Pope Urban II 1093 **Durham Cathedral** begun; Norman style with high ribbed vaulting 1096–1120 **Abbey Church of La Madeleine** at Vézelay built; 1096 church begun, 1104 Romanesque choir and transept dedicated, 1110 nave finished, 1120 narthex begun and nave revaulted after fire, c. 1130 tympanum over central portal of narthex carved, 1132 dedicated	c. 1000 **Minstrels** convened during Lenten season at Fécamp, Normandy c. 1050 **Beginnings of polyphonic singing** 1098–1179 **Hildegard of Bingen,** poet and composer

1100

Key Events	Architecture and Visual Arts	Literature and Music
1101–1154 **Roger II** ruled Sicily 1147–1149 **Second Crusade**	c. 1100 **Sculptures of Abbey of St. Trophîme** carved c. 1130–1135 **Gislebertus** carved sculptures at St. Lazare, Autun 1168–1188 **Matteo** carved Portico de Gloria at Cathedral of Santiago de Compostela, Spain	c. 1100 *Song of Roland,* epic poem, written in Old French c. 1100 **Music school of St. Martial** at Limoges founded; developed polyphonic style 1110 **Earliest record of miracle play** being performed c. 1200 *Nibelungenlied,* German epic poem, written c. 1237–1288 **Adam de la Halle,** author and composer of *Le jeu de Robin et Marion* (c. 1280), pastoral play with sole surviving example of chanson de geste melody

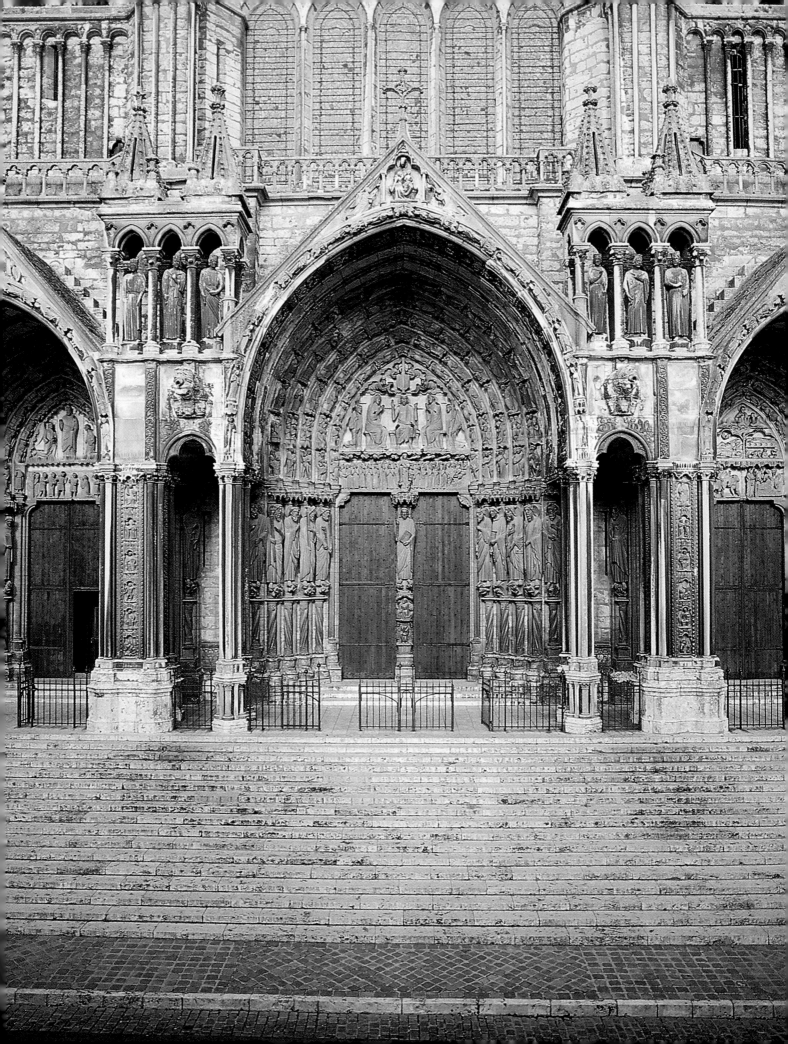

G O T H I C   S T Y L E

IN CONTRAST TO THE SHORES of the Mediterranean, where centers of culture such as Athens, Alexandria, Antioch, Constantinople, and Rome flourished for centuries, northern Europe had been little more than a rural region with a few Roman provincial outposts and, later, a scattering of castles, monasteries, and villages. Before the thirteenth century, not one medieval center north of the Alps could properly have been described as a city. Yet town life flourished from the eleventh century on, as strong regional political figures emerged and the responsibility of a king to maintain order became more accepted by the nobles. The greater civil stability was enforced by religious and secular authorities to accommodate pilgrims who increasingly traveled to towns like Chartres, where important relics were kept. Similarly, the Crusades enlarged international trade and encouraged the development of commercial centers that widened the influence of towns and boosted their patronage of the arts. As the towns grew, townspeople developed a sense of their distinctiveness in relation to the nobles and the church. Sometimes nobles were persuaded to grant charters to the towns, thereby enhancing the municipalities' political and financial independence.

PARIS AND ITS SURROUNDINGS

Toward the end of the twelfth century, Philip Augustus, king of France, set out to promote Paris as his capital. He ordered that the city be enclosed with walls and directed that some of its streets be paved with stone. His palace at the heart of the city eventually became the Louvre museum. The work continued under his successors, and by the end of the thirteenth century, Paris was the capital of a kingdom with growing financial, commercial, and cultural influence. With its splendid Cathedral of Notre Dame; its university famed for the teaching of Abelard, Albertus Magnus, Thomas Aquinas, and Bonaventura; and its flourishing mercantile trade capable of supporting about 150,000 inhabitants, Paris could well claim the status of a capital city. Like other expanding urban areas, it rapidly became a cultural center. In particular, education shifted from the monasteries of the countryside to the universities and cathedral-sponsored schools of the cities and towns.

The growth of Paris was far from an isolated instance. For a full century the town as a social unit and cultural center had been gaining importance over the manorial estate. The literature of the time mentions Ghent with its turreted houses, Lille and its cloth, Tours and its grain, and how all engaged in commerce with distant lands. Above all, the vibrancy of town and city life was symbolized by the building and decoration of Gothic cathedrals.

In the eleventh and twelfth centuries, people did not refer to their cathedrals as Gothic, but simply called them "new." The term *Gothic* came into use later, during the Italian Renaissance, as a term of contempt for architecture that seemed coarse because it excluded the elements of Roman classicism. To Renaissance eyes, the Gothic cathedrals were barbarian at heart, crude imitations of the towering German forests. Later interpreters, especially in the nineteenth century (see pp. 491–494) transformed the Renaissance insult into praise for the Gothic spirit of liberty that rejected the restrictive and shopworn rules of Rome.

In fact, traces of Roman, Early Christian, and Romanesque basilicas (see pp. 95 and 125) are still evident in the Gothic cathedral's nave, aisles, and transept. What is strikingly new, and long associated with the idea of northern European independence, is the soaring height of the Gothic cathedral, which could be seen for miles towering over the city or town that built it. The cathedrals were grand displays of community, encapsulating the physical effort, religious exaltation, and emotional and intellectual forces of the people who created them. Because the building process often spanned several centuries, few were finished according to their original builders' plans. They were,

PAST AND PRESENT

What Is a Goth?

Goths were members of a Germanic tribe who took advantage of the weakening of the Roman Empire and invaded Italy in the fifth century (see p. 117). The term *gothic* as applied to architecture only indirectly derives from the Goths. The term was first used by Renaissance scholars, looking back at the architecture of the north, which they considered inferior to classical buildings. In the seventeenth and eighteenth centuries, the word's meaning broadened to identify rude, cruel, and uncivilized behavior. For example, Ben Franklin used it to describe the British troops during the Revolutionary War. Similarly, in the early twentieth century, critics of the work of artists Henri Matisse and André Derain called them wild beasts (see pp. 557–558).

At the beginning of the 1980s, Goth subculture emerged in Britain as part of the punk rock scene. It quickly spread throughout Europe and North America. With their black clothing, body piercings, unique hairstyles, and interest in medieval-themed fantasy games such as Dungeons and Dragons, Goths were judged to be crude outsiders who renounced middle-class values. In fact, Goth culture, which persists into the twenty-first century, is composed of people whose looks do not indicate the wide variety of their ideas. Some are pacifists, whereas others are drawn to art and music that dwells on despair. Such "civilized" authors as the Renaissance poet Dante, author of the *Divine Comedy* (see pp. 232–234), and the Romantic poet Lord Byron (see p. 449) have found a new and enthusiastic audience among contemporary Goths.

in a sense, works in progress, manifestations of an ongoing struggle and dynamic urge to reach upward to embrace infinity.

ST. DENIS

The prototype of the Gothic cathedral is found in the abbey church of St. Denis, just outside Paris. This monastery was under the direct patronage of

the French kings and was their traditional burial place. Around the middle of the twelfth century, its abbot was Suger, a man whose talents were as remarkable as his origins were humble. The trusted confidant of two kings, he ruled France as regent while Louis VII was away on a Crusade. When he undertook the rebuilding of his abbey church, his great personal prestige, as well as its importance as the royal monastery and burial

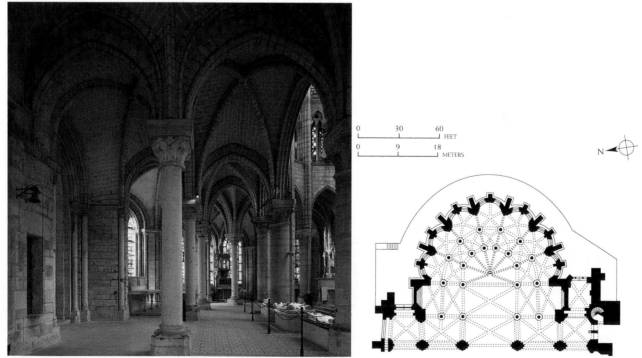

7.1   (A) Choir and ambulatory of Abbey Church of St. Denis, near Paris, France, 1140–1144. (B) Plan of Choir, Abbey Church of St. Denis.

place, enabled him to call together the most expert craftspeople from all parts of the kingdom. Suger's church became a synthesis of all the ideas that Romanesque builders had tried and found successful.

The abbot's enthusiasm for his project inspired him to write extensively about it, and his book is an invaluable source of information about the architectural thought of the time. In 1130, when St. Denis was in the planning stage, Abbot Suger made a prolonged visit to Cluny (see pp. 160–165) to learn about its recently completed church. His commentary on the iconography of the windows and sculpture of St. Denis suggests that he was directly involved in this part of the project. Yet he makes no mention of the architect or master mason who carried out the plan. Many late Cluniac Romanesque churches had used the pointed arch and the ribbed vault (see Fig. 6.26), but when Suger rebuilt the choir at St. Denis the elements were brought together in a dynamic structural interplay (Fig. 7.1).

We can only speculate on the circumstances that prompted Suger and his team of architects and designers to concoct their design. No doubt

Suger's insistence on stained glass influenced the decision to heighten the walls to let in more light. Also, the use of stained glass might have suggested the idea of thinner walls, because the windows look best when they are not set deep in thick masonry. St. Denis was one of many early twelfth-century buildings where older forms were being replaced by the "new" architecture. Suger's writings reveal that he was competitive and ready to seize the moment to create something fresh at St. Denis.

THE ÎLE-DE-FRANCE AND ITS CATHEDRAL TOWNS

The Île-de-France (see Map 7.1), with Paris as its center, was the setting in which the Gothic style originated and where, over a period approximately from 1150 to 1300, it reached the climax of its development. The name of this region referred to the royal lands under the direct control of the French king. The rest of what is now France was still under the dominion of various feudal lords. Through heredity, marriage, conquest, and purchase, the Île-de-France gradually grew into

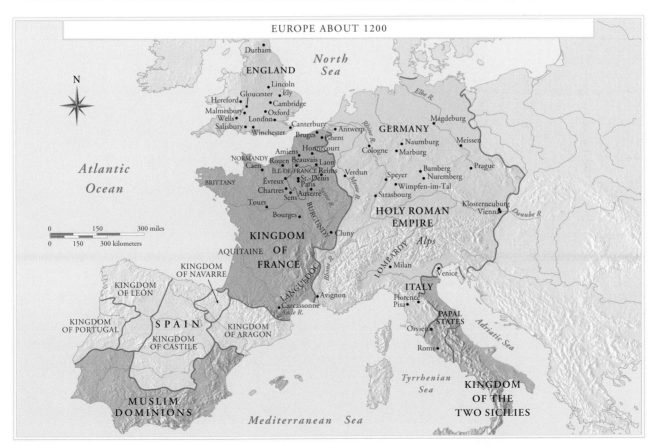

MAP 7.1

the nucleus of the future French nation. Like a wheel with Paris as its hub, it radiated outward about 100 miles, with spokes extending toward the cathedral towns of Amiens, Beauvais, Rheims, Bourges, Rouen, and Chartres.

The spires of the Gothic cathedrals rose above the rooftops of those towns and could be seen from great distances. Unlike an abbey church, a cathedral was primarily in a populated area under the administration of a bishop, whose official seat it was. Whereas the subdued exterior of an abbey church suggested lack of interest in the material world, the intricate carving on the outside of a cathedral awakened curiosity and invited entrance. As the center of a cloistered life, a monastic church was richest in its dim interior. By contrast, the elaborate exterior decoration of a cathedral helped integrate the church into the life of the city. The tall towers of the Gothic cathedral beckoned the distant traveler and directed the weary steps of the peasant homeward after a day in the fields. The bells pealed to regulate the life of an entire town and its surrounding countryside. They told of weddings and funerals and marked the times for work, rest, and prayer.

A cathedral was, of course, primarily a religious center, but in a time when spiritual and worldly affairs were closely interwoven, the religious and secular functions of a cathedral were intermingled. Its nave was not only the setting for religious services but also on occasion a town hall where the entire populace could gather for a meeting. The rich decorations that clothed the body of the cathedral told both the

7.2   Chartres Cathedral, from the air, Chartres, France, c. 1194–1260.

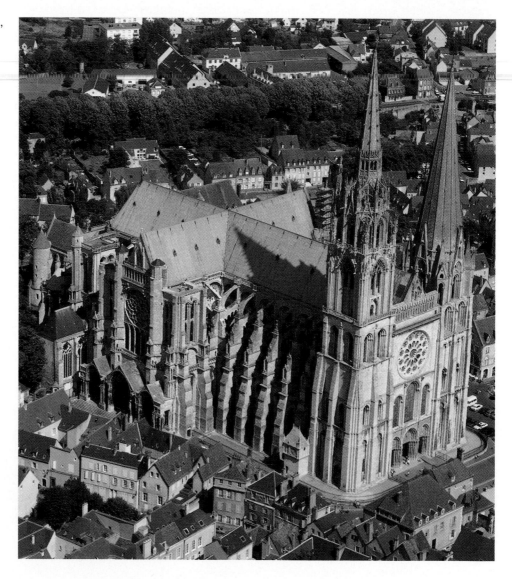

story of Christianity and the history of the town and the activities of its people.

The iconography of a cathedral dedicated to Notre Dame (Our Lady) was concerned mainly with religious subjects. Because the Virgin Mary was also the patron of the liberal arts, her cathedral often constituted a visual encyclopedia whose subjects ranged over the entire field of human knowledge. The pulpit was not only the place from which sermons were preached but also a podium for lectures and instruction. The sanctuary became a theater in which a constantly changing religious drama was enacted. The choir was the setting for liturgical song, but like a concert hall or opera house, it was also a place where intricate polyphonic choral works could be performed and the melodies of the religious dramas chanted.

Outside, the deep-set portals provided stage sets for mystery plays appropriate to the season, and the porches became platforms from which minstrels and jugglers could entertain their audiences. The stone statues and stained glass served as useful illustrations for sermons but also functioned as picture galleries to stimulate the imagination.

CHARTRES CATHEDRAL

Chartres (Fig. 7.2), unlike Paris, was never a center of commerce but rather a small town of fewer than 10,000 in the midst of a rural district southwest of Paris. Its great attraction and growth as a cultural center came from its shrine to the Virgin Mary. Thousands of people annually congregated from far and wide to celebrate the feasts of the Virgin in the grand celebrations that were unique to the Cathedral of Chartres.

Here as elsewhere, the cathedral was not only the spiritual center of the lives of the townsfolk but also the geographic center of the medieval town. Towering over all, its great shadow fell across clustering church buildings that included the bishop's palace, the cathedral school, a cloister, a hospice or lodging for travelers, and an almshouse to aid the poor. Its west facade faced one side of the marketplace, and from the cathedral square radiated the narrow streets on which were located the houses and shops of the townspeople. As members of guilds (associations of craftspeople), the people of the town contributed their labor and products to the cathedral

when it was being built, and through their guilds donated windows and statuary. They filled continuing needs, such as candles for the altars and bread for the communion service.

As years of labor and treasure were poured into a cathedral, tensions rose among leading town groups. Church-imposed taxes created lasting resentments and led to demonstrations and resistance. Nevertheless, the cathedral itself was a huge group effort of stonecutters, masons, carpenters, glassmakers, and metalworkers, all of whom gave of their time, skill, and wealth to build it. It was the greatest single product a town could produce. Appropriately, a cathedral usually could hold all the town's residents.

As a great civic monument, a cathedral was the pride of the community, and the ambitions and aspirations of citizens determined its character and contours. In those days the importance of a town could be measured by the size and height of its cathedral, as well as by the significance of the religious relics it housed. Civic rivalry thus was involved when the vaulting of Chartres rose about 120 feet. Next came the cathedral at Amiens, which achieved a height of about 140 feet. Finally Beauvais became the tallest of all, with the crowns of its high vaults soaring to about 157 feet.

The extraordinary religious enthusiasm that prompted the undertaking and construction of these immense projects is described by several medieval writers. Allowing for the enthusiasm of a religious zealot, as well as for the probably symbolic participation of the nobles in manual labor, Abbot Haimon's observations in England convey the spirit of these times:

> Who has ever heard tell, in times past, that powerful princes of the world, that men brought up in honor and wealth, that nobles, men and women, have bent their proud and haughty necks to the harness of carts, and that, like beasts of burden, they have dragged to the abode of Christ these waggons, loaded with wines, grains, oil, stone, wood, and all that is necessary for the wants of life, or for the construction of the church? . . . When they have reached the church, they arrange the waggons about it like a spiritual camp, and during the whole night they celebrate the watch by hymns and canticles. On each waggon they light tapers and lamps; they place there the infirm and sick, and bring them the precious relics of the Saints for their relief.

THE ARCHITECTURE OF CHARTRES

WEST FACADE. When one first observes the west facade of the Cathedral of Notre Dame at Chartres (Fig. 7.3A), it is difficult to imagine that so solid a monument is actually the end result of fire salvage, a long process of growth, and a good amount of improvisation. Four centuries, in fact, separate the earliest parts from the latest. The interval between saw rapid construction in times of prosperity, slower progress in times of poverty, work inspired by religious ardor, and cruel destruction by fire.

The stylistic difference between the two spires is one of the most striking features of the Chartres facade. The supporting towers, part of the previous church, are approximately contemporary. The upper part and the spire on the right, however, date from the time the later parts of the Romanesque abbey church at Cluny were being finished. The spire on the left came more than 300 years later.

Close inspection reveals some minor flaws, such as the discrepancy between the proportions of the portals and the scale of the facade as a whole, the slightly off-center rose window, and the awkward joining of the gallery and arcade of kings above it with the tower on the right. Despite these differences, the facade bears out the initial impression of unity surprisingly well. Its space is logically divided and predicts the layout of the interior (Fig. 7.3B). Horizontally, the three entrance portals lead into the nave, while the flanking towers face the aisles. Vertically, the portals correspond to the nave arcade within, the lancets to the triforium gallery, and the rose window to the clerestory level. By this means, the spatial composition maintains a close relationship between the inner and outer aspects of the structure.

Rising above the twin towers are the tall, tapering spires that seem a logical and necessary continuation of the vertical lines of the sup-

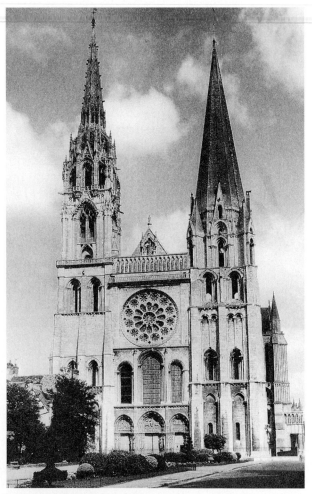
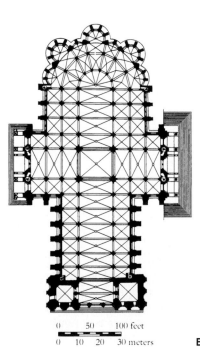

7.3   (A) West facade, Chartres Cathedral. Portals and lancet windows, c. 1145; south tower (right), c. 1180, height 344′; north spire (left), 1507–1513, height 377′. Length of cathedral 427′, width of facade 157′. (B) Plan of Chartres Cathedral.

porting buttresses below and a fitting expression of the Gothic spirit of aspiration.

THE INTERIOR.   Upon entering Chartres Cathedral through the central portal, one sees the broad nave extending toward the transept. On either side are amply proportioned aisles flanked by stained-glass windows that allow a flood of colored light to flow throughout the entire structure

(Fig. 7.4). The plan reveals that in comparison with the abbey church at Cluny, the walls are thinner and the building relies more on buttresses. Instead of running parallel to the nave, the buttresses at Chartres are at right angles to it and the area between is bridged over with vaults. This provides open space for glass to light the interior at both the ground and clerestory levels.

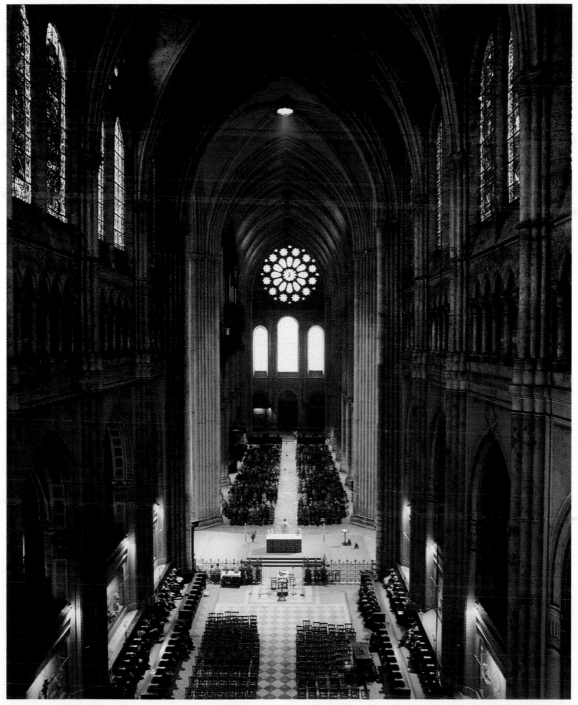

7.4   Nave and rose window, Chartres Cathedral, c. 1194–1260. Length of nave 130′, width 53′, height 122′.

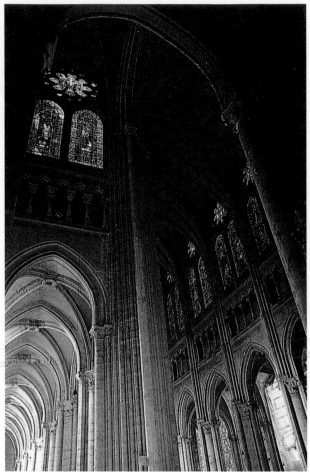

A

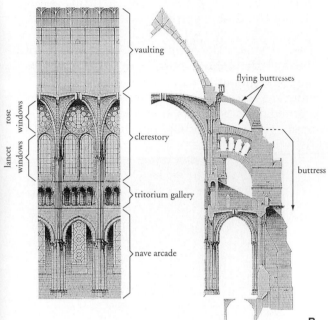

B

7.5   (A) South clerestory wall of nave, Chartres Cathedral, c. 1194–1260. (B) Transverse section of nave (left) and diagram of vaulting (right), Chartres Cathedral. Drawing by Goubert.

Through the language of form and color and in representations of religious subjects, the wall space communicates visually with the worshipers. As the sun moves across the sky, beams of tinted light emerge from the stained-glass windows and transform the floor and walls into a constantly changing mosaic of color. Together with the clerestory windows, the shafts of mysterious light accent the structural system of arches, piers, and vaults and contribute to the illusion of infinite size and upward straining. Because the eye is naturally drawn to light, the interior gives the impression of being composed entirely of windows (Fig. 7.5A).

From the center of the nave, attention is drawn to the arcade of six bays marching majestically toward the crossing of the transept and the choir beyond. Each immense **pier** consists of a strong central column with four attached **colonnettes** of more slender proportions clustered around it. As Figure 7.5A shows, piers with cylindrical cores and attached octagonal colonnettes alternate with piers with octagonal cores and attached cylindrical colonnettes. An interesting rhythm of procession and recession is set up, and further variation

is provided by the play of light on the alternating round and angular surfaces of the piers.

The space above the graceful pointed arches of the nave arcade is filled by a series of smaller open arches that span the space between the bays (Fig. 7.5B). Behind them runs the triforium gallery, a passage using the space above the internal roofing over the aisles and under the slanting external roof that extends outward from the base of the clerestory. Above the triforium runs the clerestory level, which now fully accomplishes its purpose. The triple pattern of two tall, pointed **lancet windows** below and a circular one above provides a maximum of open space for glass and a minimum amount of masonry.

The triumph of the Gothic builders was engineering the vault to cover the nave. At Chartres the broad *quadripartite,* or four-part, vaulting (Figs. 7.4 and 7.5B) rises about 120 feet above ground level. It is this principle of vaulting that underlies all Gothic architecture and, in turn, explains all the supporting facts of shafts, colonnettes, clustered columns, buttresses, and pointed arches. Each of these plays a role in directing the descending weight of the in-

ing is organized to achieve a gradual crescendo. It proceeds from the dark violet and blue lancets and rose window in the west through the brighter tones of the aisle and clerestory windows of the nave, past the flaming reds of the transept rose windows, to the high intensity of the five red and orange lancets in the apse. These apsidal windows soar above the altar and capture the rays of the morning sun.

Romanesque abbey churches were lighted mainly from within by lamps and candles, whereas Gothic interiors were illuminated by sunlight transformed through stained glass into a myriad of mysterious prismatic colors. The light activated the interior masses and voids, producing a flowing harmonious whole.

THE EXTERIOR.   At Chartres, each of the interior members has an opposite number (Fig. 7.6). The purpose of the flying buttress is to carry the thrust of the vaulting at specific points over the aisles to the outer buttresses that are set at right angles to the length of the nave. From the observer's point of view, just as in the interior of the cathedral the eye is drawn irresistibly upward by the rising vertical lines, on the outside it follows the rising vertical piers to the pinnacles, along the procession of the flying buttresses toward the roof of the transept, and on to infinity.

The extensive use of the pointed arch also becomes clearer when one observes the exterior. At Cluny, it was used mainly as a decorative motif to promote a feeling of height and elegance (see Fig. 6.6), but the Gothic architects pointed their arches to raise the crowns of the intersecting ribs of the vaulting and thus achieve a uniform height with great structural stability. A round arch tends to spread sideways under the gravitational force of the weight it bears. By contrast, a pointed arch, being steeper, directs the thrust of its load downward onto the upright supporting members (Fig. 7.7B).

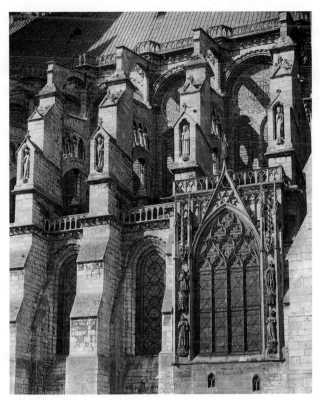

7.6   South nave exterior, Chartres Cathedral, c. 1194–1260.

tersecting ribs of the vaults toward the ground as efficiently as possible. The heavier transverse ribbing is carried past the clerestory and triforium levels by the large central shafts, while the smaller cross-ribs are borne by the groups of slender colonnettes that extend downward and cluster around the massive central piers of the nave arcade below.

Gothic interiors need little decorative detail other than the vertical lines of the structural members, the variety of representations in stained glass, and above all, the flow of light. At Chartres the light-

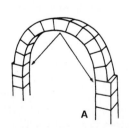
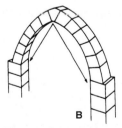
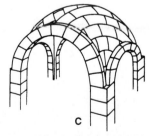
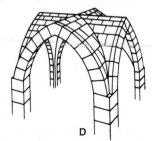

7.7   The pointed arch and ribbed groin vault are fundamental to Gothic architecture, making it a light and flexible building system that permits generous openings in walls for large, high windows. The result is well-illuminated interior spaces. Whereas the less stable, lower round arches spread the load laterally (A), pointed arches, being more vertical, thrust their load more directly toward the ground (B). Also, pointed arches can rise to any height, but the height of semicircular arches is governed by the space they span. In (C) and (D) the space, or *bay,* that has been vaulted is rectangular in shape, rather than square. In (C) the round arches create a dome-shaped vault whose forms and openings are irregular and restricted. In (D) the pointed arches rise to a uniform height and form a four-part Gothic vault with ample openings.

Through the ever-increasing skill with which they used the pointed arch, Gothic builders were able to achieve constantly increasing heights. This, in turn, led to loftier vaults and more ethereal effects.

When all these various devices—pointed arch, rib vault, flying buttress, triforium gallery, walls maintained by spacious arcades, window spaces maximized at all levels—came together in a working relationship, Gothic architects were able to bring dead masses of masonry into an lively equilibrium of weights and balances. Gothic architecture is thus a complex system of opposing thrusts and counterthrusts (Fig. 7.6) in which all parts exist in a logical relationship to the whole.

THE TRANSEPT, CHOIR, AND APSE. At Chartres the wings of the transept terminate in triple portals (Fig. 7.8) that in size and magnificence surpass those of the western facade, parts of which had survived from the previous church. The north and south portals in the thirteenth-century style are framed by row upon row of richly sculptured receding archivolts that bring a maximum of light and shadow into play. The shape of such sections was determined in part by the tastes of individual donors. The north transept, with its portals, porch, and stained glass, was the gift of the royal family of France, primarily Blanche of Castile and her son Louis IX; its southern counterpart was donated by their arch-rival, the Duke of Brittany. When the cathedral was dedicated in the year 1260, Louis IX (later canonized as a saint) was present with an immense assembly of bishops, canons, princes, and peasants.

Beyond the transepts extend the spacious choir and sanctuary, surrounded by a double-aisled ambulatory that gives easy access to the apse and its necklace of radiating chapels. The increasingly elaborate Gothic liturgy demanded the participation of more and more clerics, and the

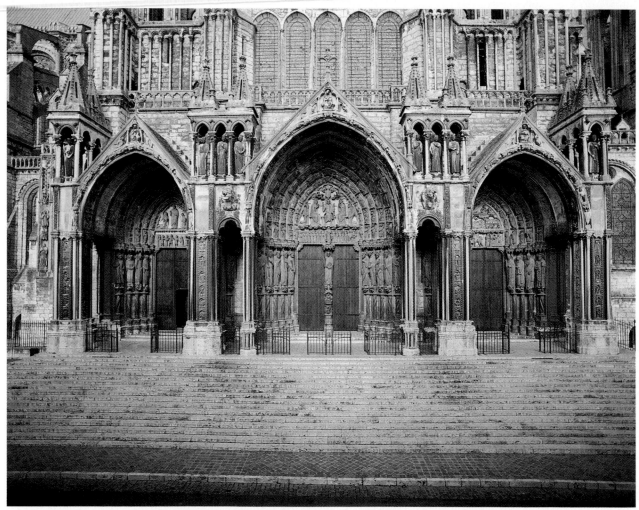

7.8 South Porch, Chartres Cathedral, c. 1210–1215.

cavernous recesses of the huge structure were needed to accommodate an ever-growing number of choristers. The apsidal chapels are also a distinctive feature of a developed Gothic plan. They provided access to the various altars where the revered relics of saints were kept in reliquaries.

The Cathedral of Notre Dame at Chartres was closely associated with the cult of the Virgin Mary, as were earlier churches that stood on the same site. Its most famous relic was the legendary veil of the Virgin, which, by tradition, had been presented to Charlemagne by the Byzantine empress Irene. Another chapel enshrined the skull of St. Anne, the Virgin's mother, which was brought back by crusaders and given to the church in 1205. This relic explains the many representations of St. Anne in statuary and stained glass and the pilgrimages in her honor, which were second only to those of the Virgin herself.

The most notable chapel in Gothic cathedrals was the *Notre Dame* (Lady Chapel), devoted to Mary, whose importance grew throughout the eleventh and twelfth centuries. She was prominently represented on tympanums and in these specially dedicated chapels. The Lady Chapel was usually placed on the main axis of the nave beyond the center of the apse, with chapels of other saints grouped on either side. All these considerations caused the parts beyond the cathedrals' transepts to expand to unprecedented proportions.

SCULPTURE AT CHARTRES

The sculptural and pictorial representations whose themes and locations contributed to the church's significance and meaning were as important to the medieval mind as the structure of the cathedral itself. In a Romanesque monastic church, sculptural elements were found in the carved tympanums over the narthex portals, on the capitals of the columns throughout the interior, and in wall paintings, especially at the apsidal end. Because such representations were designed for people who led cloistered lives, they were placed inside and the variety, subtlety, and multiple meanings of their subjects make it clear that they were meant to be pondered and carefully studied.

By contrast, Gothic sculpture faced the outside world, where it clustered around and over the porches and entrance portals to form an integral part of the architectural design. The exterior of Chartres has more than 2,000 carved figures distributed among the west facade and the north and south porches of the transepts. Sculpture at Chartres and elsewhere was closely allied with its architectural framework. Because most of it was located out of doors, the play of light and shade at different times of the day had to be considered. And although there was plenty of variety in the subjects chosen, the figures found their unity in a preconceived iconographical, or pictorial, program.

ICONOGRAPHY. A Gothic cathedral, with the all-embracing activities it housed and the all-encompassing subject matter of its sculpture and stained glass, has often been likened to a **summa,** a comprehensive summary of law, philosophy, and theology written by medieval scholars that covers both religious and secular knowledge. Cathedrals have also been described as the Bible in stone and glass or as the books of the illiterate. Nevertheless, they must also be viewed as visual encyclopedias for the educated. The key to the iconography of Chartres is the encyclopedic character of medieval thought as found in the *Speculum Majus* of the French Dominican scholar Vincent of Beauvais. He divided all learning into Mirrors of Nature, Instruction, History, and Morality. The Mirror of Nature is seen in the plant and animal forms, which are represented in comprehensive fashion. Instruction is present in the personifications of the seven liberal arts and the branches of learning taught in the universities. History is found in the story of humanity from Adam and Eve to the Last Judgment. Finally, Morality can be seen in the figures depicting virtue and vice, the wise and foolish virgins, the saved and the damned in the Last Judgment, and the hovering saints and angels and fleeing gargoyles and devils.

The sculpture is logically organized and presents a sequence of events with a beginning, middle, and end. Starting with the west facade, the life of Christ commences with his ancestors and continues through his birth, ministry, death, and ascension. The facade of the north transept is concerned with the Virgin Mary, from her ancestors to her heavenly coronation. The south transept is faced with a profusion of figures signifying human redemption. It begins with the foundation of the church; continues with its saints, great popes, abbots, and bishops; and concludes with the Last Judgment.

Each of the three porches has approximately 700 carved figures clustered in the three tympanums over the portals, the archivolts that frame them, and the columns below and galleries above. In addition to scriptural scenes and lives of the saints, the designers found a place for ancient lore and contemporary history, for prophecy and fact, for fabulous animals and the latest scientific knowledge, for portraits of princes and merchants, and for beautiful angels and grotesque gargoyles, some of which function as water spouts to drain the roof, whereas others symbolize demons fleeing from the sacred precincts of the church.

The iconography at Chartres thus stems from three principal sources: the dedication of the cathedral to Our Lady, an honor that was shared with other Notre Dame cathedrals, such as those at Paris, Rheims, Rouen, and Amiens; the presence of a cathedral school, an important center of learning, for Mary was also the patron of the liberal arts; and the preferences of such patrons as the royal family, the lesser nobility, the clergy, and the local guilds, who donated so many of the sculptures and windows.

It must also be borne in mind that sacred and secular elements in a medieval town and manor were so closely interwoven that every spiritual manifestation had a worldly counterpart. So the cathedral, as the court of Mary, Queen of Heaven, had to surpass in magnificence the grandeur that surrounded any mere earthly queen.

THE WEST FACADE OR ROYAL PORTAL. The sculptures and doorways of the west facade at Chartres are called the Royal Portal (Fig. 7.9). The central tympanum encloses the figure of Christ in Majesty surrounded by the four symbolic beasts of the Evangelists and the twenty-four elders of the Apocalypse. The tympanum over the left portal depicts the close of Christ's days on Earth and his ascension. On the right is the tympanum of the Virgin Portal (Fig. 7.10), depicting the beginning of the Savior's earthly life.

The story of the Virgin is told in three rising panels. Starting in the lower left is the Annunciation, with the figures of the Angel Gabriel and Mary. The next pair shows the Visitation. The Nativity is in the center. The shepherds in the midst of their sheep are coming from the right for the Adoration, just as their successors came in from the fields near Chartres to worship at Mary's shrine. The middle panel depicts the presentation of the young Jesus in the temple. His position on the altar foreshadows his later sacrifice. Friends approach from both sides bearing gifts. In the top panel the Virgin sits crowned and enthroned, holding her divine son and being attended by a pair of archangels. She is shown frontally, as a queen accepting the homage of the humble, who enter her court through the portal below.

THE SEVEN LIBERAL ARTS. Of great interest are the figures in the archivolts that frame the tympanum. These figures symbolize Mary's attributes. Like Athena of old, the Virgin was the patron of the arts and sciences. The German philosopher Albertus

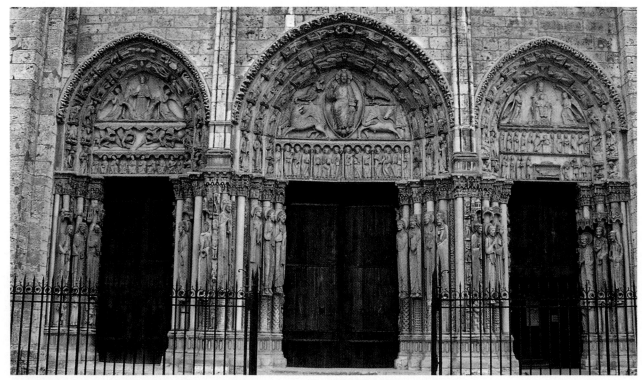

7.9 Royal Portal, west facade, Chartres Cathedral. Right, Virgin Portal, c. 1145–1170.

Magnus declared in his *Mariale* that the Virgin was perfect in the arts, and in his *Summa Theologiae,* the Italian theologian Thomas Aquinas included among his propositions the question of "Whether the Blessed Virgin Mary possessed perfectly the seven liberal arts," which he triumphantly affirmed. These representations are also reminders that this was an age that produced great scholars. Intellectual inquiry accompanied faith on the road to salvation. Indeed, Chartres was the location of one of the great cathedral schools. Before the founding of the University of Paris, Chartres shared with Rheims the distinction of being one of the best-known centers of learning in Europe.

The curriculum of the cathedral school was, of course, the seven liberal arts. These were divided into the *trivium,* which dealt with the science of words in the three subjects of grammar, rhetoric (speech), and dialectic (logic), and the higher faculty of the *quadrivium,* which was concerned with the science of numbers through the study of arithmetic, geometry, astronomy, and music.

On the archivolt, these seven arts are symbolized abstractly by female figures, somewhat akin to the ancient Muses, and below them are found their most famous human representatives. Beginning with the lower left corner of the outside archivolt, Aristotle is seen dipping his pen into an inkwell. Above him is the thoughtful figure of Dialectic. In one hand she holds a dragon-headed serpent, which symbolizes subtlety of contemplation, and in the other, she holds the torch of

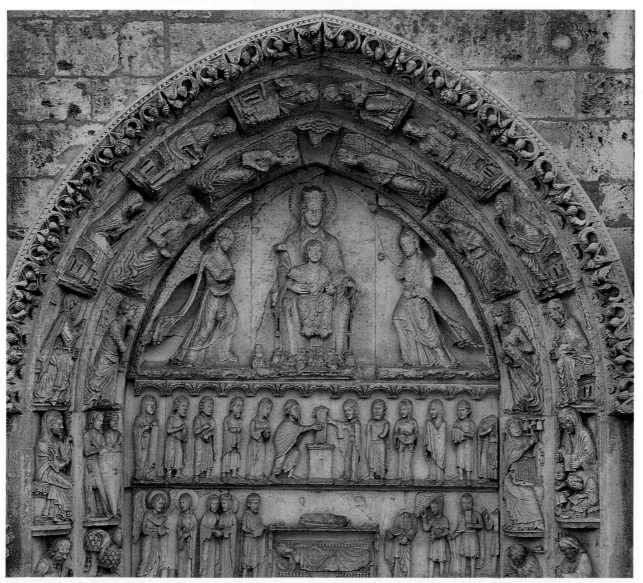

7.10 *Life of the Virgin Mary,* tympanum of the Virgin Portal, west facade, Chartres Cathedral, c. 1145–1170.

knowledge. Then comes Cicero, the great orator, and over him the figure of Rhetoric making a characteristic oratorical gesture. The next pair are Euclid and Geometry, both absorbed in calculations. In the same band, moving now from the top downward, is Arithmetic, probably personified by Boethius. Next is the stargazing figure of Astronomy, who holds a bushel basket that signifies the relationship of her science to the calendar, so important in a farming district like Chartres. Ptolemy, to whom the medievalists ascribed the invention of the calendar and the clock, is Astronomy's human representative.

The figures on the lowest level are Grammar and Donatus, the ancient Roman grammarian. Grammar (Fig. 7.11) holds an open book in one hand and a disciplinary switch in the other over two young pupils, one laughing and pulling the other's hair.

The last pair in the series of seven is adjacent to those in the inner archivolt. Below is Pythago-

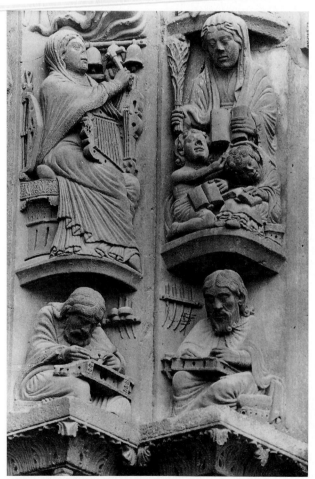

7.11   Details, Virgin Portal tympanum, west facade, Chartres Cathedral, c. 1145–1170. Music appears on the left; Grammar, on the right.

ras, the reputed founder of music theory, who is shown writing in medieval fashion with a desk over his knees. Above him is the figure of Music surrounded by instruments. At her back is a monochord, used to calculate musical intervals and to determine accuracy of pitch. A psaltery rests on her lap, and a three-stringed viol hangs on the wall. Music is striking a set of three chime bells, an allusion to the Pythagorean discovery of the mathematical ratios of the perfect intervals—the octave, the fifth, and the fourth. Both Gerbert of Rheims and his pupil, Bishop Fulbert of Chartres, are known to have taken an active interest not only in the theory of music but in its performance as well. The two figures, showing Pythagoras as the thinker and Music as the performer, signify that Chartres was an important center for the theoretical and practical aspects of music.

THE NORTH AND SOUTH PORCHES.   The north porch is far more elaborate in scope and less restrained in decorative detail than the west facade. With its three portals, it stretches to a width of 120 feet, thus spanning the transept completely. A gift of the royal family of France, its construction and decoration took place during the first 75 years of the thirteenth century, from the reign of Louis VIII and the regency of his queen, Blanche of Castile, through the reign of their son Louis IX. The north porch is dedicated to the Virgin and expands the theme of the Virgin Portal on the west facade to encyclopedic proportions. Her history, from the Annunciation and Nativity through the childhood of Jesus, is found on the left portal. The scenes of her death and assumption are depicted on the lintel over the central door, and those of her enthronement and coronation are in the tympanum above.

Mary's attributes are revealed in the archivolts through several series of cyclical representations, such as those of the fourteen heavenly beatitudes and twelve feminine personifications of the active and contemplative lives. Especially fine is the single figure of her mother, St. Anne, holding the infant Mary in her arms (Fig. 7.12). She adorns the ***trumeau,*** the post or pillar that supports the lintel and tympanum of the central portal. From the harmonious lines of the folds of her drapery to her dignified and matronly face, the work is one of the most satisfying examples of the mature Gothic sculptural style.

The arches of the portals on the south porch (Fig. 7.8) are more highly pointed than those of the west facade (Fig. 7.3A). Moreover, they are enclosed by triangular gables that further emphasize their verticality. The deep recession of the porch allows for a much greater play of light and shade on the statuary that covers every available space from the bases of the columns to the peak of the gable.

The figures on both the north and south porches, in comparison with the earlier ones on the west facade, have bodies that are more naturally proportioned; their postures show greater variety and informality, and their facial expressions have far more mobility. The representations of plants and animals are considerably closer to nature, and in comparison with the impersonality of those on the west front, many of the human figures are so individualized that they seem like portraits of living people. In the change of style, however, something of the previous symbolic meaning and monumentality has been lost, as well as the closer relationship with the architecture.

STAINED GLASS AT CHARTRES

Time has taken its toll on the exterior sculptures of Chartres. The flow of carved lines remains, and the varied play of light and shade relieves the present browns and grays, but only traces of the original colors and gilt are left to remind the observer that here was once a feast of color. In the interior, however, where the stained glass remains undimmed, the full color of medieval pageantry still exists. The wealth of pure color in the 175 surviving glass panels hypnotizes the senses. Through the medium of multicolored light, one can sense something of the emotional exaltation that inspired medieval people to create such a temple to the Queen of Heaven.

Although Chartres must share architectural and sculptural honors with its neighboring cities, the town was especially well known as the center of glassmaking. With the highest achievements of its glaziers exemplified in their own cathedral, Chartres is unsurpassed. The great variety of jewellike color was achieved chemically through the addition of certain minerals to the glass while it was in a molten state. When cool, the sheets were cut into smaller sections, and the designer fitted these into a previously prepared outline. Details, such as the features of the faces, were applied in the form of metal oxides and made permanent by firing in a kiln. Next, the glass pieces of various sizes were joined together by lead strips. Finally, the individual panels making up the pattern of the whole window were fastened to the iron bars already embedded in the masonry. When seen against the light, the glass appears translucent, and the lead and iron become opaque black lines that outline the figures and separate the colors to prevent blurring at a distance.

ICONOGRAPHY AND DONORS.   The iconographical plan of the glass at Chartres, like that of the exterior sculptures, is held together mainly by the dedication of the church as a shrine of the Virgin. There is never any doubt on the part of those who enter that they are in the presence of the Queen of Heaven, who sits enthroned in majesty in the central panel of the apse over the high altar. Grouped around her in neighboring panels are the archangels, saints, and prophets; emblems of the noble donors; and symbols of the craftspeople and tradespeople—almost 4,000 figures in all, who honor her and make up her court. Below, on her feast days, were the crowds of living pilgrims who gathered in the nave and chapels.

An interesting commentary on the changing social conditions of the thirteenth century can be read in the records of the donors of the windows. In the lowest part of each is a "signature" indicating the individual, family, or group who bore the

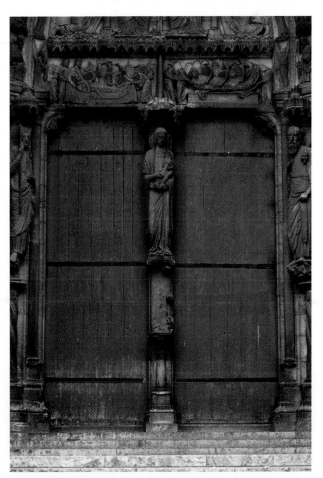

7.12 *St. Anne with the Virgin,* trumeau of Center Portal, north porch, Chartres Cathedral, c. 1250.

expense of the glass. Only a royal purse was equal to a large rose window, as evidenced by the fleur-de-lis insignia so prominent in the north rose window (see Fig. 7.14). Within the means of members of the aristocracy and the church hierarchy, such as bishops and canons, were the lancet windows of the nave and choir. The status and prosperity of the guilds of craftspeople and merchants, however, were such that most of the windows were donated by them.

Although the royal family of France and the Duke of Brittany were content with windows in the transepts, the most prominent windows of all, the 47-foot-high center lancets of the apse, were given by the guilds. Each guild had a patron saint, and a window under a guild's patronage was concerned with the life and miracles of its special saint. In the case of the nobility, the family coat of arms was sufficient to identify the donor; with a guild, the "signature" took the form of a craftsman engaged in some typical phase of work. In the windows of Chartres, some nineteen different guilds are shown; the one over the high altar was the gift of the bakers (Fig. 7.13).

THE ROSE WINDOWS.   The great rose window of the west facade dates from the early thirteenth century and thus is contemporary with the majority of examples in the rest of the church. The three lancets below it, however, like the portals and surrounding masonry on the exterior, originally were part of the previous church (Fig. 7.8). Their origin has been traced to the school that did the windows for Suger's church at St. Denis. Overall, the work on these lancets was finer grained and more jewellike, with infinite care lavished on the geometric and arabesque patterns in the borders. They are dominated by their vibrant blue background, whereas the figures and abstract patterns have been done in several shades of red, emerald green, yellow, sapphire, and white.

The great rose window of the north transept (Fig. 7.14), like the sculpture on the porch outside, glorifies the Virgin Mary. Together with its lancets, the composition shares with other thirteenth century glass a preference for red backgrounds instead of the earlier blue. The individual panes are larger and the borders more conventionalized. Its greatest effect comes from the large splashes of warm color that contrast with the cool tones of the lancet windows of the west facade, as well as that of the earlier glowing panel known as *Notre Dame de Belle Verrière (Our Lady of the Beautiful Window)* (Fig. 7.15).

In the Gothic period, the art of stained glass replaced the mosaics and mural paintings of the Early Christian and Romanesque churches. It was the ultimate stage in the dematerialization of interior space. Because it gives form and meaning to light, the art of the glazier is perhaps better adapted to the expression of transcendental concepts than any other artistic medium. By transforming raw sunlight into a spectrum of brilliant colors, the architect directed the interior lighting. It could be caused to flow in any manner the architect wished. This material control over an immaterial medium allowed the architects and iconographers to shape light to their structural, pictorial, and expressive needs. Here is how Abbot Suger expressed the ecstasy felt by medieval men and women in the contemplation of the precious stones that adorned the altar and the jeweled glass of the windows:

> Thus, when—out of my delight in the
> beauty of the house of God—the loveliness
> of the many-colored gems has called me
> away from eternal cares, and worthy

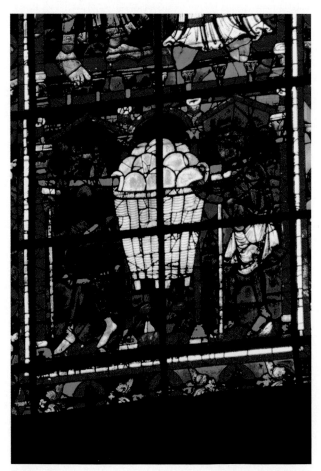

7.13   *Bakers.* Detail of stained glass window, Chartres Cathedral.

meditation has induced me to reflect, transferring that which is material to that which is immaterial, on the diversity of the sacred virtues: then it seems to me that I see myself dwelling, as it were, in some strange region of the universe which neither exists entirely in the slime of the earth nor entirely in the purity of Heaven; and that, by the grace of God, I can be transported from this inferior to that higher world in an anagogical manner.

MUSIC

Massive and magnificent as the Gothic cathedral is, it can be considered the highest achievement of its time only when associated with the many activities it was designed to house. Most important, of course, is the liturgy. As the space it enclosed increased, the cathedral grew into a vast auditorium that hummed with collective voices at communal prayer, resounded with readings and exhortations from the pulpit, and reverberated with the chanting of solo and choral song from the choir. The Île-de-France, the site of the most significant developments in architecture in the twelfth and thirteenth centuries, was also the scene of the most important musical innovations of the Gothic period. Specifically, these were the more sophisticated practices of **polyphonic,** or "many-voiced," music and their relationship with the still universally practiced **monophonic,** or unison, art of plainchant.

The practice of singing in parts originated in the north, in contrast to the prevailing Mediterranean style of singing in unison. Moreover, part singing in folk music apparently predates by several centuries its incorporation into church music. Just as the Gothic cathedral was the culmination of the long process of reconciling the northern urge for verticality with the southern horizontal basilica form, so Gothic music emerged from the union of the northern tradition of multivoiced singing and the southern single-voice tradition to form a new style of church music.

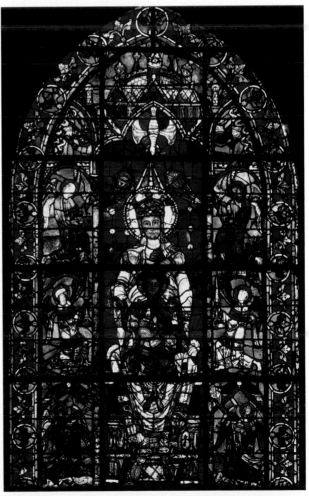

7.14   North rose window, Chartres Cathedral, c. 1220. Diameter 43′.

7.15   *Notre Dame de Belle Verrière,* stained glass window, Chartres Cathedral, c. 1170, with thirteenth-century side panels, 16′ × 7′8″.

MUSIC AT THE SCHOOL OF NOTRE DAME IN PARIS

Just as the builder of St. Denis brought together many principles that had been developed separately elsewhere and used them in a systematic whole, so too were elements of music fused into a new whole. As the growing capital of the French kingdom, Paris was the logical place for the pieces to be fitted together. The **contrapuntal,** or polyphonic, forms and textures developed in monasteries such as Cluny and in cathedral schools such as Rheims and Chartres, as well as the tradition of folk singing in several parts, were systematically organized for the first time at the School of Notre Dame in Paris.

The first great achievement of Gothic music was the *Magnus Liber Organi* (The Great Collection of Organum) by Léonin, dating from c. 1163. As its name implies, it was a great book that brought together a collection of music in two parts, arranged cyclically to provide appropriate music for all the feast days and seasons of the calendar year.

THE TENOR OR CANTUS FIRMUS. In the traditional rendering of the plainchant, some parts were sung by a soloist and answered responsorially by a chorus singing in unison. In the Gothic period, the choir still chanted the way it had for centuries, but the solo parts began to be performed simultaneously by two or more singers. Notre Dame in Paris, for example, employed four such singers. The distinction between solo voice and choir hence was replaced by the opposition of a group of individual singers and a massed chorus. With several skilled soloists available, the way was open for an art of much greater complexity than ever before.

Because the music was still intended for church performance, the traditional sacred melodies had to be used. A special part called the **tenor,** a term derived from the Latin *tenere,* meaning "to hold," was reserved for this melody, which was also known as the **cantus firmus,** or "fixed song," implying that it could not be changed. The development of Gothic music involved taking the cantus firmus as an established basis and adding one by one the other voices, called, in ascending order, the **duplum, triplum,** and **quadruplum.** Because these voices were superimposed one above the other, a definite concept of verticality is implied; this contrasted strongly with the horizontal succession of tones that characterized the older monophonic chant. The growing complexity of singing in several parts led by necessity to a new

type of time notation to define the rhythmic ratios and hold the various polyphonic voices together.

The earliest forms of Gothic polyphony are almost as rigid in their way as the old parallel organum of the Romanesque period, but they are based on the new principle of **punctus contra punctum,** that is, "note against note," or point counterpoint. *Mira Lege* illustrates one of the strictest applications of this idea. The plainchant melody is in the lower part, whereas the counterpoint above moves as much in opposition to it as possible. Although parallel movement is not against the rule, and from time to time does occur, contrary motion is preferred. A treatise written at the beginning of the twelfth century declares, "If the main voice is ascending, the accompanying part should descend, and vice versa." The name given to this newly created melodic line was the **discantus,** or descant, referring to the idea of singing against the established melody, a practice that has continued in religious and secular music.

Musical Example 7.1
Mira Lege (twelfth-century descant)

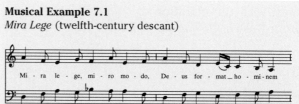

THE TWO-PART CHANT. In addition to such examples, Léonin's *Magnus Liber Organi* contains another type of counterpoint known as the **organum duplum.** The plainsong cantus firmus is found in the lower voice, but the individual tones are stretched out to extraordinary lengths. The descanting, or duplum, voice moves in free counterpoint consisting of ornate melismas over what has in effect become a relatively fixed base.

Musical Example 7.2
Organum Duplum (c. 1175; in Léonin's style)

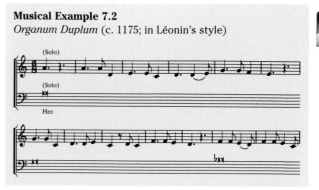

The greater melodic and rhythmic freedom that the descant assumed called for expert solo singers, and much of the descanting of Gothic times is known to have been improvised. The practice of such a freely flowing melodic line over a relatively fixed bass points to a possible origin in folk singing. Survivals are found in the instrumental music of the Scottish bagpipers, where a tune like "The Campbells Are Coming" is heard over the steady accompaniment of a droning bass note.

In performance, the slowly moving tenor, or cantus firmus, may have been sung by the choir while the soloist sang a freely moving duplum part over it. Or perhaps the tenor was played on the organ, an instrument known to have been in use at time. The organ keyboard was a thirteenth-century Gothic innovation, and many manuscript illustrations from the period point to the wide use of organs. The term *organ point,* moreover, continues to be used to refer to a musical passage in which the bass tone remains fixed while the other parts move freely over it.

THE THREE-PART MOTET

Another significant development was the addition of a third part above the other two, known as the **triplum,** from which the term *treble* is derived. This step was taken by Pérotin, who was active in Paris in the late twelfth and probably the early thirteenth centuries. In his revision of the work of his predecessor, Léonin, Pérotin moved away from polyphonic improvisational practices toward an art based on stricter melodic control and clearer rhythmic definition. By thus achieving a surer command of his material and evolving a logical technique for manipulating it, he was able to add a third voice to the original two, and in two instances there is even a fourth part. These compositions, known as ***motets,*** were independent works designed for performance in the liturgy but not part of the regular mass.

The three-part motet, like its predecessors, still had its cantus firmus in the tenor, which was the lowest part and held the *mot* (word), from which the term *motet* is probably derived. Over it, the contrapuntal voices wove a web with two different strands, each singing its independent melodic line. In the hands of Pérotin the three-part motet became the most favored and characteristic practice of thirteenth-century Gothic music.

Besides achieving ever-greater melodic independence, the two contrapuntal voices even had their own separate texts. A three-part motet thus had three distinct sets of words that were sung simultaneously: the tenor, with its traditional line, and usually two contemporary hymnlike verses over and above it. Intended as they were for church performance, the words customarily were in Latin. However, around the middle of the thirteenth century, it was not uncommon for one of the voices to sing its verses in French.

During the thirteenth century the **vernacular,** or local language, came into more frequent use in music and literature, and so did popular melodies. Above the stately tenor it was possible to have a hymn to the Virgin in Latin and a secular love song in the vernacular French being sung at the same time. Through the simple expedient of replacing the sacred melodies with secular tunes, a fully developed musical art independent of the church was not only possible but by the end of the thirteenth century had become an accomplished fact.

Gothic music exists in such close unity with other manifestations of the Gothic style that it can scarcely be understood as a thing apart. The subjects of the new hymns, especially those with the words of St. Bernard and the melodies of Adam of St. Victor, were mainly devoted to the Virgin, as were most of the cathedrals and the iconography of the sculpture and stained glass. Instead of a monolithic choir chanting in unison or in parallel organum, Gothic listeners now heard a small group of professional singers. In the case of a three-part motet, they could choose, according to their temperament or mood, to follow, or "tune into," the solemn traditional melody, the Latin commentary above it, or the French triplum in their everyday mode of speech. This allowance for diversity of musical taste is part of the general shift from the homogeneity of monastic life to the heterogeneity of city life, expressed by the cathedral. The new melodic, rhythmic, and textural variety implied a congregation of people from all walks of life, as did the diversified imagery of the sculpture and stained glass.

Musical Example 7.3
Triplum (thirteenth century; in Pérotin's style)

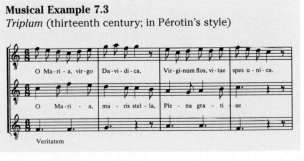

O Ma-ri-a, vir-go   Da-vi-di-ca,   Vir-gi-num flos, vi-tae   spes u-ni-ca.

O   Ma-ri-   a,   ma-ris stel-la,   Ple-   na gra-   ti   ae

Veritatem

Individual voices were superimposed one above the other, yielding an *aural,* or listening, impression of verticality. The ear, like the eye, needs fixed points to measure rises and falls. In Musical Example 7.1 *(Mira Lege),* the intervals in the lower part established the point over which the descant moved in contrary motion. In the case of the *Organum Duplum* (Musical Example 7.2), the soaring upward and plunging downward movement of the melody could be heard above and against the long sustained tenor. In addition to this vertical feeling, all types of counterpoints achieved a sense of rhythmic progress. Against a relatively static or stable point, other voices measured rapid movement. Melodies and intervals clashed as separate texts were sung at the same time. Thus, Gothic music was able to build a sense of mounting tension that set it apart as a distinctive new style.

IDEAS

In the century between the dedication of the Romanesque abbey church at Cluny (1095) and the beginning of Chartres Cathedral (1194), much more than a change in artistic styles occurred. A mighty shift in social and political institutions and in basic modes of thought took place. The resulting changes in church, secular, and artistic life brought into the open sharp divisions of opinion. Old conflicts, long restrained by the medieval divinely ordered social structure, now burst into flames, and new ones as well. Intellectual disputes grew hot and bitter as emotional tensions deepened.

In this critical situation, the rational methods of scholastic philosophy were brought to bear to evaluate the strong points of opposing arguments. In fact, the Gothic is best summarized as a clashing and dissonant style in which opposite elements were maintained in a state of uneasy equilibrium. With the eventual dissolution of the Gothic synthesis in the following century, the basic oppositions became so impossible to reconcile that some of them led to the battlefield. Others resulted in schisms, that is, divisions within the church, and produced growing philosophical and artistic conflicts.

GOTHIC OPPOSITIONS AND DIVISIONS

In the Gothic era, the age-old struggle between church and state, evident in Romanesque times in the endless quarrels between popes and Holy Roman emperors, shaped up as a conflict between traditional ecclesiastical authority and the growing political power of northern European kingdoms, especially France and England.

The prevailing monastic and feudal organizations of Romanesque times tended to separate society into widely scattered cloisters and manors, isolating many of the sources of social strain. In the Gothic era, the towns began to grow into cities and differing worldviews were brought into a common center, making confrontation possible. Also, tensions mounted between the landed aristocrats and the volatile urban groups, as well as between the monastic orders and the growing secular clergy. In the towns, residents saw at close range the bitter rivalries between abbot and bishop, lord and burgher, clergy and laity.

For the common people, a strong contrast had always existed between the squalor in which they lived and the luxury of their lords, bishops, and ab-

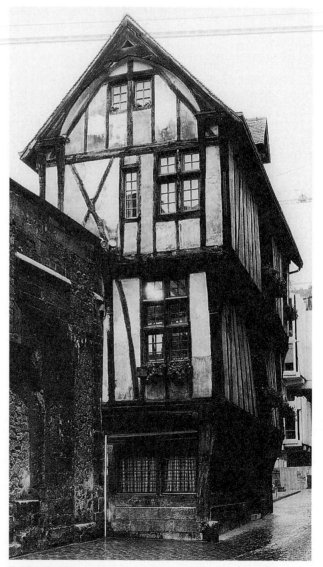

7.16   Gothic half-timbered house, Rouen, France, fifteenth century.

bots. This disparity was amplified by the gap between the poverty of their daily lives and promises of heavenly glory.

DUALISM AND THE ARTS

The arts were also torn by conflicting aspirations. Artists accepted a relatively anonymous status in the service of God, yet through the guilds and other activities, they actively competed for worldly recognition and rewards. Aristocratic and church patrons had to contend with the increasingly influential and affluent middle class and guilds. The rising power of the middle class is well illustrated by their dwelling places, such as the Gothic half-timbered houses at Rouen (Fig. 7.16) and the splendid residence of the banker Jacques Coeur at Bourges (Fig. 7.17).

In architecture, strong opposing forces produced a new visual vitality, especially the interplay of interior and exterior in Gothic cathedrals. Masses and voids played against one another, as did the thrust and counterthrust of vaults and buttresses. In sculpture, the conflict between the particular and the universal was expressed in the remarkable feeling for human individuality that contrasted with the dignified impersonality found in rows of saints and prophets who lined the doorways of churches. At Chartres, these opposing tendencies are apparent in the lifelike figures of Grammar and Donatus on the Virgin Portal tympanum (Fig. 7.11), whose rounded high relief stands out against the stiffly posed ***jamb,*** or doorway, figures of Old Testament kings and queens on the west facade (Fig. 7.9).

In literature, the cleavage between Latin and the vernacular languages was increasingly evident in the developing distinction between sacred and secular musical styles. In music, abstract academic discussions about the hypothetical nature of the music of the spheres contrasted with the escalating importance of the actual sounds heard in the choirs of the churches. Similarly, the singing of monophonic choruses alternated with groups singing polyphonically. In short, Gothic music displayed all the inherent oppositions of an art based on the principle of point counterpoint.

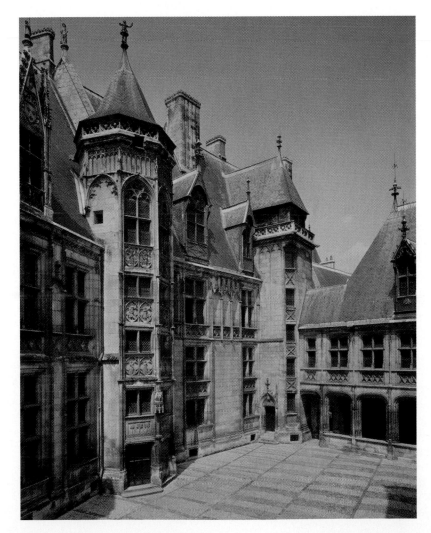

7.17 Hotel Jacques Coeur, courtyard, Bourges, France, 1443–1451.

SCHOLASTIC SYNTHESIS

In the face of so many differences, it seems astonishing that the Gothic style was able to effect even a momentary synthesis. In fact, a method for keeping differences in suspension was devised by scholars, a kind of pro-and-con dialogue followed by a resolution. To the scholastic philosopher, God, as the Creator of a world based on principles of reason, was approachable through the logical power of the mind. Hence, the key to understanding the universe was in the exercise of the rational faculties. Philosophical truth or artistic value was determined not by factual evidence but by how well an idea fitted into a logically ordered system. The results of this dialectical thought infiltrated the Gothic monarchy, university, encyclopedia, summa, and even the cathedral.

Abelard's *Sic et Non (Pro and Con)* was an early manifesto of Gothic dualistic thinking and a prime example of scholasticism at work. Abelard posed one pertinent question after another, then lined up authorities from the Scriptures and church fathers for and against each. His purpose was to expose some of the fissures in the thought of sanctioned authorities. However, Abelard contradicted scholastic practice and did not reconcile his oppositions.

THOMAS AQUINAS'S *SUMMA THEOLOGIAE*. The scholastic successors of Abelard debated whether ultimate truth was to be found through faith or reason, blind acceptance of authorities or the evidence of the senses, determinism or free will. In their search for a synthesis, Thomas Aquinas and others found an answer in the dialectical method of argument. Thomas's synthesis, as demonstrated in his **Summa Theologiae** *(Summation of Theology),* was a comprehensive attempt to bring together all Christian articles of faith into a rational system.

Thomas faced the problem of how to adapt Aristotle's philosophy to Christian theology. He also tried to harmonize such differences as truth revealed by God in the Scriptures and truth arrived at by human learning, the classical and Christian traditions, and the mystery of faith and the light of reason. He proposed to reconcile Abelard's pros and cons through a subtle intellectual maneuver.

His *Summa Theologiae* was as intricately constructed as a Gothic cathedral and had to embrace the totality of a subject, systematically divided into propositions and subpropositions, with inclusions deduced from major and minor premises. Every logical proposition was fitted exactly into place like each stone in a Gothic vault. If one of the premises were to be disproved, the whole structure would fall like an arch without its keystone.

AESTHETICS AND NUMBER THEORY

From Aquinas's highly rationalistic viewpoint followed a scholastic definition of beauty. He said that the mind needed order and demanded unity above all other considerations. Even though seeing and hearing played an increasingly important role in art and music, mathematical calculation and symbolism had to be called upon.

In the cathedral schools and later in the universities, music was studied mainly as a branch of mathematics. Bishop Fulbert of Chartres emphasized theory in the training of singers, saying that without it "the songs are worthless." His view was generally held throughout the Gothic period. As one theorist put it, a singer who is ignorant of theory is like "a drunkard who, while he is able to find his home, is completely ignorant of the way that took him home." The academics tended to suppress the sensuous beauty of tone and emphasize the mathematical, theoretical, and symbolic aspects of the musician's art.

At Chartres, as at other cathedral schools, arithmetic, geometry, music, and astronomy—the quadrivium of the seven liberal arts—were carefully and closely studied. Plato's theory of the correspondences between visual proportions and musical harmony (see p. 50) was kept alive in Early Christian times by both St. Augustine and Boethius in their books on music. In his *De Musica,* Augustine wrote that both architecture and music are the children of numbers. For him, architecture was the mirror of the cosmos, whereas the tonal art was the echo of the music of the spheres. These two books, along with parts of Plato's *Timaeus,* were widely studied in medieval monasteries and universities.

The mystical number 3 played a major role in music, architecture, and philosophy. Since antiquity, uneven numbers had been considered male and even numbers female. The number 1 was the symbol of the progenitive force and creative principle, and the number 2 was the female equivalent. The two joined together to form the first whole—or complete—number, 3. In addition, the number 3 was associated with Plato's trinity of truth, goodness, and beauty. Its Christian symbolism of Father, Son, and Holy Spirit would have been obvious to all. The number 3 also referred to the three parts of creation: hell below, the Earth, and the heavens above.

In the plan and cross section of Chartres Cathedral (Figs. 7.3B and 7.5B) the number 3 was all-pervasive. There are the triple entrance portals. The facade rises in three steps, from the level of the doorways, through the intermediate story, to the rising towers intended to elevate the thoughts of the worshipers and direct their aspirations heavenward. In the interior there are three corresponding levels: the nave arcade, the triforium gallery, and the windowed clerestory. In the clerestory itself, each bay has two lancets and one rose window. Then there is the tripartite division of the floor plan into the nave, transepts, and choir sections; the three semicircular chapels in the apse; and so on indefinitely.

In philosophy, encyclopedias and summas were divided into three parts. The triple rhyming plan of Latin poetry, as in the *Dies Irae* (p. 231) and the **terza rima** stanzas that Dante wrote in the *Divine Comedy* (pp. 232–234), serve as literary examples. In music, Gothic composition favored the three-part motet and the **ternary,** or three-beat, rhythm, which was called the **tempus perfectum** because of its Trinity symbolism.

Whereas the number 3 designated the spirit, the number 4 stood for matter, because the material elements composing the universe were considered to be fire, earth, air, and water. The sum of the two numbers is 7, which symbolized the human being, whose dual nature was made up of spirit and matter, soul and body. At Chartres, the number 7 also referred to Mary as the patron of the seven liberal arts. The number 9 was also a Marian symbol, because the Virgin was considered the seat of wisdom, and by analogy, knowledge was the root of power (3 being the square root of 9). As Dante wrote, "The Blessed Virgin is nine, for she is the square of the Trinity." Chartres has nine entrance portals, three in the facade and three in each of the transepts. According to the original plan, the cathedral was to have had nine towers— pairs on the west facade and on each of the transepts, two flanking the apse, and one over the crossing of the nave and transepts. In sum, numbers were thought to be the key to the divine plan and the link between the seen and the unseen.

THE FEMININE IN GOTHIC THOUGHT

Hovering above all these earthly concerns was the figure of Mary. The worship of Mary also had its worldly counterpart, as Gothic chivalry and courtliness partially replaced the might-makes-right code of Romanesque feudalism. Just as the clergy sang the praises of Notre Dame, the knights praised their ladies in particular and Our Lady in general. The high place of womanhood in secular circles was the courtly parallel of the religious cult of the Virgin.

In the poetry of the time, a knight's ladylove is always a paragon of feminine virtue and charm. To woo and win her, he had to storm the fortress of her heart by techniques far more intricate and subtle than those needed to take a castle. When successful, he became the vassal of his mistress and she his liege lady to command him as she would. As one of the troubadours sang, "To my lady I am vassal, lover, and servant. I seek no other friendship but the secret one shown me by her beautiful eyes." The concept of romantic love originated in the Gothic period and came to full flower in the complex code of chivalry.

SOME BROADER RESOLUTIONS

The rise of national monarchies in France and England began to limit the international authority of the papacy and to curb the provincial power of the feudal lords by increasing the centralization of civil authority. In England, a political resolution between king and nobles and between nobles and commoners was made in the Magna Carta, a document that not only outlined civil liberties but also became the basis for parliamentary government. In France, the establishment of a working relationship between the king and the urban middle class accomplished a similar purpose. King Louis IX of France was so skillful at strengthening his own kingdom while maintaining good relations with the popes that he was canonized. In the cities the guilds brought patrons and craftspeople together; meanwhile, the system of apprenticeships and examinations ensured a high standard of quality and workmanship.

The Gothic universities were set up as institutions to bring together diverse disciplines and controversial personalities and to fit all the various intellectual activities into a single universal framework. Scholasticism became the common mode of thought and its dialectic the common method of solving intellectual problems.

The structural uniformity of Gothic vaulting and buttressing was, in effect, the Gothic builder's answer to Romanesque experimentation. Ample allowance for urban diversity was made in the iconography of each cathedral and in the differences between cathedrals in different towns and countries.

Gothic architecture tried to synthesize the interior and exterior of the cathedral. Externally, the eye follows the numerous rising vertical lines to the spires and pinnacles and then to the sky. Inside, the experience is similar: the vertical lines rise to the window levels and from these through the glass to the space beyond. By contrast, the inward-turning monastic church was based on the notion of excluding the outside world. The Gothic cathedral attempted an architectural union of the inner and outer worlds as the exterior and interior flowed together through the glass-curtained walls. The thrust and counterthrust of the interior vaulting was paralleled on the outside by that of the piers and flying buttresses; the sculptural embellishments of the exterior were repeated in the iconography of the glass in the interior. Through the medium of stained glass, the iconographers transformed physical light into metaphysical and mystical illumination.

The various European languages and dialects found a place in secular literature, but Latin was championed by the church and universities as the language of scholarship. In music, Latin and the language spoken by the common people were reconciled in the multiple texts of the motet. Gothic music also attempted a synthesis of theory and practice. Through these separate manifestations, the Gothic spirit was revealed, whether in the systematic logic of St. Thomas, in the heightened sense of time achieved by the musicians, or in the visual aspirations and linear tensions of the builders.

No one of these resolutions was final, and the Gothic style must be viewed as a dynamic process rather than an end result. By contrast, a Greek temple or even a Romanesque abbey is a completed whole, and in the observer's eye can eventually come to rest. The appeal of the Gothic lies in the restlessness that prevents this sense of completion. The observer is caught in the stream of movement and from the initial impulse desires to continue it. The completion, however, can occur only in the imagination, because each cathedral lacked something, such as a tower or a spire.

The nineteenth-century French archeologist Viollet-le-Duc once conjectured what a complete cathedral would look like. He gave it seven spires—one pair on the west facade, others on the north and south transepts, and a climactic spire over the crossing of the nave and transept (Fig. 7.18). None of the real cathedrals was completed to this degree. Incompleteness was not limited to architecture: Vincent's encyclopedia and Thomas Aquinas's *Summa Theologiae* were never finished.

Gothic unity is therefore to be found mainly in such methods and procedures as the use of dialectic in philosophy, strict structural principles in architecture, and techniques of writing in literature and music. No more effective processes could have been devised to deal with the specific inconsistencies that confronted the Gothic mind. They were, in fact, the only ways to reconcile the seemingly irreconcilable, to arrive at the irrational by ingenious rational arguments, and to achieve the utmost in immateriality through material manifestations.

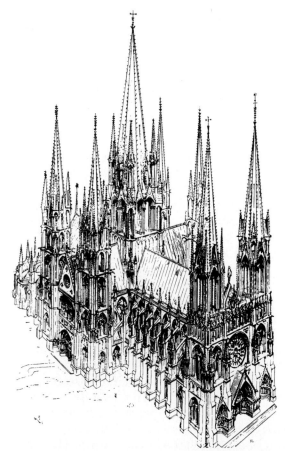

7.18   Eugène Viollet-le-Duc. Drawing of a Gothic cathedral with full set of seven spires.

YOUR RESOURCES

- ***Exploring Humanities CD-ROM***
  - ○ Interactive Map: Europe about 1200
  - ○ Architectural Basics: The Gothic Rib Vault
  - ○ Readings—Peter Abelard, Prologue to *Sic et Non;* Thomas Aquinas, Part 1, Question 2, Article 3 of *Summa Theologiae*

- ***Web Site***

  http://art.wadsworth.com/fleming10
  - ○ Chapter 7 Quiz
  - ○ Links

- ***Audio CD***
  - ○ *Mira Lege*
  - ○ *Organum Duplum*
  - ○ *Triplum*

GOTHIC PERIOD IN FRANCE

Key Events	Architecture	Literature and Music
c. 1088 **University of Bologna** founded 1095–1291 **Crusade period;** Christians and Muslims fought over Holy Land; trade routes opened		

1100

Key Events	Architecture	Literature and Music
1137 **Louis VII King of France;** married Eleanor of Aquitaine	c. 1136 **Abbey Church of St. Denis,** prototype of Gothic cathedrals, begun by Abbot Suger	c. 1130 **Abelard** (1079–1142) wrote *Sic et Non,* taught at School of Notre Dame, Paris

1140

Key Events	Architecture	Literature and Music
c. 1150 **University of Paris** founded		c. 1149 **Abbot Suger** (1081–1151) wrote account of building and decoration of St. Denis c. 1150 **Adam of St. Victor** wrote hymns with St. Bernard of Clairvaux c. 1150 **Troubadours** flourished c. 1150 **Léonin** active as composer at Cathedral of Notre Dame, Paris

1160

Key Events	Architecture	Literature and Music
c. 1163 **Oxford University** founded	1163–1235 **Cathedral of Notre Dame** in Paris built	1170 *Lancelot and Perçeval,* romance of courtly love, by Chrétien de Troyes

1180

Key Events	Architecture	Literature and Music
1180–1223 **Philip Augustus** reigned as king of France; enclosed Paris with walls; Paris became capital city	1194–1260 **Chartres Cathedral** built after fire destroyed earlier Romanesque cathedral; 1260 new cathedral dedicated by Louis IX	c. 1183 **Pérotin** active as composer at Cathedral of Notre Dame, Paris c. 1185 *Tristan et Iseult,* Celtic epic, written

1200

Key Events	Architecture	Literature and Music
1200 **Cambridge University** founded 1215 **Magna Carta** signed by King John in England 1223 **Louis VIII** crowned king of France 1226 **Louis IX** king of France under regency of mother, Blanche of Castile, until 1234	1210 **Rheims Cathedral** rebuilt 1220 **Amiens and Rouen cathedrals** begun 1225 **Beauvais Cathedral** begun; 1272 choir finished 1243 **Ste. Chapelle,** royal chapel of French kings, begun in Paris	1236 *Roman de la Rose* written c. 1250 **Vincent of Beauvais** (died 1264) wrote encyclopedic *Speculum Naturale, Historiale, Doctrinale* 1250 **Albertus Magnus** (c. 1193–1280), scholastic philosopher, taught at University of Paris 1273 *Summa Theologiae* written by Thomas Aquinas (1225–1274) 1275 **Scholastic philosophy** at height c. 1280 **Adam de la Halle** (c. 1237–1288), author and composer of *Le Jeu de Robin et Marion,* pastoral play with music

1300

Key Events	Architecture	Literature and Music
	1334–1362 **Palace of Popes** built at Avignon	

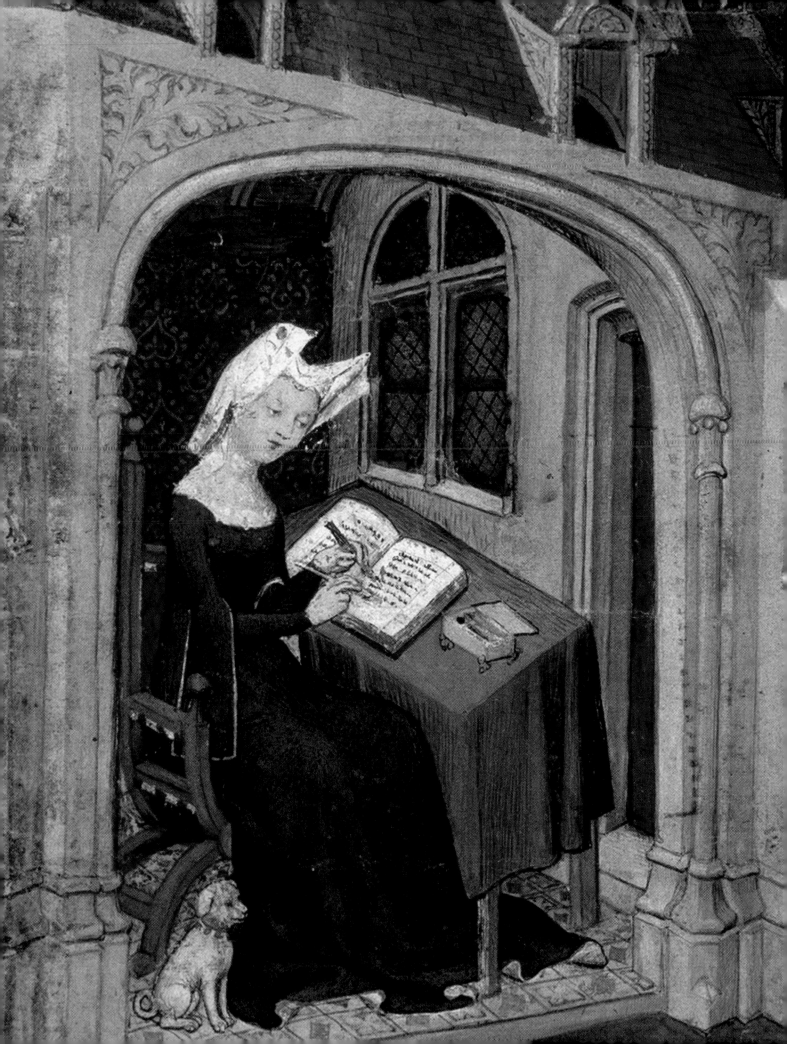

8

I N T E R N A T I O N A L   S T Y L E S
I N   T H E   L A T E
M E D I E V A L   P E R I O D

THE GREAT GOTHIC BUILDING WAVE that engulfed central France soon became an international style. Even while Chartres and other Île-de-France cathedrals were still being built, some of the French schools of stonemasons crossed the English Channel to work on building the great cathedral complexes at Canterbury and Salisbury in England. Thereafter the Gothic moved across the Rhine River into Germany, over the Alps into Italy, and across the Pyrenees into Spain. As the Gothic style spread, it encountered new social, political, religious, and cultural forces that were destined to give all the arts new shapes and directions. The French Gothic oppositions that had been maintained in a state of uneasy equilibrium (see pp. 208–209) by the application of scholastic logic and strict structural balances were to break into open conflict during the fourteenth century.

THE DEVELOPMENT
OF INTERNATIONAL GOTHIC

While Gothic cathedrals were still being built in the north, classical art was reinvigorated in the south. Thunderous threats of fire and brimstone and fear of the Lord were hurled from church pulpits one day, only to be followed the next day by comforting Franciscan parables and assurances of divine love and mercy. University professors still argued with the icy logic of scholastic philosophy, whereas the followers of St. Francis were persuading people with simple human truths. Some painters designed images of doomsday filled with warring angels and demons while others portrayed biblical stories as seen through the eyes of simple folk. People wondered whether the world they lived in was a moral trap set by the devil to ensnare the unwary, or a pleasant place that a loving Creator designed for their enjoyment.

The new Franciscan and Dominican orders rarely kept to their cloisters. Instead, they took to the road as itinerant preachers to all who would gather and listen. The great Italian writers Dante and Petrarch became exiles from their native cities, and their works were written during extended stays in half a dozen centers. Like them, the great painters were journeymen, traveling to wherever their work called them. Giotto, the leader of the Florentine school, painted *fresco* cycles that occupied him for several years in Rome, Assisi, and Padua, as well as in his home city. Simone Martini was active in Siena, Naples, and Assisi; he spent his last years at Avignon. Internal church dissensions were such that even the popes had to flee from their traditional seat in Rome to hold court in widely scattered residences, most notably at Avignon in southern France. Here the papal court attracted the best and most progressive writers, artists, and musicians from all of Europe. Indeed, Avignon became one of the main centers of the International Gothic style in the fourteenth century. Instead of a single dominant cultural center, as had existed during the Roman era, many cultural centers emerged in prosperous towns and cities throughout Europe. In these areas the clashes that were developing between and among townspeople, church people, and the nobility were to become louder and more insistent.

THE ENGLISH TRANSFORMATION OF GOTHIC

Salisbury (Fig. 8.1) is unique among English cathedrals because it was substantially finished within a short period, from its beginning in 1220 to its consecration in 1258. All the others were in a constant state of construction and alteration, depending on the changing fortunes and needs of their constituent cities. Set in a magnificent park on the banks of a river, the structure gives the impression of unity from every angle. If one imagines the church before the grand central tower (404 feet), still the loftiest in England, was added in the four-teenth century, its differences from the French Gothic style become apparent. In its breadth and hefty masses, Salisbury recalls the Norman Romanesque (see Fig. 6.23A). The towers and spires of its west facade seem to hug the Earth more than soar toward heaven. In sum, despite the international popularity of the Gothic style and its positive associations with royalty and learning, different regional and cultural values shaped it in regions outside the Île-de-France. At Salisbury, for instance, the English liturgy's reliance on stately processions was accommodated by a long nave of ten bays (compared with six at Chartres). Behind the wall that extends from the facade are an at-

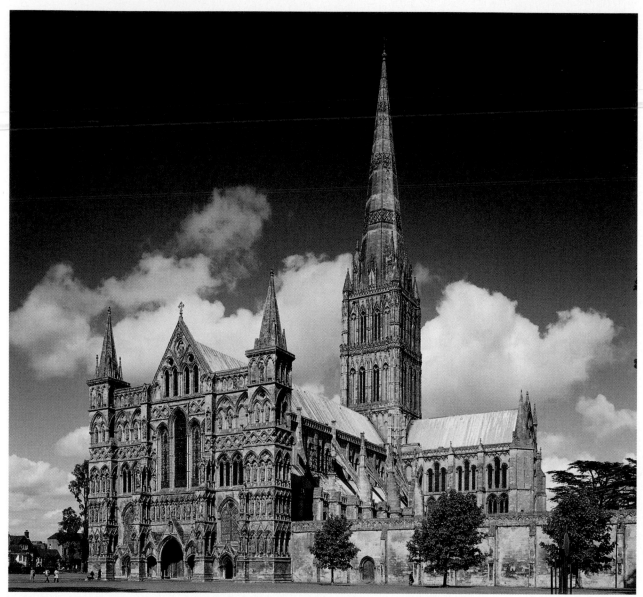

8.1 Salisbury Cathedral, 1220–1258. Length 473′, width 230′, height of spire 404′.

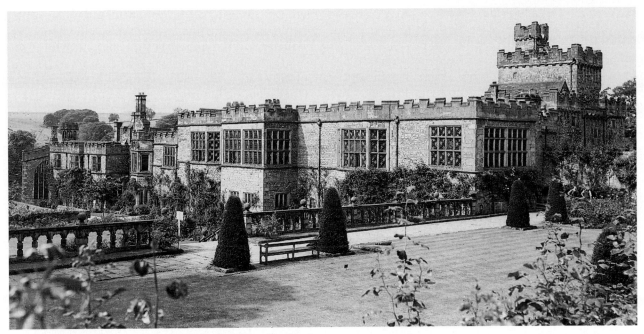

8.2 Exterior view of Haddon Hall, Derbyshire, England.

tached cloister and chapter house to serve a monastic community, a typical architectural practice in England.

The Gothic style was recast as "English architecture" in that country, partly to acknowledge its differences from French Gothic and partly to distinguish it from the earlier Norman style. With various mutations (known as the Early English, the Decorated, the Perpendicular, and the Tudor), the Gothic continued as the dominant mode of construction, permeating English life into the seventeenth century. There were Gothic chapels, parish churches, castles, manor houses, schools, colleges such as those at Oxford and Cambridge, guildhalls, market halls, inns, hospitals, townhouses, country cottages, bridges, fortifications, castles, and even barns, stables, and furniture.

Haddon Hall in Derbyshire is a manor house in the English Gothic tradition. Its similarity to the sturdy Tower of London is apparent (see Fig. 6.23A). Set on the side of a hill amid pastoral surroundings, the house overlooks verdant fields where sheep and cattle graze (Fig. 8.2). Its spacious banqueting room (Fig. 8.3), with its timbered ceiling, large arched windows, and huge fireplace, is particularly impressive. The rest of the stately structure includes a long gallery, a chapel the size of a small church, ample living and sleeping quarters, and exterior terraces and extensive gardens.

Entertainment in the courtly banqueting halls of Europe during the internationalization of Gothic was illustrated on the January page of the richly illustrated *Book of the Hours,* created by the Limbourg Brothers for the Duke of Berry, brother

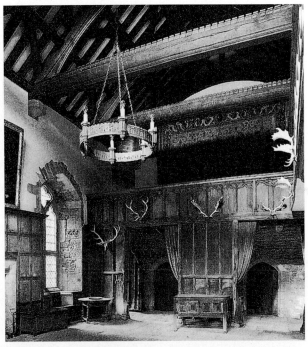

8.3 Haddon Hall Banqueting Hall, fourteenth century.

to the king of France (Fig. 8.4). The scene is a celebration of Epiphany, or Twelfth Night, the day the Three Wise Men, following the star of Bethlehem, found the infant Jesus in the manger and brought gifts of gold, frankincense, and myrrh. The Duke of Berry, in a rich robe and fur hat, turns to receive greetings and gifts. The large, circular, gold-colored fire screen behind him resembles a halo. It

is as if the artist has put him in the place of the Christ child, but in an elegant setting much removed from the poverty of the Nativity stable. Incidentally, the central figure with the monk's tonsured head is thought to be a self-portrait of the artist, Paul de Limbourg.

In the English countryside, where trees were plentiful, a modest type of wooden domestic

8.4 January: The Feast of the Duke of Berry. Illuminated manuscript page from *Les Très Riches Heures de Duc de Berry,* 1416. Ms. 65; folio 1V. Musée Condé, Chantilly, France.

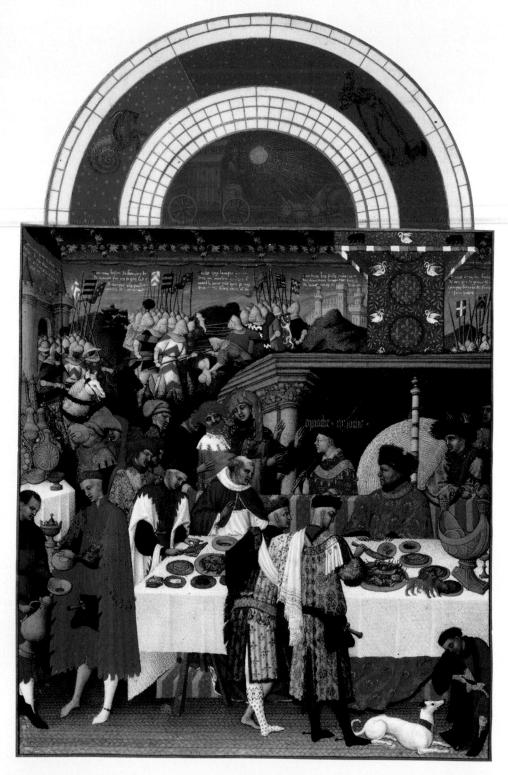

dwelling also developed along Gothic lines. This house style—with raftered ceilings and steep-pitched Gothic gabled roofs—traveled to America with the early colonists, who built the kinds of homes they knew and remembered best.

The arts of sculpture and stained glass were also incorporated into English architecture, but never to the extent of their French counterparts. Both arts suffered considerable destruction during the break from Roman Catholicism in the time of Henry VIII, and much of what remained was destroyed during Cromwell's Puritan revolution in the seventeenth century. The fragments that survive show that these arts were similar in quality and character to those in thirteenth-century France.

English Literature: Geoffrey Chaucer

London resident Geoffrey Chaucer painted a vivid verbal picture of fourteenth-century life in the verses of his *The Canterbury Tales*. The time is spring and the place a London tavern. A varied group of people, ranging from a knight to a plowman, gather before setting out on a pilgrimage to honor the martyred saint Thomas à Becket, the archbishop who had been murdered in the cathedral at Canterbury.

> And specially from every shire's end
> Of England they to Canterbury wend,
> The holy blessed martyr there to seek
> Who helped them when they lay so ill and weak.

Pilgrims, according to tradition, told tales to amuse one another during their long treks. Chaucer lets his pilgrims talk in conversational English as it was spoken in his day. The stories range from moral tales and fables to outright farce. Religious beliefs are treated with a sophisticated slant and good-humored irony. In the General Prologue, Chaucer introduces an amiable cross section of medieval society. The group includes the bawdy wife of Bath, who has buried five husbands and is still looking for another; a poor Oxford student; an earthy miller; a fraudulent doctor; a flamboyant young squire with a roving eye for the ladies; a rich, busybody lawyer; a fastidious prioress whose inclinations are far more worldly than a nun's should be; and finally a knight, who draws the shortest straw and thus gets to tell the first tale:

> He said: "Since I must then begin the game,
> Why, welcome be the cut, and in God's name!
> Now let us ride, and hearken what I say."

Unlike today, when reading is usually a private and silent activity, Chaucer's poetry was read aloud, usually to a group. Indeed, he fashioned *The Canterbury Tales* for listeners, carefully describing locations, pacing the language for maximum emotional effect, and contriving characters who not only tell tales but also reveal their personalities in conversation with other pilgrims. Sadly, Chaucer died before he was able to finish the vast work he planned. Until time obscured the accessibility of the English in which he wrote, he was considered one of England's greatest poets.

GOTHIC ART AND ARCHITECTURE IN GERMANY

In Germany the new Gothic style had to battle for acceptance with the traditional Romanesque style that became thoroughly entrenched during the Holy Roman Empire (see pp. 150–151). Slow in evolving, German Gothic ultimately acquired a distinctly national character of its own.

The builders of the Cathedral at Ulm (Fig. 8.5), a prosperous and politically influential German city,

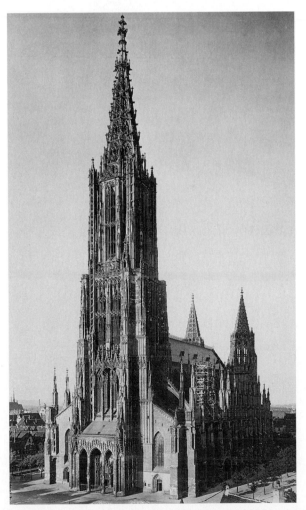

8.5 Ulm Cathedral, Ulm, Germany, begun 1377; tower designed 1482; spire nineteenth century.

eventually abandoned the balanced, two-tower design common to the west facade of earlier Gothic churches, such as Chartres (see Fig. 7.3A). An extravagant, thickset single tower and spire achieved an unprecedented height of 620 feet. The spectacular structure seems to be not only leaping into the heavens but also pushing the bulky church into the ground. The west tower had to wait for its final flourishes until the nineteenth century, when its builders could use cast-iron construction.

The Cathedral at Ulm is often cited as the tallest church tower in the world. Similarly, the great cathedral complex at Cologne, planned to rival the height and size of French Gothic cathedrals, had a long, drawn-out history. Begun in 1248, its choir and transept stood for centuries at one end of the site, with the stubs of the two facade towers at the other end and a yawning chasm between. The cathedral was not completed until 1880, after interest in medieval architecture led to the discovery of the original building plan. The new wealth of Cologne during the Industrial Revolution finally provided the funds for the cathedral's completion.

German Gothic sculpture also shows a distinctive regional character. In the choir of the Naumburg Cathedral, the donors and founders are depicted in solemn procession (Fig. 8.6). The figures portrayed were from the historical past, but the skillful sculptor created them with great particularization of features, as if they had modeled for their likenesses. The stocky Margrave Ekkehard, military governor of the region, appears as a self-confident, haughty aristocrat whose hand is never far from his sword. Uta, his beautiful wife, is regally poised.

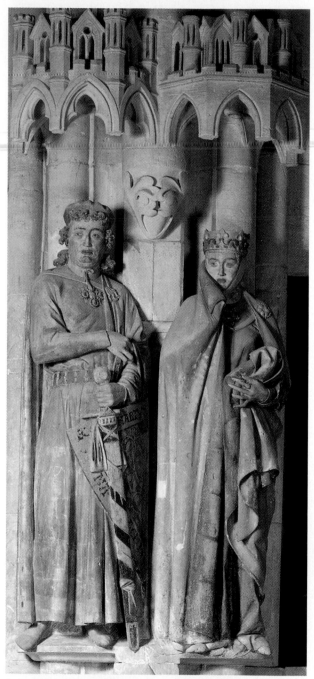

8.6 Ekkehard and Uta, c. 1249–1255. Limestone, approx. 6′2″ high. Naumberg Cathedral, Naumberg, Germany.

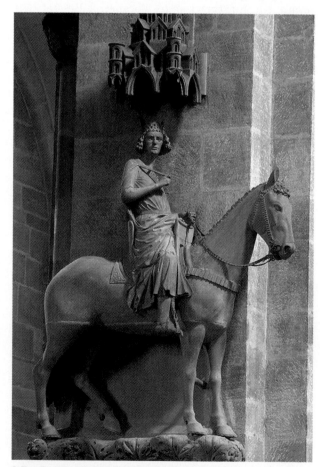

8.7 *Bamberg Rider,* 1235–1240. Sandstone, 7′9″ high. Bamberg Cathedral, Bamberg, Germany.

With graceful gestures, she draws her collar across her face with one hand while gathering the ample folds of her gown with the other. As with classical sculpture, the curves of the arm and modeling of the breast reveal how the artist distinguishes the drapery from the body beneath. Both statues retain bits of pigment that hint at the extensive use of color that once graced Gothic cathedral sculptures. Likewise, at Bamberg Cathedral the so-called Bamberg Rider, in a niche on the exterior, is splendidly carved and lifelike (Fig. 8.7). The rider's facial features and physique suggest that this might be a portrait. Sitting high in the saddle, this Gothic knight might be preparing to participate in some medieval tournament or to leading his victorious soldiers into some vanquished city.

GOTHIC ART AND ARCHITECTURE IN ITALY

When the Gothic reached Italy, it underwent a radical transformation. The tall spires found in French and Gothic churches were rejected. Italian

churches were conceived of as cool retreats from the southern sun, so there was less need for illuminated interiors than in the north. Stained glass never played a major role in the Italian interpretation of Gothic. The Italians favored the mural arts of mosaic making and fresco painting, which still flourished in the decoration of Italian churches and public buildings. Surrounded by the remains of classical civilization, Italian artists had models from antiquity to inspire them. Nevertheless, northern influence on architecture, sculpture, and the handling of pictorial space is evident in many instances. The Milan Cathedral (Fig. 8.8) seems to have synthesized the linear thrusts of French Gothic and the horizontal sturdiness of English models, such as Salisbury Cathedral, with the Italian heritage, especially the basilica form.

Although the elements of Gothic were introduced in Italy by members of the Cistercian monastic order, the style's emphasis on structural equilibrium, visible both within and outside of French Gothic cathedrals, was not highly influential there. For example, the Doge's Palace, the center of government in the wealthy city of Venice, used

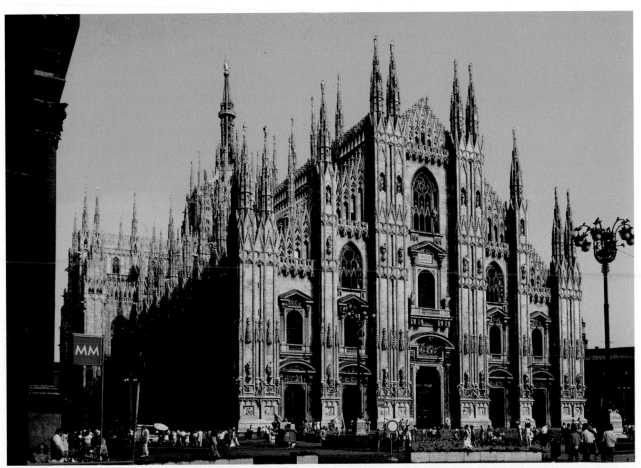

8.8   Milan Cathedral, Duomo, Milan, Italy. Begun 1386. Height 350′.

pointed arches, ribbed arches on the ground level, and a conglomerate of French and Islamic elements on the floor above. Together with the pink-and-white pattern marble of the upper stories, the effect is of a delicate, airy confection far removed from the gray chill of northern Gothic (see Fig. 12.1). Likewise, at Assisi, the large thirteenth-century basilica of St. Francis incorporated pointed arches and ribbed vaults, yet the aesthetic effect and the structural relationships differ greatly from the French prototype.

THE BASILICA OF ST. FRANCIS AT ASSISI

The town of Assisi was built on a rocky hill in the midst of a gentle and lush countryside. This provincial location would never have emerged as a cultural center if Francis, one of the most beloved medieval saints, had not been born there. After the completion of Assisi's great pilgrimage basilica in the midthirteenth century, many of the outstanding artists of the age came to decorate its walls.

A large city might have produced a great orator and organizer, capable of moving minds to bring about a new social order. Francis of Assisi, however, recognized the dangers of inflammatory oratory. Francis accomplished his pastoral mission with the sweet persuasion of simple parables and the eloquence of his own exemplary life. Whereas the mature life of Francis fell within the thirteenth century, the collection of tales that made him a living legend, as well as the full development of the Franciscan movement, belongs to the fourteenth century. Formerly, the clergy who received their training in the universities and the scholarly orders of monks had never influenced a broad segment of society. The Franciscans, however, found a way into the hearts and minds of the multitudes by preaching to them in their own language, rather than Latin, and in the simplest terms. Franciscan voices were heard more often in village squares than in the pulpits of churches.

The essence of the Franciscan idea is contained in the mystical marriage of the saint to Lady Poverty, the subject of one of the Assisi frescoes. When a young man approached Christ and asked what he should do to ensure eternal life, the answer came, "Go and sell that thou hast, and give to the poor, and thou shalt have treasure in heaven: and come and follow me" (Matthew 19:21). Francis took this directive literally. In his will he described his early life and that of his first followers. "They contented themselves," he wrote, "with a tunic, patched within and without, with the cord and breeches, and we desired to have nothing more. . . . We loved to live in poor and abandoned churches, and we were ignorant and submissive to all." He then asked his followers to "appropriate nothing to themselves, neither a house, nor a place, nor anything, but as pilgrims and strangers in this world, in poverty and humility serving God, they shall confidently go seeking for alms."

Had St. Francis's vow of complete poverty been followed strictly, no great art movement would have developed at Assisi. A building program involved the accumulation and expenditure of large sums, and immediately after Francis's death, this matter created dissension among those who had been closest to him. Brother Elias wanted to build a great church as a fitting monument to his friend and master. Others believed that Francis should be honored by the closest possible adherence to his simple life pattern. Erecting the monument Brother Elias had in mind would require a vast treasure, and many of his fellow friars were shocked when Elias set up a marble vase to collect offerings from pilgrims who came to Assisi to honor Francis. Yet only 2 years later, at the very time he was declared a saint, a great basilica and monastery were begun on the hill where Francis had wished to be buried. No doubt, Pope Gregory IX's interest and funds hastened the construction of the project, which was built in a state under papal control.

Taking advantage of the natural contours of the site, the architects designed a structure that included two churches, one above for pilgrims and one below for the Franciscan monks. At Assisi, the differences from French Gothic are easily seen. Despite their comparatively large size, both the upper and the lower churches lack side aisles, which were common in northern examples. The central naves of the upper and lower churches terminate in apses beyond small transepts. The large interior areas are spanned by spacious quadripartite ribbed vaults, partially supported by rows of columns that are set against the walls rather than freestanding, as in French Gothic. Italian Gothic, contrary to the northern style, did not accent well-lighted interiors in which the walls were almost completely replaced with stained-glass windows. The southern sun made shade more welcome, and the interiors were refuges from the brightness of the world outside.

In both the upper and lower churches at Assisi, the absence of a nave arcade and side aisles and the small number of stained-glass windows allowed ample wall space for the brightly colored fresco paintings that cover them. Lighted principally by the clerestory, the walls of the upper church are decorated with scenes from the life of St. Francis. More than anything else, it is these murals that bring the twin churches their most special distinction. The names of the artists who worked here read like a roster of the major painters of the period: Cimabue and Giotto of Florence and Simone Martini and Pietro Lorenzetti of the Sienese school.

GIOTTO

On the walls of the nave of the upper church at Assisi are a series of frescoes depicting the life of Francis (Fig. 8.9). These are attributed to Giotto, but the attribution has long been debated. Although his exact role remains unknown, it seems safe to say that if Giotto did not actually paint at Assisi, either he supervised assistants or his approach was adopted by those who worked there. The date generally assigned to the work is the

4-year span just before the jubilee year of 1300. Knowing that more pilgrims than ever before would be traveling to Rome for the celebrations, the artists at Assisi made every effort to cover the bare walls of the upper church in time. The frescoes for the friars' own lower church were not completed until the midfourteenth century.

Like other master artists of his period, Giotto learned to work in a variety of techniques. In addition to frescoes, he did mosaics, painted altarpieces in tempera on wood, and was a sculptor. Several years before his death, he was named the chief architect of Florence, and in this capacity he designed the **campanile,** or bell tower, of the cathedral (see Fig. 9.1), still popularly called "Giotto's Tower." Giotto's greatest and most enduring fame, however, rests on the three fresco cycles in Assisi, Padua, and Florence.

The fresco medium calls for the rapid and sure strokes of a steady hand and for vibrant, colorful

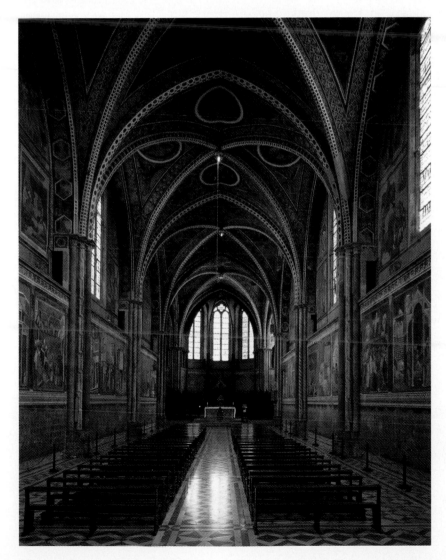

8.9   Nave, Upper Church of St. Francis, Assisi, Italy, 1228–1253.

designs that harmonize with the architectural scheme. After first covering the entire wall with a layer of rough plaster and allowing it to dry thoroughly, the artist makes a preliminary drawing in charcoal, called a *cartoon,* on the surface. Then, selecting an area that can be finished in a single day, the artist smoothes on a thin layer of wet plaster and, if necessary, retraces the original drawing. Next, earth pigments (colors) are mixed with water, combined with egg white as a binder, and applied directly to the fresh plaster—hence the term *fresco,* meaning "fresh."

The pigments and wet plaster combine chemically to produce a permanent surface. Artists sometimes paint over the surface after it is dry, but this repainting usually flakes off in time. If corrections are necessary, the entire section must be knocked out and redone. Fresco, therefore, is a medium that does not encourage time-consuming, subtle types of expression. It is best adapted to bold designs and simple compositions. The emotional depth, the communicative value, and the

masterly execution Giotto achieved in his fresco cycles rank them among the highest achievements in world art.

THE ASSISI SERIES. Even though it is unclear whether Giotto actually painted at Assisi, the first two panels of the series seem inspired by his methods. On the right, after one passes through the entrance portals, is the *Miracle of the Spring* (Fig. 8.10), and on the left is the well-known *Sermon to the Birds.* These two images were placed on either side of the entrance, probably to impress pilgrims at the outset with the most popular Franciscan legends. One shows the saint ministering to the poor and humble; the other demonstrates his kinship with all God's creatures, including those he called his "brothers the birds."

The literary source for the *Miracle of the Spring* is the *Legend of the Three Companions,* which tells of Francis's journey to the monastery of Monte la Verna. A fellow friar, a peasant, and his donkey accompanied him, but the way was steep and the day hot. Overcome by thirst, the peasant cried out for water. Kneeling in prayer, the saint turned to him, saying, "Hasten to that rock and thou shalt find a living water which in pity Christ has sent thee from the stone to drink." Pilgrims entering the church were thirsty for spiritual refreshment, and the placement of this picture assured them that they had arrived at a spring that would nourish the soul.

The composition is as simple as it is masterly. St. Francis is the focal center of two crisscrossing diagonal lines like the letter X. The descending light from the rocky peak in the upper right reveals the contours of the mountain in a series of planes. It reaches its greatest intensity in its union with Francis's halo, diminishing in his shadow, where his two companions and the donkey stand. The dark mountain at the upper left moves downward toward the shadowy figure of the drinking peasant at the lower right, as if to say that he is still in spiritual darkness. But because Francis is also on this diagonal line, the way to enlightenment is suggested.

Perhaps the most dramatic of the series is *St. Francis Renouncing His Father and Worldly Goods* (Fig. 8.11). In his haste to abandon the material world, Francis casts off his garments and stands naked before the townspeople, saying to his father, "Until this hour I have called thee my father upon earth; from henceforth, I may say confidently, my Father who art in Heaven, in whose

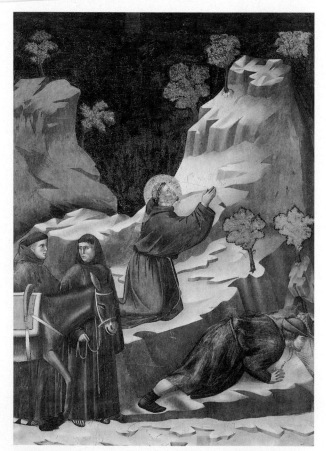

8.10 Giotto (?). *Miracle of the Spring,* c. 1296–1300. Fresco. Upper Church of St. Francis, Assisi, Italy.

hands I have laid up all my treasure, all my trust, and all my hope." The bishop covers Francis with his own cloak and receives him into the church.

The gestures and facial expressions of the various figures make this fresco a study of contrasting human attitudes. The angry father has to be physically restrained by a fellow townsman, yet his face shows the puzzled concern of a parent who cannot understand his son's actions. His counterpart on the other side is the bishop, who becomes the new father of the saint in the church. Disliking such a scene, his glance shows both embarrassment and sympathy. These opposing figures are supported respectively by the group of townspeople, behind whom is an apartment house, and by the clergymen, behind whom are church buildings. Giotto concocted a pictorial geometry to unify the picture and resolve the tension. The two opposing groups, symbolizing mate-

rial pursuits and spiritual aspirations, become the base of a triangle. Between them, the hand of Francis points upward toward the apex, where the hand of God emerges through the clouds.

On September 27, 1997, an earthquake shook the Basilica of St. Francis. Part of the vaulting collapsed, taking with it frescoes by Giotto or his assistants and students. It will take decades to restore the dust and fragments to an approximation of their original condition.

THE ARENA (OR SCROVEGNI) CHAPEL IN PADUA.   Unlike the frescoes in the Basilica of St. Francis in Assisi, Giotto's work in Padua is well documented. Padua, a prosperous city-state in northeast Italy, had flourished since Roman times as an agricultural, banking, and commercial center. One measure of Padua's wealth is reflected in the chapel built by Enrico Scrovegni next to his palatial residence. Not since

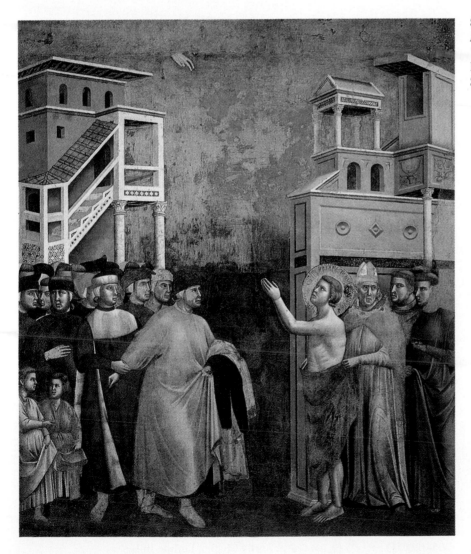

8.11 Giotto (?). *St. Francis Renouncing His Father and Worldly Goods*, c. 1296–1300. Fresco. Upper Church of St. Francis, Assisi, Italy.

Roman emperors paid for religious art out of their own pockets (assuming their togas had pockets) had a citizen lavished so much on a private place of worship. The church and the nobility were the usual patrons of art, followed by towns and cities.

Giotto and his patrons seem to have been fond of marvelous mountains, such as those that form the background of *Joachim Returning to the Sheepfold* (see Fig. 8.21), the *Flight into Egypt,* and the *Pietà* (Fig. 8.12). Structurally, the mountains advance and recede to form niches for the figures. Their hardness and heaviness complement the figures' compassion and expressiveness. The mountains and architectural backgrounds are not naturalistically correct; rather, they exist to form volumes and masses in Giotto's pictorial designs. Scattered trees, looking like bouquets of artichokes, serve mainly as spatial accents.

Giotto's spatial proportions are psychologically rather than actually correct. As they did in Byzantine representation, human beings loom large against their backgrounds, in keeping with their greater expressive importance. Splashed with light that seems more theatrical than natural, the principal figures in the *Pietà* fully occupy their foreground stagelike space. The deeply shadowed folds

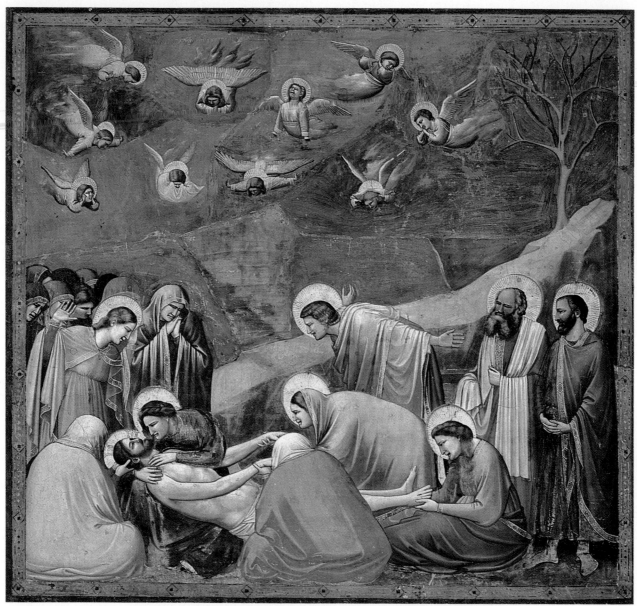

8.12 Giotto. *Pietà (Lamentation),* 1305–1306. Fresco, 6′6¾″ × 6′6¾″. Arena Chapel, Padua, Italy.

of their garments not only model their bodies but also enhance the grief that creases their faces. By contrast, the ashen figure of the dead Christ is limp. In the sky, a company of angels weep. More miserable than the rest, the central angel, dressed in white, strains upward, as if calling on God to reverse the dreadful scene below.

SCULPTURES OF NICOLA AND GIOVANNI PISANO

At the cathedral complex in Pisa, two outstanding sculptors carved impressive pulpits. That of the father, Nicola Pisano, stands in the baptistry, whereas a generation later, that of his son Giovanni graces the nave of the cathedral. The panels of both depict scenes from the New Testament. Contrasting the work of the father with that of the son reveals both the enduring influence of classical sculpture in Italian art and the adaptation of late Gothic aesthetic qualities.

Nicola's panel of the *Annunciation and Nativity* (Fig. 8.13) clearly draws on the classical relief sculpture that he knew so well from his formative years spent near Rome (see Figs. 4.3, 4.4, 4.11, and 4.12). The Virgin, wearing Roman dress and coifed in a Roman hairdo, appears as a dignified Roman matron. In the upper left, Gabriel, the angel of the Annunciation, is posed against a classical temple and dressed in a Roman toga, as are many of the figures. To tell the story of the Annunciation, the Nativity, and the Adoration of the Shepherds, Nicola uses the simultaneous mode of narration. The Virgin makes appearances in the Annunciation scene in the upper left; in the Adoration of the Shepherds (damaged) in the upper right; and in the central scene, which shows the Christ child being washed. The relief as a whole projects a mood of monumental calm. It is interesting to note that Nicola, who designed the pulpit, also signed and dated his work.

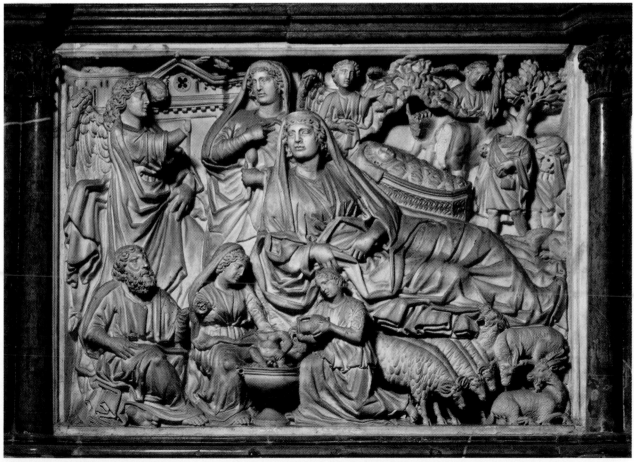

8.13 Nicola Pisano. *Annunciation and Nativity,* detail of pulpit, 1259–1260. Marble. Baptistry, Pisa, Italy.

The work of Nicola's son, Giovanni, seen in his *Nativity and Annunciation of the Shepherds* (Fig. 8.14), moved away from his father's classicism into the late French Gothic style. His figures are slim and smaller in scale. They fit more naturally into their surrounding space. Greater animation and agitation of line replace the serene repose of the father's style. The virgin's slender form, her youthful, smiling face, and the muted S-curve of her reclining body show late Gothic influences. Nevertheless, the panels by both father and son display a sense of human warmth and response and closely resemble the spirit of Giotto's frescoes.

PATRONAGE AND PAINTING IN THIRTEENTH-CENTURY ITALY

Two rival cultural centers, Florence and Siena, both enjoyed prosperity in the thirteenth century. Florence was a stronghold where power was held by rich merchants and craftsman guilds. In Siena, by contrast, most of the wealth and patronage was in the hands of the aristocracy, who owned the ter-tile countryside. The openness of Florentine leaders to change and innovation—the result, perhaps, of the flexibility required of traders and bankers—promoted a similar outlook among artists who worked in Florence. Siena, however, remained a bastion of tradition. Two worlds, the realm of agriculture plus the land-based wealth of the aristocracy and the church, alternately collaborated with and opposed the realm of the city, whose wealth was based on commerce.

Cimabue, the leading Florentine artist of the late thirteenth century, was succeeded by the formidable figure of Giotto, whose painting points clearly to the coming Renaissance. In Siena, the great Duccio was followed by Simone Martini and the Lorenzetti brothers, who continued in the more conservative Byzantine tradition that had been introduced into Italy many centuries earlier via such cultural centers as Ravenna and Venice. Despite its ongoing respect for tradition, the Sienese school was able to combine the old medieval and late Gothic styles in a final flowering of Italo Byzantine painting.

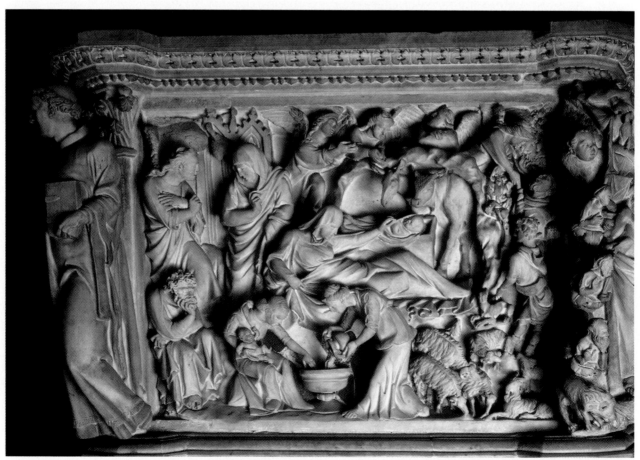

8.14 Giovanni Pisano. *Nativity and Annunciation of the Shepherds,* detail of pulpit, 1302–1310. Marble. Cathedral, Pisa, Italy.

Four altarpieces for Florentine churches—similar in purpose, theme, and form but different in style—illustrate these integrations. Cimabue's *Madonna Enthroned with Saints and Prophets* (Fig. 8.15), designed for the high altar of Santa Trinità in Florence, demonstrates that in addition to classical influences, Byzantine aesthetics persisted in Italy. The predominant use of gold recalls the mosaics of Ravenna (see Figs. 5.15 and 5.16). The Byzantine heritage is also apparent in the Madonna's frontal pose and the linear quality achieved by the use of gold streaks to emphasize the folds of her garment and that of the infant. The Christ child conforms to the theological image of the miniature patriarch born knowing all things. At the same time, Gothic verticality governs the two-story composition, with four solemn prophets below displaying their scrolls and the ascending ranks of eight angels above. Cimabue also suggests recessive space in the shadowing of Mary's wooden throne, which is painted to look as if it were inlaid with gems.

Duccio, the great Sienese master, painted the so-called Rucellai Madonna (Fig. 8.16) for the Florentine church of Santa Maria Novella in a lighter, more buoyant, and decorative vein. Although Duccio undoubtedly knew Cimabue's monumental style, his kneeling angels are airier, as if they were gently settling down after a heavenly flight. In this picture the grace and elegance characteristic of the courtly late Gothic style merge with Byzantine elements. The deeply folded, heavy textile backdrop may allude to the wool industry of Florence. The undulating edges of the Madonna's robe; the slightly off-center angle of the throne; and the gauzy transparency of the Child's mantle, which has casually slipped down, all produce a late Gothic linear delicacy.

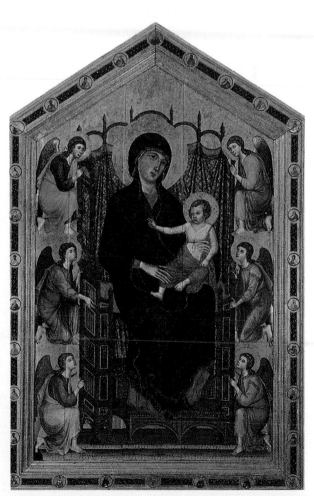

8.15 Cimabue. *Madonna Enthroned with Saints and Prophets*, c. 1280–1290. Tempera on wood, 12'7" × 7'4". Galleria degli Uffizi, Florence, Italy.

8.16 Duccio. *"Rucellai" Madonna,* 1285. Tempera on wood, 14'9" × 9'6". Galleria degli Uffizi, Florence, Italy.

Duccio's student Simone Martini fused the Byzantine and the Gothic in his elegant *Annunciation* (Fig. 8.17). The slim, flat, pointed arches and miniature spires are as elegant as they are far removed from the rugged, soaring sense of earlier northern forms. The regal Madonna is draped in a French-style blue gown, rendered in pigment made from powdered lapis lazuli. Disturbed in her reading by the sudden appearance of the Archangel Gabriel, his robes and wings aflutter, the startled Virgin recoils in fear and astonishment as she hears the words that appear in relief: "Hail Mary . . . the Lord is with thee." The composition is a masterly combination of vivid colors and curvilinear design, as revealed in the folds and swirls of the costumes, the angel's transparent wings, and the vase of curving white lilies that symbolize Mary's purity.

The fresh direction that the early Renaissance would take is foreshadowed in Giotto's *Madonna Enthroned* (Fig. 8.18), which was painted for the Church of Ognissanti about 20 years after the work of Cimabue and Duccio. The gold background and pointed arches of the roofed throne occupied by the Madonna harken back to the Byzantine and the Gothic. At the same time, Giotto fashioned a forward-looking illusion of depth. The two kneeling angels in the foreground serve a function similar to that of the bulky robed figures in the immediate foreground of his *Pietà* (Fig. 8.12). Their rounded shapes appear three-dimensional, and they seem to "push" the main subject backward into space. The angels of the heavenly choir are placed one in front of the other to create a sense of space expanding into the distance. Similarly, two of the six somber saints in the background are visible

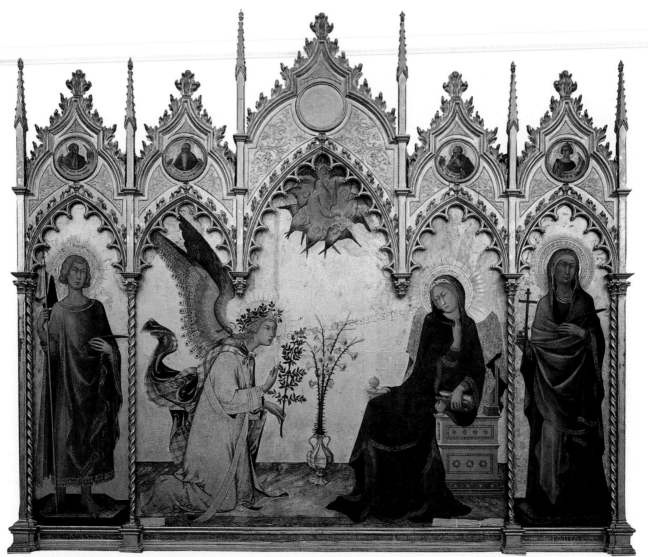

8.17 Simone Martini. *Annunciation*, 1333. Tempera and gold leaf on wood, approx. 10′1″ × 8′8¾″ (center panel). Galleria degli Uffizi, Florence, Italy.

through the arches of the Madonna's throne. The Madonna is not aloof but meets the gaze of her beholders. Her figure is heavier than a Byzantine figure would be, and her breasts are prominent, because the Madonna's robe is modeled in light and shadow to delineate the flesh beneath. In addition, the Child is in a more natural posture.

LATE MEDIEVAL MUSIC AND LITERATURE

The contrast between the gloomy, threatening medieval worldview, evident in the tympanum at the Cathedral of Autun (see Fig. 6.1), and the joyful Franciscan spirit is illustrated by two thirteenth-century songs. The *Dies irae,* which reflects the prevailing medieval spirit, is traditionally attributed to the great Latin stylist Thomas of Celano, who may have written it a few years before he met St. Francis and became one of his friars. Thomas entered the

Franciscan order about 1215 and enjoyed the friendship of St. Francis for several years. Pope Gregory IX chose him to write the official biography of Francis shortly after he was declared a saint in 1228. The second song, the *Canticle of the Sun,* is by St. Francis himself.

THE *DIES IRAE*

In the triple stanzas and fifty-seven lines of the *Dies irae,* the medieval Latin poetic style reaches a high point. Its content invokes the vision of the final dissolution of the universe, the sounding of angelic trumpets calling forth the dead from their tombs, and the overwhelming majesty of the coming of Christ as king to judge the living and the dead. The grandeur of its language and the perfection of its poetic form are equal to this solemn theme. The images and moods range from anger and terror to hope and bliss before coming to a close with a plea for eternal rest. A sense of its vivid verses can be gained from the following stanzas:

> Day of Wrath! O day of mourning!
> See fulfilled the prophets' warning,
> Heaven and earth in ashes burning!
> Wondrous sound the trumpet flings;
> Through earth's sepulchres it rings;
> All before the Throne it brings.
> Guilty, now I pour my moaning,
> All my shame with anguish owning;
> Spare, O God, Thy suppliant groaning!
> While the wicked are confounded,
> Doomed to flames of woe unbounded,
> Call me, with Thy saints surrounded.

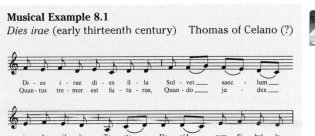

Musical Example 8.1
Dies irae (early thirteenth century) Thomas of Celano (?)

Di - es   i - rae di - es   il - la   Sol - vet___ saec - lum___
Quan - tus tre - mor est fu - tu - rus, Quan - do___ ju - dex___

in   fa - vil - la,   Te - ste___ Da - vid___ cum Si - byl - la.
est ven - tu - rus, Cunc - ta___ stri - cte___ dis - cus - su - rus.

Although the colorful language and verbal rhythms of the Latin original have a music all their own, the *Dies irae* is inseparable from its melodic setting. Both the poem and its melody found their way into the liturgy as important parts of the mass for the dead. Later this melody was to become famous as a symbol of medieval hellfire in the nineteenth-century Romantic Movement (see p. 495–497).

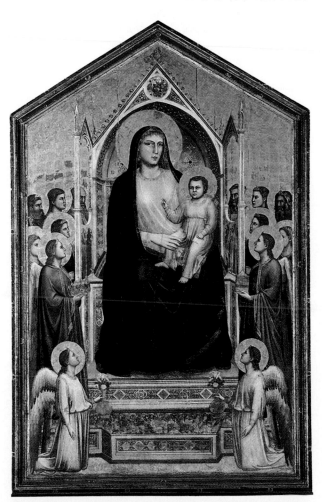

8.18 Giotto. *Madonna Enthroned,* c. 1310. Tempera on wood, 10′8″ × 6′8″. Galleria degli Uffizi, Florence, Italy.

LAUDS AND THE *CANTICLE OF THE SUN*

The most characteristic Franciscan contribution to poetry and music is found in a body of informal hymns called ***laudi spirituali***—songs of praise, or simply "lauds"—that are traceable directly to St. Francis and his immediate circle. The practice of spontaneous hymn singing continued from his time onward, and in the fourteenth century, it was firmly established as the most popular form of religious music.

In music, as in his religious work, Francis drew together the sacred, courtly, and popular traditions. The lauds thus were a poetic bridge between the traditional music of the church, the music of the castle, and the music of the streets. The words always had a religious theme. Often they were mere variations of psalms and prayers sung to popular tunes. Above all, they were music and poetry that the people could both sing and feel with their hearts.

Contrapuntal choral music, whether in the form of a church **motet** or a secular ***madrigal,*** was a sophisticated musical medium that required the voices of skilled professionals. By contrast, the lauds were folklike in spirit, were simple and direct in their appeal, and were sung either as solos or with others in unison. Just as the skilled monastic choir was characteristic of the Cluniac movement and the contrapuntal chorus the musical counterpart of the northern Gothic spirit, the lauds became the characteristic expression of the Franciscans.

The Canticle of the Sun by St. Francis is at once the most sublime of all the lauds and the most original. Legend has it that when St. Francis was recovering from an illness in a hut outside the convent of St. Clare, the nuns heard from his lips this rapturous new song. The informality, even casualness, of its composition and its rambling rhythms and rhymes make it as simple and unaffected as the dialect of Umbria (the region of central Italy, including Assisi) in which it is written. Sincerity and deep feeling dominate the unequal stanzas of St. Francis's songs of praise, rather than any attempt at learned communication or poetic elegance. It goes, in part:

> Praised be my Lord God with all his creatures, and especially our brother the sun, who brings us the day and who brings us the light; fair is he and shines with very great splendor; O Lord, he signifies to us Thee!
> Praised be my Lord for our sister the moon, and for the stars, the which He has set clear and lovely in heaven.

> Praised be my Lord for our sister water, who is very serviceable unto us and humble and precious and clean.
> Praised be my Lord for our brother fire, through whom thou givest us light in the darkness; and he is bright and pleasant and very mighty and strong.

Although the original melody of the *Canticle of the Sun* is lost, countless lauds survive, some dating back to shortly after St. Francis's time. Jacopone da Todi, a Franciscan monk who died in 1306, was one of the greatest writers of lauds. His most famous hymn is the *Stabat Mater Dolorosa,* which was officially incorporated into the liturgy in the eighteenth century to be sung on the Feast of Seven Sorrows. This remarkable man, like St. Francis before him, was of Umbrian origin, and after a succession of such diverse careers as lawyer, hermit, and Franciscan preacher, he became a poet and composer. His hymns readily found their way into the texts of the early miracle plays, which dramatized episodes in the life of a miracle-working saint or martyr, and his music became the foundation of the laudistic tradition. The following example is a part of one of his lauds. Its rhythmic complexity, emotional intensity, and stylistic character mark it as typical of the early Franciscan movement.

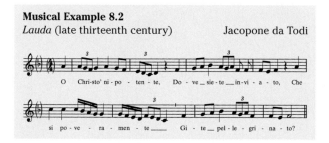

Musical Example 8.2
Lauda (late thirteenth century)   Jacopone da Todi

O Chri-sto' ni-po - ten - te, Do - ve_ sie - te_ in-vi - a - to, Che

si po-ve - ra - men - te____ Gi - te_ pel - le - gri - na - to?

DANTE'S *DIVINE COMEDY*

At the summit of the Middle Ages, Dante Alighieri composed the soaring verses of his *Divine Comedy.* This *summa* of diverse philosophical, theological, and political worldviews became at once a great human document, the outstanding book of the medieval period, and a prophecy of the Renaissance. In one stroke, Dante established the Italian spoken by the common people as an expressive language and gave his country its most enduring literary masterpiece. The work is not only a synthesis of scholastic and Franciscan philosophy but also a summation of the thought of the medieval period and of Greco-Roman antiquity as its author knew it. Classical figures such as Aristotle, Cicero, Ovid, and Virgil rub shoulders with Boethius, Thomas Aquinas, St. Francis, and Giotto himself, who in turn portrayed Dante in a *Paradiso* of his own, painted in the Chapel of Palazzo del Podèsta in the Bargello at Florence (Fig. 8.19).

Although the poem is elaborately allegorical, full of symbolism, and meant to be read on more than one level, the reader should not be intimidated. Dante tells a broad, compelling story, as well as stories within stories. Allegory, after all, interprets experience by means of visual and verbal images and symbols. Symbols are just generally agreed-on signs that stand for something else, as $ stands for "dollar."

The form of the poem is divided into a three-part structure—Hell, Purgatory, and Heaven—and one of its building blocks is the medieval mystical number 3: Each stanza has three lines, and the rhyming scheme is the melodious *terza rima*: aba, bcb, and so on. In turn, Dante is terrified by three animals personifying the three sins he must overcome to progress upward. Each time, he is saved by the mediation of three holy women. To enter the three realms, he must pass through three gates. Each section contains thirty-three cantos, the number of Christ's years on Earth. The introductory canto, added to the 3 times 33 others, brings the total to an even 100—that number having the quality of wholeness and perfection. Nine as the multiple of three also plays its part. Hell and Purgatory each have nine circles while in Paradise there are nine categories of angels in their nine different spheres.

The allegorical journey through these vast spaces symbolizes the soul in its quest for self-knowledge and spiritual illumination. The path, which passes from Hell to Heaven, also runs the gamut from despair to hope, sin to grace, hate to love, ignorance to enlightenment. Dante's vision is concerned not only with life after death but with the course of human life from birth in original sin, through the purgative process of experience, to the knowledge of ideal goodness, truth, and beauty. As Dante says in the opening lines, "Midway in our life's journey, I went astray from the straight road and woke to find myself alone in a dark wood."

From this dark and sunless forest, he plunges into the depths of the Inferno, where he encounters the fearsome inscription, "Abandon All Hope Ye Who Enter Here":

> Here sighs and cries and wails coiled and
>   recoiled
> on the starless air, spilling my soul to
>   tears.
> A confusion of tongues and monstrous accents
>   toiled.

In the lowest pit of Hell he encounters the monstrous body of Lucifer, who, as his name implies, is the fallen angel of light now dwelling in eternal darkness. From this point onward, Dante begins the ascent from darkness to light.

The next state is Purgatory, where light begins to dawn:

> Now shall I sing of that second kingdom given
> the soul of man wherein to purge its guilt
> and so grow worthy to ascend to Heaven.

Here he glimpses the pure radiance of the eastern star while encountering a strange spirit, who asks:

> Who led you? or what served you as a light
> in your dark flight from the eternal valley,
> which lies forever blind in darkest night?

Up to this point, Dante has been guided by the Roman poet Virgil, who must now leave him because only Christians may enter the sacred precincts of Paradise. From here onward, his guide will be Beatrice, his lifelong love, inspiration, and spiritual ideal. In real life, Dante met Beatrice only a few times, but in the poem, she becomes the "blessed and glorious Beatrice," the personification of divine grace.

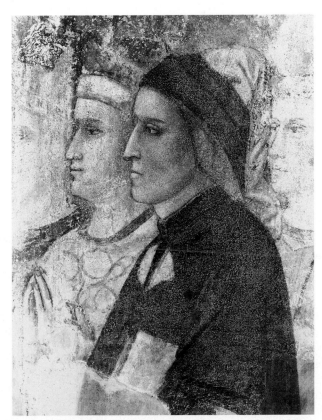

8.19   Giotto (?). *Portrait of Dante,* detail of fresco, c. 1325. Chapel of Palazzo del Podèsta, Bargello, Florence, Italy.

Dante then climbs the mount of Purgatory, where sunrise and sunset are transitory phases before progression into the ultimate realm, the presence of God, where sunlight never fades.

> The glory of Him who moves all things rays forth
> through all the universe, and is reflected
> from each thing in proportion to its worth.
> I have been in that Heaven of His most light,
> and what I saw, those who descend from there
> lack both the knowledge and the power to write.

Not only was Dante a gifted writer, but he also had a musician's ear for sound. His verses have a music of their own. He also had a painter's eye for detail. His images are a feast for the inner eye of the imagination. Although spiritual light concerned him most, he nonetheless conjured up its vision in familiar everyday impressions. He sings of sunlight, firelight, starlight; the sparkle of precious stones; the gleaming rays of a lamp in the darkness; the translucent effects of light filtered through water, wine, glass, and jewels; rainbows and the colored reflections from clouds; the ruddy glow of infernal flames and the pure radiance of Paradise; the light of the human eye and that of halos surrounding the heads of saints. As a result,

light becomes the divine spark that leads from reason to revelation. Finally, each of the three cantos of the poem ends on the word *stelle* (stars). The last words of the Paradise mirror the ultimate, ineffable vision of divinity as "[t]he love that moves the sun and other stars."

THE BLACK DEATH AND ITS IMPACT

All went well in Italy during the first third of the fourteenth century. Townspeople prospered, and the arts flourished. Beginning in 1340, however, a series of disasters occurred, starting with local crop failures and continuing with the miseries of famine and disease. The climax came in an outbreak of plague in France and Italy during the catastrophic year 1348. The so-called Black Death killed more than half the population of such cities as Florence, Siena, and Pisa. A chronicler of Siena, after burying five of his children, said quite simply, "No one wept for the dead, because everyone expected death himself." In due course, the plague swept through Germany, middle Europe, Scandinavia, and Britain. It recurred throughout Europe for almost 30 years.

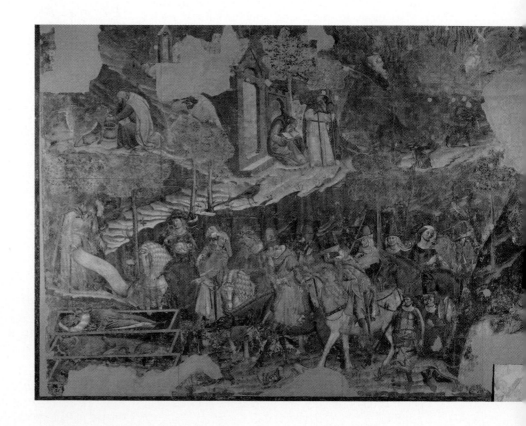

An event so calamitous was bound to have a deep effect on social and cultural trends. Many survivors found themselves suddenly made poor or, through unexpected inheritances, vastly enriched. Eventually, thousands of residents in the relatively safe countryside flocked into the cities to take the places of those who had died. The lives of individuals underwent radical changes. For some, it was the "eat, drink, and be merry" philosophy, exemplified in Boccaccio's *Decameron;* for others, it was moral self-accusation and repentance, as seen in the purgatorial vision of the same author's later *Corbaccio.*

Driven by fear and a sense of guilt, people felt that something had gone disastrously wrong and that the Black Death, like the biblical plagues of old, must have been sent by an angry God to chastise humanity and turn people from their wicked ways. In the literary world, both Boccaccio and Petrarch adopted this view after having penned earlier, more worldly writings. What was true of literature was true also of painting.

REACTION TO THE PLAGUE

The response to the plague may have been illustrated in one of the frescoes on the inner wall of the Camposanto in the Pisa Cathedral group. *The Triumph of Death* (Fig. 8.20), whose post-1348 date has been disputed, is nonetheless an epic statement with much detail crowded into every bit of space. Like the sermons of the time, some parts warned of the closeness of death and the terrors of hell if the soul was claimed by the devil. Others showed the bliss of being carried off by angels.

On the left, a group of mounted nobles sets out for the hunt, but instead of the game they were pursuing, they find only death. Inside three open coffins, serpents consume the corpses of the one-time great of the Earth. In a poem also titled "Triumph of Death," the contemporary poet Petrarch speaks of death as the great leveler when he notes that neither "the Popes, Emperors, nor Kings, no enseigns wore of their past hight but naked show'd and poor," and then asks, "Where be their riches, where their precious gems? Their miters, scepters, robes and diadems?"

Near the coffins a bearded hermit monk unfolds a prophetic scroll that warns them to repent before it is too late. The only relief from the scene of horror and desolation is found in the upper left, where some monks are gathered around a chapel, busying themselves with their duties. Apparently only those who renounce the world can find relief from its general turmoil and terror of death. The

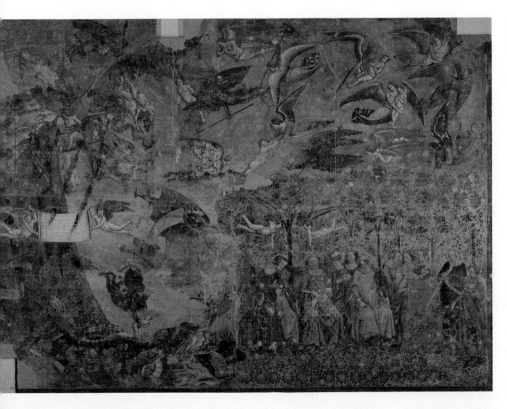

8.20 Master of the Triumph of Death. *The Triumph of Death*, c. mid-1330s (partially destroyed, 1944). Fresco. Campo Santo, Pisa, Italy.

sheer horror and desolation of this scene harken back to the carved Last Judgments in earlier medieval churches.

The long-lasting psychological effects of the plague were not illustrated as clearly as the physical effects of the disease. Nevertheless, the plague ravaged worldviews as well as villages. The medieval ideal of a neatly stacked social order was challenged as it became increasingly apparent that neither the rich, the royal, nor the wealthy could stand against the catastrophe. Fear replaced fealty, doubt challenged faith, and civil unrest pitted region against region and class against class.

IDEAS

The late medieval period had one foot planted in the Middle Ages and the other in the emerging Renaissance. These opposing worldviews were reflected in a number of situations, especially the power struggle between the landed aristocracy and the growing cities; the incompatibility of Gothic architecture and the Classical/Byzantine heritage in Italy; the presence of medieval devils and genuine human types in Giotto's frescoes; the opposing visions of the Inferno and Paradise in Dante's *Divine Comedy;* and the different attitudes expressed in poetry and painting before and after the Black Death.

The tug-of-war between and among differing ideas found expression in the life of St. Francis, whose otherworldly self-denial contrasted with his worldly love of natural beauty. For him, fire was created not to roast the souls of sinners in hell but to offer light in darkness and warmth on a cold night.

The Romanesque St. Peter Damian had said, "The world is so filthy with vices, the holy mind is befouled by even thinking of it." In contrast, the Gothic encyclopedist Vincent of Beauvais exclaimed, "How great is even the humblest beauty of this world!" In his *Canticle of the Sun,* St. Francis found evidence of God's goodness everywhere— in the radiance of the sun, in the eternal miracle of springtime. He saw all nature as a revelation of divinity, and his thought foreshadowed a departure from the medieval dualism that opposed the flesh and the spirit. After a lifetime of self-denial and self-inflicted pain, St. Francis humbly begged pardon of the body for the suffering he had caused it to endure.

LATE MEDIEVAL NATURALISM

In both the north and south of Europe, the abstractions of the scholastic mind found a new challenge in the down-to-earth reasoning of philosophers who called themselves **nominalists.** Late scholasticism had, in fact, become a strained exercise in logical gymnastics. It disregarded the real world and the facts necessary to give substance to thought.

On their road to knowledge, the nominalists turned the scholastic ways upside down. They insisted that generalities must be built from the bottom up, first by gathering data and sorting out particular things and events, then by putting like with like. Only in this way, they said, was it possible to classify things and give a name to those that grouped together (hence the term *nominalists,* from the Latin word meaning "to name"). The question was whether to start with an assumption determined beforehand and then look for the supporting data, as the scholastic thinkers did, or to assemble the facts first. These two methods approximate the difference between deductive and inductive thought, the latter pointing toward the experimental method of modern science.

As it gained a foothold, the nominalist viewpoint weakened medieval authoritarianism, in which the word of Aristotle and the church fathers was accepted without question. Correspondingly, it initiated the modern practice of finding facts through firsthand observation. Particular things became more important than universal forms. For example, a plant was a vegetable or flower that grew in a garden rather than the manifestation of a universal idea of a plant existing in the mind of God.

The result of this new mental orientation was a renewed interest in a tangible reality that would have important consequences in art and scientific inquiry. In the fifteenth century it would lead to the representation of figures in natural surroundings, the rendering of the body with anatomical accuracy, the modeling of figures three-dimensionally by means of light and shadow, and the working out of laws of linear perspective for foreground and background effects.

While these systems of logic were being argued in the universities, the friars of St. Francis were bringing his message to town and country folk. With them, religious devotion became a voluntary, spontaneous relationship between human beings and God rather than an imposed obligation. Religion, they asserted, should be based on love rather than on fear. The Franciscans also sought to establish a common bond between individuals, whatever their station in life, thus implementing the golden rule, "Love thy neighbor as thyself." Franciscan ideas represent an important shift from the vertical feudal organization of society, in which individuals were related to those above and below them by a hierarchical authority, to a horizontal or level ethical relationship that bound people to one another.

NOMINALISM AND THE ARTS

St. Francis saw evidence of God's love in everything, from the fruits and flowers of the Earth to the winds and the clouds in the sky, a concept that was to have great consequences for the arts. The birds to which St. Francis preached, for instance, were the birds that were heard chirping and singing every day, not the symbolic dove of the Holy Spirit or the apocalyptic eagle of St. John.

Although this tendency toward naturalism was already noticeable in the thirteenth-century sculpture of Chartres and elsewhere, it became widespread in the fourteenth century. As this view of the natural world gained ascendance over the supernatural, it released the visual arts from the perplexing problems of how to represent the unseen. The love of St. Francis for such simple things as grass and trees, which could be represented as they were observed in nature, opened up new subjects for artists to explore.

St. Francis's message was taught in parables and simple images of life that all could understand. Giotto succeeded in translating these into pictorial form. In this favorable naturalistic climate, both found a balance between the abstract and the concrete, between divine essence and human reality.

Giotto moved away from medieval mysticism. To him, the saints were not remote ethereal spirits but human beings who felt all the same emotions, from joy to despair, as the people in the Italian towns he knew so well. Even his contemporaries could see that Giotto was blazing new trails. Although Giotto undoubtedly showed a love of nature, he never accentuated it to the point where it might overshadow or weaken his primary human emphasis. His interest was less in nature for its own sake than in its meaning in the lives of his subjects.

In viewing a picture by Giotto, one does well to begin with the people and be concerned only secondarily with their natural surroundings. His subjects create their own environment through their expressive attitudes and dramatic placement. Although his work shows an increasing concern with problems of natural space, space is less important than his expressive intentions. His

use of color and shading gives his figures a sense of depth and volume that brings them to life. In this way, both human nature and nature as such achieve an intimate and distinctive identity in Giotto's art.

FRANCISCAN HUMANITARIANISM

Long before the trend toward naturalism, the monastery at Cluny had changed the character of monasticism by uniting cloistered life with feudalism. The new orientation of the Franciscan order was no less revolutionary. St. Francis did not confine his monks in cloisters but sent them out into the world. The idea of evangelical poverty, humility, and love for humanity expressed through living and working with simple people resulted in a union with, rather than a withdrawal from, society. The Franciscans did not avoid the world as much as they avoided worldly pursuits. The Cluniacs were, in the proper sense of the word, an *order;* that is, their discipline required a strict hierarchical organization. By contrast, the Franciscans were, in every sense of the word, a *movement.*

The frigid intellectualism of the late medieval universities was bound to thaw in the warmth of Franciscan emotionalism and attention to nature. Also, self-denial held little appeal for an increasingly prosperous urban middle class. The mathematical elegance of Gothic structures began to yield to more informal types of buildings. The logical linear patterns of the surviving Byzantine pictorial style gave way to the physical fullness and emotional warmth of Giotto's figures. The stylized faces of Byzantine saints paled in the light of the human tenderness found in a smiling mouth or tearful eye in a Giotto picture. The formal architectural sculpture and abstract patterns of Gothic stained glass were replaced by the colorful informality of mural paintings in fresco. In his music, as in his religious work, St. Francis drew the sacred and popular traditions closer together, and in the lauds he encouraged people to sing. He gave people a music that they could feel in their hearts without having to understand it with their brains.

HUMANITARIANISM AND THE ARTS

When Dante declared that Giotto's fame outshone that of Cimabue and Boccaccio proclaimed that Giotto revived painting after it had "been in the grave" for centuries, they were recognizing in his art a new spirit and style. This new spirit was also apparent in Boccaccio's *Decameron,* which mocks the manners and ways of Gothic knights, abbots, and monks and the outmoded feudal ideal to which they clung.

Likewise, new feeling was apparent in music. In France, Philippe de Vitry published a musical treatise in 1316 with the title *Ars Nova (New Art),* which he opposed to the *ars antiqua,* or "old art," of the Gothic thirteenth century. He ardently promoted the idea of bringing lively new dancelike rhythms into church music. His book gained such popularity that it attracted the anger of conservative church leaders in the form of a papal criticism issued by Pope John XXII in 1325.

A new spirit of freedom was in the air, a release from tradition. St. Francis had earlier struck out in a new religious direction, and Giotto, by translating the saint's life into pictures, avoided the traditional biblical subjects and their traditional stylized treatment. Giotto was working on an almost contemporary subject, as well as rendering it in a new manner. In addition, he painted subjects that came within the iconographic tradition, such as *Joachim Returning to the Sheepfold* (Fig. 8.21) and the *Pietà* (Fig. 8.11), far more dramatically than others. In general, his figures moved about in the space he created for them with greater suppleness than those in earlier pictures. His world was marked by a new, emotional relationship between human beings, their natural environment, and God.

Portrayals of Christ as a human infant in the arms of his mother began to replace the image of Christ in majesty from the Gothic period. Along with growing interest in the cycle of Christ's infancy, legends of Mary's life became increasingly prominent. The emotional element in the Passion was largely conveyed through compassion for the Virgin as the mother of sorrows. This was as true for Giotto's cycle in Padua, as for Jacopone da Todi's *Stabat Mater Dolorosa.*

The adoption of the language of ordinary people in literature, the informal treatment of fresco painting, and the folk spirit in music all make it apparent that works of art were being addressed to a new group of patrons. Furthermore, one of Giotto's statements reveals the artist's new conception of himself. Each man, he said, "should save his soul as best he can. As for me, I intend to serve painting in my own way and only so far as it serves me, for the sake of the

8.21 Giotto. *Joachim Returning to the Sheepfold,* 1305–1306. Fresco. Arena Chapel, Padua, Italy.

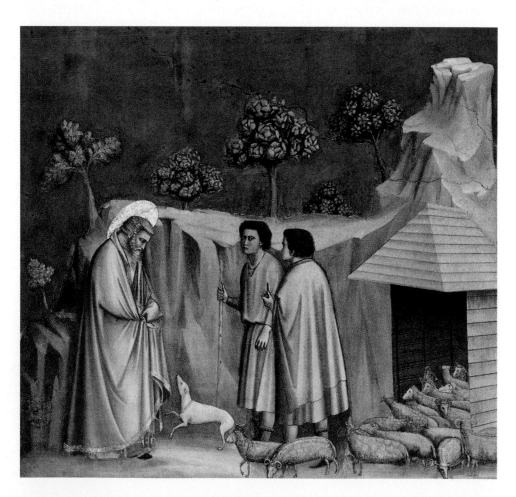

lovely moments it gives at the price of an agreeable fatigue." Because it claimed so many lives, even the horrific Black Death had some beneficial effects for artists after Giotto's time. It decreased authority in many realms, including the conservative guilds, and thereby allowed the younger masters to assert their independence and develop new ideas and techniques.

THE SURVIVAL OF CLASSICISM

A renewed interest in classical antiquity began to be seen, heard, and read in the works of the artists and writers of the fourteenth century. The panels of Nicola Pisano's pulpit show the classical Roman influence of sarcophagi and narrative reliefs such as Trajan's Column (see Fig. 4.11). However, what seems to be a revival of Roman classical forms is also a survival of those forms. Nicola Pisano's sculpture certainly seems to be closer to the art of ancient Rome than to the Gothic. Because Roman sculpture was present everywhere in Italy, no Italian sculptor could avoid seeing it. Likewise, because Dante was writing an epic poem, his obvious model was Virgil's *Aeneid,* which had never ceased to be read.

Although a growing consciousness of the classical in the works of Dante and his contemporaries should not be overlooked, it must be seen from the fourteenth-century point of view—as a continuation of a cultural tradition rather than as a sudden rebirth of classicism. The influence of the classical authors and classical art was not as neglected or dead as many historians have supposed. Virgil, Cicero, and certain works of Aristotle were as widely read and written about in medieval times as they were in the fourteenth and fifteenth centuries.

This is not to deny that a new spirit of curiosity enlivened the search, begun by Petrarch and Boccaccio, in monastic libraries for manuscripts by other Greek and Roman authors besides those who bore the sacred approval of church tradition. This probing went hand in hand with the discovery in Rome of some long-buried antique sculpture and with the study of Roman building methods.

Even though Petrarch was crowned in Rome with the laurel wreath, the ancient token of immortal fame, and even though he wrote his cycle of *Triumphs* with the Roman triumphal arch in mind, it is doubtful that he or Dante or Boccaccio did more than bring the ancient world a little closer to their own time. Even though Giotto spent some time in Rome, the joyous humanistic spirit that permeates his work is much closer

to the new Franciscan outlook and the continuous tradition of Roman relief sculpture and fresco painting than to any conscious reappraisal of classical culture as such. It is necessary, then, to dissociate fourteenth-century Franciscan humanitarianism from the more self-conscious, text-based revival of Greco-Roman antiquity that would characterize developments in fifteenth-century Florentine and early sixteenth-century Roman humanism.

Especially in the late fourteenth century, the weakness of classicism allowed new perceptions to take hold. For example, Boccaccio was among the first modern writers to recognize and describe the feats of accomplished women in history. His popular *Of Famous Women* (1362), inspired by Petrarch's *Lives of Famous Men,* told the stories of 106 women. Moreover, he deliberately addressed the book to female readers. Some versions of the work contained illustrations of legendary and historical figures, such as Marcia, who was, according to tradition, a painter and a Roman Vestal Virgin (Fig. 8.22). Interestingly, the illustrator chose

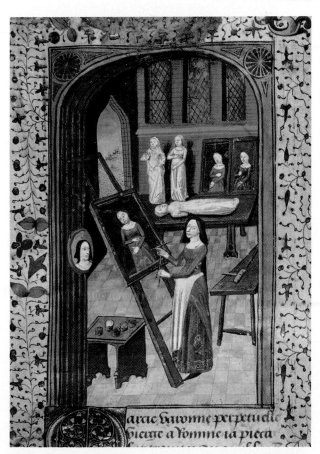

8.22 Giovanni Boccaccio. *Marcia.* Illustration for *Of Famous Women.* Ms. 33; folio 37v, France, c. 1470. The New York Public Library, New York.

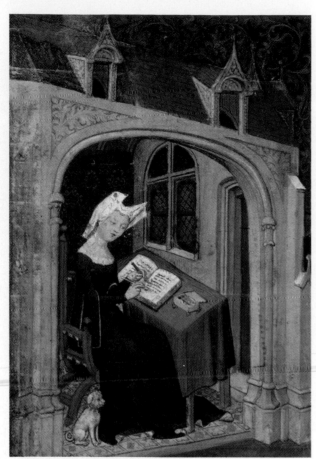

8.23   *Christine de Pisan Writing in Her Study,* frontispiece to her *Livre de la Mutacion de Fortune,* early fifteenth century. Harl. 4431; folio 4 Min, France. British Library, London, England.

to depict her not in classical garments but in early fifteenth-century dress. In France, Christine de Pisan, daughter of an Italian doctor, wrote the *Book of the City of Ladies* (1405) (Fig. 8.23). The book not only celebrated talented women but also argued for the equal education of women and men. It imagined an ideal place, the city of women, where women lived their lives fully.

Of course, these texts did not instantly reverse existing assumptions about gender, but they did broadcast intriguing, fresh ideas before the revival of classicism in the Renaissance brought with it a heritage that intensified gender roles and differences. When Renaissance intellectuals examined the Roman historian Plutarch's book, *Lives of Virtuous Women,* and found classical authority for the notion that women could work in traditionally male professions without losing their femininity, they did so with recent precedents in mind. Like so many other Gothic challenges to received ideas and established authority, feminism was a product of the progressive towns, and like these challenges, it was a phenomenon that would not go away.

YOUR RESOURCES

- **Exploring Humanities CD-ROM**

  - Readings—*The Decameron,* Introduction; *The Divine Comedy: Inferno,* Cantos 1–5, *Paradiso,* Canto 33

- **Web Site**

  http://art.wadsworth.com/fleming10

  - Chapter 8 Quiz

  - Links

- **Audio CD**

  - *Dies irae*

LATE MEDIEVAL PERIOD

Key Events	Architecture	Visual Arts	Literature and Music
c. 1140 **War begins** between the Guelphs (supporters of papal sovereignty) and Ghibellines (supporters of the German emperor); at root was a struggle between the newly minted middle class and aristocratic power	1174–1184 **Canterbury Cathedral choir** built by William of Sens		1170–1220 **Wolfram von Eschenbach** ❏, poet, Minnesinger
1182–1226 **St. Francis of Assisi;** 1210 founded Franciscan order, 1223 confirmed by pope, 1228 declared saint			c. 1200 **Walther von der Vogelweide** ❏, poet, Minnesinger
1198–1216 **Innocent III,** pope; church reached pinnacle of power			

1200

Key Events	Architecture	Visual Arts	Literature and Music
			1203 **Wolfram von Echenbach** wrote *Parzifal*
			c. 1214–1294 **Roger Bacon** ○, Franciscan monk and scientist
	1220–1258 **Salisbury Cathedral** built	c. 1220–1284 **Nicola** (d'Apulia) **Pisano** ●	c. 1225–1274 **Thomas Aquinas** ○, scholastic philosopher
	1228–1253 **Basilica of St. Francis** built at Assisi	1230–1240 **Bamberg Rider** carved	1225 **St. Francis** wrote *Canticle of the Sun*
		1240–c. 1302 **Giovanni Cimabue** ▲	
	1248 **Cologne Cathedral** begun, finished in nineteenth century	1250–1260 **Ekkehard** and **Uta** carved at Naumburg Cathedral	1229 **Thomas of Celano** wrote *Life of St. Francis*
		c. 1250–c. 1317 **Giovanni Pisano** ●	1262 **St. Bonaventura** wrote *Life of St. Francis*
	1278–1283 **Campo Santo** at Pisa built by Giovanni di Simone	c. 1255–1319 **Duccio di Buoninsegna** ▲	1265–1321 **Dante Alighieri** ◆
		c. 1260 **Pulpit in Pisa Baptistry** carved by Nicola Pisano	c. 1285–c. 1349 **William of Occam** ○, Franciscan monk and nominalist philosopher
		c. 1266–1337 **Giotto di Bondone** ▲	1291–1361 **Philippe de Vitry** ❏
		c. 1285–1344 **Simone Martini** ▲	
		c. 1290–c. 1349 **Andrea Pisano** ●	
		c. 1296 **Frescoes on life of St. Francis** painted at Assisi	

1300

Key Events	Architecture	Visual Arts	Literature and Music
1309–1376 **Popes** in residence at Avignon		c. 1305–1309 **Giotto** painted frescoes on life of Virgin at Padua	1304–1374 **Petrarch** (Francesco Petrarca) ◆
		1305–1348 **Pietro Lorenzetti** ▲ active	1306 **Jacopone da Todi** ❏ died
		1308–1311 **Duccio** painted Maestà altarpiece, Siena Cathedral	1313–1375 **Giovanni Boccaccio** ◆
			1314–1321 **Dante** wrote *Divine Comedy*
		c. 1320 **Giotto** painted Bardi Chapel frescoes in Santa Croce, Florence	1316 ***Ars Nova,*** treatise on new music written by Philippe de Vitry
		1321–1363 **Francesco Traini** ▲ active	c. 1325–1397 **Francesco Landini** ❏, organist-composer at Florence
		1317–1348 **Ambrogio Lorenzetti** ▲ active	1332 ***Little Flowers of St. Francis*** compiled
		1330–1336 **Bronze doors of Florence Baptistry** cast by Andrea Pisano	c. 1340–1400 **Geoffrey Chaucer** ◆
			1341 **Petrarch** crowned poet laureate in Rome
1348 **Black Death** swept Europe		c. 1334 **Andrea Pisano** and **Giotto** collaborated on sculpture for Florence Cathedral	1348–1353 ***Decameron*** written by Boccaccio
	c. 1350 **Haddon Hall** built	c. 1350 ***Triumph of Death*** painted in Campo Santo, Pisa, by Traini	c. 1354 ***Triumph of Death*** written by Petrarch
1378–1417 **Great Schism** between rival popes	1377 **Ulm Cathedral** begun		1364–c. 1430 **Christine de Pisan** ◆, French writer who promoted women's participation in the arts.

❏ - Musician ▲ - Painter ○ - Philosopher ● - Sculptor ◆ - Writer

1200

Franciscan Order founded, 1209
Dante, 1265–1321, *The Divine Comedy*

1300

Black Death, 1348–mid-1350s
Hundred Years' War, 1337–1453

1400

Columbus arrives in West Indies, 1492
Invention of movable metal type by Johann Gutenberg, c. 1445
Conquest of Constantinople by Turks, 1453
Medici expelled from Florence, 1494

1500

Protestant Reformation begins, 1517
Council of Trent, 1545–1563

PART THREE

RENAISSANCE AND REFORMATION

The Renaissance was a period of commercial and cultural exploration and expansion that took many new directions: the advancement of humanistic and scientific knowledge, the discovery of new worlds by navigating the globe, the continued growth of towns and cities, increasing wealth in the hands of the merchant class, the development of national states, and an unparalleled outburst of productivity in the arts.

During the Renaissance, humanistic scholars thought of themselves as participating in a vast intellectual awakening, following a long medieval period of darkness. They searched the monasteries for neglected volumes and freed themselves intellectually to study the Greco-Roman classics without the pretext of looking only for Christian values. After the fall of Constantinople, many Greek scholars found refuge in Italy, bringing with them their learning and ancient manuscripts. The humanists rediscovered the beauties of life in the here and now, rather than in the hereafter. Their outlook changed to a more human-centered one, reaffirming the ancient belief that "nothing is more wonderful than man." In the midfifteenth century, the invention of printing made books more readily available, aiding in the spread of knowledge. Merchants and bankers rapidly increased the numbers of middle-class people, whose wealth and influence was self-made, and books enlarged the ranks of people who had access to the power of learning. In the 50 years after Gutenberg first published his Bible in 1456, more books were printed than had been copied by hand in the previous 1,000 years.

More broadly, humanism promoted a revival of interest in the affairs of the everyday world, reasserted people's faith in themselves, and reinforced the role of individuals in all spheres. Writers, dramatists, visual artists, and musicians flourished. Architects were inspired by the geometric clarity and harmonious proportions of the ancient Roman style. Sculptors and painters studied geometry, optics, and anatomy to achieve accurate three-dimensional representation of the world, objects, and human figures as the eye beholds them.

In northern Europe, Renaissance humanism expressed itself less in a revival of antiquity and more in scientific observation and careful study of natural phenomena. In the arts, this meant a shift away from heavenly visions toward the integration of symbols in careful representations of the natural world, and even the study of nature for its own sake.

The position of the church, both as a powerful political force and as an institution increasingly concerned with worldly affairs, came under close scrutiny. Abuses among the clergy set the stage for the Reformation, as did the papal interest in winning victories on the battlefield rather than caring for human souls. Led by Martin Luther, John Calvin, and others, the "Protestant" reformers rejected the central authority of the church and the mediation of the priesthood. They held that by reading the scriptures, individuals could know and interpret the word of God for themselves.

In Europe during the Renaissance, the merchant and artisan classes rose to challenge the entrenched position of the nobility. The expansion of the urban middle class was strengthened by the increase of trade that followed in the wake of exploration. The increasingly wealthy merchant families demanded and received greater political power in business organization, city government, and church circles.

In these momentous developments in thought, science, religion, exploration, statecraft, and the arts, we can recognize the beginnings of the modern era.

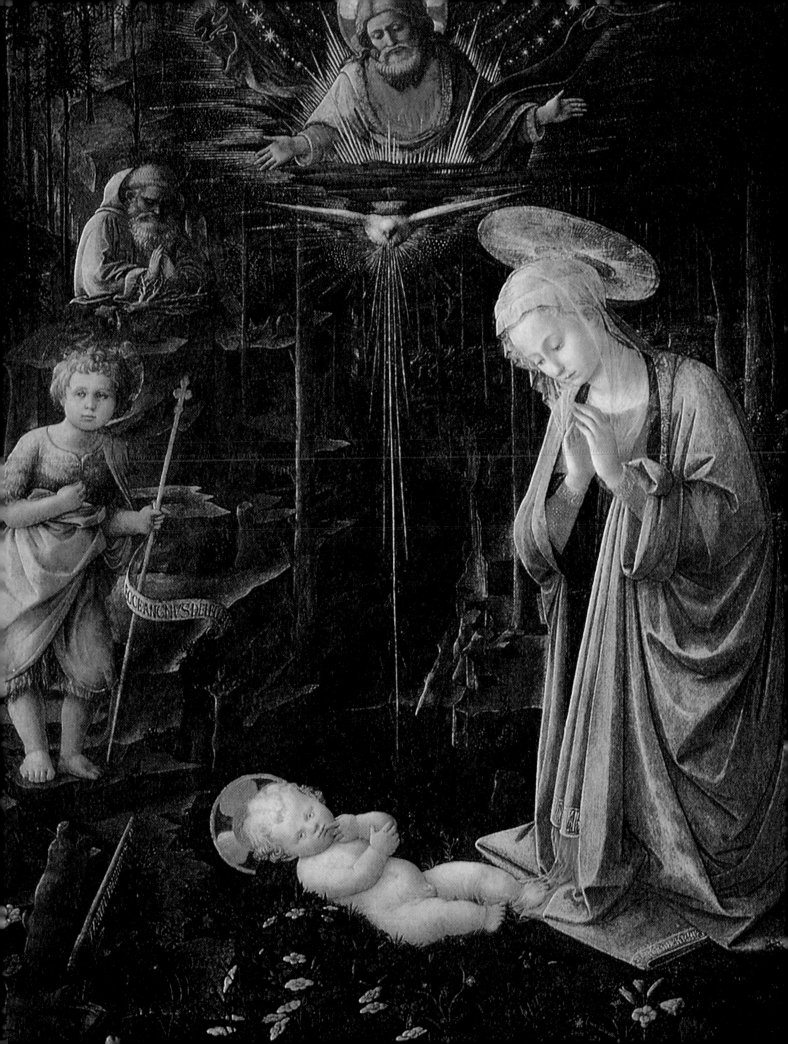

FLORENTINE
RENAISSANCE STYLE

LIVELY FESTIVALS WERE THE DELIGHT of all Florentines, but March 25, 1436, was a special occasion that would linger long in the memory of these prosperous people. The dedication of Florence's newly completed cathedral (Figs. 9.1A and 9.2A) brought together an unprecedented number of church dignitaries, statesmen, and diplomats. In their wake were famous artists, poets, scholars, and musicians. The white-robed Pope Eugene IV, crowned with the triple tiara and attended by seven cardinals in bright red and no fewer than thirty-seven bishops and archbishops in purple vestments, made a triumphal progress through the banner-lined streets, accompanied by city officials and guild leaders with their honor guards.

Appropriately enough, the cathedral was christened Santa Maria del Fiore (Holy Mary of the Flower), because Florence (derived from the word

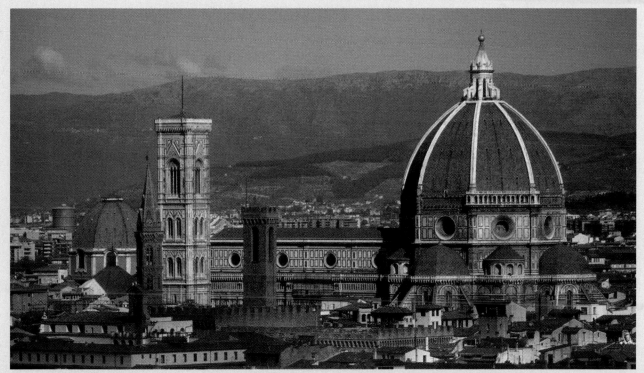

A

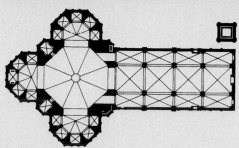

B

9.1 (A) Florence Cathedral group. Cathedral begun by Arnolfo di Cambio, 1296; dome by Filippo Brunelleschi, 1420–1436; present facade, 1875–1887. Length of cathedral 508′; height of dome 367′. Campanile begun 1334 by Giotto, continued by Andrea Pisano, 1336–1348; height 269′. Baptistry (lower right), 1060–1150. (B) Plan of Florence Cathedral.

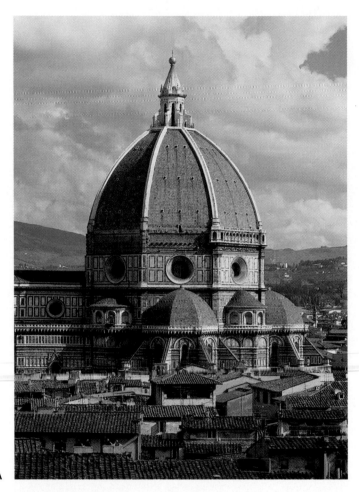

A

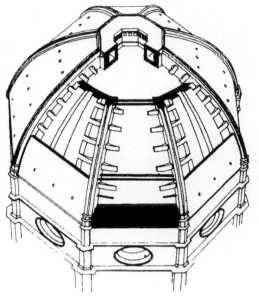

B

9.2 (A) Filippo Brunelleschi. Dome of Florence Cathedral, Florence, Italy, 1420–1436. (B) Internal structure of Brunelleschi's Dome, Florence Cathedral.

flora) was the city of flowers. March 25 was also the Feast of the Annunciation, and the Annunciation and the Nativity were favorite subjects of Florentine art.

FLORENCE IN THE FIFTEENTH CENTURY

The colorfully costumed citizens of this flourishing Tuscan town lined the streets for the grand procession and crowded into the vast nave of the cathedral. At a time when many feudal aristocrats still dwelled in cold, fortresslike castles, Florentine patrician families lived in a style that could well have been the envy of kings. The working members of the population belonged to the various guilds and trade organizations, of which the most important were those dealing with the carding, weaving, and dyeing of wool and silk for the internationally famous Florentine textile industry. Metal crafts and stonework followed in importance, and so on down to the butchers, bakers, and providers of goods for everyday life. The masters of the principal guilds were the influential citizens from whose ranks the members of the Signory, or city council, were chosen and from which many merchant and banking families emerged.

The most renowned of these families was the Medici, whose head at this time was Cosimo. Through a combination of political understanding and keen financial ability, he dominated the government of the city. Cosimo never assumed a title or other outward sign of authority. Instead, he was the political boss, ruling from behind the scenes with the support of the guilds, which knew that a stable government and peaceful relations with their neighbors (see Maps 9.1 and 9.2) were the best safeguards of their prosperity.

The Medici were the papal bankers and received deposits of church funds from England, France, and Flanders. From their branch offices in London, Lyon, and Antwerp, they lent this money at high rates of interest to foreign heads of state. With the papal revenues, they bought English wool, had it processed in the Netherlands, shipped it to Florence to be woven into fine fabrics, and exported these at a handsome profit. It was Cosimo who made the florin the soundest currency in Europe.

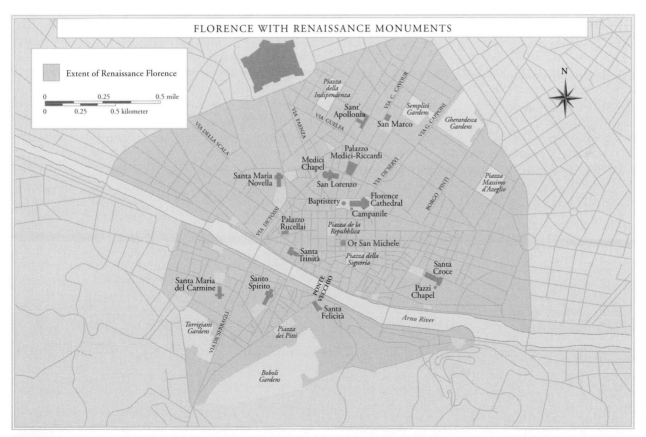

ITALY ABOUT 1400

KINGDOM OF FRANCE

HOLY ROMAN EMPIRE

DUCHY OF SAVOY

Turin

Milan

DUCHY OF MILAN

Verona

Vicenza

Venice

Mantua

Padua

REPUBLIC OF VENICE

MARQUISATE OF MANTUA

Ferrara

DUCHY OF FERRARA

Modena

Bologna

Genoa

DUCHY OF MODENA

REPUBLIC OF GENOA

Lucca

Pistoia

Pisa

Florence

REPUBLIC OF LUCCA

REPUBLIC OF FLORENCE

Urbino

Siena

PAPAL STATES

REPUBLIC OF SIENA

Orvieto

Avignon

CORSICA (Genoa)

Rome

Appenines

Adriatic Sea

KINGDOM OF ARAGON

KINGDOM OF NAPLES

Naples

SARDINIA (Aragon)

Tyrrhenian Sea

Mediterranean Sea

Palermo

KINGDOM OF SICILY (Aragon)

0   100   200 miles

0   100   200 kilometers

MAP 9.1

FLORENCE WITH RENAISSANCE MONUMENTS

Extent of Renaissance Florence

0   0.25   0.5 mile

0   0.25   0.5 kilometer

VIA DELLA SCALA

VIA FAENZA

VIA GUELFA

Piazza della Indipendenza

Sant' Apollonia

San Marco

Semplici Gardens

VIA C. CAVOUR

VIA G. CAPPONI

Gherardesca Gardens

Palazzo Medici-Riccardi

Medici Chapel

Santa Maria Novella

San Lorenzo

VIA DE' SERVI

Baptistery

Florence Cathedral

Campanile

BORGO PINTI

Piazza Massimo d'Azeglio

VIA DE' FOSSI

Palazzo Rucellai

Piazza de la Republica

Or San Michele

Santa Trinità

Piazza della Signoria

Santa Croce

Santa Maria del Carmine

Santo Spirito

PONTE VECCHIO

Pazzi Chapel

Santa Felicità

Arno River

Torrigiani Gardens

VIA DE' SERRAGLI

Piazza dei Pitti

Boboli Gardens

MAP 9.2

But political power and high finance were not the only pursuits of this ambitious banker. A serious student of Plato, Cosimo became one of the founders of the Neoplatonic Academy—not a school as such, but a circle of scholars, intellectuals, and artists that had enormous intellectual influence. From all the parts of Europe where his financial interests extended, he commissioned works of art. At home, he gathered a library of rare manuscripts, which he made available for study and translation.

Through Cosimo's generosity, a group of Dominican monks moved into the monastery of San Marco, which was rebuilt for them by his personal architect, Michelozzo. Among the monks was Fra Angelico, whom Cosimo encouraged to decorate the monastery walls with his famous frescoes. Other artists also benefited from Cosimo's patronage. Filippo Lippi, the future teacher of Botticelli, looked to him for commissions. Cosimo also took the advice of the sculptor Donatello and collected antique statuary. He placed it in his gardens and encouraged young sculptors to work there. Small wonder, then, that the Signory voted him the posthumous title *Pater Patriae,* "Father of His Country."

THE CATHEDRAL OF FLORENCE

On the day of the cathedral's dedication, the eyes of all Florentines were directed upward to the mighty **cupola,** which still gives the city its characteristic profile. Although begun in the late thirteenth century, the building's construction had long been delayed because no architect possessed the necessary knowledge to span such an enormous (140-foot wide) octagonal space (Fig. 9.2B).

BRUNELLESCHI'S DOME

It is unclear whether Filippo Brunelleschi, the architect who solved the problem, had ventured to Rome to study the Pantheon and other ancient monuments, where he might have observed the construction of domes. Yet it appears that he was aware of the basic principles of dome construction. Starting at a level some 180 feet above ground, he boldly sent eight massive ribs soaring skyward from the angles of the supporting octagon to a point almost 100 feet higher, where they converged at the base of a lantern, that is, a small turretlike tower. Concealing them from external view, he added two minor radial ribs between each pair of major ribs, twenty-four in all, to make the inner shell. After reinforcing these with wooden beams and iron clasps at key points, he had the necessary support for the masonry of his inner and outer shells. The structure is, in effect, an eight-sided Gothic vault. By concealing the functional elements and shaping a smooth external silhouette, Brunelleschi abandoned a central tenet of Gothic functionalism—that the structural elements of a building must be visibly logical. Brunelleschi's dome became the prototype for all massive domes and a bridge to a new Renaissance architecture.

Opposite the facade of the cathedral is the older Romanesque baptistry (Fig. 9.1, lower right), which was adorned with Ghiberti's gilded bronze doors. The handsome north doors were already in place, and the sculptor was well on his way to completing the east doors (see pp. 252–254), which Michelangelo was later to hail as worthy of being the "Gates of Paradise." Helping him cast these doors in his workshop at various times were the architect Michelozzo, the sculptor Donatello, and the painters Paolo Uccello and Benozzo Gozzoli. At about the same time, Donatello was working on a series of statues of prophets to be placed in niches on the exterior of both the cathedral and the campanile, known as "Giotto's Tower" (see pp. 223–224).

In Pope Eugene's company at the dedication of the cathedral were some of the leading Florentine humanists, including the artist-scholar Leone Battista Alberti, who had just completed his book *On Painting* and was working on his influential study *On Architecture.* On hand to provide music for the occasion was the papal choir, whose ranks included the foremost musician of his generation, Guillaume Dufay, who composed the commemorative motet for the occasion. Antonio Squarcialupi, an organist at the cathedral and a private master of music in the Medici household, is thought to have composed the solemn High Mass.

An eyewitness account of the procession noted the perfume of the flowers and incense and the bright-robed company of viol players and trumpeters, "each carrying his instrument in hand and arrayed in gorgeous cloth of gold garments." In appropriately flowery language, the observer recorded that "the whole space of the temple was filled with such choruses of harmony, and such a concert of diverse instruments, that it seemed (not without reason) as though the symphonies and songs of the angels and of divine paradise had been sent forth from Heaven to whisper in our ears an unbelievable celestial sweetness."

THE DOME AND THE DEDICATION MOTET

The eyewitness was referring in part to Guillaume Dufay's dedicatory motet, *Nuper rosarum flores* (Flowers of Roses). In this choral work the cathedral is praised as "this mighty temple" and its dome as a "magnificent artifice" and a "marvel of art."

Brunelleschi and Dufay were the most important representatives of their crafts in Florence during the first half of the fifteenth century. Brunelleschi's first biographer, Manetti, states that he had studied Vitruvius (see p. 104) and that he thought in terms of the ancient musical proportions. Both the dome and the motet were constructed using late medieval methods. The dome included Gothic elements, and the music used **isorhythmic** symmetries incorporating strict rhythmic progressions and formal proportions. Isorhythmic motets consist of a series of sections that are unified by the use of identical rhythmic relationships but not necessarily the same melodic patterns. Such music was not intended only to please the ear or stir the emotions; rather, in the manner of ancient music theory (see pp. 49–50), it aimed to mirror the hidden harmonies of the universe. In Dufay's conception, however, the universe was populated with shapely melodies, warm harmonic colors, and a rich variety of rhythmic forms. Dufay clothed the austere skeletal structure of the composition with smooth melodic lines and a fluency of sound that made it a joy to the ear as well as to the mind.

THE PAZZI CHAPEL

The analogy that Renaissance theorists drew between audible and visual proportions was an undercurrent in all their designs. It bore witness to their profound belief in the harmonic–mathematical basis of creation. Music also had a strong attraction for Renaissance architects, because it had always been considered a mathematical science and had been studied as such in antiquity and in the medieval universities. Mathematical relationships are easy to see in Brunelleschi's Pazzi Chapel, where he had complete control of the whole plan (Fig. 9.3A). The central axis, as seen in the ground plan (Fig. 9.3B), is based on three circles signifying the domed spaces above, and the relationship of the two smaller circles to the larger one is in the ratio of 2:1. Similarly, the two smaller squares above have an octaval relationship (based on the number eight) to the large square surrounding the central dome.

The fruits of Brunelleschi's studies of ancient Roman buildings are even more in evidence in the facade, where the break with the Gothic tradition is complete. The harmonious spacing of the columns of the porch, the treatment of the walls as flat surfaces, and the balance of horizontal and vertical elements make his design the prototype of the Renaissance architectural style. The entablatures above the columns and below the roof give further evidence of classical influence. The curved pattern above comes directly from ancient Roman sarcophagi, whereas the elegant carving

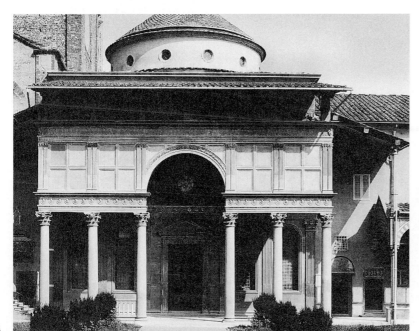

A

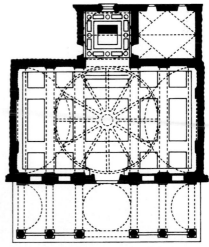

B

9.3 (A) Filippo Brunelleschi. Facade, Pazzi Chapel, Cloister of the Church of Santa Croce, Florence, Italy, c. 1429–1433. (B) Plan of Pazzi Chapel.

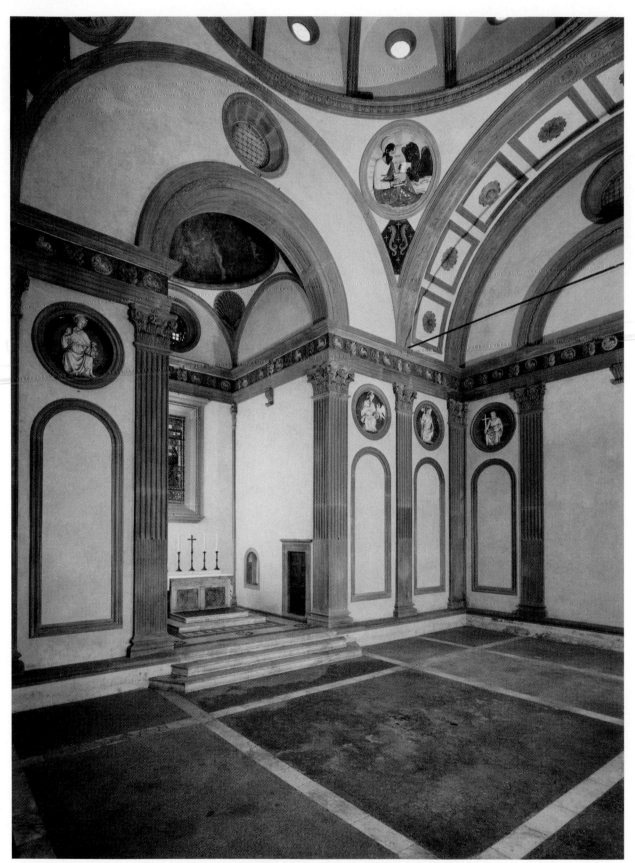

9.4   Filippo Brunelleschi. Interior, Pazzi Chapel, Cloister of the Church of Santa Croce, Florence, Italy, c. 1440. Length 59′9″, width 35′8″.

of the Corinthian capitals, the Composite pilasters, and other design details reveal Brunelleschi's early training as a silversmith and his interest in authentic Roman originals.

The interior continues the classical theme (Fig. 9.4). Lacking Gothic mystery, height, and shadowy indefiniteness, the pilastered walls give the viewer a cool, crisp, lucid impression. Frames of dark-colored stone divide the surfaces into clear geometric forms. Barrel vaults (see Fig. 4.22C) cover the rectangular room, and a low dome on pendentives (see Fig. 5.11) rises in the center at the point of intersection. The simplicity of its design made the Pazzi Chapel a highly influential prototype throughout the Renaissance. The unity of its centralized organization under a unifying dome became the point of departure for the later church plans of Alberti, Bramante, and Michelangelo.

THE MEDICI–RICCARDI PALACE

When Cosimo de' Medici decided to build a new house, he is said to have rejected a grand plan submitted by Brunelleschi with the shrewd observation that envy is a plant that should not be watered. For the Medici–Riccardi Palace (Fig. 9.5), he chose instead a less pretentious design submitted by Brunelleschi's disciple Michelozzo. (The palace has a dual name because it was bought from the Medicis by the Riccardi family in the seventeenth century.)

Like many buildings of its type, the palace was a continuation, rather than a revival, of the multi-storied ancient Roman city apartment house. The heavily **rusticated** masonry of the first story (many of the rough-cut stones protrude more than a foot) has the threatening aspect of a medieval fortress. But as the eye moves upward, the second and third floors present an increasingly elegant appearance. The accent on horizontal lines, seen in the molding strips that separate the three stories and in the boldly projecting cornice at the roof level, is neither Roman nor medieval. A classical motif can be seen in the semicircular arches that frame the windows (the pediments over those on the lower story are a somewhat later addition). Details such as the colonnettes of the windows on the second and third floors, as well as the egg-and-dart pattern and the dentil range that appear in the cornice frieze just under the roof, are derived from the classical patterns adapted by Renaissance architects and builders.

Cosimo's worries about public display stopped with the palace's exterior; inside the doors everything was on a princely scale. Frescoes by Benozzo Gozzoli and an altarpiece by Filippo Lippi decorated its second-floor chapel. Easel paintings by Uccello and Botticelli hung on salon walls. Antique and contemporary bronze and marble statues stood in the courtyard and gardens. Collections of ancient and medieval carved gems and coins filled cabinets. Precious metal vessels and figurines adorned tables. Priceless manuscripts, including the works of Dante, Petrarch, and Boccaccio, could be found in the library. In effect, the Medici–Riccardi Palace was one of the first and richest museums in Europe.

Cosimo's palace was also the meeting place of the Neoplatonic Academy, where authors, philosophers, and artists discussed new ideas and gave expression to them in their works. Briefly, Neoplatonism was an interpretation of Plato's notion of the eternal forms (see p. 56). It held that the eternal absolutes of truth, goodness, and beauty existed only in the divine mind. Such absolutes are not wholly within human grasp. Nevertheless, through learning, observation, and creativity, mortals could catch occasional hints of them. Truth was pursued through scientific knowledge. Goodness might be glimpsed in the performance of good deeds and through the experience of physical and, more important, spiritual love. Beauty was sought in nature and the experience of great works of art.

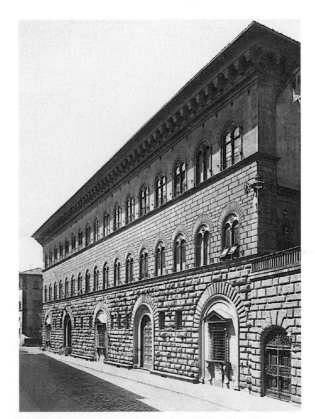

9.5 Michelozzo. Facade, Medici–Riccardi Palace, Florence, Italy, 1444–1459. Length 225′, height 80′.

AN ART CONTEST: GHIBERTI VERSUS BRUNELLESCHI

In the year 1401, the Wool Merchant's Guild held a competition to determine who should be awarded the contract for the new north doors of the baptistry. As in the earlier south doors by Andrea Pisano, the material was to be bronze, and the individual panels were to be enclosed in the **quatrefoil,** or four-lobed, pattern. For the purpose of the contest, the subject was to be the Sacrifice of Isaac. Some half-dozen sculptors were invited to submit models; among them were Brunelleschi and Lorenzo Ghiberti.

Both men were in their early twenties and were skilled workers in metal and members in good standing of the Goldsmiths' Guild. Despite these shared characteristics, their work reveals many significant differences of viewpoint and technique (Figs. 9.6 and 9.7). Brunelleschi's composition shows the influence of Gothic verticality in the way the design is built in three rising planes. Ghiberti's composition is almost horizontal, and his two scenes are divided diagonally by a stylized mountain in the manner of Giotto (see Fig. 8.12). Brunelleschi's panel is crowded, and his figures spin out toward the sides of the frame. By contrast, Ghiberti's is uncluttered, and all his figures and details converge toward a center of interest in the up-

per right, formed by the heads of the principal figures. Brunelleschi accents dramatic tension, with Abraham seizing the screaming Isaac by the neck and the angel staying his hand at the last moment. Ghiberti sacrifices intensity for poise and decorative elegance. Brunelleschi shapes Isaac's body as a series of angular and awkward bends. Ghiberti models it with the smooth lines and grace of a late Greek or Hellenistic statue. In fact, Ghiberti's *Commentaries,* arguably the first autobiography by an artist in Western culture, mention the discovery near Florence of the torso of an ancient classical statue, on which he modeled his Isaac. Finally, Brunelleschi cast his relief in separate sections, mounting these on the bronze background plate. Ghiberti, with greater technical command, cast his in a single mold. The decision in Ghiberti's favor showed the way the aesthetic winds were blowing at the dawn of the fifteenth century. Ghiberti set to work on the twenty panels of the north doors, which were to occupy the major part of his time for the next 24 years.

GHIBERTI'S EAST DOORS

Ghiberti's north doors were no sooner in place than he was commissioned, this time without competition, to execute another set. The famous east doors (Fig. 9.8), on which he worked from 1425

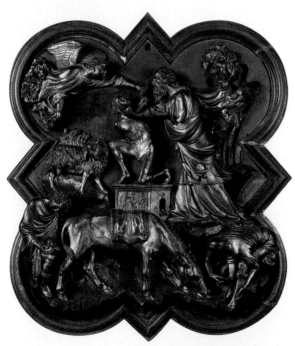

9.6   Filippo Brunelleschi. *Sacrifice of Isaac,* 1401–1402. Gilded bronze, 1′9″ × 1′5″. Museo Nazionale del Bargello, Florence, Italy.

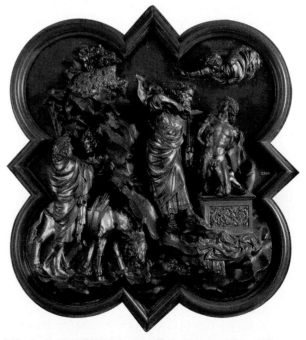

9.7   Lorenzo Ghiberti. *Sacrifice of Isaac,* 1401–1402. Gilded bronze, 1′9″ × 1′5″. Museo Nazionale del Bargello, Florence, Italy.

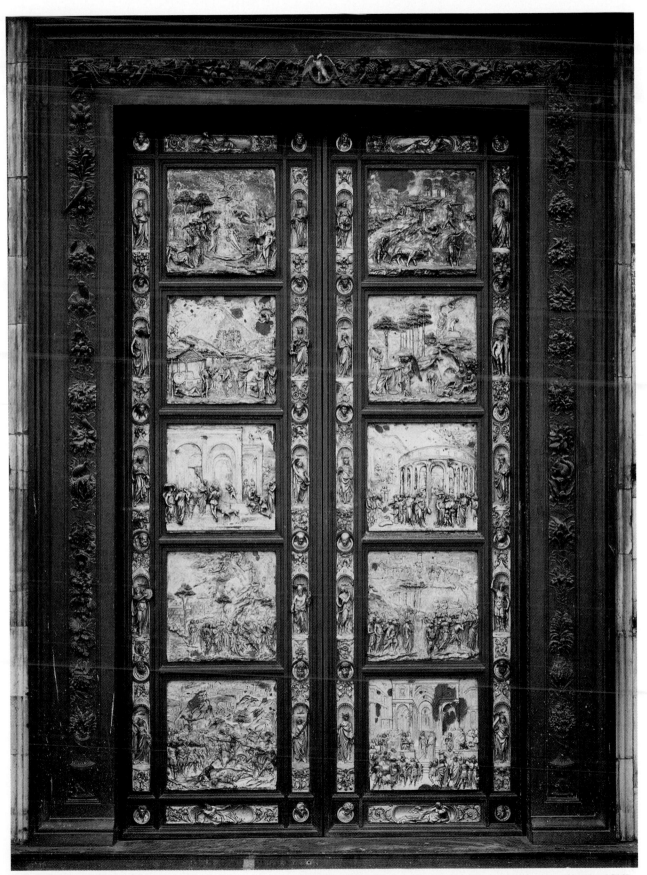

9.8 Lorenzo Ghiberti. *Gates of Paradise,* east doors of Baptistry, Florence, Italy, 1425–1452. Gilded bronze, height 18′6″.

to 1452, tell their own tale. The Gothic quatrefoil frames of the competition panels had become a thing of the past. In addition, whereas his north doors were conceived of in terms of their architectural function, the east doors served as a convenient framework for decoration. They disregard techniques appropriate to the three-dimensional medium of relief sculpture and are more like pictures painted in gilded bronze.

Ghiberti attempted daring perspectives far in advance of the painting of the period. Some figures, such as those in the center panel of the left door, are in such high relief as to be almost completely in the round. In the Adam and Eve panel at the top of the left door (Fig. 9.9), he uses three receding planes. The high relief in the lower foreground tells the story of the creation of Adam (lower left) and Eve (center) and the expulsion from the Garden of Eden (right). The immediate past is seen in the half-relief of the middle ground showing the Garden of Eden. In the low relief of the background, God and his accompanying cloud of angels seem to be dissolving into the thin air of the remote past.

On either side of the pictorial panels Ghiberti included a series of full-length figurines alternating with heads that recall Roman portrait busts (see Fig. 4.15). Hebrew prophets on the outer sides are set opposite pagan sibyls, all of whom were supposed to have foretold the coming of Christ. The figure beside the second panel from the top on the right door is that of the biblical strongman

Samson, but his stance and musculature are those of a Hellenistic Hercules. Ghiberti mentions in his *Commentaries* how he sought to imitate nature in the manner of the ancient Greeks when molding the plant and animal forms of these door frames.

The care and delicate craftsmanship Ghiberti lavished on these and other details make the east doors a high point in the metalworker's art. The influence of Ghiberti's Goldsmiths' Guild was felt in many aspects of Florentine art, not only in such door moldings but also in pulpits, wall panels, window brackets, columns, pilasters, and cornices, all of which were executed with a wealth of fine detail.

DONATELLO

Donatello's personality and career contrast strongly with Ghiberti's. A man of fiery temperament and bold imagination, Donatello scorned the fussy details that allied Ghiberti's work with that of a jeweler. Whereas Ghiberti studied local examples of antique sculpture and read Vitruvius's books, Donatello journeyed to Rome to study the finest surviving classical statuary.

Ghiberti remained a specialist in bronze, whereas Donatello was at home with all materials: marble, wood, painted terra-cotta, and gilded bronze. He was equally comfortable in all mediums—relief and in the round, small scale and heroic size, architectural embellishment and independent figure—and in all subjects—sacred and secular, historical scenes and portraiture. Whereas Ghiberti had a single personal style, Donatello had many. His tremendous power of epic expression, enormous energies, sweeping passion, and impetuosity make him the representative sculptor of his period and the immediate artistic ancestor of Michelangelo.

The Prophet (Fig. 9.10), also known as *Lo Zuccone,* which means "pumpkin head" or "bald pate," is one of a series of marble statues that Donatello was commissioned to sculpt for the Florence Cathedral in 1424. Designed for a third-story niche of the campanile, it was intended to be seen about 55 feet above ground level. Consequently, the deep-cut drapery and lines of the face took into account the distance from the viewer as well as the angle of vision and the lighting. Donatello sought to produce a powerfully expressive figure rather than a handsome one. He achieved this through the boniness of the huge frame, the powerful musculature of the arms, the convulsive gesture of the right wrist, the tension of the muscles of the neck, and the intensity of the face.

The statue represents an Old Testament prophet (either Habakkuk or Jeremiah). The figure

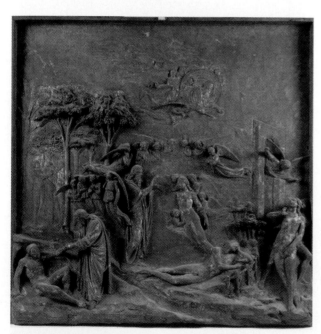

9.9   Lorenzo Ghiberti. *The Creation of Adam and Eve,* detail of east doors, Baptistry, Florence, Italy, c. 1435. Gilded bronze, 2'7¼" square.

is full of inner fire and fear of the Lord; it portrays a seer who was capable of fasting in the desert, dwelling alone on a mountaintop, or passionately preaching to an unheeding multitude from his niche. The classical influence is seen in the heavy folds of drapery, an adaptation of the toga, and in the rugged features and baldness, which recall realistic Roman portraiture. With *Lo Zuccone,* Donatello created a unique figure of strong individuality, not one of the traditional iconographic types.

In his bronze *David* (Fig. 9.11), Donatello worked in a more lyrical vein. As a figure meant to be seen from all angles, *David* departs from the Gothic

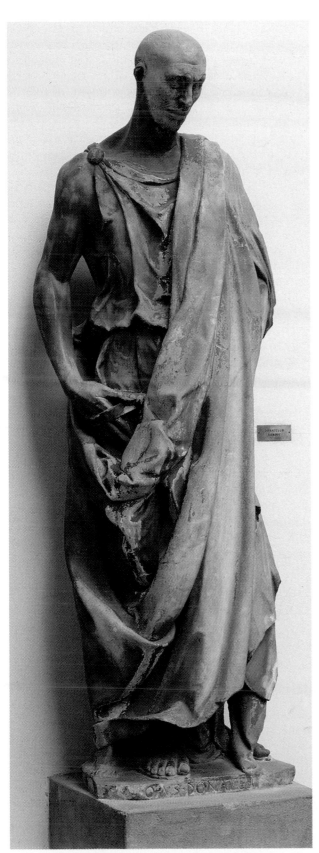

9.10 Donatello. *The Prophet (Lo Zuccone),* from campanile, Florence Cathedral, 1423–1425. Marble, height 6′5″. Original in Museo dell'Opera del Duomo, Florence, Italy.

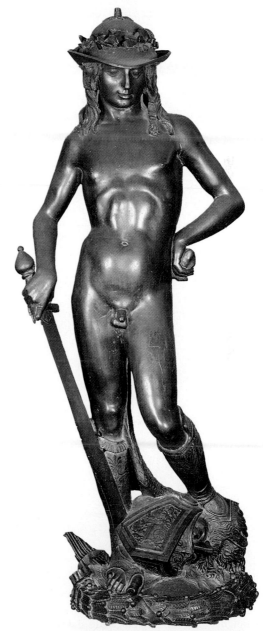

9.11 Donatello. *David,* c. 1430–1432. Bronze, height 5′2¼″. Museo Nazionale del Bargello, Florence, Italy.

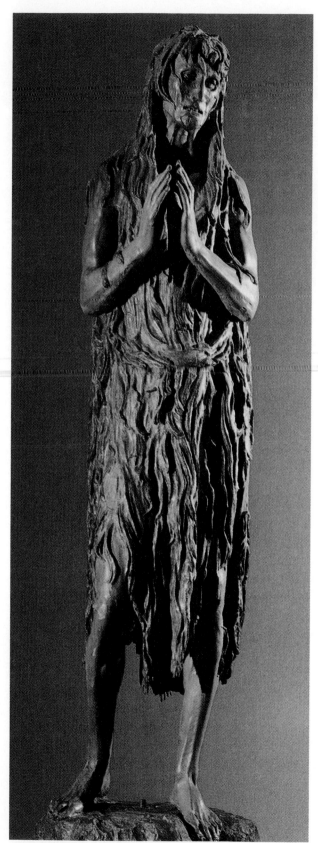

9.12   Donatello. *Repentant Magdalene,* 1454–1455. Wood, height 6′2″. Museo dell'Opera del Duomo, Florence, Italy.

tradition of sculpture in niches and as architectural embellishment. *David* was the first life-size bronze nude in the round since antiquity, and as such, it marks the revival of classical nude statuary.

David stands alone in the confident attitude of the victor over the vanquished, a sword in his right hand, a stone in his left. His weight rests on his right foot, whereas the left foot is on the severed head of the conquered Goliath. The curving posture is familiar from Greco-Roman antiquity (see Fig. 2.21 [Doryphorus]). The serenity of the classical profile, together with the languid stance and modeling of the youthful body, also shows the sensual awareness of Hellenistic culture. A local touch is provided by the Tuscan shepherd's hat, which throws the smooth, delicate-featured face into strong shadow and serves to accentuate the adolescent body. From its first days in the courtyard of the Medici Palace, Donatello's *David* raised eyebrows and provoked questions. In commissioning the statue, did the Medici family seek to display a symbol of their power, taking into their private domain a Biblical figure associated with the city of Florence? Is *David,* the savior of his people, an allusion to the youthful promise of Cosimo's grandson, Lorenzo? More intimately, is the daringly nude *David* an allusion to Donatello's sexual preference?

At the opposite end of Donatello's emotional range—and far less ambiguous—is the wraithlike *Repentant Magdalene* (Fig. 9.12). The emaciated, cadaverous figure originally stood in the Florence Baptistry as a reminder of the original sin that is washed away by baptism and of the universal presence of death among the living.

HUMAN ANATOMY INVESTIGATED: POLLAIUOLO AND VERROCCHIO

Quite another attitude is revealed in the work of the next generation, especially Antonio Pollaiuolo and Andrea del Verrocchio. The work of Pollaiuolo is dominated by scientific curiosity, especially in regard to human anatomy. He is known to have dissected corpses in order to study musculature and bone structure. Trained in his father's goldsmith shop, he specialized in athletic figures such as the cast-bronze *Hercules and Antaeus* (Fig. 9.13), of which he made both painted and sculptural versions.

Legends about ancient strongmen like Hercules provided excellent subjects, permitting the artist to bring out the musculature of the male figure in action. In this instance, Hercules overcomes his enemy, the giant Antaeus, by raising him off the Earth, the source of his strength. Antaeus struggles desperately to release the stranglehold Hercules has on him. The muscles in Hercules's legs noticeably bear the weight of both bodies. Pollaiuolo also painted a series of pictures depicting the Labors of Hercules. Like his works in bronze, they are studies of muscular tension, full of athletic energy and unrelieved by gracefulness.

Verrocchio, a contemporary of Pollaiuolo, was frequently given commissions from the Medici family. For this powerful family he designed everything from tournament trophies and parade gear to portraits and tombs. Verrocchio paid homage to the city of Florence with his bronze statue of David (Fig. 9.14). Verrocchio's *David* contrasts with that of Donatello (Fig. 9.11) in a number of ways. The clothed Verrocchio version is a self-assured adolescent athlete, proud of his victory over the giant, whose severed head lies at his feet. The youth's developing musculature is accurately

observed to the very veins in his arms and hands. In Verrocchio's interpretation, David looks with satisfaction on the gratitude of his audience. His self-assurance is apparent in his open, outgoing stance. Donatello's *David* is more meditative and psychologically unavailable, with his eyes half-hidden under his hat. One portrayal emphasizes physical action; the other, contemplation.

Like Pollaiuolo, Verrocchio was also a painter at a time when sculpture led the field in experiments with perspective, anatomy, and light and shadow. Whereas Ghiberti and Donatello had been more classically oriented, Pollaiuolo and Verrocchio were primarily scientifically minded. Leonardo da Vinci trained in Verrocchio's workshop and carried on the searching scientific curiosity of his master, whereas it remained for Michelangelo, stimulated by Donatello's art, to carry the humanistic ideal into the next century.

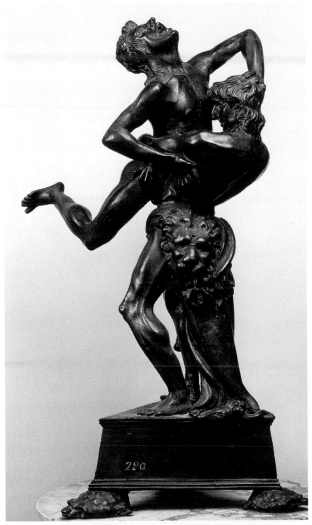

9.13 Antonio Pollaiuolo. *Hercules and Antaeus,* c. 1475. Bronze, height approx. 1′6″. Museo Nazionale del Bargello, Florence, Italy.

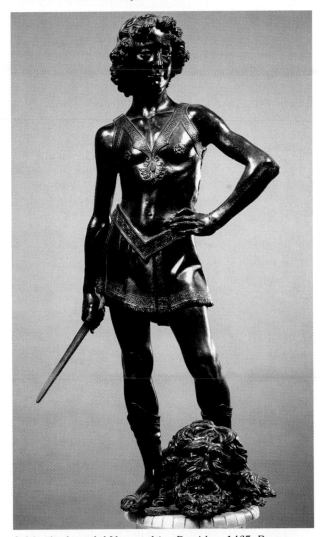

9.14 Andrea del Verrocchio. *David,* c. 1465. Bronze, height approx. 4′1″. Museo Nazionale del Bargello, Florence, Italy.

PAINTING

THE PREMATURE LOSS OF THE GENIUS OF MASACCIO

With Brunelleschi and Donatello, the third member of the trio of early fifteenth-century innovators was Masaccio. The importance of his series of frescoes in the Brancacci Chapel of the Church of Santa Maria del Carmine, where he worked with his older and more conservative colleague Masolino da Panicole, can hardly be overestimated. In the *Expulsion from the Garden* (Fig. 9.15), he chose one of the few subjects in which the nude human body could be portrayed in churches.

By defining the light as coming diagonally from the right and having Adam and Eve approach it, Masaccio invented a way to show them casting natural shadows. In addition, he surrounded his figures with soft, hazy light, thereby situating them in the space. Moreover, he modeled them in light and shadow as a sculptor would, so that they appear as if seen in the round with all the weight and volume of living forms. Masaccio thus achieved one of the most important innovations in painting: **atmospheric perspective.**

Masaccio seems well aware of the drama inherent in the expulsion from Paradise. The full force of this first moral crisis in human history is expressed by the body alone, with almost no reliance on surrounding details. Eve, aware of her nakedness and sensing her future, cries aloud, while Adam, ashamed to face the light, expresses his remorse by covering his face. Even the avenging angel who drives them out of the garden reflects the tragedy of the fall from grace with an expression of human concern and compassion so unlike the passive angels and fiendish devils of medieval sculpture (see Fig. 6.1). The curved line of Adam's right leg may have been drawn to indicate the hurried motion of the expulsion, but the proportions of his arms and the drawing of Eve's lower hand are anatomically incorrect. Such flaws, however, are minor when one considers the impact of Masaccio's treatment of light, which puts figures in a new, vital relationship to their spatial environment.

The Tribute Money (Fig. 9.16), another of the Brancacci Chapel frescoes, further illustrates the principle of atmospheric perspective. The figures are well modeled in light and shade, and each occupies its appointed space in the front and middle planes with ease and assurance. Approached by the tax collector, Peter and his fellow apostles question the propriety of Christian believers paying tribute to the Roman authorities, whereupon

Jesus responds, "Render therefore unto Caesar the things that are Caesar's; and unto God the things that are God's" (Matt. 22:21). Jesus then tells Peter that the first fish he catches will have a coin in its mouth. The simultaneous mode of presentation is used, with St. Peter appearing first in the center, then at the left fishing, and finally at the right paying the debt.

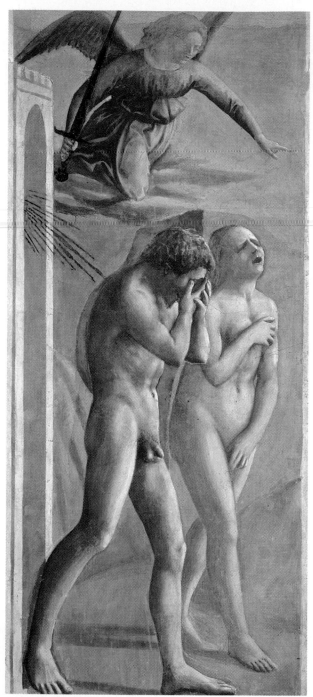

9.15 Masaccio. *Expulsion from the Garden,* c. 1425. Fresco, 7′ × 2′11″. Brancacci Chapel, Santa Maria del Carmine, Florence, Italy.

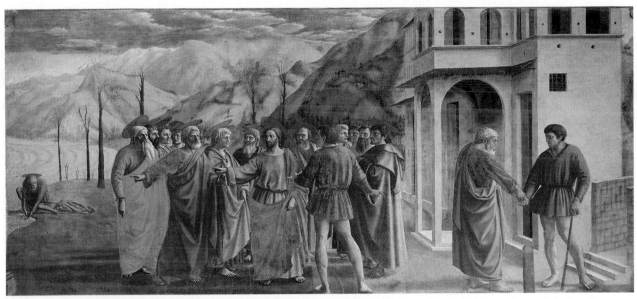

9.16   Masaccio. *The Tribute Money,* c. 1427. Fresco, 8′1″ × 19′7″. Brancacci Chapel, Santa Maria del Carmine, Florence, Italy.

Masaccio's colors, the bulky forms, and the placement of a figure in the immediate foreground remind one of Giotto's pioneering techniques (see Fig. 8.12). Yet Masaccio created greater psychological depth and differentiation in his figures. Moreover, he subjected his picture to a rigorous formulation of perspective. All the **orthogonals**— that is, lines leading to the vanishing point—end not at a point on the horizon but at the head of Christ (the orthogonals and the vanishing point can be revealed by placing a ruler along the angles

of the projecting roof on the building at the right in Fig. 9.16). Masaccio's death at the age of 27 cut short the promise of his innovative career.

LINGERING GOTHIC: FRA ANGELICO

Fra Angelico was in many respects a late Gothic artist who never painted anything but religious subjects. But although he dwelt lovingly on the older forms, he often treated them within the new frame of reference. His *Annunciation* (Fig. 9.17), painted for

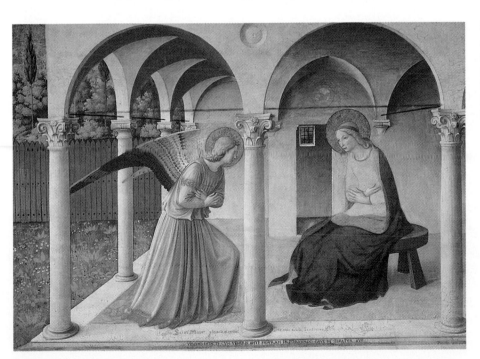

9.17   Fra Angelico. *Annunciation,* c. 1445–1450. Fresco, approx. 7′6″ × 9′9″. From former Monastery of San Marco, Florence. Museo di San Marco, Florence, Italy.

the upper corridor of the monastery of San Marco in Florence, is a blend of old and new elements.

Fra Angelico seemed to have found angels as real and interesting as human beings. Although he always painted with the deepest religious sentiment, the figures in the *Annunciation* appear within the new conception of space. The perspective and the fifteenth-century architectural details are so exact that the event could well be taking place in a corner of the San Marco cloister that Michelozzo recently had rebuilt. Moreover, the native Tuscan flowers seen in the garden are depicted accurately enough to satisfy a botanical expert. The lighting, however, is far from the natural illumination of Masaccio. Fra Angelico's rendering of the Virgin's form retains the late Gothic fascination with line. The Archangel Gabriel's mul-

ticolored wings recall those of the angels who surround the throne of Cimabue's *Madonna* (see Fig. 8.15). Yet the archangel's robes are modeled in light and shade, suggesting that the friar looked to Roman sculpture or the illusionistic techniques being explored in Florence.

AT HOME IN THE WORLD: BENOZZO GOZZOLI AND FILIPPO LIPPI

Unlike Fra Angelico, his principal pupil, Benozzo Gozzoli, was focused firmly on this world. With Cosimo's son Piero as his patron, Benozzo painted the *Journey of the Magi*, a favorite subject for pomp and pageantry. Here his talents were more than equal to their task: a fresco cycle on three walls of the chapel in the Medici Palace.

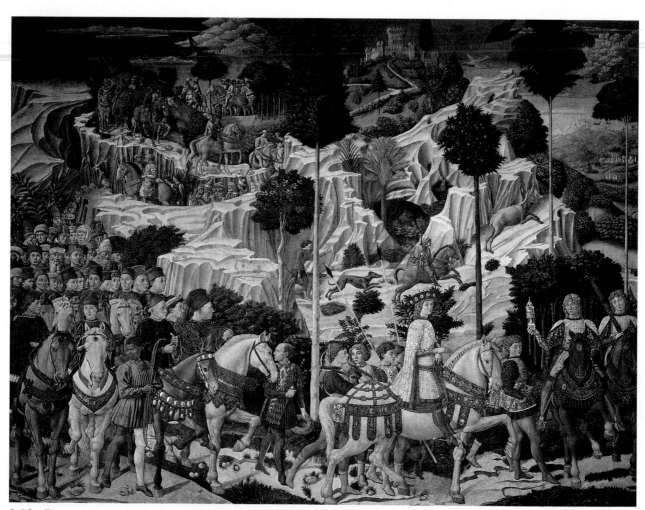

9.18   Benozzo Gozzoli. *Journey of the Magi,* detail, c. 1459–1463. Fresco, length 12′4¼″. Chapel, Medici–Riccardi Palace, Florence, Italy.

In the detail (Fig. 9.18), a richly costumed young Wise Man sits astride a splendid horse. At the head of the retinue, Benozzo portrays three generations of the Medici family. Patrons sometimes were painted in attendance at a scene, yet they were more clearly differentiated from the religious story. Here the Medici and the Magi mingle as equals.

At the far right, Piero de' Medici (in profile) appears at the head of the procession. Displayed on the lower part of the harness of his white horse is the motto *Semper* (Forever), a part of the Medici coat of arms, each letter appearing in the center of one of the jeweled rings that make a continuous chain. Beside him is the elderly Cosimo (also in profile) seated on a gray mule, with a black groom at his side. The youthful Giuliano and his older brother, the future Lorenzo Il Magnifico (the Magnificent), are on horseback at the extreme left. Bringing up the rear are various intimates and retainers of the Medici court, with the artist himself in the second row back, identified by a cap band that reads *Opus Benotii* (Work of Benozzo). Other faces may represent the philosopher Pico della Mirandola, the poet Poliziano, and Fra Angelico.

The procession winds through mountains reminiscent of Giotto's choppy peaks, yet tall umbrella pines and needle cypresses recall the Tuscan landscape. The convoy terminates at the fourth wall of the chapel, where Fra Filippo Lippi's altarpiece, the *Adoration* (Fig. 9.19), is situated. The linear emphasis of Lippi's drawing,

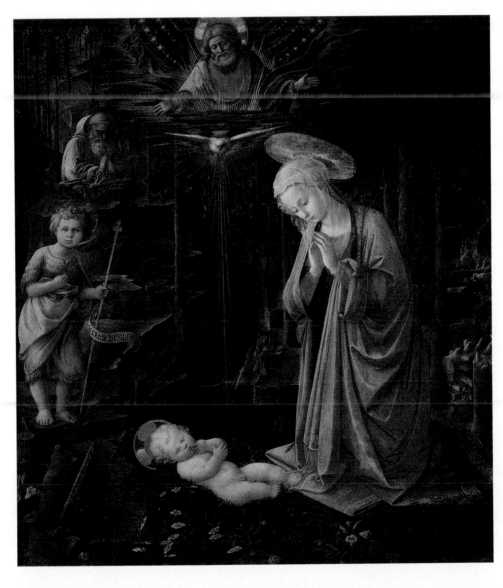

9.19 Filippo Lippi. *Adoration,* c. 1459. Tempera on wood, 4'2" × 3'10". Staatliche Museen zu Berlin, Berlin, Germany.

softened by pastel hues, had a decisive influence on the art of his famous pupil, Botticelli. In his *Adoration,* the pictorial space is divided symmetrically by the Trinity, with God the Father imparting a blessing on his Son through the descending rays of the Holy Spirit. The rays find an earthly echo in the vertical lines of the tree trunks that rise by steps in the background, thus creating niches for the figures of the Madonna on the right and the youthful St. John. Farther up the mountain, St. Bernard of Clairvaux is shown bowing in prayer. His Nativity sermons provide the keys that help unlock the picture's complex iconography.

THE PURSUIT OF LINEAR PERSPECTIVE: PAOLO UCCELLO AND PIERO DELLA FRANCESCA

To decorate one of the rooms of the Medici Palace, Cosimo called on Paolo Uccello. As a student of spatial science, Uccello tried to solve the problem of **linear** perspective, that is, the formula for arranging lines on a two-dimensional surface so that they converge at a vanishing point on the horizon, thereby promoting the illusion of recession in depth. One of his three scenes in his *Battle of San Romano* (Fig. 9.20), a skirmish in 1432 in which the Florentines put the Sienese army to flight, shows his pioneering effort in applying Euclidean geometry to pictorial mechanics.

Uccello laid the lances and banners out on the ground as if on a chessboard. He was evidently so absorbed with his lines that his bloodless battle is staged more in the manner of a dress parade than a clashing conflict. Also, he did not delve into the possibilities of modeling with light and shade, so his merry-go-round–like horses, despite the variety of their postures, remain as flat as cardboard cutouts. For all his scientific curiosity and intellectual effort, the solution to the linear problem eluded him. In this respect, he was always a pupil and never a master.

Another artist interested in perspective, Piero della Francesca, was also in Florence during the 1440s. As an assistant to Domenico Veneziano (whose last name indicates that his family was from Venice), he absorbed lessons in perspective as well as in the richness of color that characterized Venetian painting. By studying the work of Masaccio, he learned about atmospheric perspective and how to model figures in light and

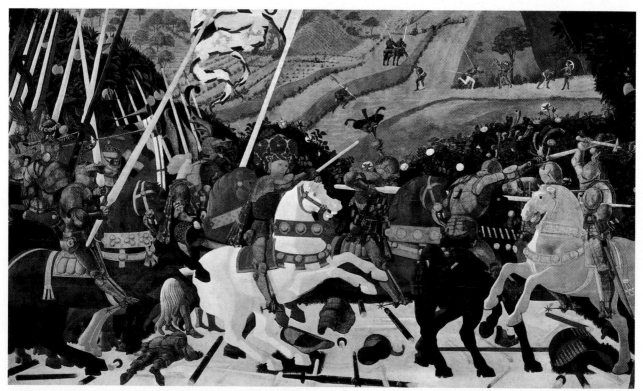

9.20 Paolo Uccello. *Battle of San Romano,* c. 1455. Tempera on wood, 6′ × 10′5″. National Gallery, London, England.

shade. Through his association with Ghiberti, Brunelleschi, Alberti, and Paolo Uccello, he eventually became a master of linear perspective and later wrote an essay on the subject.

Piero's *Resurrection* (Fig. 9.21), painted for the chapel of the town hall of his native Umbrian town of Borgo San Sepolcro, is one of his most sophisticated works. His clarity of design is seen in the compact pyramidal composition that builds up from the sarcophagus and the sleeping soldiers (the second from the left is generally thought to be a self-portrait) to the figure of Christ, which was modeled like a classical statue, holding a triumphant banner.

Color contrasts, as well as light and shade, play important roles in both the pictorial mechanics and the symbolism of this Resurrection. The somber tones of the soldiers' costumes are offset by the radiant pink of Christ's robe. Furthermore, the dark-clad soldiers, paralleled by the shadowy earth, set up an alternating rhythm with the flowing figure of Jesus against the Easter dawn. The barren earth on the left yields to the springtime rebirth of the fields on the right. The brightening sky above and the radiant spirit of Christ, with his piercing, almost hypnotic gaze, are reflected on the faces of the soldiers below.

CLASSICISM AND COLOR: BOTTICELLI

In creating a signature style of his own, Sandro Botticelli became the representative artist of humanistic thought at the end of the fifteenth century. Botticelli enjoyed the patronage of the Medici

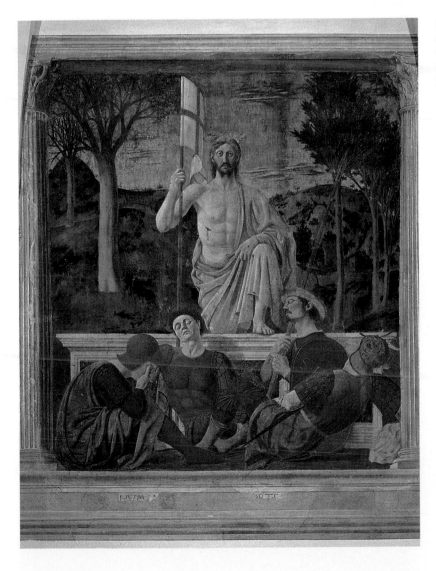

9.21 Piero della Francesca. *Resurrection,* c. 1463. Fresco, 7′5″ × 6′6½″. Pinacoteca, Palazzo Communale, Borgo San Sepolcro, Italy.

family, and in his *Adoration of the Magi* (Fig. 9.22), he portrays the clan engaged with religious figures, as had his predecessor, Benozzo Gozzoli (Fig. 9.18). Among the admirably arranged figures one finds the elderly Cosimo kneeling at the feet of the Christ child. Also kneeling are his two sons, Piero and Giovanni. To their right, standing against the ruined wall, is the profiled figure of Giuliano, the handsome grandson of Cosimo and the younger brother of Lorenzo the Magnificent, who is to be found in the extreme left foreground. His opposite number at the right, looking intently at the viewer, not at the Holy Family, has been identified by some as Botticelli himself.

Although the colors are bright—ranging from the cool sky blue of the Virgin's robe and the dark green and gold embroidery of Cosimo's costume to the ermine-lined crimson cloak of the kneeling Piero and the bright orange of Botticelli's mantle—they create a harmonious pattern. The Roman ruins in the background and the coffered ceiling of the shed where the Holy Family is sheltered indicate not only Botticelli's attention to the classical heritage but also his interest in symbolizing the end of the Roman Empire, foreshadowed by the birth of Christ.

Botticelli was not a popular painter of pageants like Benozzo Gozzoli and his contemporary Ghirlandaio, but he was a member of the sophisticated group of humanists who gathered around the Medici. In this circle, which included the poet Angelo Poliziano, the philosophers Marsilio Ficino and Pico della Mirandola, as well as Lorenzo the Magnificent and his cousin Pierfrancesco di Lorenzo de' Medici, classical myths were constantly discussed and interpreted. The dialogues of Plato, the collected works of the Roman philosopher Plotinus (known as the *Enneads*), and Greek musical theory were all thoroughly explored. As in Botticelli's *Adoration,* references to ancient works were frequent.

La Primavera. Botticelli's *La Primavera,* or *Allegory of Spring* (Fig. 9.23), is one of the most eloquent, intricate, and ultimately mysterious expressions of Renaissance thought. It was probably painted for the wedding of a young cousin of Lorenzo de' Medici, who numbered among his tutors Poliziano and Ficino. The eight figures, with Venus in the center, form an octaval relationship, that is, one consisting of eight forms. Together they run a gamut of mythological references and metaphors, which are more or less clear individually, even if the ultimate collective meaning of the work is obscure. The narrative reads from right to left. The gentle, blue-toned south wind, Zephyr, pursues the shy nymph of springtime, Chloris. As he impregnates her, flowers spring from her lips, and she is transformed into Flora in an appropriately flowery robe. This figure also refers to Florence, an allusion that was not lost on the citizens of the city of flowers.

9.22 Sandro Botticelli. *Adoration of the Magi,* c. 1475. Tempera on wood, 3'7½" × 4'4¾". Galleria degli Uffizi, Florence, Italy.

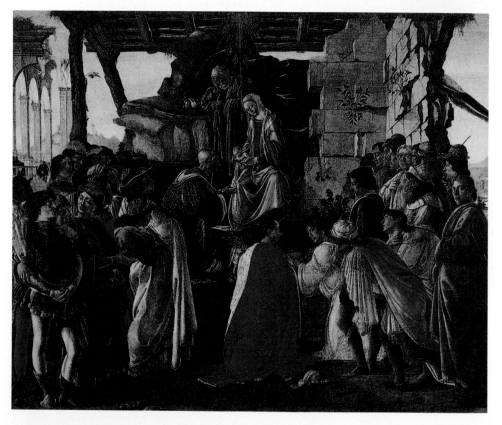

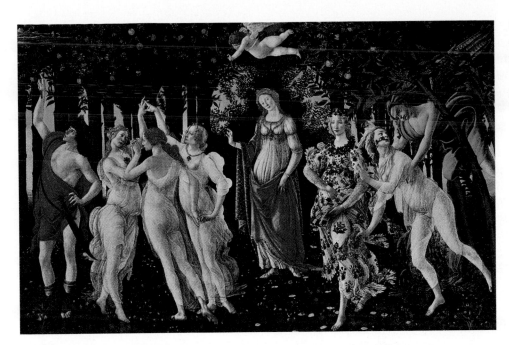

9.23 Sandro Botticelli. *Allegory of Spring (La Primavera),* c. 1478. Tempera on wood, 6′8″ × 10′4″. Galleria degli Uffizi, Florence, Italy.

Above, the blind Cupid shoots an arrow toward Castitas (Chastity), the youthful central dancer of the three graces. Her partners are the bejeweled Pulchritudo (Beauty) and Voluptas (Passion). Their transparent, gauzy drapery vibrates with the movements of their dance and creates rhythmic flowing lines. (In his *Pagan Mysteries of the Renaissance,* historian Edgar Wind saw this dance as the initiation rites of the virginal Castitas into the fullness of beauty and passion.) At the far left stands Mercury, both the leader of the Three Graces and the fleet-footed god of the winds. Lifting his magic staff, the Caduceus, he completes the circle by directing Zephyr to drive away the wintry clouds and make way for spring. Symbolically, Mercury dispels the clouds that veil the intellect to allow the light of reason to shine through. Presiding over the entire story, whose meaning is much disputed, is the figure of the goddess of love.

THE BIRTH OF VENUS. Botticelli painted another aspect of the goddess of love in his *The Birth of Venus* (Fig. 9.24). This composition was inspired by ancient descriptions of a lost masterpiece, *Venus Anadyomene,* by Apelles, the famous Greek painter who is said to have done portraits of Philip of Macedon and his son, Alexander the Great (see pp. 63–64). Here there are four figures instead of eight. Venus's nudity and modest posture express the dual nature of love, the sensuous and the chaste. These motifs are carried out on the left by the blowing winds, which Poliziano called amorous zephyrs. Flora reappears, wearing a flowery dress and carrying a flower-strewn robe forward toward Venus.

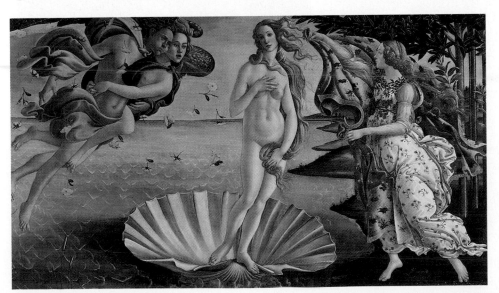

9.24 Sandro Botticelli. *The Birth of Venus,* c. 1482. Tempera on canvas, 5′8″ × 9′1″. Galleria degli Uffizi, Florence, Italy.

Venus seems to be floating gently across the green sea on her pink shell. The fluttering drapery of the side figures creates a sense of lightness and movement and leads the eye toward Venus's head, which is surrounded by an aura of golden hair. The clarity of outline, the balletlike choreography of lines, and the pattern of linear rhythms, especially in the lime-green waves, recall the techniques used in gold work and shallow relief sculpture.

In this painting, Botticelli demonstrated his profound connection with the Florentine Renaissance humanists, who were concerned with the revival of classical forms, figures, and imagery. Botticelli's break with the past is not quite complete. The composition of his *Allegory of Spring* echoes with the traditional Christian iconography of the Madonna surrounded by saints and angels. Also, *The Birth of Venus* hints at the baptism of Christ as he stands in the Jordan River with St. John on one side and an angel on the other. On the other hand, the artist's break with the painterly present is remarkable. It is as if he absorbed recent experiments with natural light and the rendering of three-dimensional figures on the picture plane, only to reject further naturalism as too limiting to the imagination. His graceful, elongated figures with their sweetly ideal faces have

a trace of late Gothic styles, but they are still his invention, as is the sensuous appeal of color that helped make him famous.

MASTERMIND: LEONARDO DA VINCI

Trained in Verrochio's workshop, Leonardo da Vinci rejected the classical humanistic scholarship that prevailed in Florence in favor of firsthand investigation, observation of nature, and constant experimentation. Many of his theories and speculations pushed at the frontiers of contemporary knowledge. A music lover and performer, he was first received at the court of Milan as a lute player and singer. In a letter to the Duke of Milan, he outlined his skills, noting that he could "vie successfully with any in the designing of public and private buildings, and in conducting water from one place to another. . . . I can carry out sculpture in marble, bronze, or clay." He then casually men-

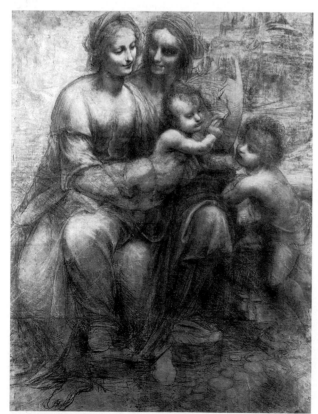

9.25 Leonardo da Vinci. Cartoon for *Madonna and Child with St. Anne and the Young St. John*, c. 1505–1507. Charcoal and white chalk on paper, approx. 4'6" × 3'3". National Gallery, London, England.

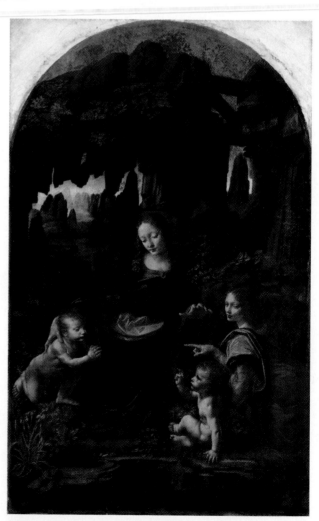

9.26 Leonardo da Vinci. *Madonna of the Rocks*, begun 1483. Oil on panel (transferred to canvas), approx. 6'3" × 3'7". Louvre, Paris, France.

tioned that "in painting I can do as well as any man." The voluminous notebooks he kept throughout his long life testify to his wide-ranging interests, including the flight of birds, the flow of water, the force of winds, the movement of clouds, and the invention of machines. His elegant, precisely observed drawings in all these fields and in human anatomy qualify him as the founder of modern scientific illustration.

Leonardo's point of departure in painting was not the graceful linear approach of Botticelli but the natural lighting, atmospheric perspective, and sculpturesque modeling of Masaccio. His treatise on painting advises artists to observe faces and figures in the softer light of dawn, dusk, and cloudy weather rather than in full daylight. This yielded greater delicacy of expression and a special quality of warmth and intimacy. In his masterly cartoon (preliminary drawing) for the *Madonna and Child with St. Anne and the Young St. John* (Fig. 9.25), all sharp lines are eliminated. He used the technique of modeling shapes in shades of dark and light, called *chiaroscuro,* so subtly that it became a language of its own through which he could suggest fleeting intuitions and states of mind. In this portrayal of three generations, the grandmotherly St. Anne becomes the personification of benign tranquility, whereas Mary is the image of grace and maternal concern. Although children, Christ and St. John exhibit the thoughtful gravity of those on whom the salvation of the world will depend.

MADONNA OF THE ROCKS. In *Madonna of the Rocks* (Fig. 9.26), the forms seem to emerge out of the surrounding darkness. Diffused rays of light shape

the bodies three-dimensionally and illuminate the landscape background. More important than mere physical light, however, is the spiritual illumination that shines from each face. Here Leonardo carries chiaroscuro one step further, into what is called **sfumato,** whereby all hard lines disappear and the figures are revealed in a hazy, almost smoky atmosphere. The central part of the picture is built three-dimensionally like a pyramid, one of Leonardo's most significant contributions to pictorial form. The Madonna's head becomes the apex, and the two children give just the right weight and volume to the base. The hands play an expressive part as Mary embraces the young St. John, the representative of humanity in need of protection. Her other hand seems to hover in space as it forms a halo for the infant Jesus. The hand of the angel points to St. John as the forerunner of Christ, while that of the infant Jesus is raised in blessing.

Leonardo's great interest in nature plays a prominent role in this painting. Around the pool in the foreground and throughout the cave are flowers, grasses, and plants that are observed and painted with minute accuracy. The stalagmites, stalactites, and other rock formations are rendered with the precision of an expert in geology. The overall tone of the grotto setting is melancholy, seeming to foreshadow the tomb that awaits the Savior at the end of his earthly mission.

THE *LAST SUPPER.* The *Last Supper,* a fresco on the wall of the monks' refectory, or dining hall, at Santa Maria delle Grazie in Milan (Fig. 9.27), is a masterpiece of dramatic power and pictorial

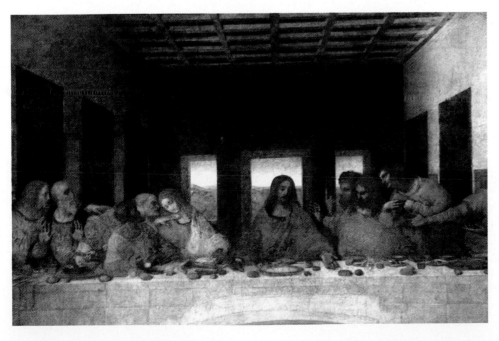

9.27 Leonardo da Vinci. *Last Supper,* 1495–1498. Oil and tempera on plaster, 14′5″ × 28′¼″. Refectory, Santa Maria delle Grazie, Milan, Italy.

9.28 Diagram of Leonardo da Vinci's *Last Supper* showing vanishing point (one-point) perspective.

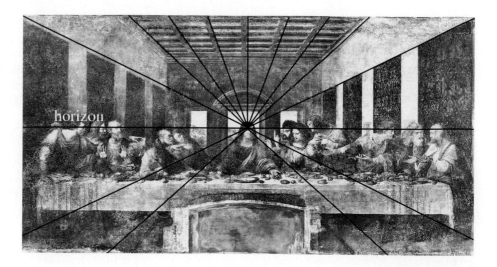

horizon

logic. Leonardo has chosen to depict the moment when Jesus said, "Verily I say unto you, that one of you shall betray me." The apostles "were exceeding sorrowful, and began every one of them to say unto him, Lord is it I?" (Matt. 26:21–22). The reactions run the gamut of human feeling, from fear, outrage, and doubt to loyalty and love. As each apostle responds, his mental and emotional state is reflected in searching facial expressions and eloquent gestures (see Fig. 9.27). In the process, the defiant Judas is isolated. He draws back, his face in deep shadow, his hand clutching the moneybag containing the fatal thirty pieces of silver. Of him Jesus said, "Behold, the hand of him that betrayeth me is with me on the table" (Luke 22:21).

To contain this highly charged scene, Leonardo devised a setting of spaciousness and stability. As in Masaccio's *The Tribute Money* (Fig. 9.16), all the lines of the walls and ceiling beams converge in the exact middle, directly behind the head of Christ, in perfectly realized linear perspective (Fig. 9.28). The light from the center window with the curved pediment above functions as a halo around his head. At the table, the revealing gestures of the hands also focus attention toward the center. As an underlying motif, Leonardo draws on the Florentine understanding of harmony as expressed in numbers—in this case, the symbolism and properties of the number 12. The twelve apostles appear in four groups of three on either side of the lonely central figure. There are four wall hangings on each side and three windows, alluding to the four gospels and the Trinity. Twelve also relates to the passage of time—the hours of the day and months of the year—in which human salvation is to be sought.

Always thoughtful and deliberate in his working methods, Leonardo found the usual fresco technique of rapid painting on wet plaster uncongenial. Instead, he experimented by mixing oil pigments with tempera to lengthen the available painting time, to obtain deeper colors, and to produce more shadow effects. Unfortunately, the paint soon began to flake off the damp wall. Over the years it has been restored and repainted so often that only a shadow of the original remains.

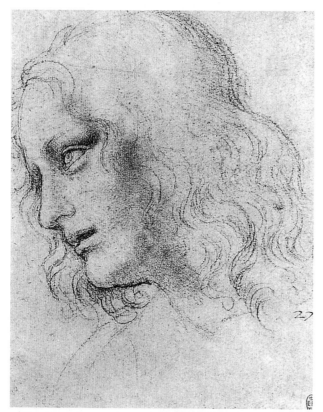

9.29 Leonardo da Vinci. Study of St. Philip for the *Last Supper,* c. 1495–1496. Black chalk on paper. Royal Library, Windsor Castle, London, England.

Nevertheless, it is still possible to admire the overall design, the dramatic gestures of the figures, and some of the color tones. The original intensity of the facial expressions can be glimpsed through the few preparatory drawings that have survived. The profile of Philip, who is standing third to the right of Christ (Fig. 9.29), is particularly poignant.

Leonardo's ambitions, conceptions, and projections far exceeded his capacity to realize them in tangible form. None of his buildings progressed beyond the planning stage, his sculptures have all perished, and only about seventeen generally accepted paintings remain. These include four that are unfinished, and the others exist in varying states of preservation, restoration, and repainting.

POETRY AND MUSIC

LORENZO AS POET AND PATRON

The principal poets of the Florentine Renaissance were Lorenzo de' Medici and Poliziano. In retrospect, Lorenzo's title, Il Magnifico, seems to recognize his activities not only as an international banker but as a poet; humanist; philosopher; discoverer of genius; patron of the arts and sciences; and advisor to writers, sculptors, painters, and musicians (see Fig. 9.31).

Under the guidance of his grandfather Cosimo, Lorenzo was educated by Pico della Mirandola and other scholars to be the type of philosopher-ruler Plato had described in the *Republic*. Social conditions, however, had changed considerably since Cosimo's time. Whereas his grandfather had been a banker with intellectual and artistic tastes, Lorenzo became a powerful leader whose power rested on philosophical prestige and leadership in matters of taste as well as on his banking fortune.

Lorenzo maintained embassies at all the principal courts to which he made loans. He was willing to finance foreign conflicts, provided that he saw a substantial profit. By having the services of the greatest humanists under his command, he ensured that he could also fight a war of words in the form of elegantly turned phrases, veiled threats, and verbal thunderbolts.

As the fifteenth century progressed, conditions affecting the arts and artists changed significantly. During the early decades, Ghiberti had been employed by the Signory and his work was intended for public view. Later, the major commissions came from a few wealthy families. Under Lorenzo, the arts took on a more courtly character

and the audiences grew correspondingly smaller and more elite. Some painters were able to make a living outside the charmed circle, depicting scenes of births and marriages for a growing upper-middle-class clientele, but pictures like those of Botticelli, with their intricate classical references, were meant mainly for the humanistic intellectuals of the time.

RENAISSANCE FESTIVALS

Although he was a political, business, and intellectual leader, Lorenzo had the instincts of a popular ruler. He participated actively in the Florentine festivals (see Fig. 9.18 for a glimpse of the pageantry) by composing new verses for traditional folk tunes, encouraging others in his circle to do the same, and holding competitions among composers for better musical settings of the songs.

Lorenzo thus gave new impetus to popular literature in the native dialect. In a commentary on four of his own sonnets, he went to considerable lengths to defend the expressive possibilities of Tuscan Italian. After comparing it with Hebrew, Greek, and Latin, he found that its harmoniousness and sweetness outdid all the others. Although he continued to write sophisticated sonnets, Lorenzo also wrote popular verses that have, in addition to their beauty and literary polish, the spontaneous freshness, humor, and charm of folk poetry. He even uses the rustic dialogue of true country folk in some of his pastoral poems. Few poets could rival the lyricism of his *canti carnascialeschi,* or "carnival songs," one of which contains these oft-quoted lines:

> Fair is youth and free of sorrow,
> Yet how soon its joys we bury!
> Let who would be, now be merry:
> Sure is no one of tomorrow.

THE MUSIC SCENE IN FLORENCE

Popular music-making in Florence and other Italian cities was as much a part of the good life as any of the other arts. Yet it was mainly an art of performance; little music was ever written down. When the time came to appoint a successor to Squarcialupi as private master of music in the Medici household after his death in 1475, Lorenzo chose the rapid and productive composer Heinrich Isaac, a native of Flanders. Florence immediately became a second home to this cosmopolitan figure, who combined native Italian idioms with elements from his own background and training.

PAST AND PRESENT

Listening to Music

Lorenzo de Medici and his circle were unusual in their attraction to folk tunes (see p. 269). Outside of church, kings, courtiers, and commoners typically listened to different kinds of music. The royals and the wealthy seldom heard what the people heard, and the people did not have access to the music heard by the upper classes. The rich and the powerful employed composers and requested music to be played at special events, such as weddings, funerals, and state dinners. This music was written down, which made it possible to circulate to distant courts. As a consequence, music produced in Italy or France could dominate court taste in other European countries.

Peasant music tended to remain local, with regional variations in tune and lyrics. Love songs, for instance, were sung and played by friends at family gatherings or in taverns. Instruments, like music, were locally made. District languages and dialects prevailed in lullabies, children's songs, and the chants sung by workers while gathering agricultural crops.

Today, more than a century since the invention of recorded sound, rich and poor alike are able to listen to the same music. Moreover, recordings of local and national musical styles from around the world have increasingly influenced each other. The rhythms and sounds of traditional Indian music, known as *ragas,* can be heard in Western music. Afro-pop, a blend of African music and rock, is popular worldwide. Music is no longer linked solely to formal occasions or to work but can be heard at all hours of the day, every day, and wherever listeners choose to listen.

Isaac's duties included those of organist and choirmaster at the Florence Cathedral as well as at the Medici Palace, where Lorenzo is known to have had no fewer than five organs. Together with Poliziano, he was also the teacher of Lorenzo's sons, one of whom was destined to be the music- and art-loving Pope Leo X. Most important, Isaac collaborated with Lorenzo on songs written for popular festivals. He thus became co-creator of one of the many kinds of popular secular music that eventually led to the sixteenth-century **madrigal.** The madrigal, often about love and designed for home performance and entertainment, was a well-liked type of vocal chamber music in the polyphonic style.

Dufay's settings of Lorenzo's verses have been lost, but many by Isaac still exist. In one of these he shows the tendency away from complex counterpoint and toward simple harmonic texture. He created music in the style of the Florentine *frottola,* a carnival song for dancing as well as singing. The collaboration of Lorenzo and Isaac resulted in both a meeting of minds and a merging of poetic and musical forms. Lorenzo's verses were a union of the courtly *ballata* and popular poetry, whereas Isaac succeeded in Italianizing the Burgundian *chanson,* or song. In this instance, Italianizing meant simplifying, omitting all artificiality, and enlivening a rather stiff form with graceful Florentine folk melodies and rhythms. This cultural tendency worked both ways, raising the level of popular poetry while simultaneously giving new life to more sophisticated poetic and musical forms through popular idioms.

IDEAS

The Florentine Renaissance clustered around three concepts: classical humanism, scientific naturalism, and Renaissance individualism. In their broadest meanings, these concepts were far from new. When classical humanism first took shape in Italy, it was as much the survival of ancient influences as a true revival in the sense of a reinterpretation and new adaptation of older Greco-Roman forms.

Naturalism, in the sense of faithfulness to nature, appears in a well-developed form both in northern Gothic sculpture and in the poetry of St. Francis. By the fourteenth century, representations of people and nature alike had lost their primary value as otherworldly symbols. Rather than being content with describing the world as seen by the eye alone, fifteenth-century naturalism took a noticeably scientific turn. Careful observation of natural events and the will to reproduce objects as the eye sees were evidence of a developing empirical attitude. Likewise, dissection of corpses to see the structure of the human body revealed a spirit of free inquiry. In addition, the study of mathematics to put objects into proper perspective involved a new concept of space. Clearly, a new scientific spirit was stirring.

The distinctive features of Florentine individualism were largely attributable to the access this small city-state gave to artists, who could come into immediate contact with their patrons and audience. Competition was keen; desire for personal fame was intense; and a high regard for individual personality is seen in the portraiture, biographies, and autobiographies of patrons and artists.

Humanism in the humanitarian Franciscan sense was a carryover from the thirteenth and fourteenth centuries (see p. 237). Naturalism stemmed from late Gothic times, and, of course, some form of individualism is almost always present in any period. It should therefore be clear that the Florentine Renaissance was characterized by no sharp division from the past and that its special flavor lies in the quality of its humanism, in the direction of its naturalism, and in the distinctive nature of its individualism.

CLASSICAL HUMANISM

The term *Renaissance,* implying as it does a rebirth, is a source of some confusion. To the early sixteenth-century historian, it meant an awakening to the values of ancient classical arts and letters after the long medieval night. But just what, if anything, was reborn has never been satisfactorily explained. Because all the principal ideas were present in the Gothic period, one might do better to speak of the cultural conditions that encouraged the maturing of certain tendencies that were present in late medieval times. Yet there was a specific drive that gave an extraordinary stimulus and color to the creative life and thought of this small Tuscan city-state in the fifteenth century. It is important to discover what specific factors gave humanism in Florence its special flavor.

Although Florentine humanism evolved from the Franciscan spirit, it took on a consciously classical coloration that was not part of the Franciscan outlook. Here again, however, a word of caution is necessary when speaking of a "rebirth" of the spirit of antiquity. In Italy, much more than in northern Europe, the classical tradition had been more or less continuous. Roman remains were everywhere in evidence. Many Roman arches, aqueducts, bridges, and roads were still in use, and fragments of ancient buildings were reused as building materials.

In the late thirteenth century, Nicola Pisano's sculptural models were the Roman remains he saw all around him. By the fifteenth century, the revival of the classical male nude as an instrument of expression was seen in the work of Ghiberti, Donatello, Pollaiuolo, and Verrocchio. At the beginning of the sixteenth century, Michelangelo had developed such a formidable sculptural technique that his *David* (Fig. 9.30) rivaled the work of ancient sculptors such as Praxiteles (see Fig. 2.22).

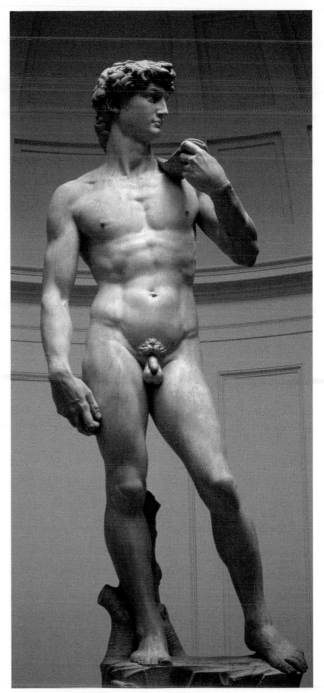

9.30 Michelangelo. *David*, 1501–1504. Marble, height 18′. Galleria dell'Accademia, Florence, Italy.

Aristotle was studied, and ancient musical theory continued to be taught. What was new to Florence was the study of the Greek language, the use of Roman Latin rather than medieval church Latin, and a passionate interest in Plato. Despite a concern for antique books and works of art, however, the net result was less a revival of things past than a step forward. The Renaissance was a search for past examples to justify new practices.

Much has also been written about the pagan aspect of the appeal to antiquity. Here again it was less anti-Christian than it seems on the surface. Florentine interest in Plato was a conscious departure from scholastic thought, but it was mainly a substitution of the authority of Plato for that of Aristotle. Marsilio Ficino spoke of Plato as the Athenian Moses. He added "Saint" Socrates to the litany of saints and may have burned a candle before a bust of Plato. In this light, his thought appears more as a reinterpretation of Christianity in Platonic terms than a revival of paganism as such.

When the Florentine philosopher Pico della Mirandola said that "there is nothing to be seen more wonderful than man," he was picking up exactly where the ancient Greek thinkers had left off (see p. 58). Pico's famous *Oration* exalted human dignity. He placed humanity at the center of the universe and considered the human being "the intermediary between creatures, the intimate of higher beings and the king of lower beings, the interpreter of nature by the sharpness of his senses, by the questing curiosity of his reason, and by the light of his intelligence, the interval between eternity and the flow of time." According to Pico, humans have the possibility of descending to the level of brute beasts or the power to rise to the status of higher beings, which are divine. This confident picture of human potential and destiny animates the spirit of the great humanistic artists Botticelli, Michelangelo, and Raphael, and it is one of the most important keys to the interpretation of their works.

SCIENTIFIC NATURALISM

The two basic directions taken by the naturalism of the fifteenth century led to a new experimental attitude and a new concept of space. A close partnership between art and science developed, with architects needing to be mathematicians, sculptors becoming anatomists, painters learning geometry, and musicians studying acoustics.

The spirit of free inquiry was by no means confined to the arts. It penetrated all the progressive aspects of life of the time, from a reexamination of the forms of secular government to Machiavelli's candid reflections on how people behave under certain political circumstances. This searching curiosity reached its full fruition in the early years of the sixteenth century in Machiavelli's political handbook *The Prince*. Like Thucydides, the Athe-

nian historian he admired, Machiavelli attempted to create a dispassionate, chronological account of near-contemporary events and underlying causes in his *History of Florence* (see p. 274). The scientific observations in Leonardo's notebooks, which cover everything from astronomy to zoology, show a similar passion for inquiry.

Well within the fifteenth century, the same spirit continued to manifest itself. Ghiberti's *Commentaries* pointed to the mathematical proportions of the human body as the basis of its beauty, and he wrote the first essay in Italian on optics. Brunelleschi, a diligent student of the Roman architect Vitruvius, was concerned with the mathematical and harmonic proportions of his buildings. Alberti, in his books on painting, sculpture, and architecture, stressed the study of mathematics as the underlying principle of all the arts. Leonardo also took up this theme by demonstrating the geometric proportions of the human body in his well-known drawing (see Fig. 2.39).

The sculptors and painters who followed the leadership of Antonio Pollaiuolo and Verrocchio were animated by the desire to express the structural and muscular forms of the body beneath its external appearance. Their anatomical studies opened the way to the modeling of the movements and gestures of the human body. The result was the reaffirmation of the expressive power of the nude.

In painting, naturalism meant more faithful representations based on detailed and accurate observation. Even Fra Angelico showed an interest in the exact reproduction of Tuscan botanical specimens in the garden of his *Annunciation*. Under the influence of Pollaiuolo and Verrocchio, Botticelli combined the objective examination of nature with imaginative subjects. The culmination of this line of thought was reached in the work of Verrocchio's pupil Leonardo da Vinci, who considered painting a science and sculpture a mechanical art. Leonardo's scientific probing went beyond the physical and anatomical into the metaphysical and psychological aspects of human nature.

In music, interest in Greek theory continued, coupled, however, with experiments. The compositions of Dufay and others of the northern school applied mathematical laws to such aspects of composition as rhythmical progressions, formal proportions, and the development of technical devices.

The exploration of geographic space that began with the voyages of Columbus, led to the development of trade routes and commerce and the tapping of distant sources of wealth. In architecture, the concentration on space is reflected in the raising of Brunelleschi's cupola almost 370 feet high. In painting, it is seen in a number of advances. Among them are the placing of figures in a more normal relationship to the space they occupy and the use of landscape settings. Other steps forward include Masaccio's development of atmospheric perspective, in which figures are modeled in light and shade, and the working out of rules for linear perspective, whereby the illusion of depth on a two-dimensional surface is achieved by defining a point at which lines converge. **Foreshortening,** the reduction in the size of figures and objects in direct ratio to their distance from the **picture plane,** is yet another element of progress toward more naturalistic portrayals.

Because the subject matter of medieval art was drawn from the spiritual world, naturalistic representation was not a major goal. But during the Renaissance, art entered a new phase of self-awareness as artists began to ponder purely aesthetic problems, modes of presentation, and pictorial mechanics. In medieval music, the emphasis had been on perfect intervals and mathematical rhythmic ratios to please the ear of God. Renaissance musicians were willing to render sounds that would delight the human ear. The new spirit was also heard in the extension of the range of musical instruments into both higher and lower registers, thus broadening the scope of tonal space. The development of pleasant harmonic textures, the softening of dissonances, and the writing of singable melodies and danceable rhythms all contributed to the period's new outlook.

In the trend toward scientific naturalism, the arts of painting and sculpture became firmly allied with geometric and scientific laws, a union that lasted until twentieth-century Expressionism and abstract art. Indeed, the fifteenth-century Florentine artists reveled in the perspective, optical, and anatomical discoveries of their day. When the basic research, experiments, and discoveries were decisively under way, it was left for their successors—Leonardo da Vinci, Michelangelo, and Raphael—to explore the full possibilities.

RENAISSANCE INDIVIDUALISM

In the Renaissance, the desire for personal prestige through art was a prime concern. Wealthy families and individuals commissioned artists to build memorial churches and chapels and to create statues and paintings. The high regard for individual personality was also mirrored in the number and quality of portraits painted during this time. Because artists were so eagerly sought after, their social status rose accordingly, and sculptors and painters became important thinkers who developed distinctive styles.

Private patronage began to rival church patronage. Brunelleschi built the Pazzi Chapel, Masolino and Masaccio decorated the Brancacci Chapel, and Benozzo Gozzoli and Fra Filippo Lippi did the paintings for the Medici Chapel, all on commission from private donors as memorials to themselves and their families. San Lorenzo, the parish church of the Medici, was rebuilt and redecorated by Brunelleschi and Donatello—but the money came from Cosimo, not from the church. Fra Angelico decorated the corridors of the monastery of San Marco, which was under the protection of the Medici family, and Squarcialupi and Isaac were on the payroll of the Medici when they played the organ in the cathedral, in a church, or in the family palace. Piousness and the desire for spiritual salvation were not the only motives for such generosity. The donor's lasting fame depended on building monuments and choosing distinguished artists to decorate them.

Certain technical considerations within the arts themselves point toward individualization and recognition of the viewer. The development of perspective drawing, for example, implied that the subject in the picture—whether a Madonna, a saint, or an angel—was definitely placed in this world rather than symbolically in the next. Hence, the figure was on a more equal basis with the observer. The unification of space through the convergence of all the lines at one point on the horizon tended to flatter the spectator. Through its clear organization of lines and planes, linear perspective makes it seem that everything is seen from a single optical vantage point—that of the observer. The artist visually implies that nothing of importance lies outside the painting and that the entire picture can be taken in at a glance.

Human figures, whether rendered as prophets or as portraits, tended to become more personal and particularized. Each statue by Donatello, be it *Lo Zuccone* or his *David,* was an individual person who made a powerful, unique impression. Even the pious Fra Angelico gave that most ethereal of creatures, an angel, the bodily weight of a gravity-bound human. Whether the medium was marble, terracotta, paint, words, or sounds, a new emphasis was placed on human individuality. Whether the picture was a barely disguised family group, like Botticelli's *Adoration of the Magi,* or a personal portrait, like

Verrocchio's bust of Lorenzo (Fig. 9.31), the figures were differentiated personages rather than stylized abstractions. Even though Lorenzo de' Medici was the most powerful political figure in Florence, Verrocchio saw him as a man.

The high social status of Florentine artists was evident in the inclusion of self-portraits in such paintings as that of Benozzo Gozzoli in his *Journey of the Magi* and the prominent position Botticelli allowed himself in his *Adoration of the Magi*. Ghiberti's personal reminiscences in his *Commentaries* were probably the first autobiography of an artist in history. His inclusion of the lives and legends of his famous fourteenth-century predecessors were the first biographies of individual artists. He also included a self-portrait in one of the round medallions in the center of his famous doors. Signatures of artists on their works were becoming the rule, not the exception. The culmination of this trend came when Michelangelo realized that his style was so highly individual that he no longer needed to sign it. The desire for personal fame grew to such an extent that Benvenuto Cellini no longer was content to let his works speak for him and wrote a lengthy autobiography filled with self-praise. The painter Giorgio Vasari likewise took up the pen to record the lives of the artists he knew personally and by reputation.

In late medieval and early Renaissance times, artists were mostly seen as practitioners of crafts. They were trained as apprentices to grind pigments, carve wooden chests, make engravings, and prepare wall surfaces for frescoes, as well as to carve marble reliefs and paint pictures. In the late fifteenth and early sixteenth centuries, however, handwork was not enough for artists. They had to know the theory and history of art and the place of art and the artist in the intellectual and social atmosphere of their period.

RENAISSANCE SELF-IMPROVEMENT BOOKS: CASTIGLIONE AND MACHIAVELLI

Two Italian literary works published early in the sixteenth century round out the picture of Renaissance humanism and individualism: Machiavelli's *The Prince,* written in 1513 and published in 1532, after his death, and Castiglione's *Book of the Courtier* (1518). One is a handbook for achieving success as a political leader; the other is a manual of courtly manners and etiquette. Niccolò Machiavelli's very name has become a part of our language. To act in a "Machiavellian" manner denotes devious and manipulative behavior. This negative ascription, however, overlooks Machiavelli's monumental intellectual honesty and his status as one of the founders of modern political science. Since its appearance, *The Prince* has remained high on the list of recommended reading for every would-be politician, political observer, and entrepreneur.

Machiavelli declared that "a prince must not keep faith when by doing so it would be against his self-interest." But he also pointed out that "the voice of the people is the voice of God." Like a good scientist, Machiavelli isolated his subject from extraneous considerations to study and describe it more precisely. In practice, this meant divorcing politics from ethical and religious considerations. As a pragmatist, Machiavelli held that whatever works in the power game is good and whatever fails is bad. Well versed in the classics, Machiavelli had as a starting point Aristotle's dictum that "man is a political animal." From his own experience as a diplomat for his native Florence and from his keen powers of observation, he concluded that people are primarily self-seeking and basically evil. In matters of statecraft, he held

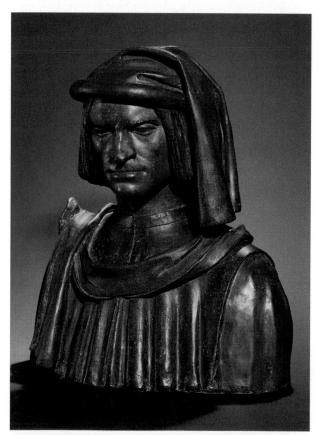

9.31 Andrea Del Verrocchio, *Lorenzo de' Medici,* c. 1478. Terra-cotta, 2′1⅛″ × 1′11¼″ × 1′⅛″. National Gallery of Art, Washington, D.C., Samuel H. Kress Collection.

that the end justifies the means and that what is morally right or wrong is beside the point. He believed that a ruler must be cunning as a fox and fierce as a lion: "The one who knows best how to play the fox comes out best, but he must understand well how to disguise the animal's nature and must be a great simulator and dissimulator. So simple-minded are men and so controlled by immediate necessities that a prince who deceives always finds men who let themselves be deceived." Machiavelli counseled that "it is much safer for a prince to be feared than loved."

In any state, the rights of the people are important if domestic peace and stability are to be maintained. However, when dissenters appear, the people can be managed only by a hardheaded ruler who knows how to utilize factions to his own best advantage. Divide and conquer was Machiavelli's guiding principle. He also believed that princes needed to maintain a style befitting their position. He saw the arts as useful to propaganda, and writers, painters, and musicians as valuable instruments to impress a ruler's rivals as well as his own subjects.

Baldassare Castiglione's *Courtier* was written at the glittering court of Urbino. In the form of a lively dialogue recalling Plato's *Symposium,* its subject is the deportment and accomplishments expected of the lords and ladies who participated in courtly life. Courtiers, Castiglione wrote, should be persons of wide humanistic learning. Unlike Machiavelli, he also required of them high ethical standards. In addition to mastery of martial arts and physical skills, a courtier should be a connoisseur of the arts; a wise and witty conversationalist; a poet; and a graceful dancer, singer, and musician. Some of these qualities shine through Raphael's dignified portrait of Castiglione (Fig. 9.32). Castiglione also explored the role of women in high social circles. He held that men and women should be equally educated except in the arts of war and that women should be able to lift their voices in song, participate in discussions, and be knowledgeable about literature and painting.

In many ways, the lot of Renaissance women resembled that of women in ancient Rome. Marriages of noble and upper-class women were used to forge political and commercial alliances. The rich costumes, jewelry, and other paraphernalia in marriage portraits of wealthy women catalogued the assets as well as the gentility they would bring to the union. The education of women was increasingly deemed necessary for the role of mother. As in medieval times, women in religious orders often had access to large libraries. Women of means influenced political and business decisions and were

sometimes patrons of the arts in their own right, as well as with their spouses. Of course, poor women continued to serve as caregivers and co-workers in family businesses and farming. In the arts, the female figure presented an ideal of beauty.

Nevertheless, the narrow scope of women's collective presence and the widely accepted disparaging attitude toward women's abilities prompted scholars of the late twentieth century to pose the question, "Did women have a Renaissance?" Women were largely excluded from the animated humanism of Pico della Mirandola and Machiavelli, both of whom encouraged men to use their willpower to improve themselves and broaden their interests. Generally speaking, exertions of this very kind would have been judged unsuitable or even dangerous to a woman's femininity.

Nevertheless, in the sixteenth century, notions of self-improvement through the humanities began to be applied to highborn women. Among a few noble and wealthy families, women not only studied but occasionally wrote about the arts. Science and mathematics, cornerstones of Renaissance art, were still considered too masculine for the feminine sensibility. In the northern Italian town of Cremona, the talented daughter of a noble

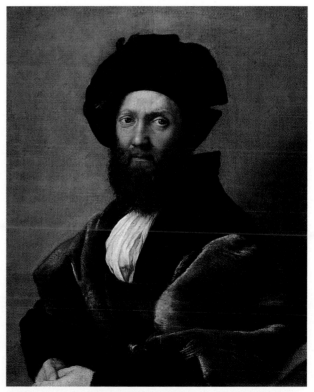

9.32   Raphael. *Baldassare Castiglione,* 1514–1515. Oil on panel (transferred to canvas), approx. 2′6¼″ × 2′2½″. Louvre, Paris, France.

family, Sofonisba Anguissola, and her sisters were educated in music and painting. While raising some conventional doubts about the coexistence of femininity and talent, Vasari dubbed her a *virtuosa*—that is, an exceptional woman. Her eye-teasing self-portrait, presenting herself as if she were being painted by a male artist, highlights her confidence and ability (see Fig. 12.17). She achieved an international reputation as a court painter to King Phillip II of Spain, where her social class and education allowed her to serve as a lady in waiting to the queen.

One of the qualities most admired by Castiglione and other Renaissance writers was *virtù*. Virtù revealed itself in the confidence, stamina, and self-actualizing ability that led to the achievements of a Lorenzo the Magnificent or the breathtaking conceptions of a Michelangelo. To achieve virtù, Renaissance artists could no longer be completely satisfied with a single specialty; rather, they sought to become universal in their interests and activities. For example, in addition to being one of the leading lights of Renaissance architecture, Brunelleschi was also a goldsmith, sculptor, engineer, and mathematician.

Castiglione articulated the Renaissance ideal of the **uomo universale,** the universal man, who embodied all the aspects of Renaissance humanism and individualism in one person. An artist who approached this ideal was Leon Battista Alberti, who in his youth excelled in feats of athletic strength and extraordinary horsemanship. In maturity, he mastered mathematical skills and scientific knowledge. He was a noted Latin stylist and a practicing musician, painter, sculptor, architectural designer, and city planner. His work was summed up in three influential treatises on painting, sculpture, and architecture, which provided the foundation of the Renaissance theory of art.

Alberti believed that all people can do all things if they have the will to do so. He was not only a universal man himself but the prototype for his high Renaissance successors, Leonardo da Vinci and Michelangelo. In Leonardo, Renaissance universality reached a peak. Michelangelo shunned courtly life in favor of his studio, preferring to deal with popes and princes as equals and rejecting all offers of noble titles. He realized his potential by becoming the ranking sculptor, painter, poet, and architect of his day. When people began calling him "the divine," the cycle was complete.

The later years of the fifteenth century were dark ones for Florence. After Lorenzo's death in 1492, his son and heir Piero (aptly called "the Unfortunate") made a series of political blunders that led to the conquest of Florence by the French king Charles VIII. In 1494, Piero was forced to leave the city. In his wake, the fiery monk and reformer Savonarola came to power. He held bonfires on a regular basis to burn earthly vanities, including priceless manuscripts and works of art. For several years, Florence waned as a center of cultural invention. All its major artists with the exception of Botticelli, whose ties to the Medicis continued for decades, fled to other centers, particularly to Rome, where the popes were embarking on ambitious building projects that demanded all manner of sculptural and painterly embellishments.

YOUR RESOURCES

- ***Exploring Humanities CD-ROM***

  ○ Interactive Map: Italy around 1400, Renaissance Florence

  ○ Readings—Niccolò Machiavelli, *The Prince,* selected chapters

- **Web Site**

  http://art.wadsworth.com/fleming10

  ○ Chapter 9 Quiz

  ○ Links—Online readings: *Book of the Courtier*

FIFTEENTH-CENTURY FLORENCE

Key Events	Architecture	Visual Arts	Literature and Music
	1377–1446 **Filippo Brunelleschi** 1396–1472 **Michelozzo di Bartolommeo**	1374–1438 **Jacopo della Quercia** ● 1378–1455 **Lorenzo Ghiberti** ● 1386–1466 **Donatello** ● c. 1395–1455 **Fra Angelico** ▲ 1397–1475 **Paolo Uccello** ▲	1304–1374 **Petrarch (Francesco Petrarca)** ◆ 1313–1375 **Giovanni Boccaccio** ◆

1400

Key Events	Architecture	Visual Arts	Literature and Music
1406 **Pisa** comes under Florentine rule 1434 **Pro-Medici government** elected; Cosimo de' Medici began rule 1434–1443 **Pope Eugene IV** resided in Florence 1439–1442 **Council of Florence** nominally united eastern and western churches 1447 **Parentucelli,** Florentine humanist elected as Pope Nicolas V	1404–1472 **Leone Battista Alberti** 1420–1436 **Brunelleschi** built dome of Florence Cathedral c. 1429 **Pazzi Chapel** begun by Brunelleschi 1436 **Florence Cathedral** dedicated by Pope Eugene IV (begun 1298) 1444–1459 **Medici–Riccardi Palace** built by Michelozzo	c. 1400–1461 **Domenico Veneziano** ▲ 1400–1482 **Luca della Robbia** ● 1401–1428 **Masaccio** ▲ 1401 **Competition for Florence Bapistry** north doors held c. 1402 **Donatello** studied ancient sculpture in Rome 1403–1424 **Ghiberti** worked on Bapistry north doors c. 1406–1469 **Filippo Lippi** ▲ c. 1416–1492 **Piero della Francesca** ▲ c. 1419–1457 **Andrea del Castagno** ▲ 1420–1497 **Benozzo Gozzoli** ▲ 1425–1452 **Ghiberti** worked on Florence Bapistry east doors ("Gates of Paradise") c. 1432–1498 **Antonio Pollaiuolo** ● 1435–1488 **Andrea del Verrocchio** ● 1444–1510 **Sandro Botticelli** ▲ 1449–1494 **Domenico Ghirlandaio** ▲	1400–1474 **Guillaume Dufay** ❏ c. 1410–1497 **Jean de Ockeghem** ❏ 1416–1480 **Antonio Squarcialupi** ❏ 1433–1499 **Marsilio Ficino** ○ 1436 **Dufay** wrote choral motet for dedication of Florence Cathedral 1440–1521 **Josquin Desprez** ❏ 1449–1492 **Lorenzo de' Medici** ◆

1450

Key Events	Architecture	Visual Arts	Literature and Music
1453 **Constantinople** falls to Ottoman Turks; end of Eastern Roman Empire 1464–1469 **Piero de' Medici** ruled after Cosimo's death 1469–1492 **Lorenzo de' Medici** ruled 1478 **Pazzi** family's unsuccessful revolt against Medici; Giuliano de' Medici died, Lorenzo consolidated power 1489 **Savonarola** (1452–1498) preached moral reform 1490 **Aldine Press** in Venice began printing works of Plato and Aristotle 1492 **Lorenzo de' Medici** died 1494 **Medici** exiled from Florence; government dominated by Savonarola 1497 **Bonfires** of "Vanities" 1498 **Savonarola** burnt at stake	c. 1485 **Alberti's treatise** *On Architecture* printed	c. 1450–1523 **Perugino** ▲ 1452–1519 **Leonardo da Vinci** ▲ c. 1457–1504 **Filippino Lippi** ▲ 1475–1564 **Michelangelo Buonarroti** ▲ c. 1485 **Alberti's treatises printed;** *On Painting* (1436), *On Sculpture* (1464) 1489 **Michelangelo** apprenticed to Ghirlandaio	c. 1450–1517 **Heinrich Isaac** ❏ 1454–1494 **Angelo Poliziano (Politian)** ◆ c. 1457–1505 **Jacob Obrecht** ❏ c. 1460–1480 **Lorenzo de' Medici** wrote poetry, including carnival songs 1462 **Cosimo de' Medici** founded Platonic Academy 1463–1494 **Pico della Mirandola** ○ 1466–1482 **Marsilio Ficino's** translations of Plato's *Dialogues* 1467 **Squarcialupi** organist in Florence and music teacher to Medici household 1469–1527 **Niccolò Machiavelli** ○ 1478–1529 **Baldassare Castiglione** ◆ c. 1480 **Heinrich Isaac** succeeded Squarcialupi as organist at Florence Cathedral; also served as court composer for Lorenzo de' Medici and teacher of his children

1500

Key Events	Architecture	Visual Arts	Literature and Music
		1501–1504 **Michelangelo** carved *David*	1518 **Baldassare Castiglione** wrote *The Courtier* 1532 **Machiavelli** published posthumously *The Prince*

❏ - Musician ▲ - Painter ○ - Philosopher ● - Sculptor ◆ - Writer

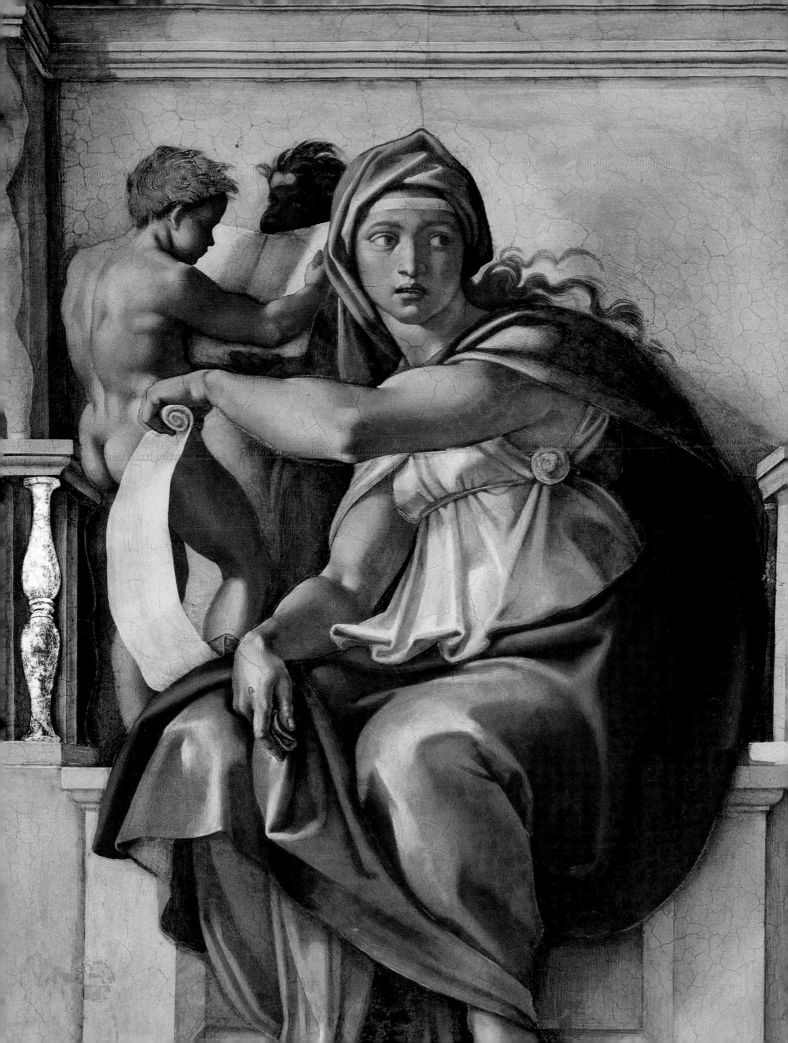

CHAPTER

10

ROMAN RENAISSANCE STYLE

ON APRIL 18, 1506, WHEN the foundation stone of the new Basilica of St. Peter was laid (Fig. 10.1), Rome was well on its way to becoming the major artistic, intellectual, and cultural capital of the Western world. Pope Julius II was gathering about him the foremost artists in all fields, and together they continued the transformation of the Eternal City from its medieval past into the brilliant Rome of today.

Donato Bramante, originally from Urbino but educated in Lombardy, was the architect at work on the plans for the new St. Peter's, the cen-

tral church of the Christian world. Michelangelo Buonarroti from Florence was collecting the marble for a monumental tomb for Pope Julius and was about to begin painting the Sistine Chapel ceiling. Soon Raffaello (Raphael) Sanzio of Urbino would be summoned from Florence to decorate rooms in the Vatican Palace. At about the same time, the Florentine Andrea Sansovino was carving a cardinal's tomb in one of Julius II's favorite Roman churches, Santa Maria del Popolo, where the Umbrian Pinturicchio was covering the choir vaults with a series of frescoes. The

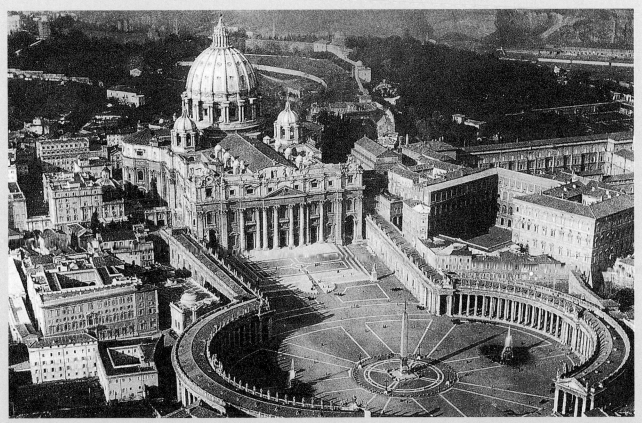

10.1 St. Peter's Basilica and the Vatican, Rome. Apse and dome by Michelangelo, 1547–1564; dome completed by Giacomo della Porta, 1588–1592; nave and facade by Carlo Maderno, 1601–1626; colonnades by Gian Lorenzo Bernini, 1656–1663. Height of facade 147′, width 374′, height of dome 452′.

singer-composer Josquin Desprez, who had been a member of the papal choir for 8 years, recently left to become choirmaster to the king of France.

The papal court under Julius II and his successor, Leo X, was such a powerful magnet that for 3 years the three greatest figures of the Renaissance –Leonardo da Vinci, Michelangelo, and Raphael—were working for the Vatican. In 1517, however, the aged Leonardo left Rome to join the court of Francis I of France.

The flight of the Medici from Florence in 1494 (see p. 276) had signaled a general exodus of artists from that city. Many found temporary havens in the ducal courts of Italy, but Rome proved an irresistible attraction. Hence, during the days of the two great Renaissance popes, Julius II and Leo X, the cultural capital shifted from Florence to Rome. Because Leonardo, Andrea Sansovino, Michelangelo, and Pope Leo were from Florence and because Bramante and Raphael had absorbed the Florentine style and ideas during extended visits there, Florentine influence was felt in the art of Rome. At the same time, the shift from Florence to Rome encouraged artists to branch out.

Large projects such as the building of the world's biggest church and the construction of Julius II's tomb, as well as the painting of the Sistine ceiling and of the Vatican Palace walls, were found only in Rome. The cardinals, who maintained Roman palaces that rivaled the brilliance of the papal court, were also generous patrons of the arts. Nowhere else were commissions of such magnitude available.

The interest in antiquity animated many other Italian cultural centers, but as the Renaissance got under way in Rome, it was, so to speak, on home soil. When antique statues were excavated elsewhere, they caused a considerable stir. In Rome, however, many renowned ancient monuments were still standing. Moreover, as a result of the revived interest in archeology, a veritable treasure trove was revealed. First the *Apollo Belvedere* (see Fig. 3.20) and then the *Laocoön Group* (see Fig. 3.17) came to light and stimulated the work of Michelangelo and other sculptors. The frescoes from Nero's Domus Aurea and the Baths of Titus provided the first important specimens of ancient painting. Although the art of painting on fresh plaster had never died out, the techniques

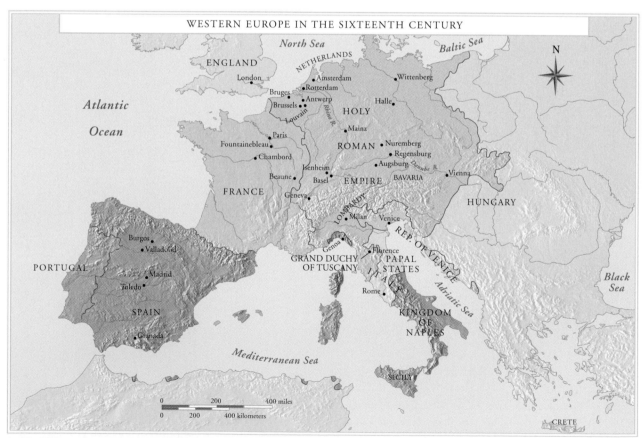

WESTERN EUROPE IN THE SIXTEENTH CENTURY

MAP 10.1

and themes in these ancient Roman fragments gave fresco painting a new impetus.

Julius II had received most of his training in diplomacy and statecraft from his uncle, Pope Sixtus IV. Fortunately, a passionate love of the arts was included in his education. It was Sixtus who had built the chapel that subsequently carried his name, and who had installed there the group of papal singers that has ever since been known as the *Cappella Sistina,* or Sistine Chapel Choir. It remained for Julius to establish a chorus to perform in St. Peter's—one that still bears his name, the *Cappella Giulia,* or Julian Choir. This latter group corresponded to the Early Christian Schola Cantorum (school for singers) and prepared the singers for the Sistine Choir. Both received strong papal support.

Essentially a man of action, Julius II was an expert with the sword as well as the bishop's staff. The spectacle of the pope riding into battle had a demoralizing effect on his enemies. As one of the principal architects of the modern papacy, he also saw the need for a setting on a scale with the importance of the church founded by St. Peter, and he made it a matter of policy to command artists as well as soldiers. At the end of his career,

Julius II became the subject of one of Raphael's most penetrating portraits, showing the Pope bent down by time and the stress of rebellion among his cardinals and bishops (Fig. 10.2).

When Leo X ascended the papal throne, a popular saying went, "Venus has had her day, and Mars his, now comes the turn of Minerva." Venus symbolized the reign of the Borgia pope, Alexander VI; Mars, of course, referred to Julius II; and Minerva, the Roman equivalent of Athena, was Leo. As the son of Lorenzo the Magnificent, he brought to Rome the intellectual spirit of Florence, a latter-day Athens. Michelangelo, whom Leo had known since his childhood at the Medici palace, was unfortunately bound by the terms of his contract to serve the heirs of Pope Julius. Fortunately, the suave and worldly Raphael was available, and he was more congenial to the personal taste of Pope Leo than the gruff Michelangelo. Once again, Raphael served as papal portraitist in a diplomatically adept yet frank study that shows the pope with two cardinals who are, not coincidentally, his nephews (Fig. 10.3).

Heinrich Isaac, Leo's old music teacher, wrote the six-part motet that commemorated his accession. In turn, Isaac's pupil became one of the most

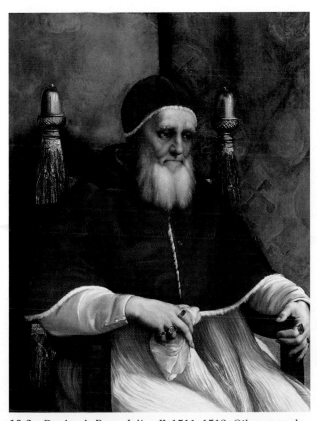

10.2 Raphael. *Pope Julius II,* 1511–1512. Oil on wood, 2′½″ × 2′7½″. National Gallery, London, England.

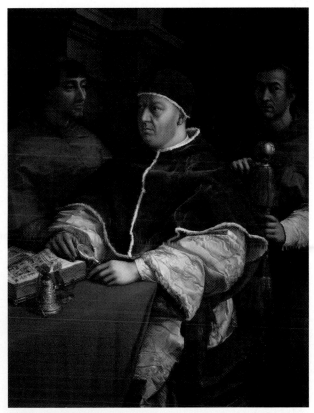

10.3 Raphael. *Leo X with Two Cardinals,* c. 1518. Oil on wood, 5′⅝″ × 3′8⅞″. Galleria degli Uffizi, Florence, Italy.

liberal of all Renaissance patrons of music. Other princes of Europe had difficulty keeping their best musicians because the Pope's love of music was so well known. Leo collected lute and viol players, organists, and the finest singers. Chamber music was avidly cultivated at the papal palace, and a wind ensemble performed at papal dinners. Leo's encouragement of music put it on a par with literary pursuits, causing irritated murmurings among poets and writers. As a competent composer in his own right, Leo knew the art from the inside as few patrons knew it. As a philosopher, writer, and collector, his patronage, like that of his father, Lorenzo the Magnificent, was accompanied by active participation in many of the pursuits that he sponsored.

SCULPTURE: MICHELANGELO

Despite his many masterpieces in other media, Michelangelo always thought of himself first and foremost as a sculptor. He undertook other projects reluctantly. On the contract for the painting of the Sistine Chapel ceiling, for example, he pointedly signed *Michelangelo scultore* (Michelangelo the sculptor) as a protest. His first visit to Rome at the age of 21 coincided with the discovery of some ancient statuary, including the *Apollo Belvedere* (see Fig. 3.20). His most important statues from this early period illustrate the pull of pagan and Christian ideals that affected his aesthetic thought throughout his long career.

10.4 Michelangelo. *Pietà,* 1498–1499. Marble, height 5′9″. St. Peter's Basilica, Rome, Italy.

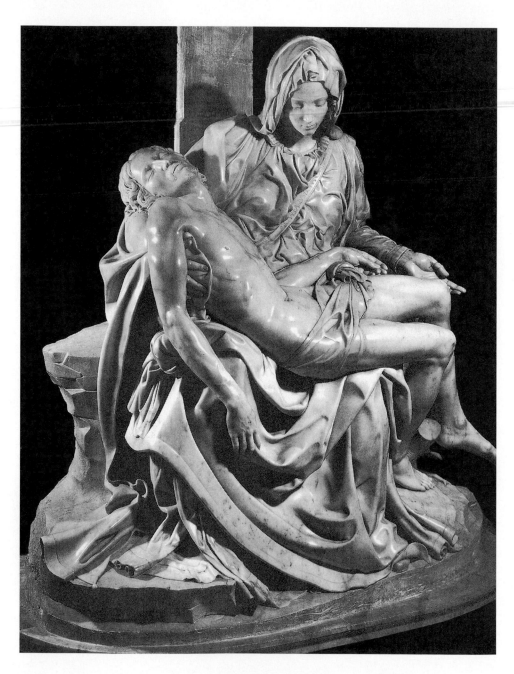

THE *PIETÀ*

The *Pietà* (Fig. 10.4), now in St. Peter's, was commissioned in 1498 by Cardinal Villiers, the French ambassador to the Vatican. Its beauty of execution and delicacy of detail reveal Michelangelo's debt to the Florentine Renaissance. Its pyramidal composition follows a type worked out by Piero della Francesca (see Fig. 9.21) and by Leonardo da Vinci, seen in his drawing for *Madonna and Child with St. Anne and the Young St. John* (see Fig. 9.25). Michelangelo uses the voluminous folds of the Virgin's drapery as the base of the pyramid and her head as the apex.

Michelangelo cast the figure of Christ in the form of a Greek god. The Madonna, although overwhelmed by grief, maintains a classical composure. No tears, no outcry, no gesture mar this conception of Mary as the stoic mother of sorrows. Yet Michelangelo broke with classical ideas when he took symbolic liberties with the proportions of his figures to heighten their expressive effect and enhance the harmony of design. The extensive drapery exists to increase the brilliant execution of folds and sweeping lines. The horizontal body of Christ is far shorter than that of the vertical Madonna, but the disproportion makes the composition more compact. The triangular shape, as a self-sufficient form, holds the attention within the composition and makes external framing devices such as niches or architectural backgrounds unnecessary. In a sense, the *Pietà* is a sculptural declaration of independence, and it bears the distinction of being the only work Michelangelo ever signed (see the sash in Fig. 10.4).

A TOMB FOR A POPE

After finishing the *Pietà,* Michelangelo went home to Florence, where he worked on his *David* (see Fig. 9.30). In 1505, however, he was summoned back to Rome by the imperious Julius to discuss a project for a colossal tomb. In the original conception of this gigantic composition, the artist's imagination for once met its match in his patron's ambitions. Julius's monument was conceived as a small temple within the great new temple—St. Peter's—that was being built. It was to rise pyramidally from a massive quadrangular base and include more than forty statues (Fig. 10.5).

When Julius died in 1513, only parts of the project had been finished and a new contract with his heirs had to be negotiated. Further revisions were made later, each reducing the proportions of the project and eliminating more of the unfinished statues. In its final form of 1545, the monument had shrunk to the relatively modest wall tomb now in the aisle of the church of San Pietro in Vincoli.

Tombs of the popes, like the triple tiaras with which they were crowned, were traditionally

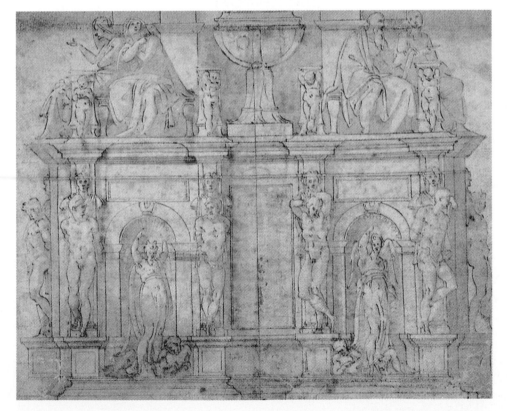

10.5 Michelangelo. Projected Tomb of Julius II. Drawing. Gabinetto dei Disegni e delle Stampe, Gallerie degli Uffizi, Florence, Italy.

constructed in three rising zones symbolizing earthly existence, death, and salvation. For the original project, Michelangelo translated these divisions into Neoplatonic terms that represent the successive stages of the liberation of the soul from its bodily prison. For the final project, the monument lapsed into more traditional stages. In the original scheme, the lowest level was to have figures symbolizing those who are crushed by the burden of life and those who rise above the bonds of matter. This idea was retained in some of the later revisions. Six of the so-called Slaves or Captives and one so-called Victory survive in various stages of completion.

On the second level of the original project there were to have been heroic figures of the leaders of humanity, those who pointed the way toward the divine goal of reunion with God. Moses and St. Paul were to represent the old and new laws, whereas Rachel and Leah would personify the active and contemplative ways of life. Of these, only the *Moses* was finished by Michelangelo himself.

The three figures that date from the years 1513 to 1516, when Leo X was pope, are the two Slaves now in the Louvre, and the *Moses. The Bound Slave* (Fig. 10.6) is the more nearly finished of the two, and it seems to represent a sleeping adolescent tormented by a dream rather than the "dying captive" it is sometimes called. The imprisoned soul, tortured by the memory of its divine origin, has found momentary peace in sleep. The cloth bands that bind the figure are only symbolic, because Michelangelo was not concerned with the visible aspect of captivity but rather with the internal torment. Here is the tragedy of the human race, limited by time but troubled by the knowledge of eternity; mortal but with a vision of immortality; bound by the weight of the body yet dreaming of a boundless freedom.

This tragedy of the tomb was understood only too well by Michelangelo himself, who had the conception of his great project in mind but was doomed to see only a few fragments of his dream completed.

In a later version of the tomb, Michelangelo sustained the Platonic idea of the human soul confined in the bonds of flesh (Fig. 10.7). In the *Captives,* the imprisonment of the spirit by matter is almost total. Unconscious, clasped in stony wombs, they struggle and writhe to emerge from their bondage. Their unfinished state offers an interesting glimpse into Michelangelo's methods, which resemble techniques used to create relief sculpture. To Michelangelo, the finished statue was a potential form hidden in the block of marble awaiting the hand of the master sculptor to re-

lease it. "The greatest artist has no single concept which a rough marble block does not contain already in its core," he wrote in a sonnet. The artist-creator, he continues, must discover, "concealed in the hard marble of the North, the living figure one has to bring forth. (The less of stone remains, the more that grows)." The Neoplatonic implication is clear: the soul is entombed in the body and can be perfected into pure being only by a higher creative power.

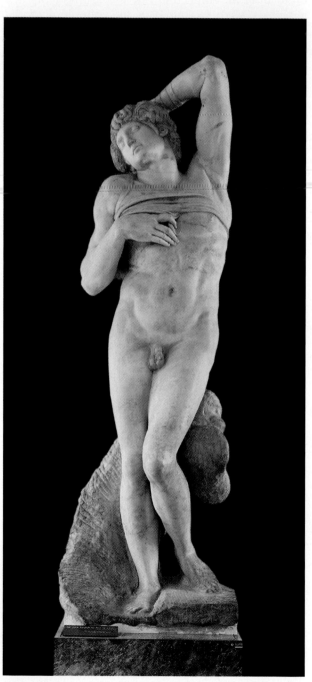

10.6 Michelangelo. *The Bound Slave,* 1513–1516. Marble, height 7′5″. Louvre, Paris, France.

Moses (Fig. 10.8) is the only statue completed entirely by Michelangelo to find its place in the finished tomb. Both Julius II and Michelangelo possessed the quality of **terribilità,** or "awesomeness," that is embodied in this figure. Julius was known as *il papa terribile,* meaning the "forceful pope" or "powerful pope." Michelangelo conceived his *Moses* as the personification of Julius's commanding will. It was also an idealized portrait of the determined Julius, who, as the formulator of a code of church laws, had something in common with the ancient Hebrew lawgiver Moses. In addition, Moses seems to be portrayed as the personification of elemental natural forces. He is the human volcano about to erupt with righteous wrath, the dead center of a hurricane of emotional fury, the messenger of those thunderous "Thou shalt nots" of the Ten Commandments. The smoldering agitation revealed through the drapery, the powerful musculature of the arms, the dominating intelligence of the face, the fiery mood, and the twisting of the body are characteristic of Michelangelo's style. An interesting detail is the carved irises of the eyes, found earlier in his *David* (see Fig. 9.30), which Michelangelo did to express a look of fixed determination. When he wanted to convey the qualities of dreaminess, gentleness, and resignation, as in his Madonnas, he left the eyes untouched. The curious horns on Moses's head were an iconographic tradition from medieval days. They stem from a mistranslation in St. Jerome's Latin version of the Old Testament, which should have read "rays of light."

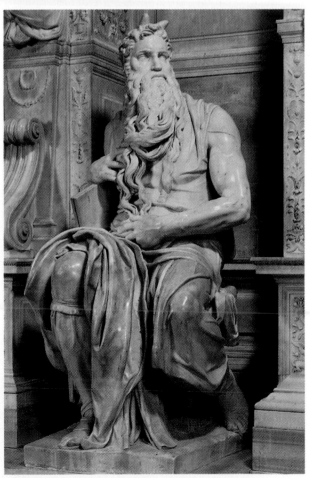

10.7 Michelangelo. "Boboli Captive," c. 1530–1534. Marble, height 7′6½″. Galleria dell'Accademia, Florence, Italy.

10.8 Michelangelo. *Moses,* 1513–1515. Marble, height 8′4″. San Pietro in Vincoli, Rome, Italy.

Michelangelo worked when examples of antique statuary were being unearthed and admired, and his work was often compared favorably with that of the classical sculptors. Michelangelo, like the Greco-Roman artists, saw men and women as the monarchs of creation, yet he was indifferent to their natural environment. His early art affirmed the supreme place of humanity in the universal scheme of things. His world was populated by godlike beings at the peak of their physical power, full of vitality, creativity, and self-confidence.

As Michelangelo's art matured, the men and women he portrayed were beset with quite unclassical tensions, doubts, and conflicts. Unlike those of antiquity, his figures are armed with mental and moral powers that imply the hope of victory in the struggle against fate. Having successfully rivaled the art of the Greco-Roman sculptors as well as that of his own time, not only in his technical mastery but in his expressive power, Michelangelo was regarded with awe by his contemporaries. In his biography of the artist, Giorgio Vasari wrote, "The man who bears the palm of all the ages, transcending and eclipsing all the rest, is the divine M. Buonarroti, who is supreme not in one art only but in all three at once."

PAINTING

MICHELANGELO PAINTS THE SISTINE CEILING FRESCOES

When Michelangelo left Rome out of frustration over the plans for Julius II's tomb, the pope resorted to every means from force to diplomacy to

10.9 Sistine Chapel, viewed toward Michelangelo's *Last Judgment* over the altar, 1473–1480. Height of ceiling 68′. Vatican Palace, Rome, Italy.

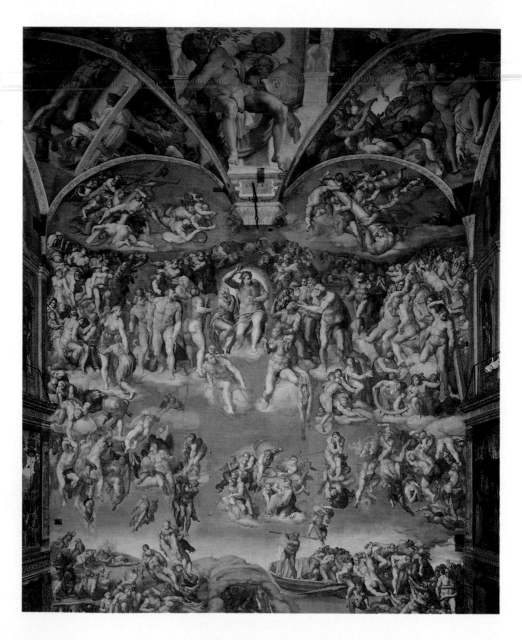

get him to return. Knowing he had a restless genius on his hands, Julius conceived some interim projects to keep Michelangelo busy until the problems with his tomb could be solved. Thinking it could be done quickly, the pope set Michelangelo to paint the ceiling of the Sistine Chapel.

THE SISTINE CEILING.   The building itself, whose roof can be seen paralleling the nave on the right of St. Peter's in Figure 10.1, was built by Julius's uncle, Pope Sixtus IV, as the private chapel of the popes. The interior consists of a single rectangular room 44 feet wide and 132 feet long (Fig. 10.9). Frescoes painted by the foremost fifteenth-century artists, including the Florentines Ghirlandaio (one of Michelangelo's teachers), Botticelli, and Perugino (the teacher of Raphael), decorated the walls.

Six windows were above the frescoes in the side walls. Overhead, the barrel-vaulted ceiling extended 68 feet above the floor, with 700 square yards of surface available for decoration. Using the traditional fresco technique (see pp. 223–224), Michelangelo set to work.

The artist conceived the Sistine ceiling as an organic union of philosophy and design (Fig. 10.10). Its iconography is a fusion of traditional Hebrew–Christian theology and the Neoplatonic philosophy that Michelangelo knew from his days in the Medici household. The ceiling space is divided into painted geometric forms, such as the triangle, circle, and square, which in Plato's philosophy were the eternal forms that furnish clues to the true nature of the universe. Next is a three-way division into zones, the lowest consisting of eight concave triangular

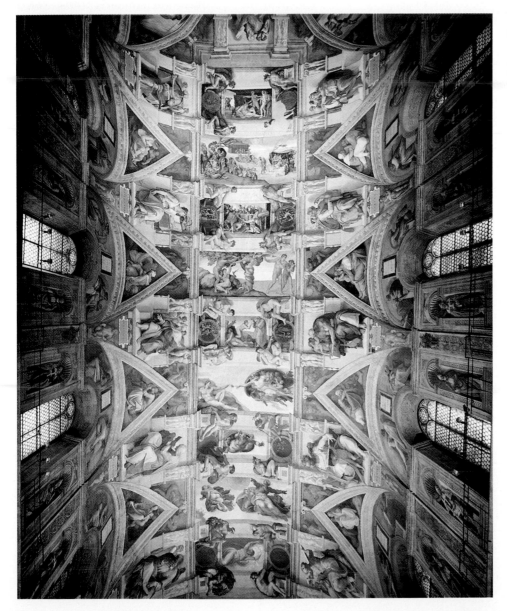

10.10 Michelangelo. Ceiling, Sistine Chapel, 1508–1512. Fresco, 44′ × 128′. Vatican Palace, Rome, Italy.

spaces above the windows and four domed corner spaces. The intermediate zone includes all the surrounding space except that given to the nine center panels, which in turn form the third zone.

Symbolically, these divisions correspond to the three Platonic stages: the world of matter, the world of becoming, and the world of being. Plato also thought in threes when he divided society into classes: workers, free citizens, and philosophers, symbolized by brass, silver, and gold, respectively. Each stratum had its characteristic goal: the love of gain, the development of ambition, and the pursuit of truth. Learning was similarly broken down into the three stages of ignorance, opinion, and knowledge. In addition, Plato's theory of the human soul was tripartite in nature, consisting of the appetitive, emotional, and rational faculties, located in the abdomen, breast, and head, respectively. Of these only the rational part could aspire to immortality.

On the lowest outside level, Michelangelo placed unenlightened men and women imprisoned by their physical appetites and unaware of the divine word. In the intermediate area are the inspired Old Testament prophets and pagan sibyls, whose writings and prophecies impart knowledge of the divine will and who act as intermediaries between humanity and God. In the central section are the panels that tell the story of men and women in their direct relationship to God.

THE LOWER AND INTERMEDIATE LEVELS. The eight border triangles tell the dismal tale of people without vision, who, as St. Luke says, "sit in darkness and in the shadow of death," awaiting the light that will come when the Savior is born. In the four corners are depictions of the heroic men and women whose acts secured temporary deliverance for their people: David slaying Goliath, Judith beheading Holofernes, Haman's punishment through Esther, and Moses's transformation of his rod into a serpent that devoured the similarly transformed rods of the Egyptian priests.

These figures serve as an introduction to the representations of the seven Hebrew prophets, who

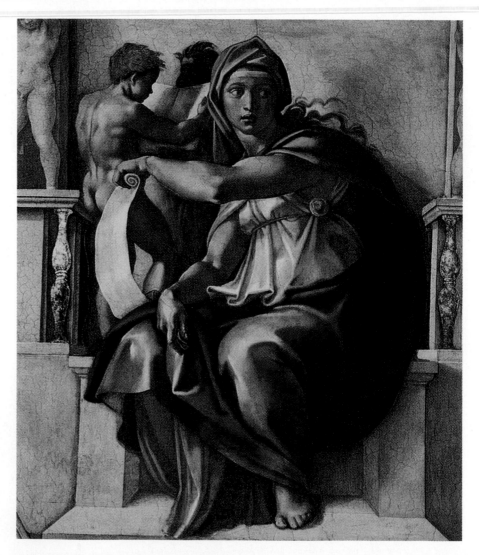

10.11 Michelangelo. *Delphic Sybil,* detail of Sistine Chapel ceiling, 1509. Fresco. Vatican Palace, Rome, Italy.

alternate with five pagan sibyls. The *Delphic Sibyl* is the first of the series (Fig. 10.11). In the Greek tradition, she was the priestess of Apollo at Delphi. As Michelangelo depicts her, she is a young woman possessed by the spirit of prophecy. In the grip of divine fury, she turns her head toward the voice of her inspiration. Although she is clothed in classical Greek garments, her beauty recalls that of Michelangelo's early Madonnas.

Above each of the prophets and sibyls and framing the central panels are **ignudi** (nude youths), seen in Figure 10.10. In the Christian tradition, these figures would have been represented as angels. In the Platonic view, however, they personify the rational faculties of the sibyls and prophets, by means of which they contemplate divine truth and are able to bridge the gap between the physical and spiritual, or earthly and heavenly, regions. Thus, all the prophets and sibyls have a single figure below to denote the body, a pair of nudes behind them to signify the will, and a heroic *ignudo* to personify the immortal soul. These three levels correspond to Plato's three-part conception of the soul—the appetitive, the emotional, and the intellective faculties. Aesthetically, these symbolic figures also serve to soften the contours of the architectural design.

THE CENTER PANELS.   Instead of starting at the beginning and proceeding chronologically as in Genesis, Michelangelo conceives the story of creation in reverse order, as the ascent of humanity from its lowest estate back to its divine origin. In this return to God, the soul in its bodily prison gradually becomes

aware of God and moves from finiteness to infinity, from material bondage to spiritual freedom. Immortality, in this sense, is not the reward for a passive and pious existence but the result of a tremendous effort of the soul struggling out of the darkness of ignorance into the light of truth.

The first of the histories in the nine central panels is *The Drunkenness of Noah.* As in the Slave figures of the Julius tomb, the picture of Noah is that of a mortal man in an abysmal condition, the victim of bodily appetites. Noah's servitude is symbolized on the left, where he is seen tilling the parched soil. He is still strong physically, but his spirit is overwhelmed by the flesh. His sons, powerfully built adolescents, do not seem to be discovering their father's nakedness, as related in the Bible. Instead, they are subject to the tragic fate of all mortals, who must work, grow old, and die. Noah's reclining posture recalls that of the ancient Roman river gods, but in this instance his head has sunk forward on his chest in what seems to be a premonition of death. After this picture of Noah as the prisoner of his own baser nature, the next panel represents *The Deluge,* which shows the plight of men and women when beset by forces of nature beyond their control. In the third panel, *Noah's Sacrifice,* human dependence on God is implied for the first time.

The story of *The Fall and Expulsion from Paradise* follows. The last five panels show various aspects of God's divine nature. In *The Creation of Eve,* God appears as a benign paternal figure closed within the folds of his mantle. In *The Creation of Adam* (Fig. 10.12), God is seen in the skies, with his mantle surrounding Him like a cloud as

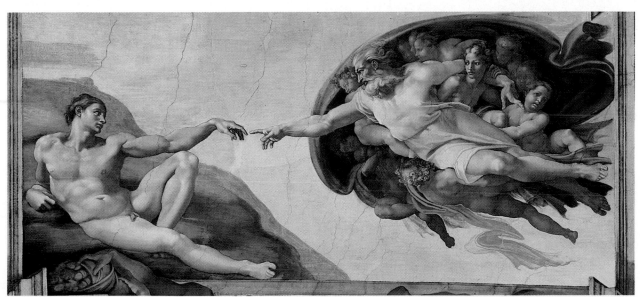

10.12   Michelangelo. *The Creation of Adam,* detail of Sistine Chapel ceiling, 1511. Fresco, approx. 18′8″ × 9′2″. Vatican Palace, Rome, Italy.

He moves downward toward Earth and the inert body of Adam. The creative force is likened to the divine fire that flashes like lightning from the cloud to Earth. Adam's body is one with the rock on which he lies, not unlike the unfinished Slaves of the Julius tomb. In keeping with the Platonic idea of life as a burden and imprisonment, Adam is awakening to life reluctantly rather than eagerly. With his other arm, God embraces Eve, who exists at this moment as an idea in the mind of God. She resembles Michelangelo's Madonna types and looks with fear and awe on this act of creation. God's fingers point to the coming Christ child, whereas behind Him are the heads of unborn generations of human beings.

After *The Gathering of the Waters* comes *The Creation of the Sun and Moon* (Fig. 10.10, right). Here the figure of God becomes a personification of the creative principle, whereas in *God Dividing the Light from Darkness* (Fig. 10.10, far right), the final panel of the series, the light of pure being is attained. Here clarity emerges from chaos, order from the void, existence from nothingness. Light is the symbol of enlightenment and the knowledge that brings

freedom from the darkness of ignorance and bondage. Only through the light of wisdom can an individual attain the highest human and divine status. "You shall know the truth and the truth shall make you free," says the Bible (John 8:32); "Know thyself," the Delphic oracle told Socrates.

Explanations for the total program of images and idea in the Sistine Chapel ceiling run from the practical (Michelangelo adjusted the size of his figures in midcourse to make them more visible from the chapel floor) to the psychosocial (through religious imagery, the iconography of the ceiling expresses the subtle power alliances of church and worldly powers as Michelangelo perceived them). Michelangelo's absorption with merging Christianity and Neoplatonism may also clarify the order and significance of the images.

The conception of God progresses from the paternal human figure of *The Creation of Eve*, to a cosmic spirit in the intervening panels, and then to a swirling abstraction in the realm of pure being. The Neoplatonic goal of the union of the soul with God has been achieved through gradual advancement from the bondage of blind humanity,

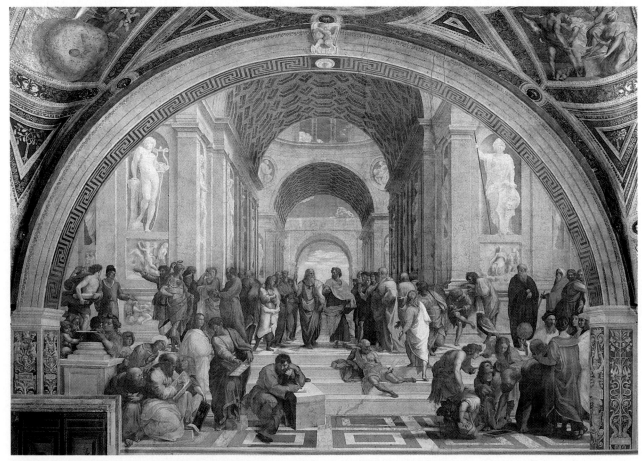

10.13 Raphael. *School of Athens,* 1509–1511. Fresco, 19′ × 27′. Stanza della Segnatura, Vatican Palace, Rome, Italy.

through the prophetic visions of the seers and the ascent of the ladder of the histories into the pure light of knowledge, to the point of dissolving into the freedom of infinity. In the words of Pico della Mirandola, the human being "withdraws into the center of his own oneness, his spirit made one with God." The weight of expression, story content, and philosophical meaning are carried entirely by Michelangelo's placement and treatment of more than 300 human figures in a great variety of postures.

Although he later returned to the Sistine Chapel to paint the *Last Judgment* on the altar wall (Fig. 10.9) and worked on another group for the Pauline Chapel in the Vatican, Michelangelo never succeeded in recapturing the optimism and creative force of the Sistine ceiling frescoes.

RAPHAEL'S FRESCOES FOR THE VATICAN WALLS

At the same time that Michelangelo was painting the Sistine ceiling, his younger contemporary Raphael was working on the murals of the Vatican Palace. In *School of Athens* (Fig. 10.13), Raphael presents a visual philosophy that places him in league with Michelangelo as an artist-scholar. Raphael's fresco is full of both intellectual and pictorial complexities. Yet because of the deepening and widening of the space and the skillful arrangement of the more than fifty figures, the design is clear and uncluttered. Raphael placed Plato and Aristotle on either side of the central axis of the fresco, with the vanishing point slicing backward between them. The book Plato holds in his hands is his *Timaeus,* and he points skyward to indicate his idealistic worldview. Aristotle carries his *Ethics* and indicates by his earthward gesture his greater concern with the real world.

In the spacious hall the various schools of thought argue or ponder the ideas put forth by the two central figures. On Plato's side, a niche contains a statue of Apollo, patron of poetry. On Aristotle's side there is one of Athena, goddess of reason. This division of the central figures balances the picture, with the metaphysical philosophers on Plato's side and the physical scientists on Aristotle's.

Spreading outward on either side are groups corresponding to the separate schools of thought within the two major divisions, each carrying on the philosophical arguments for which they were famous. The figure of Plato is thought to be an idealized portrait of Leonardo da Vinci. In the group at the lower right, Raphael portrayed his architect friend Bramante as Euclid demonstrating on his slate a geometric proposition. At the extreme right, Raphael painted a self-portrait in profile next to his friend, the painter Sodoma. The intriguing figure near the left center is sometimes identified as the Greek philosopher Heraclitus. Legend has it that it is also a portrait of Michelangelo. In *School of Athens,* Raphael captured the intellectual atmosphere and zest with which Renaissance ideas were argued.

THE DOME OF ST. PETER'S

The cornerstone of the new St. Peter's (Fig. 10.1) was laid in 1506, when Michelangelo was starting work on the plans for Pope Julius's tomb. Comparatively little progress had been made in the stormy years that followed, despite the succession of brilliant architects working on the project. Michelangelo favored the centralized church plans of Brunelleschi and Alberti, just as his predecessor Bramante had done. The latter's design, however, was to have culminated in a low dome, modeled after that of the Pantheon (see Fig. 4.20A), but with a series of columns at the base and a lantern tower on top.

Michelangelo accepted Bramante's Greek cross ground plan with a few alterations of his own (Fig. 10.14), but he projected a loftier dome rising over the legendary site of St. Peter's tomb. This cupola was to be of such monumental proportions that it would not only unify the interior spaces and exterior masses of the building but also serve as a symbol of the liturgical, religious, and artistic forces united by Roman Catholicism.

Michelangelo's first problem was an engineering challenge: determining whether the masonry

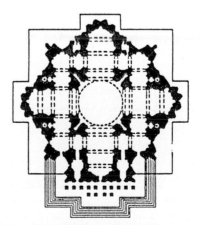

10.14 Michelangelo. Plan of St. Peter's.

was strong enough to support such a dome. He concluded that it was not and set about reinforcing the four main piers until each was a massive 60 feet square. This square understructure was encircled by pendentives, upon which the cylindrical drum was placed. Meanwhile, Michelangelo made a large model of the dome itself so that it could be built by others in case of his death. He lived just long enough to see the drum finished. After his death, two of his associates completed the dome (see Fig. 10.17) without making substantial alterations.

At about this time, there were calls for reforms within the church itself, along with a new spirit of conservatism that frowned on anything that might be considered pagan. A new wave favored a return to traditional Latin cross planning. In the early seventeenth century, Carlo Maderno undertook the lengthening of the nave (Fig. 10.15) and the design of the facade (Figs. 10.1 and 10.16).

Liturgically, the new nave provided more space for grandiose processions. Practically, it provided room for larger congregations. Historically, it ab sorbed all the area formerly occupied by Constantine's basilica, which was demolished to make way for the new structure. Aesthetically, however, the proportions suffered, and the climactic effect of the great dome was lessened. Nevertheless, the scale of the interior had been steadfastly set by Michelangelo's huge piers beneath the dome, and Maderno was bound to continue the same proportions. The vaulting thus rises a little more than 150 feet above the pavement, and the enormous interior covers more than 25,000 square yards.

The exterior of the church Michelangelo planned can best be seen from the apse and the interior from beneath the dome, where it still looks like the compact unified structure he wanted. From the apse of the completed church (Fig. 10.17), where the lengthened nave does not detract, the effect is still substantially as Michelangelo intended it to be. From this vantage point, the building seems like a great podium for the support of the vast superstructure. From ground level to the base of the dome, there is a rise of about 250 feet. The cupola then continues upward to the top of the

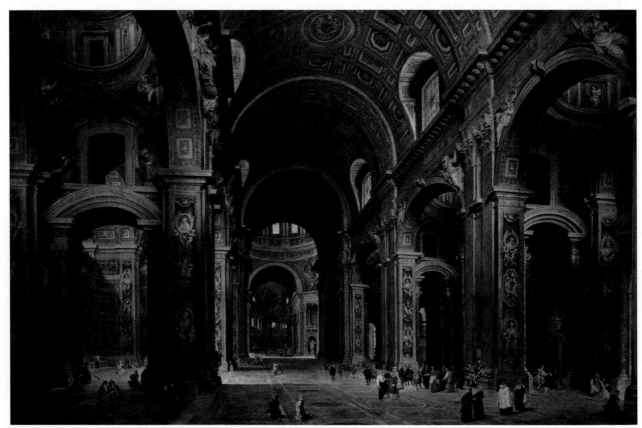

10.15   Giovanni Paolo Pannini. *Cardinal Melchoir de Polignac visiting the basilica of Saint Peter's, Rome,* 1730. Oil on canvas, approx. 5′¾″ × 6′5½″. Louvre, Paris, France.

lantern tower, where its ultimate height of 452 feet is attained.

JOSQUIN DESPREZ AND THE SISTINE CHAPEL CHOIR

In a book on Dante published in 1567, a Florentine literary historian wrote,

> I am well aware that in his day Ockeghem was as it were the first to rediscover music, then as good as dead, just as Donatello discovered sculpture in his; and that of Josquin, Ockeghem's pupil, one might say that he was a natural prodigy in music, just as our own Michelangelo Buonarroti has been in architecture, painting, and sculpture; for just as Josquin has still to be surpassed in his compositions, so Michelangelo stands alone and without a peer among all who have practiced his arts; and the one and the other have opened the eyes of all who delight in these arts, now and in the future.

Almost half a century after his death, Josquin Desprez was regarded as a figure comparable to Michelangelo. A Florentine could bestow no higher praise. This opinion, moreover, was also held by musicians. The distinguished theorist Glareanus wrote that the work of Josquin was "the perfect art to which nothing can be added, after which nothing but decline can be expected." The so-called ***ars perfecta,*** or "perfect art," rested on the assumption that the most advanced level of development has been achieved by the arts in antiquity. The Renaissance composers sought to regain the perfection of ancient music.

Italians took great pride in the achievements of their own architects, sculptors, and painters. Nevertheless, they universally acknowledged the supremacy of the northern composers. The spread of the northern polyphonic art dated from the period when the papacy was centered in Avignon. Later, the taste for polyphonic music led to the establishment of the Cappella Sistina in 1473, which was dominated by Flemish, Burgundian, and French musicians. Their influence spread over the entire Christian world. From this time forward, the contrapuntal writing of these artists became the standard of perfection.

Under Pope Sixtus IV, church music had progressed from its status as a modest servant of the liturgy to a position of major importance. The grandeur of the Roman liturgical displays called for music of comparable magnificence. Owing to the prevailing taste of the time, musicians from the great singing centers of Antwerp, Liège, and Cambrai flocked to Rome. The highest honor for a musician was an appointment to the Sistine Choir, which performed on occasions when the pope officiated.

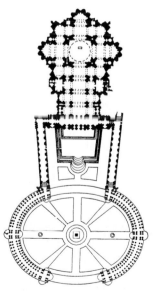

10.16　St. Peter's. Plan of present complex.

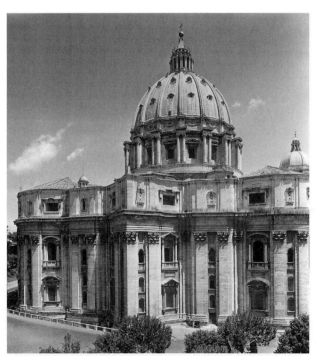

10.17　Michelangelo. View of apse and dome, St. Peter's, Rome, Italy, begun 1547. Height of dome 452′.

Membership in the Sistine Choir was highly selective, totaling from sixteen to twenty-four singers, except during the time of Pope Leo, who increased it to thirty-six. These singers were divided into four parts: boy sopranos, male altos, tenors, and basses. Normally they sang **a cappella**—that is, "in the chapel manner," without instrumental accompaniment—a practice that was considered exceptional rather than usual at the time.

The quality of this choir can be deduced from the list of distinguished people who made their reputations in its ranks. In the archives are numerous masses, motets, and psalm settings composed by Josquin Desprez during his service there from 1486 to 1494. Giovanni Palestrina, who studied Josquin's contrapuntal technique, became a member in 1551 and brought the organization to the pinnacle of technical perfection.

In Josquin's compositions the stark, barren intervals of Gothic polyphony and all traces of harshness in the harmonies are eliminated. He allows dissonance to occur only on weak beats or as suspensions on the stronger ones. His rhythms and forms are based on strict symmetry and mathematically regular proportions. Like much music stemming from northern traditions, his writing is characterized by imitation of a melody by successive voice parts, in the manner of a **canon,** as well as other complicated contrapuntal constructions. He manages these devices masterfully, and his tremendous compositional technique never intrudes on the expressive content.

Although Josquin was at home in all Renaissance musical forms, he excelled in his motets and in his solo and choral songs. In Rome, where his talent was influenced by the warm, liquid smoothness of Italian lyricism, Josquin's music mellowed until it achieved a level of incomparable beauty, clarity, and expressiveness.

Josquin's four-part motet *Ave Maria* is an admirable illustration of his art. Like Michelangelo's early *Pietà* (Fig. 10.4), it has a perfectly self-contained form, emotionally restrained and full of luxuriantly flowing lines. Even the short excerpt reproduced in Musical Example 10.1 shows his love of canonic imitation between the voices and the smoothness of contour that comes with stepwise melodic motion.

Josquin treats all four voices with balanced impartiality but prefers to group them in pairs, as in the example, to achieve a transparency of texture and purity of sound. Darker sides of Josquin's emotional spectrum can be found in his requiem masses and his setting of the psalm *De Profundis.*

Although Josquin enjoyed universal acclaim as the greatest musical mind of the early sixteenth century, the very perfection of his art implied that it was on the verge of becoming outdated. A number of composers in the succeeding generation carried his art to its logical conclusion. Palestrina served as master of St. Peter's Julian choir and enjoyed the title of "Master of Composition" to the papal chapel until his death later in the century. Meanwhile, Tomás Luis de Victoria carried the style to Spain, William Byrd brought it to England, and through Philippe de Monte and Orlande de Lassus, it spread throughout France and Germany. In the seventeenth century, although the art was still studied, it became known as the "antique style," in contrast to baroque music, which was called the "modern style." Within its limitations the style has never been surpassed.

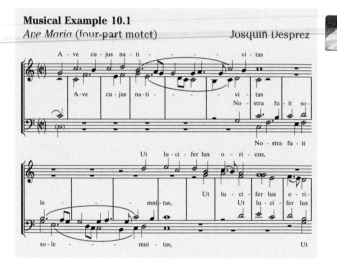

Musical Example 10.1
Ave Maria (four-part motet)   Josquin Desprez

IDEAS: HUMANISM

REVIVAL OF CLASSICAL FORMS

Florentine humanism and its Roman aftermath rested on a reappraisal of the values of Greco-Roman antiquity. An attempt was made to reconcile pagan forms with Christian practices, to reinstate the philosophy of Plato, and to reinterpret that of Aristotle. Above all, Renaissance humanists used antiquity to discover the nature of this world and human values. They were not primarily religiously or scientifically minded and tended to substitute the authority of respected classical writers for that of the Bible and church dogma. They found more convenient and convincing precedents in the civilizations of Greece and

Rome than in the medieval past. Lorenzo de' Medici, for instance, saw a new orientation for secular government in Plato's *Republic*. Niccolò Machiavelli found a model for writing history in Thucydides's accounts of his own time. Bramante made a new adaptation of the Greco-Roman temple for Christian worship.

Bramante's Tempietto (Fig. 10.18) was a conscious revival of the rounded structures of antiquity (see Figs. 4.20A, 4.21, and 4.25). This temple in miniature, coming as it did at the outset of the sixteenth century, became the architectural prototype for the Roman Renaissance, just as Brunelleschi's Pazzi Chapel (see Figs. 9.3 and 9.4) had been for the fifteenth-century Florentine Renaissance. Placed in the cloistered courtyard of the Church of San Pietro in Montorio, the little temple rests on the site where St. Peter is supposed to have been crucified.

Bramante chose the simple yet monumental Doric architectural order. He held to the classical principle of the module, whereby all parts of the building are either multiples or fractions of the basic unit of measure. He also promoted the feeling of balance and proportion by making the height and width of the lower floor equal to that of the upper story. The only formal decorative element is in the Doric frieze, with regular triglyphs alternating with metopes that employ a shell motif.

Above all, Bramante wished to demonstrate the cohesiveness and compactness of the centralized plan under the unifying crown of a cupola. Later, when Pope Julius entrusted him with the design of the new St. Peter's, Bramante had a chance to build on a monumental scale. Here again he turned to antiquity for inspiration and is reputed to have declared, "I shall place the Pantheon on top of the Basilica of Constantine."

The humanists preferred purer versions of classical art forms to the adaptations that had been made in the thousand-year period between the fall of Rome and their own time. The members of the Florentine humanistic circle learned to read and speak ancient Greek under native tutors. Marsilio Ficino translated the dialogues of Plato, and Angelo Poliziano translated Homer from the original Greek into Italian and wrote essays in Latin on Greek poetic and musical theory. Other scholars catalogued and edited books for the Medici library, and Squarcialupi compiled the musical compositions of the preceding century.

The interest in cataloguing, editing, translating, and commenting was pursued with such enthusiasm that it all but blotted out the production of new literature. The Latin of Renaissance schol-

ars was that of the Roman orator Cicero rather than medieval Latin, which they believed had become corrupted over time. The architects read Vitruvius and preferred central-plan churches modeled on the Pantheon to the rectangular basilica form that had evolved over the centuries. They revived the classical orders and architectural proportions in more authentic forms. Decorative motifs were derived directly from ancient sarcophagi, reliefs, and carved gems. Sculptors reaffirmed the possibilities of the nude, and it became the chief expressive vehicle of Michelangelo's art. Painters, lacking major models from antiquity, used mythological subjects and literary descriptions of ancient works.

Musicians reinterpreted Greek musical thought, and some actually attempted to put into practice the theories expounded in Euclid's essay on music. The Greek assertion that art imitates nature was universally acknowledged, but in architecture and music this had to be applied in the general sense of nature as an orderly and regular system conforming to mathematical proportions and laws. Josquin Desprez was hailed as a modern Orpheus who had regained the perfect art of antiquity, although the

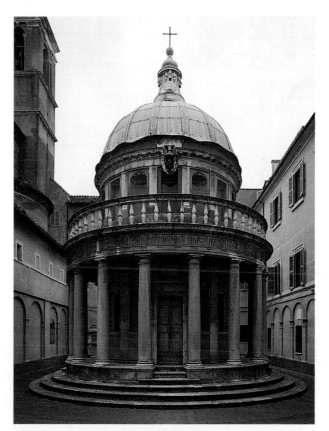

10.18 Donato Bramante. Tempietto, San Pietro in Montorio, Rome, Italy, 1502(?). Marble, height 46', diameter of colonnade 29'.

Greeks and ancient Romans would have been bewildered by his musical style. Josquin's less enthusiastic admirers pointed out that the trees and stones did not follow him the way they had followed the Orpheus of mythology. His art, however, like that of Michelangelo, was thought by the humanists to be a path back to a classical paradise.

PAGAN VERSUS CHRISTIAN IDEALS

Both Botticelli and Michelangelo set out to produce works in the classical spirit. The literary ancestry of Botticelli's *Allegory of Spring (Primavera)* and *The Birth of Venus* (see Figs. 9.23 and 9.24) has been traced through the poetry of Poliziano back to that of the Roman poets Lucretius and Horace. Their philosophical ancestor, however, is the Plato of the *Symposium,* who deals with the nature of physical and spiritual love and the function of beauty. According to Plato's theory, human beings have forgotten their divine origin. Falling in love with a beautiful person reminds them of their natural affinity for beauty. From physical attraction and fleeting loveliness they are led to thoughts of the lasting beauty of truth and, finally, to contemplation of the eternal verities of absolute beauty, truth, and goodness. Venus is, of course, the image of this transcendent beauty, and the way to approach it is through love.

Michelangelo's Plato, however, was the Plato of the *Timaeus,* who dwells on the creation of the world, the spiritual nature of the human soul, and the return to God. Unlike Botticelli, who had a dream of fragile beauty, Michelangelo had a vigorous vision of the creative process itself. When Botticelli came under the influence of the fiery moralist Savonarola, with his resurgence of medievalism, he repented of his paganism and painted only religious pictures.

Botticelli never tried to combine paganism and Christianity as Michelangelo did; for him, they remained separate compartments. Michelangelo, however, had the mind to assimilate Platonic abstractions, the overwhelming urge to express his ideas, and the technical skill to translate them into dramatic visual form. But the voice of Savonarola spoke loudly to him, too, and Michelangelo wrestled with the two essentially irreconcilable philosophies for the rest of his life. Leonardo da Vinci, by contrast, kept the religious themes of his painting and his scientific inquiries in separate intellectual compartments.

Michelangelo's Madonnas reveal the accord between mortal beauty and eternal beauty, his *Moses* links human moral power with eternal goodness, and his organic compositions connect the truth of historical time with eternal truth. His triple divisions symbolizing the Platonic stages of the soul as it progresses from its bodily tomb to its liberation and reunion with God are a constantly recurring theme. Even in the abstract architectural forms of St. Peter's this concern with the progress of the soul is apparent. The pilasters, like imprisoned columns, are the "slaves" held down by the weight of the heavy burden they must carry. Overhead soars the lofty dome in the geometric perfection of the circular form, symbolizing the paradise that humanity has lost and must somehow regain. The whole building is thus conceived of as an organic system of upward pressures and tensions, reaching its highest point at a cupola that ascends toward the divine realm.

─────── **YOUR RESOURCES** ───────

- *Exploring Humanities CD-ROM*

  ○ Interactive Map: Europe in the Sixteenth Century

  ○ Readings—Vasari, excerpts from *Life of Michelangelo,* excerpts from *Life of da Vinci*

- *Web Site*

  http://art.wadsworth.com/fleming10

  ○ Chapter 10 Quiz

  ○ Links—Online Readings: Tasso, *Jerusalem Delivered*

- *Audio CD*

  ○ Josquin Desprez, *Ava Maria*

LATE FIFTEENTH-CENTURY AND EARLY SIXTEENTH-CENTURY ROME

Key Events	Architecture	Visual Arts	Literature and Music
			c. 1440–1521 **Josquin Desprez** ❑
	c. 1444–1514 **Donato Bramante** ★	c. 1450–1523 **Luca Signorelli** ▲	
	1473–1480 **Sistine Chapel** built	1452–1519 **Leonardo da Vinci** ▲	
		1452–1513 **Bernardino Pinturicchio** ▲	
		c. 1467–1529 **Andrea Sansovino** ●	1469–1527 **Niccolò Machiavelli** ◆
1471–1527 **Roman Renaissance;** art and humanism at climax	1475–1564 **Michelangelo Buonarroti** ★	1475–1564 **Michelangelo Buonarroti** ●▲	1474–1533 **Ludovico Ariosto** ◆
1471–1484 **Sixtus IV** (della Rovere) pope		1481–1482 **Sistine Chapel** side-wall frescoes painted by Rosselli, Ghirlandaio, Botticelli, Perugino, Signorelli, Piero di Cosimo	1478–1529 **Baldassare Castiglione** ◆
1484–1492 **Innocent VIII** (Cibò) pope			1483–1546 **Martin Luther** ◆
1492–1503 **Alexander VI** (Borgia) pope		1493–1506 **Ancient Roman** frescoes and statues uncovered; *Apollo Belvedere, Laocoön Group* excavated	1483–1520 **Raphael (Raffaello Sanzio)**
			1486–1492 **Josquin Desprez** in Sistine Chapel choir
		1496–1501 **Michelangelo** in Rome working on *Bacchus* and *Pietà* statues	

1500

Key Events	Architecture	Visual Arts	Literature and Music
1503–1513 **Julius II** (della Rovere) pope		1500–1571 **Benvenuto Cellini** ●	
	1506 **New Basilica of St. Peter** begun by Bramante; Old St. Peter's razed	1505–1545 **Michelangelo** worked on Julius II's tomb	
		1508–1511 **Raphael** painted Vatican Palace frescoes	1511–1574 **Giorgio Vasari** ◆
		1508–1512 **Michelangelo** painted Sistine Chapel ceiling	1513 **Capella Giulia** founded to perform in St. Peter's
1513–1521 **Leo X** (Medici) pope		1513–1516 **Leonardo da Vinci** in Rome	1515 **Ludovico Ariosto** wrote *Orlando Furioso (Madness of Roland)*
1517 **Protestant Reformation** began in Germany with Luther's 95 Theses			1515–1564 **Michelangelo** wrote sonnets and other poems
1521 **Luther** excommunicated			c. 1521–1603 **Philippe de Monte** ❑
1523–1534 **Clement VII** (Medici) pope		1523 **Michelangelo** worked on Medici tombs in Florence	c. 1525–1594 **Giovanni da Palestrina** ❑
1527 **Rome** sacked by Emperor Charles V; Pope Clement VII imprisoned			1528 **Baldassare Castiglione's** *The Courtier* published
1534–1549 **Paul III** (Farnese) pope		1534–1541 **Michelangelo** painted *Last Judgment* fresco in Sistine Chapel	c. 1532–1594 **Orlande de Lassus** ❑
			1532 **Niccolò Machiavelli's** *The Prince* published
1534 **Church of England** separated from Rome; reaction to Renaissance humanism began		1542 **Michelangelo** painted frescoes in Pauline Chapel	1534 **Reaction to Renaissance humanism** began
			1544–1595 **Torquato Tasso** ◆
	1546 **Michelangelo** named architect of St. Peter's		1548–1600 **Giordano Bruno** ◆
	1556–1629 **Carlo Maderno** ★		1550 **Giorgio Vasari's** *Lives of the Most Eminent Painters, Sculptors, and Architects* published
			c. 1550 **Philippe de Monte** in Rome; first book of madrigals published 1554
	1590 **St. Peter's dome** completed by Giacomo della Porta		1551 **Orlande de Lassus** in Rome
	1607–1614 **Carlo Maderno** completed nave and facade of St. Peter's		1562 **Torquato Tasso** wrote *Rinaldo*
			1575 **Tasso** wrote *Jerusalem Delivered*

★ – Architect   ❑ – Musician   ▲ – Painter   ● – Sculptor   ◆ – Writer

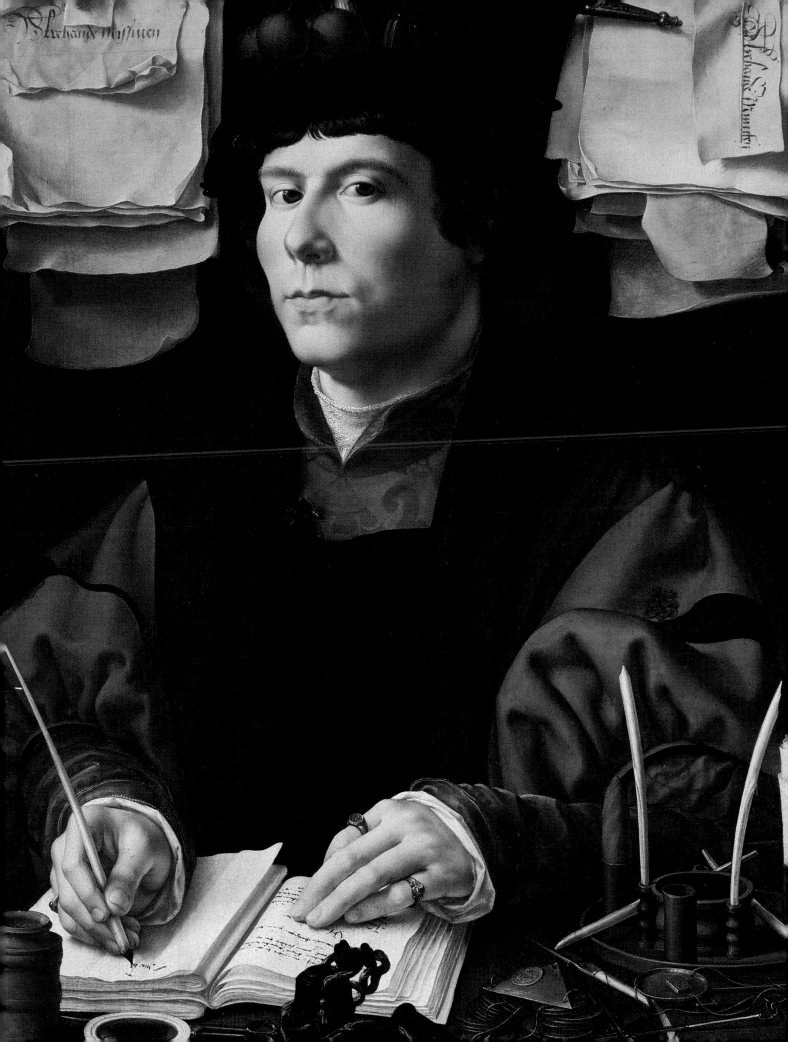

C H A P T E R

11

N O R T H E R N   R E N A I S S A N C E
A N D   R E F O R M A T I O N   S T Y L E S

THE RENAISSANCE DEVELOPED MORE GRADUALLY and diffusely in the northern countries than in the South. There were no sudden, distinctive regional manifestations of a new style, as there had been in Florence. Nor did the North experience the presence of classical antiquity as a foremost inspiration, as did Italy. Renaissance thought and action in the North was a selective maturation of ideas present in the late Middle Ages, such as the use of symbols to enhance the meaning of an image. In the North, artists tended toward increased awareness of the natural environment and acute observation of the visible world. They were fascinated with what the eye could see, the mind could comprehend, and the heart could feel and attempt to represent. Also, women painters in the North were somewhat freer to join guilds and to pursue a full-time profession in art. For example, Caterina van Hemessen, who was trained by her father, a painter, emerged as a prominent figure in Antwerp, and eventually at the Spanish court (Fig. 11.1). She was adept at bringing out the rich tonalities and luster that oil paints, a Northern invention, brought to the visual experience of art.

The early fifteenth century saw a variety of reactions against the excesses and worldly interests of the upper echelon of church officials. The so-called modern devotion, a lay movement with its roots in the fourteenth century, gripped parish priests and believers. It proclaimed that individuals could and should interpret the Bible for themselves rather than relying solely on the clergy. In addition, modern devotion questioned the need for the Virgin and the saints to intercede with God on behalf of sinners. This "protestant" faction produced leaders like Martin Luther and John Calvin, who challenged the church to reform itself. In the North, strong feelings about how reform should take place resulted in civil unrest and open conflict. Ultimately, the Church of Rome lost its hold on much of Northern Europe and England. The Eu-

ropean religious unity that had prevailed for many centuries collapsed, and a new outlook on humans' relationship to God and authority emerged.

The church reacted with its own reform movement, formulated at the Council of Trent, a city in northern Italy. In a series of meetings beginning in 1545 and lasting until 1563, church officials attempted to wipe out abuses of power and money. At the same time, they reinforced the necessity for priests and the sacraments. Moreover, they underscored the importance of the Virgin and the saints. The Council of Trent concluded that the arts should function within a narrow scope, literally

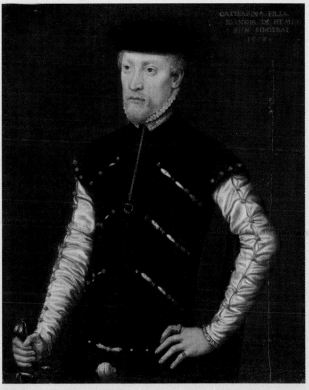

11.1 Caterina van Hemessen. *Portrait of a Man,* c. 1550. Oil on wood, approx. 1′2″ × 11½″. National Gallery, London, England.

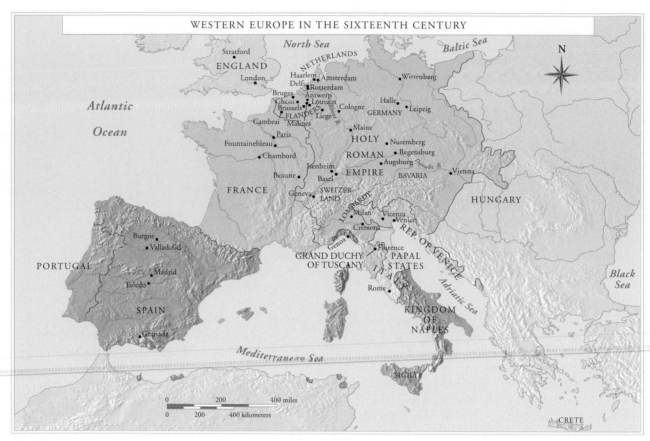

MAP 11.1

depicting Bible stories and other sacred texts. In 1542, even before the Council of Trent, a church commission that became known as the Inquisition set about rooting out heresy. Soon it turned to trials and torture to enforce religious conformity. In large part, the orthodoxy of the Council of Trent and the violence perpetrated by the Inquisition further severed the North from the South.

The center of gravity of northern Europe was in the Low Countries, especially in Flanders. Because of the discovery of America, as well as the establishment of Atlantic trade routes to Asia, commercial activity began to shift from the Mediterranean to the Atlantic coast. Through a combination of fortuitous circumstances and political skill, Philip the Good, the Duke of Burgundy, had brought most of this territory under his rule. His decision to make the Flemish seaport city of Bruges his capital was a momentous one, both for commerce and for the arts. Soon the term *Flemish* came into common usage to describe all the peoples of the Low Countries, including the schools of painters and musicians for which the region was so famous. Later in the sixteenth century, through a series of dynastic marriages and territorial consolidations, the Low Countries came under the dominion of the formidable Emperor Charles V, who was also the king of Spain, lord of the Spanish overseas empire, ruler of Germany and Austria, and conqueror of Italy. Meanwhile, England under Henry VII and Henry VIII had already achieved nationhood, with London as its flourishing political and cultural center.

THE NORTHERN SCENE

Northern artists and composers lived in an adventuresome age. As journeymen seeking commissions, they traveled all over Europe. The Flemish painter Jan van Eyck was active at the courts of both John of Holland and Philip of Burgundy. The German artist Albrecht Dürer's home was in Nuremberg, but he traveled extensively in Italy and the Low Countries. His countryman Hans Holbein the Younger, who was born in Augsburg, made his career in Switzerland and at the court of Henry VIII in England. John Dowland, the English lutenist and foremost songwriter of his time, worked mainly in London, but he traveled widely in Italy and Germany and held posts at the courts of the Duke of Brunswick and the king of Denmark. The great Flemish-born composer Orlande de Lassus was a complete cosmopolitan, active in Sicily, Naples, Rome, and Antwerp before settling at the ducal court at Bavaria.

THE COMMERCIAL REVOLUTION IN THE NORTH

The importance and prosperity of the Low Countries stood on two main pillars. First was the flourishing textile trade, evidenced by the fine wool and linen cloth that was sent all over Europe. On a more limited and luxurious level, the region was also renowned for its tapestries, lace, rugs, cloth of gold, and costly glazed pottery and dishes. Next, its sea and river ports were busy scenes of shipping, distribution, and bartering for goods from all over the known world. With the rapid growth of the northern cities, the commercial center of gravity began to shift from the Mediterranean ports of Venice, Genoa, Marseilles, and Barcelona to those of the North Sea. For example, Dutch merchant ships carried their cargoes south to Lisbon, where they picked up spices and imported goods from India and Africa and transported them back north. The cities of Bruges, Antwerp, and Cologne were the main marketplaces for the exchange of goods, and as a result, they were the principal financial centers of northern Europe.

The accumulation of wealth by the merchant class began to reduce the importance of land ownership as the primary source of wealth. Of course, land continued to produce the food supply and raw materials, but commercial growth favored the merchants. The large fortunes amassed by some families gave them both increasing political importance and the means to become patrons of the arts.

The growing importance of the commercial revolution is graphically captured by Jan Gossaert in his *Portrait of a Merchant* (Fig. 11.2). Pen in hand, the merchant works on a ledger. Nearby are the tools of his trade: an inkpot, scissors, scales to weigh the coins, some sealing wax, and extra quill pens. Miscellaneous letters are seen above and left on the wall, and on the right are various business drafts. The painting itself reveals the deep coloring of the oil medium, which was being developed in the North.

EXPANDING HORIZONS

In the northern universities, scientists and humanistic scholars were freer in their inquiries and speculations than their counterparts in Italy and Spain, where the church imposed stricter controls. The beginnings of scientific geography, for instance, received great impetus from the expansion of northern commerce and the opening of new trade routes, and particularly from the discoveries of the great navigators. Observing the winds and sea currents, mapping shorelines and landmarks, studying the

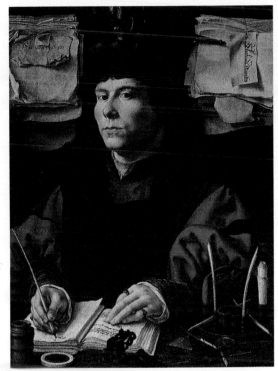

11.2   Jan Gossaert. *Portrait of a Merchant,* c. 1530. Oil on panel, 2′1″ × 1′6¾″. National Gallery of Art, Washington, D.C.

stars and developing mathematics, and inventing mariners' instruments were all activities related to a vastly expanding experience of the world.

The spread of such learning by means of the new printing presses that sprang up in southern Germany, Bruges, Amsterdam, and London became one of the crowning achievements of the Northern Renaissance. The production of books soon became an industry. Gutenberg's beautiful Bible was printed around 1456. The English printer William Caxton published the first book in English at Bruges in 1474. Through printing, *Imitation of Christ,* probably written by Thomas à Kempis, became Europe's most popular book after the Bible. Printing also quickly spread scientific knowledge. In 1543, Flemish scientist Andreas Vesalius revolutionized the study of anatomy with his book *On the Structure of the Human Body.* In the same year, the astronomer Copernicus turned the reigning worldview inside out by showing in his book *On the Revolution of the Celestial Bodies* that Earth was but one of several planets revolving around the sun, instead of vice versa. Of course, the major revolution brought on by printing was a quiet one: education by means of books gave more people access to knowledge and hastened the development of a middle class.

Printing by means of wooden blocks or metal casts was invented in China and Korea centuries before it appeared in Europe. It is unclear whether

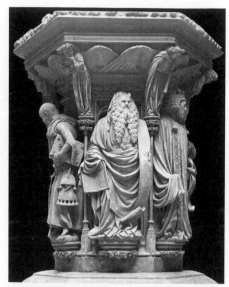

11.3 Claus Sluter. *Well of Moses,* detail of Moses, 1395–1403. Height 10′6″, height of figures approx. 6′. Chartreuse de Champmol, Dijon, France.

printing was developed independently in Europe or whether it was learned through contact with Asia. Similarly, the compass and gunpowder are Asian inventions that Europeans used extensively. The compass enabled northern sailors to set out on distant oceans, and cannons and firearms supported the expansion of trade and the establishment of colonies.

Turbulent times shaped the Northern Renaissance. Although artists from the North and the South continued to view each other's work, in general the North affirmed cultural independence from the dominance of the Mediterranean South, which had begun in Greco-Roman times and continued through the Middle Ages, augmented by the power of the Church of Rome. In commerce, the North wrested control of shipping and trade from the southern ports. In addition, tensions grew between the prosperous towns and the feudal landholding nobles. In political life, the international outlook of the Church of Rome (and its secular

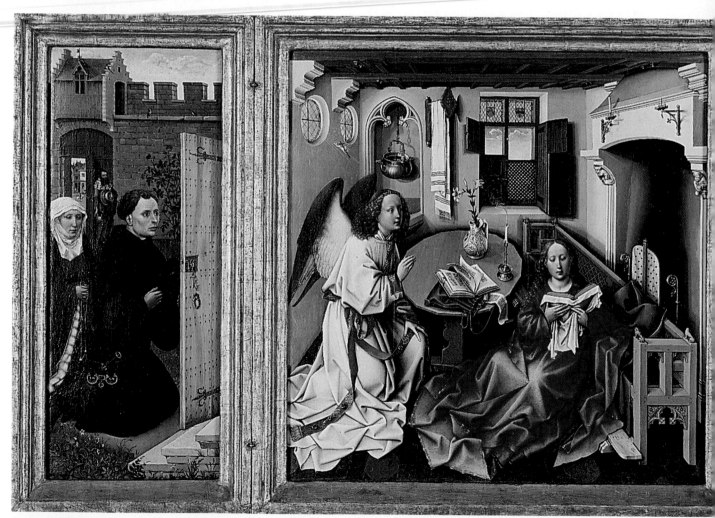

11.4 Robert Campin (Master of Flémalle). *Merode Altarpiece* (open), c. 1425–1428. Tempera and oil on wood, center panel approx. 2′1″ × 2′1″. Metropolitan Museum of Art, New York, Cloister Collection Purchase.

arm, the Holy Roman Empire) confronted the rising tide of national movements in the Low Countries and England. In religion, a tumultuous series of splits among the various Protestant movements in Germany, the Low Countries, and England set factions against one another and against those loyal to Rome. Bitter as they were, these tensions and conflicts did not stifle the arts. The Flemish and German painters Jan van Eyck, Hugo van der Goes, and Albrecht Dürer and the Flemish composers Guillaume Dufay, Josquin Desprez, and Orlande de Lassus became powerful influences all over Europe, including France, Italy, and Spain.

Architecture continued to develop along late Gothic lines, influenced only minimally by the striking innovations associated with the Italian Renaissance. Painting also flourished in a unique way, especially in the artists' acute and accurate observations of nature. Except in the case of Dürer, there were few traces of southern classicism. The important technical breakthrough of oil painting, however, swept all before it. With oils, painters could achieve deep, glowing colors; intense tonalities; and striking lighting effects. Northern oil techniques soon spread far and wide, especially to various Italian centers. Flemish paintings were also in demand in international centers, including Italy, where collectors included the ducal courts of Naples, Ferrara, and Urbino as well as Lorenzo de' Medici in Florence. Productivity in literature, except in England, was more restricted. The struggle between the reformers and Roman Catholics led to tight censorship of printed materials under the Spaniards and the Holy Roman emperors. In music, Flemish composers were the acknowledged leaders throughout Europe. Throughout the period, central tensions arose from a new critical humanism, itself a product of the Reformation movement.

ART IN THE NORTH

When Philip the Bold, the Duke of Burgundy and grandfather of Philip the Good, founded a Carthusian monastery outside his capital city of Dijon, he summoned skilled craftspeople throughout Europe. Among them was Claus Sluter from Haarlem in Holland, who brought the carver's art to new heights of expression. His works include a group of life-size figures surrounding a well in the middle of a courtyard (Fig. 11.3). This so-called *Well of Moses* consists of a group of Old Testament prophets who carry scrolls foretelling the Passion and Death of Christ. The carving reveals an extraordinary receptiveness for naturalistic detail. Likewise, the voluminous, deep-cut drapery creates a rhythm of curved lines that animates the surrounding space. The prophets' grave, expressive faces are not generalizations but rather seem like portraits of living individuals. When originally painted in lifelike colors (one of them had actual gold-framed eyeglasses), the figures must have created an overwhelming impression. The monumentality and grandeur of Sluter's work sets him apart as a figure comparable to Donatello (see Fig. 9.10). His work was known throughout the Low Countries, and his influence on painting was as profound as it was on sculpture.

Painting in Flanders

The vigilant political management enforced by Philip the Good and his successors on Flanders's rich commercial centers did not extend to control of the visual arts. Outstanding among fifteenth-century works is the *Merode Altarpiece* (Fig. 11.4), long identified with the anonymous Master of Flémalle, a town in the region. It is now generally

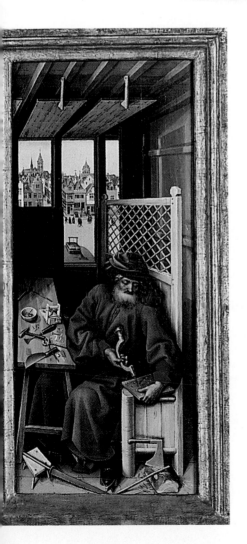

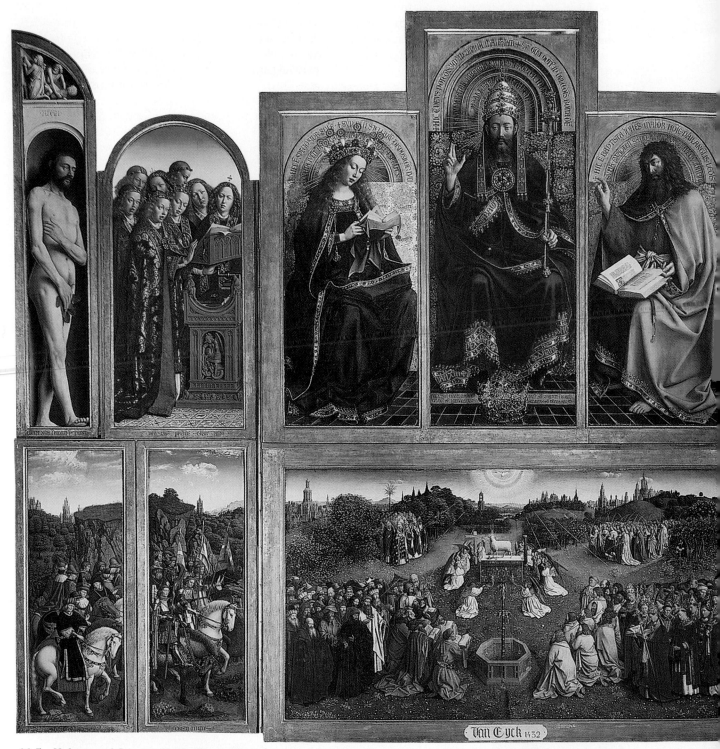

11.5 Hubert and Jan van Eyck. *Ghent Altarpiece* (open). "Adoration of the Lamb," detail, completed 1432. Oil on wood, approximately 11′6″ × 15′1″. Cathedral of St. Bavo, Ghent, Belgium.

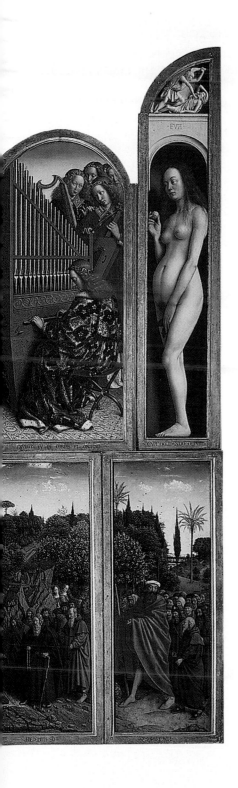

attributed to the painter Robert Campin. The subject is the Annunciation, as seen in the center panel. Mary is absorbed in her reading, seemingly not yet aware of the angel's presence. On the left in a courtyard garden are the kneeling donors, who look through the open door to view the event occurring within. On the right panel, Joseph is portrayed in his carpenter shop next door. The central scene is set in a comfortable middle-class chamber with soft light flowing in through the windows. The painter has succeeded in representing a supernatural event in familiar, contemporary surroundings. Even the conventional haloes have been omitted.

Yet beneath the apparent story is a subtle, extensive program of religious symbols that originated in medieval times but were brought up to date in an everyday domestic setting by the artist. For example, the lily-filled vase on the table refers to Mary's purity, and the rosebush and flowers in the courtyard are also sacred to the Virgin. Part of the program is derived from Isaiah, the Old Testament prophet who foretold the coming of the Messiah. It is from this book that the Madonna seems to be reading the words, "Behold a virgin shall conceive and bear a son" (Isaiah 7:14). The water jug and towel on the back wall denote the Virgin as the "vessel most clean" and may also allude to baptism.

On the right, Joseph has an ax, a rod, and a saw, which are noted in Isaiah 10:15. The ax "laid into the root of the trees" refers to the fate of sinners (Matthew 3:10); the rod is Joseph's, the one that bloomed miraculously in the Temple to signify that he was chosen to be Mary's spouse. The saw refers to the grisly death of Isaiah himself. Thus, the picture can be appreciated on many different levels.

A CHALLENGE TO NATURE: JAN VAN EYCK

The continuing exchange between Northern and Southern artists was verified by Giovanni Santi, a painter and the father of the Italian master Raphael, who remarked that the art of Jan van Eyck "challenges nature itself." Indeed, van Eyck's fame rests on his sensitivity to color, his eye for precision, his exquisite description of the minutest detail, and his technical innovations in the oil medium. He was fortunate to enjoy the patronage and friendship of Philip the Good, for whom he executed delicate diplomatic missions as well as commissions for paintings. He also received commissions from Joos Vijd, a minor noble who earned his wealth from the wool trade. Vijd sponsored the *Ghent Altarpiece.*

This magnificent altarpiece, signed by Jan van Eyck and his brother Hubert, is housed at the Cathedral of St. Bavo in Ghent (Fig. 11.5). The genesis of the work is still a matter of scholarly controversy, but the evidence seems to point to Hubert as the sculptor of the sumptuous Gothic tabernacle that once surrounded it, whereas Jan painted the twenty panels. Hubert's framework was demolished in the religious strife of the late sixteenth century. Forewarned, the clergy hid the painted panels, which have survived. Shorn of its frame, the work still stands in its original place, the memorial chapel sponsored by its donor and his wife. The form is that of a **polyptych** with many hinged panels that open and close like the pages of a book. The glowing luminosity and technical brilliance of the painting are undiminished by time. Like the *Merode Altarpiece,* it is simultaneously a visual feast and an intellectual exercise in church doctrine and symbolism.

When the great altarpiece is open, deep, radiant hues greet the viewer's eye with the Adoration of the Lamb in the lower middle section. The overall theme is the union of God and humanity as in the apocalyptic vision of St. John: "Behold, the tabernacle of God is with men, and he will dwell with them, and they shall be his people" (Revelation 21:3). The upper level is on the heavenly plane, whereas the lower represents the New Jerusalem of the book of Revelation. Above is the dominating figure of Christ. Robed in rich scarlet with gold trim and sparkling jewels, He wears a triple tiara like that worn by the pope. The three-part crown also indicates the three-part nature of God and His dominion over heaven, Earth, and the underworld. At his feet is a golden crown signifying that He is lord of lords and king of kings. The Virgin Mary, enthroned at his right, is clothed in bright blue with a crown of twelve stars from which spring lilies and roses, symbols of purity and love. John the Baptist is at his left, with an emerald green cloak over his camel hair undergarment. Spreading outward on both sides are choirs of angels in brocaded velvet gowns, singing and playing the organ, harp, and other instruments. It is unusual to find Adam and Eve on the heavenly level, but here, splendidly modeled, they represent redeemed humanity and God's love for humankind.

On the central axis, reading downward from God the Father, is the dove of the Holy Spirit in the sky below; the Lamb on the altar, connoting the redeeming sacrifice of Jesus, completes the Trinity. Then come the Fountain of Living Waters and the stream that flows through the green, flower-bedecked meadow: "And I John saw the holy city, new Jerusalem, coming down from God out of heaven . . . [and the angel showed me] a pure river of water of life, clear as crystal, proceeding out of the throne of God and of the Lamb" (Revelation 21:2–22:1).

From the four corners of Earth come the faithful, moving toward the altar of the Lamb. In the side panels are delegations symbolizing the four cardinal virtues: the judges stand for Justice; the knights on horseback, Fortitude; the pilgrims, Prudence; and the hermits, Temperance. Around the Fountain of Life on the left are the kneeling apostles and a group of red-robed martyrs. On the right are the evangelists with their gospel books and a group of prophets. The holy virgins come from the right background and the holy confessors from the left, while a chorus of angels encircles the altar. Taken as a whole, van Eyck's realization of the New Jerusalem is the summation of Christian aspirations.

A MARRIAGE OF NORTH AND SOUTH

Jan van Eyck's *The Marriage of Giovanni Arnolfini and Giovanna Cenami* (Fig. 11.6) is a reminder of the close ties between North and South. The shrewd and calculating Arnolfini, the Bruges agent of the Medici of Florence, was active in business and banking circles. He had risen to the rank of counselor to the Duke of Burgundy, who was also one of van Eyck's patrons. Both he and his bride were from the Italian town of Lucca in Tuscany. The picture is a record of their marriage vows. Before the Council of Trent made it one of the seven sacraments, marriage could be contracted in pri-

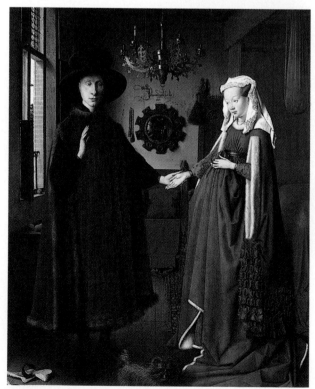

11.6 Jan van Eyck. *The Marriage of Giovanni Arnolfini and Giovanna Cenami,* 1434. Oil on wood, 2'8" × 1'11½". National Gallery, London, England.

vate by joining hands and pledging faith. The artist himself was a witness, as his beautifully lettered signature on the wall testifies: *Jan de Eyck fuit hic. 1434* (Jan van Eyck has been here, 1434).

At first glance, the picture seems to be a straightforward double portrait of nearly photographic realism. The meticulous rendering of every detail; the deft handling of perspective; and the contrasting textures of cloth, wood, fur, and metal are all depicted with naturalistic precision. Warm light coming from the open window accents the faces and hands of the subjects as well as the black velvet and apple green of their fashionable Burgundian costumes and the highly polished brass candelabrum and mirror. Gradually the light fades into the shadowy background. Van Eyck draws the viewer into the room with the device of the convex mirror that reflects the backs of the figures and two witnesses (one perhaps a self-portrait of the artist). Behind them, the doorway and wall complete the intimacy of the enclosed space.

Beyond this surface play, however, is an intricate and intriguing program of symbolism. In one influential interpretation, the dog stands for fidelity (*fides* in Latin; hence the popular name Fido). The apples refer to Adam and Eve in the Garden of Eden, the fall of man, and original sin. The ten miniature scenes surrounding the mirror tell of Christ's Passion, His death, and human salvation. The whisk broom represents domestic care. The statuette above the chair at the back is of Margaret, the patron saint of childbearing women (note that Giovanna's left hand is over her womb). The single lighted candle in the chandelier not only represents a Flemish marriage custom but also signifies the all-seeing eye of God, the light of the world.

In recent years, historical investigations have chipped away at the conventional view, pointing out that some of the symbolic references were not current at the time the picture was painted. As to the persistent question about whether the bride was pregnant, neither the conventional nor the new interpretations find any justification for it. In the custom of the time, the bride would have been a virgin. She has lifted her voluminous outer garment, whose extravagance indicated her wealth, perhaps to signal her consent to the marriage and its consummation.

A MEDICI TRIPTYCH: THE WORK OF HUGO VAN DER GOES

In the latter half of the fifteenth century, Tommaso Portinari, a shipowner and representative of the Medici banking interests in Bruges, commissioned an altarpiece for the Portinari Chapel in Sant'Egidio, Florence. Hugo van der Goes, the artistic heir of van Eyck, painted it in the form of a **triptych** (Fig. 11.7). In the left wing, he portrays the donor and his two sons kneeling and praying. Over them loom the large-scale figures of their patron saints, Anthony and Thomas, in melancholic and brooding attitudes. On the right side in similar postures are his wife and daughter with their saints, Margaret and Mary Magdalene.

The central panel depicts the adoration of the shepherds. Like van Eyck, Hugo closely observed naturalistic details, from the weather-beaten faces of the shepherds to the rich brocaded cloth of the angels' robes. The artist, however, created some spatial discrepancies to achieve dramatic effect: The floor tips slightly upward to project the figures forward. Hugo also observed the practice of depicting important people on a large scale. In this work, Mary, Joseph, and the shepherds in the middle ground loom larger than the angels in the foreground.

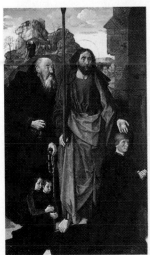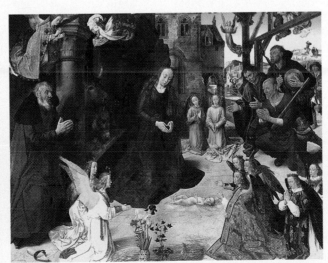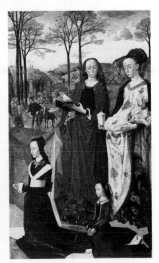

11.7 Hugo van der Goes. *Portinari Altarpiece,* c. 1476. Oil on wood, 8′3½″ × 10′ center panel, 8′3½″ × 4′7½″ each wing. Galleria degli Uffizi, Florence, Italy.

For Hugo, like van Eyck, details have symbolic significance. The building behind Mary is the palace of David, identified by the harp carved in the tympanum over the doorway. It refers to the fact that Mary and Jesus stemmed from the house of David. The presence of spring flowers in the dead of winter casts a miraculous atmosphere over the event. The sheaf of wheat alludes to Bethlehem, which means "house of bread" in Hebrew. The reference is also to the bread of the Eucharist, while the jar refers to the wine. The white lilies symbolize Mary's purity, the red roses refer to blood and suffering, and the irises ("swordflowers" in northern parlance) point to the pierced heart of the Madonna as the mother of sorrows. A psychological intensity characterizes the picture as a whole. Especially through the reading of symbols, the joyousness of Christ's birth is dampened by a sense of foreboding that foreshadows His sacrifice on the cross.

When the altarpiece reached Florence, its realism and depiction of human expression excited the painters who saw it. Domenico Ghirlandaio even adapted van Eyck's depiction of the humble shepherds for one of his pictures of the Nativity.

ART AND ALCHEMY: HIERONYMUS BOSCH

Hieronymus Bosch took his name from the last syllable of s'Hertogenbosch, the Flemish town where he was born and worked all his life. His was a time of social tension and religious unrest, a period in which people believed in witchcraft, sorcery, alchemy, and the coming of the antichrist. Bosch's art holds up a mirror not to nature but to humanity. It reflects the subconscious desires and drives that motivate human behavior. For the sources of his bizarre imagery, scholars have searched many sources, including the Bible, the lives of the saints as told in Jacobus de Voragine's *Golden Legend*, bestiaries, mystery plays, the writings of the mystics, Flemish proverbs and folklore, books on alchemy, drawings in manuscripts, and the fiery sermons and moralistic tracts of his time. His pictures have been interpreted as pre-Freudian psychoanalytic dreams, as premonitions of surrealism and fantastic art, and as satiric commentaries on the vanities and follies of his time. These enigmatic images can also be enjoyed for the way they delight the eye and challenge the imagination.

In the triptych *Garden of Earthly Delights* (Fig. 11.8), the viewer enters a world of magic and mystery conjured up by Bosch's inexhaustible imagination. When the wings are closed, one sees a giant sphere enclosing the world as it was on the third day of creation, when the dry land had been divided from the waters and the earth had brought forth grass, herbs, and trees. The colors are neutral grays and greens. In the upper left-hand corner, God is seen uttering the words, "For he spake and it was done" (Psalm 33:9). When the triptych is open, the spectator beholds a bright-colored vision, a phantasmagoria of fascinating forms. In the left panel, God has created Eve and brings her to the awakening Adam with the words, "Be fruitful, and multiply, and replenish the earth" (Genesis 1:28). Around them is a Noah's ark of

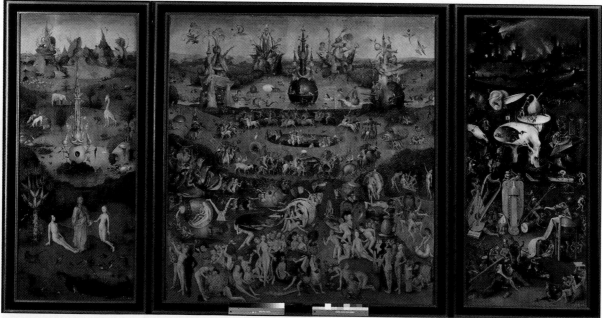

11.8 Hieronymus Bosch. *Garden of Earthly Delights* (open). *Creation of Eve* (left wing), *Hell* (right wing), 1505–1510. Oil on wood, 7′2⅝″ × 6′4¾″. Museo del Prado, Madrid, Spain.

animals, some natural, others imaginary. A spiraling flock of blackbirds flies out of a strange hollow rock; a dragon fights with a wild boar. The Fountain of Life, shaped like an intricately carved tabernacle, yields its waters, and a wise owl peers out from the pupil of the eye below. Nearby is a palm tree encircled by a serpent.

The garden of love that gives the triptych its name is depicted in the center panel. God's command to Adam and Eve to be fruitful and multiply is abundantly realized. Nude young men and women disport themselves in the crystal-clear light, making love in the alluring pastel-tinted spring landscape. They eat luscious fruits and gigantic strawberries, such as might have been imagined to exist at the beginning of the world. In the center, male riders, mounted on exotic animals as on a carousel, circle a pool filled with maidens who await their amorous advances. Strange, hornlike rock structures are silhouetted against the sky. Crustaceans, birds, and fish of both normal and monstrous size abound. Curiously enough, there are no children.

A grim and awesome day of reckoning is portrayed in the right panel, depicting Hell, where the lush dreams have now become arid nightmares. Here all nature is dead, and the spectral barkless trees accent the lifeless atmosphere. Below are the objects of sin: dice, cards, a backgammon board, a brothel scene, and a drunken brawl. Above are enormous musical instruments, allusions to the seductive power of music and dance, which have become objects of torture. One naked soul is tied to a lute, another enmeshed in the strings of a harp, and still another crammed into the bell of a large horn. The image of a man with an egg-shaped torso with decaying tree trunks for legs and boats for shoes is terrifying. On his head is a bagpipe, an obvious sexual symbol. On the far right, a devil makes a pact with a man who is goaded on by a monster whose legs are attached to his helmet. Nearby a man is tempted by a sow clothed in a nun's veil. Above, two huge ears are pierced by a lance with a projecting knife blade.

Although its format recalls that of a church altarpiece, the picture was obviously intended for a sophisticated lay patron, much as Sandro Botticelli's pagan classical allegories were in Florence (see Figs. 9.23 and 9.24). Philip II of Spain was one of Bosch's greatest admirers, and in 1593 this work was added to the royal collection.

THE WORK OF "PEASANT BRUEGEL"

Pieter Bruegel the Elder was the heir to Bosch's style, and many of his early paintings were directly inspired by the older master. Bruegel's main fame, however, rests solidly on the vivid scenes of rustic life that gave him his nickname, "Peasant Bruegel." Far from a peasant himself, he was a well-educated, prosperous painter who was welcome at the imperial court and numbered the cardinal-archbishop of Malines among his many patrons. His pictures depicting the pleasures and activities of farming people helped establish genre scenes as an important category of painting, one that carried over into the Dutch School of the seventeenth century.

The Peasants' Wedding (Fig. 11.9) is set in a barn stacked with hay. The bride sits on the right,

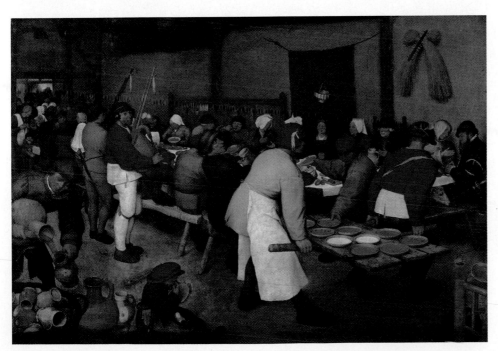

11.9 Pieter Bruegel the Elder. *The Peasants' Wedding* , c. 1568. Oil on wood, 3′8⅞″ × 5′4⅛″. Kunsthistorisches Museum, Vienna, Austria.

under a paper crown and against an improvised cloth of honor that is hung from a rope and fastened on the left by a pitchfork stuck in the hay. Grooms at such Flemish weddings were less important, and this bridegroom could be the figure stuffing himself in the center background. More likely he is the young man seated at the end of the table serving bowls of cereal from the unhinged door that serves as a tray. (It was the custom at the time for the groom to wait on the bride's family on such occasions.) The entertainers are playing bagpipes, the typical peasant instrument; one of them stares at the food with hungry eyes. At the far right, the bearded man in a black costume with a sword at his side has sometimes been identified as a self-portrait of the artist, based on resemblance to an earlier engraving. The crowded scene with its deep diagonal accent captures all the sturdy, stolid, and earthy qualities of people who live close to the soil.

Peasant life, however, was only one aspect of Bruegel's complex personality. He also devoted much attention to intricately constructed landscapes, such as *Hunters in the Snow* (Fig. 11.10), one of a projected series that would have depicted all the months. The bleak open spaces are enlivened by the interplay of sporting activities, with the tired hunters and their dogs in the foreground and skaters on frozen ponds in the background. In addition, Bruegel painted penetrating religious and moral allegories such as the *Fall of the Rebel Angels, The Deadly Sins,* and the grim *Triumph of Death,* as well as fantastic scenes dwelling on human folly such as *The Blind Leading the Blind.* He also pioneered the field of printmaking with many etchings and engravings.

PAINTERS IN GERMANY

In southern Germany, painters of great originality, imagination, and individuality rose to command international acclaim. Among them were Albrecht

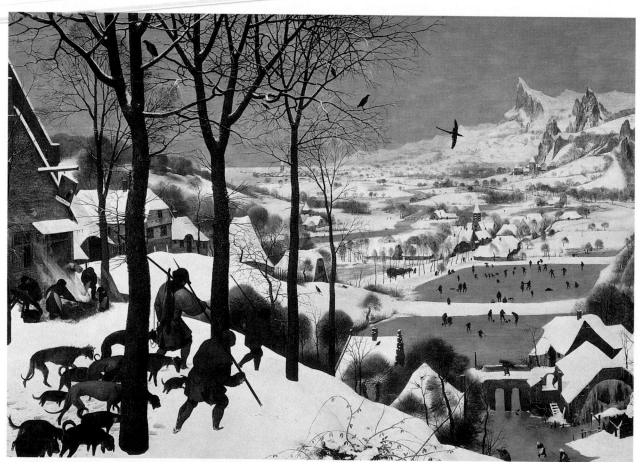

11.10   Pieter Bruegel the Elder. *Hunters in the Snow,* 1565. Oil and tempera on panel, approx. 3'10" × 5'4". Kunsthistorisches Museum, Vienna, Austria.

Dürer from Nuremberg; Matthias Grünewald, who was active in Mainz and other centers; and Hans Holbein the Younger, who worked in Switzerland and England.

INTERNATIONAL STUDY AND FAME: ALBRECHT DÜRER. Many German artists were attracted to the twin cultural centers of Bruges and Ghent, but in addition to studying the art of the North, Dürer blazed a trail over the Alps into Italy. He emerged as the primary interpreter of the classical Renaissance in the northern countries. His enormous productivity after his return from Italy is reflected in the woodcuts and engravings that poured from his own presses and led him to international fame.

Dürer created his first self-portraits as a teen, and he continued the practice throughout his life. His *Self-Portrait* (Fig. 11.11) bears the legend, "I made this according to my appearance when I was 26." His long curly hair frames his serious, searching expression. Dürer depicts himself against a background that is closed on one side; the other side opens out into a landscape painting with high mountains. Are these the Alps over which he traveled to study art in Venice? Or do they suggest a more sinister symbolism, perhaps of Germany itself, which endured a tortured century of peasant wars, internal dissents, and religious reformation? In either case, Dürer reveals himself not only as a confident, successful young master but also as thinker and writer concerned with meaning and subtlety.

Dürer's lifelong preoccupation with the accurate rendering of nature is seen in his *The Great Piece of Turf* (Fig. 11.12), in which he depicted a mundane clump of new spring vegetation at about life size. He resisted any urge to glamorize or dramatize this subject, which was literally below the gaze of most artists and viewers. The dandelions are a few days past their showy peak. Some strands of grass and a few broad furry leaves seem mired in the muddy clod, which Dürer has not disguised or excluded.

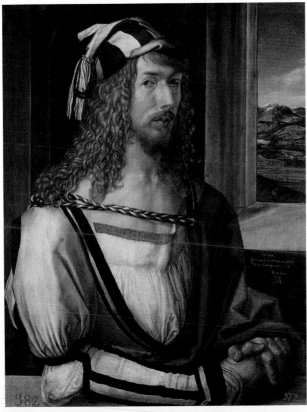

11.11   Albrecht Dürer. *Self-Portrait,* 1498. Oil on wood, 1′8½″ × 1′4⅛″. Museo del Prado, Madrid, Spain.

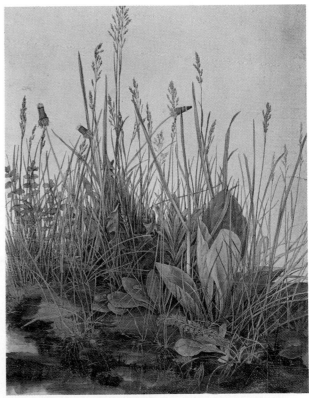

11.12   Albrecht Dürer. *The Great Piece of Turf,* 1503. Watercolor and tempera on paper, 1′4″ × 1′½″. Graphische Sammlung Albertina, Vienna, Austria.

Dürer's mature masterpiece, *Four Apostles* (Fig. 11.13), can be read as a visual manifesto of the Reformation. The governing board of Nuremberg, like those of other towns and cities, had to resolve the religious crisis between Roman Catholicism and Protestantism. When it adopted Lutheranism, Dürer presented the two panels to be hung in the city hall as his legacy to his native town and as a memorial to himself.

The artist revered Martin Luther as "that Christian man who has helped me out of great anxieties." Several quotations from Luther's German translation of the New Testament are found beneath the figures. Dürer once told Philipp Melanchthon, the Protestant humanist and close associate of Luther, "When I was young I craved variety and novelty; now, in my advanced years, I have come to see . . . that simplicity is the ultimate goal of art." In *Four Apostles,* he purged extraneous detail and superfluous ornamentation so that the individuality and integrity of the characters could shine through with the utmost clarity and conviction. The over-life-size figures represent John the Evangelist and St. Peter on the left, with Mark and Paul on the right. St. John was Luther's favorite evangelist. Interestingly, St. Paul was viewed as the spiritual father of

11.13 Albrecht Dürer. *Four Apostles,* 1526. Oil on wood, two panels, each 7′1″ × 2′6″. Alte Pinakothek, Munich, Germany.

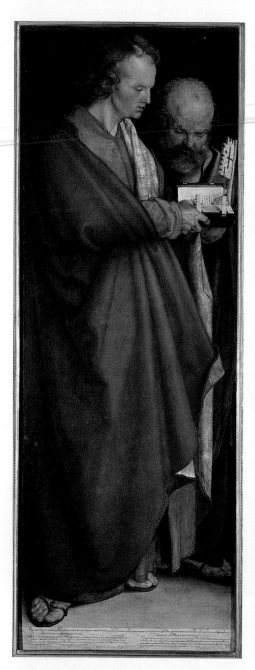
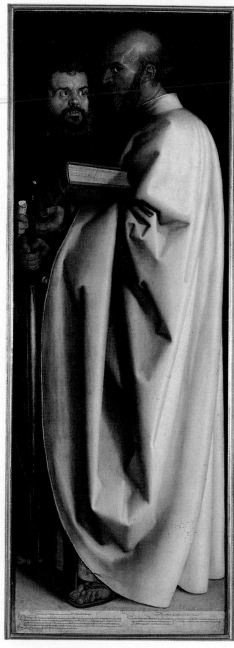

the Protestant movement, so much so that Catholic theologians referred to the Reformationists as the Paulines. Peter, with his keys to the Kingdom, the oldest of the apostles and the one most associated with Roman Catholicism, is still present, though now in the background.

The balanced composition is replete with naturalistic detail down to the stitches and layers of leather in the sandals. But far more important is the powerful psychological portrayal of these religious leaders. Johann Neudörfer, Dürer's friend, colleague, and early biographer, noted that the four apostles stand for the four temperaments. St. John, with his ruddy complexion and glowing red robe, is the warm, outgoing **sanguine** type. The white-robed St. Paul, with his symbolic sword

as soldier of Christ, stands as his opposite number in the psychological as well as the pictorial sense. He represents the **melancholic** side with his piercing hypnotic eye and stern, unyielding demeanor. The bowed head and downcast eyes of Peter and his withdrawn and resigned attitude bespeak the **phlegmatic** character. St. Mark, with his rolling eyes and fiery visionary look, represents the **choleric** temperament. Together they constitute the four basic aspects of religious experience, and the picture itself becomes a monument to Reformation thought.

FEAR AND TRIUMPH: MATTHIAS GRÜNEWALD'S *ISENHEIM ALTARPIECE*. Grünewald completed the celebrated *Isenheim Altarpiece* (Figs. 11.14 and 11.15) for the

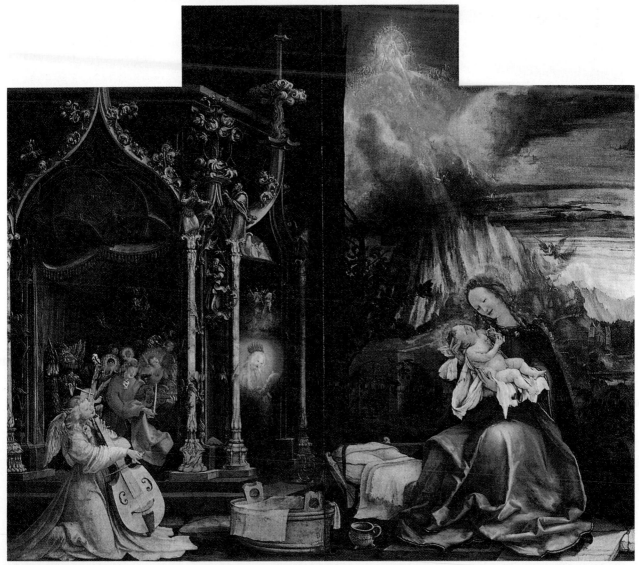

11.14 Matthias Grünewald. *Nativity,* center panel, front opening of *Isenheim Altarpiece,* completed 1515. Oil on wood, approx. 8'6″ × 21'4″. Musée d'Unterlinden, Colmar, France.

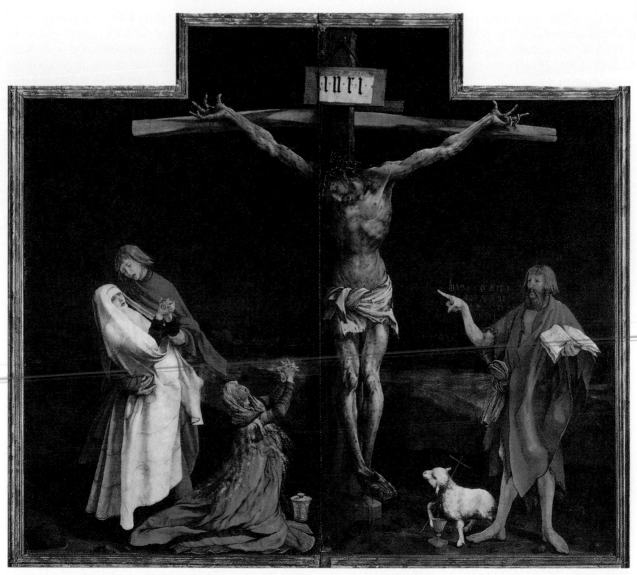

11.15 Matthias Grünewald. *Crucifixion,* center panel exterior of *Isenheim Altarpiece,* completed 1515. Oil on wood, approx. 8′6″ × 21′4″. Musée d'Unterlinden, Colmar, France.

monks of St. Anthony, a religious order that maintained hospitals for the sick and the poor. The work consists of a cycle of scenes painted on the front and back of two sets of folding panels, with immovable side wings, paired one behind the other. This intricate form resembles a book, opening leaf after leaf so that the stories of the Christian calendar can pass in review. Earthly, heavenly, and infernal beings alike are present to worship, witness, horrify, and tempt. The moods range from the ecstatic joy of the music-making angels in the Nativity panel to the depths of despair in the Crucifixion. The narrative extends from the Annunciation and Nativity, through the Passion and Entombment of Jesus, to the fantastic ordeals of St. Anthony, the legendary prophet of Christian monasticism.

The unusual and obscure iconography is derived from a number of sources, including the scriptures, the mystical writings of St. Bridget of Sweden, and pictures by Grünewald's contemporaries, not the least of whom was Dürer. The strange *Nativity* (Fig. 11.14) omits the traditional St. Joseph, the crib, the animals, and the shepherds. The *Crucifixion* (Fig. 11.15) includes St. John the Baptist, rare in this context. In this Nativity, Mary appears twice, on the right as the more familiar Madonna with Child, and on the left kneeling in prayer in a Gothic templelike chapel. Her head is surrounded by heavenly light. St. Bridget described such a scene in her *Revelations.* The allusion also suggests the Magnificat in St. Luke (1:46–55), in which the Virgin prays, "My soul doth magnify the Lord, and my spirit hath rejoiced in God my Saviour." The images of the prophets and musicians as well as the Venetian glass pitcher at her feet may point to the Revela-

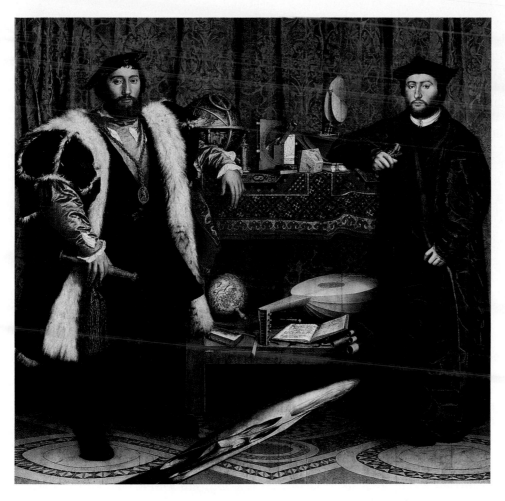

11.16 Hans Holbein the Younger. *Jean de Dinteville and Georges de Selve* ("The Ambassadors") 1533. Oil and tempera on wood, approx. 6'8" × 6'9½". National Gallery, London, England.

tion of St. John, in which the twenty-four elders of the Apocalypse appear with jars to symbolize their prayers and with musical instruments to signify their praises of the Lord.

In his *Crucifixion* (Fig. 11.15), Grünewald depicts the Baptist on the right side of the cross, St. John the Evangelist on the left, and Sts. Sebastian and Anthony on the side wings. With this plan he managed to include the interceders for the principal maladies treated at the hospital: St. Sebastian for the plague, the two Johns for epilepsy, and St. Anthony for St. Anthony's fire (thought to be the feverish, infectious inflammation of the skin known as *ergotism,* a disease caused by eating contaminated grain). No gentle Italian harmonies soften the grim agony of the crucified Christ. Festering sores and dried blood cover the ghastly dying flesh. Such vivid details may have been naturalistic, but they bear little relation to southern Renaissance practice. Grünewald, like Hugo van der Goes, followed the ancient way of proportioning his figures according to their religious or dramatic importance. Compare the size of the kneeling Magdalene's hands with those of the Savior.

The Temptation of St. Anthony, with its ghoulish and monstrous apparitions, reminded the suffering patients of the horrible ordeals endured by their patron saint. With its all-encompassing range of human feeling, Grünewald's altarpiece is one of the most moving documents in art history. In the late nineteenth and early twentieth centuries, the painting's vivid imagery helped inspire the Expressionist movement (see pp. 551–557), as well as Paul Hindemith's opera and symphony *Mathis der Maler* (Mathias the Painter).

PAINTING IN ENGLAND

THE COURT OF HENRY VIII. With Hans Holbein the Younger the scene shifts to Tudor England. He served as painter at the court of Henry VIII, where poetry, drama, and music flourished. Among Holbein's surviving portraits are those of Henry's son, the future Edward VI, and three of Henry's wives: Jane Seymour, Anne of Cleves, and Catherine Howard.

Jean de Dinteville and Georges de Selve ("The Ambassadors") (Fig. 11.16) is one of Holbein's most courtly, subtle, and intriguing works. It portrays a pair of envoys bringing a letter from the French king to Henry VIII. Underlying the surface play of elegant costumes, rich drapery, and still-life objects is a profound interplay of signs and symbols. Reading from bottom to top, each figure stands on the tiled marble pavement with one foot in a circle, indicating his spiritual aspirations, and the other foot in the central square, denoting the worldly realm and humanity's physical nature. The objects in the middle are arranged on two levels. On the terrestrial plane are a globe of the world, a compass, some flutes, a lute, and a hymnal open to Luther's translation of the hymn *Veni creator spiritus*. Above them are a spherical map of the skies, some navigational instruments, and some geometric forms, including a square and a circle, which echo the pattern on the floor. Together they signify various attributes of the traditional seven liberal arts, particularly the quadrivium—mathematics, geometry, music, and astronomy—which were the humanistic pursuits of the scholarly gentlemen represented.

There is, however, a more somber side to the painting, because all these things are but vanities when viewed under the aspect of eternity. The theme seems to be *sic transit gloria mundi* (thus passeth worldly glory). The richly costumed subjects and their attributes represent the wealth and power of the state and church, whereas the sundial and the lute with its broken string indicate the brevity of life and the inevitability of death. Confirming this interpretation are a medallion with a skull in the left figure's cap, and a strangely distorted image of a skull on the floor, which can be seen only when viewed from the extreme lower left of the picture. It is a *memento mori* (remember you must die)—a reference to death as the great leveler. It comes as a chilling footnote to the human dignity and achievement that are depicted above.

MUSIC

"The man that hath no music in himself, nor is not mov'd with concord of sweet sounds, is fit for treasons, stratagems, and spoils . . . let no such man be trusted.—Mark the music." Shakespeare's words testify to the high esteem in which music was held in the northern countries. Music, in fact, was closely woven into the fabric of daily life for all social classes, from the rustic bagpipers in Bruegel's *Peasant Wedding Feast* (Fig. 11.9) and the wind players in town bands available for civic occasions, to middle-class house music, to courtly

entertainments. Very little music was written down, and most of what was has been lost. A great impetus to the spread of music was the invention and development of printing. Published anthologies made songs and dances readily accessible. Printed music also stimulated composers to write for wider audiences.

The greatest body of surviving music is, of course, music for churches, which was performed where everyone might hear it. Outside the church, however, printed collections of solo and group songs with lute accompaniment (Fig. 11.17), madrigals, rondos, and motets for special celebrations (such as state visits, military victories, births, marriages, and other ceremonies) became available. These works were mainly for professional performers or educated amateurs.

The Courtier, Baldassare Castiglione's popular etiquette book (see pp. 274–275) was translated and published in England in 1561. It makes the point that "music is not only an ornament, but also necessary for a courtier." Besides knowing how to read music at sight, Castiglione advised that every gentleman should also be a musician and "have skill on sundry instruments." Gradually the pleasures of such music making were adopted in middle-class households, where music after dinner became a popular form of entertainment. Each household had its own printed or hand-copied scores. Music masters were called on for instruction in reading notes or playing on the lute, recorder, keyboard, and viols. The Elizabethan madrigal composer Thomas Morley chronicled the story of a young man at a social gathering who was called upon to sing a part. When he protested that he could not, everyone surmised that he had been badly brought up.

FLEMISH COMPOSERS

The great fame of the Flemish composers of this period spread throughout Europe in church and courtly circles. Among others, Guillaume Dufay was the dominating force in early fifteenth-century Italy (see pp. 248–249), as was Josquin Desprez later in the century (see pp. 293–294). Orlande de Lassus completed the illustrious line that practiced what was called the "perfect art" of polyphony in the sixteenth century. Trained in his native Flanders and in Italy, he was active all over the Continent. Eventually he settled in Munich, where he was ennobled by Emperor Maximilian II and enjoyed every honor fame could bestow—including such accolades as "prince of musicians" and "the divine Orlande." Lassus was adept at

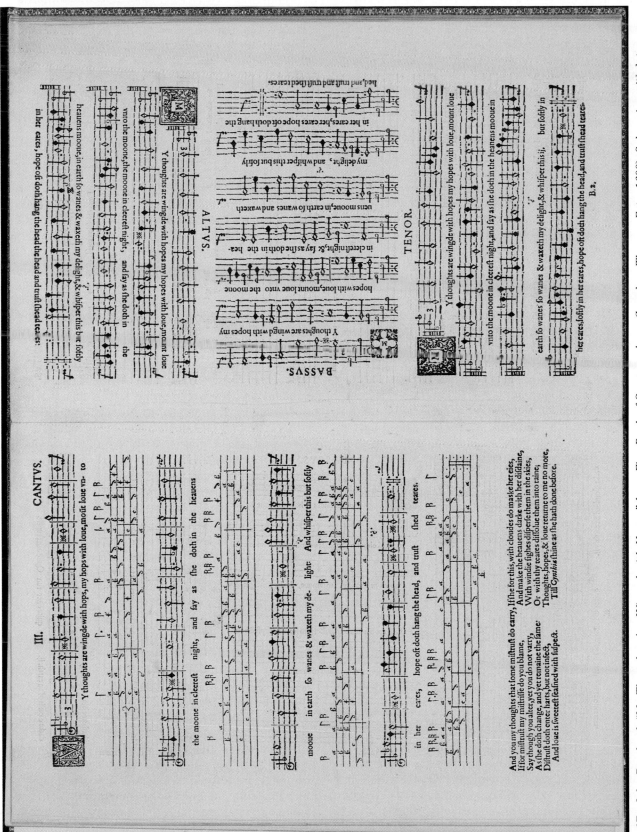

11.17   John Dowland. "My Thoughts Are Winged with Hopes" from *First Book of Songs or Ayres* (London: Thomas Este, 1600). Solo voice with lute accompaniment in tablature (left), optional arrangement for voices (right).

writing in any style and could set texts in French, Italian, and German. He took special delight in the sounds of particular words and was sensitive to every nuance of his text. Musically, his writing is characterized by purity of sound, close knitting together of the various voices, clever use of imitations, and clarity of texture. The moods of his chansons range from bawdy burlesque to profoundly moving serious sentiments. "Susanne un jour" and "Bonjour mon coeur," the one derived from the Old Testament story of Susanna and the Elders, the other a touching love song, were the most popular of his many-voiced songs during his lifetime. They have since been arranged in every way, from solo lute and voice settings to madrigals and full choruses.

COMPOSERS IN TUDOR ENGLAND

Henry VIII—himself a composer—attracted the best Flemish, Italian, and English composer-performers to his court. His son Edward VI played the lute, and his daughter Elizabeth I was an expert performer on the virginal, a small harpsichord-like instrument. England also had its share of great contrapuntal composers, chief among them Thomas Tallis and William Byrd. The crowning achievement of the period was the madrigal, a type of part-song for several individual voices, and the **ayre,** or solo song, in which lyric poetry and melody combined to create a delicate and appealing art form.

John Dowland was outstanding among composer-poets. His ayres range in mood from plaintive lamentation to passionate intensity and dramatic power. The published arrangement of Dowland's "My Thoughts Are Winged with Hopes" (Fig. 11.17) shows how they were printed for home music making.

The book opened so that the performers could be seated at a table. In this case, the principal singer and lute player would sit together, as shown in the left-hand score. The music can also be sung by two voices, with the second singer seated around the table at the right. Many such songs were arranged for vocal quartet with a lute accompaniment that duplicated the three lower parts, allowing great flexibility in performance.

Depending on the number of available singers, these arrangements could be sung as solos with lute accompaniment, a cappella (that is, for four voices without accompaniment), as duets, as lute solos, as instrumental pieces with viols instead of voices, as a combination of voices and viols, as instrumental ensembles with doublings of the parts, with wind instruments substituting for the voices and viols, and so on. Indeed, music had to

be adaptable to the size, skill, and instrumental capabilities of any group that might gather for an evening of musical pleasure in the home. These works were the popular music of the period.

DRAMA: SHAKESPEARE

The towering achievement of the Renaissance in England was in the field of drama. By the midsixteenth century, plays emerged as a popular form of entertainment for both the nobility and the general public. The growing demand led to the formation of traveling troupes of actors who played in the provinces as well as in London. The usual place of performance was the courtyard of an inn. When more permanent theaters, such as the old Globe Playhouse in London (Fig. 11.18), were built, their design recalled the layout of a courtyard inn, with its open-air center surrounded by roofed galleries. People of all classes attended these performances; the more prosperous were seated in the galleries with a view of the stage, whereas others stood in what was called the *pit* or *ground.* The stage itself had doorways for the entrances and exits of the players; otherwise, it was quite barren of scenery. The poetry of the text described the setting and carried on the action of the play. The Globe was the playhouse of William Shakespeare and others until it burned down in 1613 during a performance of Shakespeare's *Henry VIII.*

Born in the provincial town of Stratford-upon-Avon, Shakespeare's early life is clouded in obscurity. Like that of most great artists, however, his biography is found in his life's work—nearly 40 plays and some 150 sonnets. At the end of the reign of Queen Elizabeth I, he was associated with a group of players known as the Lord Chamberlain's Men. Such groups performed not only in public places but also in aristocratic households, including the royal court. A number of Shakespeare's plays were performed before Queen Elizabeth, whom he gracefully referred to in *A Midsummer Night's Dream* as "a fair vestal throned by the west." Queen Elizabeth is said to have been so delighted with the character of Sir John Falstaff in the *Henry IV* dramas that she expressed the wish to see a play with Falstaff in love. The result was *The Merry Wives of Windsor.* After 1603, Shakespeare's plays were often performed at the court of James I, who was flattered by Macbeth's allusions to his writings on witchcraft. Under James I, Shakespeare's actors were honored as the King's Men, with the title of Grooms of the Chamber.

The scope of Shakespeare's early plays ranges from the rollicking *Comedy of Errors* and *Taming of the Shrew,* through the tragedy *Romeo and Juliet,* to such great comedies as *Much Ado about Nothing and Twelfth Night.* The historical dramas range from ancient Roman times in *Julius Caesar* to the reigns of various English monarchs. The climax of Shakespeare's prodigious output was attained in his mature years with the tragedies *Hamlet, Othello, Macbeth,* and *King Lear,* all profound works that examine the perennial questions of life and death, love and hate, sanity and madness, ambition and human error. In later plays, he still sought new dramatic directions and explored the borderline between comedy and tragedy.

Shakespeare's stage not only mirrored the values and customs of the Elizabethan era but also rendered a vision of human qualities and flaws that would appeal to subsequent generations. Because his works can be read on so many different levels, new meanings and interpretations are constantly brought to light. There are as many Shakespeares as there are actors, directors, scholars, critics, historians, and audiences, as each interprets, appraises, and enjoys the plays in his or her own way. As his contemporary and fellow dramatist Ben Jonson summed it up, "He was not of an age, but for all time."

BEAUTY AND THE BEAST: SHAKESPEARE'S *THE TEMPEST*

The Tempest is one of Shakespeare's last plays, and its construction borders on technical perfection. The classical unities of time, place, and action are observed, and it follows the five-act form of ancient Roman drama. Essentially, it is a pastoral play, concerned with the opposition of nature and art. One of the central characters, Prospero, is a man of learning, with power over the environment and over himself. In Shakespeare's time, Prospero's magic would have been understood as the special knowledge derived from books, such as Francis Bacon's *Advancement of Learning* (1603).

By contrast, Caliban, like the shepherds in pastoral plays, is a man of nature, akin to the ignorant beasts of the field. It is Caliban, however, against whom all the other figures are measured. He is portrayed as existing at the simple level of the senses, feeling pleasure without knowledge, experiencing lust without love, and being unable to distinguish good from evil. The "civilized" characters, beneath their polished exteriors, have within themselves in varying degrees some of Caliban's baser instincts.

The fairy-tale plot tells of Prospero, the rightful Duke of Milan, who is exiled with his lovely daughter Miranda to a tropical island. The only other inhabitants are Caliban—"a freckled whelp . . . not honor'd with a human shape"—and the "ayrie spirit," Ariel. Learning through his magic powers that his old enemies are sailing past, Prospero conjures up a tempest that shipwrecks their boat and scatters the survivors about the island. There Ferdinand, the handsome young prince of Naples, finds Miranda. After many trials, plots, and subplots, the lovers are united and their marriage celebrated. Prospero regains his dukedom, and forgiveness and reconciliation prevail.

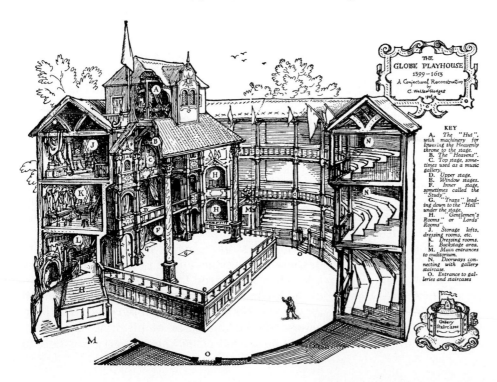

11.18 Globe Playhouse, London, England. Conjectural reconstruction by C. Walter Hodges.

THE GLOBE PLAYHOUSE 1599–1613 A Conjectural Reconstruction by C. Walter Hodges

KEY
A. The "Hut", with machinery for lowering the Heavenly throne to the stage.
B. The "Heavens".
C. Top stage, sometimes used as a music gallery.
D. Upper stage.
E. Window stages.
F. Inner stage, sometimes called the "Study".
G. "Traps" leading down to the "Hell" under the stage.
H. "Gentlemen's Rooms" or "Lords' Rooms".
J. Storage lofts, dressing rooms, etc.
K. Dressing rooms.
L. Backstage area.
M. Main entrances to auditorium.
N. Doorways connecting with gallery staircase.
O. Entrance to galleries and staircases

Interpretations of *The Tempest* abound. In recent years there have been productions playing up the adversarial relationship between Prospero and Caliban as representing the colonial powers exploiting the natives of distant lands. This view is not without some justification. Elizabethan England was already a major rival of Spain in the colonization of the New World. Walter Raleigh's and Francis Drake's accounts of their voyages had already been published. Just at the time of *The Tempest*'s first performance in 1611, the public was enthralled by the adventures of a group of colonists who had been shipwrecked in Bermuda on their way to the yet unnamed state of Virginia.

The religious and ethical implications of the meeting of settlers and natives were the subject of hot debate. Shakespeare certainly knew about these developments. The name *Caliban,* for instance, is almost an anagram for *cannibal,* which at the time referred to the natives of the Caribbean, not to eaters of human flesh.

In other views, the drama is seen as symbolizing the four elements, with Caliban as Earth and brute force, Prospero as the fire of imagination, Ariel as the fancy-free spirit of air, and the sea as the environmental waters that surround them. It can also be interpreted as an allegory of fall and redemption, revenge and resolution.

The rhythm and musicality of Shakespeare's verse became an open invitation and challenge to composers from his time to the present. In fact, the plays contained songs, such as the touching "Willow Song" in *Othello.* An anonymous setting from the time survives, but there is no way of knowing whether it was actually performed in a Shakespeare production. The first known setting of a Shakespeare lyric is Robert Morley's "It was a lover and his lasse" from *As You Like It,* but again there is no record of its performance in the play. Shakespeare's contemporary Robert Johnson's settings of two lyrics from *The Tempest*—"Full fathom five" and "Where the bee sucks"—survive and are generally thought to have been composed for the production of 1611, although they were not printed until 1660.

The Tempest's alliance with music is illustrated by the inclusion in Act IV of a full-scale **masque.** These spectacles predate opera and were designed for courtly entertainment. This masque's second known performance was in 1613, for the betrothal of James I's daughter Elizabeth to an important German prince. It was performed by the King's Men, the royal acting troupe of which Shakespeare was a member. The masque, a play within the play, begins with a prologue to set the theme, in this case

reconciliation and forgiveness. It continues with songs, dances, and instrumental interludes and finally with the revels, in which the audience participates. The reconciliation is completed in the last act of *The Tempest,* in which Miranda speaks the oft-quoted lines, "O brave new world, / That has such people in't." Even Caliban joins in with the words, "I'll be wise hereafter / And seek for grace."

One of the most intriguing interpretations of the play is that Prospero is Shakespeare himself. His lines toward the end of the masque may function as Shakespeare's farewell to the theater, when he was leaving London for retirement at Stratford:

Our revels now are ended. These our actors,
As I foretold you, were all spirits and
Are melted into air, into thin air:
And, like the baseless fabric of this vision,
The cloud-capp'd towers, the gorgeous palaces,
The solemn temples, the great globe itself,
Yea, all which it inherit, shall dissolve
And, like this insubstantial pageant faded,
Leave not a rack behind. We are such stuff
As dreams are made on, and our little life
Is rounded with a sleep.

IDEAS

CRITICAL HUMANISM

The new learning in England, France, and the Low Countries, evidenced by the books of Thomas More, François Rabelais, and Desiderius Erasmus, was pursued vigorously in the early sixteenth century. Inevitably it became entangled in Reformation theological controversies. Italian thinkers, too close to Rome for comfort, had to veil some of their criticism of the church. They deflected attention by projecting a past golden age in antiquity and reviving Plato in opposition to Aristotelian scholasticism. Northern scholars could view church and social abuses more openly and objectively. They also tended to fix on the observation of nature and the world about them. In Northern thought, criticism of the church and the inherited social order assumed two main directions. One way led to the projection of imaginary idealized societies on the model of Plato's *Republic,* the other to holding up the mirror of satire and ridicule to the outmoded medieval heritage.

Thomas More, a lawyer by profession, rose to become Lord Chancellor of England under Henry VIII. When he refused to recognize Henry as head of the English church, he was tried and executed for treason. His widely read *Utopia* was a disguised exposé of the injustices of his time. In *Utopia,* which means "no place," all property was held in common, because only without personal property could there be social equality. All towns had the same plan, all houses were exactly alike, and all religions were tolerated. Each family made its own clothing, yet all men and women dressed alike. A chosen few, like the Platonic Guardians (see p. 26), were called to pursue learning. Those who governed were picked from this group. There was a kind of representative democracy modeled on the parliamentary system and a ruler chosen by indirect election. The ruler served for life but could be deposed if he turned to tyranny. Life in More's *Utopia* may have been an improvement on the present, but it certainly was dull.

Far more lively reading was provided by the satirists. In France, Rabelais was a professed monk of broad humanistic learning who took up the pen to ridicule the stagnant, lingering medieval outlook of his period and human folly in general. In his *Gargantua* and its sequel, *Pantagruel,* the bawdiness and ribaldry of his tales and his unbridled zest for living sometimes obscure his essentially serious concerns with politics, education, and philosophy. His real purpose was to liberate men and women from their foolishness so that they could realize their higher potential as human beings.

The most influential thinker of all was Erasmus of Rotterdam, who was universally admired for his great knowledge, sharp wit, and brilliant writing style, as well as for the breadth of his humanistic worldview. He was also a connoisseur of art and a friend of Holbein the Younger, who painted several portraits of him and illustrated many of his books. Erasmus lived and worked in Germany, France, and England. His many letters serve as records of his era, and his *Colloquies* take up popular issues.

In "The Godly Feast," one of his *Colloquies,* Erasmus discusses how nature and art complement each other in two gardens—one real, the other painted. "In one we admire the cleverness of nature, in the other the inventiveness of the painter." In *In Praise of Folly,* Erasmus's biting wit cuts into the pretensions and hypocrisies of his time. Folly narrates the book. Her satire targets people in all walks of life. All are dependent on her, for who can marry or mate without Folly? Held up to ridicule are the monks who "compute the time of each soul's residence in purgatory," the theologians with their endless disputes about the Trinity and incarnation, and the friars who calculate "the precise number of knots to the tying of their sandals." Bishops, cardinals, and popes are castigated for having little religion in them, and it is suggested that even religion is a form of folly.

Visual artists also engaged in satire. Holbein's *Dance of Death,* a series of woodcuts portraying humanity from the Creation to the Last Judgment, is really a comedy about life. Everyone from popes and emperors to common sailors and peasants is eventually leveled off by Death, who appears as a skeleton. Holbein also did a series of drawings for the 1515 printing of Erasmus's *In Praise of Folly.* On the last page (Fig. 11.19), Folly, dressed in a

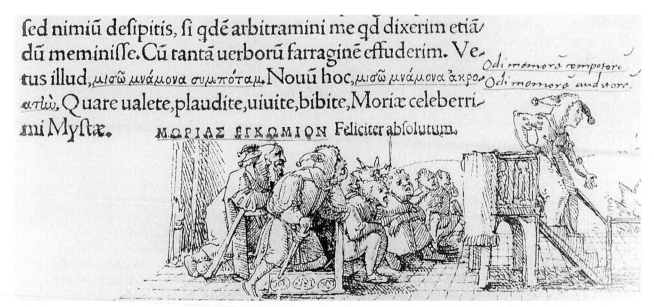

11.19   Hans Holbein the Younger. Marginal drawing for the last page of Erasmus's 1515 Basel printing of *In Praise of Folly,* facsimile reproduced from the original in the Offentliche Kunstsammlung Basel (H. Oppermann, 1931). The George Arents Research Library at Syracuse University.

joker's cap and bells, has been preaching to her audience of fools. She descends from the pulpit, saying, "And now fare ye well, applaud, live, and drink, ye votaries of Folly."

An ordained priest, Erasmus nonetheless opposed pilgrimages, papal indulgences, the mediation of saints, the power of the clergy, the sacramental system, and the literal interpretation of the Bible. Thus, the road to the Reformation was paved by the northern humanists, whose articulation and advocacy of reason in human affairs served to underscore the corruption of the Church of Rome. Erasmus hoped that his reforms would lead to a new golden age of the arts, but, as has been remarked, he laid the egg that Luther hatched. When he beheld the chick, Erasmus remarked bitterly that "wherever Lutheranism reigns there is the death of letters." He resolved (as did More and Rabelais) to stay with the Church of Rome, and it remained for Luther to sharpen the issues and bring the Reformation to a head.

LUTHER AND THE REFORMATION

The reforms initiated by Martin Luther became the dominating force of the sixteenth century. Luther did not merely change the map of Europe; he also transformed the way people thought of themselves, their associates, and the world about them. During the dark days of his inner struggle to clarify his beliefs, he was struck by St. Paul's words, "The just shall live by faith." Justification by faith became Luther's motto, but it was a faith that every person had to find for himself or herself. Luther held that the individual conscience was the ultimate moral authority and proclaimed the priesthood of all believers. By this he meant that through prayer each believer could address God directly without the mediation of priestly authority, the Roman Catholic Church, or the intercession of the saints.

The word of God, Luther taught, was not necessarily to be found in the writings of the church fathers or in Roman Catholic doctrine, but in the Bible itself. Consequently, it became imperative to translate the Scriptures from Latin into the languages ordinary people knew. Again, the development of printing played a major role in spreading both the Gospel and the writings of the reformers. No longer were the Bible and other books the private preserve of the clergy, the learned, or the well-to-do. Luther held that the Bible spoke directly and clearly. Learning to read and understand was the necessary prelude to faith and salvation. Although Luther was motivated by religious ideas, others promoted the use of vernacular languages to create national awareness. For instance, François I of France made French the official language of politics and business in his realm.

The psychological impact of Lutheranism lay in shifting the burden of thinking from the authority of the priesthood to the individual. Although Luther himself wrote many commentaries, he allowed ample scope for individual opinion and interpretation.

THE EFFECTS ON THE ARTS.   The Reformation had an enormous impact on the arts. At first, there was a disruption in the sources of patronage. Funds from the Roman Church for architectural projects, complete with sculptural and decorative programs, were no longer forthcoming in the Reformation countries. However, with the rise of nation-states and the growing power of merchant and shipping families, a reorientation of the patronage system gradually took place.

Architecture also had to take the new religious direction into account. For the most part, the Church of England retained elaborate liturgies, so the heritage of the Gothic structures continued to suffice. On the Continent, however, the Protestants objected to ceremonial pomp. They redecorated their churches and reoriented their services. At first, Protestants on the Continent simply took over and adapted existing Roman Catholic churches, tearing out the sculpture and paintings, whitewashing the walls, and keeping decorative details to a minimum. When new churches were built, they tended to resemble university lecture halls because of a new emphasis on preaching.

Lutheranism recognized only two sacraments: communion and baptism. The communion altar was retained, but it no longer displayed relics of the saints and was no longer the center of attention. The baptismal font also remained, but no longer in a separate chapel. The new order focused on the pulpit, with appropriate seating for the congregation and a prominent place for the choir and organ loft.

In the representational arts, sculpture suffered the most because its lifelike three-dimensionality was believed to bring it close to idol worship and because graven images were forbidden by the second commandment. Painted altarpieces were also out of the question.

One of the darkest aspects of sixteenth-century history was the wholesale destruction of church art. Protestant extremists in England, France, and Germany smashed stained-glass windows, demolished statuary, decapitated sculptured figures on Gothic porches and facades, and destroyed choir screens that they believed separated the faithful from the altar. Paintings were ripped out and burned. Fortunately, Luther disapproved of this wanton destruction and warned his more zealous followers that it was not necessary "to swallow the Holy Ghost feathers and all."

The views of Reformation leaders on the proper place for the arts varied from partial acceptance to total exclusion. John Calvin, a leader of the Reformation in Switzerland, initially said, "I approached the task of destroying images by first tearing them out of my heart." He modified his position somewhat by saying that crucifixes and images of the saints were "praiseworthy and to be respected," but for memorial purposes only. However, he remained rigid in his disapproval of works of art and the worship of images.

Luther scorned the worship of icons and images, but he was not an iconoclast, that is, someone who promotes the destruction of images. "If it is . . . a good thing for me to bear the image of Christ in my heart," he asked, "why should it be a sin to have it before my eyes?" He sat for innumerable portraits (Fig. 11.20) and numbered the painter Lucas Cranach the Elder among his friends

and Dürer and Bruegel among his admirers. In general, though, Luther was more sensitive to the spoken word and music than to the visual arts.

In the pictorial arts, new themes and a new iconographic tradition gradually emerged. Up to the Reformation, the emphasis had been on history painting, with mainly biblical and mythological subjects. The Reformation brought other categories to the fore. Iconography shifted from universals to particulars. Luther's reorientation of religion toward the subjective, private individual favored the development of portraiture. Genre scenes telling of everyday experiences, personal feelings, and reactions received new impetus. Dürer's engravings and Bruegel's paintings of peasant life are cases in point.

Another major change was the increased attention to landscape for its own sake rather than merely as a background for figures. For the Reformationists, landscape was a reflection of increasing interest in the exploration of nature as such, an expression of God's bounteous creation, and a confirmation that God exists in a simple clod of earth like that painted by Dürer (Fig. 11.12). Albrecht Altdorfer's view of the Danube (Fig. 11.21)

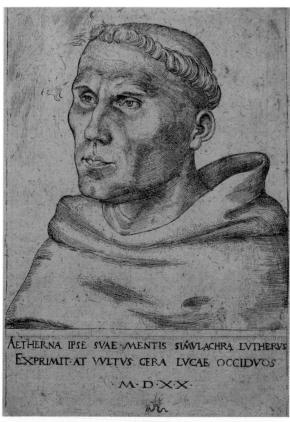

11.20 Lucas Cranach the Elder *Luther as Augustinian Friar,* 1520. Copper engraving, 5⅞" × 4⅝". British Museum, London, England.

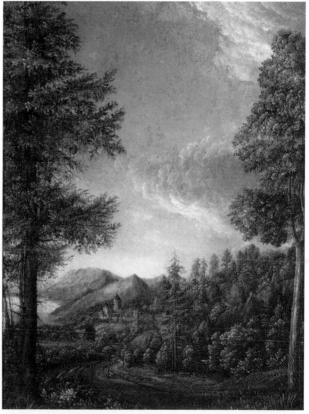

11.21 Albrecht Altdorfer. *Danube Landscape near Regensburg,* c. 1522–1525. Panel, 11" × 8⅝", Alte Pinakothek, Munich, Germany.

combines keen observation of color and light with a perception of nature infused by the supernatural. Still life also began to come into its own. The new middle class took special delight in the tangible objects that represented the good life, but their consciences demanded a moral message. Thus, representations of crockery, mirrors, jewelry, and the like were meant to recall a well-known phrase from the Bible (*vanitas vanitatus, omnia vanitas*; Ecclesiastes 1:2), which stresses the delusion of worldly riches. Flowers, fruit, dead animals, and skulls were classed as memento mori, reminders of the passage of time, the brevity of life, and the inevitability of death.

Above all, a lively market developed for prints, both alone and as illustrations in books. These were media that had not before been associated with idolatry or popery. Indeed, book illustration soon became an art in its own right, one that was acceptable in both Protestant and Catholic circles and one that would attain importance.

The Reformation also opened up many possibilities for music. Luther himself wrote the stirring words and perhaps the music for "A Mighty Fortress Is Our God," the anthem that became the marching song of the Reformation. His reorganization of the German Mass opened the doors to new directions in choral and organ music and to the forms of the cantata and oratorio (see pp. 408–409 and 428–430).

Both congregational and professional singing were woven into the Mass.

In general terms, the Reformation was a conflict between North and South, the Germanic and Latin cultures, nationalism and internationalism, personal conviction and hierarchically organized religion. No one side could be declared the winner. In the long run, the principal casualty would be the Renaissance style in both the North and the South. The stage would soon be set for an adjustment of the arts in an era of spiritual conflict and mannerism.

YOUR RESOURCES

- ***Exploring Humanities CD-ROM***

  ○ Interactive Map: Europe in the Sixteenth Century

  ○ Readings—Shakespeare Modules: *A Midsummer Night's Dream, Henry IV, The Merry Wives of Windsor, Twelfth Night, Hamlet, Othello, King Lear, The Tempest,* Erasmus, *In Praise of Folly*

- ***Web Site***

  http://art.wadsworth.com/fleming10

  ○ Chapter 11 Quiz

  ○ Links

NORTHERN RENAISSANCE

Key Events	Visual Arts and Reformers	Literature and Music
	c. 1324–1327 Jean Pucelle active ▲	
	c. 1330–1384 John Wycliffe ✚	
1337–1453 Hundred Years' War between England and France	1369–1415 **John Huss** ✚	
	c. 1375–c. 1425 **Limbourg Brothers:** Pol, Herman, and Jehanequin ▲	
	c. 1378–1444 **Robert Campin** (Master of Flémalle) ▲	
	1379–1471 **Thomas à Kempis** ✚	
	c. 1379–1406 **Claus Sluter** active ●	
1384 Philip of Burgundy acquired Flanders	c. 1385–1426 **Hubert van Eyck** ▲	
	c. 1390–1441 **Jan van Eyck** ▲	c. 1390–1453 **John Dunstable** ❑

1400

Key Events	Visual Arts and Reformers	Literature and Music
	c. 1400–1464 **Rogier van der Weyden** ▲	1400–1474 **Guillaume Dufay** ❑
	c. 1405–c. 1445 **Conrad Witz** ▲	1427 **Thomas à Kempis,** probably wrote *Imitation of Christ*
1414 Council of Constance began church reform; declared church councils as supreme authority, not pope; John Huss condemned as heretic	c. 1415–1475 **Dick Bouts** ▲	
	c. 1420–1481 **Jean Fouquet** ▲	c. 1430–1495 **Johannes Ockeghem** ❑
1420–1436 Philip the Good of Burgundy made Bruges his capital	c. 1430–1494 **Hans Memling** ▲	c. 1440–1521 **Josquin Desprez** ❑
	c. 1435–1498 **Michael Pacher** ▲	c. 1446–1506 **Alexander Agricola** ❑
1429 Joan of Arc defeated English at Orleans; Charles VII crowned at Rheims	c. 1440–1482 **Hugo van der Goes** ▲	1450–1505 **Jacob Obrecht** ❑
	c. 1450–1491 **Martin Schongauer** ▲	c. 1450–1517 **Heinrich Isaac** ❑
1440 Johannes Gutenberg developed press with movable type; 1456 Gutenberg Bible printed	c. 1450–1516 **Hieronymus Bosch** ▲	1470 **Voragine's** *Golden Legend* (Lives of Saints) first printed in Cologne
	c. 1460–1523 **Gerard David** ▲	1473–1543 **Nicholas Copernicus** ◆
1455–1485 Wars of Roses in England; 1485 Henry VII (Tudor) ascends throne	c. 1460–1531 **Tilman Riemenschneider** ●	1478–1535 **Thomas More** ◆
	c. 1465–1530 **Quentin Metsys** ▲	c. 1490–1553 **François Rabelais** ◆
1474 Caxton printed first book in English *(Histories of Troy)* at Bruges	c. 1465–1524 **Hans Holbein the Elder** ▲	c. 1497–1563 **Johann Neudörfer** ⁂
	1466–1536 **Erasmus of Rotterdam** ✚	c. 1505–1585 **Thomas Tallis** ❑
1488 Diaz rounded Cape of Good Hope	1471–1528 **Albrecht Dürer** ▲	1509 **Erasmus** wrote *In Praise of Folly*
1492 Columbus reached America	1472–1553 **Lucas Cranach the Elder** ▲	1514–1564 **Andreas Vesalius** ⁂
1493–1519 Holy Roman Emperor Maximilian I ruled; patron of Dürer	c. 1475–1528 **Mathias Grünewald** ▲	c. 1521–1603 **Philippe de Monte** ❑
	c. 1475–1532 **Jan Gossaert** ▲	1521–1531 **Luther** translated Bible into German
1497–1499 Vasco da Gama voyaged to India	c. 1480–1538 **Albrecht Altdorfer** ▲	c. 1532–1594 **Orlande de Lassus** ❑
1500–1700 Overseas empires created by Spain, Portugal, Holland, England, and France	1483–1546 **Martin Luther** ✚	1533–1592 **Michel de Montaigne** ◆
	1484–1531 **Ulrich Zwingli** ✚	1536 **Calvin** published *Institutes of Christian Religion*; 1541 founded Protestant church at Geneva
1517 Luther posted 95 Theses condemning church practices	c. 1485–c. 1540 **Jean Clouet** ▲	
1519 Charles I of Spain elected emperor; until 1555 ruled Spain, Low Countries, Germany, Austria, Italy as Charles V	1489–1556 **Thomas Cranmer** ✚	1543–1623 **William Byrd** ❑
	c. 1497–1543 **Hans Holbein the Younger** ▲	1543 **Copernicus** published *On the Revolution of the Celestial Bodies;* **Vesalius** wrote *Structure of the Human Body*
1519–1522 Magellan's expedition circumnavigates globe	1497–1560 **Philipp Melanchthon** ✚	
1521 Diet of Worms convened; Luther refuses to retract teachings, declared outlaw by Charles V's Council; Luther excommunicated by Pope Leo X, burns papal bull, translates New Testament into German	c. 1508–1575 **Pieter Aertsen** ▲	1546–1601 **Tycho Brahe** ⁂
	1509–1564 **John Calvin** ✚	1549 **Cranmer** compiled first *Book of Common Prayer,* revised 1552
	c. 1510–c. 1565 **Jean Goujon** ●	
1524–1525 Peasants' revolt in Germany	c. 1525–1590 **Germain Pilon** ●	c. 1552–1599 **Edmund Spenser** ◆
1534 Church of England founded under Henry VIII	c. 1527–1569 **Pieter Bruegel the Elder** ▲	1554–1586 **Philip Sidney** ◆
1545–1563 Council of Trent called to reform church from within; censorship of books begun; Inquisition established to try to condemn heretics	1528–1587 **Caterina van Hemessen** ▲	

1550

Key Events	Visual Arts and Reformers	Literature and Music
1555 Diet of Augsburg convened by Charles V; ordered Protestants to state beliefs; Augsburg Confession became Lutheran creed; each ruler could decide faith of his people		c. 1557–c. 1602 **Thomas Morley** ❑
		1561–1626 **Francis Bacon** ◆
1555 Charles V abdicates; son Philip II ruled Spain, Low Countries, Mexico, Peru; brother Ferdinand ruled Austria, the Germanys		1561 **John Knox's** *Book of Discipline* established church constitution for Scotland
		c. 1563–1626 **John Dowland** ❑
1572 Dutch war of liberation begun; 1576 Provinces of Netherlands united		1564–1593 **Christopher Marlowe** ◆
		1564–1616 **William Shakespeare** ◆
1572 St. Bartholomew Day Massacre of Huguenots (French-Calvinists)		c. 1565–1640 **Giles Farnaby** ❑
		1567–1620 **Thomas Campion** ❑
1577–1580 Drake sailed around world		c. 1570–1638 **Francis Pilkington** ❑
1583 William of Orange became ruler of northern Netherlands		1571–1630 **Johannes Kepler** ⁂
		1572–1637 **Ben Jonson** ◆
1588 Spanish Armada defeated by British		1582–1616 **Beaumont** and **Fletcher** active ◆
1598 Edict of Nantes gave Huguenots freedom of conscience, private worship, and civil rights		1583–1625 **Orlando Gibbons** ❑
		1594–1613 **Shakespeare** wrote plays
1603 Elizabeth I succeeded by **James I**		1604 **Francis Bacon** published *Advancement of Learning*
		1611 **Bible** appears in King James Version

❑ - Musician   ▲ - Painter   ✚ - Religious Reformer   ⁂ - Scientist   ● - Sculptor   ◆ - Writer

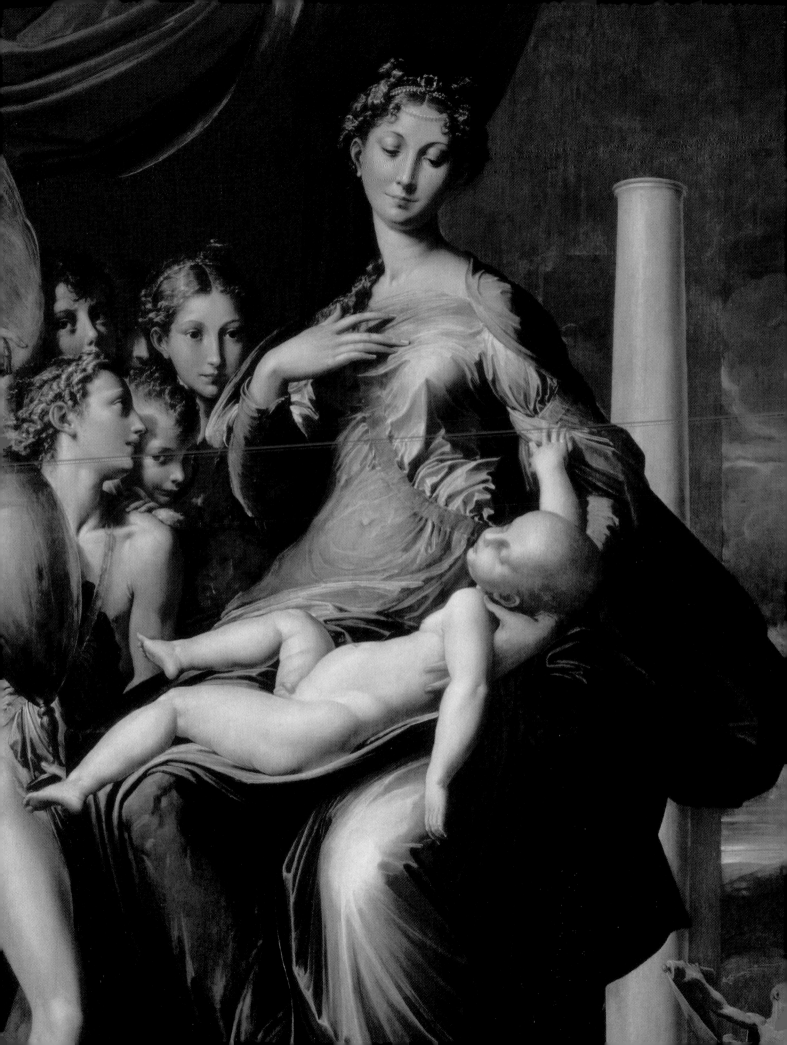

CHAPTER

THE VENETIAN RENAISSANCE AND THE RISE OF INTERNATIONAL MANNERISM

A GLIMPSE OF VENICE AS it looked at the threshold of the sixteenth century can be seen through the eyes of the painter Gentile Bellini. His reporting in *Procession in St. Mark's Square* (Fig. 12.1) is so accurate that architectural historians can make reconstructions of buildings long since destroyed and researchers can study the mosaics and sculptures of St. Mark's Basilica as they were before later restorations.

St. Mark's Basilica proclaims Venice as a cultural center where East and West met. Begun in the tenth century, it is the product of centuries of community effort. Indeed, an early law required every Venetian ship to bring back materials for the construction or decoration of the church. As a result, fragments from many Mediterranean countries can be found somewhere in its fabric—from the Greco-Roman bronze horses of the first century CE over the central portal (Fig. 12.2) to the many-colored marble columns from Alexandria

and the Greek alabaster windows. The plan is that of a Greek cross, with smaller domes covering each of the four wings and a large cupola in the center.

To the right in Bellini's painting is a corner of the Doge's Palace where the doge—the chief official of Venice—and his guests are seated on the second-story arcade. This striking variation of a Gothic town hall rises in two stories of open pointed arches surmounted by a third story notable for its diamond-shaped design in brilliant pink marble tiling. Across the square on the left is the old library, from which many spectators are watching the activities. This building, with its curious chimney pots, also dates from medieval times.

As remarkable as the library's architecture is the institution itself. Donors chose Venice as a safe repository for books because the water-bound city was less at risk of fire than other places. Venice

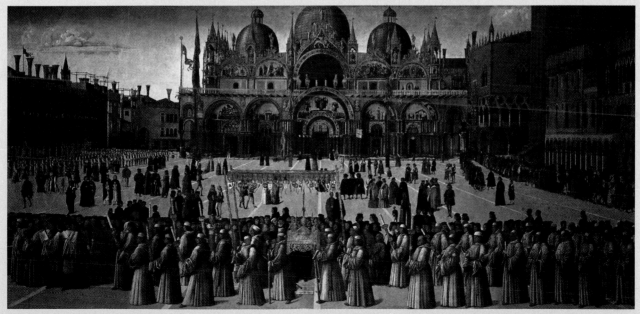

12.1 Gentile Bellini. *Procession in St. Mark's Square*, 1496. Oil on canvas, 12′ × 24′. Galleria dell'Accademia, Venice, Italy.

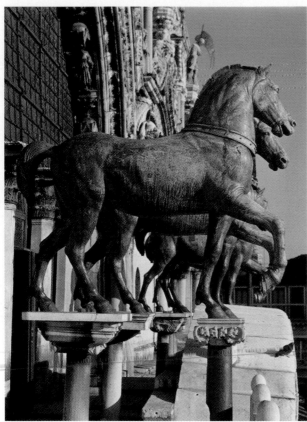

12.2 Four horses of Greek origin. First century CE. Gilt bronze, life-size. St. Mark's Basilica, Venice, Italy.

treasured the great collections of books that had been bequeathed by the poet Petrarch, the Greek scholar Cardinal Bessarion, and others. In addition to these collections, the library housed all the specimens of the city's elegant printing and bookmaking industry. They included fine but inexpensive editions of classics, which were published here for the first time by the famous Aldine Press and contributed to the spread of learning throughout the educated world. In the sixteenth century these collections were transferred to the handsome building across the square, designed by Sansovino especially to house them (Fig. 12.3).

VENICE IN THE SIXTEENTH CENTURY

Bellini depicted not only the look of St. Mark's Square but also the feeling of public life and the freedom of social movement found in Venice during the sixteenth century. The independence of Venice and the prosperity of its citizenry were due in many respects to the city's unusual situation. Built on a group of island lagoons at the head of the Adriatic Sea, Venice was what a Florentine

poet described as "a city in the water without walls." Reasonably secure from attack either by land or sea as a result of possessing the largest navy then in existence, Venice carried on an active commerce that afforded its citizens a quality of life unrivaled in its time for comfort and luxury.

The fall of Constantinople to the Turks in 1453 and the rising power of the Ottoman Empire produced competition for Venice's commercial empire. Also, the traditional shipping upon which the Venetian economy rested was upset by the benefits gained by regions along the Atlantic coast from the findings of Spanish, Portuguese, Dutch, and English navigators and explorers. Despite the unsettled world situation, the Venetians were preparing to reassert their economic and cultural supremacy. They embarked on an ambitious program of building and decorating to enrich their city while impressing their competitors.

ARCHITECTURE

A NEW LIBRARY FOR THE CITY. Jacopo Sansovino was awarded the commission to build the new Library of St. Mark (Fig. 12.3). Trained in both sculpture and architecture in his native Florence, he had been active in Tuscany and Rome before settling in Venice in 1527. His library design recalls such Renaissance city palaces as those built for the wealthy families of Florence and Rome (see Fig. 9.5), but with an important difference. Instead of relying on flat surfaces, rusticated masonry, and fortresslike facades, Sansovino molded his masses and voids as if they were sculpture. The structure has two stories, with a spacious foyer below and a great staircase leading to a well-lighted reading room above.

The dignified Doric arcade of the lower story serves as a base for the increasingly rich adornment of the upper parts. The deep-set arched windows of the second floor are unified by the regularity of the Ionic columns, and the poses of the sculptured nudes in the spandrels provide variety. A high-relief frieze of cherubs holding garlands runs above, alternating with small, deep-set windows. At the top a **balustrade**—a row of short posts topped by a rail—encircles the roof and supports a line of statues silhouetted against the skyline. The overall impression is one of spaciousness and openness that invites entry and promises an equally significant interior.

THE THEORY AND PRACTICE OF ARCHITECTURE. Sansovino's designs influenced Andrea Palladio, the greatest architect associated with the Venetian style. The author of the highly influential *Four Books of Architecture,* first published in Venice in

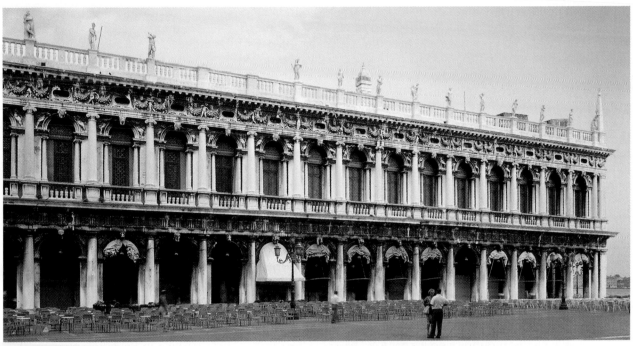

12.3 Jacopo Sansovino. Library of St. Mark, Venice, Italy, begun 1536. Length 290', height 60'.

1570, Palladio left a detailed discussion of his philosophy. In the preface to this work, Palladio paid eloquent tribute to his ancient Roman guide Vitruvius, whose writings stimulated his study of the classical buildings in Rome. "Finding that they deserved a much more diligent Observation than I thought at first Sight," he noted, "I began with the utmost Accuracy to measure every minutest part by itself."

Palladio's *Four Books of Architecture,* with their sketches and drawings, was more influential in France, England, Ireland, and America than were his buildings. The English translation, published with notes by his disciple Inigo Jones, helped establish the Georgian tradition in England (see Fig. 14.16).

In the United States, Thomas Jefferson carried on Palladio's insights in the designs he prepared for his residence at Monticello and the Rotunda of the University of Virginia (see Fig. 17.11), both of which are adaptations of Palladio's Villa Rotonda (Fig. 12.4A). Jefferson also wanted to build the White House in Washington, D.C., using the same plan, but his proposal, submitted anonymously, was rejected. However, even in its present form, the White House has a Palladian design, with a classical Ionic entrance portico in the center and two equal wings spreading outward.

Palladio's ideas were based on both Roman classical architecture and some of the more progressive trends of his Renaissance contemporaries.

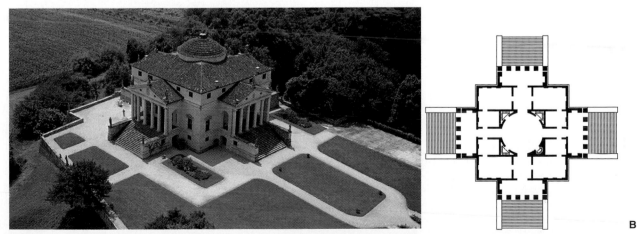

12.4 (A) Andrea Palladio. Villa Rotonda, Vicenza, Italy, begun 1550; 80' square, height of dome 70'. (B) Plan of Villa Rotonda.

He also saluted his immediate predecessor, Sansovino, whose library he praised as "perhaps the most sumptuous and the most beautiful edifice . . . since the time of the Ancients."

Palladio's architecture can be studied in Vicenza, then a part of the Venetian Republic's holdings on the mainland. Just outside Vicenza is the Villa Rotonda (Fig. 12.4A), a country house in the grand style and the prototype of many later buildings. The plan is a cube enclosing a cylindrical core surmounted by a low saucer dome (Fig. 12.4B).

On four sides, grand flights of steps lead to Ionic porches that project forward. The pediments are those of a classical temple, with statues on either side and above. Each porch provides entrance into the imposing round reception room that gives the villa the name **Rotonda.** This central salon is as high as the house itself and rises to the cupola above. Alcoves left over from the parts between the round central hall and the square sides of the building allow space for four winding staircases and for no less than thirty-two rooms in the adjoining corners, all lighted both from the outside and from the eight round windows at the base of the cupola. Below, a basement includes ample storerooms, servants' quarters, and kitchens. Palladio thus designed a house that is spacious but simple in plan.

As with Brunelleschi and Alberti in Florence (see p. 248), musical proportions played a major role in Palladio's spatial thinking. The ground plan (Fig. 12.4B) is a marvel of geometric clarity, with the central circle signifying the dome. Grouped around the dome are reception rooms; the larger of which are positioned on the corners and designed in a rectangular shape. Palladio insisted that the harmonic ratios be preserved in the relationships of each room to the others. He also designed an additional harmony between length, width, and height.

Palladio was thoroughly conversant with the musical ideas of his contemporary, Gioseffo Zarlino, the Venetian theorist who synthesized all knowledge of music in a famous sixteenth-century compendium. In this great age of counterpoint, Zarlino based his system on the **hexachord,** or six-note scale from do to la. The number 6 also comes to the fore as the basic module in Palladio's thought. For example, if a room is 6 feet wide, then the length would be 12 feet and the height would be the mean between them (that is, 9 feet). Palladio also favored rooms measuring 18 by 30 (both divisible by 6) or 12 by 20 (both divisible by 4), each making a ratio of

12.5 (A) Andrea Palladio. Il Redentore, Venice, Italy, 1576–1592. (B) Plan of Il Redentore.

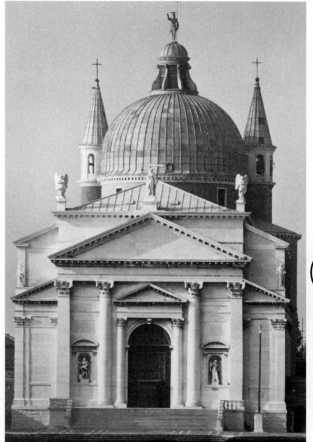

A

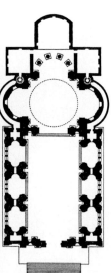

B

3:5. Musically, 3:5 comes out as the interval of the major sixth. "Such harmonies," wrote Palladio, "usually please very much without anyone knowing why, apart from those who study their causes."

When advancing years limited Sansovino's activities, Palladio was called to Venice to construct several buildings, among them the Church of Il Redentore, "The Redeemer" (Fig. 12.5A). Palladio challenged himself to reconcile the Greco-Roman temple with the traditional oblong Christian basilica plan (Fig. 12.5B). Because a classical temple is of uniform height with a simple shed roof, whereas a Christian basilica has a Latin-cross ground plan with a central nave rising high above two side aisles, his solution to this age-old problem shows great ingenuity.

The central part of the facade of Il Redentore becomes the portico of a classical temple complete with columns and pediment, which faces the central nave. The acute angles of a fragmentary second pediment face the side aisles. The pediment theme is repeated in the small triangle above the entrance and in the side angles at the roof level, making in all two complete and two incomplete pediments. This **broken-pediment** motif would later appear in much baroque architecture. To create the feeling of deep space, Palladio alternated square pilasters with round columns and arranged the pediments in a complex intersecting design.

To create the impression of spatial depth in the interior of Il Redentore (Fig. 12.6), Palladio

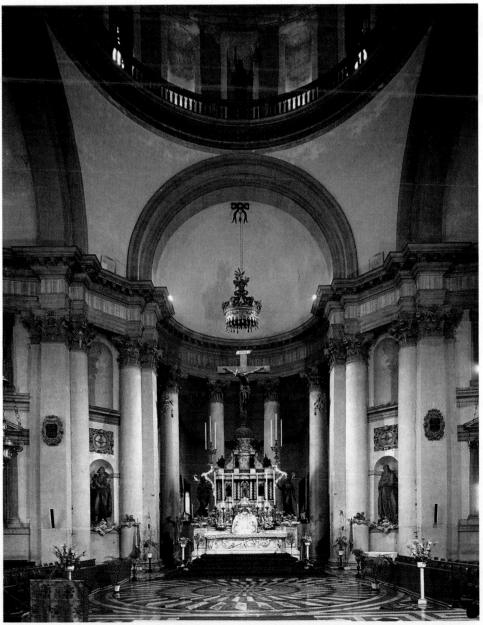

12.6 Andrea Palladio. Interior, Il Redentore, Venice, Italy, 1576–1592.

eliminated the solid-walled apse that usually closes the space around the altar. In its place he used a semicircular open colonnade against clear glass windows. The effect leads the viewer's eye past the altar and into the distance.

The last building Palladio undertook was the Olympic Theater at Vicenza (Fig. 12.7). He had only begun this project the year he died, and Vincenzo Scamozzi finished the construction using Palladio's designs. Palladio's design called for the use of an ingenious device to give the feeling of deep space: a ramp. The ramp is flanked by building facades and rises through the central arch from which actors made their entrance. Although the ramp recedes only about 50 feet, it creates the illusion of a long avenue leading to an open city square in the distance. Inspired by ancient Roman amphitheaters, the Olympic has, in turn, been the inspiration for many later theaters, including one of London's largest, the Palladium.

A NEW KIND OF PAINTING

Venice has always been a visual paradise. Palaces rise like lace out of the waters. The mercurial movements of the winds and clouds cast constantly changing reflections and colors on the canals. There seems to be no borderline between dream and reality. Venice's fulfillment as a major visual arts center, however, awaited the development of oil paints.

Mosaics served well in Byzantine times, but they were not adaptable to the subtler aspects of Renaissance art. Fresco murals painted on plaster were too impermanent in such a damp climate. Tempera on wood panels also proved to be short-lived. When the technique of oil on canvas was developed in the north, particularly in Flanders in the middle and late fifteenth century, the Venetians quickly took it up and made it their own.

The oil medium opened up many new possibilities. In contrast to the hard resins used by the Flemish painters, the Venetians mixed their pigments with oil and flexible resins, giving themselves greater freedom of brushwork. This new technique also made it possible to work directly on canvas without having to make extensive preliminary drawings, either on paper or on the canvas itself. Also, the range of color and blended color was vastly increased. Dramatic use of high intensities to spotlight principal figures and deeper shadow for subordinate ones became more attainable. In addition, subtle modeling of figures, softness of contours, and various atmospheric effects came under greater control.

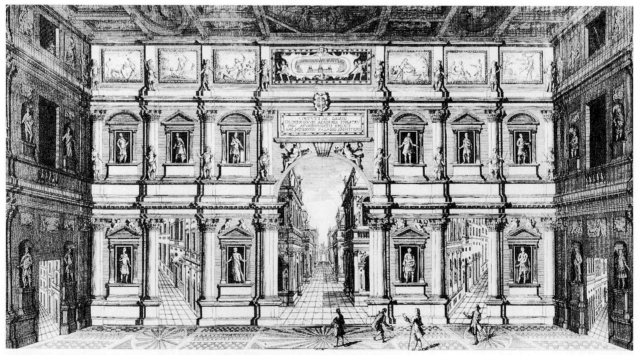

12.7　Andrea Palladio. Interior, Teatro Olimpico, Vicenza, Italy, 1580–1584.

The success of the Venetian mode of painting spread throughout Europe. It was quickly taken up in Italy, and El Greco carried it with him to Spain (see pp. 377–380). Peter Paul Rubens brought it to northern Europe. From there, both Rubens and Anthony Van Dyck introduced the technique to England, from whence it traveled to America.

A STAR IN THE FAMILY BUSINESS: GIOVANNI BELLINI. When the young German painter Albrecht Dürer first visited Venice in 1495, Gentile Bellini was working on his *Procession in St. Mark's Square.* His brother Giovanni was doing a series of altarpieces for Venetian churches. Of all the Venetian painters, Giovanni Bellini's work commanded Dürer's highest admiration. This first impression was confirmed on a later trip in 1506, when he praised Giovanni as "still the supreme master."

The root of Giovanni Bellini's art was a harmonious blend of his father Jacopo's early-Renaissance heritage and the special contributions of his brother Gentile and his brother-in-law Andrea Mantegna of Mantua. But the beautiful branches of this family tree were Giovanni's own paintings, which embraced an emotional range from the silent suffering of his *Pietàs,* through the melancholy meditations of saints and hermits (Fig. 12.8), to the lyrical grace and joyous maternity of his

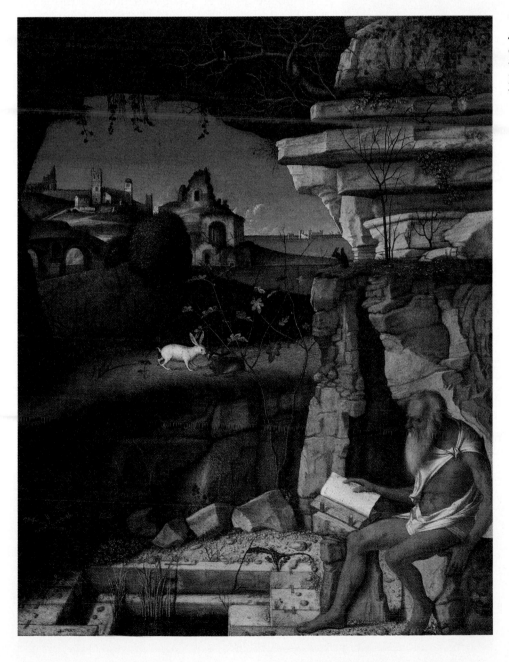

12.8 Giovanni Bellini. *Saint Jerome Reading,* c. 1480–1490. Oil on wood, 1′7¼″ × 1′3½″. National Gallery of Art, Washington, D.C.

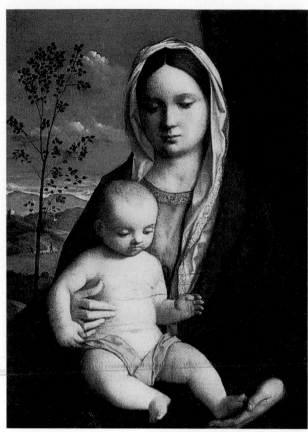

12.9 Giovanni Bellini. *Madonna and Child,* 1505. Oil on wood, 1′7⅜″ × 1′4⅛″. Galleria Borghese, Rome, Italy.

Madonnas (Fig. 12.9). All are set in poetic landscapes filled with the soft, golden light that brings all of nature into a warmly glowing unity.

Giovanni Bellini developed a special treatment of space, dividing the viewer's attention between the closed setting of foreground figures and a receding landscape background. Like the gentle, warm light he used, this spatial treatment became a distinctive part of the Venetian artistic vocabulary. In fact, for later painters it was to become practically a formula for religious subjects and portraiture.

POETRY OF COLOR: GIORGIONE AND TITIAN. The full development of Venetian painting is evident in the poetic pictures attributed both to Giorgione and to his close associate, Titian. In the *Concert Champêtre,* or *Pastoral Concert* (Fig. 12.10), the eye is first attracted to the quartet of figures on the picture plane, then led leisurely toward the middle ground, where a shepherd is tending his flock. The eye finally comes to rest on the gleaming water of the distant horizon. This pastoral idyll, or interlude, is enlivened by several oppositions of figures. Among them are the clothed male figures and the female nudes; the pairing of the polished courtier and stately lady on the left with the rustic shepherd and shepherdess on the right; the attitudes of the two women—one gazing intently at

12.10 Giorgione? Titian? *Concert Champêtre (Pastoral Concert),* c. 1510. Oil on canvas, 3′7¼″ × 4′6⅜″. Louvre, Paris, France.

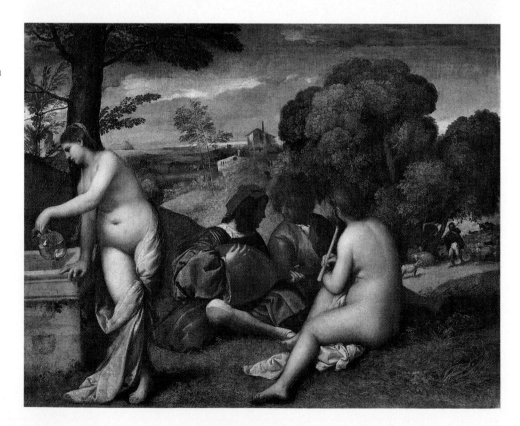

her lover, the other turning gracefully away; the lute, symbolizing lyric poetry; and the flute, pastoral poetry.

The Tempest (Fig. 12.11) is even less concerned with storytelling and more with pictorial construction than the *Concert Champêtre*. A sunny foreground and human figures define the picture plane. Iconographically, a soldier usually personifies fortitude, whereas a seated mother nursing her child represents love or charity. But the main interest of this work lies in the landscape, which reveals itself as the eye is led in receding planes into deep space and the threatening sky in the distance. Stability is maintained through the careful balance of vertical (standing figure, broken columns, trees, buildings) and horizontal (unfinished wall, bridge) lines.

Both the *Pastoral Concert* and *The Tempest* create a mood rather than communicate a specific story or meaning. A puzzle, perhaps, to contemporaries who were accustomed to the usual iconographic subjects, the paintings may be more understandable to the modern observer, who is used to seeing a picture as complete within itself rather than as an illustration of a religious or literary theme.

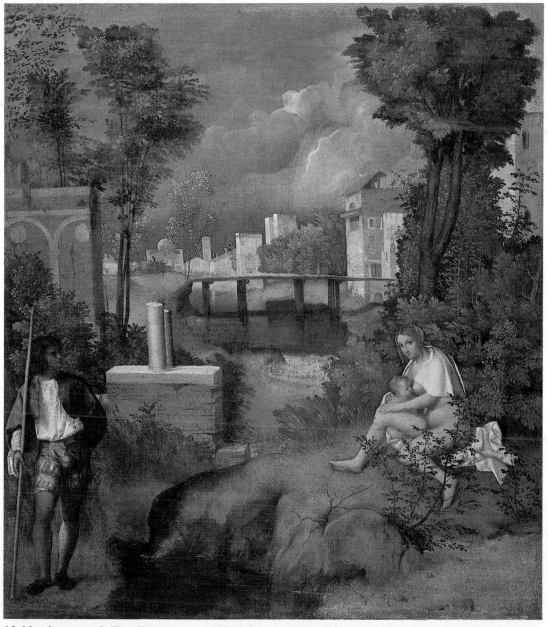

12.11   Giorgione? *The Tempest*, c. 1505. Oil on canvas, 2′8¼″ × 2′4¾″. Galleria del'Accademia, Venice, Italy.

Unlike the modest-sized *Pastoral Concert* and *The Tempest,* Titian's large altarpiece *Assumption of the Virgin* (Fig. 12.12), an altarpiece for the church of Santa Maria dei Frari, is filled with heroic-sized figures. It was intended to catch the attention of anyone entering through the nave portal about 100 yards away. The painting's dynamic vertical movement fits well into the Gothic style of the church.

In this dramatic composition, heavenly and earthly spheres converge momentarily. The apostles are grouped below, in deep shadow; they are raising their arms toward the intermediate zone and the ascending Madonna, whose gesture, in turn, directs the eye to the dazzling brightness above. The upward motion is arrested by the descending figure of God surrounded by angels. Titian skillfully adapted linear movement and gradations of light, as well as transitions of color from somber shades to light pastel hues, to convey the idea of a human spirit soaring triumphant over the gravitational pull of earthly considerations. In this work, Titian created a new pictorial type that was to have a profound influence on the painter El Greco (see Figs. 13.18, 13.19, and 13.20), the baroque sculptor Gian Lorenzo Bernini (see Fig. 13.11), and a number of seventeenth-century painters.

Titian's rich coloring also became the model for later Venetians, such as Tintoretto, and for baroque masters, such as Rubens and Velázquez. In *Bacchus and Ariadne* (Fig. 12.13), Titian depicts the god's return from India accompanied by his mixed band of revelers. On seeing the lovelorn Ariadne, who has been deserted by her lover Theseus, Bacchus leaps from his panther-drawn chariot, his pink drapery aflutter, to wed her. A fascinating visual rhythm based on the repetition of the V-shaped tree near the center pervades the composition. In inverted form, it is echoed in the limbs of Bacchus and Ariadne. The pattern continues across the canvas with the legs of the leopard, the dog, the young faun, and each of the dancing bacchantes.

Titian devised a slashing diagonal direction for the sharp downward plunge of Bacchus. A subtle touch of visual counterpoint can be seen in the sky, where the incident is reenacted by clouds whose shapes echo the drapery and gestures of the principal figures and where the starry crown of immortality awaits Ariadne.

The frenzied Bacchus contrasts with the serene modern goddess of love whom Titian created for the Duke of Urbino (Fig. 12.14). Although she is called Venus, it is more likely that she was a fashionable courtesan, fully at home in her sensuality and her luxurious surroundings. The warm, winey tones of the painting, including the color of Venus's hair, which has for centuries been called *titian red,* introduce a world like that portrayed in *Bacchus and Ariadne,* where the moral concerns of mortals are absent but not missed.

THE ORIGINS OF MANNERISM: TINTORETTO. The paintings of Titian's younger colleague, Tintoretto, added a new dimension to the sensuous qualities of Venetian tones. Tintoretto wedded the vigor of Michelangelo's drawing to the color range of Titian. His violent contrasts of light and dark, together with his off-center diagonal directions, moved away from the harmonious Renaissance composition of a work like Titian's *Assumption.* Tintoretto also rejected the

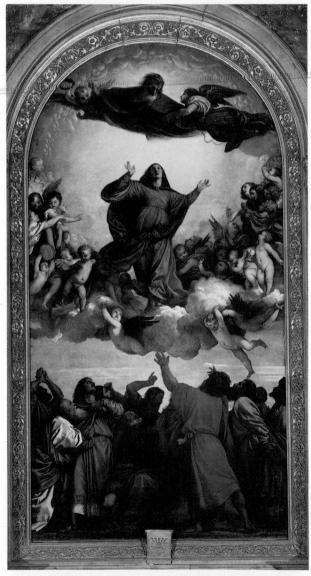

12.12 Titian. *Assumption of the Virgin,* 1516–1518. Oil on canvas, 22′6″ × 11′8″. Santa Maria dei Frari, Venice, Italy.

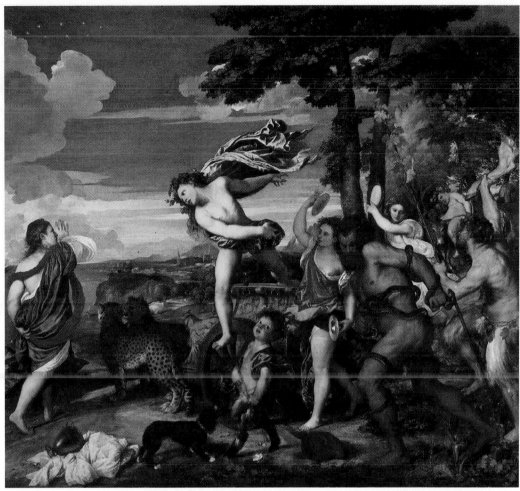

12.13   Titian. *Bacchus and Ariadne,* c. 1520. Oil on canvas, 5′8″ × 6′⅞″. National Gallery, London, England.

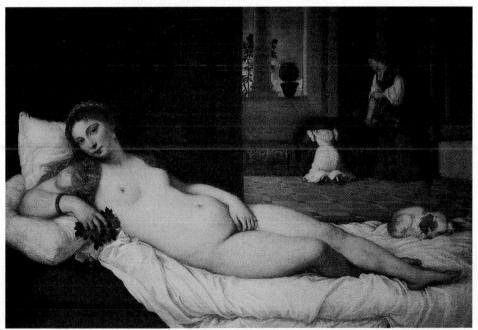

12.14   Titian. *Venus of Urbino,* 1538. Oil on canvas, 4′ × 5′6″. Galleria degli Uffizi, Florence, Italy.

Renaissance notion that an image should be reasonable, that is, that it should appear clear, orderly, and directly legible to a viewer. He teased viewers by placing principal figures on the edge of the action and contriving intricate space-penetrating designs that directed the eye along several different routes. Similarly, he favored a dramatic interplay of the natural and the supernatural, the earthly and the unearthly, the human and the divine.

In his *Last Supper* (Fig. 12.15), Tintoretto represents the miraculous moment when Jesus offers the bread and wine as the sacrificial body and blood of human redemption. To depict this unfathomable mystery of faith, Tintoretto bathes his canvas in a supernatural glow that seems to come partly from the figure of Christ and partly from the flickering flames of the oil lamp. The smoke is transformed into a hovering angelic choir and ends in a burst of light around the head of Christ. The drastic diagonals of the floor are paralleled by those of the table, but instead of directing the eye to the head of Christ, as they would in Renaissance paintings like those of Masaccio (see Figs. 9.15 and 9.16), the lines lead to an indefinite point in the upper right and to space beyond the picture.

Tintoretto's design for *The Marriage of Bacchus and Ariadne* (Fig. 12.16) is more lyrical yet equally complex. He created a rotating movement in which the figures seem to be floating weightlessly in space.

In this work the seated Ariadne personifies Venice, crowned with the stars of immortality. Bacchus represents the good life, providing the fruits of the earth that flowed from the city's prosperous maritime trade. The hovering Venus, goddess of love, binds both together. The ship on the horizon recalls the grand aquatic ceremony that took place each year, when the doge cast a golden ring into the water to symbolize Venice's marriage to the sea.

This is one of four panels originally painted for the ambassadorial waiting room in the Doge's Palace. It is likely that each conveyed a political message to visitors. One depicts Vulcan in his forge producing armor, to signify Venice's industrial might. In another, Minerva with her wisdom repulses the war god Mars to proclaim Venice's love of peace. A third shows the doge between figures symbolizing peace and justice.

It is interesting to note that Tintoretto trained his talented daughter, Marietta Robusti, as a painter. Unlike Sofonisba Anguissola (Fig. 12.17), whose education was shaped by her noble family's implementation of suggestions for the education of women outlined in Baldassare Castiglione's *Book of the Courtier* (see pp. 274–276), Robusti received an education typical of that given to male painters in the midsixteenth century. Similarly, Lavinia Fontana, who studied with her father Prospero, achieved a reputation in her own right.

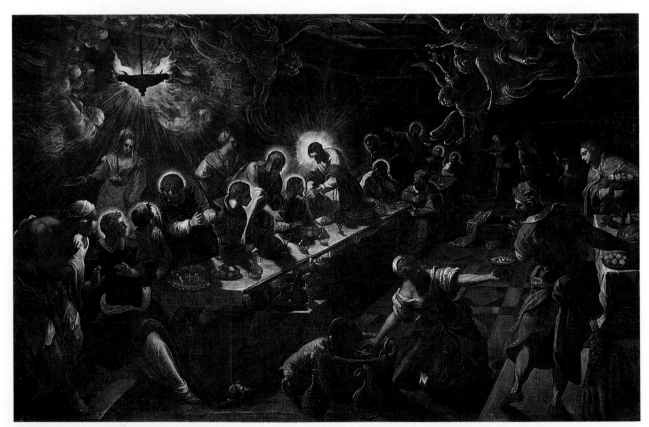

12.15 Tintoretto. *Last Supper,* 1592–1594. Oil on canvas, 12′ × 18′8″. San Giorgio Maggiore, Venice, Italy.

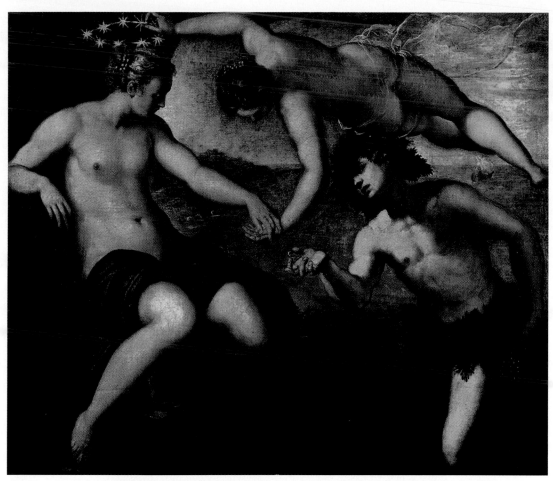

12.16 Tintoretto. *The Marriage of Bacchus and Ariadne,* 1577–1588. Oil on canvas, 4′9″ × 5′5″. Doge's Palace, Venice, Italy.

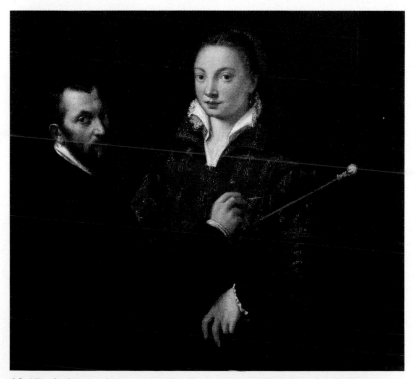

12.17 Sofinisba Anguissola, *Bernadino Anguissola Painting Sofonisba Anguissola,* late 1550s.

Her gender prevented her from attending an art academy, but she found ample work painting portraits and creating religious art (Fig. 12.18). Although few in number, successful sixteenth-century women artists, and the activities of women patrons like the formidable Isabella d'Este, marchioness of Mantua, may have helped other women think not only of making art but also of making money while making art.

A PAINTER'S PAINTER: VERONESE. Paolo Cagliari, known as Veronese, did not scale the heights and plumb the depths as did his colleagues Titian and Tintoretto. Instead, his searching eye sought out the rich and varied surface play of the Venetian scene around him. A painter's painter, Veronese is known for his bravura with the brush, the sensuousness of his surfaces, and the tactile strength of his drawing. In his *The Dream of Saint Helen*

12.18 Lavinia Fontana, *Consecration to the Virgin,* 1599. Musée des Beaux-Arts, Marseilles, France.

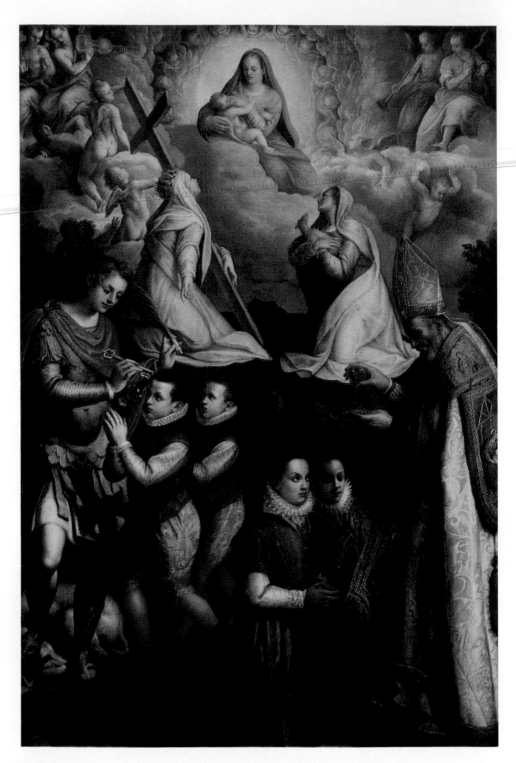

(Fig. 12.19), he is not so much concerned with her inner vision as he is with the colorful splendor of his canvas. Helen was the mother of the Emperor Constantine, who converted to Christianity in 313. According to tradition, it was she who first found a relic of the true cross of Christ and in a vision beheld the location of the Holy Sepulchre. As Veronese portrays her, she is clad in a queenly robe of satin brocade and wears a bejeweled crown. Veronese revels in the play of light and shadow around the rich folds of the drapery, the glow of the golden crown, and the shimmer of the pearls. He excels in rendering the contrasting textures of the marble column, the gilt-bronze figure in the niche, the wood of the cross, and the nude flesh of the angel.

Of all his subjects, the most congenial to Veronese's approach was celebration. Painted with the primary object of engaging and entertaining vision, his canvases succeeded in capturing an important part of Venetian life: the pleasure and

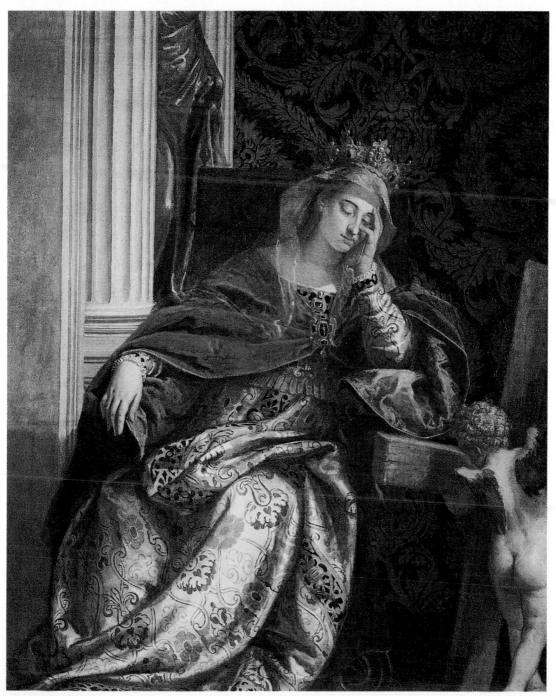

12.19   Paolo Veronese. *The Dream of Saint Helen,* c. 1580. Oil on canvas, 5′5⅓″ × 4′4¾″. Vatican, Pinacoteca, Italy.

amusement of large social gatherings and the love of rich surroundings embellished with fruits, flowers, animals, furniture, draperies, and jesters. *The Feast in the House of Levi* (Fig. 12.20) was originally painted as a Last Supper for the refectory of a Venetian monastery. The composition is held in tight control by the three arches of the loggia setting, which Veronese adapted from the designs Sansovino had made for the interior of the library and the Loggetta at the base of the campanile in St. Mark's Square (Fig. 12.1).

Questions were soon raised about the propriety of the painting's content. By tradition, a Last Supper scene portrayed only Christ and the twelve apostles, but Veronese had included more than fifty figures (including the twelve apostles). This departure from tradition resulted in his being brought before the court of the Inquisition (see p. 362). The inquisitors were disturbed not only by the number of figures but also by the presence of a dog and a cat, which Veronese painted in the foreground. Even more troublesome was the inclusion of German soldiers sitting on the staircase at the very time when the Roman Catholic Church was experiencing a theological confrontation with the Lutheran Reformation in Germany. One of the most remarkable documents in the history of painting—a summary of the painter's actual testimony intended to justify his work—reveals much about this picture and about Veronese's conception of art in general:

Question. Did anyone commission you to paint Germans, buffoons, and similar things in that picture?

Answer. No, milords, but I received the commission to decorate the picture as I saw fit. It is large and, it seemed to me, it could hold many figures.

Q. Are not the decorations which you painters are accustomed to add to paintings or pictures supposed to be suitable and proper to the subject and the principal figures or are they just for pleasure—simply what comes to your imagination without any discretion or judiciousness?

A. I paint pictures as I see fit and as well as my talent permits.

Q. Does it seem fitting at the Last Supper of the Lord to paint buffoons, drunkards, Germans, dwarfs and similar vulgarities?

A. No, milords.

Q. Do you not know that in Germany and in other places infected with heresy it is customary with various pictures full of scurrilousness and similar inventions to mock, vituperate, and scorn the things of the Holy Catholic Church in order to teach bad doctrines to foolish and ignorant people?

A. Yes, that is wrong; but I return to what I have said, that I am obliged to follow what my superiors have done.

Q. What have your superiors done? Have they perhaps done similar things?

A. Michelangelo in Rome in the Pontifical Chapel painted Our Lord, Jesus Christ, His Mother, St. John, St. Peter, and the Heavenly Host. These are all represented in the nude—even the Virgin Mary—and in poses with little reverence.[1]

---

[1]Elizabeth G. Holt, ed., *Literary Sources of Art History: An Anthology of Texts from Theophilus to Goethe* (copyright © 1947, 1975 by Princeton University Press). Reprinted by permission of Princeton University Press.

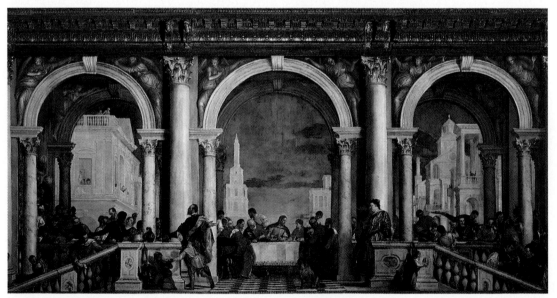

12.20 Paolo Veronese. *The Feast in the House of Levi,* 1573. Oil on canvas, 18′2″ × 42′. Galleria dell'Accademia, Venice, Italy.

In a Last Supper, the figures seated with Jesus at the table should be the twelve apostles, but Veronese could specifically identify only two. He pointed out St. Peter on Christ's right, in robes of rose and gray, who according to the painter is "carving the lamb in order to pass it to the other end of the table," and St. John on Christ's left. When questioned about the other figures, Veronese claimed that he could not recall them, given that he had "painted the picture some months ago." Yet only 10 months had passed, and the iconography of the Last Supper was very well known.

The Inquisition's verdict required Veronese to make certain changes in the picture. Rather than comply, he simply changed the title to *The Feast in the House of Levi,* thereby placing it outside the iconographic tradition of Last Supper pictures. This controversy is a landmark in art history. In defending his work, Veronese raised aesthetic and formal values above those of subject matter.

MUSIC

The peak of Renaissance musical development was the polyphonic style of the Netherlandish composers. The general admiration for this art at the beginning of the sixteenth century was summed up by the Venetian ambassador to the court of Burgundy, who remarked that three things were of the highest excellence in the area: first, the finest, most exquisite linen of Holland; second, the tapestries of Brabant, most beautiful in design; and third, the music, which certainly could be said to be perfect. With such sentiments being expressed in official circles, it is not surprising to find that in 1527 a Netherlander and a leading representative of the polyphonic art, Adrian Willaert, was appointed to the highest musical position in Venice: choirmaster of St. Mark's.

This admiration for northern musical forms is another instance of the internationalism of the Venetians. Under Willaert and his successors, Venice became a center of musical progress while Rome remained a fortress of tradition. Its relative freedom from religious authority predisposed it to new developments, and among the results were a number of new musical forms and radical changes in older ones. In vocal music, this meant promotion of the madrigal, modification of the church motet, and development of the **polychoral style,** which made simultaneous use of two, three, and sometimes four choirs. Instrumental music found new forms in the organ **intonazione** (short prelude), **ricercare** (contrapuntal composition), and **toccata** (brilliant showpiece) for keyboard solo

and in the **sinfonia** and early **concertato** and **concerto** forms for orchestra.

In Venice, the "modern style" was linked with Giovanni Gabrieli and his organ music, with early orchestral writing, and with the development of the polychoral style. In Florence, it was associated with Vincenzo Galilei, Peri, and Caccini and their solo songs and early opera experiments. In Rome, it was associated with Girolamo Frescobaldi and his virtuoso organ works. In Mantua and Venice, the madrigals and operas of Claudio Monteverdi became the basis of the new baroque music.

MUSIC AT ST. MARK'S CATHEDRAL. The musical development begun by Willaert culminated in the work of Giovanni Gabrieli, who held the position of first organist at St. Mark's from 1585 until his death in 1612. His principal works were published under the title *Symphoniae Sacrae* in 1597 and 1615.

The domed Greek cross plan of St. Mark's, with its choir lofts placed in the transept wings, seems to have suggested some unusual acoustic possibilities to composers. When a choir was concentrated in the compact space beyond the transept, as in the traditional Latin-cross church, the body of sound was unified. When it was divided into two or more widely separated groups, as at St. Mark's, the interplay of sound led to experiments that resulted in the so-called polychoral style. In effect, it dissolved the traditional choruses and heralded a new development in the choral art.

These **chori spezzati**—literally, "broken choruses"—as they were called, added the element of spatial contrast to Venetian music, and a variety of new effects were created. One of these effects was the echo device, which became central to the baroque tradition. Composers could alternate two contrasting bodies of sound, such as chorus against chorus, single line versus full choir, solo voice opposing full choir, or instruments pitted against voices. Instrument groups could be contrasted, high and low voices alternated, soft sound played against loud sound, fragments played against a continuous musical line, and block chords made to stand out against a flowing counterpoint.

The resultant principle of duality, based on opposing elements, is the basis for the concertato or concerting style. The word appears in the title of some works Giovanni Gabrieli published jointly with his uncle Andrea in 1587: *Concerti. . . per voci e stromenti* (Concertos . . . for voices and instruments). The term later came to be widely used, with such titles as *Concerti Ecclesiastici* (Church Concertos) appearing frequently.

The motet *In ecclesiis,* written as the second part of the *Symphoniae Sacrae,* is an example of Gabrieli's mature style. Although the specific occasion for which it was intended is unknown, the motet is of the processional type and as such is appropriate music for ceremonies similar to that depicted in Bellini's picture (Fig. 12.1). Moreover, the choirs arranged in groups, as well as a brass ensemble, are similar to Bellini's details (Fig. 12.21).

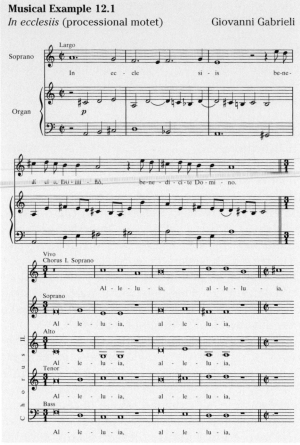

Musical Example 12.1

In ecclesiis (processional motet)   Giovanni Gabrieli

The structure of Gabrieli's motet is based on the word *alleluia,* which functions as a **refrain,** or recurring section, and acts as a divider between the verses. The alleluias also are set in the more stationary triple meter, suggesting a pause in the procession, whereas the stanzas have the more active beat of footsteps, as in march time.

A gradual buildup of volume can be heard in the sequence of sopranos and full chorus; tenors and full chorus; the instrumental sinfonia, first alone, then in combination with tenors and altos; and the instrumental color against the chorus with organ support. The cumulative climax is brought about by the final grandiose union of all vocal and instrumental forces, ending in a solid cadence radiating with musical color and producing the huge sonority necessary to bring the mighty work to its close.

THE MUSICAL EXPERIMENTS OF MONTEVERDI. Although Gabrieli's tonal works became the precedent for the later *colossal baroque,* it remained for his successor, Claudio Monteverdi, to probe the inner spirit of the new style. With Monteverdi, the transition to the baroque becomes evident. Appointed master of music of the Most Serene Republic of Venice in 1613 after serving as court composer at Mantua for 23 years, Monteverdi achieved a working combination of Renaissance counterpoint and all the experimental techniques of his own time.

At Mantua, Monteverdi had already written his *Orfeo* (1607), a complete opera in the modern sense, with overture, choruses, vocal solos and ensembles, instrumental interludes, and ballet sequences. At Venice, where the first public opera house was established in 1637, he continued with a series of lyrical dramas, of which only the last two survive: *Return of Ulysses to His Homeland* (1641) and *The Coronation of Poppea* (1642). Today all three operas remain in the repertory of international opera houses and can be seen and heard through visual and aural media.

In addition, Monteverdi gave a new twist to the Renaissance madrigal, a type of music for two or more singers, each of whom has a separate part. The madrigal with lyrics devoted to the delights of love and the beauties of nature reached a high point of popularity in sixteenth-century Italy and in the England of Queen Elizabeth. With Monteverdi, however, the madrigal took on a special emotional and dramatic character that paralleled developments in visual mannerism (discussed in the next section).

The new emotional orientation is stated in Monteverdi's *Eighth Book of Madrigals* (1638):

> I have reflected that the principal passions or affections of our mind are three, namely, anger, moderation, and humility or supplication; so the best philosophers declare, and the very nature of our voice indicates this in having high, low, and middle registers. The art of music also points clearly to these three in its terms 'agitated,' 'soft,' and 'moderate' [**concitato, molle,** and **temperato**].

The collection has the significant subtitle "Madrigals of War and Love." Monteverdi declared

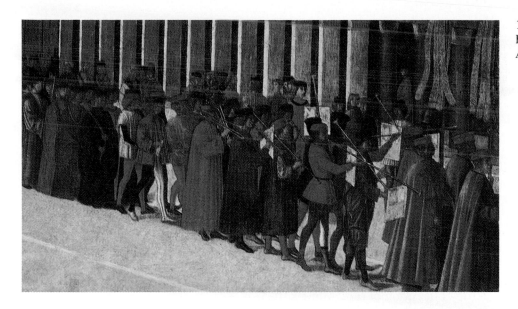

12.21 Gentile Bellini. Brass Ensemble. Detail. Accademia, Venice, Italy.

that he wanted to depict anger, warfare, entreaty, and death as well as the sounds of brave men engaged in battle. According to Monteverdi, vocal music of this type should be "a simulation of the passions of the words." Descriptive melodies in this **representative** style reflected the imagery of the poetic text. In Monteverdi's madrigal "Zefiro torna" (Return, O Zephyr), the word *l'onde* (waves) is expressed by a rippling melody, whereas *da monti e da valli ime e profonde* (from mountains and valleys high and deep) is rendered by sharply rising and falling lines.

Musical Example 12.2
"Zefiro torna" (Return, O Zephyr)   Monteverdi

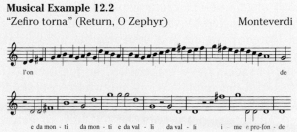

MANNERIST EUROPE IN THE SIXTEENTH CENTURY

In the sixteenth century, Europe was in a state of acute crisis. A series of catastrophic events shocked major cultural centers. Every aspect of life—religious, scientific, political, social, economic, personal, aesthetic—was destined to undergo reexamination and radical change.

In England, Henry VIII broke with Rome and established the Church of England. On the Continent,

the moral zeal and desire for reform of Martin Luther, John Calvin, and others divided Europe into Reformation and Counter-Reformation camps. Territorial ambitions and the lust for conquest resulted in a clash of wills between Emperor Charles V and King Francis I of France. Feeling his country caught in a giant squeeze play, Francis tried to fortify his position by invading northern Italy, but the king proved to be no match for the powerful Holy Roman Emperor.

The voyages of the great navigators and the exploits of the colonizers who followed in their wake had brought much of North, Central, and South America under Spanish control. With a monopoly on the Asian spice trade and with the gold and silver mines of the New World pouring fabulous riches into its treasury, Spain was rapidly emerging as the most powerful country in the world. With the Spanish crown on his head and the lordship of Holland, Flanders, Germany, and Austria firmly in his grasp, Charles next turned his attention to Italy. One by one the formerly independent Italian duchies and city-states came under his domination.

Opposition from any quarter was not tolerated. In 1527, Charles's mercenaries marched on Rome, sacking and plundering. Eight days later the Eternal City was a smoking ruin, the Vatican a barracks, St. Peter's a stable, and Pope Clement VII a prisoner at Castel Sant'Angelo. The Sack of Rome was a psychological and a physical blow to its citizens, who believed that they no longer lived at the thriving center of the Western world. Many took the fact that the Eternal City could be vanquished as a portent of worse things to come. It seemed to be a sign that the city and the church were being punished for indulging in worldly vices. Resident artists fled; among them were Sansovino (to Venice), Parmagianino (to Parma), and Benvenuto Cellini (to France).

The pope had no choice but to submit to Spanish policy. A Spanish viceroy ruled in Naples, and a Spanish government was installed in Milan. Through the Gonzagas in Mantua, the Estes in Ferrara, and the Medici in Florence, the Spaniards controlled all important commercial and cultural centers. With Spanish rule came Spanish severity and religiosity mixed with etiquette and courtly elegance, all of which quickly began to shape Italian cultural life. The new scientific theories and discoveries were equally unsettling. In 1543, the astronomer Copernicus brought out his book *On the Revolution of the Planets in Their Orbits,* a work that was destined to change the conception of the cosmos from an Earth-centered to a sun-centered universe. Shock and anger followed the publication as people began to realize that they inhabited one of several planets whirling through space and were no longer at the center of creation. (Almost 75 years later, the Italian astronomer Galileo was tried for heresy because he made a similar claim. He was sentenced to prison and released only when he disavowed his teachings and writings.) The combined effect of Copernicus's claim and other scientific findings weakened the prevailing belief in miracles and divine intervention in human affairs.

Peasant revolts, invasions by the Ottoman Turks, piracy at sea, trials by the dreaded Inquisition, the burning of heretics, and religious and civil wars completed the turbulent picture. Such a seething of currents and crosscurrents, new and old directions, and inner anxieties and contradictions was bound to find expression in the arts.

THE DEVELOPMENT OF MANNERISM

As a historical phenomenon, **mannerism** ran an erratic course from about 1530 to 1590, sandwiched between the fading Renaissance and the emergence of the baroque style. Like the crisis it incorporated, mannerism points in many directions. Any discussion of mannerism should probably refer to *mannerisms,* because so many different cultural centers, conflicting trends, varieties of patrons and personalities, and individual idioms were involved. The word itself has several meanings. *Maniera* in Italian denotes "manner" or "style." In English, *mannered* indicates a somewhat derogatory, idiosyncratic, affected, or exaggerated mode of behavior. In the arts, *mannerism* implies fluency, virtuosity of execution, a high degree of sophistication, and a sense of stylishness, which often leads to overrefinement and self-consciously contrived attitudes.

Living in the shadow of such unrivaled masters of the immediate past as Leonardo da Vinci, Michelangelo, and Raphael created a dilemma for the younger generation of painters. They were very much aware that a golden age had preceded them and that there was little hope of their improving on the concepts and craft of their famous predecessors. These young artists found themselves at a crossroads. Following the old paths meant selecting certain ideas and techniques of their precursors. Striking out in new directions meant taking for granted such perfected technical achievements as linear and atmospheric perspective, mathematically correct foreshortening, and anatomically correct renderings—if only to deliberately and visibly break these rules with telling and dramatic effects.

The first course required working "in the manner" of the giants of the past. In part, the reverence for the past led to the founding of academies to transmit the traditional techniques to young artists. When Giorgio Vasari, a disciple of Michelangelo, used the term *de maniera,* he meant working in the manner of Leonardo, Michelangelo, and Raphael. By reducing their art to a system of rules, he could work quickly and efficiently. His fondest boast was that whereas it took Michelangelo 6 years to finish one work, he could complete six works in 1 year.

Some artists accepted the fact that the era of experimentation was over and the era of fulfillment was at hand. This was not a time of eccentric genius or soul-searching prophecy, only a period of competent craftsmanship. Such was the course followed by Vasari, Palladio, and Veronese. In Florence, Vasari was instrumental in founding an academy of design in 1561. At Bologna in 1585, the Carracci family established an institute with the word *academy* in its name, where courses in art theory and practice were offered.

The mannerist artists did not turn to nature for their models, as Leonardo had done, but rather studied great works with the thought of mastering the artistic vocabularies of the late Renaissance geniuses. Art, in other words, did not hold up a mirror to nature but rather reflected the art of the past. At the lowest level, this implied well-schooled technicians and a style based on conventions—a free borrowing and reassembling without the original creative synthesis. At the highest level, this approach could lead to virtuosity of execution. In no way did it rule out inspiration. In the work of the Florentine mannerist Rosso Fiorentino, who followed in the footsteps of Michelangelo, the results are evident. Rosso's tumultuous *Moses Defending the Daughters of Jethro* (Fig. 12.22), with its muscular male nudes, is a typical example of this aspect of mannerism. The development of mannerism can, in fact, be traced to some of Michelangelo's late work, such as the *Last Judgment* (see Fig. 10.9), and the architecture of the Medici Library in Florence.

With the architecture of Palladio, a more academic mannerism came to terms with the classical orders of Vitruvius. By adapting Roman architectural forms to his contemporary needs, he cooled the Venetian love of lavishness and curbed the excesses of overdecoration. Similarly, through the symmetry of his designs, his closed forms, and the organizing function of his architectural backgrounds, Veronese was able to handle large crowds and bustling movement without detracting from his pictorial unity, as in *The Feast in the House of Levi* (Fig. 12.20). Although Gabrieli's music broke up the unity of the Renaissance choir—encompassing and increasing the scope of musical space—his support of the traditional Renaissance polyphony kept his work under strict control.

Thus, one important type of mannerism was an extension, codification, and academic adaptation of the ideals of the High Renaissance. The more striking aspect of mannerism, however, is found in its strong reactions to and bold, dramatic departures from Renaissance rules and decorum. Loyal followers of the Renaissance saw this trend as the collapse of an ideal order and the adoption of an "affected manner" by highly idiosyncratic artists. The rapid rise of Mannerism's popularity in the courts of Italy and France suggests that the style appealed to those who wanted to show their superior taste and connoisseurship.

The second type of mannerism was originated by artists who, unlike their Renaissance forebears, were no longer excited by the mathematics of linear perspective or the challenge of finding the proper size and relationship of figures to their surrounding space. Instead, they discovered excitement in breaking established rules and violating Renaissance assumptions. In their work, naturalism gave way to the free play of the imagination. Classical composure yielded to nervous movement, which would emerge as a hallmark of the baroque style. Clear definition of space succumbed to a jumble of picture planes crowded with twisted figures. Renaissance symmetry and focus on the central figure were replaced by off-balance diagonals that made it difficult to find the protagonist of the drama amid the numerous directional lines. Backgrounds no longer contained the picture but were instead vaguely defined or nonexistent. Also, the norms of body proportion were distorted by the unnatural elongation of figures. **Chiaroscuro,** the art of modeling with light and shade, now served to create optical illusions, violent contrasts, and theatrical lighting effects. Finally, strong, deep colors and rich

costumes faded to pastel hues and gauzy, fluttering drapery. In short, the Renaissance dream of clarity and order became the mannerist vision of anxious, warped space. Some of these tendencies had been present in the late High Renaissance. Giorgione's puzzling pictures (Figs. 12.10 and 12.11) broke with iconographic tradition and confused his contemporaries. In Leonardo's *Madonna and Child with St. Anne and the Young St. John* (see Fig. 9.25), the figures are uncomfortably superimposed on each other; how St. Anne supports the weight of the Madonna and what they are sitting on is left to the viewer's imagination. The symbolism of the work, which shows the genealogy of Christ and His ancestry in the developing cult of St. Anne, is overwhelmed by the powerful, naturalistic representation. In the black terror and bleak despair of Michelangelo's *Last Judgment* (see Fig. 10.9), clarity of space no longer exists: there are crowded parts and bare spaces, the size of figures is out of proportion, and one cannot even be sure who are the saved and who the damned.

What was the exception in the High Renaissance became the rule under mannerism, which quickly, although briefly, was taken up in several international cultural centers. Florentine mannerists such as Rosso Fiorentino and Benvenuto Cellini

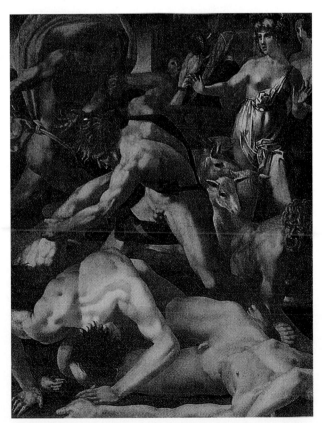

12.22   Rosso Fiorentino. *Moses Defending the Daughters of Jethro,* 1523. Oil on canvas, 5′ × 4′. Galleria degli Uffizi, Florence, Italy.

12.23 Jacopo Pontormo. *Joseph with Jacob in Egypt,* 1518. Oil on canvas, 3'2" × 3'7⅛". National Gallery, London, England.

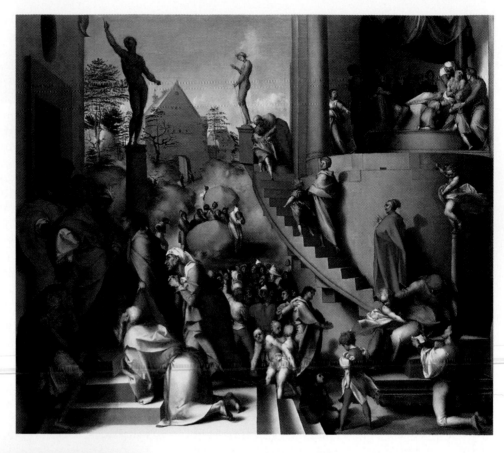

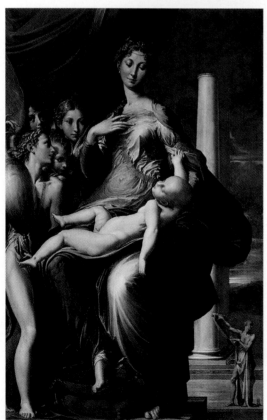

12.24 Parmigianino. *Madonna with the Long Neck,* 1534–1540. Oil on wood, 7'1" × 4'4". Galleria degli Uffizi, Florence, Italy.

were summoned to Paris to become court artists of Francis I. Raphael's prolific pupil Giulio Romano was appointed the official architect of the Duke of Mantua.

Despite their desire to dazzle and their whimsically contrived tricks, these artists had no intention to deceive. Their complicated art was addressed to the sophisticated few who were well aware of the new practice and could enjoy the witty turns and startling twists. This courtly phase of the mannerist style, however, was too restricted to a single class and too refined and self-conscious in its aestheticism to endure for long.

PAINTING: PONTORMO, PARMIGIANINO, AND BRONZINO

Pontormo's *Joseph with Jacob in Egypt* (Fig. 12.23) was painted on commission for a bedroom in a Florentine palace. The appropriately dreamlike canvas is a picture puzzle, the parts of which do not quite fit together. The story is told in three scenes, with Pharaoh's dream in the upper right, the finding of the cup in Benjamin's sack in the center, and Joseph's reconciliation with his brothers at the left. The Renaissance traditions of unified space and diminution of figures as they recede from the picture plane are deliberately violated. The kneeling figure in the right foreground is half the size of

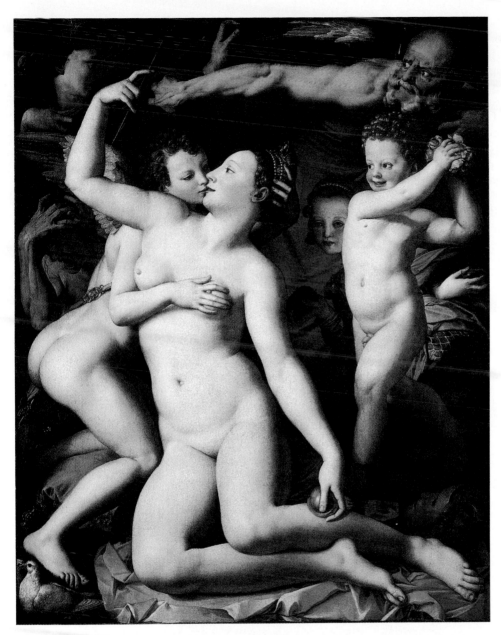

12.25 Bronzino. *Allegory of Venus,* c. 1550. Oil on wood, 4′9″ × 3′9″. National Gallery, London, England.

his counterpart on the left. The winding staircase that goes nowhere, the statues that gesticulate like actors on stage, and the capricious flickering of light and shadow over the surface of the picture all add to the strange, enigmatic atmosphere.

Gracefulness, elegance, and extreme refinement characterize Parmigianino's *Madonna with the Long Neck* (Fig. 12.24). The artist may have been inspired by a hymn to the Virgin that compares her neck to an ivory column. Even though the painting is unfinished, its oddness seems to contradict its original intent as an altarpiece. The Madonna's elongated neck is paralleled by the strange rising column that supports nothing. The exaggerated length of her hand, the delicate tapering of her fingers, and the stretched-out body of the child provide balancing

horizontal accents at the expense of naturalistic representation. The serpentine posture of Mary terminates in the unnatural elongation of her right foot and left leg. The prophet on the right (St. Jerome?) in a calculated violation of normal perspective completes this surprising excursion into artistic license. Unmistakably, Renaissance concern with clarity and accurate depiction of the human figure have been sacrificed to create a more stylish, if strange, picture.

Bronzino came by his mannerism through his training with Pontormo, who portrayed him as the boy sitting on the steps of the middle foreground of Figure 12.23. He is best known for the icy formalism of his elegant portraits of the local aristocracy. In his *Allegory of Venus* (Fig. 12.25), he makes an excursion into mythological metaphor. The number of figures is enough to fill a large-scale mural, but here they are intertwined and crowded into a cramped, claustrophobic space. The muscular arm of Time at the top, aided by Truth, is drawing a curtain to expose the **tableau vivant** below. Along with Venus's legs and the standing figures of Cupid and Folly, the arm frames the picture. The ardent caresses of Cupid certainly exceed the usual demonstrations of affection by a son to his mother. Behind them the old hag Envy clutches her hair despairingly while turtledoves bill and coo below. The innocent face of the figure identified as Fraud or Inconstancy lurks in the right background. She holds a honeycomb in a left hand that is grafted onto her right arm. Further deception is seen in her lion's legs and her coiling, scaly serpent's tail. The masks in the lower right cast the whole scene as a theater piece, perhaps creating an amoral dream world like that envisioned by Titian.

MANNERISM IN SCULPTURE

Today, Benvenuto Cellini's reputation rests more on his flamboyant, swaggering autobiography than on his surviving works. Probably as much fiction as fact, the autobiography portrays Cellini as a soldier of fortune, a statesman, and an ardent lover, as well as a sculptor. He provides an eyewitness account of Charles V's sack of Rome, where he was imprisoned because of his involvement in a violent crime. After a spectacular escape, he fled to France. Although he was first and foremost a goldsmith, only one work in gold survives that can be attributed to him, a saltcellar executed for Francis I (Fig. 12.26). The workmanship shows the overly refined side of mannerist art. Referring to the two figures, Cellini writes that Earth, the figure on the right, is "fashioned like a woman with all the beauty of form, the grace and charm,

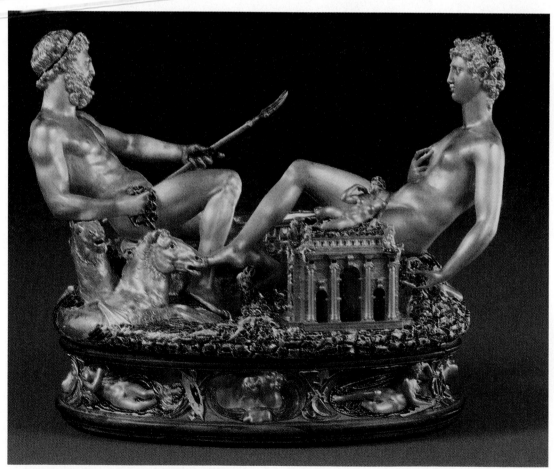

12.26 Benvenuto Cellini. Saltcellar of Francis I. 1540–1543. Gold, chased and partially enameled, base made of ebony, 10¼″ × 1′1″. Kunsthistorisches Museum, Vienna, Austria.

of which my art was capable." As Earth's limbs become erotically entwined with her opposite, Water, the two meet and merge with a promise of future fertility. Cellini also described the large-scale bronze-casting methods he used in his larger-than-life-size freestanding statue, *Perseus with the Head of Medusa* (Fig. 12.27). He chose the gruesome moment just after the decapitation, when Perseus holds high the head with its coiling, snaky locks as blood gushes forth in intricate patterns.

Elegance of design, polished craftsmanship, and fluency of line also mark the sculpture of Giovanni Bologna, also known as Giambologna. *Winged Mercury* (Fig. 12.28), with its delicate balance and extraordinary technical dexterity, was once used as the gleaming symbol of the twentieth-century communications industry. Born in Flanders and trained

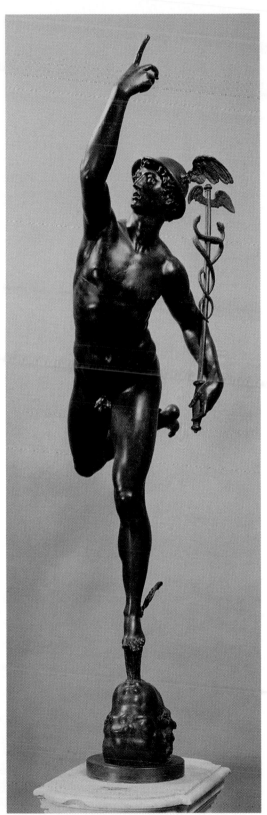

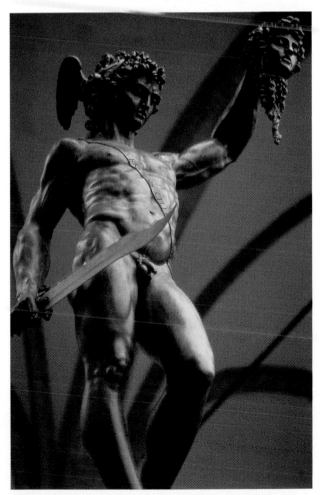

12.27 Benvenuto Cellini. *Perseus with the Head of Medusa,* 1545–1553. Bronze, height 18′. Loggia dei Lanzi, Florence, Italy.

12.28 Giovanni da Bologna. *Winged Mercury,* c. 1574. Bronze, height 5′9″. Museo Nazionale del Bargello, Florence, Italy.

in northern Europe, Bologna worked mainly in Florence, where he became a dominating force in Italian sculpture. He was, in fact, the link between Michelangelo and the baroque sculptor Bernini, and thereby between the Renaissance and baroque styles.

For the group that was later called *Abduction of the Sabine Women* (Fig. 12.29), Bologna set himself the task of probing the limits of motion and emotion that could be expressed in marble. The writhing, serpentine movement spirals upward from the crouching elderly male figure through the twisting tension of the young man's muscular body to the wildly outflung arms of the girl. Despite the violent centrifugal motion, the action is contained within an open cylindrical space. The obvious precedent is the ancient *Laocoön Group* (see Fig. 3.17), but unlike this classical model, which is frontally oriented, Bologna's work was meant for an outdoor setting where it could provide variety and interest when seen from any angle.

MANNERISM IN ARCHITECTURE: ROMANO, SCAMOZZI, AND ZUCCARI

In architecture, mannerism assumed many and varied shapes. Giulio Romano built the Palazzo del Tè, or "Tea Palace" (Fig. 12.30), outside Mantua in northern Italy for the ducal family. To enclose the formal garden, he constructed a wall of heavily rusticated masonry that was far too massive for its function. Sturdy Doric columns rise upward only to support the frieze. This dramatic overstatement, however, pales in comparison with the somewhat unnerving effect of the frieze itself, in which every third triglyph slips downward a notch, thus creating a lively syncopated visual rhythm. Small frameless windows are crowded between the closely spaced columns at the top, whereas the heavily pedimented windows below are blind. Romano's handling of the classical orders and detail recalls an aphorism in a letter to him from the witty Venetian writer Pietro Aretino, who said of his style, "Always modern in the antique way and antique in the modern way." The Tea Palace was obviously an architectural fantasy for the delight of his sophisticated clients.

In Venice, meanwhile, Scamozzi, the younger collaborator of both Sansovino and Palladio, was commissioned in 1584 to add a wing to Sansovino's library. Extending the side toward St. Mark's Square, the wing would house the Procuratie Nuove, the new civic agencies (Fig. 12.31). Scamozzi's design

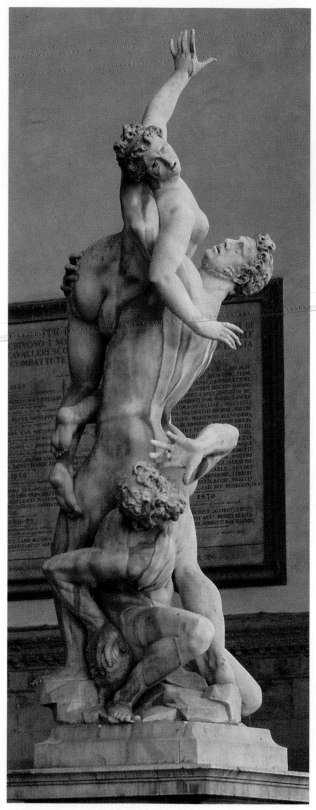

12.29   Giovanni da Bologna. *Abduction of the Sabine Women*, 1583. Marble, approx. 13′6″ tall. Loggia dei Lanzi, Florence, Italy.

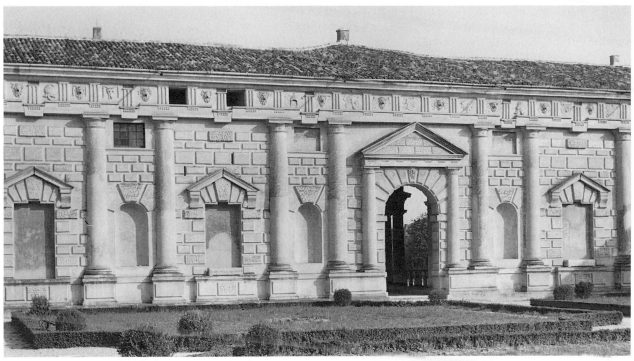

12.30   Giulio Romano. Interior courtyard facade, Palazzo del Tè, Mantua, Italy, 1525–1535.

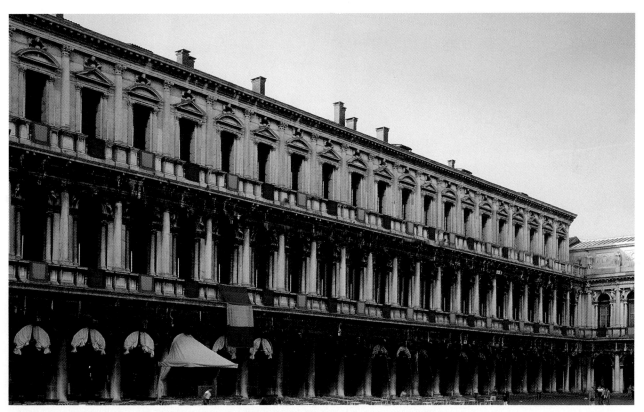

12.31   Vincenzo Samozzi. Detail of facade, Procuratie Nuove, Venice, Italy, 1584.

shows the usual Palladian sharp angularity, but he turned to Michelangelo for the alternation of semicircular and angular window brackets. He inserted a touch of manneristic whimsy in the insecurely perched nudes on top of the third-story window brackets, which he borrowed directly from Michelangelo's tombs for the Medici dukes in Florence.

In Rome, Federico Zuccari built himself a house that he described as a poetic caprice, one that carried mannerism over the edge into the grotesque. The windows, doors, and monstrous entrance portal (Fig. 12.32) broke the boundaries of expected shape.

IDEAS

DYNAMICS OF SPACE AND TIME

In both Venetian Renaissance art and mannerism, a quickening of pace and an increased sense of action became apparent. Venetian space is

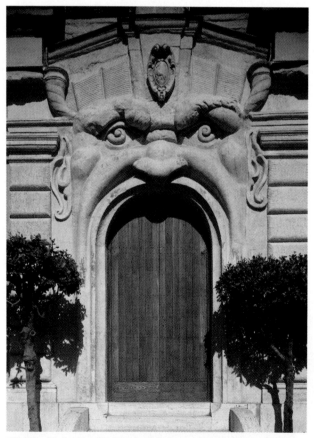

12.32 Federico Zuccari. Palazetto Zuccari, Rome, Italy, c. 1593. Detail, entrance portal.

never in repose but is restless and teeming with action. Sansovino's and Palladio's buildings, with their open **loggias,** or galleries, recessed entrances and windows, and pierced, deep-cut masonry, invite entry. Their spacious interiors allow for freedom of movement. Action is also implicit in the lively contrasts of structural elements and decorative details, such as rectangularity side by side with roundness, and the intersection of complete and broken pediments. Palladio's churches, with their open semicircular colonnades around the altar and windows in the apse, allow the eye to continue into the space beyond. The reflection of facades in the rippling waters of canals and the use of mirrored interior walls serve to activate the heavy masses of masonry and increase the perception of light and space.

Similarly, the composition of some Venetian paintings broke up Renaissance compositional unity. Dynamic design replaced stable space. Forms and figures opposed each other both on the picture plane and in the receding planes of a composition. These devices can be seen in Giorgione's *Concert Champêtre* and *The Tempest* (Figs. 12.10 and 12.11). Also, space was energized by the rising planes of a vertical organization, as in Titian's *Assumption,* and by the wheel-like rotary movement Tintoretto set up in his *Marriage of Bacchus and Ariadne* (Fig. 12.16). A dramatic diagonal slashes from the upper right to lower left in Titian's *Bacchus and Ariadne* (Fig. 12.13). In the pictures of Tintoretto and Veronese, fractures in the unity of central perspective produce a fragmentation that leads the eye simultaneously in several directions.

A comparable expression is heard in Gabrieli's "broken choirs" when parts of one group contrast with the full sound of an entire chorus. The sequence of contrasting sound progressively builds to ever-larger volumes until the climax is reached in the union of them all. The tossing back and forth of contrasting, unequal sound masses in the concerting style; the alternation of loud and soft dynamic levels of opposing groups; and the contrast of high and low parts all intensify the emotional effects of music.

A TENDENCY TOWARD THE MONUMENTAL AND THE GRANDIOSE

The increase in spatial and temporal dimensions in all the arts is also striking. Palladio's villa interiors are designed for large gatherings and to impress visitors by their spaciousness, so necessary to the grand manner of living to which his clients aspired. His preference for central plans in private dwellings, such as the Villa Rotonda, and for church buildings is, he says, because "none is more capacious than the round."

The growth in the size of paintings by Titian, Veronese, and Tintoretto is a phenomenon in itself. The dimensions alone predispose them to monumental portrayals. (The finished version of Tintoretto's colossal *Paradise* mural in the Doge's Palace includes more than 500 figures and measures about 72 by 23 feet.) The grandeur of sound produced by the vast musical resources that Gabrieli marshaled for his polychoral motets exceeded anything before their time. The Venetian ideal of the human figure is likewise large and ample. All these instances point in the direction of the grandiose.

In addition, dynamism is pervasive in the work of the mannerists, upsetting the heritage of Renaissance equilibrium. The canvases of Pontormo teem with activity, and the figures seem to be moving in all directions at once. In the crowded compression of Bronzino's allegory, the characters almost burst their bonds. Giovanni Bologna's *Mercury* speeds along with lightning swiftness, whereas his *Abduction of the Sabine Women* writhes and turns. The very space around his statues seems to be in pulsating motion.

ROADS TO THE BAROQUE

From Venice, as well as from Rome and other cultural centers where international mannerism flourished, the roads to the baroque fanned out in all directions. The thriving painting industry ensured the circulation of Venetian ideas. The writings of Palladio, as translated into English with commentary by Inigo Jones, led to the architecture of Christopher Wren and the Georgian styles and from there to the colonial and Federal styles in America. The printing of musical scores assured Venetian composers widespread prominence. By avoiding strong commitments to either side, Venetian diplomacy paved the way for the acceptance of aspects of the Venetian Renaissance and mannerist styles in both Reformation and Counter-Reformation countries.

Venetian innovations in architecture and painting were eagerly adopted in the church and court circles of Spain and France. Both the church hierarchy and the aristocracy required the impressive splendor of the arts to enhance their exalted positions. The more monumental the buildings, the more lavish the decorations, the more grandiose the musical entertainments, the better the arts served their social purpose: to impress spectators.

El Greco absorbed the Venetian and Roman versions of mannerism in his early travels and was eventually accepted by the church and court in Spain, where his art made a deep impression. Rubens spent eight years in Italy, much of the time making copies of Titian's pictures. He then took the Venetian techniques with him to his native Flanders and later to France. In turn, Rubens and his pupil van Dyck transmitted them to England, and ultimately they reached America.

In the Counter-Reformation countries, such as Italy, Spain, France, and Austria, church music remained more attuned to the Roman tradition, but Venetian music was readily accepted in secular circles. For Holland, Scandinavia, and northern Germany, which were centers of the Reformation, the greater liturgical freedom of Venetian musical forms proved adaptable to Protestant church purposes precisely because of their departure from Roman models.

J. P. Sweelinck, who studied the works of both Andrea Gabrieli and Gioseffo Zarlino, carried the Venetian keyboard style to Amsterdam. His great reputation brought him organ students from Germany, who later taught the generation of Johann Pachelbel and Dietrich Buxtehude, both major influences on the style of Johann Bach and George Handel. Francesco Cavalli, Monteverdi's successor at the Venetian opera, was called to Paris to write the music for the wedding festivities of Louis XIV. Heinrich Schütz, the greatest German composer before Bach and Handel, was a pupil of both Giovanni Gabrieli and Monteverdi. In sum, the Venetian style evolved as part of the basic vocabulary of baroque art.

During the early years of the seventeenth century, the architect Baldassare Longhena broke from the stiff rectilinear style of Palladio and Scamozzi and transformed Venetian architecture with his Church of Santa Maria della Salute (Fig. 12.33). As the name implies, the church was dedicated to the Virgin to implore her help with the health of the populace. Specifically, Venice was enduring the plague, brought on by a flourishing rat population. The church's ground plan

12.33 Baldassare Longhena.
Santa Maria della Salute,
Venice, Italy, 1631–1656. Length
200′, width 155′.

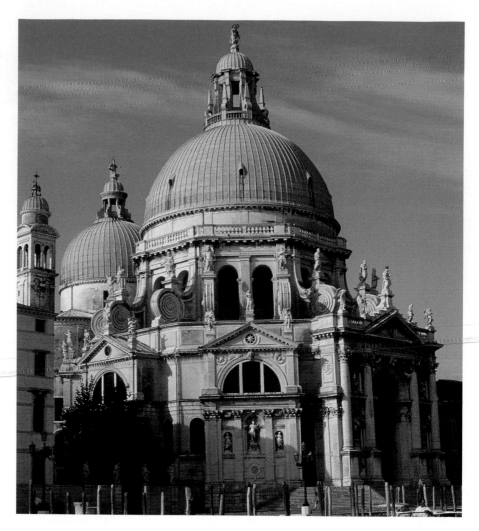

is octagonal, like a baptistry. The main entrance (on the right of the figures) is like a Roman triumphal arch with a classical triangular pediment above it. Each of the other seven sides echoes this motif. Supporting the high-pitched dome are buttresses in the form of ornamental scrolls, or volutes. The elaborately decorated exterior is held together by the good composition of the design as a whole. This building was far more to the taste of the Venetians than the restrained Palladian style, and it is one of the finest examples of the emerging early baroque.

Venice was not only a productive cultural center but also the stylistic clearinghouse for currents of thought flowing from the Italian South, the Mediterranean East, and the European North. Flemish and German merchants established trade connections and resident communities in Venice and commerce prospered. The traffic in artists

and musicians was equally active. In effect, Venice moved slowly and consistently from the glow of its Byzantine dawn through a Renaissance high noon and the brief thunderstorm of mannerism to an ornate baroque sunset.

YOUR RESOURCES

- ***Web Site***

  http://art.wadsworth.com/fleming10

  ○ Chapter 12 Quiz

  ○ Links

- ***Audio CD***

  ○ *In ecclesiis*

  ○ *Zefiro torna*

VENETIAN RENAISSANCE AND INTERNATIONAL MANNERISM

Key Events	Architecture	Visual Arts and Music	Mannerists
		c. 1429–1507 **Gentile Bellini** ▲ c. 1431–1516 **Giovanni Bellini** ▲	

1450

Key Events	Architecture	Visual Arts and Music	Mannerists
1453 **Turks** conquered Constantinople; Venetian commerce challenged 1492 **Geographical discoveries** by Spanish and Portuguese navigators weakened Venetian maritime trade 1495 **Aldine Press** began publishing inexpensive editions of Greco-Roman classics	1486–1570 **Sansovino** (Jacopo Tatti) ★	c. 1456–c. 1526 **Vittore Carpaccio** ▲ c. 1477–1510 **Giorgione** (Giorgione da Castelfranco) ▲ c. 1485–1576 **Titian** (Tiziano Vecellio) ▲ 1490–1562 **Adrian Willaert** ❏, 1527–1562 choirmaster at St. Mark's	1494–1540 **Rosso Fiorentino** (Giovanni Battista di Jacopo) 1494–1556 **Pontormo** (Jacopo Carucci) c. 1499–1546 **Giulio Romano** (Pippi)

1500

Key Events	Architecture	Visual Arts and Music	Mannerists
1501 **Odhecaton,** anthology of vocal and instrumental works by Josquin Desprez, Obrecht, Isaac, and others printed in Venice by Petrucci 1517 **Protestant Reformation** began 1527 **Sack of Rome** by Charles V; artists flee; beginning of mannerist style 1543 **Copernicus** published *On the Revolution of the Planets in Their Orbits* 1545–1563 **Council of Trent** initiated Counter-Reformation	1508–1580 **Palladio** (Andrea di Pietro) ★ 1536 **Library of St. Mark** built by Sansovino 1540 **Loggetta** at base of campanile built by Sansovino 1546–1549 **Basilica at Vicenza** built by Palladio 1548–1616 **Vicenzo Scamozzi** ★	1510–1592 **Bassano** (Jacopo da Ponte) ▲ 1517–1590 **Gioseffo Zarlino** ❏, composer, theorist, 1565–1590 choirmaster at St. Mark's 1519–1594 **Tintoretto** (Jacopo Robusti) ▲ 1528–1588 **Veronese** (Paolo Cagliari) ▲ 1532–1625 **Sofonisba Anguissola** ▲ c. 1532–1585 **Andrea Gabrieli** ❏, composer, 1566–1585 organist at St. Mark's	1500–1571 **Benvenuto Cellini** 1503–1540 **Parmigianino** (Francesco Mazzola) 1503–1572 **Bronzino** (Angelo de Cosimo di Mariano) 1511–1574 **Giorgio Vasari** 1529–1608 **Giovanni Bologna** (Giambologna) c. 1540–1609 **Federico Zuccari**

1550

Key Events	Architecture	Visual Arts and Music	Mannerists
1571 **Naval Battle of Lepanto;** Venice and Spain defeated Turks 1573 **Veronese** called before Inquisition	1550 **Villa Rotonda** near Vicenza begun by Palladio 1565 **Church of San Giorgio Maggiore,** Venice, built by Palladio 1570 **Palladio** published *Four Books of Architecture* 1576–1578 **Church of Il Redentore,** Venice, built by Palladio 1579–1580 **Olympic Theater,** Vicenza, built by Palladio 1584 **Procuratie Nuove,** continuation of Sansovino's design of St. Mark's Library, built by Scamozzi 1589 **Olympic Theater,** Vicenza, dedicated with performance of Sophocles's *Oedipus* (music by A. Gabrieli) 1596–1682 **Baldassare Longhena** ★	1552–1614 **Lavinia Fontana** ▲ 1554–1590 **Marietta Robusti** ▲ c. 1554–1612 **Giovanni Gabrieli** ❏, composer, 1586–1612 organist at St. Mark's 1567–1643 **Claudio Monteverdi** ❏, 1613–1643 choirmaster at St. Mark's	1555–1619 **Ludovico Carracci** 1560–1609 **Annibale Carracci**

1600

Key Events	Architecture	Visual Arts and Music	Mannerists
	1631 **Santa Maria della Salute** begun	1602–1676 **Francesco Cavalli** ❏, opera composer	

★ - Architect   ❏ - Musician   ▲ - Painter

1500

BEGINNING OF PROTESTANT REFORMATION, 1517
IGNATIUS LOYOLA FOUNDS JESUIT ORDER, 1534
BEGINNING OF THE REVOLT OF THE NETHERLANDS AGAINST PHILIP II OF SPAIN, 1568
PHILIP II SENDS THE GREAT ARMADA AGAINST HOLLAND AND ENGLAND, 1588

1600

GALILEO GALILEI REFINES TELESCOPE, 1609
JOHANNES KEPLER'S LAWS OF PLANETARY MOTION, 1609–1619
RENÉ DESCARTES, *DISCOURSE ON METHOD,* 1637
ISAAC NEWTON'S LAWS OF MOTION, GRAVITATION, 1687

1700

DENIS DIDEROT, *ENCYCLOPÉDIE,* 1751–1780
AMERICAN REVOLUTION, 1763–1783
NEW STEAM ENGINE PATENTED, 1769
FRENCH REVOLUTION, 1789–1795

1800

NAPOLEON BONAPARTE, FIRST CONSUL OF FRANCE, 1800
NAPOLEON CROWNED EMPEROR, 1804, ABDICATES 1814
REVOLUTION OF 1830 IN FRANCE
REVOLUTION OF 1848 IN FRANCE

PART FOUR

COUNTER-REFORMATION, BAROQUE, AND SEVENTEENTH-CENTURY STYLES

Considering the baroque period as a whole—including the Counter-Reformation, aristocratic, and bourgeois styles—it was a period during which irresistible modern forces met immovable traditional objects.

The era coincided with a time of expansion and empire building during which great wealth was pouring into European coffers from the Americas, Africa, India, the East and West Indies, and China. The arts played a major role in religion, statecraft, and the enhancement of the good life. They were also central to the movement for reform within Roman Catholicism itself. This Catholic Reform movement, later dubbed the Counter-Reformation, undertook vast building programs in the countries that remained loyal to the church. New religious orders were founded to carry on missionary work all over the world.

The Counter-Reformation and baroque era was one in which oppositions that were impossible to reconcile were forced to find a way to coexist. The rise of rationalism was accompanied by the march of militant mysticism. The aristocratic cult of majesty was opposed by bourgeois domesticity. The internationalism of Roman Catholicism conflicted with the nationalism of the Protestant sects and rising monarchies. Religious orthodoxy had to contend with freedom of thought.

The printing press made books available, while suppression by censorship took them away. The boldest scientific thinking took place alongside a reassertion of the belief in miracles and a renewal of traditional religious beliefs. Isaac Newton's *Principia* and the final part of John Bunyan's *Pilgrim's Progress* appeared in London within 2 years of one another.

The arts demonstrated similar oppositions. In Spain, the emotional involvement of El Greco was succeeded by the optical detachment of Velázquez. In France, the sensuality of Rubens was followed by the academic formalism of Poussin. In Holland, the broad humanity of Rembrandt contrasted with the cool ocular precision of Vermeer.

Such oppositions could hardly be expected to resolve themselves into a single uniform style. At best, they could achieve only a temporary resolution and a fusion of forms, such as those found in a Counter-Reformation church, the Versailles Palace, Rembrandt's visual dramatization of the Bible, and Purcell's operatic synthesis. In these works, forceful striving and restless motion are more characteristic than calm and repose. Baroque art emerged from these tensions.

Grandeur and magnificence prevailed in the baroque arts. Emperors, kings, popes, and princes vied with one another to attract great artists to their courts by offering large commissions. In the service of church and state, the arts created or renewed myths of the miraculous and the majestic. The new wealth of the bourgeois merchants and bankers became increasingly important for commissioning and collecting art.

For all its grandiosity, the baroque was also the age of reason, when minds and imaginations opened up new worlds of scientific knowledge and artistic creativity. The conflicts of the baroque world took place within a tremendously enlarged sense of space and time. Astronomers told of remote regions populated by an infinite number of stars. Pascal speculated on the mathematical implications of infinity. Copernicus turned the world upside down and inside out by establishing that the sun was the center of the solar system and the Earth was but one of several planets revolving around it. Newton's speculations on celestial mechanics led to the formulation of the laws of gravity and motion. Such a dynamic world called for a new mathematics capable of dealing with infinity and a universe of matter in motion. With Leibniz came the development of the infinitesimal, or differential, calculus.

Above all, the baroque universe was in ceaseless movement. Whether a rationalist thought of it in terms of whirling particles or a mystic saw it as full of swirling spirits, both saw their world as a whirlpool of spheres and spirals creating infinitely complex patterns of motion. In its various forms, the art of this era was the aesthetic reflection of a new conception of world order and the exuberant affirmation of a modern dynamic attitude toward life.

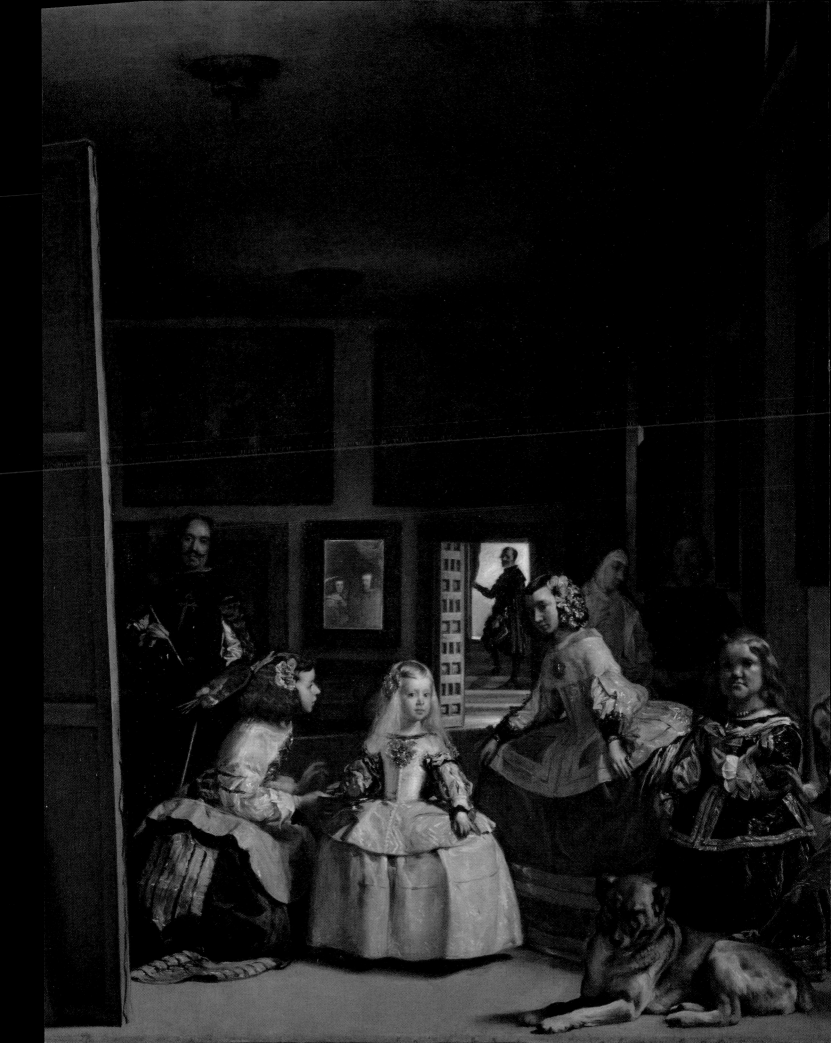

C H A P T E R

13

FROM COUNTER-REFORMATION TO BAROQUE

AT THE THRESHOLD OF THE seventeenth century, Rome was caught up in a mixture of stylistic trends ranging from the late Renaissance to mannerism. At the same time, new tendencies were emerging that pointed in the direction of a new cluster of stylistic ideas that would come to be called the *baroque*. This aesthetic inclination cannot be detached from the tumult within the Church of Rome, especially the actions taken at the Council of Trent (see the next section) to meet the challenge of the Reformation.

Because of the Council's recommendations, bold humanistic speculation was replaced by militant measures. Neoplatonic philosophy was succeeded by a return to Aristotelian scholasticism. The distant voices of pagan antiquity were drowned out by the roar of rekindled medieval

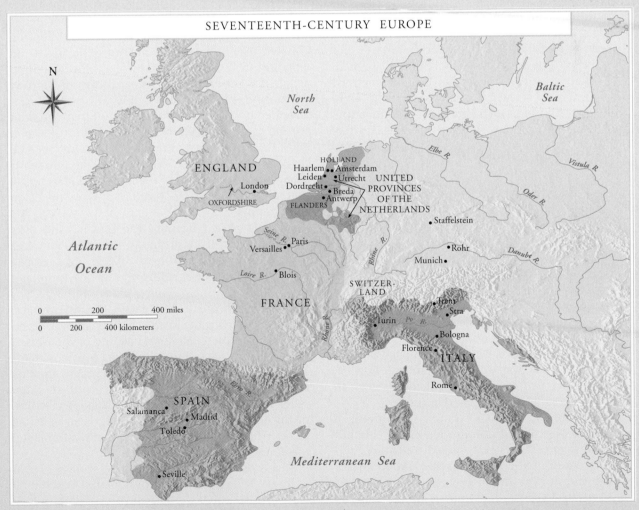

MAP 13.1

fire. Liberal religious attitudes hardened into strict church doctrines. Access to literature, knowledge, and scientific discovery through the printed word was suppressed by the Inquisition and the *Index Expurgatorius,* which listed books that good Catholics should not read. God no longer appeared as the loving Father but as a terrifying Judge. Christ was transformed from a Good Shepherd into a Great Avenger.

ROME IN THE EARLY SEVENTEENTH CENTURY

The founders of the new Counter-Reformation religious orders, which were to shape the course of Roman Catholicism in the seventeenth century, were in Rome at various times. At informal meetings in his Congregation of the Oratory, Philip Neri brought together people of all classes, from aristocrats to street urchins, and encouraged them to pray or preach as the spirit moved them. By dramatizing and setting to music familiar biblical stories and parables (the origin of the baroque oratorios), he generated a cheerful devotional spirit that stirred the hearts of the poor and humble.

Ignatius Loyola came from Spain to obtain papal sanction for his Society of Jesus, an activist order generally known as the Jesuits, who were dedicated to foreign missionary work, education, and participation in worldly affairs. Mystics like Teresa of Ávila and John of the Cross combined the contemplative and active ways of life. They wrote vital, popular literary expressions and reorganized and redirected the Carmelite orders. Also in Rome was Carlo Borromeo, the young, energetic archbishop of Milan who gave voice to the new church doctrines and wrote manuals for architects and artists, as well as for students and teachers, in the many seminaries he founded.

At a grand ceremony in the newly completed Basilica of St. Peter on May 22, 1622, Ignatius Loyola, Francis Xavier, Teresa of Ávila, and Philip Neri were canonized as saints and admitted to the honors of the altar. The architects Giacomo Vignola, Giacomo della Porta, Carlo Maderno, Gian Lorenzo Bernini, and Francesco Borromini were called on to design churches and chapels dedicated to them.

The classical harmony, stability, and poise of Renaissance art could not survive under this hot blast of reform. The overly refined, sensuous, and excessively dramatic art of mannerism could not endure the new stern religious climate. Venuses reverted to Virgins; Bacchuses and Apollos to bearded Christs. The organic form and unity of Michelangelo's Sistine ceiling were succeeded by the calculated shapelessness of his awesome *Last Judgment* (Fig. 13.1; see also Fig. 10.9). Giovanni Palestrina was conscience-stricken for having written madrigals and thenceforth wrote only Masses. Under the rulings of the Council of Trent, church art was firmly integrated with religious doctrine and the clergy were required to monitor the way artists treated religious subjects.

The new religious climate deeply affected the lives and attitudes of Counter-Reformation artists. Michelangelo's *Last Judgment* reveals some of the new soul-searching attitude, but it is mixed with Renaissance themes drawn from antiquity, such as the Apollo-like Christ and the mythological Charon who rows the souls of the dead over the Styx, the chief river in Hell. Later in the century, strict reformers judged Michelangelo's nudes to be offensive and ordered that they be covered with drapery. Only the timely intervention of a group of artists saved the *Last Judgment* from being completely destroyed by those who saw it as an affront to piety and decency.

In his last years, Michelangelo became a recluse, giving up figurative art for the abstractions of architecture and devoting himself to the building of St. Peter's, a project for which he would accept no fee. In the privacy of his own studio, he worked periodically at sculpture and brooded over his last *Pietàs,* one of them intended for his own tomb. While Michelangelo exiled himself, Palestrina was banished from his post as leader of the Sistine Choir because he refused to take the priestly vow of celibacy and give up his wife. Later, he was reinstated and asked to reform church music.

Gian Lorenzo Bernini, the busiest and most successful sculptor-architect of the Counter-Reformation and baroque styles, was closely associated with the Jesuits and regularly practiced St. Ignatius's *Spiritual Exercises* (see pp. 385–386). As the name suggests, these were mental exercises designed to keep the spirit robust. Andrea Pozzo, who painted the illusionistic ceiling of the Church of Sant'Ignazio (see Fig. 13.9), was also a member of the Society of Jesus. El Greco, Spain's greatest representative of Counter-Reformation art, was a religious mystic in whose last visionary canvases physical matter practically ceases to exist. His tall, slender figures are more spirit than flesh, his settings more of heaven than of Earth.

Likely enough, Counter-Reformation art began in Rome, the capital of Catholicism. It reached its climax in the 50-year period from about 1620 to 1670. Its consequences were felt simultaneously in

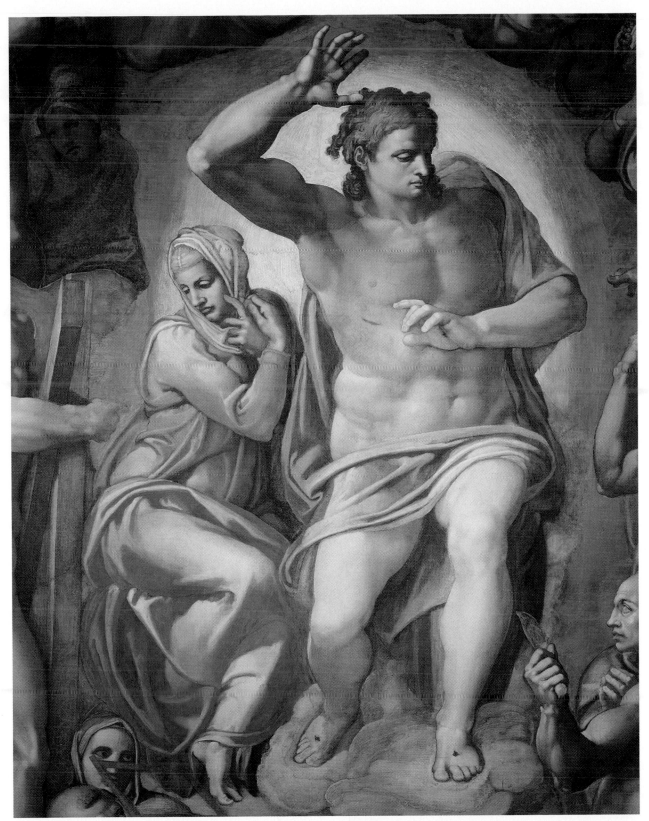

13.1   Michelangelo. *Last Judgment,* detail with Christ and the Madonna, 1534–1541. Fresco, 48′ × 44′. Sistine Chapel, Vatican Palace, Rome, Italy.

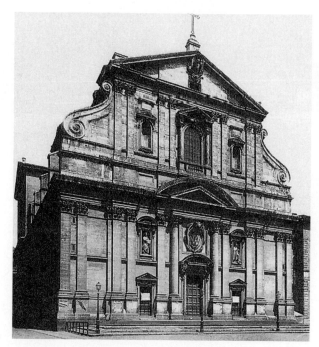

A

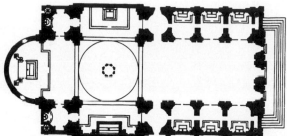

B

13.2 (A) Giacomo Vignola and Giacomo della Porta. Facade, Il Gesù, Rome, Italy, c. 1575–1584. Height 105′, width 115′. (B) Plan of Il Gesù.

Spain. Thereafter, the style spread throughout the Roman Catholic countries of Europe and traveled with the missionary orders to the Americas and elsewhere in the far-flung colonies established by Spain and Portugal.

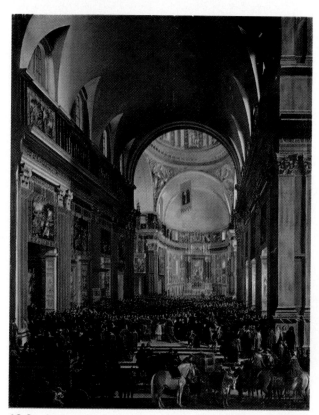

13.3 Andrea Sacchi and Jan Miel. *Urban VIII Visiting Il Gesù,* 1639–1641. Galleria Nazionale d'Arte Antica, Rome, Italy.

THE TRANSITION FROM COUNTER-REFORMATION TO BAROQUE

ARCHITECTURE

As the central monument of the Jesuit order, the Church of Il Gesù in Rome (Figs. 13.2 and 13.3) became the prototype for many Counter-Reformation churches (Figs. 13.4 and 13.5). Commissioned in 1564, Il Gesù combines classical motifs from the Renaissance heritage in a nonclassical and original way. Giacomo Vignola's design for the facade, somewhat revised after his death by his successor Giacomo della Porta, recalls a Roman triumphal arch on the ground floor, but the lean-to roofing over the side chapels is masked with graceful scrolls that swirl upward toward the triangular templelike pediment. The heart of the structure—the domed crossing of the nave and short transepts—is derived from Michelangelo's and Palladio's centralized plans (see Figs. 10.16 and 12.5B). The wide, spacious nave with no side aisles allows a large congregation to gather within sight of the high altar and within earshot of the pulpit. The altar is where the Eucharistic rite is performed, and by making it visible to the entire congregation, the architects of Il Gesù visually reinforced the participation of Catholics in the mystery of Communion with Christ. This was an explicit response to Reformation Protestants, who maintained that communion was only symbolic, not the actual transubstantiation of bread and wine into the body and blood of Christ.

Borromini's San Carlo alle Quattro Fontane (St. Charles of the Four Fountains) (Fig. 13.4A) is

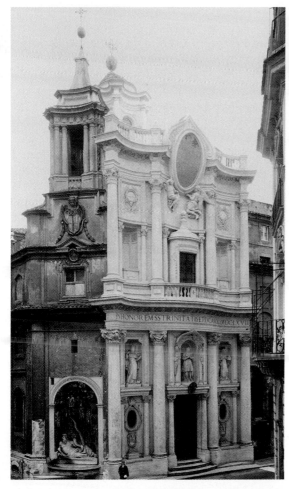

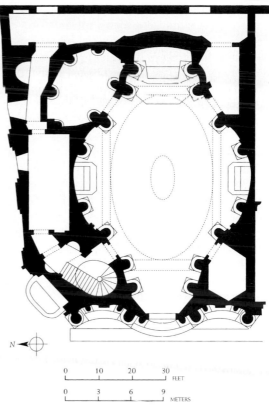

B

13.4 (A) Francesco Borromini. Facade, San Carlo alle Quattro Fontane, Rome, Italy, begun 1635, facade 1667. Length 52′, width 34′, width of facade 38′. (B) Francesco Borromini. Plan of San Carlo alle Quattro Fontane.

A

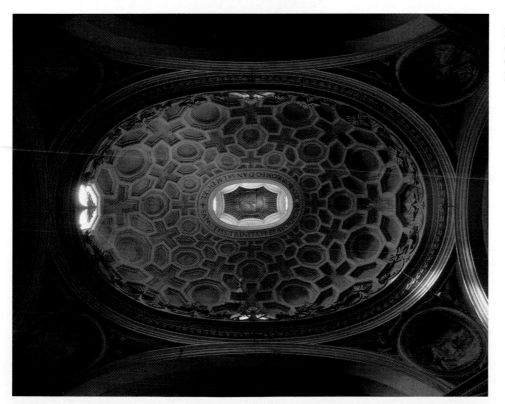

13.5 Francesco Borromini. Interior of dome, San Carlo alle Quattro Fontane, Rome, Italy, c. 1638.

one of the most original expressions of the period. It is located on a small site at an intersection of two streets with a fountain at each of its four corners. Using the location to its fullest potential, the architect devised a plan that embraced an intricate interplay of geometric shapes. The plan is formed by two equal-sided triangles joined at their bases to make a diamond-shaped rhombus, which was then softened into curved lines (Fig. 13.4B). The facade (Fig. 13.4A) is set into swaying motion by the alternating concave and convex walls and the flow of curved lines and forms, which lets a maximum of light and shade play over the irregular surface.

The inner surface of the dome is decorated with octagons and elongated hexagons that join to produce Greek crosses in the intervening spaces (Fig. 13.5). These shapes diminish in size toward the top to suggest greater height, although the dome is actually quite shallow. Partially concealed openings allow light to filter in and give the honeycomb-like pattern a gleaming brightness. The undulating movement of the facade and the illusionistic treatment of the dome illustrate two major directions of the emerging baroque style.

PAINTING AND SCULPTURE

Among the painters and sculptors who were active in post-Renaissance Rome, Michelangelo, Caravaggio, and Bernini tower above all the others. Taking his name from his native town, Caravaggio brought the northern Italian tradition of mannerism and the Venetian drama of light and shade with him to Rome. For his part, Bernini, a sculptor-architect-designer-painter, succeeded in synthesizing Renaissance, mannerist, and emerging baroque elements and brought the new baroque style to an expressive climax in the Eternal City.

Restless and rebellious, Caravaggio was always at odds with society and his patrons, whereas Bernini, despite his passionate temperament, was nevertheless a polished courtier. "It is your good luck," Bernini was told by the newly elected Pope Urban VIII, "to see Maffeo Barberini pope; but we are even luckier that Cavaliere Bernini lives at the time of our pontificate." Caravaggio's life and career were brief, solitary, and meteoric; Bernini's were long, social, and prodigiously productive. Both artists had far-reaching effects on future developments. Caravaggio, with his bold chiaroscuro, influ-

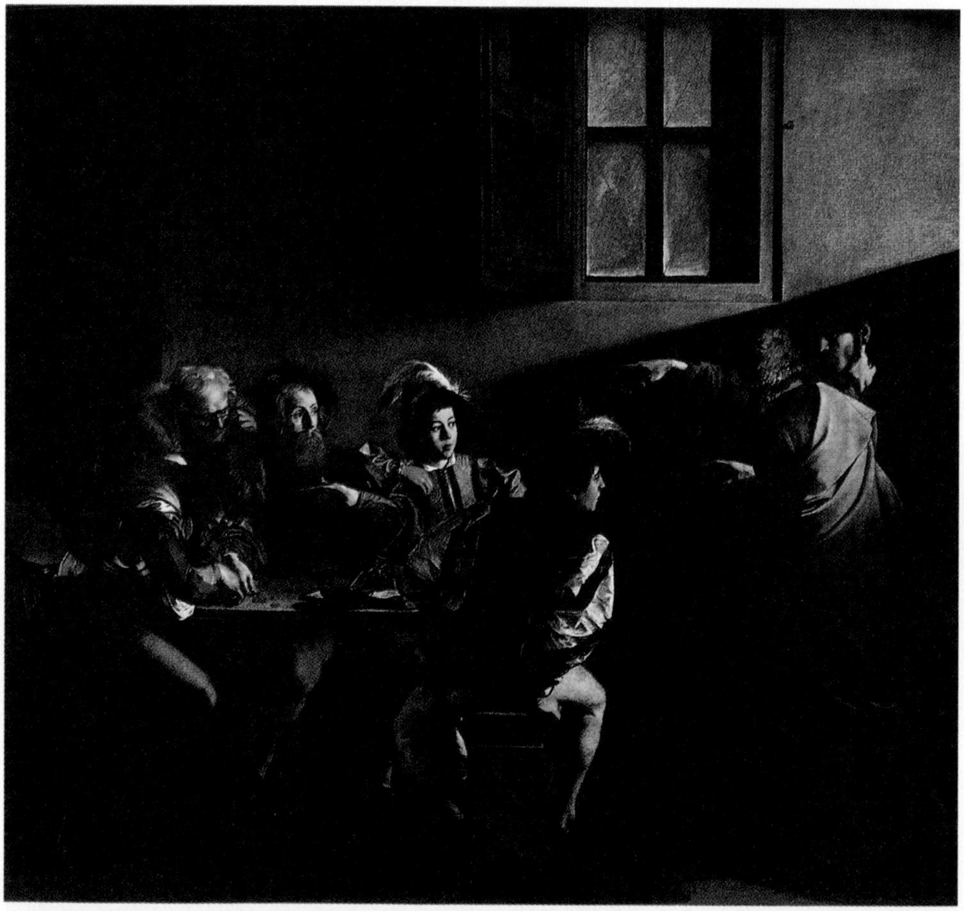

13.6 Caravaggio. *The Calling of St. Matthew,* c. 1597–1598. Oil on canvas, 11′1″ × 11′5″. Contarelli Chapel, San Luigi dei Francesi, Rome, Italy.

enced later Italian and French baroque painters, as well as Peter Paul Rubens and Rembrandt. Bernini, with his twisted columns and visionary illusionism, had a major impact on baroque sculpture and architecture.

RELIGIOUS DRAMAS IN DARK AND LIGHT: CARAVAGGIO

Caravaggio, who painted in Rome from about 1590 to 1606, scorned Renaissance correctness, dignity, and elegance and set out to depict religious subjects in a defiant yet down-to-earth way. His *The Calling of St. Matthew* (Fig. 13.6) shows the future Evangelist among a group at a public tavern. An inky darkness hovers over the table, where tax money is being counted. As Jesus enters, a shaft of light illuminates the bearded face of St. Matthew and the faces of the young men in the center. The light strikes each figure and object with a varying degree of intensity. Caravaggio thus spotlights the inner selves of his subjects. Note the hand of the Savior, which is taken directly from that of God in Michelangelo's *The Creation of Adam* (see Fig. 10.12), by this time a well-known symbol of the divine spark. *The Calling of St. Matthew* was at first refused by the church for which it had been painted because it showed the saint in a worldly situation, even though the story was told by the Evangelist himself.

In *The Conversion of St. Paul* (Fig. 13.7), Caravaggio created a blinding lightning flash to highlight the saint's inner illumination. "And

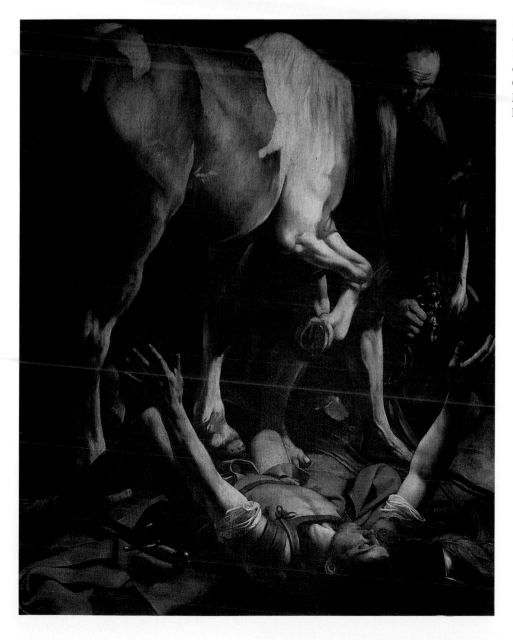

13.7 Caravaggio. *The Conversion of St. Paul*, 1601–1602. Oil on canvas, 7′6½″ × 5′9″. Cerasi Chapel, Santa Maria del Popolo, Rome, Italy.

suddenly there shined round about him a light from heaven," reads the New Testament passage, "and he fell to the earth, and heard a voice saying unto him, Saul, Saul, why persecutest thou me?" (Acts 9:3–4). Because of Caravaggio's astute design, viewers sense themselves to be located just beyond the extremely foreshortened angle of St. Paul's prone body. Just outside the range of St. Paul's upraised arms, in the darkness made all the more murky by the intense spiritual light of his conversion, viewers become theatergoers with front-row seats. The contrived space of the painting and the real space of the spectator merge. Against a background that does not situate the scene in any place, Caravaggio introduces a tense vertical rhythm with the alternation of horse's shanks and human arms and legs. Mannerist freedom can be seen in the placement of the groom's shoulders over to the right, keeping the design below undisturbed, even through there is no natural way for the man's limbs to be joined to his trunk

and shoulders. Pictorial construction and dramatic design, not naturalism, were Caravaggio's first considerations.

The influence of Caravaggio's theatrical compositions was soon seen in all parts of Europe. Among his followers was Artemisia Gentileschi, who was active in Rome, Florence, Venice, and Naples. She learned her craft in the studio of her father Orazio, a painter of repute and also an admirer of Caravaggio. Eventually her fame outshone his. Her powerful depiction of *Judith Slaying Holofernes* (Fig. 13.8) depicts the heroic daughter of Israel saving her people by beheading the invading general whose cohorts were sweeping down on her city. Like Caravaggio, Gentileschi employs the technique of **tenebrism** to create a menacing surrounding darkness for the gruesome subject. The shocking realism is brought home as Judith pulls back to avoid the spurting blood. Arguably, Gentileschi is better known today than she was in her own time because her life and career have been at the center of a debate for about

13.8 Artemisia Gentileschi. *Judith Slaying Holofernes,* c. 1620. Oil on canvas, 6′6½″ × 5′4″. Galleria degli Uffizi, Florence, Italy.

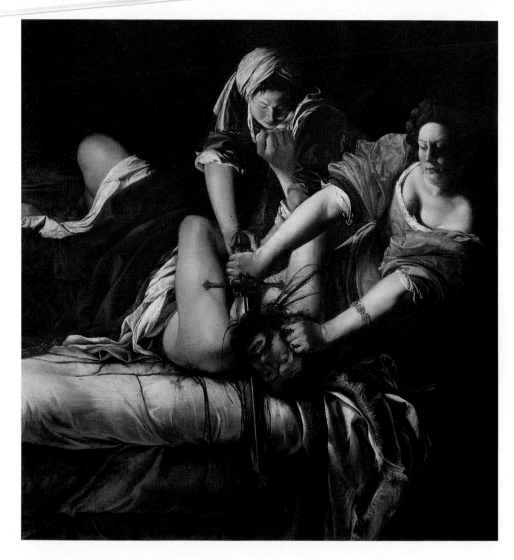

25 years. Because she was humiliated by a rape and public trial, some scholars have argued that the violence in her *Judith Slaying Holofernes* is a direct expression of her bitterness. Others point out that the subject matter was popular in the period and that she would not have produced her several paintings on this theme if it did not appeal to buyers.

In Rome, Caravaggio's efforts to situate religious subjects in contemporary settings experienced by ordinary people met with a mixed reception. Roman Catholic priests and the public both preferred ele-

gance, drama, and illusionism, which are found in ceiling murals such as those of Annibale Carracci in the Farnese Palace, Pietro Cortona in the Barberini Palace, and Pozzo in the Church of Sant'Ignazio, and especially in the work of Bernini.

HEAVENS ABOVE: ANDREA POZZO

Pozzo succeeded in capturing the new spirit of faith in his extraordinary painting on the barrel-vaulted ceiling of the Church of Sant'Ignazio (Fig. 13.9),

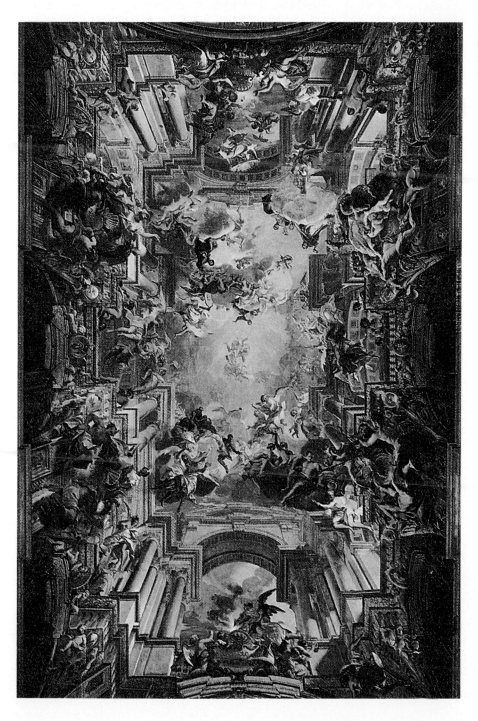

13.9   Andrea Pozzo.
St. Ignatius in Glory, c. 1691.
Fresco, nave ceiling.
Sant'Ignazio, Rome, Italy.

dedicated to St. Ignatius Loyola, the founder of the Jesuit order. When one looks up beyond the clerestory windows, the walls of the building seem to soar upward so that the vaulting of the nave becomes heaven itself. Accompanied by a heavenly host, St. Ignatius ascends in a winding spiral toward figures symbolizing the Trinity. Here all the lines converge, and beams of light radiate outward to illuminate the four corners of the world, personified by allegorical representations of Europe, Asia, Africa, and America, where the missionary work of the Society of Jesus was carried on. Asia is a woman aboard an awestruck camel; Africa is a dark-skinned woman riding a crocodile; America is an aggressive, bare-breasted native; but Europe is a serenely powerful queen whose horse is torn between the heavenly scene above and the rapture of the majesty's gaze. The painter makes it unmistakably clear that only Europe has risen to the level of civilization, an idea that suggested to many the obligation of Europeans to influence other cultures.

As his skills suggest, Pozzo was the author of a definitive book on perspective, in which he advised artists "to draw all points thereof to that true point, the Glory of God." This dramatic illusionistic approach spread rapidly in Catholic Europe and the Americas, and Pozzo's murals, with their startling foreshortening techniques, became a major influence on the course of Counter-Reformation art.

FAITH AND TRANSFORMATION: BERNINI

In Gian Lorenzo Bernini, the fiery and versatile architect, sculptor, designer, and painter, the Roman Counter-Reformation and emerging baroque found an expressive and prolific interpreter. He designed the Piazza of St. Peter's, which begins with the trapezoidal plaza in front of the basilica's facade and opens out into the mighty oval area framed by massive fourfold Doric colonnades (see Fig. 10.1). He created several of the basilica's side chapels and two monumental compositions at the climactic points of the interior: the rising baldachino underneath Michelangelo's mighty dome and the chapel at the axial center of the apse that contains the Chair of St. Peter. His open-air designs for many Roman public monuments, such as the Four Rivers Fountain in the Piazza Navona (Fig. 13.10), help give the city the unique appearance it has today.

The Council of Trent discouraged themes drawing on classical antiquity, especially for public religious buildings, but Bernini seems to have felt safe in creating the *Apollo and Daphne* (Fig. 13.11) for a private family palace. The statue ingeniously blends Renaissance reverence for antiquity with the era's preoccupation with heightened physical experience and transformation. Like many of Bernini's youthful works, this one is full of motion and tense excitement.

13.10 Gian Lorenzo Bernini. Four Rivers Fountain, Piazza Navona, Rome, Italy, 1648–1651.

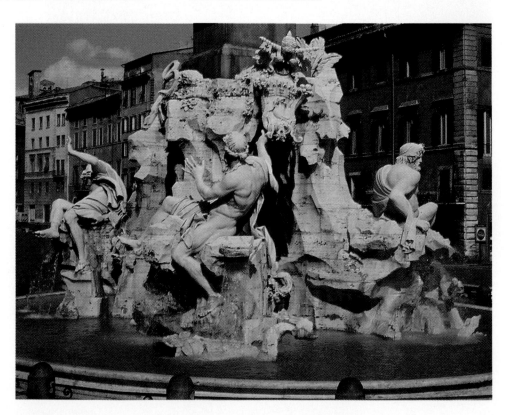

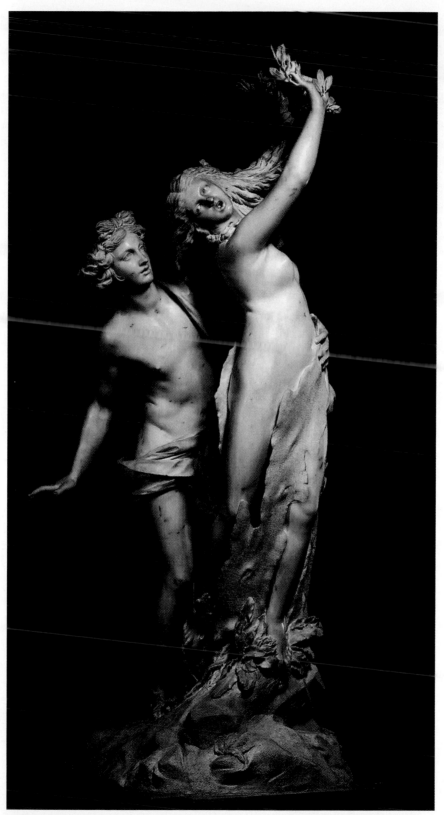

13.11   Gian Lorenzo Bernini. *Apollo and Daphne,* 1622–1625. Marble, life-size. Galleria Borghese, Rome, Italy.

According to the myth, Apollo, as the patron of the Muses, was in pursuit of ideal beauty, symbolized by the nymph Daphne. Bernini chose to portray a poignant single moment, from which the viewer may deduce the previous and forthcoming action. As Daphne flees from Apollo's ardent embrace, she cries aloud to the gods, who hear her plea and change her into a laurel tree. Root-bound, with bark already enclosing her limbs, she seems to be in quivering motion. The complex surfaces of the sculpture maximize the play of flickering light and shadow. Bernini, who attempted to "paint" with marble, carefully carved various textures, such as the smooth flesh, flowing drapery, floating hair, bark, leaves, and branches. The diagonal line running from Apollo's left leg and right hand to Daphne's leafy fingers activates the scene, leading the eye upward and outward. Although he was not representing a religious conversion, Bernini's *Apollo and Daphne* centers on a pivotal moment of transformation. In that sense, it resembles Caravaggio's *The Conversion of St. Paul.*

13.12 Anonymous. *Cornaro Chapel, Santa Maria della Vittoria, Rome,* c. 1644. Oil on canvas. Staatliches Museum, Schwerin, Germany.

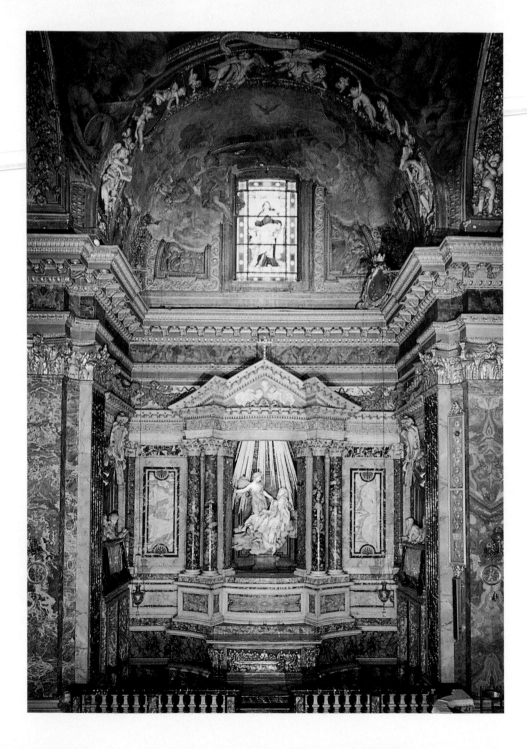

One of the essential features of emerging baroque practice is the manner in which all parts of a composition are brought into a convincing unity by some strong, linear, painterly, or rhythmic device. Renaissance compositions tended toward the isolated perfection of each part. By contrast, in baroque work, all components converge into one interdependent whole. Ideally, all the separate arts and media could be brought into play so that they would melt and merge with one another to form new and fascinating possibilities. The baroque is also noted for its emphasis on the grandiose, its theatricality, and its sweeping emotional power. An outstanding example of these qualities can be found in the chapel and sculpture Bernini fashioned for the Church of Santa Maria della Vittoria.

St. Teresa in Ecstasy is Bernini's masterpiece. The composition fills one end of a transept arm in Carlo Maderno's church of Santa Maria della Vittoria (Fig. 13.12). The arts come together in this work, which originated in a literary source, St. Teresa's writing about her intense vision. Many visual arts are called on to create the scene: architecture, sculpture, scenic design, and fresco. Moreover, Bernini assembled a rich array of materials: varicolored marbles, gilt bronze, stucco, and tinted glass. All are so artfully combined that the dividing line between media and materials disappears and a grand total effect emerges.

In the central group (Fig. 13.13), Bernini portrays Teresa in a state of ecstasy. In her

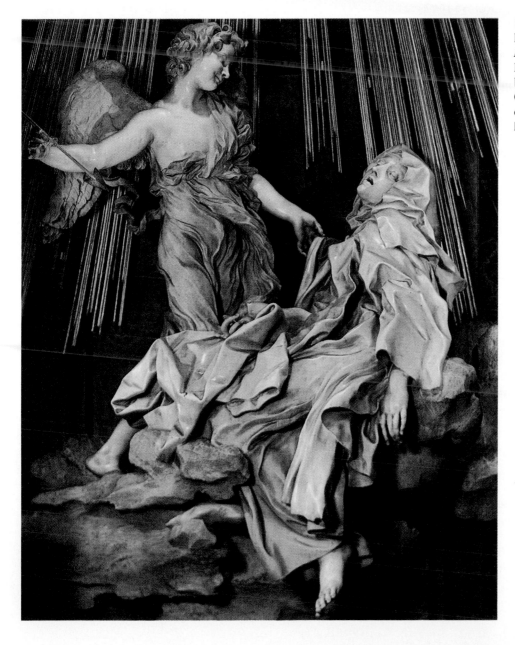

13.13 Gian Lorenzo Bernini. *St. Teresa in Ecstasy,* 1645–1652. Marble and gilt bronze, life-size. Cornaro Chapel, Santa Maria della Vittoria, Rome, Italy.

autobiography, she describes a bright angel, face aflame, who appeared to her in a vision. She wrote:

> In his hands I saw a great golden spear, and at the iron tip there appeared to be a point of fire. This he plunged into my heart several times so that it penetrated to my entrails. When he pulled it out, I felt he took them with it, and left me utterly consumed by the great love of God. The pain was so severe that it made me utter several moans. The sweetness caused by this intense pain is so extreme that one cannot possibly wish it to cease, nor is one's soul then content with anything but God. . . . So gentle is this wooing which takes place between God and the soul.[1]

St. Theresa's heart is pierced by a mix of the physical and spiritual, just as St. Paul was transformed by light that seems to center on his heart.

Throughout Bernini's composition, warm color and luminosity emphasize the sensuality and intensity of the saint's experience. From a concealed window, beams descend along gilded shafts and bathe the saint's figure in a miraculous golden glow. Marble paneling of agate and dark green frames the picture. On either side, kneeling cardinals and members of the Cornaro family, who donated the chapel, behold the vision as if from stage boxes, although they are actually kneeling at prayer desks. Caravaggio employed a similar evocation of the theatre in *The Conversion of St. Paul.* In the central niche, the figure of the cloud-borne saint floats weightlessly in a state of voluptuous ecstasy, torn between earthly emotion and divine love, rising and falling on gales of passion. An angel, the iconographic cousin of the pagan Cupid, is about to pierce her heart with his dart. High above, a ceiling fresco with three-dimensional painted stucco additions depicts an angelic choir grouped around the dove of the Holy Spirit. The sculpture group is surrounded by actual and make-believe architecture; the painted sky and the theatrical lighting form part of a single conception in which real and visionary elements blend into one.

SPAIN: FROM COUNTER-REFORMATION ART TO BAROQUE

The close alliance between Italy and Spain that had begun with the invasion of Charles V continued throughout the baroque period. Politically and economically, the Spanish crown controlled the major Italian regions through viceroys and

puppet regimes. Moreover, through its colonial exploits in North Africa and the Americas, Spain was in command of the largest land area held by any international power. Papal approval of the Jesuits allowed them to extend their influence worldwide and brought sainthood to two of the order's Spanish founding members, Ignatius Loyola and Francis Xavier. In addition, the works of two great Spaniards, St. Teresa of Ávila and St. John of the Cross, captured the Counter-Reformation spirit in literature and became the most widely read writings in the Roman Catholic world.

The personal tastes of Philip II, who succeeded his father, Charles V, were austere to the point of severity. His worldly position and ambitions, however, made it necessary that he surround himself with sufficient magnificence to command awe and respect. To unify his kingdom, take local authority away from his feudal lords, and give himself the power of an absolute monarch, Philip selected as his capital the then-obscure but centrally located town of Madrid. An enormous building program had to be undertaken to house the court and provide palaces for the aristocracy.

With riches from the Old World and the unlimited resources of the New World flowing into his coffers, Philip summoned the leading artists of Europe to build and embellish his capital. His far-flung ambassadors were under instructions to buy any available masterpiece of painting and sculpture. Although they remained in their native cities, Titian and other Italian artists continued to paint for Philip as they had for his father. But Domenicos Theotocopoulos, the Greek-born artist who had been trained in the Venetian mannerist style and had studied the work of Michelangelo and Raphael in Rome, settled in Spain, where he became known as El Greco (The Greek). The Spanish composer Tomás Luis de Victoria, although fully established in Rome, dedicated a book of Masses to Philip in the hope of receiving a court commission. Attracted by the glitter of Spanish gold, other artists, known and unknown, flocked to Madrid in search of fame and fortune.

THE ARCHITECTURE OF POWER

In planning the Escorial, Philip II was bound by his father's will to build him a tomb. He was equally bound by his solemn oath to found a monastery dedicated to St. Lawrence, on whose day he had won his great military victory over the French. Last, he was bound by his religious fervor and royal position. Philip II envisioned a vast architectural project that would coordinate these different obligations while resolving some of his inner con-

---

[1]*Life of St. Theresa,* tr. J. M. Cohen (Harmondsworth, England: Penguin, 1957), 210.

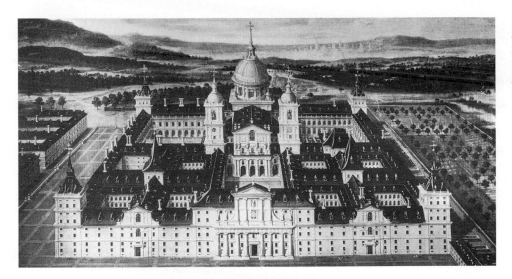

13.14 Juan Bautista de Toledo and Juan de Herrera. Escorial Palace, near Madrid, Spain, 1563–1584. Engraving after Herrera.

flicts. As the plan matured in the king's mind, he conceived of the monument as a temple to God, a mausoleum for his ancestors and descendants, a national archive of arts and letters, a dwelling place for the monks of St. Jerome, a college and seminary, a place of pilgrimage with a lodging for strangers, a royal residence, and of course, a symbol of the glory of the Spanish monarchy.

Located in the barren foothills of the Sierra de Guadarrama mountains about 30 miles from Madrid, a site named for the nearby village of Escorial was chosen for the undertaking. The original plans were drawn up by Juan Bautista de Toledo, who had studied with Jacopo Sansovino and Palladio in Venice and worked on St. Peter's in Rome under the direction of Michelangelo. After his death, the Escorial was completed by his collaborator, Juan de Herrera.

According to Philip's instructions, the monument had to embody the ideals of "nobility without arrogance, majesty without ostentation." As it stands, the Escorial is a vast quadrangle of almost 500,000 square feet, subdivided into a symmetrical system of courts and cloisters (Fig. 13.14). The form refers symbolically to the gridiron on which St. Lawrence was roasted alive. Elsewhere in the building the grill is widely used as a decorative motif.

The Escorial strikes a note of gloomy grandeur and stark magnificence, in keeping with both the Spanish spirit and the somber personality of Philip II. Each side presents a long expanse of wall, entirely lacking in decoration, its monotony broken only by the endless rows of windows (Fig. 13.15). The principal entrance (Fig. 13.14), located on the western front, is carried out in the somber, solid Doric order with only the royal coat of arms and a

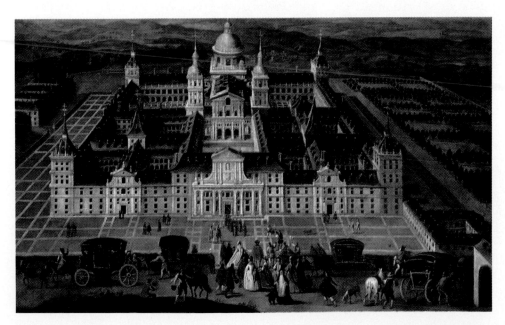

13.15 Escorial Palace, side view. Louvre, Paris, France.

colossal statue of St. Lawrence holding his gridiron to relieve the general austerity. The portal leads into the Patio of the Kings, which occupies the central place in the design. The Patio takes its name from the statues of David, Solomon, and the other kings of Israel placed over the entrance to the imposing church.

The Escorial's grandeur and concentration of functions signal the beginnings of the baroque style. Nevertheless, the restraint of Philip's taste and his strong dislike of flamboyant decoration, as well as the discipline of his architects, kept the urge to decorate within strict bounds, an important difference from the courtly or aristocratic baroque that emerged in other nations (see Chapter 14).

THE ARRIVAL OF THE CHURRIGUERESQUE STYLE

After Philip's death, a number of Spanish patrons and artists felt free to develop a more elaborate style. Indeed, some of their enthusiasm for an ornate style came as a direct reaction to the formal severity of Philip's time. Daring designs, fantastic forms, curved lines, and the spiral twist of corkscrew columns replaced the austere facades and classical orders enforced by Herrera.

The church of the Jesuit college of La Clérica (Fig. 13.16) was begun after the period of Philip and Herrera. The lower part, designed by Juan Gómez de Mora, dates from the early seventeenth century. Even though it remains faithful to the classical orders, the new decorative inclination is unmistakable in the attached Composite columns and the frieze above them, as well as in many of the other details. The towers and gable belong to the latter part of the seventeenth century and were executed by José de Churriguera, whose name is associated with the more florid aspects of Spanish baroque, the **churrigueresque** style.

Churriguera's ornate altarpiece for the Church of San Esteban is an architectural-sculptural-pictorial extravaganza (Fig. 13.17). More than 90 feet high, it combines the Composite order (see Fig. 3.21) with gilded and garlanded twisted columns that wriggle and writhe upward in rhythmic spirals.

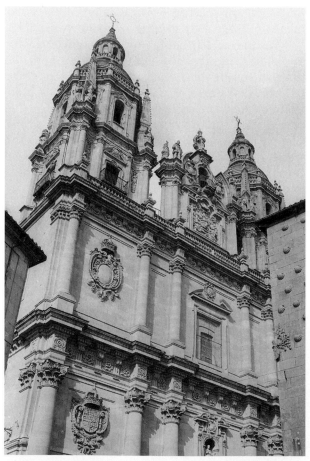

13.16 Juan Gómez de Mora. Facade, La Clérica (left), Salamanca, Spain, 1617.

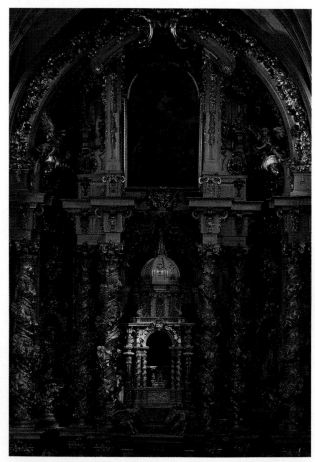

13.17 José de Churriguera. Altarpiece, San Esteban, Salamanca, Spain, 1693.

PAINTING

SPIRITUALITY AND ART: EL GRECO

While the Escorial was still under construction, Philip II commissioned El Greco to paint an altarpiece for the Chapel of St. Maurice. The painter, who was born on the island of Crete when it was a Venetian possession, had studied in Venice, possibly with Titian. El Greco carried the mannerist style to Spain, where he transformed it into an art of burning religious and spiritual incandescence. The subject of El Greco's early masterpiece, *The Martyrdom of St. Maurice and the Theban Legion* (Fig. 13.18), reflects Counter-Reformation tensions in that it depicts the dilemma of an individual caught between conflicting loyalties. St. Maurice, the figure in the right foreground, was the commander of the Theban Legion, a unit of Christians serving in the Roman imperial army. An order has just arrived commanding all members of the unit to acknowledge the traditional Roman deities or

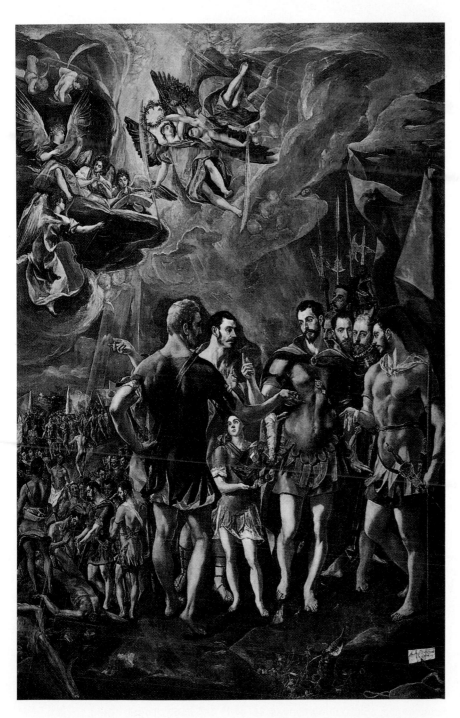

13.18 El Greco. *The Martyrdom of St. Maurice and the Theban Legion,* 1581–1584. Oil on canvas, 14′6″ × 9′10″. Escorial Palace, Madrid, Spain.

else be put to death. In the expressive gestures of their upward-pointing hands, St. Maurice and his staff officers reveal their choice.

El Greco's spiral composition conveys the conflict between the material and spiritual, the natural and the supernatural, and the earthly and the heavenly. Anxiety and hope are expressed in the twitching muscles, flamelike fingers, taut faces, and swirling upward motion of the composition. In coiled, snakelike fashion, the main organizing element winds around to the left middle ground, where St. Maurice is seen again, this time giving comfort to the men as they await their turns for beheading. The tempo is increased toward the background, where the nude figures of the soldiers seem already to have parted company with their bodies and are drawn into the center of a spiritual whirlwind that bears their souls aloft. The eye is led upward by the

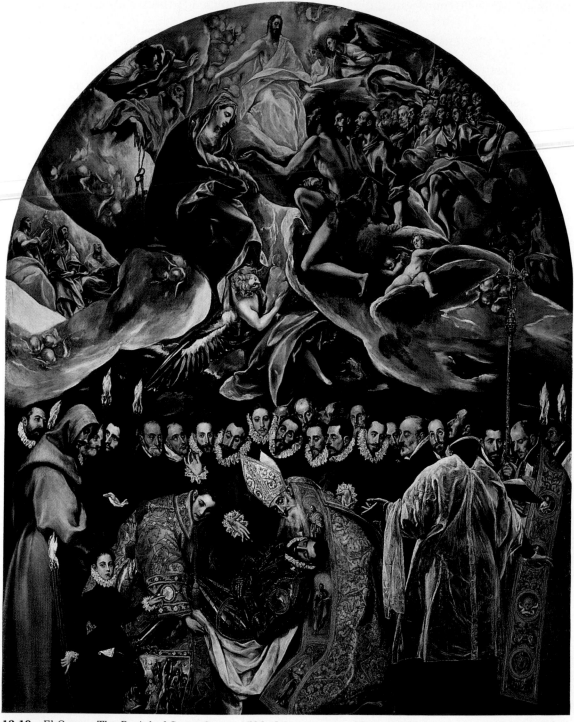

13.19 El Greco. *The Burial of Count Orgaz,* 1586. Oil on canvas, 16′ × 11′10″. Santo Tomé, Toledo, Spain.

constantly increasing light and the transition of color from the darker hues below to the vaporous pink and white clouds above. There the viewer beholds a visionary vista in which some of the angelic figures are hovering and holding crowns of martyrdom for those who suffer and die below, while others produce the sounds of celestial harmony.

Despite the repugnance of the subject, the light, transparent palette that El Greco used gives the work a celebratory feeling, found in the rose-colored banners as well as in the steel-blue and lemon-yellow costumes that shine like metal. The originality of the work, with its jolts of daring color, mannerist elongation of the figures, and lavish use of costly ultramarine blue, lost for El Greco the favor of King Philip, whose tastes ran to a more conservative style. Thereafter, El Greco painted almost exclusively for church patrons.

For his own parish church of San Tomé in Toledo, his adopted city, El Greco painted his masterpiece, *The Burial of Count Orgaz* (Fig. 13.19). The count, who rebuilt and endowed the church, was said to have been honored in 1323 by the miraculous appearance of St. Stephen and St. Augustine, who gently lowered him into his tomb, which is in the wall just below the picture. The earthly and heavenly spheres are separated by flickering torches and swirling draperies as the soul of the count is borne heavenward on angelic wings to be received by the radiant figure of Christ.

The row of mourners includes portraits of the Toledo clergy and gentry and a self-portrait of the artist with his hand raised directly above the head of St. Stephen. A note of subtle humor is struck in the portrait of El Greco's 8-year-old son Jorge Manuel as the attendant in the lower left. The boy points to the encircled white and gold rose embroidered on St. Stephen's vestment—the circle being the symbol of immortality, the rose of love. On his son's pocket handkerchief, El Greco signed in Greek, "Domenicos Theotocopoulos made me, 1578." The date is not that of the picture but of his son's birth.

In *Christ Driving the Money Changers from the Temple* (Fig. 13.20), Jesus appears as refining fire,

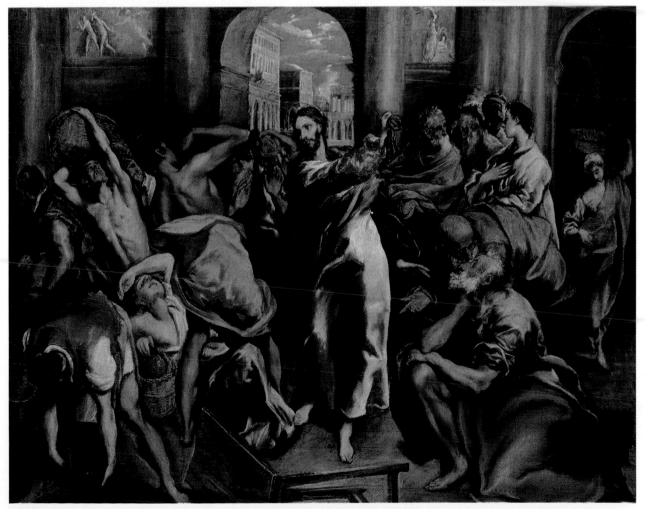

13.20   El Greco. *Christ Driving the Money Changers from the Temple,* c. 1572–1574. Oil on canvas, 3'8" × 4'9". Minneapolis Institute of Arts, William Hood Dunwoody Fund.

a vision prophesied by Isaiah. The painting and its subject constitute a manifesto of Counter-Reformation thought. Jesus is seen as a reformer fighting the commercialization of religion. As St. John's Gospel records the event, Jesus "found in the temple those that sold oxen and sheep and doves, and the changers of money sitting: And when he had made a scourge of small cords, he drove them all out of the temple. . . . And said unto them that sold doves, Take these things hence; make not my Father's house a house of merchandise" (John 2:14–16). The mood of fiery anger is displayed in El Greco's clashing colors of crimson red, pink, orange, and greenish yellow. The pictorial organization recalls Last Judgment scenes, with Christ in the center as judge, the sinners on the left, and the saints on the right (see Fig. 6.1). On one side all is turbulence and con-

fusion; on the other all is calm as the disciples ponder the meaning of the event. The picture also contains a personal element: the four heads in the lower right are those of individuals whom El Greco considered his artistic mentors. From left to right they are Titian, Michelangelo, Giulio Clovio, and Raphael.

THE PAINTER OF COURTLY LIFE: VELÁZQUEZ

When the Spanish sailing fleet, or armada, was sunk by the British Navy, Spain's ambitions to dominate Europe were also ruined. Nevertheless, there was a brief cultural flowering under King Philip IV, in part because he had the good fortune to have the great Diego Velázquez as his court painter. Whereas El Greco had concerned himself almost exclusively with religious subjects,

13.21   Diego Velázquez. *The Water Carrier of Seville,* c. 1619. Oil on canvas, 3'5½" × 2'7½". Wellington Museum, London, England.

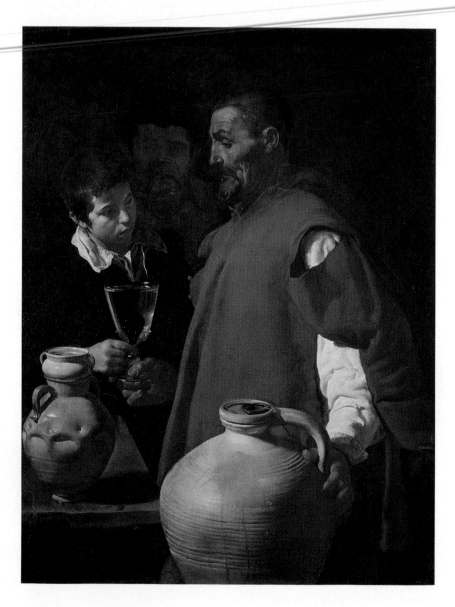

Velázquez, with few exceptions, painted scenes of courtly life. Especially in contrast to El Greco's blistering religiosity, Velázquez's world was cool and detached.

Velázquez's art does not fit into the Counter-Reformation category; it is an example of the nonreligious aristocratic baroque style, which will be discussed in the next chapter. However, because Velázquez's was Spanish, his work is more conveniently covered here.

Velázquez spent his early years in his native Seville. By the age of 20, he was skilled in painting naturalistic genre pictures, such as *The Water Carrier of Seville* (Fig. 13.21). His admiration for Caravaggio, whose work he studied, is evident in the craggy face of the water vendor and the de-

tailed realism of the drops of water that appear on the cool jug. Velázquez's work for the court is admirably summed up in his masterpiece *Las Meninas,* or *The Maids of Honor* (Fig. 13.22). The painter combines the formality of a royal group portrait with the informality of a more casual scene in his studio. In the picture, attention is distributed about evenly among the various groups. In the foreground is the daughter of Philip IV and Queen Mariana, the Infanta (princess) Margarita, dressed in a gown of white satin. On the left, a maid of honor is offering her a drink from a red cup on a gold tray. At the right is a group made up of a second maid of honor and two of the court dwarfs, one of whom is poking the sleepy dog with his foot. In the middle ground, on the left,

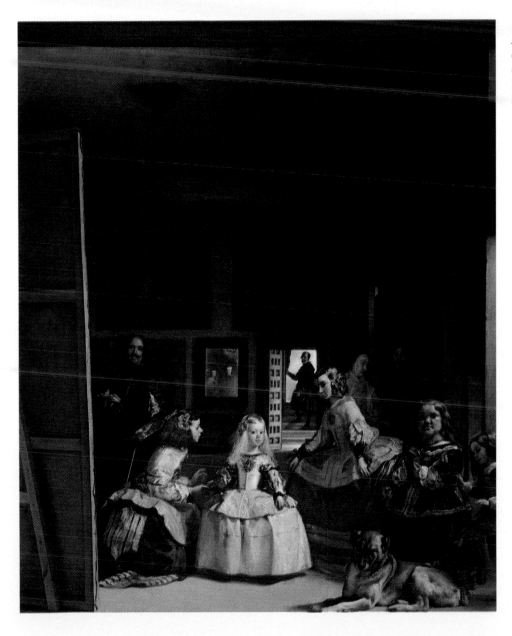

13.22 Diego Velázquez. *Las Meninas (The Maids of Honor),* 1656. Oil on canvas, 10′5¼″ × 9′¾″. Museo del Prado, Madrid, Spain.

Velázquez stands before a canvas that, by reason of its large dimensions, must be for *Las Meninas* itself.

The presence of the painter practicing his profession and the picture within the picture are like the amusing passages in Cervantes's picaresque novel, *Don Quixote,* in which the title character and Sancho Panza talk to the author about the book in which they are the principal characters. Here Velázquez looks at King Philip IV and Queen Mariana, whose faces are reflected in the mirror at the back of the room, much in the manner of Jan van Eyck's *The Marriage of Giovanni Arnolfini and Giovanna Cenami* (see Fig. 11.6). As a balance for his own figure, Velázquez paints the conversing lady-in-waiting and courtier in the right middle ground. At the rear of the room, a court attendant stands in the open doorway, pulling back a curtain, possibly to adjust the light.

Velázquez was a virtuoso in the handling of space and light. He organized the picture into a series of receding planes, and by so doing, he gave the figures their spatial relationships. The first plane is in front of the picture itself, where the king and queen and, by inference, the viewer stand. In this design the spectator becomes part of the picture, just as the king and queen do. Next comes the plane in which the principal group stands, lighted by a window at the right, which is outside the picture but provides the brilliant illumination that falls on the blond hair of the princess. The window light is balanced by light from the door at the rear, which defines the plane in the background. In between is the intermediate plane with the figures of Velázquez and the attendants, who are shown in more subdued light. The receding planes blend together through the delicately rendered atmosphere, which also makes forms in the background seem less distinct. Otherwise, the space is occupied by an abundance of rectangular shapes, such as the floor and ceiling, the window, the easel, the pictures hanging on the wall, the mirror on the wall, and the door at the back.

On another level, Velázquez's picture is a painting about the art of painting. At the time, the artist was seeking membership in the order of the Knights of Santiago. His candidacy had the powerful support of the king and of the great dramatist Lope de Vega. The ancient rules, however, forbade admission of manual workers. In this pictorial manifesto, Velázquez attempts to raise the status of painting to that of a liberal art rather than a mechanical craft. On the wall in the back, he includes copies of works by Peter Paul Rubens, who was knighted by England's Charles I for his diplomatic efforts in establishing peace between England and Spain. Rubens's subjects are those in which gods and goddesses themselves take part in the arts. In his self-portrait, Velázquez appears not in an ordinary painting smock but in the costume of court chamberlain, with the keys of his office on his belt. After he was finally admitted, he painted in the cross of the noble order at the request of the king himself.

In such a precise analytical study of space and light, which lacks both the spiritual mysticism of El Greco and the worldly grandeur of the Venetian painters, the baroque qualities are not immediately apparent. Velázquez was a master of external rather than internal vision, and his baroque traits can be located in such things as the intricate play of light and shadow, the complex spatial arrangements, the tricky suggestion that much of what is happening lies outside the picture space itself, and the subtle relationships of the subjects to each other.

MUSIC

The Roman Catholic urge for reform predisposed church music to look more to the past than to the future and to favor traditional rather than experimental forms. The papal brief authorizing Giovanni da Palestrina to undertake the reform of church music along lines laid down by the Council of Trent notes that "the Antiphonals, Graduals, and Psalters have been filled to overflowing with barbarisms, obscurities, contrarieties, and superfluities as the result of clumsiness or negligence or even wickedness of the composers, scribes, and printers." An ardent advocate of the Flemish contrapuntal style of Josquin Desprez and Heinrich Isaac, Palestrina, together with his great contemporaries Orlande de Lassus and Tomás Luis de Victoria, brought that art to its final fruition. Palestrina's prayers in song achieved a fluidity and transparency of texture, a balance of melody and harmony, a spiritual and organic unity worthy of the closing years of the *ars perfecta,* or "perfect art."

CONQUEST OF THE NEW WORLD

A momentous event in world history occurred during the reign of Charles V, the father of Philip II. This was the Spanish-sponsored expedition by Hernán Cortés to explore and conquer the New World in the wake of Columbus's discoveries. He landed in the Yucatan peninsula of what is now Mexico, where he discovered a stranded Spaniard who had learned the language of the indigenous people. Cortés and his troops were also fortunate in finding an astute woman whom they christened Marina. She spoke both Mayan and Nahuatl, the language of the Aztecs.

Cortés and his cohorts marched on to central Mexico, where they discovered the Aztec Empire ruled by Montezuma. Riding horses and using firearms, which the indigenous peoples had never seen, Cortés and his troops seemed like supermen. To the Spanish, Montezuma's city, Tenochtitlán, with its great buildings built on islands in a lake, seemed like a dream. At first, Montezuma and his court welcomed the Spanish. Then, by means of what may have been a treacherous stratagem, Cortés imprisoned and executed Montezuma.

The country was rich in gold and silver, and the land was ripe for colonization. The Spanish, repulsed by the Aztec practice of human sacrifice, thought of the people as degenerate. Instead of promoting the welfare of the conquered people, they pillaged and plundered the countryside, robbing the people of their gold, silver, and artworks, which were sent back to Spain and melted down for coinage. In an effort to erase Aztec culture, the Spanish destroyed most of the books the Aztecs had produced and blatantly proclaimed themselves the new rulers by building their capital, Mexico City, on the ruins of Tenochtitlán, destroying the palaces as well as the multifamily apartment houses made of stone and adobe that had sheltered about 200,000 people. Near Mexico City, in Teotihuacán, pyramids of the Sun and Moon

still survive. In Mexico City itself, the Spanish built a cathedral (Fig. 13.23) on the stones of a temple dedicated to the Aztec sun god.

New World treasure fueled Spain's rise as the richest nation in the world. About a decade later, another conquistador, Francisco Pizarro, set out for Peru, where he conquered the Inca Empire, which at its height had extended over an area of more than 2,500 square miles in western South America, where Peru, Ecuador, Bolivia, and northern Chile are located today. As Cortés had done in Mexico, Pizarro ultimately killed the Inca ruler, stole the gold, and enslaved the people to make them produce more. Spain was well on its way to mastering the New World, with the exception of Brazil, which was claimed by the Portuguese.

The Aztec people revered the ancient city of Teotihuacán as the place where their gods had created the universe. In fact, it was a former large metropolis peopled by the Olmec. A huge and densely populated area of about 200,000 people, the city was laid out on a grid plan like that developed by the Hellenistic Greeks (see pp. 65–66). At the same time, Rome and Constantinople had only about 50,000 inhabitants each.

The Mayan people of the Yucatan and adjacent territories drew elements of their culture from the Olmec. From about 300 to 900 CE, they built public buildings for administration, astronomical observatories, temples, dance platforms, ball courts, and pyramids. The pyramids were erected with wide flights of steep stone steps leading to small temples at the top. The finest of these is found at

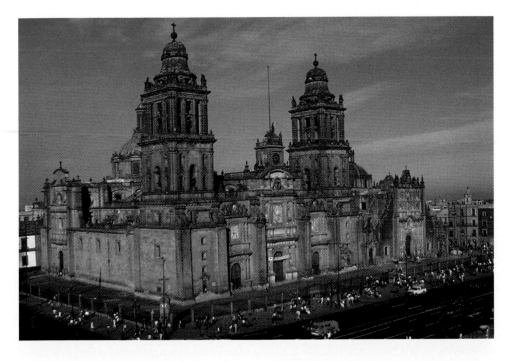

13.23 Mexico City Cathedral, 1656–1671.

Tikal (Fig. 13.24). These pyramids were positioned to coincide with the sun's movements, and religious rites involving human sacrifice were conducted to ensure that the sun would continue in its regular course. The Maya also developed a precise solar calendar of 365 days and had a sophisticated arithmetical system. Their astronomy could predict solar eclipses and chart the orbits of the planets. Moreover, they invented a type of hieroglyphic writing on paper made from the bark of fig trees. The few manuscripts that were not burned by the zealous Spanish clergy have been partially deciphered. They contain records of rulers and priests, including their ancestry, their dates of birth, and when they came to power.

Some impressive temple wall paintings have also come to light. They were first cartooned in black, then finished in fresco using many mineral and vegetable colors. The subjects are mainly ceremonial scenes and religious rites. Figure 13.25 shows a mural in which captive people are presented to the Mayan king.

Sculptures in the round and in relief existed in profusion. They depict the all-important sun and rain gods (Fig. 13.26), as well as the plumed serpent, Quetzalcoatal, who symbolized fertility and wealth. They also show a ritual ball game played on courts within the temple precincts. It is thought that the game's large rubber ball symbolized the sun. The ball game, an invention of the Olmecs, is a much-debated aspect of the cultures that flourished in Mexico, Central America, and South America. Rather than being merely a pastime, it seems to have had ritual significance. It has been argued that at the game's end the leader of the losing team was sacrificed to propitiate the sun god, but the game itself, whose rules are not known, may have been fixed so that only captives would suffer defeat and death.

IDEAS

MILITANT MYSTICISM

The Counter-Reformation vigorously asserted a mystical worldview. It was a practical mysticism of this world as well as the next, blending the active and the contemplative life. It was an intense religious experience not limited to future saints but broadened to include members of the church, laity as well as clergy, those active in worldly affairs, and those behind convent walls. The new mysticism attempted to spark the fires of faith at a time when they were threatened by Protestantism and scientific discoveries. It was a call to arms for all those willing to fight for their convictions against doctrines the Roman Catholic Church considered heresy. It was, in short, a militant mysticism of a church on the march. The "enemy" was the various Protestant movements at home plus the pagan religions of Africa, Asia, and the Americas abroad.

The Counter-Reformation was just as much an assertion of spiritual and moral values in the face of rising scientific views of the world as it was an anti-Protestant movement. The church plainly saw that if the mechanical image of the world as "matter in motion" were generally accepted, the belief in miracles would be undermined, the notion of divine intervention in worldly affairs would be destroyed, and the sense of mystery would be drained from the cosmos.

The new outlook was not so much concerned with abstract theological notions as with vivid religious experience in the here and now. The mysticism of St. Teresa and St. John of the Cross differed from medieval mysticism in its written documentation of each stage of the soul's ascent from the depths of temptation and sin to the ecstasy of union with the divine.

13.24 Temple I (Temple of the Giant Jaguar). Maya, Tikal, Petén, Guatemala, c. 700.

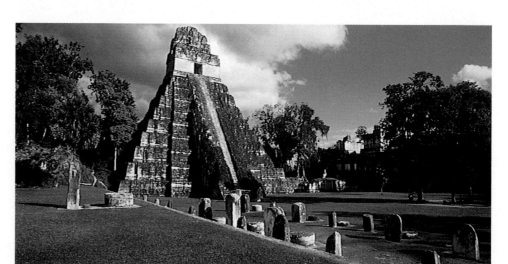

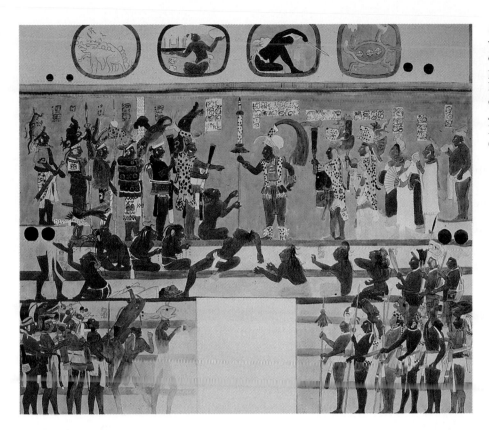

13.25 Temple mural of warriors surrounding captives on a terraced platform. Maya, from Bonampak, Mexico, c. eighth century. Watercolor copy by Antonio Tejeda. Peabody Museum, Harvard University, Cambridge, Massachusetts.

St. Ignatius Loyola and the Jesuits

The most typical expression of the militant church was the Society of Jesus, founded by that soldier and man of action, Ignatius Loyola. The Jesuits helped adapt church doctrine to modern conditions while taking an active part in education, public affairs, and missionary work. A Jesuit enlisted as a "warrior of God under the banner of the Cross" and stood ready to engage in "propagation of the faith to the Turks or other infidels even in India or to heretics, schismatics or some of the faithful." For missionary purposes, the world was divided into Jesuit provinces, and the priestly army of occupation followed in the wake of the navigators and colonizers.

The spiritual side of the Jesuit military organization is reflected in St. Ignatius's *Spiritual Exercises,*

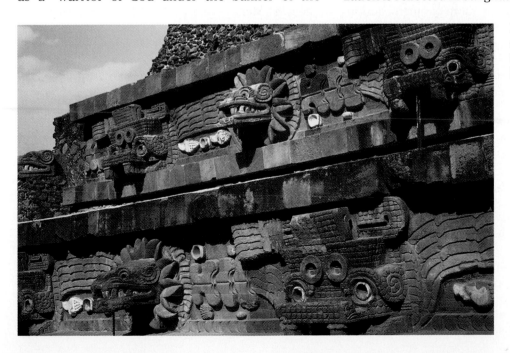

13.26 Detail of Temple of Quetzalcoatl, The Citadel, Teotihuacán, Mexico, c. third century.

a precise, disciplined exploration of the mysteries of faith through the medium of the senses. As part of the Jesuit system of education, St. Ignatius worked out a 4-week series of meditations leading to the cleansing and purifying of the soul. All the human faculties were brought into play so that the experience would become intensely personal.

Sin is the subject of the first week, and its consequences are felt through each of the senses in turn. In the "Torment of Sight," the student visualizes the terrible words engraved on the gates of Hell—Ever, Never—and sees the flames spring up all around. In the "Torment of Sound," the sinner listens to the groans of the damned, the howls of demons, and the crackle of flames as they devour the victims. With the "Torment of Smell," the reader is reminded that the bodies of the doomed retain in Hell the decay of the grave. Their "stink shall come up out of their carcasses," prophesied Isaiah (Isaiah 34:3). For the "Torment of Taste," the condemned shall suffer hunger like dogs; "they shall eat every man the flesh of his own arm" (Isaiah 9:20), and their wine shall be the "poison of dragons and the cruel venom of asps" (Deuteronomy 32:33). In the "Torment of Touch," the damned will be enveloped in flames that ceaselessly boil the blood in the veins and the marrow in the bones but do not consume the victim.

The final phases lead up to the suffering, resurrection, and ascension of Christ, and close with the contemplation of heavenly bliss. The exercises were, of course, merely the preparation for and prelude to the mystical experience itself. By proclaiming that human beings could influence their own spiritual destiny, Jesuits countered Protestant belief and made an appeal to people of action.

MYSTICISM AND THE ARTS

The strong accent on sensory experience as the means to excite religious feeling found expression in the arts. Through architectural, sculptural, pictorial, literary, and musical illusions, miracles and transcendental ideas were made to seem real to the senses. The increasing complexity of life, the rapid growth of new knowledge, and the deepening of psychological insights all shaped the emergence of baroque art. As religious, social, and economic pressures mounted, people were increasingly inclined to resolve their insecurities by turning to the cults of visionary saints or the power of the absolute state. Artists were enlisted to enhance the full power and glory of both church and state. Counter-Reformation churches were spacious, light, and cheerful. Visual artists, dramatists, and composers joined forces to make churches like theaters, where a concert of the arts performed a prelude to future heavenly bliss.

Renaissance clarity of definition and the division of space into clearly understood patterns gave way to a baroque line that relished fluidity of movement. Neat Renaissance lines, circles, triangles, and rectangles became the intertwining spirals, curves, ovals, elongated diamond shapes, rhombuses, and irregular polygons of the baroque. With Borromini, horizontal and vertical surfaces were set into waves of rippling rhythms; balance and symmetry yielded to restless, unsettled movement; walls were molded sculpturally; and surfaces were treated with a rich play of color, light, and shadow. Pictures escaped from their vertical walls and settled on spherical triangular pendentives and spandrels, concave and convex moldings, and the inner surfaces of ceilings, vaults, and domes.

With Pozzo, solid walls, vaulted ceilings, and domes dissolved into cloudy, illusionistic vistas of the great beyond. With Bernini, marble saints and angels floated freely in space. With El Greco, humans shivered with spiritual joy. St. Teresa recorded and published her ecstatic visions in sparkling Spanish prose and poetry so that a wide public could experience them vicariously. Palestrina and Victoria illuminated the hymns of the liturgical year through their counterpoint and invested their melodies with new meaning.

By adopting the baroque style as their own, the Jesuits not only brought baroque art down from the court level but also carried the new ideas with them wherever they went, thus broadening the baroque into an international style. Counter-Reformation baroque churches are found as far afield as Mexico (Fig. 13.23), South America, and the Philippines. The extraordinary vigor of the militant church succeeded in tapping new spiritual sources and vitalizing Roman Catholicism to such an extent that it emerged as a popular religious movement in the Spanish colonies.

YOUR RESOURCES

- **Exploring Humanities CD-ROM**

  ○ Interactive Map: Empires of Art: Comparing the Dutch Republic and Spanish Empire, 1500–1700

- **Web Site**

  http://art.wadsworth.com/fleming10

  ○ Chapter 13 Quiz

  ○ Links—Cervantes, *Don Quixote, Part I*

ROME AND SPAIN: SIXTEENTH AND EARLY SEVENTEENTH CENTURIES

Key Events, Rome	Key Events, Spain	Architecture and Visual Arts	Literature and Music
1491–1556 **Ignatius Loyola** ◆ received papal approval for new Jesuit order	1474–1516 **Ferdinand and Isabella** reigned; 1492 West Indies discovered by Columbus; 1498 South America discovered; expulsion of Moors and Jews from Spain	1498–1578 **Giulio Clovio** ▲	
1500			
	1516–1556 **Charles I,** king of Spain; 1519 became Holy Roman Emperor Charles V 1519–1521 **Hernán Cortés** conquered Mexico	1507–1573 **Giacomo Vignola** ★ c. 1515–1567 **Juan Bautista de Toledo** ★●	c. 1500–1553 **Cristobal Morales** ❏ 1515–1582 **Teresa of Ávila** ◆
1525			
1527 **Charles V's** mercenaries sacked Rome; Protestant Reformation in progress under Luther in Germany; Zwingli and Calvin in Switzerland; reaction to Renaissance humanism began 1530s **Society of Jesus (Jesuit Order)** founded by Ignatius Loyola 1534 **Counter-Reformation** began 1542 **Inquisition** established; censorship of printed matter began 1545 **Council of Trent** (1545–1763) undertook reform within church; reaffirmed dogma	1531 **Francisco Pizarro** conquered Peru	1530–1597 **Juan de Herrera** ★ 1532–1602 **Giacomo della Porta** ★● c. 1541–1614 **El Greco (Domenicos Theotocopoulos)** ▲ 1541–1621 **Juan Bautista Monegro** ●	c. 1525–1594 **Giovanni da Palestrina** ❏ 1538–1584 **Charles Borromeo** ◆ 1542–1591 **John of the Cross** ◆ 1544 **Morales,** composer from Seville, published his first book of Masses 1547–1616 **Miguel de Cervantes** ◆ c. 1548–1611 **Tomás Luis de Victoria** ❏
1550			
c. 1562 **Teresa of Ávila and John of the Cross** reformed Carmelite orders	1556–1598 **Philip II,** king of Spain; Spanish empire reached greatest extent 1561 **Madrid** chosen as capital	1553–1584 **Escorial Palace** built by de Toledo and de Herrera 1556–1629 **Carlo Maderno** ★ 1571–1610 **Michelangelo Merisi da Caravaggio** ▲	1554 **Palestrina,** choirmaster of St. Peter's, Rome, published first Masses 1562–1635 **Lope de Vega** ◆ 1562–1565 **Teresa of Ávila** wrote autobiographical life and treatises on prayer and visions
1575			
1575 **Congregation of the Oratory** (founded by Philip Neri) approved	1588 **English Navy** sank Spanish Armada 1598–1621 **Philip III,** king of Spain; decline of Spanish power	1575–1584 **Il Gesù** built in Rome by Vignola and della Porta 1586–1648 **Juan Gomez de Mora** ★ 1593–1653 **Artemisia Gentileschi** ▲ 1598–1680 **Gian Lorenzo Bernini** ★● 1599–1667 **Francesco Borromini** ★● 1599–1660 **Diego Velázquez** ▲	1577 **Charles Borromeo** wrote treatises on church architecture and art 1583 and 1600 **Victoria** published collection of Masses, motets, psalms, hymns, dedicated to Philip II of Spain 1587 **John of the Cross,** mystic poet, wrote *Spiritual Canticles* and began *Songs of the Soul*
1600			
1616 **Galileo** enjoined by pope not to "teach or defend" researches confirming Copernican theory; 1633 called before Inquisition 1622 **Canonization** of Ignatius Loyola, Teresa of Ávila, Philip Neri, Francis Xavier	1621–1665 **Philip IV,** king of Spain 1623 **Velázquez** appointed court painter 1648 **Treaty of Westphalia;** Spanish power in Europe	1605-1626 **Nave and Facade of St. Peter's** (Rome) built by Maderno 1617–1682 **Bartolomé Murillo** ▲ 1617 **La Clerecia facade** (Salamanca, Spain) completed by de Mora 1635–1667 **San Carlo alle Quattro Fontane** (Rome) built by Borromini 1642–1709 **Andrea Pozzo** ▲ 1656–1563 **Colonnades and sculptures** facing St. Peter's (Rome) done by Bernini 1664–1725 **José de Churriguera** ★● 1693 **Altarpiece of San Esteban** (Salamanca, Spain) completed by Churriguera	1600–1681 **Pedro Calderón** ◆ 1604 **Cervantes's** *Don Quixote,* Part I, published in Madrid (Part II, 1615) 1609 **Lope de Vega,** Spanish playwright, began his many dramas 1622 **Calderón** began writing religious plays and philosophical dramas

★ - Architect ❏ - Musician ▲ - Painter ● - Sculptor ◆ - Writer

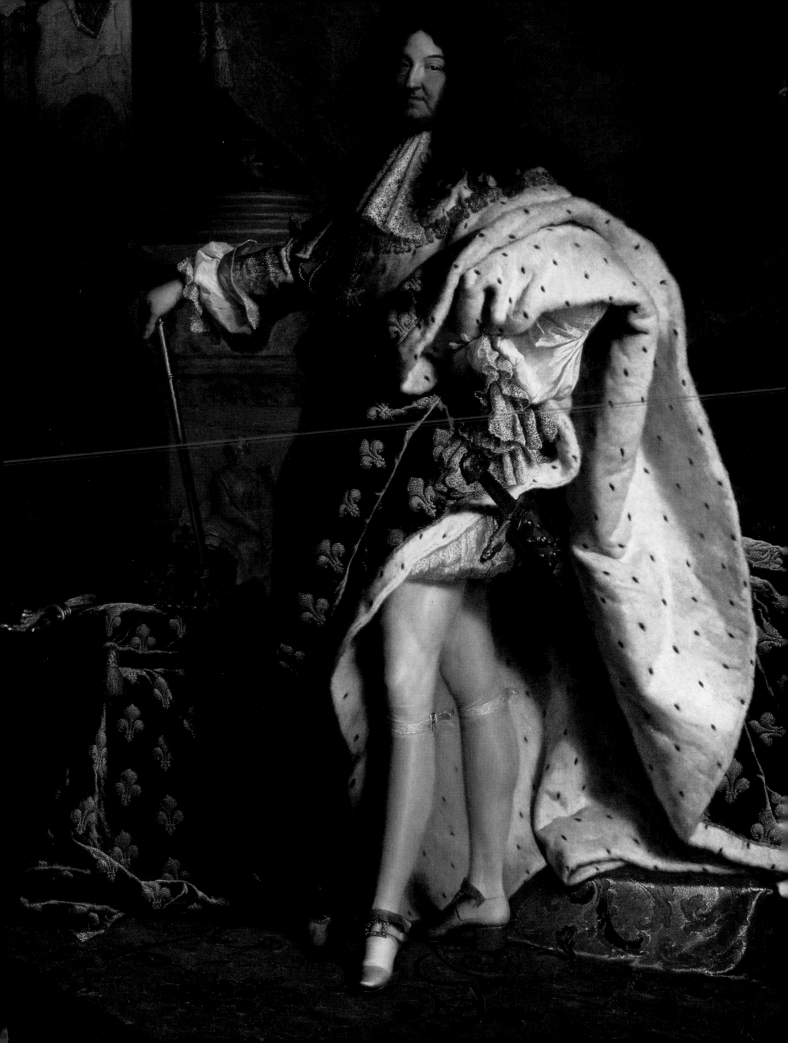

A R I S T O C R A T I C B A R O Q U E
S T Y L E I N F R A N C E
A N D E N G L A N D

DUE TO THE DEFEAT OF its armada and rampant inflation at home, Spain's supremacy was on the wane. By contrast, the power of France and of England was rapidly ascending. Advisors to the French monarchy noted that Philip II had unified Spain in two phases. First, the king created his capital city in Madrid—then a small town but strategically located in the center of his kingdom. Next, he launched a tremendous building program to glorify his monarchy and provide decades of work for his people. The French king would soon follow suit. The aristocratic baroque style burst on the scene with ruffles, flourishes, and many extravagances. Royal pomp and circumstance had started in England with the Stuart kings, but the monarchy was temporarily overthrown by Oliver Cromwell's Puritan revolution. After the restoration of the English monarchy, however, the baroque resumed its opulent course, although in a much more limited fashion under Charles II and his successors.

FRANCE: ABSOLUTE MONARCHY

With Louis XIV, the aristocratic phase of the baroque became French state policy, as everything about the king was calculated to suggest grandeur. His concept of kingship assured him the title *le grand roi,* or "the great king"; his code of etiquette made him in every sense *le grand seigneur,* or "the great gentleman"; and his reign gave his century the name *le grand siècle,* or "the great century." At the time of his portrait by Hyacinthe Rigaud in 1701 (Fig. 14.1), Louis had ruled France for a full 40 years. Dressed in his ermine-lined coronation robes with the collar of the Grand Master of the Order of the Holy Spirit draped about his neck, Louis XIV might actually be uttering the very words attributed to him: *L'etat, c'est moi* (I am the state). Because he was the personification of France, his portrait was that of an institution. His figure was as much a pillar holding up the state as is the column that supports the building in the background. Pompous and pretentious as the portrait may be, it formed part of the illusionism of a period that strove to make abstract notions, such as the divine right of kings, absolutism, and the politically centralized state, seem real to the senses and the imagination.

The triumph of centralized power is evident in the list of accomplishments during Louis XIV's

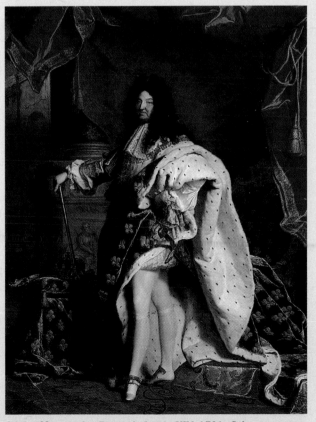

14.1 Hyacinthe Rigaud. *Louis XIV,* 1701. Oil on canvas, 9′1½″ × 6′2⅝″. Louvre, Paris, France.

reign. In the course of his kingship, the feudal power of the provincial nobles was broken and the church became part of the state. Paris arose as the intellectual and artistic capital of the world, and France was on its way to attaining a dominant position among European nations. The alliance of the arts with the absolute power of the king meant that they were valuable instruments of political propaganda at home and abroad. The arts glorified the state, impressing visiting dignitaries and stimulating export trade. They were crucial aids in creating the cult of majesty and sustaining the myth that by divine right the king could do no wrong.

With the king as principal patron, art inevitably became a department of the government. Louis was surrounded by a system of cultural satellites, each of which was supreme in a specific field. The foundation of the Academy of Language and Literature (1635), the Royal Academy of Painting and Sculpture (1648), and other institutions made it possible for Nicolas Boileau to dominate the field of literature, Charles Lebrun that of the visual arts, and Jean-Baptiste Lully that of music.

Absolutism also meant some standardization, because no artist could receive commissions or employment except through official channels. Louis was clear about his aims. In an address to his artists, he remarked, "Gentlemen, I entrust to you the most precious thing on earth, my fame." With so much at stake, he defended his favorite writers and artists and supported them generously.

The outward sign of this absolutism was the dramatization of the personal and social life of the *Roi Soleil,* or "Sun King." Louis's adoption of the sun, the center of the universe, as his symbol was understandable. Motifs like the sunburst were widely used in the decor of his palaces. As patron of the arts, Louis identified himself freely with Apollo, the sun god, who was also the Olympian protector of the Muses. In the morning, when it was time for the Sun King to rise and shine, the *lever du roi* was made as dazzling as a second sunrise. This special dawn was accompanied by a cloud of attendants who flocked into the royal bedchamber precisely at 8 AM to hand the king the various parts of his royal apparel. A similarly colorful ceremony accompanied the *coucher du roi* at precisely 10 PM, when the Sun King finally set in a golden glow of candlelight.

Throughout a reign of 72 years, Louis XIV played the leading role in this constant court drama with the effortless technique and self-assurance of an accomplished actor. Of course, a great actor needed a great audience, and a dramatic spectacle demanded a splendid stage setting. Architects were called on to plan long series of connecting salons as impressive backdrops for triumphal entries. Landscape designers were summoned to fashion grand avenues for open-air processions. Painters were commissioned to decorate the ceilings with pink clouds and classical deities so that the monarch could descend long flights of stairs as if descending from Mount Olympus, home of the Greek gods. Musicians were brought in to sound the musical salutes that accompanied the grand entrances.

It was no accident that the Louvre and Versailles palaces resembled vast theaters, that the paintings and tapestries of Lebrun seemed like curtains and backdrops, and that Bernini's, Puget's, and Coysevox's sculptural adornments took on the aspect of stage props. Nor was it by chance that the most important literary expression should be the tragedies of Jean Racine and the comedies of Jean-Baptiste Poquelin Molière and that the characteristic musical forms should be Lully's court ballets and operas.

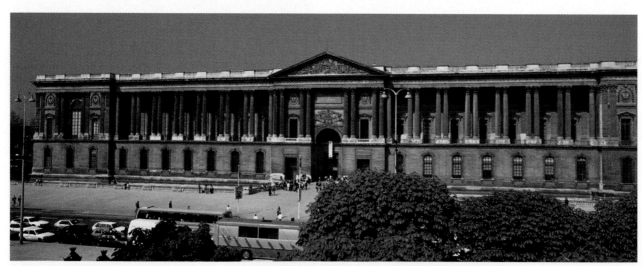

14.2   Claude Perrault. East facade, Louvre, Paris, France, 1667–1670. Length 570', height 90'.

ARCHITECTURE

THE LOUVRE PALACE

Colbert, Louis's astute finance minister, counseled him that "apart from striking actions in warfare, nothing is so well able to show the greatness and spirit of princes than buildings; and all posterity will judge them by the measure of those superb habitations which they have built during their lives." In 1665, at Colbert's insistence, the king asked the pope to permit his principal architect, Gian Lorenzo Bernini, to come to Paris to supervise the rebuilding of the Louvre Palace. When he arrived, Bernini was received with all the honor due him as the ranking artist of his day (see pp. 370–374). The design he made for the Louvre would have required replacing existing parts of the building with a grandiose baroque city palace of the Italian type. Colbert admitted that Bernini's palace was truly grand in style, but he felt that it did not house the king any better.

After a round of festivities, Bernini returned to Rome. His plan was scrapped and a French architect, Claude Perrault, was appointed to finish the job. This episode proved to be a turning point in cultural history. It marked the weakening of Italian artistic influence in France. It also indicated that Louis XIV had plans of his own for making his palace a French cultural center.

Perrault's facade (Fig. 14.2) incorporated some parts of Bernini's project, such as the flat roof concealed behind a Palladian balustrade and the long, straight front with wings extending toward the sides instead of projecting forward to enclose a court in the traditional French manner. Perrault's own contributions can be seen in the solid ground floor, which is relieved only by a series of windows. This story functions as a platform for the classi-cally proportioned Corinthian colonnade, with its rhythmic row of paired columns marching majestically across the broad expanse of the facade. The space between the colonnade and the wall of the building allows for the play of light and shadow that was so much a part of the baroque ideal. The frieze of garlands adds an ornate touch, whereas the central pediment and the classical orders of the columns and pilasters act as restraining influences.

LIFE AND POLITICS AT THE VERSAILLES PALACE

Even before Bernini went to Paris, and long before the Louvre was completed, Louis XIV had conceived the idea of a royal residence outside Paris where he could escape from the restrictions of the city and design a new way of life for himself and the many French nobles whom he gathered there. Colbert, who believed that a king's place was in his capital, advised against it, and Louis allowed the Louvre to be completed as a gesture to Paris. But his real capital was destined to be Versailles. This project was sufficiently awe-inspiring to serve as a symbol of the young king's supremacy. With such a center he could assert his power over rival nations, the aristocracy of his own country, the parliament, the provincial governments, the town councils, and the middle-class merchants. Away from Paris there would be a minimum of distraction and a maximum of concentration on his own royal person. In a wooded site almost half the size of Paris that belonged entirely to the crown, everything could be planned from the beginning and a completely new manner of living could be organized.

The grand axis, or main line of direction, of the Versailles Palace starts with the Avenue de Paris (Fig. 14.3, lower right), continues through the center

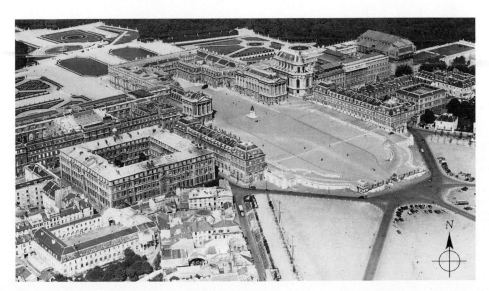

14.3 Versailles Palace, Versailles, France, aerial view, 1661–1688.

of the palace building itself, and runs along to a grand canal. As the avenue enters the palace grounds, the barracks for the honor guard, coach houses, horse stables, dog kennels, and orangeries (greenhouses for orange trees) are found on either side. The orangeries caused an ambassador from a foreign country to remark that Louis XIV must indeed be the most magnificent of beings, because he had a palace for his orange trees that was more beautiful than the residences of other monarchs.

The wide avenue narrows progressively with the parade grounds toward the marble court of honor, above which is found the heart of the plan—the state bedroom of Louis XIV. Versailles thus is an all-embracing structure, integrating a vast segment of external as well as internal space. The gardens, parks, avenues, and radiating pathways are as essential to the whole as the halls, salons, and corridors of the palace itself.

Jules Hardouin-Mansart was the architect of the two wings that extend the main building to a width of about a third of a mile (Fig. 14.3). His design is noteworthy for the horizontal accent created by the uniform level of the roofline, which is broken only by the roof of a chapel added in the early eighteenth century. The simplicity and elegance of these long, straight lines, in contrast to the irregular profile of a medieval building, proclaim the new feeling for space. From every room, vistas of the garden become part of the interior design and tell of a new interest in nature, albeit through a high degree of order and regulation. A detail of the garden facade (Fig. 14.4) reveals how freely Hardouin-Mansart treated the classical orders and how the levels become increasingly ornate, from the podium-like base below to the attic story and balustrade above with its file of silhouetted statuary. As a whole, the building is a commanding example of baroque luxuriance and grandeur modified by academic discretion and restraint.

Some of the interior rooms have been preserved or restored in the style of Louis XIV. The grandest room of the palace is the famous Hall of Mirrors, which stretches across the main axis of the building and looks out toward the spacious gardens (Fig. 14.5). Designed by Hardouin-Mansart and decorated by Lebrun, it was the scene of the most important state ceremonies. Corinthian pilasters of green marble support the ornate vault, which is covered with paintings by Lebrun and inscriptions by Boileau and Racine, all glorifying the Sun King.

The gardens, which were laid out by André Le Nôtre, are not just a frame for the building but part of the whole spatial design (Fig. 14.6). Their formality and geometric organization symbolized human dominance over nature, coupled with the idea of embracing nature rather than keeping it at arm's length. The square pools across the garden side, liberally populated with goldfish and swans, mirror the contours of the building. The statues of river gods and nymphs at the angles, designed by Lebrun, personify the rivers and streams of France.

The gardens and park form a logical system of terraces, broad avenues, and pathways radiating outward from clearings. They are lavishly embellished by fountains, pools, canals, pavilions, and grottos, all of which are richly decorated with statuary. Skilled engineers installed more than 1,200 fountains, which have jets that spout water in many patterns into the air. Each had a name, and each was adorned with an appropriate sculptural group.

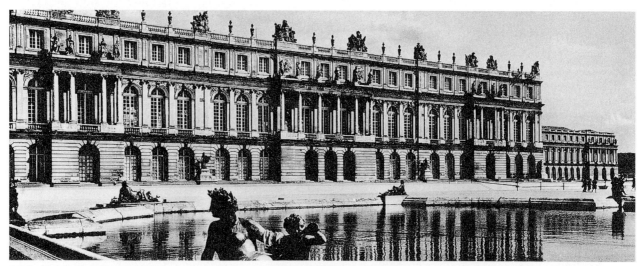

14.4   Louis Le Vau and Jules Hardouin-Mansart. Garden facade, Versailles Palace, Versailles, France, 1669–1685.

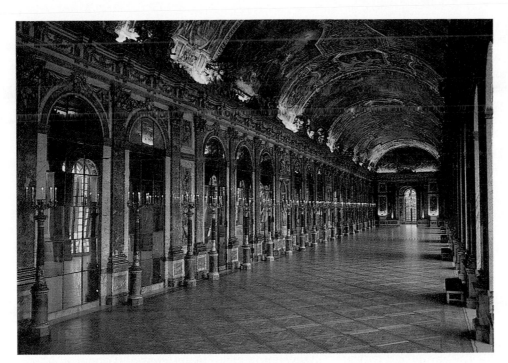

14.5 Jules Hardouin-Mansart and Charles Lebrun. Hall of Mirrors, Versailles Palace, begun 1676. Length 240', width 34', height 43'.

The Versailles Palace, in the broader political sense, was not only a monument to the vanity of Louis XIV but also a symbol of the absolute monarchy and, as such, the outstanding example of aristocratic baroque architecture. It represented a movement away from a decentralized feudal government toward a centralized modern state. As a vast advertising project, it was also a highly influential factor in the international diplomacy of the time. By urbanizing the country aristocracy and promoting court activities, Versailles built up a large and knowledgeable audience for the arts. The artistic center of gravity shifted from Italy to France. In addition, the French court was a center of style and dress. Together with its extensive programs for the training of craftspeople, France was assured the leadership of Europe in fashion and elegance.

By combining all the activities of a court into a single structure, Versailles pointed the way toward the concept of architecture as a primary means to deliberately alter existing patterns of life and create new ones. Indeed, the design of Versailles became a model for later city planning. Details of Le Nôtre's garden plan, such as the radiating pathways, were the acknowledged basis for laying out new sections of Paris; the city plan of Washington, D.C., was a direct descendant of the parks of Versailles. Modern city planners and housing developers have hailed Versailles as the origin of the contemporary ideal of placing large residential units in close contact with nature. Finally, by starting with a grand design, Versailles anticipated the planning of whole cities from the start to avoid haphazard growth and change. In this light, Versailles is one of the earliest examples of modern urbanism and city planning on a large scale.

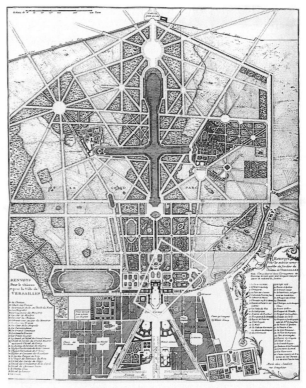

14.6 André Le Nôtre. Plan of Gardens of Versailles, 1662–1688.

SCULPTURE

While Gian Lorenzo Bernini was working on plans for the Louvre, he was overwhelmed by appeals from would-be patrons to design everything from fountains for their gardens to tombs for their ancestors. The king was first in such requests, and Bernini received a commission from Louis XIV for a portrait bust (Fig. 14.7). This by-product of the artist's visit to Paris ultimately turned out to be far more successful than his mission to design the Louvre Palace.

Dispensing with the usual formal sittings, Bernini made rapid pencil sketches of Louis playing tennis or presiding at cabinet meetings. The informal sketches were made, as he said, "to steep myself in, and imbue myself with, the King's features."

After Bernini had captured the king's individuality, he decided on the general ideas to be embodied in his sculpture: nobility, majesty, and the optimistic pride of youth. All the accessories, such as the costume, drapery, and position of the head, would play a part. After he noted the king's bearing and typical movements and settled on the general concepts, Bernini held thirteen sittings with the king to make finishing touches directly on the marble.

Bernini's fame as a sculptor rested not only on such portraits but also on religious statues, such as *St. Teresa in Ecstasy* (see Fig. 13.13), on the many fountains he designed for Rome (see Fig. 13.10); and on mythological groups such as *Apollo and Daphne* (see Fig. 13.11), which were designed to embellish aristocratic residences.

The Versailles gardens were a source of numerous major commissions for French sculptors. Some went to Italy to copy admired antiquities, such as the *Laocoön Group* (see Fig. 3.17). Replicas were then sent back and placed on pedestals along the various walks at Versailles. Notable among these sculptures were works of Pierre Puget, such as his *Milo of Crotona* (Fig. 14.8). This statue shows the ancient Olympic wrestling champion who challenged Apollo to a match. Milo was, of course, given the punishment due a mortal who dares to compete with a god—death.

PAINTING

Patronage of the arts on a lavish and international scale had been a royal privilege since the time of Francis I (see p. 280). The procession of major cultural figures to the French court, beginning in the sixteenth century with Leonardo da Vinci and Benvenuto Cellini, never ceased. Foremost among the newcomers was the celebrated Flemish painter

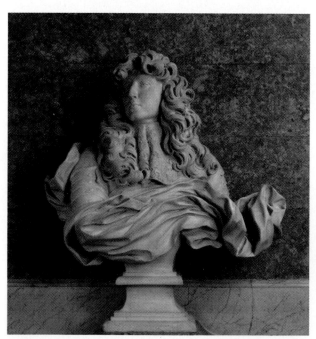

14.7 Gian Lorenzo Bernini. *Louis XIV,* 1665. Marble, height 2′9⅛″. Versailles Palace, Versailles, France.

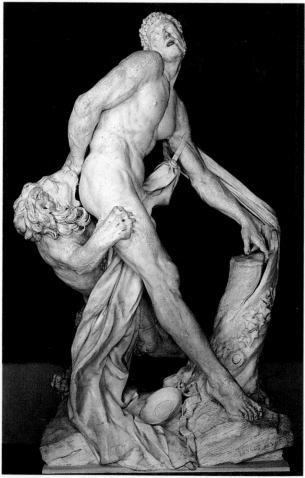

14.8 Pierre Puget. *Milo of Crotona,* 1671–1682. Marble, height 8′10½″, width 4′7″. Louvre, Paris, France.

Peter Paul Rubens. Although loyal to Flanders and Antwerp, where he maintained his studio, Rubens had studied the works of Titian and Tintoretto in Venice, as well as those of Michelangelo and Raphael in Rome. Never lacking aristocratic favor, he passed long periods in Spain and Italy, particularly at Mantua and Venice.

THE INTERNATIONAL CELEBRITY ARTIST: RUBENS

During the reign of Louis XIII, when the Luxembourg Palace was being completed for the Queen Mother, Marie de Medici, she sought a painter who could decorate one of its long gallery walls in a manner that matched the Italian baroque style of its architecture. Marie's career as Henry IV's queen and Louis XIII's regent was lacking in luster. Nevertheless, as the direct descendant of Lorenzo the Magnificent, she knew that the immortal reputations of royals often depended more on their choice of artists and their visual representations than on their skill in statecraft. Marie's choice for the gallery murals was Peter Paul Rubens.

Rubens's cycle of twenty-four large canvases gave the needed glorification to Marie's unimaginative life. As Rubens showed the story, Jupiter, Juno, and Minerva presided over the scene of *Henry IV Receiving the Portrait of Marie de' Medici* (Fig. 14.9). Minerva, goddess of peace and war, whispers words of wisdom into the king's ear. Above them Jupiter and his eagle and Juno with her peacocks bestow

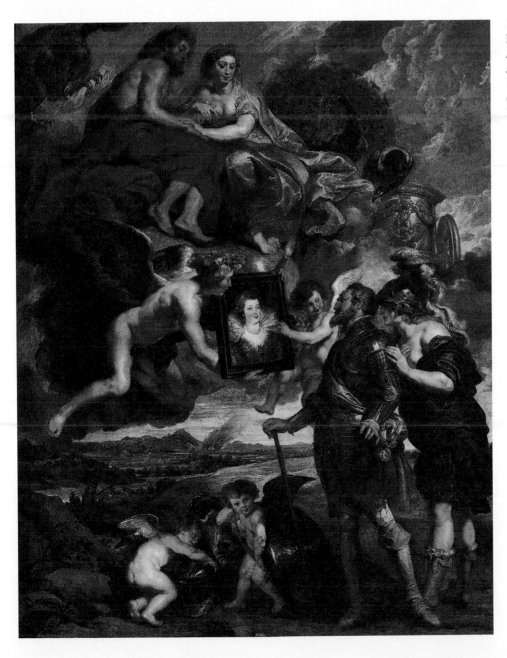

14.9   Peter Paul Rubens. *Henry IV Receiving the Portrait of Marie de' Medici*, 1622–1625. Oil on canvas, 13′ × 9′8″. Louvre, Paris, France.

their Olympian blessings, assuring viewers that marriages like this one are made in heaven.

The baroque ideal of richness and lavishness is again manifest in a picture from Rubens's later years, *Garden of Love* (Fig. 14.10). The scene of amorous revelry unfolds in a diagonal line beginning with the chubby cherub in the lower left. Rubens himself is seen urging his second wife, Helena Fourment, who appeared in many of his later pictures, to join the others in the garden of love, a long-standing symbol for human affection and fertility. The rest of the picture expands in a series of spirals mounting upward toward the figure of Venus, who, as a part of the fountain, presides over the festivities. The use of large areas of strong primary colors—reds, blues, yellows—enriches the scene and strengthens the pictorial structure.

Rubens succeeded in combining the lush color of Titian and the dramatic tension of Tintoretto with an unbounded energy and physical power. His conceptions have something of the heroic sweep of Michelangelo, although they lack the latter's thoughtfulness and restraint. His complex organization of space and freedom of movement recall El Greco, but his figures are as round and robust as the latter's were tall and thin. His success in religious pictures, hunting scenes, and landscapes, as well as mythological paintings, shows the sweep of his pictorial powers. For brilliant handling of the brush, he has rarely been equaled. His huge output of paintings owed both to his international reputation and to the squad of assistants he employed to paint the formulaic parts of his works.

FIRST PAINTER TO THE KING: POUSSIN

While Rubens was executing his murals for the Luxembourg Palace, a then-obscure French painter named Nicolas Poussin, who had been working on minor decorations, left the Luxembourg Palace for the less confining atmosphere of Rome. He soon built a solid reputation that came to the attention of Cardinal Richelieu, who bought many of his paintings and determined to bring him back to Paris. In 1640, Poussin returned to decorate the Grand Gallery of the Louvre. He received from Louis XIII a shower of favors and the much-desired title of First Painter to the King. The inevitable courtly intrigues that followed such attention made Poussin so miserable that after 2 years he returned to Rome. There he acted as France's artistic ambassador and supervised the French painters sent under government subsidies to study and copy Italian masterpieces for the decoration of the Louvre. Settled in Rome for the rest of his life, Poussin enjoyed the freedom to pursue his classical studies, the independence to work out his own principles and ideals, and the time to paint pictures ranging from mythological and religious subjects to historical canvases and architectural landscapes.

Two paintings depicting baroque attitudes toward sexuality and power indicate the differences in temperament between Rubens and his younger French colleague (Figs. 14.11 and 14.12). Poussin's scene, *Rape of the Sabine Women,* refers to the legendary founding of Rome according to the historians Livy and Plutarch. Romulus, having been

14.10 Peter Paul Rubens. *Garden of Love,* c. 1632–1634. Oil on canvas, 6′6″ × 9′3½″. Museo del Prado, Madrid, Spain.

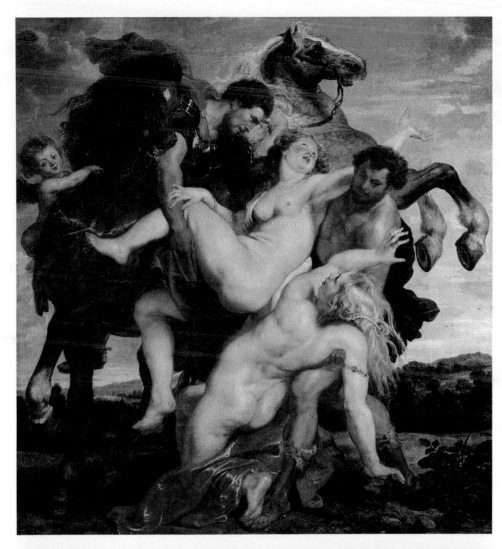

14.11 Peter Paul Rubens. *Rape of the Daughters of Leucippus*, c. 1618. Oil on canvas, 7′3″ × 6′10″. Alte Pinakothek, Munich, Germany.

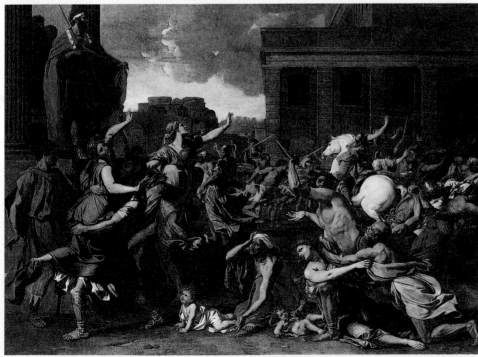

14.12 Nicholas Poussin. *Rape of the Sabine Women*, c. 1636–1637. Oil on canvas, 5′1″ × 6′10½″. Metropolitan Museum of Art, New York, Harris Brisbane Dick Fund, 1946.

unsuccessful in negotiating marriages for his warriors, has arranged a religious celebration with games and festivities as a plan to bring families from the neighboring town of Sabina to the Roman Forum. A mythological subject is the basis for Rubens's *Rape of the Daughters of Leucippus,* which shows the gods Castor and Pollux abducting the daughters of King Leucippus.

In the feminist literature of the late twentieth century, this picture and the increased number of mythological rape scenes decorating court palaces were much discussed. Such scenes worked as propaganda to reinforce the absolute power of the king. In particular, Rubens's painting probably praises the political alliances attained through two marriages arranged by Marie de Medici between her son Louis XIII and Anne, the sister of the future Spanish King, Philip IV, and between her daughter Elisabeth and Philip. The royals are presented as brothers joined by marriage and sexual pursuit. The fact that the future king of Spain was 11 years old and his bride 13 does not enter the picture. Nor does the reality that Louis and his future bride were 15 influence the painting's concept.

The more studious Poussin, in his efforts to recreate the classical past, turned to Roman museums for models of many of his figures and to Vitruvius for his architectural setting. From his prominent position on the porch of the temple at the left, Romulus is giving the prearranged signal of unfolding his mantle, whereupon every Roman seizes a Sabine maiden and makes off with her. The contours of the figures are as clearly defined as if they had been chiseled out of stone. Although the subject is one of sexual violence, Poussin manages to maintain an orderly composition through a careful arrangement of opposites. The smooth, marblelike flesh of the women contrasts with the bulging muscles beneath the bronzed skins of the Romans. The anger of the outraged victims contrasts with the purposive calm of Romulus and his attendants. Romulus believed that the future of his city depended on the formation of families and that the end justified the means. The turbulent human action is also counterbalanced by the repose of the architectural and landscape background.

Poussin's obsession with ancient sculpture is readily seen when the group in the right foreground is compared with the Hellenistic *Gaul and His Wife* (see Fig. 3.6). Poussin's male figure derives from the ancient statue, with the position of the left arm and right hand constructed as he thought they ought to have been made. This group reveals the close study the artist made of ancient architecture and statuary in Rome's libraries and museums. The building at the right, for instance, is taken from a description of a Roman basilica in Vitruvius's book on architecture (see p. 58). Poussin's reconstruction of the statue and the shape of the basilica turned out to be quite wrong in the light of later, more exact archeological evidence.

Et in Arcadia Ego (Fig. 14.13) shows Poussin in a quieter and more introspective mood. The rustic figures of the shepherds might well have stepped out of one of Virgil's pastoral poems, whereas the shepherdess could be the tragic Muse in one of the dramas by contemporary playwright Pierre Corneille. As they trace out the letters of the Latin inscription on the sarcophagus, "I Too Once Dwelled in Arcady," their outlook becomes somber. They may be

14.13 Nicholas Poussin. *Et in Arcadia Ego (I Too Once Dwelled in Arcady),* 1638–1639. Oil on canvas, 2′9½″ × 3′11⅝″. Louvre, Paris, France.

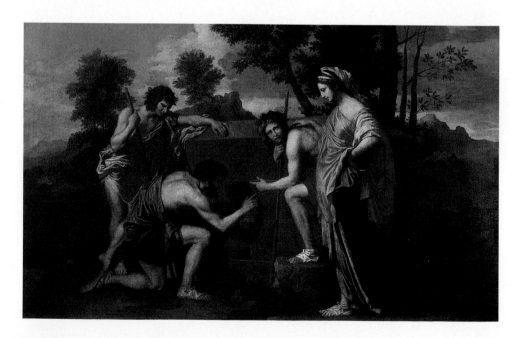

thinking about the shepherd in the tomb, who once lived and loved as they do. The inscription can also be rendered as "I, Death, also dwell in Arcady," suggesting that no place is free from ruin. In this composition of space, the female figure parallels the trunk of the tree to define the vertical axis, whereas the arm of the shepherd on the left rests on the tomb to supply horizontal balance. Subdued baroque diagonals can be traced along the back of each crouching shepherd. Each gesture, each line, follows inevitably from the initial spatial statement, which progresses with the cool logic of a geometric theorem.

The subject was obviously a sympathetic one for Poussin, who had found his own Arcadia in Italy and took a lifelong delight in the monuments of antiquity and the voices from the past that spoke through just such inscriptions. He tried to emulate the ancient Greeks and Romans, conducting his own search for truth and beauty. Like them, he also sought for the permanent in the momentary and the universal in the particular.

The stylistic differences of Rubens and Poussin admirably illustrate the free and academic sides of the baroque coin. Both painters were well versed in the classics, both were acquainted with the spirit of the Counter-Reformation, and both in their way represented the aristocratic tradition. Rubens filled his pictures with tumultuous movement, whereas Poussin pursued tranquil formal values. Rubens's figures are soft and fleshy, whereas Poussin's are hard and statuesque. Rubens sweeps up his spectators in a tidal wave of energy, but Poussin encourages quiet meditation. The Academy's championship of Poussin indicates a clear distinction between academic and unbound baroque. In the late seventeenth and eighteenth centuries, painters were divided into camps that labeled themselves either "Poussinist" or "Rubenist." Indeed, well into the nineteenth century, this distinction resonated in the controversy of classic versus Romantic styles.

LANDSCAPE AND SOFT LIGHT: LORRAIN

Like his countryman Poussin, Claude Gellée, better known as Claude Lorrain, preferred life in Italy to that in his native France. His lifelong interest was idealized landscapes, but the convention of the time demanded that pictures contain personages and have titles. Claude solved the problem by painting his landscapes, letting his assistants put in a few incidental figures, and giving the pictures obscure names, such as *Disembarkation of Cleopatra at Tarsus, Expulsion of Hagar,* or *David at the Cave of Adullam*—subjects no other artist painted. With tongue in cheek, he once remarked that he sold his figures and gave away his landscapes.

Harbor scenes like *Disembarkation of Cleopatra at Tarsus* (Fig. 14.14) were his special concoction.

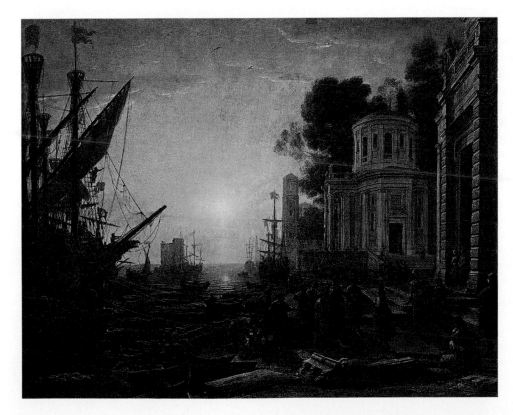

14.14 Claude Lorrain. *Disembarkation of Cleopatra at Tarsus,* c. 1647. Oil on canvas, 3′10″ × 5′6½″. Louvre, Paris, France.

In them he could concentrate on limitless space and the soft atmospheric effect of sunlight diffused in misty air. He usually balanced his compositions on either side of the foreground with buildings or trees, which are more generalized than detailed. He liked to draw the viewer's eye deep into the intervening space, along long vistas, over land or sea, toward the indefinite horizon.

MUSIC

Music and drama at the court of Louis XIV were as lavish as the other arts. Three groups of musicians were maintained, the first of which was the **chambre** group, which included the famous *Vingt-quatre Violons* (Twenty-Four String Players), the first permanent orchestra in Europe. This was the string ensemble that played for balls, dinners, concerts, and the opera. The group also included lutenists and keyboard players. Next came the **chapelle,** the choirs that sang for religious services, and the organists. The **Grande Écurie,** or military band, formed the third category, which consisted mainly of the wind ensemble and was available for parades, outdoor festivities, and hunting parties.

MUSIC AND DRAMA AT COURT: MOLIÈRE AND LULLY

Court theater flourished under the direction of the brilliant actor and playwright Jean-Baptiste Poquelin, known professionally as Molière. Molière united elements of comedy, music, and dance into a form he called *comédie-ballet.* One of the best known of these is the popular *Le Bourgeois Gentilhomme* (The Bourgeois Gentleman, about a middle-class man who wants to become a gentleman). It was first performed at court in 1670. Molière had a gift for comedy, especially when he could expose the social pretensions, affectations, and hypocrisies of his day with biting satire. *Le Bourgeois Gentilhomme* pokes fun at a newly rich businessman, a social climber who tries to imitate the aristocracy only to make a series of hilarious blunders. The play implies that wealth alone cannot change a person's social status: it is inborn.

BIRTH OF FRENCH OPERA

During Louis's youthful years, his Italian prime minister, Cardinal Mazarin, sought to bring the new Italian opera—"the spectacle of princes"—into the French court. Francesco Cavalli, a pupil of Claudio Monteverdi who had brought the Venetian lyric drama to a high point of development, was invited to Paris in 1662 to write an opera for Louis's wedding celebration. Music for the ballet sequences was entrusted to the young Jean-Baptiste Lully. Florentine by birth and French by education, at the early age of 17 he was a violinist in the *Vingt-quatre Violons.* As luck would have it, his ballet scenes proved more popular than Cavalli's opera. The ever-resourceful Lully was soon in charge of all the music at court. He collaborated with Molière by supplying the musical portions of the dramatist's comédie-ballets, including incidental music for *Le Bourgeois Gentilhomme.*

THE LYRIC TRAGEDY

It was Lully who came up with a French form of opera that he called *tragédie lyrique,* or "lyrical tragedy." One of the earliest of these operas was *Alceste,* performed in the Marble Court at Versailles on July 4, 1674 (Fig. 14.15). Lully used the *Vingt-quatre Violons* as the nucleus of his orchestra, supplementing them with wind instruments from the *Grand Écurie* for fanfares as well as for the hunting, battle, and climactic transformation scenes. The *chapelle* was also drafted into the operatic service for the choruses, and the generous dance sequences that Lully included gave the ballet group a prominent role. Dance was admired not only in theatrical performances but also as a skill required of the nobility and the well-to-do. The king was said to be an excellent dancer. The regimented physical movements of baroque dance conveyed a sense of courtly control, and can be seen as a dramatization of absolute power.

The structure of lyrical tragedies crystallized early and changed little in the following years. Each began with an instrumental number of the type that would become known as a "French overture." The first part is a march with dotted notes, massive sonorities, and resolving dissonances. The second half is livelier and contrapuntal in style and texture.

Musical Example 14.1
Alceste, Overture, bars 1–4   Jean-Baptiste Lully

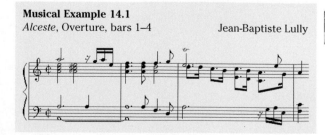

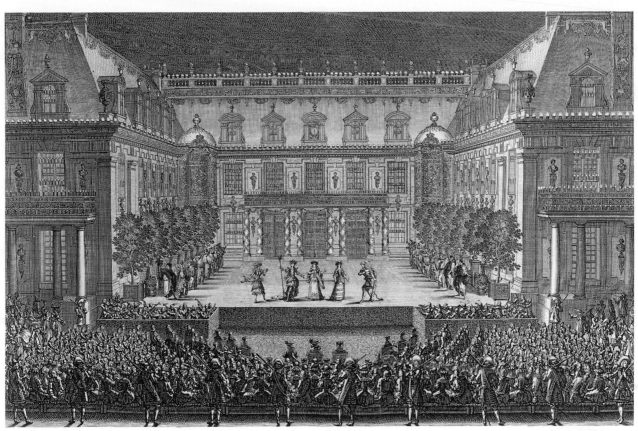

14.15   Louis Le Vau. Marble Court, Versailles Palace, Versailles, France. Engraving by Lepautre entitled "Divertissements . . . 1674" showing a performance of Lully's *Alceste,* 1674. Metropolitan Museum of Art, New York, Harris Brisbane Dick Fund, 1930.

Next came a prologue, sung in **recitative** style, a kind of free vocal delivery of lines that sets the scene, describes the action, or carries on the dialogue. It is usually sung to the accompaniment of a keyboard instrument supported by a string bass. Recitative is opposed to the more formally organized and melodic arias or airs, which are accompanied by the orchestra.

In *Alceste,* Glory enters to the tune of a triumphal march and is eventually joined by a chorus of water nymphs and pastoral divinities, whose songs and dances give assurance that France will be ever victorious under the leadership of a great hero, whose identity is never in doubt. The overture is repeated, and the five acts of a classical tragedy follow with much the same formal pattern as the prologue.

Lully insisted that the music and all other elements of the opera were the servants of drama and poetry, and he counseled singers to follow the noble and expansive intonations of the actors trained by the playwright Racine. Thus, a Lully air, unlike a formal Italian aria, follows the elastic, fluid speech rhythms and the natural recitation of

French baroque poetry and prose. After the death of Alceste, a long instrumental ***ritornel*** provides the pompous funereal strains for the entrance of the mourning chorus.

Because the hero was so closely identified with the monarch, a tragic ending was impossible. Just when all seemed darkest, a *deus ex machina* (see p. 47) descended from above to put things right. The final act brought the tragedy to a conclusion worthy of the Sun King.

Practically single-handedly, Lully brought the ballet into a unified, organic form and founded French opera. His standardization of the sequence of dances became known as the "French suite," his form of the overture was called the "French overture," and his organization of opera remained standard practice for almost two centuries.

Like Poussin's paintings, Lully's operas remained aloof, restrained, and aristocratic. The concept of opera, however, with its combination of elevated language, emotional appeal, sonorous splendor, majestic movement, and visual elegance, remains one of the most magnificent creations of the baroque era.

ENGLAND: LIMITED MONARCHY

In London during the seventeenth century, a sizable middle-class citizenry was on a collision course with the absolutist ideas of Charles I. Middle-class power was based on London's escalating commercial success as well as on England's increasing control of colonies in Asia and America. When Charles attempted to assert the divine right of kings by dissolving Parliament and ruling by royal decree, he plunged his country into a bitter civil war that ended with victory for the anti-Royalists. Charles was brought to trial and condemned to death, and his monarchy was replaced by a commonwealth based on parliamentary rule. However, the uncompromising Cromwell, who governed as "Lord Protector," continued to alienate the still-powerful aristocracy. Eventually a compromise was reached that established the Restoration regime of Charles II, who ruled as a limited monarch. The political and social struggle extended to the arts, as poets, playwrights, architects, and painters contended for patronage and audiences in both aristocratic and middle-class circles. Like French absolutism, the ostentatious French aristocratic baroque was too showy for English tastes.

REBUILDING LONDON: WREN AND ST. PAUL'S

The Great Fire of London in 1666 demolished more than 13,000 homes and more than 400 acres. About ninety churches were destroyed, among them St. Paul's. When it came time to build a new cathedral after the fire, King Charles and his principal architect, Christopher Wren, thought in terms of the richly embellished classical orders, the splendor and spaciousness of the Louvre and Versailles, and the central-type churches of Andrea Palladio and Michelangelo. The Church of England clergy and their parishioners, however, still thought of a cathedral as a tall, imposing Gothic structure. Wren wanted the new cathedral to be crowned with a dome; the church leaders thought it should have a spire. In an attempt at compromise, Wren built his dome and put a high lantern tower on top of it. Charles wanted the London parish churches to be free of Gothic gauntness and gloom, but the parishioners insisted on belfries with tall-spired steeples. Wren gave them their steeples, but with classical geometric flourishes.

A similar concession was achieved in music. Charles wanted opera in the style of Lully, but Lon-

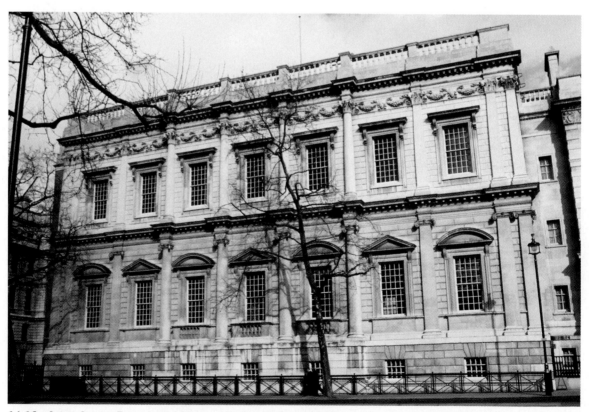

14.16 Inigo Jones. Banqueting House, Whitehall, London, England, 1619–1622. Length 120′, height 75′.

don theatergoers showed remarkable resistance toward sung recitative. They settled for a hybrid form of spoken dialogue with songs and instrumental interludes. A comparison among the three great figures of the Restoration style, Wren, John Dryden, and Henry Purcell, reveals that each tried to bring his audience up to date on the latest Continental developments while injecting something of the grandeur of the French baroque style into an English art form. Each artist proved willing to compromise to avoid parting company with English audiences.

When Wren was designing his ideal models, Dryden was writing solely for a small circle of readers, and Purcell was composing experimentally for amateurs, each could be as free as he chose. But when it came to building a cathedral, mounting a play, or composing music for the theater, many subtle and even drastic adjustments had to be made. Each of the three artists had sufficient mastery in his field and was sufficiently versatile and inventive to make those adjustments. Each preferred and developed an aristocratic style but never neglected the common touch, and each had an influence that lasted well into the next century. Wren's buildings became the backbone of the Georgian style, Dryden's works were the backdrop for eighteenth-century Augustan classicism in English literature, and Purcell's music was absorbed directly into the sacred and secular music of later generations.

In seventeenth-century England, political authority was divided between the monarch and Parliament. Literary tastes split between classical and Elizabethan traditions. French baroque architecture was at odds with the tradition of English Gothic (see pp. 216–221), and musical expression was torn between Continental developments and national preferences. Remarkably, the British achieved a synthesis of aristocratic and middle-class institutions, Roman Catholicism and Protestantism, as well as Continental and English traditions. Through the efforts of Wren in architecture, Dryden in literature, and Purcell in music, the Continental influences were merged with English traditions and transformed into a distinctive English Restoration style.

ARCHITECTURE

MORE THAN A DINING HALL: THE BANQUETING HOUSE IN WHITEHALL

London had caught a brief glimpse of Continental elegance under James I, Charles II's grandfather. James I had commissioned Inigo Jones to build the Banqueting House at Whitehall (Fig. 14.16) as the first unit of a projected royal palace. An enthusiastic admirer of Palladio, Jones had brought his theories to England with a translation of the *Four Books on Architecture* for which he wrote an introduction. The interior of the Banqueting House is 55 feet high, 55 feet wide, and 110 feet long, forming two equal cubes. These dimensions yield yet another use of musical proportions, with the double cubes forming the 1:1 and 2:1 relationship of unison and the octave.

The harmonious room (Fig. 14.17), with its ceiling murals painted by Rubens, was the frequent scene of musical activities. The Jacobean court masques were often performed here. These were "compleat entertainments" incorporating dance, song, instrumental and choral interludes, and spoken dialogue, all woven around a mythological plot. The elaborate and intricate "scenes and machines" were usually designed by Inigo Jones himself, and the writers included John Milton, Francis Bacon, and Ben Jonson.

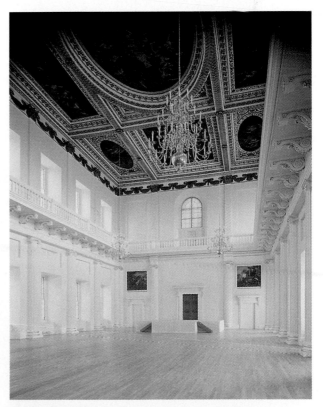

14.17   Inigo Jones. Interior, Banqueting House, Whitehall, London, England. Ceiling paintings by Peter Paul Rubens, 1629–1634.

St. Paul's Cathedral

In the crypt beneath St. Paul's Cathedral in London, a Latin inscription on a stone slab reads, "Beneath is laid the builder of this church and city, Christopher Wren, who lived more than 90 years, not for himself but for the good of the state. If you seek a monument, look around you." The most striking feature of St. Paul's (Fig. 14.18A) is its structural unity, for this is the only major cathedral in Europe to be built by one architect, by one master mason, and during the episcopate of one bishop. In contrast, it took thirteen architects, twenty popes, and more than a century to build St. Peter's in Rome (see Fig. 10.1). The last stone on the lantern tower above the dome of St. Paul's was put in place in 1710 by one of Wren's sons in the presence of the 78-year-old builder, and for another 8 years, Wren continued to supervise the completion of the last decorative details.

Even before the Great Fire, Wren was a member of a commission charged with the remodeling of Old St. Paul's. The plan had to be scrapped when a survey conducted after the fire showed that the building was beyond repair, giving Wren his great opportunity.

Like Bramante and Michelangelo before him, Wren projected a spacious centralized area from which radiated subsidiary units of space. Like his famous predecessors, he, too, preferred a central-type church based on the Greek cross. In this way a building of such monumental proportions could have both its exterior mass and interior space dominated by the all-embracing, unifying force of a dome. From a practical point of view, Wren was also aware that he was designing a Protestant cathedral that should permit as many people as possible to be able to hear the sermon-centered service of the Anglican Church.

The conservative members of the clergy wanted a long nave with aisles on either side to accommodate processions. Therefore, without sacrificing the heart of his plan, Wren lengthened the

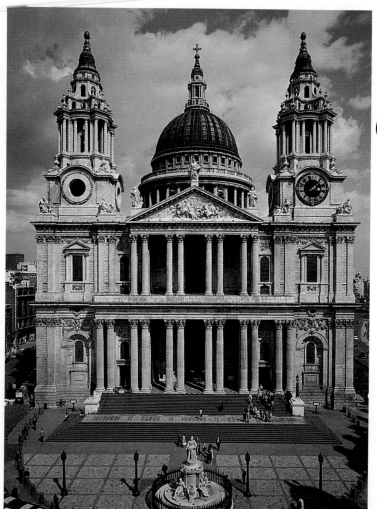

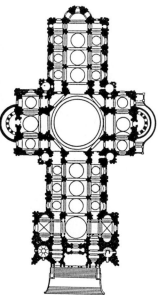

14.18 (A) Christopher Wren. Facade, new St. Paul's Cathedral, London, England, 1675–1710. Length 514′, width 250′, height of dome 366′. (B) Plan of St. Paul's Cathedral as executed.

edifice by adding an apse in the east and a domed **vestibule,** or lobby, with an extended porch in the west. His model, however, brought further objections from the clergy, necessitating still other revisions. All Wren's diplomacy, versatility, cleverness, and patience were called into play to create a workable compromise that would satisfy his difficult clients yet at the same time save the essential elements of his conception.

Wren gave the clergy their aisled nave and transepts and their deep choir, but he grouped them around the central plan of his original design (Fig. 14.18B). In so doing, he could still concentrate a great deal of space under the dome. In effect, Wren was building two churches, the clergy's and his own, a procedure that was bound to produce some architectural dissonances.

When no quarry could supply stone in the necessary lengths for the great columns of his original facade, Wren divided the facade into two stories: one with Corinthian columns and the other with Composite columns. His use of paired columns recalls Perrault's colonnade on the east front of the Louvre (Fig. 14.2). The side **turrets,** or ornamental towers, were designed after 1700. One of them was left hollow except for a circular staircase so that Wren and other astronomers could use the roof as an observatory.

The effect of Wren's plan is felt most strongly in the rotunda beneath the dome (Fig. 14.19). Geometrically, the space is bounded by a gigantic octagon, accented at the angles by the eight piers on which the cupola rests. These are bridged by a ring of connecting Roman triumphal arches, which in turn are crowned by the great dome, the culmination of the entire composition.

From this central area the arches open outward into eight spatial subdivisions that give the interior constant variety and interest. The centralization under the lofty dome, the complex divisions and subdivisions of space, and the imaginative design reveal Wren's fondness for the baroque. The restraining influences of the conservative clergy, the lack of funds, and Wren's rationalistic viewpoint demonstrate his remarkable feat in making the style acceptable to British taste.

WREN'S PLAN FOR A NEW LONDON

Wren's plan for the rebuilding of London after the Great Fire met with even stiffer resistance than his design for St. Paul's. It included laying out a series of new streets that extended outward in starlike fashion from central squares and took major traffic routes into consideration. Certain public buildings were to be situated on an axis that included the new cathedral and the Royal Exchange. The spires of the various parish churches would enhance the silhouette at certain points and reach a climax with the dome of St. Paul's.

The plan, if it had been carried out, would have gone far beyond the coordination of space that took place in the planning of Versailles. But unlike Louis XIV, Charles II was not an absolute monarch with the power to condemn property and the money to buy it. Time also worked against Wren: shopkeepers were in a hurry to rebuild and reopen their businesses. About all he could rescue were the church steeples he was called on to design.

As London's principal architect, Wren was commissioned to build more than fifty new parish churches. Discussions had to be held with the churchwardens about the problems and needs of each church. For monetary reasons the churches had to be modest affairs. Wren, in keeping with the spirit of the time, wanted to build them in the restrained baroque style based on the classical orders. His clients, however, still demanded the

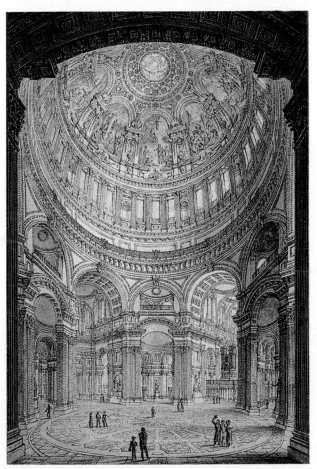

14.19 Christopher Wren. Rotunda, St. Paul's Cathedral, London, England. Engraving by John Coney.

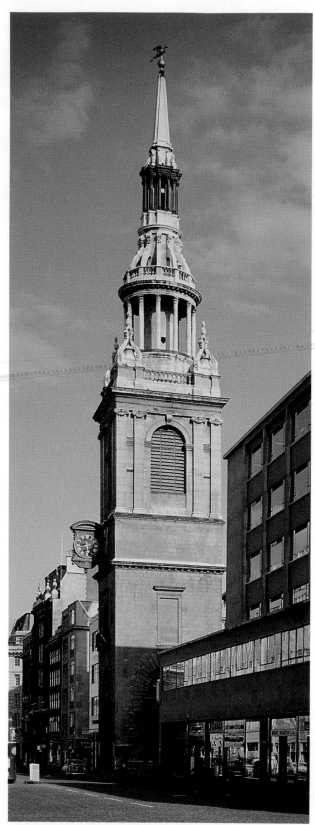

Gothic spires that not only served as symbols but also housed towers, whose bells announced services and were used by city dwellers to tell the time of day. Wren's problem, therefore, was to balance the vertical tendency of the steeple with the horizontality of his classical temple facades—again, to reconcile northern and southern building traditions. Wren's solution can be understood through another important example.

The steeple of St. Mary-le-Bow (Fig. 14.20), where the famous Bow bells once rang out, shows a mathematician's delight in the free play of geometric forms. From a solid square base it moves through several circular phases and terminates finally in an octagonal pyramid. The use of baroque scrolls and twists at various points prevent any hint of abruptness. Because the churches themselves would be hidden by the surrounding buildings, Wren lavished most of his skill on their spires,

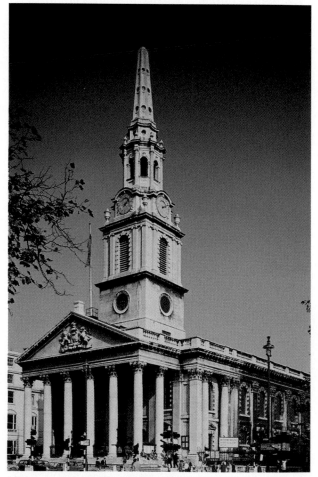

14.20 Christopher Wren. St. Mary-le-Bow, London, England, 1671–1680. Total height 216′1″, steeple 104′6″.

14.21 James Gibbs. St. Martin-in-the-Fields, London, England, 1721–1726.

James Gibbs continued Wren's ideas in the church of St. Martin-in-the-Fields (Fig. 14.21). Wren had always planted his steeples firmly in the ground, so to speak, so that they seemed to grow in an organic relationship to the whole composition. Gibbs's spire, by contrast, appears to sprout unexpectedly out of the roof. The memory of these churches and their steeples was carried to the American colonies. When Americans came to build their own churches in new cities, they turned to the designs of Wren and Gibbs for their models.

Despite his many responsibilities, Wren found the time to design some spacious and impressive houses for well-to-do middle-class clients. During the reign of William and Mary, he was also commissioned to complete the unfinished Royal Hospital at Greenwich, begun earlier by Inigo Jones, and to add a new wing to Hampton Court Palace. His patron, William of Orange, remembered the red brick of his native Holland, whereas Wren recalled the grandeur of the Louvre and Versailles palaces. Another of Wren's famous compromises is found in his design for the Fountain Court and the garden facade at Hampton Court Palace (Fig. 14.22).

Christopher Wren, professor of astronomy at London and Oxford, left off probing the mysteries of the heavens with his telescope and equations to become London's leading engineer and architect.

His works penetrate the sky above London with the majestic spires and domes that long gave the city its characteristic profile and skyline.

DRAMA AND MUSIC

DRYDEN

On the gala occasion of the formal opening of the King's Theatre in 1674, the king and London's most distinguished audience gathered for the evening's entertainment. John Dryden took advantage of the situation offered by the prologue to express his sentiments in some well-chosen words:

> 'Twere folly now a stately pile to raise,
> To build a playhouse while you throw down plays;
> Whilst scenes, machines and empty Operas reign,
> And for the Pencil you the Pen disdain;
> While Troops of famished Frenchmen hither drive,
> And laugh at those upon whose Alms they live;
> Our English Authors vanish, and give place
> To these new Conquerors of the Norman race.

Dryden was making a brave effort to stem the tide of foreign forms of opera, which, in his opinion, threatened to engulf reason with rhyme. He believed that the dramatic logic of plot development would be arrested and overwhelmed by the music

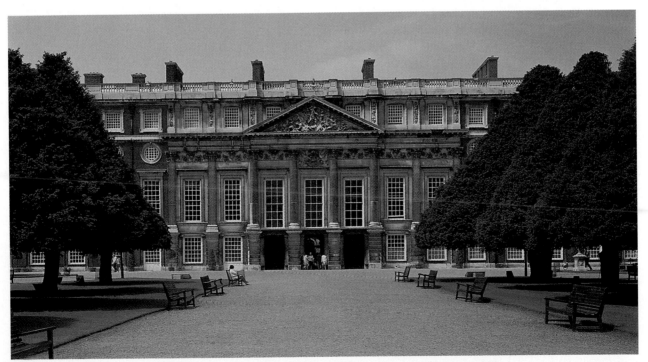

14.22   Christopher Wren. Garden facade, Hampton Court Palace, Surrey, England, c. 1690.

and that the high art of poetry would yield to jingling rhymes for the convenience of singers. Demand, however, was flowing far too strongly, and Dryden himself was soon collaborating with one of those fashionable Frenchmen and writing some fancy "scenes and machines."

Dryden tried to squeeze some content into those "empty Operas." In his preface to *Albion and Albanius,* for instance, he was more than a little apologetic about having to write so as "to please the hearing rather than gratify the understanding."

INTERNATIONALIZING ENGLISH OPERA

England's greatest composer, Henry Purcell, attempted to fuse Venetian and French techniques into English opera. In 1789, he wrote and staged his miniature operatic masterpiece, *Dido and Aeneas.* Designed for a small space, the school for young gentlewomen at Chelsea where he was music master, it is restricted to a few characters and employs a small orchestra limited to stringed instruments and continuo.

The opera opens with a dignified overture written in the style of Lully. Throughout the opera, recitatives and arias are based on models developed by Monteverdi and his successor at the Venetian opera, Cavalli. Purcell makes bold use of the "representative style," a type of word painting by which the descriptive imagery of the text is reflected in the shape of the melodic line. Words such as "Shake" (a), and "Storms" (b) are rendered in an appropriately shaky and stormy fashion. Aeneas's entrance is announced by a vocal line that takes the shape of a trumpet fanfare.

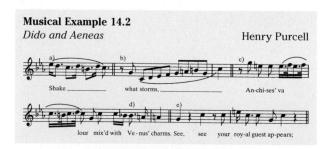

Musical Example 14.2
Dido and Aeneas   Henry Purcell

The arias show a considerable variety of type, ranging from Italian **ostinato aria**—built over a short repeated bass pattern—to the ever popular baroque **da capo aria.**

Purcell also added the aural effects of a Venetian echo chorus (see p. 343) to the mix. A set of

witches, dedicated to the downfall of Dido, meet in front of a cave to weave their nefarious spells. As they sing, "In Our Deep Vaulted Cell," an offstage chorus softly voices "-ed cell." The spell is completed in the "Echo Dance of Furies," in which an offstage instrumental group echoes the principal orchestra to enhance the feeling of mystery and deep space.

The tragedy is carried through to its predetermined conclusion with growing eloquence and mounting emotion. There is no *deus ex machina* to bring it to a happy ending in the manner of the French court style of Lully. As Dido prepares to die, her farewell becomes an extraordinarily moving moment, combining passionate feeling with the dignified restraint demanded of a tragic heroine out of Virgil's *Aeneid.* It is cast in the form of an ostinato aria with its descending, repetitive bass pattern, implying the physical lowering of a body into the earth.

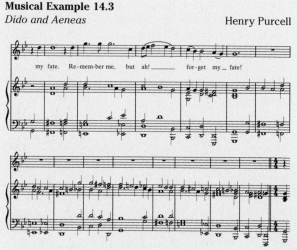

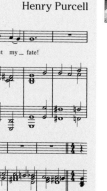

Musical Example 14.3
Dido and Aeneas   Henry Purcell

OPERA AND ORATORIO: HANDEL

Early in the eighteenth century, another great composer, George Frideric Handel (Fig. 14.23), brought the delights of Italian opera to English audiences. In his native Germany, Handel had been music director at the court of the Elector of Hanover, who succeeded Queen Anne on the British throne as George I. Coming just after the newly crowned king, Handel was assured of his position in London. Handel oversaw his own opera company, which was part of the Royal Academy of Music. He brought in famous singers to star in his Italianate opera series, written over a period of 30 years for London audiences.

Operas such as *Guilio Cesare in Egitto (Julius Caesar in Egypt)* relied on grand historical, mythological, and fictional protagonists, with arias in the *da capo* tradition. Despite their beauty, the Italian operas enjoyed only limited success in London. The bottom dropped out of the Italian opera market when Handel's listeners, reacting to the latest fad, discovered a new type of musical theater, known as *ballad opera,* in John Gay's *The Beggar's Opera* of 1728.

When that door was closed, Handel turned to large-scale oratorios with English texts. Like operas, oratorios had instrumental overtures and interludes, recitatives, solo arias, and choruses. However, they were usually presented in concert form without scenery, costumes, and dramatic action. Handel's oratorios were written to both sacred and secular texts and were primarily intended for public performances in theaters and large halls rather than in church. They were, in fact, promoted as "Grand Musical Entertainments." Such works as *Semele, Messiah,* and *Israel in Egypt* have won a place in the contemporary international repertory.

Many oratorios are based on religious subjects, and Handel's *Messiah* is the most popular and most frequently performed of the oratorios. It celebrates the major events of the Christian calendar: Advent, with the coming birth of Christ; the Lenten season, with the suffering, death, and resurrection of Jesus; and the triumph of Christianity over death. Despite its familiarity and fame, *Messiah* is not a typical Handel oratorio. It is the only one based on the New Testament, and it is composed of a series of meditations rather than actions. In Handel's time it was described as an entertainment, that is, a secular theater piece, not a religious experience. *Messiah* contains many elements commonly found in baroque musical practice: the French overture; dance, pastorale, and Sicilian rhythms; *da capo,* strophic, and rage arias; as well as madrigal, fugal, and anthem choruses. Handel made his most unforgettable impression with the power and breadth of the jubilant sound of his choruses. Audiences regularly reacted to the thundering streams of choral sound. In his energetic oratorios, both Handel and his London audiences found a ready identification with Old Testament and New Testament events and characters, which reflected the heroism of their own empire-building leaders.

The inward orientation and lyrical qualities of *Messiah* contrast strongly with the outward actions and sweep more common in Handel's other oratorios. In his mighty *Israel in Egypt,* Handel makes liberal use of the representative style. The

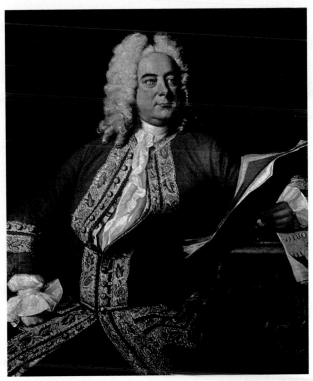

14.23   Thomas Hudson. *George Frideric Handel,* 1748–1749. Oil on canvas, 3′11⅛″ × 3′3″. Staats-und Universitäts-Bibliothek, Hamburg, Germany.

musical representations of the plagues sent upon the Egyptians to persuade them to free the Israelites contain many notable pictorial passages. The "Chorus of Flies" is abuzz with insects, the "Hailstone Chorus" describes a fire running on the ground in the bass lines, and "He smote all the first-born of Egypt" gives the orchestra potent hammer strokes to punctuate the destruction of the Egyptians' first-born sons.

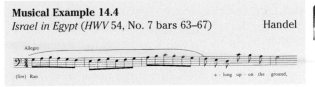

Musical Example 14.4
Israel in Egypt (HWV 54, No. 7 bars 63–67)   Handel

The scope of his choral writing in such a massively designed work as *Israel in Egypt* summarizes and completes the practice of the two prior centuries. Handel's synthesis of German polyphony with Italian operatic practice, French dance forms, and English choir music, combined with his use of the English language for an English audience, established an oratorio tradition that continues today.

IDEAS

The aristocratic baroque style embraces three distinct yet interrelated and interwoven ideas: absolutism, academicism, and rationalism.

ABSOLUTISM

The concept of the modern unified state, which first emerged in Spain under Philip II, was adapted to French political purposes by Cardinal Richelieu and ultimately reached its full realization under Louis XIV. "It is the respect which absolute power demands, that none should question when a king commands," was how Corneille stated the doctrine in 1637 in his heroic drama *The Cid*. As the principal personification of monarchical absolutism and the centralized state, Louis XIV, the Sun King, assumed the authority to replace natural and human disorderliness with a reasonable facsimile of cosmic law and order. All human and social activities came under his protection, including the arts, which he caused to serve the cult of majesty. Versailles became the symbol of absolutism, the seat of absolute monarchy, and the personal glorification of the king.

UNIFICATION OF THE ARTS. Just as political absolutism meant unifying all social and governmental institutions under one head, its aesthetic counterpart implied bringing together all the arts into a single rational plan. Although Louis's reign produced some buildings, statuary, paintings, literature, and music that command attention in their own right, they spoke most impressively in their combined forms.

It is impossible to think of Versailles except as a combination of all the arts into a unified pattern that grew out of the life and institutions of the absolute monarchy. The parks, gardens, fountains, statuary, buildings, courtyards, halls, murals, tapestries, furnishings, and recreational activities are all parts of a single coordinated design. Versailles accomplished the daring feat of unifying all visible space and all units of time into a spatial-temporal setting for the aristocratic way of life. Indoor and outdoor space are inseparable; even music and the theater went outdoors at Versailles.

The same tendency toward unification can be seen in opera. Indeed, all the arts were mirrored in the operatic form, with its literary lyricism, orchestral rhetoric, dramatic recitation, instrumental interludes, dancing, architectural stage settings, mechanical marvels, and picturesque posturings. In Lully's hands, opera became a microcosm of court life, a form in which all the separate parts related closely to the whole.

The spirit of absolutism was directly revealed in the drama surrounding the life of the monarch. All the arts took the cue, becoming theatrical and seeking to surprise and astonish. Often the simple human element was buried under an avalanche of palatial scenery, pompous wigs, props, and protocol. The architecture of Versailles, the statuary of Bernini and Coysevox, the murals of Lebrun (Fig. 14.5), the tragedies of Racine, and the operas of Lully were all designed to promote the illusion that Louis XIV and his courtiers were beings of heroic stature, powerful will, and grandiose utterance. Yet in Molière's satires, Jean de La Fontaine's moralizing fables, and the secret memoirs of the period, it is possible to catch glimpses of the reality behind the scenes of courtly life.

ACADEMICISM

Although the academic movement began formally with the first French Academy during the reign of Louis XIII, it was not until later in the century that the implications of academicism were fully mobilized. Both Louis XIV and his minister Colbert believed that art was much too important to be left exclusively in the hands of artists. The various academies, therefore, became branches of the government and the arts were incorporated into the civil service. An administrative organization was instituted, headed by the king and director and including professors, members, associates, and students. Approved principles were taught and theoretical and practical knowledge communicated through lectures, demonstrations, and discussions.

Boileau as head of the Academy of Language and Literature, Lebrun of the Academy of Painting and Sculpture, Hardouin-Mansart of the Academy of Architecture, and Lully of the Academy of Music were directly subject to the king and were absolute dictators in their respective fields. As such, they were the principal advisors to the king and his ministers and were responsible for carrying out the royal will. Control of patronage was centered in their hands. Theirs was the final word in determining who would receive commissions, appointments, titles, licenses, degrees, pensions, prizes, entrance to art schools, and the privilege of exhibiting in the salons.

The academies were the means of transmitting the idea of absolute monarchy from the political to the aesthetic sphere. Academicism invariably implied an authoritarian principle, whereby regularly constituted judges of taste placed their stamp of approval on the products of the various art media. These interpreters of the official point of view tended not to take chances and thus inevitably became highly conservative.

For example, under Lebrun, the Academy of Painting and Sculpture favored the restrained style of Poussin over the passionate emotionalism of Rubens. Poussin's pictorialism was quickly reduced to a system of formal values based on geometric principles. Rubens's approach, however, was so intense, sensuous, and violently emotional that it was attacked for its imbalanced preference for bright color and vivid emotion. Academics tried to tame baroque enthusiasm and reduce it to formulas and rules. Nothing eccentric or unpredictable was allowed to creep in and destroy the general impression of orderliness. The Academy always remained somewhat skeptical of feeling and color, because neither was subject to scientific laws.

The pictorial standards of the Academy were therefore based on formal purity, clear mathematical relationships, logical definition, and rational analysis. These qualities brought academic art the designation *classic,* a term that was defined at the time as "belonging to the highest class" and hence approved as a model. Because similar standards were generally to be found in Roman antiquity, classic and Roman art became accepted models.

From the start, French academicism was an unqualified practical success. Under the academies, the artistic dominance of Europe passed from Italy to France, where it effectively remained through much of the nineteenth century. The hundreds of skilled artists and artisans who were trained on the vast projects of Louis XIV became the founders and teachers of a tradition of high technical excellence. The influence of the academy does not mean that aesthetic disagreements were totally avoided. Toward the end of the seventeenth century, the famous quarrel between the ancients and the moderns set those who believed that classical art was the best model for contemporary work against those who believed that modern artists had improved on ancient art. In a microcosm, this dispute pointed toward the beginnings of a much larger argument that pitted proponents of absolute power against those members of the nobility and the middle class who wanted more of a say in politics and commerce.

In Spain, by contrast, the only successor to El Greco and Velázquez was the lonely figure of Goya (see pp. 489–491). In Flanders there were no outstanding followers of Rubens and van Dyck except Jean-Antoine Watteau, who made his entire career in France. In France, however, painting continued on a high level throughout the eighteenth and nineteenth centuries. By setting rigorous technical standards, academicism was a determining force even in nonacademic circles. The works of Perrault and Hardouin-Mansart in architecture, Boileau in criti-

cism, Molière in comedy, Racine in tragedy, and Lully in opera were absorbed directly into a tradition that successfully set up measuring rods of symmetry, order, regularity, dignity, reserve, and clarity.

In England, academies were founded under royal charter and supported by state subsidies. The oldest of these was the Royal Society for Improving Natural Knowledge, founded about 1660. Its interests were mainly scientific, and it numbered Isaac Newton, Christopher Wren, and Robert Boyle among its founding members. The Royal Academy of Arts came later, in 1768; it was established "for the purpose of cultivating and improving the arts of painting, sculpture, and architecture." It was followed in 1822 by the Royal Academy of Music, whose function was to support opera and concerts as well as to instruct young musicians. Various learned societies—scientific, archeological, literary, and so on—were founded and carried on by private collective efforts. These served as supplements to the state-supported institutions and remain devoted to gathering, collating, and disseminating scholarly research and knowledge.

BAROQUE RATIONALISM

Stimulated by the explorations of navigators, the scanning of the skies by astronomers, and the advances of inventors, scientists reassessed the world and the place of human beings in the universe. Galileo's telescopes confirmed Copernicus's theory of a solar system in which the Earth revolved around the sun rather than vice versa. The Aristotelian concept of an unmoving universe yielded to one that was full of whirling motion.

Because the Earth was no longer considered a fixed point located at the center of the cosmos, human beings could no longer be regarded as the sole purpose of creation. There was some consolation in knowing that this strange, new, moving universe was subject to mechanical and mathematical laws, and therefore to a considerable extent predictable. Copernicus, Johannes Kepler, and other scientists were convinced of its unity, proportion, and harmony. They also believed that the human mind could probe the innermost secrets of nature.

The rationalism of the seventeenth century was based on the position that at long last the universe could be understood in logical, mathematical, and mechanical terms. This worldview had far-reaching consequences. It tended to drive God out of the day-to-day workings of nature. It prepared intellectual culture for the coming theories of positivism and materialism, the doctrines of deism and atheism, and the mechanical and industrial revolutions.

Whereas Greek rationalism had been based on the perception and measurement of a stable, immobile world, baroque rationalism came to terms with a dynamic universe. Scientific thought was concerned with movement in space and time. The need for a mathematics system capable of understanding a world of matter in motion led René Descartes to his analytical geometry, Blaise Pascal to the study of cycloid curves, and both Gottfried Leibniz and Isaac Newton to the simultaneous but independent discovery of integral and differential calculus.

Baroque invention also led to refinements in navigation, improvements in the telescope and microscope, and the invention of the thermometer and the anemometer. Astronomers were occupied with the study of planetary motion, William Harvey discovered the circulation of the blood, and physicists experimented with the laws of thermodynamics and gravitation.

Newton's concern with mass, force, and momentum; his speculations on the principles of attraction and repulsion; and his calculations on earthly and heavenly mechanics led him to a monumental synthesis that he presented to the British Royal Society in 1686 and published in London a year later. His *Principia,* as it was called, embraced a complete and systematic view of an orderly world based on mechanical principles, subject to mathematical proof and accurate prediction. Newton's work was, in fact, a scientific *summa,* or complete summation, that established the intellectual architecture of the new view of the universe.

Such a changed worldview was bound to have important consequences for the arts, which responded with a ringing reassertion of human supremacy. The application of rationalistic principles to aesthetic expression was by no means accidental or casual. Before he became an architect, Wren was a mechanical inventor, an experimental scientist, and a professor of astronomy at London and Oxford. As a founder of the Royal Society, he was in close contact with such men as Boyle and Newton.

John Milton's *Paradise Lost* was also concerned with knowledge and reason, but in relation to the continuing presence of the Divine in the world. Milton's adaptation of the story of Adam and Eve ranges cosmically from Heaven to Hell, as if he were painting in words an illusionistic baroque ceiling like that of Pozzo (see Fig. 13.9). Through the multilayered symbols of darkness and light—also central to baroque painting—Milton explored sin and redemption as well as ignorance and knowledge. Along the way he created a Satan who stands out in his suffering, wounded pride, and facile sophism as one of the most memorable characters in Western literature. However much he

may have believed humans to be reasonable creatures, Milton also recognized the human capacity, even in Paradise, for suspicion, egotism, and vanity. When the fallen Adam and Eve walk hand in hand from Paradise, they are more moderate in their urges and humbly hopeful for redemption.

The fellows of the Royal Society appointed John Dryden to a committee whose purpose was to study the English language with a view toward linguistic reforms. They believed that English prose should have both purity and brevity so that verbal communication could come as close to mathematical plainness and precision as possible. In this context, Dryden's obvious embarrassment in writing an opera that was designed to please the ear rather than gratify the intellect is therefore understandable.

The music of Bach, Lully, Purcell, and Handel was based on a system of complex contrapuntal principles and tonal logic in which given premises, such as sequences or repeated ground basses, are followed by predictable conclusions. Moreover, it is characterized by intellectual discipline, symmetry, clarity, and a sure sense of direction. Their forms are models of brevity, in which each part has its place, no loose ends are left dangling, and the cadences bring everything to a positive finish.

Like the architecture of Perrault and Hardouin-Mansart in France and that of Wren in England, the musical art of Lully, Purcell, and Handel reflects an assured self-confidence. Theirs was an inventive spirit that gave birth to new forms, an exploration of novel visual and acoustic ideas, and a conviction, in keeping with the new worldview, that a work of art should be a reflection of an orderly and lawful universe.

YOUR RESOURCES

- ***Exploring Humanities CD-ROM***
  - Reading—Francis Bacon, *Novum Organum*

- ***Web Site***

  http://art.wadsworth.com/fleming10
  - Chapter 14 Quiz
  - Links—Online Readings—Milton, *Paradise Lost;* Bunyan, *Pilgrim's Progress,* Vol. 15, Part 1

- ***Audio CD***
  - Lully, *Alceste*
  - Purcell, *Dido and Aeneas*
  - Handel, *Israel in Egypt*

SEVENTEENTH-CENTURY FRANCE AND ENGLAND

Key Events	Architecture and Visual Arts	Literature and Music, France	Literature and Music, England
	1571–1626 **Salomon de Brosse** ★		1561–1626 **Francis Bacon** ◆
	1573–1652 **Inigo Jones** ★		1564–1593 **Christopher Marlowe** ◆
	1577–1640 **Peter Paul Rubens** ▲		1564–1616 **William Shakespeare** ◆
1589–1610 **Henry IV,** king of France	1594–1665 **Nicolas Poussin** ▲	1596–1650 **René Descartes** ◆, philosopher	1572–1631 **John Donne** ◆
	1598–1680 **Gian Lorenzo Bernini** ★●		1572–1637 **Ben Jonson** ◆
			1588–1679 **Thomas Hobbes** ◆

1600

Key Events	Architecture and Visual Arts	Literature and Music, France	Literature and Music, England
1603–1625 **James I** (Stuart), king of England	c. 1604–1682 **Claude Lorrain (Claude Gellée)** ▲	1602–1676 **Francesco Cavalli** ❑, Venetian opera composer	1604 *Advancement of Learning* by Francis Bacon
1610–1643 **Louis XIII,** king of France, with his mother Marie de Medici (1573–1642) as regent during his minority	1612–1670 **Louis Le Vau** ★	1606–1684 **Pierre Corneille** ◆, dramatist	1608–1674 **John Milton**
	1613–1688 **Claude Perrault** ★	1621–1695 **Jean de La Fontaine** ◆, wrote fables	1611 **King James Bible**
1618–1648 **Thirty Years' War;** Spain and Austria defeated; France became dominant European nation	1613–1700 **André Le Nôtre** ★	1622–1673 **Molière (Jean-Baptiste Poquelin)** ◆, wrote comedies	1620 *Novum Organum* by Francis Bacon
	1615–1624 **Luxembourg Palace** built for Queen Mother by Salomon de Brosse	1623–1662 **Blaise Pascal** ◆, philosopher	1628–1688 **John Bunyan** ◆
1624–1642 **Cardinal Richelieu** (1585–1642), prime minister	1619–1621 **Banqueting House Whitehall** built by Inigo Jones	1632–1687 **Jean-Baptiste Lully** ❑, wrote operas	1628 *Treatise on Terrestrial Magnetism and Electricity* by William Gilbert ⚬; William Harvey discovered circulation of blood
1625–1649 **Charles I** reigned; after 1629 ruled England without Parliament	1619–1690 **Charles Lebrun** ▲	1635–1688 **Phillipe Quinault** ◆, librettist	1631–1700 **John Dryden** ◆
	1620–1694 **Pierre Puget** ●		1632–1704 **John Locke** ◆
1642–1660 **English Civil War**	1621 **Rubens** commissioned to paint murals in Luxembourg Palace	1635 **French Academy of Language and Literature** established	1633–1703 **Samuel Pepys** ◆
1643 **Theaters closed** by Parliament	1628–1715 **François Girardon** ●	1636–1711 **Nicolas Boileau** ◆, poet, academician	1651 *Leviathan* by Hobbes
1643–1661 **Cardinal Mazarin** (1602–1661), prime minister	1632–1723 **Christopher Wren** ★	1639–1699 **Jean Racine** ◆, dramatist, wrote tragedies	1652–1715 **Nahum Tate** ◆
1643–1715 **Louis XIV,** king of France; ruled without prime minister from 1661	1640–1720 **Antoine Coysevox** ●	1666 **Academy of Sciences** established in France	c. 1659–1695 **Henry Purcell** ❑
	1640 **Poussin** returned from Rome to decorate the Louvre Palace		1661 *The Sceptical Chymist* by Boyle ⚬ (1627–1691)
1649 **Charles I** executed; England proclaimed Commonwealth	1646–1708 **Jules Hardouin-Mansart** ★	1668–1733 **François Couperin le Grand** ❑, harpsichordist, organist, composer	1662 **Royal Society of London** founded; Newton, Wren, Boyle, Dryden charter members
	1648 **Royal Academy of Painting and Sculpture** founded in London	1669 **Royal Academy of Music** (Paris Opera) established	1667 *Paradise Lost* by Milton
1653–1658 **Oliver Cromwell** (1599–1658) ruled	1659–1743 **Hyacinthe Rigaud** ▲		1678 *Pilgrim's Progress,* Part I, by Bunyan; 1684 Part II
1660 **Restoration of English monarchy**	1661–1688 **Versailles Palace** built by Le Vau and Hardouin-Mansart; 1682–1754 **James Gibbs** ★	1674 *Alceste,* lyrical tragedy by Quinault and Lully, performed at Versailles; Boileau's *Art of Poetry* published	1679 **Purcell** appointed organist at Westminster Abbey; named composer-in-ordinary to king
1660–1685 **Charles II** reigned	1699–1708 **Chapel added**		1685–1759 **George Frideric Handel** ❑
1664–1665 **Black Death** (bubonic plague) swept London	1662 **Christopher Wren** appointed deputy surveyor-general to king; 1665 in Paris to observe remodeling of Louvre; met Bernini, Perrault, Hardouin-Mansart	1682 *Venus and Adonis,* chamber opera by John Blow, performed at court	1685 *Albion and Albanius,* opera by Dryden and Purcell, performed in London
1665–1683 **Colbert** (1619–1683), French minister of finance	1665 **Bernini** came to Paris to rebuild the Louvre Palace; French Academy in Rome established	1683–1764 **Jean-Phillipe Rameau** ❑, wrote keyboard music, operas, theory of harmony	1687 *Mathematical Principles of Natural Philosophy* by Newton ⚬ (1642–1727)
1666 **Great Fire of London**	1667 **Wren** appointed royal surveyor-general		c. 1689 *Dido and Aeneas,* opera by Purcell
1682 **Government and ministries of France** installed at Versailles	1667–1674 **East facade of the Louvre Palace** built by Perrault		1690 *Essay Concerning Human Understanding* by John Locke
1685–1688 **James II** reigned	1671 **Academy of Architecture** established		1691 *King Arthur . . . A Dramatick Opera* by Dryden and Purcell
1688 **Glorious Revolution;** James II deposed; William of Orange and Mary (Stuart) became limited monarchs	1671–1680 **St. Mary-le-Bow** and other London parish churches built by Wren		
	1675–1710 **St. Paul's Cathedral** built		
1689–1702 **William and Mary** reigned	1690 **Wing of Hampton Court Palace** built by Wren		

1700

Key Events	Architecture and Visual Arts	Literature and Music, France	Literature and Music, England
1702–1714 **Queen Anne** reigned	1722 **St. Martin-in-the-Fields** built by Gibbs	1704 *Opticks* by Newton ⚬	

★ - Architect ❑ - Musician ▲ - Painter ⚬ - Scientist ● - Sculptor ◆ - Writer

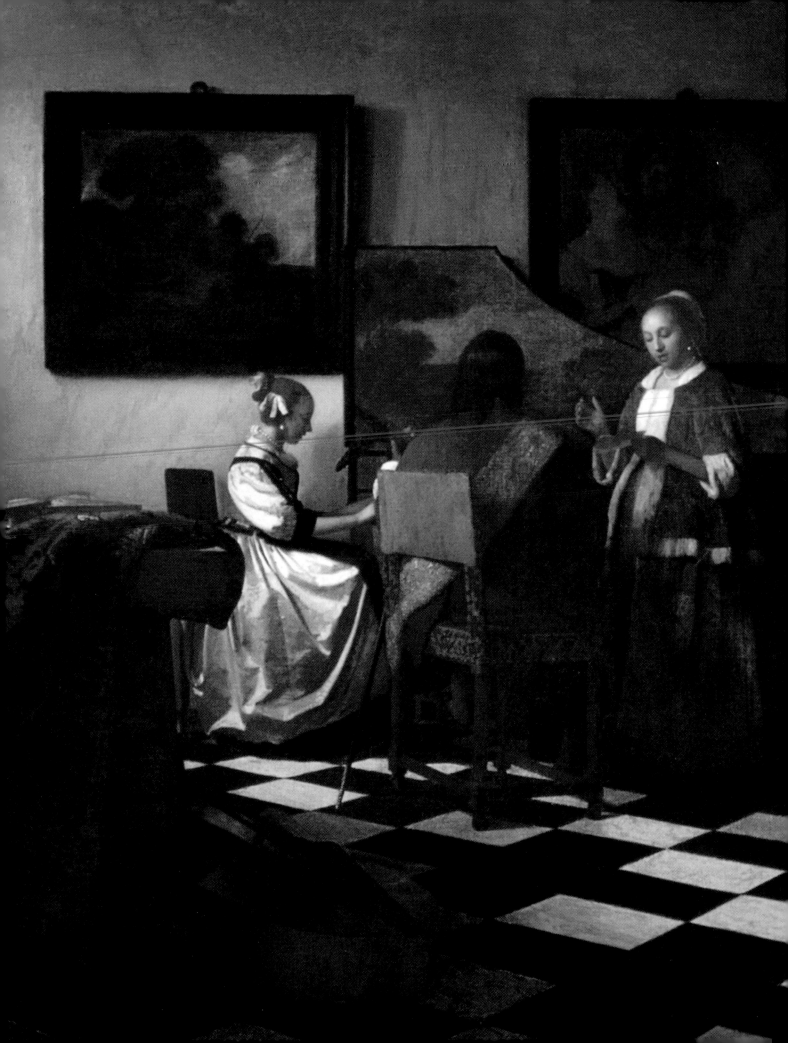

B O U R G E O I S   B A R O Q U E   S T Y L E

IF VISITORS TO SEVENTEENTH-CENTURY Amsterdam—or any other prosperous Dutch town, for that matter—looked about for triumphal arches or vast military monuments, they would be disappointed. Especially during the first half of the century, the Dutch, like Americans of the early twenty-first century, identified with a bourgeois, or middle-class, outlook. That does not mean that most seventeenth-century Dutch or early twenty-first-century Americans were members of the middle class. Dutch families ranged from extremely poor to very wealthy, and the difference between the lowest and highest classes grew even greater as the Dutch prospered after 1648, when they essentially achieved independence from Spain. At the same time, though, occupations such as banking and seafaring commerce allowed a substantial economic middle class to emerge.

The Dutch wars of independence, geographic isolation, the constant struggle against the advances of the sea, the harsh climate, the seafaring economy, Calvinist Protestantism, and individualism combined with the other circumstances of Dutch life to produce a focus on hard work and home, which emerged as basic middle-class ideals. Predictably, some families accumulated more than others, and by means of the wealth concentrated in their hands they became a ruling class. These so-called **regent families** were the ones from whose ranks the members of the town councils and mayors were selected. They were, however, an upper-middle-class group rather than a hereditary, landed aristocracy. Their power, together with that of the professional and merchant guilds, depended on exercising a maximum of local authority.

In fact, after they achieved independence in 1648, the Dutch organized a government with a minimum of centralization and a maximum of diversity. The land became the Dutch Republic, although it was not a democracy. The titular leader was a *stadtholder,* or governor. This office was held for a time by various princes of Orange, perhaps because their forebears had led the Dutch to victory over the Spanish. The stadtholder's power was often challenged and successfully limited by the regents, who doubtless wanted government to make decisions that favored commerce.

AMSTERDAM IN THE SEVENTEENTH CENTURY

The residents of Amsterdam shared a fondness for the events and rhythms of daily life and a desire to see it depicted. When Jacob van Ruisdael painted *Quay at Amsterdam* (Fig. 15.1), he showed more than just a view of the old fish market at the end of the broad canal known as the Damrak. In this local variant of the international academic style, he pictured an important element of the bourgeois way of life. The scene depicts thrifty women gathering provisions for their dinner tables. A part of the moored fishing fleet is seen at the left. Anchored in the distance are the merchant vessels used by the Dutch to create efficient modern commerce. Merchants like these traded clay pipes, glazed tiles, and Delft pottery for sugar, spices, fabrics, and other wares. The introduction of these goods spurred further international commerce, and with it the shameful enlargement of the slave-trade circuit, from Africa to the New World and Europe.

This decentralization favored the growth of universities—those at Leyden and Utrecht became the most distinguished in Europe—and promoted the careers of such noted native humanists as Constantijn Huygens, friend and patron of Rembrandt, and Hugo Grotius, founder of the new discipline of international law. The freedom to think and work attracted foreigners, such as the French philosopher René Descartes, who resided in Holland for almost 20 years, and the parents of Baruch Spinoza—one of the most profound intellects of all time—who found refuge in Amsterdam after the persecution of the Jews had made life intolerable for them in their native Portugal.

15.1   Jacob van Ruisdael. *Quay at Amsterdam,* c. 1670. Oil on canvas, 1'8¾" × 2'2". Frick Collection, New York.

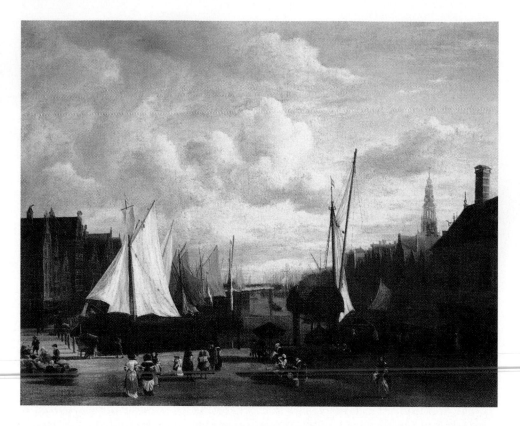

The architectural expression of this bourgeois way of life is found in commercial structures such as warehouses, banks, counting houses, and the market building seen on the extreme right in Figure 15.1. Above all, it is manifest in the long rows of gabled brick houses, like those seen on either side of the canal in the same picture. Dating from earlier times were ecclesiastical buildings such as the Oudekerk, or "Old Church," whose Gothic tower is silhouetted against the sky in the right background. Originally Roman Catholic, the building was taken over by the Dutch Reformed Church after the Reformation. As organized under the precepts of John Calvin, the Reformed Church held that religious truth was not the exclusive possession of any individual or group and that the word of God was available to each person without the mediation of priestly authority. Following the development of the printing press, every family could have its own Bible, and the prevailing high degree of literacy, even among the poor, meant that almost everyone could read it.

The Dutch took literally the idea of the home as a religious center. Much important religious activity took place in the home, through family devotions, hymn singing, and Bible reading. According to the teachings of Calvin, the reason for going to church was to hear a sermon and sing the praises of the Lord. No architectural embellishments, statuary, paintings, and professional choirs or orchestras should distract the worshipers' attention.

Because art and music commissions no longer came from the Catholic Church, artists had to seek outlets for their work in other circles. The prosperous Dutch families desired an art that would reflect their robust materialism and reveal their outlook, their institutions, and their country just as they were—solid, matter-of-fact, and without airs. Patronage was spread on a sufficiently broad basis that many homes had at least a small collection of pictures.

MUSIC AND THE OTHER ARTS

Under Calvinistic austerity, only three groups of professional musicians survived: the church organists; the hired singers and instrumentalists who performed for weddings, banquets, and parades; and the music teachers who taught the younger members of the family to sing and to play the lute (see Fig. 15.12), viols, and keyboard instruments such as the virginal and spinet (see Fig. 15.18). Music, like other aspects of Dutch life, was centered largely in the home. During the Renaissance, Holland and Flanders dominated European music with the polyphonic masterpieces of their distinguished composers. Only one musical genius of universal stature was left in Amsterdam in the early seventeenth century: Jan Pieterszoon Sweelinck, whose career brought to a brilliant close the radiant chapter of Dutch music that had dominated the Renaissance.

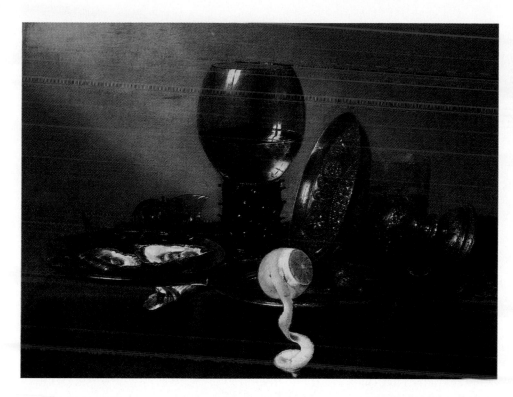

15.2 William Claesz Heda. *Still Life with Oysters, Rum Glass and Silver Cup,* 1634. Panel approx. 1′5″ × 1′10⅜″. Museum Boymans-van Beuningen, Rotterdam, the Netherlands.

All the arts were centered in the home. The simple and unpretentious Dutch dwelling with its polished tiled floors, tidy interiors, and window boxes was the modest setting for this bourgeois way of life. Unless ceramics are included, there was little sculpture other than a few figurines on the mantelpiece and an occasional statuette.

Daily life followed the routines of the business establishment, the marketplace, and the household. It was a reality in which nothing was too small to be noticed and appreciated. All things, even the most trivial, were considered gifts of God. As such, they were studied in the smallest detail.

PAINTING

TYPES OF PAINTING

The Dutch produced work in all categories of painting, but always with a characteristic national and personal touch. In **history scenes,** Greco-Roman mythological allegories were mostly avoided because they recalled the aristocratic court life under which the Dutch had been suppressed for so long. Also shunned were the traditional Roman Catholic subjects, such as the life of the Virgin Mary and representations of Christ's suffering, death, and resurrection. Instead, the Protestant accent was on the stories and parables of the New Testament and Jesus's teaching and preaching (see Fig. 15.7).

Landscape had a strong attraction because the Dutch had fought the sea and the Spanish for their land. Paintings of fields, mills, and cottages appealed to their sense of ownership. Typically horizontal in orientation, views of the level Dutch landscape were frequently enlivened by windswept skies. They also included human figures tilling the soil, an image that emphasized that precious acres had been wrested from the ocean and bogs and were now under cultivation to contribute to the good life of their hard-won country.

Genre scenes—that is, scenes from everyday life—were particularly popular because their casualness, informality, and human interest harmonized with the Dutch focus on domestic surroundings. Such pictures portrayed people going about their daily activities within defined spaces. Their subjects ranged from the tranquil atmosphere of well-ordered home life, peasants at their farming chores, and young musicians playing or singing at the family hearthside, all the way to roguish and ribald tavern scenes. Such studies were often rendered with meticulous visual description of minute details.

Still-life compositions also found favor, because quiet arrangements of fruit, flowers, oysters, herrings, ceramics, drinking glasses, and textiles were visible evidence of the good life. In these studies, objects were rendered with almost scientific precision, as seen in a still life by William Claesz Heda (Fig. 15.2). Often a somber note was sounded in these representations of the joys of possession,

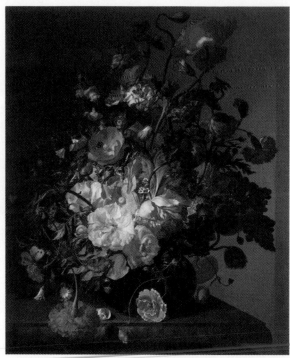

15.3 Rachel Ruysch, *Flower Still Life,* after 1700. Oil on canvas, 2′6″ × 2′. The Toledo Museum of Art, Toledo (purchased with funds from the Libbey Endowment, gift of Edward Drummond Libbey).

because worldly goods were also symbols of life's vanities. These *memento mori,* or reminders of death, took the form of symbolic objects, in the manner of Flemish masters like Jan van Eyck (see pp. 305–307). In Dutch still life, an empty place setting indicated absence, a trumpet alluded to Judgment Day, a lute with a broken string signified the transitory nature of time, and playing cards with the ace of spades visible told of death.

Flower painting was situated in the fertile terrain between science and art. It manifested Dutch concern with the observable world as a source of both knowledge and aesthetic pleasure. As happened increasingly throughout Europe, women were involved in the gathering and rendering of botanical specimens. The scientific research and depictions of plant and insect life painted by Anna Maria Sibylla Merian were published in richly illustrated folios. Amsterdam's Rachel Ruysch enjoyed a long career as a flower painter (Fig. 15.3). Her pictures exemplify how the Dutch skill in bringing out the buttery richness of oil paint developed hand in hand with careful observation of the visible world.

Portraiture was the most popular type of painting. The Dutch burghers and burgesses wanted

15.4 Judith Leyster. *Self-Portrait,* c. 1635. Oil on canvas, 2′5⅜″ × 2′1⅝″. National Gallery of Art, Washington, D.C. Gift of Mr. and Mrs. Robert Woods Bliss.

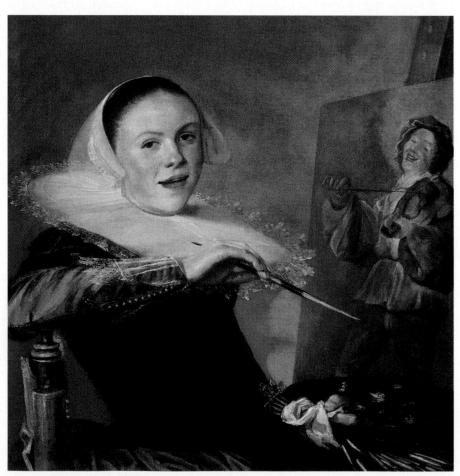

family portraits for their living rooms. These might be commemorative pictures of events such as christenings and weddings, paintings of quiet interiors with the wife and daughter performing some household chore, or images of a talented family member playing a musical instrument (see Fig. 15.18). A piquant example is found in Judith Leyster's *Self-Portrait* (Fig. 15.4). Leyster enjoyed a high reputation in her native Haarlem, where she was the only woman member of the Painters' Guild. She may have submitted her *Self-Portrait* to gain admission. Leyster competed with Frans Hals (who will be discussed later) for commissions. In her *Self-Portrait,* the loose brushwork depicting her paint rag and brushes, as well as the edges of her large collar and the lace of her sleeve, shows her confidence as a painter. In her clever composition, she poses, brush in hand, as a kind of mirror image of the violinist's pose in the painting at her easel. Leyster also painted flowers, including prize tulips, which were the rage in Holland during the 1630s. (Tulipomania—the faddish investment in tulip bulbs—was an important, if fleeting, economic phenomenon.)

Dutch men liked to be portrayed along with their co-workers in what are called **corporation pictures.** In these group portraits, the men were seen in the company of their fellow directors or board members in panels designed to be hung on the walls of some guild hall, professional society, officers' club, or charitable trust.

PAINTER OF AN INNER LIGHT: REMBRANDT

Like his contemporaries, Rembrandt painted portraits, genre scenes, historical subjects, and landscapes; but unlike them, he refused to specialize and succeeded magnificently—and voluminously—in each medium. He brought a new psychological depth to his portraiture, a liveliness to his genre scenes, a dramatic intensity to his religious pictures, and a broad sweep to his landscapes. Above all, Rembrandt used light, in all its varying degrees, to illuminate character both from without and from within, to define space by varying degrees of brightness, and to give life to that space through the flowing movement of shadows.

Rembrandt's art as a whole shows a steady growth in his capacity to penetrate appearances, to discover and reveal the spiritual forces that lie beneath. Soon after he settled in Amsterdam, the 26-year-old painter received his first important assignment from the local Guild of Surgeons and Physicians. The result was *Dr. Tulp's Anatomy Lesson* (Fig. 15.5), a composition that combines group portraiture of the so-called corporation type with

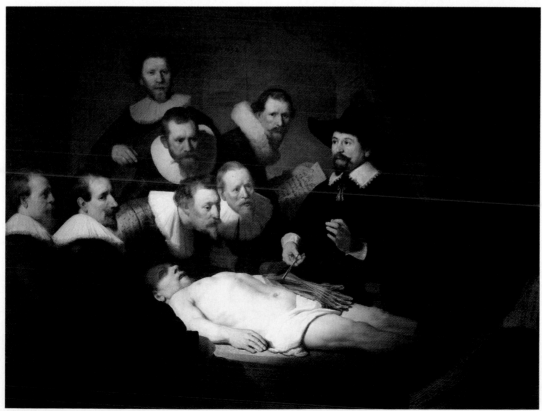

15.5 Rembrandt. *Dr. Tulp's Anatomy Lesson,* 1632. Oil on canvas, 5'3⅜" × 7'1¼". Mauritshuis, The Hague, the Netherlands.

scientific pictures. The subjects in this case were the heads of the guild and other prominent citizens, whose names are recorded on the sheet of paper held by the figure in the center.

Rembrandt grouped the figures on different levels to achieve a sense of candor and informality. Through the use of light, he narrated the essential drama of the situation and he composed the facial expressions to show a variety of reactions, from intense concentration to casual indifference. The fullest light is focused on the corpse and on the hands of Dr. Nicholas Tulp, the professor of anatomy who is giving the lecture. The large open book at the feet of the corpse is possibly an edition of Vesalius's *Anatomy.* This universally recognized authority was the work of the Dutch scientist Andries van Wesel (1514–1564), who had taught and held just such demonstrations at the University of Padua. Because Dr. Tulp styled himself *Vesalius redivivus* ("Vesalius revived"), the reference is appropriate. In effect, Rembrandt's dramatization of the spirit of scientific inquiry is a vivid product of a period that has been aptly called the Age of Observation.

Exactly one decade elapsed between the *Anatomy Lesson* and the *Sortie of Captain Banning Cocq's Company of the Civic Guard* (Fig. 15.6), Rembrandt's masterpiece of the corporation type. Group portraits of military units that had fought against the Spaniards were common. Once their original purpose in the struggle for independence was gone, many of these companies continued as parts of the civic guard and as officers' clubs, available for anything from emergency duty to a holiday parade. By 1642, most members had become prosperous shopkeepers who hugely enjoyed dressing up occasionally in their dashing uniforms, polishing their shooting irons, and posing as warriors in holiday processions or civic celebrations.

These military units were usually shown in convivial situations, for example, gathered around a banquet table. However, to get life and movement into his picture, Rembrandt discarded this formula and chose to show Captain Cocq's company in action, as if responding to a call to genuine duty. Because life-size figures are seen moving outside the city gate and because the painting was

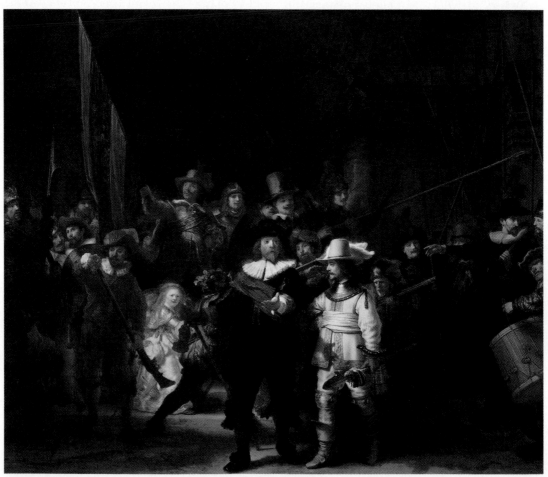

15.6 Rembrandt. *Sortie of Captain Banning Cocq's Company of the Civic Guard,* 1642. Oil on canvas, 12′2″ × 14′7″. Rijksmuseum, Amsterdam, the Netherlands.

once soiled with dirt and darkened varnish, it has been popularly called "The Night Watch."

The light flows freely throughout the composition, filling every corner with dynamic gradations from dark to bright. It becomes most intense in the center, where Captain Cocq is explaining the plans to his lieutenant, whose uniform catches the rays of the morning sun. As a counterbalance, Rembrandt places the unexplained figure of a young girl in gleaming cream-colored satin at the captain's other side. Strung from her belt are a powder horn and a white cockerel, possibly a pun on the captain's name. The shadow of Captain Cocq's hand falling across the lieutenant's uniform defines the source of light, which, in turn, relates all the other figures to the central pair by means of the intensity with which it illuminates them. Such skill in the handling of light and shadow was one of Rembrandt's unique achievements, and it was also evident in the great number of his prints that have survived.

Rembrandt lived during the first great period of printmaking. The **etching** *Christ Healing the Sick* (Fig. 15.7), familiarly known as the "Hundred Guilder Print," is an example of Rembrandt's many works in what was then a popular medium in the visual arts. The price of this etching, which became its popular name, was a record high. The relatively modest price of most of his etchings assured Rembrandt some income—and reasonably wide distribution of his work—at times when his paintings piled up unsold in his studio. Like other Dutch artists, Rembrandt often created his paintings before buyers saw them. This practice, more in keeping with Dutch capitalism, marked the decline of commissions and the beginning of artists' recreation of themselves as businesspeople.

Technically, the etching medium provided Rembrandt an opportunity to explore the qualities of light in simple line patterns independent of color. By scratching a coated metal plate with a sharp, penlike stylus, an artist makes a linear pattern that is etched, or bitten, into the metal when the plate is plunged into an acid solution. The coating is then removed and the plate inked. An etching is made by transferring the inked impression on the metal plate to paper. In *Christ Healing the Sick,* the gradations of light and dark run from the inky blackness behind the figure of Christ to the whiteness of the untouched paper, like that of the large rock in the extreme left.

Rembrandt was raised in a family that tried to live according to strict biblical teachings. His religious subjects are conceived of from a Protestant point of view and reveal an intimate knowledge of the Scriptures. Because he was not painting for churches and was under no compulsion to conform to the Roman Catholic iconographic traditions of

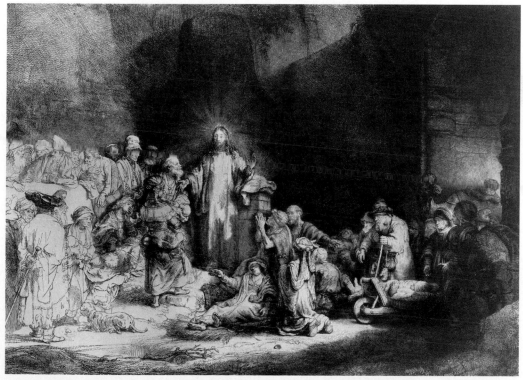

15.7   Rembrandt. *Christ Healing the Sick* (Hundred Guilder Print), c. 1649. Etching, 10⅞" × 1'3⅜". Metropolitan Museum of Art, New York. Bequest of Mrs. H. O. Havemeyer, 1929. The H. O. Havemeyer Collection.

the Madonna and Child or the Crucifixion, Rembrandt was free to develop new themes and new points of view. Much of the intimacy and effectiveness of such works is due to the fact that they were not conceived of as public showpieces. Rembrandt was primarily interested in Old Testament subjects. He also loved to explore the Amsterdam ghetto, and it was there that he found subjects for his art among the Jewish descendants of the people who created the Old Testament. Indeed, recent speculation suggests that the Dutch may have seen themselves and their history to be like that of the Jews in the Bible, making Jewish themes popular.

SELF-PORTRAITS. Rembrandt is known to have painted at least sixty-two self-portraits. His motivation, however, may have come more from a strong tendency to look inward than from personal vanity.

Extending from young manhood to his last year, his likenesses of himself read like a pictorial autobiography. After successfully establishing himself in Amsterdam and after his marriage to Saskia van Uylenburgh, daughter of a wealthy family, Rembrandt enjoyed a period of material prosperity. He depicted himself in cavalier clothes, with his young wife sitting on his knee as he lifts his glass in a toast (Fig. 15.8). Rembrandt and his friend, the painter Jan Lievens, devised this style of painting, in which acquaintances, relatives, or painters were shown in unusual and colorful costume.

From 1640 on, Rembrandt suffered a series of tragedies, beginning with his mother's death, which was followed 2 years later by that of his wife, shortly after the birth of their son Titus. He also suffered public embarrassment when an alienated lover initiated court proceedings in an attempt to

15.8   Rembrandt. *Self-Portrait with Saskia,* c. 1634. Oil on canvas, 5′3½″ × 4′3½″. Gemäldegalerie Alte Meister, Dresden, Germany.

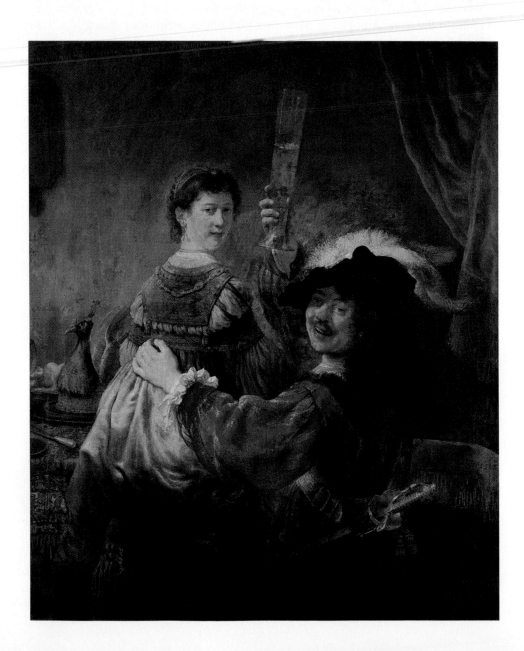

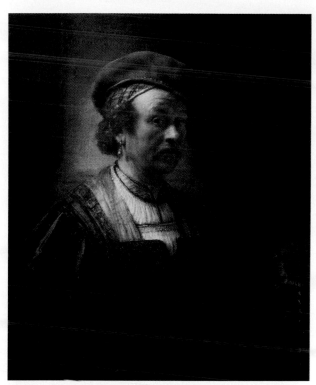

15.9 Rembrandt. *Self-Portrait,* 1650. Oil on canvas, 3′¼″ × 2′5¾″. National Gallery of Art, Washington, D.C. Widener Collection, 1942.

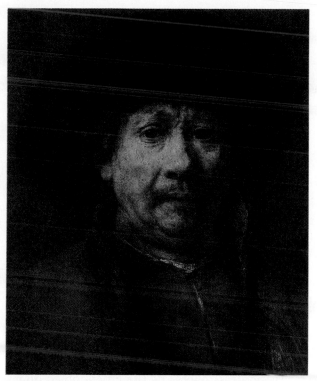

15.10 Rembrandt. *Self-Portrait,* 1656–1658. Oil on wood, 1′8″ × 1′4″. Kunsthistorisches Museum, Vienna, Austria.

gain financial support. Moreover, by 1650, artistic tastes had changed, but Rembrandt did not bow to fashion. The penetrating look in the self-portrait reproduced in Figure 15.9, glowing with an internal light, seems to peer into the depths of his own character. From this time on, Rembrandt realized more and more that his mission was to explore the world of the imagination and leave the world of appearances to others. His face shows the serenity of a man who, having chosen his course, knows that there is no longer any turning back.

Rembrandt's financial troubles increased as his debts piled up, and from 1656 to 1660 the artist experienced bankruptcy. His fine house, with its furnishings and his collection of paintings, prints, armor, and artistic props, was sold to satisfy creditors. Although his circumstances were reduced, he still maintained an appreciative clientele. At this point, the searching gaze of the glowing eyes in his *Self-Portrait* (Fig. 15.10) turns inward in what may be self-appraisal. His last years were saddened by the deaths of his faithful friend and housekeeper Hendrickje Stoffels (1662) and his son Titus (1668). Still working continuously, Rembrandt in his last self-portrait shows the familiar face marked by illness and resignation but still full of the deep compassion that characterized his life and art (Fig. 15.11). The intensity of Rembrandt's self-portraits has made them seem inexhaustible. Yet

despite almost four centuries of research, interpretations remain mostly subjective. Meager documentation supports no definitive readings of these intriguing works.

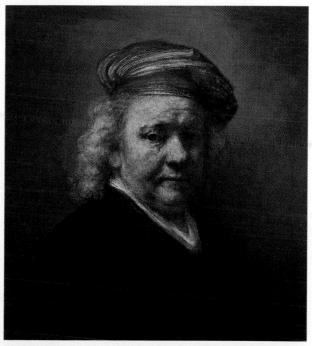

15.11 Rembrandt. *Old Self-Portrait,* 1669. Oil on canvas, 1′11¼″ × 1′8¾″. Mauritshuis, The Hague, the Netherlands.

PAINTERS OF EVERYDAY EXPERIENCE: HALS, DE HOOCH, AND RUISDAEL

Whereas Rembrandt sought to portray the spirit of the whole person, Frans Hals excelled at capturing human individuality in a fleeting glance. A close look at his early work reveals that he was able to indicate light and texture, often with a flick of the brush. In this sense, he foreshadows the work of the French Impressionists (see pp. 529–535). The infectious gaiety of his *Lute Player with Wine Glass* (Fig. 15.12) is typical of Hals's carefree early period. With mussed hair and cap cocked at a jaunty angle, the subject might well be an entertainer at a public tavern. The glass of sparkling wine cleverly reveals the source of light, which strikes both face and instrument. In similar pictures, Hals studied physical attributes and behavior in his native city of Haarlem, creating lively portrayals of quarreling fish sellers, reveling officers, and tipsy merrymakers. Later, when he came under the influence of Rembrandt's soul-searching, he gave up his vivid colors and light touch for somber hues and serious subjects.

By contrast, Pieter de Hooch ennobled down-to-earth incidents from everyday life. His *Mother and Child* (Fig. 15.13) is a quiet domestic study. The woman is carefully picking lice from the head of the child. Today, this subject would indicate neglect and ill health, but in the period it was a necessary and routine part of grooming, and it is consistent with household tidiness.

Like so many Dutch painters in the period, de Hooch knew that light was the magnet that attracted the eye and that its vibrations intimated life and movement. But he chose to work with a soft light that matched the tranquility of his subject matter. Sunlight streams inward from the open Dutch door at the back and the window at the upper right. By this means, the artist separated his space into three receding planes, while accentuating the contrasting textures of the tile flooring, the transparency of glass, the sheen of varnished wood surfaces, the soft surface of textiles, and the metallic brilliance of the copper bed warmer. De Hooch's figures are less animated than Hals's, yet each of his interiors has the timeless essence of a still life, with figures and objects blending together to create a compositional whole.

Jacob van Ruisdael's *View of Haarlem from the Dunes at Overveen* (Fig. 15.14) belongs to the

15.12 Frans Hals. *Lute Player with Wine Glass,* 1626. Oil on canvas, 3′ × 2′5″. Mansion House, London, England.

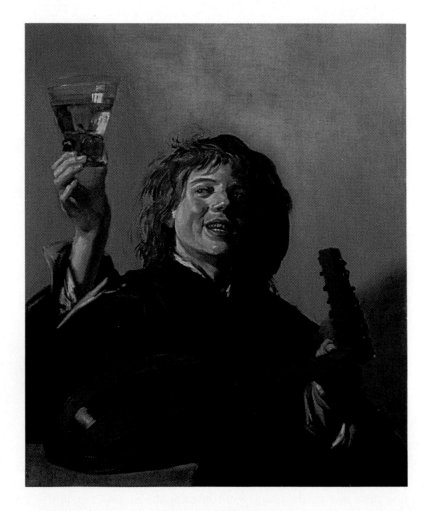

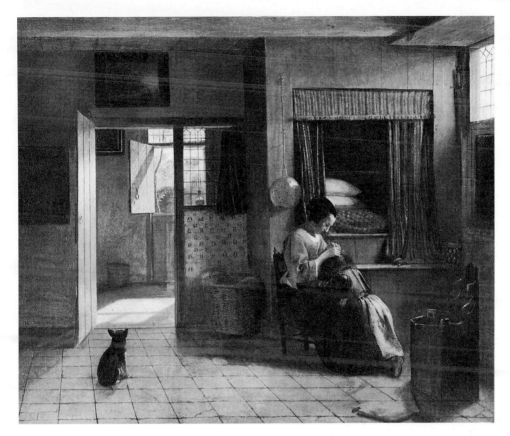

15.13 Pieter de Hooch. *Mother and Child,* c. 1660. Oil on canvas, 1′8¾″ × 2′. Rijksmuseum, Amsterdam, the Netherlands.

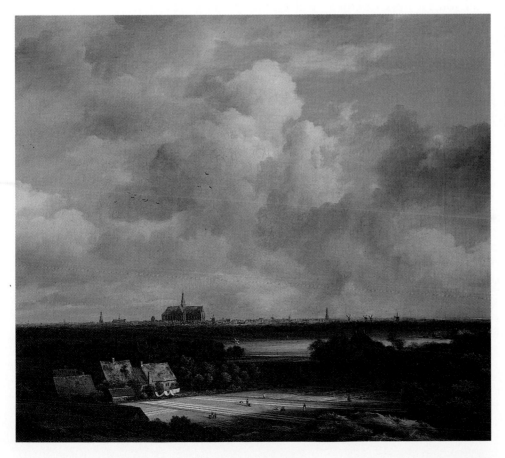

15.14 Jacob van Ruisdael. *View of Haarlem from the Dunes at Overveen,* c. 1670. Oil on canvas, approx. 1′10″ × 2′1″. Mauritshuis, The Hague, the Netherlands.

15.15   Jan Vermeer.
View of Delft, c. 1658.
Oil on canvas,
3′2¾″ × 3′10¼″.
Mauritshuis, The Hague,
the Netherlands.

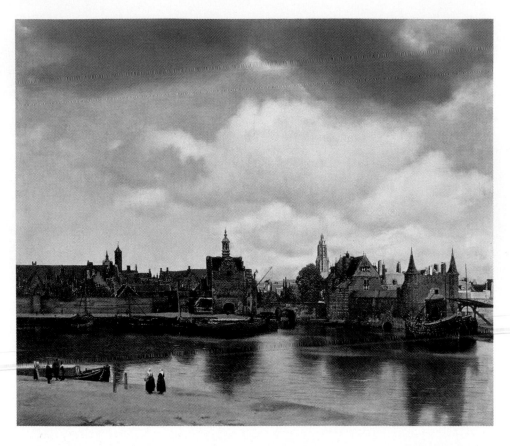

category of landscapes that meant so much to the Dutch people, who had fought persistently for their country against the Spanish oppressors. Whereas his *Quay at Amsterdam* (Fig. 15.1) is a forthright cityscape, Ruisdael instilled his *View of Haarlem from the Dunes at Overveen* with the unique Dutch relationship to the land wrested not only from foreign domination but also from the sea and swamps. The picture places a Dutch farmstead in direct relation to Saint Bavo, Haarlem's towering landmark that had become a Protestant church. The long strips of cloth hanging near the house and stretched along the ground are probably linen. This textile, derived from the flax plant, yielded grayish-yellow fibers that after weaving could be bleached white in the sun. The cottage industry depicts the focal points of Dutch life: the land, the city, the church, the home, and especially the sea, whose close proximity is indicated by the large, moisture-bearing clouds.

PHOTOGRAPHY BEFORE PHOTOGRAPHY: THE PAINTINGS OF VERMEER

In his *View of Delft* (Fig. 15.15), Jan Vermeer van Delft painted a profile of his native city. From the people strolling in the lower left foreground, the eye is carried across the canal, along the line of commercial buildings and houses behind the city wall on the left, past the stone bridge in the center with the steeple of the church rising in the background, to the moored boats and drawbridge on

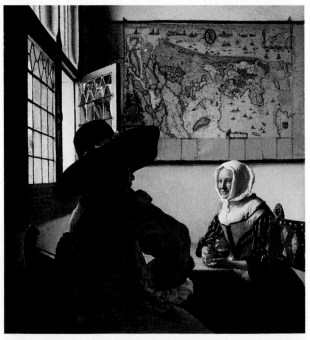

15.16   Jan Vermeer. *Officer and Laughing Girl,* 1655–1660. Oil on canvas, 1′7⅞″ × 1′6⅛″. Frick Collection, New York.

the extreme right. Vermeer's unusual and inventive handling of pictorial space is seen in this horizontal sweep, which makes no attempt to direct the eye toward a single vanishing point.

The effectiveness of *View of Delft* is greatly increased by the subtle treatment of light and color. As the sunshine filters through the broken clouds, the light falls unevenly over the landscape, varying from the shadowy foreground and the dull red of the brick buildings, through the flame and orange tones in the sunny distance, to the brilliant gleam of the church tower in the distance. More than half the area of the picture is given to the ever-changing Dutch sky, where patches of blue alternate with the silvery and leaden grays of the clouds, while the waters below reflect the mirror image of the town. Scholars have argued that Vermeer achieved his unique effects through the use of a drawing aid called a **camera obscura.** The tiny flecks of white light, such as those on the water and the boat on the right, which are observable only at close range, could have been isolated and studied by this means.

Vermeer also painted a group of interior scenes, such as *Officer and Laughing Girl* (Fig. 15.16). Here

the angularity of Vermeer's logical organization of rectangles and intersecting surfaces is relaxed by the importance given to the conversing couple. The daring perspective projects the figure of the officer forward and gives greater size to his large slouch hat and head than to the figure of the girl. His red coat and sash contrast noticeably with the cooler colors of the girl's white cap, black-and-yellow bodice, and blue apron, which allow her figure to recede. The map on the wall is painted with the greatest care in relation to the light and the angle of the wall. Its Latin title is quite clear and reads, "New and Accurate Map of all Holland and West Friesland." The warm, rich, natural light that streams in from the open window gives both unity and life to the severe division of planes. It bathes every object and fills every corner of the room, starting with the maximum intensity of the area around the source and tapering off by degrees into the cool, bluish tones of the shadows in the lower right.

The Art of Painting (Fig. 15.17) is a work that may have had deep personal significance for Vermeer, as he is said to have kept it in his studio during his

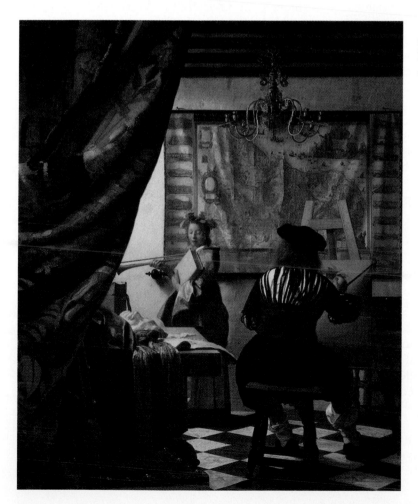

15.17 Jan Vermeer. *The Art of Painting,* c. 1665–1670. Oil on canvas, 4′ × 3′8″. Kunsthistorisches Museum, Vienna, Austria.

lifetime. After his death, his wife also made every effort to keep it in her possession. The sixteenth-century costume of the painter places the action in the past, and the lovely model, crowned with laurels, represents Clio, the muse of history. The large volume she holds is thought to be the *Schilderboeck,* a book written by Karel van Mander about the lives of Dutch painters. The trumpet probably signifies Fame. In addition, the trumpet, book, and death mask on the table allude to music, literature, and sculpture, and as in Dutch still lifes, the mask is an obvious reminder of death. The map on the wall indicates the pride of the Dutch in their country as well as in its sailors and navigators. In sum, the painting is a visual allegory that defines the arts to include not only painting, literature, and music but also history and science.

The contrast between Rembrandt's restless, searching spirit and Vermeer's sober, objective detachment is fully as great as the disparity between El Greco and Velázquez or Rubens and Poussin. Rembrandt's light is the glow of the human spirit, whereas Vermeer's is the light that floods in through an open window. Rembrandt tried to penetrate the world of appearances, whereas Vermeer studied that world exhaustively. Rembrandt was concerned with moral beauty, whereas Vermeer dwelled on physical reality, especially the perception of light and atmosphere. Rembrandt's dramas need only the crescendo of a single color from deep brown to golden yellow, or in an etching, from black to white, whereas Vermeer's subdued dramas were rendered through the entire spectrum of colors. Like a philosopher, Rembrandt laid bare the human soul in his moving characterizations, whereas Vermeer, like a jeweler, delighted the eye with his unique perception of space and the texture of things.

MUSIC

INTERNATIONAL HONORS: SWEELINCK

Jan Pieterszoon Sweelinck was the last great representative of the brilliant period during which Dutch and Flemish composers dominated the European musical scene (see p. 355). A lifelong resident of Amsterdam, he held the post of organist at the Oudekerk for more than 40 years. Public music in Calvinist Holland was centered on the church. Whereas strict Calvinistic church music allowed only for the congregational singing of psalms and hymns, Dutch tradition favored the organ. Sweelinck was allowed to play preludes before and postludes after the service, and as the official organist of Amsterdam, Sweelinck had the additional responsibility of performing public concerts. Large audiences crowded the Oudekerk, taking delight in his improvisations and variations on sacred and secular themes: the baroque flourishes of his Venetian toccatas, his fantasies "in the manner of an echo," and the choral preludes and fugues he built on Protestant hymn tunes.

The Dutch also embraced the widespread custom of domestic music making. As a result, a large body of literature was composed for the home rather than for public performance. Printed scores circulated internationally and could be obtained from Venice and London. In addition, Holland was noted as a center for the manufacture of musical instruments.

The domestic musical practices of the times can be vividly reconstructed by combining the surviving scores and musical instruments with the rich visual evidence in paintings of the period. Vermeer's *The Concert* (Fig. 15.18) shows a typical musical moment in the home. The trio is made up of a young woman, who reads her song part from the score she holds in her hand; a seated man, who supplies the harmonic background on his theorbo, a type of lute; and a girl, who sits at a spinet, a small kind of harpsichord, playing the keyboard part. On the floor is a viola da gamba, an instrument somewhat like the modern cello. This instrument could be used to duplicate the bass line of the keyboard part in a combination known as the **continuo.**

Sweelinck attracted students from all over northern Europe. Through such noted pupils as Samuel Scheidt of Halle, a direct line extended to Germany, where Johann Sebastian Bach and George Frideric Handel were born in the year 1685.

BACH AND THE REFORMATION TRADITION

Although his work lies outside the purview of the cultural center of Amsterdam, no examination of the arts of the baroque would be complete without considering the all-encompassing musical art of Johann Sebastian Bach. His travels were limited to an area little more than 60 miles from his birthplace, and he was a strong advocate of music making in the home. He was equally comfortable writing music for princes, for emperors, and for the church. Although the Reformation imposed restrictions on the visual arts, German Lutherans were generally more liberal than the Dutch Calvinists concerning music. Bach composed chamber music, instrumental dance suites, and concertos for middle-class and aristocratic patrons, in addition to a vast quantity of sacred music, consisting of cantatas, oratorios, and organ pieces.

As a performer, Bach was considered the greatest keyboard player of his generation. As a composer, he not only was prolific but also had the rare ability to view European styles of music and translate them into compositions that represented his personal outlook. Many of his compositions are organized into sets that give an overview of current European musical practice. One such set is a group of six concertos, known today as the Brandenburg Concertos, written as a gift for a nobleman, the Margrave of Brandenburg.

Each concerto contains the basic principles of the baroque **concerto grosso:** three movements of contrasting tempos performed by two groups that differ in size and tone color. Each concerto is unique, investigating different possibilities of tone color and form. For example, the second concerto is scored for a group of strings against a smaller group consisting of recorder, oboe, violin, and small, high-sounding trumpet. At first glance, the use of a special small trumpet that is capable of reaching great heights seems an unusual choice. Yet Bach's ear was sure, and the ensemble is unified.

In his time, Bach's reputation as a keyboard player outshone that of his compositions. Although he pursued his career in German provincial centers, his final post at Leipzig—a university town of

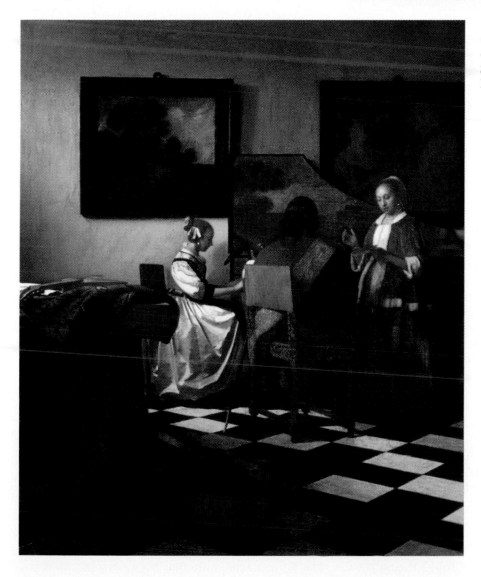

15.18 Jan Vermeer. *The Concert,* c. 1660. Oil on canvas, 2′4″ × 2′¾″. Isabella Stewart Gardner Museum, Boston.

some standing in Germany—was an important one. Bach's duties required him to teach at the St. Thomas school and to provide music for church services. The latter included composing and performing large-scale oratorios for Christmas, Passion Week, and Easter; occasional music for marriages, funerals, and important civic occasions; and a cantata for each Sunday of the church year, for all of which he conducted the soloists, choir, and a small orchestra.

Special occasions required music on a larger scale. For the great church festivals, Bach produced oratorios containing many of the same musical elements as those by Handel, such as recitatives and arias, and they include an emphasis on the chorus. However, he designed these oratorios for performance as part of a religious, rather than secular, event. Bach composed a *Christmas Oratorio,* which consists of a series of six cantatas, for weekly presentations during Advent, a period of anticipation beginning 4 weeks before Christmas, with the last one scheduled for the day after Christmas. Similarly, the Passion oratorios grew out of the liturgical dramas performed during the week preceding Easter, particularly on Good Friday. In this special type of religious oratorio, the text is taken from one of the four gospels of the New Testament, telling the events surrounding Christ's crucifixion.

Bach's *St. Matthew Passion* is one of the milestones of the choral literature, showing his skill at dramatic organization. Bach organized the *St. Matthew Passion* into twenty-six sections, with a design somewhat like that of many baroque operas. For example, the action takes place largely in a recitative, with balancing reactions in the form of arias or chorales. Text describing the action is restricted to quotations from the gospel of St. Matthew. It is given to a tenor soloist representing Matthew, designated in the score as "Evangelist."

The *St. Matthew Passion* is scored for soloists, orchestra with continuo, and a double chorus. Two large-scale double choruses enclose the work. The first describes Christ carrying the cross while groups look on and comment. Three metaphysical levels are described: the earthly here and now, the church, and another plane that stands physically and spiritually apart, soaring over the other musical forces. This chorus sings a traditional passion chorale to the text *O Guiltless Lamb of God.* At the close of the work, a double chorus laments at the tomb of Christ.

The magisterial sweep of the *St. Matthew Passion* carries the congregation through the betrayal of Judas, the judgment of Pilate, the crucifixion, and the events that follow it. During the course of the work, the recitatives, solos, and ensembles present the dramatic action, which is balanced by the contemplative choral sections. The solo passages represent individual reactions, and at various times, the chorus symbolizes the crowd and the body of faithful Christians. The congregation is free to join in singing the chorales, which are interspersed throughout the work.

Even in such a large-scale work, a domestic intimacy associated with family gatherings persists in Bach's Protestant treatment of biblical stories. In a sense, the Christmas story and the Passion become counterparts to family life: birth, marriage, suffering, and death. In Bach, the Protestant Reformation reached its highest musical fulfillment.

IDEAS

The many related elements of the Dutch worldview, such as commercialism, Protestantism, antiauthoritarianism, nationalism, individualism, the passionate championing of personal rights and liberties, and the practical application of scientific discoveries, sprang from and supported the middle-class outlook. The interplay between exploration and commerce fostered navigational adventure and the exploration of distant lands. Yet the Dutch conquests were mainly those of businesspeople, not those of armies. Their empire was based on corporate enterprise, and their kingdoms were those of banking houses and holding companies. Hard work and industriousness, coupled with thrift, led to a widespread accumulation of wealth in the hands of the middle class.

The Protestant church permitted no embellishment in its buildings and little musical elaboration in its services. Although both the Anglican and Lutheran reform movements modified and preserved much of the traditional Roman Catholic liturgy, Calvinistic Protestantism was marked by its austerity. A strict interpretation of Calvinism would lead directly to a gloomy form of asceticism, but their honest enjoyment of material pleasures saved the Dutch from a thoroughly orthodox application of this doctrine. Religious mandate, moral principle, and scarce land drove the Dutch to direct their desire for aesthetic pleasure toward the home.

During the first half of the seventeenth century, wealthy burghers mostly did not build palatial showplaces, although they certainly had the means to do so. They were content with comfortable multistoried houses. Fighting the Spanish crown for independence and resisting the growing menace of Louis XIV's absolute state had made the Dutch look with disfavor on courtly pomp and display. But after midcentury conspicuous consumption afflicted the very wealthy, who built lavish city homes and country villas, some with ornate gardens. Amsterdam's Town Hall was begun by architect Jacob van Campen in 1648, the year the new Dutch Republic was proclaimed. It echoes the restrained classicism evident in Italy that would soon find expression in the Louvre and Versailles (see Figs. 14.2 and 14.13). The Town Hall's interior was sumptuously decorated with marble and many carvings. In its time it was the largest public building in Europe.

The Protestant movement fortified Dutch hostility to authority and intensified nationalist consciousness. Middle-class merchants particularly resented the draining off of their provinces' wealth in the direction of Rome or Madrid. Protestantism took root and became identified with patriotism in the Dutch mind. Protection of national rights and individual freedoms further focused attention on the home.

OBSERVATION

Philosophy, social theory, and the natural sciences flourished in Dutch universities. These intellectual pursuits theorized the existence of an ordered and regulated universe in which everything could be measured and understood. Dutch citizens distrusted the physical and emotional forces that could render their world chaotic and unpredictable. Hence, an ideal, ordered, and comprehensible universe appealed to those whose security and comforts could be perpetuated by it.

René Descartes's rational theory of the universe, his equally rational psychology, and Baruch Spinoza's mathematically provable ethical system paralleled the middle-class concept of reasoned organization. Descartes sounded the call of reason with the declaration, "I think; therefore I am." His skepticism was revealed in his remark that the only thing that cannot be doubted is doubt itself. His optimism was revealed in his statement that only things that the mind perceives clearly are true.

Although the Dutch acknowledged the existence of a rational universe, they also insisted on tangible, observable facts. Human anatomy was a subject of intense interest, and with Vesalius's

Anatomy as a point of departure, dissection was carried over into other fields. Books had titles such as *Anatomy of Melancholy, Anatomy of Wit, Anatomy of Abuses,* and *Anatomy of the World.* In this age of observation, the restless human eye extended by the telescopic lens could explore many worlds. Optical instruments were developed by the skilled lens makers of Holland, whose ranks included the philosopher Spinoza. An astronomical observatory was built at the University of Leyden. Conversely, the microscope opened up a new world in miniature. More things were seen in heaven and on Earth than had ever been dreamed of before, and the cumulative effect was to diminish the hold of older, inherited models of the universe, such as those proposed by Aristotle.

Although their eyes were on the heavens, Dutch scientists did not neglect earthly applications of their discoveries. Astronomical calculations led to the discovery of triangulation and the spiral balance, both of which were of vast value to navigation. The pendulum was applied to the keeping of time, and the pocket watch added punctuality to daily life.

DOMESTICITY AND THE ARTS

The Dutch worldview and material prosperity placed artistic patronage in the hands of a well-to-do middle class. Outside such public buildings as town halls, churches, and commercial structures, Dutch architecture was, for all intents and purposes, domestic architecture. In the early seventeenth century, these houses were about the same size as today's middle-class homes, providing no room for monumental sculpture. The major domestic aesthetic expressions occurred, therefore, in painting and music, together with all the minor decorative arts that added to the comfort and beauty of the home.

Destined for interior house walls, pictures were correspondingly smaller than those painted for palaces and public halls. The number of professional artists multiplied with the increasing demand, which, in turn, led to a degree of artistic specialization. In portraiture there were painters of the proper family types, of drinkers in public taverns, and of corporation pictures. There were landscapists, seascapists, skyscapists, and even those whose specialty was cows. Especially in the second half of the century, when the gap between the well-off and the poor widened, patrons were drawn to works like those provided by Jan Steen in his boisterous tavern scenes and rowdy

15.19 Jan Steen. *The Happy Company,* c. 1663. Canvas, approx. 4′4¾″ × 5′4″. Mauritshuis, The Hague, the Netherlands.

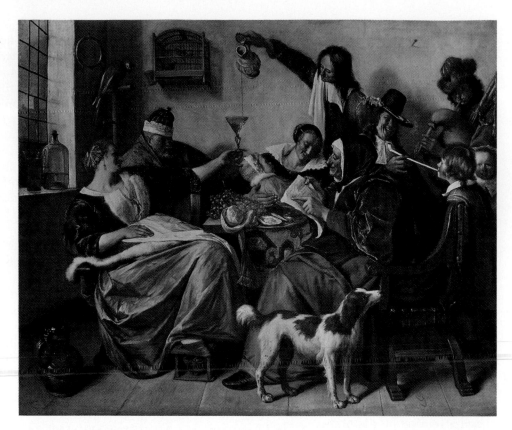

domestic interiors (Fig. 15.19). Frans Hals found some of his subjects among fish sellers and fruit peddlers. De Hooch and Vermeer depicted scenes in proper middle-class homes.

The home shaped art forms and gave them an intimate character. The home was the dominant architectural form as well as the place where pictures were hung, books read, and music played. Dutch domestic architecture, painting, and music were designed to be lived with and enjoyed by middle-class people who took a frank delight in their physical comforts and the arts that enriched their lives.

Large canvases designed for altarpieces or palace ceilings, colossal choral compositions for cathedrals, and operatic performances for palaces could produce grandiose utterances but had no place in the middle-class home. The more modest dimensions of a painting or etching intended for the wall of a living room, or of a chamber sonata or solo keyboard piece meant to be played in the same type of room, succeeded in encouraging a more intimate and personal form of communication.

In Holland and the northern countries generally, the baroque style was adapted both to Protestantism and to the tastes of the middle class. The bourgeois aspect of baroque art found its unity in the cult of the home, and domesticity is the key to its interpretation.

YOUR RESOURCES

- ***Exploring Humanities CD-ROM***

  ○ Descartes, *Discourse on Method,* Descartes module

- ***Web Site***

  http://art.wadsworth.com/fleming10

  ○ Chapter 15 Quiz

  ○ Links—Online Readings—Descartes, *Principles of Philosophy,* Selections

- ***Audio CD***

  ○ Bach, *St. Matthew Passion*

SEVENTEENTH-CENTURY HOLLAND

	Key Events	Visual Arts	Literature and Music
			1469–1536 Desiderius Erasmus ◆
1500			
	1517 **Protestant Reformation** began in Germany		
	1536 ***Institutes of Christian Religion*** published by John Calvin (1509–1564); Dutch Reformed Church established later along Calvinist lines		c. 1540–1623 **William Byrd** ❏ (English School)
1550			
			1562–1621 **Jan Pieterszoon Sweelinck** ❏
			c. 1562–1628 **John Bull** ❏ (English School); 1617–1628 organist at Antwerp, friend of Sweelinck
	1566 **Revolt of Netherlands** against Spain began		1570–1638 **Francis Pilkington** ❏ (English School), author of *First Booke of Ayres*
	1575 **University of Leyden,** first Dutch university, founded by William the Silent, Prince of Orange	c. 1581–1666 **Frans Hals** ▲	1578–c. 1644 **Henry Peacham** ❏ (English School), author of *Compleat Gentleman*, teacher and composer
			1583–1625 **Orlando Gibbons** ❏ (English School)
			1583–1645 **Hugo Grotius** ◆, founder of international law
			1585–1672 **Heinrich Schütz** ❏ (German School)
			1587–1654 **Samuel Scheidt** ❏ (German School), pupil of Sweelinck
			1587–1679 **Joost van den Vondel** ◆, Dutch dramatist, author of *Lucifer*, poem similar to Milton's *Paradise Lost*
			1596–1650 **René Descartes** ◆
			1596–1687 **Constantijn Huygens** ◆, poet, humanist, diplomat
			1596–1663 **Heinrich Scheidemann** ❏ (German School), pupil of Sweelinck
1600			
	1602 **Dutch East India Company** organized	1606–1669 **Rembrandt van Rijn** ▲	
	1609 **Holland and Flanders** given virtual independence in truce with Spain	1607–1674 **Jan Lievens** ▲	
		1609–1660 **Judith Leyster** ▲	
	1618–1648 **Thirty Years' War**	1617–1681 **Gerard Terborch** ▲	
	1621 **Dutch West India Company** founded		1623–1722 **J. A. Reinken** ❏ (German School), successor of Scheidemann at Hamburg and influencer of J. S. Bach
1625			
		1626–1679 **Jan Steen** ▲	1628–1648 **René Descartes** ○ resided in Holland
		c. 1628–c.1682 **Jacob van Ruisdael** ▲	1629–1695 **Christian Huygens** ◆
	1630–1687 **Limited public art patronage** dispensed through Constantijn Huygens	c. 1629–1683 **Pieter de Hooch** ▲	1632–1677 **Baruch Spinoza** ◆
		1630–1693 **Maria van Oosterwyck** ▲	1637 ***Discourse on Method*** published by Descartes in Leyden
	1642 **Dutch explorer Tasman** discovered New Zealand	1632–1675 **Jan Vermeer** ▲	1644 ***Principles of Philosophy*** published by Descartes in Amsterdam
	1648 **Independence of Netherlands** recognized by Treaty of Westphalia		
1650			
	1652–1674 **Anglo-Dutch commercial wars**		
		1663–1750 **Rachel Ruysch** ▲	1670 **Spinoza** published *Tractatus Theologico-Politicus*
			1685–1750 **Johann Sebastian Bach** ❏ (German School)
			1685–1759 **George Frideric Handel** ❏ (German School)

❏ - Musician   ▲ - Painter   ○ - Philosopher   ◆ - Writer

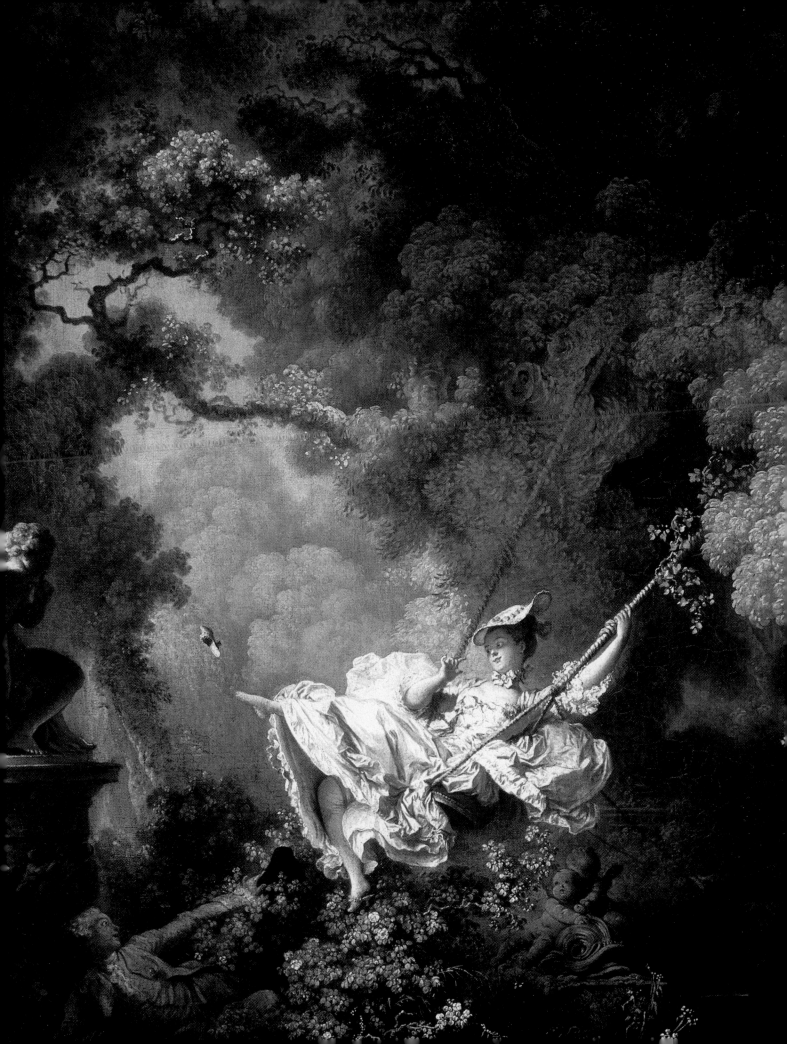

C H A P T E R

16

THE ENLIGHTENMENT

DURING THE EIGHTEENTH CENTURY, THE newly prosperous middle class challenged the nobility's right to rule. At the same time, fresh ideas about human nature and society were widely debated. The century began with the European landed aristocracy firmly in control of government and resources. Soon the smoky beginnings of the industrial era were visible, and the accompanying migration of people from the country to the cities presaged the radical social changes that culminated in the revolutionary upheavals of the late eighteenth century. As the century progressed, the continued rise of the middle class to wealth, education, and social prominence was accompanied by a decline in aristocratic dominance. In 1776, the world heard the ringing words of the American Declaration of Independence, which proclaimed that "all men are created equal, that they are endowed by their Creator with certain inalienable Rights, that among these are Life, Liberty and the pursuit of Happiness." In 1789, these sentiments were echoed in the French Declaration of Human Rights, with its ideals of liberty, equality, and fraternity.

In Western Europe and North America, the period from the early eighteenth century to the revolutionary era is called the Enlightenment. Its optimistic attitude about individual and societal improvement was summed up in 1784 by the

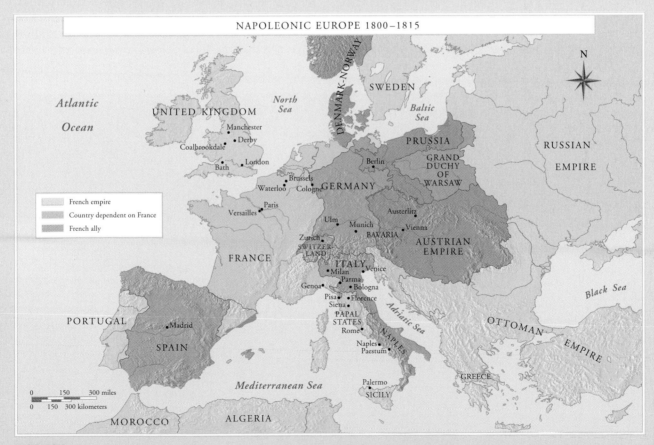

MAP 16.1

German philosopher Immanuel Kant. "Dare to know!" he challenged. "Have courage to use your understanding! That is the motto of Enlightenment." The movement was not based in one cultural center but traversed the entire Western world. Its regional accents did not significantly disrupt the nucleus of ideas at its core.

In a sense, the Enlightenment was the flowering of notions planted during the Renaissance and in antiquity. The gradual accumulation of mathematical and scientific knowledge over many centuries encouraged belief in the ability of humans to know and shape a better world. This human-centered attitude flourished throughout the Renaissance, although not with as much secular fervor as during the eighteenth century. It challenged the entrenched power of religion and government with the authority of knowledge. It propagated new notions of human rights and new visions of the human future. Some Enlightenment thinkers, although by no means all, considered that humans were fundamentally good at heart but greatly diminished by circumstances such as poverty, slavery, and political oppression. They found the aristocracy and the well-to-do irresponsible in their frivolity and callous waste of financial resources on monuments to personal power like Versailles (see pp. 391–393). Because many Enlightenment thinkers believed in progress, they did not automatically accept the continuation of hereditary political power or the divine right of kings, especially for self-indulgent rulers. Indeed, they saw a role for government in making the world a better place, although nothing like the involvement that would characterize much of the twentieth century.

For artists and writers, the Enlightenment meant setting up rational rules of expression that would guarantee excellence. For members of the audience, it meant the cultivation of taste and judgment. Taste, as the French savant Voltaire defined it, meant "attaining a quick discernment, a sudden perception which, like the sensations of the palate, anticipates reflection; like the palate it relishes what is good with an exquisite and voluptuous sensibility, and rejects the contrary with loathing and disgust." Without knowledge of the rules, the person of taste could not appreciate the subtle and often inspired deviations from the norm, and for such discernment one needed more than an elementary education. In other words, taste was mostly an attribute of the aristocracy and the upper middle class—people with the time and funds to pursue learning and aesthetic pleasure. In London, Paris, and other European cities, some wealthy and powerful women dubbed themselves "learned women" while vying to have the most famous and witty people attend their *salons*. These social gatherings included not only the upper classes but also artists, writers, composers, and scientists. Salons gave artists access to potential patrons and intro-

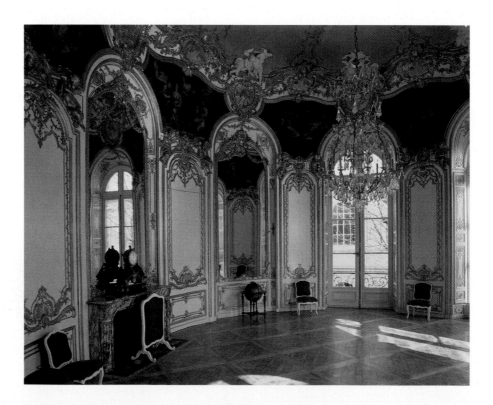

16.1   Germain Boffrand. Salon de la Princesse, Hôtel de Soubise, Paris, France, c. 1740. Oval, 33′ × 26′.

duced the wealthy to middle-class intellectuals, scientists, government officials, traders, and lawyers.

Art activity during this fruitful time moved in several seemingly contradictory stylistic directions. There was the aristocratically oriented **rococo,** or gallant style, and its opposite, **sensibility,** which reflected middle-class sentiments and aspirations. The 1770s brought the ***Sturm und Drang*** (Storm and Stress) movement, an outburst by artists who angrily chafed at the artificial restraints of both academic rules and the restrictive codes of polite society. They sought to broaden artistic expression by making it more sensitive to the scope of emotional responses. Eventually, these competing styles met and merged in the late eighteenth- and early nineteenth-century syntheses of classicism and Romanticism.

ROCOCO

With the death of Louis XIV in 1715, the aristocratic baroque style moved into its final, or rococo, phase. The regent for his young successor closed the majestic Versailles Palace and reestablished the royal residence in Paris. When Louis XV came of age, he hustled the court back to Versailles, but artistic patronage was no longer the near-monopoly of the court that it had been for his father. Arriving in Paris during the year that the Sun King died, the painter Antoine Watteau looked for patrons among a broad group drawn from both the nobility and the upper middle class. Throughout the century the operas of Jean-Philippe Rameau, Christoph Willibald Gluck, and Wolfgang Amadeus Mozart were composed for public opera houses where aristocrats rubbed shoulders with the bourgeoisie. In effect, the arts were extending their reach from the marble halls of kings into the elegant salons (Fig. 16.1), where subtlety and charm were considered higher aesthetic virtues than sumptuousness and grand display.

The rococo was by no means confined to Paris. To some degree, European courts became cultural suburbs of the City of Light. French fashions in architecture, painting, furniture, costume, and manners were imitated in far-off places like the courts of Catherine of Russia and Maria Theresa in Vienna. Whether a prince ruled a province in Poland or a duchy in Denmark, members of his family were more likely to speak French than the language of his native country. In Prussia, Frederick the Great built a rococo palace at Potsdam and called it *Sans-souci* (Carefree), the king of Saxony commissioned the jewellike Zwinger pleasure pavilion in Dresden, and the prince-bishop erected a handsome residence in Würzburg (see Fig. 16.6). French authors such as Voltaire and Jean-Jacques Rousseau found an international reading public; French dances dominated the balls, and French plays, the theaters.

In southern Germany and Austria, Italian influence remained strong. At the court in Vienna, an Italian architect finished the Schönbrunn Palace for Maria Theresa; Italian paintings decorated its walls. Pietro Metastasio was the imperial poet, playwright, and opera librettist, and only plays and operas in Italian could be performed in the royal theaters.

The word *rococo* apparently was a pun on *barocco,* the Italian word for "baroque," and on *rocailles* and *coquilles,* the French words for "rocks" and "shells," which were widely used as decorative motifs in the rococo style (Fig. 16.2). It achieved its designation during the era of the French Revolution, when whimsical, pleasure-seeking art was scorned along with the aristocratic class that enjoyed it. The rococo was not so much a new style as a modification or variation of the baroque. It was a domesticated baroque, better suited to fashionable townhouses than palace halls, but used in both.

SALONS OF THE EIGHTEENTH CENTURY

The rococo style suited the intimate salon life of wit and subtle conversation. The style affected both the major art forms and the decorative arts. Typical of the time is an engraved drawing by Watteau that uses the shell as a prominent motif (Fig. 16.2). Such a design could be applied to furniture, paneling, stage curtains, ceramics, or fabrics. In comparison to a Louis XIV interior (see Fig. 14.5), the rococo

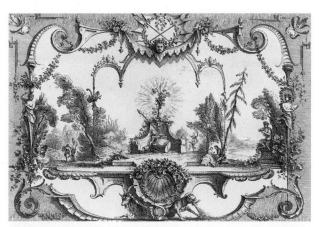

16.2 Antoine Watteau. *Gardens of Bacchus.* Etching by Gabriel Huquier, 10¼" × 1'3". Cooper-Hewitt National Museum of Design, Smithsonian Institution.

16.3   Salon, Hofburg Palace, Vienna, Austria, c. 1760–1780.

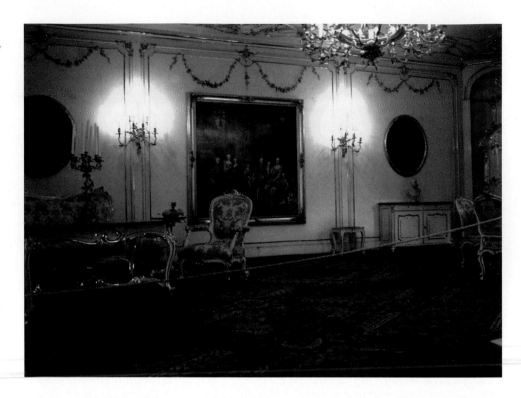

rooms of Vienna's Hofburg Palace (Fig. 16.3) are more delicate, light, and charming. Monumentality, stateliness, and pompous purples are replaced by refinement, elegance, and pastel shades.

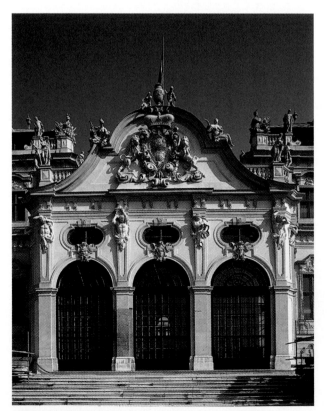

16.4   Lukas von Hildebrandt. Detail of facade, Belvedere Palace, Vienna, Austria, 1724.

At the Belvedere Palace in Vienna, the rococo burst outdoors into a lavish exterior design (Fig. 16.4). Details that the French architects confined to interiors moved to the garden facade of a summer palace begun in 1713 by Lukas von Hildebrandt for Prince Eugene of Savoy. Palladian academic restraint was cast to the winds. On either side of the windows were highly ornate double Composite pilasters; over the entrance figures that resemble Atlas, the mythological figure who holds up the Earth, struggle in a perpetual ballet. Otherwise, the architectural orders all but disappeared. The repose created by Renaissance triangular pediments and window brackets of the academic style dissolved into flowing curves and broken decorative rhythms.

The fusion of the arts that created mystical–emotional excitement, like that found in Gian Lorenzo Bernini's *St. Teresa in Ecstasy* (see Fig. 13.13), came to a climax in the churches of Austria and Bavaria. By this time, though, the Roman baroque extravaganzas of Andrea Pozzo, Francesco Borromini, and Gian Lorenzo Bernini (see pp. 369–374) transformed into popular rococo fancies. Churches such as Dominikus Zimmermann's Wieskirche (Church in the Meadow) appeared in rural surroundings where the faithful believed that a saint or angel had come to minister to those in distress or to deliver the local people from some impending evil. They became known as *pilgrimage churches* because they attracted visitors from far and near. Such shrines indicated the continuation of strong religious fervor. In many minds, they were images of the city of God.

On entering the oval nave of the Wieskirche, the pilgrim was swept up in swirls of curvilinear forms and crescendos of brilliant color, as if borne aloft on the wings of smiling cherubs and dancing angels (Fig. 16.5). These forms culminate in the choir loft and ceiling, where the tones of the organ mingle with the concealed chorus and float upward past terra-cotta angels perching gracefully

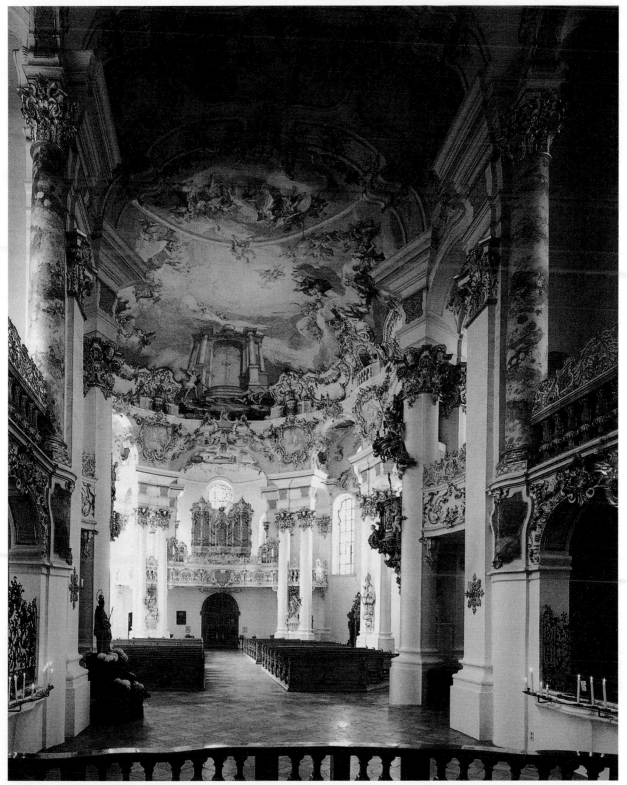

16.5   Dominikus Zimmermann. Wieskirche, Upper Bavaria, Germany. View of nave toward entrance portal, 1745–1754.

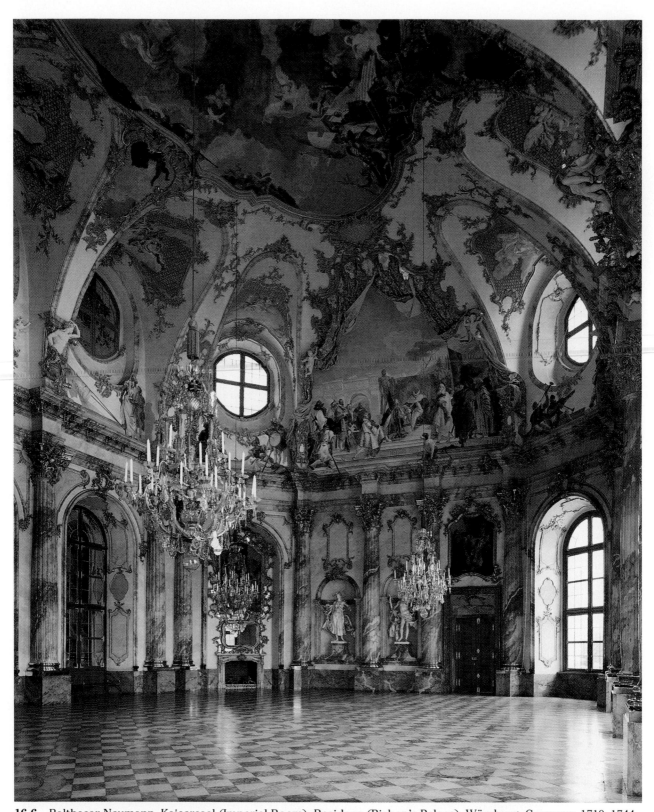

16.6 Balthasar Neumann. Kaisersaal (Imperial Room), Residenz (Bishop's Palace), Würzburg, Germany, 1719–1744.

on stucco clouds. The vanishing point is reached in the vast atmospheric perspective of the painted vaulting. Liturgy and music fused harmoniously with the arts to produce a complete work of art in which architecture, sculpture, and painting combined to render a unified worldview. Colors, lights, sounds, surfaces, lines, and shapes melt and merge into a single whole impression.

Elsewhere in southern Germany, aristocrats built themselves pleasure palaces, such as that of the Prince-Bishop of Würzburg. His architect, Balthasar Neumann, created in the Kaisersaal (Imperial Room) a complex synthesis of the arts (Fig. 16.6). The supple undulating movement of the decorative details leads the eye upward toward the flowing lines, wavy curves, and visionary vistas of the illusionistic ceiling mural by the Venetian painter Giovanni Battista Tiepolo, which includes stereotypical figures of Asia, Africa, and America, much in the manner of Pozzo (see Fig. 13.9). In this stately, aristocratic room, where Mozart once played, rococo and gallant-style music were comfortably at home.

FÊTES AND FANTASIES: PAINTING AND SCULPTURE

Antoine Watteau's *The Music Party* (Fig. 16.7) is a *fête galant,* or "elegant entertainment." Such canvases depicted imaginary visions of well-dressed young people enjoying themselves in idyllic gardens and spacious landscapes. A comparison of this rococo picture with the sensuous baroque *Garden of Love* by Peter Paul Rubens (see Fig. 14.10) reveals the hallmarks of the new style. The dimensions of the pictures alone tell their story. Rubens's *Rape of the Daughters of Leucippus* is roughly 7 feet square. Watteau, by contrast, made small easel paintings for the drawing room rather than murals for a grand gallery. Watteau, like Rubens, was Flemish, and he was an ardent admirer of the work of his older countryman. In Watteau's pictures, however, Rubens's massive figures are trimmed down to graceful and slender proportions. In effect, Rubens's lusty revelers have been made to dance a graceful minuet.

In *The Music Party,* a group has gathered on a terrace for a pleasant afternoon of musical

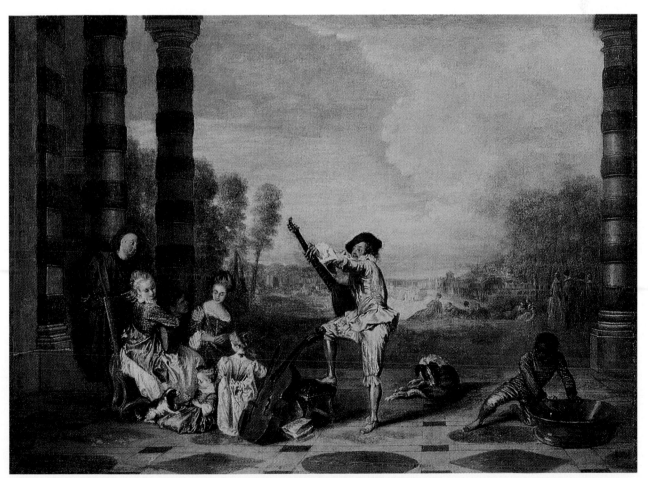

16.7   Antoine Watteau. *The Music Party,* c. 1719. Oil on canvas, 2′1½″ × 3′¼″. Wallace Collection, London, England.

instruction, entertainment, and perhaps some amorous interchanges. The cello has been laid aside, the score is still open, and the lady who has just had her lesson lets her elbow rest on her guitar. The music master is tuning his theorbo (a type of long lute) before he begins to play. A young black servant seems to be chilling bottles of wine in a copper tub. A mood of melancholic anticipation and slow time prevails. Like his baroque forebears, Watteau built his picture like a stage set, even to the point of making the background ambiguous. Is it meant to resemble a painted backdrop, or is it an idealized landscape? The fondness of Flemish painters for including figures with symbolic value may have influenced Watteau, whose renderings of dogs may signal sexual assignations among the music makers.

Although he began as a genre painter specializing in scenes of Flemish village life, in Paris Watteau became associated with decorators and designers of theater scenery and took an interest in the elegant world of fashion. He combined these elements with the baroque interest in theatrical effects, creating a new style in which the fantasy of the stage and the reality of everyday life mingled, playing out a comedy of love and desire.

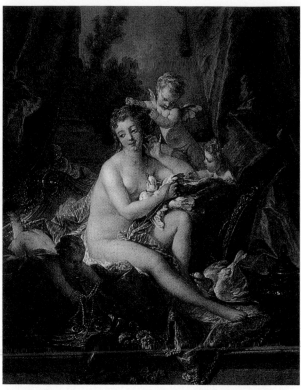

16.8 François Boucher. *The Toilet of Venus,* 1740. Oil on canvas, 3′6⅜″ × 2′9½″. Metropolitan Museum of Art, New York. Bequest of William K. Vanderbilt, 1920.

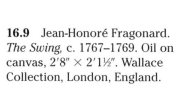

16.9 Jean-Honoré Fragonard. *The Swing,* c. 1767–1769. Oil on canvas, 2′8″ × 2′1½″. Wallace Collection, London, England.

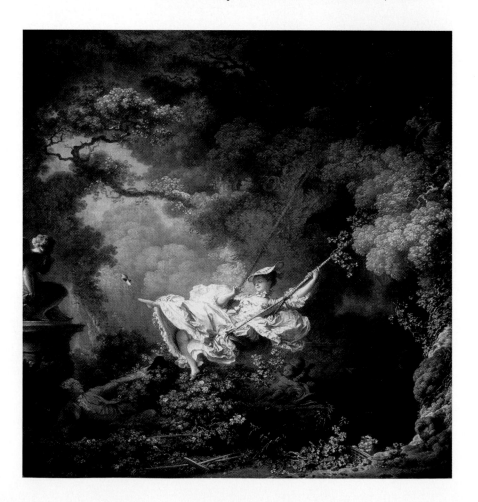

Sparkling with skillful brushwork, fanciful color, and charming imagery, Watteau's art achieved a freedom from prior models through the use of distinctive feathery brushstrokes. A poetic feeling, gentle irony, and elusiveness permeate these scenes, as in the works of Giorgione (see Figs. 12.10 and 12.11). In *The Music Party,* the misty, vaporous, blue-tinged landscape conveys subtle, elusive moods for which there are no words. Like characters in the pastoral novels of the time, elegant ladies and lovers stroll through lush gardens like the imaginary Arcadian shepherds so popular in antiquity.

François Boucher, the favorite painter of Louis XV's mistress, Madame de Pompadour, worked in a lighter vein than Watteau. *The Toilet of Venus* (Fig. 16.8) portrays the eighteenth-century concept of feminine charm in all its amoral artificiality. Love is no longer the robust passion it was with Rubens but rather a sophisticated flirtation. Like Watteau, Boucher favored youthful figures. His productivity matched his popularity: during his career he produced about 1,000 paintings.

Boucher's successor, Jean-Honoré Fragonard, became a leading painter of the French rococo. *The Swing* (Fig. 16.9), which was commissioned by the young aristocrat shown in the lower left, portrays the frivolous, sexually charged, pleasure-seeking pursuits of his class. The patron has concealed himself in the shrubbery while his love swings. As her skirts and petticoats billow on the breeze, her silken slipper flies off toward the statue of Cupid, who enters the conspiracy by putting a finger to his lips. In the picture, all of nature has become a burbling extravaganza of fecundity, no doubt signifying the sexual attraction of the lovers. The artist's fine feeling for fantastic artificial colors rather than objectively observed and rendered hues and his ingenious composition with its dynamic crisscrossed diagonals save the picture from the twin perils of overrefinement and triviality.

In the field of portraiture, Élisabeth Vigée-Lebrun was in great demand by royal families and nobility all over Europe (Fig. 16.10). She was commissioned to paint the likeness of Louis XVI's

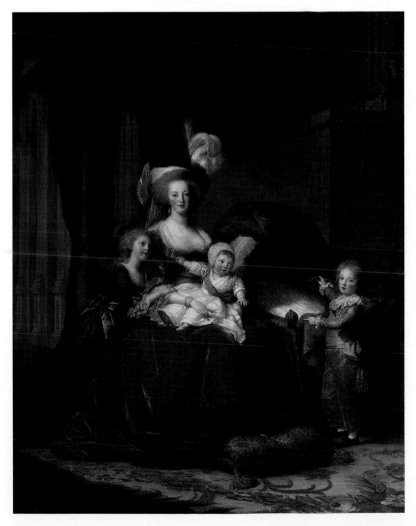

16.10 Élisabeth Vigée-Lebrun. *Marie Antoinette of Lorraine-Hapsburg, Queen of France, with Her Children,* 1789. Oil on canvas, approx. 8′10½″ × 6′4¾″. Musée de Versailles, Versailles, France.

wife, Marie Antoinette. Marie Antoinette's reputation for profligate spending and other excesses sullied the reputation of the king, whose own activities would not withstand much scrutiny. On the advice of the king's ministers, Vigée-Lebrun was asked to create a propaganda picture that would sweeten the queen's reputation by portraying her as a tender mother, both of her children and, by extension, of the nation. The lavish result deliberately played on the public's emotions, especially by casting light into an empty cradle, an unsubtle reference to the death of a baby daughter.

A spirit of elegance and charm animates the sculpture of Falconet and Clodion. Terra-cotta, that is, clay, is inexpensive and can be modeled quickly. It was a receptive medium to capture the fleeting rhythms of Clodion's *Intoxication of Wine* (Fig. 16.11), in which a follower of Bacchus, god of wine and dance, cavorts with a faun, the sexually uninhibited half-man/half-goat forest creature from antiquity. Rococo figurines like these, based on classical themes, adorned tables and mantles. They were sometimes more candidly erotic than the paintings of the period.

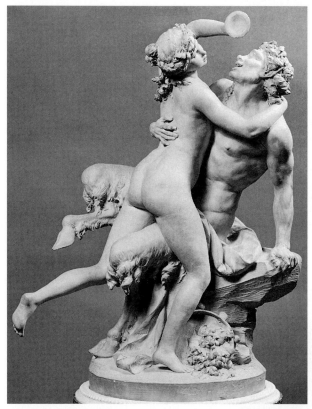

16.11 Clodion. *Intoxication of Wine (Bacchante and Faun),* c. 1775. Terra-cotta, height 1′11¼″. Metropolitan Museum of Art, New York. Bequest of Benjamin Altman, 1913.

SENSIBILITY

To the sturdy, hardworking, socially responsible members of the middle class, the frills of the rococo were too trivial and vain. The heroic attitudes of mythological gods and goddesses and the rustic loves of charming shepherds and shepherdesses signified the idle pleasures of the nobility. The growing middle-class patrons of art demanded more down-to-earth subjects that reflected their experience. The style known as *sensibility* evolved as an answer to this demand in England; in France, it was known as *sensibilité,* and in Germany, as *Empfindsamkeit.* Within this concept, two key words were *nature* and *natural.* In the eighteenth-century sense, nature was the opposite of the artificial, a departure from affectation, liberation from the pretentious manners and lifestyles of a narcissistic, nonworking class of people, and a reflection of the idea of an ordered universe in which all things had their proper place. Sensibility found expression in the painting, literature, and music of the period.

In France the painter Jean-Baptiste Greuze drew his clientele mainly from the middle-class ranks, as was the case in England with William Hogarth. In literature the novels of Samuel Richardson, Henry Fielding, and Oliver Goldsmith targeted the growing English middle-class audience. Alexander Pope's mock-heroic poem, *The Rape of the Lock,* a tongue-in-cheek account of the theft of a strand of hair from the head of an outraged lady, pilloried the pretense and etiquette of the idle rich. In *The Dunciad,* a later work, Pope took aim at his critics, dubbing them dunces in a send-up of Homer's *The Iliad.* Pope's career, and that of other writers, flourished at a time when newspapers and journals formed an ongoing, if quarrelsome, salon in print to which any and all readers were invited.

Theater also flourished. Plays such as Gotthold Lessing's *Miss Sara Sampson* (1755) in Germany and Denis Diderot's *Natural Son* (1757) in France established what came to be known as the *bourgeois drama.* A similar shift occurred in musical life. The collective patronage of audiences attending performances in the newly opened public concert halls replaced music making in courtly and church circles. Instead of aiming to please one patron, composers and performers now tried to win the favor of many. Mozart, for one, felt confident enough to break with his tyrannical archbishop patron and strike out as an independent composer. It is far from an accident that his operatic masterpiece *Don Giovanni*

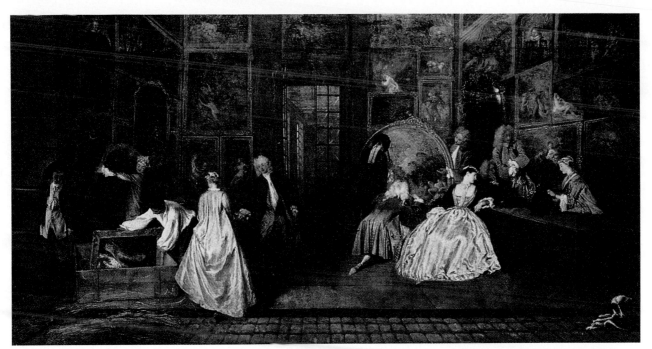

16.12 Antoine Watteau. *Gersaint's Signboard,* 1720–1721. Oil on canvas, 5′3⅞″ × 10′1″. Staatliche Museen, Berlin, Germany.

was commissioned by the municipality of Prague rather than by the royal capital of Vienna.

PAINTING BOURGEOIS REALITY

One of Watteau's most significant pictures (Fig. 16.12) was painted as a signboard for a Paris art dealer named Gersaint. The project was proposed by the artist himself, who was dying of tuberculosis and wanted, as the story goes, to get the stiffness out of his fingers by painting. Watteau idealized his sponsor to the extent of showing him as the owner of a gallery-like showroom filled with the fashionable elite of Parisian society, although this was more wish than reality. On the right, Gersaint praises the virtues of a Watteau-like oval painting to a lady and gentleman, who view it through their lorgnettes. On the left, the picture being packed away is a portrait of Louis XIV. This act symbolizes a farewell to the old regime, and it also works as a visual pun on the name of Gersaint's shop, *Au Grand Monarque.* The scene (cut in half sometime after 1750) constitutes an elegant stage setting in which real characters act out the drama of gentile life in eighteenth-century Paris.

The popularity of genre pictures with casual subjects was part of the eighteenth-century middle-class reaction against aristocratic posturing. They parallel the scenes from ordinary life produced in Holland a century before (see Figs. 15.1–15.16).

Jean-Baptiste-Siméon Chardin portrayed the lives of common folk going about their daily routines or indulging in quiet pleasures (Fig. 16.13). In his many still-life compositions, he glorified everyday household objects, such as bottles, cups, jugs, fruit, and

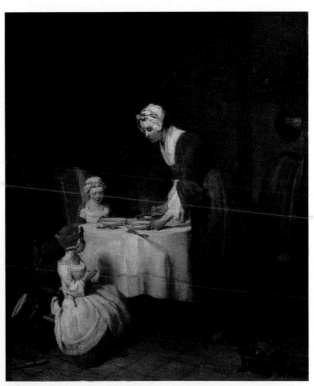

16.13 Jean-Baptiste-Siméon Chardin. *Saying Grace,* 1740. Oil on canvas, 1′7″ × 1′3″. Louvre, Paris, France.

vegetables for the dinner table (Fig. 16.14). Beyond Chardin's modest subject matter and deceptive simplicity is a thoughtful relationship between and among these objects. Through his careful arrangements, contrasts of textures, and subtle choice of colors, these became symbols of the good life, just as fine fabric, simulated nature, and sexual innuendo symbolized the good life for the nobility. Oddly enough, Chardin's work was collected by the aristocracy, including Madame de Pompadour. The French philosopher and critic Denis Diderot, one of Chardin's ardent admirers, wrote that he "is the one who understands the harmony of colors and reflections." Diderot pointed out that it was not the colors he mixed, but "it is the very substance of objects, it is the air and light you take with the tip of your brush and fix on the canvas." Chardin's geometric clarity and pictorial harmony became the model for many modern masters, notably Édouard Manet, Paul Cézanne, and Henri Matisse (see Figs. 19.9, 19.29, 20.9, and 20.10).

The English painter William Hogarth was in good company with other distinguished eighteenth-century social satirists. Like Swift's *Gulliver's Travels,* John Gay's *Beggar's Opera,* and Voltaire's *Candide,* Hogarth's series of eight pictures titled *Marriage à la Mode* is a merciless exposé of the environment and customs of his time, modified by the saving grace of a brilliant wit. As Charles Dickens, Émile Zola, Francisco Goya, and Honoré Daumier were to do in the nineteenth century, Hogarth dramatized the conditions he saw and issued a challenge to society to do something about them. In this case it was the evil of putting young men and women on the auction block of marriage.

Hogarth's *Marriage Contract* (Fig. 16.15) introduces the characters as in the first scene of a play. The gouty nobleman points with pride to the family pedigree as he is about to sell his social standing, in the person of his son, to pay off the mortgage on his ancestral estate. The merchant who is marrying off his daughter carefully inspects the dowry settlement through his spectacles, just as he would in any other hard-driven bargain. The pawns in this game, the ill-matched bride and groom, sit with their backs to each other. The lawyer, Counselor Silvertongue, begins a flirtation by flattering the future Lady Squanderfield while her fiancé takes a pinch of snuff.

The other five scenes show the unhappy consequences of this doomed union as it progresses from boredom and frivolity to infidelities, a duel, and death. In *The Countess's Levée* (Fig. 16.16), Lady Squanderfield entertains some of her friends as she makes her morning toilette. Counselor Silvertongue, now her lover, shows her tickets for a masked ball that evening. A French barber dresses her hair, a servant passes cups of chocolate, and a little black pageboy points gleefully to the horns of a doll, indicating that she is cuckolding her husband. The corpulent singer may be Farinelli, the famous castrato, who was then performing soprano roles in London opera. The infatuated fan beside him has been identified as

16.14 Jean-Baptiste-Siméon Chardin. *Still Life: Bowl of Plums, a Peach and Water Pitcher,* c. 1728. Oil on canvas, 1′5¾″ × 1′10⅜″. Phillips Collection, Washington, D.C.

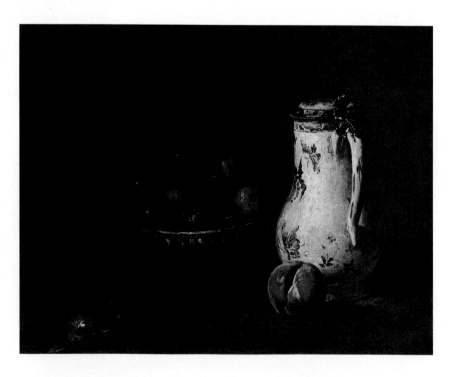

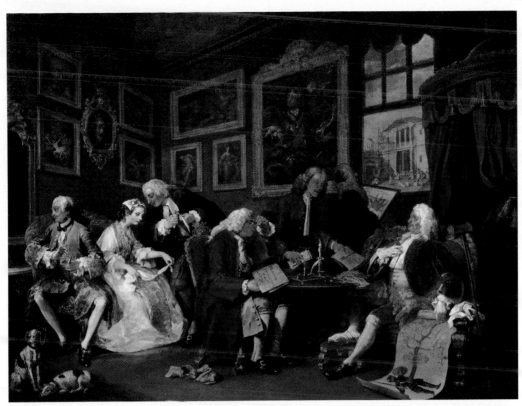

16.15   William Hogarth. *Marriage Contract* (*Marriage à la Mode,* Scene I), 1744. Oil on canvas, 2′3″ × 2′11″. National Gallery, London, England.

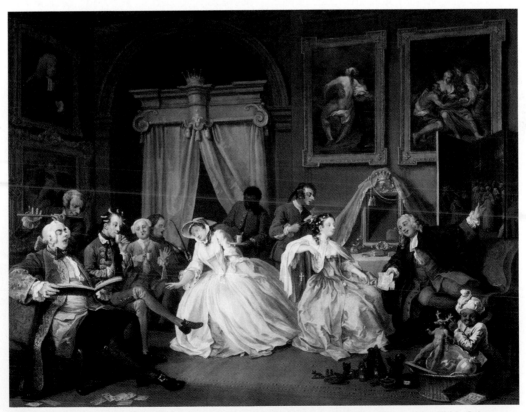

16.16   William Hogarth. *The Countess's Levee* (*Marriage à la Mode,* Scene IV), 1744. Oil on canvas, 2′3″ × 2′11″. National Gallery, London, England.

a socialite who once exclaimed, "One God, one Farinelli!" This and such other series, such as *The Harlot's Progress* and *The Rake's Progress,* were first made as paintings and then copied in the form of copper engravings. The prints were widely sold by subscription, and group patronage made them financially successful.

Similarly, French sensibilité upheld moral standards, although not with such biting satire. According to Diderot, the arts should celebrate the victory of virtue and the defeat of vice. He criticized the sensual fantasies of Boucher because they were not ethically enlightening. Moral instruction was explored by the painter Jean-Baptiste Greuze, who titled some of his pictorial sermons *The Paralytic Cared for by His Children, Young Girl Weeping over Her Dead Bird,* and *The Father's Curse.* His *Village Bride* (Fig. 16.17) depicts the moment when the father of the bride hands over her dowry to the groom. Such pictures are like living tableaux and scenes from a play. Sensibility here comes close to sentimentality.

SCULPTURE FOR THE MIDDLE CLASS

As might be expected, bourgeois sculptural expression was at home in the domain of portraiture. Jean-Antoine Houdon's fine feeling for characterization is obvious in his bust of Voltaire (Fig. 16.18), one of several likenesses he did of the famous French philosopher and dramatist. In the tilt of the head and the humorous gleam of the eye, Houdon

captures the amused look of the philosopher as he comments on the follies of other mortals. To chisel a glance of amiable skepticism in hard marble is no small feat. Leaving a rough edge in the outline of the pupil of the eye, the artist was able to produce a special glint that gives just the desired effect. Houdon captured a fleeting moment of animated conversation in which the philosopher might have coined one of his famous epigrams. His work was sold in reproductions of various sizes to those who admired the work of the Enlightenment thinkers.

Houdon's subjects included many Americans, including Thomas Jefferson, John Paul Jones, Robert Fulton, and Benjamin Franklin. The latter statue was carved while Franklin was serving as ambassador to the court of Louis XVI. In 1785, on the invitation of Jefferson, Houdon crossed the Atlantic with Franklin and spent several weeks at Mount Vernon making studies for a statue of George Washington, now in the State Capitol in Richmond, Virginia (Fig. 16.19).

THE TRIUMPH OF THE NOVEL

In English novels, sensibility explored personal feelings and a spectrum of emotional reactions to familiar social situations. Samuel Richardson's 1740 novel *Pamela* portrayed a poor but proud young woman who had to seek her fortune by working in the residence of a well-to-do bachelor. She takes his fancy but resists his sexual overtures until frustration provokes him into proposing marriage. This

16.17 Jean-Baptiste Greuze. *Village Bride,* 1761. Oil on canvas, 3′ × 3′10½″. Louvre, Paris, France.

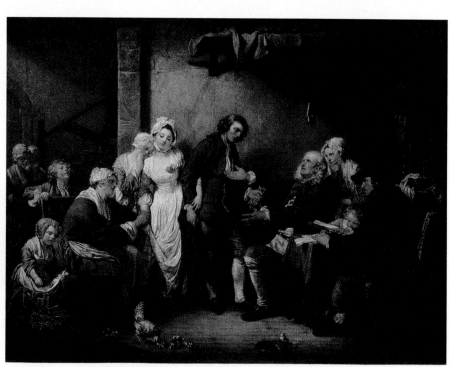

victory of virtue over vice was celebrated in the press and pulpit, winning wide popularity for the author. In Oliver Goldsmith's *Vicar of Wakefield,* the trials and troubles of a country parson push him nearly to the breaking point. He loses his modest capital to a rascally traveling salesman, his beloved daughter is ravished by a villain, and his son's military career is ruined by false accusations. Despite suffering deep mortification and calamity, he manages to hold his head high. In the end, of course, all turns out well.

Toward the end of the eighteenth century, Jane Austen had the last word in her *Sense and Sensibility.* This witty comedy of middle-class manners portrays two sisters. Elinor is the one who has good sense and "strength and understanding. . . . Her feelings were strong, but she knew how to govern them." Marianne, however, "was eager in everything; her sorrows, her joys, could have no moderation . . . she was everything but pru-

dent." In an ironic twist, Elinor marries for love and Marianne learns that prudence and common sense are the foundation of family happiness.

REACTIONS TO ENLIGHTENMENT

Those who believed that the exercise of reason could solve all political, social, religious, and personal problems took an optimistic view of human nature and the future. In contrast, those who surveyed the dismal conditions that surrounded them

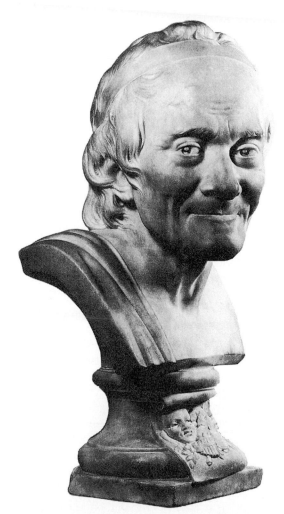

16.18 Jean-Antoine Houdon. *Voltaire,* 1781. Marble, height 1′8″. Victoria and Albert Museum, London, England.

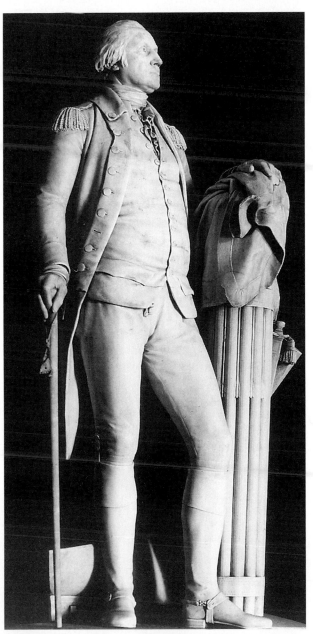

16.19 Jean-Antoine Houdon, *George Washington,* 1785–1796. Marble. 6′2″. State Capitol, Richmond, Virginia.

favored a pessimistic outlook. Jonathan Swift, for instance, questioned the assumption that human nature was essentially good. In his view, men and women were animals capable of reason, but more often than not they used their faculties "to aggravate man's natural corruptions." Coining the phrase "man's inhumanity to man," his sharp pen exposed the social evils and inequalities he beheld all around him, most famously in *Gulliver's Travels*. Swift carried his convictions to the grave, which bears his self-written epitaph: "He has gone where savage indignation can tear his heart no more."

Voltaire, a central figure of the French Enlightenment, believed in both the power of reason and the freedom of thought. His incisive critical intelligence, however, led him to satirize the pursuit of pure reason. If, as the seventeenth-century rationalist Baron Leibnitz believed, the human race was all good and its progress inevitable, human beings must inhabit the best of all possible worlds. In his masterpiece, *Candide*, Voltaire satirizes Leibnitz as Dr. Pangloss, the tutor of the naïve Candide, whom he escorts on a grand tour. Along their way they experience one social and natural disaster after another—rape, murder, slavery, shipwrecks, and earthquakes. In the end, Candide has returned to his farm, heeding the advice of his friend Martin: "Let us work without theorizing, it is the only way to make life endurable." Voltaire's parting words are, "We must cultivate our gardens."

STORM AND STRESS

By far the most tempestuous reaction to the Enlightenment took place in Germany with the *Sturm und Drang* movement. Its central figure was the poet and dramatist Johann von Goethe. In his university days, Goethe was greatly attracted to the philosopher Johann Gottfried Herder, who had studied with Kant and was conversant with the ideas of Enlightenment rationalism. Under the spell of Rousseau, however, Herder concluded that reason was not the key that unlocked the universe. Throwing off the restraints of academic rules, he believed that only nature could provide the answers. He found nature in folklore as the voice of the people, in Gothic architecture with its myriad imaginative forms, in Shakespeare's plays, and in the *sublime*. The sublime was a concept that the English philosopher Edmund Burke projected as a counterbalance to beauty. Beauty was achieved through order, clarity, symmetry, and the judicious balancing of opposites, but the sublime was to be found in the wild and awesome aspects of nature—tempests and tor-

rents, impenetrable forests, avalanches, and Alpine scenery. The sublime suggested that the terrifying, the fearsome, the mysterious, and even the ugly could become the material of art. In the canon of Storm and Stress, rules were not made to be broken elegantly and politely, but with shattering and shocking effect.

Herder became Goethe's model for the characterization of Faust, the title figure in the drama that occupied him for much of his life. *Faust* was based on a medieval legend about a philosopher who sold his soul to the devil in exchange for magical knowledge that would unlock the secrets of the universe. Goethe's devil, Mephistopheles, is a very sophisticated evil spirit with a cynical sense of humor and an ironic eye for human follies and foibles. In Goethe's original version, Faust concludes that the world cannot be known through theory alone but only through experience, feeling, and emotion. Faust's tragedy is that in the fulfillment of his love for Margaret he brings about the destruction of the woman he loves. Margaret's tragedy is that when she experiences love with all its tender feeling, and when she achieves fulfillment by bearing a child, she is condemned as an unwed mother by the customs and laws of a strict society. Faust's constant search for new experiences and emotional involvements is also the inherent tragedy of human life, because only by seeking the unattainable can the divine spark ignite and illuminate the course of human existence. For both Faust and Margaret, the road to salvation and redemption lies in continuous striving and struggling, not in fixed attainment. After his Storm and Stress period, Goethe wrote a philosophical sequel in which Faust finally finds redemption through the prayers and love of Margaret and his service to humanity.

The Storm and Stress movement is evident in the pictures of the Swiss-born artist Henry Fuseli. Trained for the ministry and ordained at the age of 20, he made a rebellious escape into the world of art. He hailed Shakespeare and Michelangelo as his "twin gods." Fuseli sought psychological insights into the dark, irrational realm of dreams, and he added a nightmarish dimension to Storm and Stress expression, populating his pictures with witches, goblins, ghosts, and ghouls. In *The Nightmare* (Fig. 16.20), he conjured up the fantastic dream world. The work inspired a long poem by the natural scientist Erasmus Darwin, grandfather of the well-known Charles. One verse of it reads:

> On her fair bosom sits the Demon-Ape Erect,
>   and balances his bloated shape;
> Rolls in their marble orbs his Gorgon eyes,
> And drinks with leathern ears her tender cries.

THE MOZARTIAN SYNTHESIS

Wolfgang Amadeus Mozart's most mature music, written in Vienna during the last decade of his life, brought together many aspects of the Enlightenment. Mozart continued to compose chamber music for aristocratic salons and German comic operas for the popular musical theater, but his art attained its highest expression in the works he created for the public opera houses and concert halls, where nobles and commoners gathered together for their mutual recreation. Here Mozart's musical genius found its widest scope, here he could explore the endless variety of tragic and comic situations that give his operas their boundless humanity, and here his dramatic power could make its greatest impact. These qualities carried over into the less direct and more abstract forms of his symphonies and concertos, giving these compositions their dramatic intensity.

The spirit of the Enlightenment shines in the logical clarity and unified structure of Mozart's musical and dramatic forms. His letters show his enthusiasm for Rousseau's naturalness, and his music's explosive energy displays his knowledge and connection to Storm and Stress literature. In opera he found a medium in which he could combine all these ideas and styles into one grand, endlessly changing yet well-ordered pattern.

Mozart understood that an opera is not a drama *with* music but a drama *in* music. For him, an operatic character had no existence apart from the music. The character is awakened to life through melody and rhythmic patterns. More-over, Mozart carried his characters through situations by the direction of a melodic line and developed the most intricate interactions with the other characters by means of harmonic modulation and contrapuntal complexity. Mozart's emotional range was enormous. His music is by turns spirited and profound, serene and agitated, ethical and diabolical—all within a short span of time. Yet everything takes place within an ordered framework.

THE LIFE AND DEATH OF DON JUAN: MOZART'S *DON GIOVANNI*

Like the Faust legend, the Don Juan story was far from new. For his updated treatment of the legendary lover, Mozart chose as his librettist Lorenzo da Ponte, a skillful writer with a real theatrical flair. Mozart subtitled his opera ***dramma giocosa*** (comic drama), but he also referred to it as an "opera buffa in two acts." In fact, it is a mixture of both comic and dramatic elements that create a high-spirited eighteenth-century comedy of manners blended with Storm and Stress demonology.

The pace of the opera is breathtaking. The first scene alone includes an attempted seduction, a challenge and duel, the dying gasps of an outraged father, blasphemy, the escape of the culprit, and oaths of vengeance. The drama centers around Don Giovanni, who breaks the bonds of civilized restraint, defies all social conventions, sweeps aside every barrier in his way, and stands alone against the world. The other

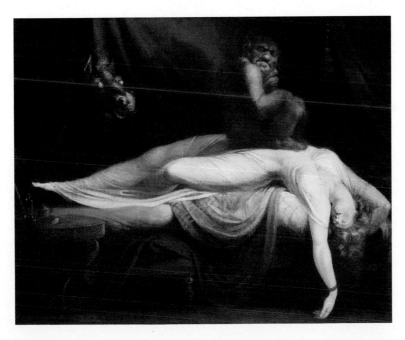

16.20 Henry Fuseli. *The Nightmare,* 1781. Oil on canvas, 3′4″ × 4′2″. Detroit Institute of Arts.

characters are like the spokes of a wheel, existing only in relation to the hub, Don Giovanni.

Opposite Don Giovanni are the three female leads, each of equal importance. Two—Donna Anna and Donna Elvira—are the Don's social equals, whereas the third—Zerlina—is a peasant girl. Chronologically, Donna Elvira surfaces first, because she has been seduced and deserted before the curtain rises. Hers is the fury of a woman scorned, mixed with the desire to forgive, forget, and regain Don Giovanni's affections. The emotional life of Donna Anna, who first appears near the beginning of the opera in a rage at Don Giovanni's attempted seduction of her, is no less complicated. Full of righteous wrath and filial affection for her murdered father, she swears vengeance on his assassin. Her gentlemanly fiancé, Don Ottavio, joins her in this resolve. Together they constitute the serious couple, a type often found in Italian opera buffa. Because Don Ottavio is the opera's lone champion of lawful love, his appropriately aristocratic gallant-style music inevitably paints him as a somewhat pale and conventional character within these highly charged surroundings.

The naïvely flirtatious Zerlina is torn between loyalty to her rustic bridegroom Masetto and the flattering attentions of the glamorous upper-class Don Giovanni. In their music together, Zerlina and the Don are given a musical characterization in which the division of the melody between the voices and the subtle melodic variants point up their respective attitudes. The Don is tender yet still the lordly aristocrat; Zerlina is feminine and doubtful of his intentions, but enjoying every moment.

On the male side, Don Giovanni has no Romantic competition, only a very substantial shadow in the form of his stock opera-buffa comic servant Leporello. Leporello repeatedly expresses his earthy cynicism, one example of which is the famous "Catalogue Aria," in which he lists the master's amorous female conquests throughout Europe, including 1,003 in Spain alone.

In the finale to Act I, all the characters are onstage. Don Giovanni is throwing a large party at which both upper-class and peasant guests are present. He schemes to add Zerlina to his list of conquests. Fine dramatic contrast is provided by Don Giovanni's joyous drinking song, which sparkles like the wine he is ordering, and the sullen resentment of Zerlina's fiancé Masetto, who senses that his bride-to-be is much too interested in this glamorous member of the privileged class.

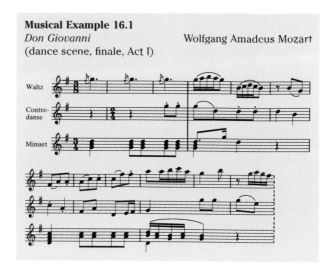

Musical Example 16.1
Don Giovanni
(dance scene, finale, Act I)
Wolfgang Amadeus Mozart

The scene climaxes with the dance music. No fewer than three instrumental groups appear on stage, in addition to the main orchestra in the pit. At the time, everyone would have recognized this as a scene from a typical Viennese public ball, for which Mozart frequently composed music. To accommodate everyone's taste, minuets might be played in one room, waltzes in another, and so on. Here the three groups play different dances. The first group plays an aristocratic minuet, the second plays a type of square dance known as a **contredanse,** and the third ensemble plays a type of old-fashioned German waltz known as a **Ländler.** The obvious separation of social levels is implied, with the masked figures of Donna Anna and Don Ottavio doing the aristocratic minuet, the peasants stamping out the vigorous *Ländler* meter, and Don Giovanni and Zerlina meeting on the middle-class ground of the *contredanse.*

In a cemetery—a scene designed to foreshadow the finale of the opera—Don Giovanni confronts the equestrian statue of Donna Anna's father, the Commendatore, whom he killed in the duel at the beginning of the opera. In ominous tones, a voice from the ghostly statue reproaches him for his wickedness, and Don Giovanni, as a grim joke, responds by inviting the statue to dinner.

The final scene is set at the fateful dinner. Like many nobles of his time, Don Giovanni has his own house orchestra standing by to play dinner music. This wind group plays snatches from two popular Italian operas by Mozart's rivals. Mozart also introduced a delightful bit of humor by quoting a popular aria from his own *Marriage of Figaro,* which happened to be a hit tune of that season, not the classic it is now.

Uninvited, Donna Elvira enters and makes a final unsuccessful attempt to compel Don Giovanni to change his life and save his soul. In an agitated state, she rushes out, and at the door her shriek indicates that she has seen the statue's approach. With fatefully heavy footsteps, the monument sings a rigid musical line reinforced by the funereal sounds of trombones, instruments long associated with solemn church festivals and burial services. The contrast between the living and the dead is brought out by the statue's stiff melody, around which all the other characters react in ways that vary from farce to frustration and tragedy.

When Don Giovanni takes the hand of his marble guest, the Storm and Stress horror music that was foreshadowed in the overture is heard. Strings play spine-tingling scale figures upward and downward, alternately soft and loud. Thunder roars, demons shout, and flames shoot upward. The Don, unrepentant to the last, goes to his doom on a descending scale. The other characters arrive breathless, too late for the excitement but in time to sing a final quintet to these words: "Sinner, pause, and ponder well / Mark the end of Don Juan! / Are you going to Heaven or Hell?"

CHINOISERIE

Ever since Marco Polo's time, China had been pictured in the West as an exotic dreamland of rising pagodas, silk fabrics, and fragrant teas. The Dutch East India Company's international success, which included trade with China, did not alter that image and increased the taste for Chinese imports and rococo fantasies based on what were thought to be Chinese themes. A vogue for things Chinese, called *Chinoiserie,* took England by storm in the mideighteenth century. The importation of fine porcelain objects and tableware so different from the pottery made in Europe made a great impression in the West. Indeed, the very word *china* is now used to refer to the plates and cups from which we eat and drink. Poets sang the praises of this fabled land, and the popularity of Chinese tea grew so quickly that it rapidly became the English national drink. In well-to-do circles, tea drinking became a daily ritual. Some great houses decorated special rooms in Chinese fashion for the ceremony. England's most famous furniture designer, Thomas Chippendale, published an illustrated catalogue that featured Chinese chairs and tables for use at teatime. Upon returning from China, William Chambers, one of the leading architects of the century, built a tall pagoda for London's park at Kew Gardens (Fig. 16.21). Soon thereafter, pagodas and

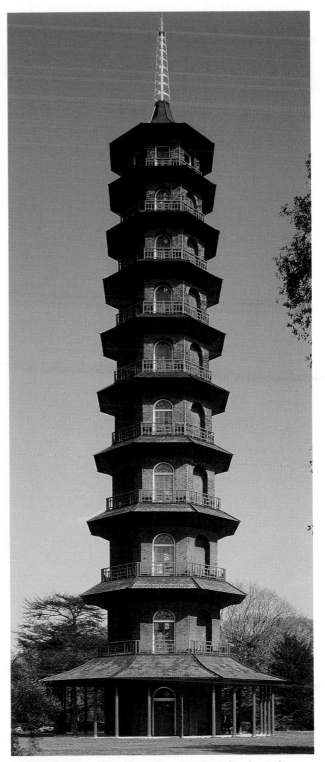

16.21 William Chambers. Pagoda, Kew Gardens, Surrey, England.

Chinese-inspired gazebos for afternoon tea sprang up in the gardens of country houses throughout England.

In addition, collectors began purchasing works of Chinese art. The Chinese invented a process of making prints from woodblocks. Their drawings and paintings, particularly their superb landscapes, commanded world admiration. The Chinese art collected in the West dwelled on nature. Even when human figures are included, the people do not stand out independently but rather become an integral part of their natural surroundings.

According to Kung Hsien, a seventeenth-century landscapist, pictorial content should include "clouded mountains, mist-enveloped trees, steep rocks, cool springs, plank bridges and rustic dwellings." He also delighted in mountain scenery and the warm relationship between people and the land. The role of the painter, according to Hsien, was to reveal the spirit of nature (Fig. 16.22).

Many Chinese paintings are not meant to be seen all at once; rather, they are revealed gradually as on unfolding screens or unwinding scrolls (Fig. 16.23). A temporal dimension is established as the observer's eye travels over the details, producing an almost cinematic experience. Poetic commentaries in elegant Chinese characters are often included; in fact, the Chinese consider calligraphy to be one of the fine arts.

IDEAS: EIGHTEENTH-CENTURY RATIONALISM AND THE ENLIGHTENMENT

Baroque rationalism had been the province of a few outstanding minds. Isaac Newton had projected his image of a universe in which all phenomena obeyed certain predictable cosmic laws. John Locke taught that all knowledge comes through the experience of the senses, including common sense. He suggested that the human mind at birth was a *tabula rasa*—a blank slate to be written on by the social environment. He also helped formulate what became Western *empiricism,* that is, the gathering of facts and observations as primary steps in securing knowledge. René Descartes made his famous pronouncement, "I think; therefore I am," while pointing out that only the things he observed clearly and distinctly could be true.

In the eighteenth century, scientific knowledge became the common property of the educated, a diverse and growing group that ranged from amateur scientists among the well-to-do to members of the middle class, who often used learning as a ladder up the economic slope. Accordingly, baroque rationalism broadened its base and its scope of ideas, evolving into the Enlightenment, an intellectual movement that embraced rationalism, scientific inquiry, an inventive spirit, an optimistic worldview, and a belief in progress.

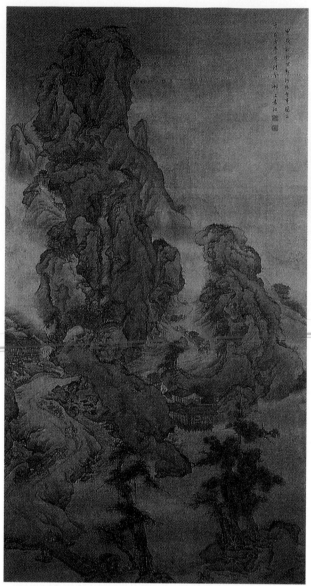

16.22 Yuan Chiang. *Carts on a Winding Mountain Road,* 1694. Hanging scroll (laid down on panel), ink and color on silk, 5′11¼″ × 3′¾″. Ch'ing Dynasty (1644–1911). The Nelson-Atkins Museum of Art, Kansas City, Missouri.

As the streams of rationalism and academicism met, one of the most characteristic expressions of the Enlightenment became the seventeen-volume *Encyclopédie* edited by Denis Diderot and Jean d'Alembert. In this *Classified Dictionary of the Sciences, Arts, and Trades,* some 180 outstanding minds made available in clear language all the knowledge that before then had existed only in obscure scientific treatises. Most of the major French intellectuals contributed their expertise, with Voltaire writing the historical parts, Montesquieu those on political science, Rousseau the sections on music, Diderot himself the philosophical and critical articles, and so on down the list. The encyclopedists were convinced

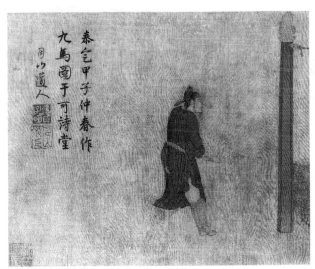

16.23 Jen Jen-fa. *Nine Horses (Chiu ma),* detail, 1324. Hand scroll, ink and color on silk, 1′⅝″ × 8′7″. Yuan Dynasty (1271–1368). The Nelson-Atkins Museum of Art, Kansas City, Missouri.

that the world was knowable if only knowledge could be gathered, classified, and most important, distributed. To them, men and women were rational beings, held back only by political oppression, economic tyranny, and religious superstition.

The Enlightenment spirit of free scientific inquiry was so opposed to religious dogmatism that it came close to becoming a substitute religion. For a time, **deism** became the rational replacement for traditional Catholicism. To the deists, God was a kind of cosmic clockmaker who had created a mechanical universe, wound it up for all eternity, and let it go. In other words, God was not directly involved in the day-to-day workings of the universe. The experimental method of laboratory science became the liturgy of this new orientation, the encyclopedia its bible, nature its church, and all rational people its congregation.

The Enlightenment was also accompanied by a healthy spirit of optimism and a belief in progress and human perfectibility. Theologically, the Christian viewpoint was based on the fall of humanity and the doctrine of original sin dating from the expulsion of Adam and Eve from the Garden of Eden. Philosophically, Plato's theory of knowledge was founded on a doctrine of perfection before birth and the subsequent acquisition of knowledge by the process of remembrance. Humanists, such as the historians Edward Gibbon and Johann Joachim Winckelmann, believed in the intellectual and artistic paradise of ancient Greece and Rome, yet they wrote books analyzing their declines and endings, as if to point out that nothing—not even the best things—are permanent.

Without denying the greatness of the ancient writers and artists, the champions of the Enlightenment were well aware that they had gone far beyond classical science and believed that if they applied rational processes properly they would eventually surpass it. This view was a continuation and expansion of the late seventeenth-century French quarrel between the so-called ancients, who believed that classical art was the best model for contemporary work, and the so-called moderns, who held that modern artists had improved on ancient art (see p. 411). Kant enthusiastically hailed Rousseau as the Newton of the moral world, and Condorcet, in his *Progress of the Human Spirit,* listed the ten stages by which humanity had raised itself from ignorance and savagery to the threshold of perfection. Material progress was an observable fact, and because the many secrets held by nature could be unlocked by reason, eventually rational humans could control their environment. If all mental and moral powers were used to their fullest extent, the argument ran, human development could go in one direction only: onward and upward.

Although the fruits of rationalism became the common property of the middle class, *reason,* in the vocabulary of the eighteenth century, implied much more than cold intellectuality. Reason was considered to be a mental faculty shared by all who chose to cultivate it through the exercise of good judgment and the development of taste. As applied to the arts, *reason* meant the search for expressive forms and sentiments that were sufficiently universal and valid for all who supported the principles of good taste and judgment. With the broadening of the bases of wealth and education, the middle class was able to rise and challenge the authority and privileges of the aristocracy. Through the power of knowledge released by the Enlightenment, the age-old chains of superstition, intolerance, and fear began to be thrown off. The ideals of freedom championed by reasonable people were eventually written into the American Declaration of Independence and Bill of Rights and became the moving force behind the French Revolution. Increasingly, it was the middle class who wrote and read books, constructed and lived in buildings, painted and bought pictures, and composed and listened to music.

The philosophy of the Enlightenment did not, however, go unchallenged. Undercurrents of irrationalism were found in movements that anticipated nineteenth-century Romanticism. Rousseau, for example, gave sensibility a deeper emotional tone. In France, England, and Germany, sensibility meant tugging at the heartstrings of readers, observers, and listeners. This tendency was also evident in the

Storm and Stress movement. Although the Enlightenment was trying to tame nature and bring it under human control, the *Sturm und Drang* authors reveled in nature's unbridled power and how it worked its obscure and mysterious will on humanity. During the height of the Enlightenment, for instance, Storm and Stress artist Henry Fuseli powerfully portrayed the blinded mythological giant Polyphemus (Fig. 16.24) in a pose modeled on one of the damned souls in Michelangelo's *Last Judgment,* just as Rodin was later to do for his *Thinker.* Fuseli portrays a helpless humanity struggling vainly to realize its strength and potential. Blinded by ignorance, it cannot see the light of self-knowledge. Similarly, in Goethe's early drama, Faust was a rebel against all accepted forms of wisdom, especially those arrived at through mathematical or scientific formulas. Both Faust and Don Giovanni were engaged in a quest for emotional truth and succeeded in unleashing the infernal forces that eventually consumed them. Goethe's characterizations of Faust and Prometheus and Mozart's adaptation of Don Juan show these individuals to be independent human beings. They defied convention and demanded a range of inner and outer experience, even if they had to pay the penalty of eternal torment.

The truth such figures sought was one of feeling rather than logic, and their curiosity was boundless. By bursting the bonds of civilized restraints, they were in full rebellion against hereditary aristocratic privilege as well as stern middle-class morality. Their freedom was far from that of Enlightenment thought. It was, in fact, an antirationalistic, antiuniversal, powerfully individualistic freedom that bordered on self-destruction and anarchy.

The eighteenth century as a whole was marked by a quickening of the pulse of human affairs. The flood of material from the printing presses alone made it all but impossible to keep up with the pace set in philosophy, literature, and music. The spread of wealth led to the development of urban centers and widespread building projects. Writers, painters, and musicians no longer aimed their output exclusively at one social group.

Although it is often called the Age of Reason, the eighteenth century gave birth to some of the most bizarre and irrational beings, real or imaginary, ever conceived by the mind or imagination. The passionate disputes begun in the seventeenth century continued, but on the surface at least the divisions did not appear to be so sharp. The unresolvable oppositions of the baroque were softened in subtle satires, gentle ironies, witty verbal dueling, and nostalgic melancholies. What appeared to be a period of comparative quiet, however, was but the calm before the storm, the prelude to a social explosion that brought the aristocratic rococo to a violent, revolutionary end and hurled into the next century the conflicting forces of reason and emotion it had generated.

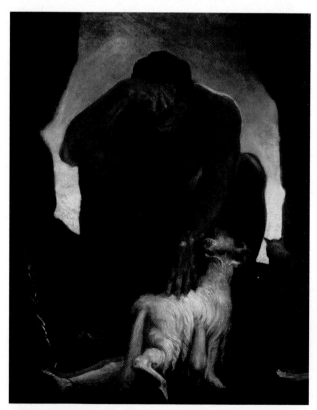

16.24 Henry Fuseli. *The Blinded Polyphemus, at the Entrance to His Cave, Strokes the Ram under Which Odysseus Lies Concealed,* 1803. Oil on canvas, 2'11¾" × 2'4". Swiss Institute for Art Research.

YOUR RESOURCES

- ***Exploring Humanities CD-ROM***

  ○ Interactive Map: Napoleonic Europe, 1800–1815

  ○ Comparing Early Modern Art Module

  ○ Comparing Early Modern Architecture Module

  ○ Readings—Montesquieu, selected books from *The Spirit of Laws*

- ***Web Site***

  http://art.wadsworth.com/fleming10

  ○ Chapter 16 Quiz

  ○ Links—Online Readings—Swift, *Gulliver's Travels*

- ***Audio CD***

  ○ Mozart, *Don Giovanni*

THE EIGHTEENTH CENTURY

Key Events	Architecture and Visual Arts	Literature and Music
	1656–1723 **Johann Fischer von Erlach** ★	
	1664–1726 **John Vanbrugh** ★	
	1667–1754 **Germain Boffrand** ★	1667–1745 **Jonathan Swift** ◆
	1668–1745 **Lukas von Hildebrandt** ★	1668–1733 **François Couperin** ❑
	1684–1721 **Antoine Watteau** ▲	1683–1764 **Jean-Philippe Rameau** ❑
	1685–1766 **Dominikus Zimmermann** ★	1688–1744 **Alexander Pope** ◆
	1687–1753 **Balthasar Neumann** ★	1689–1761 **Samuel Richardson** ◆
	1696–1770 **Giovanni Battista Tiepolo** ▲	1694–1778 **Voltaire (François-Marie Arouet)** ◆
	1697–1764 **William Hogarth** ▲	1698–1782 **Pietro Metastasio** ◆
	1698–1782 **Ange-Jacques Gabriel** ★	
	1699–1779 **Jean-Baptiste-Siméon Chardin** ▲	

1700

Key Events	Architecture and Visual Arts	Literature and Music
1704 **Marlborough** defeats Louis XIV in battle of Blenheim	1703–1770 **François Boucher** ▲	1707–1754 **Henry Fielding** ◆
1705 **Blenheim Palace** begun by Vanbrugh	1714–1785 **Jean-Baptiste Pigalle** ●	1712–1778 **Jean-Jacques Rousseau** ◆
1709 **Ancient Herculaneum** discovered	1716–1791 **Étienne Falconet** ●	1712 *The Rape of the Lock* by Alexander Pope (revised 1717)
1715 **Louis XIV** died	1723–1796 **William Chambers** ★	1713–1784 **Denis Diderot** ◆
1715–1774 **Louis XV,** king of France	1724 **Belvedere Palace, Vienna,** finished; Hildebrandt, architect	1714–1788 **Carl Philipp Emanuel Bach** ❑
		1714–1787 **Christoph Willibald Gluck** ❑
		1717–1768 **Johann Joachim Winckelmann** ◆
		1724–1804 **Immanuel Kant** ◆

1725

Key Events	Architecture and Visual Arts	Literature and Music
	1725–1805 **Jean-Baptiste Greuze** ▲	1726 *Gulliver's Travels* by Jonathan Swift
	1732–1806 **Jean-Honoré Fragonard** ▲	1728 *Beggar's Opera* by John Gay (1685–1732) performed in London
	1732 **Hotel de Soubise, Paris,** begun; Boffrand, architect	1728 *The Dunciad* by Alexander Pope
	1738–1814 **Clodion (Claude Michel)** ●	1729–1781 **Gotthold Ephraim Lessing** ◆
1740–1780 **Maria Theresa,** empress of Austria	1741–1825 **Henry Fuseli** ▲	1730–1774 **Oliver Goldsmith** ◆
1740–1786 **Frederick the Great,** king of Prussia	1741–1828 **Jean-Antoine Houdon** ●	1732–1799 **Pierre-Augustin Caron de Beaumarchais** ◆
1748 **Pompeii** discovered, excavations begun	1744 **Schönbrunn Palace** built in Vienna (begun 1696 by Fischer von Erlach)	1732–1809 **Joseph Haydn** ❑
	1745–1754 **Wieskirche** built near Steingaden	1737–1794 **Edward Gibbon** ◆
		1744–1803 **Johann Gottfried von Herder** ◆
		1748 *Spirit of Laws* by Montesquieu
		1749–1832 **Johann Wolfgang von Goethe** ◆
		1749–1838 **Lorenzo da Ponte** ◆

1750

Key Events	Architecture and Visual Arts	Literature and Music
		1751–1772 *Encyclopédie, or A Classified Dictionary of the Sciences, Arts, and Trades,* published by Denis Diderot
1754 **Thomas Chippendale** published *Gentleman and Cabinet Maker's Directory,* which included models for Chinese chairs and cabinetry	1755–1842 **Élisabeth Vigée-Lebrun** ▲	1752 **Pergolesi's** *Serva Padrona* performed in Paris; Guerre des Bouffons, "war" in Paris over serious versus comic opera
	1757 **William Chambers** published *Designs of Chinese Buildings, Furniture, Dresses, etc.*	1756–1791 **Wolfgang Amadeus Mozart** ❑
1762–1796 **Catherine the Great,** empress of Russia	1762 **William Chambers** built Pagoda in Kew Gardens, London	1759–1805 **Friedrich von Schiller** ◆
1774–1792 **Louis XVI,** king of France	1762–1768 **Petit Trianon, Versailles,** built by Louis XV for Mme. Dubarry; Gabriel, architect	1759 *Candide* by Voltaire
		1762 *Social Contract* by Rousseau; Gluck's *Orpheus* performed in Vienna
		1774 **Gluck's** *Orpheus* and *Iphigenia in Aulis* performed in Paris

1775

Key Events	Architecture and Visual Arts	Literature and Music
1776 **American Declaration of Independence**		1775–1817 **Jane Austen** ◆
1780–1790 **Joseph II,** emperor of Austria		1775 **Beaumarchais's** *Barber of Seville* presented in Paris
1789 **French Revolution** begun		1776 *Storm and Stress,* play by Maximilian Klinger (1752–1831), gave name to art movement
1789 **Washington** elected president		1781 **Mozart** settled in Vienna; *Critique of Pure Reason* by Kant
1793 **Louis XVI** executed; France declared republic		1784 **Beaumarchais's** play *Marriage of Figaro* presented; 1786 Mozart's opera *Marriage of Figaro* performed in Vienna
		1787 **Mozart's** *Don Giovanni* performed in Prague; 1788 performed in Vienna
		1790 *Faust, a Fragment* by Goethe, published in Leipzig
		1794 *Progress of the Human Spirit* by Condorcet
		1797 *Sense and Sensibility* by Jane Austen; published in 1811

★ - Architect ❑ - Musician ▲ - Painter ● - Sculptor ◆ - Writer

1800

CHARLES DARWIN, *ORIGIN OF SPECIES,* 1859
AMERICAN CIVIL WAR, 1861–1865
PARIS COMMUNE, 1870–1871

1900

SIGMUND FREUD, *THE INTERPRETATION OF DREAMS,* 1900
ALBERT EINSTEIN, THEORY OF RELATIVITY, 1905–1915
WRIGHT BROTHERS' FIRST FLIGHT, 1903
WORLD WAR I, 1914–1918
RUSSIAN REVOLUTION, COMMUNIST REGIME, 1917–1921

1925

STOCK MARKET CRASHES, 1929
THE GREAT DEPRESSION, 1930s
RISE OF NAZISM IN GERMANY, 1930s
SPANISH CIVIL WAR, 1936–1939
WORLD WAR II, 1939–1945
EXISTENTIALISM, 1930–1950s

1940

UNITED NATIONS ORGANIZED, 1945
ATOMIC BOMB DEVASTATES HIROSHIMA AND NAGASAKI, 1945

1960

FIRST MANNED SPACE FLIGHT, 1961
JOHN F. KENNEDY ASSASSINATED, 1963

1989

OPENING OF BERLIN WALL, 1989, COLLAPSE OF SOVIET UNION
GULF WAR, 1990s

2000

HUMAN DNA SEQUENCE ESTABLISHED
SEPTEMBER 11, 2001, ATTACKS ON THE UNITED STATES
GULF WAR II

PART FIVE

REVOLUTIONARY PERIOD

The modern age swept in on a tidal wave of rapid change in the fundamental aspects of life, knowledge, and work. Industrial, social, political, technological, scientific, and cultural transformations gathered strength and speed, overwhelming traditional ways of life. Fundamental beliefs were washed away. Ideas about society, the processes of nature, and the structure of the universe were changed. In the age of reason, scientific knowledge had been greatly expanded but remained largely theoretical. But in the modern world, scientific principles were applied to practical problems; machinery revolutionized agriculture, manufacturing, communications, mining, and warfare, altering the Western world.

"Man is born free and is everywhere in chains," Rousseau wrote in his *Social Contract.* The slogan was echoed in the midnineteenth century in the words of Karl Marx: "Workers of the world, unite. You have nothing to lose but your chains." The fetters were those of ignorance, superstition, poverty, and a social structure based on hereditary privilege, class distinction, and the divine right of kings. Rousseau and other philosophers were heartened by the American Revolution. The American colonies showed that political freedom, religious tolerance, and the goals of life, liberty, and the pursuit of happiness could co-exist. The French Revolution, with its ideals of liberty, equality, and fraternity, soon followed.

A swift sequence of inventions throughout the nineteenth century sped up the production and marketing of manufactured and raw goods. Initial advances such as the railroad and the steamboat were followed in the twentieth century by the automobile and airplane. The harnessing of electricity helped relieve human labor. Moreover, it led to mass media, first with high-speed presses and radio, then with sound recordings, motion pictures, television, and the Internet. Mass production, automation, laser beams, satellites, space exploration, and the computer transformed the conditions of human life in less than a century.

As awesome as the consequences of the Industrial Revolution were the effects of the scientific revolution on the understanding of nature. In the midnineteenth century, Darwin revolutionized the life sciences by demonstrating that creation was a continuous evolutionary process. In the struggle for existence, species needed constantly to adapt to their environment, he wrote. Through Herbert Spencer's popularizing of Darwin's work and words, natural selection came to be understood as the survival of the fittest.

In the twentieth century, Einstein's theory of relativity and the development of quantum theory produced a revolution in physics. Einstein created the picture of the universe as a four-dimensional, space-time continuum. Space and time as separate absolutes were replaced by space-time in the light of relativity; light was joined to time, and time to space, opening up a new concept of nature, not only for the starry cosmos but also for the ultimate tiny particles that are the basic building blocks of the universe.

Twentieth-century artists have been constantly producing revolutions of their own. As in all previous periods, the arts have reflected emotional and intellectual trends, continuing to give voice to the eternal hopes and fears of humanity.

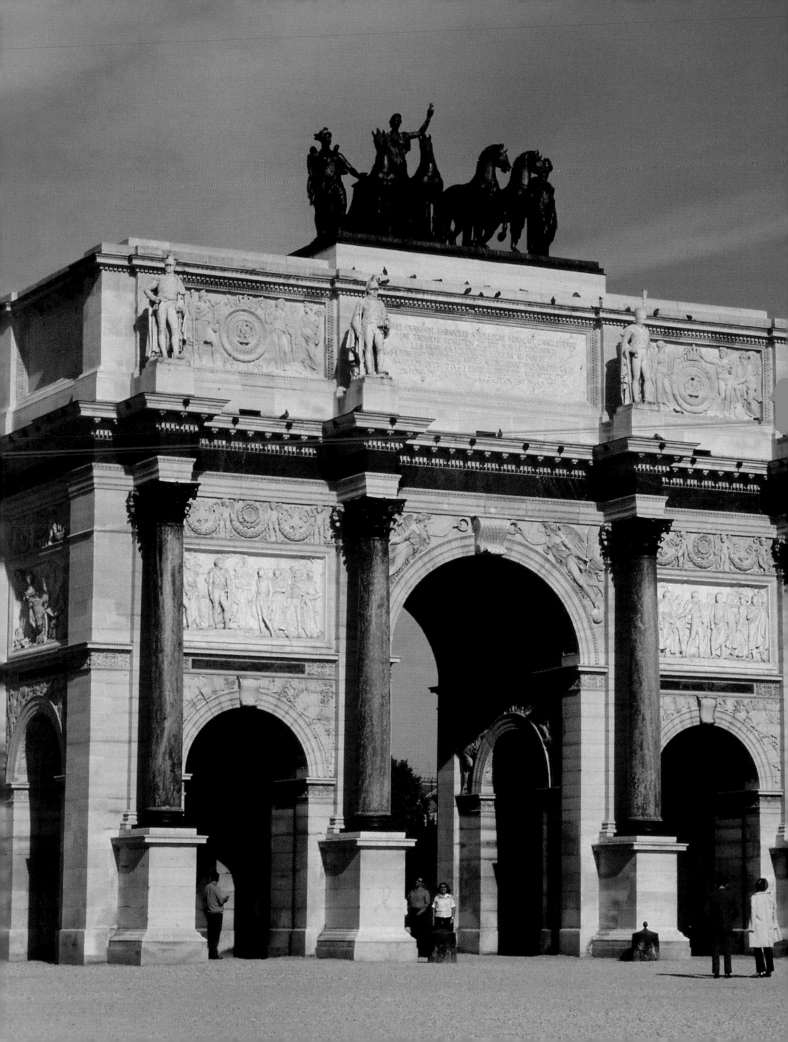

N E O C L A S S I C I S M :
S T Y L E   A N D   R E A C T I O N

PARIS WAS THE EUROPEAN STAGE on which dramatic fluctuations in political thought, governmental forms, and styles of art were played out during the latter part of the eighteenth and early nineteenth centuries. The overture to this great drama came with two world-shaking events: the American Declaration of Independence from Britain in 1776 and the French Revolution, which began the process of overthrowing the monarchy, in 1789. In a set of dizzying reversals, the confident optimism that accompanied the events of 1789 and impressed progressives throughout Europe was promptly followed by the weak constitutional government and mayhem that ultimately became known as the Reign of Terror because of the imprisonment and execution of many individuals suspected of anti-Revolutionary sentiments. At roughly the same time, France pursued war with Austria and Prussia and then with a coalition of other European nations.

In response to this social turbulence, various forms of government alternated with each other in quick succession. After 1789, France experienced three types of monarchies, two kinds of constitutional republics, and six coups d'état. In one of these coups the successful military leader, Napoleon, came to power, declaring an end to the Revolution. The period of his rule, first as consul and then, after 1804, as emperor, witnessed a mix of progressive reform and self-righteous authoritarian rule.

THE EMERGENCE
OF NEOCLASSICISM

Even before these vast upheavals, leaders in art and architecture, as well as government, increasingly turned to ancient Greece and Rome for precedents. The urge to locate a more perfect world in antiquity, especially one of art and literature, had possessed the ancient Romans, who prized Greek statues, pottery, and writing. In a sense, Roman culture was the first to create a *neo*classical era. In Western culture, the term **neoclassical** is generally applied to the period in European and North American thought that extends from about the middle of the eighteenth century to the early nineteenth century. At the time, it was referred to as the "true style." Neoclassicism overlaps the Enlightenment, of which it was a product. Since this era, classical themes and visual sources have waxed and waned but have never vanished from Western culture or those areas of the world that have been colonized or influenced by it. Greco-Roman mythology still underlies much contemporary astronomy, poetry, and even popular culture. (The Nike brand took the name of a minor Greek goddess.) Classical columns continue to adorn buildings around a world in which athletes still compete in the Olympic Games.

During the eighteenth century, two important books about art made a timely appearance. In 1762, Stuart and Revett, English scholars who had visited Greece, published *Antiquities of Athens,* which made a much-needed differentiation between Greek and Roman architecture. Two years later, Johann Joachim Winckelmann's highly influential landmark, *History of Ancient Art,* was published and has remained in print ever since. Winckelmann declared that "the principal and universal characteristic of the masterpieces of Greek art is a noble simplicity and a quiet grandeur." Moreover, he linked the spirit of the art to the inner life of the Greeks: "As the depth of the sea remains always at rest, however, the surface may be agitated, so the expression in the figures of the Greeks reveals in the midst of passion a great and steadfast soul."

Winckelmann's words provided critics of the rococo style with aesthetic ammunition to fire at what they found frivolous and immoral in the subject matter of paintings by François Boucher and Jean-Honoré Fragonard (see Figs. 16.8 and 16.9).

During revolutionary times, the voice of Enlightenment philosopher Denis Diderot was prized, especially his opinion that the major function of art was to make "virtue adorable and vice repugnant."

Ancient Rome became a symbol of revolutionary dissent. In politics, this meant admiration for a republican rather than a monarchical form of government. In religion, a tolerant paganism was promoted as an alternative to Christianity. (For a brief time after the French Revolution, the Cathedral of Notre Dame in Paris was rededicated to the "Goddess of Reason.") In political and economic life, veneration of Rome entailed supporting the weak against the strong and equalizing the possession of wealth, even though Republican Rome was far from a democracy.

This spirit is captured in Angelica Kauffmann's *Cornelia Pointing to Her Children as Her Treasures* (Fig. 17.1). As the story goes, a friend had been displaying her jewels to Cornelia. When asked to show hers, Cornelia pointed to her two sons, who grew up to become social reformers in ancient Rome. They eventually led the effort to repossess public lands that had been taken over by the rich in order to redistribute them to the poor. The severe simplicity of the composition is in keeping with neoclassical ideals. Kauffmann was a Swiss-born, Italian-trained painter who became one of the leading figures of neoclassicism. She met Winckelmann in Rome, made his portrait, and was inspired by his enthusiasm. Unlike many women painters, who were confined to flower painting, still lifes, and portraiture, Kauffmann pursued the male-dominated business of history painting, that is, painting that draws its subjects from mythology, religion, or historical events. Because of her international success, she became one of only two women who were admitted to the Royal Academy of Arts in London.

Heroism and self-sacrifice, rugged resolve, and Spartan simplicity became hallmarks of the revolutionary spirit. Reflections of these qualities were easily found in Roman literature and art. The political writings of Cicero and Seneca were widely read and quoted to confirm the principle that sovereignty resided in the people and that government ought to be based on a voluntary agreement among citizens. Political pamphlets were studded with quotations from the Romans Tacitus, Sallust, and Horace, and the oratory of the period imitated that of Cicero.

The convention hall where French revolutionary legislators met was lined with laurel-crowned statues of Solon, Camillus, and other ancient statesmen. In debates, the speakers relied on apt phrases from Cicero to clinch important points. They referred to their followers as Brutuses and Catos and to their opponents as Catilines, that is,

17.1 Angelica Kauffmann. *Cornelia Pointing to Her Children as Her Treasures,* c. 1785. Oil on canvas, 3′4″ × 4′2″. Virginia Museum of Fine Arts, Richmond, Virginia. The Adolph D. and Wilkins C. Williams Fund.

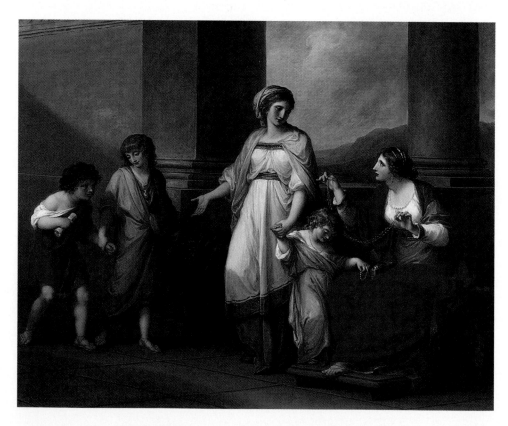

enemies of Rome. They modeled their postures and gestures on those of Roman statues, and their oaths were sworn on the head of Brutus or by the immortal gods.

All those who could read became biography-conscious and spoke like living characters out of Plutarch's *Parallel Lives*. (On the day she murdered the revolutionary hero Marat, Charlotte Corday spent her time reading Plutarch.) Never before had public personalities seemed so obviously to have walked straight out of books and art galleries. Many of the symbols of the French Revolution were borrowed directly from antiquity. The cap of liberty was a copy of the Phrygian cap worn by liberated slaves in Rome. The French Revolutionaries also adopted an emblem of Roman authority, the **fasces,** a bundle of sticks bound with an ax whose blade protruded. In ancient Rome it had been carried in front of a magistrate to signify political power vested in the common bond that united the people (see Fig. 16.19).

DAVID AND NEOCLASSICISM

The most articulate champion of revolutionary fervor and ancient Roman heroism was Jacques-Louis David, a painter whose temperament and technique were suited to the spirit of the times. A reformer by nature and a classical enthusiast by nurture, David painted pictures whose austerity was a conscious reaction to the rococo extravagances exemplified in the work of his cousin, François Boucher. By virtue of his studies in Rome, David absorbed all that was necessary for the enthusiastic French readers of Plutarch's *Parallel Lives* and Winckelmann's *History of Ancient Art.* Influenced by Diderot and other stern moralists during the days before the French Revolution, David did not conceive of a painting as a pleasure but rather as a spur to moral rectitude and political action. Bourgeois by birth and upbringing, David frankly addressed his art to the newly established middle-class social order.

ANCIENT ROMAN SUBJECTS IN SERVICE OF THE REVOLUTION

David's first great success was *The Oath of the Horatii* (Fig. 17.2), commissioned by one of the Louis XVI agencies while he was still on the throne. The subject, one of the legends about the founding of the Roman Republic, may have been suggested by Pierre Corneille's ballet *Les Horaces* (The Horatii), although the specific scene does not appear in the dance. The three arches of the severely simple setting separate the figures like niches for statuary. In the center stands Horatius Proclus, dedicating the swords of his three sons, who swear to defend the Roman Republic against the plotting Curiatii,

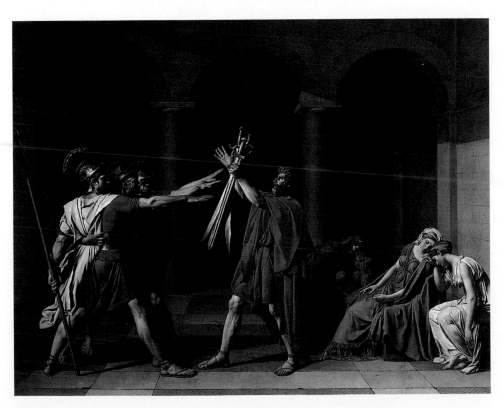

17.2   Jacques-Louis David. *Oath of the Horatii,* 1784. Oil on canvas, 10'10" × 14'. Louvre, Paris, France.

one of whom is the fiancé of their grief-stricken sister on the right. Manly virtue literally stands up to the test of courage, whereas feminine sensitivity, a clear symbol of overly refined rococo emotion, caves in with tears and terrors. David acknowledged his debt to the past. "If I owe my subject to Corneille," he said, "I owe my picture to Poussin." Clarity of contour, sculptural sharpness of modeling, and the hard, clear handling of light and shadow characterize this stark but heroic canvas.

David's *The Lictors Bringing Back to Brutus the Bodies of His Sons* (Fig. 17.3) bears the date 1789, the fateful year the French Revolution commenced. One finds the same strict spirit of self-sacrifice in this painting that appears in *The Oath of the Horatii*. This severity of style appealed to eyes that were weary of the fussy rococo. The somber setting spiked the interest of those who were reading about the archeological discoveries at Pompeii and Herculaneum. Over time, this painting came to be seen as David's bold way of flaunting the stern, do-or-die virtues of Roman republicanism under the noses of his aristocratic patrons. Nevertheless, it was painted for Louis XVI, who thought that paintings could improve moral behavior. David again chose for his subject an incident from the days soon after the founding of the Roman Republic. Lucius Junius Brutus (foreground left), one of the consuls, discovered that his own sons were involved in a plot to restore the recently overthrown monarchy. Having ordered their executions, he is shown as an isolated figure sitting in the shadow of the goddess Roma. Behind him are the lictors, Roman officers, bearing the dead bodies of his sons, and a third group is formed by his grieving wife and daughters. As in *The Oath of the Horatii,* men bear the brunt of action in the political world, whereas women are too weak and emotional to make decisions and act on them. Many people who were living through the trying times of the Revolution could see something of themselves in Brutus, a figure of stoic resolution, torn between public duty and private grief.

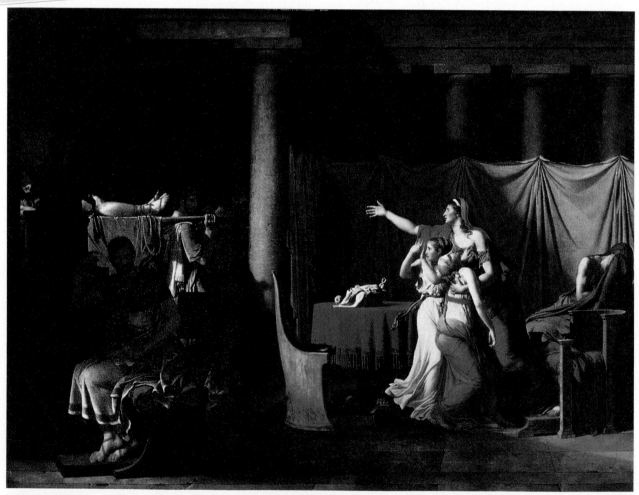

17.3 Jacques-Louis David. *The Lictors Bringing Back to Brutus the Bodies of His Sons*, 1789. Oil on canvas, 10′8″ × 13′10½″. Louvre, Paris, France.

DAVID'S PORTRAITURE

David's portraiture was much in demand. A sensitive example is his portrait of Madame Récamier (Fig. 17.4). One of the most fascinating and intelligent women of the period, she had furnished her salon in the popular Pompeian style. Here she reclines in the classical manner on a chaise lounge, just as she might have done on the days when she received her guests. Her flowing white gown is draped with deep folds reminiscent of antique statuary. The only other pieces of furniture are the footstool and bronze lamp, both drawn from Pompeian originals. The clarity with which David handles the outlines of the figure and the silhouette of the head combine with the austere setting to create an orderly, elegant effect, which is all the more wonderful because Madame Récamier came late to sitting so often that David abandoned the painting unfinished.

After the French Revolution, David took on the role of power broker, with far-reaching effects. He was among those who voted for the death of Louis XVI. In addition, his interests in Greek and Roman antiquities influenced the official art of Europe and America well into the nineteenth century. David's craftsmanship was on a par with that of any of the master painters of the past. Moreover, he influenced future painters like Picasso, who owed some of the cool, objective character of their work to the neoclassical art of David.

IMPERIAL CLASSICISM

When Napoleon Bonaparte rose to power, he shared the popular enthusiasm for antiquity. His chosen models were Alexander the Great and Julius Caesar—especially the latter, because he believed that Caesar's career and his own had many parallels. Napoleon first became a republican consul. Later he ruled France through a tribune. Then, after a plebiscite, he emerged a Roman emperor. The fasces became his emblem of authority. He made the eagles of the Roman legions the insignia of the French battalions. The forms and images of ancient glory had a vast appeal to this man of modest birth.

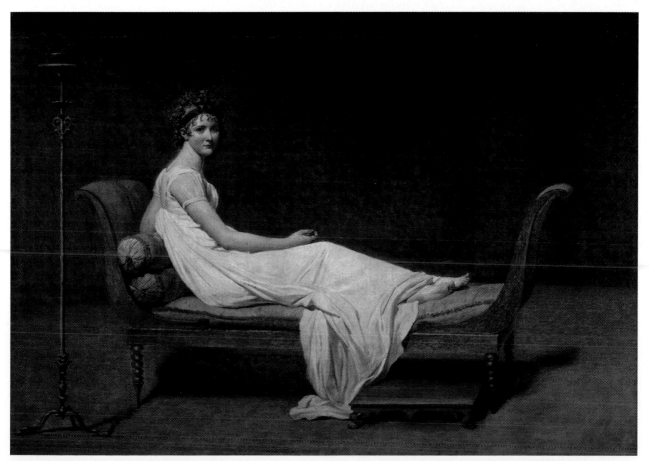

17.4   Jacques-Louis David. *Madame Récamier,* 1780. Oil on canvas, 5′8″ × 7′11¾″. Louvre, Paris, France.

During his brief period on the stage of history, Napoleon envisioned France as the leader of a new Roman Empire. His proclamation to the Italian people on the eve of his invasion of their country exemplifies his view. "We are the friends of all nations," he claimed, "especially the descendants of Brutus, the Scipios, and of the great men we have chosen for our own model." He took frequent pains to point out that he was embarking on a cultural as well as a military mission. He was no barbarian, Attila the Hun, storming the citadel to sack it—he was a conqueror who came in the company of a group of art experts who were aware of the value of antiquities and ready to pack those items up for the trip to France.

In 1796, a petition signed by all the important French artists actually had been sent to the Directory, the regime that ruled France from 1795 to 1799. The petition claimed that the Romans had become civilized by confiscating the art of ancient Greece. The petitioners argued that France would likewise flourish by bringing original works to Paris. Although this returning would-be Caesar brought no human captives back with him, his victory celebration was enlivened by the presence of distinguished "prisoners of war," such as the *Apollo Belvedere* (see Fig. 3.20), many paintings by Raphael, and rare treasures plundered from the Vatican and other Italian collections.

The invasion of Italy, however, had another rationale. The country's northern provinces were under Austrian control. The reactionary monarchists there threatened to invade France not only to avenge the execution of their princess, Marie Antoinette, but also to combat the spread of French revolutionary ideas in their own territories.

ARCHITECTURE AND CITY PLANNING

Napoleon reorganized the government, remade the constitution, and rewrote the laws on the model of the Roman Empire. Apparently, he was determined that Paris should be replanned as a new Rome. He undertook the ordering and commissioning of buildings with the same vigor that marked his activities in other fields.

PARIS: THE NEW ROME

The plan for the heart of the new city maintained the spacious center around the old Place Louis XV, which under the Directory had been renamed the Place de la Concorde (Fig. 17.5). Its axis began on the left bank of the Seine River with the old Palais Bourbon, now the Chamber of Deputies, which was to have its face lifted by a Corinthian colon-

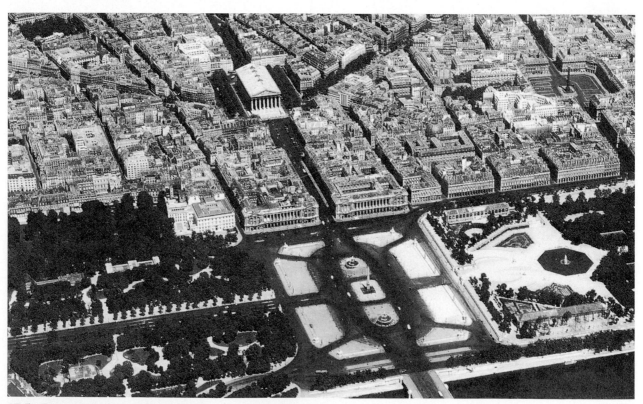

17.5   Place de la Concorde, Paris, France, aerial view.

nade. It continued across the river, via the bridge begun in early revolutionary days (lower center), to the center of the Place, where some statuary was to cover the spot where the guillotine had done its grim work. The end of the axis was to be the unfinished Church of La Madeleine at the end of the Rue Royale, scheduled to be rebuilt in the form of a Roman temple (upper center).

Jacques-Louis David, who worked for Napoleon, introduced him to the architect Pierre F. L. Fontaine. Soon Fontaine and his partner Charles Percier became Napoleon's favorite architects, and he commissioned them to redesign the Rue de Rivoli, which intersected the axis at right angles and ran parallel to the Seine River (middle right). Elsewhere throughout Paris, triumphal arches and monumental columns were erected to fortify the image of Paris as the new Rome. In his memoir, Fontaine recalled discussing possible alterations to the Louvre with Napoleon. The emperor swiftly halted the exchange with the conclusion that what is big is always beautiful.

A TEMPLE OF GLORY

Napoleon envisioned La Madeleine, the uncompleted church that had been started under Louis XVI, as a pagan Temple of Glory with a dedicatory inscription: "From the Emperor to the soldiers of the Great Army." For this project Napoleon chose a plan by Pierre Alexandre Vignon that would cast the church as a large-scale Roman temple of the Corinthian order (see Fig. 4.20A). After Napoleon's downfall, it was completed as a Christian church; however, the structure itself was finished according to Vignon's design (Fig. 17.6). In the Roman manner, La Madeleine stands on a podium 23 feet high and is approached by a flight of steps in the front. It is surrounded by 63-foot Corinthian columns, eighteen on each side and eight on each end, with an additional row of four in front that supports the cornice.

The interior cella of an ancient temple was never intended as a gathering place and was always dark and mysterious. Hence, of necessity, Vignon had to depart from precedent and design

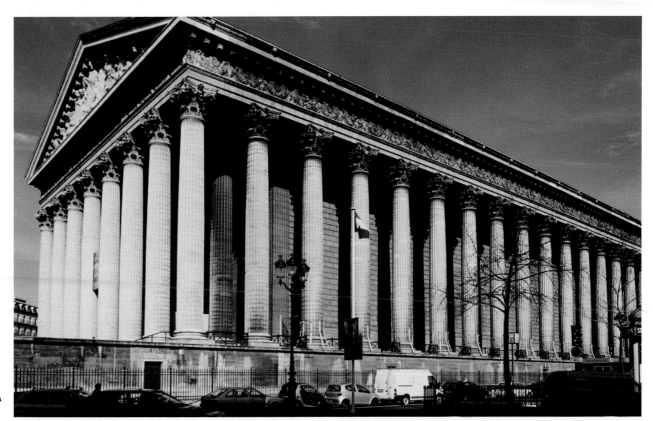

A

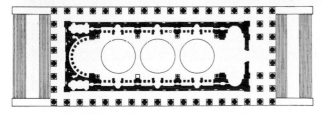

B

17.6 (A) Alexandre-Pierre Vignon, La Madeleine, Paris, 1806–1852. Length 350′, width 147′, height of podium 23′. (B) Plan of La Madeleine.

17.7 Pierre Antoine Demachy. Interior of the Church of the Madeleine, Paris, France. Musée Carnavalet, Paris, France.

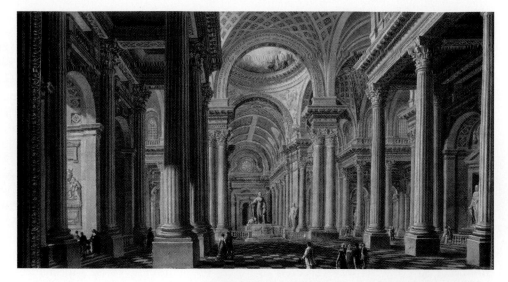

something new. The surprise that awaits the visitor who passes through the massive bronze doors is complete, for the interior and exterior actually amount to two different buildings.

The aisleless nave is divided into three long bays and a choir (Fig. 17.7), which are not roofed in timber as in a Greek temple or vaulted in the Roman manner but rather are crowned with three low saucer-shaped domes on pendentives. The nave ends in a semicircular apse that is roofed by a semidome. Chapels are located in the recesses cre-

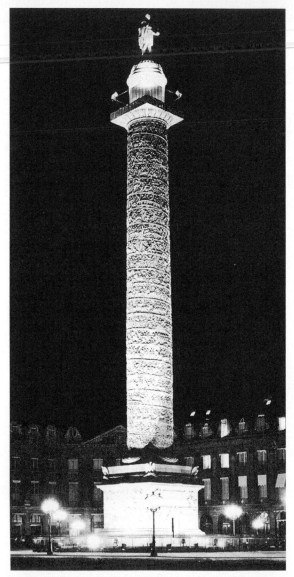

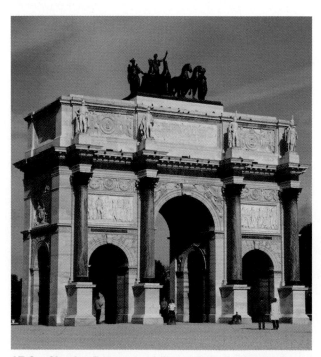

17.8 Charles Percier and Pierre F. L. Fontaine. Arc de Triomphe du Carrousel, Paris, France, 1806. Width 63′6″, height 48′.

17.9 Charles Percier and Pierre F. L. Fontaine. Vendôme Column, Paris, France, 1810. Marble with bronze spiral frieze, height 140′, diameter 13′.

ated by the buttresses that support the domes, and two classical orders—the Corinthian and Ionic—form the basis of the decorative scheme.

ARCHES OF TRIUMPH

In 1806, after winning military victories in Germany and Austria, Napoleon entrusted Percier and Fontaine with the building of a triumphal arch. Now known as the Arc de Triomphe du Carrousel (Fig. 17.8), it was designed as a gate of honor to the Tuileries Palace. It turned out to be a rather slavish imitation of the Arch of Septimius Severus in Rome (compare with Fig. 3.21), although of more modest proportions. Standing on the platform above it, however, was one of Napoleon's proudest battle trophies—the group of four bronze horses taken from St. Mark's in Venice (see Fig. 12.2). Owing to the shifting fortunes of war, Venice later got the horses back as a result of a peace treaty, and a triumphal chariot drawn by horses of considerably later vintage was installed in their place to celebrate the fall of Napoleon and restoration of the old line of Bourbon kings in the person of Louis XVIII. The face of the triumphal arch is decorated with undistinguished carvings in low relief depicting such scenes as the Battle of Austerlitz, the surrender of Ulm, the Peace of Tilsit, and Napoleon's triumphal entries into Munich and Vienna.

When finished, the result did not measure up to Napoleon's imperial ambitions, and a still grander arch was commissioned for the Place de l'Étoile (now Place de Gaulle). In this familiar Paris landmark, the architect Jean François Chalgrin achieved more life and elasticity by freely adapt-

ing rather than copying a known model. French baroque precedents, Roman classical inspiration, and academic correctness of execution merge harmoniously. To give a monumental effect, Chalgrin relied on bold proportions and a grand scale. Later, after Napoleonic times, the severity of the general outline was relieved by the skillful placement of high-relief sculptures by Cortot and Rude (see Fig. 18.6) on a scale comparable to the immense size of the arch.

Still not content, Napoleon ordered a monumental Doric column to be erected in the Place Vendôme (Fig. 17.9). In size and style of ornamentation, it was a conscious copy of Trajan's Column in Rome (see Fig. 4.11). The principal difference was that its spiral relief images were done on a bronze strip made from the guns and cannons captured from the defeated Prussian and Austrian armies. The sculpture recounts the story of the campaign of 1805 in scenes such as Napoleon's address to his troops, the meeting of the three emperors, and the conquests of Istria and Dalmatia.

THE RETURN OF ACADEMIC ART

When Napoleon was deposed in 1814, the Academy was reestablished and Jean-Auguste-Dominique Ingres became the leading figure in the academic art world. He not only championed the arts in official circles but also became a French senator. The idea of placing an official stamp of approval on writers and painters finds full expression in Ingres's huge painting, *Apotheosis of Homer* (Fig. 17.10), which linked French cultural achievement to the classical past.

17.10 Jean-Auguste-Dominique Ingres. *Apotheosis of Homer,* 1827. Oil on canvas, 12′8″ × 16′10¾″. Louvre, Paris, France.

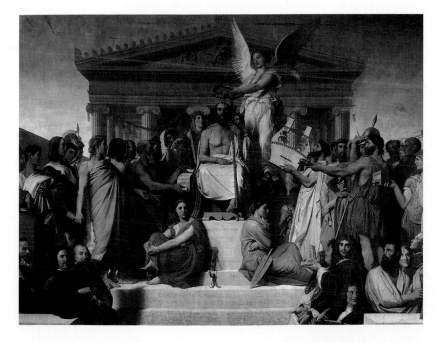

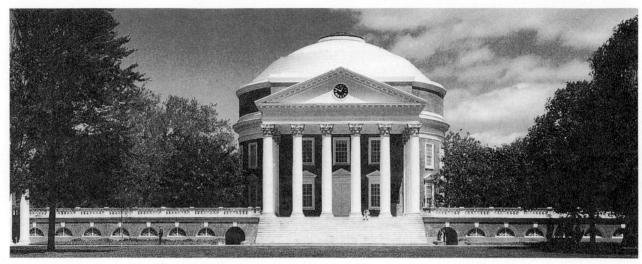

17.11   Thomas Jefferson. Rotunda, University of Virginia, Charlottesville, Virginia, 1819–1826.

Ingres treats his subject, the deification of Homer, as a meeting of the immortal leaders of literature, art, philosophy, and music. In their midst sits the enthroned Homer, the father of poetry. Behind him is the facade of an Ionic temple. Winged Victory holds the laurel wreath above his brow. At his feet are personifications of his epic poems, *The Iliad* and *The Odyssey*, and around him are his successors, who have carried the torch for poetry and art throughout the ages. In this exclusive society, Aeschylus is seen unfolding a scroll listing his tragedies, the poet Pindar holds up his lyre in tribute, Virgil and Dante (extreme left) represent epic poetry, and Longinus is standing up for philosophy. More recent French luminaries have joined the throng. Nicolas Boileau is recognized for his contributions to criticism. At the lower right, Jean Racine and Molière, in the courtly wigs of the time of Louis XIV, make an offering of tragic and comic masks. Raphael, the profiled figure in the upper left, represents Renaissance painting. Below him in the foreground is Nicolas Poussin, and behind him, William Shakespeare.

Ingres's composition exemplifies the neoclassical ideals of clarity, order, and symmetry, while its content calls on the artists of his day to carry on the achievements of their counterparts in the past. He builds his composition by means of precise

17.12   Robert Mills. Treasury Building, Washington, D.C., 1836–1842.

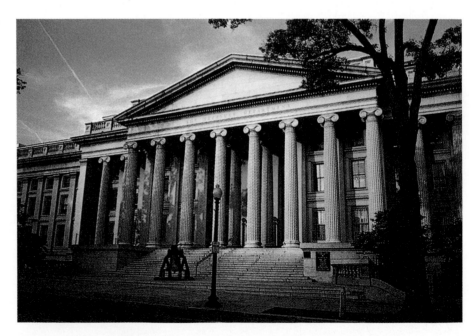

lines, which he organizes into a series of receding planes. Ingres's technical skill in drawing is seen in the sharply defined figures. Like his contemporaries, he accepted what he understood to be the Greek aesthetic of art as a representation of nature, but he insisted that the artist must endow wild nature with orderliness through selection and rearrangement. Given his hard-nosed attitude about the exclusive superiority of Greek art, it is surprising to note that he also produced some of the nineteenth century's most exotic images (see Fig. 18.23).

THE INTERNATIONAL CLASSIC REVIVAL

The wave of enthusiasm for classical architecture and extensive city planning was by no means confined to Paris. Germany, England, and the United States each experienced classical revivals in the eighteenth century. During the early nineteenth century, the Roman revival was strongest in the countries identified with Napoleon's empire, whereas the Greek revival was adopted in the nations that opposed Napoleon, notably England and Germany. In London, public buildings such as the British Museum were strongly Greek in character. In Berlin, the Brandenburg Gate was modeled after the Athenian Propylaea.

After achieving independence, the United States witnessed a wave of public building programs, especially in state capital cities and the new national capital, Washington, D.C., Thomas Jefferson served as ambassador to France during George Washington's presidency. There he became familiar with the neoclassical movement. Jefferson used the Roman Pantheon as the prototype for the design of the Rotunda at the University of Virginia (Fig. 17.11). His model for the Virginia state capitol in Richmond was also based on an ancient Roman temple, the Maison Carrée in Nîmes (see Fig. 4.13), which he studied during his travels in France. The rotunda of the Virginia state capitol became the setting for Jean-Antoine Houdon's life-size representation of George Washington (see Fig. 16.19). Washington rests an arm on the adapted Roman symbol of unity, the fasces (see p. 463), and the simple plow behind him reminds viewers that, adhering to the biblical injunction to beat swords into plowshares, he returned to his estate to farm. In Washington, D.C., other architects revealed Roman influence in the familiar dome-shaped structure of the national capitol, whereas the Treasury Building (Fig. 17.12), with its crisp contours, displays Greek influence in its splendid Ionic colonnade and the pediment above its entrance portico.

SCULPTOR TO THE EMPEROR

The sculptor Antonio Canova, who in his day enjoyed a reputation second to none, was summoned from Rome to Paris by Napoleon to execute statues

PAST AND PRESENT

The Return of Cultural Treasures

During his conquests, Napoleon sent experts to Egypt to select and bring back to France wagonloads of antiquities. He also directed his staff to acquire hundreds of paintings and sculptural works such as the *Laocoön* (see Fig. 3.17) from the Vatican in Rome. In other words, he practiced the age-old custom of taking spoils. Roman aristocrats regularly enriched themselves through the process, yet the well-known phrase, "to the victor belong the spoils," was not coined until the 1830s. The spoils of war include not only art and religious objects but other forms of wealth, such as the South American gold that fueled the Spanish Empire and building projects such as the Escorial palace (see Figs. 13.14 and 13.15). By the early twenty-first century, Western museums and private collections were filled with treasures taken from cultures that had been conquered by war or subjugated through colonization.

Efforts to repatriate cultural treasures have gained strength in recent decades. Greece has never stopped petitioning Britain to return the so-called Elgin marbles, sculpture taken from the Athenian acropolis (see, for example, Fig. 2.12). Many art objects appropriated from Jewish families by the Nazis before and during World War II have been returned. Native American objects acquired in the eighteenth, nineteenth, and twentieth centuries continue to be returned to the cultures that produced them.

Yet the return of cultural treasures is not as simple a matter as it may seem. Around the world, in areas such as India and South America, scores of tribal people disappeared long ago or were absorbed into subsequent cultures. The social and religious customs that inspired their art objects vanished with them. Who, then, should put in a claim for their return? Do the countries where these extinct cultures once lived have a greater claim than the countries that acquired the objects many centuries ago? Until these large issues are resolved through international efforts, it seems that the victors will continue to hold the spoils.

of the emperor and his family. Through his neoclassical eyes, the Italian artist saw Napoleon's mother as the matronly Agrippina of old, Napoleon's sister Pauline—not without some justification—as Venus Victorious (Fig. 17.13), and Napoleon himself as a Roman emperor (Fig. 17.14).

Canova was accompanied to Paris by his brother, who recorded the conversations between artist and patron. From these talks one learns that Napoleon had a few qualms about being portrayed in the "heroic altogether" and suggested an appropriate costume. To this Canova grandiosely replied, "We, like the poets, have our own language. If a poet introduced into a tragedy, phrases and idioms used habitually by the lower classes in the public streets, he would rightly be reprimanded. . . . We sculptors cannot clothe our statues in modern costumes without deserving a similar reproach."

The sculptor's arguments prevailed, and except for the suggestion of a toga draped over his shoulder and a fig leaf, Napoleon stands naked, holding in his right hand an orb surmounted by Winged Victory and in his left, a staff of authority in place of a scepter. His head is idealized but recognizable; the body, with the shifting of the weight toward one side, is clearly based on Praxitelean models (see Fig. 2.22).

Canova's reclining statue of Napoleon's sister Pauline Bonaparte Borghese, entitled *Venus Victorious* (Fig. 17.13), had a Hellenistic model and was a scandalous work that would have reminded those few viewers who were allowed to see it of Etruscan tomb sculpture (see Fig. 4.6). Although it is similar to David's *Madame Récamier* (Fig. 17.4),

the statue conveys much less of the individuality of its subject than does the painting.

Although practically nothing of ancient painting was known to David, museums and collections were filled with well-preserved ancient statues that Canova could study. As a result, the painter was freer to create a new style, but the sculptor had to conform to existing models. Like a good academician and follower of Winckelmann, Canova advised his students on a "scrupulous adherence to rules" and against "arbitrary and capricious errors."

The British Parliament invited Canova to London to evaluate the Parthenon sculptures before purchasing them from Lord Elgin (see Figs. 2.16 and 2.17). After feeling the full force of these originals, the Italian sculptor might have realized their superiority to his previous Roman models. Instead, he found in them the justification of his own life's work and seized the opportunity to point out how wrong his critics had been. He did show good judgment, however, in refusing to attempt a restoration of the original sculptures. History also proved him correct in his observations on the differences between the real Greek sculptures and the works designed for the Roman market.

MUSIC

NAPOLEON AS PATRON

Musicians in Paris were as active as the architects and painters. "Among all the fine arts," Napoleon said, "music is the one which exercises

17.13 Antonio Canova. *Pauline Borghese as Venus Victorious,* 1805. Marble, life-size. Galleria Borghese, Rome, Italy.

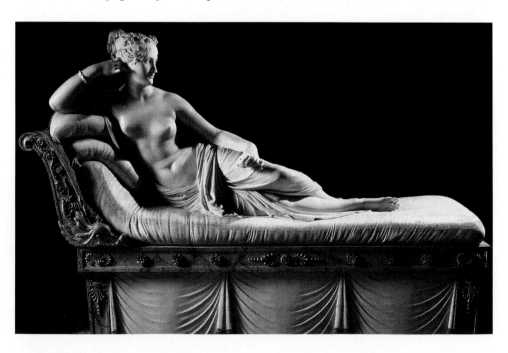

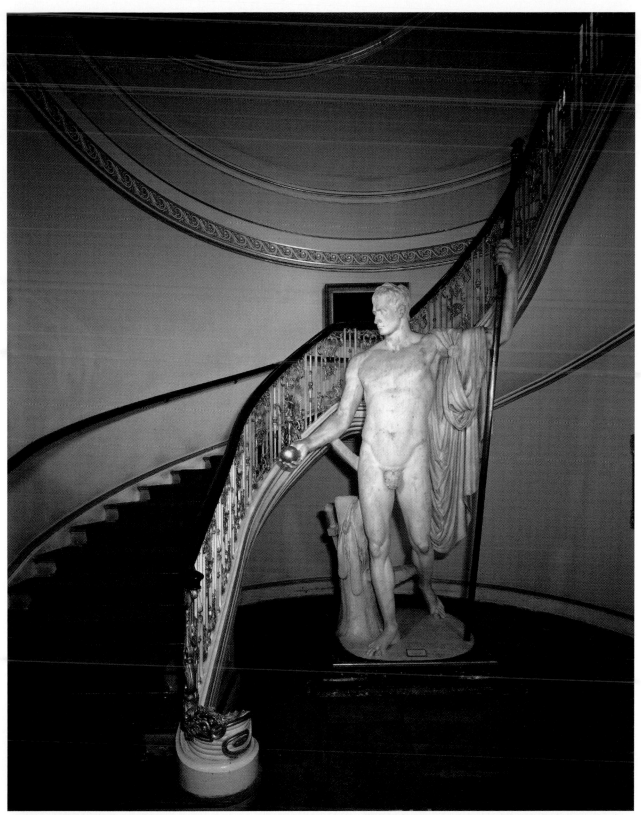

17.14   Antonio Canova. *Napoleon Bonaparte as Mars Pacificator,* 1802–1810. Marble, height 11′8″. Apsley House (Wellington Museum), London, England.

the greatest influence upon the passions and is the one which the legislator should most encourage."

The production that most closely caught the spirit of the new empire was Spontini's opera *La Vestale* (The Vestal Virgin). Appearing in 1807, at the height of Napoleon's military successes, it had the necessary pomp and pageantry to whip public enthusiasm to a frenzy. It had the right Roman setting, and the spectacle of a vestal virgin's struggle between her desire for personal happiness and her vows of service to the state was sufficient to ensure more than 100 performances in its first season in Paris. The plot stressed glory on the battlefield, and Spontini supplied the necessary triumphal marches.

BEETHOVEN: THE HEROIC IDEAL

Unknown to Napoleon, the essence of the heroic ideal was captured in musical form in Austria, one of the countries he had conquered. Ludwig van Beethoven's Third Symphony, which the composer entitled the *Eroica* (Heroic), was never heard by the man whose career had suggested it, nor was it played in Paris until 1828, a quarter of a century after it was composed.

The colossal symphony was the result of Beethoven's desire to honor the heroic Consul Bonaparte and was dedicated to him. But the year in which the symphony was completed was also the year in which Napoleon accepted the title of emperor. Beethoven, feeling that the former apostle of liberty had become both a traitor and a new tyrant, erased the name from the title page and inscribed it instead "to the memory of a great man." That memory stirred Beethoven deeply, for from the days of his youth he had been a lifelong enthusiast for the ideals of the French Revolution—liberty, equality, and fraternity. It was Napoleon's championing of these principles, his opposition to hereditary privilege, and his will and ability to translate these ideals into action that moved Beethoven profoundly.

The Third Symphony is not focused narrowly on Napoleon; it is a broad elaboration of the idea of heroism. When writing music for the theater, Beethoven invariably chose subject matter involving the quest for individual liberty and the cause of popular freedom. For example, in his only opera, *Fidelio,* he selected a story that would reflect high moral purpose and steadfast resolve. However, it is in the fluid forms of his instrumental compositions that the ideals of liberty, equality, and fraternity reached their most abstract and universal expression. Beethoven used the power of his art to convey the spirit of these great human declarations and to urge humanity toward progress and perfectibility. Through the *Eroica* Beethoven gave tangible shape to the goals of a large part of humanity during those thrilling times. He condensed the titanic struggle between the opposing attitudes of submission and assertion, passivity and activity, acceptance and challenge.

The length of the symphony is unprecedented, and Beethoven also expanded the orchestra somewhat. Nevertheless, Beethoven never fell into the trap that many of the French composers of the revolutionary period did when they equated enormous size with grandeur of expression. Although the French revolutionists wrote their choruses for a thousand voices accompanied by cannons and three or four combined orchestras, Beethoven added just one horn to his usual brass section.

THE MOVEMENTS OF THE *EROICA*.   The opening movement is cast in **sonata form,** which might be described as a dramatic reconciliation of opposites or, more technically, as a strategy of thematic and key relationships. Perfected in the late eighteenth century by Haydn and Mozart, this balanced classical design, with its Aristotelian beginning, middle, and end, unfolds with an opening section called an **exposition.** This is followed by a transition to the central core, the **development,** and the movement then concludes with a **recapitulation.** Optionally, a prologue, or **introduction,** and an epilogue, or **coda,** may be added. The exposition presents an abstract dramatic encounter between a protagonist, consisting of related motifs, themes, or subjects within a principal key center (the tonic), and an antagonist, composed of contrasting material in a different key center (the dominant) in the relative major or minor, and so on. The development or working-out portion follows, in which the previously presented materials oppose or conflict and interact with one another. The subjects or themes may be broken up into fragments or segments, new tonal territories may be explored by modulating to new key centers that are close or remote, and themes may be combined in overlapping contrapuntal lines. Finally, the materials are reassembled in the recapitulation, which reveals their altered character in a kind of dramatic reconciliation.

Each of the four movements shattered precedent in its own way. The first is distinguished by its restless, surging character and its enormous expansion of the sonata form to include a development section of unprecedented proportions.

The use of a funeral march as the second movement of the symphony was another innovation. Its heroic proportions, as well as its poetic conception as a glorification of the hero, link it with the first movement. The effect of this march is that of a glowing lamentation for heroes who give up life itself so that the ideals for which they fought may live. The stately measured rhythms and muffled sonorities also reminded the listener of Beethoven's time that contemporary heroes, as well as such ancient ones as Socrates and Jesus, often suffered martyrdom at the hands of a society that did not understand them.

The title "Scherzo" over the third movement appears for the first time in a formal symphony, although it had been used earlier in piano sonatas and chamber music. Beethoven once more reveals himself as a man of the revolutionary period by substituting a robust movement for the traditional minuet.

THE THEME OF PROMETHEUS. The *Eroica* might have been called the Promethean Symphony in honor of Prometheus, who stole divine fire from the hearth of the gods on Mount Olympus and brought it down to animate the bodies and souls of men and women and release them from the bonds of darkness. Fire brings warmth and light, and with light comes enlightenment. Prometheus was adopted as the prime symbol of the Enlightenment in philosophy and social thought, as well as in poetry, art, and drama. He represented for Beethoven, as the poet Percy Bysshe Shelley put it, "the type of the highest perfection of moral and intellectual nature impelled by the purest and truest motives to the best and noblest ends."

Over time, a musical idea associated with Prometheus began to take shape in Beethoven's notebooks. It first saw the light as a simple, popular dance tune, then, in 1801, as a prominent number in his full-length ballet *The Creatures of Prometheus.* The year 1802 saw its use as a theme for an extended set of piano variations. In its most exalted form it at last became the basic material for the great finale of the *Eroica,* where it was transformed into a monumental set of orchestral variations. The music becomes an arch of triumph through which a liberated humanity joyously passes in review.

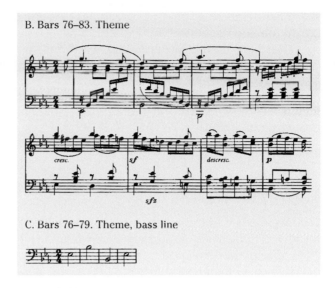

B. Bars 76–83. Theme

C. Bars 76–79. Theme, bass line

The last movement of the *Eroica* begins with a fiery plunging figure for strings, a motif taken from the ballet, in which Prometheus descends from Mount Olympus with torch in hand. The form of the finale is a series of variations that are unequal in length and strongly contrasted in style. The theme itself is unique in that its bass line appears first and is developed. The melody enters later, at which time both elements are combined (see Musical Example 17.1).

By this additive process, Beethoven built this theme into the cumulative structure needed for the victory finale. Some of the variations are aristocratic in sound, whereas others reflect popular idioms of the time. Elegant sonorities contrast with boisterous band music; fugues that use sophisticated contrapuntal devices contrast with a sturdy German chorale.

This vast variety of forms—dances, songs, fugues, chorales—is arranged sequentially in the manner of a procession that eventually leads to the rousing triumphant climax. At this point, Beethoven throws in all his orchestral forces, including the brasses and drums, to bring about the image of the ultimate achievement of the heroic ideal.

In the finales of three of his symphonies, Beethoven envisioned the emergence of a strong and free human society, and all three start with themes in the popular style of his time. In the *Eroica,* it is a modest little country dance; in the Fifth Symphony, a simple marching tune; and in the Ninth Symphony, an unpretentious hymn. All build to epic proportions. Through the use of an immense variety of styles, episodic deviations, a wide range of keys, and shifting orchestral color,

Musical Example 17.1
Ludwig van Beethoven, Symphony No. 3

A. Fourth movement *Allegro molto*, bars 1–5. "Promethean" subject

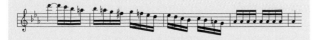

the music embraces multiple levels and reaches out to include the entire human panorama.

The fiery spirit of creation exhibited by Beethoven at the height of his powers has never been surpassed. The *Eroica* symphony was as much a revolution in music as the American and French revolutions were in the fields of political thought and action.

IDEAS

THE ARCHEOLOGICAL IDEAL

The Napoleonic era was a mixture of forward and backward tendencies. At the very time when the social hopes of the revolutionary period were about to be realized in democratic forms, Europe was confronted with Napoleon's militant revival of ancient Roman imperial authority. The spirit of eighteenth-century individualism that helped stimulate the struggle for freedom was engulfed by regimentation and uniformity, presented as necessary to maintain the hard-fought social gains. Revolutionary ideals were partially eclipsed by Napoleonic actualities: the desire for freedom collided with the need for order, the rights of individuals conflicted with the might of authority, and spiritual well-being was pitted against material considerations. New scientific and technological advances competed for attention with revivals of ancient glories. Napoleon boasted of a new culture, yet he clothed it in a Roman toga.

Neoclassicism in the eighteenth and nineteenth centuries was by no means unique in its revival of a bygone era. Numerous periods in Western art have witnessed a resurgence of classical ideas and motifs. Throughout history, classical revivals have been associated with many and contradictory purposes. For Napoleon and other rulers before him, appeals to Roman history could be fashioned as justifications for extending power beyond a particular region or nation. Indeed, in Napoleon's view, briefly put, Rome equaled Europe. Those looking to find a historical precedent with which to support or challenge the course of events and ideas combed the literature of antiquity. When the Roman emperor and philosopher Marcus Aurelius wrote his *Meditations* in Greek, he did so in part to validate his thoughts with a demonstration of his deep learning. The revival of classical literature in the Renaissance had many motivations, among them the authoritative confirmation of a human-centered universe that implicitly challenged the church's view of humankind as tainted by original sin. Florentine Renaissance humanists, in their reaction to medieval scholastic thought and the traditional church interpretation of Aristotle, turned to the beauties of antiquity in general and to the philosophy of Plato in particular. Late eighteenth- and early nineteenth-century neoclassicism was adopted by a wide range of users. Revolutionaries found precedents in republican Rome, just as Napoleon fashioned an imperial classicism.

In other words, each period chose those elements from the past that harmonized with its specific ideals and goals. The Renaissance revival of classicism was confined to several intellectuals and artists. By contrast, late eighteenth- and early nineteenth-century neoclassicism became the official, government-approved art style. Baroque classical interests reflected an aristocratic image of society and were restricted to courtly circles. Louis XIV and his associates identified themselves with the gods of Mount Olympus, and their moral standards, like those of the ancient deities, were the ethics of a highly privileged class who could break the rules they made. On the contrary, Napoleonic neoclassicism was directed toward the middle class, which saw a comfortable image in the living standards of ancient Pompeii and Herculaneum but tempered luxury with the stricter moral standards of a revolutionary regime. The new interest in classical sculpture, architecture, and painting was also a bourgeois criticism of the artificiality and extravagance of courtly life as mirrored in the rococo. Without the moral overtones of this revived interest in the ancient world, the choice of conservative classical art forms would have been extremely odd for such a revolutionary period.

FAITHFULNESS TO ANTIQUE MODELS

The Romans' desire to own and display Greek sculpture prompted them to import whatever objects they could and to copy many works. Statues found on the bottom of the ocean along the routes between Greece and Rome (see Fig. 2.38) attest to the profitability as well as the dangers involved in transporting works of art. The Romans seem to have preferred marble copies of Greek originals, whether the originals were in stone or metal. They also do not appear to have applied paint to the bodies and facial features of their copies, as the Greeks did. Consequently, when artists like David and scholars like Winckelmann went to Rome to seek Greek culture, they found a Roman interpretation, a white world substituted for a polychrome one. In Western culture, weather-bleached monochrome architecture and sculpture quickly became symbols of harmony, simplicity, and purity, which they were not in Greek society.

When Winckelmann went to the Vatican collection and elsewhere, he saw mostly Roman copies of Greek statues, such as the *Apollo Belvedere*. From these sources he reconstructed Greek culture as an ideal. He believed that he could read the values of Greek society in its works of art. He never visited Greece, nor did he travel through Asia Minor or the chain of islands between the two where Hellenic and Hellenistic culture flourished. In addition, Winckelmann interpreted Greek art as having been invented solely by the Greeks. He repeatedly denied any influence from other cultures, particularly that of Egypt (see, for example, Fig. 2.26). Winckelmann's isolation of ancient Greek art and culture from that of surrounding Mediterranean societies was possibly the most influential aspect of his study. It remains a hot-button issue in twenty-first-century art history, archeology, and cultural studies. On the other hand, Winckelmann helped create modern art history by ignoring artistic biographies like those written by Giorgio Vasari (see p. 274) in favor of a broad-based history of art that linked it to the values of the culture that produced it. In addition, Winckelmann was justly appalled by the disorder and secrecy that prevailed at archeological sites like those at Pompeii and Herculaneum. He fought for a more methodical approach to archeological research, storage, and preservation.

Enthusiasm for antiquity sometimes led other artists into pitfalls. As models for the heads of figures in his early pictures, David used ancient Roman portrait busts instead of live models. In the baroque period, when Poussin and Claude Lorrain painted Rome, they usually did so in terms of picturesque ancient ruins, but David painted archeological reconstructions. Madame Récamier was a nineteenth-century Parisian socialite, but David made her into a fancy-dress reincarnation of a Pompeian matron. In poetry, a similar maneuver can be found in the work of the poet-hero of the French Revolution, André Chénier. For his odes and elegies as well as his pastoral idylls and epics, he drew directly on Homer, Pindar, Virgil, and Horace. "Let us upon new thoughts write antique verses," he urged.

Because musicians and composers did not have an abundance of ancient music at hand, they developed their own style, which has had more lasting general appeal than the other neoclassical arts. Unencumbered by reconstructions of ancient music, Beethoven achieved a sinewy expressive style that was heroic and not merely theatrical.

Late neoclassicism had other critics as well. Ingres, an ardent defender of the style, began to loosen its grip in paintings that linked the Greek style to exotic and erotic subjects that would have raised Winckelmann's eyebrows (see Fig. 18.23). Similarly, Benjamin West, the American-born English resident who helped found the British Royal Academy and served as its second president, was at once a proponent and a critic of the style. His painting *The Death of General Wolfe* (Fig. 17.15), which illustrates the 1759 Battle of Quebec in which

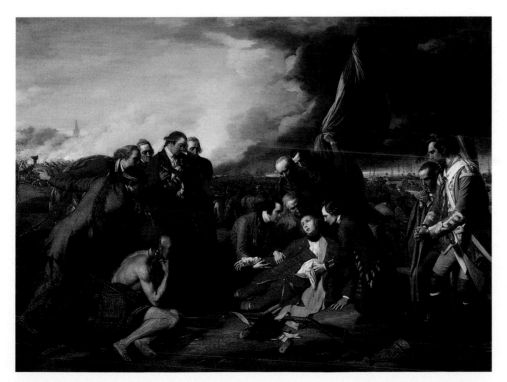

17.15 Benjamin West. *The Death of General Wolfe,* 1770. Oil on canvas, 5′ × 7′. National Gallery of Canada, Ottawa.

the British decisively defeated the French, was criticized by the Royal Academy's first president, Joshua Reynolds. Reynolds's collected lectures to Academy students, called *Discourses,* counseled them to generalize from imperfect nature and to seek excellence by copying models from antiquity as well as the Renaissance. Although Reynolds believed in using imagination, he frowned on giving in to whims. To him, West had crossed the line into sensational realism by depicting a contemporary subject and showing people in contemporary dress. West countered that the Greeks and Romans could not be models for painting in the New World and that he would not perpetrate what he called "classical fictions." West did, however, borrow the pose of a pietà, like that found in Giotto's *Lamentation* (see Fig. 8.12), to underscore the sacrifice made by Wolfe. Like Ingres, he also included an exotic element in the figure of the Native American who ponders the scene. Moreover, West made known his admiration for the painting and poetry of William Blake, as well as for the elusive images of J. M. W. Turner (see pp. 506–508), testifying to his appreciation for feeling and sentiment.

Perhaps neoclassicism's proponents tried so hard to purify a "true style" because it was easy to slip into a romantic longing for a perfect past. Certainly, neoclassicism was hard pressed to express the range of emotions surrounding the experience of the French Revolution. In addition, because of the archeological interests furthered by Stuart and Revett, as well as Winckelmann, more and more objects from the classical era were retrieved. The publication of information about widely different works of classical art cooled the claim that all Greek art displayed, in Winckelmann's famous phrase, "noble simplicity and a quiet grandeur."

Because of political troubles, the increasing numbers of people making the Grand Tour—that is, an extended visit to European cultural centers—did not usually visit Greece. Nevertheless, travel exposed many of the well-to-do, the new middle class, artists, and amateur archeologists to a variety of regional and historical art styles, as well as to the nucleus of neoclassicism, the city of Rome. Those traveling to Florence might visit nearby museums of Etruscan art, which was already being collected and studied in the early eighteenth century.

In France, the influence of scholarly expeditions in Egypt sponsored by Napoleon led to what was later called "Egyptomania," the use of Egyptian-themed designs for all manner of costly things, including furniture, table services, and wallpaper. Fanciful interpretations of Egyptian court life undermined the insistent cultural purity of neoclassicism. This trend persisted throughout the nineteenth century and into the film era of the early twentieth century. Possibly the best-known example of art based on Egyptian themes is Giuseppe Verdi's opera *Aïda,* first performed in Cairo in 1871, with a plot suggested by the renowned Egyptologist Auguste Mariette, who also designed some of the costumes.

Although neoclassicism has never completely disappeared, it lost its moral force by the midnineteenth century because it was no longer the language of progressive thought and it could not give voice to human feeling. Revolutionary activity persisted throughout the nineteenth century, and it found little nourishment in a style so closely associated with the regimentation of the academy and the hopelessness that followed the decision of the once-heroic Napoleon to begin his imperial reign.

--------------- **YOUR RESOURCES** ---------------

- **Web Site**

  http://art.wadsworth.com/fleming10

  ○ Chapter 17 Quiz

  ○ Links

- **Audio CD**

  ○ Beethoven, *Symphony No. 3*

LATE EIGHTEENTH CENTURY AND EARLY NINETEENTH CENTURY

Key Events	Architecture and Visual Arts	Literature and Music
	1716–1809 Joseph Marie Vien ▲	1714–1787 Christoph Willibald Gluck ❑
	1723–1792 Joshua Reynolds ▲	1740–1816 Giovanni Paisiello ❑
	1732–1808 Carl Gotthard Langhans ★	1741–1813 André Ernest Modeste Grétry ❑
	1738–1820 Benjamin West ▲	
	1739–1811 Jean François Thérèse Chalgrin ★	
	1741–1807 Angelica Kauffmann ▲	
	1743–1826 Thomas Jefferson ★	
	1746–1828 Francisco Goya ▲	
	1748–1825 Jacques-Louis David ▲	
	1748 **Excavations** begun at Pompeii and Herculaneum	
1750		
	1753–1837 John Soane ★	1760–1837 Jean-François Lesueur ❑
	1757–1822 Antonio Canova ●	1760–1842 Salvatore Cherubini ❑
	1762–1853 Pierre F. L. Fontaine ★	1762 *Antiquities of Athens* published by Stuart and Revett
	1763–1828 Pierre Alexandre Vignon ★	1764 *History of Ancient Art* published by Winckelmann (1717–1768)
	1764–1838 Charles Percier ★	1766 *Laocoön* published by Gotthold Ephraim Lessing (1729–1781)
	1770–1844 Bertel Thorvaldsen ●	1770–1827 Ludwig van Beethoven ❑
	1771–1835 Antoine Jean Gros ▲	1774–1851 Gasparo Spontini ❑
		1774 Gluck's *Orfeo* produced at Paris Opera
1775		
1776 **American Declaration of Independence**	1780–1867 Jean-Auguste-Dominique Ingres ▲	
1789 **French Revolution** began	1780–1867 Robert Smirke ★	
1792–1794 **First French Republic**	1781–1855 Robert Mills ★	
1796 **Napoleon's** first Italian campaign	1784–1864 Leo von Klenze	
1798 **Napoleon's** campaign in Egypt; Battle of the Pyramids	1785–1820 **Federal style** in the United States	
	1785–1799 **Virginia State Capitol** built by Thomas Jefferson	
	1788–1791 **Brandenburg Gate** in Berlin built by Langhans	
	1791–1824 Théodore Géricault ▲	1792–1822 Percy Bysshe Shelley ◆
1799 **Napoleon** became First Consul	1798–1880 Phillippe Joseph Henri Lemaire ●	1797–1828 Franz Schubert ❑
1800		
1802 **Napoleon** made Consul for life		
1803 **Napoleonic Code of Laws** issued		
1804 **Napoleon** crowned emperor	1805–1852 Horatio Greenough ●	1804 **Beethoven** finished *Eroica* symphony
1814 **Napoleon** abdicated; Bourbons restored to French throne	1806 **Temple of Glory** (later La Madeleine) begun by Vignon; **Arc de Triomphe du Carrousel** begun by Percier and Fontaine; **Arc de Triomphe de l'Étoile** begun by Chalgrin	1871 **Verdi's** *Aïda* performed in Cairo; plot and some costumes designed by Egyptologist Auguste Mariette (1821–1881)
1814–1821 **Louis XVIII,** king of France	1810 **Elgin Marbles** first exhibited in London	
1815 **Napoleon** defeated in Battle of Waterloo	1816 **Elgin Marbles** purchased by Parliament, placed in British Museum	
1821 **Napoleon** died	1819–1826 **University of Virginia** built by Jefferson	
1824–1830 **Charles X,** king of France	1836–1842 **U.S. Treasury,** Washington, D.C., built by Robert Mills	
1830 **July Revolution**		
1830–1848 **Louis Phillipe,** king of France, constitutional monarch		

★ - Architect   ❑ - Musician   ▲ - Painter   ● - Sculptor   ◆ - Writer

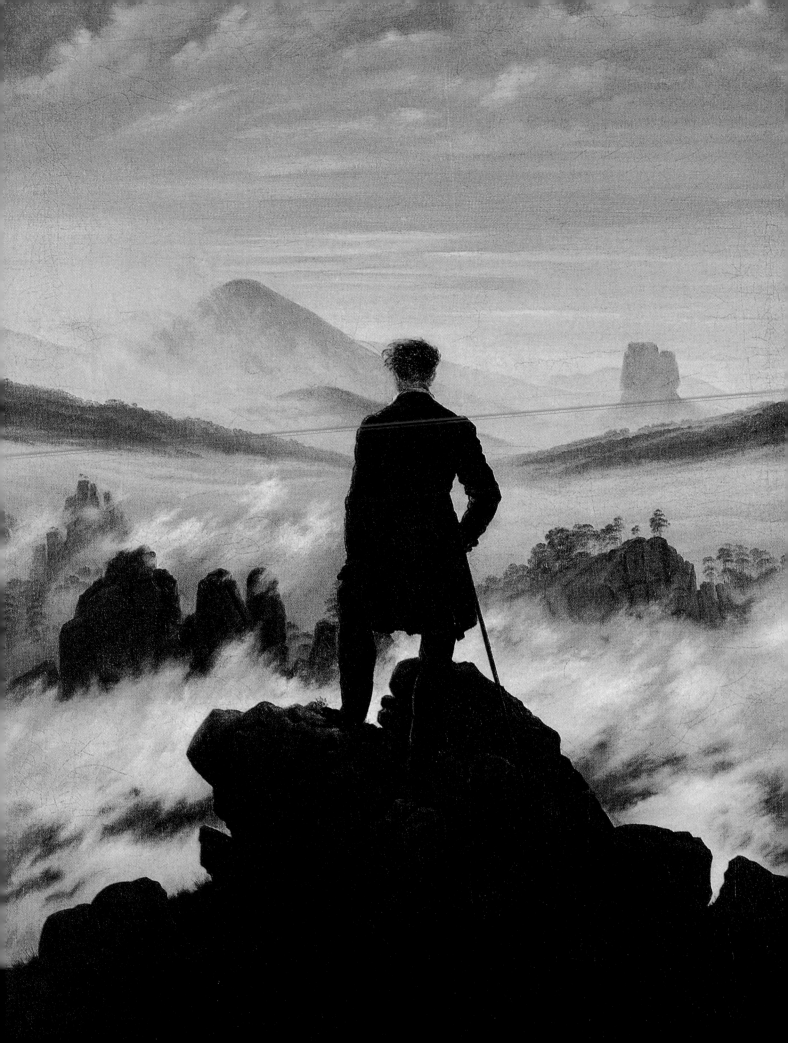

CHAPTER

ROMANTIC STYLE

THE SLOGAN OF THE AGE of Reason and the Enlightenment had been Descartes's declaration, "I think; therefore I am." The neoclassical painter David revealed a similar attitude when he proclaimed, "Art should have no other guide than the torch of Reason." For the post-Enlightenment generation, Descartes's dictum became "I *feel;* therefore I am." These self-proclaimed "Romantics," the first in Western art to pick their own designation, believed that the "heart has reasons that Reason does not know." The Romantic Movement grew slowly at first, primarily in literature, but became more prominent in the early 1800s during the imperial phases of neoclassicism.

By 1820, the word ***romantic*** was a familiar buzz word. The movement was composed of artists who exalted emotion over intellect, subjective response over objective observation, mystery over reason, passion over restraint, freedom over rules, and the supremacy of the individual over that of the crowd. The creative life of the English painter and poet William Blake fused elements of the neoclassical and the new Romantic perception. Blake created his own mythological creatures from biblical and classical sources. Reading Joshua Reynolds's *Discourses* (see p. 478), he lashed out at the painter's coldness and questioned what reason might have to do with the art of painting. Against the neoclassical ideal, he proposed inspiration and inner vision.

Like Blake, the Romantics thought the artist should transcend the boundaries of logical thought and rise above the limitations imposed by reason. The excesses of the French Revolution had revealed the limitations of reason, the power of the irrational, and the devastating role chance plays in human affairs. The crimes committed in the name of liberty during the Reign of Terror and the massacre of equality and fraternity under Napoleon's dictatorship were still fresh in the minds of the Romantics. Also, as science continued to progress, the universe seemed to grow more mysterious and less predictable. The Romantics observed that major thinkers such as Immanuel Kant, Voltaire, Jonathan Swift, and Henri Rousseau had become increasingly skeptical of Enlightenment thinking and had introduced many modifications that suggested new directions of philosophical inquiry.

Romanticism, like neoclassicism, was an international movement. In England, France, Germany, and the United States, the seeds of Romanticism were planted in the eighteenth century. For example, sensibility had strongly stressed personal feelings in the novels, paintings, and music of the time (see pp. 444–445). The rebellious Storm and Stress movement had been built on breaking formal restraints and unleashing violent emotional outbursts (see p. 450). Edmund Burke had proposed a powerful aesthetic force, the sublime, that when coupled with the awesome aspects of nature transcended the confines of beauty and suggested territory for the arts to explore. The early development of the Gothic novel was destined to come to full fruition in the Romantic works of Walter Scott, Victor Hugo, and Edgar Allan Poe. Rousseau's "back to nature" movement did not mean taking to the woods as much as it meant avoiding too much intellectualizing and opening the mind instead to instinctive emotional experience. Yet the Romantic landscape painters, for their part, took Rousseau literally and looked for inspiration in unspoiled natural surroundings.

Romantic artists began to work in a greater variety of forms than before, and poets and musicians wrote shorter works. Even when a composer like Hector Berlioz wrote symphonies, the results were no longer the all-embracing universal structures of Beethoven, but rather sequences of pieces strung together by a literary program or some recurrent motif that gave them a semblance of unity.

Also new was the idea that an art medium was not unique but shared certain qualities with other media. Some artists attempted to overcome the arbitrary limitations and technical rules of their separate crafts. For example, the literature of the period was filled with musical references, and musicians drew on literature for their program pieces. Architects were called on to build dream castles like those described in the novels of Horace Walpole,

Scott, and Hugo. Indeed, it is difficult to think of Eugène Delacroix's painting or Berlioz's music without Virgil, Dante, Shakespeare, Johann Wolfgang von Goethe, and Lord Byron coming to mind.

The effect on music was the invention of new, hybrid forms, such as the program symphony and the symphonic poem. The tonal art had been associated from its beginning with words, and program music was by no means an invention of the nineteenth century. No other period, however, built an entire style on this mixture.

There is also a considerable distinction between the setting of words to music, as in a song, or the musical dramatization of a play, as in an opera, and basing a purely instrumental form on the spirit of a poem or the sequential arrangements of episodes taken from a novel. Berlioz wrote overtures to such novels as Scott's *Waverley* and *Rob Roy.* Felix Mendelssohn composed *Songs without Words* for the piano, leaving the imagination to supply the text, and Berlioz's *Fantastic Symphony* and *Harold in Italy* were operas without words. Berlioz's later works, such as *Romeo and Juliet,* which he called a "dramatic symphony," and *The Damnation of Faust,* which he dubbed a "dramatic legend," were scored for soloists and chorus as well as orchestra. In effect, Berlioz wrote concert operas in which the costumes and scenery were left to the listener's imagination. This tendency continued until it reached a climax in Richard Wagner's music dramas, which he conceived as *Gesamtkunstwerke,* complete or total works of art.

The animated spirit of Romanticism cannot be captured in a single attitude. It included a variety of aesthetic approaches, stylistic tendencies, and divergent directions. One of these is *Romantic realism* (see Fig. 18.1), which may be seen in works that dramatized current events. Another was the medieval revival, which challenged the neoclassical emphasis on Greco-Roman antiquity. A different inflection occurred in Carl Maria von Weber's opera *Der Freischütz,* the great success of the 1826 season in Paris. It dwelled on the darker aspects of nature. Much is made of the sinister powers of the night, and the forces over which it rules are effectively presented in the eerie "Wolf's Glen" scene. Nature, here as well as in Goethe's *Faust,* exposed its terrifying as well as its inspiring aspects and portrayed both awesome elemental forces and magical and fantastic characters. In addition, Romantic painters and poets often deified nature. All of these tendencies furthered the European fascination with exotic aspects of Asia and Africa.

In England and Germany, Romanticism was mainly a movement of the intellectuals, poets, novelists, painters, and musicians. As the style gained momentum in France, however, it penetrated into wider social and political circles. Eventually the Romantic Movement contributed to the forces that overthrew the intransigent Bourbon monarchy in the July Revolution of 1830, and thus Romanticism became the official style of France.

THE ROMANTIC REVOLUTION

Well before the July Revolution of 1830, new ideas were stirring the minds and imaginations of the intellectuals and artists of Paris. In 1827, as the new movement was spreading, Victor Hugo published

PAST AND PRESENT

What Is Genius?

In the Romantic era, Berlioz's huge output and intense emotional sensitivity marked him in the public mind as a genius. During the early nineteenth century, genius was a literary and philosophical concept, applied primarily to artists, composers, and writers, as well as to a few extraordinary scientists, such as Isaac Newton. By the early twentieth century, genius had become a number, an intelligence quotient (IQ), which measured potential, not actual accomplishment. With their emphasis on analytic skills, IQ tests labeled far more people as geniuses than had ever been considered to be so.

Are there really more geniuses now than in the past? Those who argue for the presence of more geniuses point out that access to higher education grew enormously throughout the last century, permitting more people to develop their innate talents and make a contribution to society. In particular, women increasingly participated in the arts, the sciences, and the professions. But does the early twenty-first century have towering figures like Mozart, Berlioz, and Beethoven?

Scholars who study the occurrence of genius suggest that today's scientific inquiries are so complex that they cannot be worked out by a single individual, such as Newton reckoning the notion of gravity or Einstein estimating the theory of relativity. Today's scientific genius is likely to be a group of talented people, not just one person. But in the arts, the question remains open. Who were the geniuses of the twentieth century, and who are the emerging geniuses in the twenty-first century?

Cromwell, a drama with a preface that served as the manifesto of Romanticism. François Guizot was lecturing at the Sorbonne on the early history of France. François Rude, destined to be the principal sculptor of the period, returned from exile in Belgium. Painter Eugène Delacroix observed in his journal that when he went to the Odéon Theater to see Shakespeare's *Hamlet,* he met the writers Alexandre Dumas and Victor Hugo. Harriet Smithson played the part of Ophelia in that production; she later became the wife of the composer, Hector Berlioz. Gérard de Nerval's French translation of Goethe's drama *Faust* appeared that autumn and inspired Berlioz to compose *Eight Scenes from Faust,* which achieved popularity in a later revision, retitled *The Damnation of Faust.* Delacroix was already at work on a set of lithographs to illustrate the 1828 French edition of Goethe's play.

All in all, the 1820s in Paris was an inspiring cultural moment. When Théophile Gautier later came to write his history of Romanticism, he looked back on his youthful years with nostalgia:

> What a marvelous time. Walter Scott was then in the flower of his success; one was initiated into the mysteries of Goethe's *Faust,* which as Madame de Staël said, contained everything. One discovered Shakespeare, and the poems of Lord Byron: *The Corsair; Lara; The Giaour; Manfred; Beppo;* and *Don Juan* took us to the orient, which was not banal then as now.

All was young, new, exotically colored, intoxicating, and strongly flavored. It turned our heads; it was as if we had entered into a strange new world.

ART AND REVOLUTION: *LIBERTY LEADING THE PEOPLE, 1830*

The life and work of Eugène Delacroix exemplify the meshing of talent with the spirit of the time. His *Liberty Leading the People, 1830* (Fig. 18.1) gave incandescent expression to those glorious July days. The canvas is dominated by the fiery allegorical figure of Liberty, seen as the spirit of the French people, whom she leads onward to triumph. This robust, energetic reincarnation of the revolutionary spirit of 1789 is no serene neoclassical goddess. She has muscular arms that are strong enough to hold both a bayoneted rifle and the tricolored banner of the republic. Although bare-breasted, she betrays no sign of softness or sensuality, and her powerful legs stride over the street barricades as she leads her followers forward through the oncoming forces. She does not hover over the action on wings, as so many other artists depicted her; instead, she is in the midst of the turmoil with her feet on the ground. While Delacroix intended her to be a symbolic figure, he portrayed her as a distinctive personality. Only the Phrygian cap and the near-classic profile

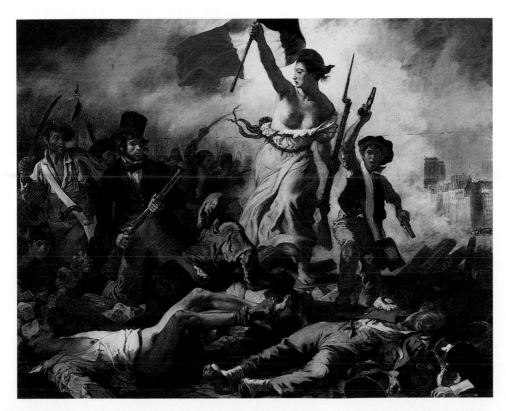

18.1 Eugène Delacroix. *Liberty Leading the People, 1830.* Oil on canvas, 8'6" × 10'10". Louvre, Paris, France.

indicate her significance. This energetic, stern liberty influenced Frédéric-Auguste Bertoldi's later work, the Statue of Liberty, which was given to the American people by the French in 1884.

Liberty's followers include both impulsive students and battle-scarred soldiers who have heeded her call and renounced their reactionary king. On the right, a boy from the Paris streets holds a pistol in each hand. This youthful figure functions not only as a representative of the downtrodden but also as an agent of the future. In the background are the remnants of the old guard from revolutionary days, still carrying on the struggle. Two main social classes are represented. The boy stands for the impoverished working class. In the shadows on the extreme left, the man armed with a saber may be black, representing France's reach into Africa. In front of him toward the center, the more prominent figure in the fashionable frock coat, top hat, and sideburns is a bourgeois gentleman who has grabbed his musket and joined in the general confusion. It was this class that controlled the fighting and stamped its image on the new monarchy in the person of Louis Philippe, the "Citizen King."

Although the July Revolution was essentially a palace revolt that replaced a reactionary Bourbon with his more liberal cousin, no aristocrats are shown taking part. In the shadow below, the wounded and dying are strewn on the loose cobblestones looking toward Liberty—their inspiration and reason for being. The twin towers of Notre Dame show through the smoke on the right.

Unlike David, who represented contemporary revolt indirectly, employing a Roman legend in his *Oath of the Horatii* (see Fig. 17.2), Delacroix had a timelier frame of reference. A contemporary viewer would recognize the familiar shirts, blouses, trousers, rifles, pistols, and other nineteenth-century equipment. Consequently, the picture has sometimes been described as realistic. Nevertheless, the spirit of the work rises above the event itself, and because the artist infused reality with emotion, the picture is in the Romantic style.

More eloquent than any page in a history book, the canvas captured the feeling and the facts that made up the incident. It is as if Delacroix had been roused from his dreams of the past and, suddenly wide awake, applied his expressive techniques to one of the stirring happenings of his own time.

As always with Delacroix, color plays an important part in the communication of mood. Here a striking instance of the use of color is seen in the way he takes the red, white, and blue of the banner (the symbol of patriotism) and merges them into the picture as a whole. The white central strip, signifying truth and purity, blends with the

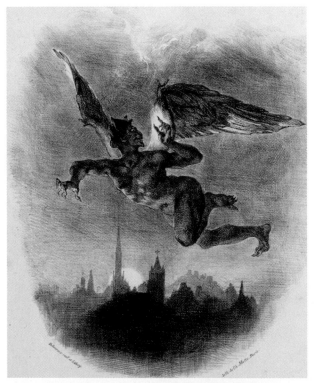

18.2 Eugène Delacroix. *Mephistopheles Flying,* illustration for Goethe's *Faust,* 1828. Lithograph, 10¾″ × 9″. Metropolitan Museum of Art, New York. Rogers Fund, 1917.

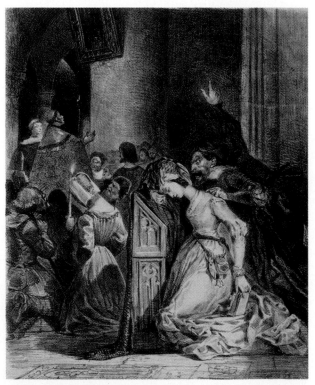

18.3 Eugène Delacroix. *Margaret in Church,* illustration for Goethe's *Faust,* 1828. Lithograph, 10½″ × 8¾″. Metropolitan Museum of Art, New York. Rogers Fund, 1917.

purifying smoke of battle. The blue, denoting freedom, matches the parts of the sky that are visible in the top corners through the smoke. The red in the flag high above balances the blood of those below who have fallen for the ideal of liberty. Thus, the symbolism of the banner blends into the color scheme, and both combine with the dramatic lighting to define the emotional range. All these, in turn, expand the patriotic theme into a formal pictorial unity. When the new bourgeois king purchased this picture in the name of the state during the Salon of 1831, he gave the seal of official approval to the Romantic style.

EUGÈNE DELACROIX AND EXOTICISM

Delacroix, a leading French Romantic, usually looked to the literary world for the sources of his pictorial visions. Titles such as *The Death of Sardanapalus, Mazeppa, Giaour and the Pasha,* and *The Shipwreck of Don Juan* point to motifs contained in the poetic writings of Lord Byron. Delacroix's illustrations for Goethe's *Faust* (Figs. 18.2 and 18.3) won the admiration of the author himself, who believed that their clarity and depth of insight could not be surpassed. Delacroix's imagination had been haunted by *Faust* ever since he first saw it on the London stage. In a letter to a friend in Paris, he commented particularly on its diabolical aspect. The **lithographs,** or prints, that eventually resulted demonstrate his mastery of illustration

and prove that Delacroix was proficient in small works as well as large ones.

Despite his close kinship with Byron and Goethe, Delacroix was not always sympathetic toward the work of his Romantic Parisian contemporaries. In his diary he spoke of Meyerbeer's opera *Le Prophète* as "frightful" and referred to Berlioz and Hugo as those "so-called reformers." "The noise he makes is distracting," he wrote about Berlioz's music; "It is a heroic mess." Of all musicians, he admired Mozart the most, and among his contemporaries only Frédéric Chopin measured up to his standards of craftsmanship.

Delacroix's sophisticated color technique energized his emotional and highly charged subject matter. As he declared, "gray is the enemy of all painting . . . let us banish from our palette all earth colors . . . the greater the opposition in color, the greater the brilliance." His admitted models were the lush canvases of Peter Paul Rubens (see Figs. 14.9 and 14.10) and the dramatic pictures of Rembrandt, with their emphasis on the dynamics of light (see Figs. 15.5 and 15.6). Among his contemporaries, he admired the mellow landscapes and subtle coloring of the English painter John Constable (see Figs. 18.26 and 18.27).

Delacroix's own art was built on principles of color, light, and emotion rather than line, drawing, and form. This is illustrated in his early masterpiece *Dante and Virgil in Hell* (Fig. 18.4), which attracted wide attention when it was exhibited in the

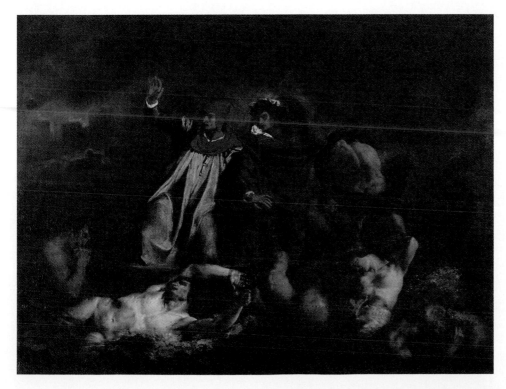

18.4 Eugène Delacroix. *Dante and Virgil in Hell,* 1822. Oil on canvas, 6'1½" × 7'10½". Louvre, Paris, France.

Salon of 1822. The revival of Dante's *Divine Comedy* (see pp. 232–234) was one of the Romantic literary enthusiasms. Likely enough, *The Inferno,* with its tales of the demonic and macabre, as well as descriptions of the tortures of the damned amid hellfire and brimstone, held the greatest appeal.

In *Dante and Virgil in Hell,* Delacroix depicted the realm of eternal suffering. The central figure is that of Virgil. In the crimson robe of a medieval Florentine and crowned with a laurel wreath, Virgil stands with dignified monumentality as a symbol of classic calm. Dante appears on the left, wearing a red hood. In contrast to Virgil, Dante is vividly caught up in his grotesque and gruesome surroundings. He looks with terror on the damned who swirl all about him.

The wake of the boat is filled with the writhing forms of the condemned, who ceaselessly hope to reach the opposite shore by trying to attach themselves to the craft. One attempts to climb aboard; the gnashing teeth of another bite into the edge of the boat. Despite their efforts, they are plunged back into the dark waters. Distress and despair abound. On the right, Phlegyas, the ghostly boat-man, is seen from the rear as he strains at the rudder to guide the boat across the River Styx to the flaming shores of the city of Dis, visible in the distant background between the clouds of sulfurous fumes.

When first exhibited, the picture aroused storms of protest, which helped immeasurably in bringing the young artist critical attention. One defender of David's academic tradition called it a "splattering of color." In the 1830s, the painting's intensity was novel and somewhat incomprehensible. Today, the work is readily understood as part of the macabre aspect of the Romantic style. Even the nude figures, as muscular as those of Michelangelo and Rubens, function here more as color masses than as forms modeled three-dimensionally. Delacroix's use of color was to have far-reaching effects on later painting.

PAINTING THE NEWS

Delacroix's initial inspiration for the *Dante* picture came from his older contemporary, Théodore Géricault, whom he thought of as his master.

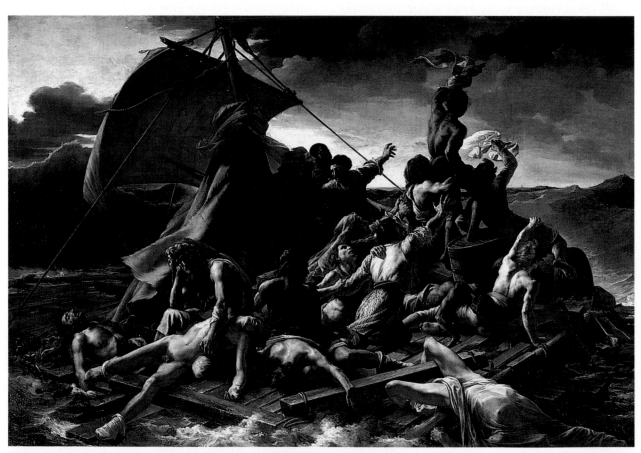

18.5   Théodore Géricault. *Raft of the "Medusa,"* 1819. Oil on canvas, approx. 16′ × 23′6″. Louvre, Paris, France.

While Géricault was painting his *Raft of the "Medusa"* (Fig. 18.5), Delacroix posed for the dying youth lying facedown in the center foreground. The vast canvas created a sensation because its subject was a controversial topic of current interest. The French government frigate *Medusa* had foundered off the West African coast. The captain, a reactionary royalist, and his officers seized the lifeboats and cast almost 150 hapless passengers and crew adrift on an improvised raft.

The event was a political scandal of major magnitude, which Géricault dramatized with great passion and intensity. The superbly modeled figures were based on Géricault's studies of Michelangelo's nudes in Rome. As such, they do not realistically depict how the passengers would have appeared after 12 days of enduring hunger, thirst, exposure, and cannibalism. Only fifteen of the passengers were finally rescued, and Géricault interviewed some of them. The huge canvas depicts a scene held together by a tight pyramidal composition, with the line of interest rising from the lower left to the waving young sailor at the top.

Shipwrecks, events in which the human will is powerless in the face of the awesome forces of nature, were a favorite subject of Romanticism in literature and art. These confrontations with brute nature provided settings that Romantics exalted for their spine-chilling sublime qualities rather than their beautiful elements. Géricault dealt with the elemental animal will to survive. This powerful work soon emerged as a manifesto against the restored monarchy. Among other forces, it led to the overthrow of the Bourbons during the July Revolution of 1830.

ROMANTICISM, CLASSICISM, AND HEROISM: THE SCULPTURE OF FRANÇOIS RUDE

The Departure of the Volunteers of 1792 by François Rude (Fig. 18.6) is one of the dominating sculptural works of the Romantic style. It achieved its stature through its impassioned expression and sustained heroic mood. Its prominent location on one side of the Arc de Triomphe in Paris assured it the largest possible audience. Carved in bold high relief, the dimensions of the composition alone—rising to a height of 42 feet and spreading to a width of 26 feet—make its proportions truly colossal. The conception and commission of this work date from the wave of patriotic emotion associated with the July Revolution and the memories it stirred of earlier struggles for freedom. This source of inspiration was shared by both

Delacroix and Rude, whose design certainly owes much to Delacroix's *Liberty Leading the People.* It took Delacroix only 1 year to get his painting before the public, but a sculptural work of these proportions took Rude 6 years to complete.

The scene is that of a band of volunteers rallying to the defense of the newly established French Republic when it was threatened by a foreign invasion in 1792. The five determined figures in the foreground, presented as Romans, are uniting to meet the common danger and receiving mutual inspiration from Bellona, the winged Roman goddess of war, who also alludes to the French figure of Liberty. A fine rhythm is established by the compact grouping of the figures; it is quickened by the repetitive movement of their legs below. All combine to weld the composition together in a lively yet majestic march, which successfully blends neoclassical elements into a vigorous Romantic conception.

These representatives of the humanity so recently liberated by the French Revolution are self-motivated protectors of their newly won liberty,

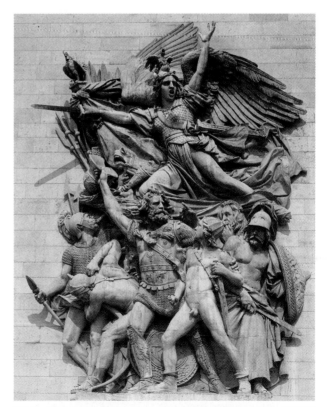

18.6 François Rude. *Departure of the Volunteers of 1792 (La Marseillaise),* 1833–1836. Height 42′, width 26′. Right stone relief, Arc de Triomphe de l'Étoile, Paris, France.

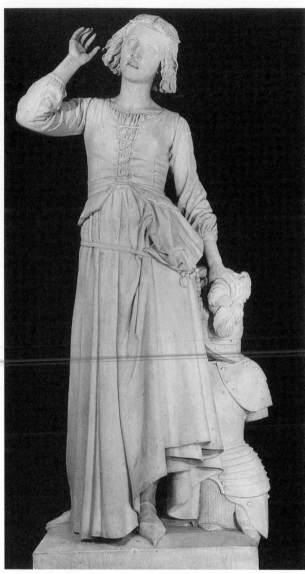

18.7 François Rude. *Joan of Arc Listening to the Voices,* 1845. Marble, life-size. Musée des Beaux-Arts, Dijon, France.

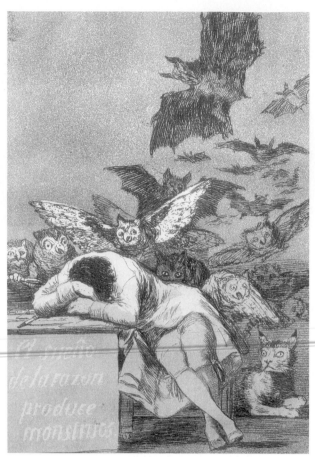

18.8 Francisco Goya. *The Sleep of Reason Produces Monsters,* from *Los Caprichos,* 1796–1798. Etching and aquatint. Museo del Prado, Madrid, Spain.

equality, and fraternity. The full force and power of four of the mature volunteers contrast with the potential strength of the finely carved nude figure of the idealistic youth who literally looks up to them. The waning ability of the old man behind him is such that he can only point out the direction to the others and wave them on. The surging power of shared ideals urges the volunteers ever onward with driving force and momentum. Because Rude designed the *Departure* for a Napoleonic arch of triumph, his motifs are Roman in origin. The soldiers are outfitted with Roman helmets and shields. The avoidance of any contemporary costumes and sym-

bols in this representation of an event that had taken place less than a half-century before points to Rude's tendency to draw on the past for inspiration.

Popularly called "*The Marseillaise* in stone," the *Departure* represents an inventive sculptural use of a musical motif in suggesting the great revolutionary song, which serves to unify the patriotic spirit of the group. The anthem, with its stirring words "To arms, O citizens," was practically forgotten during the days of Napoleon's empire, and under the Bourbon restoration it was officially banned. Credit for its rediscovery and revival goes to the composer Berlioz. Stirred to patriotic frenzy by the events of July 1830 (although avoiding direct participation), this eccentric genius contented himself with scoring the song for double chorus and orchestra, asking "all who have voices, a heart, and blood in their veins" to join in.

In a later work, *Joan of Arc Listening to the Voices* (Fig. 18.7), Rude combines emotionalism and medieval subject matter. Originally executed in 1845 as part of a series on famous French women, the life-size statue represents the Maid of Orleans in peasant costume with a suit of armor at her side. In this way the sculptor indicated both her rural origin and her heroic mission. The mystic element is suggested as she lifts her hand to her ear to hear the angelic voices that guide her. By trying to capture the intangible sounds of these heavenly voices as Joan listens with upraised head, Rude strains the marble medium to its expressive limits.

Rude, who had grown up in revolutionary times, was always thoroughly in sympathy with the liberal spirit. He accepted exile in Belgium in 1815 rather than live under a Bourbon ruler. *Action* was his aesthetic watchword. "The great thing for an artist," he once said, "is to *do*." The sheer energy and power of his carving broke with academic tradition. By liberating sculpture from many outworn classical clichés and conventions, Rude revealed himself as a true Romantic.

SPAIN'S ROMANTIC ORIGINAL: FRANCISCO GOYA

Francisco Goya's work defies stylistic classification. His art cannot be separated from the conflicting crosscurrents of ideas, political upheavals, and stylistic trends of Spain in the late eighteenth and early nineteenth centuries. His early work in the Spanish royal tapestry studios mirrors the carefree, lighthearted aristocratic rococo. He also shared the Enlightenment opposition to religious fanaticism, social injustice, and senseless cruelty. As happened to so many others, his optimistic faith in the power of reason to solve human and artistic problems ended in disillusionment.

The first of his series of etchings, titled *Los Caprichos* (Fig. 18.8), bears the inscription, "The sleep of reason produces monsters." This can be understood both as an endorsement of rationalism and as a warning that the surrender of reason can result in disorder and misery. Alternatively, it can be read as a sign that the faith in reason to solve human problems had ended only in nightmares.

Goya parted company with the ideal of "noble simplicity and quiet grandeur." His break with the typical neoclassical treatment of mythological subjects was signaled in the bitterness and horror of *Saturn Devouring One of His Children* (Fig. 18.9). This painting, made late in life for his own dining room, accentuates the blood and gore of ancient myths as an antidote to the glamour and glory of

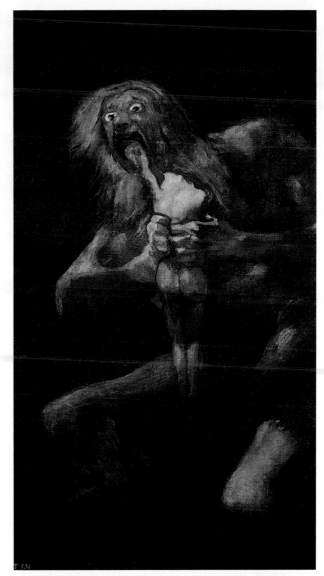

18.9 Francisco Goya. *Saturn Devouring One of His Children,* 1819–1823. Wall painting in oil detached on canvas, 4′9⅞″ × 2′8⅝″. Museo del Prado, Madrid, Spain.

neoclassicist idealism. With the other works that Goya created directly on the plaster walls of his home, the *Saturn* has been dubbed one of the "black paintings." These fourteen works seem to exemplify Goya's fearless confrontation with evil. But, in 2003, the authenticity of the *Saturn* and the other works was called into question. It may be more than a decade before a conclusion is reached.

There is no question that Goya witnessed the sufferings of his subjugated countrymen during Napoleon's invasion of Spain in 1808. His *Executions of the Third of May, 1808*

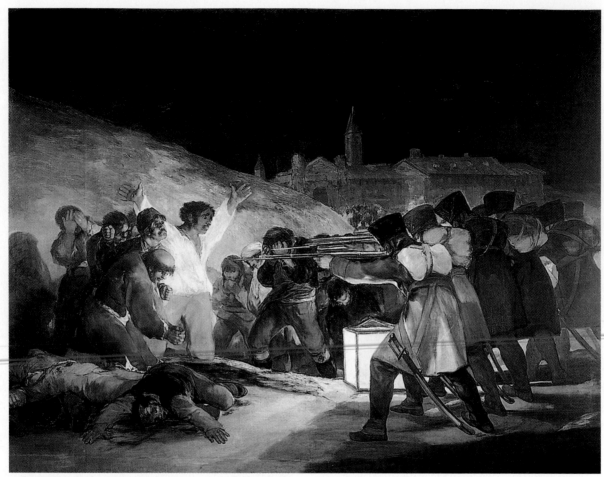

18.10 Francisco Goya. *Executions of the Third of May, 1808,* 1814–1815. Oil on canvas, approx. 8′9″ × 13′4″. Museo del Prado, Madrid, Spain.

(Fig. 18.10) was painted some years later, when Spain had regained its independence after Napoleon's downfall. Goya saw no positive aspects of warfare, only the desolation of his country and the accompanying misery and bloodshed. In fact, *Executions of the Third of May, 1808* is his response to the heroic posturing of Napoleon's official painters. The spectator's sympathy is directed toward the defenseless, terrified civilians, who have been rounded up at random to avenge a guerrilla attack on the French forces the day before. The work is in the Romantic realistic vein of Delacroix and Géricault, although it predates them by some years.

Intended for public exhibit, the picture was to memorialize those who had lost their lives in the conflict. It is filled with savagery. From Goya's point of view, the Enlightenment, represented by the lantern, was to have brought reason and order into society. Christianity, symbolized by the church in the background, the tonsured monk, and the crucifixion-like posture of the victim awaiting execution, should lead to the unity of humankind. Yet under Napoleon the revolutionary ideals of lib-

erty, equality, and fraternity failed. Only the artist's vision and power to expose human martyrdom emerge to create meaning and reassurance.

Goya's sympathies were briefly revived in his *Allegory on the Adoption of the Constitution of 1812.* This short-lived document declared the people sovereign and reduced the king to a figurehead. Still seeing nothing but brutality and misery around him, Goya then withdrew from public life. In the final paintings of his so-called black period, he explored the dark and terrifying world of the subconscious (Fig. 18.11). Evil was now no longer to be attributed to the devil but to humanity itself. During the nineteenth century Goya was thought to be a Romantic painter, but twentieth-century Surrealists and Expressionists saw him as one of their own.

A MEDIEVAL REVIVAL

Romantic architecture received its initial thrust from the popularity of so-called Gothic novels in the late eighteenth century. Romances and

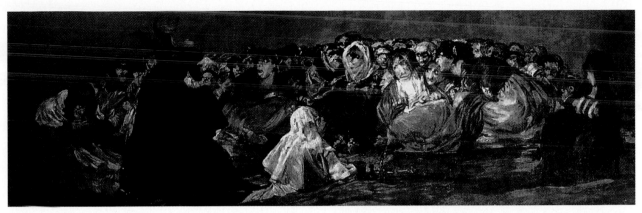

18.11   Francisco Goya. *Witches' Sabbath,* c. 1819–1823. Oil on canvas, 4′7⅛″ × 14′4½″. Museo del Prado, Madrid, Spain.

plays of this type published in England were variously titled *The Haunted Priory; The Horrid Mysteries; Banditti, or Love in a Labyrinth; Raymond and Agnes, or The Bleeding Nun of Lindenberg;* and *Castle of Otranto,* subtitled *A Gothic Tale,* by Horace Walpole.

The settings for these stories were large baronial halls or decayed abbeys, liberally equipped with mysterious trapdoors, sliding panels, creaking gates, animated suits of armor, and ghostly voices emanating from ancient tombs. Such scenes served as backdrops for the injured innocence of helpless heroines and the fearless, if somewhat reckless, courage of dashing heroes. These tales played their part in the redefinition of the word *Gothic*—which Voltaire had called a fantastic compound of rudeness and filigree—into something

more mystical, tinged with weirdness and bordering on the fantastic.

THE GOTHIC REVIVAL IN ENGLAND AND THE UNITED STATES

The imaginary castles of these novels first took concrete form in England as the architectural whims of wealthy eccentrics. Horace Walpole, the well-to-do son of a powerful prime minister, indulged his fancy in a residence that gave its name to one aspect of the Romantic style, "Strawberry Hill Gothick." William Beckford, whom Byron called "England's richest son," had the architect James Wyatt construct a residence called Fonthill Abbey (Fig. 18.12). Its huge central tower rose over a spacious interior hall that was approached by a

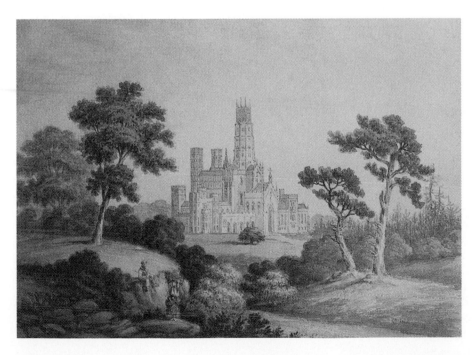

18.12   James Wyatt. Fonthill Abbey, Wiltshire, England (no longer standing), 1796–1807. Height of tower 278′. Contemporary lithograph by Francis Danby.

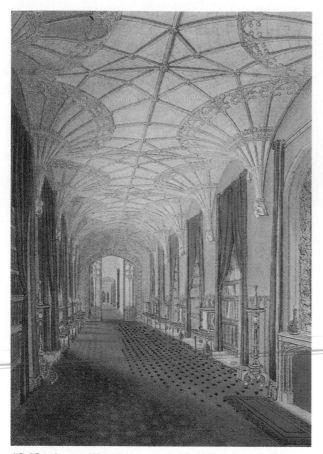

18.13 James Wyatt. Interior of St. Michael's Gallery, Fonthill Abbey, Wiltshire, England. Length 25′, width 35′. Contemporary lithograph from John Rutter's *Delineations of Fonthill.*

massive staircase (Fig. 18.13). The rest of the interior was a maze of long, drafty corridors that provided the wall space for the proprietor's pictures and tapestries as well as a suitable setting for his melancholy musings.

In his frenzy to have Fonthill Abbey completed, Beckford drove the workers day and night to the point where, in their haste, they neglected to provide an adequate foundation for the tower. Only a few years after its completion, the tower of Beckford's dream castle fell to the ground, taking most of the building with it. However, because ruins were greatly admired at the time, this catastrophe served to enhance the abbey's picturesque Gothic appearance.

In the early 1820s, Fonthill Abbey became so enormously popular that newspapers wrote articles on "Fonthill mania." Up to 500 visitors made the pilgrimage each day. Many in particular wanted to view Beckford's spectacular landscaping, which involved transplanting more than 1 million trees to create a forest setting. The effect commanded the admiration of the painter Constable, who lived nearby, as well as that of poets such as Byron and Poe.

The Gothic novel in literature and the Gothic revival in architecture steadily gained momentum. Jane Austen's *Northanger Abbey,* a delicious satire on the movement, was published just as Walter Scott's historical novels were bringing their author such huge acclaim. Scott's novels were translated into French beginning about 1816. In turn, they paved the way for the romances of Hugo

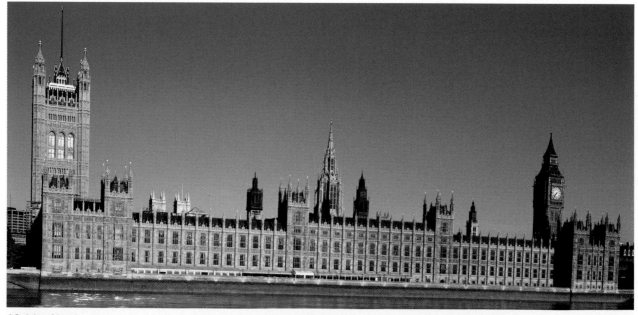

18.14 Charles Barry and A. W. N. Pugin. Houses of Parliament, London, England, 1840–1860. Length 940′.

and Dumas. Gothic novels, plays, and operas also had their serious side, as they explored the social responsibility and commitment of individuals to righteous causes.

Moreover, the Gothic revival included intellectual and political overtones. In England especially, it gained impetus through opposition to Napoleon's attempt to establish a new Roman Empire that would dominate the entire continent. Gothic was seen as an indigenous English style, associated with the founding of universities at Oxford and Cambridge. In the political world it was linked with the establishment of parliamentary rule when the Magna Carta was signed in 1215. Hence, when the new Houses of Parliament (Fig. 18.14) were designed by Charles Barry and A. W. N. Pugin, and the new Law Courts were planned by George Street, the Gothic style seemed particularly appropriate.

The medieval revival also found a home in the United States, which had no medieval heritage. In New York the Gothic spire of Trinity Church rose among lower Broadway's skyscrapers. Two churches by James Renwick—Grace Church (Fig. 18.15) and St. Patrick's Cathedral—also show the American fascination with the style. Many American colleges and universities, in their eagerness to be identified with ancient learning and honorable causes, were built in the neomedieval style. Scattered throughout the country are half-timbered houses, castle residences, railroad stations, banks, and other public buildings that reveal the wide influence of the medieval revival on American architecture.

THE GOTHIC REVIVAL IN GERMANY AND FRANCE

As early as 1772, the young German poet Goethe, under the guidance of his trusted university guide Johann Gottfried von Herder, wrote in praise of the builder of the Strasbourg Cathedral, Erwin von Steinbach. The book, titled *Von Deutscher Baukunst (On German Architecture)*, stressed the German soul of Gothic. Later, Goethe placed his drama about the medieval Faust legend in a Gothic setting. In the nineteenth century, German literary interest in neomedievalism became the background for Wagner's operas *Tannhäuser, Lohengrin,* and *Parsifal.* The momentum of the Romantic Movement also led to the completion of the Cologne Cathedral after the discovery of the original plans, a project that had lapsed for several centuries (see p. 220).

In France, architectural energies were diverted toward the preservation of the many medieval monuments still in existence. Less than a year after the July Revolution, Hugo published his *Notre Dame de Paris* (known to the English-speaking world as *The Hunchback of Notre Dame*). The fact that the real hero of the novel is Paris's Gothic

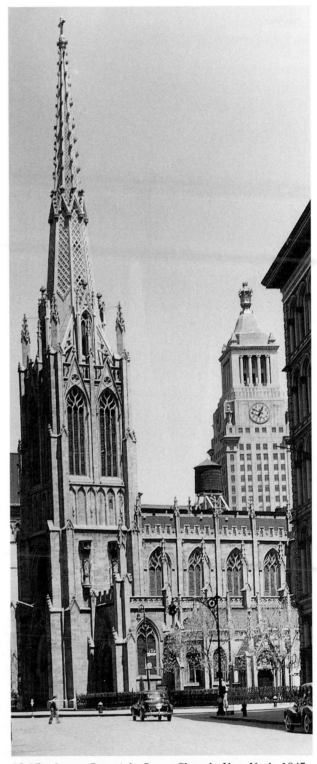

18.15   James Renwick. Grace Church, New York, 1845.

cathedral fanned into flames the enthusiasm for the restoration of churches, castles, and abbeys. Support for the reconstruction of Notre Dame was soon forthcoming from François Guizot, the historian who was then prime minister. It was he who in 1837 founded the Commission for the Conservation of Historic Monuments.

In France, as previously in England and Germany, Romantic architecture was associated with the upsurge of patriotic and nationalistic sentiment, in which cultural achievements were used to rationalize political identity. Romantic architecture channeled French national energies into new flights of imagination and provided an escape from the dreams of Roman imperial glory that had become the nightmare of Napoleonic defeat.

The precise scholarship of the French academic mind found a ready outlet in the establishment of the new science of medieval archeology, which resulted in the restoration of such buildings as Sainte Chapelle and the Cathedral of Notre Dame in

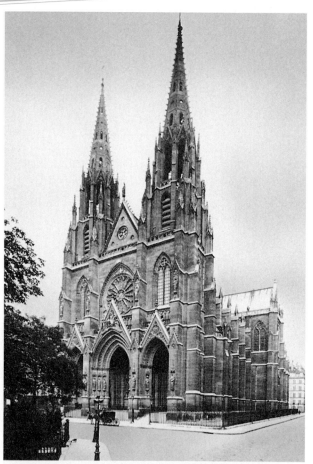

18.16 François-Christian Gau and Théodore Ballu. Ste. Clotilde, Paris, France, 1846–1857. Width 105′, height 216′.

Paris. In his essay on medieval architecture, Eugène Viollet-le-Duc called attention to the engineering logic of medieval builders and demonstrated the organic unity of the Gothic structural system, in which each stone played its part and even the decorative details served useful purposes. The belief that everything was necessary and nothing was used merely for effect not only revised nineteenth-century architectural thought but also encouraged the twentieth-century return to functional building.

As comparative latecomers to the medieval revival, French architects were in no hurry to leave their reconstructions and design new buildings. Although the Church of Sainte Clotilde (Fig. 18.16) was planned at the same time that Hugo, Delacroix, and Berlioz were producing their neomedieval works, it was not until 1846 that ground for it was broken. Designed by François-Christian Gau, a native of Cologne but a naturalized French citizen, the project was completed after his death by Théodore Ballu. Built principally of white stone, Sainte Clotilde received the distinctive technical innovation of cast-iron girders added to the vaulting to assure strength and durability. The girders were disguised by blocks of stone, but the fact that a building of medieval design used materials developed during the nineteenth-century industrial revolution commanded considerable interest.

When an original Gothic monument like the Cathedral of Chartres (see Fig. 7.2) is compared with the Church of Sainte Clotilde, the new church seems too consciously designed, overly symmetrical, and academically frigid. But when viewed in the context of its times and combined with the reflections of the medieval fervor of Hugo, the emotionalism of Rude's sculpture, the expressive color of Delacroix's painting, and the fantastic imagery of Berlioz's music, it catches some rays of their glowing warmth.

THE WRITINGS OF VICTOR HUGO

Of the three great literary figures who influenced the writings of Victor Hugo, Dante and Shakespeare came from the past. Only his elder contemporary, Goethe, lived in Hugo's time. As he states in the preface to his play *Cromwell,* these writers pointed out that the sources for the grotesque elements were to be found everywhere, "in the air, water, earth, fire, those myriads of intermediate creatures which we find alive in the popular traditions of the Middle Ages; it is the grotesque which impels the ghastly antics of the witches' revels, which gives Satan his horns, his cloven feet and his bat's wings. It is the grotesque, still the grotesque, which now casts into the Christian hell the frightful faces which the severe genius of Dante and Milton will evoke."

The *Inferno* section of Dante's *Divine Comedy* inspired Hugo's 1837 poem *Après une lecture de Dante*, which closely parallels Delacroix's picture of Dante (Fig. 18.4): "When the poet paints the image of hell," Hugo wrote, "he paints that of his own life." Hugo sees Dante as surrounded by ghosts and specters, groping blindly through mysterious forests as weird forms block his dark path. Lost amid thick fog, with each step he hears lamentations and the faint sounds of the grinding of white teeth in the black night. All the vices and scourges, such as vengeance, famine, ambition, pride, and avarice, darken the scene still more. Farther on, the souls of those who have tasted the poison of cowardice, fear, and treason mingle with the grimacing masks of those whom hatred has consumed. The only light amid this general gloom is the voice of the eternal artist, Virgil, who calls, "Continue onward."

In Petrarch's writing, Hugo admired *The Triumph of Death;* in Boccaccio, he favored the vivid descriptions of the Black Plague; in Shakespeare's works, he dwelled on the macabre scenes from *Hamlet* and the boiling and bubbling of the witches' cauldron in *Macbeth;* and in Goethe's *Faust,* he was fond of the descriptions of the Walpurgis Night. Collectively, these constitute a carnival of the macabre.

Hugo's transition to a new psychology was apparent as early as 1826. At this time he brought out a new edition of his *Odes,* to which he added fifteen *ballades,* with the fourteenth titled "La Ronde du Sabbat," or "Rondo of the Witches' Sabbath." He explained his fascination in his introduction. The odes, he wrote, were derived from his purely religious inspirations, cast in classical meters. But those titled "ballad" were of a more imaginative character than the odes and included pictorial fantasies, dreams, and legends of superstition. The latter came to him, he continued, under the inspiration of medieval troubadours.

"Witches' Sabbath" begins with a description of a Gothic church at midnight. The clock in the belfry tolls twelve, and the witching hour begins. Strange lights flash, and the holy water begins to boil in the fonts. Shrieks and howls are heard as from all directions come those who answer Satan's call—ghosts, dragons, vampires, ghouls, monsters, and the souls of the damned from their tombs. As Satan sings a Black Mass, an imp reads the Gospel

and the whole fantastic congregation performs a wild dance:

> All in unison moving with swift-circling feet
> While Satan keeps time with his crozier's beat,
> And their steps shake the arches colossal and
>   high,
> Disturbing the dead in their tombs close by.

Both the technique and the imagery of Hugo's ballad are related to the fantastic sections of *Faust,* and both poems, in turn, have a common ancestor in the witches' scene from Shakespeare's *Macbeth.* The similarity of metrical plan and black magic imagery is unmistakable. The same rhythmic language stimulates the ear and the imagination in the Walpurgis Night scene from *Faust.* The scene is filled with witches riding he-goats and giant owls, the earth crawls with salamanders and coiling snakes, and bats fly around and glittering fireflies provide the illumination. As Mephistopheles describes the ghostly dance, all manner of gruesome and awesome night creatures

> . . . crowd and jostle, whirl, and flutter!
> They whisper, babble, twirl, and splutter!
> They glimmer, sparkle, stink, and flare—
> A true witch-element! Beware!

ROMANTIC MUSIC: HECTOR BERLIOZ

At the dawn of Romanticism, Paris's salons were populated with poets, playwrights, journalists, critics, architects, painters, sculptors, musicians, and utopian political reformers. Heinrich Heine, a poet and journalist from northern Germany, and composers Chopin from Poland and Franz Liszt from Hungary mixed freely with French artists and intellectuals such as Hugo, Théophile Gautier, Alphonse Lamartine, François-Auguste-René Chateaubriand, Alfred de Musset, Dumas, and George Sand. Social philosophers such as Félicité-Robert de Lamennais, Pierre-Joseph Proudhon, Auguste Comte, and Henri de Saint-Simon gave a political accent to the artists' aesthetic debates.

Even in the supercharged atmosphere of the Paris salons, Hector Berlioz must have appeared as an authentic apparition, embodying in the flesh the wildest Romantic dreams and nightmares. One contemporary described him as a young man trembling with passion, whose large umbrella of hair projected like a movable awning over the beak of a bird of prey. Berlioz combined qualities that made him a great composer, the ranking orchestral conductor of his day, a brilliant journalist, and an autobiographer. As a conductor, he was caricatured by

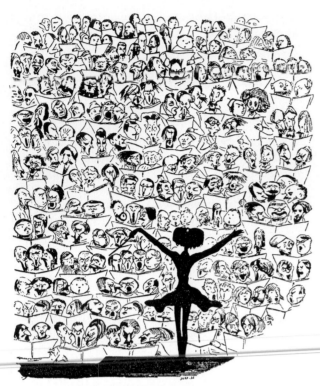

18.17   Gustave Doré. *Berlioz Conducting Massed Choirs,* nineteenth-century caricature.

the painter Gustave Doré as the mad musician (Fig. 18.17). At the first performance of one of his overtures, when the orchestra failed to give him the effect he demanded, he burst into tears, tore his hair, and fell sobbing on the kettledrums.

From Berlioz's lively *Memoirs* one gathers that his development was jarred by a series of emotional shocks that he received from his first contact with the literature and music of his time. The fires of his explosive imagination were ignited by Goethe's *Faust,* which resulted in his "Dramatic Legend," *The Damnation of Faust.* The poetry of Byron became a symphony for viola and orchestra, *Harold in Italy.* Shakespeare's tragedy inspired his *Romeo and Juliet Symphony,* and Dante's *Divine Comedy* was the inspiration for his *Requiem.*

Berlioz's *Fantastic Symphony,* first performed in 1830, contains a complex of many ideas gathered from the musical and literary atmosphere that surrounded him. Its subtitle, "Episode in the Life of an Artist," tells the listener that it is based on a story. In Berlioz's detailed program notes, it is clear that he took the idea of poisoning by opium from English author Thomas De Quincey's sensational *Confessions of an English Opium Eater,* a recent best-selling book.

The musical form of the first movement ("Reveries—Passions"), with its slow largo intro-

duction and vigorous allegro continuation, is in the symphonic tradition of Beethoven. Its principal claim to technical originality is the use of an *idée fixe,* or "fixed idea," through which Berlioz conveys the notion of the beloved, who is present in every thought. The changing shape of the theme on its appearance in each of the five movements fulfills a dual purpose: it provides an appearance of unity in the sequence of mood pieces, and it expresses, through its mutations, the necessary dramatic progress.

In the succeeding movement, "A Ball," the hero beholds his beloved dancing a brilliant concert waltz in all the glamour and glitter of a great social occasion. The slow third movement, "Scene in the Country," brings out both benign and malignant aspects of nature as the hero seeks refuge and consolation in a true evocation of the Romantic sublime.

Prior to the fourth movement, the hero dreams that he has murdered his beloved. After being condemned to death, he is led to the guillotine. The final bars sound the idée fixe in the piercing, high register of the clarinet. It is suddenly cut off as the blade falls. After a dull thud and a roll of the drums, the crowd roars its bloodthirsty approval.

The symphony ends with the diabolical "Dream of a Sabbath Night," a grisly scene that serves as both a climax and an unresolved end. This movement, which fully justifies the adjective *fantastic,* is divided into three distinct sections. The first suggests a weird landscape with strange creatures described by high woodwinds and accompanied by the ominous roll of the kettledrums. The heroine appears at the witches' Sabbath, in which the idée fixe is now distorted and transfigured. Was she a witch all along and disguised in desirable human form only in the hero's imagination, or is this merely another manifestation of her "bewitching" power? The entrance at this point of his beloved on her broomstick, accompanied by a pandemonium of sulfurous sounds, settles the matter. The hero gives a shriek of horror. After the shocking revelation, she executes a few capers and subsides for the moment.

The second section of the final movement begins with the tolling of bells, recalling the opening lines of Hugo's ballad. The foreboding *Dies irae* is solemnly intoned, first by the brass instruments. The offbeat syncopations injected into this Gothic liturgical melody fulfill Berlioz's promise that he would compose a "burlesque parody" on the *Dies irae.* Besides serving Berlioz as an evocation of the fire-and-brimstone aspects of medieval Christianity, it also introduces a form of macabre humor. This parody of a sacred melody caused considerable comment at the time. Might it be Romantic irony, or might Berlioz have conceived of this use of the *Dies irae* in the same way that Dante called his work a "divine comedy?" The devil is conceded to be a clever theologian, and in Goethe's drama he is found in the sacred precincts of the church, whispering in Margaret's ear as she listens to the choir chant the *Dies irae* (Fig. 18.3).

The third and final section is titled "Rondo of the Witches' Sabbath," after Victor Hugo's neomedieval, bloodcurdling, Black Mass ballad. It was also the subject of one of Goya's paintings, *Witches' Sabbath* (Fig. 18.11). A dance fragment hinted at earlier now becomes the "Rondo of the Sabbath." A series of fugal entrances begins with the cellos and double basses, followed by successive entries, each with a different instrumental combination. It must be noted that when Berlioz wrote his wildest and most fantastic images, his mind was fully in command. As he expressed it, "One must do coolly the things that are most fiery."

Finally, the *Dies irae* makes a reappearance, joining the fugue subject in a skillful interweaving of the thematic materials. With final bloodcurdling shrieks, flying images, and a blast from the brasses, the symphony is brought to a vivid close.

After the *Fantastic Symphony,* use of the *Dies irae* became a symbol of the macabre, and it has been used countless times since. Liszt's *Totentanz (Dance of Death)* for piano and orchestra is a set of variations on it. It appears again in Gustav Mahler's Second Symphony and in Sergey Rachmaninoff's *Rhapsody on a Theme of Paganini.* With this final movement, Berlioz also established a style that brought the demonic element—and a chain of harmonic and psychological dissonances—into music to stay. Both Modest Musorgsky's *Night on Bald Mountain* and Camille Saint-Saëns's *Danse Macabre* are cut from the same cloth. Finally, in the music dramas of Richard Wagner the influence of Berlioz's orchestration and his experiments in combining voices and orchestral music in dramatic symphonies and oratorios is all-pervasive.

THE WAGNERIAN SYNTHESIS

Wagner's art matured later than that of his younger contemporaries, giving him the advantage of being able to review the entire Romantic scene and create a synthesis of Romantic elements. Beethoven, he believed, had blazed a new trail in bringing vocal soloists and a chorus into his great Ninth Symphony, and his genius for developing motifs was unparalleled. Schubert's union of poetry and instrumental music in the *Lied,* or art song, was on too small a scale. Carl Maria von Weber had made a

brave beginning toward establishing a national German opera, but it did not go far enough. Robert Schumann's Romanticism was perhaps too refined and obscure, but it had a certain attraction. Niccolò Paganini and Liszt were sensational virtuoso performers, but personal skill was a perishable commodity. Chopin's urbane and polished style was restricted to the piano, but his chromatic harmony proved good grist for the Wagnerian mill. Liszt's programmatic symphonic poems, with their drama and thematic development, pointed in the right direction. Berlioz's original experiments in combining drama, symphony, and opera would be very useful to Wagner. When Wagner peered backward into history, the dramatic power and sweep of Shakespeare and the colossal baroque qualities of George Frideric Handel did not escape his notice. In Wagner's view, none of these approaches was sufficiently successful in itself. Still, all contained enough vital elements to ensure success if carefully selected, blended, and combined in the proper proportions. Ultimately, Wagner projected a synthesis of all these tendencies wrapped up in a package he called the *Gesamtkunstwerk,* the complete work of art, including symphony, mythology, poetry, and drama.

The self-declared musico-dramatic successor to Shakespeare and Beethoven took most of his material from German mythology. *Tannhäuser, Lohengrin,* and *Parsifal* come from the poetry and legends of the thirteenth-century minnesingers. *Tristan und Isolde* stems from a Gothic romance, whereas *The Ring of the Nibelung* derives from an early Germanic epic, the *Nibelungenlied* (see p. 175). *The Mastersingers of Nuremberg,* on the other hand, is set in Renaissance times.

Wagner's mature music dramas are closer to the symphonic idea than they are to Italian operatic conventions. The principal lyrical element is transferred to the orchestra, and the general effect is that of a vast symphonic poem with visualized stage spectacle and vocalized running commentary on the orchestral action by the singers. Because the music of his mature operas runs on in unbroken continuity, arias and recitatives effectively disappear as such. Only rarely is a self-contained aria introduced.

In lieu of aria, recitative, or ensemble numbers, the essential convention in Wagnerian music drama becomes the **leitmotifs,** or leading motifs. These aphoristic fragments vary in length from short phrases to melodies and are designed to characterize individuals, aspects of personality, abstract ideas, the singular properties of inanimate objects, and the like. Wagner was astoundingly skillful in his capacity to create such musical-dramatic characterizations with minimal means.

Musical Example 18.1
Richard Wagner, *Ring of the Nibelung*
A. Young Siegfried
B. Mature Siegfried
C. Siegfried as hero
D. Siegfried's death

These motifs are by no means static entities; they undergo constant development. The carefree 9/8 time of Siegfried's jaunty horn call (Musical Example 18.1A) portrays the buoyant mood of the youthful hunter. But when this child of nature reaches manhood, the rhythm is transformed into that of a march with incisive offbeat accents (Musical Example 18.1B). When Siegfried attains his true heroic stature, the same theme is amplified by full harmonies and reinforced by the whole brass choir and rolling drums (Musical Example 18.1C). Finally, as the hero lies treacherously slain, the tempo slackens and the theme is heard in a mournful minor key (Musical Example 18.1D).

With a fairly large number of such motifs to work with, the orchestra's participation in the drama is vastly enlarged. Moreover, a motif sounded in the orchestra can recall an earlier event and clarify the motivation behind a given action on the stage. In the *Ring,* which takes four evenings to complete, events of the first night *(Das Rheingold)* can be recalled by this means in subsequent installments. Similarly, the orchestra can anticipate the future for the listener. At the end of the second evening *(Die Walküre),* for instance, when Wotan puts Brünnhilde to sleep on a mountain ringed with magic fire with the promise that only an intrepid and fearless mortal will awaken and claim her, the orchestra first announces (and Wotan then takes up) the motif that will subsequently be associated with Siegfried as hero. At this point in the drama Siegfried is not yet born, but in the world of mythology the prediction can safely be made.

The orchestra can also interpret states of mind that are not yet explicit in overt action on stage. Thus, when Siegmund and Sieglinde meet (Act I of *Die Walküre),* the orchestra makes clear that they are falling in love, although their conversation indicates that they themselves are as yet quite unaware of it. Finally, the leading-motif system proves its efficacy at the end of the cycle in *Die Götterdämmerung (The Twilight of the Gods).* In Act III, when the mortally wounded Siegfried recalls his past and in the subsequent orchestral funeral oration, all the motifs previously associated with him pass by in biographical review: fate; his mother, Sieglinde; the heroism of his paternal ancestors, the Wälsungs; the sword; Siegfried's own theme; Siegfried as hero; and finally the women in his life, Brünnhilde and Gutrune. Such a procedure lends itself to biography in music and at the same time summarizes the entire dramatic cycle.

In Wagner's music, the intellectual trends, the technical devices, and the emotional directions of Romanticism come together. In addition to summing up the past and synthesizing the nineteenth-century system of writing motifs, Wagner pushed the frontiers of Western harmony to their outermost limits. This sensuous, seductive **chromaticism,** with its tangled web of motifs, never-ending chains of chordal progressions, and complex counterpoints carried through to a rapturous conclusion, was destined to have profound effects on the future course of music.

Recognizing the essential symphonic core of Wagner's writing, many post-Wagnerian composers dispensed with stage business altogether and wrote dramatic music in other mediums. Johannes Brahms clung to the symphonic form developed by Beethoven, but Anton Bruckner, Gustav Mahler, and Richard Strauss translated the Wagnerian idioms into the program symphony and symphonic poem. Similarly, César Franck translated these idioms into organ and orchestral works; Hugo Wolf, into songs for voice and piano; and Arnold Schoenberg, into program chamber music such as *Verklärte Nacht (Transfigured Night)* and orchestral song cycles such as his *Gurrelieder (Songs of Gurre).*

ROMANTIC INDIVIDUALISM AND NATIONALISM

Romantic social and political thought viewed people as individuals first and members of society second. The Romantic period was also the age of the emancipation of the individual and the era of the great hero who attained such heights through personal effort. Napoleon stamped his image on the age—as the corporal who became a general, as the bureaucrat who became emperor, and as the individual who for a time completely dominated the European scene. His rise fired the ambitions of aspiring artists to conquer their own worlds in poetry, painting, sculpture, architecture, and music. Similarly, the continued rise of the middle class, fueled particularly by the Industrial Revolution in England and France, created a milieu in which the rough-around-the-edges self-made individual was honored for willpower and grudgingly admired for amassing a fortune. In turn, these newly rich individuals pressured government for greater input and influence.

Artists vied with each other for positions on the top rung of the ladder in their respective fields. For sheer technique in letters it would be difficult to surpass Hugo, who could write with mastery in any style. Viollet-le-Duc and other architects could duplicate any building in the history of architecture. The feats of such bravura composer-performers as the violinist Paganini and the pianist Liszt are legendary.

All this was, perhaps, an assertion of the diminishing self in the face of the growing organization of society under collective control. Each work of art was associated with the personality of a distinctive individual. It was no longer enough for an artist to be merely the master of a craft, no matter how high the degree of skill. The artist also had to be a great personality, a prophet, and a leader, with what today is called a signature style.

Consequently, the Romantic era was one of autobiography, confessions, memoirs, portraiture, and the dramatic stroke. The preoccupation with living a "life" worthy of recording in biography took so much time that it could be a real handicap to artistic production.

The place of the artist in society had been a matter of vital concern to artists such as David and Beethoven, who combined the moralistic fervor of revolutionary thought with a sense of social responsibility. David's championship of the cause of art in the French legislature and Beethoven's behavior toward his patrons as their social equal reveal both men as modern artists who placed the aristocracy of genius on a higher plane than that of birth.

The force of national identity also entered the picture. Chopin, with his polonaises and mazurkas and his "Revolutionary" étude, became the champion of Polish nationhood. Liszt with his Hungarian rhapsodies emerged as a national hero of his native country. Giuseppe Verdi's operas, especially *Nabucco (Nebuchadnezzar)*, became chapters in the book of Italian nationalism. In *Nabucco*, the plight of the children of Israel was a thinly disguised picture of Italy under foreign control. Its famous chorus became a revolutionary anthem and

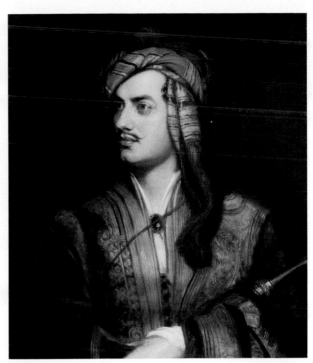

18.18   Thomas Phillips. *Lord Byron in Albanian Costume*, 1814. Oil on canvas, 2′5½″ × 2′½″. National Portrait Gallery, London, England.

the letters of Verdi's name were understood to be an acronym for political union under one Italian king: **V**ictor **E**mmanuel **R**e **d'I**talia.

Byron, Delacroix, and others were compelled to bend their energies and talents to the cause of liberating the oppressed Greek people from Turkish rule. Lord Byron's meteoric career became at once the living symbol of Romantic melancholy and the personification of freedom and political liberalism. He was idealized as a champion of oppressed peoples everywhere (Fig. 18.18). He first visited Athens in 1809 and immediately identified himself with the goals of Greek independence. On that first visit he translated a famous ancient Greek war song, giving it a contemporary twist by substituting Turkey for the old Persian enemy:

> Sons of the Greeks! let us go
> In arms against the foe. . . .
> Then manfully despising
> The Turkish tyrant's yoke,
> Let your country see you rising, And all her
>   chains are broke.

In a more melodious and lyrical vein, he penned these lovely lines:

> Maid of Athens, ere we part,
> Give, oh give me back my heart!
> Or, since that has left my breast,
> Keep it now and take the rest!

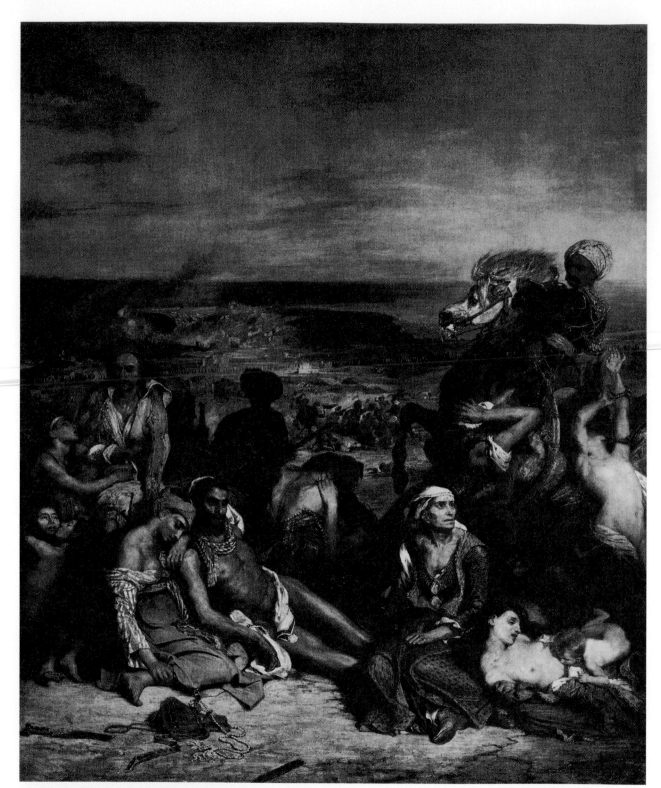

18.19   Eugène Delacroix. *Scenes of the Massacre at Chios: Greek Families Awaiting Death or Slavery,* 1824. Oil on canvas, 13′7″ × 11′10″. Louvre, Paris, France.

In 1823, while residing in Italy, Byron joined the London Greek Committee in furthering the cause of Greek independence. He then chartered the ship *Hercules,* financing the campaign partly with his own fortune, and sailed to Missolonghi in western Greece, where he died of a fever in 1824 while trying to bring the feuding factions together.

Eugène Delacroix was a constant reader of Byron's works. As he remarks in his journal, "To set fire to yourself, remember certain passages from Byron." His *Massacre at Chios* (Fig. 18.19) was inspired by one of the most gruesome episodes in that messy war. In a naval battle off the shores of Chios, the Greeks had set fire to the Turkish flagship, burning to death the crew and a detachment of soldiers. As an act of reprisal, the Turks rounded up 25,000 innocent bystanders on the island, burned their town, slaughtered most of them, and sold twice their number into slavery. This brutal incident outraged all of Europe. Delacroix's painting reflected this wave of indignation while it was still fresh.

The canvas is heroic in its proportions: almost 14 feet high and more than 11 feet wide. The entire foreground and all of the middle-distance figures are life-size. The full title is *Scenes of the Massacre at Chios: Greek Families Awaiting Death or Slavery.* The French writer and critic Théophile Gautier commented on the "feverish convulsive drawing and the violent coloring." These were the very qualities that inflamed Delacroix's critics, who dubbed it "The Massacre of Painting." Particularly apparent is the sensuous treatment of the women's bodies, especially the bound figure in the right middle ground. This softness strongly contrasts with the force, muscularity, and cruelty seen in the face and form of the Turkish cavalry officer. Also eloquent is the sense of defeat, apprehension, and despair written on the grandmotherly face of the woman in the foreground. The distant background, with the smoking town and threatening sky, contributes to the sense of doom.

An artist could fashion a self-image in classical terms as a Prometheus or in the medieval vocabulary as a knight championing the weak against the strong. Interestingly, while the industrialization of labor created foul slums and great human suffering in cities near at hand, artists were generally more interested in researching and depicting the past. Some located national identity in folk tales and ballads of a particular locale; others did so in collections and variations of Spanish epics, Scottish ballads, and German fairy tales; still others, in the writing of Italian symphonies, Hungarian rhapsodies, and Polish mazurkas. In part, nationalism,

like the medieval revival, was a northern declaration of cultural independence from the Mediterranean tradition, fired with opposition to Napoleon in England and Germany. Berlioz's nationalism is expressed in a much more subtle way, but his symphonic operas without words, concert overtures, and music dramas were as distinct a departure from the prevailing Italian operatic tradition as were those of Weber in Germany.

EXOTICISM

As European countries expanded their colonial empires, the exotic terrain of Asia and Africa held endless fascination for poets, novelists, and artists, as well as their readers and audiences. Spain had started the process with its vast holdings extending from the Americas to the Philippine Islands. England followed with the conquest of India and large parts of Africa. The French claimed Algeria and parts of central Africa. Shrewd business leaders opened up new foreign markets, while missionaries tried to bridge the gap between Christian and non-Christian regions. Artists captured the popular imagination with scenes of exotic mysteries associated with far-off lands and peoples.

The striking *Portrait of a Black Woman* (Fig. 18.20) by Marie-Guillemine Benoist, painted

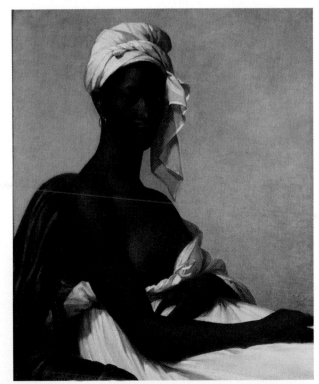

18.20 Marie-Guillemine Benoist. *Portrait of a Black Woman,* 1800. Oil on canvas, 2′8″ × 2′1½″. Louvre, Paris, France.

in 1800, shows how exoticism quietly seeped into neoclassical aesthetics. Benoist studied with Vigée-LeBrun (see pp. 443–444) and worked in David's studio along with several women. In the same year that David painted the portrait of Madame Récamier (see Fig. 17.4), Benoist exhibited her *Portrait of a Black Woman*. Benoist's cool drawing is reminiscent of David, but the sensitive individualization of the sitter is not. Against a gleaming cream background, the unknown sitter seems relaxed and elegant. Her white dress, cinched under the bust in the Empire style, has been slipped off her shoulder to display her breast. In a period when women of color were often portrayed as ignorant, dissipated, or promiscuous, the sitter displays gravity and grace. At the same time, though, the blackness of her skin is deliberately exaggerated against the light dress and background, and despite the artist's possible intentions, the work may have appeared exotic to viewers. Benoist's career was cut short when her husband achieved a high-ranking political office and she was obliged to give up painting.

Benoist is thought to have founded a workshop for women painters, about which little is known. Another painter, Adélaïde Labille-Guiard, who ran a studio for women, was admitted to the Royal Academy at the same time as Vigée-LeBrun. During her short professional life, she actively campaigned within the Academy to give women greater access to art training and to increase the number of women who could be admitted to more than four. Labille-Guiard helped open the Academy's salon to younger women like Benoist.

ORIENTALISM

"Enough of Greece and Rome: Th'exhausted store / of either nation now can charm no more." So went the prologue of Arthur Murphy's play of 1759, *Orphans of China.* Thus, Asia took its turn in the West's repertory of imagined places. Its image in one guise or another has been incorporated in the arts to the present day. Reflections of this early phase can be found in operas such as Gluck's *Unforeseen Meeting, or The Pilgrims to Mecca* (1764) and Mozart's *Abduction from the Seraglio* (1785), with its setting in a Turkish harem, and in William Beckford's Oriental novel *Vathek* (1786).

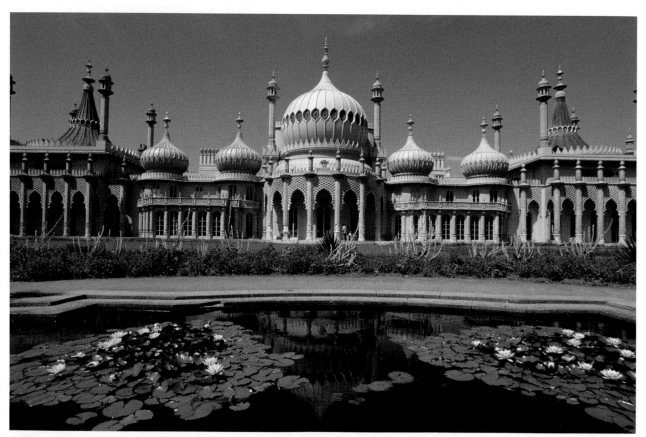

18.21   John Nash. Royal Pavilion, Brighton, England, 1815–1822. Lithograph.

Kew Gardens, a public park in London, was studded with fanciful structures revealing a wide imaginative range. Some paths led to little rococo pavilions; others led to Greek temples or Gothic chapels. There was a Muslim mosque, a Moorish palace, and a "house of Confucius." A pagoda, built by the Palladian architect William Chambers, is the only one of these fancies that has survived (see Fig. 16.21).

In England, the tale *Thalabor the Destroyer* (1799), by Robert Southey, included chapters called "The Desert Circle" and "Life in an Arab Tent." Drawing rooms were hung with wallpaper depicting scenes of Mandarin China, and hostesses poured tea at Chinese Chippendale tables. The Prince Regent of England commissioned his architect to build a fanciful Royal Pavilion at his favorite seaside resort of Brighton (Fig. 18.21). John Nash, who had previously built an exotic country house for a gentleman who had lived in India, came up

with an Arabian Nights extravaganza in a style that was then referred to as "Indian Gothic." The exterior is an exotic fantasy of minarets and cupolas, pinnacles and pagodas, all constructed over cast-iron frames. A domed ceiling painted like a spreading palm tree covers the dining hall (Fig. 18.22). Completing the decor are water-lily chandeliers suspended from the cast-iron claws of scaly dragons, along with lotus-blossom lamps, Asian lacquerware, and Chinese Chippendale furniture.

Colorful Japanese prints that found their way to Europe after Commodore Matthew C. Perry's voyage of 1852–1854 had an important effect on painting (see p. 530). In 1860, Gautier published a popular book called *L'Orient,* which was based on his travels. At this time, Delacroix was painting one of his last pictures, *The Lion Hunt,* which vividly portrayed the violent struggle of men and horses against the unbridled ferocity of wild animals. Charles-François Gounod's opera

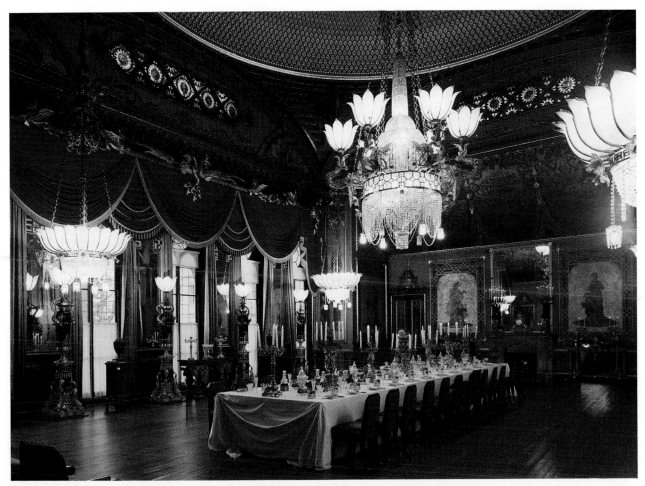

18.22   John Nash. Banqueting Room, Royal Pavilion, Brighton, England, 1815–1821.

The Queen of Sheba was produced in 1862, at about the same time Jean-Auguste-Dominique Ingres was finishing his fleshscape *The Turkish Bath* (Fig. 18.23), one of many painted harem fantasies. These images of sexually promiscuous women helped justify colonial expansion on the ground that some cultures promoted immoral activities and needed Western guidance.

The search for exotic settings eventually reached its climax in two of the greatest works for the lyric stage: Verdi's *Aïda* (1871), set in ancient Egypt and premiered in Cairo in celebration of the opening of the Suez Canal, and Bizet's *Carmen* (1875), set in Spain and based on a short story by Prosper Mérimée. Toward the end of the century exoticism began to pall, and the realist novelist Émile Zola made fun of his Romantic colleague Gautier because "he needed a camel and four dirty Bedouins to tickle his brains into creativity."

BACK TO NATURE

Rousseau sounded the call of "back to nature" in the late eighteenth century. In so doing, he challenged the image of so-called civilized life with his notion of the noble savage whose integrity was achieved by shunning society and communing with nature.

For his own part, Rousseau was perfectly willing to be received in courtly circles. His rustic opera, *Le Devin du Village (The Village Soothsayer),* was performed for Louis XVI at Versailles with great success. In fact, his ideas were partly responsible for the country cottage, complete with a dairy and mill, that Queen Marie Antoinette had built for herself amid the formal gardens of Versailles (Fig. 18.24).

The back-to-nature idea grew steadily and became one of the more popular nineteenth-century escape mechanisms for city dwellers who dreamed

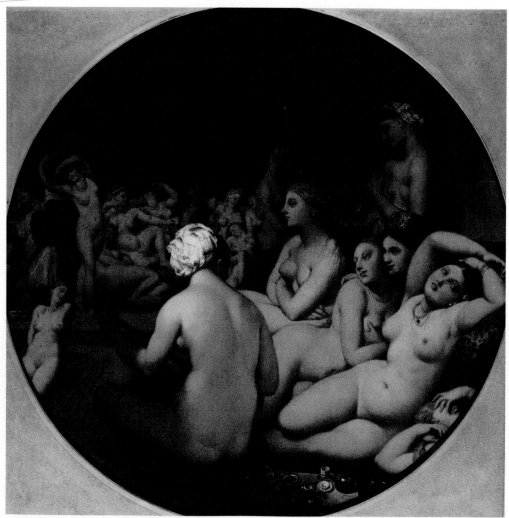

18.23 Jean-Auguste-Dominique Ingres. *The Turkish Bath,* c. 1852–1863. Oil on canvas, diameter 3′6½″. Louvre, Paris, France.

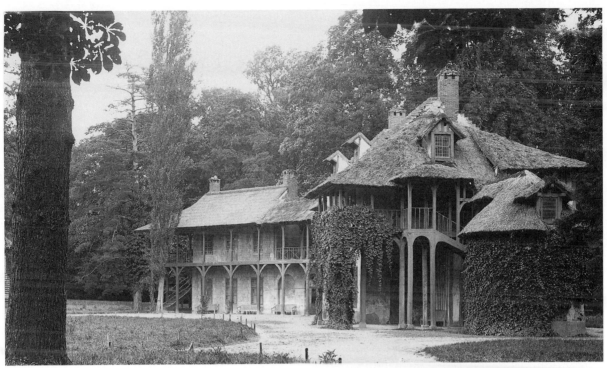

18.24   Richard Mique. Marie Antoinette's Cottage (Le Hameau), Versailles, France, 1783–1786.

of an idyllic country life that they could not or would not live. Aristocratic and middle-class audiences delighted in reading poetry that was full of nature imagery and in hearing folk ballads and fairy tales. In the preface to his second collection of *Lyrical Ballads,* the English poet William Wordsworth argued for a truth of nature based on the experience of simple, rustic life. Poetry to him was not the stilted, decorous language of the salon but, as he phrased it, "the spontaneous overflow of

powerful feelings . . . recollected in tranquility." The new urban well-to-do and middle classes hung landscapes by Camille Corot on the walls of their apartments and townhouses. Beethoven's *Pastoral Symphony* and Wagner's "Forest Murmurs," as well as dozens of piano pieces and songs, sounded the proper rustic note in music.

Rosa Bonheur achieved her greatest fame for her pictures of horses. The sweeping canvas *The Horse Fair* (Fig. 18.25), now at the Metropolitan

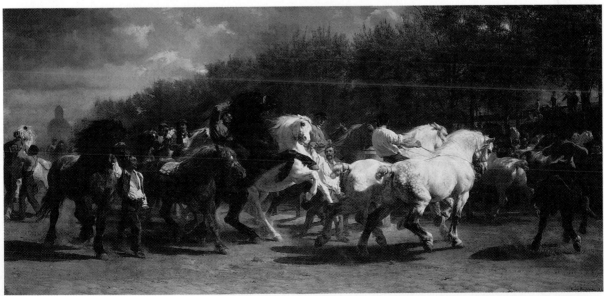

18.25   Rosa Bonheur. *The Horse Fair,* 1855. Oil on canvas, 8′1¼″ × 16′7½″. Metropolitan Museum of Art, New York. Gift of Cornelius Vanderbilt, 1887.

Museum of Art in New York City, created an international sensation and became the best-loved animal picture of the nineteenth century. She said that she was first inspired by the frieze of men and horses on the Parthenon (see Fig. 2.13). The dramatic lighting, the release of animal energy, and the keen and accurate rendering of equine anatomy all commanded wide attention, and engraved reproductions were eagerly acquired by a wide audience.

John Constable's studies of the English countryside, such as *Hay Wain* (Fig. 18.26) and *Salisbury Cathedral from the Bishop's Garden* (Fig. 18.27), recorded the look and especially the light of everyday scenes. Constable's major pictorial interests were in capturing unpredictable and fleeting changes of atmosphere; the infinitely varied intensities of light on clear, showery, or foggy days; sunshine filtered through translucent green leaves; and the changing reflections of the sky and passing clouds on water. To capture these effects, Constable made numerous oil sketches outdoors and later finished his pictures in his studio. When his paintings were exhibited in Paris, their freshness, warmth, and spontaneity created a considerable stir. Delacroix

admired Constable's bold use of color. His descriptive powers and technical innovations had an important influence on the Impressionists.

In contrast to Constable's goal of accurately depicting natural phenomena, the works of J. M. W. Turner, also English and a contemporary of Constable, were poetic invocations and emotional experiences tinged with Romantic melancholy. In his early pictures, Turner did variations on the landscapes and seascapes of Claude Lorrain, whom he admired above all other artists. Turner's style, however, gradually transformed his history paintings to emphasize purely visual and painterly effects. His grays and browns yielded to thin glazes of soft pastel hues and sparkling yellow and orange tonalities. Turner's titles, such as *Snowstorm: Hannibal and His Army Crossing the Alps, Shade and Darkness: The Evening of the Deluge, Wreck of a Transport Ship,* and *Fire at Sea,* indicate his zeal to capture on canvas some of the elemental forces of nature and link them to dramatic historical events. In one of his late works, *Rain, Steam, and Speed: The Great Western Railway* (Fig. 18.28), the viewer feels the impact of headlong movement in the Edinburgh Express as it crosses a bridge in a driving storm.

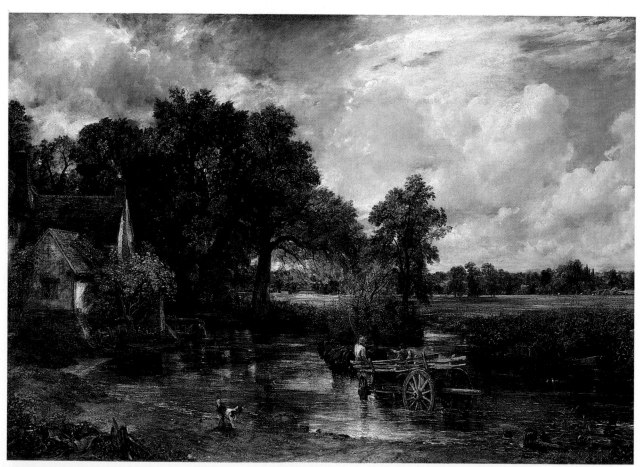

18.26 JOHN CONSTABLE. *Hay Wain,* 1821. Oil on canvas, approx. 4′2½″ × 6′1″. National Gallery, London, England.

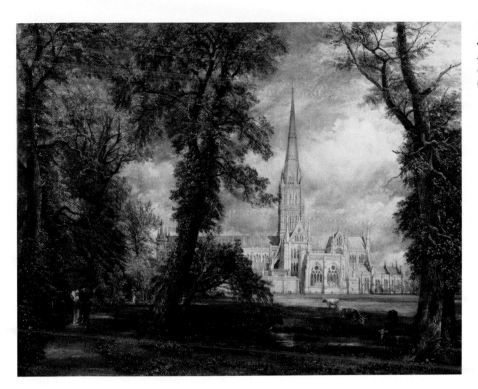

18.27 John Constable. *Salisbury Cathedral from the Bishop's Garden,* 1826. Oil on canvas, 2′11″ × 3′8¼″. Frick Collection, New York.

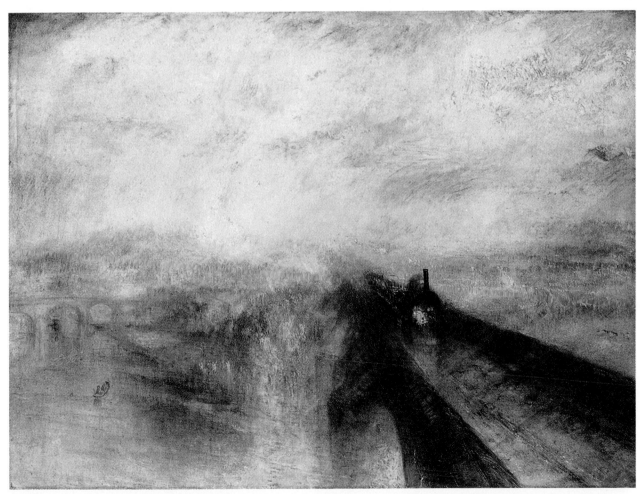

18.28 Joseph Mallord William Turner. *Rain, Steam, and Speed: The Great Western Railway,* 1844. Oil on canvas, 2′11½″ × 3′11⅝″. National Gallery, London, England.

The rabbit racing ahead of the train symbolizes both speed and the Romantic vision of modern technology as a threat to nature. Amid the swirling, spiraling storm of wind and rain, the engine's firebox glows with hot, flamelike color that contrasts with the dark blue of the passenger cars and the flecks of light blue in the sky. Constable once criticized Turner for his "airy visions painted with tinted steam," but in retrospect Turner's glowing canvases, many-colored light, and ethereal atmospheric effects proclaim him one of the most daring colorists in the history of painting. He pioneered the use of light and color as a language for conveying mood, yearning, and intuitive glimpses of unfathomable forces beyond the intellect's reach.

Although Turner's subjects were not usually political, his *Slavers Overthrowing the Dead and Dying, Typhoon Coming On* (Fig. 18.29) was an exception. Based on a grisly incident that took place in 1783, the painting indistinctly shows dead and dying slaves being thrown overboard so that the captain of the slave ship could claim an insurance loss. Slaves who drowned at sea were insured, but those who were among the many who simply died at sea because of neglect were not insured. The painting itself is like a raw wound. Blood-red colors slash across the middle. In the foreground, shackled bodies struggle against churning, burnt-looking waves and a host of odd predatory fish. Turner knew his audience would be familiar with the incident, so he did not need to detail the event. Instead, he created a shocking spew of color to symbolize the moral calamity. The painting was shown in 1840, during the summer salon of the Royal Academy. This work, and other more detailed documentary images of slavery, helped rouse the first meeting of the British and Foreign Anti-Slavery Society in London, 1 month after *The Slave Ship* was exhibited.

In Germany the Romantic landscape painters were closely associated with poets and philosophers. Caspar David Friedrich's *The Wanderer above the Mist* (Fig. 18.30) presents an image of man alone amid the awesome expanse of nature, guided only by his inner light. Like the transcendental philosophers of the Romantic period, Friedrich believed that God revealed himself in nature. Here the haunt-

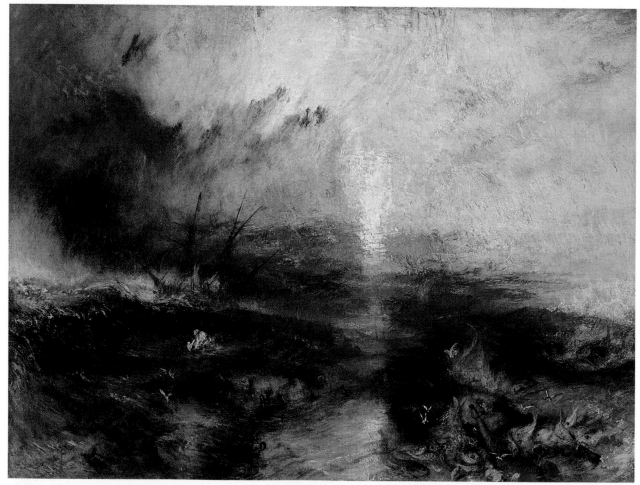

18.29 Joseph Mallord William Turner. *Slavers Overthrowing the Dead and Dying, Typhoon Coming On,* 1840. Oil on canvas, 2'11¹¹⁄₁₆" × 4'5⁵⁄₁₆". Museum of Fine Arts, Boston. Henry Lillie Pierce Fund.

ing space and mood of brooding melancholy recall the lyric poetry of Wilhelm Müller, as set in Franz Schubert's poignant and powerful song cycle *Die Winterreise (Winter's Journey)*.

The American painter Thomas Cole was the leading landscapist of the Hudson River School. For him, nature was a Bible and painting was the revelation of God's handiwork. The sweeping grandeur of the America he portrayed was wild and untamed, a rugged wilderness far from the tame and familiar European countryside. In his pictures the viewer was drawn into a magnified version of the Catskill Mountains, complete with craggy cliffs, fallen trees, and gushing streams. Cole's vision is captured in his own words: "Seated on a pleasant knoll, the mind may travel far into futurity. Where the wolf roams, the plough shall glisten; on the gray crag shall rise temple and tower; mighty deeds shall be done in the pathless wilderness; and poets yet unborn shall sanctify the soil." In other words,

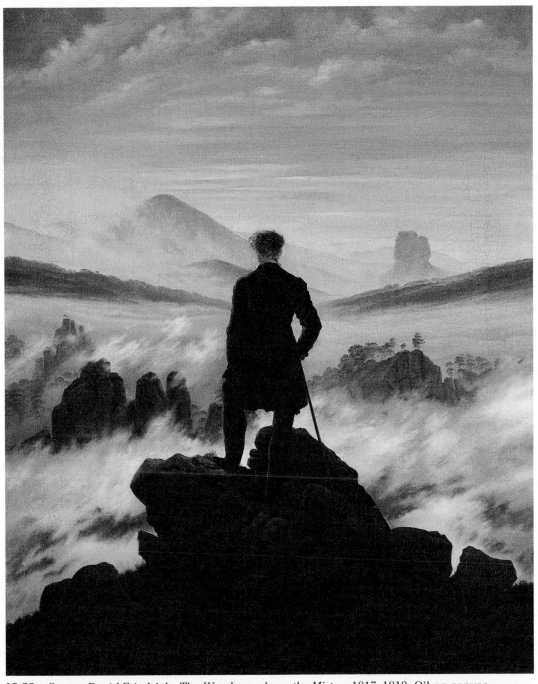

18.30   Casper David Friedrich. *The Wanderer above the Mist,* c. 1817–1818. Oil on canvas, 2′5½″ × 3′1¼″. Kunsthalle, Hamburg, Germany.

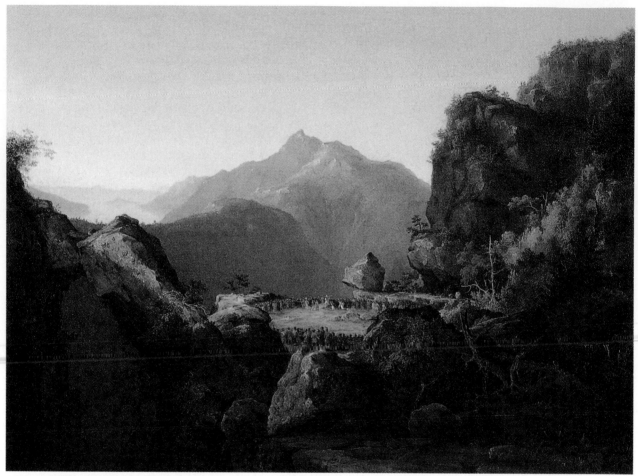

18.31   Thomas Cole. *The Last of the Mohicans,* 1827. Oil on canvas, 2′1″ × 3′1″. New York State Historical Association, Cooperstown, New York.

he thought the pristine quality of American nature would soon yield to the plow and the city.

In his *The Last of the Mohicans* (Fig. 18.31), Cole painted a scene from James Fenimore Cooper's popular novel of the same name. If not the first, then certainly it is among the earliest American paintings taken from an American novel. A viewer who did not know the novel's plot would gain little from the painting, whose tiny figures are engulfed in light in the midst of wild nature. In the scene, a white woman and an Indian man argue their opposing values. Both Cole and Cooper created landscapes that equated the United States with wilderness and natural law. In their works, nature is the main character.

IDEAS: ROMANTIC HISTORICISM

History, in the scholarly sense, originated in the late eighteenth and early nineteenth centuries. The newly awakened interest in earlier periods and peoples began with archeological discoveries in Pompeii and Herculaneum in the eighteenth cen-

tury and continued with French and British discoveries in Egypt. In the northern European countries, awareness of medieval sagas, poetry, and romances found literary expression in fanciful Gothic novels. In architecture, it took the form of building neo-Gothic castles and reconstructing and preserving medieval abbeys, churches, and cathedrals. There were even architects who specialized in building picturesque ruins.

The dynamics of the revolutionary period, with its social, political, and industrial upheavals, confronted artists with the image of a rapidly changing world. No longer were the arts produced only for a small, sophisticated group of aristocrats. Instead, they were addressed to a larger and more anonymous public, mainly the middle class. Indeed, most of the artists of this period were themselves from the middle or lower middle classes. They knew that their audience was not hungering for subtle symbolism and arcane innuendo. In addition, an architect could seldom count on one patron for a single monumental project but rather had to cater to many clients with smaller buildings.

The concept of a divinely regulated universe controlled by a cosmic clockmaker no longer seemed valid in a world of constant change. The Romantic period had come to grips with the drive of emotion and the force of fanaticism. Even the new scientific discoveries seemed to make the world more, rather than less, mysterious and beyond the grasp of ordinary folk. Artists began to reach beyond logic and delve deeply into subconscious states of mind beyond rational controls.

Romanticism, then, is a blanket term that covers a whole spectrum of social trends, individual attitudes, and artistic responses. Like neoclassicism, it was not concentrated in one cultural center but was a fully fledged international movement, modified, of course, by regional and national accents. The high degree of individualism ruled out a single stylistic direction. Personal hopes, fears, beliefs, and feelings were mirrored in the work of each individual artist, and the consequences were profound and far-reaching. Above all, the Romantic view included a sense of history. Creating imaginary places far apart from workaday situations proved a welcome refuge from the increasingly industrialized and mechanized world. It was now not sufficient for an artist to be a fine craftsperson; it was necessary to become a great personality and perhaps a champion of epic causes as well.

A sense of history pervaded almost all aspects of thought and activity in the Romantic Movement. In France, England, and Germany the medieval past in particular was associated with the foundations of nationhood. The French turned toward their beginnings in the preservation of their Gothic past in architecture, painting, and literature. In England, the neo-Gothic Houses of Parliament recalled the origin of their constitution with the signing of the Magna Carta in 1215. In Germany, memories of past grandeur pointed back to the Carolingian and Ottonian periods.

In such unstable and drastically changing times, historical precedents were cited in all fields—social, political, economic, and aesthetic—to promote a feeling of continuity and stability. The philosophical and social systems of both Georg Hegel and Karl Marx were based on the dynamics of history. Even scientific thinking looked backward to the origins and evolution of species. Meanwhile, the reading public turned the historical novels of Walter Scott, Victor Hugo, Alexandre Dumas, and James Fenimore Cooper into best-sellers. Medieval motifs and imagery animated the spirit of Goethe's *Faust,* Delacroix's paintings, and Berlioz's *Fantastic Symphony* and *Requiem.*

The expanding educational system, which divided architecture into polytechnical schools on the one hand and schools of fine arts on the other, also contributed to historical awareness—or the lack of it. Because engineers were educated in one school and architects in another, construction techniques tended to be divorced from the stylistic aspects of architecture. When architects did begin using cast iron and other industrial materials, it was to build dream castles and neomedieval cathedrals. Likewise, when musicians began writing for the improved horns and trombones of the nineteenth century, it was to sound the call of Judgment Day and introduce a rain of fire and brimstone into their symphonies.

While they were willing to use the fruits of the Industrial Revolution as aids in the production and distribution of their artistic wares, many artists were convinced that the new technologies were not making their world more beautiful. Thus, the gulf between usefulness and beauty widened. Refusing to reconcile themselves to reality, some artists sought ever more fanciful ways to avoid it. Certainly they knew what was going on in their world. As intellectuals they were better educated and informed than similar groups in other times had been. However, "Any time but now, and any place but here" became one of the battle cries of Romanticism. The yearning for past periods, whether ancient Greco-Roman or medieval, was expressed in the various revivals. It remained for later artists to exploit the full significance of the Industrial Revolution.

Neoclassicism attempted to revive the past, and the passion for precision soon divided antiquity into separate Greek and Roman revival movements. Through historical novels and Romantic imaginations, interest in medieval times was awakened. Scholars extended their studies into the medieval periods, and artists delved deeper into the Middle Ages. Revivals of Gothic, Romanesque, and Byzantine styles followed next. The Romantic love for times past was expanded into admiration for the Renaissance and baroque periods. In their exteriors, at least, both the Library of Sainte Geneviève in Paris (see Fig. 19.14) and the Boston Public Library were interpretive revivals of Renaissance architecture. The Paris Opéra, begun in 1861, revived Louis XIV's Versailles. Wagner composed the opera *Rienzi* after a novel by the English writer Edward Bulwer-Lytton about a ruler of the Roman Renaissance. Felix Mendelssohn rediscovered Bach's choral music and in 1829 conducted the first performance of the *St. Matthew Passion* since the composer's death.

In retrospect, the nineteenth-century separation of the arts into classical and Romantic has been resolved, because scholars now understand both as parts of a broader trend. The artists who lived on into the post-Napoleonic period drew their inspiration from Greco-Roman or medieval times with ease. John Nash, for example, built himself a neoclassical townhouse in London and a Romantic Gothic castle in the country. Rude made statues of Roman nymphs and of Joan of Arc. Ingres painted the impressive *Apotheosis of Homer* and later a picture of the Maid of Orleans. John Keats wrote "Ode on a Grecian Urn" and also "The Eve of St. Agnes." Victor Hugo included neoclassical odes in the same volume with his medieval ballads. Berlioz admired Virgil as well as Dante and wrote *The Trojans,* an opera based on the *Aeneid.*

After neoclassicism and Romanticism had run their courses, the revival idea yielded, in the later nineteenth century, a broad **eclecticism** that allowed artists to choose from a variety of sources. An architect might build in any past style, a painter do a portrait or historical canvas in the manner of Titian or Rubens, a poet employ any form of metrical organization with ease, and a composer quote a Renaissance or baroque source.

England and Germany both claimed the Gothic style as their own. To them it was a conscious departure from the Greco-Roman ideals of antiquity as well as their rebirth in the Renaissance, baroque, and neoclassical styles. In England especially, the Gothic revival was closely bound up with the wave of prosperity caused by industrial expansion, national pride, and a reaction against the Napoleonic threat. The English clergy and their congregations demanded a turning away from Greco-Roman architectural forms and a restoration of medieval liturgies, which required appropriate architectural settings.

In Germany the Gothic revival took the form of a vision of past national glory associated with Charlemagne, whom the Germans adopted as their national hero Karl der Grosse. The relative security and fame of Germany under the rule of the Holy Roman Empire had continued intermittently up to the sixteenth-century reign of Charles V, the last of the powerful emperors. The past thus played an important role in the nineteenth-century revival of German power, based as it was on the memory of an empire dominated by the north. Stung into action by the abolition of the Holy Roman Empire under Napoleon, German nationalism took root during the nineteenth century, eventually bearing fruit in Otto von Bismarck's statesmanship, which reminded Teutonic experts of earlier leaders such as Attila the Hun, Alaric, and Frederick Barbarossa.

From the Renaissance through the aristocratic baroque tradition and the eighteenth century, French art was closely bound to traditional Greco-Roman forms. During the Revolution of 1789 and its aftermath, a wave of opposition to the Roman Catholic clergy's interference in public affairs led to the actual destruction of some medieval buildings. The neoclassicism of Napoleon's empire continued through the early years of the nineteenth century and, although weakened under the Bourbon restoration, had at least official approval right up to the July Revolution of 1830.

Beneath the surface, however, the destruction of medieval monuments during the French Revolution indirectly stimulated certain groups to preserve parts of these works in museums. When the glories of their own medieval past were brought to the attention of the French people at a time when the wave of neomedievalism was gathering momentum in England and Germany, there were bound to be consequences.

Significantly, it was not until French national power had been thoroughly subdued under the coalition that defeated Napoleon in 1815 that the Romantic style took a firm hold on the French mind and imagination. For the first time, France began to look within and rediscover the roots of nationhood in early medieval times. Even so, this interest in medievalism and Romanticism officially lasted less than a generation, that is, between the revolutions of 1830 and 1848. Then, under the new emperor, Napoleon III, imperial ambitions rose once more. A later phase of neoclassicism became the official style, and realism emerged as its opposition.

In retrospect, Romanticism, in its many manifestations and various guises and disguises, proved its durability. Many of its central tenets persisted throughout the nineteenth century, chief among them the value of individual subjective response and the notion of artistic genius. Romantic literature continues to be read with pleasure; Romantic painting and architecture are admired. Romantic music is heard in concert halls and opera houses, and on recordings it is more widely heard today than it was in its own historical setting.

--- **YOUR RESOURCES** ---

- ***Web Site***

  http://art.wadsworth.com/fleming10

  ○ Chapter 18 Quiz

  ○ Links—Online Readings—Keats, *Selected;* Hugo, *Notre Dame de Paris;* Balzac, *Old Goriot, Part 1*

- ***Audio CD***

  ○ Berlioz, *Symphonie fantastique*

  ○ Wagner, *Ring of the Nibelung*

MIDNINETEENTH CENTURY

Key Events	Architecture and Visual Arts	Literature, Music, and Ideas
	1723–1796 William Chambers ★	1717–1797 Horace Walpole ◆
	1746–1828 Francisco Goya ▲	1749–1832 Johann Wolfgang von Goethe ◆
	1746–1813 James Wyatt ★	
	1749-1803 Adélaïde Labille-Guiard ▲	
1750		
	1752–1835 John Nash ★	1760–1825 Henri de Saint-Simon ○
	1768–1826 Marie-Guillemine Benoist ▲	1766–1817 Germaine de Staël ◆
	1771–1835 Antoine Jean Gros ▲	1768–1848 François-Auguste-René Chateaubriand ◆
	1774–1840 Caspar David Friedrich ▲	1770–1850 William Wordsworth ◆
		1771–1832 Walter Scott ◆
		1772–1834 Samuel Coleridge ◆
1775		
	1775–1851 Joseph Mallord William Turner ▲	1782–1871 Daniel F. E. Auber ❏
	1776–1837 John Constable ▲	1782–1854 Félicité-Robert de Lamennais ○
	1780–1867 Jean Auguste Dominique Ingres ▲	1782–1840 Niccolò Paganini ❏
	1784–1855 François Rude ●	1783–1842 Stendhal (Henri Beyle) ◆
	1787–1843 John Pierre Cortot ●	1784–1859 Louis Spohr ❏
	1790–1853 François-Christian Gau ★	1785-1859 Thomas De Quincy ◆
	1791–1824 Théodore Gericault ▲	1786–1826 Carl Maria von Weber ❏
	1795–1860 Charles Barry ★	1787–1874 François Guizot ◆
	1796–1875 Antoine-Louis Barye ●	1788–1824 George Gordon, Lord Byron ◆
	1796–1875 Camille Corot ▲	1788–1860 Arthur Schopenhauer ◆
	1798–1863 Eugène Delacroix ▲	1789–1851 James Fenimore Cooper ◆
		1791–1864 Giacomo Meyerbeer ❏
		1792–1822 Percy Bysshe Shelley ◆
		1795–1821 John Keats ◆
		1797–1856 Heinrich Heine ◆
		1799–1850 Honoré de Balzac ◆
1800		
	1801–1848 Thomas Cole ▲	1802–1870 Alexandre Dumas, Sr. ◆
	1802–1878 Richard Upjohn ★	1802–1885 Victor Hugo ◆
	1808–1879 Honoré Daumier ▲	1803–1869 Hector Berlioz ❏
	1812–1852 A. W. N. Pugin ▲	1803–1870 Prosper Mérimée ◆
1814 **Fall of Napoleon;** restoration of the monarchy under Louis XVIII	1814–1875 Jean-François Millet ▲	1804–1876 George Sand ◆
	1814–1879 Eugène Viollet-le-Duc ★	1809–1847 Felix Mendelssohn ❏
1821 **Napoleon** died	1817–1885 Théodore Ballu ★	1809–1865 Pierre-Joseph Proudhon ○
1824 **Louis XVIII** succeeded by Charles X	1818–1895 James Renwick ★	1810–1849 Frédéric Chopin ❏
	1822–1899 Rosa Bonheur ▲	1810–1856 Robert Schumann ❏
	1824–1881 George Street ★	1811–1872 Théophile Gautier ◆
		1811–1886 Franz Liszt ❏
		1813–1901 Giuseppe Verdi ❏
		1813–1883 Richard Wagner ❏
		1818–1893 Charles-François Gounod ❏
1825		
1830 **July Revolution** overthrew old line of Bourbons; Louis Philippe began reign as limited monarch		1833–1897 Johannes Brahms ❏
1837 **Commission for the Preservation of Historical Monuments** founded by Louis Philippe		1838–1875 Georges Bizet ❏
1837–1901 **Victoria,** queen of England		
1840 **Guizot,** French historian and statesman, became prime minister of France		
1848 **February Revolution** overthrew Louis Philippe's government; Second Republic proclaimed; Louis-Napoleon, nephew of Napoleon I, elected president		
1852 **Louis-Napoleon** elected emperor; reigned as Napoleon III		
1871 **Napoleon III** abdicated after unsuccessful conclusion of Franco-Prussian War; Third Republic proclaimed		

★ - Architect   ❏ - Musician   ▲ - Painter   ○ - Philosopher   ● - Sculptor   ◆ - Writer

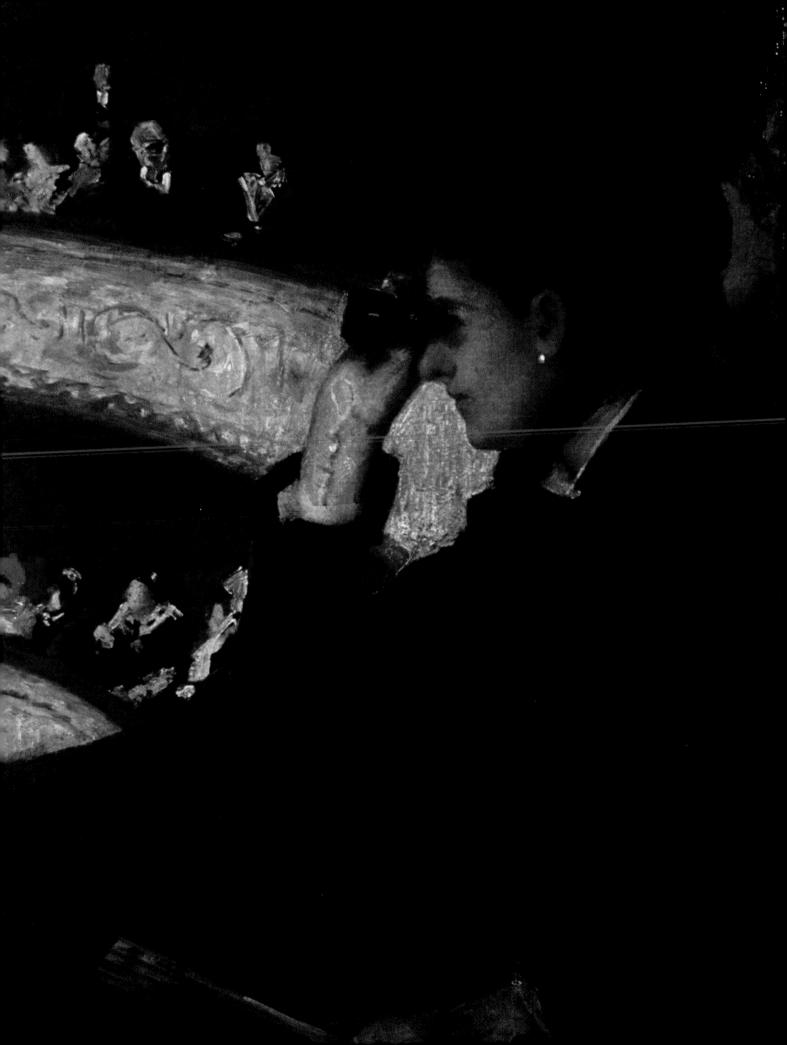

R E A L I S M , I M P R E S S I O N I S M ,
P O S T - I M P R E S S I O N I S M ,
A N D S Y M B O L I S M

REALISM

Realism emerged in the midnineteenth century, in part as a reaction to Romanticism's flights of fancy. Equally important in its formation were the multiple aspects of modern life, which Romanticism did not address. A new world of visual experience waited to be discovered in the pulse of urban life, in the machines that revolutionized manufacturing, in the growth of industry, and in the facility of railway transportation. The growth of factories and the new machine-driven methods of production instigated a profound social shift from farming to an industrial economy, which was accompanied by the migration of large numbers of people from the country to the cities. Rapid changes were also taking place in the minds of people whose lives now moved at a faster pace, prompting new social attitudes and insights as well as many problems of adjustment. Fresh philosophical concepts addressing the flow of time and the expansion and contraction of space infiltrated literature and music as

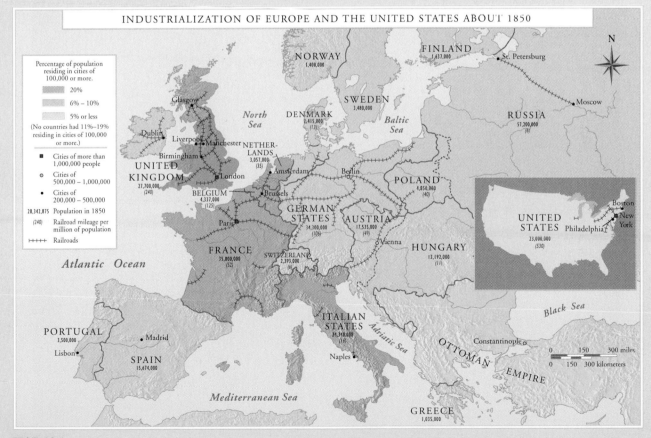

MAP 19.1

well as architectural and pictorial space. In addition, art deepened its partnership with the new scientific ideas and technologies.

Writers reveled in the rapidity of the printing presses, musicians marveled at the mechanical and acoustical improvements of their instruments, and painters delighted in the brilliant coloristic possibilities of synthetic chemical pigments. Low-cost reproductions such as lithographs and other print techniques, and especially photography, made possible the wide distribution of pictures to a growing public. For the architects, new materials such as cast iron aided in the rapid construction of buildings. New manufacturing methods made quick and cheap mass production of complicated decorative objects possible.

The application of scientific knowledge to industrial progress opened up many new possibilities, but it also raised many questions. Governments sought constitutional formulas that would strike a just balance between social rights and material progress. Religious denominations tried to reconcile time-honored scriptural truths with the new scientific knowledge. Social theories explored the ways in which political liberalism could evolve side by side with traditional religious views. Philosophers attempted a new resolution between the fixed absolutes of idealism and the dynamic thought underlying the theory of evolution.

Architects wondered how their work could still remain in the realm of the fine arts and yet make use of the new materials and technological methods now available. Sculptors such as Rodin asked whether traditional mythological and historical themes could be replaced by more contemporary subjects. The Realist and Impressionist painters sought a way to incorporate into art the new physical discoveries concerning the nature of light and its perception by the human eye.

Likewise, novelists such as Émile Zola tried to establish an agreement between scientific and literary methods. Poets and playwrights such as Stéphane Mallarmé and Maurice Maeterlinck searched for a middle ground between the realities of rapid change and the traditional limitations of poetic expression. Composers such as Claude Debussy tried to harmonize discoveries involving the physics of sound with accepted concepts of tonality and musical form.

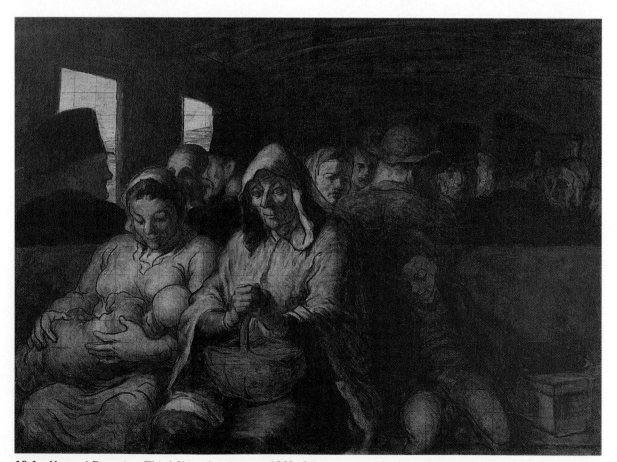

19.1   Honoré Daumier. *Third-Class Carriage,* c. 1862. Oil on canvas, 2′1¾″ × 2′11½″. Metropolitan Museum of Art, New York. H. O. Havemeyer Collection, bequest of Mrs. H. O. Havemeyer, 1929.

The attention of artists was diverted from historical and exotic subjects to everyday life and seemingly trivial occurrences. The novels of Honoré Balzac and Charles Dickens focused on social conditions, as did some of the most talked about imagery created by Honoré Daumier. The ordinary people of Paris live on in works like *Third-Class Carriage* (Fig. 19.1), in which Daumier's observations mix with social criticism. Three generations of poor patrons occupy the cheap mode of transportation, along with the viewer, who implicitly sits across from them. In art, ugliness, violence, and shock techniques began to be reoriented away from *Sturm und Drang* terror toward arousing concern for the underclass.

Collectively, social and aesthetic developments oriented artists toward the new world of the city. Built environments replaced natural ones, and urban entertainments rivaled the delights of nature. The ordinary dominated the unusual; the here and now deflated the Romantic there and then. In the accelerated pace of modern life, styles were exhausted more quickly than in the past. Realism found a rival in Impressionism, and Symbolism challenged them both. As happened with neoclassicism, a style's peak of popularity was not followed by its disappearance. Since the eigh-

teenth century, styles had tended to overlap, and even when their initial rush was played out, they remained available for later artists to explore and mine.

THE INVENTION OF PHOTOGRAPHY

Photography, which became a fundamental challenge to the arts, was made known to the world in 1839. In fact, two photographies were disclosed. The first, created in France, was the **daguerreotype,** named for its inventor, Louis-Jacques-Mandé Daguerre. It produced a highly detailed, mirrorlike image on a metal plate. The daguerreotype was a unique, singular image that could not be easily copied or reproduced (Fig. 19.2). The second was photography on paper, which was invented in England by William Henry Fox Talbot, who quickly realized that it could be used to make duplicate prints and eventually set up a business to do just that. In his book, *The Pencil of Nature,* Talbot speculated on multiple uses of photography, such as depicting botanical specimens, reproducing works of art, and, he speculated, someday even taking surveillance pictures in the dark. Talbot argued that the seventeenth-century Dutch practice of making scenes from everyday

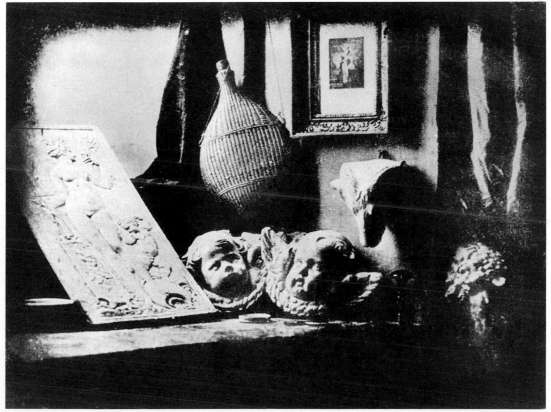

19.2   Louis-Jacques-Mandé Daguerre. *Still Life in Studio,* 1837. Daguerreotype. Collection Société Française de Photographie, Paris, France.

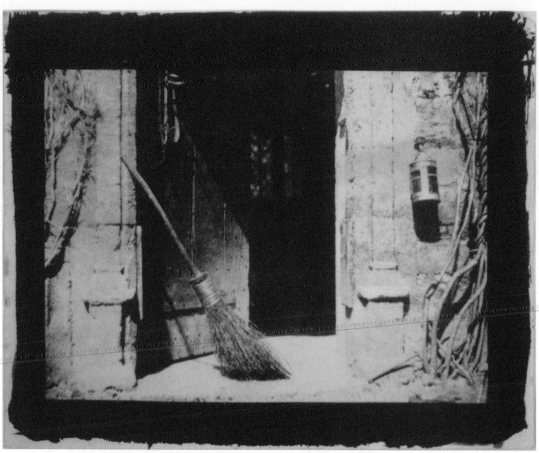

19.3   William Henry Fox Talbot. *The Open Door*. Salt print from a calotype negative, 1844. Plate 5 from *The Pencil of Nature,* 1844–1846, 5′7⁄16″ × 6′5⁄8″. J. Paul Getty Museum, Los Angeles.

life had set a precedent for photography as a fine art. He included his image, *The Open Door* (Fig. 19.3), composed for the camera, as an example.

People could choose either the daguerreotype or the paper photograph until the late 1850s, when the descriptive qualities of paper photography improved and slowly put daguerreotypists out of business. One might think that the clarity and detail of the daguerreotype would make it the first choice for what would later be called *documentary imaging*. However, the paper photograph, with its suggestive masses of dark and light, was selected by the French Commission for the Conservation of Historic Monuments. The daguerreotype was thought to have a cold, metallic tinge, whereas paper photography's contrasts were more evocative. The notion of photographic truth, much discussed in our era of digital manipulation of images, was not as keenly felt in the nineteenth century as it was in subsequent eras. When Edouard Baldus, a photographer hired by the Commission for Historic Monuments, recorded the condition of the cloister at Saint-Trophime at Arles (see Fig. 6.3), he joined several negatives and drew in parts of the vaulting that did not show up clearly in the original.

Photography challenged the established visual arts while reflecting on the styles created in them. After photographs of the Holy Land became well known, fanciful images like those produced by Claude Lorrain lost their credibility. Some photographers, such as Gustave Le Gray, who also photographed for the Commission, were influenced by the Barbizon School, a group of painters who sought a new subject in the ordinary landscapes of field and forest. Le Gray decided that an art photograph, rather than the highly detailed kind, might be more aesthetically pleasurable if it were slightly out of focus. Le Gray also combined negatives from two different pictures. He was sure that photography did not have to record optical reality exactly. In his writing, he supported the Romantic notion of individuality and superior sensitivity, declaring that only an artist or a person of taste could achieve good results in art.

Because photography was relatively easy to learn and did not have to respond to an entrenched academic establishment, as did the other arts, it invited practitioners from all social classes. So-called cheap jacks traveled the countryside, often offering inferior work. At the same time, photog-

PAST AND PRESENT

Having a Portrait Made

When the mosaic artists at San Vitale in Ravenna, Italy, created the image of the Empress Theodora, they probably never met her nor did they have drawings of her to which they could refer (see Fig. 5.16). Rather than capturing her unique features, the artists were commissioned to make an image that conveyed royalty, dignity, and luxury. They created an image of the empress that stood taller than her attendants, and they gave her a long neck with which to support an elaborate crown. Her face is blank and expressionless. By contrast, the Roman couple represented in Figure 4.15 is individualized and bears the marks of age. But had they chosen to, they could have been as idealized and regal as Augustus Caesar (see Fig. 4.1), whose great height and godlike looks did not indicate his real age or appearance.

Royal or not, portrait sitters hired artists who were known to minimize a sitter's physical flaws and to render the client youthful and beautiful. During the eighteenth century, sitters even helped artists achieve the desired result by powdering their faces and wearing rouge. Lead was the major ingredient in a popular powder, and cinnabar, which contained mercury, helped redden cheeks. Makeup could be deadly!

The invention of photography extended portraiture to millions, yet it did not fundamentally change people's attitudes toward portraiture. While viewers of early photographs claimed to enjoy studying the exact features of their friends and relatives, for themselves they often attempted to improve on nature.

Today, routine photographs such as baby pictures, yearbook photographs, and wedding pictures use lighting techniques, makeup, backgrounds, and digital retouching to enhance a sitter's looks. Then and now, everyone seems to understand that a portrait need not be a likeness.

---

raphy became a patrician hobby, and informal clubs of amateurs exchanged prints and comments. Women and men set up darkrooms and ventured outdoors, where the light was brighter, to make images. Julia Margaret Cameron photographed many of the famous artists, writers, and scientists of her time. She also composed tableaux based on biblical scenes, literary sources (Fig. 19.4), and contemporary ideas like those advanced by the Pre-Raphaelite Brotherhood.

By the 1850s in Europe and the United States, photography's advocates were facing criticism. The painter Eugène Delacroix (see pp. 483–486) used photography as an aid in posing models and was a founding member of the French photographic society. Nevertheless, he condemned photographic images that were true to the eye but not the mind. Photography's most stinging critic was probably the poet Charles Baudelaire, who wrote that photography could be endured for its note-taking capacity but not as art, because it vulgarized taste by making optical reality the measure of aesthetic excellence.

However much photography was accused of deadening aesthetic judgment, its effects outside the arts were indisputable. For the first time, people from the lower and middle classes were able to have multiple images made of family members. Moreover, as photography proliferated, it stirred a liking for photographs of celebrities, such as politicians, artists, and even famous criminals. Photographs from the American Civil War, which were available to the public both in galleries and in drawings based on photographs that were published in newspapers, gave viewers a sense of living history much more directly than even realist paintings

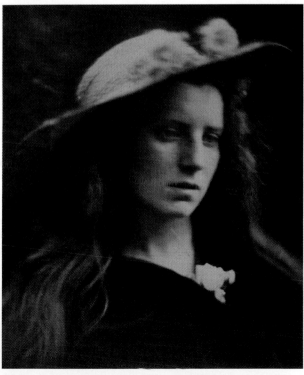

19.4   Julia Margaret Cameron. *Ophelia,* Study no. 2, 1867. Albumen print, approx. 11″ × 10½″. George Eastman House, Rochester, New York.

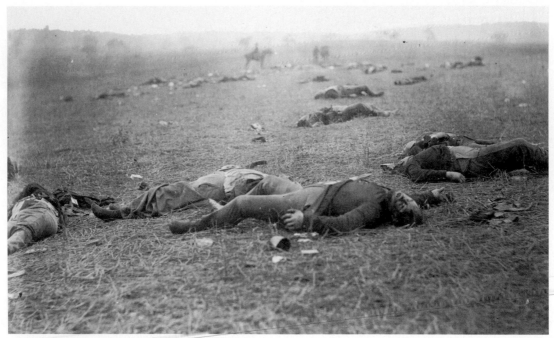

19.5 Alexander Gardner. *The Harvest of Death,* Gettysburg, Pennsylvania, July 1863. Library of Congress, Washington, D.C.

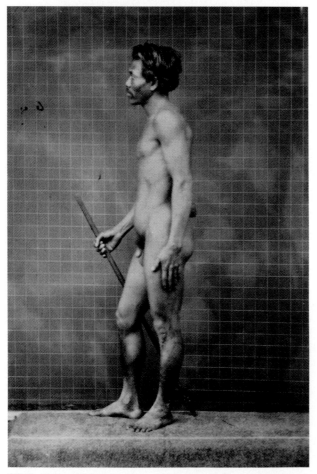

19.6 John Lamprey. *Front View of a Malayan Male,* 1868–1869. Royal Anthropological Institute of Great Britain and Ireland.

did (Fig. 19.5). Photographers circled the globe to supply scientific information of all kinds, as well as images of exotic people and places. Through photography, social scientists and the general public confirmed their belief in the inferiority of non-Western cultures (Fig. 19.6).

PARIS, LONDON, AND BEYOND

PAINTERLY REALISM

Around the middle of the nineteenth century, some young painters rejected Romantic flights of the imagination as well as academic glorification of the heroic past. They began to redefine painting as a language with which to capture the physical world, and thus they ruled out pursuing the metaphysical and invisible.

"SHOW ME AN ANGEL"

The French artist Gustave Courbet was in the vanguard of the realist painters. With a keen eye and a desire to record accurately what he saw about him, he consciously set out to build his art on commonplace scenes. His painting was concerned with the present, not the past; with bodies, not souls; with the material, not the spiritual. His nudes were not nymphs or goddesses but models who posed in his studio. When asked why he never painted angels, he replied, "Show me an angel and I'll paint one."

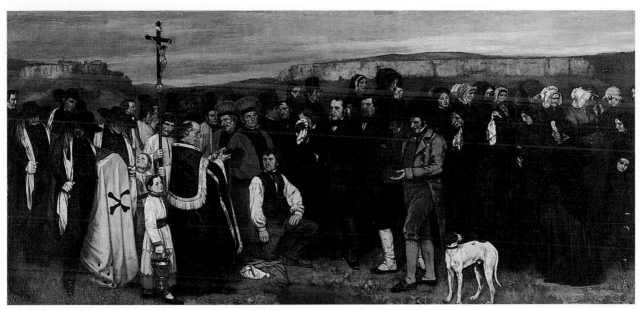

19.7   Gustave Courbet. *A Burial at Ornans,* 1849. Oil on canvas, 10′3½″ × 21′9″. Musée d'Orsay, Paris, France.

Consequently, Courbet did not idealize the villagers in *A Burial at Ornans* (Fig. 19.7), which depicts his grandfather's burial. A priest routinely reads the committal service, and the gravedigger casually waits his turn to complete the job. An altar boy, bored with the proceedings, tugs at the priest standing beside him. No one betrays much grief, and the skull and bone at the grave's edge add a realistic rather than a macabre touch. Courbet could be as passionate about the commonplace as his prede-

cessors had been about the beautiful and the sublime. However, he and Édouard Manet, who came under his influence, were occasionally caught up in a strong emotional interest in their subject matter.

REALISM AND SCANDAL: MANET

Édouard Manet's candid depiction of *Olympia* (Fig. 19.8) caused a major furor because she was not a goddess but recognizably a model in his studio

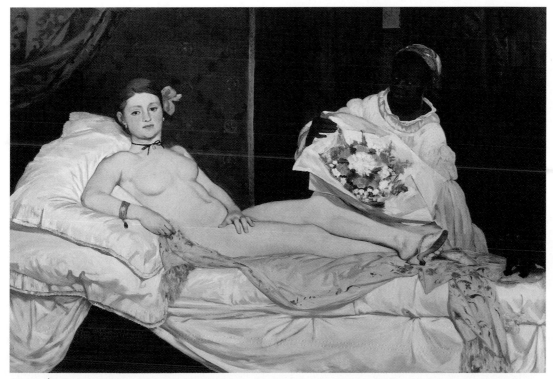

19.8   Édouard Manet. *Olympia,* 1863. Oil on canvas, 4′3¼″ × 6′2¾″. Musée d'Orsay, Paris, France.

posing as a courtesan. Critics howled that she looked like a monkey, a balloon, and a cadaver. Like the *Venus of Urbino* (see Fig. 12.14), whose pose Manet seems to have had in mind, Olympia is virtually nude. She looks unashamedly at a visitor, presumably the viewer, who has startled the cat at the foot of the bed. Throughout the painting are attributes of her success, a maid, and flowers sent, presumably, by an admirer.

Manet's approach was criticized by the press and public, who found it difficult to understand the painting. Nevertheless, Manet found an ardent champion in Émile Zola, a writer of realistic sociological novels. Manet depicted Zola seated at his desk and surrounded by the tools of his trade, as well as with references to the realistic movement in painting (Fig. 19.9). On the wall are pictures within the picture. One is a Japanese print of an actor, referring to the prints from that country that were so much admired for their bright colors, flat patterns, and informal subjects. Another is Manet's own *Olympia*, placed in front of one of Velázquez's masterpieces, *Bacchus, or The Drinkers*. Behind the quill pen on the desk are the manuscript pages of Zola's defense of Manet's art. Manet picked the monograph as the spot on which to sign the painting.

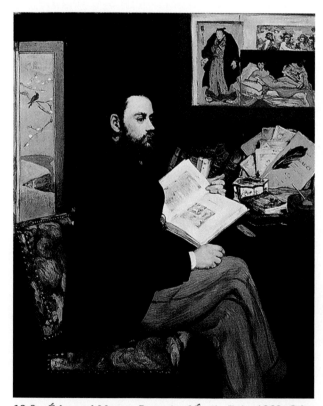

19.9 Édouard Manet. *Portrait of Émile Zola,* 1868. Oil on canvas, 4′10″ × 3′8½″. Louvre, Paris, France.

REALISM AND GEOMETRY

Unlike Courbet and his contemporaries, Edgar Degas was interested in unusual angles of vision. His command of line, meticulous draftsmanship, and accuracy of detail are all evident in *The Cotton Exchange at New Orleans* (Fig. 19.10). Degas's mother and her family were from New Orleans. On an extended visit to his uncle and brothers, who were in the cotton business there, he painted this tightly knit composition. "Everything attracts me here," he wrote back to a Paris friend. "I look at everything." The painting is a study in geometry as well as realism. Figures are framed by the open windows and occupy an appointed place in relation to the receding planes. Each figure is also a portrait study in itself. Some are intent on inspecting the cotton; others are at their work; and still others lounge in casual attitudes, awaiting developments. Degas's keen eye always seemed to catch the exact moment that revealed individual character and personality, whether the individual was a casual stroller in a park, a dancer executing arabesques, or a merchant at work. Degas eventually moved toward the lighter tonality and more brilliant color palette of the Impressionists, particularly in his famous studies of ballet dancers. However, his deliberate approach, emphasis on line, and carefully constructed composition made his relationship to the Impressionists a peripheral one.

REACTION TO MODERN REALISM: THE PRE-RAPHAELITE BROTHERHOOD

Reactions to realism quickly made themselves manifest, beginning in 1848 with a group of young English painters who called themselves the Pre-Raphaelite Brotherhood. In the academies and art schools of the time, Raphael was held to be the perfect painter whose work students should emulate. The Pre-Raphaelites, however, insisted that there were other valid ways of painting that had prevailed both before and after Raphael's time. They also shunned realism, materialism, and the ugliness brought about by the Industrial Revolution. Art, they believed, should uplift and convey a moral message, so they borrowed the authority of literary and historical subjects, but like the realists they believed that their paintings should render optical details meticulously.

At first glance, Pre-Raphaelite John Everett Millais's *The Carpenter Shop* (Fig. 19.11) seems like a genre scene set in an everyday workshop. But the painting also bears the title *Christ in the House of His Parents*. As such, it is an allegory replete

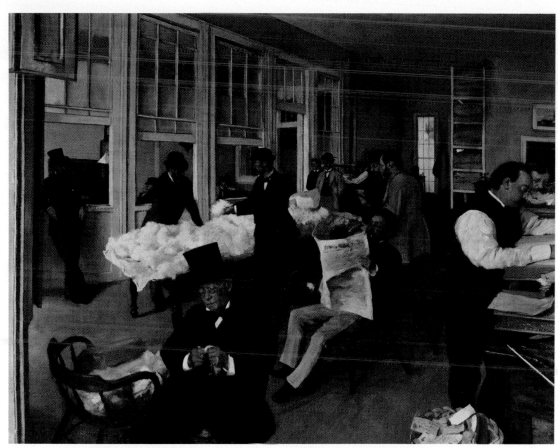

19.10   Edgar Degas. *The Cotton Exchange at New Orleans,* 1873. Oil on canvas, 2′4⅜″ × 2′11⅜″. Musée des Beaux-Arts, Paris, France.

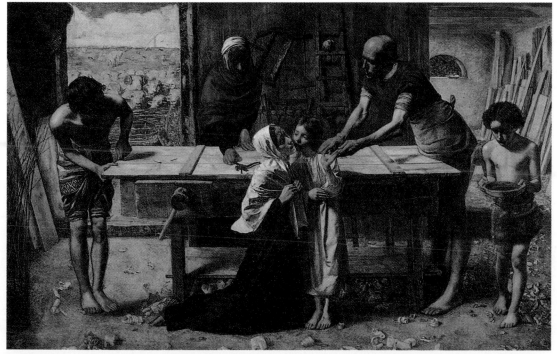

19.11   John Everett Millais. *Christ in the House of His Parents (The Carpenter's Shop),* 1850. Oil on canvas, 2′9½″ × 4′6″. Tate Gallery, London, England.

with symbolism. For instance, the picture foretells Christ's crucifixion. The composition is based on the upright wall in back and the horizontal table in front, which form a cross. The child Jesus, who has cut His hand on a nail (foreshadowing His later suffering), is being comforted by His mother Mary, while John the Baptist brings a bowl of water to cleanse the wound. The ladder in back refers to the descent from the cross; outside, the sheep representing the future Christian faithful safely graze.

The Pre-Raphaelite response to realism was mostly limited to England. Other responses came later, in the theory and practice of the French Impressionists and Post-Impressionists.

REALISM IN LITERATURE

The literary dimension of realism is found in a host of international writers. The increasing level of education and rising literacy of the population created an ever-larger readership. Many who wrote in the realistic vein found inspiration in everyday events and real-life experiences. Honoré de Balzac created a complete fictional bourgeois world in his *Human Comedy*. Gustave Flaubert depicted Madame Bovary's struggles against the banalities of humdrum bourgeois existence, which drove her into a succession of ruinous tawdry affairs. In England, Charles Dickens exposed the plight of those condemned to debtor's prisons, workhouses, and factories. In Russia, Fyodor Dostoyevsky delved into the subconscious motivations of human behavior and sought the psychological motivations of his characters and the reasons for their alienation from society.

Zola and Norwegian dramatist Henrik Ibsen analyzed their characters much as a social worker might examine a client's motivations and surroundings. Zola filled notebooks with jottings about the world of work, how railroads ran, and how laundry was done in communal washhouses. Nevertheless, he felt sympathy for the oppressed and flawed subjects of his novels. In the spirit of a reformer, he found it necessary to bring social ills into the sunlight of public exposure in order to effect their cure. Ibsen was more coolly calculating than Zola. In plays like *A Doll's House* he charted the despair and awakening of a once-happy wife who discovers the insignificance of her home life.

SCULPTURAL REALISM: RODIN

Among the sculptural exhibits at the Paris Salon of 1877 was a statue of a nude youth entitled *Age of Bronze* (Fig. 19.12), which the academic critics assailed as too lifelike. Other sculptors started rumors that Auguste Rodin was trying to pass off a statue taken directly from plaster casts of a living model. In official quarters the gossip was given sufficient credence to cause the hasty withdrawal of the work. To refute one and all, Rodin had casts and photographs made of the model who had posed for him, and the following year, with official explanations and apologies, *Age of Bronze* was again on exhibition. A short while later it was bought by the state for placement in Paris's Luxembourg Gardens.

Like others of his forward-looking contemporaries in other fields, Rodin turned from the heroic. The poses of his figures began to reveal

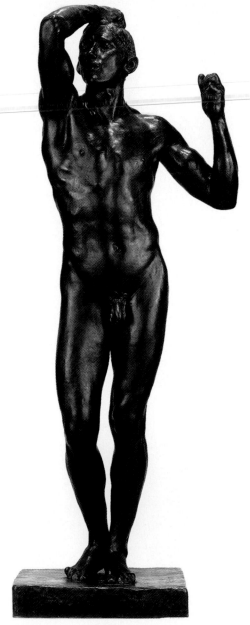

19.12   Auguste Rodin. *Age of Bronze,* 1876–1877. Bronze, height 5′11″. Minneapolis Institute of Arts, John R. Van Derlip Fund.

the inner torments of those who have to struggle with anxiety and feel the hellish tortures of their daily lives.

First commissioned as door panels for a projected building to house the Paris Museum of Decorative Arts, Rodin's *Gates of Hell* (Fig. 19.13) had as their point of departure the portals of the Florence Baptistry, Lorenzo Ghiberti's *Gates of Paradise* (see Fig. 9.8), and the writhing nudes of Michelangelo's *Last Judgment* (see Fig. 13.1), as well as Dante's *Divine Comedy* and the Symbolist poetry of Charles Baudelaire's *Flowers of Evil*. "Dante is not only a vi-sionary but a sculptor," wrote Rodin. "His expression is lapidary in the good sense of the word." By "lapidary" Rodin implied that Dante's words and images were carved as if on stone. Above Rodin's doors broods the figure of *The Thinker*—a man, not Christ, there to judge.

Most details for the *Gates of Hell* were worked out between 1880 and 1887, except for readjustments that went on until 1917. *The Thinker*, Rodin's best-known work, and *Three Shades* (Fig. 19.13, top) were derived from his original inspiration for the *Gates of Hell*.

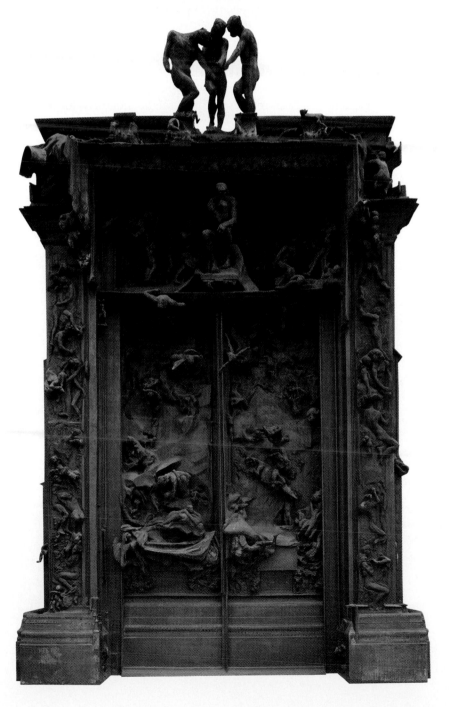

19.13 Auguste Rodin. *Gates of Hell,* 1880–1917. Bronze, height 18′, width 12′, depth 2′9″. Kunstgewerbemuseum, Zurich, Switzerland.

Because Rodin preferred the natural over the heroic, he always acknowledged his material frankly, seeking neither to disguise it nor to escape from it. In many of his works the figures seem to be emerging from their stony wombs. The significance of his work was caught by the philosopher Henri-Louis Bergson, author of *Creative Evolution,* who saw it as "the fleeting moment of creation, which never stops." Bergson's theme reflected the speeded-up modern experience (discussed later). It suggested that nothing is ever quite complete; that everything takes place in the flow of time; that matter is the womb continuously giving birth; that creation is never ending. This interpretation lent Rodin's conceptions a bold and daring quality.

REALISM IN ARCHITECTURE

Throughout the nineteenth century there was a sharp division of thought about the work of an architect. Was the architect primarily an artist or a builder, a designer, or an engineer? Should the architect be concerned more with decoration or with structure? Was the architect's place in a studio making drawings or in the field working with materials? Those who practiced architecture primarily as a fine art could produce on their drawing boards a design based on any known building from the past. Late in the century, all the historical styles had been so carefully catalogued and documented that the range of choices was almost unlimited. What had begun as a revival of special periods now included them all.

The term for such freedom of choice is *eclecticism,* and it best describes the architecture of the period. The sole limitation on eclecticism was the generally accepted appropriateness of the styles of certain periods to special situations. The classical style was considered best for commemorative buildings and monuments, but "classicism" now included anything from Mycenaean Greek to late Imperial Roman. Medieval was the preference for churches, but this might mean Byzantine, Romanesque, or early or late Gothic. For public buildings, Renaissance style was thought to be the most suitable choice.

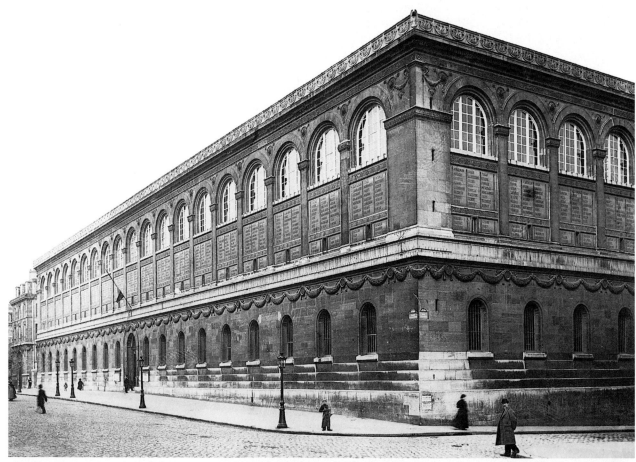

19.14 Henri Labrouste. Library of Ste. Geneviève, University of Paris (Sorbonne), France, 1843–1850. Length 336′.

At the same time, industry produced new methods and materials that opened up novel possibilities. The potential of cast iron, for example, had been perceived by engineers and industrialists long before architects began to speculate on its creative applications. The structural use of iron actually dates from the latter part of the eighteenth century, although at first it was found in bridges or cotton mills and other functional structures, where it was usually combined with brick, stone, or timber.

Using cast iron and steel, nineteenth-century architects and builders could span broader widths, enclose more space, and project greater heights than hitherto thought possible. In effect, the new materials and structural principles were both a threat and a challenge to the traditional pictorially oriented designers.

RENAISSANCE AND IRON: LABROUSTE'S LIBRARIES

In the early nineteenth century, iron columns and girders were used by John Nash in the exotic Royal Pavilion (see Figs. 18.21 and 18.22) at Brighton, marking one of the first instances of their use in a large residential building. At midcentury, François Gau also used iron girders, but he masked them with stone facings to reinforce his Church of Sainte Clotilde in Paris (see Fig. 18.16).

At about the same time, but with more penetrating insight into the possibilities of the new material at his command, Henri Labrouste went one step further in his Library of Ste. Geneviève (Fig. 19.14). A first glance at its exterior reveals simply a well-executed Renaissance revival building indebted to a fifteenth-century Italian church in Rimini designed by Alberti. A closer inspection, however, shows that the ground floor is conceived of as a plain, sturdy space, whereas the bold arcade of windows above gives promise of light and air within. Symbolically, the Renaissance supports the future of learning. Nevertheless, the stone exterior outside gives no hint that the interior is constructed of iron.

Because the building was a library, it needed a practical relationship between the closed storage space for the books below and the open reading room above. By utilizing the strength of metal, Labrouste was able to replace the massive masonry ordinarily required for such a large reading room (Fig. 19.15) while providing a maximum of open space and brilliant illumination. The room is vaulted with two series of arches made of cast iron, which form two parallel barrel vaults. An open leafy pattern related to the

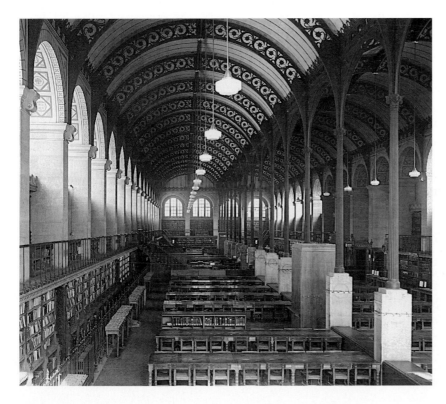

19.15   Henri Labrouste. Reading Room, Library of Ste. Geneviève, University of Paris (Sorbonne), France, 1843–1850. Length 330′, width 60′, height 42′.

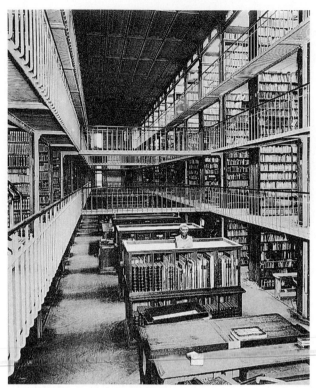

19.16 Henri Labrouste. Stacks, Bibliothèque Nationale, Paris, France, 1858–1868.

classical acanthus motif is used as a decorative theme, and the vaults are supported by tall, thin, fluted Corinthian colonnettes, also made of iron. Labrouste used metal to its fullest, yet allowed the iron colonnettes to assume a form associated with carved stone piers.

What Labrouste began in the Library of Ste. Geneviève he brought to brilliant fulfillment in his later masterwork, the Bibliothèque Nationale, the National Library of France (Fig. 19.16) (replaced in 1998 by a much larger complex of buildings). Storage space for books was conceived of as the very heart of the library, and as such it was brought out into the open, alongside the reading room. Although it was closed to the public, a full view of it was possible through a glass-enclosed archway. All superfluous ornamentation was omitted in favor of the function for which it was designed. Except for the bookcases and the glass ceiling, everything was of cast iron.

By dividing his space into five stories, four above and one below the ground level, Labrouste provided housing for about 1 million volumes. The floors were of open grillwork, which allowed a free flow of light to reach all levels. Frequent stairways provided rapid communication between floors,

and strategically placed bridges allowed freedom of access between the two wings. In both libraries, Labrouste took a bold step toward the realization of the potential of modern materials. His work as a whole is a contribution to the development of a new architecture.

THE GREAT EXHIBITION OF THE WORKS OF INDUSTRY OF ALL NATIONS

The same year that Labrouste was completing his first library, a new and original structure was going up in London that made no pretensions of being either a Roman bath or a Renaissance palace. The *London Times* referred to it as "Mr. Paxton's monstrous greenhouse." Indeed, it was conceived and carried out by a landscape gardener skilled in the construction of conservatories and nurseries.

The occasion was the Great Exhibition of the Works of Industry of All Nations, where the latest mechanical inventions, as well as raw materials, were to be brought together with the finished products of industry. Machinery of all sorts was to take its place beside the manufactured arts and crafts that were being turned out by the new factories. The Crystal Palace's (Fig. 19.17) light and airy structure was rectangular—408 feet wide and, in a neat bit of symbolism to coincide with the year of the exhibition, 1,851 feet long. It rose by means of a skeleton of cast-iron girders and wrought-iron trusses and supports, all bolted together. Its walls and roof enclosed 33 million cubic feet of space.

The rapid construction of the Crystal Palace was remarkable because the whole structure had been accurately analyzed and separated into a large number of prefabricated parts. It was so well planned that 18,000 panes of glass were put in place by eighty workers in one week. Begun at the end of September 1850, it was ready for the grand opening on May 1, 1851.

Contrary to expectations, the Crystal Palace turned out to be a thing of surprising beauty and brilliance, as inexpensive in its construction as it was daring in its use of materials. No applied decoration marred the forthright character of the exterior. Whereas the iron columns of the interior paid lip service to their classical ancestors, the enormous scale of the structure made such details incidental.

At the inauguration ceremonies, Albert, husband of Queen Victoria, stood by a crystal fountain and restated the purpose of the exhibition: to present "a living picture of the point of development at which the whole of mankind has ar-

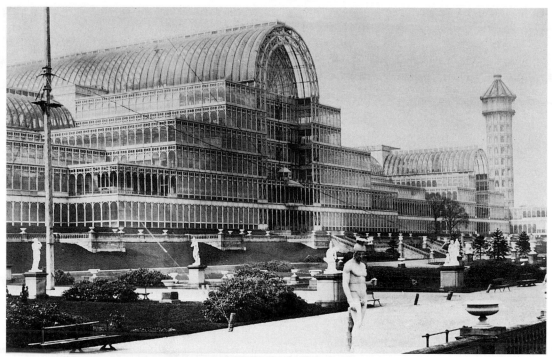

19.17 Joseph Paxton. Crystal Palace, London, England, 1850–1851. Cast iron and glass, width 1851'. Lithograph. Victoria and Albert Museum, London, England.

rived . . . and a new starting point from which all nations will be able to direct their further exertions." Everything seemed set for the Victorians to step out of their self-created pseudo-Gothic gloom into the new industrial age. Yet Paxton and his greenhouse had to wait more than half a century before architects caught up with them.

IMPRESSIONISM

Closeness to nature and realism combined to form a strong incentive for artists to go outdoors. Rather than working in the studio from sketches, painters could observe light and color while painting. Throughout the century a new optical realism slowly emerged that dwelled on the experience of vision itself. In 1874, Claude Monet exhibited a picture called *Impression—Sunrise*, which gave the new movement its name. At first, **Impressionism** was a term of critical contempt. Over time, the word lost its sting and came to imply the unfinished, the incomplete, an act of instantaneous vision, a sensation rather than a perception.

Impressionist painters were stimulated by the new discoveries in the science of optics, color theory, and the nature of light, as well as recent knowledge about the physiology of the eye. Physi-

cists such as Hermann Helmholtz made discoveries about the component prismatic parts of white light and pointed out that the sensation of color has more to do with a reaction in the retina of the eye than with objects themselves. Wider use of the color wheel demonstrated that two separate hues on a wheel at rest are fused by the eye into a third hue when the wheel is in rapid motion. Moreover, when all the colors of the spectrum are rotated, the eye sees them as tending toward white.

In addition, painters speculated on the nature of the visual experience. Form and space, they reasoned, are not actually seen but implied from varying intensities of light and color. Objects are not so much things in themselves as they are agents for the absorption and refraction of light. Hard outlines do not exist in nature. Shadows, they maintained, are not gray or black but tend to take on a color complementary to that of the objects that cast them. For instance, shadows on grass are not black but greenish. The chief concern of the painter, they concluded, should be light and color rather than objects and substances.

For the Impressionists, a painting should consist of a breakdown of sunlight into its component parts. Brilliance should be achieved through the use of the primary colors that make up the spectrum. Instead of greens mixed by the painter on the palette, separate dabs of yellow and blue should be placed close together and the mixing left to the spectator's eye. What seems to be confusion at close range is clarified at the proper distance. By trying to increase the brightness of their canvases to convey the illusion of sunlight sifted through a prism, the Impressionists achieved a veritable carnival of color in which the eye seems to join in a dance of vibrating light intensities. They also used color for its own sake rather than merely to describe objects. As a result of this reexamination of their technical means, the Impressionists invented a new method of visual representation.

JAPANESE ART IN EUROPE

Another aspect of the new style can be seen in the discovery of Japanese art. In 1867, when Impressionism was in its formative stages, the Paris Universal Exposition included exhibits of Japanese woodcuts, colored prints, and other objects. What particularly caught the eyes of the young painters was the delicacy of their pastel coloring and their different approach to perspective.

From Renaissance times to the late nineteenth century, Western painting had been tied to the tradition of linear perspective. As taught in the academies, a picture had a foreground plane, and figures and objects diminished in size as they receded until the vanishing point was reached on the horizon. In the arts of both China and Japan, nature has lines that point simultaneously in many different directions. Japanese prints demonstrated how a picture could be composed with multiple points of interest. In the conventions of these Asian countries, the perspective viewpoint is often high in the air, not grounded as in Western systems. An area of limited three-dimensionality may be introduced by successive bands of contrasting color and tone.

The Impressionists became avid collectors of Japanese prints, whose influence was pervasive. Manet, for instance, included one in his *Portrait of Zola,* and Monet painted a portrait of his wife in a silk kimono surrounded by a pattern of multicolored fans. Its title was *La Japonaise* (Fig. 19.18).

In Japan the arts play a role in daily life, from visits to pagodas and temples to the tea ceremony, gardening, and flower arrangements. Prints were first developed with an eye to the large market of people who collected them to decorate their dwellings. Technically, they are woodblock prints made with black ink on white paper, and most were colored afterward by hand. Favorite subjects were birds, flowers, portraits of actors, and young women clad in intricately patterned kimonos. One of the outstanding artists was Katsushika Hokusai, whose masterpiece was the *Thirty-Six Views of Mount Fuji.* His *The Great Wave at Kanagawa* (Fig. 19.19) from the series captures the essence of the ocean's power as it tosses the boats around while creating a frame for the calm snow-clad Mount Fuji in the distance.

PAINTER OF AIR AND MIST: MONET

Claude Monet was the central figure of Impressionism. His *La Gare Saint Lazare* (Fig. 19.20) renders the humid atmosphere, the mixture of steam and smoke, the hazy sunlight filtering from the open background and transparent ceiling glass. He refused to tell stories about

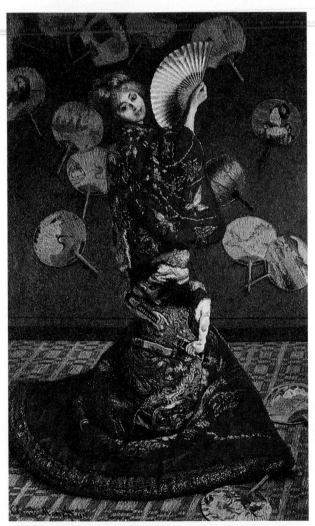

19.18 Claude Monet. *La Japonaise,* 1876. Oil on canvas, life-size. Museum of Fine Arts, Boston.

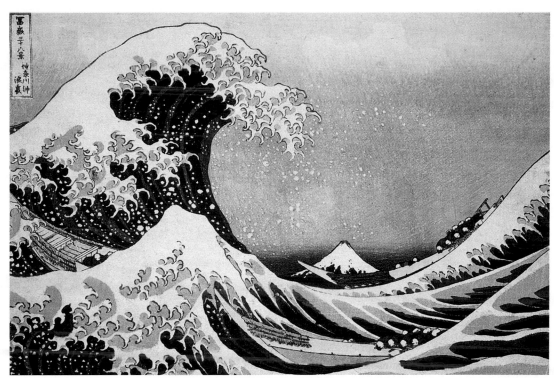

19.19   Katsushika Hokusai. *The Great Wave at Kanagawa,* from the series *Thirty-Six Views of Mount Fuji,* 1829–1833. Woodblock print, ink and colors on paper, 9⅞″ × 1′2¾″. Museum of Fine Arts, Boston.

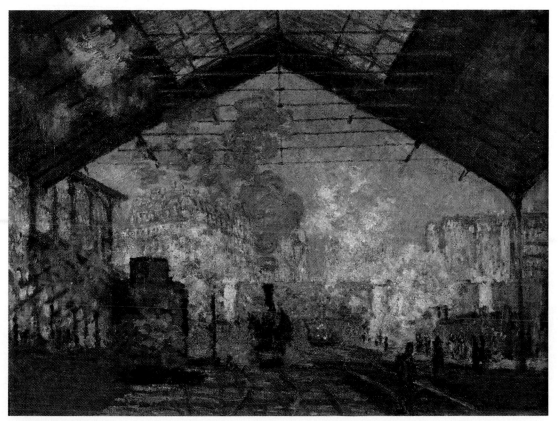

19.20   Claude Monet. *La Gare Saint Lazare,* 1877. Oil on canvas, approx. 2′5¾″ × 3′5″. Musée d'Orsay, Paris, France.

arriving or departing people. Instead, his figures, represented by thick dabs of paint, file from the waiting room toward the train, and the working people, similarly depicted in this shorthand way, go about their tasks. As it materializes for the viewer, the picture becomes an atmospheric study in blues and greens.

The full development of Monet's broken color technique is seen more clearly in *Japanese Bridge at Giverny* (Fig. 19.21), which was painted in the garden of his home outside Paris. Here he broke up the light into a spectrum of bright colors that form shimmering patterns in and around the leaves and lilies. The eye follows an irregular line of water reeds toward the end of the pool. Japanese influence is noted in the sharp tonal differences of the foreground and background, as well as in the splash of white blossoms toward the upper right of the painting. Water imagery recurs repeatedly in Impressionistic painting. The perpetual play of changing light makes water ideal to convey the insubstantial, impermanent nature of visual experience.

In order to capture a particular moment, Monet would paint a succession of canvases during a single day: one showing the garden at dawn, an-

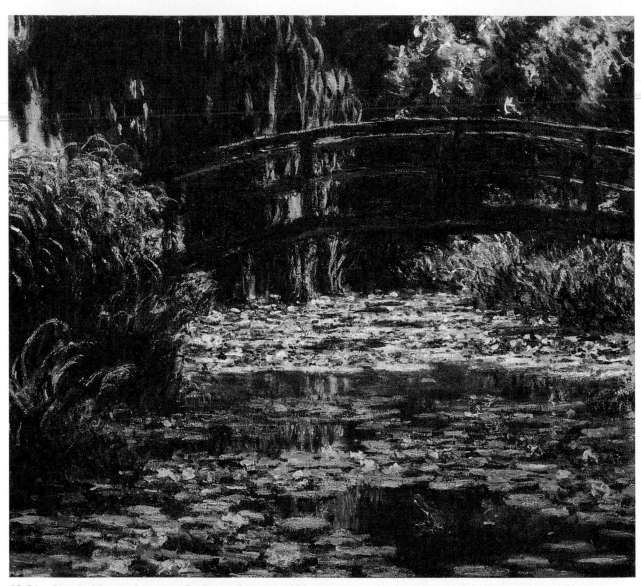

19.21 Claude Monet. *Japanese Bridge at Giverny,* 1900. Oil on canvas, 2′11⅜″ × 3′3¾″. Art Institute of Chicago. Mr. and Mrs. Lewis Larned Coburn Memorial Collection.

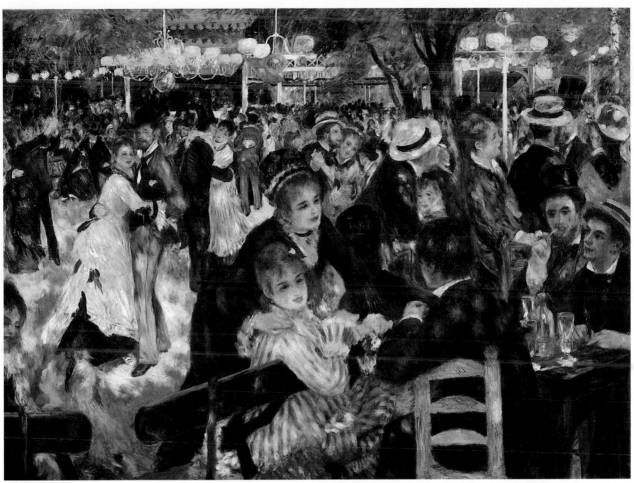

19.22   Pierre Auguste Renoir. *Le Moulin de la Galette,* 1876. Oil on canvas, 4′3½″ × 5′9″. Louvre, Paris, France.

other in full morning light, and a third in a late-afternoon glow. The following morning he would take up the dawn scene where he had left off the day before and, when the light changed, set it aside for the next canvas, and so on. With scientific detachment he tried to maintain the constancy of his subject matter by painting several versions of *Haystacks, Rouen Cathedral,* and *St. Lazare Train Station* in a series, so as to focus exclusively on the variables of light and atmosphere. Each version varies according to the season, day, or hour. As the painter Paul Cézanne once remarked, "Monet, he's only an eye, but my God, what an eye!"

PARIS AS IMPRESSIONIST SUBJECT: RENOIR

While Monet concentrated mostly on landscapes, Auguste Renoir depicted casual, lighthearted city scenes, such as his rendering of a gaslit evening

at a popular Parisian cafe, *Le Moulin de la Galette* (Fig. 19.22). The full force of Impressionistic color is felt in the rainbow of brilliant hues, especially the variations of blue, and in the opalescent quality of filtered gaslight that Renoir rendered. The whirling movement of dance explodes with color and light. The Moulin was open only on Sundays and was frequented mostly by working-class families on their one day off, as well as artists and students. Renoir was a regular. He found his models among the dressmakers, milliners, and florists, cajoling their mothers into letting the young women pose for him.

MANET AS AN IMPRESSIONIST

Manet's later work was in the style of Impressionism, with cityscapes constructed of interrelated planes tinted with a rainbow of luminous

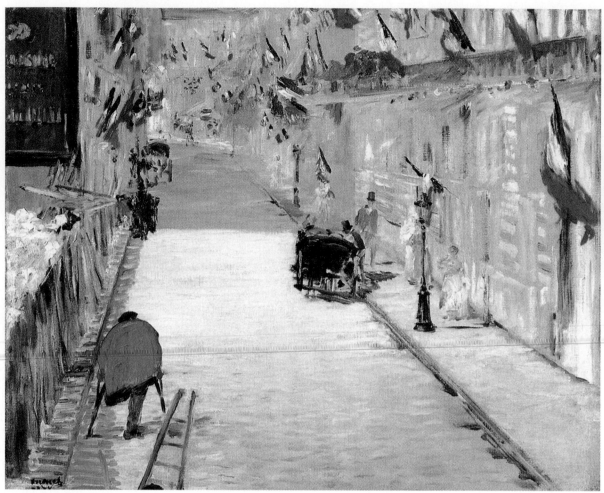

19.23 Édouard Manet. *Rue Mosnier, Paris, Decorated with Flags on June 30, 1878,* 1878. Oil on canvas, 2′1½″ × 2′7½″. Collection of the J. Paul Getty Museum, Los Angeles.

color intensities, as in his view of Rue Mosnier (Fig. 19.23). The street is decorated for a holiday known as the Festival of Peace, which remembered the sacrifices made during France's nineteenth-century wars, including the bloody civil strife during the uprising known as the Commune. The festival also recalled the recent Paris world's fair, called the Exposition Universelle. Wind-rustled flags are indicated with just a few touches of the brush. In the lower left, Manet introduced a contemplative note in the figure of the blue-smocked amputee hobbling on crutches toward the festivities. He may have been a casualty of a war whose memory now is more celebratory than sad. To his left, behind the fence, is debris from a building torn down to make way for the construction of a railroad. In effect, Manet developed a composition that tells about the passing of time and remembrance.

Manet's last large-scale work, *Bar at the Folies-Bergère* (Fig. 19.24), is a technical tour de force. The barmaid looks straight out at the viewer, as if she is waiting patiently to take the viewer's order. The real customer, however, is the top-hatted, goateed gentleman in the upper right, whose face is reflected in a mirror behind the woman. The audience is also reflected in the mirror, and in the upper left the legs of a trapeze artist are visible.

For correctness, the barmaid would have to stand almost sideways to cast such a reflection, but with poetic license Manet lets her face forward. Scholars have argued that Manet deliberately confused real and reflected space in the picture and that no resolution is possible. Yet in some ways the composition is tightly structured, with the double image of the patient waitress and the bottles of the stunningly painted still life in

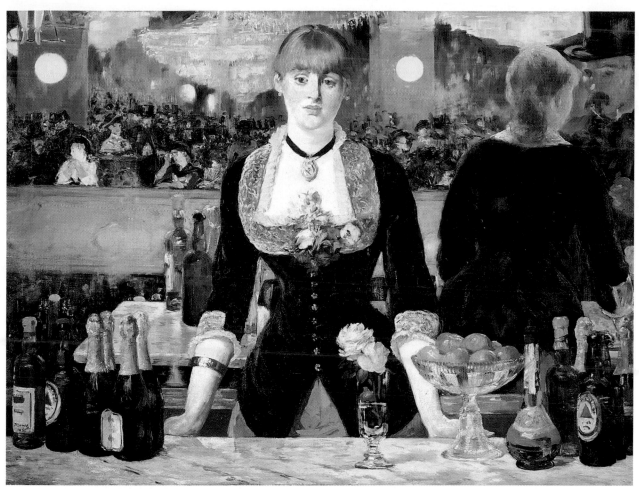

19.24 Édouard Manet. *Bar at the Folies-Bergère,* 1881–1882. Oil on canvas, 3′1½″ × 4′3″. Courtauld Institute Galleries, London, England.

the foreground defining the vertical rising lines. The marble counter at the picture plane, its reflected image, and the mirrored ledge of the balcony contribute horizontal balance.

The scene is bathed in glaring gaslight, glints of which are caught by the crystal chandeliers, assorted bottles, the vase, and the compote dish, and the balcony scene is reflected in the shimmering expanse of the mirror. Except for the barmaid, all the figures are suggested rather than defined. With a few bold strokes Manet creates women with opera glasses, ladies in colorful costumes, and bearded men in stovepipe hats, and above all captures an evening's merry mood. The intricate composition may have been suggested by Velázquez's *Las Meninas* (see Fig. 13.22), which Manet studied in Madrid. There, the king and queen stand unseen in front of the picture, and their images are reflected in the background mirror.

AN AMERICAN IN PARIS: CASSATT

Philadelphia-born painter Mary Cassatt absorbed the tenets of Impressionist color and atmospheric effects but added the dimension of fine drawing and carefully controlled composition. Cassatt, together with her Parisian friend Berthe Morisot, worked closely with the Impressionist painters and helped create the ideas generated by the movement. Although Cassatt is remembered for her pictures of women's activities, mostly domestic interiors and scenes of child care, she also pushed Impressionism in a direction different from that represented by Monet and Renoir. She incorporated a sociological twist, resembling that established in Zola's novels. Moreover, she created a visual critique aimed at one of Impressionism's favorite subjects: women in public spaces like bars, nightclubs, theaters, and city streets.

Cassatt's *At the Opera* (Fig. 19.25) puts the viewer in the chair next to a woman observing a performance. Although the viewer of the painting looks at her, her opera glasses prevent her from seeing that she is the show for a man using opera glasses to view her. The painting's complicated composition triangulates the viewers and the viewed. Using this painting as a guide, one can look back through Cassatt's images of women in public spaces to see that they usually imply an active viewer. In effect, Cassatt took the Impressionist interest in seeing and used it to construct what amounts to a gender interpretation of looking and being observed.

DOTS OF LIGHT AND COLOR: SEURAT

Sunday Afternoon on the Island of La Grande Jatte (Fig. 19.26) by Georges Seurat carries Impressionist theory to an almost mathematical finale. Light, shadow, and color are still the major concerns, and the subject is the familiar Impressionistic urban scene. Here a relaxed group of middle-class Parisians are on a Sunday outing. Instead of misty, indistinct forms, details such as a bustle, a parasol, or a stovepipe hat are as stylized and geometric as in a Renaissance fresco.

Unlike the earlier Impressionists, who improvised their outdoor pictures, Seurat carefully com-

19.25 Mary Cassatt. *At the Opera,* 1878–1879. Museum of Fine Arts, Boston.

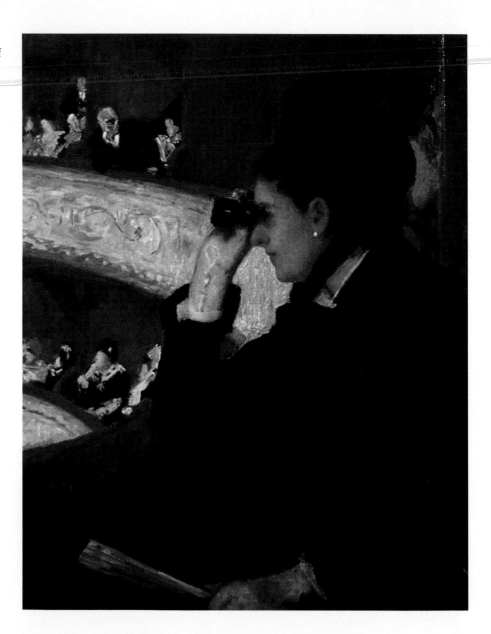

posed his large canvas in his studio over a period of years. Instead of quickly painting patches of broken color, Seurat worked out a system called **pointillism,** in which thousands of dots of uniform size were applied to the canvas in a calculated and painstaking way so that the most subtle tints were brought under the painter's control. Moreover, the picture was divided into areas, and graduating shades blended tonalities into a total unity.

ART AND THE CITY

Impressionism was an art of urban people whose self-concept incorporated a fast pace, mounting tensions, and sudden change. Their lives were buffeted by impermanent forces. Impressionist painters purposely chose everyday subjects such as street scenes, children at play, and life in a café. When they did go to the country, it was mostly to the leafy suburbs, in the manner of city folk on a short holiday. Impressionist artists were intoxicated by light and life. They saw the world as made up of myriad mirrors that refracted a constantly changing kaleidoscope of color and varying intensities of light. They lived in a visual world of reflections and appearances, in which visual values replaced tactile ones.

To reproduce fleeting atmospheric effects, the Impressionists worked directly from nature, speeding up the process of painting to a point where working with oils approached the more rapid technique of watercolor. They wanted their paintings to have an improvised, fragmentary look. They intended to paint not so much *what* is seen but *how* it is seen. Instead of formally composing a work, which implies arranging things, they sought to isolate a single aspect of experience and explore it to the utmost. Their art was one of analysis more than synthesis, sensation more than perception, sight more than insight. As such, the cool objectivity of Impressionism could be said to represent the triumph of technique. As a result of their apparent spontaneity, they were occasionally accused of hasty work and careless craftsmanship.

POST-IMPRESSIONISM

Romanticism was a name chosen by many of its founders (and rejected by some of them as well). *Impressionism,* on the other hand, was a term of derision that quickly became a positive identification. The term **Post-Impressionism,** however, was coined in 1910 by the art critic Roger Fry, well after the appearance of the paintings it attempted to identify. The term has stuck, implying greater consistency in French painting after the era of Impressionism than actually exists. The directions taken by Post-Impressionists are varied, but they have in common a sense that Impressionism could not accommodate psychological depth, emotional involvement, or further aesthetic exploration.

Scarcely more than a dozen years after Monet had shown his *Impression—Sunrise,* the movement

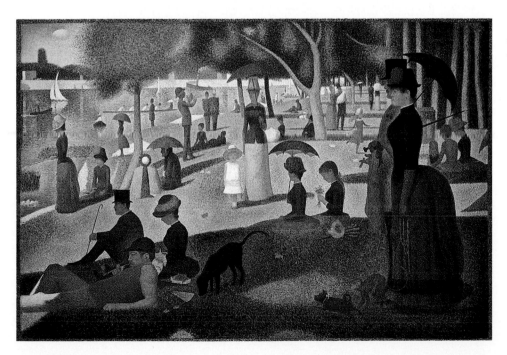

19.26   Georges Seurat. *Sunday Afternoon on the Island of La Grande Jatte,* 1884–1886. Oil on canvas, 6′9″ × 10′3⁄8″. Art Institute of Chicago. Helen Birch Bartlett Memorial Collection, 1926.

had lost its momentum. Even though no one painted an *Impression—Sunset* to commemorate the event, Impressionism in its original form came to an end, to all intents and purposes, with the last Impressionist exhibit in 1886. Three figures—Vincent van Gogh, Paul Gauguin, and Cézanne—translated Impressionist ideas into a far more expressive language. They also directed Impressionism away from the temporal and fugitive into the search for deeper meaning and universal values.

Vincent van Gogh's *Starry Night* (Fig. 19.27) is an intense personal testament, an emotionally wrought version of the view from his room in a mental institution. In the last decade of his tempestuous life he found his vocation in painting. His letters to his brother Theo tell of his burning desire to capture the spirit of life and his "terrible need of—shall I say the word—religion." A feverish worker, he threw himself into his art with the zeal of a medieval saint. *Starry Night,* one of his last pictures, reaches upward from the sleeping earth by way of the writhing, twisting, flamelike forms of the cypress tree, church steeple, and heaving hills to merge with the incandescent sky in a mystical union reminiscent of Counter-Reformation fervor.

In his own way, Paul Gauguin was as restless as van Gogh. A stockbroker by trade, he took up painting, and along with it, the footloose, romantic longing for places far away from modern urban life. He traveled to Tahiti, where he integrated local mythology into his work. Gauguin's *Mahana No Atua* (Fig. 19.28), or *Day of the God,* uses large areas of flat color in two-dimensional decorative designs to portray what he thought was a timeless culture fully integrated into nature. Indeed, the reflections on the water's surface mimic the fetal shapes of the dreaming nudes on the shore. In 1888, Gauguin expressed his theory of the correspondence between natural form and artistic feeling when, during an outdoor painting session in Brittany, he interrogated and advised a younger colleague, Paul Sérusier, in the following way: "How do you see that tree? . . . Is it quite green? Then put on green, the finest green on your palette;—and that shadow, is it a bit blue? Don't be afraid to paint it as blue as possible."

The process Gauguin recommended was one that synthesized the facts of nature with the artist's own aesthetic intuition: the artist's sense of organizing lines, colors, shapes, and textures to have an intended effect. In an article published in 1890, Maurice Denis, a fellow student of Sérusier, formulated Gauguin's ideas into a statement that became fundamental to all understanding of modern art: "A picture—before being a warhorse, a

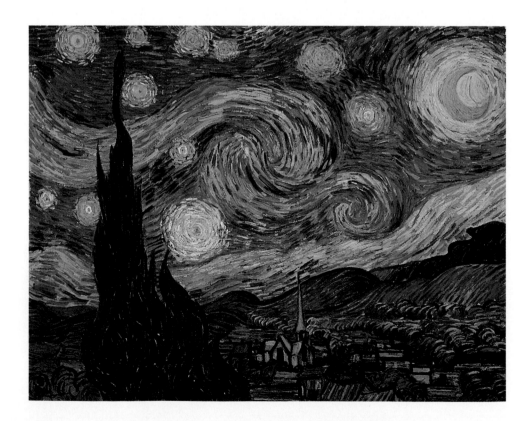

19.27   Vincent van Gogh. *Starry Night,* 1889. Oil on canvas, approx. 2′5″ × 3′¼″. Museum of Modern Art, New York. Acquired through the Lillie P. Bliss Bequest.

nude woman, or some sort of anecdote—is essentially a surface covered with colors arranged in a certain order." In other words, form and design, much more than actual subject matter, have the greatest potential for giving a picture expressive content. Because they were willing to distort the image of nature to make each painting express the artist's feelings, Gauguin and his associates paved the way toward Expressionism in modern art.

In the late 1870s, Paul Cézanne became dissatisfied with the prismatic color palette of the Impressionists. His discontent signaled a major turning point in the history of painting. For him, the superficial beauty of Impressionism did not provide a firm enough base on which to build a significant art. The delight in the transitory tended to exclude permanent values.

Instead of severing connections with the past, Cézanne announced that he now wanted "to make of impressionism something solid like the art of the museums." Nicolas Poussin (see pp. 397–399) was the old master he chose to follow, and his expressed desire was to recreate Poussin in the light of nature. His pictures, unlike those of the Impressionists, were not meant to be comprehended immediately. For Cézanne, painting and its interpretation should not simply be acts of the eye but mental feats. If painting aimed only at the senses, any deeper problem of human psychology would be eliminated. Light is important in itself, but it can also be used to achieve inner illumination. Color as such is paramount, but it is also a means of describing masses and volumes, revealing form, creating relationships, separating space into planes, and producing the illusion of projection and recession.

Cézanne retained both light and color as the basis of his art, but not to the extent of eliminating the need for line and geometric organization. He believed that analysis was necessary for simplification and to reduce a picture to its bare essentials. His canvases tend to be more austere than sensuous, more sinuous than lush. His pictures are dominated by order, repose, and a serene color harmony, yet they can rise to the very highest points of tension and grandeur.

The forms Cézanne chose were from his daily experience—apples, mountains, houses, trees—constants by which it is possible to measure the extent of his growth. "You must paint them to tame them," he once remarked. Mont Ste. Victoire, a rising rocky mass near his home in Aix-en-Provence, was for Cézanne a recurring motif, and it became a symbol of his ambitions.

Comparing an early and a late version of Cézanne's favorite mountain provides an interesting index to his artistic development. The first

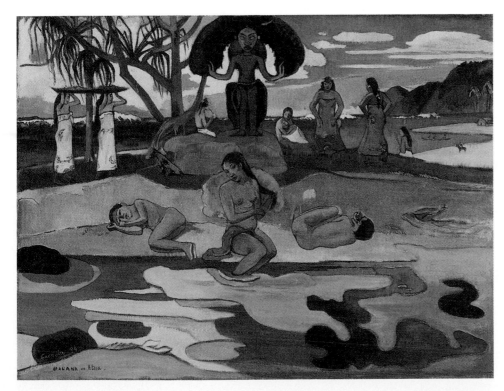

19.28 Paul Gauguin. *Day of the God (Mahana no Atua)*, 1894. Oil on canvas, 2′3⅜″ × 3′. Art Institute of Chicago. Helen Birch Bartlett Memorial Collection, 1926.

Mont Ste. Victoire (Fig. 19.29) dates from between 1885 and 1887. Another version (Fig. 19.30) was done between 1904 and 1906. Both are landscapes organized into a pattern of planes by means of color. Both show Cézanne's way of achieving perspective not through converging lines but through intersecting and overlapping planes of color. In the first version, there is a complementary balance between the vertical rise of the trees and the horizontal line of the viaduct. In the second, these details are omitted and a balance is achieved between the dense green foliage of the lower foreground and the purple and light green jagged mass of the mountain in the background. In the earlier version the mountain descends in a series of gently sloping lines; in the later it plunges steeply downward. In the former, details such as the road, houses, and shrubs are quickly recognizable. In the latter, all is reduced to the barest essentials, and only such formal contours as the cones, cubes, and slanting surfaces remain. Both show Cézanne's desire to mold nature into a meaningful pattern in order to unite the inanimate world of things and the animate world of the mind.

In a still life such as *Basket of Apples* (Fig. 19.31), Cézanne worked in a more intimate vein. The search for pure formal values continued, however. In one of his letters he remarked that nature reveals itself in the forms of the cylinder, the sphere, and the cone. Here his cylinders are the horizontally arranged biscuits, his spheres the apples, and his cone the vertically rising bottle. They are balanced in this case by the forward-tilting ellipse of the basket and the receding plane of the tabletop. An almost imperceptible feeling of diagonal motion is induced by the distribution of the fruit from the upper left to the lower right. This compositional momentum is brought to an equally imperceptible stop by means of the pear-shaped apple at the extreme right. In contrast to the Impressionists, Cézanne brought a measure of form and stability into a visual world where everything was change and transition.

SYMBOLISM IN THE ARTS

With the idea of creating a stream of suggestive ideas, a Symbolist prose poem flows by in a sequence of images that sweeps the reader along on a swift current of words that scarcely leaves time to ponder their meaning. Like the Impressionist painters, the Symbolists reveled in sensory data, and like the realistic novelists, they looked for their material among the seemingly trivial occurrences of daily life. But in their attempt to endow such happenings with profundity, they went a step further.

Whereas painters found sustenance in the physics of light and novelists discovered a new world in the social sciences, the Symbolists investigated recent discoveries in psychology. By purposefully leaving their poetry in an inconclu-

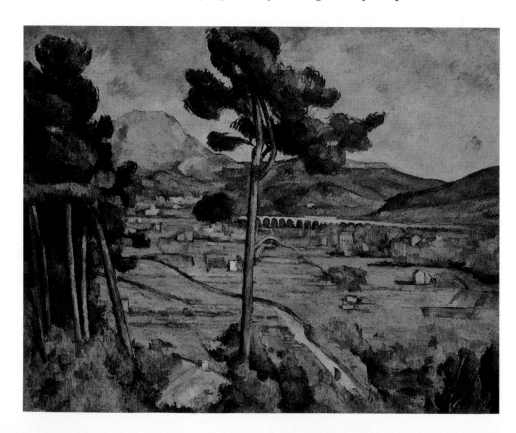

19.29 Paul Cézanne. *Mont Ste. Victoire*, 1885–1887. Oil on canvas, 2'1⅜" × 2'7⅞". Metropolitan Museum of Art, New York. H. O. Havemeyer Collection, bequest of Mrs. H. O. Havemeyer, 1929.

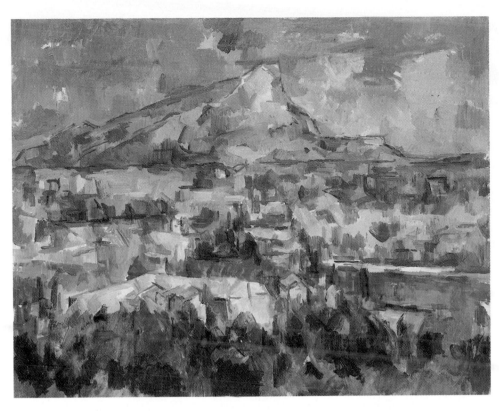

19.30 Paul Cézanne. *Mont Ste. Victoire,* 1904–1906. Oil on canvas, 2'4⅞" × 3'1¼". Philadelphia Museum of Art, George W. Elkins Collection.

sive and fragmentary state, they were making use of the psychological mechanism of reasoning from the part to the whole. Because the poets did not define the whole, the reader's imagination was given plenty of room for interpretation.

Just as the Impressionist painters left the mixing of color to the eye of the observer and the relation-ship of the subject matter to the mind of the viewer, so the Symbolists left the connection, order, and form of their verbal still lifes to be completed by the reader. They also found a new world to explore in "listening" to colors, "looking" at sounds, "savoring" perfumes, and all such mixtures of separate sensa-tions, known to psychology as *synesthesia.* This

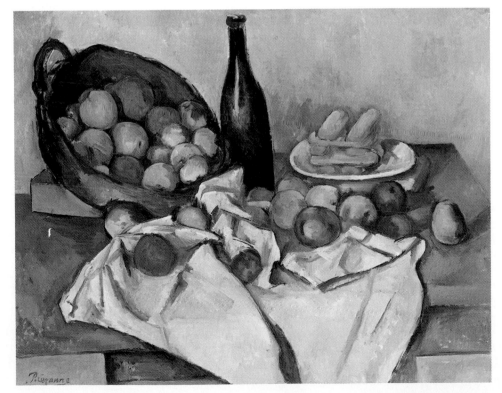

19.31 Paul Cézanne. *Basket of Apples,* c. 1895. Oil on canvas, 2'⅜" × 2'7". Art Institute of Chicago. Helen Birch Bartlett Memorial Collection, 1926.

fusion of sensations by which the awakening of one sense impression sets up a chain reaction of others is vividly expressed in Baudelaire's "Correspondences," a poem from his *Flowers of Evil.*

> Like those deep echoes that meet from afar
> In a dark and profound harmony,
> As vast as night and clarity,
> So perfumes, colors, tones answer each other.
> There are perfumes fresh as children's flesh,
> Soft as oboes, green as meadows.

By developing a hypersensitive tonal palette, the composer Claude Debussy, like his Symbolist colleagues, was able to sound a range of images, including volatile perfumes *(Sounds and Perfumes Turn in the Evening Air),* fluid architecture *(The Engulfed Cathedral),* sparkling seascapes *(La Mer),* exotic festivities *(Ibéria; Fêtes),* and gaudy fireworks *(Feux d'artifice).* The Symbolists pushed outward to the limits of perception to develop more delicate sensibilities and stimulate the capacity for new and peripheral experiences. They moved about in a twilight zone where sensation ends and thought begins. The very word *symbolism,* however, implies that the images are revelations of something beyond sense data. This is where the Symbolists parted company with the objectivity of the realists and the optical experiments of the Impressionists.

MAETERLINCK'S SYMBOLIST DRAMA

Maurice Maeterlinck made an interesting attempt to translate the aims of the Symbolist poets into dramatic form. His *Pelléas et Mélisande,* a play that was first performed in 1892, brings about a synthesis of the material world and the world of the imagination. In it Maeterlinck denies the importance of external events and explores the quiet vibrations of the soul. His symbols function as links between the visible and the invisible, the momentary and the eternal. The tangible fragments of common experience, the seemingly trivial everyday occurrences furnish clues to the more decisive stuff of life. "Beneath all human thoughts, volitions, passions, actions," he wrote in one of his essays, "there lies the vast ocean of the Unconscious, the unknown source of all that is good, true, and beautiful. All that we know, think, feel, see, and will are but bubbles on the surface of this vast sea." The sea, then, is the symbol of the absolute toward which all life is reaching but that can never quite be grasped. What the senses perceive are only the ripples on the surface of life.

In his drama the sea, the forest, the fountain, and the bottomless well are the **dramatis personae** in a deeper sense than the human characters, who are but shadowy reflections of real people. In spite of the settings in which they appear, Maeterlinck's characters belong neither to the past nor to the future. They hover in an extended present, seeming to have no existence in space and no volume. Not much is acted out; what plot there is seems to unfold within the characters. One overhears rather than hears the dialogue, and so little happens in the ordinary sense that a kind of dramatic vacuum is created that must be filled by the imagination of the spectator. Just as the viewer's vision is implied in creating scenes like Manet's *Bar at the Folies-Bergère* and Cassatt's *At the Opera,* in a Maeterlinck play the observer must participate in creating the work of art by connecting the metaphors, uniting the flow of scenes, filling each pause, and supplying emotional depth to the surface play of symbols.

DEBUSSY'S LYRIC DRAMA

It was Maeterlinck's good fortune to find a composer who could fill his silences with atmospheric sounds, give voice to the "murmur of eternity on the horizon," and write the music that linked dream to dream. Indeed, it was as if the music of Debussy was created for the very purpose of providing a tonal envelope to enclose Maeterlinck's "ominous silence of the soul."

For *Pelléas et Mélisande,* Debussy made the sea sing "the mysterious chant of the infinite." In his score, references to the ocean on which all the characters are floating toward their unknown destinies are handled with special sensitivity. In one guise or another, water is present in practically every scene, in the form of a spring in the forest, a well in a courtyard, a fountain in a park, or the stagnant pools in underground caverns.

This ever-present water imagery symbolizes the flowing, fleeting nature of experience. As an unstable medium without form of its own, water becomes the means of capturing atmospheric effects and reflecting changes of mood. The course of Mélisande's life is conveyed by means of these changing waters. She comes from over the sea, is found by a dark pool in the forest, discovers her love for Pelléas at a fountain in the park, and as she dies, asks that the window be opened so that she can once more view the sea.

Other symbols play their parts. Mélisande weeps in the first scene over the loss of a golden crown, symbolic of her happier state of childhood innocence. Later she tosses her wedding ring up and down beside the fountain, signaling that she is taking her marriage vows lightly. When the ring falls into a bottomless well and disappears, it means that her marriage has dissolved. Only the circles on the surface of the water remain. As the ripples expand, they foretell developments to come.

Debussy's style first took shape in the songs he wrote on texts by the Symbolist poets, but Maeterlinck's drama provided him with the necessary lyric material to ripen it into maturity. His methods were in many ways the opposite of conventional operatic techniques. He followed Wagner in giving the orchestra the main task of carrying on the sequence of the drama. As a result, his work became more of a symphonic poem with running commentary by the singers than a conventional opera. Debussy believed that melody stopped rather than promoted the dramatic progress. "I wished—intended, in fact—that the action should never be arrested; that it should be continuous, uninterrupted," he commented.

In considering recitative the most important element of the lyric drama, Debussy allied himself with his famous predecessors Jean-Baptiste Lully and Jean-Philippe Rameau (see pp. 400–401), but whereas their characters spoke in the stylized accents of baroque theatrical bombast, his speak in rhythmic flows of sound more closely approximating modern conversational French. "The characters in this drama endeavor to sing like real persons," the composer wrote. By bringing their language closer to everyday speech and allowing the flow of dramatic action to proceed without interruption, his opera is far more realistic than is common in such a highly artificial medium. Debussy's recitative takes on the flexible character of psalmodic chant. The rhythms are free, and the absence of regular accentuation allows the words to flow.

Debussy's musical motifs parallel Maeterlinck's shifting, fragmented literary symbols. They suggest rather than define atmospheric effects, and are associated with the mood of a character. They are much closer to Wagner's system of leitmotifs than Debussy was willing to admit (see pp. 497–498).

The harmonic method Debussy used was also well suited to rendering the ambiguities and obscurities of the Symbolist poets. His key centers lose their boundaries; progressions move about freely in tonal space; everything is in a state of flux, always on its way but never quite arriving. Debussy's sensitivity to the **timbre,** or distinctive quality of sound, borders on the uncanny. He thought of Mélisande's voice as "soft and silky," and thus the woodwinds dominate the orchestral coloration with their peculiarly poignant and penetrating quality. Above all, performers must know how to make this intangible music live and breathe, how to render its rhythms with the proper elasticity, and how to fill its silences with meaning.

Debussy's evocation of Maeterlinck's pale, shadowy world is one of those rare instances of the indissoluble union of literature and music. Debussy worked on *Pelléas* over a period of 10 years and

was constantly worrying about the audience's reaction to his fragile lyric drama. Contrary to his expectations, the opera ultimately was a success and is still performed.

IDEAS

Any interpretation of the complex interplay of forces that underlie and motivate the diverse tendencies of the latter part of the nineteenth century faces the danger of oversimplification. Nevertheless, two of the most prominent ideas provide insights into the relationship of the several arts: the influence of the scientific method on the arts, and the interpretation of experience in terms of time.

THE ALLIANCE OF ART AND SCIENCE

Artists in all fields were aware of the extraordinary success of the scientific method. Realism and Impressionism brought a new objective attitude into the arts, together with an emphasis on the technical side of the crafts and a tendency for artists to become specialists pursuing a single aspect of their media.

Architects began to look to engineers for the more advanced developments in building. Cézanne thought of his pictures as visual-research problems. In sculpture, Rodin sought a new synthesis of matter and form. The literary realists cultivated a scientific detachment in their writing and developed a technique that would enable them to record the details of their observations of everyday life with accuracy and precision. Zola, by means of his experimental novel, introduced a modified social-scientific observation to fiction. In addition to his poetic dramas, Maeterlinck wrote popular nature studies such as *The Life of the Bee* and *The Magic of the Stars.* For his part, Debussy spoke of some of his compositions as his "latest discoveries in musical chemistry."

Many of the scientific discoveries opened up new vistas in the arts. Experiments in optical physics revealed secrets of light and color that painters could explore. New chemical syntheses provided brighter pigments. Increased knowledge of the physiology of the eye and of perception led to a reexamination of how observers look at a picture and what they perceive. Rodin took Darwin's theory of evolution and transformed it into a poetic understanding of how form emerges from matter and how the inanimate becomes animate. Helmholtz's *On the Sensation of Tone as a Physiological Basis for the Theory of Music* stirred Debussy and other composers to speculate on the relation of tone to overtone and consonance to dissonance in their various harmonic techniques.

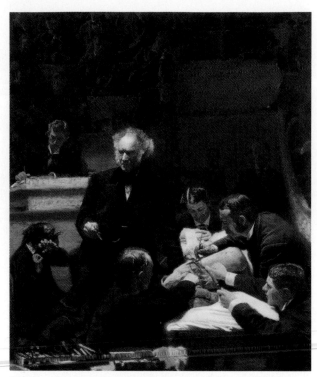

19.32 Thomas Eakins. *The Gross Clinic,* 1875. Oil on canvas, 8′ × 6′6″. Jefferson Medical College of Thomas Jefferson University, Philadelphia.

Despite his art training in Paris, the American Thomas Eakins was determined to meld his interests in science and art. His *The Gross Clinic* (Fig. 19.32) was painted for the Jefferson Medical College in his native Philadelphia, where he had dissected cadavers in his student days. Although an obvious antecedent is Rembrandt's *Anatomy Lesson* (see Fig. 15.15), Eakins focused on an actual surgical procedure in progress. The noted surgeon Dr. Gross makes his point with a bloodied hand while the students show various attitudes—close attention, indifference, or boredom. The mother of the patient turns away from the grisly scene. In other pictures Eakins captured the American love of sports in scenes of boat races, boxing matches, and hunting. In addition, he helped Eadweard Muybridge create influential photographic studies depicting how humans and animals move.

The Impressionist painters were convinced that pictures were best made from light and color, not line and form; the Symbolists claimed that poetry was made with words, not ideas; and composers believed that music should be a play of varied sonorities rather than a means of evoking programmatic associations. By pursuing this general line of thought, artists made a number of discoveries. Monet revealed a new concept of light and color and their interdependence; Rodin, an at-mospheric extension of solid three-dimensional form. The Symbolists found a new world of poetry; Debussy, a new concept of sound. In his famous Paris landmark, the Eiffel Tower, Gustave Eiffel incorporated light and air into the design, achieving a new relationship between inner and outer space.

This mechanistic phase, however, could lead only so far, and artists were soon trying to push beyond it. Cézanne's path led into a new concept of pictorial geometry that anticipated and paved the way for twentieth-century abstract art and Cubism. Maeterlinck attempted to humanize science and describe it in poetic terms. In his case the result was a kind of animism that brought life to inanimate objects such as trees, stones, and fountains and gave them speech and souls of their own. In an essay, "Intelligence of Flowers," he tried to establish more sympathetic ties between people and nature. In his stage fantasy, *The Bluebird,* Sugar and Bread are among the live characters. Cézanne also felt the living force of the objects he placed in his still lifes; in a conversation with a friend he remarked that there are people who say a sugar bowl has no soul, yet it changes every day.

In addition, the Symbolists tried to bring about a synthesis between the phenomenal world and that of the imagination. Their metaphors hinted at the existence of a more profound world of ideas and were based on a view that life was something more than the sum of its molecular parts. Debussy, too, turned away from the physical elements of sound toward the deeper psychological implications of tonal symbolism.

CONTINUOUS FLUX

The arts of the late nineteenth century were bound together by their common tendency to interpret experience in terms of time. The idea of progress carried over from the late eighteenth century and found fertile ground in evolutionary theories, like that of Darwin. Material progress continued to be an indisputable fact, but the disassociation of material progress from political, moral, spiritual, and artistic progress was also becoming apparent.

With industrialization came specialization, in which people were concerned more with fragments than with wholes. Industrial workers were rapidly forfeiting to the machine their place as the primary productive unit. With this loss of control came a corresponding shift from a rational worldview toward an increasingly irrational one. With industrialization also came a flourishing capitalistic economy in which the lives of workers were controlled by external forces that were difficult to fathom.

Two centuries earlier, the baroque mind was shaken by Copernicus's revolution that the sun—not the Earth—was the center of the universe. The mind-set of the late nineteenth century was similarly altered by evolutionary theories, which taught that creation was an ongoing process rather than an accomplished fact. As a result, the onward-and-upward concept of progress was revised to one of continuous flux and change. In effect, the lingering optimism of the Enlightenment, which attached itself to the promise of the machine, was reduced to a perception of relentless societal instability rather than continual social improvement.

The literary and visual realists concentrated on the momentary, the fragmentary, the everyday occurrence. Even when they planned their works in more comprehensive schemes, the effect was more of a broad cross-section than of a complete three-dimensional structure. For 20 years, Balzac worked on parts of his *Human Comedy,* Wagner on his *Ring* cycle, Rodin on his *Gates of Hell,* and Marcel Proust on his *Remembrance of Things Past.* None, however, is a systematic, organic, or logical whole. Instead of having all-embracing unity, they are easily broken down into collections of fragments, motifs, genre scenes, scraps, and pieces. The late nineteenth century produced no comprehensive metaphysical systems such as those of Thomas Aquinas, Gottfried Leibniz, Immanuel Kant, or Georg Hegel, each of whom tried to encompass all experience in a single universal structure.

BERGSON'S THEORY OF TIME

A thinker who came close to making a clear picture of constant change was the French philosopher Henri-Louis Bergson. His point of departure was a remark by the pre-Socratic philosopher Heraclitus, who had said that one cannot step into the same river twice. Bergson cited Heraclitus in support of his theory that time is more real than space and that becoming is closer to reality than being.

Existence, according to Bergson, is never static. Rather, it is a transition between states of being and between moments of duration. Experience is thus durational, "a series of qualitative changes, which melt into and permeate one another, without

precise outlines." His conclusions were underscored by the time photography of Étienne-Jules Marey (Fig. 19.33), which showed movement as a series of small changes, flowing ever forward.

Bergson was critical of the intellect because it tended to reduce reality to immobility. He favored intuition as a higher faculty than reason, because through it one could perceive of the course of time as well as the dynamic qualities of motion and change.

Art for Bergson was a force that frees the soul, and one through which one can grasp "certain rhythms of life and breath" that compel the individual "to fall in with it, like passersby who join in a dance. Thus they compel us to set in motion, in the depth of our being, some secret chord which was only waiting to thrill." Convinced that reality is mobility, or "incipient change of direction," Bergson believed that to look at or listen to a work of art was to perceive the mobile qualities of the objects or sounds presented. For him, the aesthetic experience was an experience in time, which necessitates an "anticipation of movement." Such thinking ahead permits the spectator or auditor "to grasp the future in the present." His theory of art is based on what he called "spiritualistic materialism," through which finely perceived material activity awakens spiritual echoes.

Past, present, and future, in Bergson's thought, are molded into an organic whole, as "when we recall the notes of a tune melting, so to speak, into one another." Time, therefore, is "the continuous progress of the past, which gnaws into the future and which swells as it advances." Bergson's concept of time is not clock time with its divisions into seconds, minutes, and hours; nor is it concerned with the usual groupings of past, present, and future. Time cannot be measured in such arbitrary and quantitative ways; it is a quality, not a substance.

BERGSON AND THE ARTS

Bergson often cited the motion picture as an example of what he meant by the perception of duration. The separate frames in a motion picture film are still, but when the series is run through a

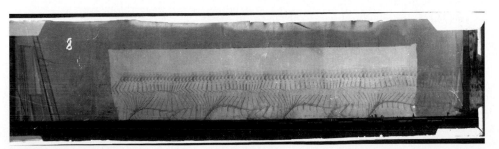

19.33 Étienne-Jules Marey. *Joinville Soldier Walking,* 1883. Negative print. Collège de France, Paris, France.

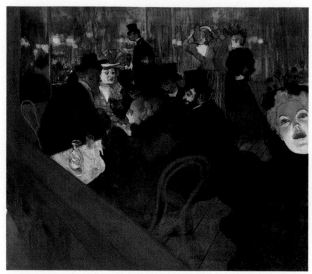

19.34 Henri de Toulouse-Lautrec. *At the Moulin Rouge*, 1892–1895. Oil on canvas, 4'⅜" × 4'7½". Art Institute of Chicago. Helen Birch Bartlett Memorial Collection, 1928.

projector the eye and mind meld them together in a continuous flow and they appear to be animated. Similarly, human consciousness blends the separate colors on an Impressionist canvas, the separate metaphors in a Symbolist poem, the separate scenes in a Maeterlinck play, the separate chords in a Debussy progression. In Impressionism, the eye mixes the colors; in a Symbolist poem, the mind supplies the connecting verbs for the so-called fragments; in a Maeterlinck play, the imagination gives the irrelevancies of speech and action a dramatic meaning; in Debussy's music, the ear expectantly bridges over the silences.

This ceaseless flux leads toward the improvisatory, the deliberately incomplete. For the Impressionists, pictorial substance disintegrated, becoming an airy mixture of color sprays, fleeting shadows, and momentary moods. Cézanne sometimes painted so thinly that parts of the canvas are actually bare, and at other times the texture is so thin as to be almost transparent. Rodin likewise left parts of the stone surrounding his figures uncut. Some of the most important buildings of the time were open to the air and sky and were conceived of as temporary exposition structures, such as the Crystal Palace and the Eiffel Tower. In Debussy's *Pelléas et Mélisande* the personalities are lightly sketched; what they feel has to be in-

ferred by the spectator. Through perception, imagination, and memory, the audience participates in the creative act.

The sense of creating for the moment is well illustrated in the sketches, color lithographs, posters, and paintings of Henri de Toulouse-Lautrec. Amid the surface play of flickering gaslight in *At the Moulin Rouge* (Fig. 19.34) the artist captured with sure, deft strokes the mood and character of his subject, which includes a self-portrait (the small bearded man in front of the tall top-hatted figure in the upper center).

Both the awareness of science and the accentuation of the flow of time became important means by which the arts at the end of the nineteenth century established the basis for the transition to the various modern styles.

The functional architecture of Labrouste, Paxton, and Eiffel became the foundation of contemporary architecture. Rodin's convex and concave surfaces and his concern with the atmospheric problems of light and shadow led to important new developments in sculpture. The fragmentary style of the Symbolists anticipated stream of consciousness and other techniques of modern literature. Debussy's concept of relative rather than absolute tonality, together with his harmonic experimentation, pointed toward some of the significant musical developments of the twentieth century.

YOUR RESOURCES

- **Exploring Humanities CD-ROM**

  ○ Interactive Map: Industrialization of Europe and the United States about 1850

  ○ Comparing Modern Art Styles Module

  ○ Readings—Darwin, *On the Origin of the Species;* Charles Dickens, excerpts from *Hard Times*

- **Web Site**

  http://art.wadsworth.com/fleming10

  ○ Chapter 19 Quiz

  ○ Links

- **Audio CD**

  ○ Debussy, *Pelléas et Mélisande*

LATE NINETEENTH CENTURY

Key Events	Architecture and Visual Arts	Literature, Music, and Ideas
	1760–1849 **Katsushika Hokusai** ▲	
	1801–1875 **Henri Labrouste** ★	1799–1850 **Honoré de Balzac** ◆
	1803–1865 **Joseph Paxton** ★	1809–1865 **Pierre-Joseph Proudhon** ◆
	1808–1879 **Honoré Daumier** ▲	1812–1870 **Charles Dickens** ◆
	1809–1891 **Georges-Eugène Haussmann** ★	1813–1883 **Richard Wagner** ❑
	1819–1877 **Gustave Courbet** ▲	1818–1883 **Karl Marx** ◆
	1822–1899 **Rosa Bonheur** ▲	1820–1903 **Herbert Spencer** ◆
		1821–1867 **Charles Baudelaire** ◆
		1821–1881 **Fyodor Dostoyevsky** ◆
		1821–1880 **Gustave Flaubert** ◆
		1822–1890 **César Franck** ❑
		1824–1896 **Anton Bruckner** ❑

1825

Key Events	Architecture and Visual Arts	Literature, Music, and Ideas
	1825–1898 **Charles Garnier** ★	
	1827–1875 **Jean-Baptiste Carpeaux** ●	1828–1906 **Henrik Ibsen** ◆
	1829–1896 **John Everett Millais** ▲	1828–1910 **Leo Tolstoy** ◆
1830–1848 **Louis Philippe,** constitutional king of France	1832–1923 **Gustave Eiffel** ★	1833–1897 **Johannes Brahms** ❑
1837–1901 **Victoria,** queen of England	1832–1883 **Édouard Manet** ▲	1835–1921 **Camille Saint-Saëns** ❑
1848 **February Revolution;** Louis-Philippe overthrown; Second French Republic proclaimed; *Communist Manifesto* issued by Marx and Engels	1834–1917 **Edgar Degas** ▲	1838–1875 **Georges Bizet** ❑
	1834–1903 **James Abbott McNeill Whistler** ▲	1839 **Daguerre and Talbot** published findings on photography; daguerreotype and calotype processes revealed
	1839–1906 **Paul Cézanne** ▲	
	1840–1926 **Claude Monet** ▲	1840–1893 **Peter Tchaikovsky** ❑
	1840–1917 **Auguste Rodin** ●	1840–1902 **Émile Zola** ◆
	1841–1895 **Berthe Morisot** ▲	1842–1898 **Stéphane Mallarmé** ◆
	1841–1919 **Pierre Auguste Renoir** ▲	1842–1912 **Jules Massenet** ❑
	1844–1926 **Mary Cassatt** ▲	1844–1900 **Friedrich Nietzsche** ◆
	1844–1916 **Thomas Eakins** ▲	1845–1924 **Gabriel Fauré** ❑
	1848–1903 **Paul Gauguin** ▲	
	1848 **Pre-Raphaelite Brotherhood** founded by group of English artists	

1850

Key Events	Architecture and Visual Arts	Literature, Music, and Ideas
1851 **Louis-Napoleon,** president of Second Republic, became dictator by coup d'état	1851 **Great Exhibition of the Works of Industry of All Nations** in London; Crystal Palace by Paxton was one of the buildings	1850–1893 **Guy de Maupassant** ◆
1852–1870 **Louis-Napoleon** reigned as Emperor Napoleon III	1852–1926 **Antonio Gaudi** ★	1856–1866 *Physiological Optics* published by Helmholtz (1821–1894)
1853 **Commodore Perry** opened Japan	1853–1890 **Vincent van Gogh** ▲	1857 *Les Fleurs du Mal (Flowers of Evil)* published by Baudelaire
1861 **American Civil War** began	1854–1875 **Bibliothèque Nationale** built by Labrouste	1859–1941 **Henri-Louis Bergson** ◆
1862 **Bismarck** became Prussian premier	1859–1891 **Georges Seurat** ▲	1859 *Origin of Species* published by Darwin
1864–1886 **Ludwig,** king of Bavaria	1863–1944 **Edvard Munch** ▲	1860–1956 **Gustave Charpentier** ❑
1863 **Abolition of slavery** proclaimed in United States	1864–1927 **Paul Serusier** ▲	1862–1918 **Claude Debussy** ❑
1869 **Suez Canal** opened	1864–1901 **Henri de Toulouse-Lautrec** ▲	1862–1949 **Maurice Maeterlinck** ◆
1870–1871 **Franco-Prussian War;** Napoleon III abdicated; Third French Republic established; Germany united as empire	1874 **First Impressionist exhibit** held	1863 *Life of Jesus* published by Renan
		1863 *On the Sensation of Tone as a Physiological Basis for the Theory of Music* published by Helmholtz
		1870–1925 **Pierre Louÿs** ◆
		1871–1922 **Marcel Proust** ◆
		1871 *Descent of Man* published by Darwin

1875

Key Events	Architecture and Visual Arts	Literature, Music, and Ideas
		1875–1937 **Maurice Ravel** ❑
1888 **Wilhelm II,** emperor of Germany	1889 **La Grande Exposition Universelle** held in Paris; Eiffel Tower was one of the buildings	1892 *Pelléas et Mélisande,* drama by Maeterlinck, presented in Paris
1899–1902 **Boer War** between British and Dutch in South Africa began		1896 *Matter and Memory* published by Bergson
		1902 **Debussy's opera** on Maeterlinck's *Pelléas et Mélisande* produced in Paris
		1907 *Creative Evolution* published by Bergson

★ - Architect   ❑ - Musician   ▲ - Painter   ● - Sculptor   ◆ - Writer

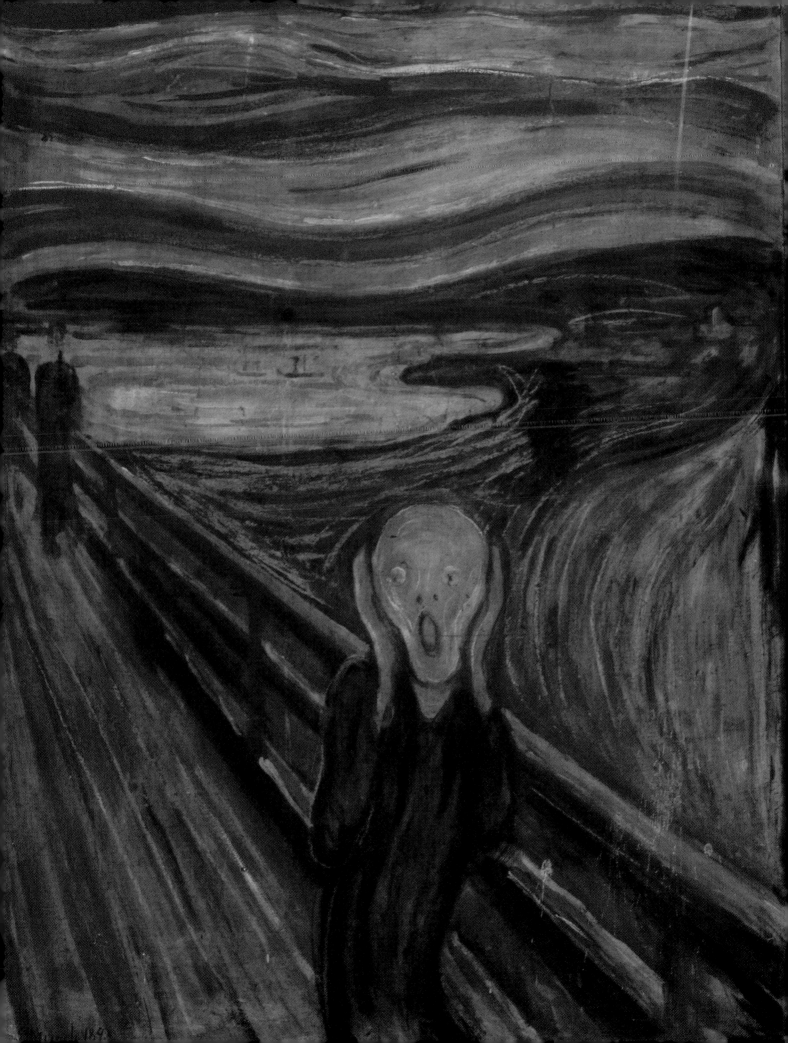

T W E N T I E T H - C E N T U R Y
M O D E R N I S M ,   P A R T   I :
A R T   P R I O R   T O   W O R L D   W A R   I

THE DECADES BEFORE WORLD WAR I (1914–1918) teemed with new ideas and new art that actively engaged the question of what it meant to be "modern." Although the concept of modernity began its steady infiltration of the arts during the Renaissance, it was the prewar generation of artists whose work became associated with **Modernism.** Unlike previous movements, including the seventeenth-century quarrel between the ancients and the moderns (see p. 411), early twentieth-century artists consciously allied themselves with what they perceived to be the basic trends and promises of contemporary life. Instead of longing for another time like the Romantics, Modernists embraced the swift pace of the present and attempted to make art that responded to it and enlarged its implications.

The beginnings of modern art still challenge viewers, listeners, and readers. To clear the way for new modes of expression, some artists found it necessary to ridicule and destroy the concepts

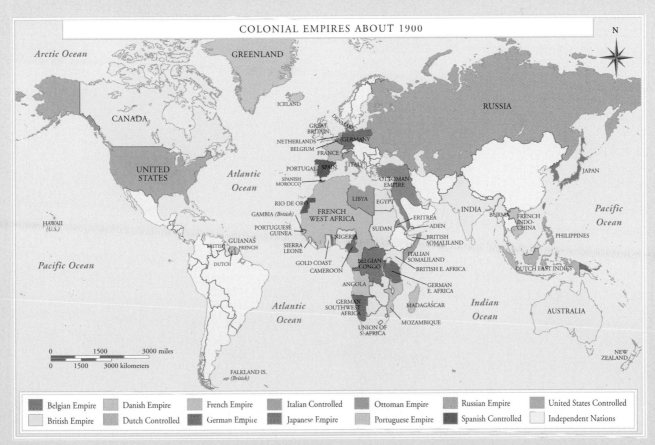

MAP 20.1

and practices of the past and invest their work with shocks and surprises. When Marcel Duchamp's *Nude Descending the Staircase, No. 2* was exhibited at the 1913 Armory Show in New York, it elicited howls of outrage (see Fig. 20.24). One critic likened it to an explosion in a shingle factory. Similarly, the audience for the first performance of Igor Stravinsky's ballet *Rite of Spring* loudly heckled it, and critics called it ugly and perverse.

The tempo of change continued its acceleration to a point where audiences had difficulty keeping pace with artists and scientists. Fashions, fads, and fancies succeeded each other with bewildering speed. However, along with passing trends came the solid accomplishments of artists of major stature. The innovations of Pablo Picasso and Wassily Kandinsky in painting and of Arnold Schoenberg and Igor Stravinsky in music rank as major breakthroughs in cultural history. Ironically, these rebel artists arc now thought of as the old masters of modern art.

Modern materials and methods opened up many new possibilities in the arts. Ferroconcrete, structural steel, glass, and laminated wood took their place alongside bricks and mortar; cantilevering extended the reach of post-and-lintel construction. Modern architects constructed facilities ranging from airline terminals and suspension bridges to low-cost public housing in entirely new capital cities such as Brasilia and Chandigarh. Side by side with the steel-and-glass

20.1 Edvard Munch. *The Scream,* 1895. Lithograph on red paper, 1'2½"× 9⅞". National Gallery, Oslo, Norway.

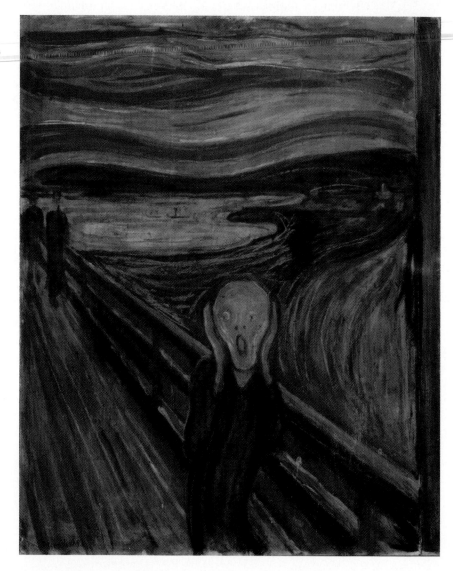

office buildings and urban-planning projects of the industrialized society, twentieth-century architects were called on to build bold new churches and temples. Sculptors discovered the welding torch to replace the traditional hammer, chisel, and metal-casting methods, and complicated metal alloys began to supersede marble and bronze materials.

The arbitrary distinction between the so-called major and minor arts, fine arts and crafts, beauty and utility narrowed to a point where architect and engineer, sculptor and furniture designer—once thought to be poles apart—were brought together in the modern unity of form and function. Drama expanded from the live theater to include films and eventually television. New language concepts were explored, with words used as syllabic sounds in abstract poetry.

During the early decades of the twentieth century, modern art battled for acceptance with provocative manifestos, verbal epithets, and critical thunderbolts. There were street demonstrations against museums and art galleries that refused the Modernists recognition. The ultimate victory of Modernism, however, had to wait until after World War II.

EXPRESSIONISM

Expressionism looked inward to a world of emotional and psychological states rather than outward to a world of fleeting light and shadow, as Impressionism did. These artists turned away from naturalistic representation, investing their forms with emotionally provocative colors and shapes. With Vincent van Gogh and Paul Gauguin as their point of departure, they distorted outlines, applied strong colors, and exaggerated forms to convey their intentions (see Figs 19.27 and 19.28).

Expressionists left behind the classical idea of art as imitation of nature. They closed their eyes to explore the mind, spirit, and imagination. They insisted that there were worlds to be explored that were not visible to the eye or organized according to logic. They welcomed Freud's writings on the subconscious, which revealed a realm of dark drives, hidden terrors, and self-serving motivations underlying human behavior. The Norwegian artist Edvard Munch became one of the prophets of Expressionism with studies of stark human terror, haunting anxieties, and nightmarish fears like *The Scream* (Fig. 20.1). The lines radi-

ating outward from the head of the screaming figure seem to continue the piercing cry into a pattern of shattering shock waves. Munch remarked that he deliberately made the clouds the color of blood.

Expressionistic pictures attempted to describe the intangible through the use of discordant colors and distorted shapes. The clashing dissonances of Expressionistic music were intended to arouse rather than soothe the listener. Expressionistic literature startled the reader with revelations of neurotic, psychic, and often psychotic states. To describe their reactions to physical, psychic, and spiritual events, the Expressionists altered, distorted, and colored their images according to the intensity of their feelings. Expressionism, then, may range from depression, through sudden fright and hysterical outbursts, to shattering nightmares. The movement embraced stylistic variations such as Neoprimitivism, Fauvism, and a variety of other trends in France and Germany. Unmoored from its original impetus, the usual vocabulary of Expressionism persisted for a century. It found its way into early films, such as *The Cabinet of Dr. Caligari,* as well as late twentieth-century art movements, such as the Italian *transavantguardia* (see p. 635).

THE INFLUENCE OF AFRICAN ART ON WESTERN PRIMITIVISM

Twentieth-century Expressionists deliberately integrated many visual ideas that they found in non-Western art, including the native arts of the South Sea Polynesian Islanders, the wood carvings of African tribes, and pre-Columbian American art. Samples of these non-Western arts were on view in the collections of the Trocadéro Museum in Paris. **Primitivism** consisted of conscious adaptations by European and American artists of authentic specimens of Oceanic, African, and other non-Western art. Early twentieth-century Western artists mistakenly assumed that a timeless spirituality and emotional openness underlay all African art. They were therefore only dimly aware of specific cultural differences among African people and did not acknowledge that African art, like art around the world, changed over time in response to the same sorts of social forces that altered Western art.

African art promised a new beginning for Western art because it was seen as depicting a wealth of ingenious geometric descriptions of the human figure that were free from Western

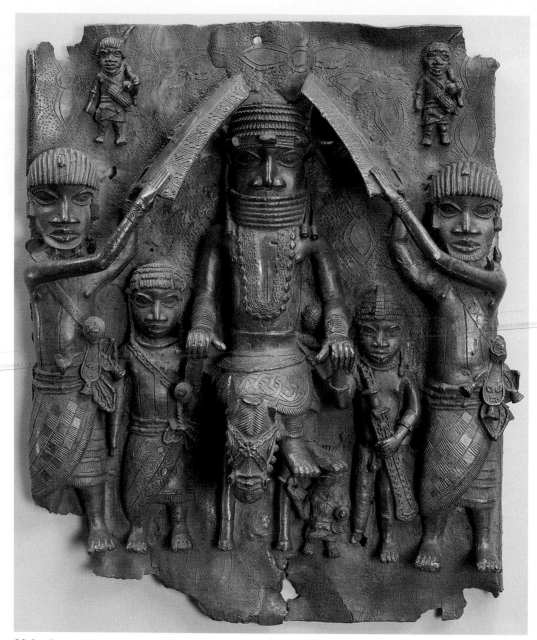

20.2 Benin Wall Piece. From Benin, Nigeria, c. 1550–1680. Bronze, 1'7½" high. Metropolitan Museum of Art, New York. Michael C. Rockefeller Memorial Collection, gift of Nelson A. Rockefeller.

stereotypes and academic conventions (Figs. 20.2, 20.3, and 20.4). The animistic attitudes of the carvers, who divined the spirit of wood, metal, and stone and expressed it in the grains, textures, and shapes of their materials, suggested possibilities for art making outside the confines of the Western tradition.

The expressive power of African tribal art was felt not only by artists, anthropologists, and ethnologists but also by collectors who gathered it for museums. Especially prized was work from Benin, not the modern state of the same name but an area now absorbed into Nigeria. The skilled Benin ivory

carvings, and most of all their outstanding metalwork, were first encountered by Portuguese navigators in the fifteenth century. Benin art of the sixteenth century was court art, produced by artists who were members of guilds. Most of the surviving objects were intended for religious purposes, including ancestor worship. On the finely detailed plaque shown in Figure 20.2, which was probably attached to a house post or wall, the king is the most important figure, indicated by his disproportional large size

An ancestral altar served both as a place of worship and as a historical record. In Figure 20.3,

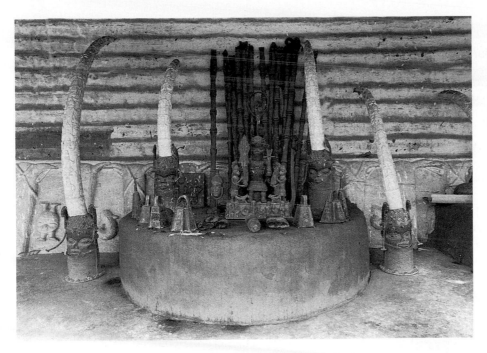

20.3 Benin, Nigeria, royal ancestral altar. Clay, copper alloy, wood, and ivory. Photographed in 1970. Eliot Elisofon Photographic Archives, National Museum of African Art. Smithsonian Institution, Washington, D.C.

four cast copper heads hold carved elephant tusks on which major events in the life of a ruler are depicted. Tall wooden staffs in the background and large bells in the foreground were used to make music that was thought to beckon ancestral spirits.

Most African sculpture is made of wood in a variety of forms produced by different cultures. The stylized sitting couple in Figure 20.4 was created by a master sculptor of the Dogon people of modern Mali. It apparently represents the mythic ancestors of humanity. The composition consists of vertical tubular shapes balanced by the horizontal lines of the bench and the extended arm of the male figure. Delicately carved geometric patterns appear on the bodies of the two figures.

THE ARTS AND THE WORLD BEYOND THE WEST

Paul Gauguin was one of the first major artists to employ exotic patterns and motifs in woodcuts and paintings in pictures like *Mahana No Atua* (see Fig. 19.28), which was painted during his extended stay in Tahiti. Examples of Polynesian handicrafts, such as oars, arrows, and harpoons, had been collected by traders and were shown in the Paris expositions of 1878 and 1889. Later, when expeditions went to the interior of Africa, carved wooden objects were brought back for display, where their influence was felt by Picasso, Georges Braque, and other Cubists.

In 1890, James Frazer began publishing *The Golden Bough,* a multivolume digest of primitive

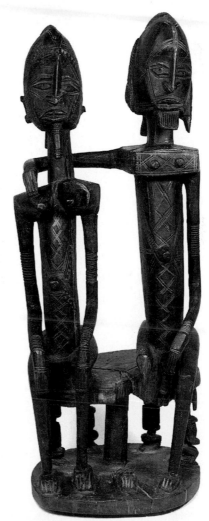

20.4 Couple, Dogon, Mali. Wood, height 2′4″. Barnes Foundation, Merion Station, Pennsylvania.

customs, folklore, magical practices, and taboos collected from around the world. This monumental work became a resource for artists as well as one of the foundation stones of modern anthropology.

When Amedeo Modigliani came to Paris in 1906, he fell under the spell of African tribal sculpture. For a time he traded the brush for the chisel and produced work like *Head* (Fig. 20.5), which was influenced by the art of Ivory Coast. In his paintings he used similarly stylized oval faces and elongated shapes, such as those in *Yellow Sweater* (Fig. 20.6).

The elemental simplicity of Constantin Brancusi's post–World War I sculpture found inspiration in ancient Romanian masks, African art, and the bold innovations of the Fauve painters (see pp. 557–558). Brancusi's objective was to free sculpture from everything nonessential and get down to ultimate essences. "What is real," Brancusi remarked, "is not the external form, but the essence of things." One egg-shaped marble piece, for instance, is called *Beginning of the World*. His *Bird in Space* (Fig. 20.7) is fashioned from bronze with such a high copper content that it approaches the glossy brilliance of gold. He molded it into a graceful curvilinear form and gave it a high polish to make it an abstraction of the movement of both a bird and a feather in flight. Brancusi also tried to increase the sense of motion in sculpture by placing his figures on slowly rotating turntables.

The influence of "primitive" sculptural forms was carried over into the later decades of the century in the work of Henry Moore, who also responded to prehistoric forms like Cycladic figures, Egyptian sculpture, Etruscan motifs, pre-Columbian Mexican carvings, and African and Oceanic art. He also studied the ways in which wind and water shape trees and erode boulders. "Truth to material," Moore once wrote, is "one of the first principles of

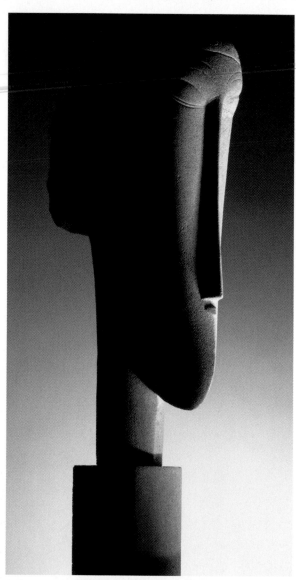

20.5 Amedeo Modigliani. *Head,* c. 1911–1912. Limestone, approx. 2′1″ × 5″ × 1′2″. Tate Gallery, London, England.

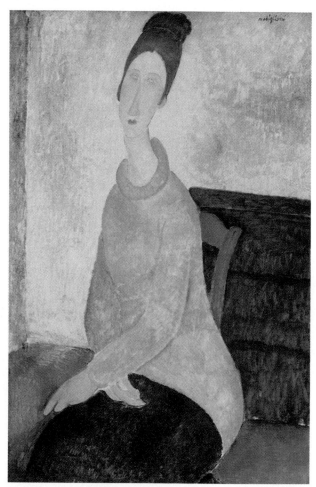

20.6 Amedeo Modigliani. *Yellow Sweater (Portrait of Mme. Hebuterne),* 1919. Oil on canvas, 3′3⅜″ × 2′1½″. Solomon R. Guggenheim Museum, New York.

art so clearly seen in primitive work. . . . The artist shows an instinctive understanding of his material, its right use and possibilities."

Moore's reclining figures sometimes seem like ancient fertility goddesses (Fig. 20.8). The curves and intricate windings rise above the human form and become part of the heaving hills and plunging valleys of a rolling landscape. Many of Moore's figures are pierced by holes and hollows so that they have an interior as well as an exterior existence. In his *Reclining Figure,* the natural grain of the elmwood surface creates a pattern that suggests the ebb and flow of the tides as well as the action of wind and weather.

THE JAZZ AGE

Knowledge of non-European musical systems increased rapidly during the late nineteenth century. The orchestrations of Claude Debussy and Maurice Ravel were influenced by the strange and exotic gong sounds of gamelan orchestras from Java, which both composers heard at the International Exposition of 1889. By far the strongest of these new influences, however, was American jazz. Looking back, the American writer F. Scott Fitzgerald dubbed the period "The Jazz Age."

Jazz was born when African slaves brought their heritage of strong, driving rhythms and group singing with them to America, where they encountered Western harmonic and melodic forms, as well as Christian hymns. A mixture of these memories and new encounters produced music of tremendous invention and vitality. From the first,

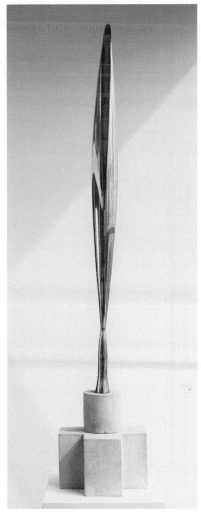

20.7   Constantin Brancusi. *Bird in Space,* 1928. Bronze, height 4′6″. Museum of Modern Art, New York.

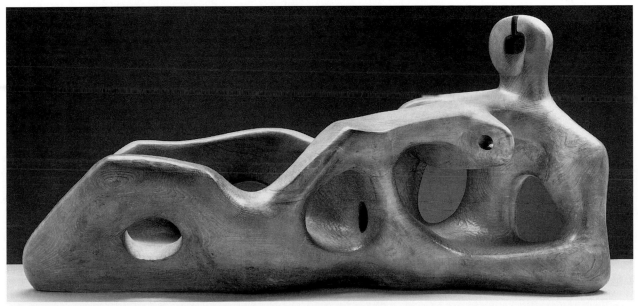

20.8   Henry Moore. *Reclining Figure,* 1939. Elmwood, height 3′1″, length 6′7″, depth 2′6″. Detroit Institute of Arts.

improvisation was part of jazz. Singers and instrumentalists were free to be spontaneous and create riffs around melody and words. This particular aspect of jazz produced unique virtuosos, such as composer-performer Scott Joplin, and singers, such as "Ma" Rainey and Bessie Smith. Improvisation was a major characteristic of the work of later musician-composers such as Duke Ellington, Charlie Parker, and Thelonious Monk.

From its origins in blues and ragtime in New Orleans and along the Mississippi Delta, jazz quickly spread to such centers as Chicago, St. Louis, and New York in the 1920s. With the various forms of rock, it continues to be nationally and internationally popular. This rich source of expression was soon recognized by major composers. In Paris, Debussy, Ravel, and Darius Milhaud worked elements of jazz into their compositions. Later, in the United States, George Gershwin, Aaron Copland, and Leonard Bernstein based a major part of their output on jazz.

Igor Stravinsky, whose music reflects many style trends, achieved the sophisticated musical counterpart of Picasso's *Les Demoiselles d'Avignon* (see Fig. 20.13) in the ballet *Rite of Spring*, which

he wrote in Paris for the Diaghilev company in 1913. Subtitled *Scenes from Pagan Russia*, the opening "Dance of the Adolescent Girls" (Musical Example 20.1) uses repetitive rhythms and syncopated accents somewhat like those of American jazz. Sharply angular melodies have complex textures created by multiple rhythms. The dance combines traditional ballet with unusual geometric movements, combining the Western interpretation of Primitivism with the emerging Cubist sensibility.

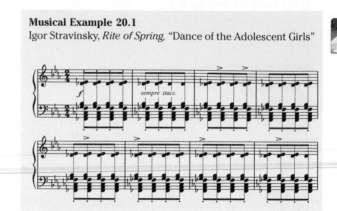

Musical Example 20.1
Igor Stravinsky, *Rite of Spring*, "Dance of the Adolescent Girls"

20.9   Henri Matisse. *The Green Stripe (Mme. Matisse)*, 1905. Oil on canvas, 1′4″ × 1′¾″. Royal Art Museum, Copenhagen, Denmark.

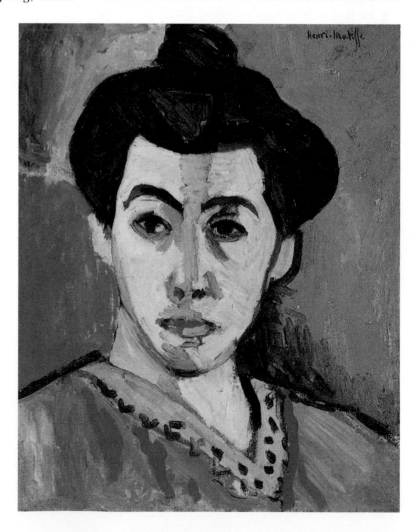

FRENCH AND GERMAN EXPRESSIONISM

Expressionists dwelled on subjective reactions instead of representing objective realities and asserted the supremacy of the human imagination over the representation of nature. At about the same time that Picasso was learning about tribal sculpture, other groups championed Expressionism in painting as a reaction against the cool atmospheric effects and objectivity of Impressionism.

In the late nineteenth century, van Gogh pointed the way with his frenzied canvases, passionate pictorial outbursts, saturated colors, and evangelical fervor. His *Starry Night* (see Fig. 19.27), with the dark green flames of the cypress trees, the rolling rhythms of the hills, and the cosmic explosion of the Milky Way, set the imaginations of Expressionists on fire. Gauguin's color juxtapositions were also seized upon as means for producing lively emotional responses. The Expressionists also looked more distantly at the luminous colors of medieval stained glass and the imaginative inventiveness of Romanesque sculpture. The arts of Polynesia and Africa played a part here too.

THE WILD BEASTS

The violent color clashes and visual distortions of the French Expressionist painters in the Paris Salon of 1905 caused a sensation comparable to that of the first Impressionist show. When an outraged critic saw paintings by Henri Matisse and others grouped around a Renaissance-like statue, he remarked that it looked like "Donatello in a cage of wild beasts [*fauves*]." Fauve painters like André Derain boasted about the "deliberate disharmonies" of their colors. If there was ever anything "wild" about Matisse (Figs. 20.9 and 20.10), it was his reveling in brilliant color for its own sake and his inventive composition. Still, he was a Fauve without ferocity. One of his most enduringly influential pictures from that show (Fig. 20.9) was

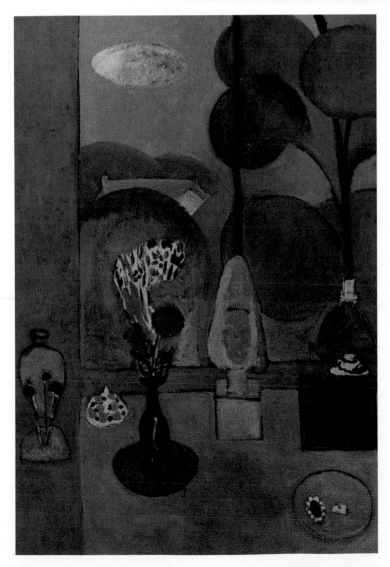

20.10 Henri Matisse. *The Blue Window*, 1913. Oil on canvas, 4'3½" × 2'11⅛". Museum of Modern Art, New York. Abby Aldrich Rockefeller Fund.

a portrait of his wife, now titled *Green Stripe.* It is a rainbow of vivid reds, oranges, and blues. Especially striking is the startling bright-green stripe going from her forehead to the end of her nose.

The Blue Window (Fig. 20.10) is composed as an abstract still-life study merging subtly into a stylized landscape. The hatpins in the cushion on the left unite with the empty vase behind them, the flowers in the other vase grow into the foliage and the roof of the painter's studio outside, the small statue in the center leads the eye to the vertical division of the casement window, and the lines formed by the contours of the lamp continue with those of the tree trunk in the garden. The bedroom table and its objects are united with the trees and sky beyond, making the interior and exterior elements parts of one design. Depth and recession are suggested only by a slight lessening of the color intensities. In this picture, Matisse approached his dream of an "art of balance, of purity and serenity devoid of depressing subject matter." For Matisse, Expressionism did not apply to the content of his canvases or to the communication of an emotional message, but rather to the entire formal management of his pictorial pattern. "Expression to my way of thinking," he remarked, "does not consist of the passion mirrored upon a human face or betrayed by a violent gesture. The whole arrangement of my picture is expressive."

EXPRESSIONISM IN GERMANY

In the decade preceding World War I, German Expressionism was allied with the French Fauves. A distinguished group of artists who gathered in Munich added further dimensions to the Expressionist movement. In 1912, they published a book of articles titled *Der Blaue Reiter (The Blue Rider),* edited by Franz Marc and Wassily Kandinsky. The volume included works by some of the French Fauves and Paul Klee, in addition to those by Marc. Kandinsky's short book, *On the Spiritual in Art,* quickly emerged as the seminal work that promoted art not as representation but as the expression of deep emotional truth. Kandinsky argued that color could set the soul vibrating. The Viennese composer Arnold Schoenberg contributed a chapter on parallel Expressionist developments in music. Marc's art, as seen in his *Great Blue Horses* (Fig. 20.11), is a swirl of pulsating rhythms, curvilinear design, and lyrical movement.

Kandinsky was an international figure who first painted in his native Russia, worked in the Post-Impressionist and Fauve styles in Paris, and joined in founding the Blue Rider group in Munich. Works of his Blue Rider period, such as *Improvisation No. 30 (Cannons)* (Fig. 20.12), still contained sketchy references to natural, human, and animal figures. He recalled that he painted it "subconsciously and

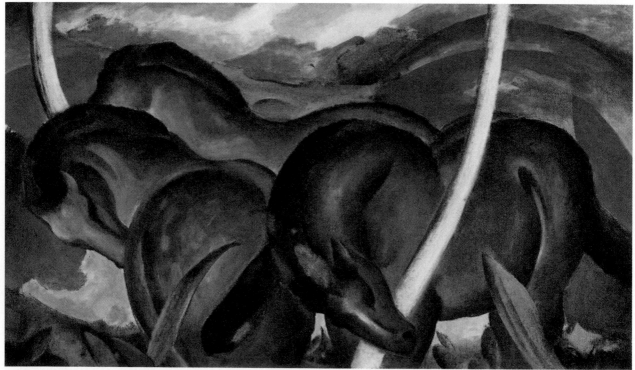

20.11 Franz Marc. *Great Blue Horses,* 1911. Oil on canvas, 3′5⁵⁄₁₆″ × 5′11¼″. Collection Walker Art Center, Minneapolis. Gift of the T. B. Walker Foundation, Gilbert M. Walker Fund, 1942.

in a state of strong tension" during 1913, when rumors of World War I were circulating. This, he added, explains the presence of the two cannons in the lower right and the explosive forms.

By eliminating objects and figures, dissolving material forms, and improvising, Kandinsky hoped to create a universal language of color and shape. He reached the frontiers of nonobjective art before World War I and set the stage for the Abstract Expressionism of the 1940s and 1950s, in which painting was "liberated" from nature. Commenting on his later, completely abstract paintings, Kandinsky stated that their content is "what the spectator lives or feels while under the effect of the form and color combinations of the picture." For him, color was a universal language.

Kandinsky, who published art theory, poetry, plays, essays, and an autobiography, also recognized the affinity of his painting to music. In his own words, he strove to reproduce on his canvases the "choir of colors which nature has so painfully thrust into my very soul." He believed that a painting should be "an exact replica of some inner emotion." He used musical terms for his art. Works that required "an evenly sustained pitch of inner emotional uplift sometimes lasting for days" he called "compositions." Spontaneous shorter works, sketches, and watercolors that "do not last the span of a longer creative period" he termed "improvisations."

MUSICAL COUNTERPARTS TO EXPRESSIONISM

Some of the earliest and most violent outbursts of musical Expressionism are found in Richard Strauss's operas *Salome* (1905) and *Elektra* (1909), which he wrote in Munich while the Blue Rider movement was developing. *Salome* is an operatic voyage into the realm of abnormal psychology. Strauss lures listeners with sensuous sounds and radiant orchestral colors, then horrifies them with the spectacle of Salome singing an erotic soliloquy to the gory severed head of John the Baptist. This combination of simultaneous attraction and repulsion produced emotional excitement. The sensational nature of the play by Oscar Wilde that Strauss adapted as his text, together with the famous "Dance of the Seven Veils," caused the opera to be banned temporarily in New York, Boston, and London. *Elektra,* adapted by Hugo von Hofmannsthal from Aeschylus's tragedy, is a similarly intense effort, filled with emotional climaxes and lurid orchestral sounds.

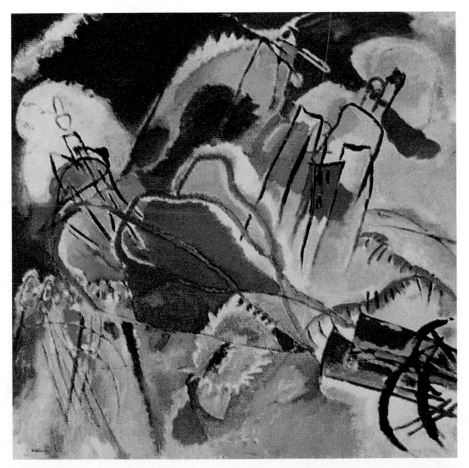

20.12 Wassily Kandinsky. *Improvisation No. 30 (Cannons),* 1913. Oil on canvas, approx. 3'7¼" square. Art Institute of Chicago. Arthur Jerome Eddy Memorial Collection, 1931.

Arnold Schoenberg's Expressionistic song cycle *Pierrot Lunaire,* written for singing narrator and small chamber ensemble, explored the weird world of Freudian motivations. The series of twenty-one songs based on poems by Albert Giraud offers an Expressionistic view of a sad *commedia dell'arte* figure who is literally out of this world. In the cycle, Schoenberg explores a new and special use of the human voice, called *Sprechstimme,* which requires a vocalist to recite within widespread pitch areas, rather than singing specific note pitches (see "x" marks on notes in Musical Example 20.2). In the eighth song, night is likened to the wings of a giant moth.

Musical Example 20.2
Arnold Schoenberg, *Pierrot Lunaire*

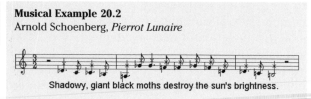

Shadowy, giant black moths destroy the sun's brightness.

Alban Berg also created an Expressionist high point in his opera *Wozzeck* (1925) (see p. 581).

Composers of the late nineteenth and early twentieth centuries worked up to their musical climaxes gradually, generally starting low in pitch and volume and mounting upward in an extended melodic, harmonic, and dynamic crescendo. In addition, they often treated musical dissonances as chains of sequences that eventually were resolved. Schoenberg and Berg compressed the process. Their music became all climax, with the extremes of low and high, soft and loud following each other suddenly by leaps instead of in a gradual progression. They believed that dissonance exists for its own sake, so that the anxiety it produces leaves the listener hanging in the air, with harmonic expectations unfulfilled.

ABSTRACTION

Abstraction implies analyzing, detaching, and selecting before distilling the essence of experience. In earlier centuries, a picture was a reflection, in one way or another, of the outside world. In twentieth-century abstraction, however, artists freed themselves from representation. Natural appearances play little part in their designs, which reduce a view to a system of geometric shapes, patterns, lines, angles, and patches of color. The artist's imagination and invention concentrate on pictorial mechanics and the arrangement of patterns, shapes, textures, and colors. From the semiab-

stract Cubist art, in which objects are still discernible (see Fig. 20.13), abstraction moved toward nonobjective art, in which a work has no representational, literary, or associational meaning outside itself. In effect, the picture becomes its own self-defining referent (see Fig. 21.4).

In the early years of the century, physicists were formulating a fundamentally new view of the universe based on a rejection of absolute time in favor of the notion that time is modified by motion and by the observer. In effect, science proposed many "times" and in fact was edging toward the concept of relativity. X-rays, developed before World War I, were not only medical tools but also amusements in department stores and carnivals. In painting, artists explored the Cubist system of multiple visual viewpoints, whereby several sides of an object could be presented at the same time in two-dimensional space. In sculpture, a new theory of volume was developed in which open holes or gaps in the surface suggested the interpenetration of several planes and the existence of other sides and surfaces not immediately in view. In architecture, the International Style used the vocabulary of steel and glass to incorporate into a structure the simultaneous experience of outer and inner space. Similar developments occurred in literature and music, which found new ways of presenting materials in the time dimension. In literature, the stream-of-consciousness technique merged objective description and the subjective flow of images. In music, the so-called atonal method of composition dismissed fixed tonal centers in favor of a state of continuous flux and variation. Abstraction thus includes a wide variety of developments, such as Cubism, Futurism, nonobjective art, the twelve-tone method of musical composition, and the International Style of architecture.

THE ORIGINS OF CUBISM

Just as the discovery of the rules of linear perspective had revolutionized painting in the Florentine Renaissance, so **Cubism** brought about a new way of looking at things in the twentieth century. First worked out in painting, the consequences of Cubism were echoed directly in sculpture and architecture and indirectly in literature and music. A strong shove in the direction of abstraction had come from the large retrospective exhibit of Paul Cézanne's paintings held in Paris in 1907, where painters were struck by the artist's pictorial architecture. In the catalogue of the exhibit, they noted a quotation from a letter in which Cézanne remarked that natural objects can be reduced to the forms of the cylinder, the

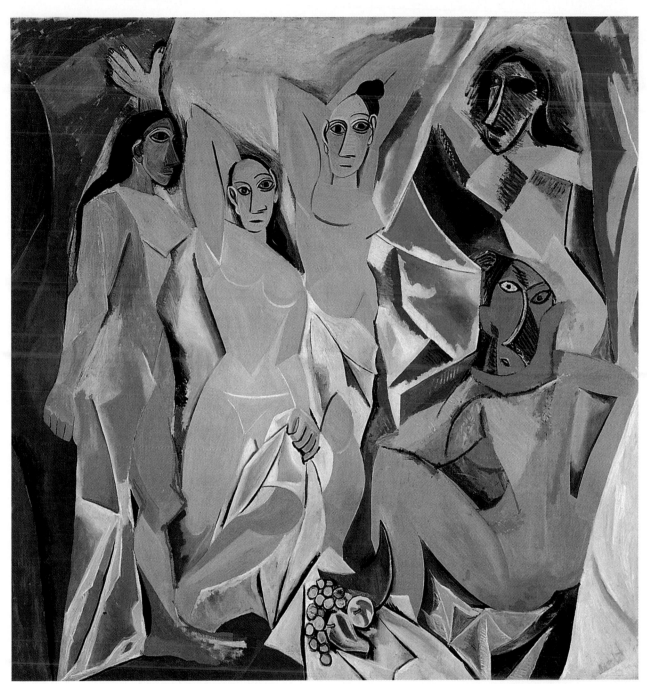

20.13   Pablo Picasso. *Les Demoiselles d´Avignon,* 1907. Oil on canvas, 8′ × 7′8″. Museum of Modern Art, New York, acquired through the Lillie P. Bliss Bequest.

sphere, and the cone. Art, they reasoned, is not an imitation of nature in the usual sense but an imposition upon nature of geometric forms derived from the human mind. As a result, Cubist painting became a play of planes and angles on a flat surface. Cézanne's famous sentence, it should be pointed out, never mentioned cubes at all. His cylinders, spheres, and cones are all rounded forms. By contrast, Cubist design is predominantly angular and rectilinear.

The ideal Renaissance composition depicted a scene from a single point of view. However, Cubist theory engaged the fragmentary and discontinuous contemporary worldview, in which objects are perceived hastily in parts rather than leisurely as wholes. Cubist paintings viewed the world from many points of view rather than from a single viewpoint. In Picasso's *Les Demoiselles d'Avignon* (Fig. 20.13), for instance, the faces of the second and third figures from the left are seen frontally, whereas their noses appear in profile. Just as the Crystal Palace (see Fig. 19.17) pointed the way toward the interpenetration of inner and outer aspects of architectural space, so the art of the Cubists undertook to move inside as well as outside an object, below and above it, in and around it.

In addition, the Cubists were convinced that pictorial space, limited as it is by the two dimensions of the flat canvas, was something quite apart from natural space. From the Renaissance onward, the accepted procedure had been to produce the illusion of three-dimensionality through some form of linear perspective derived from the principles of Euclidean geometry. Cubist painters, however, approached their canvases as architects to construct their pictures. Instead of trying to create the illusion of depth, they built

their pictures on the straight lines of the triangle and the T-square by which they defined the planes of their surfaces.

The expression of volume, as achieved by the modeling of objects in light and shade, was also modified by the Cubists, and so was the tactile feeling and structural solidity of Renaissance painting. Instead of representing objects in the round, the Cubists analyzed them into their basic geometric forms, broke them up into a series of planes, and then collected, reassembled, and tilted them at will into a new but strictly pictorial pattern of interlocking, interpenetrating, and overlapping surfaces and planes.

Cubist color at first was purposely confined to the rather neutral tones of gray, green, olive, and ochre. The emphasis was on design and texture, and unity was found in the picture itself rather than in the objects represented.

Pablo Picasso's *Les Demoiselles d'Avignon* (Fig. 20.13) incorporated so many of the ideas of the early twentieth century that it became a landmark of modern art. Picasso was impressed by the comprehensive Cézanne retrospective of 1907 and with various expositions of African tribal art. As a result, he reexamined his pictorial approach, turning away from representational conventions toward tighter geometric controls, and began to acquire his own collection of the African sculpture that he so much admired.

Les Demoiselles d'Avignon began as an allegory. A man seated amid fruit and women was to have represented Vice, whereas a woman entering on the left holding a skull in her hand was to have represented Virtue. The original plan was abandoned, and the picture developed in another direction, depicting women striking suggestive poses in a brothel. The figures, the background drapery, and the still life below blend into the design, but so much so that they are absorbed into angular abstraction. The woman on the left pulling back some curtains is a series of overlapping planes and geometrically arranged contours. Her pose, with one foot forward, resembles that found in classical sculpture. The head of the figure in the upper right resembles a mask from Etoumbi (Fig. 20.14) (which at the time was located in the French Congo), whereas the head just below and the profile of the figure on the left also show African influence. In other words, the figure on the far left seems to be walking away from the classical tradition toward the primitive values perceived in African art.

Indeed, Picasso's preliminary drawings reveal his fascination with the oval-shaped heads, long

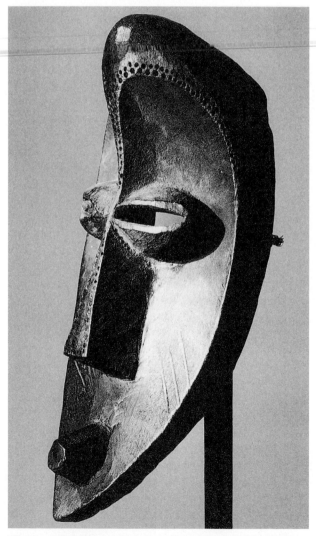

20.14   Mask, Etoumbi region, People's Republic of the Congo, c. 1775. Wood, height 1′2″. Musée Barbier-Müller, Geneva, Switzerland.

noses, small mouths, and angular bodies that characterize the sculpture of West Africa. The painting's color, with its vivid pink and orange hues blending into one another, creates the effect of an emotional crescendo, whereas the formal arrangement of the figures suggests the jagged rhythms of a tribal dance.

Les Demoiselles is a pivotal picture. Its heightened colors, combined with its dynamism and energy, make it a summary of the avant-garde Paris school of painting at the turn of the century. It also marks an important step toward abstraction. When Georges Braque first saw *Les Demoiselles,* he perceived that both he and Picasso had been assimilating Cézanne's geometry of cones, spheres, and cylinders and his principles of pictorial construction. As co-inventors of Cubism, Picasso and Braque undertook a new definition of pictorial space in which objects were represented simultaneously from many visual angles, in wholes or in parts, opaque and transparent. Over 4 years they worked out the language of Cubism. However, during Picasso's long creative life he painted in so many successive styles that he defies classification in any one of them. We will encounter his work again.

Braque's oval *Still Life with Violin* (Fig. 20.15) shows Cubism in its more developed form. This form of Cubism, usually called *Analytical Cubism,* is one in which the artist used recognizable objects as a point of departure, analyzing and focusing on their formal properties. Still-life components such as the table, violin, and sheet music are broken up so that they can be reassembled in a design determined by the artist.

Analytical Cubist pictures tended to be cold, impersonal studies in abstract design. However, later works like Picasso's *Three Musicians*

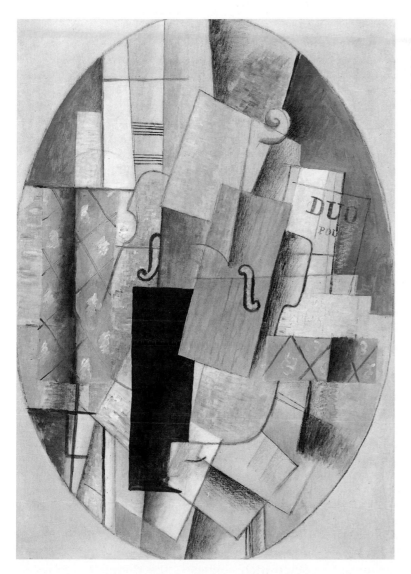

20.15 Georges Braque. *Still Life with Violin,* 1914. Oil on canvas, 3'½" × 2'2". Los Angeles County Museum of Art, purchased with funds provided by the Mr. and Mrs. George Gard de Sylva Collection and the Copley Foundation.

20.16 Pablo Picasso. *Three Musicians,* 1921. Oil on canvas, 6′7″ × 7′3¾″. Museum of Modern Art, New York, Mrs. Simon Guggenheim Fund.

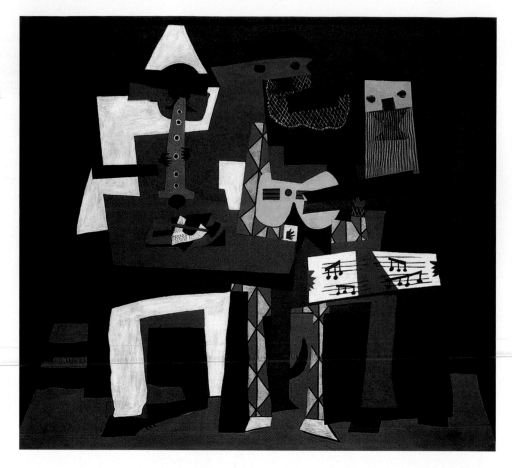

(Fig. 20.16) introduced a greater creative confidence, bright coloration, and generally more easily identified subjects. The three masked figures sitting at a table are the same commedia dell'arte figures that regularly recur in Picasso's canvases, Cubist or otherwise; these come from his love of circus and theatrical performances in which clowns and other performers dress in festive carnival costumes. The figure on the left playing a clarinet is a Pierrot, the center one with the guitar is a Harlequin, and the more solemn monklike figure on the right holds a musical score.

Picasso translated Cubist principles into the three-dimensional medium of sculpture in works like *Woman's Head* (Fig. 20.17). The figure is a geometric analysis of the structure of the human face, emphasizing the most important planes and surfaces. Through this process of analysis and reduction, the head could be organized into a number of different facets, each of which casts its own shadow. This brings variety and a sense of movement to the composition.

The sculptures of Jacques Lipchitz were also three-dimensional adaptations of Cubism in its mature phase. *Man with Mandolin* (Fig. 20.18) creates a repetitive pattern of rough stone textures,

diagonal lines, tilted planes, and irregular rectangles and triangles. Lipchitz breaks down the traditional distinction between solids and voids, convex and concave surfaces, and the relationship between wholes and parts in an intricate interlocking design.

MUSIC UPSIDE DOWN

The musical counterpart of Cubist space was invented when composers began breaking up traditional tonality and searching for new musical resources and mediums of expression. As a strict follower of the principles of order, Stravinsky had observed that "tonal elements become musical only by virtue of their being organized." The **twelve-tone system** of musical composition that Arnold Schoenberg developed in about 1920 was a strict form of tonal organization. Where the Cubists reduced natural objects into their most basic forms, Schoenberg chose to begin from music's most basic element: notes. For each new composition he created a basic row made up of the twelve different chromatic pitches that exist within the octave. Each new row for each new composition contained the rhythmic, harmonic,

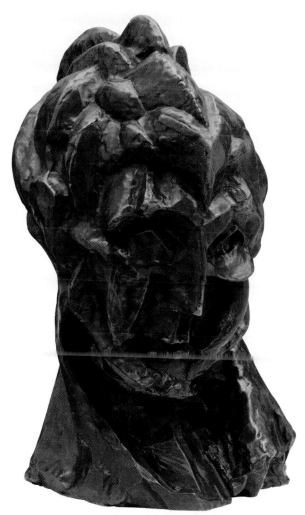

20.17 Pablo Picasso. *Woman's Head,* 1909. Bronze,
1′4¼″ × 9¾″ × 10½″. Museum of Modern Art, New York.

Musical Example 20.3
Arnold Schoenberg, *Suite for Piano*

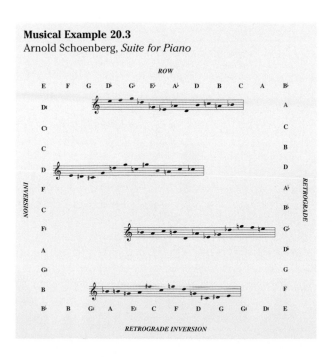

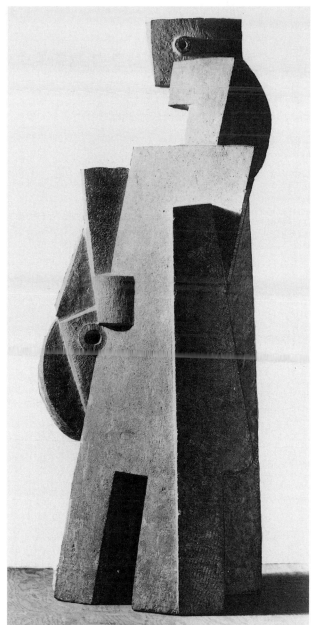

20.18 Jacques Lipchitz. *Man with Mandolin,* 1917.
Stone, height 2′5¾″. Yale University Art Gallery, New
Haven, Collection Société Anonyme.

melodic, and tone color potential for that composition. Once the row was stated, it could then be manipulated in endless ways—performed as a whole or in part with various notes clustered into chords; played serially, one note after another as a melody in normal order; presented successively in contrapuntal sequences; appear upside down in melodic inversion, backward in retrograde motion, or upside down and backward in retrograde inversion (Musical Example 20.3). All in all there are an estimated half a billion different possible combinations.

The twelve-tone method has generally been referred to as **serialism,** but Schoenberg preferred to call it simply a method of composing with twelve tones that are related only to one another. Tonality is thus relative rather than absolute, because there is no single tonal center. Tonality in the usual sense, however, is not excluded; rather, the system encompasses tonality and rises above it.

ART AND THE FUTURE

The movement known as **Futurism** began in Italy before World War I under the leadership of the poet and dramatist Filippo Tommaso Marinetti. Agreeing with Friedrich Nietzsche's remark that history is the process by which the dead bury the living, Marinetti declared in his *Manifesto* of 1909 that Futurism was being founded to "deliver Italy from its plague of professors, archeologists, tourist guides, and antique dealers." The Futurists wanted to destroy museums, libraries, academies, and universities to make way for their particular view of the future. "A roaring motorcar, which runs like a machine gun," they said, "is more beautiful than the winged Victory of Samothrace."

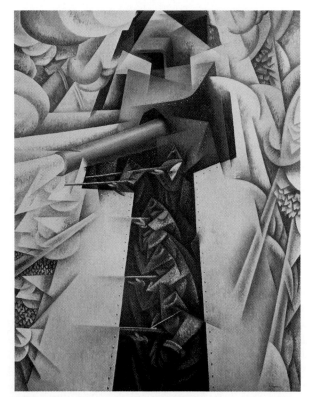

20.19 Gino Severini. *Armored Train in Action,* 1915. Oil on canvas, 3′9⅝″ × 2′10⅞″. Museum of Modern Art, New York, gift of Richard S. Zeisler.

Above all, the Futurists projected an art for a fast-moving, machine-propelled age. They admired the motion, force, speed, and strength of mechanical forms, and in their pictures they wanted more than anything else to include the dynamic sensation of motion. A galloping horse, they said, has not four legs but twenty. Deriving his inspiration from automobiles, airplanes, trains, and machine guns, Gino Severini painted *Armored Train in Action* (Fig. 20.19), with its diagonal lines and plumes of smoke suggesting speed, and gunfire adding the dimension of rapid action. Futurist photographer Anton Giulio Bragaglia interpreted Futurism in a hazy image that depicts sequential pictures of the painter Giacomo Balla lecturing on his humorous picture, titled *Dynamism of a Dog on a Leash* (Fig. 20.20).

THE CITY AND THE MACHINE

In the twenty-first century, after devastating world wars, threats of global warming, and fear of terrorism, it is difficult to understand the fervent optimism of the early twentieth century, when many people hoped that the machine would alleviate the hardship of human labor and help create an equitable society. Alfred Stieglitz's *The Hand of Man* (Fig. 20.21) is a visual boast of industrial accomplishments, visible in the telephone lines, locomotive engine, factory chimney, and train tracks. Stieglitz was a cosmopolitan American who not only promoted photography as an art but also organized exhibitions in his famous New York gallery that introduced Americans to the work of Matisse, Cézanne, Auguste Rodin, Henri Toulouse-Lautrec, and Brancusi. In other words, he allied himself with progressives, envisioning

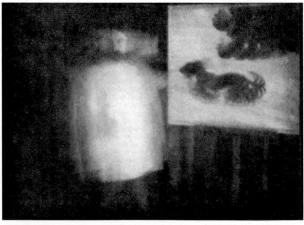

20.20 Anton Bragaglia, *The Futurist Painter Giacomo Balla*, 1912. From *Fotodinamismo Furista,* Rome, Italy.

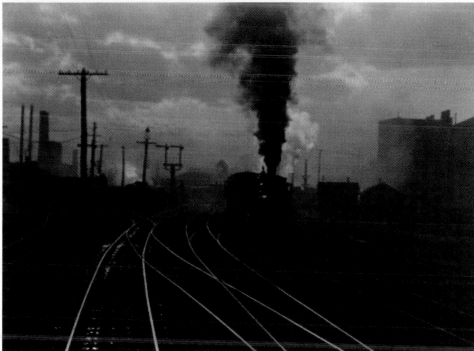

20.21 Alfred Stieglitz. *The Hand of Man,* 1902 negative; c. 1933 print. Gelatin silver print, 3¼″ × 4⁷⁄₁₆″. The J. Paul Getty Museum, Los Angeles.

a better world through the fruits of industrialization and art.

Stieglitz was an eclectic Modernist who promoted artists with diverse approaches to modern art. Among them was Georgia O'Keeffe, whose simplified forms derived not from the industrial landscape, but from nature. O'Keeffe was what those in the prewar era in the United States called "a new woman," who took advantage of women's greater freedom to enter art schools and to think of art as a full-time, life-long career. When he photographed her, Stieglitz posed her in front of one of her nearly abstract charcoal drawings and had her bend her fingers in sharply angular shapes that suggested the modern fascination with geometry (Fig. 20.22).

In general, the machine aesthetic assumed that automation and industrial projects and products would eventually free humanity from its dependence on nature. Many of the later Cubist movements, such as Vorticism in England, professed a love of the machine. The Vorticists hoped to blast away the remnants of the past with Cubism's angular geometry and Futurism's dynamic movement. The first abstract photography, created by American-born Alvin Langdon Coburn, was produced by photographing

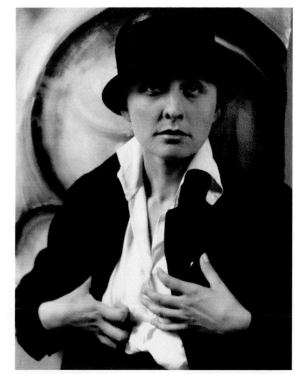

20.22 Alfred Stieglitz. *Georgia O'Keeffe: A Portrait,* 1918. Gelatin silver print, 9½″ × 7¾″. The J. Paul Getty Museum, Los Angeles.

20.23   Alvin Langdon Coburn.
Vortograph, 1917. Printed
c. 1950s. Gelatin silver print,
approx. 8″ × 6″. George
Eastman House, Rochester,
New York.

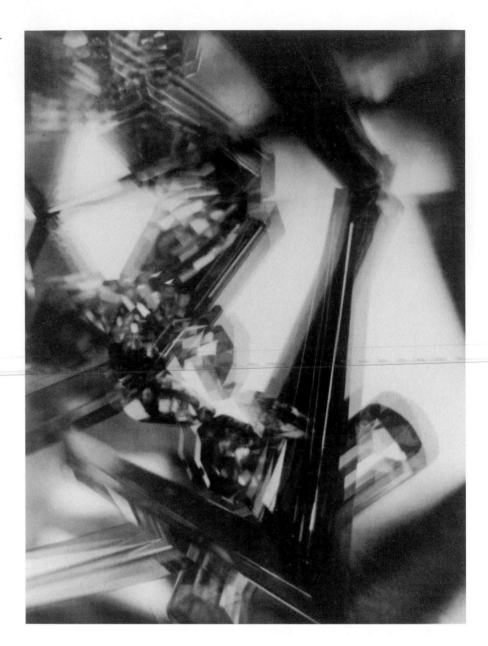

abstractions made with a kaleidoscope-like system of mirrors (Fig. 20.23).

Composers also took up the idea of the machine and its implications for music. In 1917, Stravinsky composed a piece for player piano titled *Étude for Pianola.* France's Arthur Honegger gave voice to a triumphant song of the machine in a work called *Pacific 231.* Its title, an allusion that only locomotive buffs would immediately grasp, refers to the standard arrangement of drive wheels in a locomotive's engine. The piece was designed to evoke the sounds of the railroad, complete with the powerful grinding of the wheels and the penetrating shriek of the steam whistle. George Antheil composed a score for Fernand Léger's silent film, *Ballet Mécanique* (see

pp. 573–574), that could not be used because it was twice the length of the film. He included instruments in the piece such as pianos, electric doorbells, and an airplane propeller.

Perhaps the most successful musical realization of the mechanical style is found in the works of Edgard Varèse. Technically trained in two fields, Varèse was as much a physicist as a musician, and the titles of his works sound as if they came from a laboratory: *Integrales, Density 21.5* (the specific gravity of the platinum of the flute for which it was composed), and *Ionisation.* The last is constructed in a series of interlocking planes of sound that suggest but do not directly imitate the rhythms of modern city life. Varèse's expressed aim was to build a music that would embrace the realities of the industrial world rather than try to escape from them.

The pre–World War I world was not without its critics. One of the era's most famous paintings, Marcel Duchamp's *Nude Descending a Staircase, No. 2* (Fig. 20.24), combined Cubism, the jerky motion of early movies, and the look of time-study photographs like those produced by Marey (see Fig. 19.33) to create a speed-blurred mechanical figure obviously lacking the sensuous appeal of conventional nudes. This commentary of the path of science and industry became comic fodder for cartoonists throughout the twentieth century. More direct criticisms of city life and industrial practice were gathered by the American photographers Jacob Riis and Lewis Hine, whose work showed how progress was achieved through the work of poor immigrants and child laborers (Fig. 20.25) in Carolina cotton mills.

In Europe during World War I, faith in the machine collapsed into cynicism and despair as cultural centers were starved and ravaged and the toll of dead, wounded, or missing soldiers and civilians, which reached about 40 million people, devastated families and nations. Machines like tanks and planes and technologies like poison gas blunted faith in the potential of industry to make a better world.

Although Americans fought in the war, they did not enter it until the last 6 months; this minimized losses of American soldiers, and because the war was fought in Europe, it did not transform

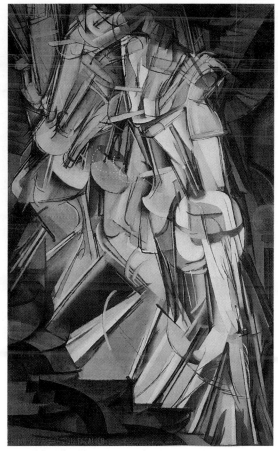

20.24 Marcel Duchamp. *Nude Descending a Staircase, No. 2,* 1912. Oil on canvas, 4′9⅞″ × 2′11⅛″. The Louise and Walter Arensberg Collection, 1950. Philadelphia Museum of Art, Philadelphia.

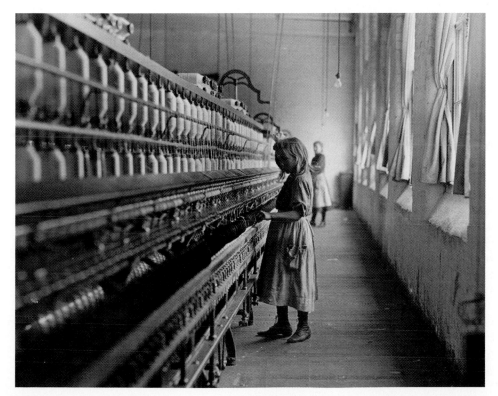

20.25 Lewis Hine. *Girl Worker in Carolina Cotton Mill,* 1908. Gelatin silver print, 7½″ × 9½″. The Museum of Modern Art, New York.

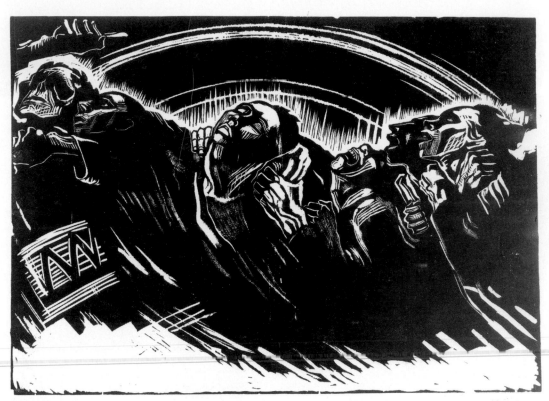

20.26   Käthe Kollwitz. *The Volunteers* from *War Series,* 1922–1923. Woodcut, approx. 1′1¾″ × 1′7¼″.

the American landscape as it did abroad. No artist living in Europe could ignore the war, and many were shaken by it for the rest of their lives. Käthe Kollwitz, whose son was killed early in the conflict, spent the war years in Berlin. An independent Expressionist and active feminist, she worked primarily in print media. In a unique style that drew on her training as a painter, she was among the few to depict the effects of industrialization on the working poor. During the 1920s, she began a series of woodcuts that dramatized the effects of the war on ordinary people (Fig. 20.26). In dramatic black-and-white smears, she exposed children's hunger and widows' anguish. In *The Volunteers* (Fig. 20.26), part of her *War Series,* she depicted doomed young military recruits marching to the drumbeats of a skeleton-like figure. Images like these haunted the postwar generation. Some despaired that art had any purpose after the savagery of trench warfare. Others decided that Modernism had not gone far enough in understanding how humans could sink to such brutality.

YOUR RESOURCES

- **Exploring Humanities CD-ROM**

  ○ Interactive Map: Colonial Empires about 1900

  ○ Aspects of Modernism: The Visual Arts 1863–1939 Module

  ○ Readings—Freud, excerpts from *The Interpretation of Dreams*

- **Web Site**

  http://art.wadsworth.com/fleming10

  ○ Chapter 20 Quiz

  ○ Links—Online Readings—T.S. Eliot, selected works; Shaw, *Man and Superman;* Stein, *Three Lives*

- **Audio CD**

  ○ Smith, *Back Water Blues*

  ○ Stravinsky, *Rite of Spring,* "Dance of the Adolescent Girls"

  ○ Schoenberg, *Pierrot Lunaire*

  ○ Varése, *Ionisation*

TWENTIETH-CENTURY MODERNISM, PART I

Key Events	Architecture and Visual Arts	Literature and Music

Key Events

1891 **Wainwright Building,** St. Louis, first skyscraper

1891–1893 **Motion-picture camera** patented by Thomas Edison; sound recording developed

1903 **Aviation age** begun by Wright brothers

1905 **Sigmund Freud** formulates psychoanalysis; first motion-picture theater opened in Pittsburgh

1905–1916 **Einstein** developed theory of relativity; becomes better known after 1919, when it is verified

1905 **Expressionism** began; "Fauve" exhibit in Paris; other Expressionist exhibits followed in Dresden and Munich

1905 **Alfred Stieglitz** opened the gallery that became known as "291" on 5th Avenue, New York; showed photography and French Modernists, Cézanne, Picasso, and Braque; 1903–1917 published the influential journal *Camera Work*

1907 **Picasso** and other Paris artists discovered power of African tribal art at Trocadéro Museum of Man

1907–1914 **Cubism** developed in Paris by Picasso and Braque

1908 **Model T** (touring car) introduced by Henry Ford

1909 **Wireless radio** developed by Marconi; Peary reached North Pole; 1911 Amundson reached South Pole

1909 **Futurist** movement developed in Italy

1911 **Der Blaue Reiter (Blue Rider)** group formed in Munich with Kandinsky, Marc

1911–1912 **Chirico** and **Chagall** exhibited proto-Surrealist pictures in Paris

1913 **New York Armory Show** brought controversial European art works to United States, including Duchamp's *Nude Descending the Staircase, No. 2*

1914–1918 **World War I**

1916–1922 **Dada** art founded in Zurich, Switzerland; spread quickly to Berlin, Paris, New York

1917 **Russian Revolution** began; Lenin triumphed

1917 *De Stijl* magazine published in Holland; gave name to International Style architecture

1919 **Treaty of Versailles**

1919–1933 **Weimar Republic** ruled in Germany

1920 **U.S. women won right to vote**

Architecture and Visual Arts

1838–1886 H. H. Richardson ★

1844–1910 Henri Rousseau (le Douanier) ▲

1849–1914 Jacob Riis ▲

1856–1924 Louis Sullivan ★

1861–1944 Aristide Maillol ●

1863–1944 Edvard Munch ▲

1864–1946 Alfred Stieglitz ▲

1866–1944 Wassily Kandinsky ▲

1867–1945 Käthe Kollwitz ▲

1867–1956 Emil Nolde ▲

1867–1959 Frank Lloyd Wright ★

1869–1954 Henri Matisse ▲

1870–1938 Ernst Barlach ●

1870–1953 John Marin ▲

1871–1958 Giacomo Balla ▲

1871–1958 Georges Rouault ▲

1874–1940 Louis Hine ▲

1874–1954 Auguste Perret ★

1876–1957 Constantin Brancusi ●

1879–1940 Paul Klee ▲

1880–1966 Hans Hofmann ▲

1880–1916 Franz Marc ▲

1881–1955 Fernand Léger ▲

1881–1955 Max Pechstein ▲

1881–1973 Pablo Picasso ▲

1882–1916 Umberto Boccioni ▲

1882–1963 Georges Braque ▲

1882–1966 Alvin Langdon Coburn ▲

1883–1969 Walter Gropius ★

1883–1962 Ivan Mestrovic ●

1883–1949 José Clemente Orozco ▲

1883–1966 Gino Severini ▲

1883–1954 William van Alen ★

1884–1950 Max Beckmann ▲

1884–1920 Amedeo Modigliani ▲

1886–1966 Jean (Hans) Arp ●

1886–1980 Oskar Kokoschka ▲

1886–1957 Diego Rivera ▲

1886–1969 Ludwig Mies van der Rohe ★

1887–1964 Aleksandr Archipenko ●

1887–1985 Marc Chagall ▲

1887–1965 Le Corbusier (Charles-Édouard Jeanneret-Gris) ★

1887–1968 Marcel Duchamp ▲

1887–1986 Georgia O'Keeffe ▲

1888–1978 Giorgio de Chirico ▲

1889–1975 Thomas Hart Benton ▲

1890–1977 Naum Gabo ●

1890–1963 J. J. P. Oud ★

1890–1976 Man Ray ▲

1891–1976 Max Ernst ▲

1891–1973 Jacques Lipchitz ●

1892–1942 Grant Wood ▲

1893–1967 Charles Burchfield ▲

1893–1959 George Grosz ▲

1893–1983 Joan Miró ▲

1894–1964 Stuart Davis ▲

1898–1976 Alexander Calder ●

1898–1967 René Magritte ▲

1898–1986 Henry Moore ●

1898–1969 Ben Shahn ▲

1900–1955 Yves Tanguy ▲

1901–1966 Alberto Giacometti ●

1901–1970 William H. Johnson ▲

1904–1989 Salvador Dali ▲

Literature and Music

1842–1910 William James ◆

1856–1939 Sigmund Freud ◆

1856–1950 George Bernard Shaw ◆

1858–1924 Giacomo Puccini ❑

1859–1952 John Dewey ◆

1860–1911 Gustav Mahler ❑

1863–1938 Gabriele d'Annunzio ◆

1864–1949 Richard Strauss ❑

1866–1925 Erik Satie ❑

1868–1917 Scott Joplin ❑

1869–1951 André Gide ◆

1871–1945 Paul Ambroise Valéry ◆

1872–1915 Aleksandr Scriabin ❑

1873–1943 Sergei Rachmaninov ❑

1874–1951 Arnold Schoenberg ❑

1874–1946 Gertrude Stein ◆

1875–1955 Thomas Mann ◆

1875–1937 Maurice Ravel ❑

1876–1946 Manuel de Falla ❑

1876–1944 Filippo Tommaso Marinetti ◆

1878–1967 Carl Sandburg ◆

1879–1936 Ottorino Respighi ❑

1881–1945 Béla Bartók ❑

1882–1941 James Joyce ◆

1882–1967 Zoltán Kodály ❑

1882–1971 Igor Stravinsky ❑

1883–1965 Edgard Varèse ❑

1883–1945 Anton von Webern ❑

1885–1935 Alban Berg ❑

1885–1951 Sinclair Lewis ◆

1886–1939 "Ma" Rainey (Gertrude Malissa Nix Pridgett) ❑

1887–1962 Robinson Jeffers ◆

1888–1965 T. S. Eliot ◆

1888–1953 Eugene O'Neill ◆

1889–1963 Jean Cocteau ◆

1890 James Frazer's *The Golden Bough* first published

1891–1953 Sergey Prokofiev ❑

1892–1955 Arthur Honegger ❑

1892–1974 Darius Milhaud ❑

1894–1937 Bessie Smith ❑

1895–1963 Paul Hindemith ❑

1896–1966 André Breton ◆

1897–1962 William Faulkner ◆

1898–1937 George Gershwin ❑

1899–1961 Ernest Hemingway ◆

1899–1963 Francis Poulenc ❑

1905–1980 Jean-Paul Sartre ◆

1913–1960 Albert Camus ◆

★ - Architect ❑ - Composer or performer ▲ - Painter or photographer ● - Sculptor ◆ - Writer

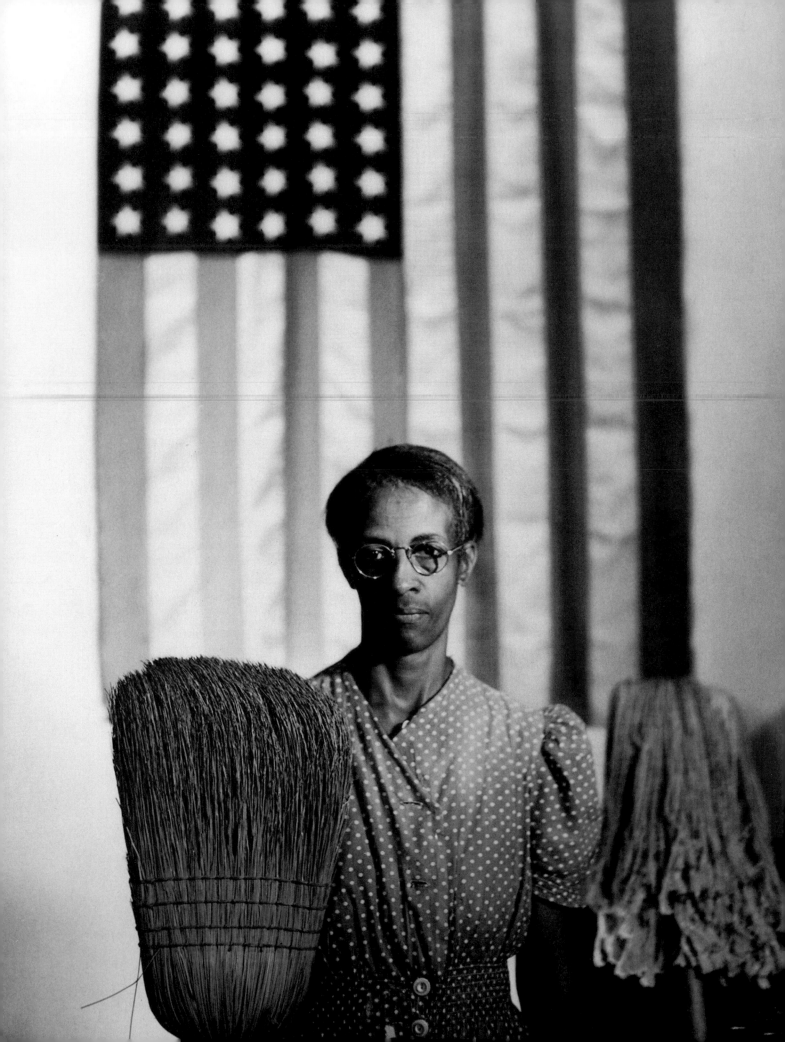

CHAPTER

21

TWENTIETH-CENTURY MODERNISM, PART II: ART BETWEEN THE WORLD WARS

THE MAGNITUDE OF THE DEATH and destruction caused by World War I brought about a new vision of the world. Those who brokered the peace did so in global terms, founding the League of Nations, which after World War II became the United Nations. With the exception of the United States, which became the world's largest manufacturing power in 1914, the war weakened the economics and governments of the combatant nations, spurring new ideas for recovery and reform. In Russia, the new socialist government that had fought the Germans continued to fight a bloody civil war while trying to industrialize the country. Around the world, Soviet Russia was seen by some as an emerging ideal and by others as a threat to peace and prosperity.

Oddly enough, the slaughter wreaked by new instruments of war—tanks, planes, rapid-fire machine guns, and the dreaded mustard gas—did not thoroughly destroy faith in the ability of machines to bring about better living conditions. The French painter Fernand Léger, who fought in World War I and spent a year recovering from a mustard gas attack, believed that the experience has changed his notions of what was important in art. He came to believe that machine guns had a greater reality than still-life or landscape painting. Moreover, he believed that painting should be accessible to the viewer. He developed a style in which precise and neat parts all fit into an appointed place, as in *The City* (Fig. 21.1). Léger

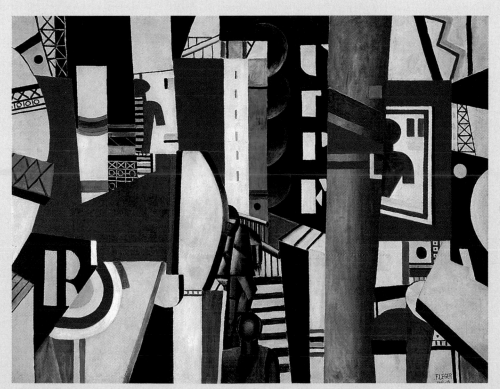

21.1 Fernand Léger. *The City,* 1919. Oil on canvas, 7′7″ × 9′8½″. Philadelphia Museum of Art. A. E. Gallatin Collection.

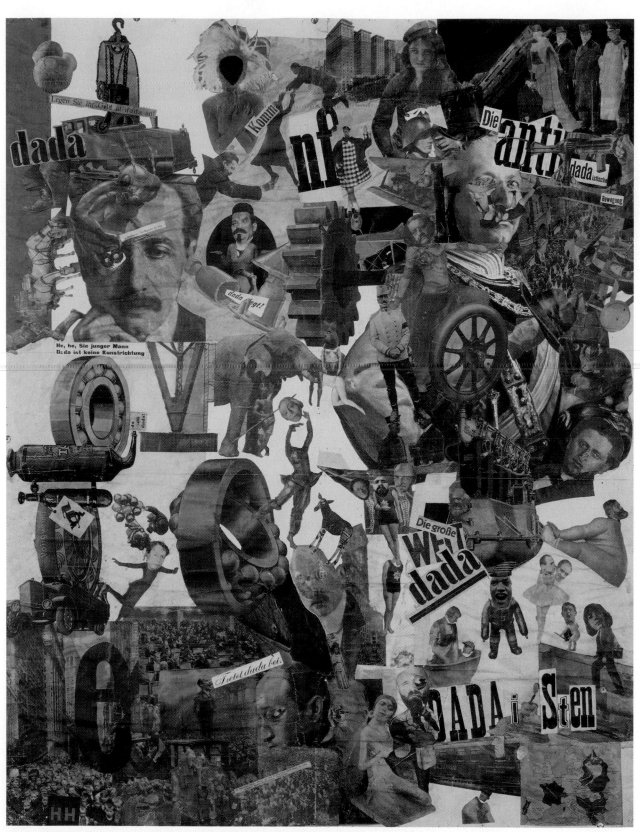

21.2 Hannah Höch. *Cut with the Kitchen Knife Dada through the Last Weimar Beer Belly Cultural Epoch of Germany,* 1919–1920. Photomontage, 3′9″ × 2′11½″. Neue Nationalgalerie, Staatliche Museen, Berlin, Germany.

loved crankshafts, cylinder blocks, and pistons, all painted in gleaming primary colors. Taking Paul Cézanne's statement about cylinders, spheres, and cones more literally than did the Cubists, he drew curved forms and modeled them in light and dark. His is a world without sentiment or criticism, populated by people whose parts are geometric shapes. Human forms are introduced only for their design contribution and remain inexpressive. In 1924, Léger made an abstract silent film called *Ballet Mécanique* in which machine forms mostly replace human beings and their activities. An airplane propeller, an electric doorbell, and a player piano perform scenes. Léger's was a unique response to the war; other artists reacted with bitterness and cynicism.

DADA AND PHOTOMONTAGE

During the war the rising death toll and destruction brought expressions of horror from a group of artists who gathered in Zurich, Switzerland, a country that was neutral during the conflict. The year was 1915, and these artists believed that the cultural heritage of such a sick civilization should be shattered. In other words, they defined art's task as destruction, not creation. For reasons that remain unclear, they called their movement by the nonsensical word **dada.** Another group of like-minded dada artists met in Berlin toward the end of the war. They were more politically oriented and more aware of the influence of mass media in daily life. They developed a form of art know as **photomontage,** gathering words and images from newspapers and magazines and arranging them in symbolic rather than representational groups. Although they did not acknowledge a direct influence from cubist collage, where painters added bits of newspaper, tickets, or menus and the like to their canvases, the look is similarly angular and nonnarrative. Hannah Höch's *Cut with the Kitchen Knife Dada through the Last Weimar Beer Belly Cultural Epoch of Germany* (Fig. 21.2) contains several references to dada interspersed with sarcastic political references that contemporary Berliners would instantly recognize. The work contrasts the past and the modern, symbolized by draft horses and automobiles and women in traditional roles compared with fashion models in chic clothing. *Cut with the Kitchen Knife* recognized that with the

modern comes an enhanced consumer society. In the center, above the headless dancer, floats the head of Käthe Kollwitz (see p. 570), the renowned Berlin artist and feminist who was greatly admired by progressives. Here she appears to be the symbolic pivot around which the dada world, whose style she did not adopt, seems to turn.

Dada, an international movement, sprang up in Paris after the war. There, to make a point about the futility of Western culture, Marcel Duchamp irreverently drew a moustache and goatee on a reproduction of Leonardo da Vinci's *Mona Lisa* (Fig. 21.3), giving it the title *L.H.O.O.Q.,* a French graffito meaning "She has hot pants." This sardonic, anti-romantic, prankster attitude was seen earlier in France in the musical compositions of iconoclast Erik Satie. Satie titled his three piano pieces of 1913 *Desiccated Embryos* and included absurd instructions for its performance, such as calling on the pianist to play a melody "like a nightingale with a toothache."

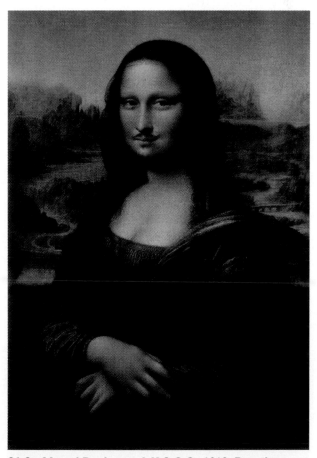

21.3 Marcel Duchamp. *L.H.O.O.Q.,* 1919. Pencil on reproduction of Leonardo's *Mona Lisa,* 7¾" × 4⅞". Private collection.

Dada was a nihilistic movement whose artists were distrustful of order and reason. They challenged polite society and protested the pretense of fine art by concocting nonpictures from the contents of wastebaskets and gutters. Their bitter humor, aggressive nonsense, and attacks on respected institutions were aimed at the hypocritical pomposities of bureaucrats. By reducing the role of art to absurdity, they cleared the air for the other experiments and innovations of the postwar period.

ART AND REVOLUTION

The Russian Revolution of October 1917 had immediate and profound implications for the arts. In one blow, the taste of the czars was wiped out and experimental art put in its place by the Bolshevik leadership, who thought that a revolutionary party ought to promote avant-garde art. Some artists were given jobs or put on government salaries so they could create art for the future.

Expressionism, Futurism, and Cubism had been known in prerevolutionary Russia, and they became the platform upon which the postrevolutionary artist built. Kazimir Malevich developed an approach that he called **suprematism,** which he believed was a universal language of basic geometric shapes to which all people could respond (Fig. 21.4). Like Malevich, a number of women artists had been investigating the new trends before the Revolution, often linking the modernist simplification of form to the legacy of Russian folk art. Painter and theorist Liubov Popova created paintings in which she attempted to define a purely painterly space that resulted from line and color relationships on the canvas and that was not a generalization or an abstraction of the world of visual experience (Fig. 21.5).

Vladimir Tatlin put forward a bold plan for a building to house the congress of the new

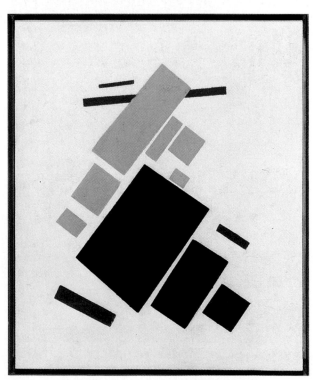

21.4 Kazimir Malevich, *Suprematist Composition: Airplane Flying,* 1915 (dated 1914). Oil on canvas, 1′10⅞″ × 1′7″. Museum of Modern Art, New York.

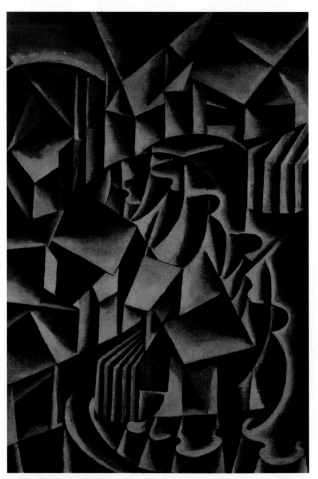

21.5 Liubov Popova, *Birsk,* 1916. Oil on canvas, 3′5¾″ × 2′3⅜″. Solomon R. Guggenheim Museum, New York. Gift of George Costakis, 1981.

Soviet state (Fig. 21.6). The building was never constructed, but the model indicates how Tatlin planned to employ open, functional architecture like that of the Eiffel Tower in his plan. From outside, the building spirals upward, as if toward better prospects for Soviet citizens. Inside, there were to be meeting rooms and offices based on cubes, pyramids, semicircles, and cylinders, each of which would turn at a different speed.

Artist-photographer Aleksandr Rodchenko believed that a new society must be founded, literally, on a new vision. His photographs were deliberately taken from odd, unsettling angles, so that the viewer could not be a passive recipient of the image but had to ponder it to understand its meaning (Fig. 21.7). In the Soviet state, linkage between a new vision and a new society was deeply felt, to the point that many art makers rejected the word *artist*, with its connotations of self-expression, and opted to describe themselves with words like *engineer* and *builder*. They turned toward designing functional items such as dinnerware, clothing, books, and posters. El Lissitzky projected the ideal merger of art and engineering in his work, *The Constructor*, a self-portrait superimposed on graph paper

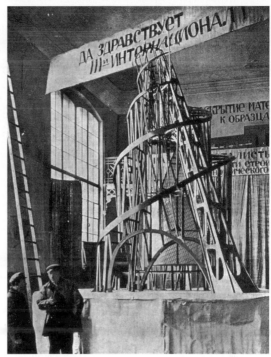

21.6 Vladimir Tatlin. *Monument to the Third International,* 1919–1920. Model in wood, iron, and glass. Recreated in 1968 for exhibition at the Moderna Museet, Stockholm, Sweden.

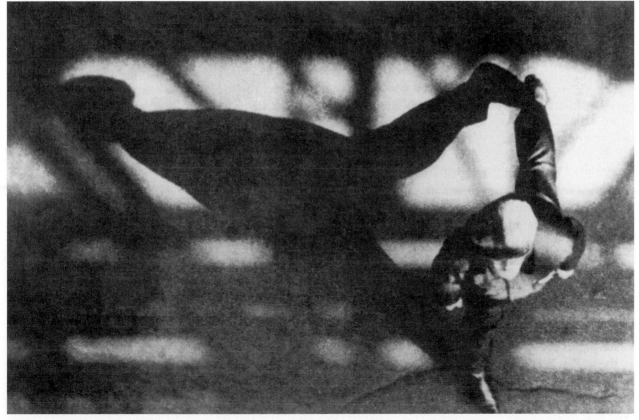

21.7 Aleksandr Rodchenko. *Untitled,* 1928. Gelatin silver print. Rodchenko & Stepanova Archive, Moscow, Russia.

21.8 El Lissitzky. *The Constructor,* 1924. Photomontage, Getty Research Institute, Los Angeles.

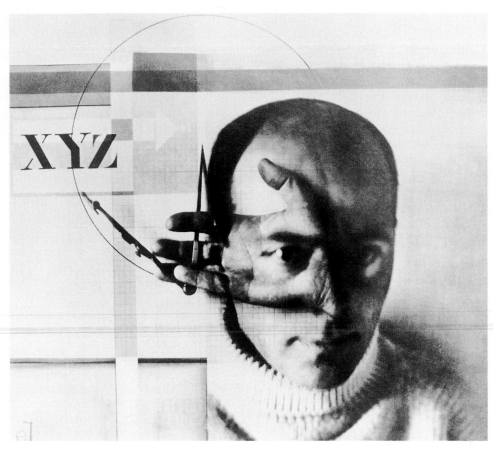

(Fig. 21.8). The artist's fingers hold a compass that has drawn a circle above his head in the manner of a halo. Although these Soviet artists were at best a loose alliance, the term **Constructivism** has been used to describe their efforts.

The prospect of revolutionary art was short-lived. Even during the early 1920s, some artists became disillusioned with the ability of abstract art to communicate with Soviet workers and peasants. The end of experimental art followed on the heels of Joseph Stalin's accession to the leadership of Russia. Stalin favored what became known as Socialist Realism, representational art that could more easily be used to inspire and instruct the Russian people.

SURREALISM

The *Surrealist Manifesto* of 1924 proclaimed that the art was based on "pure psychic automatism by means of which one sets out to express, verbally, in writing, or in any other manner, the real functioning of thought without any control by reason or any aesthetic or moral preoccupation." Surrealism suggests a greater reality underlying, yet often symbolized by, the physical world. Members of the group believed in the superiority of altered conscious-ness, whether the dream state, fantasy, or subconscious maneuverings. André Breton, the author of the manifesto, spoke of "convulsive beauty," a rare and desirable moment when reality quakes and a brief moment of superreality issues forth. Praising the cleansing forces of the irrational, the Surrealist poet Paul Éluard insisted that "a poem should be the debacle [ruination] of the intellectual."

The painter Salvador Dali associated himself with the group in 1929 and became one of its leading advocates. His pictures swarm with phobias, delusions, and aspects of abnormal psychology. Like Giorgio Chirico and Marc Chagall, Dali was haunted by the mystery of time. In his *Persistence of Memory* (Fig. 21.9), logical clock time has become limp and infected with insects in a primordial landscape of icy sun and a snoozing, crypto-sexual monster. Similarly, Meret Oppenheim's famous *Object*, a fur-lined cup, saucer, and spoon, resonates with dada hijinks and flickers with sexual suggestion (Fig. 21.10).

The versatile Swiss-German painter Paul Klee emerged as an independent artist whose images have surreal echoes. Like the Surrealists, he admired the straightforward, unrefined perceptions of children and used these perceptions in his deceptively simple images that mask subtle meanings. At first glance, for example, the pink-toned *Twittering*

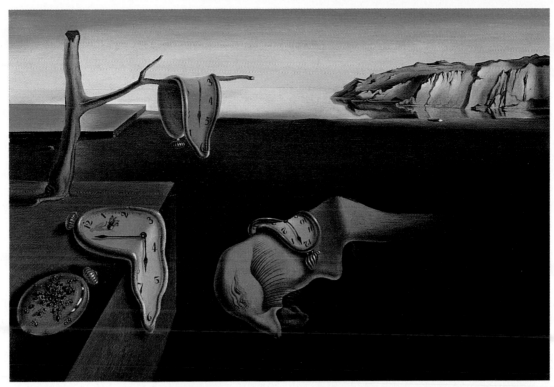

21.9   Salvador Dali. *Persistence of Memory,* 1931. Oil on canvas, 9½″ × 1′1″. Museum of Modern Art, New York (given anonymously).

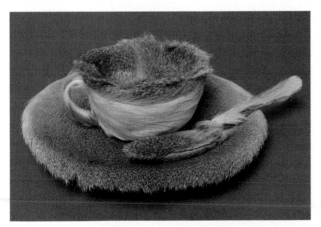

21.10   Meret Oppenheim. *Object,* 1936. Fur-covered cup, 4⅜″ in diameter; saucer, 9⅜″ in diameter; spoon, 8″. Museum of Modern Art, New York (purchase).

Machine looks like a child's rendering, complete with water stains and fingerprints (Fig. 21.11). This, however, is mere surface play in Klee's world of unstable meanings. Four creatures with birdlike feet and eyelike heads perch on the stem of a crank. Presumably, when the handle is turned, their tongues will clack. Below them there seems to be a rectangular pit. Is this a device for trapping some creature that inhabits Klee's eerie, nearly two-dimensional world? The meaning is not explicit, yet with a few fragile lines Klee succeeds in drawing the viewer

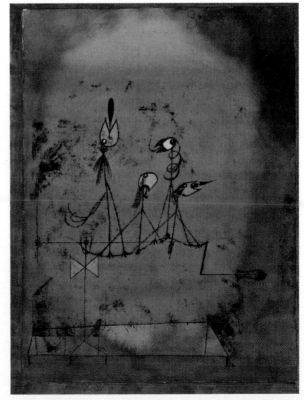

21.11   Paul Klee. *Twittering Machine,* 1922. Watercolor and pen and ink, on oil transfer drawing on paper, mounted on cardboard, 2′1″ × 1′7″. Museum of Modern Art, New York.

into an alternative reality where appearances, though plain, cannot be fathomed.

Klee consciously set out to look at the world through the eyes of a child to achieve a spontaneity untroubled by reason. "I want to be as though newborn, knowing nothing," he said. He gave his drawings the casual quality of doodles and the impulsiveness of improvisations. Klee stuck mainly to small forms and the techniques of watercolor and ink, pencil, and crayon. His mastery of line was so complete that his work should never be confused with carelessness.

Joan Miró, a Spanish artist working in Paris, was an independent like Klee, and like Klee he was drawn to an art of invention that eluded logic or reason. He used techniques popular with the Surrealists, such as automatic writing, which required

him to still his senses, enter a trance, and allow his pen to be guided by his subconscious rather than his conscious mind. He also randomly selected and cut paper to suggest nonrepresentational shapes. In *Painting* (Fig. 21.12), animated, amoeba-like forms float and swim in the turgid atmosphere of an unearthly landscape. As in Klee's work, there is barely a suggestion of three dimensions.

Alberto Giacometti represents Surrealism's sculptural dimension. In *Palace at 4 A.M.* (Fig. 21.13) he uses a thin, geometric, cagelike framework to house spectral and skeletal forms. With its slender size and animal-like forms, it seems like a Klee painting pumped up to a skimpy three-dimensionality. The phantom figures in their interpenetrating open and closed spaces produce a haunting sensation of barrenness and isolation.

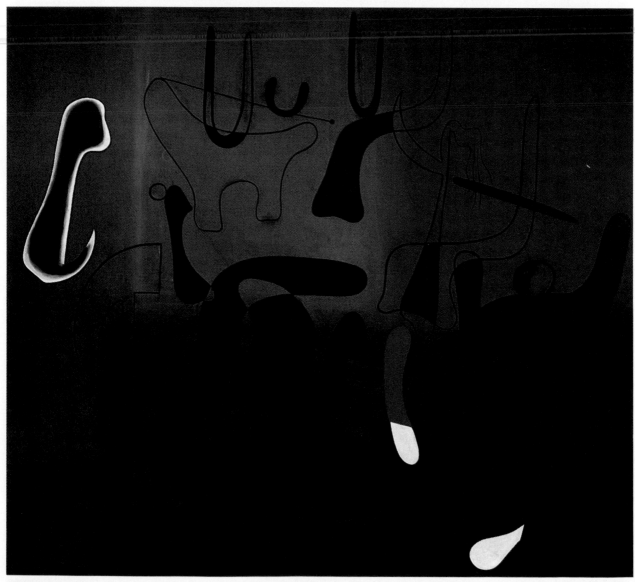

21.12 Joan Miró. *Painting,* 1933, 5′8″ × 6′5″. Museum of Modern Art, New York. Loula D. Lasker Bequest by exchange.

LITERATURE AND MUSIC

In the years immediately after World War I, literary landmarks like T. S. Eliot's poem *The Wasteland* incorporated the era's plummeting faith in human nature and Western culture. Flawed human characters were alienated not only from the upbeat worldview of the prewar years and the utopian dreams of socialists but also from one another. Anxiety-riddled subjectivity and hopelessness also prevailed in Czech writer Franz Kafka's tales about individuals caught up in the capricious, malevolent power of rulers that they cannot identify or understand. That puzzled, suffering, alienated outlook was directly related to the World War I experience by German novelist Erich Maria Remarque, whose 1929 book *All Quiet on the Western Front* portrayed, in the first person, the chilling events in the life of an ordinary soldier during the conflict.

Both James Joyce and Gertrude Stein tried to establish a method for automatic writing as a way to tap the reservoir of the subconscious mind. The result was the stream-of-consciousness technique, notably exemplified in James Joyce's *Ulysses* (1922). In this work, Joyce deals with the thoughts, feelings, and spiritual states of his characters without regard to logical argument or chronological or narrative sequence. His style has the timelessness and quick switchbacks of dreams.

The Austrian composer Alban Berg emerged from service in World War I with strong antimilitary convictions. His expressionist opera *Wozzeck* revealed his disillusionment with the military. Based loosely on short scenes from a play by the early nineteenth-century author Georg Büchner, *Wozzeck* reflects the postwar mood of depression and loss of traditional values. The title character, a career soldier, is a man alone, despite acquaintances and relationships. Everyone in his life inflicts physical or psychological injury, gradually crushing his spirit, until in a mad outburst (Act 3, Scene 2) he kills his wife, Marie, near a small pond outside the town. Fearing that he may have left some evidence there, he returns to the scene of the crime and accidentally drowns. The morning after, while the young child of Wozzeck and Marie is seen playing alone outside, the news arrives that Marie's body has been discovered by the pond. As village children run to see the sight, the young child naïvely follows them, leaving the stage empty.

The era's fascination with the world of childhood found a very different and lyrical counterpart in Maurice Ravel's opera of 1925, *The Child and the Sorceries (L'Enfant et les Sortilèges)*. In Colette's text, a nasty child breaks some bric-a-brac and toys in a temper tantrum. Suddenly the objects come to life to seek revenge. A Wedgwood teapot and a china cup converse in broken English while dancing a foxtrot,

21.13   Alberto Giacometti. *Palace at 4 A.M.,* 1932–1933. Wood, glass, wire, and string, 2′1″ × 2′4¼″ × 1′3¾″. Museum of Modern Art, New York (purchase).

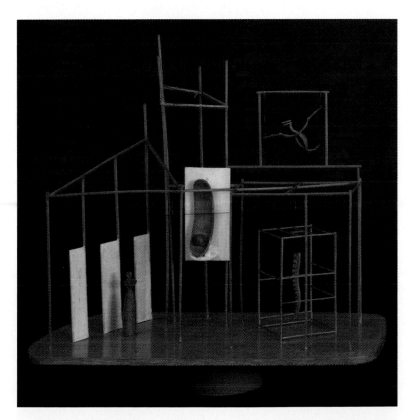

a little old man pops out of nowhere and sings multiplication tables and story problems with wrong answers, two cats mew a duet, and all that is left of the torn picture of the fairy princess in a storybook is "a golden hair and the debris of a dream." Ravel's clever orchestration adds whistles, wood blocks, and friction instruments such as cheese graters to the usual ones for a full range of effects.

THE NEOCLASSICAL INTERLUDE

In a time of immense social stress, when Western culture was under great scrutiny, neoclassicism made a probable appearance in an attempt to calm the anxious spirit with a sense of the enduring value of the classical past. Before World War I, the artistic scene had been severely shaken by the explosions of pictorial Expressionism and outbursts like Stravinsky's *Rite of Spring*. In the aftermath of war, order and clarity were appealing. In 1927, Stravinsky turned to a classical subject, *Apollo and the Muses,* and created a warm, audience-friendly ballet score.

In 1922, an adaptation of Sophocles's *Antigone* by Jean Cocteau was performed in Paris. Pablo Picasso designed the scenery and masks, and the incidental music for harp and oboe was supplied by Arthur Honegger. An opera called *The Eumenides* by Darius Milhaud, based on Paul Claudel's translation of the tragedy by Aeschylus, was written in the same year. In 1924, the Diaghilev dance company presented a ballet titled *Mercury,* with music by Erik Satie and costumes and set designs by Picasso.

Three years later, Stravinsky completed his opera-oratorio *Oedipus Rex.* Diaghilev was the producer, and Jean Cocteau's text, based on Sophocles' tragedy, was translated into Latin so that it would be in a "petrified" language that produced sounds that seemed like unintelligible words to the audience. The motionless stance of the actors was intended to make them as static as Greek columns, and the chorus was placed behind a low relief where only their heads were visible. Such collaborative productions continued occasionally throughout the 1930s, when Stravinsky worked with André Gide on a work for orchestra, chorus, and tenor called *Persephone* (1934).

21.14 Pablo Picasso. *Three Women at the Spring*, 1921. Oil on canvas, 6′8¼″ × 6′8½″. Museum of Modern Art, New York. Gift of Mr. and Mrs. Allan D. Emil.

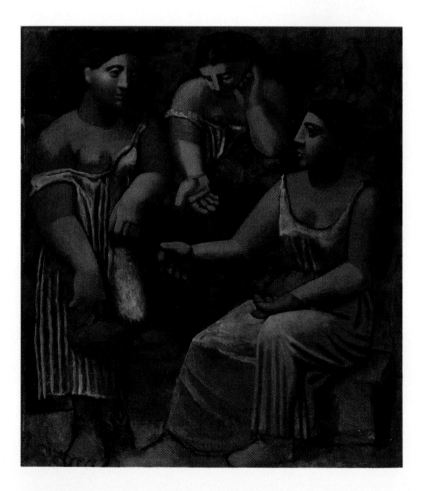

NEOCLASSICISM IN THE VISUAL ARTS

Picasso embraced classicism in the 1920s. His pictures are characterized by elegant line, sculpturesque modeling of bodies, and reduction of pictorial elements to the bare essentials. The *Three Women at the Spring* (Fig. 21.14) are larger than life size, and their robes seem to be turning into fluted columns. Their massiveness, which is not characteristic of Greek or Roman sculpture, was designed to indicate the weight and importance of classical art in Western culture. Similarly, in the neoclassical interlude the statues of Maillol reasserted the expressive importance of the nude figure. Maillol's stable, calm

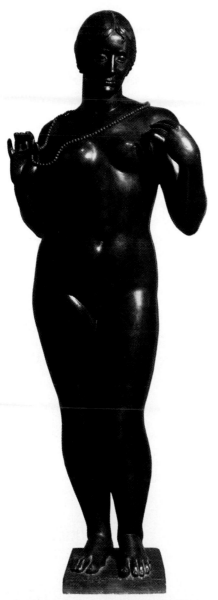

figures seem to weigh against the era's anxiety. His *Venus with a Necklace* (Fig. 21.15), with its Praxitelean curve and stance (see Fig. 2.30) and its merger of antiquity and modernity, achieves a quiet monumentality.

Abstraction was caught up with this new classicism that was not directly derived from ancient models but subtly appealed to them as a source for purifying art, much as eighteenth-century neoclassicism attempted to rid art of rococo frivolity. Piet Mondrian, whose art evolved from the concrete to the abstract, believed that art could become a universal language and font of spiritual strength if it were to become totally nonobjective. In his early years Mondrian painted landscapes and quiet interior scenes in the tradition of his native Holland. He helped found the movement and magazine called *De Stijl (The Style)*. His later work, though completely abstract, owes much to the cool geometric precision of his great predecessor Vermeer (see Figs. 15.16 and 15.17).

The new art, Mondrian believed, should not be individual, but collective, impersonal, and international. All references to the "primitive animal nature of man" should be rigidly excluded to reveal "true human nature" through an art of "balance, unity, and stability." He strove to realize this goal by using "only a single neutral form: the rectangular area in varying dimension." His colors are likewise abstract—black lines of various widths against white backgrounds, or primary colors (red, blue, and yellow) in as pure a state as possible (Fig. 21.16).

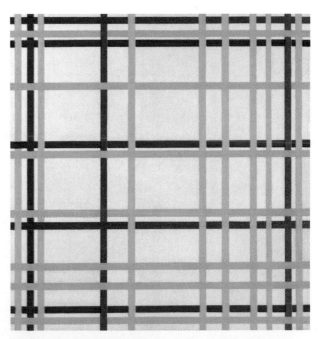

21.15   Aristide Maillol. *Venus with a Necklace,* 1918–1928; cast 1930. Bronze, 5′9″ × 2′ × 1′3¾″. Tate Gallery, London, England.

21.16   Piet Mondrian. *New York City I,* 1942. Oil on canvas, 12′ × 10′. Sidney Janis Gallery, New York.

With El Lissitzky, Mondrian believed that a work of art should be "constructed," and he approached a canvas with the objectivity of a draftsman making a blueprint. The result of this pictorial engineering is the series of pure, two-dimensional studies of space for which he is best known. His visual patterns have a repose that is based on a precise balance of horizontal and vertical elements, and they appear clean to the point of being antiseptic. His pictures have had a great influence on modern design, especially advertising layouts, posters, and rugs.

LITERARY NEOCLASSICISM

One of the most consistent patterns of twentieth-century literature and drama, especially in France, was the reinterpretation of Greek myths as subtle devices for pointing out modern moralistic or political parallels. This tendency runs regularly through the works of André Gide, from the early *Prometheus Drops His Chains* (1899) to the autobiographical story *Theseus* (1946). It can also be found in Franz Werfel's antiwar play *The Trojan Women* (1914) and in Jean-Paul Sartre's *The Flies* (1943). The latter was staged in Paris during the Nazi occupation, and the reference to the plague of flies that sucked Orestes' blood in Aristophanes' bitter comedy could have escaped no one in the audience.

Poets have sometimes adopted classical subjects so that they could create fragmentary works such as ancient ruins. Paul Ambroise Valéry's 1922 trilogy, for instance, contains a poem called "Frag-ments of Narcissus." T. S. Eliot's "Sweeney Agonistes" (1932), in which the grandeur of the past is contrasted with the drabness of the present, likewise is incomplete and bears the subtitle "Fragments of an Aristophanic Melodrama." Freud's use of the names of characters from Greek literature—Oedipus, Electra, Narcissus—as symbols of recurrent subconscious drives also found its way into literature.

James Joyce's *Ulysses* uses classical mythology to give his ordinary characters universal significance. Originally, the eighteen chapters bore titles alluding to similar episodes in Homer's *The Odyssey*. The "Calypso" chapter refers to the goddess with whom Odysseus, or Ulysses, lived for seven years, just as Joyce's antihero Leopold Bloom resided for several years with Molly. In "Hades," Bloom is attending the funeral of a friend, an allusion to Ulysses' descent into the underworld. "Scylla and Charybdis," those hazardous rocks in the Straits of Messina that Ulysses had to navigate, is set in a library where Bloom and his friend Stephen Dedalus find similar pitfalls and contradictions in the books they consult. "Sirens" takes place in a pub where the barmaids are singing bawdy ballads interspersed with popular opera arias. "Circe" is the brothel scene, in which the madam turns men into swine, like her mythical counterpart in *The Odyssey*.

These views of the heroic past serve to heighten the squalid picture of the present that the novel paints. The entire action of *Ulysses* occurs in Dublin in a single 24-hour period to preserve the classical unities of place, time, and action. The plot

21.17   José Clemente Orozco. *The Epic of American Civilization: Gods of the Modern World* (Panel 17), 1932–1934. Fresco, panel, 12′ × 9′11″. Hood Museum of Art, Dartmouth College, Hanover, New Hampshire.

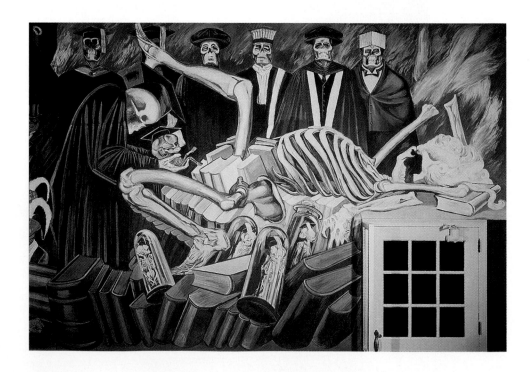

tells the tale of a wanderer who voyages through the treacherous terrors and temptations of Dublin's streets while on his way home to his wife and son. This journey becomes the modern counterpart to Odysseus's efforts to return to Penelope and Telemachus. In the larger sense, *Ulysses* is concerned with the eternal search for the meaning of life.

SOCIAL REALISM AND DOCUMENTARY

During the late 1920s and the 1930s, when a worldwide depression worsened conditions for agricultural and industrial workers, several projects were initiated to record economic and social injustice as well as to build solidarity among the working class. José Clemente Orozco, one of the Mexican muralists deeply involved in his country's revolution, identified with the struggle of the illiterate masses as they tried to break the chains of their landowning and capitalist exploiters. His grim satire also extends to the academic community, pictured in one of the frescoes he made for the Baker Library at Dartmouth College. *The Epic of American Civilization: Gods of the Modern World* (Fig. 21.17) is a macabre comment on the sterility of higher education. It depicts a skeleton giving birth while one professor acts as a midwife and others pompously witness the ghastly event.

Another Mexican artist, Frida Kahlo, moved in a different direction than the Mexican muralists. Although her work has been associated with the Surrealists, she was an independent like Klee and Miró. Using the visual vocabulary of Mexican folk art, she drew directly on the events of her life, particularly the accident that left her partly crippled and in pain. In *Self-Portrait with Thorn Necklace and Hummingbird* (Fig. 21.18) the prickly thorns represent the ache of body and soul. The monkey and the cat refer to the jungle and the fact that she was part Indian. The hummingbird that hangs around

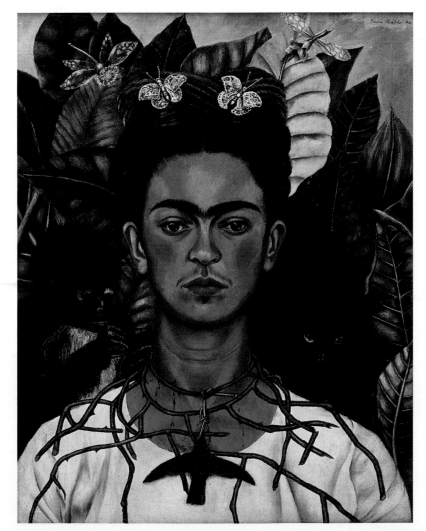

21.18   Frida Kahlo. *Self-Portrait with Thorn Necklace and Hummingbird,* 1940. Oil on canvas. Harry Ransom Humanities Research Center, University of Texas, Austin, Texas.

her neck is a symbol of those who have lost love. In particular, it refers to her recent divorce from muralist Diego Rivera, whom she soon remarried.

PHOTOGRAPHY AND FILMMAKING

Photography played a major role in social documentation in the interwar years. In Europe, groups calling themselves worker-photographers organized their picture-taking efforts to depict working conditions and their effects. In Germany, *Der Arbeiter-Fotograf (The Worker-Photographer)* published their efforts. In England, an organization called Mass Observation targeted the preconceptions of academic sociologists, government bureaucrats, and mass-circulation magazine editors with a panoply of photographs, paintings, and verbal descriptions that the organization thought of as an anthology of real life. Traveling through Poland, Russia, Hungary, and Romania during the 1930s, the Russian photographer Roman Vishniac carried on documentary work to raise money to help the beleaguered Jews in the area.

In 1937, a U.S. government agency known as the Farm Security Administration (FSA) hired pho-

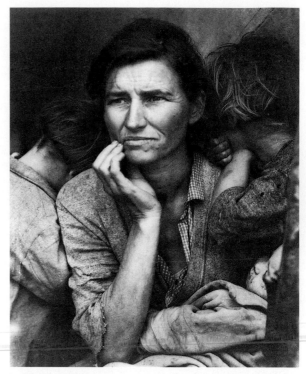

21.19 Dorothea Lange. *Migrant Mother,* 1936. Gelatin silver print, 1'1⁷⁄₁₆″× 10⁹⁄₁₆″.

21.20 Gordon Parks. *Ella Watson,* 1942. Gelatin silver print. Library of Congress, Washington, D.C.

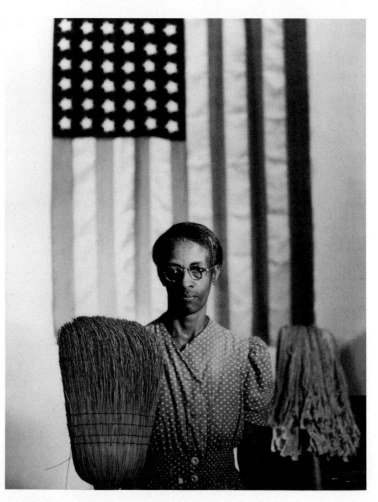

tographers to record the agency's efforts to assist small farmers suffering the effects of the Depression. One of those photographers, Dorothea Lange, made the best-known photograph of the Depression: *Migrant Mother* (Fig. 21.19). Among the last photographers hired at the FSA was Gordon Parks, who subsequently became a filmmaker as well. His pictures of the life of Ella Watson, who cleaned the FSA offices, contrast American dream and American reality (Fig. 21.20).

Documentary films, such as American Robert Flaherty's *Nanook of the North*, were box-office hits during the Depression era. In Russia, Dziga Vertov mounted a camera on a small truck and produced the exhilarating, fast-paced chronicle *Man with a Movie Camera*. Picture magazines were also extremely popular, especially in Europe. Arriving late on the scene, *Life* magazine hit the ground running with its 1936 issue, featuring photographs recounting the building of Montana's Fort Peck Dam, then the largest earth-filled dam in the world. The cover photograph (Fig. 21.21) was made by Margaret Bourke-White, the era's best-known photographer, whose images ranged from celebrations of industry and industrial workers to portraits of the rural poor.

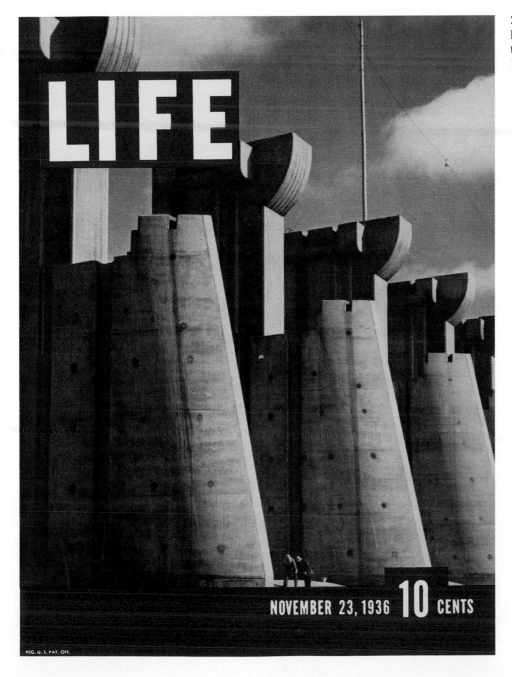

21.21 Margaret Bourke-White. Cover of the first *Life* magazine, 1936.

THE HARLEM RENAISSANCE

The Harlem Renaissance, or New Negro Movement, grew out of African-American efforts to study and express their heritage. In the philosophy of Alain Locke, one of the movement's leaders, blacks should look to Africa the way Western culture looks to Greece. In 1934, painter Aaron Douglas, who was influenced by Locke's emphasis on the African heritage of blacks, received a commission from the Work Progress Administration (WPA) to create a series of murals for the New York Public Library. Like the Farm Security Administration, the WPA was a government organization set up to provide assistance during the Depression. Among other programs, it sponsored public art projects. Douglas took his commission to mean that he should educate viewers about African-American accomplishments and influences, including the use of visual ideas derived from African sculpture by leading artists like Picasso and the central place of jazz in American and European culture (Fig. 21.22).

Like many Americans living abroad, painter William H. Johnson returned to the United States on the eve of World War II. Merging Cubism's flat planes and angularity and the characteristics of folk art, Johnson strove to portray the lives and history of African Americans. *The Chain Gang* (Fig. 21.23) is a powerful and anguished statement about the plight of blacks, as well as Johnson's personal struggle for recognition.

ANTIWAR ART: PICASSO'S *GUERNICA*

Picasso's *Guernica* (Fig. 21.24) is probably the era's most monumental statement, as well as a dramatic manifesto against the brutality of war. It was created in reaction to the death and terror caused by the twentieth century's first saturation air raid, which targeted a whole community, not just military sites. The raid was carried out as a military experiment by the German air force against the defenseless Basque town of Guernica, and was a central event in General Francisco Franco's suc-

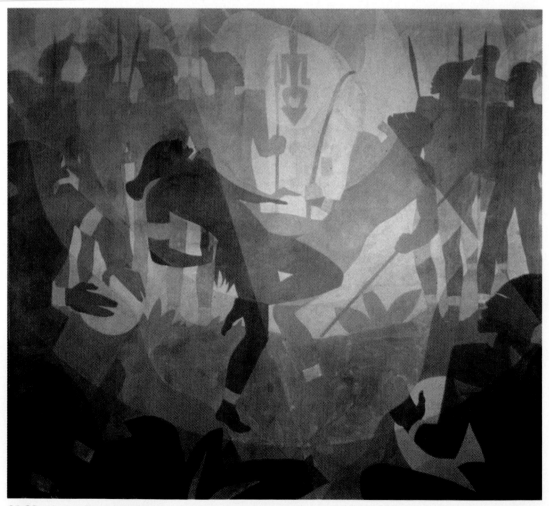

21.22 Aaron Douglas. *Aspects of Negro Life: The Negro in an African Setting*, 1934. Oil on canvas, 3′1″ × 3′4½″. Arts and Artifacts Collection. Schomburg Center for Research in Black Culture. The New York Public Library, New York.

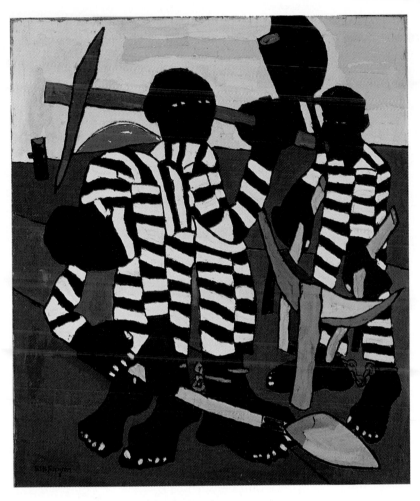

21.23   William H. Johnson. *The Chain Gang*, c. 1939–1940. Oil on plywood, 3′9¾″ × 3′2½″. Smithsonian American Art Museum, Washington, D.C.

cessful rebellion against the legally elected government of the Spanish Republic.

Picasso, a Spanish loyalist, was in Paris to paint a mural for the Spanish pavilion of the World's Fair of 1937. Just two days after the news of the bombing reached Paris, he began work. The huge canvas, accomplished in a matter of weeks, took up one wall of the Spanish pavilion, where it made an unforgettable impression on the thousands of visitors who saw it. Picasso

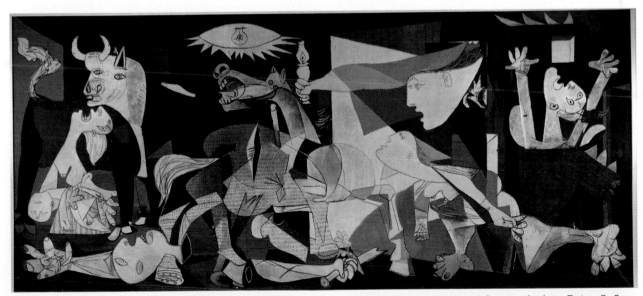

21.24   Pablo Picasso. *Guernica,* 1937. Oil on canvas, 11′5½″ × 25′5¾″. Museo Nacional Centro de Arte Reina Sofía, Madrid, Spain.

used a combination of expressionist and abstract techniques to protest a cruel and inhuman act.

Guernica is a picture in the grand tradition of historical painting. Like Géricault's *Raft of the "Medusa"* (see Fig. 18.5), it was intended to shock and horrify its audience. It also recalled the apocalyptic visions of Romanesque Last Judgments (see Fig. 6.1). The principal action begins in the lower right, where a woman dashes forward, her hands in an attitude of despair. The triangular composition then mounts to its apex at the point where the lamp, the horse's head, and the eye of day (with the electric bulb of night as its pupil) come together. From this climax the viewer's eye moves downward to the head of the dismembered warrior at the lower left.

Picasso made an effort to explain some of the symbolism. The horse with the spear in its back, the inevitable victim of bullfights, signifies victimized humanity overwhelmed by brute force. The bull, standing for brutality, is the only triumphant figure in this symbolic struggle between the forces of darkness and those of light, between barbarism and civilization. Above, an arm reaches forward to hold the lamp of truth over the whole gruesome scene. Amid the general havoc, the artist sounds one soft note of optimism. Above the victim's severed arm and broken sword in the bottom center is a tiny plant in bloom to signify the force of renewal.

Guernica appeared at a time when many earlier pictorial experiments could be combined. It employs all the exaggerations, distortions, and shock techniques developed by expressionistic drawing, but it omits ghastly coloration in favor of the somber shades of mourning combined with the colors of the newspapers that reported the disaster: black, white, gradations of gray, and a few accents of color. The abstract design, the overlapping planes on a two-dimensional surface, and the absence of modeling are all derived from Cubism. The Cubist principle of simultaneity operates in the head of the bull, which is seen both from the front and the side at the same time, and in the sensation of inner and outer space, by which the observer is at once both inside and outside the burning buildings.

After making a hundred sketches, Picasso worked in a disciplined and selective manner that showed him to be in complete command of his medium. By combining so many twentieth-century artistic techniques, Picasso gave powerful expression to the chaos and conflicts of this bloody century.

ARCHITECTURE

More than any of the other twentieth-century arts, modernist architecture achieved wide popular acceptance. Experimental architecture is possible, but unlike a painting, a building must fulfill some practical purpose. This demand kept architects from some of the wilder flights of fancy seen in twentieth-century painting, sculpture, literature, and music.

The needs of a complex, modern, urbanized society and the availability of new materials and structural methods promoted a new architecture. **Ferroconcrete,** cement with wire mesh or iron rods embedded in it, has the strength of both steel and stone without their weaknesses or expense. It can span broader spaces than marble and can carry the weight of steel. The **cantilever**—the extension of a slab or beam horizontally into space beyond its supporting post—is an ancient principle that had to await the development of ferroconcrete.

During the period between the world wars, the American architect Frank Lloyd Wright represented one point of view, whereas Europeans Walter Gropius and Le Corbusier proposed opposing ideas. Wright spoke in romantic terms of the union of nature and humans that could be realized through his "organic architecture." By contrast, Gropius and Le Corbusier were champions of the International Style and its emphasis on building for the machine age.

ORGANIC ARCHITECTURE IN THE UNITED STATES

American architect Louis Sullivan proposed that in an ideal building, form follows function. The criterion for a successful building should be not just what it looks like but how well it fulfills its purpose. This notion is subject to a variety of interpretations, but the line of thought it provoked led to an important international reevaluation of architectural forms in relation to human activities. It also prompted a reevaluation of basic architectural methods, materials, and purposes. Sullivan's disciple, Frank Lloyd Wright, and the architects identified with the International Style embraced the principle that stone should behave like stone, wood like wood, and steel like steel. They pointed to the absurdity of people catching trains in Roman baths, working in Renaissance office buildings, banking money in Doric temples, living in Tudor houses, and attending services in Gothic churches.

Among the earliest and boldest instances of modern architecture, the skyscraper, was made possible by steel skeleton construction and the elevator. It emerged in the American Midwest as a solution to the need for centralization of commercial activities. In the hands of Louis Sullivan, who designed the Wainwright Building in St. Louis in 1891 (Fig. 21.25), the skyscraper was a "proud and soaring thing," reflecting the pride of business-people in their work, as well as the power of a technologically oriented society.

Picking up where Sullivan left off, Wright saw both the advantages and the drawbacks of the sky-scraper. With his characteristic nature imagery, he described his eighteen-story skyscraper in Bartles-ville, Oklahoma, as having a "taproot" foundation, growing upward like a tree, whereas its floors and walls are cantilevered outward like branches from its central trunk (Fig. 21.26). Wright was convinced that skyscrapers did not belong in congested cities but out in the open, where they could have room to cast evocative shadows. His philosophy was that architecture should be a liberating force, both for occupants and for the architect.

For Wright, a dwelling had to be a home for the spirit as well as for the body. A house, he thought, should express warmth, protection, and seclusion. The heart of the home, according to Wright, is the hearth, in the form of a central fire-place, and all the other rooms should be built around this. Interior space, moreover, should not confine but expand without interruption from the inside to the outside so as to bring people closer to nature.

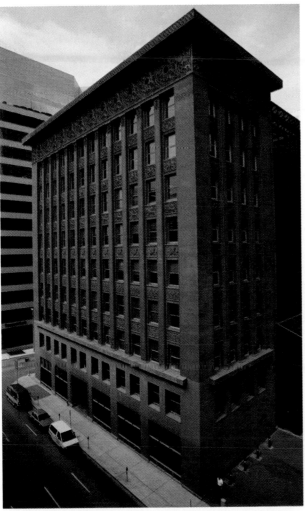

21.25 Louis Sullivan. Wainwright Building, St. Louis, 1890–1891.

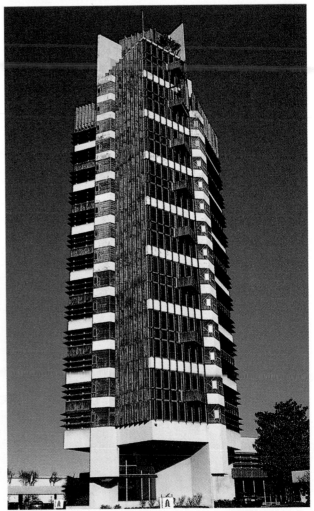

21.26 Frank Lloyd Wright. Price Tower, Bartlesville, Oklahoma, 1953.

Fallingwater (Fig. 21.27), which Wright built for Edgar J. Kaufmann in Bear Run, Pennsylvania, is an animated combination of reinforced concrete material, cantilevered construction, and a dramatic site. The house comes close to realizing Wright's ideal of a structure growing organically out of its setting. Wright's client loved the waterfall and wanted to live near it. Fallingwater therefore incorporated both the stream and the waterfall. The ledge of natural rock under the water is paralleled by the concrete shelf above it, whereas the jutting slab on top is placed at right angles to repeat the direction of the moving water. The site, like the building, consists of a series of terraces reaching outward from a stone core.

The main focus of Fallingwater is a large room opening out onto the terraces and porches. The horizontal planes of these porches are balanced by the vertical volumes of the fireplace. The local stone used in this chimney mass is related both in color and texture to the rock of the river bank. As on the outside, the inside space radiates around the central core, with advancing and receding areas promoting what Wright called the "freedom of interior and exterior occupation."

ART DECO STYLE

Before Wright's organic architecture and the functionalism of the International Style became widely accepted, the dominant approach of the 1920s and 1930s was what these architects scornfully labeled "modernistic," and is now called ***art deco,*** after a Paris exhibit of 1925, *Exposition Internationale des Arts Décoratifs et Industriels Modernes.*

Art deco reflected the vitality of the jazz age and remained popular during the more sober 1930s. It was inspired by the speed and streamlined design of the automobile and airplane. It found expression in everything from soaring skyscrapers and luxury ocean liners to streamlined statuettes, overstuffed furniture, jukebox designs, radio cabinets, toasters, and other kitchen gadgetry. Art deco manifested the frantic faith in mechanized modernity that emerged so illogically out of World War I. It also combined new building materials, such as polished aluminum, with glass, steel, and chrome.

Extravagant examples of art deco were found in public buildings like department stores and, particularly, movie houses (Fig. 21.28). These "people's palaces" were the stuff dreams were made of.

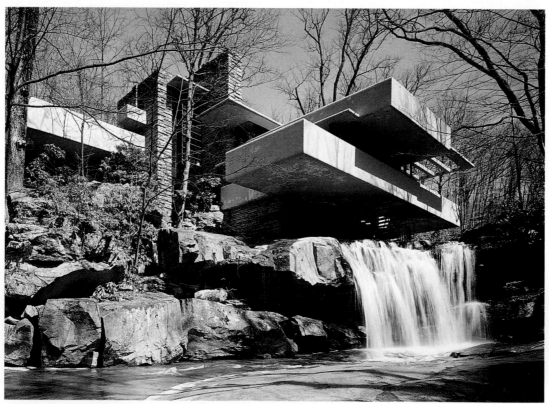

21.27 Frank Lloyd Wright. Fallingwater, Edgar Kaufmann residence, Mill Run, Pennsylvania, c. 1937. Reinforced concrete and stone, depth 64′, width 62′.

Here one found release from drudgery, boredom, and the humdrum activities of daily life. Audiences could revel in romances played by beautiful screen idols, hear the peals of mighty Wurlitzer organs, and relax to the luxuriant sounds of real symphony orchestras that rose up on stage elevators while playing hit tunes from Broadway musicals. The architecture of these theaters was improvisational fantasy, mixing Persian gardens, Egyptian temples, and Chinese pagodas. There were imaginary recreations of King Solomon's temple, Babylonian towers, Muslim mosques with minarets, and Mayan jungle pyramids.

Art deco also produced less ornate and more enduring architectural masterpieces, such as the Chrysler Building (Fig. 21.29), long the symbol of New York City before the Empire State Building (also in art deco style) eclipsed it in height and size. It was designed by William van Alen and completed in 1930. As the structure rises well over 1,000 feet, there is a pause at the thirtieth floor for a brick frieze featuring an abstract pattern that suggests automobiles with decorative hubcaps and huge winged radiator caps serving as gar-

goyles. The culmination of the structure is the familiar stainless-steel sunburst tower with its overlapping projections pierced by sharply pointed triangular windows, which terminates in a soaring cadmium-plated spire.

The rich art deco interior is equally remarkable, with its three-story entrance hall leading to a triangular lobby of African marble with stainless-steel trim. Each detail participates in the exuberant design, from the elevator doors to the marble floors. Even the elevator cabs, with their inlaid

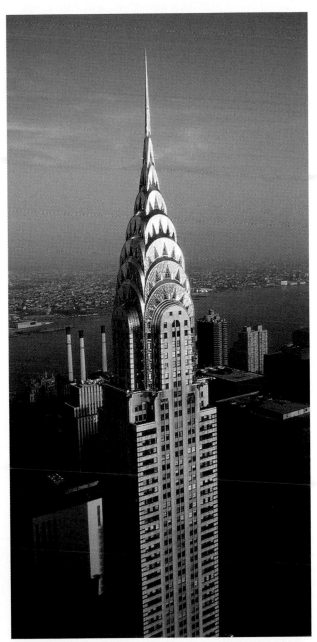

21.28 Timothy Pfluegger. Interior, Paramount Theater, Oakland, California, 1931 (restored).

21.29 William Van Alen. Chrysler Building, New York, 1930. Height 1,048'.

wood and intricate geometric patterns, are perfectly appointed small art deco rooms.

Frank Lloyd Wright, Walter Gropius, Le Corbusier, and Mies van der Rohe fussed and fumed about art deco, seeing it as a false approach to the modernist challenge. Proponents of the International Style insisted on a functional and structural architecture, free of decoration. They sniffed at art deco artists as embroiderers and lace makers and theorized that lack of decoration was a sign of spiritual strength. If there was to be decoration at all, it should not be applied to surfaces; rather, it must grow out of the materials and functions of the design itself.

THE INTERNATIONAL STYLE

The International Style crystallized in Germany with the work of Walter Gropius and Ludwig Mies van der Rohe, in France with that of Le Corbusier, and in the Netherlands with that of J. J. P. Oud. When Gropius was commissioned to reorganize a German art school after World War I, he renamed it the *Bauhaus* (Building Institute) and made it a technical school of design with special emphasis on the industrial arts and the study of modern materials and methods. He brought together the complex of studios, machine shops, administrative offices, and professors' houses into a single group of interlocking and interrelated cubes. Smaller units had bland facades; others, like the machine shop (Fig. 21.30), were open structures with curtain walls, that is, non-weight-bearing walls mostly filled with glass.

As a champion of the International Style, Gropius started with the open box as the basic unit of space, varied its volume, and grouped several units in a related pattern of cubes. The machine shop shows how he treated the building as an open volume rather than as a closed mass. By means of cantilevering, he allowed the building to project several feet outward over its supporting piers. The horizontal emphasis thus established was carried out in the concrete base and repeated at the roof level. Between the parallel lines of the base and roof hang the glass curtain walls. The resulting transparency permits details, such as the spiral staircase and the skeletal structure of the interior, to remain open and visible from the exterior. The Bauhaus complex proved to be among the most influential buildings of its decade.

In addition, the Bauhaus exploration of materials and industrial processes led to many new approaches in printing, pottery, metalwork, weaving, and stagecraft. Students were taught never to forget the purposes their products were designed to serve. A chair, in other words, was made to be sat on, a lamp to provide efficient lighting. As a result, the Bauhaus became the fountainhead of the new industrial design. Such innovations as tubular steel chairs, indirect lighting fixtures, and streamlined appliances were designed for mass production and are part of every modern household today. To counterbalance the utilitarian side, however, Gropius added the painters Kandinsky, Klee, and Lyonel Feininger to his distinguished faculty to uphold the expressive and creative aspects of drawing and painting. Mondrian and the architect Mies van der Rohe also maintained close relations with the Bauhaus.

Le Corbusier thought of houses as machines for living, containers for families, and extensions of public services. His commissions ranged from country villas to entire cities, from private dwellings to apartment blocks, and from temporary exposition structures to pilgrimage churches. Architecture for him was the play of masses brought together in the light. Cubes, cones, spheres, cylinders, and pyramids, he said, are the great primary forms that reveal themselves in sun and shadow. While Frank Lloyd Wright's buildings expressed harmony with nature, Le Corbusier raised his structures on piers to assert the "independence of things human." Wright rather tartly called Le Corbusier's cubistic buildings "boxes on stilts."

Le Corbusier's L'Unité d'Habitation (Union for Living) is an apartment house in Marseilles that brings together in a single structure a community of 1,600 people with complete facilities for living, shopping, and recreation (Fig. 21.31). Remembering the dismal mass dwellings in Paris, which he called "disastrous architectural fortifications

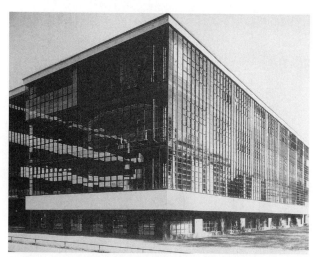

21.30 Walter Gropius. Bauhaus machine shop, Dessau, Germany, 1925–1926. Length 167', width 49'.

where thousands of families never see the sun," Le Corbusier set out to build apartments vibrating with color, light, and air. To achieve his goal, he cantilevered a gigantic structure of rough-textured concrete over a double row of massive supports, called *pylons*. The outside staircase is both functional and decorative. Set at an oblique angle to the horizontal axis, it relieves the rectangular masses with its rising motion.

The exterior is honeycombed with shallow balconies that have sunbreaks tinted in many colors on the inner sides. These sunbreaks proved so effective in protecting the tall living rooms from the sun's glare that they have since become commonplace in warm climates. Each floor has duplex apartments served by a skip-stop elevator system. At the halfway point an entire floor is allotted to shops, whereas a day school for children, a gymnasium, and a theater are located at the roof level.

IDEAS: RELATIVISM

The only thing that is permanent is change. This seeming contradiction points at the very heart of twentieth-century thought, whether expressed in philosophical, scientific, or aesthetic terms. No static absolute can provide a satisfactory view of the dynamic world of today. Even the age-old principles of mathematics can no longer be regarded as eternal truths, but, like art, are expressions relative to the time and place of their creation. The firmest articles of religious faith and political doctrine are subject to far more commentary and modification from time to time than their followers would care to admit.

The shift from a stable world order to the present dynamic view of the universe, which began with Copernicus and Galileo, swept all before it. Those who believe in orderly progress toward a definable goal interpret this flux as some form of evolution. Those who accept it at face value, as most scientists do, simply believe in change. In his observations of physical phenomena, Albert Einstein saw that in a world where everything moves, any calculation or prediction, to be valid, must be based on the relative position of the observer. Newton's absolute space, which was immovable, and his absolute time, which flowed on uniformly—both of which were "unrelated to any outward circumstance"—had to be discarded and replaced by the theory of relativity. All space, in the modern view, is measured by mobility and change of relative position, and all time by the duration of movement in the space traveled across. The world becomes a space-time continuum; all matter, energy, and events are related in the dimensions of space-time.

Anthropologists' studies of the life and customs of distant peoples have shown how ethical considerations are relative to tribal customs as well as to social and economic conditions. The

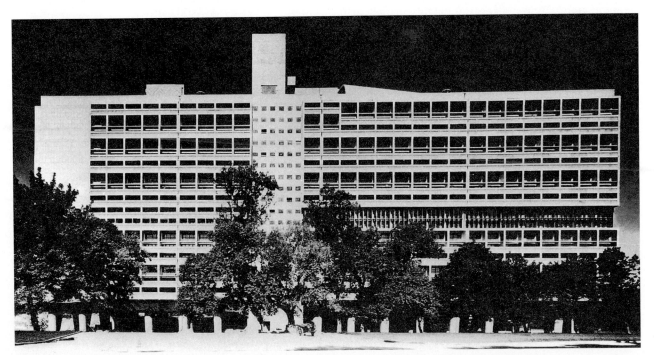

21.31 Le Corbusier. L'Unité d'Habitation, Marseilles, 1947–1952. Length 55', width 79', height 184'.

pragmatic philosophers William James and John Dewey took a long look at history and a wide view of the world and concluded that when an idea is effective, it must be true; when it ceases to work, its truth is no longer valid and another solution must be discovered.

Such a relative world, in which all things appear differently to each person and each group depending on their educational, geographic, historical, ethnic, and psychological backgrounds, can be understood only in terms of many frames of reference. Any absolutism—such as the rigidly stratified society of Plato's *Republic,* a modern police state, or a military dictatorship—insists on a maximum of conformity to ensure the stability of government. A relative world is a pluralistic one populated by men and women who see themselves in multiple roles and express themselves in many different styles.

RELATIVISM AND THE ARTS

In this relative world, the Cubists disintegrated the objects in their paintings so that they could reintegrate them in patterns of their own choosing. Each picture created its own unique spatial relationships. It is impossible to make any precise analogy between Cubist principles and the mathematics of space-time, yet such a relationship, however unsystematic it may be, can be found in the Cubist concept of several viewpoints existing at the same time and showing objects from many sides at once. By representing bodies at rest or in successive stages of motion, a Futurist painting sets up a space-time continuum of its own. In music, the experience of dissonance is freed from its dependence on consonance so that it does not demand preparation, anticipation, or resolution. The absolutes of tonality, rhythmical regularity, and musical form have yielded to a host of tonal relativisms. Composers may choose to change meter in every measure, employ several rhythms simultaneously, and/or make use of two or more tonalities simultaneously.

In *Ulysses,* James Joyce created a simultaneous cross section of the life of a city. In this maze-like literary space-time continuum, all events, whether memories of the past or premonitions of the future, flow together into a kind of extended present. There is no distinction between before and after. Whereas the single day and night and city in which all the action takes place have some relationship to the Greek unities of time, place,

and action, there is no beginning, middle, or end to Joyce's structureless realm. Readers can begin at almost any place in the book and the continuity will not be broken. The series of fleeting images are simply recorded. Entrance to the sphere of free association of words and thoughts is left open, allowing readers to supply the transitions between moods and fragments and thus create their own relative order. The end is a conclusion in which nothing is concluded.

For artists working in the interwar period, historical relativism provided an unparalleled number of choices of styles and techniques from the past and the present, as well as an anticipated future. A Picasso exhibit or a Stravinsky concert can present a bewildering assortment of styles. Picasso drew inspiration from ancient Iberian sculpture, African masks, Romanesque wall frescoes, and medieval stained glass, as well as from many different contemporary sources. His paintings also include provocative variations on Velázquez's *Las Meninas,* Delacroix's *Pietà,* and other masterpieces that caught his eye. His mediums included pencil drawings, collages constructed of cloth and paper, ceramics, painted pottery, and woodcuts, as well as oils and watercolors. Sources for Stravinsky included the free rhythms of medieval plain chant, the dissonant counterpoint of the fourteenth century, the operas of Mozart, and the multiple rhythms of African music. For these artists, historical relativism provided complete freedom of choice without the necessity of sacrificing either their originality or their principles.

Philosophers of history, such as Oswald Spengler and Arnold Toynbee, showed that the past still exists within the living present. From the point of view of historical relativity, then, tradition can be as potent a factor as innovation.

YOUR RESOURCES

• **Web Site**

  http://art.wadsworth.com/fleming10

  ○ Chapter 21 Quiz

  ○ Links—Online Readings—Sandburg, *Collections;* O'Neill, *Beyond the Horizon,* Three Plays

• **Audio CD**

  ○ Ravel, *L'Enfant et les sortileges*

TWENTIETH-CENTURY MODERNISM, PART II: ART BETWEEN THE WORLD WARS

Key Events	Architecture	Visual Arts	Literature and Music
1922 **Fascist revolution** in Italy	1838–1886 **H. H. Richardson** ★	1844–1910 **Henri Rousseau (le Douanier)** ▲	1842–1910 **William James** ◆
1924 *Surrealist Manifesto* published in Paris	1856–1924 **Louis Sullivan** ★	1863–1944 **Edvard Munch** ▲	1856–1939 **Sigmund Freud** ◆
1927 **Lindbergh's** solo flight across Atlantic	1861–1944 **Aristide Maillol** ●	1866–1944 **Wassily Kandinsky** ▲	1856–1950 **George Bernard Shaw** ◆
1928 **First complete talking film**	1867–1959 **Frank Lloyd Wright** ★	1867–1956 **Emil Nolde** ▲	1858–1924 **Giacomo Puccini** ❑
1929 **New York stock market collapses;** Great Depression begins	1870–1938 **Ernst Barlach** ●	1869–1954 **Henri Matisse** ▲	1859–1952 **John Dewey** ◆
1929 **Stalin** becomes Russian dictator; 1934–1939 he purges opposition	1874–1954 **Auguste Perret** ★	1870–1953 **John Marin** ▲	1860–1911 **Gustav Mahler** ❑
1933 **Nazi** take over in Germany; Adolf Hitler becomes dictator	1876–1957 **Constantin Brancusi** ●	1871–1958 **Giacomo Balla** ▲	1863–1938 **Gabriele d'Annunzio** ◆
1935–1940 **WPA** art project in United States	1883–1969 **Walter Gropius** ★	1871–1958 **Georges Rouault** ▲	1864–1949 **Richard Strauss** ❑
1936–1939 **Spanish Civil War;** General Franco's dictatorship begins	1883–1962 **Ivan Mestrovic** ●	1872–1944 **Piet Mondrian** ▲	1866–1925 **Erik Satie** ❑
1939–1945 **World War II**	1883–1954 **William van Alen** ★	1878–1935 **Kazimir Malevich** ▲	1869–1951 **André Gide** ◆
1941 **Japanese bomb Pearl Harbor, Hawaii;** United States enters World War II	1886–1966 **Jean (Hans) Arp** ●	1879–1940 **Paul Klee** ▲	1871–1945 **Paul Ambroise Valéry** ◆
1945 **United Nations** organized	1886–1969 **Ludwig Mies van der Rohe** ★	1880–1916 **Franz Marc** ▲	1872–1915 **Aleksandr Scriabin** ❑
1946 **Cold War** begins between the USSR and Western powers	1887–1964 **Aleksandr Archipenko** ●	1880–1966 **Hans Hofmann** ▲	1873–1954 **Colette (Sidonie-Gabrielle Colette)** ◆
1946 **First Computer** (ENIAC) invented in Philadelphia; 1948 followed by UNIVAC; the machines that changed the world	1887–1965 **Le Corbusier (Charles-Édouard Jeanneret-Gris)** ★	1881–1955 **Fernand Léger** ▲	1873–1943 **Sergei Rachmaninov** ❑
1948 **Transistors** begin replacing vacuum tubes in computers, etc.	1890–1977 **Naum Gabo** ●	1881–1955 **Max Pechstein** ▲	1874–1951 **Arnold Schoenberg** ❑
	1890–1963 **J. J. P. Oud** ★	1881–1973 **Pablo Picasso** ▲	1874–1946 **Gertrude Stein** ◆
	1891–1973 **Jacques Lipchitz** ●	1882–1916 **Umberto Boccion** ▲	1875–1955 **Thomas Mann** ◆
	1898–1976 **Alexander Calder** ●	1882–1963 **Georges Braque** ▲	1875–1937 **Maurice Ravel** ❑
	1898–1979 **Aaron Douglas** ●	1883–1949 **José Clemente Orozco** ▲	1876–1946 **Manuel de Falla** ❑
	1898–1986 **Henry Moore** ●	1883–1966 **Gino Severini** ▲	1876–1944 **Filippo Tommaso Marinetti** ◆
	1901–1966 **Alberto Giacometti** ●	1884–1950 **Max Beckmann** ▲	1878–1967 **Carl Sandburg** ◆
		1884–1951 **Dziga Vertov** ▲	1879–1936 **Ottorino Respighi** ❑
		1884–1920 **Amedeo Modigliani** ▲	1880–1936 **Oswald Spengler** ◆
		1885–1953 **Vladimir Tatlin** ▲	1881–1945 **Béla Bartók** ❑
		1886–1957 **Diego Rivera** ▲	1882–1941 **James Joyce** ◆
		1886–1980 **Oskar Kokoschka** ▲	1882–1967 **Zoltán Kodály** ❑
		1887–1968 **Marcel Duchamp** ▲	1882–1971 **Igor Stravinsky** ❑
		1887–1985 **Marc Chagall** ▲	1883–1924 **Franz Kafka** ◆
		1887–1986 **Georgia O'Keeffe** ▲	1883–1965 **Edgar Varèse** ❑
		1888–1978 **Giorgio de Chirico** ▲	1883–1945 **Anton Webern** ❑
		1889–1975 **Thomas Hart Benton** ▲	1885–1935 **Alban Berg** ❑
		1889–1978 **Hannah Höch** ▲	1885–1951 **Sinclair Lewis** ◆
		1889–1924 **Liubov Popova** ▲	1887–1962 **Robinson Jeffers** ◆
		1890–1976 **Man Ray** ▲	1888–1965 **T. S. Eliot** ◆
		1891–1976 **Max Ernst** ▲	1888–1953 **Eugene O'Neill** ◆
		1891–1956 **Aleksandr Rodchenko** ▲	1889–1963 **Jean Cocteau** ◆
		1892–1942 **Grant Wood** ▲	1889–1975 **Arnold Toynbee** ◆
		1893–1983 **Joan Miró** ▲	1891–1953 **Sergey Prokofiev** ❑
		1893–1959 **George Grosz** ▲	1892–1955 **Arthur Honegger** ❑
		1893–1967 **Charles Burchfield** ▲	1892–1974 **Darius Milhaud** ❑
		1894–1964 **Stuart Davis** ▲	1895–1963 **Paul Hindemith** ❑
		1895–1965 **Dorothea Lange** ▲	1896–1966 **André Breton** ◆
		1896–1954 **Robert Flaherty** ▲	1897–1962 **William Faulkner** ◆
		1898–1967 **René Magritte** ▲	1898–1937 **George Gershwin** ❑
		1898–1969 **Ben Shahn** ▲	1898–1970 **Erich Maria Remarque** ◆
		1900–1955 **Yves Tanguy** ▲	1899–1961 **Ernest Hemingway** ◆
		1901–1970 **William H. Johnson** ▲	1899–1963 **Francis Poulenc** ❑
		1904–1989 **Salvador Dali** ▲	1905–1980 **Jean-Paul Sartre** ◆
		1907–1954 **Frida Kahlo** ▲	1913–1960 **Albert Camus** ◆
		1913–1985 **Meret Oppenheim** ▲	

★ - Architect   ❑ - Musician   ▲ - Painters, Photographers, Filmmakers   ● - Sculptor   ◆ - Writer

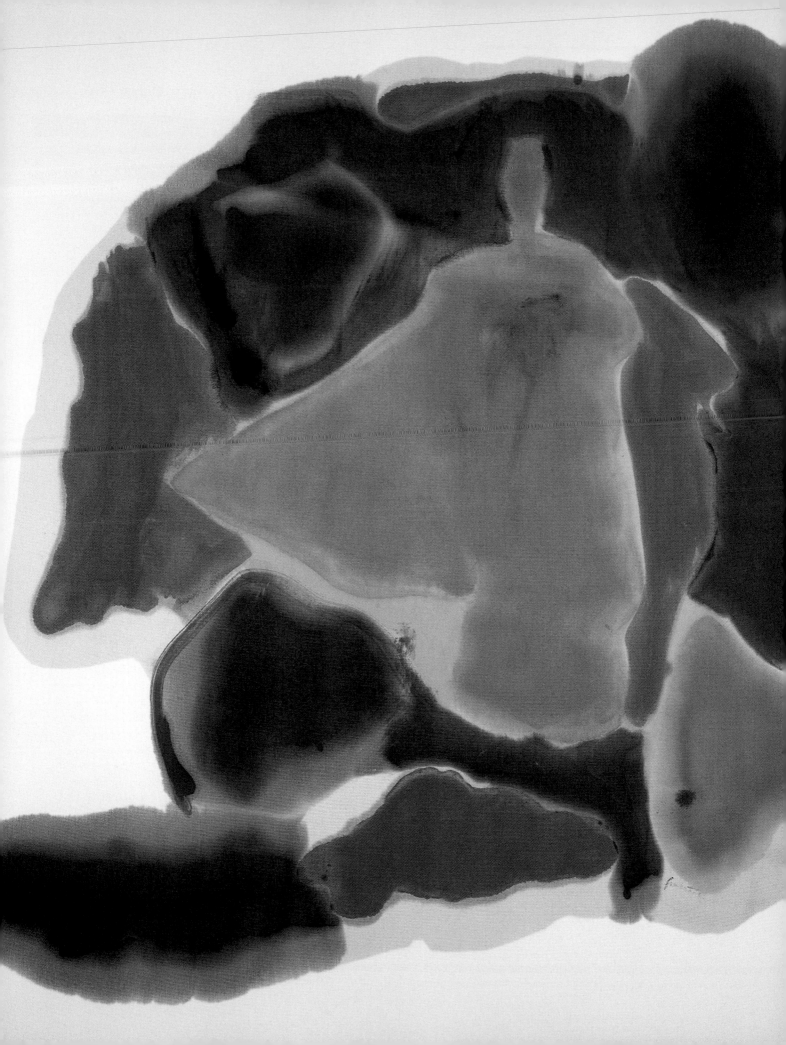

M I D T W E N T I E T H - C E N T U R Y
S T Y L E S

A REVOLUTIONARY SPIRIT CONTINUED DURING the middle part of the twentieth century, bringing rapid changes in science, technology, politics, and economics as well as in the arts. The increased acceptance of cultural relativism and the notion of a pluralistic society continued to wear down absolute values. Artists' styles ranged from abstraction to realism and from objectivity to expressionism.

Developments in space exploration and electronic communications, increasingly sophisticated computer techniques, automation, and robotics began to alter the human outlook as much as the Industrial Revolution had done two centuries earlier. Through electronic eyes, people could watch the whole world while the whole world watched them. Through satellite transmitters and dishes capable of sending and receiving thousands of beams, communications expanded dramatically. Information quickly transcended national boundaries. News reached closed societies in such capacity that mandated censorship became nearly impossible to enforce. The Earth began to seem like a huge planetary city—what media critic Marshall McLuhan called a global village—where national and regional units functioned as provinces within a vast global complex. At the same time, however, the post–World War II period was filled with disorder, disruption, and anxiety

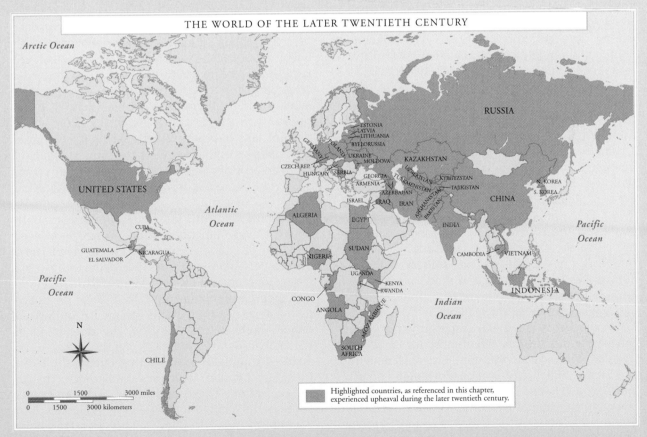

THE WORLD OF THE LATER TWENTIETH CENTURY

Highlighted countries, as referenced in this chapter, experienced upheaval during the later twentieth century.

MAP 22.1

springing from fear of nuclear warfare and worry that the Cold War between the capitalist and communist countries would erupt into a world war of unprecedented proportions.

MODERNISM IN THE UNITED STATES

DESTINATION USA

During the dark days of World War II, from 1939 to 1945, the United States gave refuge to towering figures in the arts. Prior to America's entry into the war, the originator of relativity theory, Albert Einstein, came to the United States from Adolf Hitler's Germany. Later, American physics was enriched by the arrival of Enrico Fermi from Italy and Niels Bohr from Denmark. Employing the ideas of these three scientists, teams of researchers succeeded in splitting the atom and ushering in the nuclear age.

Formerly of the Bauhaus in Germany, the renowned International Style architects Walter Gropius and Ludwig Mies van der Rohe began to teach and build in the United States while architects Eliel Saarinen and his son Eero left Finland to work there. Literary figures such as Thomas Mann and Aldous Huxley moved to southern California. The composers Igor Stravinsky and Arnold Schoenberg also worked and taught in California, whereas Paul Hindemith joined the music faculty of Yale University.

A similar emigration from Europe was seen among painters and sculptors. The influential French dada painter Marcel Duchamp was already established in New York. Piet Mondrian from Holland and the abstractionist Josef Albers, of the Bauhaus faculty, also arrived. When the war clouds darkened and the Nazis occupied France, leading figures from Paris also found in New York a sanctuary where they could live and work. Among those who moved to New York were the sculptor Jacques Lipchitz and painters such as Fernand Léger, Marc Chagall, and Max Ernst. Peggy Guggenheim, an American who was more content in the art circles of Paris and London, returned to the United States and in 1942 founded New York's Art of This Century Gallery, where she not only presented European modern art to New Yorkers but also gave one-person shows to artists of the emerging New York School.

In the 1920s and 1930s, aspiring young American artists and musicians had sailed for Paris in the wake of writers Gertrude Stein, Ernest Hemingway, and Henry Miller and composers Virgil Thomson and Aaron Copland. Now a reverse migration was changing the relationship between European and American artists. After the war, some European artists returned to the Continent, where avant-garde art understandably had lost momentum. American artists were at last free to effect their own creative syntheses of European and American styles in a country whose cities were not as ravaged by war as those of Europe and whose manufacturing base and economy, unlike those of Europe, were more or less intact.

ART AND SOCIAL CHANGE

Before World War II, the United States was a major world power; after the war, it rapidly became the world's greatest political and economic force. Still, the threat of Soviet communism and nuclear war loomed large in American life. The ominous and threatening atmosphere encouraged conformity, and the notion that "you've got to go along to get along" emerged as an operational philosophy in politics, business, and academia. The crosscurrents of the period were obvious in *The Family of Man*, a 1955 photographic exhibition at the Museum of Modern Art. It presented about 400 black-and-white photographs from sixty-eight countries, organized according to universal themes such as birth, love, work, and death. To underscore the idea of a shared humanity, Edward Steichen, the organizer, originally hoped to open the show simultaneously in New York, Europe, Asia, and Latin America. That plan was not realized, but Steichen's antiwar and antinuclear positions were made clear. At the end of the exhibition, visitors were funneled into a darkened area where they found the show's only color image: a 6-by-8-foot backlighted image of a hydrogen bomb explosion. As the visitors exited, they passed a huge photograph of the United Nations General Assembly and, finally, a series of images showing children at play. Admirable as Steichen's effort was, it did not take into account the particular struggles and histories of the people in the photographs.

The American civil rights movement took some of its impetus from the rhetoric of freedom promulgated during the war and began organizing against racism, especially in the American South, where blacks demanded voting rights and desegregation of schools. Setbacks in the civil rights movement—such as those that occurred in 1963, when four children were killed in the bombing of a church, or when police set dogs on peaceful protesters—sullied the optimistic outlook of many Americans. In addition, the deepening involvement of the United States in the Vietnam War sparked rounds of protests that eventually led to President Lyndon Johnson's decision not to run for reelection. These and other political events, such as the 1963 assassination of President John F. Kennedy, reached directly into American living rooms through the medium of television, which developed rapidly in the postwar era.

THE NEW YORK SCHOOL

The designation *New York School* was coined in the mid-1940s to distinguish American painters and sculptors from the multitude of artists who had lived and worked in Paris during the first four decades of the twentieth century. Their brilliant innovations had made the French capital the center and symbol of achievement in modern art. Just as the School of Paris had embraced the Spaniards Pablo Picasso, Juan Gris, and Joan Miró, the Italians Amedeo Modigliani and Giorgio Chirico, and the Russian Chagall, in addition to Georges Braque and Henri Matisse, so too the New York School comprised an international group.

The German master Hans Hofmann was already in his fifties when he established an art school in Greenwich Village. The Dutch-born Willem de Kooning had moved to New York in the late 1920s, as had Mark Rothko from Russia by way of Portland, Oregon, and Arshile Gorky from Turkish Armenia. Jackson Pollock was born in Wyoming and raised in California; Franz Kline grew up in the coal-mining country of Pennsylvania; Robert Motherwell hailed from San Francisco; Clyfford Still was born in Spokane, Washington; and the sculptor David Smith first lived in Indiana. Adolf Gottlieb, Lee Krasner, and Barnett Newman were from the New York area.

Like the New York School, the phrase *Abstract Expressionism* became popular in the late 1940s to differentiate this widely diverse group of painters working in the New York City area from other American artists. For the first time in history, an international style was developing in the United States. While a stricken Europe rebuilt, New York emerged as the global cultural capital, whose art influenced the rest of the world.

In 1943, Newman, Rothko, and Gottlieb published a statement in the *New York Times* declaring that "there is no such thing as a good painting about nothing. . . . [T]he subject is crucial and only that subject matter is valid which is tragic and timeless." They asserted that the "impact of elemental truth" called for the "simple expression of the complex thought, and the importance of the large shape because it has the impact of the unequivocal."

Hofmann also helped supply a philosophy for artists struggling to free themselves from tradition and consciously create a new world art in an American setting. Steeped in European culture, Hofmann nonetheless maintained that an artist should work unrestrained by preconceived notions of what a painting ought to be. For him, a painting was a dynamic abstraction, the product of a highly individualized process of creation. As such, it was a unique presentation of form and color that were brought into dynamic interplay. Although scholars have debated their exact dates, Hofmann made some of the earliest drip paintings, in which he spontaneously dribbled and streamed pigment onto the canvas like words gushing forth impulsively during a session of Surrealist automatic writing (Fig. 22.1).

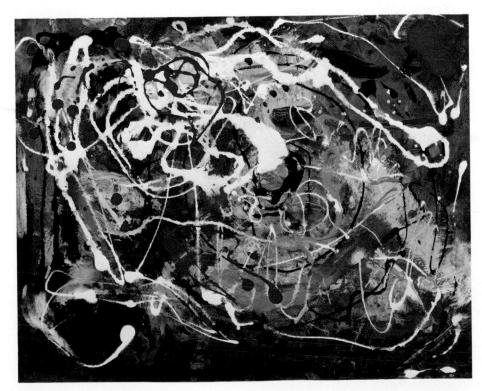

22.1 Hans Hofmann. *Spring,* 1944–1945, dated 1940. Oil on wood panel, 11¼″ × 1′2⅛″. Museum of Modern Art, New York. Gift of Mr. and Mrs. Peter A. Rübel.

Many of the Abstract Expressionist artists, photographers, and writers lived or had studios near the New York City neighborhood Greenwich Village, and they tended to gather in coffeehouses, clubs, and bars. Several were members of "The Artists' Club," or "The Club," which sponsored lectures and discussions. Hofmann was a major figure in the club. The avant-garde composer John Cage might give "A Lecture on Nothing" or silently sit before a keyboard for a prescribed period of time. The Welsh poet Dylan Thomas came to read his lyrics. W. H. Auden, the British-born poet who settled in New York in 1939, would drop in to discuss the thinness of modern life that shaped the dialogue in his long 1947 poem *Age of Anxiety.*

The painters of the New York School insisted on originality; spontaneity; intensity of feeling; and a vast range of individual choices, materials, and situations. In practice, they borrowed from European accomplishments, synthesizing Cubist and Surrealist techniques and themes. From Cubism they learned the method of abstracting the essence from familiar shapes and forms. They also mastered the Cubist techniques of analyzing and dissecting the subject matter of a painting to rearrange the parts into a satisfactory design for pictorial purposes. Like the Cubists, they frankly acknowledged the two-dimensionality and shape of their canvases and made no attempt to create the illusion of deep space and fully rounded forms. As their teacher and guide Hans Hofmann put it, "The essence of pictorial space is flatness."

Much as they would have liked their work to be totally unique, the Abstract Expressionists also discovered the spontaneous and random quality of the Surrealists' free-association techniques of psychic automatism (see pp. 578–579). As one of the group expressed it, "I want to keep a balance just on the edge of awareness, the narrow rim between the conscious and the subconscious, a balance between expanding and contracting, silence and sound." Once psychic automatism had released a free flow of creativity, the artist could work over, revise, and realize from the doodling

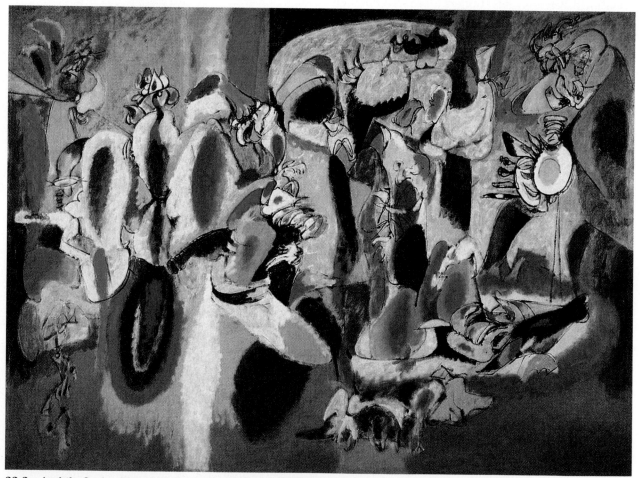

22.2   Arshile Gorky. *The Liver Is the Cock's Comb,* 1944. Oil on canvas, 6'1¼" × 8'2". Albright-Knox Art Gallery, Buffalo, New York. Gift of Seymour H. Knox, 1956.

some designs of a more controlled sort. Arshile Gorky's nightmarish picture *The Liver Is the Cock's Comb* (Fig. 22.2) illustrates the heritage of Surrealism. In this painting, Gorky conjures up fantastic images of skeletal shapes jostling imaginary creatures with sharp, toothlike claws.

Psychic automatism gave priority to process, that is, the act of doing. It emphasized impulse over premeditated composition. The Abstract Expressionists soon expanded automatism from the Surrealist process of generating images and applied it to the act of painting itself so that they could preserve freshness, cultivate accidents, and present evidence of spontaneity and creative vigor.

Surrealism also pointed the way for the Abstract Expressionists to discover memory fragments and instincts, thought to be buried in the subconscious. Through Surrealist techniques, the Abstract Expressionists attempted to come to grips with the elemental, profound, and universal aspects of human emotion. They tried to develop a visual language of signs and symbols with which to depict pictorial equivalents of deeply hidden human experience. In the process of artistic creation they sought metaphors for the myths of universal genesis, as Newman did in *Genesis—The Break* (Fig. 22.3). The stark blacks and whites in his vision of the primal creative force suggest God separating light from darkness and bringing order out of chaos. It looks as if a celestial body is taking shape out of nothingness.

The Abstract Expressionists' notions of painting as a heroic gesture and the artist as alienated genius hearken back to the Romantic Movement. Unlike the Romantics, however, these painters did not rely on depiction of the real world; rather, they sought to create art in purely pictorial terms. They wanted to take abstraction to its ultimate end: the elimination of subject and the substitution of the painting as a thing in itself and as a trace of individual temperament at the moment of creation. Ideas like these unite the Abstract Expressionists far more than the individual look of their paintings. Nevertheless, Abstract Expressionism fell into two general groups: action painting and chromatic abstraction.

ACTION PAINTING. In 1943, Jackson Pollock's first one-person show at Peggy Guggenheim's Art of This Century Gallery in New York was an event that commanded international recognition and focused worldwide attention on the Abstract Expressionists. Pollock's explosive canvases revealed a teeming vitality, frenetic energy, and creative invention that heralded a new era in painting. Pollock was later dubbed the original "action painter." He spread enormous canvases on the floor so that he could feel more directly involved with his painting and also so that he could create a work that could be viewed from all directions (Fig. 22.4).

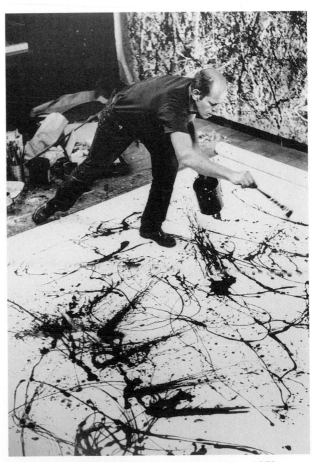

22.4   Jackson Pollock at work in his studio, 1950.

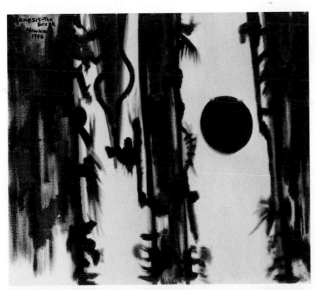

22.3   Barnett Newman. *Genesis—The Break,* 1946. Oil on canvas, 2′ × 2′3″. Dia Art Foundation, New York.

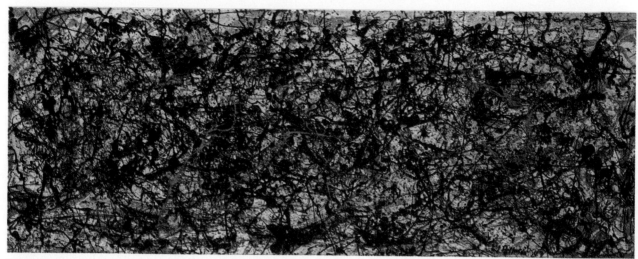

22.5 Jackson Pollock. *Lucifer,* 1947. Oil, enamel, and aluminum paint on canvas, 3′5″ × 6′9″. Collection of Harry W. and Mary Margaret Anderson.

With commercial paints, house-painting brushes, basting syringes, sticks, and trowels, he performed a kind of ritualistic dance as he dripped, squirted, dribbled, and flung. His "poured paintings," as they have been called, had no predetermined pattern. They were simply energy made visible, the result of a trancelike choreography. In *Lucifer* (Fig. 22.5), for example, the viewer confronts a web of nervous rhythms pulsating with dynamic energy and a perpetual motion of lines and colors. The result is a complex network of interwoven lines, colors, and motifs similar in its effect to musical counterpoint.

Despite its spontaneous origins, Pollock's painting shows his skill in curvilinear drawing. He developed the pouring techniques so that he could achieve improvisational continuity while overlapping lines in the process of applying paint. He insisted, "I can control the flow of paint. There is no accident."

Fundamental as color was to many of the Abstract Expressionists, black runs like a leitmotif through much of their painting. Scientifically, black is the total absorption or absence of light, which is the medium of color. Thus, through the reduction of pigmentation to basic simplicity, black could be seen as an abstraction from color. For others, black symbolized renunciation, grief, or despair.

Franz Kline, for instance, created huge, angular black figures on white backgrounds. Many of

22.6 Franz Kline. *Untitled,* 1961. Acrylic on canvas, 6′½″ × 8′10″. National Museum of American Art, Smithsonian Institution, Washington, D.C.

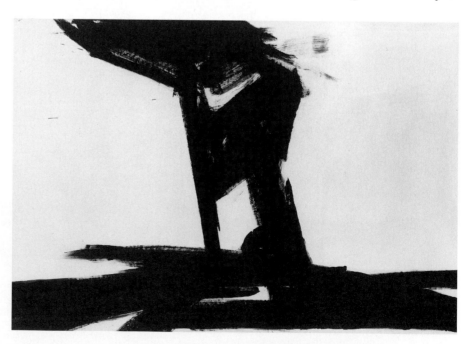

his works seem like drawings blown up to the scale of large paintings, because he actually used an overhead projector to study enlarged details. He reveled in the metallic skeletal forms characteristic of the urban scene. *Untitled* (Fig. 22.6) grows mysteriously in swift, sooty strokes, revealing the structural stresses of opposing forces such as those found in the skeletons of iron bridges and railway trestles in the coal country of the artist's birthplace. The image, then, is personal, nostalgic, and self-revealed memory.

CHROMATIC ABSTRACTION.   Pollock and Kline are often regarded as the representatives of "action painting," whereas painters such as Adolph Gottlieb, Mark Rothko, and Barnett Newman appear as color, or chromatic, abstractionists. A comparison of Pollock's and Kline's works with Rothko's *Green and Maroon* (Fig. 22.7) or Newman's *Vir Heroicus Sublimis* (Fig. 22.8) reveals why the distinction has been made. Kline's painting (Fig. 22.6), with its blacks and whites, reproduces well on the printed page. To a lesser extent, Pollock's *Lucifer,* with its accent on line, would also survive in a black-and-white illustration. The works of Rothko and Newman, however, would be incomprehensible without their subtle and sensitive ranges of color intensity. Rothko's *Green and Maroon* consists of several irregular rectangles floating in an atmospheric blue space. The rectangles are of unequal size with unstable contours, and are painted in luminous hues brushed on with such delicacy that flickering light seems to radiate from the films of color. As the eye runs over the painterly edges of the rectangles,

22.7 Mark Rothko. *Green and Maroon,* 1953. Oil on canvas, 7'6¾" × 4'6½". Phillips Collection, Washington, D.C.

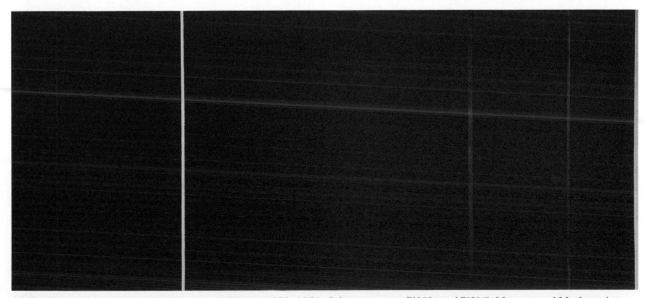

22.8   Barnett Newman. *Vir Heroicus Sublimis,* 1950–1951. Oil on canvas, 7'11⅜ × 17'9¼". Museum of Modern Art, New York. Gift of Mr. and Mrs. Ben Heller.

the delicate harmonies of the colors set off vibrations that make the shapes appear to breathe and shimmer within the color-suffused space. Similarly, Barnett Newman's *Vir Heroicus Sublimis,* which might be translated as "The Heroic and Sublime Man," has but one vivid hue—red—expanding horizontally with syncopated interruptions by lean vertical bands that seem to march across the huge canvas. These "zips," as Newman called them, cut into the great field of color and shock it into waves of visual energy that roll back and forth between the bands and the edges. These bands can also be read as abstract figures standing out against their color-field environment.

Both Pollock and Newman created paintings of immense proportions. They considered small-easel painting to be an obsolete and dying art form. Small canvases, they reasoned, had to be seen in relation to their setting and in conjunction with other pictures on the same and surrounding walls. By contrast, large-scale murals consumed the viewer's entire peripheral vision. They were complete in themselves, making their own environment.

ABSTRACTION AND SCULPTURE: SMITH

The sculptor David Smith knew the Abstract Expressionists and shared their goal of realizing new forms and a new style of abstraction and expression. He began as a painting student at the Art Students League of New York but in the early 1930s switched to sculpture after seeing reproductions of works by Picasso and others who had used an inventive new technique of joining and welding metal pieces and parts into abstract Cubist assemblages. Smith's experience as a welder in automobile and locomotive factories drew him to this approach.

Throughout his career, Smith felt a great fascination for the basic attributes of steel. "The metal," he wrote, "possesses little art history. What associations it has are those of this century: power, structure, movement, progress, suspension, destruction, brutality." Thus, Smith chose to construct sculpture rather than to carve it from stone or cast it in bronze. To accommodate a machine-shop studio large enough to construct works on an architectural scale, and to acquire an ample environment for their display, Smith moved to a farm at Bolton Landing in upstate New York. There he accomplished the epic scale of his *Cubi* works (Fig. 22.9).

Some of Smith's constructions retain the rough blackness of iron; others have been painted bright

hues. In the *Cubi* series, Smith scored the stainless steel surfaces to make them flash, dazzle, and all but dissolve in refracted sunlight. This technique created a sense of lightness that contradicted the heavy, solid appearance of the monumental forms. Smith's iron and steel constructions, like those in the *Cubi* series, create open and closed spaces that interpenetrate their environment, defining space, volume, movement, and color as they stand silhouetted against trees, buildings, or sky. These

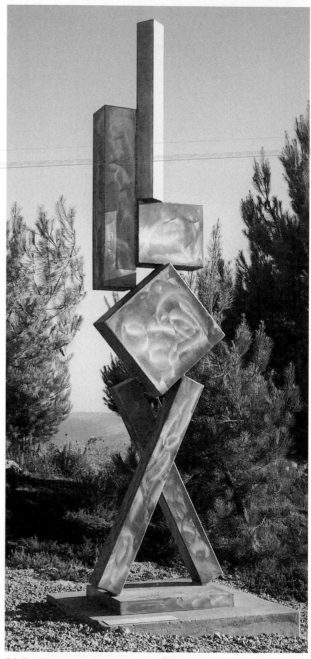

22.9   David Smith. *Cubi VI,* 1963. Stainless steel, height 9'10½". Israel Museum, Jerusalem, Israel. Donated by Mr. and Mrs. Meshulam Riklis.

sculptures have such strong silhouettes and transparent interiors that they seem like "drawing-in-space" and sometimes evoke the human figure. In addition, Smith frequently transformed standard industrial units or "found" objects from junkyards, integrating the parts into new wholes.

THE MUSEUM AND AMERICAN ART

Calling themselves "The Irascibles," several Abstract Expressionists waged a lengthy campaign in 1951 against the exclusion of contemporary American art from an exhibition at the Metropolitan Museum of Art. This protest brought them national media attention. During the 1950s, Abstract Expressionist art was polarized by the critics, who either praised it for fostering American values like freedom and individuality or condemned it as evidence of the decadence threatened by communism. In either case, it received a good deal of press attention, which the painters learned to manipulate. Also in 1951, the Museum of Modern Art recognized the movement with an exhibition entitled "Abstract Painting and Sculpture in America," and in 1958 the museum organized and circulated a large show through Europe called "The New American Painting." By the end of the 1950s, Abstract Expressionism was accepted worldwide as the stunning American contribution to modern art and the trend to emulate. Success came to the "loft rats," but it was not a harbinger of the good

life to come. After losing many paintings in a fire, enduring injury in an automobile accident, and sustaining other illnesses, Gorky committed suicide in 1948. Pollock perished in an automobile accident in 1956, as did David Smith in 1965. Kline died in 1962, at the age of 51, and Rothko killed himself in his studio in 1970.

WOMEN AND ABSTRACT EXPRESSIONISM

Although The Club originally excluded women, it soon admitted at least two and generally opened up to women and also to writers, composers, critics, and dealers. Lee Krasner, who later married Jackson Pollock, attended club functions. Her work combined visual and symbolic imagery derived from her lifelong interest in ancient lettering forms, such as cuneiform clay inscriptions and hieroglyphics. She tried to evoke in the viewer an intuitive recognition of basic, timeless patterns in human thought (Fig. 22.10). By contrast, the early Abstract Expressionists did not acknowledge the sculpture of Louise Bourgeois (see Fig. 22.30), whose totem and fetish figures from the 1940s explored the same primal urges that the painters did.

Throughout the 1950s, more women artists, such as Joan Mitchell and Helen Frankenthaler, took up the ideas and methods of the Abstract Expressionists and were able to find galleries and buyers for their work. Frankenthaler pioneered a

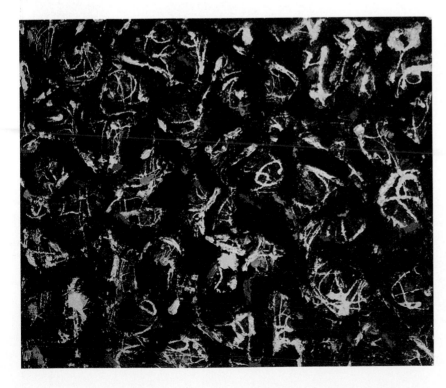

22.10   Lee Krasner. *Abstract No. 2,* 1946–1948. Oil on canvas, 1'8½" × 1'11¼". Collection of IVAM, Valencia, Spain, courtesy of the Robert Miller Gallery.

new approach to drip painting by allowing pigment to assume its own shapes and stains as it flowed directly into raw canvas. *Formation* (Fig. 22.11) shows her technique of staining, dyeing, and washing the canvas with waves of various hues in the manner of a watercolor.

THE BEAT GENERATION

Throughout the mid-1940s and early 1950s, disaffected writers, poets, and filmmakers on the East and West Coasts of the United States formed the nucleus of what would later be called the *beat genera-*

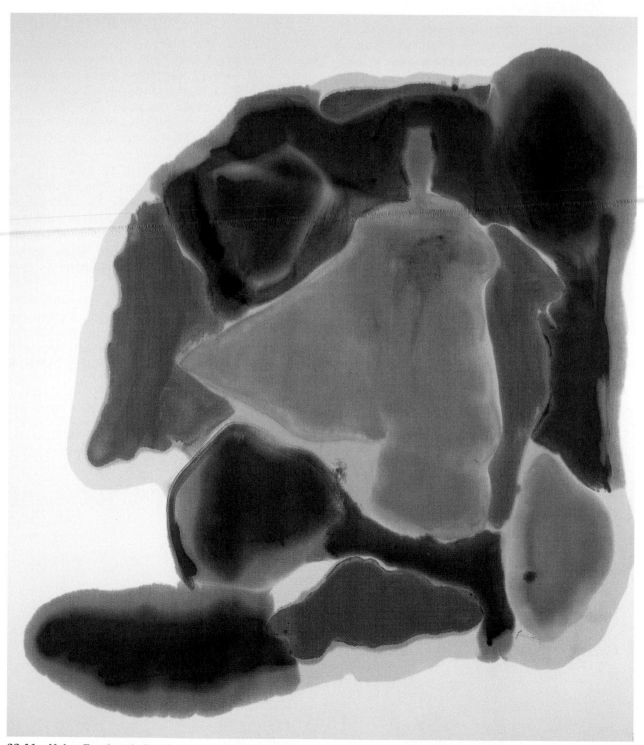

22.11   Helen Frankenthaler. *Formation,* 1963. Acrylic on canvas, 6′4″ × 5′5″. Collection of Mr. Alexis Gregory.

tion. Like the Abstract Expressionists, they saw the modern artist as an alienated, truth-seeking individual whose resolute insistence on self-expression was a flickering light in the darkness of conformist, postwar America. This attitude could be seen in Robert Frank's book *The Americans,* which portrayed people blinded by patriotism and commercialism and stuck in the solitude of their vacant psyches (Fig. 22.12). Gathered on several road trips around the United States, the pictures were first published in Paris because no American publisher would take a chance on a book that suggested that America's postwar prosperity was an empty achievement.

With his poem *Howl,* Allen Ginsberg became the irreverent poetic voice of the beat generation:

> I saw the best minds of my generation
>   destroyed by madness, starving hysterical
>   naked,
> Dragging themselves through the negro streets
>   at dawn looking for an angry fix,
> Angelheaded hipsters burning for the ancient
>   heavenly connection to the starry
> Dynamo in the machinery of the night,
>   who poverty and tatters and hollow-eyed
>   and high sat up smoking in the supernatural

darkness of cold-water flats floating across
    the tops of cities contemplating jazz.[1]

Ginsberg first read *Howl* to an audience in San Francisco. When the poem was printed, authorities tried to bring obscenity charges against the publisher. Instead of repressing them, these events encouraged public poetry readings and contributed to the concept of the so-called happenings and environments of the 1960s, which will be discussed more fully later in this chapter.

Today *Howl* is praised for its forthright reflections on homosexuality, but in the 1950s it was understood as the anthem of those who were stifled by postwar uniformity and fear. Ginsberg's friend Jack Kerouac, who wrote the famous novel *On the Road* and traveled through part of the United States with Robert Frank, is credited with giving the writers and poets of the era their lasting name, the *beat generation.* Like the word *romantic, beat* is suggestive and imprecise. Kerouac said that it simultaneously referred to the

---

[1]Allen Ginsberg, *Collected Poems 1947–1980* (New York: Harper & Row). Copyright © 1984 by Allen Ginsberg. Reprinted by permission of HarperCollins Publishers, Inc.

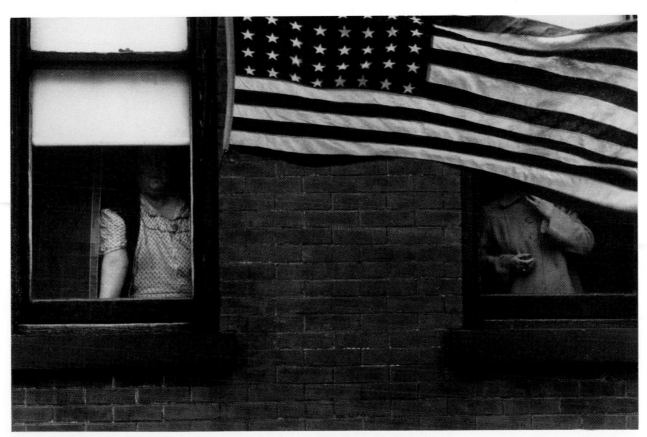

22.12 Robert Frank. "Parade—Hoboken, New Jersey," 1955, from *The Americans.*

iconoclastic beat of jazz and to artists who have been beaten down by mass culture.

ART AND LIFE

Throughout the 1950s, artists and writers attempted to merge art and life. Abstract Expressionists insisted on making their intuitive experience the center of art. Writers such as Ginsberg based their poetry on their personal impressions and experiences. Robert Rauschenberg, a New York artist, began making what he called "combines," that is, neither painting nor sculpture but a three-dimensional collage composed of discarded materials he found on the streets. His *Monogram* (Fig. 22.13) is composed of found objects. A stuffed angora ram is encircled by an automobile tire and other bits of miscellaneous debris; photographs, cutout letters, and pigment have been freely applied in an approach adapted from the work of the first generation of Abstract Expressionists.

In the mid-1950s, Louise Nevelson, who had studied with Hans Hofmann, was finally recognized for her large sculptures. She assembled her sculptures from pieces of discarded wood that she painted a uniform color, often flat black, gold, or ivory. Unlike Rauschenberg's combine paintings, whose individual items usually remain recognizable, Nevelson's works transformed debris into a whole that was greater than the sum of its parts. Her intricately contrived *Sky Cathedral—Moon Garden + One* (Fig. 22.14) is composed of asymmetrical boxes that vary in shape and size and are filled

with what looks like construction wreckage. Among these found objects are chair slats, fragments of furniture, and the newel post from a staircase. Whereas Rauschenberg's combines remain assemblages of found objects, Nevelson's work converts her materials to create a brooding, yet solemn, monument.

MUSIC AND DANCE IN THE 1950S AND EARLY 1960S

Robert Rauschenberg's friend, the composer John Cage, felt hemmed in by the strict mathematic rules of twelve-tone music advocated by Schoenberg and Berg (see pp. 564–566). Instead, he responded to Rauschenberg's interest in collecting random objects from the environment and fitting them together to make a work that merges art and life.

Cage was also a devotee of the early twentieth-century French composer Erik Satie (see p. 575). In 1948, Cage staged a performance of Satie's theater piece *The Ruse of Medusa.* Cage's friend, the utopian architect Buckminster Fuller, appeared in the work. Cage played the piano, Merce Cunningham danced, and Willem de Kooning designed the set. Soon Cage was investigating the potential of randomness. For *Theater Piece No. 1,* he assigned a specified amount of time to performers and asked them to do whatever they chose to do.

Cage believed in the value of human intuition. As a student of Zen Buddhism, he embraced the idea of the universe's essential oneness and whole-

22.13 Robert Rauschenberg. *Monogram,* 1955–1959, 5′4½″ × 3′6″ × 5′3¼″. Moderna Museet, Stockholm, Sweden.

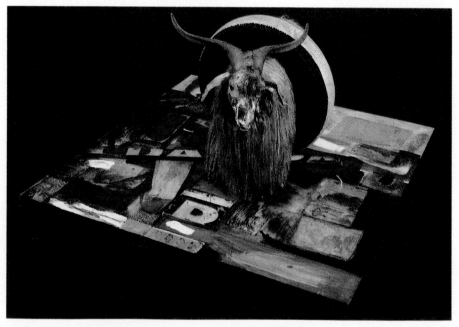

ness. In his view, one sound was no better or worse than another, and chance noises, such as automobile horns and birdsong, were the equal of musical instruments. In his 1951 work *4'33"*, a pianist sits at the instrument, not playing but turning pages of the score for 4 minutes and 33 seconds. The piano lid is opened and closed to indicate where movements begin. The music that the audience hears is the sound that occurs in the auditorium: rustling clothes, creaking chairs, and clearing throats.

In 1953, Cage and Rauschenberg collaborated on *Automobile Tire Print,* during which Cage drove a Model A Ford car. Rauschenberg had applied black ink to one of the car's tires so that as the tire passed over sheets of drawing paper it left what Cage called a musical score of the performance. In later works, Cage expanded his musical palette to include electronic sounds, radio, speech, and other vernacular sources such as matches, pins, Slinkys, and pipe cleaners.

Cage asked the serious question, "What is music?" Part of his answer is what he called **aleatory** music. The word is derived from the Latin *alea,* meaning "dice," and Cage proposed to roll the dice, that is, to create chance music. This notion was borne out for him in the *I Ching,* an ancient Chinese book about the importance of chance. Improvisation, of course, is as old as music itself, but Cage's pieces avoid the conventional sense of a beginning and an end. At a given point one begins to hear sounds, and after a while they stop. Through his

challenge to the accepted understanding of the musical experience, Cage prompted composers and audiences to reexamine the basic nature of music, its place in society, and its purposes as an art form.

Choreographer-dancer Merce Cunningham, who worked with both Cage and Rauschenberg, invented ways to introduce chance into the world of dance. Like Cage, he did not distinguish between the extraordinary and the ordinary or between strictly prescribed dance movements that occur in ballet and casual, unpremeditated human actions like walking. He did not require dancers to pace their steps and body movements to the beat of the music, nor did he insist that the most important part of a dance be performed at center stage. Cunningham allowed dancers to move in the way that Frankenthaler flowed paint onto the canvas, taking advantage of unpredictable and accidental juxtapositions.

The midtwentieth century saw the production of many enduring mainstream musical works, such as the Hungarian composer Béla Bartók's *Concerto for Orchestra.* From Russia came Sergey Prokofiev's epic opera *War and Peace* and his ballet *Romeo and Juliet,* while Dmitri Shostakovich regularly produced symphonies. On the American scene, Aaron Copland's nostalgic ballet score *Appalachian Spring* achieved popularity, as did Leonard Bernstein's theater pieces *Candide* and *West Side Story* and his haunting symphony *Age of Anxiety.*

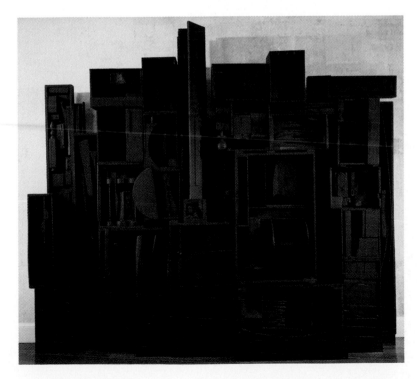

22.14 Louise Nevelson. *Sky Cathedral— Moon Garden + One,* 1957–1960. Wood painted black, 9'1" × 10'10" × 1'7" (without base). Pace Wildenstein Gallery, New York.

Happenings, Environments, and Performances

In the late 1950s and the 1960s, the Abstract Expressionists' emphasis on spontaneous art creation, which collapsed the gap between art and life, combined with Cage's concept of unpremeditated music. The result was a series of international experiments that rejected traditional art media and shunned the museum as a dusty warehouse for old art. In the United States, Allan Kaprow, one of Cage's students, encouraged the staging of **happenings,** unrehearsed performances without a central focus, presented in nontraditional locations such as street corners, shop windows, and the countryside. Happenings blended several art media, such as music and painting, with theatrical performance. The audience could join the performers, and the performers could infiltrate the audience, bringing art close to life. When the happening was over, it intentionally left no product.

Other artists wanted to create happenings but did not object to creating a product or even scripting the event. In France, Yves Klein daubed the body of a model with blue paint and used the woman's torso as a brush to apply paint to a canvas that rested on the floor. Claes Oldenburg created plastic molds of an odd array of items, ranging from an octopus to women's dresses, and then displayed them for sale in an environment he called *The Store.* As individual items were sold, he quickly made duplicates.

Fluxus, a loose coalition of artists in the United States, Europe, and Asia, was influenced by Cage's understanding of nontraditional sounds as music. They conceived of events that emphasized *flux,* that is, a quick succession of changes. They referred to their preparations as creating a score. At a Fluxus event one might watch water drip or snow fall. The Fluxus philosophy centered on ongoing processes like creation and destruction. In Germany, Joseph Beuys combined his experiences during World War II with the notion of the happening and with Fluxus's emphasis on the fluidity of time, death, and regeneration. He produced

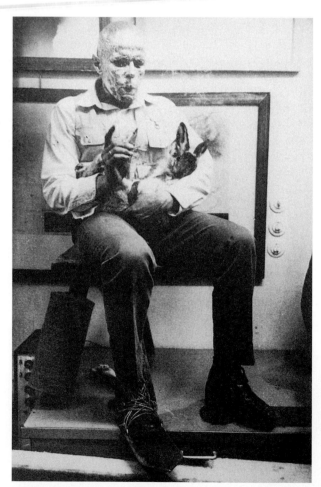

22.15   Joseph Beuys. *How to Explain Pictures to a Dead Hare,* 1965. Photograph of performance art. Schmela Gallery, Düsseldorf, Germany.

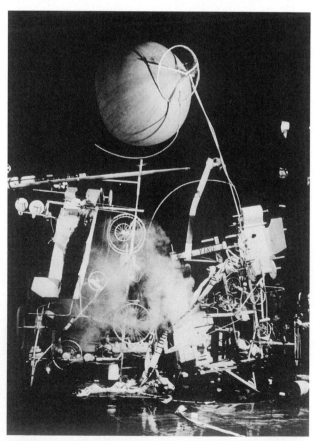

22.16   Jean Tinguely. *Homage to New York,* 1960, just before its destruction in the garden of the Museum of Modern Art, New York.

what he called *social sculpture.* "Art," he said, "is a basic metaphor for all social freedoms. . . . it should be a true means, in daily life, to enter and transform the power fields of society." Among his tangible works is a reliquary box filled with mementos from the Auschwitz concentration camp. Another, which references his near-death experience during wartime, consists of a row of survival sleds equipped with blankets, canned rations, and flashlights, all being unloaded from the back of an actual Volkswagen minibus. More intangible was his 1965 event, *How to Explain Pictures to a Dead Hare* (Fig. 22.15). In a gallery in Düsseldorf, Beuys, who believed in the spiritual power of animals, assumed the role of a shaman, or tribal priest. He covered his head and face with honey and gold leaf and spoke tenderly for 3 hours to a dead rabbit cradled in his arms.

Although he was not directly connected with Fluxus, the Swiss-born artist Jean Tinguely picked up their ideas while living in Paris. He jerry-rigged machines from miscellaneous trash items, such as weather balloons and gear wheels. His *Homage to New York* (Fig. 22.16), introduced to an elite crowd

of onlookers in the courtyard of the Museum of Modern Art, was advertised as a device that would create an instant abstract painting and then destroy itself. It failed to do so, which may have been an accident or the artist's original intent.

POP ART AND ITS INFLUENCES

During the late 1950s and early 1960s, artists such as Rauschenberg and Oldenburg highlighted postwar American prosperity and increased consumer spending by using household waste items in art or accentuating the desire to consume. By contrast, the British artist Richard Hamilton combined advertising images for mostly American products, such as television sets and vacuum cleaners. His collage, *Just what is it that makes today's homes so different, so appealing?* (Fig. 22.17), is a bittersweet comment on Britain's postwar economic recession and the longing for consumer goods, symbolized by American products and attitudes toward conspicuous consumption. Hamilton's work introduced **Pop Art,** which he defined as being popular,

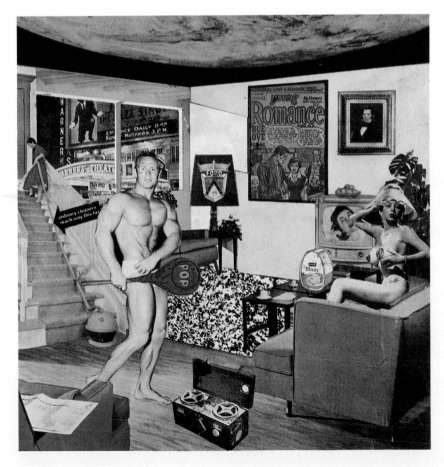

22.17 Richard Hamilton. *Just what is it that makes today's homes so different, so appealing?,* 1956. Collage, 10¼″ × 9¾″. Kunsthalle Tübingen, Germany.

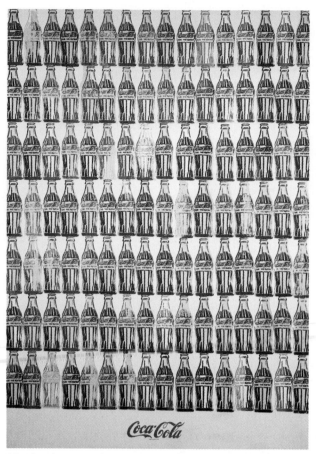

22.18 Andy Warhol. *Green Coca-Cola Bottles,* 1962. Oil on canvas, 6'10¼" × 4'9". Whitney Museum of American Art, New York. Gift of the Friends of the Whitney Museum.

transient, expendable, low cost, mass-produced, youthful, witty, sexy, gimmicky, glamorous, and the product of big business.

In the United States during the 1960s, the Pop artists accepted mass-produced commodities as part of the landscape of modern life. Pop Art offered easily recognizable subjects to which everyone could relate. Andy Warhol presented still lifes of identical soup cans and Coke bottles arranged in a manner similar to the way they would appear on supermarket shelves or in advertising (Fig. 22.18). Jasper Johns chose common items, such as shooting-gallery targets and American flags, for his subjects, painting them with heavily applied tinted wax in the manner of Abstract Expressionism (Fig. 22.19). Roy Lichtenstein's work was based on the techniques of comic-strip art (Fig. 22.20). Later in his career, Oldenburg created his own mode of Pop Art with large, soft sculptures of common items, such as hamburgers and typewriters.

As Pop Art gathered strength, it encouraged artists to think in terms of visual facts rather than the expression of inner feelings. **Photorealism** emerged during the mid-1960s and commanded attention for more than a decade. As the movement's name implies, the look of photographs supplied the visual language of Photorealism. In Richard Estes's cityscapes, such as *Downtown* (Fig. 22.21), surfaces are sharply defined and crisply portrayed, revealing the self-created urban environ-

22.19 Jasper Johns. *Flag,* 1954–1955, dated on reverse 1954. Encaustic, oil, and collage mounted on plywood, 3'6¼" × 5'⅝". Museum of Modern Art, New York. Gift of Philip Johnson in honor of Alfred H. Barr, Jr.

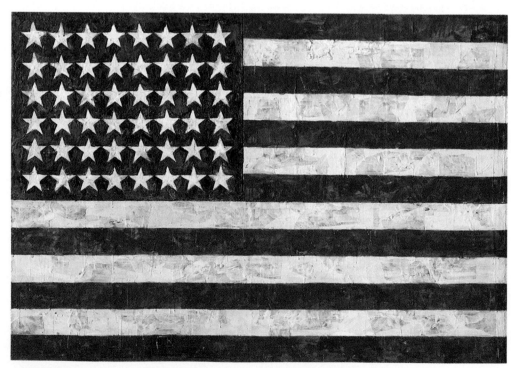

ment that people choose to live in. For *Downtown,* Estes took more than seventy-five exposures of the general view and details in various lighting and weather conditions. In the studio he produced a **photomontage,** or pasteup of photographic details, as an overall working model. In the process, the photographic images were redrawn, the positions of buildings and objects were shifted, and the processes of selection and elimination came into play to tighten and clarify the composition. As Estes remarked in an interview, "I can select what to do or not to do from what's in the photograph. I can add or subtract from it. Every time I do something, it's a choice . . . it's a selection from the various aspects of reality." Estes's images share with Pop Art a neutral vision of banal objects.

In its emphasis on fact and detail, Duane Hanson's sculpture corresponds to Estes's Photorealism. Hanson portrayed the people we all observe in everyday life. His figures probe into the soulless social conditions that help shape human lives.

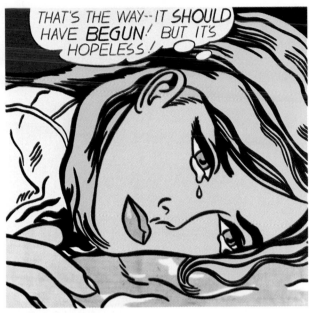

22.20 Roy Lichtenstein. *Hopeless,* 1963. Oil on canvas, 3′8″ × 3′8″. Kunstmuseum, Basel, Switzerland.

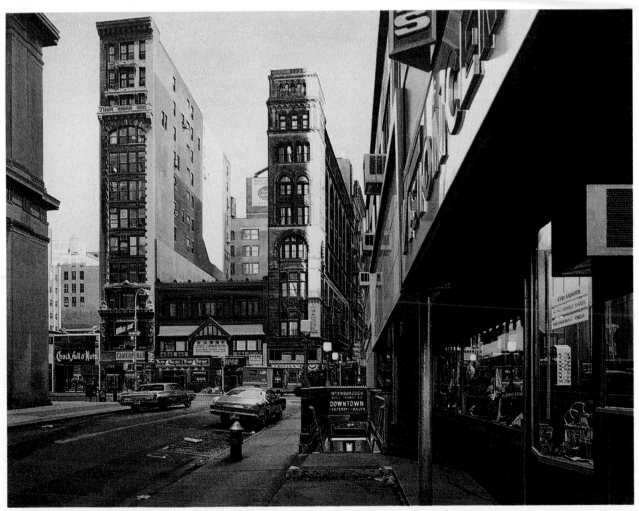

22.21 Richard Estes. *Downtown,* 1978. Oil on canvas, 4′ × 5′. Museen Moderner Kunst, Vienna, Austria. On loan from the Collection Peter Ludwig, Aachen, Germany.

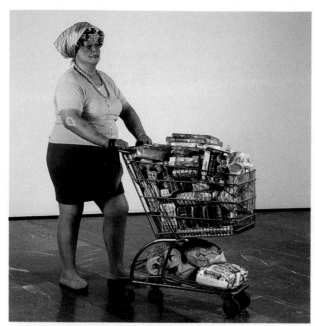

22.22 Duane Hanson. *Supermarket Shopper,* 1970. Life-size. Nachfolgeinstifat, Neue Galerie, Sammlung Ludwig, Aachen, Germany.

Supermarket Shopper (Fig. 22.22) is an embodiment of conspicuous consumption. As the artist commented, "She began my satirical period. She is a symbol of excessive consumption, pushing a cart filled with every kind of imaginable item available in a supermarket." To create this work, Hanson did not generalize from a number of views as Estes did. Instead, he used live models and made a flexible mold of each section of the body. He then assembled the parts and shaped them into a posture. Details such as wigs, clothes, eyeglasses, and accessories are all real in Hanson's work.

22.23 Frank Stella. *Mas o Menos (More or Less),* 1964. Metallic powder in acrylic emulsion on canvas. Musée National d'Art Moderne, Centre Georges Pompidou, Paris, France.

Hanson dwelled on ordinary moments in the lives of people who live rather dull lives. As he comments, "I prefer to stay away from unusual looking people and try to produce a figure people can be confronted with in their everyday lives." Yet he lifted ordinary people to symbolic status. The honesty and intensity he put into his work brings both the absurd and serious aspects of life into focus.

MINIMALISM AND AFTER: OP ART, CONCEPTUALISM, AND EARTH ART

Minimalism, the art that accompanied Pop Art and eventually succeeded it, looked nothing like its contemporary. Minimalist painting and sculpture rejected recognizable subject matter and emphasized pure form. In fact, Minimalism is sometimes called *ABC art* because of its interest in elementary structures such as squares and cubes. It was, in a sense, a new or neoclassical movement, not because it sprang from eighteenth-century neoclassicism but because Minimalists shared with the past an interest in purifying art forms and a predilection for basing art in mathematics and logic.

Frank Stella's paintings of the late 1950s and early 1960s are intellectual exercises in the reduction of a work of art to its basic elements. In *Nunca Pasa Nada* (nothing ever happens), parallel white lines follow the shape of the canvas (Fig. 22.23). Without a subject or a point of focus, the painting becomes an object. Making art that could not escape its objectness was also at the center of Donald Judd's philosophy of art. Working primarily with hollow metal boxes, Judd fashioned works that looked as if they came from a

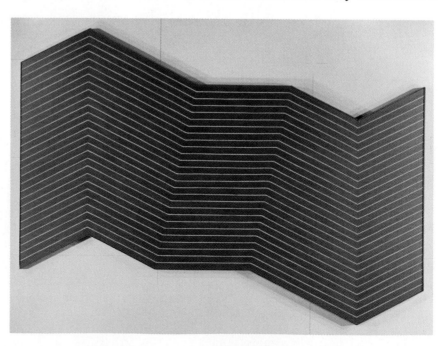

factory, because they did. Judd simply sent instructions to the metalworkers who would cast his work. He used industrial techniques in an effort to eliminate an expression of personality that might appear in handwork. His outlook was poles apart from that of Abstract Expressionists like Jackson Pollock, who believed that he had to be "in" a painting.

Minimalism shared with Pop Art an antielitist attitude and a rejection of museum art. Consequently, Minimalist sculpture was made to stand on the floor or rest against a wall, rather than being placed on a pedestal. In addition, Minimalists like Judd and Pop artists like Warhol had in common an appreciation for industrial design and for presenting visual ideas in series. Both Judd and Warhol used assistants extensively and produced work that seems aloof from its maker.

Op, or optical, art emerged in the mid-1960s and can be understood as a type of action painting, with the action taking place in the viewer's eye. Bridget Riley's *Current* (Fig. 22.24) illustrates how stable lines seem to shift and deceive. Indeed, Op artists sometimes called their work *perpetual abstraction*. Different responses are induced as the eye scans various sectors of the surface; the illusion of faster–slower and forward–backward movement occurs. The sense of perception is confused as eye and brain signals get their wires crossed. The viewer feels certain sensations, varying from disorientation and discomfort to giddiness and exhilaration. Op art quickly became the darling of the popular press, serving as a sign of the "Swinging Sixties" interest in sensual pleasure and altered states of consciousness. It was dropped just as quickly in the late 1960s because it did not ade-

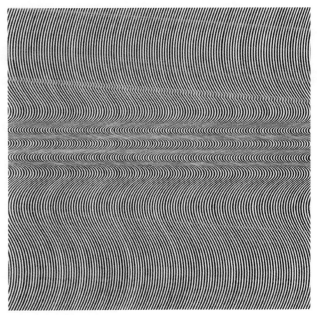

22.24 Bridget Riley. *Current,* 1964. Synthetic polymer paint on composition board, 4′10⅜″ × 4′10⅞″. Museum of Modern Art, New York. Philip Johnson Fund.

quately describe the era's protests against racism, sexism, and the Vietnam War.

As Minimalism gained strength, it became the art against which other artists and critics dissented. In the language of the period, it was called a "cop out," that is, an irresponsible rejection of the artist's role as interpreter of the times. Others felt hemmed in by its mathematical exactness. Eva Hesse began using flexible materials such as cloth and wire in works that seem close to a parody of the mathematical exactness of Minimalist sculpture. For example, in *Untitled* (Fig. 22.25) she placed

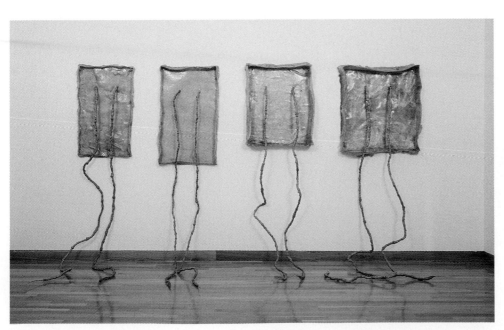

22.25 Eva Hesse. *Untitled,* 1970. Fiberglass over wire mesh, latex over cotton and wire. Overall dimensions: 7′6⅛″ × 3′6½″ × 12′4⅝″. Des Moines Art Center, Iowa.

22.26 Joseph Kosuth. *One and Three Chairs,* 1965. Wolden folding chair, photographic copy of a chair, and photographic enlargement of a dictionary definition of a chair. Chair, 2′8⅜″ × 1′2⅛″ × 1′8⅞″; photo panel, 3′ × 2′⅛″; text panel, 2′ × 2′⅛″. Museum of Modern Art, New York. Larry Aldrich Foundation Fund.

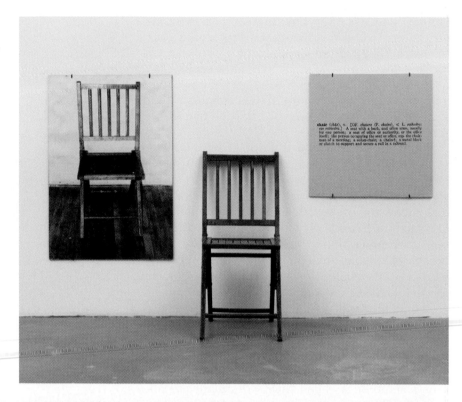

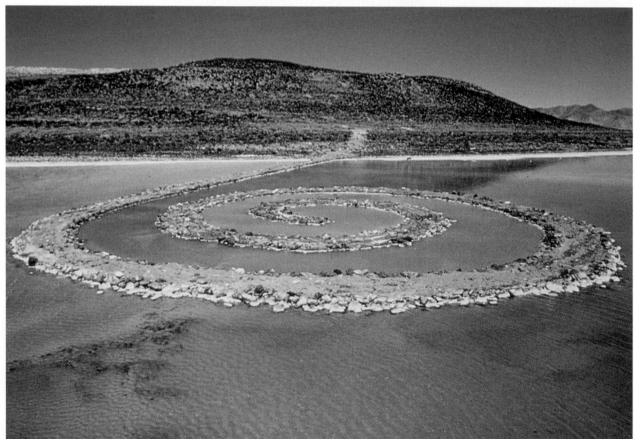

22.27 Robert Smithson. *Spiral Jetty,* 1970. Black rock, salt crystals, earth, red water (algae) at Great Salt Lake, Utah, 1,500′ × 15′ × 3½′. Estate of Robert Smithson; courtesy James Cohan Gallery, New York; collection of Dia Center for the Arts, New York.

four irregularly shaped rectangles on a wall. From each hang two thick, curling strands that reach the floor. Although it has no overt feminist content, Hesse's work was interpreted as an assault on the doctrinaire formalism of the Minimalists, which seemed to exclude social concerns.

Conceptual art grew out of the Minimalists' theoretical interests. For the Minimalist, the object was central; for the Conceptualist, the idea reigned supreme. Joseph Kosuth questioned the nature of the object and representation in his influential work, *One and Three Chairs* (Fig. 22.26), which consisted of a folding chair, a photograph of the folding chair, and a wall card displaying the dictionary definition of a chair. In an echo of Plato's concern with the illusion of reality, Kosuth's work emphasized that an idea does not reside in an object or in its verbal and visual representation. Instead, ideas exist in the mind, the perfect home for art. Other Conceptualists were adamant about eliminating the object altogether, or at least using inexpensive materials that were available to most people.

Earth, or environmental, art also emerged out of Minimalism. It, too, attempted to slip the bonds of convention and the precincts of the gallery and the museum by moving outdoors. Robert Smithson's *Spiral Jetty* (Fig. 22.27) is probably the best-known—and one of the most geographically remote—examples. Smithson constructed a spiral that turns in on itself, a form that suggested itself to him as he looked at the site. As the name suggests, Walter de Maria's *The Lightning Field* (Fig. 22.28) was constructed to attract flashes of lightning. It is located in a remote part of the New Mexico desert, where only a few visitors are allowed to observe it. Beginning in the late 1950s, the Bulgarian-born artist Christo and his French-born wife Jeanne-Claude de Guillbon began wrapping buildings and parts of the natural environment, hiding structures and places so that they might be seen afresh in both their covered and uncovered states. Their 1972 *Valley Curtain* stretched a translucent orange fabric across a much traveled highway that runs between two slopes of the Rocky Mountains. It was about 1,368 feet wide and 365 feet high at its climactic

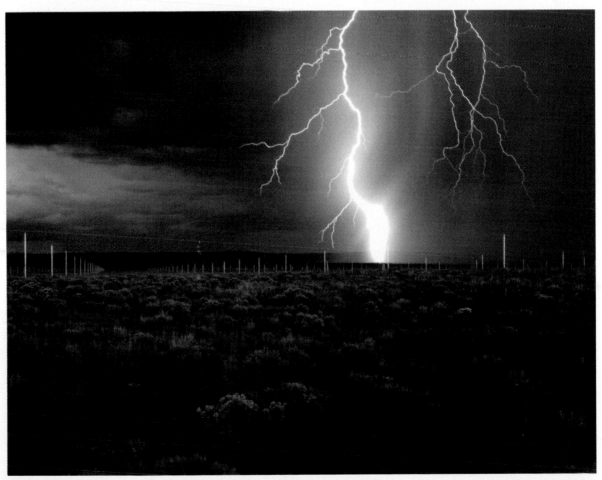

22.28   Walter de Maria. *The Lightning Field*, 1977. Quemado, New Mexico. Dia Center for the Arts, New York.

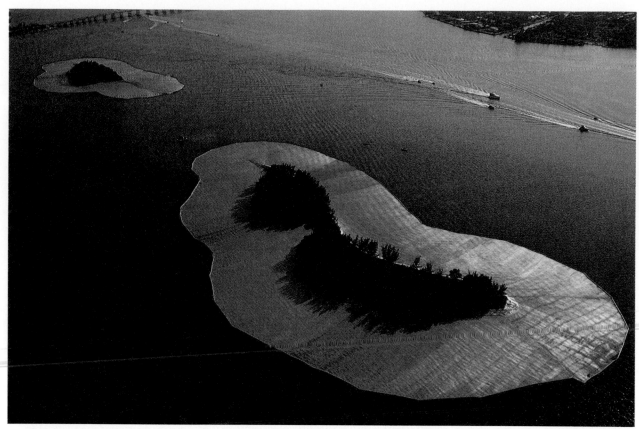

22.29 Christo and Jeanne-Claude de Guillbon. *Surrounded Islands,* Biscayne Bay, Greater Miami, Florida, 1980–1983, 6.5 million square feet of fabric floating around eleven islands.

22.30 Louise Bourgeois. *Cumul I,* 1968. White marble, approx. 1′8″ × 4′2″ × 4′. Musée National d'Art Moderne, Centre Georges Pompidou, Paris, France.

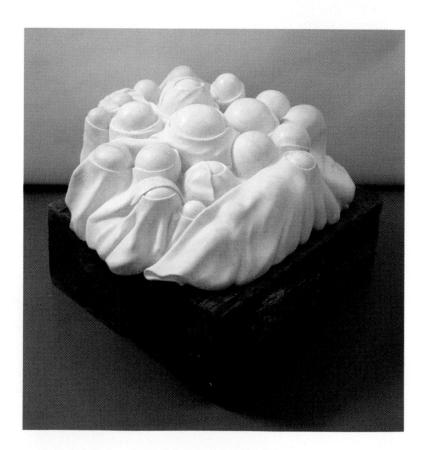

point. *Running Fence* was an 18-foot-high gleaming nylon fabric strung on cables supported by *Islands* steel poles that ran across almost 25 miles of northern California landscape. For their *Surrounded* (Fig. 22.29), finished in 1983, Christo and de Guillbon assembled 6.5 million square feet of pink woven polypropylene fabric and had it sewn into different patterns to encircle eleven islands in Biscayne Bay near Miami, Florida. The huge effort involved specialists such as marine biologists and ornithologists, government officials, and a workforce of close to 500 people. The islands were temporarily encircled with bright pink skirts that made them stand out in the blue water of the bay. The average life span of a Christo work like this is only about 2 weeks, either because it could be environmentally hazardous or socially inconvenient or because natural forces like wind and water destroy the work.

The development of Earth Art occurred at about the same time that astronauts landed on the moon, which, in turn, yielded photographs that unexpectedly focused attention on the solitary, fragile existence of the blue–green earth. At the same time, the environmental movement was gathering strength and pointing out how the rapid consumption of natural resources posed a serious threat to human life.

THE ART OF OTHERS: ANTIRACISM AND FEMINISM

Eva Hesse was not alone in creating art that highlighted the shortcomings of Minimalism. In contrast to the geometric shapes favored by the Minimalists, Louise Bourgeois attended to rounded, sensuous forms, as in *Cumul I* (Fig. 22.30), a nonrepresentational piece that reminded viewers of male and female genitalia. African-American artists such as Betye Saar, Romare Beardon, and Faith Ringgold used representation in their work, which focused on racism. Stereotypes of race found in the mass media were frequently targeted, as in Saar's *The Liberation of Aunt Jemima* (Fig. 22.31).

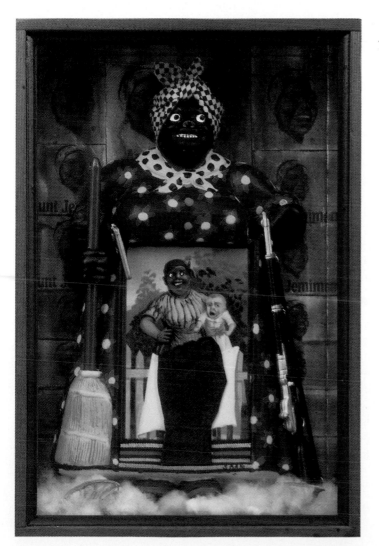

22.31 Betye Saar. *The Liberation of Aunt Jemima,* 1972. Mixed media, 11¾″ × 8″ × 2¾″. University of California, Berkeley Art Museum.

Cultural institutions such as the Studio Museum in Harlem were founded to collect art and provide venues for African-American artists.

The success of the civil rights movement in the decades after World War II helped inspire feminist activity in society and the arts. Art historian Linda Nochlin's 1971 article "Why Have There Been No Great Women Artists?" blasted the exclusionary practices of art history, which ignored the social impediments that faced women artists in the past. Ntozake Shange's play, *for colored girls who have considered suicide/when the rainbow is enuf,* opened on Broadway in 1975 and was performed frequently around the United States. The feminist dialogue of the 1960s and 1970s centered on whether there were inborn female qualities or whether feminine behavior was learned through social interaction. Essentialists—those who believe in the existence of inherent qualities and the responsibility of the female artist to address them—squared off with social constructionists—who held that gender is socially created. The argument has continued into the twenty-first century.

More Modern Musical Developments

During the 1960s, musical expression moved in diverse directions that occasionally interacted: some composers, intrigued with the notion of Minimalism, reinterpreted the potential of Schoenberg's twelve-tone method of musical composition; others were influenced by the nonlinear attributes of happenings and explored the possibilities of Cage's aleatory music. Interest in non-Western musical theory and sound increased dramatically.

The appearance of the synthesizer, an electronic device that collects, stores, and shapes sounds and is capable of performing the results, compressed the labor involved in composition and performance. The synthesizer's offspring, such as computerized keyboards, not only create purely electronic sound but also sample sounds, such as those made by a particular musical instrument. These devices allow composer-players to manipulate sound in ways never before possible.

Both Philip Glass and Steve Reich were closely allied with experimental art. Reich created a music-based happening at New York's Whitney Museum in 1969; Glass moved in avant-garde circles on both the East and West Coasts. Glass and Reich also shared an interest in Minimalist mu-

sic, and they both introduced elements of non-Western music into their compositions.

Reich brought in Indonesian notions of music, such as basing the duration of sound on the breath patterns of the performer; Glass spent time in Paris copying music for the Indian sitar player Ravi Shankar and came away with a new understanding of repetition and change that continues to influence his music. Although comprised of minimal sound modules that often repeat, these composers' music has proved accessible and popular with audiences.

Reich became known for compositions that investigated complex and interesting rhythmic elements. He is one of a large number of composers to write memorial compositions for World War II. During the conflict, he lived on and off in Los Angeles and had vivid memories of the train trips he took between New York and California. These trips meshed with the train trips that carried victims to the concentration camps. Reich's *Different Trains* (1988) is divided into three parts: "America—Before the War," "Europe—During the War," and "After the War." It included the recorded voices of his governess, a retired Pullman porter, and three Holocaust survivors, as well as recorded train sounds and music written for a string quartet.

The theater collaborations of Philip Glass and dramatist and stage designer Robert Wilson have been very successful. They produced a trilogy of operas: *Einstein on the Beach* (1976), which dramatized the revolution wrought by science; *Satyagraha* (1978), which featured Gandhi's movement to promote racial equality in South Africa; and *Akhnaten* (1984), which portrayed the struggles of a pharaoh who attempted to change the polytheistic religion of ancient Egypt (see pp. 15–16). Each opera used an ancient language: archaic Hebrew for *Einstein,* classical Sanskrit for *Satyagraha,* and Egyptian hieroglyphics for *Akhnaten.* Although these subjects may seem like history lessons, they are theatrical experiences infused with mystery and ambiguity.

John Adams, another American composer, combines some elements of Minimalism with traditional Western procedures. His *Harmonielehre* (1985) takes its title from Schoenberg's monumental treatise on harmony, written in 1911, just as Schoenberg was making his radical breakthrough into atonality and twelve-tone serialism. The word *harmony* in Schoenberg's title also refers to harmony in the larger sense, that is, as spiritual and psychological accord.

Adams's neo-Romantic orchestral work is made up of three visions. In Part I, the composer interprets a dream in which he "watched a gigantic supertanker take off from the surface of San Francisco Bay and thrust itself into the sky like a Saturn rocket." Part II comes from Adams's study of Carl Jung's views on medieval mythology and is titled "The Anfortas Wound." Part III, titled "Meister Echhardt and Quackie," returns to the composer's dream world and to his daughter Emily, who was called Quackie as a toddler. In the dream she rides perched on the shoulder of the medieval mystic Meister Echhardt and they hover among the heavenly bodies.

Unlike Schoenberg, Adams is a tonal composer. Because his music remains in a single key over time, any change comes with startling force. As he notes, "What actually interests me is the relationship of one key to another . . . the immense emotional power that's brought about by a modulation."

Adams's sense of humor—a trait he shares with a number of contemporary composers—is evident in his *Short Ride in a Fast Machine,* written for a large woodwind and brass group, an immense percussion group, a synthesizer, and strings. Composed as a fanfare to open a summer festival concert, the composition exhibits an atmosphere of celebration, surging with Minimalist rhythmic patterns and displays of brilliant orchestral color. Adams explained the title with the question, "You know how it is when someone asks you to ride in a terrific sports car, and then you wish you hadn't?"

Adams also based operas and other works on recent historical events. His *Nixon in China* (1987) dramatized the 1972 visit of a president to the capital of the world's most populous country, whose civilization dates back thousands of years. The work marks the coming together of West and East and the establishment of political and commercial relationships. His *Death of Klinghoffer* (1991) refers to the 1985 hijacking of a Mediterranean cruise ship and the cruel murder of a helpless wheelchair-bound passenger.

MODERN ARCHITECTURAL DEVELOPMENTS

After 1945 the arguments between the functionalism of the International Style of architecture and the more human scale of Frank Lloyd Wright's organic structures were muted. Both sides gave ground as they confronted environmental problems and increasing urbanization.

Gordon Bunshaft, Mies van der Rohe, and Philip Johnson provided postwar continuity for the International Style. Bunshaft's Lever House (Fig. 22.32) is cantilevered out beyond its structural supports to allow a great rise of translucent glass walls that reflect the city and sky with mirrorlike brightness. By omitting the ground floor and reducing the supporting steel shafts to a minimum, the architect could use the space for a small public garden and open passageway at street level.

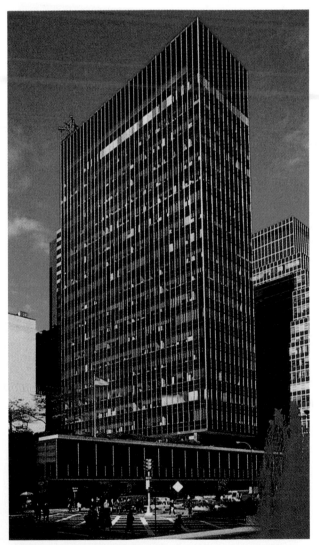

22.32 Gordon Bunshaft with Skidmore, Owings & Merrill. Lever House, New York, 1952.

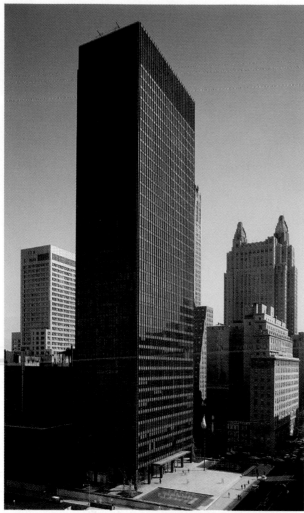

22.33 Ludwig Mies Van der Rohe and Philip Johnson. Seagram Building, New York, 1958.

Mies van der Rohe and Philip Johnson designed the Seagram Building (Fig. 22.33), which has been called the "Tower of Light." Open at the ground level, the building is supported by stilts. Its severe functionalism is offset by outdoor pools and gardens sunk into a pink granite platform. The tower of smoky amber glass is cantilevered over bronze-colored steel piers to impart airiness to the soaring mass. Mies van der Rohe went beyond mere practicality, producing aesthetically pleasing proportions and taking advantage of the beauty of materials. The bronze finish of the Seagram Building is alternately smooth and textured, providing a contrapuntal pattern.

During the closing years of his career, Frank Lloyd Wright finally received a commission to construct a building in New York City: the Solomon R. Guggenheim Museum (Fig. 22.34). For Wright, a museum could never be a group of boxlike compartments. Instead, he envisioned a continuous flow of floor space in which the eye would encounter no obstruction. To realize this concept he designed a single round room of reinforced concrete 100 feet in diameter at the base, with a hollow cylindrical core surmounted by a wire-glass dome 92 feet above the ground (Fig. 22.35). Spiraling upward around the room for a distance of a quarter of a mile is an open six-story cantilevered ramp rising at a 3 percent grade and broadening from a width of 17 feet at its lowest level to almost 35 feet at the top.

Groups of spectators can be accommodated without congestion as they move easily up or down the ramp. Visitors can take the elevator to the top level and wind downward at leisure, or

22.34 Frank Lloyd Wright. Solomon R. Guggenheim Museum, New York, 1957–1959. Reinforced concrete, diameter at ground level 100′, height of dome 92′.

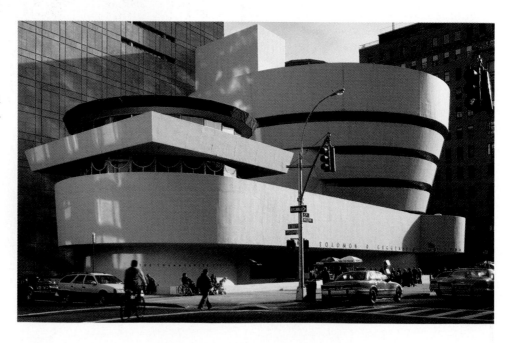

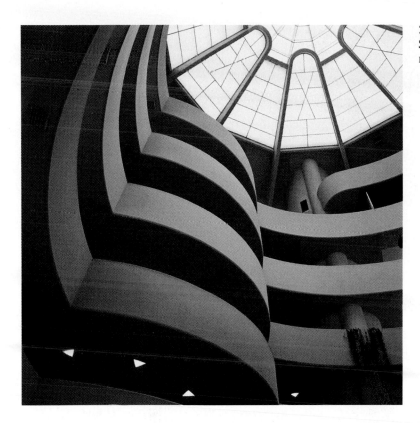

22.35 Frank Lloyd Wright. Interior, Solomon R. Guggenheim Museum. Ramp more than one-quarter mile long.

they can start at the bottom and walk up. They can inspect part of the exhibit at close range and at eye level or view three levels simultaneously across the open room.

In his later work, Le Corbusier (see pp. 594–595) allowed more color and freedom of design in his architecture. His pilgrimage church of Notre-Dame-du-Haut at Ronchamp (Fig. 22.36), high up in the Vosges Mountains of southeastern France, is a fantasy of free sculptural forms in ferroconcrete and stained glass. A prowlike roof harks back to the Early Christian meaning of the word *nave,* which signified a ship steering its way through the stormy seas of life toward a haven of refuge.

The grandeur of the exterior of Ronchamp has the power to rival the splendid natural setting, but

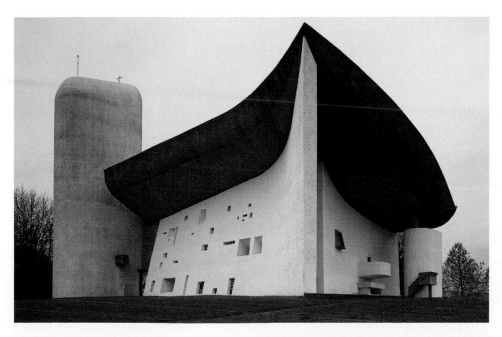

22.36 Le Corbusier. Notre-Dame-du-Haut, Ronchamp, France, 1950–1955. View from southeast.

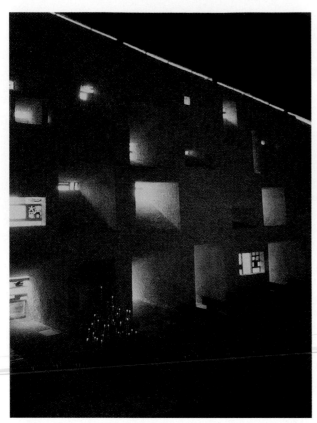

22.37 Le Corbusier. Interior, south wall, Notre-Dame-du-Haut.

the interior (Fig. 22.37) offers the intimacy of the human scale. Years before, Le Corbusier and his associates had devised a proportional system based on 7.5 feet (2.2 meters), the approximate height attainable by an average person when standing with an arm raised. Using this dimension as a basic *module,* or unit of measure, the architect felt confident of achieving in his structures a scale suited to human beings.

The south wall of the interior (Fig. 22.37) suggests strength and vitality through its pitch, curve, and massiveness. Here and there on the stained glass has been painted the prayer to the Virgin: *Je vous salute Marie, pleine de grâce* (Hail Mary, full of grace). At Ronchamp, Le Corbusier achieved a rich and complex structure, appropriate to its function.

FUNCTION AND BEAUTY

Through imaginative solutions to modern architectural problems, Eero Saarinen and Joern Utzon provided for functional needs without sacrificing beauty of design. For his Trans World Airlines Terminal at Kennedy International Airport in New York (Fig. 22.38), Saarinen invented flowing concrete forms and dynamic stresses to convey the idea of flight. Four large concrete shells resting on supports of abstract shape enclose an interior whose elegance and grace make the building seem like a massive sculpture. The outstretched wings of the building are reminiscent of a bird or plane, and the whole effect is a visual metaphor for flight.

Three major Modernist buildings commanded international acclaim: the Sydney Opera House in Australia; the Pompidou National Center for Arts and Culture in Paris, commonly called Beaubourg; and the East Building of the National Gallery in Washington, D.C. Each operates as an active cultural center.

Utzon's Sydney Opera House (Fig. 22.39), a performing arts and recreation center, stands astride a point jutting out into Sydney Bay, one of the world's busiest harbors. Its unique shape looms up as a massive piece of outdoor sculpture. From some angles it suggests a group of interlocking shell formations, from others a group of large white sails skimming over the rippling water.

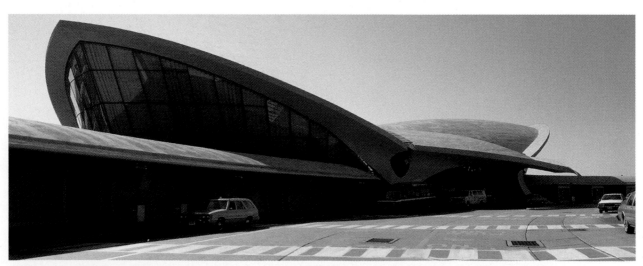

22.38 Eero Saarinen. Trans World Airlines Terminal, Kennedy International Airport, New York, 1962.

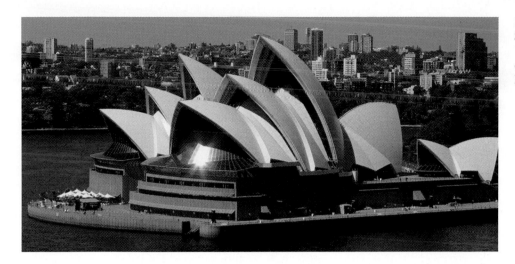

22.39 Joern Utzon. Sydney Opera House, 1959–1972. Reinforced concrete, height of highest shell 200′.

The Danish-born Utzon won the international competition for the Sydney Opera House in 1957. His daring design, however, proved to be far ahead of the technology needed to construct it. The building was one of the most difficult construction jobs ever undertaken, calling for daring feats of structural technology. The immense poured-concrete foundation was first put in place on the natural sandstone bedrock of the site. Over this rise the three sets of roof vaults, or shells, of enormous size and bold curvature. If the structure had been built from the ground up, the price would have been astronomical. To reduce cost, a system of prefabricated units was devised by which precast segments made on the spot were hoisted into place by cranes. The sections are held together by tensioned cables.

Except for the elegance and quality of the materials and the free play of structural forms, there is no conscious attempt at decoration as such. In the tradition of Saarinen's Trans World Flight Center, Le Corbusier's church at Ronchamp, and Wright's Guggenheim Museum, the whole building is an ornament in itself. The building has become a symbol for both Sydney and Australia, taking its place with the Eiffel Tower for Paris, the Empire State Building for New York, and the Gateway Arch for St. Louis.

FUNKY FUNCTIONALISM

Since its 1977 opening in Paris, the Pompidou National Center for Arts and Culture (Fig. 22.40) has been a popular success. Indeed, its stated purpose was to be so inventive that it would draw the cultural center of gravity away from New York and back to Paris. Designed by the Italian

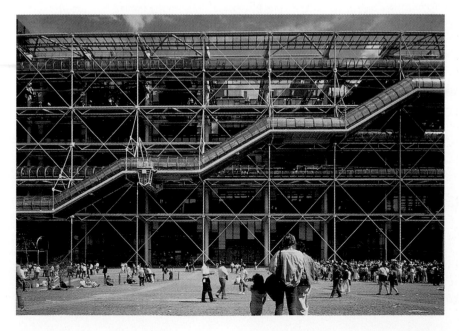

22.40   Renzo Piano and Richard Rogers. Georges Pompidou National Center for Arts and Culture (Beaubourg), Paris, 1977.

architect Renzo Piano and his British colleague Richard Rogers, the building quickly joined the Eiffel Tower as an attraction for Parisians as well as for millions of tourists around the world. In fact, in its first 20 years the building attracted so many visitors that it had to undergo 2 years of major rebuilding. It reopened in 2000.

Named for the plateau it occupies, the Beaubourg is an open glass box supported by steel skeleton scaffolding. It looks like a building turned inside out. Things that normally are hidden in a basement or central core—building supports, heating and air conditioning ducts, freight elevators—are transferred to the exterior, painted in strong colors, and made visible to viewers standing outside the building. The colors are coded: green for the water ducts, blue for the air-conditioning units, yellow for the electrical work, and red for the escalators and movements of people. The interior was not broken up into rooms, and only temporary partitions can be used to enclose space.

The Beaubourg was conceived of as a people's palace that would break down the barriers between art and life, and as a cultural supermarket where both artists and visitors could get into the act. Together with the interior activities and lively exterior plaza where jugglers, fire-eaters, and folksingers perform, it has become a perpetual happening. The "boiler-room facade," as it has been called, moves continuously as freight elevators rise and fall and people ride up and down the Plexiglas-enclosed escalators. With its bubble dome, transparent glass walls, whirring machinery, and spectacular lighting, it has been dubbed the first building of the space age.

The National Gallery's East Building in Washington, D.C., is a structure whose interplay of geometric unity and variety originated in the trapezoid-shaped site the building occupies. The architect, I. M. Pei, first divided the area diagonally into two triangular sections: one to house the art collection and the other for the newly established Center for Advanced Study in the Visual Arts, complete with a library and six-story reading room. Taking later motifs from this basic division, Pei created startling diagonal accents.

Inside, the drama heightens as the space expands into a triangular court (Fig. 22.41) where tall trees alternate with massive sculptures to provide a simultaneous indoor–outdoor feeling. Smaller alcoves branch out from this central hall to provide space for viewing smaller works of art. The large court is ornamented by a Joan Miró tapestry, a Henry Moore bronze, and a welded metal sculpture by Anthony Caro, all scaled to harmonize with the space. A huge Alexander Calder mobile

22.41 I. M. Pei. East Wing, National Gallery of Art, Washington, D.C., 1978. Interior view of the triangular court with mobile by Alexander Calder.

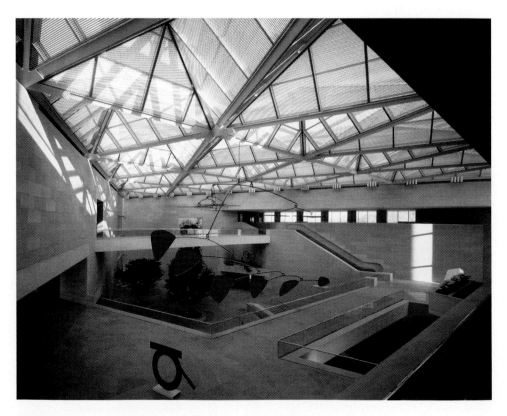

hangs from the roof. The constant circular movement of the mobile against the structure's sharp geometric patterns provides a dramatic dimension of its own.

IDEAS: EXISTENTIALISM

As happened after World War I, the death and destruction of World War II set off a round of questioning of Western values. Religion, culture, and political ideas all seemed powerless to prevent extensive desolation and left humans standing alone without consolation or direction in the midst of dread and nothingness. Technology and science, which had instigated hope for the betterment of humankind, had caused catastrophe and seemed ready to trigger nuclear holocaust. The postwar paintings of the English artist Francis Bacon are filled with this postwar anguish and disillusionment (Fig. 22.42). He stripped the human image of pretense, illusion, and dignity, leaving the figure to scream with terror and anxiety. For many years Bacon had been haunted by Velásquez's portrait of the wily seventeenth-century Pope Innocent X, whose interests were more worldly than spiritual. Here he shows a screaming pope surrounded by butchered beef carcasses dripping with blood, bitter references to the carnage of war.

But existentialism was not simply a philosophy of despair. The failure of traditional values served to highlight the fact that an individual may create his or her own meaning for life—to work or play, protest or acquiesce, love or hate, notice or ignore, or tend one's garden and let the world go by. For the French existentialist Jean-Paul Sartre, existence precedes essence: first one must exist, then project a self-image or define oneself through actions taken. Ironically, human beings are condemned to be free; the only limit to their freedom is freedom itself.

For Sartre, existence meant making choices that are not casual but creative. They lead to life commitments that become positive forces in the face of the inevitable negation of death. Indeed, the confrontation with extinction can be the greatest challenge to the affirmation of life. Not meekly accepting the status quo, but living on the brink and making each moment count, were tasks that not everyone welcomed. Sartre's 1945 play *No Exit* introduces three characters whose inaction and hesitation have managed only to create their own hell. Its most famous line, "Hell is other people," shows how far the midtwentieth-century outlook

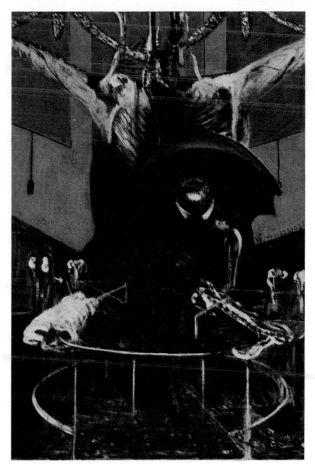

22.42 Francis Bacon, *Painting,* 1946. Oil and pastel on linen, 6′5⅞″ × 4′4″. Museum of Modern Art, New York (purchase).

had moved from the confident humanism of the Renaissance and the Enlightenment.

For Sartre, no one is more aware of the challenge to create than the twentieth-century artist, whose will to create and to continually experiment was a model for infinite possibilities in human attitudes, insights, and lifestyles. In a similar vein, French philosopher André Malraux pronounced that art had replaced religion as the last defense against death.

Sartre believed that human experience was best expressed in myth and metaphor, as well as in literature and art. For him, novels, plays, artworks, and music were better vehicles to communicate ideas than philosophical treatises and formal arguments. In its embrace of freedom of choice, existentialism is the philosophy that comes closest to capturing the experimental thrust of midtwentieth-century art. Yet it is difficult to say how many experimental artists were directly influenced by existentialist writers, or whether philosophers and artists were affected by similar events and cultural perceptions.

Many people took from existential philosophy the notion that life was essentially absurd. When the notion of the absurd appears in existentialist art and drama, it has a grim quality. Samuel Beckett's *Waiting for Godot* (a paraphrase of the existentialist philosopher Martin Heidegger's "waiting for God") is a classic example of theater of the absurd. It unfolds in a series of inconsequential episodes that reveal the endless boredom and futility of life (Fig. 22.43). Godot, of course, never arrives. As the characters wait, their terse, brittle dialogue explores the nagging, niggling nuisances, trivialities, and irrelevancies of daily life:

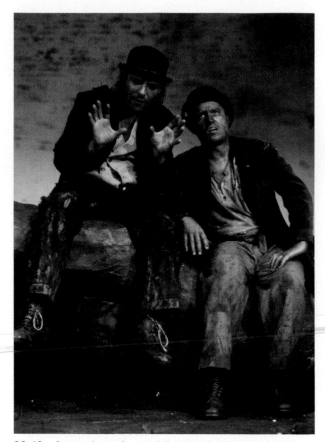

22.43   Scene from Samuel Beckett's *Waiting for Godot.* Production at the Queen's Theatre, 1991.

Vladimir:	I get used to the muck as I go along.
Estragon [after prolonged reflection]:	Is that the opposite?
Vladimir:	Question of temperament.
Estragon:	Of character.
Vladimir:	Nothing you can do about it.
Estragon:	No use struggling.
Vladimir:	One is what one is.
Estragon:	No use wriggling.
Vladimir:	The essential doesn't change.
Estragon:	Nothing to be done. . . .[2]
Estragon:	What do we do now?
Vladimir:	I don't know.
Estragon:	Let's go.
Vladimir:	We can't.
Estragon:	Why not?
Vladimir:	We're waiting for Godot.[3]

For Sartre, death is the ultimate absurdity. As Pozzo says in Beckett's play, "[Humans] give birth astride of a grave, the light gleams an instant, then it's night once more." Both Sartre and Beckett would agree with Leonardo da Vinci, who observed that just when he thought he was learning to live, he was only learning to die. Paradoxically, one cannot know life until one is confronted with death or experience affirmation until one encounters negation. All life, human or otherwise, has a death sentence hanging over it. There can be no sunshine without shadow, no light without darkness.

In a sense, existentialism is the ultimate humanism. One must constantly ask, What does it mean to exist? What is human existence like? How does it feel to be human? In a world of infinite possibilities, everything can be but nothing has to be or must be. In the existentialist worldview, all works of art are creative acts in the face of nothingness.

YOUR RESOURCES

- **Web Site**

  http://art.wadsworth.com/fleming10

  ○ Chapter 22 Quiz

  ○ Links—Online Readings—T.S. Eliot, selected works; Shaw, *Man and Superman;* Stein, *Three Lives*

- **Audio CD**

  ○ Adams, *Short Ride in a Fast Machine*

---

[2]Samuel Beckett, *Waiting for Godot* (New York: Grove Press, 1954), 14, 31. Copyright © 1954 by Samuel Beckett. Reprinted by permission of Grove Press Books.
[3]Ibid., p. 57.

MIDTWENTIETH CENTURY

Key Events	Architecture	Visual Arts	Music and Dance
	1867–1959 Frank Lloyd Wright ★	1864–1946 Alfred Stieglitz ▲	1873–1943 Sergei Rachmaninov
	1883–1969 Walter Gropius ★	1879–1973 Edward Steichen ▲	1882–1971 Igor Stravinsky
	1886–1969 Ludwig Mies van der Rohe ★	1880–1966 Hans Hofmann ▲	1891–1953 Sergey Prokofiev
	1887–1965 Le Corbusier (Charles-Édouard Jeanneret-Gris) ★	1887–1968 Marcel Duchamp ▲	1892–1974 Darius Milhaud
	1891–1979 Pier Luigi Nervi ★	1887–1986 Georgia O'Keeffe ▲	1896–1989 Virgil Thomson
	1892–1970 Richard Neutra ★	1888–1976 Josef Albers ▲	1898–1937 George Gershwin
	1895–1983 R. Buckminster Fuller ★	1898–1979 Peggy Guggenheim ▲	1899–1963 Francis Poulenc
	1898–1976 Alexander Calder ●		
	1899–1988 Louise Nevelson ●		

1900 ───

Key Events	Architecture	Visual Arts	Music and Dance
1926–1927 **First motion pictures** synchronized with sound	1902–1981 Marcel Breuer ★	1901–1985 Jean Dubuffet ▲	1900–1990 Aaron Copland
1939–1945 **World War II**	1903–1975 Barbara Hepworth ●	1903–1974 Adolph Gottlieb ▲	1906–1975 Dmitri Shostakovich
1942 **Nuclear fission;** release of atomic energy achieved	1904–1988 Isamu Noguchi ●	1903–1970 Mark Rothko ▲	1908–1992 Olivier Messiaen
1945 **Atomic bomb** developed; **United Nations** organized; **New York City** became international art and music center; **commercial TV** begins	1906– Philip Johnson ★	1904–1948 Arshile Gorky ▲	1908– Elliott Carter
	1906–1965 David Smith ●	1904–1997 Willem de Kooning ▲	1910–1981 Samuel Barber
	1910–1961 Eero Saarinen ★	1904–1980 Clyfford Still ▲	1911– Gian Carlo Menotti
	1912– Nicolas Schöffer ●	1905–1970 Barnett Newman ▲	1912–1992 John Cage
1947–1950 **UN headquarters** established in New York	1917– I. M. Pei ★	1908–1984 Lee Krasner ▲	1913–1976 Benjamin Britten
1948 **LP recordings** available	1918– Ronald Bladen ●	1909–1992 Francis Bacon ▲	1913–1994 Witold Lutoslawski
1950–1953 **Korean War**	1918– Joern Utzon ★	1910–1962 Franz Kline ▲	1916– Milton Babbitt
1951 **Electric power** produced by nuclear energy	1921–1986 Joseph Beuys ●	1911– Louise Bourgeois ▲	1918– George Rochberg
	1922– Richard Hamilton ●	1912–1963 William Baziotes ▲	1919– Merce Cunningham
1957 **First earth satellite** launched into orbit by USSR; **U.S. satellite** follows in 1958	1924– Anthony Caro ●	1912–1962 Morris Louis ▲	1923– Ned Rorem
	1925–1996 Duane Hanson ●	1912–1956 Jackson Pollock ▲	1925– Luciano Berio
1958 **European Economic Community (EEC)** established; stereophonic sound recordings produced	1925–1991 Jean Tinguely ●	1913–1967 Ad Reinhardt ▲	1925– Pierre Boulez
	1927– John Chamberlain ●	1914–1988 Romare Beardon ▲	1926– Hans Werner Henze
	1928–1994 Donald Judd ●	1915–1991 Robert Motherwell ▲	1928– Karlheinz Stockhausen
	1928– Sol LeWitt ●	1922–1993 Richard Diebenkorn ▲	1929– George Crumb
1960 **Laser technology developed;** new era in communication science begun	1928–1973 Robert Smithson ●	1922– Jules Olitski ▲	1933– Krzysztof Penderecki
	1929– Claes Oldenburg ●	1923– Ellsworth Kelly ▲	1939– Ellen Taaffe Zwilich
1961 **First satellite with human** put into orbit by USSR; U.S. satellite with crew followed in 1962	1931– Robert Morris ●	1923–1997 Roy Lichtenstein ▲	1941– Robert Wilson
	1933– Mark di Suvero ●	1923– Larry Rivers ▲	1947– John Adams
1962 **Telstar,** American communications satellite, put into orbit	1933– Richard Rogers ★	1924– Robert Frank ▲	
	1935– Carl André ●	1924– Kenneth Noland ▲	
1964 **Gulf of Tonkin Resolution** escalated Vietnam War	1935– Christo ●	1924–2000 George Segal ▲	
1964–1975 **Vietnam War**	1936–1970 Eva Hesse ●	1925– Robert Rauschenberg ▲	
1969 **U.S. astronauts** on moon	1937– Renzo Piano ★	1926– Betye Saar ▲	
1974 **Completion of Skylab series** photographing the solar system and surveying the resources of the earth	1939– Richard Serra ●	1927– Allan Kaprow ●	
	1945– Joseph Kosuth ●	1928– Helen Frankenthaler ▲	
	1958 **UNESCO building** constructed in Paris by Breuer, Nervi, and Zehrfuss, with art by Calder, Miró, Moore, Noguchi, Picasso, and others	1928– Robert Indiana ▲	
1976 **U.S. spacecraft** transmit pictures and data from Mars		1928–1987 Andy Warhol ▲	
		1930– Jasper Johns ▲	
1984 **Personal and home computers** widely available; growth of robotic technology		1930– Faith Ringgold ▲	
	1962–1966 **Lincoln Center** built in New York City; Library and Museum of Performing Arts by Skidmore, Owings, and Merrill; New York State Theater by Johnson; Metropolitan Opera House by Wallace K. Harrison; Philharmonic Hall by Abramowitz; Vivian Beaumont Theater by Saarinen; paintings by Chagall, Johns, and others; sculpture by Calder, Moore, and others	1931– Bridget Riley ▲	
		1933– James Rosenquist ▲	
		1935– Jim Dine ▲	
		1936– Richard Estes ▲	
		1936– Frank Stella ▲	
		1940– Chuck Close ▲	

★ - Architect   ▲ - Painter or photographer   ● - Sculptor

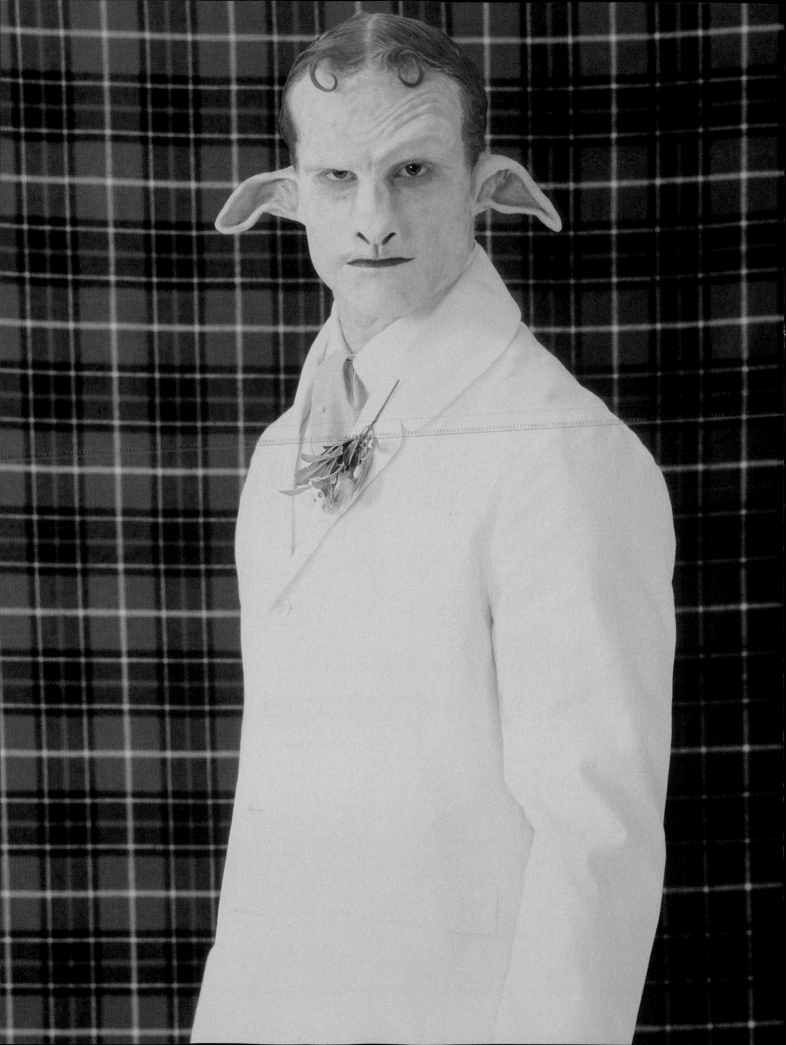

INTO A NEW MILLENNIUM

FROM A LATE TWENTIETH-CENTURY perspective, modern art was a period style, a historical fact. This does not mean that Modernism was gone or forgotten, just that it was no longer modern. Wright and Le Corbusier, Matisse and Picasso, Proust and Joyce, Schoenberg and Stravinsky were viewed as old masters, like Beethoven and Rembrandt. Their buildings became influential models, their books and manifestos were discussed in textbooks, their pictures hung in major museums, and their music became part of the standard repertory of symphony orchestras.

Aspects of Modernism aged at different rates. Some Modernist works, such as James Joyce's *Ulysses* and Béla Bartók's string quartets, still challenge contemporary understanding. At the same time, derivatives of drip painting decorate the walls of public buildings like airports and fast-food restaurants without attracting much notice. Yet the rejection or acceptance of individual works or particular approaches tells us little about Modernism's decline. After all, Modernism was a set of ideas about how art changes and what art's relationship to society ought to be. In the post–World War II period, these ideas met with mounting, multiple objections.

Modernist artists generally believed that progressive art should renounce conventional and academic art, as well as art that was popular with the masses. The avant-garde stood for aesthetic renewal and social renovation, achieved by contesting the entrenched beliefs of the establishment. Modernist artists did not care if their art was understood by ordinary people; instead, they preferred acknowledgment and patronage by educated elites. The long-term trend in modern art was movement away from representation to an emphasis on purely artistic matters, such as line, form, and color. The inclination toward reduction and abstraction diminished the presence in art of the social world and its concerns. Of course, not all modern artists subscribed to these ideas. The

Dadaists, for example, were interested in using the resources of the mass media to critique notions of consumption and personal identity.

During the post–World War II period, several Modernist ideas came under fire. Although not overtly political, the Abstract Expressionists nonetheless wanted to merge art and life. Similarly, those who created happenings tried to move outside the exclusive precinct of the museum and into the streets or the countryside. Yet, color abstractions and happenings were not accessible to ordinary people, but Pop Art, with its origins in advertising and vernacular texts like comic books, was immediately familiar, even banal. It was in a sense also realistic, because unlike abstraction it favored recognizable figures and landscapes. This popular and populist art set the stage for the return of realism.

THE RETURN OF REALISM AND EXPRESSIONISM

The late 1970s through the early 1980s was a period of artistic pluralism in which many approaches coexisted. Because some of these movements seemed to borrow ideas and appearances from the past, critics used the prefix *neo* (new) to identify them. For example, the terms *neorealism* and *neo-Expressionism* gained currency. Instead of dubbing these movements new, one could say that realism and expressionism never vanished, but remained constant, if minor, approaches throughout the late nineteenth and twentieth centuries.

The term *neo-Expressionism* was forged in the late 1970s to describe mostly European artists who rejected the Minimalists' interest in geometric shapes. Neo-Expressionists pursued a variety of figurative styles, but they often used the broad brushstrokes associated with earlier Expressionist painting, including Abstract Expressionism. German artist Anselm Kiefer, who studied with Joseph Beuys (see pp. 612–613), is a major neo-Expressionist,

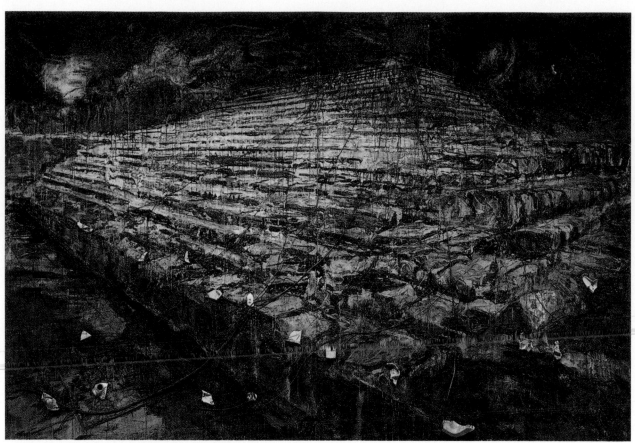

23.1   Anselm Kiefer. *Osiris and Isis,* 1985–1987. Diptych, mixed media on canvas, 12′6″ × 18′4½″ × 6½″. San Francisco Museum of Modern Art, purchased through a gift of Jean Stein, by exchange, the Mrs. Paul L. Wattis Fund and the Doris and Donald Fischer Fund.

23.2   Gerhard Richter, *Man Shot Down,* 1988, from his series *18 Oktober 1977.* Oil on canvas, 3′3½″ × 4′7¼″. Museum of Modern Art, New York. The Sidney and Harriet Janis Collection, gift of Philip Johnson, and acquired through the Lillie P. Bliss Bequest (all by exchange); Enid A. Haupt Fund; Nina and Gorden Bunshaft Bequest Fund; and gift of Emily Rauh Pulitzer.

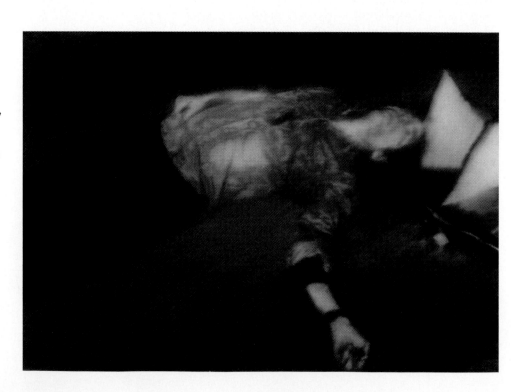

but in his work, unlike that of the Abstract Expressionists, the personal is political.

Kiefer's pictures are haunted by the ancient and modern history of Germany, particularly its guilty heritage of Nazism, the Holocaust, and the carnage of World War II. Kiefer often turns to mythology to express the psychological and social problems of modern life, especially those having to do with despair and renewal. In *Osiris and Isis* (Fig. 23.1), his subject is the ancient Egyptian story of the god Osiris, who was murdered, dismembered, and brought back to life by his wife, the goddess Isis. As in many of his other works, Kiefer mixes media; here, in addition to pigment, he uses lead, clay, copper wire, and porcelain. He explains, "I see myths living, like the parts of Osiris gathered up to make a new energy." His paintings do not evade twentieth-century German history, but focus on the possibilities for spiritual rejuvenation and the positive transformation of culture achieved by facing the horrors of the past.

The German painter-photographer Gerhard Richter is also concerned with the past, including painting's past and the way photography influences human recall. In *Man Shot Down,* a painting from his series *18 Oktober 1977,* Richter references an incident in which political prisoners died suspiciously in jail (Fig. 23.2). The gray tones of the painting approximate those of black-and-white news photography. Rather than a crisp image, the picture is blurry, perhaps symbolizing how memory, unlike photographs, does not remain sharp and how the present reshapes history. Blurriness also characterizes the surfaces of Kiefer's work. For both Kiefer and Richter, blurriness seems to suggest the passing of time and a sense of lost idealism.

In addition, Italian neo-Expressionism, also referred to as the *transavantguardia,* looked to the past, including the classical past. Sandro Chia deliberately incorporates past styles of painting, such as Italian Futurism, and past subjects, such as classical mythology. In his *Idleness of Sisyphus,* a modern figure takes the place of the legendary Sisyphus, who was doomed for eternity to roll a rock up a hill and then watch it roll down again. In *Water Bearer* (Fig. 23.3), fish emerge from the colorful waves and the traditional waterbag sprouts a huge whale-like head, of the sort envisioned by medieval artists as the mouth of hell. Many of Chia's figures from the 1980s are both menaced and challenged by their situations.

More than the other *transavantguardia* painters, Carlo Mariani dwells on the classical past and its

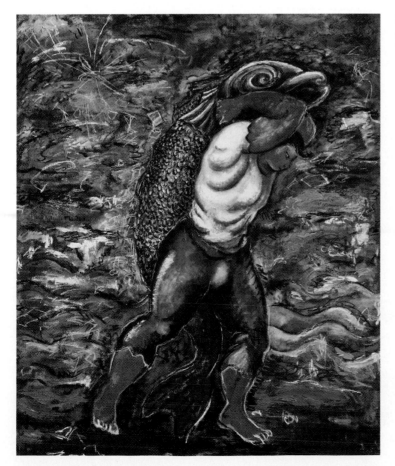

23.3 Sandro Chia, *Water Bearer,* 1981. Oil and pastel on canvas, approx. 6'9¼" × 5'7". Tate Gallery, London, England.

interpretation in neoclassical art. He is futilely trying to rewrite art history by putting painting on a different road than the path toward Modernism. In the 1970s, Mariani invented a fictional School of Rome inhabited by the poet Goethe, the art historian Johann Winckelmann, and the painter Angelica Kauffmann, whom Mariani adopted as his muse.

Mariani centers his work on the act of creation. His mythological ideal is Prometheus, who stole the flame of life from the hearth of the gods. The protagonists of his pictorial dream dramas—gods, demigods, putti—are all artists, with palettes and brushes. His allegorical approach is seen in *It Is Forbidden to Awaken the Gods* (Fig. 23.4). Two Apollo-like figures, crowned with laurel wreaths signifying immortal fame, are asleep. A drowsy Cupid is at their side, as is the broken head of a Venus. The huge hand with its commanding gesture is taken from a fragment of a colossal statue of a Roman emperor represented as the god Jupiter. The flesh is softly and sensuously modeled, and the setting is like an empty stage flooded with a luminous glow that intensifies the deep shadows cast by the figures and the folds of their drapery. Mariani's nostalgia for a past time includes a longing for beauty as a sustaining quality in art, which is to say, a time before Robert Rauschenberg gathered cast-off items to make art, and prior to Andy Warhol's gleeful acceptance of commercialism.

In the United States, neo-Expressionist artists did not attempt to escape painting's recent past to the degree that Mariani did. For example, Julian Schnabel used the heavy drips of Jackson Pollock and the eclecticism of Rauschenberg's mixed media. For *Death Takes a Holiday* (Fig. 23.5), he reached further back, searching the medieval past for his imagery. At the same time, he undercut the seriousness of his work by painting on velvet, a technique used in inexpensive works sold on street corners. The mythic skeletal personification of death presides in a picture whose broad brushstrokes seem to indicate the kinetic energy and deep emotional involvement of Expressionism. Yet Schnabel does not believe that he is expressing himself; instead, he claims to use only the visual languages and themes of the past, including those of Expressionism.

Susan Rothenberg's paintings have also been categorized as neo-Expressionist, partly because they include recognizable figures and are rendered in observable brushstrokes applied repeatedly to correct and finish the work. Since the mid-1970s Rothenberg has been making images of horses. Despite its rough surface, *Tattoo* (Fig. 23.6)

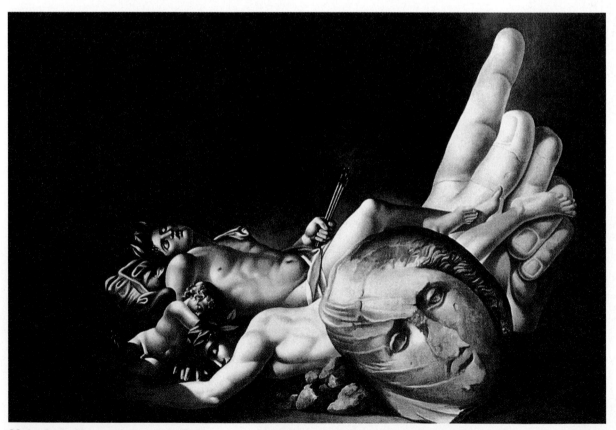

23.4   Carlo Maria Mariani. *It Is Forbidden to Awaken the Gods*, 1984. Oil on canvas, 8′2″ × 6′6″. By permission of the artist.

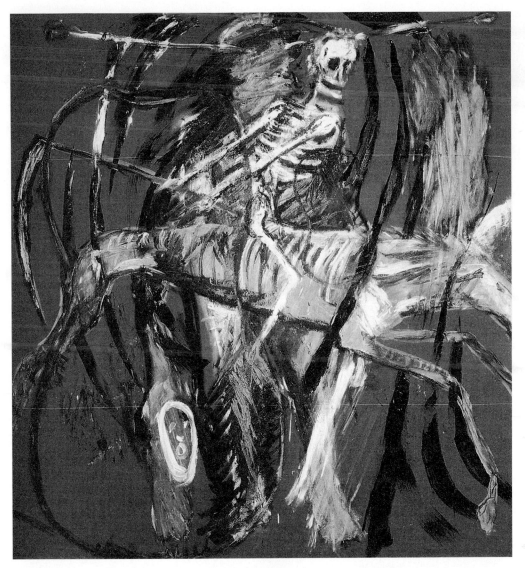

23.5 Julian Schnabel. *Death Takes a Holiday,* 1981. Oil on velvet, 7′6″ × 7′. Pace Wildenstein Gallery, New York.

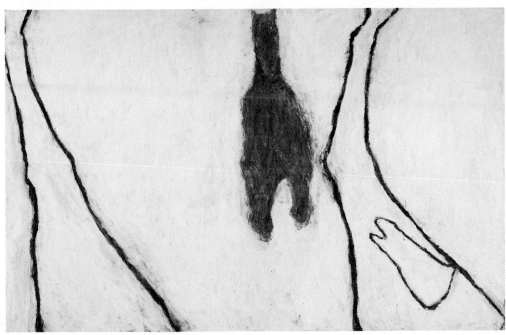

23.6 Susan Rothenberg. *Tattoo,* 1979. Acrylic, flashe on canvas, 5′7″ × 8′7⅛″ × 1¼″. Collection Walker Art Center, Minneapolis. Purchased with the aid of funds from Mr. and Mrs. Edmond R. Ruben, Mr. and Mrs. Julius E. David, the Art Acquisition Fund, and the National Endowment for the Arts, 1979.

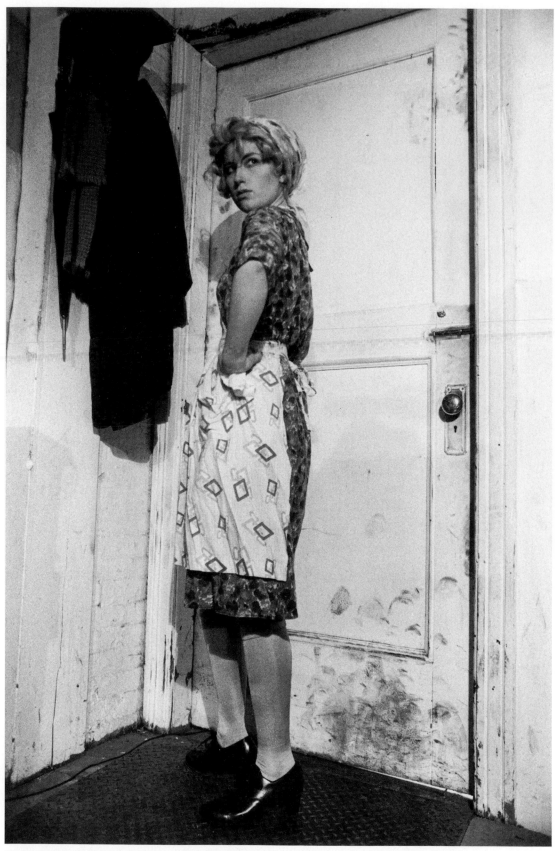

23.7   Cindy Sherman. *Untitled,* 1979. Black and white photograph, 8″ × 10″.

is reminiscent of illusionistic painting. Is the blue horse charging at the viewer, or is it merely a mark on the flank of a figure that may be equine or human? Like many painters of her generation, Rothenberg deliberately concocts irony and ambiguity as features of her work.

CRITICIZING MODERN MEDIA

The works of the neo-Expressionists may not look similar, but they are connected by an interest in memory and history. At about the same time that neo-Expressionism emerged, another group of artists began to look at how mass media manipulates human behavior. Despite the fact that television quickly became the most influential mass medium in the second half of the twentieth century, many artists working since the mid-1970s have chosen photography to explore the experience of living in a world of images. Artist and writer Richard Prince cut, cropped, rearranged, and reprinted pictures from magazine advertisements, hoping to show how they spark desire. Similarly, Cindy Sherman created photographs in which she posed herself in costumes and situations that look as though they were cut from B-movies made in the 1950s. By making her tired, anxious, or vulnerable persona the subject of the viewer's gaze, she tried to show how women have been trivialized and disparaged in mass media representations (Fig. 23.7).

In an effort to confront viewers with the same power as advertising, Barbara Kruger used her skills as a designer to create large posters using strong graphics and pithy slogans (Fig. 23.8). Perhaps the era's most devastating photo-based piece

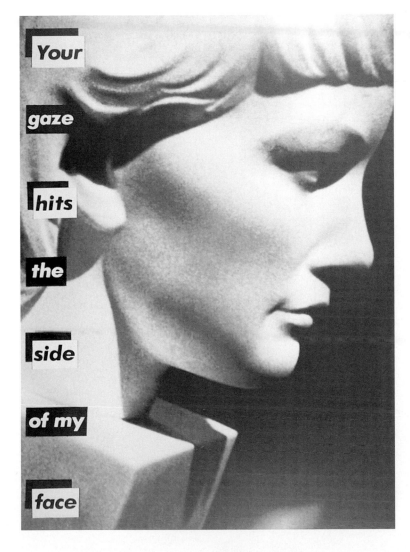

23.8 Barbara Kruger. *Untitled (Your Gaze Hits the Side of My Face)*, 1981. Lithograph, silkscreen/paper, 4′7″ × 3′5″. Courtesy Mary Boone Gallery, New York.

about human identity was made by French artist Annette Messager, who underscored the idea that there is no intrinsic maleness or femaleness. Her work, *Mes Veux (My Vows)* (Fig. 23.9) consists of many photographs depicting women's body parts. They are suspended from strings of different lengths. From a distance, the resulting construction seems like a complete circle, but as the viewer moves closer, the parts appear as pieces that do not add up to a whole.

Media criticism in the last decades of the twentieth century presented issues of gender identity in a different way than feminist artists such as Judy Chicago did in the early 1970s. Conceived of in 1971, Chicago's large installation, *The Dinner Party* (Fig. 23.10), praises women and their accomplishments. It consists of three tables arranged in a triangle. Thirty-nine individual place settings celebrate women in history, such as Hatshepsut, who ruled Egypt as a pharaoh, writers such as Virginia Woolf, and painters such as Georgia O'Keeffe. The names of other notable women are also inscribed on the base that supports the tables. The work is replete with sexual imagery, used

23.9 Annette Messager, *Mes Veux (My Vows),* 1990. Black and white photographs, strings. Diameter approx. 6'5¾". Courtesy Marian Goodman Gallery, Paris, France.

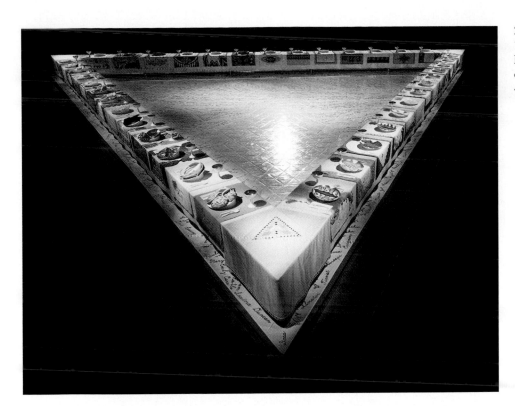

23.10 Judy Chicago. *The Dinner Party,* 1979. Multimedia, including ceramics and stitchery, 48′ × 48′ × 48′ installed.

to honor women, not to stereotype them. *The Dinner Party* resembles other feminist works of the 1970s in its use of crafts, such as embroidery, quilt-making, and beading, which have traditionally been women's work.

In late twentieth-century art, racial stereotypes were also a subject of examination and critique. Lorna Simpson's work combined words and photographs to show how simple gestures and aspects

of appearance are taken to indicate an individual's personality. In *Stereo Styles* (Fig. 23.11), two rows of figures with different hairstyles face away from the camera. In the center, words such as "daring" and "sensible" seem to invite the viewer to sum up the sitter's character in one word, as in a fill-in-the-blank test. Humor has also been frequently used to puncture simplistic assumptions. For example, London-born, Nigeria-raised Yinka Shonibare has

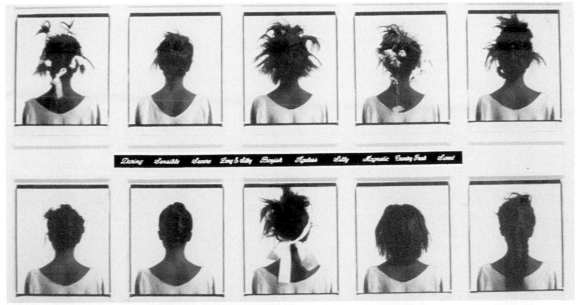

23.11 Lorna Simpson. *Stereo Styles,* 1988. Ten black and white Polaroid prints and ten engraved plaques, 5′4″ × 9′8″ overall. Collection of Raymond J. Learsy, Sharon, Connecticut.

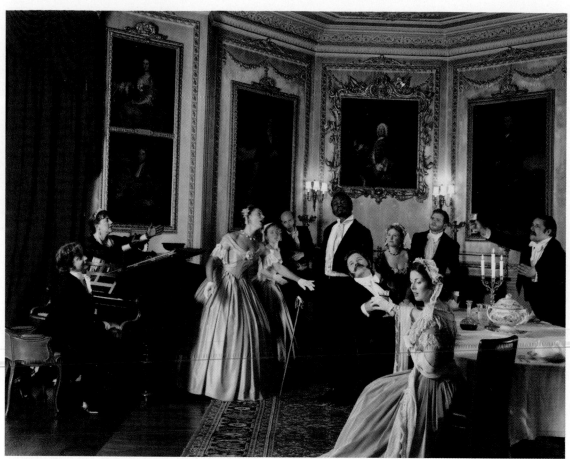

23.12   Yinka Shonibare. *Diary of a Victorian Dandy: 19.00 hours,* 1998. C-type print, 6′ × 7′½″. Edition 1 of 3. Commissioned by inIVA.

posed himself in settings that recall eighteenth-century paintings of well-to-do house parties (Fig. 23.12). But instead of acting the role of servant, as a black person would in centuries past (see, for example, Fig. 16.16), he is an honored and sought-after guest.

NEW ART MEDIA

During the late 1960s and the 1970s, artists began to explore the possibilities of video as a means to move away from traditional art media. Early videos reflected the interests of the time. The gradual rejection of Minimalism in favor of subject and narrative encouraged artists like Nam June Paik and Bruce Nauman to perform for the camera. Paik soon began using television sets as the basic material for his sculpture, stacking them like cubes and rewiring them to show odd and disturbing images. In addition, Dara Birnbaum's compilation of clips appropriated from the *Wonder Woman* television series subverted the pop sexuality of the show and made it an anthem of feminism.

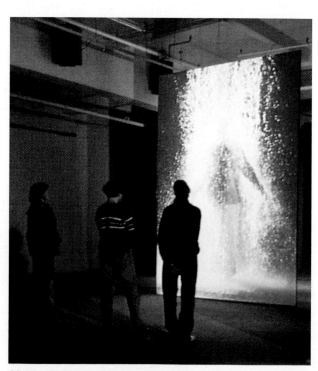

23.13   Bill Viola. *The Crossing,* 1996. Installation with two channels of color video projection onto 16′-high screens.

Video became part of performance and installation art during the 1980s. Through the use of sophisticated technology, the once crude and jumpy images became lush and smooth. Artists were able to control color and make it more expressive. At the same time, technological advances allowed them to create interactive works. Bill Viola's video installations dwell on the natural environment. Using large screens and simultaneous projection of images, Viola surrounds his viewer with opulent visual effects reminiscent of baroque art (Fig. 23.13). Other artists, such as Tony Oursler, remain concerned with the mind-altering consequences of mass media. Oursler's videos project his trademark large heads and huge eyes onto unusual "screens," such as spheres scattered around the gallery.

Although art video never achieved the pervasive presence of popular films, it has been integrated into galleries and museums. Moreover, the Hollywood-like production values of Matthew Barney's (Fig. 23.14) *Cremaster* films, which feature the artist in vivid guises as he and his characters enact ambiguous scenes in a complex mythology of the future, draw new art audiences into museums and movie houses for special showings. Indeed, other artists such as Cindy Sherman and Julian Schnabel have made big-budget films.

Without a doubt, the most influential art medium to emerge in the last part of the twentieth century was the computer, with its link to the World

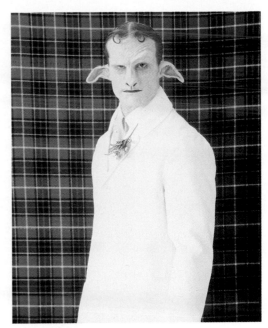

23.14   Matthew Barney. *Cremaster 4,* 1994. Production still. Courtesy Barbara Gladstone Gallery.

Wide Web. Two digital-imaging pioneers, Suzanne Bloom and Ed Hill, who work together under the name MANUAL, greeted the computer as a device that promised to jolt humanity forward into a new age. For an installation called *Community Forest* they created a series of photographs that merged nature with geometric forms (Fig. 23.15). The show

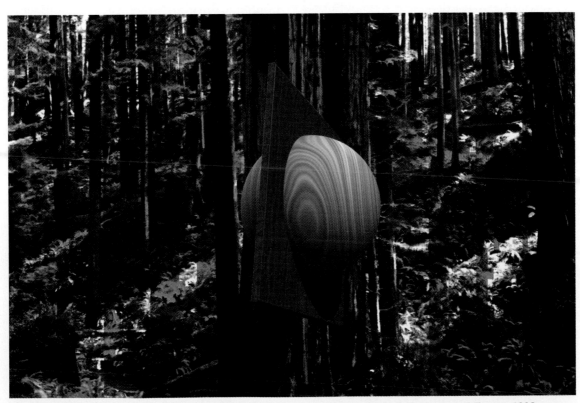

23.15   MANUAL (Ed Hill and Suzanne Bloom). *Community Forest,* from *A Constructed Forest, 1993.*

23.16 Pedro Meyer. *The Temptation of the Angel,* 1991. Digital color print. California Museum of Photography, Riverside, California.

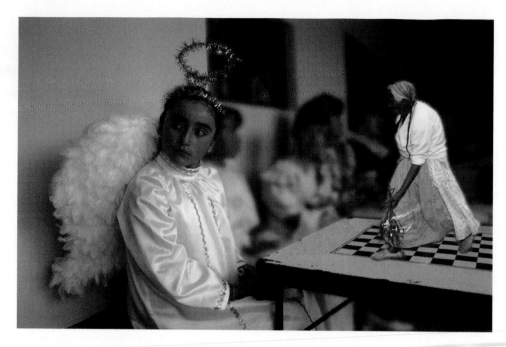

borrowed Lissitzky's enthusiasm for progressive social change brought about by engineering (see pp. 577–578).

Digital imaging means many things to different artists. For Pedro Meyer, it is a device that allows him to convincingly join the past and the present, as well as the mythological and the real (Fig. 23.16). Other artists, however, use digital media to point out that blind faith in the digital future is as misplaced and ominous as the earlier twentieth-century trust in nuclear power and space travel. To underscore the dangers of digital media, Aziz & Cucher created large

digital portraits of people whose eyes, mouths, and ears have been sealed with "digital skin" (Fig. 23.17). For these creatures, the computer did not amplify their experiences but diminished their senses, and consequently their minds.

ARCHITECTURE

Contemporary architecture reaches beyond the functional efficiency of the International Style, with its steel-and-glass, high-rise boxes on stilts

PAST AND PRESENT

The Threat and Promise of Computers

In 1982, an issue of *National Geographic* featured a picture of the Egyptian pyramids in which these mighty buildings had been digitally moved closer together. The pictures became the focus of mounting public fear about the capacity of computer-enhanced pictures to tell lies. To some, it seemed that the objectivity of photographs and the public's right to know was being threatened.

Today, some digital worries have faded into acceptance. The average drugstore photography counter now offers customers the capability to do what the *National Geographic* did: move figures, alter backgrounds, and change color.

Although digital art has been practiced since the 1970s, it is still in its infancy. Just as artists needed more than a century to fully explore the capacity of oil paints, so too will digital art require time to discover the computer's power. Together with related technologies, such as broadband transmission, digital technologies will continue to provoke varieties of angst and ardor. Some cultural critics accuse artists and musicians of rapidly abandoning the real and desensitizing humans from the direct perception of nature. Others express the hope that digital technologies will bring closer the old dream of democratizing arts, that is, creating the means by which more people can see and hear the art of the past and even create their own art and music.

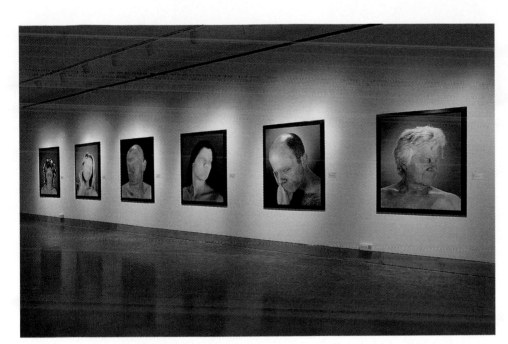

23.17 Aziz & Cucher. *Dystopia* series, 1994. Digital prints. View of Installation, Ansel Adams Center, San Francisco.

and glazed-in shopping malls. The Modernist movement in architecture was to have brought about a utopian future, but it disregarded human and environmental concerns, often yielding sterile, repetitive, and dehumanized buildings.

Contemporary architects gratefully use the technological breakthroughs that accompanied Modernism, but they add color, decoration, and sculptural and painterly embellishments to give their structures special meaning and identity. They have once again entered into partnerships with painters, sculptors, and mosaicists. Well-placed sculptural groups, frescoes, or mosaics create points of interest in a design, define exteriors and interiors, and serve as symbols of human involvement.

An early example of the new approach is New York's AT&T building, designed by Philip Johnson and John Burgee (Fig. 23.18). Nicknamed the "Chippendale skyscraper," it is crowned by a split-level cornice that visually alludes to a typical design frequently used by the eighteenth-century furniture designer Thomas Chippendale. The building departs from impersonal functionalism, displaying a human touch with its resemblance to a huge grandfather clock.

Architect Robert Venturi wrote several influential books, such as *Complexity and Contradiction in Architecture, Learning from Las Vegas,* and *Learning from Levittown,* in which he declared that vernacular architecture holds the key to making buildings that people want and like. He studied highway strip malls and subdivi

sions to learn why and how their popular features functioned in a real environment. Working with John Rauch and Denise Scott Brown, Venturi dismissed functionalism and introduced humor and history. In the group's design for a country house, they merged modern windows with witty

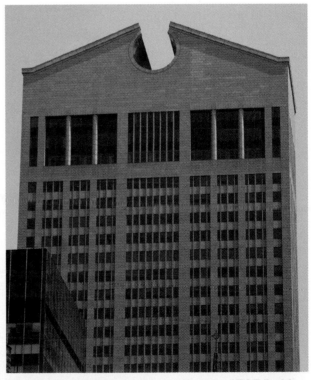

23.18 Philip Johnson and John Burgee. AT&T Building pediment, Madison Avenue, New York, 1973–1984.

23.19   Robert Venturi, John Rauch, and Denise Scott Brown. House in Delaware (west elevation), 1978–1983.

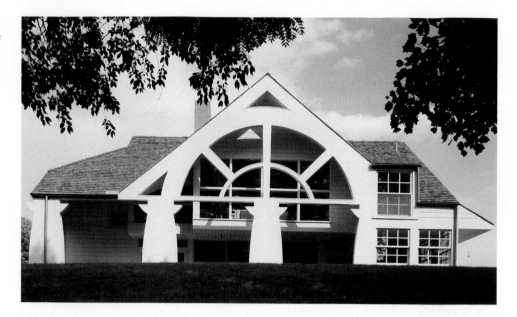

cut-out columns and arches and added a low cottage roof (Fig. 23.19).

For a public office building in Portland, Oregon, Michael Graves created an arresting design (Fig. 23.20). Reacting to the repetitive glass, concrete, and steel box structures that dominate modern city centers, Graves invents buildings that contain architectural allusions and spatial symbolism. The Portland structure delights the sophisticated taste without losing the common touch. In a cumulative historical synthesis, the massive bright red pilasters and central keystone recall ancient Rome, whereas the fiberglass garlands allude to art deco. The skyscraper silhouette is derived from the International Style. The original design was to have included a huge statue of Portlandia, an invented neo-Roman goddess signifying civic aspirations. The general effect of the whole complex is of a piece of gigantic collage sculpture, yet it has all the stately grace and monumentality of an ancient temple.

23.20   Michael Graves. Portland Public Service Building, Portland, Oregon, 1980.

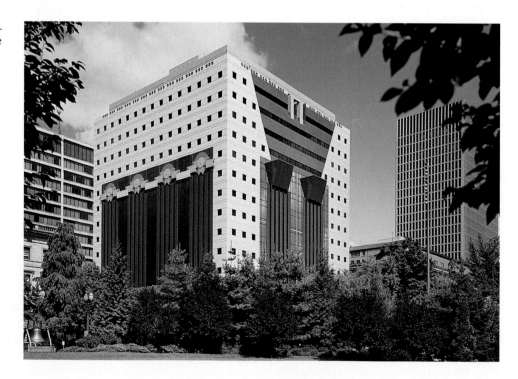

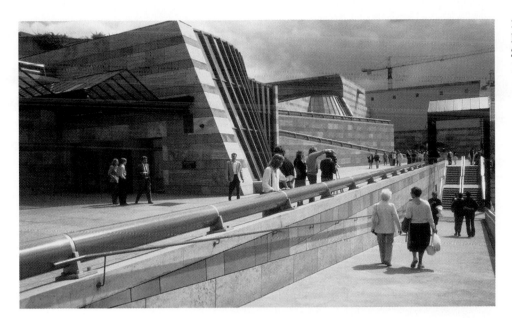

23.21 James Stirling. Neue Staatsgalerie, Stuttgart, Germany, 1977–1984.

DECONSTRUCTIVIST ARCHITECTURE

Architects such as Frank Gehry, James Stirling, and Zaha Hadid launched a strong rebellion against functionalism, unity, and uniformity in favor of freedom and diversity. Stirling's design for a new museum in Stuttgart, Germany, mixes manufactured color, such as the pink of the railing, with the natural colors and textures of stone (Fig. 23.21). As visitors walk toward the arched entryway, the angled brownstone insert on their left creates the illusion that they are descending while actually walking on level ground. Other tilted sections of the structure also serve to disorient viewers and encourage them to look at the museum in a new way. Meanwhile, the multiple ramped sections of the building indirectly refer to the graded ramps of ziggurats (see Fig. 1.8) and other ceremonial pathways typical of ancient architecture.

Frank Gehry designed the Guggenheim Museum in Bilbao, Spain, as a work of abstract sculpture on a large scale (Fig. 23.22). Its metal-plated walls curve and sway; its atrium glass window tilts inward and sideways. Like the surface of a polished metal sculpture, the Guggenheim's "skin" reflects the sun, creating the

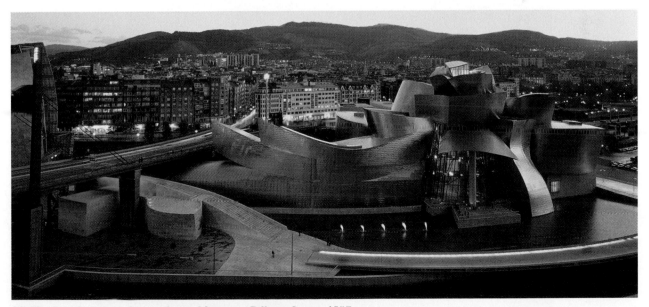

23.22   Frank Gehry. Guggenheim Museum, Bilbao, Spain, 1997.

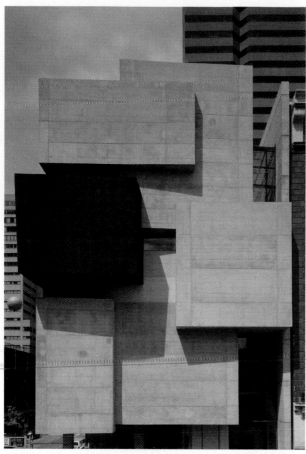

23.23 Zaha Hadid. Cincinnati Art Center, Cincinnati, Ohio.

appearance of moving asymmetrical masses. The building presents itself as an odd, living organism whose pulse is regulated by nature's lights and shadows. Zaha Hadid's design for the Contemporary Arts Center in Cinncinnati, Ohio (Fig. 23.23) also mirrors and models light like a large sculpture. Blocks of space, stacked each upon the other, define the interior galleries. Hadid's major influences came from the philosophy of the Russian Constructivists, who combined pure geometric form with the notion of functionalism (see pp. 577–578).

Light and lightness emerged as strong visual themes in contemporary architecture. The bridges designed by Spanish architect and engineer Santiago Calatrava, such as those in Bilbao, Jerusalem, and Rome, echo Brancusi's interest in soaring flight, indicated through abstractions of birds' wings and bodies (see Fig. 20.7). Calatrava's design for a new transportation hub near the World Trade Center site (Fig. 23.24) has been widely praised for the way in which it symbolizes hope through its lofty reach and its structural openness, which let natural light penetrate down into the underground subway station.

While Calatrava's design was widely applauded, proposals for rebuilding at the World Trade Center site were not. Some thought that the entire site should be left as a memorial to those who perished; others believed that the Twin Towers should be re-

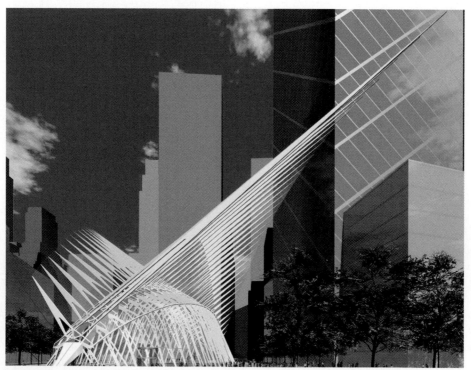

23.24 Santiago Calatrava. Design of transportation hub near World Trade Center site, 2004. Wing height, 150′.

built exactly as they were as a sign of defiance against terrorism. The master plan for the site, conceived by architect Daniel Libeskind, who designed the Jewish Museum in Berlin, Germany, includes an office building called Freedom Tower. Under the direction of architect David Childs, Freedom Tower will reach a symbolic height of 1776 feet and will be capped by a spire whose offset position echoes the upraised arm of the Statue of Liberty. A competition held to design a separate memorial that recognizes each of the nearly 3,000 people who died at the site was won by Michael Arad. His plan, called "Reflecting Absence," calls for two pools of water surrounded by scattered tall pine trees.

MUSIC

Like architects and visual artists, today's composers draw on a rich historical palette ranging from strict or modified serialism to aleatory chance music, traditional modes of harmony and counterpoint, and non-Western musical systems. They routinely draw on popular musical genres and use electronic instruments to make and mix their music. In like fashion, rock musicians feel free to draw on the classical heritage.

In the last decade of the twentieth century, a wide range of musical styles mirrored the diversity of the visual arts. A new generation of composers revisited the classical traditions that had long entertained and enlightened audiences. Some returned to more traditional tonality and harmony, and a sense of history once again permeated much contemporary music. For example, Ellen Taafe Zwilich reexamined baroque orchestral practice in her *Concerto Grosso 1985* for violin and orchestra. Subtitled *To Handel's Sonata in D,* it includes subject matter from that violin sonata. Similarly, John Corigliano's *Fancy on a Bach Air* (1996) for cello solo recalls the theme from Bach's "Goldberg" Variations as well as his suites for solo cello. Britain's Thomas Adès mixed recollections of baroque music-room elegance with the bristly harmonies often found in contemporary chamber music in his *Sonata da Caccia* (1994).

Two dramatic theater works of the 1990s were commissioned by New York's Metropolitan Opera: Philip Glass's *Voyage* and John Corigliano's *The Ghosts of Versailles.* In both operas, history is intertwined with imaginary elements. *Voyage,* inspired by Doris Lessing's sophisticated science fiction, is a parable about the force that drives people to travel and explore and the cultural conflicts that occur as a result. In the first act, an alien spacecraft lands on Earth during the last ice age; in the

second, Columbus makes contact with the New World; and in the third, a projection shows earthlings departing in quest of new life somewhere in outer space.

Corigliano, writing in traditional harmonic, vocal, and orchestral language, chose for his hero the French eighteenth-century playwright Pierre-Augustin Beaumarchais, whose plays, such as *The Marriage of Figaro,* formed the basis for the librettos of operas by Wolfgang Amadeus Mozart and Gioacchino Rossini. The work contains three interacting atmospheres: one of ghosts, one of the theater, and one of history. The spirit characters of Beaumarchais, Marie Antoinette, and Figaro interact while the music courses through parodies of eighteenth-century historical styles, twelve-tone serialism, and nineteenth-century Romantic sentimentality.

THE AFTERMATH OF WAR AND CONCERN FOR HUMANITY

After World War II a large number of antinuclear and antiwar compositions appeared. Polish composer Krzysztof Penderecki symbolized the devastation caused by the atomic bombs dropped on Hiroshima and Nagasaki in *Tren* (*Threnody "For the Victims of Hiroshima,"* 1960), for fifty-two stringed instruments. The American composer Nancy Van de Vate wrote an antiwar opera, *All Quiet on the Western Front* (1998), based on the novel by Erich Maria Remarque (see p. 581). The Russian composer Alfred Schnittke produced the orchestral *Ritual* (1985), both to mark the liberation of Belgrade at the end of World War II and to memorialize the victims of that war. Schnittke also joined thirteen other composers representing countries that had been on opposite sides of the war, including the American John Harbison, the Italian Luciano Berio, and the Pole Krzysztof Penderecki, to collaborate on the *Requiem for Reconciliation,* commissioned by the German conductor Helmut Rilling.

Disasters other than war were also commemorated in musical works. Nancy Van de Vate's searing *Chernobyl* (1987), for a large orchestra, recalled the Russian nuclear catastrophe and its aftermath by means of tone clusters, strong percussive passages, and a motif of mourning. Her *Katyn* (1989), scored for large choral and orchestral forces, memorialized the Polish victims executed by Soviet forces during World War II. The AIDS epidemic sparked compositions reflecting sadness and loss, among them John Corigliano's *Symphony No. 1* (1989), one movement of which is entitled "Of Rage and Remembrance."

Serious concerns about the environment and the future of the planet brought reactions from a number of quarters. One effective commentary was the film *Koyaanisqatsi* (1982), directed by Godfrey Reggio and featuring a sensitive score by Philip Glass. The title is from a Hopi expression that can be translated as "life out of balance." The film moves wordlessly from Hopi cave paintings to a vast panorama of magnificently photographed, pristine landscapes. Earth-digging machines signal the appearance of human intervention, followed by mining explosions, electric-line complexes, war machines, atomic bombs, and rockets soaring into space. The film then plunges into fast-forward, with cityscapes containing mobs of people and vast numbers of cars, buildings torn down, and mass production and consumption. The music suddenly becomes subdued as we are made aware of the destitute and outcasts of society. In the end, a space rocket blows up and the film returns to its beginning, with Hopi cave images.

More recently, in response to the events of September 11, 2001, John Adams composed *On the Transmigration of Souls* for orchestra and chorus, a work he describes as neither a memorial nor a requiem but a "memory space . . . a place where you can go and be alone with your thoughts and emotions." The text contains quotations from memorials and missing-persons notices posted at and near the World Trade Center, and tape recordings sporadically recite lists of names of the dead, sounds of New York streets, a siren, and the sound of footsteps. Perhaps because music is more ephemeral than architecture, Adams's composition was not received with the heated debate that greeted the plans for the new buildings and memorial to be constructed on the Twin Towers' site. It has proved difficult to envision a comprehensive design that functions symbolically as a sign of loss yet affirms the value of life and the continuation of history.

Pop Go the Classics

During the last decades of the twentieth century, the interaction between classical and popular musical idioms increased. American Michael Daugherty is one of the many composers who strove to revitalize the former with infusions of the latter. Born in Iowa and classically trained in both the United States and Europe, Daugherty has embraced popular icons from across the art world for his often witty, tongue-in-cheek compositions. The chamber work *Dead Elvis* (1993) offers a set of variations on the opening phrase of the medieval sequence *Dies irae* (see p. 231). It gives a promi-

nent role to the bassoonist, who is dressed as an Elvis impersonator, and includes a sly reference to the song *It's Now or Never,* made popular by Presley in the 1960s.

Daugherty's fascination with celebrity continued in the opera *Jackie O* (1997), "in which the events are based on history but are largely imaginary or metaphorical." It imagines the period during which Jacqueline Kennedy reemerged after a period of mourning for her husband and married the Greek shipping tycoon Aristotle Onassis. As with Daugherty's other compositions, the opera is based on traditional tonality and combines popular music idioms with, in this case, traditional operatic practice. The cast of characters is peppered with celebrities: actresses Elizabeth Taylor and Grace Kelly, opera diva Maria Callas, and pop artist Andy Warhol. The lines between the reality of history and the events of the opera are purposely blurred in this part-Broadway musical, part-serious opera.

Mixing Media

The late twentieth-century explosion of technology that affected all the arts opened the potential for combining multiple artistic disciplines. The overlapping of visual, audio, computer, and sampling devices helped bridge the gap between older and younger generations of musicians and widened the experience of the arts for both.

One such multimedia "event" was the product of Steve Reich and his wife, videographer Beryl Korot. Concerned about the Israeli–Arab conflict in the postwar world and wishing to find a venue that might help surmount obstacles between Jewish, Muslim, and Christian points of view, Reich and Korot turned to the Old Testament account of Abraham, Sarah, Hagar, Ishmael, and Isaac. The result was *The Cave* (1993), a documentary video opera in three acts. The title refers to the Cave of Machpelah in the city of Hebron, where the biblical brothers Isaac and Ishmael were reunited to bury their father, Abraham.

Each of the three acts features interviews with Israelis, Palestinians, and Americans. Each interviewee was asked to comment on the importance to them of the various Old Testament figures, and their answers were videotaped and projected onto large screens, with Jewish and Islamic sacred texts interpolated and musical commentary provided by a vocal quartet and a chamber ensemble of strings, winds, percussion, piano, sampler, and computer keyboard.

Since the late 1970s, Philip Glass has been involved with film. In the early 1990s, he began to approach film not as a medium complete in itself but as the basis for constructing larger musical works. One such project involved the French poet, writer, artist, and filmmaker Jean Cocteau. In 1994, Glass wrote a new score for Cocteau's 1946 film *Belle et la Bête (Beauty and the Beast)*, creating vocal parts out of the film's dialog. The film is shown without sound on a screen behind the performers, who sing the dialogue while instrumentalists play the background music.

In 1991, Glass wrote a new score for the 1931 horror film classic *Dracula*, using the medium of the string quartet. In its original version, music plays a minimal role in the film. In Glass's version, music is present throughout, weaving a transparent web of darkness underlying the grim drama. All this can be experienced in the home today through DVD, which allows the viewer to watch the film as it originally appeared or with the new Glass score.

MUSIC AS INTERNATIONAL COMMUNICATION

In the early twenty-first century, music has acquired a true global perspective. For example, Helmut Rilling, director of the German Bach Academy, commissioned Passion settings of each of the four gospels by four different composers to commemorate the 250th anniversary of the death of Johann Sebastian Bach. The Passion setting of St. Matthew was carried out by the Chinese composer Tan Dun, that of St. Luke by the German Wolfgang Rihm, that of St. John by the Russian Sofia Gubaidulina, and that of St. Mark by the Argentinian Osvaldo Golijov.

Although all four composers brought strong personal and national elements to their settings, the most international approach was that of Golijov in his *La Pasión Según San Marcós (The Passion According to St. Mark)*. Brought up in a Roman Catholic country by parents who represented the opposing religious views of atheism and Orthodox Judaism, Golijov was well qualified to bring an ecumenical approach to the traditional musical setting of the final days of Christ. He asked the questions, "How would Jesus live and act in Latin America?" and "How would Bach compose a Passion if he lived in South America at the end of the twentieth century?"

Golijov's work consciously avoids the traditional European approach to Passion settings, in which Biblical texts form the basis for meditative commentary and dramatic episodes. As he explained, "Our way of entering the story, instead of stopping everything and putting in an aria like Bach, is dancing. Latin America is a place where things are danced and acted; it's a violent place, very different from the Germany of Bach where people could sit at a table and meditate."

The main language of Golijov's Passion is Spanish, with additional phrases in Hebrew and Aramaic; the music is an intoxicating mixture of South American, Cuban, Spanish, and African rhythms, arias, folk songs, and hymns. In addition to more traditional instruments (trumpet, trombone, double bass), guitars, accordions, and a wide variety of Brazilian percussion are joined by Afro-Cuban dancers, two female soloists (one a jazz singer), and a large choral group.

In contrast to the European classical tradition, individual characters are not assigned to specific singers. Golijov envisioned "a dark Jesus . . . not a pale European Jesus," and wrote his text so that "most of the time the voice of Jesus would be the choir, because for me Jesus represents the people transformed into a collective spirit. At other times, his voice will be the male soloist and sometimes the female soloist." For example, in the section set in the Garden of Gethsemane, titled "Agony," Jesus leaves the disciples below as he moves away to pray that his death may be postponed. His words, pleading and deeply expressive, are sung alternately by the soprano and the chorus to an accompaniment of accordion and guitars.

Golijov admits to a variety of European influences, from Monteverdi to Rembrandt to Stravinsky, but in *The Passion According to St. Mark*, he acknowledges that the musical impetus comes from the wider world. His compositional goal is "that instrumentalists and singers and choirs in the world will realize that these types of expression are part of the nature of human music making. People will say, 'Hey, I have to sing that way, too.'"

IDEAS

POST-MODERNISM

Virtually all the works of art, music, and architecture discussed in this chapter have been labeled *postmodern*. At first glance, it is difficult to understand how the playful historical references in a Michael Graves building might relate to a critique of racial stereotyping such as that fashioned by Lorna Simpson. It is important to note that there is no postmodern "look," the way there was a shared rococo appearance in the visual arts. Post-Modernism simply means "after Modernism," and one problem in understanding it is that there have been several definitions of Modernism.

For historians, *modern* generally refers to the period during and since the Renaissance, but in art it is a collective term describing the major art movements from the middle of the nineteenth century to the 1970s. Over the long run, modern art seems to have become more and more concerned with pure form and less with subject matter. Within this framework one could say that modern art ended with Minimalism, as illustrated by Donald Judd's rectangular boxes (see p. 616), which compressed the difference between art and object.

Modern art mostly coincided with the shift in the Western world from an agriculture-based society to an urban industrial one. That momentous shift was accompanied by the growth of a middle class, whose tastes, rather than those of kings and the church, became central to commerce and to art. Modern social theory and modern art theory shared a belief in progress. In particular, modern art was understood to advance by means of a confrontational avant-garde whose role was to re-orient and refresh art. This artistic avant-garde had its parallels in the social vanguard and in science and technology, which also seemed to be continually refining and changing dominant ideas as well as producing a higher material standard of living.

One of the late twentieth century's most influential books was François Lyotard's dense, short 1979 text *The Postmodern Condition* (English translation 1984), which argued that what we perceive as post-Modernism is not a split from Modernism, but just its next stage. As part of this profound transformation, long-standing social rationales, such as progress, must decline so that they can be replaced by new unifying ideas.

Post-Modernism, then, covers several different tendencies, directions, and styles in late twentieth-century art and thought. Although it means "after Modernism," it usually implies an attitude set against some feature of Modernism. For example, where Modernism had been deliberately elitist and exclusive, post-Modernism was more populist and inclusive. It freely used images and motifs from popular culture and non-Western cultures, including those produced by mass media like film, photography, and television. In addition, postmodern art embraced contradictions by employing complexity and ambiguity, paradox and irony, cynicism and whimsy.

Although some post-Modernists, such as those who fashioned critiques of gender and racial bias, hoped to banish traces of the past, others looked forward and discarded only what they considered to be late Modernism's limited repertoire of tools and ideas. In either case, postmodern art placed more emphasis on recognizable content and a wealth of symbols and connotations. The postmodern interest in the world of optical experience included a new alliance with nature and a fresh reappraisal of the human form. Post-Modernism liberated artists from Modernism's pure utility and abstraction and allowed them to again explore the illusion of three dimensions on canvas, with the camera, or on screen.

During the postmodern era, architects, artists, writers, and musicians reasserted history's role to provide a sense of human continuity and a context for meaning. In addition, stylistic pluralism emerged as a reflection of a pluralistic society and a world of global connections and influences.

THE PASSING OF POST-MODERNISM

Post-Modernism was a fleeting connection of different art trends, all of which attempted to break the hold of Modernist art. Like a juggler who has too many balls in the air, its balance and momentum could not hold. Critics began to forecast its demise during the 1980s, suggesting that its critical force was being diluted by fashion and what was then a thriving art market. In the end, post-Modernism became another art-historical moment, the very thing that it was initially set against. On the other hand, it left its mark on art at the dawn of the new millennium. The displacement of modern art and its certitudes has left a healthy residue of relativism and a thriving interest in art outside the Western world.

GLOBALISM

The long-term, worldwide convergence of political systems, integration of economic networks, and combination of cultural creations has accelerated rapidly during the last two centuries. Today, with the speed of jet travel, major cities around the world are only hours away from one another. Electronic impulses and satellite relays transmit thoughts in fractions of a second. Such unprecedented closeness has encouraged a transnational or global perspective at the same time that cultural differences and ethnic origins play a crucial role in world politics.

Art, of course, has been affected by globalization. World music, a blend of Caribbean, African, and other local music styles, is heard around the planet. Biennial art exhibitions, once the province of Western culture, now have an international reach and take place in sites across the globe. In addition, global issues have been taken up by artists. For example, photographer Sebastião Salgado roams the world, recording the conditions under which poor workers suffer. He also pictures current, large migrations brought on by unemployment, food shortages, and changing climate

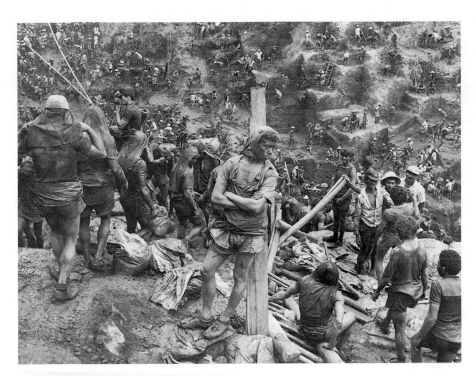

23.25 Sebastião Salgado. *Serra Pelada, Brazil,* from his book, *An Uncertain Grace,* 1990.

conditions. Perhaps his best-known images are those that chronicle the backbreaking labor of gold miners in Brazil (Fig. 23.25).

Global warming is an international problem to which artists have responded in various ways. Some, like Andy Goldsworthy, create objects of natural materials and then allow them to decay, underscoring natural cycles and the fragility of the natural world. Others, like Robert ParkeHarrison and Wolfgang Laib, have returned to the ancient role of artist-shaman, creating mystical rituals to heal nature. Laib uses natural materials and brings non-Western views of nature to bear on his efforts. In particular, he works with pollen, underscoring nature's fecundity and fragility in arrangements of the yellow powder that are so delicate that they can be destroyed by a light breeze, or even a human breath (Fig. 23.26).

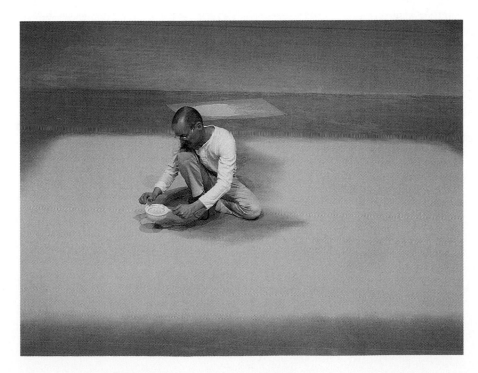

23.26 Wolfgang Laib. Installing *Pollen from Hazelnut, 1992,* 11′5¾″ × 13′1½″. Courtesy Sperone Westwater, New York.

ART AND IDEAS IN THE NEW MILLENNIUM

As more and more precise scientific instruments and theories have been produced, more and more uncertainties have appeared. Quantum physics has demonstrated that there can be no absolute knowledge. As a result, theoretical physics and mathematics have become increasingly philosophically oriented and open to new ideas.

The modern movement in art had been geared to the idea of scientific objectivity, invention, and progress—not only an increase in knowledge but also scientifically driven social change. Like science, modern art was experimental, concerned as it was with the invention of new facets and forms. Impressionists had been preoccupied with the science of optics, Cubists with dynamic geometry and Einsteinian relativity, and Surrealists with Freudian psychological discoveries. The Minimalists delved into the methods and materials of the industrial world. In short, the Modernist quest was for purity, predictability, and the clarity of an ordered world. The high point of Modernism coincided with the era of space exploration and the lunar landing.

Astronomers theorized that the galaxies surrounding the Earth had been produced by one or more cosmic explosions that yielded our solar system as a mere by-product. Similarly, biochemists speculated that life is the result of one or more biological accidents. Postmodern artists and composers understood that in spite of computer technology, real life defies the precision of mathematical calculations.

At the twentieth century's end, technology and greed led to pollution of the Earth's atmosphere and depletion of its natural resources. Space was rapidly becoming a junkyard and an arsenal. Globally, there was an ever-widening breach between rich and poor, and in parts of the world the population explosion continued unabated. In addition, civil war and political terrorism were frequently in the headlines.

At the dawn of the twenty-first century, Western art ranged from that made by artist-shamans with perishable natural materials, through the traditional art media, to works created with cutting-edge computers and other scientific instruments. In the past, this division would have been viewed as a split between the developed and the developing world. One might think that a threatening present would defeat art at its roots, chilling the urge to make art as well as the audience's interest in listening and looking. But the availability of art in the Western world has grown and so have audiences. New museums, themselves works of art, have appeared, and gallery and concert attendance has increased. More people make a living making art than ever before in history. In addition, much of the world's art is available from virtual sources, such as books, videos, and, of course, the World Wide Web. In a sense, all art has become contemporary, and contemporary people can move easily from a postmodern building to the Parthenon. Likewise, recordings have made the world's historical and contemporary music widely available. The outlines of the past, present, and future have become blurred. The old is new and the new is ever new.

Humans look to art as evidence of humanity's creative power in the face of inexhaustible chaos. If any message comes through the mists and mazes of history, it is that we should never underestimate the power and creative force of the human mind and heart. The challenge remains to the artist, scientist, and philosopher to envision the invisible and to comprehend the incomprehensible.

YOUR RESOURCES

- **Web Site**

  http://art.wadsworth.com/fleming10

  ○ Chapter 23 Quiz

- **Audio CD**

  ○ Daugherty, *Dead Elvis*

  ○ Golijov, *Passion According to St. Mark*

LATE TWENTIETH CENTURY

Key Events	Architecture and Visual Arts	Literature and Music
1961 **Berlin Wall** constructed	1901–1974 **Louis I. Kahn** ★	1889–1951 **Ludwig Wittgenstein** ◆
1962 **Second Vatican Council** opened in Rome	1903–1972 **Joseph Cornell** ●	1900–1990 **Aaron Copland** ❑
1965 **National Endowment for Arts and Humanities** established	1914–1988 **Romare Bearden** ▲	1901–1981 **Jacques Lacan** ◆
1969 **U.S. astronauts** landed on moon	1925– **Robert Venturi** ★	1905–1980 **Jean-Paul Sartre** ◆
1974 **Mariner** photographed Venus	1926–1992 **James Stirling** ★	1906–1989 **Samuel Beckett** ◆
1976 **U.S. Episcopal churches** approved ordination of women as priests and bishops	1927– **Alfred Leslie** ▲	1910–1976 **Jacques Monod** ◆
1976 **Vikings I, II** explored Mars	1929– **Frank Gehry** ★	1918–1990 **Leonard Bernstein** ❑
1977 **First manned test flight** of U.S. space shuttle	1929– **Philip Pearlstein** ▲	1923– **Gyorgy Ligeti** ❑
1977 **Complete genetic structure** of living organism made	1930– **Denise Scott Brown** ★	1925–2003 **Luciano Berio** ❑
1979 **Voyager** explored Jupiter moons	1931– **Carlo Maria Mariani** ▲	1926–1984 **Michel Foucault** ◆
1980 **Electronic synthesizers** available to composers, performers	1932– **Richard Estes** ▲	1928– **Karlheinz Stockhausen** ❑
1980 **Facsimile (Fax) machines** extended electronic communication	1932– **Nam June Paik** ▲	1930– **Jacques Derrida** ◆
1981 **Voyager** explored Uranus, its rings, and its moons	1932– **Gerhard Richter** ▲	1931– **Sofia Gubaidulina** ❑
1989 **Voyager** explored Neptune and its moons	1934– **Michael Graves** ★	1932– **John Updike** ◆
1989 **Cold war** ended	1935– **Ed Hill (MANUAL)** ▲	1932– **Umberto Eco** ◆
1989 **Berlin Wall** torn down	1935– **Pedro Meyer** ▲	1933– **Krzysztof Penderecki** ❑
1992 **Soviet Union** dissolved	1935–1993 **Charles Moore** ★	1934– **Peter Maxwell Davies** ❑
1992 **Eastern European countries** freed from Soviet control	1937– **David Hockney** ▲	1934– **Alfred Schnittke** ❑
1992 **Earth Summit meeting** held in Rio de Janeiro; 178 countries represented	1939– **Judy Chicago (born Judy Cohen)** ▲	1935– **Terry Riley** ❑
1993 **Maastricht Treaty** ratifies the European Union	1940– **Chuck Close** ▲	1936– **Steve Reich** ❑
1994 **Church of England** approved ordaining women as priests	1941– **Thomas Hall Beeby** ★	1937– **David del Tredici** ❑
1995 **Dayton Peace Accords** end civil war in Bosnia	1941– **David Childs** ★	1937– **Philip Glass** ❑
1995 **World Trade Organization** established	1941– **Bruce Nauman** ▲	1938– **John Corigliano** ❑
1997 **Kyoto Protocol** proposes ways to minimize global warming	1943– **Suzanne Bloom (MANUAL)** ▲	1938– **John Harbison** ❑
2000 **Human DNA sequence** established	1943– **Annette Messager** ▲	1938– **Joyce Carol Oates** ◆
2001 **Attack on the World Trade Center** in New York and **Pentagon** in Washington, DC; **crash of United Airlines Flight 93** near Shanksville, Pennsylvania	1944– **Sebastião Salgado** ▲	1939– **Ellen Taafe Zwilich** ❑
2003 **United Nations authorizes sanctions** against Iraq	1944– **Bernard Tschumi** ★	1947– **John Adams** ❑
	1945– **Anselm Kiefer** ▲	1952– **Wolfgang Rihm** ❑
	1945– **Susan Rothenberg** ▲	1954– **Michael Daugherty** ❑
	1946– **Dara Birnbaum** ▲	1957– **Tan Dun** ❑
	1946– **Sandro Chia** ▲	1960– **Oswaldo Golijov** ❑
	1946– **Daniel Libeskind** ★	1971– **Thomas Adès** ❑
	1946–1989 **Robert Mapplethorpe** ▲	
	1949– **Richard Prince** ▲	
	1950– **Zaha Hadid** ★	
	1950– **Wolfgang Laib** ▲	
	1951– **Santiago Calatrava** ★	
	1951– **Julian Schnabel** ▲	
	1951– **Bill Viola** ▲	
	1953– **Carrie Mae Weems** ▲	
	1954– **Cindy Sherman** ▲	
	1958– **Sammy Cucher** ▲	
	1958–1990 **Keith Haring** ▲	
	1960– **Lorna Simpson** ▲	
	1961– **Anthony Aziz** ▲	
	1962– **Yinka Shonibare** ▲	
	1968– **Robert ParkeHarrison** ▲	
	1970– **Michael Arad** ★	
	1977– **Tony Oursler** ▲	

★ - Architect ❑ - Musician ▲ - Painter, photographer, mixed media artist ● - Sculptor ◆ - Writer

GLOSSARY

abacus In an architectural column, the uppermost member of the capital; the slab upon which the architrave rests.

abstraction In the visual arts, the process of subordinating the real appearance of forms in nature to an aesthetic concept of form composed of shapes, lines, colors, values, etc. Also the process of analyzing, simplifying, and distilling the essence from nature and sense experience. See *nonrepresentational*.

a cappella Italian for "in chapel style." Choral music without instrumental accompaniment. The music supporting soloist or group of performers; music subordinate to the melody.

acro From the Greek meaning "high," as in *acropolis*, or "high city."

acropolis The upper, often fortified, hilltop of an ancient Greek town or city.

agora In ancient Greek cities, an open marketplace where the population could assemble and hold meetings.

aleatory From the Latin meaning "dice," a music that is uncontrolled or left to chance. Whatever the elements introduced by the composer, their arrangement is left to the performer or to circumstance.

ambulatory A covered passage for walking found around the apse or choir of a church, in a cloister, or along the peristyle of an ancient Greek temple.

amphitheater From the Greek meaning "two" or "both," plus theater. In Roman architecture, a round or oval building used for public events.

antiphony and antiphonal psalmody Music in which two or more groups of voices or instruments alternate with one another; *antiphonal psalmody* refers to verses sung alternately.

antiquarianism Concern with things old and rare.

apse A large nichelike space—usually semicircular in shape and domed or vaulted—projecting from and extending the interior space of such architectural forms as Roman and Christian basilicas. Most often found at the eastern end of a church nave and serving to house the high altar.

apsidal chapel Chapels created within apses.

arcade A series of arches supported by piers or columns; a passageway with an arched roof.

archetype A universal pattern or model.

architrave In post-and-lintel architecture, the lintel, or lowest, division of the entablature that rests directly on the capitals of columns.

archivolt The molding that frames an arch.

aria An elaborate solo song with instrumental accompaniment used usually in cantatas, oratorios, and operas. A da capo aria has the basic ternary form ABA. The first section (A) concludes on the tonic and is followed by the second section (B), which is contrasting in key and character. The singer then returns to the beginning (da capo), repeating the A section, usually with some improvisation. A *continuo aria* is an aria with continuo accompaniment.

ars perfecta Latin for "the perfect art." A name used to describe the music of Josquin Desprez and other fifteenth-century Flemish composers.

art deco A style of art and decoration from the 1920s. Uses flat shapes, curves, and geometric shapes.

assemblage The technique of creating three-dimensional works of art by combining a variety of elements, such as found objects, into a unified composition.

assonance In literature, the use of similar sounds or words.

atmospheric perspective See *perspective*.

atomism The belief that all elements in the universe are reducible to small, indivisible parts.

atonality A type of music in which no particular pitch serves as the tonic, or key, note.

atrium An open court constructed within or in relation to a building; found in Roman villas and in front of Christian churches built from late antiquity through Romanesque times.

auditorium In ancient Rome, a public meeting place often used for performances of music or drama.

aulos In ancient Greece, a flutelike instrument.

avant-garde Vanguard or advance guard; a term used to designate innovators whose experimental art challenges the values of the cultural establishment or even those of the immediately preceding avant-garde styles.

ayre, or air In music, a simple, often popular song.

background In pictorial arts, that part of the composition that appears to be behind forms represented as close to the view; the most distant of the three zones of recession in linear perspective.

ballata, or ballad A narrative song usually set to relatively simple music.

balustrade An architectural form that is a continuous row of abbreviated shafts (balusters) surmounted by a handrail to make a low fence.

barrel vault A vault, or room, whose upper portion is created in the shape of an arch.

basilica A rectangular-plan building, with an apse at one or both ends, originating in Roman secular architecture as a hall and early adopted as the form most suited to the needs of Christian architecture.

bay In architecture, the space defined at four corners by the principal upright structural members, with the character of the space usually established by the need to sustain aloft the great weight of a vault.

bestiary, or bestiaries A collection or collections of stories using animals as principle characters.

broken pediment A pediment in which the top part of the triangular structure has been omitted for decorative affect.

buttress, buttressing A support, usually an exterior projection of masonry or wood for a wall, arch, or vault, that opposes the lateral thrust of these structural members.

cadenza In music for solo voice or instrument, a free or florid passage inserted by the composer or improvised by the performer, usually toward the end of an aria or movement, whose purpose is to display the performer's technical brilliance.

camera obscura A device used since the Renaissance to aid drawing. Originally a room-sized structure, it was reduced in size in subsequent centuries. It consists of a box, a small lens opening, and a section of translucent glass upon which an image is cast by a mirror.

campanile In Italy, a bell tower, especially one that is freestanding, often next to but separate from a church building.

canon A body of principles, rules, standards, or norms; a criterion for establishing measure, scale, and proportion. In music, a type of strict imitative counterpoint, wherein the melody stated by one voice is imitated in its entirety by a second voice, which enters before the previous one has finished.

cantata Italian for music that is "sung," as opposed to music that is played, which in Italian goes by the term *sonata*. In the seventeenth-century sense of Bach, Scarlatti, and Handel, a multimovement composition for solo voices, chorus, and orchestra consisting of recitatives and arias for performance in church or chamber. Briefer than oratorio but, like oratorio, differs from opera in being mainly nontheatrical.

cantilever In architecture, a lintel or beam that extends beyond its supports.

cantus firmus Latin for "fixed song," a preexisting melody that medieval and Renaissance composers used as the basis for polyphonic pieces in which they added new melodies above and/or below the cantus firmus.

capital The upper member of a column, serving as transition from shaft to lintel or architrave.

cartoon A full-scale preparatory drawing for a pictorial composition, usually a large one such as a wall painting or a tapestry. Also a humorous drawing or caricature.

caryatid A sculptured female figure standing in the place of a column.

catacombs In ancient Rome, underground burial places.

cathedra An episcopal throne, or throne for a bishop; also known by its Latin name *sedes*, meaning "see."

cathedral The official church of a bishop containing his cathedra, or throne; a church that traditionally has been given monumental and magnificent architectural form.

cella An enclosed windowless chamber, the essential feature of a classical temple, in which the cult statue usually stood.

central plan In architecture, an organization in which spaces and structural elements are ordered around a central point.

chamber music Music for small groups.

chambre From the French for "room," it is used to define art, like chamber music, intended for small rooms rather than large auditoriums.

chanson de geste French for "song of heroic deeds"; an epic poem written in Old French during the eleventh to thirteenth centuries and designed to be performed by minstrels and jongleurs.

chant A single liturgical melody for voice or chorus that is monophonic, unaccompanied, and in free rhythm. Various types are Byzantine, Gregorian, Ambrosian, Milanese, Visigothic (Mozarabic), and Gallican.

chapelle, or chapel A small church or compartment within a church, castle, or palace containing an altar consecrated for ritual use.

chiaroscuro The art of modeling figures or objects in light and shade to achieve a three-dimensional effect on a two-dimensional surface.

choir An organized group of singers or instrumentalists of the same class. In church architecture, the complex at the east end beyond the crossing, which could include apse, ambulatory, and radiating chapels.

choleric In medieval and subsequent theories of alchemy, an irritable human disposition.

choral That having to do with chorus.

chorale A hymn tune introduced in the German Protestant church by Martin Luther, who frequently wrote the texts and sometimes the melodies.

chord Any combination of three or more tones sounded simultaneously.

chori spezzati From the Italian, meaning broken choruses. In Venetian music, the practice of placing choruses in different parts of a building to create an echo effect.

chorus In ancient Greek drama, a group of singers and dancers commenting on the main action. In modern times, a choir or group of singers organized to perform in concert with one another. Music composed for such a group.

chromaticism Raised or lowered notes introduced into diatonic music, or used instead of the normal diatonic degrees of the scale, are called chromatic notes; chords involving their use are chromatic chords; harmony saturated with chromatic chords is chromatic harmony; and music overgrown with chromaticism is chromatic music. The chromatic scale is a twelve-note scale dividing the octave into twelve half-tone intervals—the seven diatonic tones plus the five altered degrees, as C, C-sharp, D, D-sharp, E, F, F-sharp, G, G-sharp, A, A-sharp, and B.

cithara In ancient Greece, a musical instrument similar to a lyre.

citharoedus A musician who plays a cithara while singing.

churrigueresque An ornate Spanish baroque style named for José de Churriguera.

clerestory A row of windows in the upper part of a wall; also, in church architecture, the upper portion of the interior walls pierced by windows for the admission of light.

cloister A monastic establishment; more particularly, a covered passage, usually arcaded, at the side of or surrounding a courtyard within a monastery.

coda Italian for "tail"; a section at the end of a movement of a composition that serves as a "summing up" by using previously heard thematic material. A short coda is often known as a codetta.

coffer In architecture, a recessed panel in a ceiling. Coffering can lighten both the actual and apparent weight of a massive ceiling and provide a decorative effect.

collage From "papiers collés," French for "pasted papers"; a composition deriving from Cubism and made by pasting together on a flat surface such originally unrelated materials as bits of newspaper, wallpaper, cloth, cigarette packages, and printed photographs.

colonnade A row of columns usually spanned or connected by lintels.

colonnette A small column that serves both a decorative and structural function.

column A cylindrical post or support that often has three distinct parts: base, shaft, and capital.

comedy A light and amusing play or other literary work whose purpose is to arouse laughter in the beholder.

composite A classical order of temple architecture combining elements from Ionic and Corinthian orders, as the acanthus leaf motif of the Corinthian order topped by the volutes of the Ionic.

composition An organization or arrangement imposed upon the component elements within an individual work of art.

concertato In baroque music, the style of groups of instruments playing against each other.

concerto An instrumental composition featuring a soloist (violin, piano, cello, flute, etc.) pitted against a full orchestra and usually written in three movements.

concerto grosso An orchestral composition in which the instruments are divided into two contrasting tonal bodies: a large (ripieno, or grosso) and a small (concertino) ensemble.

concitato An instruction to a musician to play a section of music in an agitated manner.

connoisseurship A discriminating knowledge of the qualities of art works and their styles.

Constructivism A twentieth-century art movement that arose in Russia; it emphasized geometric shapes and urges the use of industrial materials.

continuo (basso continuo) A contrapuntal concept favored by baroque composers. It is a continuous bass line defined sharply enough to function as a clearly distinguishable level within the musical complex. The continuo bass line is commonly played on a keyboard instrument by the left hand while the right hand supplies filler parts improvisationally. Because numbers are often placed beneath the bass line to guide the player in realizing the filler parts, the continuo is also called figured bass. The continuo is a bass complex, so other bass instruments (lute, viola da gamba, cello, bassoon) usually supplement (or may substitute for) the keyboard.

contrapuntal The adjectival form of counterpoint.

contredanse, or **contredance** A dance in which the participants face each other, as in a square dance. Also the music for such a dance.

convention A formula, rule, or practice developed by artists to create a usage or mode that is individual to the artist yet communicable to the culture of which he or she partakes. Conventions exist in both form and subject matter, and they constitute the vocabulary and syntax of the artist's language.

Corinthian The classical order of temple architecture characterized by slender fluted columns topped by highly carved, ornate capitals whose decorative forms derive from the acanthus leaf.

cornice Any horizontal architectural member projecting from the top of a wall; in classical architecture, the crowning member of the entablature.

cornu A Roman instrument like a tuba.

corporation picture counterpoint The combination of two or more independent melodic lines into a single musical fabric; polyphony.

crescendo A continuous increase in loudness.

crossing In a cruciform church, the space formed by the intersection of nave and transept.

cross vault, or **cross vaulting** A vault composed of two tunnel vaults intersecting each other at right angles.

cruciform Arranged or shaped like a cross.

crypt A vaulted chamber wholly or partly underground; it usually houses a chapel and is found in a church under the choir.

cuneiform The wedge-shaped characters of ancient writing in Mesopotamia, Assyria, and Persia.

Cubism A twentieth-century art movement in which natural forms are reduced to geometric shapes and planes.

cuirass A piece of medieval armor that protected the body from the neck to the waist.

cupola A small structure on top of a building or dome, which houses bells, lights, or serves to provide a good view

da capo Italian for "from the beginning"; return to or repetition of the beginning.

da capo aria See *aria.*

Dada A post–World War I European art movement whose adherents emphasized nihilism.

daguerreotype An early form of photograph in which the image is produced on a silver-coated plate.

dance A rhythmic and patterned succession of bodily movements, usually performed to music.

deism A belief in God founded on rational sources rather than faith.

demos Greek for "people," in the sense of populace.

dentil, dentil range From the French for "small tooth"; one of a series of small decorative blocks projecting just below the cornice of an Ionic or Corinthian entablature.

deus ex machina Latin for "a god from a machine"; a device in ancient Greek and Roman drama whereby a god is introduced by means of a crane to solve a plot that has thickened to such an extent that human solutions are impossible. Figuratively, any sudden and contrived solution to what appears to be an impossible situation.

development See *sonata form.*

diakonikon Greek for a side chapel on the south side of a Byzantine church. Also known as a vestry.

diatonic The seven tones of a major (or minor) scale that correspond to the piano's white keys in an octave. Diatonic chords are chords built of diatonic notes; harmonies composed mainly of such chords are diatonic harmonies. The opposite of chromatic.

diminution Decreasing (usually halving) the note values of a phrase or section to achieve a quickening effect.

discantus (also **discant** and **descant**) A melody, often sung above a musical theme.

dissonance A discord or interval that creates a feeling of tension that demands resolution.

dome A hemispherical vault; theoretically, an arch rotated on its vertical axis.

Doric the oldest of the classical styles of temple architecture; characterized by simple, sturdy columns that rise without a base to an unornamented, cushionlike capital.

dramatis personae Actors or characters in a drama.

dramma giocosa Literally, "comic drama."

drawing A process of visualization by which an artist, using media such as pencil, chalk, or watercolor, delineates shapes and forms on a surface, typically paper or canvas.

drum or drums In architecture, a cylindrical component of a column; in music, a percussion instrument.

duplum The second voice part counting upward from the tenor or cantus firmus in medieval organum.

echinus The round cushionlike part of a Doric capital.

eclecticism The practice of selecting from various sources, usually to form a new system or style.

empirical, empiricism Based on experiments, observation, and practical experience without regard to theoretical conjecture.

engraving A form of printmaking in which grooves cut into a metal plate are filled with ink and the plate is pressed against absorbent paper after its surface has been wiped clean.

ensemble A group of two or more musicians performing the same composition.

entablature In architecture, that portion of a building between the capitals of the columns and the roof, including in classical architecture the architrave, frieze, cornices, and pediment.

entasis The slight convex curving of classical columns to correct the optical illusion of concavity, which would result if the sides were left straight.

epic poem A long narrative poem that tells the tale of a hero.

epilogue Greek for the closing section of a play or other work of art.

etching A form of printmaking in which a metal plate coated with an acid-resistant wax is scratched to expose the metal to the bite of the acid. Lines eaten into the plate by the acid are subsequently filled with ink and transferred to paper after the surface of the plate has been wiped clean of excess ink.

ethos Greek meaning "character." In art, that which gives a work tone or character and distinguishes it from other works. Also understood to mean the ideal or an ethical character.

evangelist One of the authors of the four Gospels in the Bible: Matthew, Mark, Luke, and John. Respectively, their symbols are an angel, a lion, an ox, and an eagle.

ex cathedra Literally, "from the bishop's chair." See *cathedra.*

exedra (pl. ***exedrae***) From the Greek meaning a recess in a wall or similar structure.

exodus A mass movement of people; in the Bible, the movement of the Israelites from Egypt under the direction of Moses.

exposition See *sonata form.*

expression Having to do with those factors of form and subject that together give the work of art its content and meaning.

Expressionism A late nineteenth- and early twentieth-century art movement that stressed the emotional content of an art work.

expressive content The fusion of form and subject that gives art its meaning and significance.

facade Usually the front of a building; also the other sides when they are emphasized architecturally.

fasces In Roman culture, a bundle of wood and an ax, used as a symbol of official power. Adopted by the French Revolutionaries at the end of the eighteenth century.

fauves Literally, "the wild beasts." A term used to describe early twentieth-century artists known for their vivid use of color.

fealty A medieval concept referring to a vassal's loyalty to a lord.

ferroconcrete A building material composed of concrete with rods or webs of iron or steel embedded in it. Also known as reinforced concrete.

finale The final movement of a large instrumental composition; in opera, the ensemble terminating an act.

flower painting As the term implies, the rendering of flowers. It became popular in the seventeenth century.

fluting Vertical channeling, concave in shape, used principally on columns and pilasters.

flying buttress A masonry support or segment of an arch that carries the thrust of a vault to a buttress positioned away from the main portion of the building; an important element of structure in the architecture of Gothic cathedrals.

foreground In the pictorial arts, that part of the composition that appears to be closest to the viewer. See *middle ground, background,* and *picture plane.*

foreshortening The effect of three-dimensionality made in two dimensions by basing representation on the principle of continuous decrease in size along the entire length of a form whose bulk is intended to be seen as receding in space.

French overture An introductory instrumental piece first used at the seventeenth-century French courts and characteristically in two sections: a slow stately march with dotted rhythms in duple meter and a livelier mood with fugal texture and triple meter.

fresco (pl. **frescoes**) A process of painting on wet or dry plaster wherein the pigments are mixed with water and become one with the plaster; a medium perfected during the Italian Renaissance.

frieze The central portion of the entablature between the architrave and the cornice; any horizontal decorative or sculptural band.

frottola A carnival song for dancing and singing.

Futurism An early twentieth-century art movement, originating in Italy, that stressed the dynamic quality of industry and machines.

fugal See *fugue.*

fugue A polyphonic composition characterized primarily by the imitative treatment of a single subject or subject complex.

gallery A long and narrow room or passage, such as that in the nave walls above the aisles of a church. See *triforium.*

genre, genre scene In the pictorial arts and sculpture, the casual representation of everyday life and surroundings. Also a type, style, or category of art.

Gesamtkunstwerk German for a "complete," "total," or "consummate work of art"; a term Richard Wagner coined in the late nineteenth century to characterize his music dramas, in which he brought about an alliance of all the arts—music, literature, theater, and the visual arts—to realize a program of ideas.

glaze In oil painting, a transparent film of paint laid over dried underpainting; in ceramics, a thin glassy coating fused to a clay body by firing in a kiln.

Gospels Ascribed to Matthew, Mark, Luke, and John, the four biblical accounts of the birth, life, death, and resurrection of Jesus Christ.

Grande Écurie Military band; Consisted mainly of the wind ensemble and was available for parades, outdoor festivities, and hunting parties.

graphic Demonstration and description by visual means.

Greek cross A cross in which all arms are the same length.

groin vault See *barrel vault.*

ground A coating, such as priming or sizing, applied to a support to prepare the surface for painting; also background.

ground bass See *ostinato.*

gymnasiarch The chief educator in an ancient Greek city, such as Pergamon.

hall of justice A place where courtroom and other legal offices are housed.

happenings A spontaneous or barely planned event, often taking place in a public area.

harmony The vertical or chordal structure of musical composition; the study of all relationships that can exist between simultaneously sounding pitches and the progressions of chords.

hedonism The theory that pleasure is the principal goal and greatest good in life, a doctrine held by the Epicurean philosophers.

hexachord From the Greek word for "6," a series of six tones, with a semitone between the third and fourth tones.

hexameter From the Greek word for "6," a line of verse with six beats.

hierarchy A system of persons or things that has higher and lower ranks.

hieroglyphic A picture or a symbol of an object standing for a word, idea, or sound; developed by the ancient Egyptians into a system of writing.

high relief See *relief.*

history scenes, history painting Paintings devoted to great events.

Hospice (pl. **Hospices**) A place of lodging for travelers, often run by a religious order.
humanism An emphasis in art and thought on individual creativity and capability.
hue The property of color that distinguishes one color from another as red, green, violet, etc. See *value.*
hymn A religious song meant to give praise and adoration.
hypostyle In Egyptian temple architecture, columns with a flat roof resting directly on them to create a hall.

icon Greek for "image"; used to identify panel paintings made under Greek Orthodox influence that represent the image of a holy person—Christ, Mary, or a saint; such works often imbued with sanctity.
iconography In the pictorial arts and sculpture, the meaning of the images and symbols depicted; subject matter.
iconostasis In Byzantine church architecture, a wall or screen separating the altar from those who attend mass; often highly decorated or housing icons.
ideal The representation of objects, individuals, and events according to a stylized, perfected, preconceived model; a kind of aesthetic distortion of perceived reality.
idealize See *ideal.*
idée fixe French for "fixed idea." Berlioz's name for a recurring melodic motif identified with the heroine in his *Fantastic Symphony.* In each movement, the motif varies slightly to coincide with the musical and programmatic circumstances.
idol A representation or symbol of a deity used as an object of worship.
ignudi A nude figure.
imperator An ancient roman commander or emperor.
illusion See *illusionism.*
illusionism The attempt of artists to represent as completely as their formal means permit the visual phenomena of a palpably real world, even if imaginary, as in a scene of muscular and voluptuous bodies floating high in the sky.
image A representation of an object, an individual, or event. An image may also be an evocation of a state of being in representational or nonrepresentational art.
imagery In the visual arts, the particular subjects and objects chosen by an artist for depiction in a work; or, in the instance of totally abstract or nonrepresentational art, the particular forms and shapes with which the artist has composed a work.
Impressionism A nineteenth-century art movement originating in France. Impressionist painters dwelled on the affect of light on shapes and solid forms.
improvisation On the spur of the moment, spontaneous musical composition for voice or an instrument. Also, in the performance of music, adding to the basic composition decorative embellishments such as chords and new melodies; a major aspect of baroque music and jazz.
individualism A belief in the rights and responsibilities of the individual human being.
instrument In music, a mechanism capable of generating the vibrations of musical sound.
instrumental See *instrument.*
intensity In the visual arts, the relative purity or brilliance of a hue. In music, the relative softness or loudness of a tone.
interval In music, the distance between two notes as determined by pitch. A melodic interval occurs when two notes are sounded successively; a harmonic interval occurs when two notes sound simultaneously.
intonazione Italian for "intonation." The sixteenth-century name for a prelude in which organists, before a motet was sung, established the pitch and mode for the choir by running their fingers rapidly over the keys and coming to a definite chordal cadence.
intrinsic Belonging to a thing by its very nature.
introduction In literature and music, a beginning that announces the themes of the work.
inversion In musical composition, a means of imitation by which the original ascending (or descending) voice is imitated by a descending (or ascending) voice at an equivalent intervallic distance.
Ionic One of the Greek classical styles of temple architecture. It was developed in Ionia and Asia Minor and is distinguished by slender, fluted columns and capitals decorated with volutes or scrolls.
isocephaly In pictorial composition, figures arranged so that all heads align at the same level.
isorhythmic Polyphonic music in which the forms are compounded of sections unified by an identity of rhythmic relationships but not necessarily of melodic patterns.

jamb The upright piece forming the side of a doorway or window frame; on the portals of Romanesque and Gothic church architecture, the place where sculptural decorations sometimes appear.
jazz A type of American music, originating in the black community early in the twentieth century. Players improvise on a melodic theme, expressing it in a highly personal way with syncopated rhythms and contrapuntal ensemble playing.
jongleur See *minstrel.*

ka In ancient Egypt, the belief in an aspect of the self that is immortal.
katharsis, or **catharsis** In ancient Greek drama, affecting the purgation of emotion in a view.
keep A fortress, secure area, or prison in a castle.
keyboard The arrangement of keys on instruments such as the piano, spinet, and organ; therefore, "keyboard instruments."
keystone The wedge-shaped central stone of an arch that hold all the other stones in place.

lancet window A tall, narrow, pointed window used in Gothic architecture.
Ländler An Austrian peasant dance similar to a waltz and popular in the late eighteenth and early nineteenth centuries.
landscape In the pictorial arts, the representation of scenery in nature.
lantern tower A tower added above a dome to light the interior.
Latin cross A cross in which the vertical arm is longer than the horizontal arm, through whose midpoint it passes.
laudi spirituali A hymn of praise.
leitmotif German for "leading motif"; a melodic theme introduced by Richard Wagner into orchestral writing to characterize an individual, idea, inanimate object, etc., and developed to reflect transformations in the person, idea, or thing, recalling the past, prophesying the future, or explaining the present.
Lied An art song in the German language.
line A mark left in its path by a moving point, or anything, such as an edge, boundary, or horizon, that suggests such a mark; a succession of notes or ideas, as in a melodic line or a line of thought. The linear might be considered one-dimensional, as opposed to the spatial, which is either two- or three-dimensional.
linear See *line.*
linear perspective See *perspective.*
lintel In architecture, a structural member that spans an opening between posts or columns.
lithograph, lithography A printmaking process based on the antipathy of grease and water. A grease crayon or waxy liquid is used to draw on a slab of grained limestone or on a grained metal plate. The drawing is treated chemically so that each grain of the plate touched by the drawing medium can accept a greasy ink and each untouched grain can accept water and repel the ink. When the place has been wetted and charged with ink, an image in ink is retained that essentially reproduces the drawing. The printmaker then covers the plate with a sheet of paper and runs them both through a press, which offsets the drawing onto the sheet, thus producing the print.
liturgy A rite or body of rites prescribed for religious worship.
loggia A gallery open on one or more sides, sometimes with arches or with columns.
low relief See *relief.*
lyric Of or relating to the lyre, such as a song to be performed to lyre accompaniment. In a modern sense, that which is intensely personal, ecstatic, and exuberant—even poetic. Also (in the plural) words or verses written to be set to music. The lyric theater is that involving words and music, such as opera and musical comedy.

madrigal In the early fourteenth century, a secular two- or three-voice song with a fixed form: two or three verses set to the same music plus a concluding two-line ritornello with different music. The upper voices are usually in a florid style, with the lower notes written for longer values. In the sixteenth century, a secular four- or five-voice composition based on love poetry or lyrics, with no set form but highly imitative and often homophonic in passages.
mandorla An almond-shaped halo that surrounds a religious figure.
Mannerism a late Renaissance art movement characterized by exaggerated figures and confusing spatial relationships.
masonry In architecture, stone or brickwork.
masque In drama, a play in which actors wear masks.
mass In the visual arts, the act or implied physical bulk, weight, and density of three-dimensional forms occupying real or suggested spatial depth. Also the most solemn rite of the Catholic liturgy, consisting of both sung and spoken sections. It combines sections of the Ordinary (texts that do not change) in alternation with sections of the Proper (texts that vary for certain occasions or seasons). The sung sections of the Ordinary are Kyrie, Gloria, Credo, Sanctus, and Agnus Dei. The sung sections of the Proper are Introit, Gradual, Alleluia or Tract, Offertory, Communion, and Post-Communion. A cyclical mass contains sections of the Ordinary structurally coordinated by the presence of the same melody (i.e., cantus firmus) in the tenor. A polyphonic mass is the Ordinary set to music with two or more voice parts. The requiem mass is the mass for the dead.
matroneum Gallery for women in churches, especially those of the Byzantine style.
mausoleum A shrine or burial chapel.
measure A standard of comparison; in musical composition, a regular division of time, set off on the staff by vertical bars. In rhythm and metrics, *measured* means slow and stately.
medium (pl. **media**) In general, the process used by the artist; in a more strict sense, the binding substance or binder used to hold pigments together, such as linseed oil for oil paint.
megalith A large stone, usually found in a Neolithic site.
melancholic A sad or depressed state, once through to be caused by an excess of black bile.
melismatic See *melisma.*
melodic See *melody.*
melody Single tones organized successively to create a musical line.
melodrama A play or film that emphasizes emotional effects.
meter In poetry, the scheme of accented and unaccented beats. In music, the basic grouping of beats and accents into measures (e.g., the triple meter of a waltz is recognized by recurring patterns of three beats with an accent on the first beat).
metope Square slabs with or without sculpture that alternate with the triglyphs that form the frieze of a Doric temple.
middle ground In the pictorial arts, that part of the composition that appears to exist between the foreground and the background; the intermediate of the three zones of recession in linear perspective.
mimesis Greek for "imitation," as in the imitation of nature.
miniator The person who painted small pictures in medieval manuscripts.
minnesingers Middle German for "love singers"; German musicians of the aristocratic class who composed love songs in the medieval period. See *jongleur, troubadours, trouvères.*
minor In music, a type of diatonic scale in which the interval between the first and third notes or pitches contains three semitones (as opposed to four in a major scale). A key or tonality based on such a scale.
minstrel In the twelfth and thirteenth centuries, a professional singing actor or mime in the service of a castle or wandering from town to town and from castle to castle. Also known as jongleur; in an expanded meaning, refers to troubadours, trouvères, and minnesingers.
minuet An elegant seventeenth-century French dance in moderate triple meter incorporated first into the suite and eventually into the sonata, symphony, or string quartet as the third movement. In the latter usage, a minuet is in ternary form (ABA) employing a middle section called a trio, which is followed by a repeat of the minuet.
mobile A constructed sculpture whose components have been connected by joints to move by force of wind or motion.
mode A particular form, style, or manner. In music, the ordering of pitches into a scale pattern; also a pattern of rhythm.
model See *modeling.*
modeling The shaping of three-dimensional forms in a soft material such as clay; also the representation on a flat surface of three-dimensional forms by means of variations in the use of color properties.
Modernism An inexact term generally referring to the current time rather than tradition. In the arts, Modernism embraces a variety of cultural movements, such as Expressionism and Cubism, ranging from the midnineteenth century to the midtwentieth century.
mode (pl. **modes**) In music, an arrangement of tones in an octave.
modulation Movement from one key to another.
module A standardized two- or three-dimensional unit that is intended as a unit of measure in architecture or sculpture.
molle Latin meaning "soft," referring to the note fa.
monastery A dwelling place where monks live in a community for spiritual purposes.
monastic That having to do with monks and monasteries.

monochord A musical instrument consisting of a single string stretched over a long wooden box with frets for varying the length of the string.
monochrome A single color or the value variations of a single hue.
monophonic See *monophony.*
monumental A work of art or architecture that is grand, noble, timeless, and essentially simple in composition and execution, whatever its actual size.
mosaic A decorative surface for a floor or wall made of small pieces of glass, shell, ceramics, or stone set in cement or plaster.
motet A composition that developed in the thirteenth century when words (mots) were added to the duplum (which became known as the motetus) of a melismatic organum. In the usual three-voice motets, the tenor retained fragments of the original plainchant melody, and to each of the two upper voices, new and different Latin texts were added. The sixteenth-century Renaissance motet is a four- or five-voice sacred composition developed by the Flemish composers and based on a Latin text. The musical texture is usually polyphonic, with imitation between voice parts.
motif In music, a melodic or rhythmic fragment of theme capable of being developed into different and larger contexts. In the visual arts, the subject or idea of an artwork, such as a still life or landscape, or an individual feature of a subject or form, usually one that recurs or predominates in the composition.
movement A self-contained section of a larger piece of musical composition, such as a symphony.
mural A painting on a wall, usually large in size.
mystical Having a spiritual meaning or reality that can be known only by intuition, insight, or similar subjective experience.
myth A legend or story that seems to express the worldview of a people or explain a practice or historical tradition.

narthex The porch or vestibule of a church.
nave The great central space in a church; in rectangular plans, the space extending from the entrance to the apse, or to the crossing or choir; usually flanked by aisles.
Neoclassical Literally, "new classical." Refers to a revival of Greek or Roman ideas, as well as a renewed interest in ancient architecture and the visual arts.
Neolithic The new Stone Age. The period during which agriculture was developed and settled communities were established.
niche A hollow recess or indentation in a wall for a statue or other ornament.
nominalist a person who believes in nominalism, the idea that there are no universal or abstract entities.
nonobjective A synonym for nonrepresentational art, or art without recognizable subject matter.
nonrepresentational In the visual arts, works so abstract as to make no reference whatever to the world of persons, places, and the objects associated with them; art from which all identifiable subject matter has been eliminated.
notation The system and process for writing out music in characters and symbols so that it can be read for performance.
note A musical sound of a certain pitch and duration; the sign in written music for such a sound; a key on an instrument such as the piano or organ that, when pressed, makes a specific musical sound.

octave The interval from one note to the next of the same pitch name (as from C to C), either higher or lower, which is a span of eight diatonic notes.
oculus A round eyelike opening or window.
oil painting The process of painting with a medium formed of ground colors held together with a binder of oil, usually linseed.
opera Theater in which music is the central dramatic agent. A typical opera involves a drama or play with scenery and acting, with the text usually sung to the accompaniment of an orchestra. Various types exist: opera buffa (It.) is characterized by a light, simple plot with prominent comedic elements and spoken dialogue; opera seria (It.) normally employs recitative in place of spoken dialogue and involves a dramatic or serious plot; number operas employ a sequence of self-contained musical "numbers" (arias, duets, choruses, etc.); music drama is the term used for Wagnerian operas, which substitute a continuous chain of music for musical numbers.
oratorio A musical composition written for soloists, chorus, and orchestra and usually based on a religious story or text. The latter may involve a plot or be purely meditative and non-narrative. Oratorios are usually performed in concert halls or churches, without scenery, staging, or costumes.
orchestra In Greek theaters, the circular space before the proscenium used by the chorus. Also a group of instrumentalists, including string players, joined together to perform ensemble music.
orchestration The art and technique of arranging or scoring a musical composition for performance by the instruments of an orchestra or band.
order In classical architecture, a style represented by a characteristic design of the column and its entablature; see *Doric, Ionic, Corinthian, Composite.* Also the arrangement imposed on all elements within a composition; in addition, a harmonious arrangement. To arrange or organize something; to give it order.
organic That which is living, such as plants; that which is integral to the whole; a system in which all parts are coordinated with one another.
organum From the ninth through the thirteenth centuries, the earliest form of polyphonic music, in which one or more lines of melody sound simultaneously along with the plainsong. In parallel organum (c. 800–900), an added voice runs exactly parallel and below the plainsong melody. In free organum (c. 1050–1150), the main melody occurs in the lower voice while the upper voice moves in a combination of parallel and contrary motion. In melismatic organum (c. 1150–1250), a few notes of the main chant or melody are prolonged and sustained in the lower voice while the upper voice moves freely through the melismatic melody with numerous notes occurring for each note in the main chant. Two-part organum is known as organum duplum; three-part organum as organum triplum; and four-part organum as quadruplum.
organum duplum, triplum See *organum.*
orthogonals In creating the illusion of depth in a picture, the lines imagined to span the picture plane and meet at a vanishing point.
ostinato Italian for "obstinate," which in musical composition is the persistent repetition, usually in the bass, of a clearly defined musical figure or phrase, while other parts or voices change around and above it. Also called basso ostinato or ground bass.
overture Instrumental music that typically precedes an opera, oratorio, or ballet. It may be an entity unto itself or directly related to the music that follows.

painterly Painting in which the buttery substance of the medium and the gestural aspect of paint application constitute a principal aspect of the art's quality.
painting Traditionally, painting has been thought of as an art form in which colors are applied through a liquid medium to a flat surface, called a ground or support. A dry powder called pigment is the coloring agent in painters' colors, and depending on the binding agent or binder used, pigments can produce media of paint such as oil, tempera, watercolor, fresco, encaustic, casein, and acrylic resin. These can be worked on grounds or supports such as paper, canvas, wood panel, and plaster. If the support has been given a preparatory coating by priming and sizing, the surface thus formed is considered the ground, which intervenes between the painting and its support.
Paleolithic The Old Stone Age, a period characterized by nomadic or seminomadic existence.
palette A tray or shaped planar surface on which a painter mixes colors; also the characteristic range and combination of colors typical of a painter or a style of painting.
panel Any rigid, flat support for painting, such as wood, usually prepared, with a ground. Any flat, slablike surface, usually rectangular.
pantheon Greek meaning "all the gods of a people"; a temple dedicated to them; a public building containing tombs or memorials of the illustrious dead.
parallel organum See *organum.*
part In musical composition, the writing for a single instrument or voice or a group of them; also a section of a composition.
Parthenon A Doric temple on the Athenian acropolis.
paten A shallow dish used during the mass to carry the Eucharist.
pater patriae Latin meaning "father of a country"; a title given to national heroes.
paterfamilias Latin meaning "father of a family."
pathos Greek meaning "the experience of emotion, grief, or passion." In art, an element that evokes pity or sympathy.
Pax Romana Latin meaning "Roman peace."
pediment In architecture, the triangular space or gable at the end of a building formed in the entablature by the sloping roof and the cornice.
pendentive In architecture, the triangular segment of masonry whose plane is hemispherical, four of which can form a transition from a square to a circular base of a dome.
peplos An ancient Greek garment that resembles a shawl.
personifying, personification To be the embodiment of a quality.
performing arts The arts that have their full existence only in time and that to realize full existence must be played: music, dance, and drama.
perspective A pictorial technique for simulating on a flat, two-dimensional surface, or in a shallow space, the three-dimensional characteristics of volumetric forms and deep space. During the Renaissance in Italy, a quasimathematical scheme called linear perspective developed from the fact that parallel lines moving away from the viewer must be seen as converging toward a single point on the horizon (called the vanishing point). Placed, in this system, at intervals along the assumed and converging parallels, objects are scaled in their sizes to diminish in relation to their distance from the picture plane. At about the same time in northern Europe, painters developed a perspective system known long before to the Romans and the Chinese. Called atmospheric or aerial perspective, the system used blurred outlines, loss of detail, alteration of hues toward the cool colors, and diminution of color saturation and value contrast—all in proportion to the distance of the object from the viewer. See *foreshortening.*
phlegmatic Possessing a serene or imperturbable character.
photomontage Combining photographically derived images, often from mass-media print sources.
Photorealism A late twentieth-century art movement, mostly in painting, that stressed the depiction of detail.
piano Italian for "soft" (p); pianissimo (pp) means "very soft"; pianississimo (ppp), "extremely soft."
pictorial That having to do with the flat arts of painting and drawing and, to a certain extent, with the art of low relief in that its three-dimensional subject matter and imagery are composed in relation to a flat rear plane physically parallel to and only slightly behind what would be a picture plane and whose edges constitute a frame or format of specific shape like that of a picture. Picture or pictorial space is that of the support, which is a flat surface defined by a specific shape, usually rectangular. To achieve here, at the picture plane on the support, the appearance of deep space, the artist must use illusionistic devices such as modeling, foreshortening, and perspective so that, in a still life or landscape, for instance, objects and forms seem to rest firmly on a ground plane at intervals beginning in the foreground and moving through the middle ground to the background and beyond.
picture plane An imaginary vertical plane assumed to be at the front surface of a painting. See *pictorial.*
picturesque A pictorial situation that awakens thoughts of the sublime, magnificent, quaint, vivid, or rugged as opposed to the orderly, symmetrical, or beautiful.
pier A mass of masonry rising vertically to support an arch, vault, or other roofing member.
pietà A devotional image of the sorrowing Virgin holding the dead Christ.
pigment Finely powdered coloring matter mixed or ground with various vehicles to form paint, crayons, etc.; also a term used loosely to mean color or paint.
pilaster In architecture, a shallow, flat, vertical member projecting from a wall surface and, like a column, composed of base, shaft, and capital; usually more decorative than structural.
pillar Any vertical architectural member—pier, column, or pilaster.
pitch A musical tone, or its relative highness or lowness as fixed by the frequency of the vibrations occurring per second within it.
plainchant From early medieval Christian worship, a type of sacred music or liturgical chant, monophonic in style and set to a Latin text.
plainsong Another term for plainchant.
plan An architectural drawing that reveals in two dimensions the arrangement and distribution of interior spaces and walls, as well as door and window openings, of a building as seen from above.
plane A surface that is defined and measurable in two dimensions.
plastic That which is capable of receiving physical form; therefore, the visual arts. More narrowly, that which is pliant and malleable enough to be modeled; therefore, the material of sculpture.
plasticity The three-dimensional quality of a form; its roundness and apparent solidity; the capability of material for being shaped, modeled, and manipulated.
play A literary text consisting of dialogue composed to be acted out in dramatic form for the benefit of an audience.
player One who performs.

plot In literature, the plan or scheme of the story and its unfolding actions.

podium A platform, base, or pedestal for a building or a monument.

pointillism A painting technique in which color is applied to the canvas in small dots, which blend when seen from a distance.

polychoral style Compositions in this style employ a chorus (with or without orchestra) divided into two or more groups that sing and play in alternation (antiphonally). Venetian music at the end of the sixteenth century featured this style.

polychrome Several colors rather than one (monochrome).

polyphony, polyphonic A texture created by the interweaving of two or more melodic lines heard simultaneously. Counterpoint is the technique used for composed polyphonic music.

polyptych A series of painting, often on wood, joined together by hinges.

Pop Art An art movement originating in the 1950s and 1960s that used themes and images from popular culture.

portal An imposing door and the whole architectural composition surrounding it.

portico A porch with a roof supported by columns and usually with an entablature and a pediment.

portraiture The practice of making portraits of people.

post-and-lintel In architecture, a structural system employing two uprights or posts to support a member, the lintel or beam, which spans the space between the uprights.

Post-Impressionism Literally, "after Impression." A word coined to describe the diverse styles that followed Impressionism in Europe.

prelude A musical composition designed to introduce the main body of a work—an opera; a separate concert piece for piano or orchestra, usually based on a single theme.

primary colors Colors that in various combinations are capable of creating any other color or hue. In artists' pigments, these are red, yellow, and blue; in natural or "white" light, they are red, green, and blue.

Primitivism A recurring idea of Western culture that emphasizes the purity of perception and response in people outside the developed world.

prologue An introduction or preface.

program music Broadly speaking, music that consciously imitates sound effects (bird calls, bells, etc.), describes natural or social events (thunderstorms, hunting scenes, etc.), or narrates a sequence of dramatic episodes derived from poetic and dramatic sources. In the nineteenth century, it refers principally to instrumental music based on a series of actions or a sequence of episodes designed to make narrative or dramatic sense and declared by the composer to be subject to some sort of literary, pictorial, or philosophic interpretation.

proportion The relation, or ratio, of one part to another and of each part to the whole with regard to size, height, width, length, or depth.

prosody The art of setting words to music. Also a particular system or style of versification.

protagonist A principle character in a play.

prothesis A side chapel on the north side of a Byzantine church. The Eucharist is prepared there.

prototype An original model, archetype, or primary form from which other artists make copies or adaptations.

psalter A book of the psalms (hymns) found in the Bible.

punctus contra punctum Latin meaning "point counterpoint."

putti (sing. *puto*) An angelic small child, usually male, who often appears in Renaissance paintings.

pylon In Egyptian architecture, a monumental gateway shaped in profile like a truncated pyramid and leading to the forecourt of a temple.

quadruplum See *organum.*

quatrefoil A stylized flower with four petals.

raking cornice See *cornice.*

rationalism The belief that reason is the source for human understanding of the world.

realism A midnineteeth-century style of painting and sculpture based on the belief that the subject matter of art and the methods of representation should be true to life without stylization or idealization.

recapitulation See *sonata form.*

recitative In opera, oratorio, and cantata, a form of declamation that, although highly stylized and set to music, follows the pitch and rhythms of speech more than a melodic line. Recitative tends to serve a narrative function and often leads into an aria or connects arias and ensembles.

refrain In music, a phrase or passage that is repeated.

regent families In Dutch seventeenth-century history, powerful families whose members ruled like governors.

register A range (upper, middle, lower) within the capacity of the voice, human or instrumental.

reinforced concrete See *ferroconcrete.*

relief A plane that exists three-dimensionally as a projection from a background. Also sculpture that is not freestanding but projects from a surface of which it is a part. When the projection is relatively slight, it is called bas-relief or low relief; when the projection is very pronounced, it is called high relief.

reliquary A small box, casket, or shrine for keeping sacred relics, usually made of and decorated with precious materials.

representation The depiction or illustration by the graphic means of the visual arts (lines, values, colors, etc.) of forms and images in such a way that the eye would perceive a correspondence between them and their sources in the real world of empirical experience.

representative style In music, a type of word painting by which the descriptive imagery of the text is reflected in the shape and turn of the melodic lines.

responsorial psalmody Alternate singing between a soloist and a group or choir.

retrograde A term that indicates the employment of a theme or phrase in reverse order, starting on the last note of the melody and ending with the first.

rhythm In the visual arts, the regular repetition of a form. In music, all factors pertaining to temporal organization in music, including the comparative duration of tones, meter, and tempo.

rib In architecture, a slender arched support that in a vault system typically projects from the surface along the groins where semicircular vaults intersect each other. Ribs both reinforce the vaults and unify them aesthetically.

ribbed groin vault A groin vault reinforced with ribs.

ricercare An instrumental composition that developed in the 1500s and 1600s as a counterpart to the vocal motet. It is characterized by the periodic recurrence of the first subject, and as each subsequent subject or subject complex appears, it ushers in a new section featuring contrapuntal imitations and variation techniques. The ricercare is the prototype of the later fugue.

ritornel, ritornello Italian for "refrain"; a recurrent passage in a concerto, rondo, operatic scene, etc.

rococo An art style characterized by intricate, ornate designs.

Romantic An art style that emphasized the importance of feelings and the imagination and the narrowness of rationalism. See *rationalism.*

rondo A musical form in which one main theme recurs to alternate with other themes, making a structure that can be diagrammed as ABACADA.

rotonda A round building or a round interior room.

rubricator The person who produced elaborate initials in medieval manuscripts.

rusticate, rusticated In masonry work, to build a wall of rough-hewn stone for bold texture and strong light-and-shade contrasts.

sanctuary A consecrated, sacred, or holy place; in Christian architecture, that part of the building where the altar is placed; also a refuge.

sanguine In alchemy, a cheerful temperament. Sometimes associated with a red or flushed complexion.

sarcophagus (pl. **sarcophagi**) A coffin, made of stone, clay, or other materials.

satire A witty exposure of vice and folly, the purpose of which is to entertain and effect moral reform.

scale Relative or proportional size. In music, a succession of tones usually arranged in ascending or descending order and either a whole tone or a half-tone apart.

scherzo Italian for "joke"; in sonatas, symphonies, and quartets, a movement substituted for the minuet and, like the minuet, composed in triple meter but at a faster tempo. Normally, the scherzo is linked with a trio in a sequence of scherzo, trio, and scherzo repeat.

score The written version of music, with all parts indicated both separately and in relation to one another. To prepare music in written form.

scriptorium In a medieval monastery, the workroom for the copying and illumination of manuscripts.

sculpture A type of three-dimensional art in which form is created by subtractive or additive methods. In subtractive sculpture, the form is found by removing (as in carving) material from a block or mass. In additive sculpture, the form is built up by modeling in clay, by constructing with materials as a carpenter or welder might, or by assembling such preexisting forms as found objects. Whatever the method, the final form can be cast in a material, such as bronze,

that modifies from a liquid state to a hard and permanent one. Sculpture can be freestanding or relief.

secular Not religious, but relating to the worldly or temporal.

sedes See *cathedra.*

sensibility In the cultural life of the late 1700s and early 1800s, an attitude that emphasized keen emotional responses to art, rather than analytical understanding.

sequence In musical composition, the repetition of a melody or motif at different pitch levels. Historically, sequence refers to a musical style that first came into use in the ninth century by adding text syllabically to the long melismas on the final vowel of an alleluia. Eventually the melismas were elaborated or altered musically, and the sequences became highly developed as separate compositions. All but four were banished from the liturgy by the sixteenth-century Council of Trent.

sfumato Italian for "smoked"; a misty blending of light and dark tones to create soft edges and veiled effects. A type of chiaroscuro.

shading The property of color that makes it seem light or dark. See *value.*

shape A two-dimensional area or plane with distinguishable boundaries, such as a square or a circle, which can be formed whenever a line turns or meets, as in an S or T shape.

silhouette A form as defined by its outline.

sinfonia An orchestral work; often introduces a choral work.

skene In ancient Greek theaters, which were open-air, the small building that provided for performances both a stage and a background. It is the root word for "scene" and "scenery."

skolion A Greek drinking song.

solmization The practice of using syllables to indicate notes on a musical scale—do, re, me, etc.

sonata, sonata form A structural principle used in a movement of instrumental music. It consists of three main divisions: the exposition, during which the musical materials of the movement are presented or "exposed" in the tonic key and a new key (the entire section is usually repeated); the development, in which the musical ideas of the exposition are worked out and explored in various keys to provide tension and contrast; and the recapitulation (reprise), which resolves the tension and contrast of the development by restating the exposition, but with all the themes in the tonic and usually with minor changes in orchestration or musical materials. Acoda may be added in conclusion.

song The simultaneous presentation of a literary text and a musical setting. The basic types are strophic, in which the melody is repeated over and over to different stanzas of the poem, and through-composed, in which the melody and accompaniment vary for each successive stanza.

song cycle A group or series of songs sharing a common thought, theme, or musical treatment and intended to be sung consecutively.

soprano Vocal or instrumental register with the highest range. Soloists may be designated as coloratura soprano, a vocalist with great agility in the high register, capable of performing rapid, dazzling, cadenza-like passages typical of eighteenth- and nineteenth-century operatic arias; dramatic soprano, a powerful and declamatory voice that extends downward to the mezzo region; or lyric soprano, a voice with light texture, considerable brilliance, and a capacity for sustained melodic singing.

space A volume available for occupation by a form; an extent, measurable or infinite, that can be understood as an area or a distance capable of being used both negatively and positively.

spatial That having to do with space.

spectrum The full array of rainbow colors that appear when white light (sunlight) has been refracted into its component wave lengths by means of a transparent substance, such as a prism.

squinch A device for making a transition from a square to a polygonal or circular base for a dome.

stadtholder A Dutch political leader or chief executive officer of a province.

staff The five horizontal lines and four intervening spaces on which musical notation can be written out.

stasimon In Greek tragedy, the song sung by the chorus.

stele A stone slab, often carved in relief, set upright to commemorate a person or event.

stereotype Something conforming to a fixed or general pattern.

still life In the pictorial arts, an arrangement of inanimate objects—fruit, flowers, pottery, etc.—taken as the subject of a work of art.

stoa In the agoras of ancient Greece, a one- or two-story building in the form of a colonnade or roofed porch providing space for a walkway and shops, offices, and storerooms.

stretto A narrowing or quickening process achieved by a faster tempo or diminution of the note values. In a fugue, stretto is the imitation of a subject in two or more voice parts in rapid succession so that the statements overlap, causing an increase of intensity.

string quartet An ensemble of two violins, viola, and cello; a composition in sonata form written for such an ensemble.

stringed instruments The violin, viola, violoncello (or cello), and double bass, all of which are equipped with strings capable of generating musical sound when either stroked with a bow or plucked.

Sturm und Drang From the German meaning "Storm and Stress." A late eighteenth-century cultural movement that emphasized high emotion and turmoil.

style The terms form and style, "formal analysis" and "stylistic analysis," serve interchangeably in any discussion of the way artists work or the way their art works once it has been accomplished. Both form and style are concerned with those measurable aspects of art that caused the elements, principles, and materials to come together as a composition; but they are equally concerned with the expressive content of a work. They signify a sensitive, knowing, trained, and controlled shaping and ordering of ideas, feelings, elements, and materials. Style can be the identifying characteristic of the work of a single artist, a group of artists, or an entire society or culture.

stylize To simplify or generalize forms found in nature for the purpose of increasing their aesthetic and expressive content.

stylobate In Greek temple architecture, the upper step of the base that forms a platform for the columns.

subject In the visual arts, the identifiable object, incident, or situation represented. See *iconography*. In music, the theme or melody used as the basic element in the structure of a composition, as in a fugue.

subject matter See *subject*.

sublime The representation of the violent, wild, and awesome aspects of nature as opposed to beauty, which is based on symmetry, proportion, and elegance.

suite In music, a collection of various movements without specific relationships in key or musical material. The music usually is dancelike, since suites before 1750 consisted almost invariably of four principal dance movements: the allemande, the courante, the sarabande, and the gigue. Often, simply excerpts from scores for ballet and opera.

summa An encyclopedic summation of a field of learning, particularly in theology or philosophy.

Summa Theologiae A summa (see *summa*) by Thomas More.

support In the pictorial arts, the physical material serving as a base for and sustaining a two-dimensional work of art, such as paper in the instance of drawings and prints, and canvas and board panels in painting. In architecture, a weight-bearing structural member.

suprematism An art movement originating in Russia that emphasized purity of form and emotion.

surface The two-dimensional exterior plane of a form or object.

symbol A form, image, sign, or subject standing for something else; in the visual arts, often a visible suggestion of something invisible.

syllabic A reference to the parts of a word called syllables.

symmetry An arrangement or balanced design in which similar or identical elements have been organized in comparable order on either side of an axis.

symphonic poem A term first applied by Liszt to a one-movement orchestral work of the late nineteenth century based on an extramusical idea (illustrative, literary, pictorial, etc.). The symphonic poem is a type of program music. Also called a tone poem.

symphony An orchestral composition commonly written in three or four movements. In a typical symphony, the first movement is fast and in sonata form; the second is slow and can be in sonata, binary, ternary, or variation form. The third movement (sometimes omitted) is a minuet (scherzo) and trio; the finale, usually in sonata or rondo form, is in a lively tempo.

synesthesia A combination of the senses, or an attempt to have one sense, such as sight, be stimulated by another sense, such as hearing.

syncopation Stressing a beat that normally should remain weak or unaccented.

synthesis The deduction of independent factors or entities into a compound that becomes a new, more complex whole.

tabernacle A receptacle for a holy or precious object; a container placed on the altar of a Catholic church to house the consecrated elements of the Eucharist.

tableau vivant From the French for living picture, the enactment of a historical event, scene from a painting, poem, or work of literature.

tempera A painting technique using as a medium pigment mixed with egg yolk, glue, or casein.

temperato An instruction to a musician to play a piece of music at a moderate speed.

tempo In music, the pace or rate of speed at which the notes progress.

tempus perfectum A three-part motet with a three beat rhythm, thought to reflect the three-part Holy Trinity.

tenebrism The practice of painting in "the dark manner," that is, with strong contrasts between dark and light. See *chiaroscuro*.

tenor The highest range of the male voice or an instrument with this range. In medieval organum, the voice that sustains the notes of the chant or cantus firmus. More generally, the line in musical writing corresponding to the tenor range.

tensile In architecture, structure that is capable of sustaining tension.

ternary, ternary form A common three-part musical structure consisting of three self-contained sections, with the second specifically in contrast to the first and the third a repeat or modified repeat of the first: ABA or statement, contrast, restatement.

terra cotta Italian meaning "baked earth"; baked clay used in ceramics, sculpture, and architectural decoration; also a reddish-brown color similar to fired red clay.

terribilità A word often used to describe the feelings of intense excitement and formidability produced in the viewer by the works of Michelangelo.

terza rima A rhyming scheme in poetry that follows the pattern, aba, bcb, cdc.

tesserae (sing. ***tessera***) Small bits of stone, glass, or similar material used to make a mosaic.

texture In the visual or plastic arts, the tactile quality of a surface or the representation of that surface. In music, the relationship of the melodic elements and the elements that accompany them and the particular blend of sound these create.

theme In music, a short melodic statement or an entire self-contained melody; subject matter to be treated in a composition through development, imitation, contrast, variation, expansion, juxtaposition, etc.

thermae A Roman public bath.

thrust A strong continued pressure, as in the force moving sideways from one part of a structure against another.

tibia An ancient Roman musical instrument made from the leg bone of an animal.

timbre Tone color, or the particular quality of sound produced by a voice or an instrument.

toccata Italian for "touched"; music composed for keyboard instruments, written in a free style with running passages, chords, and sometimes imitative sections.

tone In music, a note; that is, a sound of definite pitch and duration. In the visual arts, a general coloristic quality, as this might be expressed in a degree of saturation and value.

tonic The first and principal note of a key, functioning as a place of rest or home base and acting as a point of departure and return.

tragedy A serious drama or other literary work in which conflict between a protagonist and a superior force (often fate) concludes in calamity for the protagonist, whose sorrow excites pity and terror in the beholder and produces catharsis.

transept In a cruciform church, the whole arm set at right angles to the nave, which makes the crossing.

treble In music, the higher voices, both human and instrumental, the notes to whose music appear on a staff identified by a treble clef (𝄞).

triforium In church architecture, an arcaded area in the nave wall system that lies below the clerestory and above the gallery, if there is one, and the nave arcade. It can be open like a gallery or sealed (blind).

triglyph A slab divided by two vertical grooves into three bands. The panels that alternate with the metopes to form the frieze of a Doric temple.

triplum In the music of medieval organum, the third voice part counting upward from the tenor or cantus firmus.

triptych A painting consisting of three panels. A two-paneled painting is a diptych; a many-paneled one is a polyptych.

triumphal arch In Roman architecture, a large, decorated archway used to commemorate an important happening, often a military victory.

troubadours, trouvères French musicians of noble lineage who flourished in the twelfth and thirteenth centuries, composing secular songs dealing with chivalry, knighthood, the Crusades, women, and historical subjects. Troubadours stemmed from southern France; trouvères, from the north. Their German counterparts were the minnesingers.

trumeau A post or pillar placed in the center of a portal to help support the lintel above; common in medieval architecture.

tuba A valved brass instrument with a wide bell.

tune A song or melody; a musical key; the correct pitch or tonality.

tunnel vault A barrel vault.

turrets Ornamental towers.

twelve-tone technique/system A twentieth-century method of composition devised by Schoenberg in which the seven diatonic and five chromatic tones are treated equally so that no tonal center is apparent. Compositions are based on an arbitrary arrangement of these twelve tones, and their sequence is known as a tone row or series. The notes of a row must always be used in the established order but may be repeated or moved from one octave position to another. The row may also be used in inversion, retrograde form, or retrograde inversion or may be transposed to any step of the chromatic scale. A series may also be arranged vertically to form chords.

tympanum In medieval architecture, the surface enclosed by a lintel and an arch over a doorway; in classical architecture, the recessed face of a pediment.

unison The "zero" interval that occurs when two voices or different instruments simultaneously play a note or melody at the same pitch.

unity The quality of similarity, shared identity, or consistency to be found among parts of a composition; a logical connection between separate elements in a work of art; the opposite of variety.

uomo universale Literally, "universal man."

value The property of color that makes it seem light or dark; shading. In music, the duration of a note. In general, the relative worth accorded to an idea, concept, or object.

vanishing point In linear perspective, that point on the horizon toward which parallel lines appear to converge and at which they seem to vanish.

variations A musical form in which the statement of a melody or theme is followed by various modifications of it.

variety Contrast and difference; the lack of sameness among separate elements in a composition; the opposite of unity.

vault A masonry or concrete roof constructed on the principles of an arch.

vernacular The language spoken by the common people.

vestibule A room situated in front of the main room of a building.

visual arts Those arts that appeal to the optical sense—painting, sculpture, drawing, printmaking, architecture, etc.

vivace Italian for "lively" or "vivacious."

voice The sound made by the human throat or by a musical instrument; the part in music written for that sound.

void A hollow or empty space.

volume Any three-dimensional quantity that is bounded or enclosed, whether solid or void.

volutes Scroll-like spirals that characterize the Ionic capital.

votive From the Latin for "vow," an offering made to God or in his name in petition, in fulfillment of a vow, or in gratitude or devotion. A votive figure stands in for a person who has visited a shrine.

voussoir A wedge-shaped block used in the construction of a true arch. The central voussoir is the keystone.

wall In architecture, a planelike upright structure and surface capable of serving as a support, barrier, or enclosure.

waltz A dance in moderate triple meter that developed from the Austrian Ländler in the early nineteenth century.

wind instruments See *woodwind instruments, brass instruments*.

woodwind instruments The flute, oboe, English horn, clarinet, bass clarinet, bassoon, contrabassoon, and saxophone, all of which are pipes with holes in the side and can produce musical sound when blowing causes their columns of air to vibrate. Several of the woodwinds have mouthpieces fitted with reeds.

word painting See *representative style*.

ziggurat A stepped pyramid in Mesopotamian architecture.

INDEX